THE DARTNELL

ADVERTISING

MANAGER'S

HANDBOOK

THE DARTNELL

ADVERTISING MANAGER'S HANDBOOK (THIRD EDITION)

by
Richard H. Stansfield

THE DARTNELL CORPORATION
CHICAGO, BOSTON and LONDON

OTHER DARTNELL HANDBOOKS

Direct Mail and Mail Order Handbook
Office Administration Handbook
Personnel Administration Handbook
Public Relations Handbook
Sales Manager's Handbook
Sales Promotion Handbook
Marketing Manager's Handbook

The Dartnell Services

Personnel Update
Dartnell Sales and Marketing Executive Report

SECOND PRINTING—1985

Third Edition, June, 1982
Copyright 1969, 1977, 1982
in the United States, Canada and Great Britain by
THE DARTNELL CORPORATION
All rights reserved
Library of Congress Catalog Card Number 68-21480
International Standard Book Number 0-85013-128-6

Printed in the United States of America by Dartnell Press, Chicago, Illinois 60640

DEDICATION

To JANE, MARTHA, and BOB, who gave up vacations and companionship, and who never complained when the coffee pot and I disappeared into the trophy room-office. Without their encouragement, I could not have written this book. And, finally, to a host of wonderful advertising men and women who gave unselfishly of their time and advice. They are thoroughly nice people and I am deeply grateful to them.

RICHARD H. STANSFIELD

INTRODUCTION

THERE are not many 1,000-page handbooks these days, publishing costs being what they are. This one runs to slightly over that many pages. But the subject—the complex art-science-trade of advertising—requires a lot of elbow room for definitive treatment of all its aspects.

Given the elbow room by his publisher, The Dartnell Corporation, Richard H. Stansfield has come up with what I consider the first truly definitive handbook on the subject. His work will be treasured as a reference book by many different kinds of people in the field—from ad managers to copywriters to agency chairmen of the board. It is truly a panoramic view of the good practitioners at work.

Every aspect of modern advertising is treated in depth in this big handbook—campaign planning, agency selection, prospect identification, copywriting, headlines, media, research, surveys, source material, corporate image-building. All of this, and more, is easily available to the reader through the extensive index.

The text abounds in case histories—and not only of the good ads and successful campaigns. Dick Stansfield makes use of the "what not to do" training technique with some inclusions he labels Horrible Examples. The author not only tells his reader *how* something should be handled—he also tells *why*, which is something many of us have forgotten.

For the beginner in advertising, this handbook is as good as 10 years in the business. For the seasoned advertising person, it is a treasure of reference. As someone has said, we read not so much to be informed as to review what we already know. And the veteran of the advertising wars will find much here to be convinced that he or she stands with the elderly farmer who told the university agricultural extension professor, "I already know how to farm better than I'm farming now." Any one of us toiling in the advertising field could benefit from a review of Dick Stansfield's work.

Richard H. Stansfield has sat on both sides of the advertising desk. He has worked for topflight agencies serving large industrial clients, and he has dealt with agencies as manager of advertising for large industrial clients. He knows the strengths and the weaknesses of each, and how one should work with the other to accomplish the most for client and company.

While this handbook may seem oriented entirely toward industrial advertising, there actually is much here that can be fruitfully applied to consumer advertising, particularly in these days of overstress on the "hot little creative shops." While industrial advertising has displayed plenty of creativity, the "hot little shops" could learn much from the hardworking, dollar-conscious objectivity of the good industrial ad manager and agency.

This is a "gutsy" handbook. Dick Stansfield doesn't believe in sacred cows. But he's realistic enough to know there are a few around, and tells you where they might be hiding. He warns the advertising manager of the prejudices and the myths which top-management people cherish about advertising—and he offers the kind of arguments designed to overcome such obstacles. Here are the fact-packed answers to the vice-presidents and sales managers and engineers who think their company advertises only "because everyone else does."

This is not an *opinionated* handbook. Dick Stansfield knows his research, and when he's discussing the pros and cons of one ad method over another, one position over another, a choice of media or which technique, he takes a firm stand. But he offers proof from the findings of established advertising studies on the question. Dick Stansfield rests his case only upon the available evidence.

It will be a wise top-management executive who sees to it that a copy of this handbook is on the desk of every hand in the ad department. Dick Stansfield is cost-conscious on every page. Stansfield sees advertising as the handmaiden of sales, not as a direct source of sales, and he likes to see every dollar spent on advertising earn its way. Shortcuts, dollar-savers, and timesavers abound in the text.

There are nearly 350 illustrations in *The Advertising Manager's Handbook* and many helpful charts and tables.

Altogether it's a prime investment for anyone concerned with advertising, from the company president who okays the budget down to the neophyte just starting or the student who's planning a career in the most fascinating business in the world.

ZENON C. R. HANSEN
Former Chairman of the Board and President,
Mack Trucks, Inc.
One of the Signal Companies

CONTENTS

ACKNOWLEDGEMENTS

MORE THAN 300 persons in industrial advertising and the agency field helped make this handbook. They contributed case histories or other data, and were responsible for most of the illustrations. To their generous and unselfish help, the author and the publisher are deeply grateful. The names of the men and women who contributed follow, in two groups divided as to whether they are agency-media or industry people.

AGENCY AND MEDIA PERSONNEL

R. B. AMAND, Account Supervisor, Northlich, Stolley, Inc.

AMERICAN BUSINESS PRESS, INC.

DON BALDWIN, Account Executive, Batten, Barton, Durstine & Osborn, Inc.

The Late W. STORRS BALDWIN, Vice-President, Diamond T Motor Truck Co.

LEE BARTLETT, Former Vice-President, Marsteller Inc.

GENE BEAUDET, Editor-in Chief, *Iron Age*

JOHN F. BELCHER, Account Executive, Cunningham & Walsh Inc.

JACK E. BERGREN, Regional Business Manager, *Iron Age*

GRADY C. BOLES, Vice-President, Edward H. Weiss and Company

CHARLES BOWES, President, The Bowes Company (Retired)

THOMAS R. BRAMSON, President and Publisher, *Production*

HALE CAREY, District Manager, *Dun's Review*

RICHARD C. CHRISTIAN, Chairman, Marsteller Inc.

BRUCE COLE, Vice-President, General Manager, Marsteller Inc. (Chicago office)

WILLIAM CONDIT, President, Condit Corporation

WALTER G. CRUICE, Vice-President, Pohlman Studios, Inc.

VAN CUNNINGHAM, Vice-President, Fuller & Smith & Ross Inc.

JOHN DAGHLIAN, Reader Feedback Project Manager, McGraw-Hill Publications

RICHARD DIERCKS, Account Executive, Campbell-Mithun, Inc.

WILLIAM J. DWYER, District Manager, *Research/Development*

EUGENE ELDRIDGE, District Manager, *Analytical Chemistry*

THOMAS FALLON, Regional Vice-President, Chilton Company

GEORGE JOEL FINE, Promotion Manager, Visual Panographics, Inc.

JOHN T. FOSDICK, President, John T. Fosdick Associates, Inc.

MISS LINDA F. FRIEDMAN, Account Supervisor, Universal Public Relations, Inc.

JOHN A. FROST, Account Executive, Howard H. Monk and Associates, Inc.

C. A. GODING, Account Supervisor, Marsteller Inc.

KENNETH W. GOOD, Account Executive, Associated Techdata Inc.

J. J. GRAHAM, Managing Editor, *Advertising Age*

RICHARD H. GROVES, Executive Vice-President, Chilton Company

J. SANDERS HAAS, N.W. Ayer & Son

JASON HAILEY, Photographer

HENRY L. HAYDEN, Vice-President, Vernet/Hayden, Inc.

JOHN B. HOLMES, District Manager, *Product Design & Development*

JAMES J. HUGHES, Managing Editor, *Steelways*

PAT HURLEY, Public Relations Department, Gray & Rogers, Inc.

EUGENE H. JACOBS, Publisher, *Automotive Industries*

ALFRED J. JAFFE, Editor, *Marketing Forum*

JEFFERSON ADVERTISING AGENCY, creator of the Norplex ad, "It Can't Be Done."

MISS BARBARA H. KAPLAN, N.W. Ayer & Son, Inc.

MICHAEL J. KELLY, Vice-President, *Production*

ROBERT E. KENYON, JR., Executive Vice-President, Magazine Publishers Association, Inc.

ELAINE KORTAS, Media Director, Marsteller Inc.

RICHARD H. LABONTE, Director of Promotion, McGraw-Hill Publications

JOHN K. LEE, Assistant Director, Marketing Communications Research Center

ROBERT LETWIN, Editor, *Sales Meetings*

The Late T. J. LOPATKA, Vice-President, Diamond T Motor Truck Company

J. BRADLEY MACKIMM, District Manager, *Electronics*

RICHARD MANVILLE, Richard Manville Research Inc.

JAMES B. MARINE, President, The Bowes Company

ROBERT MCCANN, Traffic Manager, Papert, Koenig, Lois, Inc. Advertising

ROBERT G. MERRICK, Hal Lawrence Incorporated

CHARLES S. MILES, Assistant Publications Manager, Thomas Micro-Catalogs, Thomas Publishing Company

DAVID H. MURRAY, Account Executive, Chirurg & Cairns, Inc.

DOROTHY M. NEWMAN, Editorial Assistant, *Industrial Marketing*

MELVIN B. NYLUND, District Manager, *Construction Methods & Equipment*

DON "Antelope" OLSON, friend, hunting partner, and provider of moral support; he assured me a wise old buck was growing a pair of huge, 18-inch horns while I was writing this book, and that I would surely cut his trail when the next season rolls around in Wyoming.

WILLARD D. PEASE, President, Images West

WILLIAM A. PHAIR, Publisher, *Product Design & Development*

FRANK M. PHILLIPPS, Phillipps Associates, Inc.

FRED C. POPPE, President, Complan Inc.

CHARLES B. RAWSON, Editor, *Commercial Car Journal* (Retired)

G. BRUCE RICHARDSON, General Manager, Marsteller, Inc. (Pittsburgh office)

M. R. ROBINSON, Director, Cahners Audit, Cahners Publishing Company Inc.

FRANK ROCK, JR., Vice President, Busch and Schmitt, Inc.

ACKNOWLEDGEMENTS

RICHARD L. SCHEIDKER, Senior Vice-President, American Association of Advertising Agencies.

HAROLD SCOTT, District Manager, *Successful Farming*

J. J. SMILEY, JR., Vice-President, Graphic Service

SMITH-KLITTEN ADVERTISING (agency for Genisco)

STANLEY B. STEWART, President, Stewart, Price, Tomlin, Inc.

HOWARD A. STONE, President, Daniel Starch and Staff

CARROLL SWAN, Editor, *Media/scope*

GILBERT THAYER, Publisher, *Reseach/Development* (Retired)

FRANK W. WHITE, Account Executive, Harris D. McKinney, Inc.

E. C. WIEGAND, Jahn & Ollier Engraving Company

ROLAND WERTH, Regional Vice-President, Chilton Company

JEROME S. WILFORD, Vice-President, *Production*

DAVE WILSON, Account Executive, Marsteller Inc.

JOHN WILSON, Vice-President, Batten, Barton, Durstine & Osborn, Inc.

SPENCER ZOGG, Vice-President, Pohlman Studios, Inc.

INDUSTRY PERSONNEL

KAY ACKERMANN, Secretary, Lindberg Hevi-Duty

W. SCOTT ALLAN, Assistant Vice-President and Manager of Public Relations, Liberty Mutual Insurance Company

J. W. AMENT, Vice-President, Transue & Williams Steel Forging Division of Standard Alliance Industries, Inc.

RICHARD J. ANDERSEN, Manager, Advertising and Sales Promotion, The Ingersoll Milling Machine Company

B. E. ANDERSON, Director of Advertising and Public Relations, Bliss & Laughlin Industries.

R. F. ANDERSON, Manager, Advertising, Centralab Electronics Division Globe-Union Inc.

ROBERT S. ATCHESON, Manager, Advertising and Public Relations, Marbon Chemical Division of Borg-Warner Corporation

J. W. ATKINSON, Sales Promotion and Advertising Manager, A. B. Dick Company

JON AVRIGEAN, Director of Advertising, Wheeling Steel Corporation

J. R. BARLOW, Manager—Advertising and Sales Promotion, Chrysler Motors Corporation.

ALBERT M. BATTIS, Vice-President, DeJur-Amsco Corporation

BEN S. BEALL III, President, Lindberg Hevi-Duty Division of Sola Basic Industries, Inc.

ROSS T. BEIRNE, Advertising Manager, Giddings & Lewis Machine Tool Co.

HOWARD BERSTED, Director, Advertising and Sales Promotion, Automatic Electric Company, Subsidiary of General Telephone & Electronics

P. A. BINNEY, Manager, Public Relations, Norton Company

D. A. BLANCHARD, Director of Advertising and Public Relations, Royal Typewriter Company, Inc. A Division of Litton Industries

D. E. BOCKOVER, Advertising & Sales Promotion Manager, Carrier Air Conditioning Company

RICHARD M. BODEN, Promotion Group Supervisor, Advertising & Sales Promotion, The Babcock & Wilcox Company

M. W. BOLSTER, Manager, Commercial Products Advertising and Sales Promotion Department, Shell Oil Company

FRANCIS L. BRIA, Manager, Product Promotions, Motorola Semiconductor Products Inc.

J. S. BROWN, Advertising Manager, Reichold Chemicals, Inc.

TED BURKE, Director, Public Relations and Advertising, The Garrett Corporation

TED BUSCH, Sales Manager, Shooting Equipment, Inc.

M. V. BUZZI, Media Manager, The Firestone Tire & Rubber Company

A. W. CAMERON, Advertising Manager, ITT Semiconductors

ALEC CAMERON, Manager, Marketing Services, ITT Semiconductors

RICHARD H. CAMPBELL, Manager, Advertising and Sales Promotion, Millers Falls Co.

WAYNE E. CHAMBERS, JR., Advertising Coordinator, Aluminum Company of America

DARDEN CHAMBLISS, Director of Communications, The Aluminum Association

JOHN M. CLAMPITT, Director of Advertising, United Air Lines

ARTHUR P. CLARK, Director of Communications, Basic Incorporated

R. W. CLARK, Sales Manager, Detrex Chemical Industries, Inc.

H. WALTON CLOKE, Vice-President, Corporate Public Relations and Advertising, American Can Company

J. W. COHOE, Advertising Manager, Corporate Staff, Ex-Cell-O Corporation

CONRAD H. COLLIER, Director, Advertising and Public Relations, Tenneco, Inc.

MISS BARBARA CONWAY, Manager, Special Advertising Programs, Eastern Air Lines Incorporated

J. T. D. CORNWELL, JR., Advertising and Sales Promotion Manager, Celanese Chemical Company, A Division of Celanese Corporation

D. GREGG CUMMINGS, Advertising Manager, Electro-Motive Division, General Motors Corporation

JOHN CUNIN, Bearings, Inc.

WES CURRY, Sales Promotion Supervisor, Packard Instrument Company, Inc.

WM. B. DAUB, Advertising Manager, Industrial Products, Sun Oil Company

FRANK E. DAVIS, JR., Director of Advertising, Koppers Company, Inc.

JAMES DEAN, Advertising Manager, McGregor Division, Brunswick Corporation

JOHN L. DEFAZIO, Marketing Communications Representative, Electric Components and Specialty Products, Westinghouse Electric Corporation

E. A. DEHNER, Advertising and Sales Promotion Manager, Exide Industrial Marketing Division, ESB Incorporated

JAMES R. DEROSE, Advertising Manager, Soabar Company

MORRIS D. DETTMAN, Director, Advertising and Merchandising, Honeywell Inc.

JERRY DORFMAN, President, Protective Lining Corporation

WILLIAM T. DYER, Advertising Manager, Corning Electronics Products Division, Corning Glass Works

A. E. EGGERS, Advertising Manager, Residential Lighting Division, Thomas Industries Inc.

J. DAVID EHLERS, Advertising Manager, Mallory Battery Company, A Division of P.R. Mallory & Co., Inc.

ACKNOWLEDGEMENTS

RICHARD EHRLICH, Advertising Director, Hertz System, Inc.

JAMES ELDER, Sales Promotion Assistant, Holo-Krome Company

HERBERT H. FEINGOLD, Director, Corporate Planning, Servo Corporation of America

J. O. FERCH, Sales Department, Modern Equipment Company

G. D. FERREE, Chief, Product Information and Advertising, Chandler Evans Inc. Colt Industries

ROBERT D. FRENCH, Advertising Manager, Potlatch Forests, Inc.

B. T. FULLERTON, Director of Marketing, The Warner & Swasey Company

D. F. GAINES, Advertising Manager, The National Cash Register Company

S. M. GATES, Assistant Director of Advertising, Republic Steel Corporation

DONALD GAY, Vice-President—Sales, The Bristol Brass Corporation

MEYER GOLDBERG, General Sales Manager, Wide World Photos, Inc.

C. R. GRAHAM, Advertising Manager, Industrial Products, The Goodyear Tire & Rubber Company

JAMES W. GRAHAM, Manager Marketing Services, Brush Instruments Division, Clevite Corporation

DONALD G. HANSEN, Pitney-Bowes, Inc.

DON HARGRAVE, Advertising Manager, Siliconix Incorporated

J. E. HARTMAN, Assistant to the Director, Marketing Communications, Westinghouse Electric Corporation

HOWARD H. HAVEMEYER, Thomson Industries, Inc.

W. H. HELFRICK, Advertising Manager, Landis Machine Company

W. H. HENDERSON, JR., Director of Corporate Relations, North American Car Corp.

EDWARD D. HENDRICKSON, President, Hendrickson Manufacturing Company

DONALD F. HENRY, Marketing Services Manager, Anaconda Aluminum Company

M. M. HERRICK, Sales Promotion & Advertising Manager, Johnson Service Co.

F. LEROY HESS, Vice-President, Editorial Division, Standard Rate & Data Service, Inc.

J. R. HIGHT, Director, Public Relations and Advertising, Jones & Laughlin Steel Corp.

J. F. HOBBINS, Advertising Manager, The Anaconda Company

L. GREGORY HOOPER, Chicago Rawhide Manufacturing Company

JAMES J. HUBBARD, Account Executive, Marsteller Inc.

THOMAS G. HUBER, Director, Jeolco, Inc.

DAVID P. HUGHES, JR., Advertising Manager, E. F. Houghton Company

JIM HULL, Sales Promotion, Magcobar, One of the Dresser Industries

HENRY H. HUNTER, Vice-President, Olin Mathieson Chemical Corporation

L. J. IANNUZZELLI, Manager, Power Semiconductor Advertising, RCA Electronic Components and Devices, RCA, Inc.

GLENN F. IHRIG, President, Wellman Dynamics Corporation

JAMES G. JOHNSON, Electrowriter Sales Manager, Victor Business Machines Group, Victor Comptometer Corporation

LAURENCE S. JOHNSON, Eva-Tone, Division of American Evatype Corporation

RICHARD C. JOHNSON, Advertising Director, H. B. Fuller Company

THE DARTNELL ADVERTISING HANDBOOK

EDGAR R. JONES, Publisher

MICHAEL R. KALBS, Advertising Manager, Brinkman Instruments

C. G. KENNEDY, Manager, Marketing Services, Clark Equipment Company

V. K. KENNEDY, Vice-President, Sales, Omark-Winslow Aerospace Tool Company

CHARLES M. KENT, Advertising/Merchandising Manager, 3M Company

H. KEYS, Unitron Instrument Company

JAMES KIPPS, Advertising and Sales Promotion Manager, Dura Business Machines, Division of Intercontinental Systems, Inc.

LEONARD A. KIRSCH, Director of Public Relations, Waldes Kohinoor, Inc.

ROBERT S. KNAPP, Advertising Manager, Sperry Gyroscope Company

MISS OLGA H. KNOEPKE, Argus Chemical Corporation

WALTER P. KOVAL, Director, Advertising and Public Relations, Ametek, Inc.

R. KRAL, Advertising Manager, Electric Motor Division, A.O. Smith Corporation

G. C. KROENING, Vice-President, Sales, Norplex Corporation

DAVID A. KURR, Director of Marketing, AMAX Aluminum Co., A Division of American Metal Climax, Inc.

MRS. JOAN R. KURTZ, Public Relations Department, Eastman Kodak Company

BRUCE F. LACENTRA, Director of Advertising, Friden, Inc., Division of The Singer Co.

FLOYD C. LACY, Public Relations Supervisor, Dana Corporation

JOHN W. LAMBERT, The Photography of H. Armstrong Roberts

FRANK LINSENMEYER, Manager of Marketing Services, The Rotor Tool Company, A Division of Cooper Industries, Inc.

T. L. LAPIN, Industrial Marketing Manager, Commercial Products, Kimberly Clark Corporation

G. B. LEOPARD, Manager Corporate Communications, Brown Engineering, A Teledyne Company

RALPH LEVINE, Assistant Counsel, Carter-Wallace, Inc.

LEON LEVITT, Manager, Advertising and Public Relations, Microdot Inc.

A. J. LIBERTY, Advertising Manager, American Optical Company

PAUL H. LOBIK, Advertising Manager, Coleman Instruments Corporation

M. L. LONG, Manager, Public Relations and Advertising, Air Products and Chemicals Incorporated

ODIS A. LONG, Data Presentation Manager, Texas Instruments Incorporated

The Late THADDEUS J. LOPATKA, Vice-President, Diamond T Motor Truck Co.

NORMAN G. MACKINNON, Director of Advertising, Grumman Aircraft Engineering Corporation

DONALD G. MAIZE, Director, Advertising and Sales Promotion, Weyerhaeuser Company

DONALD R. MAKINS, Manager of Advertising, Austin-Western Division, Baldwin-Lima-Hamilton Corporation

PAUL MARCOTT, Advertising Manager, Bell Helicopter Company, A Textron Company

S.V. MARINO, Assistant Vice-President-Sales, Pinkerton's, Inc.

WILLIAM F. MAY, Chairman, American Can Company

LOWELL G. MCCLENNING, Marketing Services, Fairchild Semiconductor, A Division of Fairchild Camera and Instrument Corporation

WILLIAM E. MCKIE, Assistant Advertising Manager, Dennison Manufacturing Co.

ACKNOWLEDGEMENTS

J. R. MCMENAMIN, Director of Advertising, Uniroyal, Inc.

GEORGE A. MENTZER, Manager, Advertising Services, The B. F. Goodrich Company

ELDREDGE MILLER, Advertising Manager, Johns-Manville

WALT MILLER, Advertising Director, Sloan Instrument Corporation

J. A. MOIR, Advertising & Sales Promotion, General Electric Company

ROBERT D. MOORE, Assistant Advertising Manager, American Air Filter Company, Inc.

CHARLES J. MOSS, Manager Plastics Advertising, The Dow Chemical Company

WILLOUGHBY W. MOYER, Advertising Manager, Atlas Chemical Industries, Inc.

B. H. MUELLER, TRW Electro Insulation, TRW Inc.

JAMES H. MULLER, Sales Promotion Manager, Winchester Electronics Division, Litton Industries

DAVID L. NELSON, Marketing Manager, Micom Inc.

RAYMOND F. NEUZIL, Director of Corporate Communications, Szabo Food Service, Inc.

GAYNOR O'CORMAN, JR., Manager, Advertising Department, United Shoe Machinery Corporation

THOMAS A. O'GORMAN, Marketing Services Manager, Industrial Electronic Engineers, Inc.

R. F. OLSON, Director of Advertising, Rex Chainbelt, Inc.

WALTER J. O'NEILL, Advertising Manager, Standard Pressed Steel Company

RICHARD C. OSWANT, Advertising Manager, Chemical Division, PPG Industries, Inc.

JOHN E. OWENS, Assistant Advertising Manager, Lindberg Hevi-Duty, Division of Sola Basic Industries

FRED A. PAINE, Manager, Administration and Operations, A&SP—Marketing Services, Worthington Corporation

ROBERT M. PALMER, Vice-President—Marketing, Lindberg Hevi-Duty, Division of Sola Basic Industries

RICHARD R. PAPE, Manager, Nielsen Clearing House

R. S. PARKER, Advertising and Sales Promotion Manager, The Standard Register Co.

A. K. PARRISH, Vice-President, Automotive Group of TRW Inc.

MISS DODE PENROD, Advertising Manager, The Flying Tiger Line Inc.

ROBERT C. PIERSON, Manager, Advertising and Sales Promotion, Fairchild-Davidson, A Division of Fairchild Camera and Instrument Corporation

ARNOLD I. PLANT, H. Klaff & Company

DICK POWELL, Hamlin, Inc.

MISS GEORGIA PRASSOS, Advertising and Sales Promotion, X-acto Precision Tools

W. S. PUNTON, Commercial Advertising Manager, Mobil Oil Corporation

F. J. RASKOPF, Director of Advertising, Collins Radio Company

R. J. REES, Divisional Advertising Supervisor, Wright Hoist Division, American Chain & Cable Company, Inc.

JOHN P. READING, Director of Public Relations, Cincinnati Milacron

W. A. REEDY, Senior Editor, Advertising Publications, Eastman Kodak Company

MISS ADRIANNE REICHEG, Alcan Sales Inc.

JAMES L. RICHARDSON, Director, Public Relations and Advertising, Combustion Engineering, Inc.

N. C. RICHARDSON, Advertising Manager, Waterbury Farrel, A Textron Company

G. M. ROBERTSON, Manager, Advertising Services and Measurement, General Electric Company

L.G. ROBLYER, Advertising Manager, Bendix Motor Components Division, The Bendix Corporation

RICHARD F. ROPER, Director, Public Relations and Advertising, Computer Sciences Corporation

A. M. RUNG, Director of Public Relations and Advertising, Chicago, Burlington & Quincy Railroad Company

GERALD J. RYAN, Senior Advertising Manager, Sylvania Electric Products, Inc.

W. J. ST. ONGE, JR., Advertising Manager, The Torrington Company

K. SAITOH, Executive Vice-President, Sharp Electronics Corporation

ROBERT A. SALAMONE, Director of Operations and Marketing, Dyna-Quip, A Division of Stile-Craft Manufacturers Inc.

RICHARD J. SANDRETTI, Public Relations Coordinator, Koehring Company

D. S. SAURMAN, Advertising Manager, Simonds Abrasive Company

H. K. SAXE, International Business Machines Corporation

FRED SCHAUB, Manager, Analytical Instruments Division, LKB Instruments, Inc.

CHAS. R. SHANK, Advertising Manager, T.B. Wood's Sons Company

E. M. SHANKS, Advertising Manager, Rust-Oleum Corporation

L. R. SHAULL, Manager—Public Relations, Airtemp Division, Chrysler Corp.

J. M. SHEEHAN, Director of Advertising and Public Relations, General American Transportation Corporation

R. R. SHEPHERD, Marketing Communications Manager, Westinghouse Electric Corp.

JOHN M. SHEVIAK, Director of Advertising, Parker-Hannifin Industrial Group

J. A. SHIELDS, Vice-President, Advertising, Shaw-Walker

SUKEHIRO SHIONOYA, OSG Tap and Die, Inc.

MORTON W. SIAS, Manager, Advertising and Public Relations, Brown Company

ROBERT SILVERT, Director of Customer Relations, Perrygraf Corporation

VIRGIL L. SIMPSON, Special Assistant, E.I. Du Pont de Nemours & Company Inc.

WILLIAM J. SIMS, Department Manager, Hog Chows Advertising and Sales Promotion, Ralston Purina Company

S. A. SKILNYK, Advertising Manager, Bourns Inc.

DONALD L. SMITH, Product Marketing Manager, Warner-Chilcott Laboratories Instruments Division

D. M. SMITH, Director, Advertising and Public Relations, Burroughs Corporation

ROBERT O. SNELLING, President, Snelling and Snelling

WILLIAM J. SPADA, Advertising Manager, Walter Kidde & Company, Inc.

JAMES D. SPIVEY, Vice-President—Marketing and Sales, True-Trace Corporation

S. G. SPRAGENS, Vice-President—Marketing, Pacific Plantronics, Inc.

ANTHONY STACHELCZYK, Sales Promotion Manager, The Echlin Manufacturing Co.

J. WOOLSEY STANTON, President, Fancy Frozen Foods Company of Florida

ACKNOWLEDGEMENTS

Lawrence V. Stapleton, Vice-President, Advertising & Sales Promotion, Trans World Airlines

J. E. Starbuck, Director, Marketing Communications, Douglas Aircraft Company, Inc.

R. E. Stauffer, Jr., Advertising Manager, Grey-Rock, Division of Raybestos-Manhattan, Inc.

W. R. Sterling, Director of Advertising and Public Relations, Baker Division, Otis Elevator Company

Neil P. Stewart, Divisional Manager, Advertising & Sales Promotion, Crown Zellerbach Corporation

Parker Stough, Advertising/Sales Promotion Manager, I-T-E Circuit Breaker Co.

DeLisle Sudduth, Sales Manager, Genisco Technology Corporation

Bob Sutphen, The Dick Sutphen Studio Inc.

Don Teer, Publications Advertising Coordinator, Hewlett-Packard

George E. Tibball, Advertising Coordinator, Princeton Applied Research Corp.

M. C. Tobias, General Advertising Manager, Reynolds Metals Company

James E. Tobin, Manager of Sales Promotion, Anaconda American Brass Co.

C. F. Toll, General Manager, Advertising and Publicity, The Sherwin-Williams Co.

B. S. Tooker, Manager of Advertising, Fuller Transmission Division, Eaton Yale & Towne Inc.

William C. Tracey, Martin Marietta Corporation

C. S. Turpin, Manager, Marketing Services, AVCO Bay State Abrasives

Judd Tuttle, Advertising Manager, American Monorail

John W. Tyhacz, Advertising Manager, De Laval Separator Company

P. B. Utiger, Advertising Manager, Sinclair Refining Company

Wim van der Graaf, Advertising Department, E.I. Du Pont de Nemours & Company

J. B. Vanderzee, Advertising Manager, Autolite-Ford Parts Division, Ford Motor Co.

Theodore N. Voss, Domestic Advertising Manager, Polaroid Corporation

L. G. Waddell, Sales Manager, The Prime-Mover Company

Ed Wahl, Gits Bros. Mfg. Co.

John F. Wallace, Manager, Machinery and Allied Industries, United States Steel Corporation

J. J. Ward, Jr., Manager of Advertising, Pittsburgh Steel Company

S. D. Warren Company

Herbert N. Washburn, Advertising and Sales Promotion Mgr., International Equipment Company

C. C. Weiss, The EIS Automotive Corporation

Thomas R. Weiss, Manager, Advertising and Communications, Owens-Illinois

Richard D. Wentworth, Product Manager, Shooting Equipment, Inc.

Bob White, Jennison-Wright Corporation

Robert M. Whitney, Director of Division Advertising, Eaton Yale & Towne

George Wickstrom, Advertising Manager, Sealed Power Corporation

A. H. Widowit, Jr., Manager of Advertising, Universal Oil Products Company

R. N. Wilkinson, Advertising Manager, Caterpillar Tractor Co.

H. A. WILLIAMS, Vice-President and General Manager, Electronic Components Division, Stackpole Carbon Company

J. A. WILLIAMS, Manager, Advertising and Publicity, M&T Chemicals, Inc.

DOUGLAS WILLIAMSON, Advertising Manager, Handy & Harman

JOHN T. WILLOW, Manager, Advertising and Sales Promotion, Hammermill Paper Co.

G. H. WILSON, Manager, Sales Promotion & Advertising, Federal Products Corp.

JAMES D. WOOD, Director, Press Relations and Advertising, Sperry Rand Corp.

ROBERT S. WOODBURY, Director, Public Relations, Mathatronics, A Division of Barry Wright Corporation

R. S. YATES, Advertising Assistant, The Timken Roller Bearing Company

ED YOTKA, Sales Manager, Compix, Commercial Photography Division of United Press International

JAMES L. YOUNG, Advertising Manager, Dempster Brothers Inc.

V. J. YUNKER, Assistant to the General Sales Manager, The Mechanex Corp.

NINON DE ZARA, Sales Promotion Manager, Amphenol RF Division

I'd like to thank the following advertising people—wonderful people, one and all—for their gracious help and encouragement in revising this book. Without them, I couldn't have done the job.

THOMAS R. BRAMSON, President and Publisher, *Production*

HARRY B. DOYLE, JR., Advertising Sales, McGraw-Hill Publications, Denver

WILLIAM J. DWYER, Vice-President, Technical Publishing Company

HOWARD FISCHER, former Vice-President, Frye-Sills, Inc.

MYRA GISH, Secretary, CF&I Steel Corporation

BARBARA HANSON, Advertising and Sales Promotion Manager, Thomas Publishing Co.

WAYNE JARVIS, General Manager, Kistler Graphics, Inc.

ELISABETH M. KITTREDGE, Secretary, Technical Publishing Company

RAYMOND D. LARSON, Vice-President, *MacRae's Blue Book*

THOMAS J. McELHINNY, Regional Sales Manager, Buttenheim Publishing Corporation

WILLIAM H. NIMITZ, Advertising Department, E.I. Du Pont de Nemours, Inc.

JAMES T. QUILLINAN, President, Color Technique, Inc.

FRED STANLEY, Publisher, *Product Design & Development*

GENE WYENETH, Publisher, *Engineering News-Record* and *Construction Methods & Equipment*

And my special thanks to two great guys who have done a lot for me, on this revision and over the years:

JACK KAY, Regional Vice-President, Chilton Company

WIM VAN DER GRAAF, Supervisor, Advertising Department, E. I. Du Pont de Nemours, Inc.

Dick Stansfield
Pueblo, Colorado
1982

Chapter 1

DEPARTMENT ORGANIZATION
AND FUNCTIONS

ATTEMPTING to draw up a nice, neat organizational chart for the typical industrial advertising department is something like trying to describe the average sunset. It can't be done because there isn't any such thing.

Advertising departments are like the companies they serve. They vary widely in size and organizational complexity. This is due to differences in the number of product lines manufactured, the number of markets in which these products are sold, distribution channels, company marketing objectives, advertising objectives, the competitive climate and, of course, the size of the company.

Assume for a moment that there is such a thing as a typical advertising department in a typical company which sells a typical product through typical distribution channels to typical customers. Makeup of this department is, unfortunately for the typical company, the archaic one-man-and-a-girl operation common in industry since the birth of advertising. This one-man department almost invariably reports to the sales manager. The work load is heavy, and consists of a mixture of space ads, product literature and direct-mail pieces; thrown at him from time to time are requests to "write a nice speech for the president to give at the local lodge," and similar odds and ends. After all, he is the company's communications specialist.

Change in the Wind

Happily for industry, this casual attitude toward—and reluctance to provide sufficient funds for—a key staff function is fast becoming a thing of the past.

This is not due to a spontaneous burst of philanthropic generosity on corporate management's part, however. Rather, it is the result of the realization that, in an increasingly competitive economy something *must* be done to reduce the cost of sales and at the same time increase total sales volume.

Making generalizations is usually a time-wasting exercise, although occasionally a valid one crops up. One is that in the overwhelming majority of small- and medium-sized industrial companies the level of marketing sophistication is low when compared to the industrial giants, and even more so when compared to leading manufacturers of consumer products.

In the modest-sized industrial firms advertising is still regarded strictly as a tool "to help sell the product." And, incredible as it may seem, attitude studies consistently show that almost half of the presidents of these companies have either a negative attitude toward advertising, or have serious mental reservations as to its true effectiveness. It is inconceivable to these business executives that advertising can solve other communications problems for their companies.

This naiveté, this failure to exploit fully marketing's most versatile tool, is reflected in a simple organizational structure. The advertising manager, who is not really a member of the marketing team, generally reports to the director of sales, or, if the title exists, to the director of marketing. Advertising, such a potent and productive force when used properly, makes a minimum contribution to the sales success of such firms because it is not permitted to do otherwise. The straight-line organizational chart common in this type firm is illustrated here.

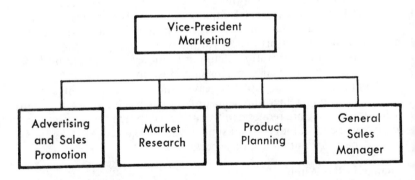

Attitudes within the company affect the organization of the advertising department and its place within the company's structure. Whether a company is marketing oriented, or product oriented, whether it is aggressive or complacent, whether it is growth minded or content to drift, are but a few of the factors affecting advertising's importance in the corporate scheme of things. They also affect how the advertising department is organized, and determine to a large extent how good a job advertising is allowed to do.

Large companies with a history of success have a large and effective marketing arm. The advertising department in such companies is highly competent and is departmentalized for maximum efficiency, as shown on page 26. It is in such surroundings, where advertising is recognized as perhaps the most important marketing service, that it makes such a significant contribution. It is here that it is permitted to.

House-Agency Advertising

Hybrid advertising departments, so called because they actually are a combination advertising department and advertising agency, are on the wane. Few really large ones exist in industry now, although they attained a considerable degree of acceptance 20 years or so ago.

Deere & Company, a leading manufacturer of agricultural, construction, and forestry equipment, lawn and garden products, and snowmobiles, is a good example of the house-agency type of operation. They have a staff of over 150 who are responsible for the administration, creation, and production of the majority of John Deere's worldwide advertising.

Administrative and supervisory personnel normally found in any industrial advertising department are present, and function in similar capacities at Deere. In addition they have personnel encountered at no other place except in a recognized agency. Copywriters, art directors, media and production personnel, traffic, all are represented.

Deere also has a large well-equipped photographic department with photographers, photographic laboratory, and studio facilities. Its staff is able to produce top-quality illustrative photos, either in the studio or at some remote location, in black and white, or color. Few advertising departments can say as much, for this is a far cry from the average ad man's ability to grab a company camera and take a product photo and save calling in an expensive commercial photographer.

Just as input, in terms of talent, is high at Deere, output of the advertising department is of a very high caliber. Space ads and collateral material are as thoroughly professional as any produced by the best Madison Avenue shop.

Deere agricultural, industrial and some international space is placed by the media section. Deere receives the customary commission on the space expenditures.

The decline and fall from favor of the hybrid department is due to a number of things. High on the list, although not necessarily at the top, is the staggering cost. Competent creative people command excellent

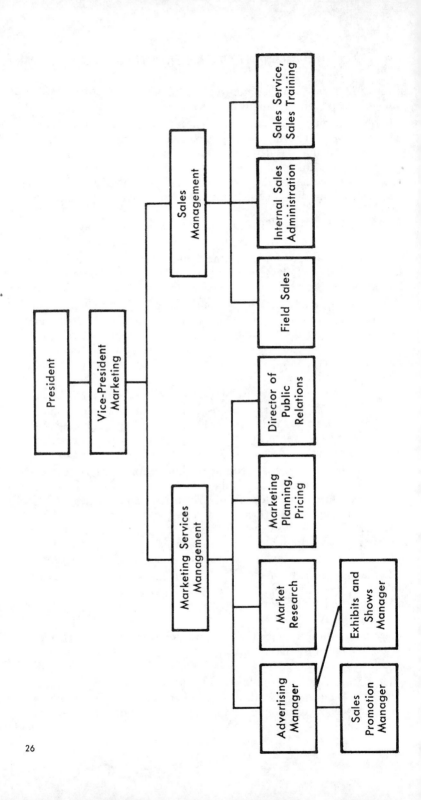

salaries, as do those in associated advertising functions. Add salaries to the fringe costs customary in industry, and the result is a cost so high few companies can, or will, bear it. This cost would not have to be tacked onto the normal cost of the department if the company went the usual route and retained an advertising agency to create and produce its material.

Even more important, however, is the lack of fresh thinking. Most companies which have tried and rejected the house-agency concept did so on this score. There's a tendency, apparently an inexorable one, for house-agency personnel to go stale. The creative people tend to take the same tack, to use the same "tried and proved" approach to different problems year after year. Ultimately the unspoken goal of some house shops seems to be to achieve a medium grade of mediocrity, to produce ads and literature that are neither good nor bad, material that cannot be faulted on any specific point. They achieve this, but also achieve a communications program with a deadly-dull sameness to it; it is certainly far from exciting and vital and alive.

Geographical locations share the blame, too. Isolation breeds stagnation. If the creative advertising man is a distance from a large metropolitan center, there is little opportunity to talk shop with fellow professionals—excepting those with whom he works. And in the house agency there is no constant infusion of new blood and new ideas as the result of personnel turnover which is accepted as normal in the agency field; in the house agency, advertising men become imbued with the company attitude in all things, including that of long tenure. In any event, lack of frequent contact with others in the field outside the company contributes an intangible something, perhaps a frame of mind, that makes the creative spark sputter.

How Du Pont Keeps on Top

At Du Pont, the Marketing Communications Department provides advertising, product information and sales aids/promotion services to the Company's Industrial and Staff Departments. It is charged with specifying the role each of these functions should play in the marketing communications program for a given product or service. It is also charged with advocating their use whenever they are likely to have a favorable impact on profits and, with equal vigor, must recommend against using them when a profitable return is unlikely.

The department is located in Wilmington, Delaware, site of Du Pont's corporate headquarters. Such centralization allows the required contact between marketing communications professionals and the marketing management responsible for the various product lines supported by the communications effort.

Because some 90% of Du Pont's products are sold to customers who combine them with other materials to make a finished product, most Du Pont marketing communications are oriented to the industrial marketplace. The product lines vary widely—including bulk chemical commodities, sophisticated electronic instrumentation, plastics, carpet fibers and many more. Such diversity provides a broad range of assignments for the department's personnel.

Corporate sales exceeded 13 billion dollars in 1980. The marketing communications support for this sales volume is large. Some 800 marketing communications budgets are prepared each year. The advertising group produces more than 840 new advertisments which appear in more than 1,000 different magazines and newspapers for a total of more than 8,000 insertions. This group also produces over 130 radio and TV commercials and over 18,000 pieces of literature. The product publicity group produces more than 650 releases, conducts more than a dozen press conferences and participates in more than 300 trade shows annually.

The organization which delivers this work is shown in the chart. Heading the department is a Director, with eight Division Managers reporting to the Director. These managers are responsible for all activities of the department.

Five of the divisions provide services to one or more industrial departments and the various products produced by these departments. Reporting to the Division Managers are some 20 Marketing Communications Managers, who have the direct responsibility for managing the communications programs for an entire department or specific division of a department, depending upon the product lines involved. Each Marketing Communications Manager, in turn, has responsibility for a number of communications professionals, of whom there are approximately 100 in the department.

Also in these divisions are groups of editors and technical writers, who produce 45 external house organs and newsletters, all of them sent to closely controlled lists of customers and prospects. Most are written and edited by those with marketing communications assignments, but a select group of senior writers and editors in the Publications Section produce the "Du Pont Magazine," "Refinisher News," and five other magazines with large circulations.

While these communications divisions are the center of the department, the expertise of Marketing Communications people working directly with industrial departments is greatly enhanced by the assistance of staff specialists within the Marketing Communications Department. A brief description of some of the departmental staff groups provides an appreciation of the versatility needed to make Du Pont marketing communications worthy to speak for the Company.

The following sections are within the Media & Marketing Communications Services Division:

The *Accounting Section* handles the accounting for all expenses and provides monthly budget status reports for the Product Marketing Communications groups. These people also provide expertise in media coordination and cooperative advertising. Media coordinators consolidate media purchases for all Du Pont advertising units and negotiate favorable rates. Cooperative advertising counselors help to develop co-op programs and then monitor customers' compliance within the terms of the contracts.

The *Audio-Visual Group* provides technicians and equipment for audio-visual presentations, maintains the Company's library of sound effects and coordinates the procurement of audio-visual materials for all Du Pont industrial and staff departments.

The *Exhibits Group* assists Marketing Communications people with trade show space and selection, booth design, construction, installation and dismantling.

The *Procurement Group* purchases advertising premiums and sales promotion materials. In addition, it contracts for services from a wide variety of specialized vendors such as coupon redemption houses, publicity agencies and merchandising manpower sources.

The *Production/Graphics Group* ensures that the quality of printed material is high and that the price for this quality is appropriate.

Another division is the Marketing Research Division, whose professionals put their expertise to work by consulting with industrial department marketing groups and Marketing Communications Department personnel on when and how to use research. An important part of their work is the design and testing of new research techniques for both advertising and marketing research. Their innovative work has earned national recognition for this division as a pioneer in research into business strategy, marketing operations, market measurement and the effectiveness of mass communications. Close relationships are maintained with consultants from the academic world, and a Fellowship allows graduate students interested in industrial marketing to spend a year working within the division.

Finally, the Personnel Division is responsible for recruiting communications personnel and also for the department's training and development program, which involves every facet of stimulating professional growth of Du Pont's communications personnel. Included are individual performance reviews, public speaking courses, workshops, management courses and other educational opportunities directed to a graduate degree, for which Du Pont pays the tuition.

In addition to handling domestic Marketing communications, the Department is responsible for the Company's *international marketing communications* as well. In recent years, Du Pont has become a truly international organization, moving from the traditional domestic-export operation it once was. Most operating departments have worldwide business managers who prepare worldwide product missions and marketing strategies. These worldwide business managers expect their local subsidiary managers to contribute to the worldwide missions and strategies by developing and executing local tactics.

Since advertising and other forms of marketing communications must reflect the marketing organizations, Du Pont is developing a worldwide organization of communications professionals.

The parent Company Marketing Communications Department has established an International Division based in Wilmington. The Division Manager-International works with the operating departments (with product profit and loss responsibility) and subsidiary management (with country responsibility). He works with the International regions and subsidiaries to determine if the business can justify local professionals. If so, the International Division Manager assists country managment in recruiting and training local nationals and in monitoring their performance. In addition, he ensures that communications people working on like businesses around the world exchange ideas and plans by communicating regularly with each other.

Du Pont communications professionals are located in six countries in Europe, with a regional manager based in Geneva. They support the businesses in Europe, Mid-East and Africa. In the Asia/Pacific Region, marketing communications people are located in Japan, Singapore and Australia, with the regional manager operating out of Tokyo. The Latin American regional manager is based in Wilmington, and there are local nationals in Brazil and Argentina.

The regional advertising agency networks are used in Europe; one working on consumer products, the other on industrial. Local agencies work with the local Du Pont nationals in the Latin American and Asia/Pacific regions.

The Full-Service Agency

By the early 1900's the full-service ad agency had arrived. As population grew, business grew. Advertising kept pace. Not only did advertising volume expand, but advertising was called upon to accept more tasks and to solve more and more business communications

DEPARTMENT ORGANIZATION AND FUNCTIONS

ADVERTISING
AGENCIES

DIRECTOR — H. LLOYD TAYLOR

DIVISION MANAGER — A. W. BALLENTINE
- INTERNATIONAL DEPARTMENT — MARKETING COMMUNICATIONS MANAGER — R. A. HOTCHKISS
- PUBLICATIONS SECTION — MANAGER — J. R. MURPHY
- STAFF DEPARTMENTS — ADVERTISING & PROMOTION SUPERVISOR — J. C. DILTS — — — — — — — — — — — — — — — AYER
- EUROPE, MID-EAST/AFRICA — PUBLIC AFFAIRS &
    ADVERTISING DEPARTMENT — DIRECTOR — J. ADSHEAD, JR. (Geneva)
- ASIA/PACIFIC — MARKETING COMMUNICATIONS MANAGER — R. E. HUTTER (Tokyo)
    DU PONT (Australia) Ltd. — MARKETING COMMUNICATIONS &
    PUBLIC AFFAIRS MANAGER — W. M. THOMSON (Sydney)
- DU PONT DO BRASIL S.A. — MARKETING COMMUNICATIONS MANAGER — J. CATARINACHO (Sao Paulo)
- DUCILO S.A. — MARKETING COMMUNICATIONS MANAGER — E. J. LERTORA (Buenos Aires)

DIVISION MANAGER — S. P. BLISH
- PHOTO PRODUCTS DEPARTMENT
    - PHOTOSYSTEMS DIVISION — MARKETING COMMUNICATIONS MANAGER — R. T. ELDRIDGE — — — — — — — — — — AYER
    - CLINICAL SYSTEMS, ANALYTICAL INSTRUMENTS AND BIOMEDICAL PRODUCTS DIVISIONS
        MARKETING COMMUNICATIONS MANAGER — T. E. MINNICH— — — — — — — — — — — — — — — — — — AYER
    - BERG ELECTRONICS AND ELECTRONIC SPECIALTIES DIVISIONS
        MARKETING COMMUNICATIONS MANAGER — C. H. WEBER — — — — — — — — — — — — — — — — — KELLY
- CARPET FIBERS, TEXTILE FIBERS DEPARTMENT
    MARKETING COMMUNICATIONS MANAGER — J. B. BRETT, JR. — — — — — — — — — — — — — — — — — — BBDO
- INDUSTRIAL FIBERS & SPUNBONDED PRODUCTS DIVISIONS, TEXTILE FIBERS DEPARTMENT
    MARKETING COMMUNICATIONS MANAGER — G. W. HALE— AYER
- TEXTILE FIBERS DEPARTMENT — AYER & BBDO
- BIOCHEMICALS DEPARTMENT
    - ENDO LABORATORIES
        MARKETING COMMUNICATIONS MANAGER — E. P. SMITH — — — — — — — — — — — — — — — — — — S & H, BC

DIVISION MANAGER — C. E. CROWLEY
- FABRICS & FINISHES DEPARTMENT
    - HOME & AUTOMOTIVE PRODUCTS — MARKETING COMMUNICATIONS MANAGER — J. S. SWAJESKI
        - AUTOMOTIVE PRODUCTS — BBDO
        - CORIAN® PRODUCTS — AYER
    - CONSUMER PAINT AND REFINISH — MARKETING COMMUNICATIONS MANAGER — J. M. MURRAY, II — — — — — — AYER
    - TEFLON® FINISHES, INDUSTRIAL FINISHES, INTERNATIONAL FINISHES,
      MAINTENANCE FINISHES, PACKAGING FINISHES, APPLIED TECHNOLOGY,
      INDUSTRIAL SPECIALTIES — MARKETING COMMUNICATIONS MANAGER — J. E. SLY — — — — — — — — — AYER
- GENERAL COMPANY — CORPORATE ADVERTISING — MARKETING COMMUNICATIONS MANAGER — R. J. ALFANO— — — — BBDO
- REMINGTON ARMS COMPANY — ADVERTISING DIRECTOR — E. J. GARRITY (Bridgeport) — — — — — — — — — — R–H

DIVISION MANAGER — H. E. DAVIS
- POLYMER PRODUCTS DEPARTMENT
    - ENGINEERING PLASTIC MATERIALS & FLUOROPOLYMERS DIVISIONS
        MARKETING COMMUNICATIONS MANAGER — H. B. HORNING — — — — — — — — — — — — — — — — — AYER
    - ELASTOMERS DIVISION
        MARKETING COMMUNICATIONS MANAGER — R. E. WILLIAMS — — — — — — — — — — — — — — — — — AYER
    - ETHYLENE POLYMERS DIVISION
        MARKETING COMMUNICATIONS MANAGER — J. H. MC DIVIT — — — — — — — — — — — — — — — — — AYER
    - INDUSTRIAL FILMS AND FLEXIBLE PACKAGING DIVISIONS
        MARKETING COMMUNICATIONS MANAGER — EILEEN SHEA — — — — — — — — — — — — — — — — — AYER
    - PLASTIC PRODUCTS DIVISION
        MARKETING COMMUNICATIONS MANAGER — J. B. BOYER — J. H. MC DIVIT — — — — — — — — — — — — AYER
    - CORPORATE AUTOMOTIVE COMMUNICATIONS
        MARKETING COMMUNICATIONS MANAGER — H. B. HORNING — — — — — — — — — — — — — — — — — AYER
- TEXTILE FIBERS, APPAREL & HOME FURNISHINGS — PRODUCT INFORMATION MANAGER — J. MORTENSON
- DU PONT CANADA INC. — MARKETING SERVICES DIVISION MANAGER — C. D. CLARANCE (Mississauga)
- PUBLIC AFFAIRS DEPARTMENT

DIVISION MANAGER — R. W. NIGHTENGALE, JR.
- CHEMICALS AND PIGMENTS DEPARTMENT —
    MARKETING COMMUNICATIONS MANAGER — J. P. SWAN — — — — — — — — — — — — — — — — — — — AYER & BBDO
- PETROCHEMICALS DEPARTMENT — MARKETING COMMUNICATIONS MANAGER — J. C. MANEVAL — — — — — — — — — AYER
- BIOCHEMICALS DEPARTMENT
    - AGRICHEMICALS MARKETING DIVISION
        MARKETING COMMUNICATIONS MANAGER — NILS KWICK — — — — — — — — — — — — — — — — — — R–H
- PRESS OFFICE
    - PRESS OFFICER — M. R. TYLER
- HOTEL DU PONT

DIVISION MANAGER, MARKETING RESEARCH — J. O. CORNER
- MARKETING RESEARCH FELLOW — I. GROSS
- MANAGER — R. C. GRASS
- MANAGER — J. B. FREY
- MANAGER — E. S. ERICKSON, JR.
- MANAGER — D. W. BARTGES

DIVISION MANAGER, MEDIA & MKTG. COMMUNICATIONS SERVICES — A. B. BAKER
- MANAGER — PRODUCTION/GRAPHICS — T. J. NIEMKIEWICZ
    - MANAGER — AUDIO-VISUAL — W. D. DAVIS
- MANAGER — ACCOUNTING — D. T. SMITH
- MANAGER — MEDIA/PROMOTIONAL AIDS — P. J. TRAINOR

PERSONNEL & EMPLOYEE RELATIONS MANAGER — C. P. SHERAN
- OFFICE SERVICES MANAGER — E. CORRIDORI

KEY TO ADVERTISING AGENCIES	
AYER	— N. W. AYER, INC.
BBDO	— BATTEN, BARTON, DURSTINE & OSBORN, INC.
BC	— BARNUM COMMUNICATIONS
KELLY	— KELLY ADVERTISING, INC.
R–H	— RUMRILL-HOYT, INC.
S & H	— SUDLER & HENNESSEY, INC.

NO. 10

The advertising department of E. I. Du Pont de Nemours & Company is large but not overstaffed in relation to its many responsibilities.

problems. Business growth accelerated, as did the investment in advertising, for one simple reason: advertising paid an outstanding return on the investment. That is why—the realization that advertising is not an expense but is an investment that returns a profit—today's investment in national advertising in the United States is more than $27 billion. This investment is larger than the gross combined sales of Xerox, Texas Instruments, Westinghouse Electric and Minnesota Mining & Manufacturing, all nice solvent enterprises.

Cynics and fast-buck misanthropic exposé artists to the contrary, one thing is certain: Advertising can legitimately claim the major share of the credit for making more goods available to more people at lower cost, for building our brand-name system, for playing a key role in creating a continuing demand for newer and better products, and for exerting a powerful influence toward development of a mass production, mass distribution, mass consumption economy. It is nothing short of sheer tragedy that there is no possible way to measure the incalculable contribution advertising has made to the growth of our economy during the last half-century. If such data could, by some magical means, be developed, advertising's detractors would be effectively and quickly silenced. It is no exaggeration to say that without advertising the world's most dynamic, most productive economy would not exist.

Signs for the Formal Gardens

Exactly what functions legitimately belong in the advertising department is a touchy subject. It is a real bone of contention in many companies, with the ad manager insisting the department is unjustly charged with chores and costs not rightly a part of the advertising program. If the problem is analyzed objectively, it is immediately apparent in most instances that the complaint is well justified.

An example which may well become a classic throughout advertising concerns the flora-fancying wife of the president of a prosperous midwestern manufacturer. This charming lady's all-consuming passion was several immaculate acres of formal gardens of flowers of all descriptions on the family acreage in rural suburbia. The flowers were fed and watered and fertilized with tender loving care by two full-time gardeners, but they were as close to the lady's heart as if she had pollinated them herself.

It's a bit difficult to detect the common denominator of formal flower gardens and an industrial-advertising program. But the advertising manager of the lady's husband's firm found it, and upon doing so he grew into a fervid flower hater. Each year before the lady entertained (catered, of course) the local garden club, new identifying signs had to be made for each blooming species throughout the estate. Nice, neat little printed signs protected by cellophane made by the gardeners looked bourgeois. No class. They clashed with the quality surroundings. So the problem fell upon the broad shoulders of the husband's company's advertising manager, as obviously it should because he was a graphic arts expert. After all, he knew all about catalogs and signs for buildings and trade shows and that sort of thing.

This hapless chap decided that only the best was good enough for the wife of the boss. That meant type. So, after wasting most of a day getting the correct spellings (English and Latin) for the flowers from the gardeners—then checking *them* against library versions—the ad manager had type set. In a burst of pure inspiration he had the typographer pull etch proofs on the shop's proof press, using choice textured enamel stock. Then he had the paper laminated onto wood and the entire assembly coated with liquid plastic, transparent and colorless and waterproof. Appropriate rust-proof-brass hardware was bought and put on by a master mechanic in the toolroom. The proud ad manager hand delivered the job to the president's wife, which took only two-thirds of a day.

Cost of the entire operation, not counting the ad manager's time, the toolroom charge, and mileage on the car, was a bit short of $2,000. What transformed an otherwise normal advertising manager into a man with the unique idiosyncrasy of detesting flowers, all flowers, was what happened when he gave the bill to the president. He was told that it should be paid out of the advertising budget. Rationale was that the company "would receive much favorable publicity from the local newspapers as the result of the impression made by the flower gardens." Try as he might, the ad manager found it a bit difficult to judge just how much this would influence industrial purchasers of his company's products—particularly those a thousand miles away.

Admittedly, this case is unusual. But it is undisputable that a vast gray area exists when it comes to what should be charged to the advertising department, for there are no hard-and-fast rules as to what is desirable or undesirable, of what is right and what is wrong. Differences of opinion are usually resolved with a liberal dose of that old bromide, company policy. Policy itself is merely precedent set by a number of people over a number of years in a number of different marketing situations. One thing is certain, though. Regardless of whether the ad manager considers his position on legitimate functions and charges tenable or untenable, he might just as well reconcile himself to engaging in a number of skirmishes on this subject every year at budget time, and with relentless regularity throughout the year. Sacred cows die hard and company attitudes don't change overnight.

What the Ad Department Shouldn't Do

Before getting into functions which rightfully fall to the advertising department, let's be negative and take a look at activities which do *not*. These items have been rejected by an overwhelming majority of well-run industrial companies, although there is by no means unanimity of thought on every one. Most are self-explanatory, although some bear discussion. It goes without saying that, while the advertising department should not be charged with many of these functions, a large number of them will be handled by the department because its personnel are the only ones in the company qualified to do the job. Functions not an integral part of advertising as far as the budget is concerned are:

Corporate advertising

Travel expense for nonadvertising personnel

> Annual reports.
> Employee welfare activity.
> Internal house organ.
> Company recreational program.
> Christmas gifts to employees.
> Christmas gifts to dealers, jobbers, or representatives.
> Company Christmas cards.
> Business cards.
> Letterheads and envelopes.
> Entertaining customers and prospects.
> Hospitality suites at conventions, shows, etc.
> Product tests.
> Boxes, packages, cartons, and labels.
> Premiums, spiffs, "deal" merchandise.
> Charitable donations.
> Salesmen's samples.
> Salesmen's sample cases.
> Binders.
> Proposal covers.

Price lists.

Price books.

Cost of distribution of literature to field force.

Corporate literature (in multidivision companies).

Signs on factories or office buildings.

Burden (rent, light, heat, maintenance of advertising-department office space).

Telephone and telegraph.

General trade-association memberships.

Reprints of magazine articles.

Showrooms.

Market research.

Office supplies.

Product displays in offices or reception areas.

Production expense of signs for president's wife's formal flower garden.

The Budget

That corporate advertising is a necessity is not disputed in reasonably sophisticated circles. Even corporate presidents, who tend to take a dim view of advertising per se, embrace it wholeheartedly. They are, after all, primarily interested in just two things: Making a profit, and making this fact known to the financial community so there will be greater awareness of the corporation as an aggressive, growing company, thus stimulating demand for the company's stock.

Benefiting the company, the stockholders, and one's self—simultaneously—has undeniable appeal. Doing so by using advertising is a tacit admission that advertising *does* work, which admission is directly opposed to the same gentlemen's scepticism as to advertising's effectiveness in other areas.

In multidivisional companies the corporate advertising program should be handled on the corporate level, not on the divisional level. It is properly the responsibility of the corporate director of advertising, if the position exists, or of the top marketing executive and the president. They customarily work directly with the advertising agency, although divisional ad managers are consulted because of their intimate knowledge of divisional advertising objectives and problems.

One sure way to gut a well-planned divisional-advertising program is to make an arbitrary assessment to provide funds for corporate advertising. When this short-sighted step is taken, the "tax bite" frequently runs around 15 percent of budget—total budget, not merely space cost—of the divisional appropriation. The first time this happens to the industrial advertising manager, he experiences a sense of bewilderment, for he is honestly unable to understand the thinking on the corporate level which led to emasculation of his program.

The traditional pattern is for the bite to continue for two or three years. Then, as the company progresses and matures, and divisional ad managers continue their strenuous protests against taxation without representation, the corporation reevaluates, reconsiders and ultimately adopts the procedure most common throughout industry. This is to earmark a certain percentage of corporate profits for the corporate promotional program, or, alternatively, to assess each division—*not* each divisional advertising appropriation—an amount based on anticipated sales volume. This assessment, as a rule, is somewhat less than ¼ of one percent of gross sales.

Although not a function or activity of the advertising department, "travel expense for nonadvertising personnel" has deliberately been included in this list because it is a significant expense item which absolutely does *not* belong in charges allocated to any industrial advertising department.

A definite correlation exists between a company's marketing naiveté and its tendency to charge off every conceivable miscellaneous expense item against advertising. In one well-known company, a potent factor in the marketplace and a leader in its highly specialized field, a cherished tradition of years' standing was for engineering, order department, sales, research and development, administrative and marketing personnel (and even *Personnel* personnel) to journey happily to far distant cities to attend trade shows at which the company exhibited. True, some were needed for their technical knowledge, although product-wise field salesmen from the immediate locality had responsibility for manning the booth. The others "increased their technical knowledge and evaluated competitive equipment." Oddly enough, it invariably required four or five days (depending on the length of the show) to accomplish this. And even more odd, their travel expenses, including the best hotels and (gourmet) meals, were charged to advertising. A new advertising manager stopped this wasteful dilution of promotional funds, though not without opposition. Few care to give up an extra week of vacation and an all-expense-paid trip on another department's expense account.

What the Ad Department Does Do

A complete listing of all functions of the busy industrial advertising department would be boringly long, including as it would activities engaged in infrequently and those which are relatively inconsequential. Instead of such an exhaustive—and exhausting—tally, the six activities of primary importance are shown, along with major breakdowns. In subsequent chapters each topic, and others, will be covered from a how-to-do-it standpoint. Following are the principal functions found in almost every industrial ad department, though not necessarily in order of importance. This would vary with individual companies.

Administration

Establish policies.

Budgeting.

Appropriations.

Expense control.

Departmental organization.

Administer salaries and departmental personnel records.

Establish efficient inquiry handling procedure.

Evaluate competitive advertising.

Evaluate own ads.

Analyze and interpret readership studies.

Make customer calls to get feel of product(s).

Coordinate advertising with other marketing activities, and with other departments.

Participate in activities of local advertising associations.

Planning

Reflect company policies with an integrated program.

Work with marketing management to establish marketing objectives and incorporate these objectives into a *written* marketing plan.

Establish communications objectives which will help achieve marketing objectives.

Develop a short-range advertising plan.

Develop a long-range advertising plan.

Develop an advertising campaign which will achieve all communications objectives and thus achieve marketing objectives.

Develop a copy platform.

Put on paper a timetable for creation and production of campaign, and for collateral material; use or develop suitable forms to organize this activity.

Demonstrate effectiveness of advertising to management and other key personnel.

Contact field sales personnel for ideas and suggestions; evaluate these carefully.

Marketing

Product analysis and familiarization.

Market research, internal and external.

Break down company markets by S.I.C.

Break down customer list by S.I.C.

Analyze past sales to determine possible trends and to verify if advertising emphasis is correctly directed.

Develop distributor (or jobber, dealer) support program.

Consult with marketing management on special problems as they arise.

Suggest new uses for existing products.

Suggest new products which research, advertising response show are salable.

Media

Analyze all potentially useful media.

Rate media quality and desirability on: editorial policy, editorial content, editorial format, circulation, publication image, readership, market potential, advertiser acceptance, services to advertisers, and space cost.

Develop a schedule of advertising insertions.

Schedule insertions.

Verify insertions through checking copy.

Purchase space (customarily done by agency when an agency is retained).

Sales promotion

Write and produce effective sales literature.

Write and produce salesmen's catalogs.

Produce instruction manuals; technical information and schematic drawings procured from product manager.

Develop point-of-purchase material for dealers, jobbers, or distributors.

Write and produce direct-mail material supplied to dealers, jobbers, or distributors for their use.

Purchase and supervise product photography, either in plant, in studio, or on location.

Direct creation and production of trade-show exhibit(s).

Direct trade shows, including followup of equipment or items to be exhibited; shipping and erection of booth; scheduling of personnel to man the booth; display of products; tear-down of booth and reshipment of products.

In conjunction with sales department, develop sales contests and incentives for field force.

Direct creation and production of movies and strip films.

Develop effective mail campaigns.

Develop high-quality lists for direct-mail use.

Direct the actual mailing, usually through a lettershop if the list is large.

Merchandise all advertising and new collateral material to management, key personnel, and to the field sales force. This includes dealers, jobbers, distributors, or representatives.

Production

Purchase art.

Purchase photography.

Purchase layout.

Purchase type.

Purchase printing.

Produce mats and electros for field use.

Direct work of outside specialists and suppliers.

Chapter 2

WHY YOU NEED AN ADVERTISING AGENCY— AND HOW TO SELECT IT

APPROXIMATELY 40 percent of all industrial advertising is produced and placed by recognized advertising agencies. The surprising figure is not the 40 percent who do, but the 60 percent who do not use agencies. In this age of sophisticated marketing it is almost inconceivable that any serious advertiser can justify the decision to go the do-it-yourself route.

The fact is, though, that out in the hinterlands the misconception still exists that it is poor business to use the talents and services of an advertising agency. The thinking is that to do so is a needless extravagance and a much more costly way of producing advertising. Exactly the reverse may be true.

And, incredible as it seems, some advertisers—and this includes top executives of otherwise reasonable well-managed companies—firmly believe that no "advertising agent" can be trusted with competitive information or company money. The concept of an agency honestly having its clients' welfare at heart, of an agency basing its business future on the premise that agency growth can come only through client growth—due to the client's increased sales and profits—is so alien that it is summarily rejected. This is all too true in too many instances.

These fallacies, along with the *we-don't-need-those-city-fellers-to-tell-us-how-to-run-our-business* philosophy are, fortunately, becoming anachronous, not so much so from an enlightened desire to reject antediluvian thinking as from realization of its impracticality.

Gradually it has dawned on even those most obdurate in resisting change that competition in the marketplace is too cutthroat and the penalty for failure too severe to accept any handicap, however slight, in competing on an equal basis. So, rather than run the risk of failure, it's been widely though reluctantly decided to accept agencies as a fact of life and hope that a good one might enable the firm to be *more* equal than the competition.

Agencies Today

There are now some 4,500 advertising agencies doing business; no firm figures can be cited at any given time because formation and dissolution of small agencies occur at a rate which must assuredly be the Eighth Wonder of the World. These 4,500 agencies employ more than 55,000 people.

Advertising Age, the trade publication which is the voice of the advertising business, lists 94 agencies which have an annual gross income of $5 million. Most agencies concentrate on consumer accounts because that's the range where the big budgets roam, although the majority also accept industrial accounts which measure up to their criteria.

There are some agencies, however, that concentrate on serving industrial accounts. Agencies of this type, regardless of their size, and assuming only that they are large enough to provide complete agency service, are probably the most fertile hunting ground for an industrial ad manager seeking a productive agency affiliation. If his account is relatively large, however, he should not overlook the large consumer-oriented agencies which actively woo—and produce excellent advertising for—the industrial advertiser. It is interesting to note that huge Batten, Barton, Durstine & Osborn, a consumer agency, has for years led all agencies in volume of industrial advertising placed in the nation's business press. And the Fuller & Smith & Ross's, D'Arcy's and Compton's and many other large, respected shops are home of a happy blend of consumer and industrial accounts, all of which benefit from the best thinking the agency can provide.

Just below the really huge agencies are found a vast number of shops in the $5- $10-million bracket, commonly referred to as "medium size" agencies. It is generally recognized that it is this size agency which feels the financial pressure the greatest; agency management in medium-size agencies know they must provide all of the "extra" services—marketing, merchandising, research and what have you—to compete successfully with the bigs. As a result, the client can often expect to pay more for these ancillary services, and for collateral material, than he would in a larger organization.

Farther down the ladder are newly-founded agencies (and many that have been around for years) that are still small, but often staffed with top talent which fled from the regimentation of the larger agencies. Often an industrial advertiser with a modest budget will find a warm welcome and top-flight creative thinking in such an agency.

At the bottom of the heap, and bearing close scrutiny if actively considered as a prospective agency, are the tiny agencies. Many are either the one-man-and-a-girl type operation, or a hybrid setup which is part agency and part art studio; seldom can these marginal operations provide other than the most rudimentary services.

Agencies Compete on an Equal Basis

There is no bargain-basement advertising. That's because agencies, to achieve "agency recognition" by media, and thus qualify for the traditional 15 percent commission on space and time purchased, must measure up to criteria established by each individual medium and/or associations formed by media. Media, incidentally, is the plural of medium. A medium is the vehicle which carries the advertising message—a magazine, newspaper, TV, radio, or even the sky in the case of skywriting.

Recognized agencies are simply those which, in the opinion of media, are equipped to perform the services clients must have, are financially responsible, and meet ethical standards.

To be recognized, an agency must convince media that:

1. The agency is a legitimate business enterprise not owned, influenced, or controlled by either an advertiser or a medium. This is essential if the agency is to be unbiased, and if it is to be able to give candid advice free from coercion or pressure which would be inimical to the best interests of the advertiser.

2. The agency must retain as earned income all commissions received from media on the purchase of space and time. There can be no fee-splitting or rebating of commissions to either advertisers or media. This provision assures advertisers that agencies will have sufficient income so that they can devote the necesary time, talent, and manpower to clients to further client interest. Also, it means that all agencies compete on an equal basis as far as costs are concerned, so there is no necessity for large agencies with large staffs to reduce the amount or quality of the services they provide in an effort to compete with cut-rate competition from less competent agencies.

3. The agency must have the depth of personnel, qualified and experienced in each of the key agency functions, to provide the necessary counsel and services. This provision obviously aids the able and acts as a hindrance to the incompetent and ill equipped.

4. The agency must provide proof of financial strength to assure its continued solvency and operation, and to assure media it is capable of paying for space and time it purchases. Long established is the principle that the agency—as the buyer—is responsible for paying media.

The agency issues space contracts or time contracts in its name to media; these are legal contracts issued by an independent contractor *in its own behalf,* not as an agent of the advertiser. So, if the agency fails to collect from the advertiser, the agency must nonetheless pay media for space and time contracted for. However, if the agency fails to honor its contract with media, media sustain the loss. It is easy to understand why, from media's viewpoint, this provision concerning agency financial strength is so important.

Procedures for Buying Space and Time

These provisions are incorporated in the four Standard Order Blanks developed by the American Association of Advertising Agencies. They are: Order Blank for Publications (on page 44), Contract for Spot Broadcasting, Contract for Spot Telecasting, and Order Blank for Transportation Advertising.

Agency Income

Approximately 65 percent of agency income derives from commission on space and time, although this varies from agency to agency, and is usually higher in agencies with a preponderance of consumer accounts on its roster of clients. The commission is paid not by the client, but by media. The balance of agency income is received directly from clients, generally in the form of fees for special services, such as market research, and as markups on services and materials the agency contracted for as part of producing a product for the client. Photography, typography, art, layout (if done outside), keyline, electros, and narration are examples. The agency quite legitimately marks up its cost of these products and services when it invoices them to the advertiser, for agency personnel have invested their time and knowledge in selecting what their experience dictates is the best to be had at a price that is acceptable. Markup ranges from 17.65 percent on prosaic purchases such as type to 40 percent or more on expensive art commissioned for the client.

While this 40-percent figure might seem exorbitant, net profit for an agency on such art usually is about on a par with other commissionable purchases. One example concerns some meticulously detailed full-color illustrations which were ordered by an agency art director for a manufacturer of huge, extremely costly machine tools. Some of the illustrations were of sufficient complexity that the agency art director and the outside artist engaged for the job had to travel from Chicago to northern Canada, to the Gulf Coast, and to Arizona, as well as three other locations to inspect installations of the advertiser's equipment. They took reference photography before the artist proceeded with the "roughs"—semicomprehensive pencil sketches to give the advertising manager a chance to make any necessary corrections before work in oils took place. Each installation differed so much from the others that it was essential that the artist actually see and ab-

Order Blank for Publications
(Copyright October 1956)

(Member of A.A.A.A.)

NAME OF ADVERTISING AGENCY
ADDRESS
CITY   STATE
TELEPHONE NUMBER

☐ IF CHECKED HERE, THIS IS A SPACE CONTRACT

☐ IF CHECKED HERE, THIS IS AN INSERTION ORDER

TO PUBLISHER OF

NO.

CITY AND STATE

DATE

PLEASE PUBLISH ADVERTISING OF (advertiser)

FOR (product)

┌──────SPACE──────┐   ┌──────TIMES──────┐   ┌──────────────DATES OF INSERTION──────────────┐

POSITION

COPY   KEY   CUTS

ADDITIONAL INSTRUCTIONS

RATE

LESS AGENCY COMMISSION   PER CENT ON GROSS   LESS CASH DISCOUNT   PER CENT ON NET

Subject to conditions stated below and on back hereof:

NAME OF ADVERTISING AGENCY, PER.....................................
CITY

Member of
AMERICAN ASSOCIATION OF ADVERTISING AGENCIES

Order Blank for Publications   Copyright October, 1956   American Association of Advertising Agencies, Inc.   *(OVER)*

Standard order blank for publications designed by the American Association of Advertising Agencies.

sorb the peculiarities of each locale to be able to capture the feeling of the individual locations. True, the artist might have gone alone and cut travel expenses in half. But the agency was responsible for the end result, and the only way it could be sure of art up to its standards was to have the account art director provide direction for the artist—on the spot. In this case the client was billed the cost of the art and an agency markup of 40 percent, plus out-of-pocket expenses incurred by the art director and the artist. The agency's only compensation for the art director's time was in the markup on the artist's invoice.

Not legitimately marked up are internal services. One agency, for example, habitually marks these up—from 17.65 percent to 60 percent or more, apparently capriciously and depending on just one factor—the agency's profit picture for the month. *This is unethical.* The advertising manager has an obligation to his company to lodge a long, loud protest if he encounters this. Agencies are entitled to make a fair charge that produces an acceptable profit on work they do internally—layout, for example—but they are *not* entitled to add a commission on their own internal charges. To do so is like putting a tax upon a tax. Incidentally, clients of this particular agency who complain about this method of milking them invariably have their invoices recalled and reduced by the exact amount of this unjustified commission. Only those ad managers who didn't realize they were being gouged and didn't raise an objection incurred this charge. This practice is not widespread, although the agency which habitually practices this form of invoice padding is still in business at the same old stand and, presumably, continues to overcharge those it can. The time an ad manager spends in carefully checking invoices is not time wasted.

Agency Commission From Media

Agency commission is given voluntarily by media, and almost all business publications allow it. Customary figure is 15 percent of the published space rate, although most media allow an additional 2 percent cash discount for prompt payment. This 2 percent is customarily passed on to the advertiser as an incentive for him to pay the agency invoices promptly; discount period is usually 10 days; although some agencies shorten it to 7, others who are all heart lengthen it to 14.

Methods of Agency Compensation

Three methods of agency compensation prevail in industrial advertising today. They are:

1. *Commission.* On space advertisements, this includes space at gross cost, and 15 percent of the cost of actually producing the ad. Production cost involves photography or art, typography, keyline, engravings, and electros.

2. *Minimum billing agreement.* This includes earned commission and a guaranteed minimum profit to the agency as compensation for handling the company's advertising. Consensus is that this system accounts for all but a tiny fraction of all formal agreements between industrial advertisers and their agencies. The figure most commonly quoted is that 98 percent of all client-agency agreements are of this type.

3. *Agreed fee.* This is arrived at by establishing a program, determining the net cost of media and production, then adding an agreed-upon fee. Other cost-and-fee arrangements have been worked out, but most are arithmetic for arithmetic's sake, or are an elaborate justification for one essential—an acceptable profit margin for the agency.

Industrial Marketing, a highly-respected trade publication which every ad manager should subscribe to, recently reported yet another fee arrangement is in use by Paul Klempter & Co., Fuller & Smith & Ross*, and other agencies. Under this arrangement, the advertiser guarantees that the agency will make a net profit on its account btween 1.5 percent and 2.5 percent on gross billings. Any profit over and above this agreed-upon amount is split equally between agency and advertiser. This is undoubtedly an equitable solution to a problem that has plagued advertising from its inception, and probably will for the foreseeable future.

All of these methods of agency compensation are workable, otherwise they would long since have departed the scene. The advertising manager should think long and carefully before departing from them. He should shy away from—in fact, avoid like the plague—any kind of a cost-plus fee arrangement where an agency's media cost and production cost are added to a fee which is theoretically a specified fraction of actual cost. Arrangements like this, whether they are a cost-plus proposition between a manufacturer of military hardware supervised by a bunch of government bureaucrats, or a cost-plus arrangement with an advertising agency, have one thing in common: they pay a premium for poor performance. The seller has no incentive to effect economies which would do just one thing—reduce profit from the job. Who voluntarily reduces profit?

How Agency Commission Is Derived

Let's take a look at what actually produces commission for the agency—a purchase of space, and since we're interested only in industrial advertising, space in a business publication.

Rates—cost of space—are based on circulation. The average business publication, "trade book" in ad terminology, with a circulation of around 65,000, charges approximately $1,000 for one full page of space. This is for a standard 7" x 10" ad, with "bleed"—an ad printed so that it runs into the gutter and/or to the top and side of the page flush with the edge—carrying an extra price tag of about 10 percent over and above the basic page price. In addition, if the advertiser wants a second color (black and one other standard color), he may specify it for an added charge of about 10 percent. A third color, or

*Now Creamer, Inc.

full four-color process, is available from many leading publications at a still higher price. Increase in readership with bleed and additional colors is discussed in depth later on.

For the sake of illustration, assume that the agency contracts for one page. Published rate (on the book's rate card) lists the space at $1,000. Agency commission is 15 percent of the gross price, or $150, which is deducted from the amount that is invoiced to the agency by the medium. Thus the agency pays the medium only $850 less, in most cases, the standard 2 percent discount for prompt payment, or another $17. This $17 is not money earned by the agency, however, for it is passed along in turn to the agency's client—the advertiser—as an incentive for him to pay the invoice promptly.

While on the subject of agency commissions, an amusing incident points up advertising's need to communicate better with company management:

The advertising manager of a nationally known company was having a routine discussion of advertising, as it applied to his major product line, with one of the company's marketing managers. To the ad man's amazement, a worried expression crossed the marketing manager's face. He got up, closed the door to his office, sat back down behind his desk and looked the ad manager in the eye. He lowered his voice and asked, in a horror-stricken tone, "Do you realize our agency is getting a kickback from magazines we advertise in?"

The ad manager was stunned, at a loss for words. Finally, he decided the marketing manager was pulling his leg. Questioning proved this was not so, however, so the ad manager proceeded quickly to explain the facts of life as far as agency commissions are concerned. When the explanation was over, the marketing expert looked relieved, and said, "I'm glad to hear that. I thought our agency people were above taking something under the table, but that's what it looked like to me. I thought we paid them to do our advertising."

This is not a fable—it's a verbatim (almost, anyway) record of a conversation. This naivete' is widespread, very much so, and every industrial ad manager will do well to remember it and explain fiscal facts about agency relationships to key people occasionally. Once won't suffice as a rule; mention it at opportune times, such as when budget discussions are being held.

A.A.A.A.

The American Association of Advertising Agencies is the national organization of the advertising agency business. Throughout the advertising world "A.A.A.A."—or "4A" is the symbol of able, ethical and responsible advertising agency service. The 534 agencies which are members of A.A.A.A. place more than 75% of all United States advertising placed through agencies. They operate more than 1,010 offices in 232 U.S. cities in 48 states and the District of Columbia. They also have 617 offices in 123 cities in 67 other countries.

Through Executive Headquarters in New York and 25 national committees, A.A.A.A. activities extend to virtually every phase of advertising. The main objectives of A.A.A.A. are:

- To foster, strengthen, and improve the advertising agency business.
- To advance the cause of advertising as a whole.
- To provide services for members which they cannot provide for themselves.

A.A.A.A. agency service standards, continuously promoted by the association, are a "delineation of fundamentals" of successful agency operation, adopted in 1918 and continued practically without change until the present time. They are as valid today as when originally adopted.

Service standards were drawn up so that "advertisers and media may know what to demand and agencies may know what may be expected of them in dealing with the problems of advertising."

Under the seven headings, the standards make clear that agency service extends from "a study of the product or service" to "cooperation with the sales work."

Advertising, they state, should be based on a plan. The plan should be based, in turn, on studies of the product or service, the present and potential market, the factors of distribution and sales, and the available media which can profitably be used.

Only after a plan has been developed and approved does the agency proceed to create the campaign and the individual advertisements, order the space or time, supply the messages (copy) in proper form to media, verify the publication or broadcast, audit and bill the client.

Following are agency service standards of the American Association of Advertising Agencies. They were first adopted on October 9, 1918, and were most recently revised on February 15, 1956:

Agency Service consists of interpreting to the public, or to that part of it which it is desired to reach, the advantages of a product or service.

Interpreting to the public the advantages of a product or service are based upon:

1. A study of the product or service in order to determine the ad-

vantages and disadvantages inherent in the product itself, and in its relation to competition.

2. An analysis of the present and potential market for which the product or service is adapted:

As to location

As to extent of possible sale

As to season

As to trade and economic conditions

As to nature and amount of competition

3. A knowledge of the factors of distribution and sales and their methods of operation.

4. A knowledge of all available media and means which can be profitably used to carry the interpretation of the product or service to consumer, wholesaler, dealer, contractor, or other factor.

This knowledge covers:

Character

Influence

Circulation...quantity...quality...location

Physical requirements

Costs

Acting on the study, analysis and knowledge as explained in the preceding paragraphs, recommendations are made and the following procedure ensues:

5. Formulation of a definite plan.

6. Execution of this plan:

   a. Writing, designing, illustrating of advertisements, or other appropriate forms of the message.

   b. Ordering the space, time, or other means of advertising.

   c. The proper incorporation of the message in mechanical form and forwarding it with proper instructions for the fulfillment of the contract.

   d. Checking and verifying the insertions, display, or other means used.

   e. The auditing and billing for service, space, preparation.

7. Cooperation with the sales work to ensure the greatest effect from advertising.

Individual agencies are, of course, free to determine with their clients just what services they will perform. Additional services routinely offered by many agencies today include package design, sales research, sales training, creation and production of sales and technical literature, designing of merchandising and point-of-purchase displays, creation and production of movies, slide and strip films, merchandising programs, and creation and production of direct-mail programs.

How much or how little an advertising manager wants his agency to do depends on his internal staff members and their ability to produce necessary material—and on his budget.

The above delineation of the fundamentals serves a useful purpose and shows what types of services should be offered by applicants for membership in the association. The more clearly agency service is understood by those who offer it and by those who receive it, the more adequate and intelligent advertising service will become, and those equipped to render a complete and effective service will be encouraged in doing so.

Qualifications for membership in the 4A are thoroughly defined by the association. The 4A says: "The qualifications are intended as a definition, by agency people themselves, of the kind of agency most likely to develop advertising *which succeeds for the advertisers*. They are based on the premise that the agency should be independent, unbiased and objective; should offer adequate staff and experience; should be ethically operated; and should be soundly financed. Only such an agency can fulfill its obligation to advertisers, to advertising media, and to the public."

Membership in the A.A.A.A. is not necessary for an agency to be good, or for it to be the right agency for your company. Membership *does* mean, however, that an agency *is* good and *is* right for its clients. In this business of intangibles, where the nebulous is weighed carefully, an affiliation such as this is more than a mere indication—it can frequently be taken as a recommendation.

To become a member of the association, individual agencies must apply on a standard form. Applicant agencies are investigated by a regional board—Eastern, East Central, Central, or Western—then voted upon. From time of application to time of final decision requires many months as a rule because the speed with which the application is processed depends entirely upon time voluntarily made available by widely scattered individuals.

Size of the agency is not a determinant. Volume of business is not a factor, although agencies must be adequately equipped to be considered eligible for membership.

To be accepted for A.A.A.A. membership, an agency must have been in the agency business long enough to demonstrate adequate experience and ability to ensure a stable operation. Two years is the minimum.

STANDARDS *of* PRACTICE *of the*
American Association of Advertising Agencies

FIRST ADOPTED OCTOBER 16, 1924—MOST RECENTLY REVISED APRIL 28, 1962

WE HOLD THAT a responsibility of advertising agencies is to be a constructive force in business.

We further hold that, to discharge this responsibility, advertising agencies must recognize an obligation, not only to their clients, but to the public, the media they employ, and to each other.

We finally hold that the responsibility will best be discharged if all agencies observe a common set of standards of practice.

To this end, the American Association of Advertising Agencies has adopted the following Standards of Practice as being in the best interests of the public, the advertisers, the media owners, and the agencies themselves.

These standards are voluntary. They are intended to serve as a guide to the kind of agency conduct which experience has shown to be wise, foresighted, and constructive.

It is recognized that advertising is a business and as such must operate within the framework of competition. It is further recognized that keen and vigorous competition, honestly conducted, is necessary to the growth and health of American business generally, of which advertising is a part.

However, *unfair* competitive practices in the advertising agency business lead to financial waste, dilution of service, diversion of manpower, and loss of prestige. Unfair practices tend to weaken public confidence both in advertisements and in the institution of advertising.

1. Creative Code

WE THE MEMBERS of the American Association of Advertising Agencies, in addition to supporting and obeying the laws and legal regulations pertaining to advertising, undertake to extend and broaden the application of high ethical standards. Specifically, we will not knowingly produce advertising which contains:

a. False or misleading statements or exaggerations, visual or verbal.

b. Testimonials which do not reflect the real choice of a competent witness.

c. Price claims which are misleading.

d. Comparisons which unfairly disparage a competitive product or service.

e. Claims insufficiently supported, or which distort the true meaning or practicable application of statements made by professional or scientific authority.

f. Statements, suggestions or pictures offensive to public decency.

We recognize that there are areas which are subject to honestly different interpretations and judgment. Taste is subjective and may even vary from time to time as well as from individual to individual. Frequency of seeing or hearing advertising messages will necessarily vary greatly from person to person.

However, we agree not to recommend to an advertiser and to discourage the use of advertising which is in poor or questionable taste or which is deliberately irritating through content, presentation or excessive repetition.

Clear and willful violations of this Code shall be referred to the Board of Directors of the American Association of Advertising Agencies for appropriate action, including possible annulment of membership as provided by Article IV, Section 5, of the Constitution and By-Laws.

2. Contracts

a. The advertising agency should where feasible enter into written contracts with media in placing advertising. When entered into, the agency should conform to its agreements with media. Failure to do so may result in loss of standing or litigation, either on the contract or for violations of the Clayton or Federal Trade Commission Acts.

b. The advertising agency should not knowingly fail to fulfill all lawful contractual commitments with media.

3. Offering Credit Extension

It is unsound and uneconomic to offer extension of credit or banking service as an inducement in solicitation.

4. Unfair Tactics

The advertising agency should compete on merit and not by depreciating a competitor or his work directly or inferentially, or by circulating harmful rumors about him, or by making unwarranted claims of scientific skill in judging or prejudging advertising copy, or by seeking to obtain an account by hiring a key employee away from the agency in charge in violation of the agency's employment agreements.

These Standards of Practice of the American Association of Advertising Agencies come from the belief that sound practice is good business. Confidence and respect are indispensable to success in a business embracing the many intangibles of agency service and involving relationships so dependent upon good faith. These standards are based on a broad experience of what has been found to be the best advertising practice.

Standards of practice advocated by the American Association of Advertising Agencies are fairly specific about such matters as false or misleading statements, authenticity of testimonials, price claims which can be substantiated, fair comparisons with competitive products, and the avoidance of statements, suggestions, or pictures which are offensive to public decency.

No agency is eligible unless the persons who control it, whether by ownership or contract, are employees of the agency.

To become a 4A agency, it is mandatory that the agency shall not own any interest in a printing, engraving, or other business supplying material to its clients, to any degree that disqualifies the agency from giving unbiased advice and service. Although ownership of any such interest by one or more of the owners, directors, officers, or employees of the agency is not ownership by the agency, it is recognized that such ownership could lead to bias. Therefore, it is most important that any substantial ownership be disclosed to the association, to the agency's clients and, in case of media interest, to other media.

Character is a quality that's difficult to measure with a yardstick, but it is vitally important. The 4A character investigation will be directed so as to determine the agency applicant's business record, its policies and principles, its ethical practices, and its reputation for honesty, integrity, and sincerity of purpose. The association aims to bring agency operations into accord with the best ethical standards of business, so it can receive into membership only those who give reasonable assurance of readiness and ability to uphold such standards. A.A.A.A. says: "It is essential to know how an agency operates in relation to certain practices, declared by the association to be unfair practices in the light of the obligation agencies have not only to their clients, but to the media they employ, to the public, and to each other. These practices are stated in the 'Standards of Practice of the American Association of Advertising Agencies'."

Adopted in 1924 and revised in April 1962, the A.A.A.A. Standards of Practice are illustrated nearby.

The Creative Code of the Association of American Advertising Agencies spells out in detail the standards which all member agencies must measure up to if they are to retain their membership in good standing. It is also illustrated.

If accepted for membership, an agency is assessed dues based on its annual volume of business in the association's fiscal year. Dues are payable quarterly and are subject to adjustment at the end of the year if the agency has ended the year in a lower or higher income bracket. An initiation fee is required of all new members amounting to 10 percent of the tentative first year's dues.

For its dues an agency receives many benefits. A.A.A.A. works to advance the cause of advertising as a whole, and with considerable success. Advertising in the United States is more and more gaining recognition as "the institution of abundance."

More and more economists and business leaders are shifting emphasis from production to marketing and consumption. There is a grow-

CREATIVE CODE
American Association of Advertising Agencies

The members of the American Association of Advertising Agencies recognize:

1. That advertising bears a dual responsibility in the American economic system and way of life.

To the public it is a primary way of knowing about the goods and services which are the products of American free enterprise, goods and services which can be freely chosen to suit the desires and needs of the individual. The public is entitled to expect that advertising will be reliable in content and honest in presentation.

To the advertiser it is a primary way of persuading people to buy his goods or services, within the framework of a highly competitive economic system. He is entitled to regard advertising as a dynamic means of building his business and his profits.

2. That advertising enjoys a particularly intimate relationship to the American family. It enters the home as an integral part of television and radio programs, to speak to the individual and often to the entire family. It shares the pages of favorite newspapers and magazines. It presents itself to travelers and to readers of the daily mails. In all these forms, it bears a special responsibility to respect the tastes and self-interest of the public.

3. That advertising is directed to sizable groups or to the public at large, which is made up of many interests and many tastes. As is the case with all public enterprises, ranging from sports to education and even to religion, it is almost impossible to speak without finding someone in disagreement. Nonetheless, advertising people recognize their obligation to operate within the traditional American limitations: to serve the interests of the majority and to respect the rights of the minority.

Therefore we, the members of the American Association of Advertising Agencies, in addition to supporting and obeying the laws and legal regulations pertaining to advertising, undertake to extend and broaden the application of high ethical standards. Specifically, we will not knowingly produce advertising which contains:

a. False or misleading statements or exaggerations, visual or verbal.

b. Testimonials which do not reflect the real choice of a competent witness.

c. Price claims which are misleading.

d. Comparisons which unfairly disparage a competitive product or service.

e. Claims insufficiently supported, or which distort the true meaning or practicable application of statements made by professional or scientific authority.

f. Statements, suggestions or pictures offensive to public decency.

We recognize that there are areas which are subject to honestly different interpretations and judgment. Taste is subjective and may even vary from time to time as well as from individual to individual. Frequency of seeing or hearing advertising messages will necessarily vary greatly from person to person.

However, we agree not to recommend to an advertiser and to discourage the use of advertising which is in poor or questionable taste or which is deliberately irritating through content, presentation or excessive repetition.

Clear and willful violations of this Code shall be referred to the Board of Directors of the American Association of Advertising Agencies for appropriate action, including possible annulment of membership as provided in Article IV, Section 5, of the Constitution and By-Laws.

Conscientious adherence to the letter and the spirit of this Code will strengthen advertising and the free enterprise system of which it is part.   *Adopted April 26, 1962*

Creative code of A.A.A.A. reveals concern with advertising standards.

ing awareness that advertising is the counterpart in marketing of the machine in production, and that advertising can and should play an ever larger role in finding customers and educating them to the enjoyment of higher standards of living. A.A.A.A. therefore carries on a continuing four-part program for the improvement of advertising, aiming to:

1. Help attract, select, train and handle more high caliber people.
2. Raise ever higher the quality and quantity of advertising research.
3. Improve advertising content.
4. Gain public understanding of advertising and its key role.

Advertising Personnel in Agencies

Each year, the A.A.A.A. estimates, the advertising-agency business needs some 3,000 new people—half of them specialized personnel. Advertising as a whole needs many more, of course.

To help meet this need, A.A.A.A. carries on a continuing program to present advertising as a career to promising young people.

The program is aimed at high-school students through some 9,000 teachers engaged in vocational guidance. It is especially aimed at young men and women on the student publications in nearly 1,000 colleges and over 10,000 accredited high schools, directly and through their faculty advisers. A booklet, *The Advertising Business and Its Career Opportunities*, is regularly offered to the students and teachers.

Closely related to this work is a 4A Plan for Cooperating with Teachers of Advertising. Local committees of A.A.A.A. agency people offer their help—visits by agency executives to the college campuses, guest lectures, invitations to teachers to attend A.A.A.A. meetings, and other planned communications to those in colleges in their areas which provide advertising courses.

Another activity assisting agency management but also benefiting advertising as a whole is the A.A.A.A. continuing study of methods of selecting agency personnel and of agency training methods.

Advertising Research

Research provides the solid floor of facts on which to practice the art of advertising. A.A.A.A. therefore engages in numerous activities to expand the field of scientific advertising knowledge.

Some of these are carries on by the association itself. The *A.A.A.A. Market & Newspaper Statistics*, issued annually since 1933, provides data on cities of 100,000 population and over and their newspapers—their circulation, rates, advertising lineage, differential between local and national rates, and circulation obtained through special prices, premiums or other inducements. The group also publishes the *A.A.A.A. Newspaper Rate Differentials*—an annual study of changes in general and retail advertising rates.

When research data are to be used by advertisers and media as well as by agencies, however, it is best carried on jointly through tripartite organizations. Agencies, advertisers, and media jointly determine the survey methods so that results are acceptable to all. Media pay all or most of the research cost, since it can be reflected in their rates and thus be shared by all users of the medium in proportion to use. A.A.A.A. cooperates with advertisers and media in two major joint research enterprises—the Advertising Research Foundation and Traffic Audit Bureau.

The Advertising Research Foundation was established by the A.A.A.A. and the Association of National Advertisers in 1936. (It was later reconstituted, in 1951, as a subscription organization to which individual media, agencies, and advertisers may subscribe. A.A.A.A. and A.N.A. continue as founder subscribers.)

Prior to 1951 the foundation worked mainly with media associations on research of print media. It conducted and published more than $1,750,000 worth of media studies which made lasting contributions to research techniques.

Since then the foundation has published some 78 studies, ranging from bibliographies on motivation research to estimates of television households in the U.S. They include a monumental 500-page study called *Printed Advertising Rating Methods*; this is of particular interest to the industrial advertising manager despite a justifiably large portion of the study being devoted to consumer advertising.

The foundation offers a consultation service that is available on a cost basis to prospective sponsors of research at any time during the planning of their projects. For media, this helps to assure acceptance of research findings. On request to subscribers, published media studies of industry-wide significance may also be appraised by the foundation.

The Traffic Audit Bureau, another joint research enterprise, certifies the circulation and space-position values of outdoor-advertising plants throughout the country.

T.A.B. was established in 1933 by the A.A.A.A., A.N.A., and the Outdoor Advertising Association of America to meet the needs of advertisers, advertising agencies, and billboard operators for uniform, reliable, and accurate information on the circulation values of outdoor media. Later the three corresponding Canadian associations joined in sponsorship and support. It is the only source on the continent for information on the outdoor medium validated by agencies and advertisers.

CONFIDENTIAL   DATE:_____

To: Secretary, ANA-AAAA Committee for
    Improvement of Advertising Content
    155 East 44th Street, New York 17, N.Y.

Interchange Case No_____Advertisement for _____ Medium_____

Description_____

The criticism of the advertisement, as received in the Interchange, is attached for your information. You are asked to give your opinion of the advertisement, however, and not simply your opinion of the criticism.

☐ If for competitive reasons you should not give an opinion on this advertisement, please check here and return form.

1. Do you believe that criticism of this advertisement is in the scope of the ANA-AAAA Interchange?

_____NO.   The problem seems to be entirely one of factual validity, involving facts not available to us.

_____YES. The problem seems to be, at least in part, whether the advertisement is in bad taste or "manifestly
              misleading" (No. 3 below) or otherwise harmful to advertising.

If "yes" please continue to check below and add any comments which may be helpful to the advertiser and the
placing agency.

2. Is there anything in the advertisement in bad taste?

Yes_____No_____Don't know _____

If "yes," what?_____

_____

_____

_____

3. Do you question the advertisement as likely to be "manifestly misleading" (i.e., based on internal evidence
   within the ad, such as visual or verbal trickery)?

Yes _____No_____Don't know_____

If "yes," in what way?_____

_____

_____

_____

(Continued on page 2)

Reproduced above and on the opposite page is the form used by members of the Joint Committee to cast their votes on advertisements submitted to the Interchange of the A.A.A.A. and the National Association of Advertisers.

Improving Advertising Content

The association works in two ways to improve advertising content: (1) By *encouraging* the highest standards in the creative output of agency people, and (2) by *discouraging* advertising which is in bad taste or otherwise objectionable.

In the first direction, aiming to stimulate creative activity, papers by outstanding creative leaders are a regular feature of the A.A.A.A. annual meetings and are supplied on request, in thousands of copies, to people in member agencies.

—2—

4. Is the advertisement for some other reason likely to be harmful to advertising?

Yes_____ No_____ Don't know_____

If "yes":

a. Is it because of disparagement of competitors?

Yes_____ No_____

Comment:_____

_____

b. Is it because you think the advertisement is unsuited to the medium?

Yes_____ No_____

Comment:_____

_____

c. If other than (a) or (b), what is the reason?

_____

_____

_____

5. Do you regard this advertisement as detrimental to advertising and requiring corrective action by the Committee?

Yes_____

No_____

Additional comments, if any:

NAME_____

Member, ANA-AAAA Committee for
Improvement of Advertising Content

Opportunity is given at the annual meetings to see exhibits of prize-winning advertising art, outstanding film commercials, and so forth. On occasion these are made available to the A.A.A.A. local councils or to individual members.

At the regional conventions—regularly at the Eastern Annual Conference and the Central Region Annual Meeting—specialized workshops, open to all member agency people, are devoted to copy, art, and general subjects. These papers are also offered to members. Local councils usually arrange meetings on creative subjects.

In another direction, the association works steadily to reduce the small percentage of advertising which is objectionable to the public and tends to lessen the effectiveness of all advertising by undermining consumer and industry confidence by offending taste.

A.A.A.A. advocates, in its standards of practice, that "The advertising agency should not recommend, and should discourage any advertising of an untruthful, indecent or otherwise objectionable character."

In addition, A.A.A.A. conducts an interchange of opinion among agencies on advertising which is outside the scope of regulatory bodies. When an agency considers an advertisement objectionable for any reason, it may submit the criticism to A.A.A.A. headquarters. Each criticism received is forwarded without identification to each of 16 members of the A.A.A.A. Committee on Improvement of Advertising Content, asking whether they agree or disagree with it. The criticism and the committee's vote and comments are then sent, unidentified as to source, to the responsible agency.

The Interchange, a biennial report of the A.A.A.A., began operations in 1946 under the auspices of a committee of the American Association of Advertising Agencies. For the first 14 years it worked only indirectly with advertisers, through their agencies. The idea behind the Interchange was simple:

- To invite advertising professionals to register their criticisms when they considered an advertisement harmful to their craft on the ground of taste or opinion.
- To supply expert evaluation of the criticism by a top-ranking committee of advertising experts.
- To give their opinions privately and in confidence to the advertiser and his agency when the committee agreed that an advertisement was harmful to advertising.

Improvement of Interchange

Early in 1960, the Association of National Advertisers was invited to explore various ways in which *both* the agency and the advertiser might work together on the problem of objectionable advertising. The way was soon found to make the Interchange a truly joint operation and it was agreed that each association would be represented by nine members and its president ex-officio; that there would be two cochairmen; a third of the committee should be appointed each year and that the two associations would share equally the out-of-pocket expenses for the Interchange operation. In September of 1960 the combined A.A.A.A.—A.N.A. Interchange came into being.

Ben Wells, former president of the Seven-Up Company, summed it up this way: "This is not an assemblage of holier-than-thou do-gooders. All of us are heavily involved in producing advertising that helps to produce sales and profits, and we realize full well that if advertising fails to do this it doesn't make any difference how socially acceptable it is or how impeccably it may be in good taste. At the same time we feel strongly that advertising which offends the canons of good taste and decency, and which deliberately misleads or that appears to smear and besmirch other advertising is not only bad advertising but bad business.''

The Interchange is set up to deal with national or regional *agency-placed* advertisements which might prove harmful to advertising as a whole. Sensitive areas include:

- Bad taste
- Suggestiveness
- Statements offensive to public decency
- Pictures or copy offensive on religious, ethnic or political grounds
- Visual trickery
- Weasel wording
- Improper disparagement of other products or industries
- Derogation of the advertising industry

The Interchange deals essentially with questions of taste and opinion. It does *not* deal with the factual validity of claims, since the committee does not have access to the facts and does not have the machinery to develop such facts through investigation, hearings, and research.

In short, the Interchange does not and should not attempt to duplicate the work of government regulatory bodies such as the Federal Trade Commission, or can it deal with problems of deception and deceit such as those covered by the better business bureaus.

Posters like this appear in agencies and offices throughout the country. They are distributed by the Interchange Committee to remind advertisers and their agencies of the need to police the ad industry for the good of all. The posters inspire many reports of objectionable advertising to the industry's joint committee.

MIND YOUR OWN BUSINESS

Report objectionable advertising to

_____

In print. Clip the advertisement and note where it appeared.
On the air. Make a note of sponsor, message, time and station.

The committee does not handle generalized complaints, but only specific objections to specific advertisements, in print, or on the air, if a complaint falls within the scope of the Interchange.

How Complaints Are Handled

The complaint itself, together with a tear sheet, radio script, or TV photocopy of the offending advertisement is sent to all 20 members of the committee together with the voting form shown in two parts. Each member votes individually and confidentially.

If a majority of the committee considers the advertisement detrimental to advertising as a whole, the criticism and the committee votes and comments—not identified by source—are sent concurrently to the advertiser and to the placing agency of record.

If a majority of the committee regards the advertising as seriously objectionable, the advertiser and placing agency are asked to respond and to take corrective action. If they fail to do so within 30 days the committee notifies the board of directors of the A.A.A.A. and A.N.A.

The committee vote is never reported to the complainant, since the committee works in confidence with the advertiser and the placing agency. It must be emphasized that the source of the complaint is never divulged to the committee or to anyone else; it is seen only by the committee secretary, who serves for three years and who processes all complaints.

The Interchange is not censorship. It is helpful criticism and must, of necessity, rely on voluntary regulation. Nevertheless it has brought about clear-cut improvement in a considerable volume of advertising including campaigns with wide public exposure.

Agencies and advertisers urge their personnel to be alert to questionable advertising by the use of posters such as this one. These posters are part of a series of bulletin-board reminders distributed by the committee over the past two years.

Complaints and their disposition during the committee's fourth and fifth years follow:

	4th year	5th year
Criticisms received	52	55
Deemed detrimental and requiring committee action	5	5

The experience in later years has followed a similar pattern. Most criticisms were received by Interchange from people in advertising agencies. This is to be expected because agency people are more familiar with the Interchange, since it was operated by A.A.A.A. before coming under joint A.A.A.A.—A.N.A. auspices. Also, agencies often forward criticisms on behalf of clients.

Some criticisms, however, come directly from advertisers. In the past some have come from media. It is still not unusual to read of a medium refusing to accept an advertisement.

A few have come from individuals outside of advertising who have heard about the Interchange. Though not actively solicited, these are welcomed and treated exactly as the others are.

Here is a typical experience of complaint reports:

From agency people	37	40
From advertisers	4	5
From people outside of advertising	7	5
From associations	4	5
TOTAL	52	55

Of the 52 criticisms received in one year and the 55 in another, the media breakdown (typical of more recent years) was as follows:

Newspaper	16	13
Television	10	11
Consumer magazines	15	14
Radio	1	2
Business publications	6	10
Transit	3	3
Direct mail	1	2

If we assume the worst—that all of the direct-mail criticisms were leveled against industrial advertising—and add those to the business-publication advertising for that particular year, we find that industrial advertising had a total of 12 criticisms out of 55.

On the surface, this seems creditable. But this is almost *one-fourth* of all criticisms when it is remembered that industrial advertising is but a tiny fraction of all advertising. It is obvious that this area could stand a good spring housecleaning.

The committee does not make general pronouncements as to the specific type of criticisms it received, although a subcommittee report stated that advertising directly attacking individual competitors seemed to be on the increase.

They stated that while vigorous competition in advertising should always be encouraged, they recommended that the A.A.A.A. take an even stronger stand against denigration of competitors, that name-calling and even name-naming should be discouraged, and that widespread derogation of competitors, even when technically true, could have a serious effect on the public's confidence in advertising.

It is interesting to note Hertz's abandonment of a particularly strong campaign in the bitterly competitive car-rental industry occurred with amazing speed. Of even more interest is speculation on the reasons why; obviously Hertz was stung enough to lash out at Avis, and from the tone of the ads it initially seemed they would run for an extended period of time.

Some members of the Interchange felt that derogation of competitors was so self-defeating that it would fall of its own weight, while others believed that each derogatory advertisement would invite retaliation, that disparagement would therefore proliferate, and that the total result might bring discredit to advertising as a whole unless a stronger stand were taken.

Subsequently, the A.A.A.A. board of directors adopted a policy statement based on the subcommittee's report.

Advertisements using sex, violence, and "suggestive" copy were the source of numerous complaints to the Interchange. A number of these involved promotion for motion pictures. At its first meeting the Interchange took note of this and voted unanimously to commend four newspapers for having tightened their standards for such advertising.

Complaints were also received on advertising which seemed to ridicule or make light of patriotic symbols, religious beliefs, and ethnic characteristics. In those cases deemed serious by a majority of the committee, the advertisements were withdrawn.

This has been the record in all cases judged detrimental to advertising by the committee—further evidence of the stature of the committee on the one hand and of the sense of responsibility by both advertisers and their agencies on the other.

In February 1966, Norman H. Strouse, chairman of the J. Walter Thompson Company, the country's largest advertising agency, responded to the presentation of the Advertising Gold Medal Award with these words:

> "We must continue our climb toward higher standards of practice, greater self-discipline, and greater sensitivity concerning the outer boundaries of public tolerance. These are responsibilities which we cannot shift to someone else. The agency initiates creative ideas—the client approves them—the media accept them in final form. All must accept responsibility for clearing the air of any advertising that offends public taste, irritates sensibilities, intentionally misleads, or denigrates a competitor."

Better Understanding of Advertising

The service that advertising performs as an economic and social force needs wide understanding. Among people engaged in advertising, such insight helps them to see the importance of their jobs to the economy as a whole. Among businessmen, it encourages proper use of advertising as a business tool. Among government officials, educators, and consumer leaders, it helps to assure that advertising is not unfairly criticized or restricted.

A notable joint enterprise in public relations, unique in American business, is *The Advertising Council.* Jointly sponsored by the 4A's, A.N.A., and four leading media groups, The Advertising Council is a demonstration of the use of advertising for the public service.

Through the council, volunteer advertising agencies contribute creative work and media and advertisers donate more than $160,000,000 per year in space and time toward the support of non-partisan public-service campaigns—for better schools, community chests, forest-fire prevention, the Red Cross, mental health, accident prevention, and many others.

In an average year, it is estimated that some 500 agency people contribute around 25,000 man-hours to prepare the campaigns. A.A.A.A. obtains the volunteer agencies, underwrites the agencies' share of council financing, names agency representatives on the council board, and distributes campaign material to advertising agencies throughout the country.

Continuing since 1941, the council's public-service program is helping to gain proper recognition for advertising among government, business, and public groups.

Another joint enterprise in public relations is the *Committee on Understanding of our Economic System,* cosponsored by A.A.A.A. — A.N.A. The Joint Committee has developed and promoted three programs of far-reaching influence:

"This Is Our Problem," which stimulated employer-employee programs of economic education in plants throughout the country, leading to the Advertising Council's "Miracle of America" campaign and booklet.

"The Future of America" which was credited by Dr. Arthur F. Burns, then economic advisor to President Eisenhower, with helping to correct "recession" psychology in 1954 and helping to bring about the economic upturn.

"Challenge to America," which explained the importance of marketing and advertising in realizing our country's economic opportunities.

In domestic economic affairs, A.A.A.A. is represented on the National Distribution Council of the Department of Commerce.

In international affairs, it sponsored the First International Meeting of Advertising Agency Leaders, attended in 1956 by leaders from more than 35 different countries throughout the world. It is regularly represented at meetings of The International Chamber of Commerce and the ICC's U.S. Council.

A TYPICAL ADVERTISING AGENCY
ORGANIZATION CHART
BY FUNCTIONS

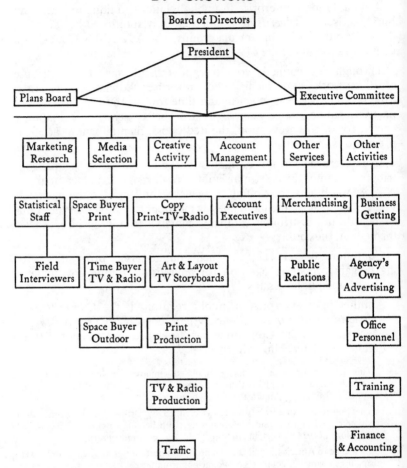

Other A.A.A.A. Committees

In addition to committees and functions already discussed, the American Association of Advertising Agencies has 15 active committees which meet either on a scheduled basis, or as necessary. They are committees on:

> Client service
> Agency management

Government and public relations
Improving advertising
Work with students and educators
Broadcast business affairs
Broadcast policy
Business publications
Consumer magazines
Direct-mail advertising
Newspapers
Out-of-home media
Print production
Fiscal control
Research

One of the greatest services the group performs for its member agencies—and for advertising in general—is its vigorous campaign to attract the cream of the crop of young people to the business. The A.A.A.A. has a continuous program of presenting advertising as a *desirable activity* to high-ranking young high-school and college graduates, and of testing them to determine their suitability for an advertising career. It has been estimated that the four branches of advertising—media, advertisers, advertising agencies, and suppliers and special services—employ around 100,000 men and women; an additional 100,000 are in related administrative and clerical activities. The four branches of advertising probably need a total of 20,000 newcomers each year, of which advertising agencies will absorb about 7,000, including novices.

What Is an Advertising Agency?

Just what is an advertising agency? How is it organized? What are its primary functions? What can it do for the industrial advertising manager and his company that he cannot do himself?

To put these questions in their proper perspective, let's look at the organizational structure of a typical agency, and glance at the functions it performs. Many of them will be discussed at greater length in the following chapters, of course.

The chart (left), by courtesy of the American Association of Advertising Agencies, shows that a typical agency has the familiar line and staff organization common throughout industry.

Except for the extremely small operation, the average agency is staffed with professionals in every facet of communications. It is a specialized creator of a custom-built, one-of-a-kind product, for each campaign and each ad within the campaign is truly unique in that it can be used by only one advertiser, and, more often than not, at only one specific time.

These skilled professionals within the agency are often multi-talented, although usually they are experts in one specific field—copy, art direction, market research, media, and so on. Each contributes his expertise to the program which the agency produces for each of its clients.

In general, most agencies have 15 areas of specialization:

1. Executive
2. Administrative
3. Client contact
4. Client services
5. Copy
6. Art
7. Radio and TV
8. Direct mail
9. Collateral material
10. Marketing
11. Media
12. Research
13. Production
14. Accounting
15. New business

Agency Organizations Most Prevalent

In most agencies today, again excluding the very small ones, one of three organizational structures and systems are used. An agency using what we shall call System 1 assigns writers, art directors, media specialists, and production and traffic people to a group of accounts. These people work only on these specified accounts and are directed by an account executive or account supervisor. When an agency uses System 1, it usually has a number of such groups of specialists working on groups of accounts. Each account group is much like a small agency in that it performs all of the necessary services for its clients. An advertiser whose agency is so set up is assured that there will be a team working on the account that *knows* the account, the products and the market; there is no question of having the work pushed off onto someone who is not thoroughly familiar with it, or of lacking service because "his or her" agency people are too busy or are out of the agency engaged in projects for another advertiser.

System 2 is known in the agency field as the "departmental system." It is departmentalized by function and consists simply of having pools of people, all talented specialists, engaging in their specialty for all of the agency's clients. In such a setup, for example, an agency would have a copy department where copy is written for all agency accounts. As a rule, the individual writers would write on the same accounts most of the time, perhaps as many as a dozen or more different accounts, but not necessarily so. Just as business problems tend to be the same in different businesses, so do copy problems. A really good copywriter can, after a brief review of material previously written—and a talk with the account executive to learn the client's desires—write on almost any product or service with equal facility. All layout artists and art directors would similarly be located in an art department, media personnel in a media department, and production specialists in a production department.

This system works well for many agencies and is probably the one most widely used. Advantages claimed for it include having work done in the various departments produced for the approval of the department head, a skilled professional in the field. Proponents of the system feel that various department heads are likely to have more knowledge and better judgment of their specialties than any individual account executive. The so-called crosspollination effect resulting from having individuals within the various departments exposed to many advertisers' problems, rather than those of just one advertiser, as found in System 1, is theoretically beneficial. There's no denying that experience broadens.

Furthermore, under System 2 it is somewhat easier to have all work reviewed by a plans board or by the agency's executive in charge of client service. Such review benefits the client by having his problems known to and considered by additional agency's personnel. This tends to preclude any possibility of the agency's not adopting the one best plan of attack for the client.

System 3 is probably the best of all for the industrial advertiser, particularly if his products are technical. It is the so-called copy-contact system, which is actually System 1 with modifications to transform it into System 3. These changes are slight, however, and involve only the account executive and the copywriter—who is one and the same individual. Many of the biggest and most successful industrial advertising agencies, Marsteller Inc., for example, are structured this way.

Rationale behind this type of organization is that the one person most closely acquainted with the advertiser's products and problems is the one who actually sees the client frequently—the account executive. The account executive gets his direction and information firsthand, right from the advertising manager. When the account executive, "A.E.," as he is commonly called, is the copywriter there is no necessity to transmit instructions and technical information and to explain the ad manager's wishes to a copywriter. thus there is far less chance of misinterpretation, false starts, and wasted time and money.

How One Firm Went Wrong

One large Chicago-based division of a national corporation recently encountered this problem. Its agency, a sizable System 1 operation, assigned a new account executive to the account at the same time a new ad manager joined the firm. With both men inexperienced, it was almost a case of the blind leading the blind. The agency made the initial mistake, of course, in not providing the necessary continuity for the client. This resulted in a great deal of floundering on the part of both parties—and considerable poor copy, poorly conceived collateral material, and wasted effort. This is a trap into which no ad manager should fall; if new on the job, he should insist that the A.E. familiar with the account stay on it until he is broken in. Sometimes, of course, the situation cannot be helped because coincidentally the A.E. left the agency at an inopportune time and was not available.

Had a copy-contact system been used in this situation, the person who actually called on the advertiser would have known whether or not he had firm and correct direction, and full and factual information. He would have been sure of the course to take. Having an inexperienced account executive relay instructions to a copywriter with whom he wasn't familiar, and an art director who had never met the ad manager (or anyone else from the company) resulted in a costly fiasco.

On the other hand, when the copy-contact man (account executive-copywriter) returns to the agency from a session with the advertising manager, he or she has this notes and his reference material—*plus a feeling* for what the ad manager wants which can only be gotten by an across-the-desk conference.

With System 3 the A.E.-copywriter has solid backing from a group, just as in System 1. He has the account supervisor who backstops him and substitutes or she as required, the group account supervisor, art director, media director, and production people, all of whom are intimately acquainted with the ad manager's account. These people are a constant, a team built by the agency to service a certain number of accounts. This system works so well that it should surely be an important influence when consideration of an agency is being entertained.

How an agency is structured is, however, of less importance to the advertising manager than whether there is the quality of service and the quality of people and creative thinking that leads to solutions of problems. If these are present, the agency is right for the company.

How to Select an Agency

With some 4,500 advertising agencies in this country to choose from, just how does an industrial advertising manager select an agency—either the first, or a new agency if the present one is not satisfactory? What can the advertising manager do to lessen the odds against an unwise choice?

One ad manager, James Dean of the MacGregor Division, Brunswick Corporation, devised a "score sheet." The sheet was given to all members of the company who viewed presentations given by a number of advertising agencies who were interested in acquiring the account. Each member of the MacGregor Division scored each agency, then the score sheets were collected and the results tabulated. The score sheets asked such questions as:

Agency ....

Date ....

Rated by ....

	Par	Score	Remarks
General background	15		

How long has the agency been in business?

(This question will help indicate whether or not the agency's operation is a stable one.)

How many accounts does the agency have?

In what industries are they?

What companies are they?

What is this agency's record of growth?

How many new accounts has this agency acquired in the last two years?
On what dates?

(This question may point up an agency being stretched too thin to handle additional accounts at this time, as far as its personnel are concerned.)

How much agency growth represents new business, and how much is due to increased billing from present clients?

(This question can show whether the agency's clients visibly benefit from agency counsel and services.)

What is the agency's record of account losses in the last five years?

(All agencies lose accounts; this question is valuable because it makes possible an evaluation of the agency's honesty and candor in answering it.)

	Par	Score	Remarks

General attitude   **15**

What kind of people are they?

What is the agency's business philosophy?

Is the agency businesslike in its approach? Do they show a genuine desire to work with us, or do they seem merely to want more business?

Physical organization   10

Does their agency seem well organized? *(A disorganized agency is the last thing an ad manager needs.)*

What is the general experience of the group with whom we talked?

What type of personnel does the agency have?

Is the agency staffed to handle our business?

Who would work on our account? On how many other accounts would these people work?

(Would they have time for us?)

Compatibility   10

Do we like these people as people? *(If they are not really liked now, while they are selling themselves to us, it is unlikely we will ever warm up to them.)*

Would we like doing business with them?

Experience   30

Has this agency solved problems similar to ours?

Can they identify problem areas?

Do they approach problems intelligently and analytically? *(If not, stop wasting time with this agency.)*

Has the agency developed any particularly effective business-publication campaigns? *(If not, it is unlikely they will start now.)*

Has the agency had experience in our field? *(This is a loaded question. Experience in a specific field is not a prerequisiste for an agency to do an outstanding job. In fact, a fresh, objective, outside viewpoint may well pay dividends in pinpointing perplexing problems and solving them most effectively.)*

	Par	Score	Remarks

Does the agency have a proved formula for effective advertising?
(If it does, steer clear! A formula is an excuse for a failure before it occurs for lack of fresh creative thinking. It presages mediocrity at best, complete and utter failure at worst.)
Does the agency experiment with new communication techniques?
(If not, it has probably gone — or is going — stale.)
Is the agency "arty" or are they marketing oriented?
Do they show a good basic grasp of desirable business practices?

Related abilities　　　　　　　　　　20
Is the agency equipped to handle our public relations?
Product publicity?
Package design?
Market research?
Make market tests?
Solve our marketing problems?
Our sales meetings?
Dealer displays?
(If not, this agency is probably too small and we would have to have additional outside sources for these necessary services.)

Par is 100, a bit high for other than a real dub golfer, but a good score for a top-notch agency to achieve on such a score sheet. According to James Dean, this system of scoring largely eliminates emotional reaction to a presentation and makes it relatively easy for company personnel to evaluate agencies to whom they have talked.

Par is 100, a bit high for other than a real dub golfer, but a good score for a top-notch agency to achieve on such a score sheet. According to James Dean, this system of scoring largely elimated emotional reaction to a presentation and makes it relatively easy for company personnel to evaluate agencies to whom they have talked.

Additional Steps in Agency Selection

Books have been written on the single subject of agency selection. One of the best is *The Critical Partnership—Standards of Advertising Agency Selection and Performance,* by Mack Hanan, managing partner of the management consultant firm, Hanan & Son. Hanan lists six steps in selecting an agency:

1. Screening　　　3. Presentation (s)　　　5. Announcement
2. Interviewing　　4. Decision　　　　　　　6. Preparation

The author of this work also added that the advertiser is responsible for 80 percent of the planning of an advertising program. He is responsible for 20 percent of the execution, and he has responsibility for a full 50 percent of the control. The agency assumes responsibility for the remaining portions in each category.

This all seems simple, but there are a number of decisions which must be made before consideration is given to talking to the first prospective agency.

First of all, the decision must be made as to who is going to make the decision of which agency will be retained. In small companies, the advertising manager is usually the man who makes the choice. However, in larger companies the trend is to make the decision by committee; the committee is usually made up of the ad manager, the marketing director, the sales manager, the assistant sales manager and, not infrequently, the company or division president.

Agency responsibility must be decided upon. This involves specifying just what the agency is expected to do for the advertiser; this may well include advertising campaigns, market research, public relations, sales promotion, collateral material—or portions of each. This must be clearly defined for the company's sake, as well as to have all agencies competing on an equal basis for the advertiser's business.

Narrowing the List

The list of prospective agencies must be narrowed down. There are simply too many to consider talking to all of them in a geographic area. Factors which enter in here are agencies with experience in products or markets similar to yours; it has long been standard practice to exclude agencies which have competitive products, or even products which are noncompetitive, but which are manufactured and marketed by a company which *does* make competitive products. However, the American Association of Advertising Agencies suggested that agencies be permitted to handle products even if they currently handle a competitor's noncompeting products. The 4A's feels that the account conflict problem inhibits agencies' growth and limits the number of agencies available to clients. The problem becomes more pressing all of the time due to mergers, company acquisitions, and the huge number of new products introduced annually. A.A.A.A.'s recommendations of this subject are found in a report titled, "The Ideal Client-Agency Policy on Account Conflicts." The Association will send a copy upon request.

Geographic location is usually quite important, although distance in this age of jet aircraft is less of a barrier than it was a few years ago.

However, it follows that the agency located close by can logically be expected to provide better service, and to call more frequently than one which is hundreds of miles away. The cost of travel being what it is, it is not profitable for the agency if too much accrues against an account. Th answer to that one is to cut the service back to where the account *is* profitable.

The amount the account bills is an important consideration. It is axiomatic in the agency business that an advertiser with a budget large enough to represent a sizable portion of the agency's total business has much "clout." This advertiser is going to get the kind of service he wants. There are many small advertisers however, who enjoy good service in giant agencies and wouldn't change for the world just as there are numbers of advertisers with huge budgets who receive fine service and first-rate thinking from small agencies, and the idea of a change is the farthest thing from their minds. Size isn't everything, but dollars still talk. And more dollars talk louder, particularly in an atmosphere where there isn't too much talking being done.

Initially, consider 25 agencies. Not talk to 25, but consider and evaluate them internally and narrow the choice down to a half-dozen or so. These finalists will be the ones chosen to make presentations to executives.

It is up to the ad manager, as the only individual in the company qualified to do so, to accumulate as much raw data about prospective agencies as possible. Sources for facts include agencies themselves; acquire a list of clients of the agencies under consideration. Evaluate them as to the type of businesses they are, decide whether your company is the same general type, and whether or not your company would feel at home in that atmosphere. Check these clients in reference works such as the Rome Report to determine approximately how large their budgets are as far as space placed through the agency is concerned. An initial evaluation of this type will reveal a number of agencies where the business climate is obviously so foreign that these agencies should be dropped from the roster of possibles.

Once the list of prospects is reduced, information about the remaining agencies should be rounded out to provide a better picture of what each could do for your company. The best advice in the world at this stage is to assume nothing. Naturally, good service, good creative thinking, good problem-solving ability are all desirable and necessary, but not every agency provides—or *can* provide—them. Many agencies stay in business without doing so.

Talk to Other Clients

The best possible way to determine what your company could logically expect to receive from the agencies under consideration is to talk to their clients. It is only common courtesy, however, to request permission to do so; needless to say, the "request" will never be turned down.

When talking with the ad manager of a company that is a client of an agency you are considering, explain your situation fully. Ask his opinion of the agency's strong points—and its weak points. All agencies have them in varying degrees. Ask him what he thinks of the agency's creativity—its ability to plan campaigns, to develop communications programs based upon marketing objectives, to produce tight, pithy copy that informs, and layouts that are arresting. Ask about the agency's role in producing collateral material such as sales literature and catalogs—whether it is weak or strong, whether the agency tackles these tasks willingly or accepts them grudgingly, and a general idea of the opinion about agency charges for these services. A frank discussion with *several* ad managers from different companies about *each* agency, with careful note-taking, will result in a very revealing profile of the capabilities of the prospective agencies.

Also, don't overlook past clients of the agency. All agencies lose accounts, of course; relationships are frequently dissolved for reasons beyond the control of either party—such as when a merger occurs, or when a company is purchased by another, for example. In such instances the account invariably goes to an agency already retained by the dominant firm in the consolidation.

Bear in mind, however, that if an agency has a history of high attrition in client relationships, of acquiring clients only to lose them a year or two later, be wary—very wary. Some agencies' major strengths—and efforts—lie in the acquisition of new business. Once an account is in the house the ad manager never again sees the personable, persuasive, hard-sell individuals who initially convinced him that *this* is *the* agency to have. Instead, an entirely different team takes over work associated with the account. They may be capable and efficient, but they are definitely the agency's second team. The first team is saved for new business presentations.

On the other hand, clients sometimes demand too much, are naturally difficult to get along with, or accounts simply are not profitable for the agency. Any of these factors, among others, can cause an agency relationship to be terminated, or cause the agency to resign the account. In fairness to all concerned, the prospective agency should be given the opportunity to rebut adverse comments from former clients.

WHY YOU NEED AN ADVERTISING AGENCY

Space Salesmen Know

Another prime source of information about the agencies being evaluated are representatives of business publications. These space salesmen make more contacts—with advertisers and agencies—in the course of a week than the ad manager makes in six months. Conscientious "reps" will usually give an unbiased and knowledgeable assessment of an agency if assured their remarks will be held in confidence. After all, they sell space to the agencies they are being asked about, so the ad manager must *not* attribute any remarks to them. Since advertising is replete with back-fence gossips to an extent probably unknown in any other business, representatives have picked up information which is strictly closed-door material; much of it is revealing, helpful, interesting—much is useless. Every bit helps round out the picture and makes an informed decision possible.

For a number of years the so-called "questionnaire approach" was considered the last word in sophistication in agency selection. An advertiser in search of a suitable agency developed a questionnaire which was sent to agencies under active consideration, and they were asked to complete and return it to the advertising manager. Many of these questionnaires had merit and asked pertinent questions in an objective way. Questionnaires of this type showed clearly and concisely what an agency expected to do, and would do, for the advertiser. They are helpful to all concerned and save everybody's time.

Some advertisers, however, in an effort to "trap" agencies into some kind of admission which would be detrimental to their cause, deliberately loaded questionnaires, wording questions in such a way that the agency executive answering them had to be psychic to come up with the "correct" reply—much in the same way that the old "have you stopped beating your wife?" question is a bit difficult to answer. The better agencies were quick to realize this was happening and today many refuse to reply to questionnaires sent to them unsolicited. Thus these advertisers, actually in need of an agency, defeated their own purpose. They put *themselves* out of the running and reduced the field from which they could select.

An alternate and much better approach is to write to the agencies being actively considered. Best make the letter relatively short, not over one page, typed and single-spaced. Ask straightforward, information-seeking questions. The answers, of course, can be either quite short, or very extensive; both types of answers will reveal much of the agency's thinking and should be analyzed thoroughly. For the most part, agencies will reply to a request such as this, whereas they may ignore a questionnaire.

The Final Contenders

By this time most of the agencies in the original list of 25 have been eliminated for one reason or another. It is now time to visit the five or six finalists and get acquainted. Phone or write for an appointment (as you'd expect if the situation were reversed). Be punctual; the agencies undoubtedly will have an array of executives on hand for the meeting and they are tying up an expensive group.

In exploratory meetings such as this, *all* agencies greatly prefer to let their prospective client do most of the talking. It is to their advantage to learn all they can at this crucial stage of the game so that they can gain some edge over their competitors. Resist this temptation; your time to talk will come soon enough. Let the agency people you're visiting carry the conversational ball. Make them sell themselves—and their agency—to you. Make them demonstrate their capabilities by showing you case histories—problem-solving programs they have prepared for other clients. Meet their people. Evaluate them—their competence, business ability, attitude, and their interest in working for you.

Ask to see their "house" ads—the advertisements they have prepared to advertise their agency. Advertising agencies, the good ones, believe in what they're doing. They advertise for the same reason that any company does. Much can be learned about an agency and its philosophy by reading what it writes about itself. Naturally you'll be welcome to take reprints of the ads with you when the meeting is over; analyze them and add comments to the files of the various agencies you've built up.

The next step is to invite the finalists—excluding any eliminated during your visits to the various agencies, of course—to make a formal presentation in your office. At this time many ad managers prefer to ask the marketing director, the sales manager, or both, to sit in on these meetings. It is now that generalities must be dispensed with and real specifics discussed. Each prospective agency should be asked to state precisely just what it will do for your company; who they will assign to the account and how much service they propose to provide. This is the time to discuss—and agree completely on—all of the details of the agency compensation. All parties must understand and concur on every detail, and they must do so *now*. Later is too late. Work out a financial arrangement that is fair to both the company and the agency. Spell it out and *write it out*. When this is done you'll find that disagreements about money—always unpleasant, frequently embarrassing, and occasionally fatal to a good working relationship—almost never crop up. The financial agreement must be discuss-

ed with all of the agencies making presentations so that all may be judged fairly and impartially.

Presentations Vary

Presentations run the gamut from full-blown "dog and pony shows" to relaxed, informal talks. Many agencies have audiovisual presentations consisting of a slide show with synchronized, taped commentary, or the comments are made by one of the agency people. Despite the possibility of being dazzled by the elaborate presentation, the ad manager is usually less likely to be talked into an affiliation that is unsuitable than are others in the company who are less familiar with agencies.

An agency presentation, whether flip-chart, show cards, audio-visual, or just conversation, should do one thing—sell the agency to those who see it. There's nothing inherently wrong with being sold, or in doing the selling. After all, it's the agency's business to help sell your product. The personality and the capability of the agency should come through loud and clear in any presentation. That, after all the dust has settled, is what you're buying.

Speculative campaigns, or ads "done on spec," merit little consideration. An agency making a presentation has had so little opportunity to learn your business and familiarize itself with your product or service—and your problems—that it is unfair to expect it to present at this time a campaign worth the artist's board it's mounted on. Any campaigns or individual ads are undoubtedly off target and are undesirable. They are a waste of time for the agency which prepared them and, most ad managers feel, reflect undisciplined thinking in the agency which prepared them.

Assuming your product is technical, and the majority of industrial products are, no agency can come armed to the teeth with knowledge of how this widget actuated that gizmo so that the product performs as promised. Nobody is justified in asking that.

Instead, the knowledgeable ad manager looks for market knowledge which proves to him that the agency understands where the product is sold and used, and how it is sold. Ability to absorb technical knowledge is vitally important, however, and should be demonstrated by agencies during their presentations. It is safe to assume, for example, that if an agency successfully prepares ad copy and collateral copy on diesel engines that it can easily do so for fork-lift trucks. Or, if it writes well on semiconductor production equipment, it can do the same for laboratory test instrumentation. It is wise to point this out to other company members evaluating presentations, for they may be unaware of this.

Score each "contestant" as previously discussed. Then compare and evaluate the scores and the other information accumulated and tabulated during this period. Make a final decision as quickly as possible. Each competing agency is understandably anxious to learn the outcome, and it is decent to notify them without delay. A little tact and thoughtfulness are in order, and the losing agencies should be let down gently and with consideration for their feelings. The courteous thing to do is to write each, thanking them for their time and effort and for considering your company as a client. Tell them what agency was selected. It is always possible that you may need another contact or quotation from another agency.

The Written Agreement

Good business practice is to get together immediately with the new agency and draw up a *written* working agreement. It should state:

1. When the agreement takes effect, and that it will be in effect until terminated. That the agreement may be terminated by either party by written notice, 30 days prior to its taking effect, is a typical clause.

2. Specific services the agency is to provide should be listed as to products or services, market areas, and any limitations are noted specifically.

3. Billing terms should be stated, with a full explanation of how the agency will bill for services and how purchases will be made for the client. A brief statement of how and when the agency pays media, together with billing and discount dates, makes it easy for the accounting department, as well as the ad manager, to handle agency invoices.

4. If for any reason the relationship is terminated by either the client or the agency, the rights and obligations of both should be stated, with particular emphasis placed on how work in process and current contracts with media are to be handled.

It is not negative to talk about termination immediately upon joining forces. It is good business for both the client and the agency to have a written agreement in the files—with both parties hoping that the day it is signed is the last time it is ever seen!

Client and Agency Relationship

It's obvious by now that selecting and appointing an agency is not undertaken lightly or done on the spur of the moment. Many have compared the client-agency relationship with marriage, and the analogy isn't an inappropriate one. Agency selection is made less emotionally and, perhaps, for better reasons, but both relationships are as important as any the ad manager is likely to experience.

A good agency is one that studies and learns the company's products and markets. It is one with a strong desire to have its clients succeed, so that it customarily does more than is expected. It is one that is a real pleasure to work with. Such an agency is a full half of the advertising team. It is far more than a placement service which buys space, issues insertion orders, and ships electros. The agency is a *partner,* and the ad manager fortunate enough to pick one that's really right should provide prompt and proper input for the agency, give it his complete backing—and cherish it.

Much has been written and will be written on the client-agency relationship. Much of it needed to be said, much didn't. The fact is that both the client and the agency have one objective which they share—to make a profit. Far too many people on the corporate side of the desk cheerfully pay lip service to "wanting our agency to make money," but too few, unfortunately, actually understand what is involved. The conscientious ad manager will familiarize himself with agency problems and costs and procedures, so that he can assure himself that his agency is getting a fair shake. Agencies, good ones, do as much or more for their clients.

At first the relationship will be formal. But people are pretty decent whether they're in corporations or agencies, and the ad manager will want to progress to a first-name basis. If all of the factors involved in the selection were evaluated correctly, a firm business friendship will develop over the years. It comes as a surprise to some ad managers — those who have endured an agency relationship that was less than productive and effective—that agencies are, by and large, inhabited by unusually talented individuals who earnestly want to make their clients successful and their ad managers look good.

It's always more pleasant to do business with friends. In the client-agency relationship the ad manager should be businesslike, should properly insist on running a tight ship; but he shouldn't be a martinet. Nobody likes a freeloader, even if he *is* a client; a good advertising manager has an expense account and he should use it. It is not right for the agency to always buy the lunch!

Few Secrets in Business

Trust the agency. Take it into your confidence. There should be no company secrets. The agency has a legitimate interest in such vital statistics as cost of manufacture of the product(s), sales volume, margins, gross profit, selling costs, marketing costs, sales projections, and the current and anticipated competitive conditions. Without this information the agency is working blindfolded.

Some advertisers say they feel this information should be withheld from the agency because it might not always be their agency. This is quite true. But they conveniently ignore the fact that there are very few secrets in business. If an agency resigns, or is terminated, some very confidential information is loose in the business community. But when a key employee resigns, or is enticed away by a competitor, just how secret is this secret information? Some things must be taken on trust.

One major goal of the ad manager as well as the agency is to make the relationship an *enduring* one. On the face of it, it is quite obvious that whether or not it endures is contingent upon the quality of service the agency provides. This would include campaign planning, copy, layout, research, merchandising, media counsel, and agency willingness and ability to become totally involved in the company's communications problems.

In addition, though, there must be an honest desire on the part of both the company and the agency for the relationship to be a long-lived one for this desire to be translated into actuality. If the agency is right for the company (if it isn't, why was it selected?), and the agency is convinced the company is the right client, all concerned should strive consciously from the very beginning to build a solid and satisfactory relationship based on mutual trust, respect for, and need of each other.

Bear in mind that a new agency is much like a new employee—or, for that matter, much like the ad manager himself when he was new on the job. It is illogical in the extreme to choose a new agency, then to expect to receive almost from the start brilliant, compelling advertising that is difficult to improve upon. This is unrealistic. A new agency, like a new ship, requires a shakedown cruise before it is truly ready to take on all that comes its way. The agency needs time to become acclimated, time to learn the products or services, time to learn the people it's involved with and establish a rapport with them. And, most important, time to think. This last is crucial if the agency is to develop a program that will achieve the desired results.

Work with the agency, give it every bit of help possible and refrain from unfavorable evaluation of initial efforts. There's plenty of time later for this sort of thing if it becomes necessary.

That Difficult Second Year

The consensus is that while building an enduring relationship is never easy, the second year is the perilous one. It is in this year that serious misunderstandings—or even a complete break—are most likely to happen. By this time it has become apparent to all that the agency is composed of hardworking, unusually competent people—not superhumans from whom frequently come blinding strokes of sheer brilliance which lay low all the problems of the past, present, and future. The ad manager and others in the company have had time to become accustomed to the advertising the agency produces. They may tend to regard it as increasingly plodding and pedestrian, rather than vigorous and vital, interesting and exciting. Sales probably have not surged dramatically, and possibly the cost of selling has not been drastically reduced by advertising, which should do just that. A psychological letdown in such a situation must be guarded against.

Now, before the situation deteriorates further so that there is nothing to be saved, is the time for the advertising manager to remember two things: (1) Breaking in a new agency is an incredibly difficult, time-consuming, and costly proposition which nobody in his right mind wants to have to do any oftener than required, and (2) It is now that the agency needs the help and encouragment of the ad manager.

Show the agency by your actions that they have your complete confidence and respect. Resist at all costs the temptation to make the mistake so many industrial ad managers with little experience make—needling, prodding, attempting to "keep the agency off balance." The ad manager who attempts to manage with such woefully misguided ideas and crude tactics is kidding nobody but himself or herself. He or she succeeds merely in getting disliked, in creating a poor impression for the company in the minds of agency personnel, and keeps the agency too busy keeping its skirts clean to do the job the ad manager must have done.

Ignore the siren songs sung by competitive agencies who want your account. There will be some who do at any given time. Talk with one, even informally, and the word inevitably will get back to your agency because the entire advertising business is a tightly knit group. What this will accomplish is to kill off all enthusiasm of your agency, instantly and probably with great finality. Then the A.E. who calls has turned into an on-guard zombie who reflects the feeling of the agency—that they've been stabbed in the back, that the client isn't to be trusted.

From then on, instead of getting the best thinking of which the agency is capable, the ad manager will receive *what the agency thinks he wants to hear—what the agency thinks it can "sell."* This input from the ad manager, polished and rewritten and fleshed out, always lacks the creative spark which distinguishes advertising created by craftsmen who believe in what they're doing from advertising cranked out because an assignment must be completed. Cost to the client is exactly the same.

Chapter 3

LAYING THE GROUNDWORK

INDUSTRY suffers from the Wilbur-and-Orville-Wright syndrome. An incredible percentage of companies whose products are sold to industry are afflicted with this debilitating syndrome, which is nothing more than flying by the seat of the pants when it comes to marketing in general and advertising in particular.

More poor ads are run, more ineffective campaigns are developed, and more money is poured down the drain—absolutely wasted—on industrial advertising that doesn't have a ghost of a chance to do its assigned job because of a dismal lack of adequate planning than for any other reason.

Planning—and the preplanning stage which we'll call laying the groundwork—are neglected much oftener than not. Perhaps it's because this is considered the least interesting activity (or *lack* of activity) the industrial ad manager encounters. But, properly done, it can be one of the most productive.

Many industrial advertising managers routinely perform the fantastically difficult feat of operating in a vacuum. They are uncommonly apt at producing advertising in the most wasteful, most ineffective way ever conceived—without an overall plan. Ads turned out one or two at a time on a hit-or-miss basis, in response to some minor panic, or possibly in reaction to a bit of pressure from sales, are far more likely to miss than to hit. And they'll waste an appalling amount of money in the process.

It's pathetic but true that this is seldom the fault of the advertising manager. He or she is a victim of circumstances, but something can be done about it.

Poor planning, or lack of *any* planning, usually starts at the top of the ladder in the small or medium-sized industrial firm. It is due either to vacillation or naivete'. Companies which don't plan are as familiar as apple pie, the corner drugstore, or the stereotype of the American-boy-makes-good success story.

Many were founded some 40 years ago by an engineering genius who had an Idea. Invariably the Idea was translated into an intricate, highly engineered product that was genuinely superior. It sold steadily because it was like the well-known mousetrap, and the company prospered. As the economy grew, so did the company. Suddenly, though, competition—serious competition—reared its ugly head.

The engineering genius, now a full-fledged business tycoon with a paneled office and private washroom, remained innocently content with simply building a better widget, never doubting for a single minute that his company would get its fair share—or more—of the market. He continued to regard his company as a production organism and continued to place primary emphasis on engineering and production. Marketing and advertising were words almost outside the corporate vocabulary for all practical purposes. What little advertising that was done was done because everybody else did it. Inevitably the company's sales deteriorated, as did its competitive position. Then the engineering genius retired to fish in Florida and control of the firm passed from his hands. As a rule, new management reversed the downtrend with smart marketing and smart advertising. Sound familiar?

The Marketing Concept

When a company is solidly product oriented, rather than embracing the "marketing concept" like a long-lost lover, it finds its position in the marketplace constantly harder to maintain. A product-oriented company thinks in terms of what *it* knows best, of what *it* wants to build, of what *it* wants to sell, of how *it* wants to distribute, of how *it* wants to provide after-sale service—rather than thinking of these basic concepts in terms of the customers' desires, or looking at them through the customers' eyes.

It is incontrovertible that successful companies, those whose performance is head and shoulders above that of their industries as a whole, are adherents to and believers in the marketing concept. Ask IBM, Xerox, Avis, P&G, 3M, or Sears, Roebuck.

The cornerstone of successful marketing strategy and getting the most out of the marketing concept is a *written* marketing plan. It is an absolute essential. This is so vitally important it bears repeating: a written plan is an absolute essential. The following letter, written by an industrial advertising manager to his boss, a vice-president of marketing, spells out just why a written plan is so necessary, what benefits derive from having it, and what happens as a result of doing without. The situation is real, incidentally, as is the letter and the advertising agency. All names have been changed for obvious reasons.

LAYING THE GROUNDWORK

Mr. John M. Wiegand
Vice-President, Marketing
Acme Engineered Products, Inc.
1234 West Boulevard Street
City, State 56789

Dear Jack:

One thing I'll say about a vacation: It lets me do something I don't have time to do at work—some random thinking.

Jack, I think it's imperative that we adopt the marketing concept if Acme is to better its competitive position. Unless we do, we'll be hard put even to retain our present position. This is elementary, I realize. But I say it because throughout the company much lip service is given to the marketing concept, yet we remain very much product oriented.

As you know, there's nothing esoteric about the marketing concept. It is simply determining exactly what our prospects want, then producing those products and selling them at a profit—preferably a fat one.

However, to realize the full potential for profit inherent in the marketing concept, it is essential that we have a written marketing plan.

Without one, we drift.

Writing a marketing plan isn't the easiest thing in the world, nor is it a terrible task.

But I think it must be done. If you agree, I suggest that you, J. Winston Johnson, and I get our heads together behind a closed door with the phone cut off.

We should discuss Acme's past performance; our position in our various markets; our major strengths; how these strengths were built up; where our weaknesses are; suggestions for overcoming them; major market trends; a rundown on what competition is now doing—and what they are likely to do; dollar volume and profitability requested by management.

Part of the preparatory work on the marketing plan is already completed. Our agency, J. Winston Johnson, has completed an internal audit, as you know.

Your knowledge of products and markets, supplemented with that of our market managers, will provide a relatively objective analysis of our desires—as the manufacturer—as well as those of our prospects.

Once these topics have been discussed and there is complete unanimity of thought, we can put words on paper.

Jack, I think our marketing plan should emphasize four major points:
1. It should describe our present position.
2. It should clearly state management's viewpoint and decisions made on products, new products, research and development, changes in the field force, changes in or additions to our present channels of distribution, and subjects for and audiences for our external communications.
3. It should establish long-range objectives, preferably five years ahead.
4. It should establish short-term goals and assign specific responsibilities to individuals—with target dates.

Some companies fall short of established goals and objectives, even when there is a written marketing plan—probably due to failure to adhere to point 4 above.

This is understandable and probably inescapable. No management expects marketing people to have extrasensory perception, nor does it expect perfection in prognosticative powers. All managements do, however, expect a good return on the investment and on the sales dollar. They usually get it when the marketing plan is right.

Jack, I know that with the guidance and direction of good, sound, written marketing plan I can make our advertising and sales promotion do a much more effective job than ever before.

Call me when we can discuss this, will you please?

Cordially,
/s/
Advertising Manager

Less Than 10 Percent Plan Properly

Most companies do not have a written marketing plan. They talk at great length about the total marketing concept and what it can do for them, but they haven't planned for it. A survey made by Cresap, Mc-Cormick and Paget, well-known management consultants, disclosed that most companies not only don't have advertising objectives, but they don't have marketing objectives. Supplementary studies made by Marsteller Inc., indicated that less than 10 percent of American industry follows formal, written marketing programs geared to marketing objectives.

If no marketing plan exists, the advertising manager is in a unique position to make a significant, recognizable contribution above his assigned responsibilities. It is one that could make a massive contribution to company growth over the years. He or she is probably the one professional in the company who can poke and prod and guide those in various areas of activity to an agreement. Then he or she can do something — *write* the plan.

The letter above covers what should be in the plan, and it can serve as a rough outline. Naturally, current and projected sales, profit margins, cost of sales, analyses of individual markets, total sales, and other items peculiar to each company will also be included. Of vital importance is having *complete* agreement of all parties on all points in the plan. To achieve this, disputed passages must be rewritten and restated until they are acceptable, without reservation, by all. Point 3 above should be particularly well thought out so that it states, clearly and concisely, management's objectives for company growth, expansion, and acquisitions. Point 4 above, which makes specific assignments to specific people with target dates, is the action area which management must watch closely. It is here that impending failure to achieve as planned will first be evident.

For the ad manager the written marketing plan is like a road map to the tourist. It helps find the right route and, once found, helps him or her stay on it. Furthermore, having the plan to refer to makes it much easier to develop an integrated promotional program that will speed achieving the set objectives. Without a written plan the ad manager is in the untenable position of working blind, of relying on conversations for direction. Those can easily be misinterpreted and even more easily forgotten.

The Other Side of the Fence

Sometimes the industrial advertising manager comes down with an affliction which closely resembles envy, except that this is a word with a poor image. Still, he or she looks wistfully at a cousin, ad manager of a company which markets nice simple little products to nice simple little customers. He or she reasons with much justification that the consumer ad person has an easier job. For one thing, the products are nontechnical. And the market is so vast it staggers the imagination; after all, everybody's a consumer, so everybody's a prospect. The manager doesn't have to try to determine who can use the product—and how—then determine the best way to communicate. The consumer ad man's story almost tells itself it seems because all that has to be done is come up with an advertising campaign with flair and style, one loaded with sure-fire appeals which trigger the right emotions, as carefully determined beforehand by the researchers and psychologists. Then dazzle 'em with four-color spreads in the mass magazines, complete with expensive art and clever, clever copy. Add appealing point-of-purchase displays, dealer tie-ins, cooperative campaigns and then, for a *coup de grace* if the budget permits (it usually does), turn to TV to beam the message to those who don't, won't, or can't read magazines. It's all very simple.

Unfortunately, the industrial advertising manager doesn't advertise nice simple little products to a mass of nice simple little consumers. This market is highly selective and the products are strictly another breed of cat, falling as they do into four main categories. These are:

1. Items or materials used, or consumed upon the premises of the manufacturer, although not consumed in the manufacturing process itself.
   Examples: sweeping compound, light bulbs, replacement V-belts, saw blades, grinding wheels, air conditioners, floor polishers.
2. Those products consumed in the manufacturing process.
   Examples: industrial adhesives, nails, flux, lacquer thinner, solder, screws, rivets, polishing compound, bolts, escutcheons.
3. Those items incorporated into the end product, either individually, or as a completed subassembly.
   Examples: upholstery fabric, transmissions, cabinet hinges and knobs, semiconductors, piston rings, tires, transistors, bricks, electric motors, window frames, valves, meters, thermocouples, batteries, compressors, radios.
4. Capital equipment used to produce the end product or service.
   Examples: machine tools, conveyors, hoists, kilns, cranes, motor trucks, draglines, heat-treating furnaces, bulldozers, dust collectors, lift trucks, computers, office copying machines, typewriters, trenching machines, diesel-electric locomotives.

Sophisticated Customers

Just as the industrial ad person's product is entirely different from those dangled enticingly before the eager consumer, so is the company different. It depends upon different distribution channels, and upon decisions of a buyer who is a unique species.

To plan an effective promotional program it is necessary to understand how the industrial buyer thinks and how buying decisions are made. You can start with the premise that he or she does not buy for own use. He or she neither eats, wears, sits on, nor rides in the products purchased, and he buys with company money. He or she makes buying decisions coldly and dispassionately and logically, aware that they influence both the future and that of his company. Impulse purchases are foreign to his or her nature and, theoretically, at least, the buyer remains emotionally detached from all decisions.

For a number of years now the magic terminology among purchasing agents—and this has, through osmosis, spread outward and upward through countless companies—is "value analysis." There's nothing esoteric about the term or the concept, for it is nothing more than an objective appraisal of a product's merit based on a meticulous analysis of its favorable and unfavorable features; entering in also is consideration of delivery schedule, reputation of the manufacturer, availability of parts and service, and price. When viewed in this light, it becomes obvious that these sophisticated buyers are really looking for *reasons why* they should buy a given item.

This, then, is the key to the thinking of the industrial buyer. The buyer wants reasons why he or she should, or should not, buy from one source as opposed to another, or why he or she should buy one brand or make in preference to others. Industrial advertising must give those reasons why.

From the industrial buyer's viewpoint, perhaps the single most compelling reason why he decides as he does is the "pocketbook reason." If an advertisement presents believable evidence to him that a product will help cut production cost of his product, reduce maintenance expense, or last longer, the ad has done its job even if he doesn't, panting with eagerness, grab the phone and call in an absolutely firm order. This happens so rarely it's akin to science fiction when it does. If the ad has left a favorable impression of the product or service, and of the advertiser, the company's salespeople will find a receptive climate when they call. They will find it easier to close a sale because they can skip several preliminary steps in the creation of a sale because advertising has partially presold the buyer.

Recognize that the purchasing agent cannot be ignored and that the wise policy is to touch all bases. The PA, however, is generally *not* the *key* buying influence. As a rule purchasing is told what to buy, or is presented with three acceptable products and asked to get prices, delivery dates, check warranties, ascertain what after-sale service policy is, and similar information so as to be able to make a reasoned buying recommendation.

Ford and Maytag Policies

Actually, the term "buyer" is a misnomer when a purchase is in the offing that involves a large expenditure. The plural of the word is much more accurate, for one individual almost never makes the decision to buy when the dollar amount is high. Such purchases are a team effort, with the final decision contingent upon recommendations by technical-level personnel to inhabitants of walnut-paneled offices.

Ford Motor Company's transmission plant at Livonia, Michigan, is a good example of multiple buying influences when capital equipment is acquired. This establishment buys new gear-cutting equipment quite frequently. Three buying offices are regularly contacted by offices of this equipment, but six other buying influences are involved in most of the purchases, including one or more individuals who decide whether *any* purchase will be made, along with several others who decide on the type of equipment Ford needs. Finally, all nine offices are involved in varying degrees when the make of equipment is decided. Only *one-third* of the buying influences were contacted by salespeople in this instance, although this is a higher percentage than usual in a capital-equipment acquisition. Bear in mind that salespeople usually call on those on the technical level, and that *they are not acquainted with and do not have an entree to buying influences in the upper echelons of management.* But advertising does.

Another example of multiple buying influences in industry is the Maytag Company, Newton, Iowa, appliance manufacturer. This firm held weekly meetings for each major manufacturing department in two plants. Topics for the discussions included budget adherence, cost and quality problems, manpower requirements, and production schedules. Solutions to problems often included proposals for process and methods changes—and equipment procurement. These meetings were chaired by the department head, and his "staff" included, among others, the vice-president of manufacturing, the works manager, his plant manager, an industrial-engineering representative, a production engineer, and any specialist who might be called in because of a problem in his area of specialization. Any of these persons, of course, might introduce an idea, or propose a solution to the problem under discussion. A purchase was involved as often as not. All of these individuals are buying influences once a course of action is decided upon. It is costly self-delusion for any company hoping to sell to Maytag—or a company its size—to adopt the complacent attitude that their salespeople call upon the decision makers in the company. They don't.

In large organizations, those with 1,000 or more employees, the involvement of less than six people in a major buying decision happens almost as frequently as salespersons walk on water. It is far more likely that the actual number would be from nine to 12, although this depends to a certain extent on just where the line is drawn as to what constitutes an influence. People who will say "yes" or "no" to the final proposal are admittedly few in number, but many times their number affects the nature of the proposal. And when we consider time as a factor—time which may delay a sale or purchase, increasing the risk of an alternate action being taken—the influences are almost countless.

Participants in buying decisions either have the technical background necessary to evaluate products under consideration, or call upon technical experts within the company. Occasionally, when extremely complex capital equipment that has not been used by the company in the past is considered, outside consultants assist in making the buying decision, particularly when an entire process is being changed. And how many salespeople call on *them?*

Urgency and Availability Factors

Time required to make a buying decision is, more often than not, affected by two factors. One of these certainly is the urgency of the need. The other is the availability of answers. These two factors have intereffects or relationships which are rather interesting. For example, a production-engineering and management group may recognize a need to expand capacity, or improve quality, or cut costs, The time required to make a buying decision will be affected by a management-imposed deadline. It can be delayed by the group's interest or willingness to probe for alternate solutions. At the same time, an answer may emerge to a need that has not been recognized. This happens when a better way to do something is made known, even though the present way has apparently been satisfactory.

Most plants did not need automation or computers until they appeared on the scene. At least, they were not actively looking for these solutions to existing problems. In a sense, invention becomes the mother of necessity.

A complete change in the production process invariably involves a lengthy purchase time, such as that which accompanied International Harvester's decision to install a numerically controlled machining line to produce cylinder blocks. This giant step forward in production machining marked a major development in the transition of numerical control from the toolroom, model shop, pilot plant, and defense-industry job to competitive commercial manufacturing.

Installed at IHC's construction equipment division plant outside Chicago, the block machining line involves 14 tape-controlled units—including a tape-controlled transfer machine—out of a total of 43 machine tools. The new automated line gave International the versatility they required, as well as a significant cost reduction. Alternate to the automated line would have involved a total of 65 machines, many so specialized they would have been idle two-thirds of the time. Changeovers for different model runs would have taken a week, compared to 16 hours; floor-space requirements would have doubled, and storage of jigs and fixtures would have created serious problems in an already overloaded plant. These considerations and many more were involved in the buying decision.

According to the works manager, the decision to go the tape-controlled route, that is, to automate, was the result of planning that began *five years* before the purchase was made, when International Harvester engineers were developing a new family of engines. As a guide to setting a course, IHC production-engineering department personnel set up five objectives:

1. No cost penalties must be incurred.
2. Maximum flexibility must be developed.
3. Minimum jigs and fixtures to be required.
4. Minimum setup or changeover time.
5. Minimize obsolescence caused by model changes.

Some free thinking was generated by these objectives, much of it gravitating toward numerically controlled machines which were considered exotic at the time. But the division accumulated experience and data, pursued various ideas, weighed and evaluated, and ultimately made the decision to buy.

The number of buying influences is almost impossible to calculate, although it certainly runs into the hundreds. How could purveyors of this sophisticated new hardware installed at IHC hope to have their salespeople call on all of these buying influences—or even a significant percentage of them—over such a long time span, and to keep in regular contact? It is an impossibility. Continuity of contact in such a situation can be maintained in only one way—through a well-planned, sustained advertising program.

Ordinarily the longer time periods are the result of a radical process change, as at Harvester. However, many companies such as NCR

Corp. have a policy that is intended to forestall perpetuation of a multiple-unit process where units are replaced one at a time. For example, a battery of six automatic screw machines may have been built up over a period of years, and the natural tendency is to begin replacing them at the rate of their deterioration or obsolescence. Such buying decisions are relatively simple and can easily be made in days or, at most, a few weeks. Where this situation exists, NCR insists that each decision to replace "kind for kind" be prefaced by a thorough examination of available alternates to the total process. NCR realizes the wisdom of finding out what is available that will possibly do a better job than the battery of six machines it now owns. Technology changes, and the company which stays tied to the past and its tried-and-proved way of doing things the same old way lags instead of leads.

Salespeople could never reach all of the buying influences at NCR when a process is being evaluated, even if they knew when this evaluation was taking place. Advertising in the right business publication does, though, communicate with all levels.

Diagram of a Purchasing Program

The evolution of a decision to buy, and how that decision was made, is graphically shown in the purchase-process diagram nearby, which is part of an extensive research study made for *Production* magazine by Harvey Research Organization, Inc. The diagram dissects the entire process, starting at Stage 1 at the time of the initial project or motivation, through Stage 7 and, finally, the issuance of a purchase order.

Since this is the most current major study of this subject, as well as one of the best that has been made to date, we should examine the diagram in detail in order to gain a better understanding of the research results.

According to the diagram, the purchase is broken down into three main increments:

I. Origination of the idea for purchase.

II. Justifying the possible purchase.

III. Receiving bids from possible suppliers, and making the final purchase decision.

In Increment I, Stage 1 consists of initial project or motivation. Only six considerations motivated all buying influences. They are:

Continuing cost reduction or profit improvement effort.

Model change or new product.

HARVEY RESEARCH ORGANIZATION, INC.

ORIGINATION OF THE IDEA FOR PURCHASE		JUSTIFYING THE POSSIBLE PURCHASE
STAGE 1 INITIAL PROJECT OR MOTIVATION	STAGE 2 BASIC OBJECTIVE	STAGE 3 ANALYZING THE PROBLEM
(Check one)	NOTE: Check one, or number in order of importance	NOTE: Check activities in which you participated
☐ Continuing Cost Reduction or Profit Improvement Effort	☐ CUT COSTS		☐ Process or Methods Comparisons
or		☐ Production Cost Analysis	☐ Product Design Review
☐ Model Change or New Product	☐ IMPROVE QUALITY		
or		☐ Parts or Process Quality Analysis	☐ Materials Evaluations
☐ Periodic Review of Equipment/ Tools or Materials	☐ ADD CAPACITY		
or		☐ Plant or Dept. Capacity Analysis	☐ Make vs. Buy Review
☐ Plant or Process Modernization	☐ NEW PRODUCT LINE		
or	☐ Other_____	☐ Other_____	☐ Plant Capacity Studies
☐ New Plant			
☐ Other_____			☐ Other_____

The seven stages of a purchase.

Periodic review of equipment, tools or materials.

Plant or process modernization.

New plant.

Other.

Stage 2 is the basic objective of the buying influences. In the research study, each was asked to check one, or number several in order of their importance. Objectives are:

Cut costs.

Improve quality.

Add capacity.

New product line.

Other.

Interviewees were asked in Stage 3, analyzing the problem, to check activities in which they participated. Activities are:

Production cost analysis.

93

PURCHASE PROCESS DIAGRAM — (WHITE SHEET A)

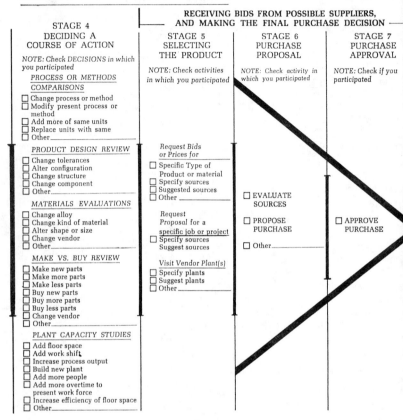

Parts or process quality analysis.

Plant or department capacity analysis.

Other.

Process or methods comparisons.

Product design review.

Materials evaluations.

Make vs. buy review.

Plant capacity studies.

Other.

In deciding a course of action, Stage 4, those questioned were asked to check the *decisions* in which they participated. Listed decisions are:

In deciding a course of action, Stage 4, those questioned were asked to check the *decisions* in which they participated. Listed decisions are:

Process or methods comparisons
    Change process or method.
    Modify present process or method.
    Add more of same units.
    Replace units with same.
    Other.

Product design review
    Change tolerances.
    Alter configuration.
    Change structure.
    Change component.
    Other.

Materials evaluation
    Change alloy.
    Change kind of material.
    Alter size or shape.
    Change vendor.
    Other.

Make vs. buy review
    Make new parts.
    Make more parts.
    Make less parts.
    Buy new parts.
    Buy more parts.
    Buy less parts.
    Change vendor.
    Other.

Plant capacity studies
    Add floor space.
    Add work shift.
    Increase process output.
    Build new plant.
    Add more people.
    Add more overtime to present work force.
    Increase efficiency of floor space.
    Other.

For Stage 5, selecting the product, those interviewed were asked to check the activities in which they participated. Those were:

Request bids or prices for
    Specific type of product or material.
    Specify sources.
    Suggested sources.
    Other.

Request proposal for a specific job or project
    Specify sources.
    Suggest sources.

Visit vendor plant(s)
    Specify plants.
    Suggest plants.
    Other.

In Stage 6, purchase proposal, those participating in the study were asked to check activities in which they participated from this list:

    Evaluate sources.
    Propose purchase.
    Other.

The short and crucial stage, Stage 7, lists only one statement to be checked:

    Approve purchase.

Space was provided for entering the respondent's name, title, company, product manufactured, name of purchased item, and a description of it.

Field work on the project involved visiting 86 plants and interviewing 145 people. Plants were selected at random from *Production's* circulation galleys. This produced a pattern closely approximating market distribution, with 76 percent of the plants in Standard Industrial Classifications 35, 36, and 37. Of these plants, 58 percent employ between 100 and 1,000, 33 percent employ more than 1,000. Of the respondents, 62 percent were in production engineering and management functions, 17 percent in purchasing, 12 percent top management, and 8 percent design engineers.

Each respondent was carefully qualified as having participated within six months in one or more purchases of capital equipment, tools, or materials. Using the diagram and questionnaire, the first contact in each plant was intervewed with respect to a specific purchase. Additional contacts, supplied by the first person, were interviewed with respect to the same purchase to the extent they were available at that time.

Based on the outline of the purchase-process diagram, here are salient points revealed by the study:

LAYING THE GROUNDWORK

I. 96 percent of the respondents stated that the purchase-process diagram represents the evolution of a purchase in their plant.

II. With respect to the successive stages, which are outlined in the following section (III), in no instance did all of the respondents participate in any one stage. A summary of activity shows that 90 percent participated in Stages 1 and 2, 85 percent in 3 and 4, 75 percent in Stage 5, 71 percent in Stage 6, and 51 percent in Stage 7.

Obviously, far more people are active in developing the information and directions upon which proposals and approvals are based than in these final stages.

III. An analysis of the factors affecting, leading to, or determining purchases, based on the purchasing-procedures diagram, follows:

Stage 1. Initial motivation of purchases:
    a. Cost-reduction programs 52%
    b. Model change or new-product development 33%
    c. Plant or process modernization 25%
    d. Periodic equipment, tools, materials review 15%
Note: More than one motivation is involved in many purchases. For example, a cost-reduction program and a model change may be initiating forces behind the same purchase.

Stage 2. The objectives of initial motivations:
    a. Cost reduction 50%
    b. Quality improvement...50%
    c. Added capacity...40%
    d. New-product production......................................30%
Note: Profit begins to appear to be a more consistent reason for production improvement than new-product tooling or materials specifications.

It is also interesting to see that more than one objective is the target of initial motivations. Scrap, for example, may be the target of both cost reduction and quality improvement. It is also apparent that any of the objectives can be the target of any of the initial motivations. Plant modernization might have the targets of both added capacity and quality improvements.

Stage 3. Analyzing the problem:
    a. Production cost analysis 40%
    b. Part or process quality analysis 40%
    c. Plant or department capacity analysis 40%
The purpose of this analysis is to define or establish the area of attack. Degrees of attention to more detailed analysis are indicated as follows:
    a. Process or methods comparisons 40%
    b. Plant capacity studies 33%
    c. Make-or-buy studies 30%
    d. Product design reviews 25%

Stage 4. Deciding a course of action:
    Decisions were made, as a result of problem analysis, to do the following things.

Note that more than one decision was made in the evolution toward a single purchase of a piece of equipment, a tool, or material.

a. Change process or method 36%
b. Change product tolerances 27%
c. Change kind of material 20%
d. Make new parts instead of buying them 24%
e. Increase floor-space efficiency 35%

Note: Many other decisions were also made. Those shown above were the most common.

Stage 5. Selecting the product:

Nearly 50 percent of those involved requested bids for a specific type of product as determined by the decisions made in Stage 4. Other activities indicated less certainty about the kind of action that the decisions made in Stage 4 called for. These activities included requests for proposed sources and visits to vendor plants.

Stage 6. Purchase proposal:

a. Evaluating sources 54%
b. Proposing purchase 48%

Stage 7. Approving the purchase:

Of those involved in the evolution of a purchase, 51 percent were also involved in the approval of the equipment, tool, or material which was finally purchased. In several instances, more than one individual's approval was necessary.

IV. *Effect of marketing influences—sales force, publication advertising, direct mail, trade shows:*

1. The time involved in the various stages of a purchase is pertinent to the marketer's decision on the use of marketing tools. From Stage 1 to Stage 4 involved anywhere from one day to two years. The most frequent intervals ranged between three months and one year. From Stage 4 to Stage 5 took from one day to six weeks, with less than three weeks involved in 40 percent of the cases. Stages 6 and 7 together required less than three weeks in more than one half of the cases. More than three months was required in only 9 percent of the cases.

2. The effect of sales representatives is felt most at Stages 4 and 5 among those buying influences that actually saw a representative. Of all the respondents involved in a purchase, 62 percent talked to a representative of the company from whom a purchase was made. Of this group, 75 percent saw the representative at Stages 4 and 5. In 72 percent of the contacts between a representative and a respondent, the contact was made at the buyer's request. In 18 percent of the cases, the contact was initiated by the salesperson.

3. The effect of advertising on buying influences is indicated by a question which asked which source of information is "most useful in keeping informed about equipment, tools and materials used in your industry."

Of the respondents, 49 percent say that industrial and trade publications are the best source of information; 26 percent say that salespeople are most useful, and 16 percent believe catalogs and literature are most useful. Direct mail and trade shows account for the balance.

Conclusions

While detailed conclusions and authoritative commentary depend on careful analysis of the purchasing-procedures study, it is apparent that industrial and trade publication advertising must play a stronger role in developing sales.

It is obvious that in the problem-solving and direction-setting stages of a purchase, the sales force has the least contact with buying influences. Advertising is important at these stages because:

1. Many of the influences do not see salespeople at all, yet they must have some kind of information in order to move from one stage to the next.

2. The greatest amount of time is spent by the buying influences in the early stages, when it would be inefficient and possibly ineffective for salespeople to be involved. Advertising is a relatively low-cost means of searching out buying influences, and of building and sustaining contact with them.

3. The time spent in the latter stages is relatively short. Because most salespeople are seen at the request of the influence, it appears that advertising is important in "bringing the customer into the store." It is also apparent, in view of the short time interval, that advertising may be important in reinforcing sales efforts at a time when contending with the competition. In some instances, it is conceivable that these latter stages may develop so rapidly that advertising may be the main contact in encouraging the customer to request a bid or to visit a vendor's plant.

Seldom does decision making follow a straight, well-marked path. A single decision does not determine if a purchase is to be made, much less *what* is to be bought. Widely accepted is the fact that at least *three* buying decisions are made—feasibility, technical, and administrative.

The feasibility decision is the easiest of three to make, and it involves less time than the other two. It is made by technical personnel concerned primarily with the economics of the situation. The criterion by which they judge is how will it affect the corporate pocketbook? Management, to whom they report, wants to know if the company can anticipate reduced costs, higher productivity, improved quality, less rejects, use of lower-priced materials, less maintenance, or other economic benefits from the proposed purchase. If the answer to these considerations is a solid affirmative, and if it is backed up with facts, the second decision is then taken up.

The second, technical decision is usually made on a relatively low level of management. It involves choosing between two or more items of the same kind. For example, a large manufacturer of earth-moving equipment needed a new overhead 20-ton crane on the main production floor of the plant. Here the technical discussion on the merits of several makes of cranes involved production foremen, superintendents, the general foreman, and the maintenance superintendent responsible for keeping production equipment in good working condition. This group compared all of the pros and cons, feature by feature, of the various makes of cranes with which they were familiar, then recommended the three which they felt best suited their needs. The customary three-bid purchasing procedure followed.

The administrative decision is the last one to be made, and it is made by top management. It differs in that it also includes consideration of whether company funds could be better invested in, say, a new mechanized paint-spray-booth system, a new wing on the office building, additional inventory, or a fleet of trucks. Capital equipment dollars are limited. No company, regardless of size and prominence, ever has enough.

Who Are the Customers?

It is axiomatic that 80 percent of a company's business is secured from 20 percent of its prospects. Scan any company's "customer list" and its record of incoming orders and this quickly becomes apparent. These "cream" accounts provide most of the business booked because they are the firms which do a large volume and have great purchasing power. This is not to say, however, that any company sells to all of the prospects it would like to. Every sales manager has target accounts he or she just itches to penetrate, but has not been able to. On the whole, the 20 percent figure is a valid one because it does not include the tremendous number of small establishments whose low business volume makes it a marginal proposition to spend much time and money trying to close sales with them.

Questions arise very quickly when developing a promotional program. Just who are our customers? Where are they located? In what businesses are they? What do they buy from us? Who are the key buying influences we must reach? What is our share of the market? From the answers to these questions come data which will influence capital investment, research and development, engineering and production decisions, new product introduction, as well as marketing programs. All of these questions must be answered in order to develop a cohesive communications program. Fortunately, the answers are easy to come by, although they are found in a number of places.

The question, "Whom do we sell to?" is partially—but only partially—answered by the customer list. All companies have one, of course, usually complete with addresses. Mere firm names assigned to smokestacks mean little, however, although this does take care of the "who" and "where" questions for the time being.

"What do they buy from us?" is usually a tough one if the company produces a diversified line of products, or products for several major markets. As a rule, there is no pat answer because customer lists are quite like Topsy—they just grew. New names are added constantly, while few are culled out even if the customers are not active ones, or if they cease doing business. Not one company in a 100 assigns this responsibility to any one individual with instructions to keep the list clean and current. The result is a long list of firm names, usually several thousand, with basic information—model number, specifications, accessories, and other pertinent data noted beside each customer. But this is still raw data, for no *pattern* has emerged. A pattern—a simple, logical arrangement that is easy to analyze—is necessary so that the advertising manager can make use of this mass of statistics.

A question that elicits blank expressions and shoulder shrugging is, "What lines of business are our customers in?" The average company simply does not know, not at company headquarters, although the field manager is familiar with the firms on which he or she calls in the territory. This is of little help, however, to the advertising manager, for if he or she queried all field personnel and waited until he received the volume of information needed, he'd be ready to file for Social Security, despite sending urgent memos requesting this data at the tender age of 31.

How to Get the Job Done

To get the job done, rather than grow senile wishing it were, add four basic reference books to the advertising department's library, and use them.

Largest and perhaps the most useful of these is *Poor's Register of Corporations, Directors, and Executives.* Currently it is in its 54th publication and is generally acknowledged as being the foremost guide to the business community and the executives who run it. Now in three volumes, it gives in straight alphabetical sequence by business name of approximately 37,000 corporations including zip codes; telephone numbers; names, titles, and functions of approximately 390,000 officers, directors and other principals; names of companies' accounting firms, primary banks and primary law firms, and so forth. Another volume gives independent listings of directors and executives totaling 72,000. Volume three is comprised of indexes including:

> Standard Industrial Classification Codes
>
> Geographic Index
>
> Obituary section
>
> New individual additions
>
> New company additions

Personnel listed include all officers and directors; other important executive personnel such as sales, advertising, general, production and traffic managers, personnel directors, engineers, and purchasing agents. To indicate company size, the number of employees and approximate sales volume is given for each company. Accuracy is practically a fetish; more than 100,000 major changes are made in the work each year, while the total number of revisions exceed 460,000. Type proofs are sent to each firm listed to verify accuracy, in itself a huge job. The book may be rented or bought outright; purchase price is $245. (1981)

A company representative is located in each metropolitan center, or the book may be ordered directly from:

> Standard & Poor's Corporation
> 25 Broadway
> New York, New York 10004

Poor's Register is kept current throughout the year by quarterly supplements which are automatically mailed to every registered holder of the book.

Other prime sources of information are the reference books published by Dun's Marketing Services, a company of The Dun & Bradstreet Corporation.

Dun's Marketing Services' three-volume *Million Dollar Directory Series* is a huge work which lists over 120,000 business enterprises in the U.S. with net worth of $500,000 and up.

The *Million Dollar Directory Series* includes the most sought-after data about manufacturers, wholesalers, retailers and industrial concerns, as well as transportation, financial and service companies. Also included are names and titles of key decision makers.

All three volumes are easy to use because they are all organized the same way and cross-referenced. You can track a company *alphabetically*, for comprehensive detail; *geographically*, to find out what businesses are in any particular city or state; or by *industry classification* to identify those companies in a particular line of business.

To help the marketer pinpoint his marketing area, and to assist him in reaching it more quickly, selected data from all of the listings in the *Million Dollar Directory Series*, are available in the following convenient forms:

> Magnetic tape
> Pressure-sensitive labels
> Cheshire labels
> 3x5 cards.

Dun's Marketing Services also publishes annually *THE BILLION DOLLAR DIRCTORY/America's Corporate Families*, *The Metalworking Directory* and *Dun's Census of American Business*. Other D&B publications available through Dun's Marketing Services include the *Canadian Key Business Directory*, *Who Owns Whom*, *Principal International Businesses*, *Australian Key Business Directory*, *Guide to Key British Enterprises*, *Guide to Irish Manufacturers*, and *Europe 5000*.

Data Universal Numbering System

According to Dun & Bradstreet, D-U-N-S, which stands for Data Universal Numbering System and also happily abbreviates to the firm's first name, is ideal for the company which uses or expects to use electronic data processing in its operation. In this system, a unique random number known as a D-U-N-S number is assigned to the 4.5 million establishments in the DUN'S MARKET IDENTIFIER (DMI) FILE. The D-U-N-S number is an eight-digit number of which the high order position is, at present, a zero. This provides for expansion when the numbering of other establishments is undertaken at a later date. The check digit—in this case the last digit—allows a computer or other automated data-processing equipment to check whether a given number is valid or contains an error, such as a transposition. It is called a "Mod 10, double-one-double-one check digit." It will detect all but the most exceptional errors.

Benefits to the advertising manager are that the system:

1. Provides an operational universal numbering system.

2. Keeps the system up-to-date through the nationwide reporting facilities of Dun & Bradstreet (maintenance is one of the biggest prob-

lems of "private" numbering systems).

3. Makes practical the imprinting of the identification number (D-U-N-S) on a company's documents, thus reducing clerical look-up time.

4. Permits intra or intercompany communication on specific accounts which may be of common interest through the use of common identification number.

5. Permits interdepartmental consolidation and evaluation of accounts which may represent both customers and suppliers.

6. Offers companies the possibility of drawing upon additional data contained in Dun & Bradstreet's computerized files.

The Data Universal Numbering System, when combined with the marked "identifiers" of DMI, discussed above—tape, tab cards, labels, or whatever form in which information can be most easily handled—provides an information system that is unique in American business. Applications in sales, market research, advertising, and sales promotion are almost limitless because they help the ad man identify his prospects so that he can reach them quicker and at lower cost.

DUN'S MARKETING SERVICES, a company of Dun & Bradstreet has offices in principal cities, or you may write directly to:

> Dun's Marketing Services
> Three Century Drive
> Parsippany, NJ 07054

The fourth text that belongs in every industrial advertising department is *Standard Industrial Classification Manual*. Standard Industrial Classification—SIC, as it's called—is the hub around which all modern industrial marketing programs now revolve. The textbook was prepared by the Technical Committee on Industrial Classification, Office of Statistical Standards of the U.S. Government. It is available in a permanent binding from:

> Superintendent of Documents
> U.S. Government Printing Office
> Washington, D.C. 20425

The price is $12.00, and your order should be accompanied by a bank draft, cashier's check, or money order to conform to government regulations.

The introduction to the SIC Manual says that SIC was developed "for use in classification of establishments by type of activity in which they are engaged; to facilitate the collection, tabulation, presentation, and analysis of data relating to establishments; and to promote uniformity and comparability in the presentation of statistical data collected by various agencies of the United States Government, state agencies, trade associations, and private research organizations.

SIC classification covers the entire field of economic activities; agriculture, forestry, and fisheries; mining; construction; manufacturing; transportation, communication, electric, gas, and sanitary services; wholesale and retail trade; finance, insurance, and real estate; services, and government." It is fortunate the last activity is included, for it is fast becoming as large as all of the others combined.

Follows Logical Principles

The following general principles were borne in mind while the classification was developed:

1. The classification should conform to the existing structure of American industry.

2. The reporting units to be classified were establishments rather than legal entities or companies.

3. Each establishment is to be classified according to its major activity or industry.

4. To be recognized as an industry, each group of establishments must have significance from the standpoint of persons employed, volume of business, and other important economic features, such as the number of establishments.

The manual describes an establishment as "an economic unit which produces goods or services—for example, a farm, a mine, a factory, a store. In most instances, the establishment is at a single physical location; and it is engaged in only one, or predominantly one, type of activity for which an industry code is applicable."

Number 3, above, and the manual's definition of an establishment should be noted well. Translating "governmentese" into plain English, it means that any given establishment may have a primary SIC, as well as one or more secondary SIC's. An example would be a large metalworking shop which is classified as, "Machine shops, jobbing, and repair—SIC 3591."

Within this metalworking shop might be a department which produces forgings, although this activity would constitute a small portion of the overall work volume and sales dollar of the establishment. In this case, then, the establishment would also be classified as a producer of "Forgings, iron and steel: light and heavy board drop and steam hammer, upset and press—not made in rolling mills—SIC 3391."

Furthermore, this establishment could also have a small metal-melting operation to produce special castings used in conjunction with some of the machined parts which are its prime product. Even though the foundry is small and might operate sporadically, the establishment would nonetheless acquire yet another secondary classification—SIC 3321, for "Foundries, gray iron and semisteel."

The SIC manual is easy to assimilate. Although a bit heavy-handed, the logic can't be faulted. Establishments engaged in essentially similar functions are arbitrarily lumped together into "Major Groups." An example is Major Group 37—Transportation Equipment. The manual says, "This Major Group includes establishments engaged in the manufacturing of equipment for transporting passengers and cargo by land, air, and water. Important products produced by establishments classified in this Major Group include motor vehicles, aircraft, ships, boats, railroad equipment, and miscellaneous equipment such as motorcycles, bicycles, and horse-drawn vehicles."

Because SIC's have four digits to permit precise classification, the next breakdown after the Major Group is the Group Number. Group Number of "Motor Vehicles and Motor Vehicle Equipment" is 371. Motor vehicles themselves are SIC number 3711. Passenger car bodies are SIC 3712, truck and bus bodies, SIC 3713. Also within Major Group 37 you'll find "Aircraft and Parts," which is Group Number 372. Within this subclassification is found aircraft, SIC 3721, aircraft engines and engine parts, SIC 3722, and so on. "Ship and Boat Building and Repairing" is Group Number 373, with ship building and repairing wearing SIC 3731, boat building and repairing 3732. Group Number 374 covers the railroad industry; locomotives and parts have SIC 3741, railroad and street cars 3742.

When you first consider it, having almost 1,000 SIC's might seem to carry things too far. But in this age of computerized marketing, when memory banks retain billions of digits on a tiny roll of tape and make detailed printouts in minutes, marketing data must be reduced to numbers—the Esperanto of computers.

"SIC-ing" Your Customer List

SIC is a key tool of the industrial advertising manager. He or she should become intimately familiar with the system, and this can easily be done. A couple of hours with the manual will enables a person to take the next important step toward identifying the market—"SIC-ing" the customer list.

This can be done internally, right in the advertising department, if sufficient clerical time is available. SIC-ing the customer list is merely a look-up operation using *Poor's Register* or one of the Dun & Bradstreet books as source material. However, if the time element is important, and it usually is, Dun & Bradstreet will do the entire job for a reasonable sum. This includes look-up and key-punching the information into IBM cards. Cost will be increased only slightly to have a separate deck of cards punched showing secondary SIC's of your customers, and this information can be identified by a separate eight digit preceding the primary SIC, or it can be coded elsewhere on the card. Secondary SIC can be vitally important information when you're trying to pinpoint a market.

When the deck of cards is returned from D & B it can then be turned over to a convenient data-processing service firm to have a printout made—assuming idle computer time is not available internally. Cards should be sorted by county and state before the final run, as well as by city if you wish; requirements vary with distribution channels and organization of the field sales force.

You will receive the printout from the tab house in six or seven working days as a rule, in the form of a continuous, perforated business form, all neatly separated and bound into a stiff paper binder, complete with two carbon copies. More carbons may be ordered when the printout is made, of course, at nominal extra cost. Cost of having a printout in triplicate of approximately 5,000 firms runs around $250 to $300 in most major cities; this is in addition to a standard setup charge of $50 to cover the cost of programming the machine to handle each specific job. Sorting charge, if necessary to have done differently than D & B provides, is relatively low.

Once the printout is on hand, you probably have for the first time an orderly analysis of whom your company sells to, with like SIC's grouped for easy tallying on an adding machine. This is far more than a group of numbers with firm names following them, however, because this printout represents the manufacturing plants that have a use for your product. They have a use for it because it solves a problem for them—one, perhaps, that your product alone can do.

This invaluable information can be put to many uses. It can be broken down by sales district or territory because it's already separated by county and state; the information can be forwarded to the district offices by making copies on the office copying machine. It can be used for direct mail. The sales department will want a copy to analyze to determine if the sales force is devoting its time to hunting ducks where the ducks actually are—instead of making useless, or nearly useless calls upon marginal prospects. Marketing will undoubtedly want to evaluate its objectives in relationship to this data, and will probably have sales review it for comment; quite possibly sales will want some district or regional managers to go over the statistics, for memories of past sales tend to be short when new ones are constantly pending. And, finally, the advertising manager will find the

SIC'ed customer list a tremendous help in planning his program, particularly when it comes to evaluating media and determining the creative approach he will take.

Since manufacturers with the same SIC make the same product, it naturally follows that those with SIC's found on your customer list printout are your best possible prospects. They obviously encounter the same problems that your present customers do, and *they* have found that your product solves their problem, or they wouldn't be your customer. So, what is needed is a complete list of all establishments with the SIC's which represent the bulk of your profitable business. (Marketing and sales management can assign weights or priorities to miscellaneous categories of establishments, although it can be assumed that the cat-and-dog accounts will be of relatively little importance.)

The Lindberg Hevi-Duty Plan

Compiling a list, possibly of 10,000 companies or more, is a time-consuming task. It should not be attempted manually due to the amount of time involved, and also because of the probability of a high percentage of errors creeping in. Inhuman computers, however, are not error prone and should be relied upon. Dun & Bradstreet can supply any desired breakdown by SIC of any type of establishments you're interested in, all with machine precision. One list used by Lindberg Hevi-Duty, Division of Sola Basic Industries, for its metal-treating market consists of approximately 8,700 metalworking firms which do on-premises heat treating. The company bought this information from D & B in a three-card deck. That is, each establishment is represented in the master deck by three IBM cards. Information about each of these 8,700 firms includes:

> Name of company
> Street address
> City
> State
> Zip Code
> Primary SIC classification
> Secondary SIC classification(s)
> Number of employees
> Annual sales volume
> Names of:
>> President
>> Executive Vice-President
>> Vice-President, Manufacturing
>> Director of Purchasing

These data, also sorted by county and state, were then printed out and the customer list checked against it. A remarkably high percentage of the company's customers were included in the master three-card deck; those who were not were then added. Lindberg Hevi-Duty then knew exactly who their customers were, and who their prospects were — including the name of the key buying influence, the director of manufacturing—for their extensive line of industrial ovens and heat-treating furnaces. The list was supplemented, of course, by names received in response to advertisements, direct mail, publicity, and from field sales before being used as the new master list for direct mail.

Baker Division of Otis Elevator Company, manufacturer of Baker fork-lift materials-handling equipment, defined its present market, projected the market potential and identified key buying influences through market research based on SIC. To do so, officials first determined where the company's sales were coming from—according to the SIC of their incoming orders and past sales. Next, the number of employees in customer companies, financial strength and similar information were analyzed to give Baker people a profile of their customers. They then projected their markets by SIC, assuming that all firms with similar SIC's as those of customers on the books were likely suspects to become new customers. The projection was made with the help of another reference volume, also available from the Government Printing Office, *County Business Patterns U.S. Summary*; this book gives the exact counts of each four-digit SIC in the United States.

Using this book, Baker Division's ad manager determined that his company could logically expect about 260,000 companies to be their total market, but they refined this massive number down to around 25,000 firms whose SIC's exactly matched their customers' in every respect, including, to be positive, cross-checking against the customer profile.

Relying on advertising to reach all 260,000 prospects, including the 25,000 target accounts, Baker qualified this smaller group by direct mail, asking each firm to tell them who the buying influences are in their companies for materials-handling equipment. Some 60 percent of the recipients of the mailing responded, giving Baker names of decision makers. These industrial buyers were reached by advertising and by well-conceived, well-executed direct mail. Dealers were sold on the program and were given the names of the recipients of Baker's direct mailings. The program was evaluated a year later—and Baker's sales were up 26 percent in the face of an industry decline, proving conclusively that prospect identification by SIC pays! It is actually the only easy, practical way to delineate a market that can run into hundreds of thousands of companies.

The Use of Trade Directories

Trade and professional directories can also provide vital market information, particularly when a company's prospects are in a market that is relatively small and stable.

This method was used by Szabo Food Service, Lyons, Illinois. Szabo sells an industrial "product"—a management service—to five major markets. One, colleges and universities, was growing at a fantastic rate due to an exploding population and a war-baby boom. This national corporation, formed shortly after World War II, achieved an annual sales volume of more than $30 million without the support of advertising or other promotion, but in an increasingly competitive market inevitably found itself on a sales plateau. The company decided to advertise to this one market, on a trial basis, to "see if advertising really works."

To get immediate results and quality sales leads, a three-pronged approach was taken—research, advertising, and merchandising.

First step was to define the market, and identify Szabo's prime prospects. To do this, all of the colleges and universities in the country with 1,000 or more on-campus students (minimum profitable size for Szabo to handle) were identified, using directories such as *College and Private School Directory of U.S. and Canada; College Blue Book; College Guide; Accredited Higher Institutions;* and *American Universities and Colleges.*

Marketing management at Szabo had determined that the business manager of each college and university was the one most important buying influence, although there were many others, including various faculty members, deans, presidents, members of boards of regents, and trustees. The individuals who were going to make the vital decision had to be identified by name and title. To accomplish this, a questionnaire was mailed to each institution's business manager. It was frank and straightforward, telling him that Szabo wanted the names of decision makers interested in student feeding so that they could be kept informed about developments in this field. A return of better than 61 percent from this qualification mailing gave Szabo the names of those pivotal individuals who would participate in making a decision of what food-service-management firm would be retained, if any, or if a change were to take place. The questionnaire is shown on the following page.

Next, four ads were written and produced, each scheduled to run twice in the best magazine in the educational field. A typical ad is reproduced here.

Please correct and complete the information below and return to:

> Mr. R. A. Longworth
> President
> SZABO FOOD SERVICE, INC.
> 4242 South First Avenue
> Lyons, Illinois   60534

From _____

_____

	NAME	**TITLE**

President _____ _____

Deans _____ _____

_____ _____

_____ _____

_____ _____

Executives
Responsible For:

Business Management

_____ _____

_____ _____

_____ _____

Food Service
Policy

_____ _____

_____ _____

_____ _____

_____ _____

From Mr. _____ Title_____

Thank you for your assistance. A stamped, addressed envelope
is attached for the return of this form.

*This is the questionnaire used by Szabo Food Service to obtain the names and titles of
individuals responsible for making food-service decisions.*

The offer of an eight-page illustrated booklet containing a wealth of information essential to an educator on the topic of student nutrition triggered an excellent response. All of the ads pulled inquiries, good ones, which were promptly followed up by the field sales force.

Key to this program, however, was merchandising the ads to the qualified prospects. When an ad ran, a letter from Szabo's president

SZABO FOOD SERVICE, INC. / STUDENT FACILITY SERVICES DIVISION

4242 SOUTH FIRST AVENUE, LYONS, ILLINOIS 60534

GENERAL OFFICES
CHICAGO PHONES BISHOP 2-3540
LONG DISTANCE HICKORY 7-8230

Mr. Robert F. Neiato
Ball State Teachers College
Muncie, Indiana

Dear Mr. Neiato:

I'm enclosing a reprint of our current advertisement entitled
"A Perfect Meal" since its subject is of vital interest to you.
Briefly, it gives you a bit of background about our organization,
and it touches on our philosophy of student feeding.

In an illustrated, 8-page booklet which we have just published,
we are able to go into greater detail about the many collateral
services our Student Facility Services Division offers.

The booklet explains how Student Facility Services Division can
provide your college with a better food service program at a
cost that is, in all probability, substantially lower than you
now find acceptable.

To get your free copy of the booklet, just return the enclosed
postage-paid reply card.

There is no obligation, of course.

Cordially,

Raymond A. Longworth
President
Szabo Food Service, Inc.

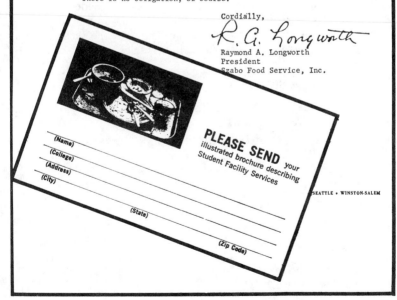

(Name)
(College)
(Address)
(City)

PLEASE SEND your
illustrated brochure describing
Student Facility Services

SEATTLE • WINSTON-SALEM

(State)

(Zip Code)

was written, reproduced on a Szabo letterhead by the multilith process, "signed" in blue ink from a signature cut, and then individually addressed to the prospect with a matching fill-in. A reprint of the advertisement was enclosed, and again the booklet was offered. A postage-paid reply card was enclosed, also mentioning the booklet, and containing a small reproduction of the illustration in the ad to remind the prospect of it. A typical letter and reply card are shown.

Response to this low-cost program (under $20,000) was outstanding. Szabo had almost 200 requests for their booklet out of a qualified list of only 800— a return of 25 percent. And many colleges checked a box on the reply card to request a no-charge, detailed survey of their requirements in student feeding, enabling Szabo to submit many more formal proposals than in any similar period in the company's history.

Szabo's sales force was understandably enthused, and management was firmly convinced that advertising *does* work because several colleges signed contracts with the management service firm as the result of this program. Each sale the company makes is substantial; when a college of 15,000 students is acquired, that adds up to 300,000 meals a week on a 20-meal-a-week basis, common in this field.

Note that success of this entire promotional program hinged on one factor—correctly identifying the market and the individual buying influences within it who made the decision of what brand to buy, in this case, what firm to retain. Here, trade directories provided the target establishments, personal knowledge the job function of the one key influence, and a mail questionnaire the names of the secondary influences. Used correctly, they resulted in new sales.

The Iron Age Checklist

Iron Age magazine has an excellent checklist of what to look for in mail questionnaires. It follows:

CHECKLIST FOR INDUSTRIAL MAIL SURVEYS

I. Has the universe (market) for the project been clearly defined in terms of:
   a. Title or function of respondents?
   b. Plants by:
      1. Industry?
      2. Size?
      3. Geographic locations?
II. Will the sample, assuming returns are representative, yield sufficiently large returns to allow classification of data according to the universe description?
III. Has the covering letter been written so as to encourage the respondent to fill out and return the questionnaire?
   a. Is it brief and to the point?

  b. Is it personal in tone?

  c. Does it stress the importance of the survey?

  d. Are any benefits to the respondent clearly described?

  e. Does it reassure the respondent of the confidential treatment of his reply if such a step is warranted?

IV. Have the questions been properly conceived in order to provide accurate and unbiased answers?

  a. Will all questions be clearly understood by all respondents?

  b. Are no undue demands made on memory or knowledge?

  c. Are the questions few enough in number to avoid aggravation or fatigue on the part of the respondent?

  d. Are open-ended questions kept to a minimum?

  e. Have leading or biasing elements in the questions been eliminated?

V. Has the physical format of the questionnaire been well planned?

  a. Do the letter and questions present an uncrowded appearance?

  b. Does the questionnaire contain as few pages as possible? (Typeface can be varied to include more data on limited space and provide a change of pace.)

  c. Does the address fill-in match the body of the letter?

  d. Does the signature appear realistic?

  e. Is the stationery of good quality?

VI. Has proper consideration been given to the reply envelope?

  a. Where highest response is needed, stamped envelopes are worthwhile.

VII. Does the nature of the survey indicate a blind letterhead (confidential) or the letterhead of the company conducting the survey?

VIII. Has a premium been considered to increase response?

  a. Is the premium of interest to the type of respondent being questioned? (A summary of the replies is often useful.)

IX. Has provision been made for a possible second mailing to nonrespondents?

  a. Are questionnaires keyed so that they can be matched with the sample?

X. Has the questionnaire been pretested for some assurance of its success?

  a. A limited mailing often uncovers the need for some rephrasing of questions and provides an indication of eventual percentage response.

  b. One or two personal calls with the proposed questionnaire may be helpful?

XI. Are the returns representative of the sample and universe?

  a. Have they been compared with the original universe characteristics?

  b. If utmost accuracy is desired, has a check of nonrespondents been made with reference to key points?

XII. *IF YOU RECEIVED THE QUESTIONNAIRE, WOULD YOU FILL IT OUT AND RETURN IT?*

If questionnaires are well written—and you should judge that by whether or not they are almost conversational in tone, not stilted, not forbiddingly technical, not depressingly dull—they will do an effective job that can otherwise be done only at great cost by personal interview. Throughout this volume other examples are given; note that they adhere strongly to this checklist, that they are as light in tone as possible considering the subject, and that they *communicate* the way most of us think.

The covering letter should also be as good a piece of copy as it's possible to produce. Hone it and whet it—refine it and rewrite it—until the letter reads as if a friend were talking to you across your desk. That's the kind of letter that pulls response in direct mail and it's the only kind to use. Few people write like that; if you can't you are in good company—with 99 44/100 percent of all industrial advertising managers. If such is the case, face it and go to a specialist in your agency, or to a direct-mail house or sales-promotion studio and pay somebody to write it for you. The cost is less than $300, as a rule, and if the letter makes the difference between a 10 percent return on your questionnaire and a 60 percent return on a mailing to 1,000 names, the cost is inconsequential.

Get the "Inside" on Your Market

Other sources of market information are open to you. For example, all first-class business publications are prime sources for the basic information the advertising manager must have to plan the program. Here's what one such magazine offers to help the advertiser define the market.

Iron Age, published by Chilton, is a leading business book which serves the vast metalworking industry. *Iron Age* has done extensive market research for many years, and has compiled a wealth of meticulously detailed market information. If a company sells only to one specific market such as metalworking, the advertising manager can cut costs and save considerable time in pinpointing the market by using data the publication will provide. He or she need have no doubt as to its being authoritative. The really good trade publication knows its market better than any company's entire marketing organization. After all, the publication lives by its market knowledge.

A census of every metalworking plant in the country has been made repeatedly by *Iron Age*. Since the magazine's census must reflect all of the changes that occur, it maintains a comprehensive and continuing roster of all metalworking plants, old and new. Plants are classified by SIC, of course.

All metalworking establishments, in *Iron Age's* breakdown, are in eight two-digit groupings, which are in turn broken down further into 214 four-digit groupings. Most sources provide only four-digit SIC groupings for advertising and marketing activities. The *Iron Age* census, with its six-digit classification, provides the most definitive breakdown available in its industry for market analysis and planning of sales and advertising. The six-digit classification was developed by *Iron Age*.

Information was obtained by mail questionnaires, telephone interviews, and every available authoritative source, including state-development commissions and private plant-finding organizations. Pertinent facts were recorded on tabulating cards, electronically processed and summarized in statistical form. This was a massive job.

The continuing plant census is an essential tool employed by *Iron Age* in its own circulation and editorial planning. In common with other business publications in which a large investment has been made by the publisher, *Iron Age* realized that sound market research and prospect identification is a prerequisite for effective selling and advertising, so makes this information available to companies in metalworking and to those selling to this industry.

The magazine's *Metalworking Data Bank Marketguide* provides a statistical summary of the *Iron Age* census. It details the size and scope of the metalworking market; summarizes the two-digit, four-digit and six-digit census data; and includes a state-by-state count of significant metal service centers. The information can be pulled from the *Metalworking Data Bank* by two-, four- and six-digit SIC, with further selections refined by employment size range (e.g., 20-99, 100 to 499, over 500); or by State, County or Zip Code selection. This makes it easy to hunt ducks where the ducks are. No wasted time chasing smokestacks.

The *Marketguide* gives specific examples of how to establish sales potentials, how to plan sales territories and prospect for sales.

The book's *Metalworking Data Bank* locates 46,329 plants with 20 or more employees. It identifies corporate headquarters, R&D locations and 2,300 metal service centers.

From time to time, *Iron Age* will take a reading, either statistically or by actual count, of major production operations performed in these plants. They cover such basic operations as:

MACHINING
    Automatic bar machining
    Drilling
    Milling
    Boring
    Sawing
    Grinding
    Tool & Die Shop
    NC Machining

HEAT TREATING
    Heat Treating
MELTING & CASTING
    Foundry - All types
    Electric Furnace Melting
FORMING
    Hot rolling
    Cold rolling
    Forging
    Stamping
    Slitting
SURFACE FINISHING
    Sand, shot or grit blasting
    Metal washing or degreasing
FABRICATING
    Plate or structural fabrication
    Screw fastening
    Welding - All types

The *Iron Age Master List of U.S. Metalworking Plants* is a two-volume listing that provides current information on the 50,000 plants covered by the census.

Volume I lists all plants alphabetically, by state. Each plant is defined by company name, division name (if applicable), full physical address with Zip Code, county code, six-digit primary and secondary SIC codes, number of employees, and activity codes designating corporate headquarters, divisional headquarters, manufacturing, R&D, and engineering.

Volume II lists these establishments by primary six-digit SIC, alphabetically by states. Provided in this numerical sequence by SIC, Volume II offers an easy way to pinpoint prime prospects. It is quick, accurate and remarkably simple to use.

To ensure accuracy, updated information is issued annually. This is a distinct improvement over the old twice in three years.

All of this information in the *Iron Age Metalworking Data Bank* is stored in a computer. It is available in a variety of forms: microfiche film; magnetic computer tape; master lists (two-volume set, or individual volumes); printouts on 3x5 cards, mailing labels or continuous labels. Partial extracts are also available at a base cost of $200 for selection and $100 per thousand for any of the printout forms.

On these pages is a picture of the total information in the *Iron Age Metalworking Data Bank*, in sample form. It suggests the kind of extracts you can make.

Laying the groundwork is simplicity itself with such precise, current information available in highly usable forms to suit individual needs. It is incredibly valuable when you determine market potentials, plan sales territories, locate new prospects and markets, and plan and direct advertising and merchandising programs.

In common with most business publications, *Iron Age* will also handle direct-mail programs, using the *Metalworking Marketguide,* extracting almost any segment or geographical entity desired. The plants may be selected on a straight national-plant-selection basis, by SIC, or by state, area, or activities code criteria. Charges for addressing,

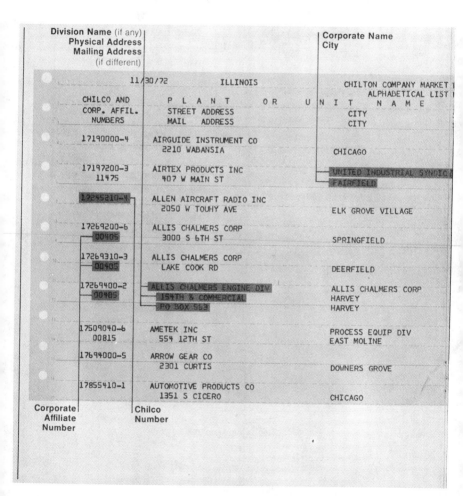

Division Name (if any) Physical Address Mailing Address (if different)				Corporate Name City
	11/30/72	ILLINOIS		CHILTON COMPANY MARKET ALPHABETICAL LIST
CHILCO AND CORP. AFFIL. NUMBERS	P L A N T STREET ADDRESS MAIL ADDRESS	O R	U N I T N A M E CITY CITY	
17190000-4	AIRGUIDE INSTRUMENT CO 2210 WABANSIA			CHICAGO
17197200-3 11475	AIRTEX PRODUCTS INC 407 W MAIN ST			UNITED INDUSTRIAL SYNDIC FAIRFIELD
12245210-4	ALLEN AIRCRAFT RADIO INC 2050 W TOUHY AVE			ELK GROVE VILLAGE
17269200-6 00405	ALLIS CHALMERS CORP 3000 S 6TH ST			SPRINGFIELD
17269310-3 00405	ALLIS CHALMERS CORP LAKE COOK RD			DEERFIELD
17269400-2 00485	ALLIS CHALMERS ENGINE DIV 154TH & COMMERCIAL PO BOX 563			ALLIS CHALMERS CORP HARVEY HARVEY
17509040-6 00815	AMETEK INC 554 12TH ST			PROCESS EQUIP DIV EAST MOLINE
17694000-5	ARROW GEAR CO 2301 CURTIS			DOWNERS GROVE
17855410-1	AUTOMOTIVE PRODUCTS CO 1351 S CICERO			CHICAGO
Corporate Affiliate Number	Chilco Number			

either by typewriter, or by affixing a four-line label, are reasonably structured and probably competitive with local letter shops. Too, the magazine will multigraph letters (on your letterhead, if supplied), insert enclosures, affix postage, sort by Zip Code, tie and deliver the mailing to the Philadelphia post office.

Many publishing companies who have in-house research departments will carry out, on a fee basis, studies to determine market potential for new products. Additionally, they customarily conduct—

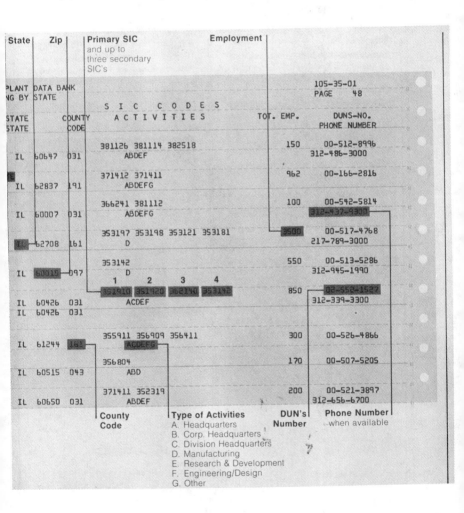

some of them almost continuously—research to determine just what individuals in companies in the industries they serve are actual buying influences. For a fee, usually relatively nominal, this information is available to the advertising manager, permitting selectivity and ability go after decision makers with a rifle approach rather than scattering material with costly abandon.

Pinpointing Influential Prospects

As a rule of thumb, it's safe to assume that the vast majority of calls made by industrial salespeople are made upon the wrong people. This is not to infer that the average salesperson, who's a pretty hardworking and conscientious member of the marketing team, is incompetent. Instead, it must be recognized that the calls are upon buying influences who are too low on the corporate ladder to approve a purchase. The talks are with influences who can recommend a purchase, which is a far cry from approving one.

Sales & Marketing Management magazine made an extensive study of this subject and stated categorically that 64 percent of all industrial sales calls were misdirected in this manner. Not only are they misdirected, but when a purchase of capital equipment is pending, salespeople simply do not have access to those executives who make the ultimate decision. It speaks well for their persistence and perseverance that, although starting low on the totem pole as they do, they are somehow able to guide many of their proposals through the chain of command and emerge with the order as often as they do. Knowing this enables the ad manager to place as much or as little credence as desirable when considering the field force's recommendations of key buying influences for use in direct mail, merchandising, or what have you.

Many business publications have research data that's free for the asking on specific products, thus eliminating many tedious steps in defining a market and its potential. Admittedly, most of these studies tend to be self-serving in that they emphasize the necessity of advertising in the publication supplying the data to achieve sales success in its market. This is not due to figure juggling or distortion of information, however, but is the inevitable result of making studies from a sampling of the magazine's circulation list. Readers of the magazine are obviously very likely to have read advertisements and editorial matter about a product simply because it is there, and because they read the magazine regularly.

A Study of pH Meters

One illuminating study was conducted by *Analytical Chemistry* magazine, a publication of the American Chemical Society, which makes advertising planning for a manufacturer of pH meters and pH electrodes somewhat less of a game of economic Russian roulette.

The study was conducted to determine:

1. The extent to which readers of the magazine use pH meters and pH electrodes.

2. Brand names of the pH meters and pH electrodes in use, and the number of each.

3. Brand names of pH meters to be purchased in the future.

4. Types of pH meters readers intend to buy during the next 12 months, and how much they expect to spend per unit.

5. Information on pH meters and pH electrodes that readers need in order to make a purchasing decision.

A letter and questionnaire were sent to a random sample of 500 readers of *Analytical Chemistry*, with 180 respondents tallied up for a 36 percent return by the time the cutoff date rolled around. Survey highlights show:

1. Of the respondents to the *Analytical Chemistry* survey, 97.78 percent have pH meters. They average 4.3 pH meters per respondent.

2. Nineteen firms were mentioned as suppliers of pH meters. However, seven firms accounted for 90 percent of all pH meters in use: Beckman (55.5 percent), Leeds & Northrup (13.4 percent), Radiometer (6.2 percent), Corning (6.1 percent), Photovolt, (3.6 percent), Coleman (3.2 percent), and Instrumentation Laboratory (2.1 percent).

3. Of the respondents to the magazine's survey, 83.33 percent intend to buy one or more pH meters during the next 12 months.

4. Of the respondents, 92.78 percent indicated the brands of pH electrodes they use. Sixteen firms were mentioned. However, six of the firms account for nearly 93 percent of all pH electrodes in use: Beckman (65.4 percent), Leeds & Northrup (9.2 percent), Corning (8.0 percent), Fisher Scientific (5.1 percent), Radiometer (2.9 percent), and Coleman (2.2 percent).

Statistical data, carefully tabulated and developed to 2 percentage points, shows that respondents mentioned as many as 22 brands in some questions. Despite this diversity of choice, one conclusion is obvious: The ad manager of a manufacturer of pH meters and pH electrodes, given these data, could analyze the leading competition and come up with some pertinent information.

He or she would find it easy to make a meaningful report on buying patterns to the sales department; to sales and engineering for an unbiased product-vs.-product evaluation, with possible needed improvements coming to light; and to marketing to help determine if a basic shift in strategy might enable the company to whittle away at the

the leader. Particularly pertinent are the answers to the question, "What features do you look for in a pH electrode?" In order of mentions, here are the features given most often by respondents:

1. Ruggedness, durability 98
2. Stability 40
3. Small size 28
4. Sensitivity 27
5. Accuracy 23
6. Temperature and pH range 22
7. Long service life 17
8. Reliability 17
9. Versatility, adaptability 14
10. Reproducibility 14
11. Fast response 11
12. Construction details 10
13. Low cost 9
14. Low sodium error 8

Objective, unbiased, completely honest opinions are frequently almost impossible to come by; salespeople are usually given erroneous answers to similar questions simply because the prospect to whom they talk wishes to spare their feelings. When the salespeople, in turn, pass this false information back to their home offices, misconceptions are born, nurtured, reared to maturity, and cherished for decades. A third-party survey turns fallacies into facts—and fast.

Then the ad manager will want to analyze the leader's advertising strategy and the collateral material. Sales literature is easily acquired, either through a friendly dealer or distributor or from a salesperson with a penchant for collecting. Possibly the leader leads because—partially, at least—of more effective advertising. If so, the reason why will become apparent and action can be taken to change the communications objectives and creative approach to negate the influence of the competitor's advertising. An advertising program should never be developed, however, merely to counter that of the competition, despite its being obvious that Avis's hurt Hertz.

It is interesting to note that when *Analytical Chemistry* readers were asked in the questionnaire to name the brands of pH meters they have and the numbers of each, the top 10 firms in both categories were also discovered to be regular advertisers of pH meters in that magazine.

Furthermore, when respondents to the survey were asked to name the firms they would contact to order a pH meter, they again chose those firms advertising pH meters in the magazine as their top 10 brand preferences. This is hardly happenstance. Coincidences do occur, but the odds against this being pure luck are astronomical.

Coincidence may indeed have a long arm, but certainly not long enough to account for the fact that *all* independent surveys, those conducted by professional research organizations, manufacturers, foundations, trade associations, and others with no axe to grind, all state that industrial advertising plays a major role in establishing and maintaining brand recognition, brand acceptance, and brand preference.

Gold Mines of Information

In one respect major publishers are like the Superstition Mountain's fabled Lost Dutchman gold mine: they are the repository of wealth in such quantity as to stagger the imagination. Instead of precious metal, however, they hold a fabulous deposit of information that's readily converted into more effective advertising to lower the cost of selling—precious stuff itself. And instead of being hidden, this deposit of data is easy to find, although it is largely untapped by the average advertising manager who has a kind of thing about asking for outside assistance for what he or she thinks should be *the* job.

As an example, the McGraw-Hill, Inc., the General Motors of business publishing, has so much to offer the industrial advertiser that the company publishes, at regular intervals, a guidebook to what is available—a vast number of marketing services for both advertisers and agencies at no cost. Others, which entail investment of considerable time by teams of specialists (for example, market researchers), are charged for on a fee arrangement agreed to beforehand.

Taking a look at a current guidebook one finds brief, concise descriptions of each of McGraw-Hill's publications. The descriptions are arranged by industry served; for example, architecture, aerospace, general business, chemical processing, computers, construction engineering and design, electronics, medical/surgical, metalworking, etc.

Each of the 70 or so publications described in the guidebook (the number of publications varies from edition to edition as publications are bought, combined, or perhaps sold off) is staffed by acknowledged industry experts in such functions as public relations, promotion, circulation, and editorial and marketing research, and these experts may be contacted by simply calling and outlining the help that is needed.

Many of the magazines, in turn, publish market letters and special statistical issues, packed and overflowing with market facts of tremendous value to the advertising/marketing executive. The approximately 40 newsletters—separate and distinct from the magazines—cover everything from the biotechnology business to fertilizer marketing intelligence to daily reports on world oil prices...a vast repository of industry information. Special issues of magazines run into the scores annually, and advanced listings of forthcoming "specials" by all publications are published annually by the McGraw-Hill Marketing Information Center (MIC). The MIC is described in detail a little further on.

Too, the guidebook features detailed outlines of services of tremendous dimension and scope; here's a brief sampling:

- economic indexes for specific industries.
- lists of manufacturers' representatives and distributors.
- a classified advertising center.
- mailing lists featuring two million-plus names of buying influences in the U.S., Canada, and abroad.
- advertising copy services (to help advertisers meet last-minute deadlines).
- advertising merchandising services.
- a Seminar Center (which conducts seminar programs—in locations around the country and abroad—for individual publications and newsletters on subjects germane to their audiences).
- an advertising/marketing techniques library.
- a centralized research service specializing in surveys of professional, business, and industrial markets.
- a Department of Economics which regularly reports and interprets business and economic trends for McGraw-Hill editors and their readers.
- a Conference and Exposition Center sponsored by McGraw-Hill publications, newsletters and other information services and which designs and manages U.S. and overseas conference programs attended by managers and technicians in the professional, financial and industrial sectors.

While the guidebook is published by McGraw-Hill, Inc., the division of McGraw-Hill that publishes mostly magazines and newsletters, it also covers the functions and services of the McGraw-Hill Book Company, the International Book Company, the Broadcasting Company, Standard & Poor's, and the Information Systems Company, whose three major groups (Regional Publishing, Product Information and Real Estate Information)—comprised of the F.W. Dodge, the Cost Information, Sweet's, Datapro Research and Multi-List Divisions—offer a comprehensive array of services and studies ranging from daily information reports to some 56;000 contractors and suppliers around the country on what new construction projects are being planned, when they will be ready for bidding, who will award the contracts, when to influence buyers, and where the jobs are—to reports on banking and retailing automation to electronic data processing management studies.

McGraw-Hill, Inc., in an effort to help advertisers and marketers narrow the information search for their day-to-day decision making, has had an information retrieval facility in daily operation for over 50 years. This facility is called the Marketing Information Center (MIC) and this center also serves as the B/PAA (Business/Professional Advertising Association) library.

The McGraw-Hill Center should be a first-stop for all fact-seeking marketers. Chances are that the facts sought have been published in the 350-plus sources that the Center has monitored continuously since 1945.

The MIC has two separate and distinct information collections from which marketers can draw the facts and ideas they need.

One collection concentrates specifically on markets—meaning *Products and Industries*. The second collection, *Marketing Techniques*, is devoted to how-to-do-it writings in the following areas: administration, advertising, international operations, marketing and selling.

Just how extensive are these collections? The *Products and Industries* database now numbers upwards of 200,000 documents. It covers well over 2,000 topics—from conventional hot-melt adhesives to exotic cryogenic gases; from estimates of solar energy requirements in the next decade to advances in bearings technology to satellite communications problems and prospects.

To keep this database completely up-to-date, more than 250 business publications, general magazines, newspapers, bank letters and the like are stripped of much of their editorial content each month. This editorial content is filed by subject, making it an easy matter to learn instantly just what is going on in any industry or to determine any product development. It is just as easy to go back in time (for a quarter of a century or more if needs be) to learn the problems, or see the engineering advances, that have affected, or may change, product markets.

To supplement these writings, most of the so-called "standard" U.S. Government statistical series are also on hand.

The *Marketing Techniques* information collection is truly unique. Here, the post World War II history of administration, advertising, marketing and selling emerges from the pages of more than 100 publications each month. And this information is available in a variety of forms: original document, microfiche, and card-abstract. There are standard cross-indexing systems, too, for locating specific documents by title and author.

From over 20,000 documents filed in chronological order by subject, and covering well over 1,000 major topics, the advertising/marketing professional can quickly review his or her knowledge of just about any administrative or marketing technique. For example: what are the characteristics of a well-read ad? How much additional readership does color obtain over black & white? At how much additional cost? In view of the extra cost of bleed, what is the gain in readership? How long may a headline or copy be before reading diminishes? How often can an ad be repeated? Just what does each element in an ad contribute to readership gains? Or, for the more marketing-inclined. How has psychographic research developed in the past 10 years? What's the latest in metamarketing? How should a product recall be handled? How can time series forecasting be used in marketing analysis? How do I write a marketing plan? And so on. It's all on record, in easily-retrieved form.

Also, the Marketing Information Center has ready access to one of the finest corporate libraries in the country and, depending on a communication manager's problem, has direct communications with over 1,000 of the country's most highly regarded business/technical editors, economists and marketing researchers. The McGraw-Hill Marketing Information Center is an excellent starting place when seeking advertising/marketing and business intelligence.

Another basic starting place for the marketing communications manager seeking information is McGraw-Hill Research.

With some 50 professionals on the Department's staff, and this figure does not include the research staffs of individual publications, McGraw-Hill Research offers advertising decision makers a number of unique services. For the sake of brevity only a few of the services will be touched upon here.

Of particular value is McGraw-Hill's *Laboratory of Advertising Performance* (LAP). The Laboratory has been in existence for more than 35 years and it has reported, in data sheet form, 100's upon 100's of research findings on a miscellany of advertising topics. In all, some 600 studies have been published and these studies pinpoint factual information on such advertising essentials as memory for advertising, the cost of a sales call (this figure is available even as far back as 1942), the value of advertising in a recession, advertising's reach among hidden buying influences, the increase in recognition which may be secured by advertising (and, conversely, how recognition diminishes when advertising is cut or stopped) and marketing costs as a percentage of sales. Additionally, research findings have been developed and published through the LAP on virtually every aspect of advertising presentation: bleed, color, size and shape of ads, copy length, placement in publication (thick vs. thin publications; front vs. back of books) ad infinitum. The cost of an LAP binder —

consisting of about 100 current studies—is presently pegged at $150. Advertising/marketing communications managers may request individual sheets at no cost; they may also request that their names be added to the LAP mailing list—to receive new studies as they are released. . . again at no cost.

McGraw-Hill Research, working with individual McGraw-Hill magazines, also provides advertisers and agencies with four opportunities to document how print advertising works. The "opportunities" are afforded by means of four performance studies — AD/Call, AD Sell, Ad Feedback and Advertising Performance—each of which measures different communications strengths.

In brief, *AD/Call* studies highlight the effectiveness of print advertising to efficiently reach purchase decision makers not called on recently by an advertiser's sales force. They report—for total readers and purchasing decision readers—the following information: basic ad readership, sales calls made on readers in the past 60 days, and actions taken. They focus attention specifically on the readership and action scores of a purchase decision reader not called on by the advertiser's sales force in the last 60 days. Nine comparative readership breakouts are included and verbatims, if offered, are reported. *AD Sell* studies are designed to measure how print advertising pre-sells readers on an advertised product/service and keeps them sold; they track how advertising establishes contact, creates awareness, arouses interest, builds preference, and keeps customers sold. Product category averages for each measurement are compared with the advertiser's own scores. A Total Performance Index ranks all ads in a given study and verbatims, if offered, are reported. *Advertising Performance Studies* underscore the ability of print advertising to communicate a message and initiate action; they measure the following involvements with advertising: attracted attention, began to read, read half or more, actions taken. Scores are provided for total readers and purchase decision readers. *Ad Feedback* studies present a qualitative approach to evaluating the communication strength of advertising; they indicate reactions and impressions to the ad message, company and product awareness, an ad's use in purchasing action, and provide a case study history of the impact of an ad. Advertisers may select patterns of verbatim questions to fit their specific communications objectives.

And this is just the beginning, for McGraw-Hill Research provides a host of other services. For example, to take just one . . . Market Directed Surveys. Market Directed Surveys are designed to help companies and publications analyze, interpret and reach markets more effectively. They provide useful intelligence for planning marketing strategy to reach and influence potential buyers. Each survey is tailor-made to fit the particular requirements and needs of each client and to provide up-to-date information in such areas as: company position (recognition, slogan association, customer attitudes, etc.); products (new marketing opportunities, design changes, brand performance, etc.); or, market potentials, share of market, user characteristics, buying intentions, etc.

McGraw-Hill Research is developing one of the biggest databases yet put together by the business press. More than 8,000 advertisments have been studied for the effects generated by some 40 physical characteristics; the findings are presently going through "number crunching." The results will provide what may be considered the most far-reaching analysis of advertising characteristics ever done; they will in all probability be communicated to the advertising world by means of the *Laboratory of Advertising Performance.*

As an additional marketing service, the Publications Company's Communications Department "packages" a plethora of research findings in booklet form. These booklets, available through local McGraw-Hill offices, cover such topics as how advertising can help condition a market for a product, how advertising builds sales and cuts costs, and how advertising increases the value of personal selling. Some titles of interest: *Businessmen and Major Media* (a study of communications exposure that develops answers to three broad questions): 1), To what extent are people with buying influence in business and industry exposed to the various communications media? 2), How, and for what purpose, do they use the various media? 3), What are the attitudes of these people toward the various media, with particular regard to their usefulness and credibility as sources of business-related information and the acceptability of their advertising contents?

Concentration (information to guide advertisers in choosing the publications and frequency schedules which provide investment concentration most effectively and economically); *Considering the Source* (Theodore Levitt's findings on how prospects for industrial products are affected by the seller's reputation); *The High Cost of Communicating in Today's Economy* (a comparison of various methods of communicating an advertiser's sales message—such as telephone, letters, personal sales calls, trade shows, and publication advertising); *How Advertising Works in Today's Marketplace* (a John Morrill study based on individual interviews among 40,000 buying influences and showing how sales calls and advertising motivate buyers' preference and share of market for specific brands in 23 product lines (also available in slide presentation form); *Advertising's Challenge to Management* (a second report based on the Morrill Study, *How Advertising Works in Today's Marketplace;* it throws additional light on the effect of advertising on brand preference, sales and the cost of selling (also available as a slide presentation); *How the Morrill Study Applies to Media Selection* (sometimes called Morrill III, it combines Morrill study findings with basic sales points to produce a tailor made concentration study); *It Pays to Repeat Good Advertisements in Business Publications* (provides answers to the questions; How often can you repeat good advertisements? How close together can you successfully schedule them); *101 Jobs Advertising Can Do* (a basic list of specific objectives for industral advertising—helpful for setting goals for campaigns); *Profit and Growth Strategies During Recession* (shows how advertising during recession periods provides advertisers with improved opportunties to reduce sales costs and increase sales, profits, market share and return on investments); *The 23-Minute Hour* (a report on the mathematics of selling; analyzes the sales person's working time, the average cost-per-call, buying influences reached and other sales problems).

In addition to such informative booklets, the Communications Department makes available many filmstrips dealing with advertising and selling on a loan basis for management conferences, sales meetings, sales training courses and so on.

These observations and descriptions of services and advertising /marketing materials available from McGraw-Hill serve only to illustrate the wealth of information that is there for the asking, though at some cost for selected services. Industrial advertising managers have a mass of data waiting for them, whether they are just laying the groundwork for a campaign, or wish to determine a market potential, or want to test a message theme, or desire to construct a DEMON (DEcision Mapping via Optimum GO-NO Networks) model for resolving the complex web of information decision alternatives encountered when marketing new products.

You can mine many a nugget of priceless information from business media with a ridiculously low cost in money and time. A bonus is that this information negates the natural human tendency to think each of our companies is unique, that each has problems the likes of which are outside the experience of mortal man. Business publishers were, perhaps, the first to recognize that this is a fallicy. They long ago established the common denominators of almost all marketing problems, many of which are, contrary to popular opinion, almost ubiquitous. Business publishers are aware of the problems most of us encounter, they've defined them, segregated them, grouped them, and solved them for the most part. They can save much time and many trials and tribulations for the ad manager who asks for their help, and make it easier to produce more and better results — in less time.

Another prime source of information about prospects, both companies and people, lies in inquiries received from advertising and editorial exposure in the trade press. Inquiries will be discussed in depth in a later chapter, but it is important to recognize that a careful analysis and tabulation of them always provides enlightening facts.

Detective Work on Prospects

Check against the customer list, check the SIC, check the printout of your mailing list; these will tell you if you have a likely prospect whose name should be bucked to the field force, or if you have a literature collector or other "nixie." As a rule, you'll find that most inquiries received via "bingo cards" (order blanks requesting literature) are valid inquiries, with one qualification: Most such inquirers are fairly low on the corporate table of organization. Granted, this is a generality, but it holds true rather consistently, especially when capital equipment is concerned.

This is not to say that inquiries, either from bingo cards or from any other source, are not worthwhile. Most of them have merit and sometimes they disclose an unusual amount of interest in a given item from a number of sources in one company. When this situation exists, it is a loud and unmistakable signal to send the first-string sales team calling *right now.* Markets do differ, and in the scientific, medical, educational, dental, and government areas, to pick some specific examples, returners of bingo cards tend to be in at least the middle echelon on the organizational chart, and frequently are higher.

Another source of information required to build a solid foundation under the communications program involves a bit of intelligence work. Unfortunately, the sleuthing is not as glamorous as that done routinely by the suave superheroes of paperbackdom, since it involves neither high living nor an overly anxious bevy of beauties. You can't have everything, though, and the information is highly important because it concerns the competition.

Competitive information is acquired in a number of ways. Sales managment, through the field force, keeps tab on what their opposite numbers say; they easily determine this via feedbacks from friendly prospects and customers. Marketing management has its sources of information. But it frequently falls to the advertising manager to tell management what the competition is officially saying, what story they are telling, what kind of creative approach they are using in their advertising, and what specific selling propositions they are stressing. In addition to keeping management posted on what competitors are doing, it is necessary for the ad manager to have this information to plan his own program.

This information is not needed to *react* to competitive advertising, for doing this merely plays right into the competition's hands. Instead, this intelligence is required so that a more forceful, more informative program can be developed that is different, that separates the company from the herd. Look-alikes are usually also-rans.

This information can be accumulated in a number of ways. Least costly, at least in terms of actual dollar outlay, is the look-up method. All industrial advertisers who use 12 or more full pages in business publications are listed in *Rome Report of Business Publication Advertising.* This reliable reference work lists companies, breaks down divisions of corporations, and then tabulates just how much advertising space they ran in the preceding year, and in what publications. Only a few minutes are required to check up on your competition to see where they appear; then, by going through back issues of applicable publications, you can quickly tear out ads for further study. If you don't have access to back issues, it is probable the public library in any large city has them; you can't tear out pages, of course, for ripping paper breaks the silence libraries love. But you can make copies on the library copying machine. The *Rome Report* is probably in your agency's library, but if you want your own, it is available from:

> Rome Reports, Inc.
> 375 Park Ave.
> New York, New York 10022

The Standard Advertising Red Books provide detailed, current information of this nature, also. *The Standard Directory of Advertisers* published by this company lists 17,000 companies doing national or regional advertising, their advertising agencies, media used, ad budgets, and also lists 80,000 executives by name and title. The classified edition of this book shows companies in 51 business classifications. It is published in April. Several arrangements are offered:

> *Standard Directory of Advertisers* (classified edition) plus nine monthly revisions, each containing all changes since publication of the directory, plus geographical index, has an annual subscription price of $173.
>
> *Standard Directory of Advertisers* (classified edition) carries a single copy price of $123.
>
> *Standard Directory of Advertisers* (classified edition) plus three issues of the *Standard Directory of Advertising Agencies* (listing 4,000 agencies, their key personnel and accounts) plus supplements and weekly bulletins, has an annual subscription price of $257.

These useful volumes may be ordered from:

> The Standard Advertising Red Books
> Skokie, Illinois 60077: 5201 Old Orchard Road

New York 10017: 20 East 46th Street
Chicago 60601: 333 North Michigan Avenue
Los Angeles 90048: 6300 Wilshire Boulevard
Atlanta 30326: 3400 Peachtree Road N.E.

Here are some related sources of advertising information which will help you. Transit Advertising Rates and Data published by Standard Rate and Data Service, Inc. Each issue contains listings arranged in geographic/alphabetical order, includes branch offices, representatives, transit lines, communities served, card requirements, advertising rates, restrictions, circulation, and so forth. Published quarterly, $18.00 a year.

How to Check the Competition

It is an oddity of business life that every company is too busy selling its own products to analyze continuously and accurately what the competition is officially saying in advertisements. The alert ad manager will read and analyze all competitive ads, possibly with the assistance of the marketing director. He or she will then submit a report, perhaps quarterly, to management on the results of this intelligence operation. Much of value may be gleaned from material that is widely disseminated if it is well analyzed and properly presented. The report should be presented much like a newspaper article—most important facts first, others arranged as to importance in descending order.

If you feel it necessary to keep a month-by-month dossier on the competition but don't have unlimited time, the best way to do it is to use a reliable clipping service.

Bacon's Clipping Bureau, among others, does an outstanding job. This firm is in a position to supply complete reading coverage of 4,000 business, trade, consumer, and farm magazines and the 500 top daily newspapers in the United States and Canada. Bacon's service covers both advertising and editorial material, or it can be limited to one or the other, as the ad manager wishes. Specialized research reading teams at Bacon's carefully read their assigned publications, picking up any articles or ads mentioning the key words relating to the subjects specified. When these readers find an article or an ad covering the subject they've been alerted to spot, they mark it and it is clipped from the publication after the reading is completed. Clippings are sorted, order by order. They are edited by Bacon's editing department to cull items which may contain the right key words, but which are otherwise not pertinent. Only edited material is submitted to the customer, who can be almost certain of getting only what is actually needed—and very close to 100% of that.

Bacon's basic rate for subject research is an $85.00 monthly service charge for the first subject checked, and $30.00 a month for each additional subject. Over and above this fee is a charge of 50 cents for each clipping. No ad manager could hope to read—or even scan hurriedly—all of these publications, even if they were received. Bacon's, therefore, can save anyone considerable time and money. Bacon's may reached at:

Bacon's Clipping Bureau
14 East Jackson Boulevard
Chicago, Illinois 60604

In the case of competitive information from publishers, the ad manager avoids drudgery and wasted time spent in detail work. The information needed is there, it's in an easy-to-understand tabulation, it's necessary, and acquiring it won't impose a strain on even the most modest budget.

A number of other firms are in the information-gathering business and provide similar information about consumer advertising in all media, including newspapers, radio, and television. They do not concern us, however, for they concentrate exclusively on the frenetic frenzy of curing headaches fast, *fast, FAST*—or of hammering home what brand of detergent should be used in washing machines twice as tall as the advertising manager's wife. They don't get into the industrial field . . . where advertising communicates with sensible, rational humans who can think.

Why People Buy Your Product

The final portion of the foundation upon which a good advertising program can be built consists of a piece of information that is always crucially important to the ad manager. It is why people buy—or *don't* buy—your product. One is as important as the other, and never mind the negative connotation.

The thing is, this information is frequently quite difficult to acquire, particularly since it must be thoroughly reliable. Far too many companies suffer from the Ostrich Complex, which is merely burying one's head in the sand and refusing to face facts. These companies blithely gloss over the difficult self-analysis entailed in developing a thoroughly objective critique of the company, its service and its product(s). Some apparently feel it is either an unnecessary waste of time, or, hugging their omnipotence to their corporate breasts, take the attitude that they know all there is to know about their company, service and products. After all it's *theirs.*

However, product weaknesses, lack of ability to accommodate to changing markets and conditions, and unwillingness to—or inability to—provide direction which will result in a uniformly high level of performance from all hands can all contribute to the reasons why sales are lost. They must be analyzed and corrective action taken before any advertising and communications program—no matter how well conceived—can stand a chance of helping to achieve the objectives.

One of the most hallowed, but still one of the best, methods of establishing attitudes toward a company or product is the survey. Customers and noncustomers should be surveryed to find out why they bought your product or service—and, in the case of prospects who did not become customers, they should be asked exactly why they did *not* buy from you.

Many cogent reasons will be unearthed, although it is extremely difficult for surveys and interviews to be completely dispassionate and objective if done by company personnel. It's far better to have your advertising agency, or a firm which specializes in industrial research, undertake the task. They can handle it without bias, without emotion and submit a meaningful report. They will let the chips fall where they may. Those who are emotionally involved with a company and its products are generally incapable of doing this. Just a hint of personal feeling, a delicate and subtle shading of a section of the report, or a desire—even a subconscious one—to shift responsibility can obscure or alter the facts and make them worse than no facts at all.

Spotlight on Product Weaknesses

In the course of such a research program actual product weaknesses may be brought to light. Some of these may almost preclude sales to certain markets, while they have little effect in others, depending upon product application. Price structure, or dealer-discount arrangements, may be such that your company operates at a strong competitive disadvantage; often this can be altered slightly to offset the edge the competition enjoys. The product may be such that salespeople have a difficult time discussing all of the user benefits, especially when prospects must keep sales calls short due to a heavy work load. Finally, and no company likes to admit it, prospects may not have heard of your product, or, at best, may be only vaguely familiar with it.

Advertising can counter all of these handicaps which limit sales. If the price cannot be lowered, advertising can present the product so favorably by stressing all of the benefits, the features which are built into it (and, by inference, lacking in competitive products), that price becomes a secondary consideration. John Ruskin remarked that quality is remembered long after price is forgotten, and this sage observation holds as true today as when it was made before the turn of the century.

Advertising has the unique capability of presenting a complex story about a complex product exactly the way you want it done, time after time. It never varies, there's no worry about how anyone may weaken the presentation. And advertising has as long a time to get the story across as the prospect wishes it to take.

If your product or service happens to be one with which the prospect is not thoroughly familiar, fine! This is advertising's forte. Among all methods of communications, word of mouth, gossip over the backyard fence, a chit carried on a forked stick, drum beats, smoke signals, or what have you, advertising alone can present a selling message about your product to thousands of people who are important to you, and do it simultaneously. Try to do that any other way.

Finally, touch bases with the sales department to verify the validity of your research findings. If the sales manager is a hard-headed realist—as most are—real support can be supplied, as well as be a valuable source of information.

Chapter 4

PLANNING A CAMPAIGN

BACK when all of this was much simpler, common practice was for the industrial ad manager to engage in a considerable amount of soul searching, crystal-ball gazing, pure unadulterated guesswork, add a pinch of hunch, and finally indulge in a profound session with the nearest Ouija board. Then, with various mysterious incantations, unsullied motives, and hopes higher than the Himalayas, he or she would bring forth a program which reflected the input received from the sales department, the marketing people (if any), and top management. As a rule it was more or less on target, even if the target was obscured by the mists of foggy thinking.

Frequently the program was responsible—at least, in part—for sales growth, reduced cost of selling, increased market penetration, or some other goal. *What* part was largely unmeasured and thus open to interpretation. *Whose* interpretation determined how effective the program was. Even today the ad manager should make a special interpretation when selling accomplishments to management.

Back then, the imagination usually had to have great elasticity to enable it to stretch enough to consider the program a campaign. A true campaign is a connected series of events or operations—closely related and carefully conceived—designed to bring about desired objectives. This, after all, is all that an advertising campaign is when stripped of excess verbiage—the complete advertising plan developed to achieve objectives spelled out in the marketing plan.

Reviewing the Groundwork

Now that we're ready to think about planning a campaign, let's take a fast look at some of the necessary groundwork which has been laid to make campaign planning possible.

1. Necessity to achieve both short-range goals and long-range objectives, as set forth in the marketing plan, is recognized and the cam-

paign is to be designed to accomplish this. Realistic objectives which can be measured must be established for the entire communications program before it is completed.

2. Industry's buying procedures are understood, and it can be taken for granted that your company's distribution channels are right for your products and your markets; that dealers and distributors (or representatives) are solvent, aggressive, in the right market locations, and that they devote sufficient time to your product(s).

3. Multiple-buying influences are a part of the scheme of things, and a varying number of individuals influence every purchase in every company, inconsequential items excepted. These buying influences are on different levels of management, but all are important and all must be communicated with.

4. Industrial purchase procedures are made in six stages—six separate increments of time—and they follow one another in sequence as inevitably as invoices arrive or personal income tax falls due. To communicate with the many influences involved in all six steps over a prolonged period of time is a job done most effectively and at lowest cost by space advertising. Advertising gives the influences information they need to move from one stage to another.

5. The market must be defined, customer and prospect companies classified by SIC, addresses and cities, then by sales territory, and the key buying influences located by name and title in each establishment. The campaign must have as one objective reaching these buying influences; this will affect media selection, budgeting, copy platform and a number of other considerations, each of which will be discussed separately.

6. Reviewed what business publishers can contribute, particularly in basic information necessary to build a campaign.

7. Realize how important it is to scout the competition to see what it has done, and what it is likely to do in the future. This can influence the tack you take in planning the advertising program, so your company capitalizes on the weaknesses of competitors and uses it to your advantage. This information influences media, budget, schedule, and creative approach.

8. The truth has been faced up to about why people buy, or don't buy, your product. Benefits people want can be stressed in advertising, whether space or broadcasting.

The next step is to develop an advertising campaign based on the above information. The campaign must be coordinated so that bits and pieces mesh together to form a coordinated whole; it must also be carefully integrated into overall marketing strategy so there's every chance it will contribute as much as is expected. Advertising must be the working partner of the field sales force and must complement these efforts, as well as those of distributors, agents and dealers.

Avoid All Generalities

The knowledgeable ad manager will want his advertising plan to be fully as specific as the marketing plan is, with generalities avoided like the plague. All too frequently advertising plans contain such solemn statements of good intention as: "This program is designed to increase sales of . . ." or, and probably even worse, business-style gobbledygook such as: "When maximized, the subsequent plan and interrelated activities are formulated to . . ." The first is akin to a ringing affirmation favoring motherhood, flag, and paying one's bills on time. Such evidence of good citizenship is highly commendable, but it doesn't pay off in sales. Advertising does. The second doesn't even deserve comment.

Nonobjective objectives cost—cost in wasted time and wasted opportunity and wasted dollars. Vague and nonspecific, they offer a haven to the fuzzy thinker who can't or doesn't want to produce. They demand that advertising handle all functions of communications, something it never pretended to be able to do. They espouse the viewpoint and desires of the advertiser, rather than those of the prospect. And, equally important, nonobjective objectives make it impossible to measure advertising effectiveness.

Following is an actual example of such fuzzy thinking. This amazing treatise is not a figment of somebody's disordered imagination. It is an actual memo to the advertising manager of a well-known company, from the marketing manager of a highly technical product line sold to an unusually sophisticated market. It was written in response to a request for marketing objectives at the start of a new fiscal year. *Not one word has been changed except the name of the company. Not one.*

TECHNICAL SALES DEPARTMENT
ADVANCED WIDGET MANUFACTURING COMPANY, INC.
MARKETING OBJECTIVES

It is the purpose of this plan to establish marketing objectives, specific and concrete in form, to firm our position in the marketplace through several media. Our objectives are focused around (1) service, (2) promotion, (3) products, and (4) advertising. A fifth topic could be our future market position, that is, to regain that percentage of the market that has been lost to the competition. However, this topic is related directly to sales activity and our goal is obviously correlated to the entire market. In outline form, some of our marketing objectives are as follows:

A. *Service*

1. To develop a service policy by virtue of a self-sustaining service organization; service personnel located in each key marketing center and manufacturing facility.

2. To supply service engineers with necessary data and information to supplement policy.

3. To provide educational facilities by methods of formalized training programs, manufacturing experience, etc., to supplement such a service organization.

4. To extend to various customers the training facility on a formalized basis to reach the technical level of management.

B. *Promotion*

1. To promote Advanced Widget Manufacturing Company product group by means of trade shows, monthly promotional mailing, PR releases, trade-journal articles, etc.

2. To promote our status with field-sales personnel by virtue of supplemental activities; i.e., gifts for the top salespersons, plaques for achievement, expense-paid trip, etc.

3. Individual customer pomotions to increase sales and/or regain as a customer.

4. To develop high morale within organization that is conducive to participation.

C. *Products*

1. To develop new products to keep pace with an ever-changing market requirement.

2. To stay abreast with "state-of-the-art" processes.

3. To substantiate the salability of existing products by research tools and analyzing the market for current needs.

4. To acquire companies that are established for additional products beyond our design capabilities providing the products fit within our present forces.

5. To increase the volume forecasts (securements of market share and profit), by means of present and future promotional activities.

6. To firm our marketing objectives by existing policy on products and present marketing approach.

D. *Advertising*

1. To analyze the market and objectives and justify programs.
2. To reach the buying powers through public relations and advertising media.
3. To promote other activities which comprise the overall marketing plan.
4. To recommend marketing appeals and strategy.
5. To be responsible for advertising matter through bulletins, brochures, and monthly promotions.
6. To be accountable for PR releases.
7. To recommend effective advertising programs and to assist in providing data for promotional activities and service training information.

The information contained herein should enable the advertising department to develop a plan and proposal to management for advertising activities derived from overall marketing objectives.

Insist Upon Realistic Goals

An advertising manager would have to be a genius of the first water to develop a program to help achieve such nonobjectives. Just what could be recommended to "increase the volume forecasts (securements of market share and profit), through present and future promotional activities," for example? Perhaps a saturation sky-writing campaign in the six largest cities in the Yukon Territory.

An ad manager faced with such a frustrating situation can, of course, attempt to translate the vague generalities into what is believed are valid marketing objectives, relying on knowledge of the company, its operation, its product, and its markets.

Chances are he or she would come quite close. But the fact remains that *the responsibility is not his.* Properly it rests with the marketing director, or, if the company is organized so that these functions are handled by a sales manager, then by that worthy person.

The advertising manager *must* have firm direction, preferably in writing, on the marketing objectives of each product line or for each market to which the company sells. These objectives may be taken directly from the company's marketing plan if one exists, although it is still prudent to check them with the individual with marketing or sales responsibilities. Making a change before a program is actually under way is easy. Afterwards, it's expensive.

The alternative, and the proper course, is to reject such lack of direction as wholly inadequate. Decline to proceed further with the development of an advertising program until legitimate objectives are received. Then, and only then, should work start on the advertising campaign planning.

So that the ad manager personally can make a significant contribution to the company's marketing success, the ad manager wants to be assured that advertising realizes its full potential—and this means that advertising must be assigned specific tasks. However, because the tasks are well defined does not mean that the program need necessarily be narrow or limited. On the contrary, it can be quite broad in scope.

How Du Pont Introduces New Products

Awareness that innovation is synonymous with success in the marketplace literally permeates E. I. du Pont de Nemours & Company. This awareness may well be the single most significant factor in the chemical giant's dominance of its industry.

This holds true in research and development, at which Du Pont excels, as well as in its advertising philosophy. Du Pont advertising thinking is solid and professional. It is built on the bedrock of well-directed research which precludes going off on tangents—at the expense of lost time and money. There's not enough of either.

The company not long ago introduced a new product, Microfoam, which was unique. Even uniqueness didn't result in that happy, happy situation where competition is nonexistent, however. Microfoam had established competition. Microfoam meets head-on with any number of older packaging materials such as crepe paper wadding and air bubble material, all used to protect various products from shipping damage. Shipping damage, incidentally, is on the increase in all modes of transportation, the result of don't-give-a-damn attitude on the part of rank and file employees.

Du Pont advertising executive William H. Nimtz supplied the rationale for positioning a new product (Microfoam) in the marketplace by use of advertising.

As Mr. Nimtz said, Microfoam joined the ranks of the thousands of products that preceded it, all of which can logically be termed "continuing innovations." Microfoam admittedly does a job that is already being done by a similar product, although not one that's a Du Pont brainchild. Even though Microfoam is a packaging product and most packaging products are paper, the fact still remains that other plastic packaging products were on the market—were, in fact, produced long before Microfoam was even thought of.

Market analysts at Du Pont took a long, hard look at the marketplace and decided to position their new product as a continuing innovation in the booming packaging market. Current theory held by up-to-date advertising practitioners holds that a product must be "positioned" so that prospective purchasers will immediately recognize the product's place in the scheme of things.

As a result, Du Pont's major communications objective was to persuade the end user, when thinking of buying a packaging product, to at least *consider* Microfoam along with others. Not considered, not bought. It's that simple.

Positioning the Product Is Critical

After discussion, the decision was made to face the competition squarely and to show—actually to show—competitive products in each Microfoam advertisement. Purpose, of course, was to position Microfoam in the mind of the reader as a logical alternative to the other packaging product shown in the ad. Du Pont people felt it very important to illustrate clearly to the reader that if he or she now used the competing product to package a widget, he could also now use Microfoam to do the very same job. And do it better.

Call it positioning, or call it what you will, after reading the ad the reader simply *must* come away with the clear understanding that instead of staying in a rut and using crepe paper wadding or bubble wrap to package a beautiful product, that person now had the option of using Microfoam. Times change, improved products appear.

If only this *one* objective were achieved, the ad would have done its assigned task. Microfoam would have been successfully positioned in the mind of the consumer of packaging products. There would be an awareness of an alternative.

An additional major role for advertising was recognized by Du Pont, of course. That role was to inform as many potential users of Microfoam as possible of its availability and of the benefits to be derived from using the new product in its various forms.

This effort would create awareness of Microfoam through mass communications and also by the very presence of the product in the marketplace help to persuade Du Pont distributors to put a push behind Microfoam—and to launch advertising and promotional programs of their own in its support. This would enable them to capitalize on the awareness created by Du Pont's advertising so that their efforts would have a synergistic effect.

A secondary role of advertising and promotion was to assist with selective promotion to high potential markets, thus increasing the effectiveness of the Du Pont sales force, as well as convincing distributors and their salespersons that it would be in their own self-interest to spend more time and effort selling Microfoam.

Incidentally, every advertiser large and small—whether of one product in a multi-product company, as well as advertisers with only one product to sell—shares a common problem. He or she is in direct competition *with every other advertiser* two things: the share of salesperson's time, and the share of mind all along the channels of distribution. If you don't get your share of those two things, you can forget everything else. Because you're doomed to bomb out.

Du Pont's other objectives were to develop programs aimed at selected markets; to back up its new emphasis on direct sales effort aimed at large volume users; and to generate inquiries for direct sales follow-up in end-user markets. This last would enlist distributor salespeople as valuable allies and stimulate them to greater efforts to develop new business—and, coincidentally, to lay claim to more of the salesperson's selling time for Microfoam.

Specific Markets and Additional Promotional Efforts

The universe with which Du Pont needed to communicate about Microfoam's benefits was broad indeed, consisting as it did of industry as a whole. Specific markets on which the company wanted to concentrate were the furniture market and the government market.

Early and enthusiastic reception of Microfoam by two well-known manufacturers of quality furniture, Thomasville and Futorian, helped substantially in introducing Microfoam to the top 100 furniture manufacturers in the country. The new product was advertised in the following media. Frequency and space size shown.

It was found that an expanded space advertising program in 1975 provided additional distributor support, as well as pounded home the fact that Microfoam was a GSA-stocked item. When the General Services Administration approves an item, further government sales accrue as a routine matter.

Various branches of the Federal Government consume incredible amounts of packaging materials and shipments made to and by the Armed Forces are so numerous the mind literally boggles when contemplating them. Fortunately we taxpayers have lots of money. And if the dollars happen to run short, there's always an ample supply of the bureaucrats' standby, red ink.

Shown nearby are the first three business publication advertisements for Du Pont Microfoam. They appear in order of insertion in media discussed above.

These are typical Du Pont ads for business books. Strong headline with user benefits, product advantages hammered home, the product clearly positioned. You'll note in the introductory ad how lower cost and better performance on the job—the two criteria by which both

YEAR MARKET	MEDIUM	CIRCULATION	SCHEDULE
1973 General packaging market	Packaging Digest	57,600	6x, b/w page
1973 General packaging market	Purchasing	70,000	4x, b/w page
1973 Electronics market	Electronics Packaging & Production	27,000	4x, b/w page
1974 General packaging market	Packaging Digest	60,000	6x, b/w page
1974 General packaging market	Package Engineering	49,000	4x b/w page

Microfoam and competitive products are judged—are hit "fustest with the mostest." Lead from strength, always. Bridge and advertising are not different in that respect.

Following in rapid-fire order are bulleted product superiorities and, in a box, additional benefits realized when the product is actually used. Each is succinct, relevant and persuasive.

These Du Pont ads put the product's best foot forward and never hesitate to tell one and all they're simply not with it if they're not using Microfoam, newest and best packaging product to come down the pike.

Hedge Your Bet With Direct Mail

It's usually a mistake to rely heavily on only one medium, even though that medium is business publication advertising, the best and lowest cost way yet devised to communicate with a specific audience. Du Pont, as a very savvy marketer, realized this fully so it also developed direct mail material to supplement its efforts in the business press, its primary communications vehicle.

Shown nearby are three of the direct mail pieces designed to look like and reflect the themes of the three ads previously illustrated. The mailers are cleverly designed to include a postpaid reply card addressed to the distributor over whose name the mailer was sent—in this case, Iroquois Paper Company, Chicago.

Supplementing the mailing pieces which supplement the space ads are illustrated post cards mailed by business publications. This is an excellent and inexpensive way to get additional exposure and generate a substantial quantity of sales leads. Cost, in 1975, was around $750 to $800 for a postcard mailing. Postcards are usually available only to display advertisers. The publication mails your card in a package,

MICROFOAM® sheeting: It's the one that protects better and costs less.

1/4" crepe paper wadding   1/8" MICROFOAM sheeting

When you specify your next protective packaging material, keep this comparison in mind: Compared to ¼" crepe paper wadding, ⅛" Du Pont MICROFOAM sheeting gives you all these advantages:

- Costs less for equal or better cushioning
- Stands up better to repeated impact
- Better protection against abrasion of product surfaces
- Sheds water like a duck
- Superior insulation properties
- Snowy white
- Can be printed, die-cut or embossed

And now Du Pont MICROFOAM sheeting is easier to use than ever (see box at right).

Why not send for some samples and work out the savings for your particular application. For samples and more information, write: Du Pont Company, Room 22987-A, Wilmington, DE 19898.

Now available in 6", 12", 18", 24" and 36" perforations.

Now you can get MICROFOAM sheeting in perforated form (6", 12", 18", 24" and 36" perforations) offering these extra advantages.

- No cutting required • Quick, easy, efficient handling • Reduced material waste and less packing room labor • Easy dispensing from overhead or under-the-bench storage • Still available in custom-sliced widths • Standard perforation lengths ideal for uniform packaging of standard-sized products • Standard 6" perforation size can be used in any multiple of 6" size sheets, because perforations *do not* affect cushioning performance.

microFoam

Note the hard-hitting copy that Du Pont used for its inaugural ad for Microfoam. Du Pont believes in strong headlines with user benefits, with product advantages hammered home.

The advertisement on the top was the second in the Du Pont series and the one immediately above was the third. Note the continuing strong headlines.

147

along with others to the book's mailing list.

You don't even have to do any printing—merely send the book camera-ready art (keyline and glossy photo) and they proceed to print your postcard. This is a real bargain in these inflationary times because you couldn't begin to print 75,000 or so mailing pieces, pay

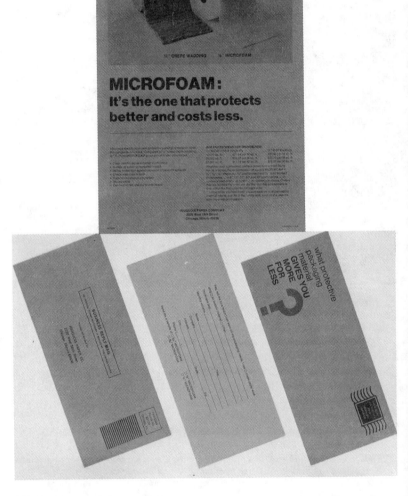

outgoing postage and handle the thing for anything near the modest cost charged. Incoming postage is an expense, of course, but the number of returns you'll receive is a tiny fraction of the number that were mailed. This cost is inconsequential. And it's bulk rate, at that.

Final sales tool in Du Pont's well-conceived introduction of its latest example of chemical wizardy is the attractive four-page sales literature shown nearby.

The familiar Du Pont logo appears prominently on the front and second pages of this two-color (black and blue) literature; for some reason that doesn't come to mind, the company was uncharacteristically modest on the other two pages and ignored the logotype.

Illustrations in the literature are conventional black-and-white halftones, along with two duotones on the front page. Duotones are a combination of halftones in black, along with a second color; a duotone is *not* a tint block laid on top of a b/w halftone, however, but has highlights that are clean.

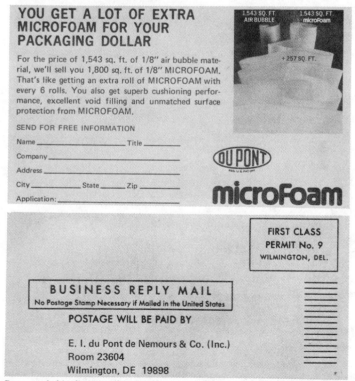

YOU GET A LOT OF EXTRA MICROFOAM FOR YOUR PACKAGING DOLLAR

For the price of 1,543 sq. ft. of 1/8" air bubble material, we'll sell you 1,800 sq. ft. of 1/8" MICROFOAM. That's like getting an extra roll of MICROFOAM with every 6 rolls. You also get superb cushioning performance, excellent void filling and unmatched surface protection from MICROFOAM.

SEND FOR FREE INFORMATION

Name _____ Title _____

Company_____

Address_____

City _____ State _____ Zip _____

Application: _____

1,543 SQ. FT. AIR BUBBLE   1,543 SQ. FT. microfoam

+ 257 SQ. FT.

(DU PONT)
REG. U.S. PAT OFF

microfoam

FIRST CLASS
PERMIT No. 9
WILMINGTON, DEL.

BUSINESS REPLY MAIL
No Postage Stamp Necessary if Mailed in the United States

POSTAGE WILL BE PAID BY

E. I. du Pont de Nemours & Co. (Inc.)
Room 23604
Wilmington, DE 19898

Du Pont used this direct mail promotion to reinforce its ads in the business press.

Good judgment was shown in the selection of the illustrations because Microfoam is seen being used, cut, stored, made into pouches and so on—in a variety of different ways. You'll note, too, that names of well-known companies which use Microfoam are casually dropped in for an implied endorsement. Strong stuff, and very effective, too.

And on the last page of the literature Du Pont discusses availability, military specifications and the comparative ratings of both Microfoam and other flexible cushioning materials. This is done in an ap-

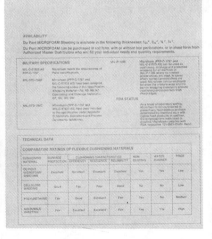

parently objective manner and it carries conviction.

Du Pont company policy prohibits disclosure of actual sales volume or percentage of market penetration. However, its advertising executives felt sure that sales targets had been hit and that Microfoam was assured of its rightful place in the sun.

Du Pont the Innovator

Having practically put plastic on the map over the last quarter-century, along with a host of other goodies such as Nylon, Dacron, Teflon and scads of others, Du Pont is not a company to rest on its laurels, Naturally, this delights my stockholder's heart because a tidy share of what the chemical giant ends up with on the bottom line accrues to us who own the company.

Recently the marketing-product, development-research types in Wilmington got their heads together and came to the conclusion that wrapping produce—and even potatoes—in transparent plastic simply wasn't the way to go. It lacked class.

Their additional conclusion was that savvy retailers are right. Every smart retailer has a bedrock belief that the shopper who can fondle, feel, see and smell the merchandise is a shopper who is going to buy that merchandise. And, as every retailer will tell you, that's the name of the game.

Du Pont's innovative people analyzed produce packaging in a number of supermarkets and immediately a number of "musts" were apparent. First of all, the package must hold the produce firmly so it won't open accidentally under the probing fingers of value-conscious female shoppers. They can *really* probe. It must present the produce so it is readily visible. It must be extremely light in weight so that at the checkout counter there won't be vociferous protests against weighing the packaging material. It must be easy to use. And, finally, it must be low in cost.

With these major considerations in mind, Du Pont teams went to work with the objective to produce a truly superior product, one with real class and one that would make a significant penetration of the market in a very short period of time.

Enter Vexar

After a suitable amount of work so that product development wouldn't appear too easy to the powers that be, there emerged an unquestionably superior new product—Vexar. Vexar is a fantastically strong, fine-mesh plastic netting. It is produced in food colors—yellow for grapefruit or lemons, for instance, or red for apples, and so on.

Vexar was a new concept, one that supermarket management was completely unfamiliar with. New concepts aren't always embraced with open arms, people have to be persuaded to accept them.

Because Vexar was a new concept, it called for exceptionally effective advertising if the corporate objective of compressing the time scale between product introduction and product profitability was to be realized.

The new Vexar was assigned to Wim van der Graaf, a solid, well-rounded advertising professional who's an alumnus of Northwestern University and that great training ground for advertising people, Montgomery Ward. The possessor of an unusually keen, analytical mind, Wim van der Graaf has a long list of outstandingly effective campaigns to his credit, along with the customary wall full of awards, plaques and so on that gravitate to topflight advertising people.

To digress for a minute, it has always seemed to me—and this has been borne out by almost three decades of management experience—that exceptional competence in industrial advertising demands an exceptionally active and inquisitive mind, one with wide-ranging interests and activities. This is in addition, of course, to a well-rounded formal education in advertising and marketing plus sufficient dedication to continue to upgrade one's knowledge of the field.

This is certainly borne out in van der Graaf's case. He's a prospector who delights in panning placer gold in rushing mountain streams in the West's high country; a dedicated ghost town buff; a first-rate tennis player; water skier and Coast Guard-certified small craft skipper; breeder and trainer of purebred dogs; music lover, New Orleans jazz *aficionado*, tape nut; rock hound and turquois connoisseur; an expert on Indian arts and crafts; skilled woodworker; shooter and handloader; a duck and goose hunter and a sportsman who exults in fair stalk for antelope and deer. All of this, although fun stuff, broadens his outlook and gives him background knowledge in many fields. Combined with his writing of magazine articles these avocations contribute to his continuing informal education; he also continues formal study, of course, as do most professional ad people.

Soon Only Advertising Tigers Will Survive

Contrast van der Graaf with a hypothetical ad person (I've actually known some like him) whom we'll call John or Jill Average. Incredibly, this Average didn't bother to finish high school; two years of high school are enough. True, this "ad person" may play golf and bowl and pub crawl and memorize the statistics of other people's accomplishments, such as those of professional athletes. This provides just about zero mental growth, of course, but such an "advertising person" sees no need for growth, no need to learn the intricacies of the chosen field. The Averages are midgets among their peers and they

THE ORANGES IN VEXAR®
GET TWICE THE ACTION FROM SHOPPERS
IN SIDE-BY-SIDE SALES TESTS.

Sold: 407 bags of oranges in Du Pont VEXAR plastic netting...
170 in plastic film. Same oranges. Same price. Side by side on the
same amount of counter space.

That's the result of a carefully controlled supermarket sales
audit over a two-week test period.*

It's no wonder that shoppers show a more than 2 to 1 preference
for oranges in VEXAR. Bags of VEXAR let the natural color and
fresh appeal of the oranges come through. There's no hazy film, no
shiny glare. Shoppers get all the convenience of bagged fruit with
the appearance of bulk display. And oranges look fresher because
they *stay* fresh longer in well-ventilated bags of VEXAR.

So the buying action goes where the VEXAR is. For you that
means faster turnover, more efficient use of precious display space,
less waste and spoilage. More consumer satisfaction and an
enhanced quality look for your entire department.

If you'd like a piece of the extra action, specify citrus and
other produce in bags of fine-mesh VEXAR plastic netting.
*details of this study on request.

FOR BETTER NET RESULTS—DU PONT VEXAR PLASTIC NETTING

*Half of these oranges is wrapped in plastic and half is wrapped in Vexar. Not only can
you see the fruit better but you can actually smell the oranges.*

rely on having a top management which knows even less about advertising than they do—or they rely on having a superior carry them because they're too lazy to learn.

With the economy in a state of flux—you'll forgive the understatement—every advertising person should hone professional skills to a razor edge. The mid-80's is no time for complacency and laziness.

To digress for just a minute more, the move to certify industrial advertising people as professionally competent—following a comprehensive certification examination—is gaining impetus. Chances are, certification will be done through the Business/Professional Advertising Association (the old Association of Industrial Advertisers). It seems likely that within just a few years industrial advertising people will fall into just two classes; those with their certification as competent professionals, and the lazies like John and Jill Average who find it just too much bother to learn the profession they've chosen. This is well and good. Industrial advertising has long been saddled with too many Averages, well meaning but inept. Come certification day, these incompetents will no longer be able to bluff or con their way because they'll be shown up for what they are—people who can't measure up to professional standards. Needless to say, an ad individual in that position will find job opportunities severely limited.

Hunt Ducks Where the Ducks Are

Wim van der Graaf had already established that the primary market for the revolutionary new fine-mesh netting was high-volume supermarkets. Some supermarkets receive their produce in reefer (refrigerated) trailers in bulk. Large burlap bags. Bushel baskets. Cardboard boxes. It's up to the store manager, through his produce manager, to repackage to give the produce as much eye-appeal as possible so that your wife and mine will buy, not pass by.

The new Vexar had to be introduced with a bang so loud the impact would be roughly comparable to that of John Wayne arriving at full gallop just in the nick of time to keep the good cowboys from being slaughtered by the black-hatted guys. It was a range war, of course, over fences and water.

After thorough analysis, it was decided to run a 13X schedule in *Supermarket News*, the leading book read by supermarket managers, their key people and the big brass at the headquarters of the country's supermarket chains.

The schedule was meticulously planned down to the last detail—including the critically important element of timing. Ads showing Vexar-wrapped (or bagged) produce and fruit were scheduled to run just prior to the time the food came into season. That is, when grapefruit was coming into its best time of year, a grapefruit-Vexar ad was run; when apples were ripe for selling, an apple-Vexar ad was inserted, and so on.

We'll look at van der Graaf's Vexar campaign in a minute, but it's only fair to mention that it has won wide acclaim. Among other kudos the campaign received was the gold medal at the Rochester, New York, Art Directors' Show. While we all realize that our primary function as industrial advertising people is to help sell more and more of the product, and to reduce the cost of selling through effective mass communications, winning gold medals is not really important. Yet who can dispute the fact there's always a warm glow around the heart when your efforts are endorsed, approved and judged *numero uno* by your peers? That's just human nature.

Shown nearby are three Vexar ads. Let's examine them and see what makes them tick—and sell.

Back in the initial planning stages of this campaign, van der Graaf realized that black-and-white ads for a packaging product enclosing such colorful items as oranges, grapefruit and apples would have all of the strength of wet spaghetti. So he decided the additional investment for four-color was both called for and justified. Four-color ads, you know, get 53 percent greater readership than do black-and-white ads.

The ad nearby that occupies a full page in this book has for its illustration a mouth-watering bin of lush California oranges. Approximately half of the oranges are conventionally wrapped in polyethyelene, in the quantity customers ordinarily purchase—or the amount that fits into the supermarket's price structure. Only thing, the oranges in plastic don't really have the visual appeal store management relies on to sell the merchandise. No getting around it, the plastic glares, reflecting back the overhead lights. This distracts. And no matter how you look at it, there is a certain amount of color degradation inherent in looking through any plastic. The vividness, the eye appeal, just don't come through.

On the left side of the illustration we see the same lot of California oranges bagged in Vexar. There's no comparison between the two. Vexar lets you see the oranges in all of their freshness, all of their lush color. And Vexar, unlike plastic, enables shoppers to *smell* the oranges. This is a superspecial subliminal fringe benefit from using Vexar. Let's take a look at what the ad says.

Like all Du Pont ads, this one is straightforward and to the point with no frills or beating around the bush. It presents Vexar in the most favorable light possible and translates product features into user benefits that supermarket managers can readily translate into extra dollars in their cash registers. The ad reads:

STORE AUDIT SHOWS
APPLES IN VEXAR® OUTSELL
APPLES IN PLASTIC FILMS BY 3 TO 2 MARGIN.

Shoppers prefer prepacked apples they can see. And smell. In a carefully controlled supermarket test they proved it. Given a choice between apples in bags of Du Pont VEXAR plastic netting and apples in plastic film, they bought 50% more of the apples in VEXAR. Same Red Delicious apples. Same price. Same counter space.

Little wonder. With bags of fine-mesh VEXAR, nothing gets between the appeal of the fruit and the shopper. No hazy film. No glare. To follow up the look of apples in plastic film. And they recognized that well-ventilated bags of VEXAR keep apples fresher (by 4 to 1).

So the buying action goes where the VEXAR is. For you that means faster turnover, more efficient use of precious display space, more impulse purchases. Less waste and spoilage. More consumer satisfaction and an enhanced quality look for your entire department.

If you'd like a piece of the extra action, specify apples and other produce in bags of fine-mesh VEXAR plastic netting.

FOR BETTER NET RESULTS—DU PONT VEXAR PLASTIC NETTING

SUPERMARKET AUDIT
SHOWS GRAPEFRUIT MOVING 100% FASTER
IN VEXAR THAN IN PLASTIC FILM.

What's the difference if you order your grapefruit in bags of Du Pont VEXAR plastic netting or packed in plastic bags?

One important difference is the way your customers react. We ran a carefully conducted sales audit in a leading supermarket to nail down the shoppers facts: in side-by-side tests shoppers preferred grapefruit in VEXAR to the same grapefruit in plastic bags by more than 2 to 1. During the same period they bought 153 bags of grapefruit in VEXAR vs. only 59 of the plastic bags.

Not surprising: bags of VEXAR let the natural color and fresh appeal of produce come through to the shopper. No hazy film, no glare gets in the way. Grapefruit looks fresh and appealing because it stays fresh in well-ventilated bags of VEXAR.

So the buying action goes where the VEXAR is. For you, the difference is faster turnover, more efficient use of precious counter space, less waste and spoilage. Plus consumer satisfaction and an enhanced quality look for your entire department.

If you'd like a piece of the extra action, specify grapefruit and other produce in bags of fine-mesh VEXAR plastic netting.

FOR BETTER NET RESULTS—DU PONT VEXAR PLASTIC NETTING

THE ORANGES IN VEXAR®
GET TWICE THE ACTION FROM SHOPPERS
IN SIDE-BY-SIDE SALES TESTS

Sold: 407 bags of oranges in Du Pont VEXAR plastic netting. . . 170 in plastic film. Same oranges. Same price. Side by side on the same amount of counter space.

That's the result of a carefully controlled supermarket sales audit over a two-week test period.*

It's no wonder that shoppers show a more than 2 to 1 preference for oranges in VEXAR. Bags of VEXAR let the natural color and fresh appeal of the oranges come through. There's no hazy film, no shiny glare. Shoppers get all the convenience of bagged fruit with the appearance of bulk display. And oranges look fresher because they *stay* fresh longer in well-ventilated bags of VEXAR.

So the buying action goes where the VEXAR is. For you that means faster turnover, more efficient use of precious display space, less waste and spoilage. More consumer satisfaction and an enhanced quality look for your entire department.

If you'd like a piece of the extra action, specify citrus and other produce in bags of fine-mesh VEXAR plastic netting.

FOR BETTER NET RESULTS—DU PONT
VEXAR® PLASTIC NETTING

The other two four-color Du Pont Vexar ads are shown nearby. Again, they stick to the tried-and-proven pocketbook appeal and promise supermarket owners and operators more profit—backing up the claims with irrefutable logic and case history data.

Take the apple ad, for example. The same illustrative technique is employed as in the orange ad—half a bin of plastic-wrapped apples, half a bin of apples bagged in Vexar. And it's again obvious that Vexar wins hands down. It isn't even a contest, it's so one-sided. Copy reads:

STORE AUDIT SHOWS
APPLES IN VEXAR® OUTSELL
APPLES IN PLASTIC FILMS BY 3 TO 2 MARGIN

Shoppers prefer packaged apples they can see. And smell.

In a carefully-controlled supermarket test, they proved it. Given a choice between apples in bags of Du Pont VEXAR plastic neting and apples in plastic film, they bought 50 percent more of

---

*Details of this study on request.

the apples in VEXAR. Same Red Delicious apples. Same price. Same counter space.

Little wonder. With bags of fine-mesh VEXAR, nothing gets between the appeal of the fruit and the shopper. No hazy film. No glare. In follow-up interviews, shoppers said they like the *visibility* of apples in VEXAR (11 to 1 over the look of apples in plastic film). And they recognized that well-ventilated bags of VEXAR keep apples fresher (by 4 to 1).

So the buying action goes where the VEXAR is. For you that means faster turnover, more efficient use of precious display space, more impulse purchases. Less waste and spoilage, more consumer satisfaction and an enhanced quality look for your entire department.

If you'd like a piece of the extra action, specify apples and other produce in bags of fine-mesh VEXAR plastic netting.

FOR BETTER NET RESULTS—DU PONT VEXAR® PLASTIC NETTING

Because one of the real keys to advertising success is repetition of major benefits and features, Du Pont's Wim van der Graaf wisely kept hitting the salient points in each ad, including the grapefruit one.

There's no need to reprint the entire copy of the grapefruit ad, but note that stress is placed on the most important parts of the message. In the headline we find, "shows grapefruit moving 100 percent faster." And in the body copy there's additional food for thought (you'll forgive that one, please), such as "in side-by-side tests, customers preferred grapefruit in Vexar by more than 2 to 1." Also that during the same period they "bought 153 bags of grapefruit in Vexar vs. only 59 in plastic bags." Then we find the no hazy film, no glare story which emphasizes the natural color of grapefruit in Vexar. And of primary importance in these days when the liberal politicians in Congress are trying their best to destroy the dollar through deficit spending, is the fact that produce in Vexar *stays* fresh due to excellent ventilation. Finally, there's the pocketbook appeal to the storekeeper of faster turnover, more efficient use of counter space, less waste and spoilage, plus more consumer satisfaction. If Du Pont can keep the price of Vexar even close to competitive with plastic film, it will have a real winner.

A Clean Campaign Look

These ads have a superb "campaign" appearance due to use of the same clean, uncluttered layout, fine illustration, and excellent typography. Incidentally, Du Pont advertising people would rather have their ads *read* than run them to impress a dwindling segment of good-hearted but misled types who haven't really done their homework when it comes to typefaces. All of these Du Pont ads, you'll notice, have a strong headline typeface—and all of them are set in a highly readable, attractive serif typeface for the body copy. Body copy set in serif type invariably receives high readership than the same copy set in a sans serif face. Cost is the same, so why penalize yourself by making it hard for the reader to read?

Fortunately, the craze for sans serif body copy type is one that is rapidly departing the scene. For far too long, far too many advertising people rushed lemminglike to join the throng whose main interest was to impress their friends, rather than have their advertisements read. Are we really trying to impress bearded, long-haired Eastern art directors in World War I army blouses and bearskin vests and sandals by using sans serif type—or are we trying to do everything possible to achieve higher readership by using serif type? Think it over.

Not All Begs In One Askit

The attractive four-color space ads we've just looked at launched Vexar with an appropriate bang. But Wim van der Graaf, seasoned old pro that he is, isn't one to put all of his begs in one askit. To rely on only one medium to carry the bulk of the load is to court disaster in the marketplace, or at the very least, to stretch out the time between product introduction and product profitability.

Back when he first developed the communications plan for the new fine-mesh netting, van der Graaf emphasized the importance of using direct mail to augment the introductory push put on by Du Pont's space advertising. Properly, however, he stressed that space ads were the primary communications vehicle because they reach more people at lower cost than any other means of communicating with the universe he had to reach.

Obviously van der Graaf could have taken the easy way out and gone with the hoary "writing them a letter" technique. He could even have carried this one step farther and used the ancient caper of mailing a letter and an ad reprint. And if he chose the ultimate in yesteryear's gambits, he'd have come up with mailing a letter and an ad reprint and a postpaid reply card. This, however, is a weak, wishy-washy and moss-grown approach to direct mail that was in its heyday around the turn of the century.

This isn't to infer that merchandising your ads is less than essential.

Just the opposite is true. The smart, dollar-conscious industrial communications man always merchandises ads because it's an effective way of assuring the message's getting the most possible readership in a target universe.

Direct mail has changed, progressed and become both more exciting and more productive in recent years. It has come of age. The dull and the trite no longer achieve their erstwhile purpose of attracting the individual's attention for a long enough time to get a message across. The average buying influence in industry receives so much direct mail now that only the truly exceptional, truly creative efforts are not consigned to the round file without a second glance.

3-D Was the Key

Knowing this, van der Graaf's conclusion was that only a "3-D" (three-dimensional) mailing would grab the recipient's attention and entice him or her into reading the enclosed message.

Moreover, there's no better way to dramatize a product, to imbue a strong curiosity about it, than to send an actual sample of it. (Remember all of the direct mail you've received from manufacturers of trousers, each with a swatch of fabric tipped onto descriptive literature?) The swatch *forced* you to read at least part of what the manufacturer had to say.

As good fortune would have it, van der Graaf had an absolute natural for a unique 3-D direct mail campaign that would achieve memorability almost akin to a Louis Armstrong blues record. Like every first-rate idea, van der Graaf's looks deceptively simple—so simple that the natural reaction is to think, "I could have come up with that." But the distinguishing mark of the true professional in this business is that he or she generates good ideas as they're needed, time after time after time.

Shown nearby is the first Vexar 3-D direct mail piece, this one on grapefruit. Name just one better way, if you can, of promoting Vexar, the fine-mesh netting for bagging produce and citrus fruits, than sending each individual on the mailing list a fresh, juicy grapefruit! My bet is you can't top this. Is there anybody who thinks this mailing wasn't noticed? That it didn't stand out from the rest of the morning mail? That it could be overlooked?

The box used for the bagged fruit was specially designed to withstand the rigors to which it would be subjected by the post office. My box of Vexar-bagged grapefruit arrived in Colorado in perfect condition and was the appetizer for the next morning's breakfast. Natural-

ly, a tastefully done piece of tie-in literature was enclosed in the box with the grapefruit; it, too, is shown nearby.

The Vexar literature enclosed with the grapefruit, neatly bagged in you know what, is also highly professional and in four-color. The model holding the bag of grapefruit is perfect for the job. She looks like the wife of one of your friends, or maybe *your* wife, but she *doesn't* look "modelish."

The headline, WOULD SHE KID YOU? can't be resisted. The supermarket owner-manager who received this mailing simply *has* to open the mailer. And when he or she does, there's a beautiful, lifelike four-color illustration of a bag of grapefruit on the left and a ready-to-eat half grapefruit complete with maraschino cherry.

Copy is conversational, convincing and persuasive. It hits the major selling points for Vexar again, emphasizing visual appeal and no spoilage. It reads:

WELL...NOT ABOUT
GRAPEFRUIT, SHE WOULDN'T

Give her half a chance and she'll double the action at your grapefruit counter.

Just don't ask her to select her fruit through the haze of plastic film. She wants to see it.

Don't suffocate it in airless film where heat and moisture can build up and lead to spoilage. She wants it fresh.

In other words, she wants grapefruit wrapped in VEXAR,® the fine-mesh plastic netting that lets her see, feel, even smell what she's buying.

We know she does, because we conducted an in-store survey of 528 shoppers and 55 percent preferred the netting while only 21 percent selected polyethylene.

Our test was made with oranges. But, if she has this thing about oranges, would she kid you about grapefruit?

FOR BETTER RESULTS—DU PONT VEXAR® PLASTIC NETTING

These fine Du Pont ads and 3-D mailers are both highly creative and exhibit superb craftsmanship. Needless to say, they met the acid test of every campaign—they sold the product.

According to Du Pont's Wim van der Graaf, results so far have "been highly gratifying." That is, no doubt, an understatement because it is Du Pont company policy to refrain from divulging information as to sales.

Du Pont has received a large number of carload orders for Vexar to be used by the growers and marketers to bag citrus fruits and produce. Thus shipped to supermarkets, Vexar will certainly dominate the shelf space because there won't be any other kind of packaging there on display!

This is in addition to sales made directly to supermarkets, of course. And speaking of supermarkets, van der Graaf reports Du Pont has been very successful in converting a major supermarket chain to 100 percent use of Vexar! Additionally, another large chain has converted at least part of its regions and it's only logical, given Vexar's superiority over plastic wrapping, that the chain will ultimately convert fully.

So satisfactory has Vexar proven in use that one large supermarket chain is contemplating using Vexar to bag lettuce! Every shopper knows, of course, that it is extremely difficult to judge the freshness of lettuce when it's encased in an armor-plating of plastic.

A fringe benefit of primary importance has been realized from van der Graaf's Vexar space ads and direct mailers, too. That is firing up the Du Pont field sales force. Enthusiastic salespersons are productive salespersons . And nothing stimulates a sales force to greater efforts than the feeling that the "home office" is giving them effective support. Advertising that does a preselling job on prospects before the salesperson calls is certainly support with an upper-case "S!"

Vexar has been successfully launched. It has achieved widespread acceptance in an incredibly short time, although Du Pont can't yet consider itself in a position to sit back and rest on its laurels. Vexar must be, and no doubt will be, promoted aggressively for some time to come before the promotional push can be reduced. Those prime prospects for Vexar—supermarket managers, produce merchandisers and buyers, along with growers of citrus fruit, potatoes and lettuce—now have awareness of Vexar and what it has to offer them. So, for that matter, do consumers.

Wim van der Graaf's advertising campaign can be credited in large part with having paved the way for near-immediate acceptance on a national basis. Without advertising it is conceivable that the same marketing objectives could have been accomplished—but most decidedly not in the same short span of time, not for the same relatively low cost. The rewarding payoff for this imaginative campaign was that in 1975 it received the coveted Direct Marketing Leader Award of the Direct Mail/Marketing Association.

Nothing has yet been devised, even with all of the technological advances that have taken place in our society, that can either replace or displace advertising.

The Story of Wheeling Steel

Advertising is a far cry from the legendary horseman who blithely leaped aboard his trusty mount and galloped off in all directions simultaneously. Advertising, to be successful, has to be specific and precise; it must have firm direction; it must have carefully planned, concrete objectives laid out point by point. Campaigns we've studied and those that follow make this quite clear.

Another example: Wheeling Steel Corporation, one of the largest producers of steel and corrugated iron. Wheeling Steel assigned a task to advertising of such magnitude that it is no exaggeration to say that the entire future of the company hinged to a large extent on advertising's ability to deliver—to achieve the objectives set for it.

In the industrial field such importance is seldom attached to advertising effectiveness. It's far from the hue and cry and partial insanity surrounding the introduction of a new cake mix, a new or improved detergent, or a new spray that is guaranteed to hold feminine hair so firmly it resists wind.

In Wheeling's case advertising *had* to produce. As Jon Avrigean, Wheeling's director of advertising, put it: "Wheeling had a big hole to crawl out of. The company was in such a fix because lackadaisical past management permitted it to drift into it. Once a major contender among the top eight steel producers, Wheeling didn't invest in modernization programs. It took the usual steel industry ho-hum attitude to customers generally. It was a very product-oriented company, it broke no records for on-time delivery. Profits slipped down and down.

"New management took over two years ago, and started to turn it around. Much investment in new facilities—nearly $200 million—many top management changes, and creation of a new marketing department took place.

"And Wheeling established a marketing policy that said, in effect, 'we're customer-oriented. Customer needs come before anything else.' "

This was a major—and critically important—series of steps in the right direction, of course. But Wheeling still faced the problem of attracting new customers, then of keeping them and retaining the goodwill—and business—of present customers while the new plant was being completed and going through its shakedown cruise.

Something, some force, had to exert a strong effect on the market—in the minds of the buying influences who specify what kind of steel will be bought and from whom it would be bought. Wheeling management assigned to advertising the twin tasks of firmly establishing in the minds of both present and prospective customers two messages:

1. That Wheeling, because of a massive expansion program and greatly expanded production facilities, was a potent new force in the steel industry—one that had grown in strength and ability to serve.

2. That Wheeling *wanted* to serve rather than merely accept orders, that the company was completely committed to the marketing concept; that Wheeling was "dedicated so strongly to the needs of customers that the company was willing to break tradition."

The steel business is no different than any other, in that service—particularly meeting delivery schedules—is near the top of the list of customer gripes when it isn't up to snuff. Wheeling formerly shared a fault that is prevalent throughout the steel industry—taking customers for granted, adopting the attitude that they had to go *some* place for steel and that a satisfactory volume of business would automatically accrue regardless of service.

Wheeling analyzed this situation correctly, then astutely established an advertising objective. It was to build an image of a customer-oriented steel producer, one from which the customer received genu-

Hustle!

Expand, innovate, promote, sell, serve, and deliver.

Have you looked at Wheeling lately?

ine service—not lip-service about service.

To create this image, Wheeling and its agency developed the now-famous "Hustle" campaign. Robert M. Morris, Wheeling president, credits the campaign with a "major contribution to the continuing task of forging Wheeling Steel into a modern, aggressive, growing, and profitable enterprise."

The ads hustle, no doubt about that. The one shown here can scarcely be confused with a shrinking violet, and it is immediately obvious that it is not an ad run by a Casper Milquetoast company. In reverse (white on black) it has what has to be one of the shortest possible headlines, followed by single-word, single-idea body copy. It reads: "Expand, innovate, promote, sell, serve, *and* deliver. Have you looked at Wheeling lately?" Short, terse, bold, and brash—and *read*. This ad set the pace and the tone for the campaign, calling attention as it did to Wheeling's activities, its expanded facilities, and its unabashed determination to capture a much larger share of the steel market.

Another Wheeling ad is dominated by an aggressive, dramatic two-word headline in type that's a full 4 7/8 " high—never mind translating that into "points." Copy reads:

PUSHY
AMBITIOUS
CALL US WHAT YOU WILL
The name of the game is hustle!
So we're hustling. And we're not embarrassed to admit it.

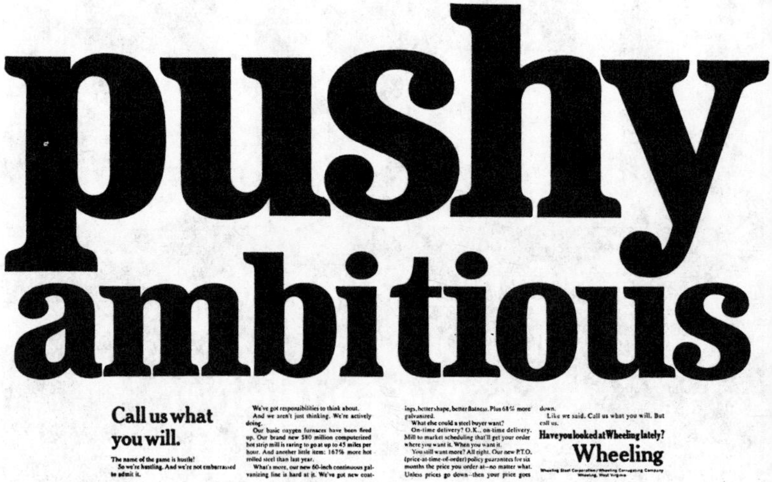

We've got responsibilities to think about.

And we aren't just thinking. We're actively doing.

Our basic oxygen furnaces have been fired up. Our brand-new $80 million computerized hot strip mill is raring to go at up to 45 miles per hour. And another little item: 167 percent more hot rolled steel than last year.

What's more, our new 60-inch continuous galvanizing line is hard at it. We've got new coatings, better shape, better flatness. Plus 68 percent more galvanized.

What else could a steel buyer want?

On-time delivery? O.K., on-time delivery. Mill to market scheduling that'll get your order where you want it. When you want it.

You still want more? All right. Our new P.T.O. (price-at-time-of-order) policy guarantees for six months the price you order at—no matter what. Unless prices go down—then your price goes down.

Like we said, call us what you will. But call us.

Have you looked at Wheeling lately?

This ad announced the bombshell that literally caused great wailing and gnashing of teeth as the rest of the steel industry went into massive flap. Wheeling was the *only* major producer to adopt this customer-first policy. The industry has traditionally accepted orders for steel, quoted a price, and shipped at another if prices happened to go up in the interval between order and fulfillment.

As Wheeling's ad director said: "While this may appear to be a small point, think back in recent history. If you placed an order in July for shipment in September (a fairly normal procedure), you would not pay the price you thought you would. Why not? Because the steel industry announced a price increase on the first of August (or just before). It was 15 cents per hundred pounds. Or $3 a ton, which is $15,000 on a 5,000 order. Many major manufacturers use that much per month. Industry screamed, and rightly so."

Here's copy on one of the now-famous ads which Wheeling produced to publicize this precedent-shattering policy. It does so so simply it's tremendously effective, in a way that everybody can grasp instantly. It says:

WOULD YOU ORDER A
SUIT FOR $75 AND PAY
$85 ON DELIVERY?

Would you order a suit for $75 and pay $85 on delivery?

Welcome to the steel industry. That's exactly what steel buyers do—order at one price then pay another (higher)—when the goods are delivered. Ridiculous? Yes.

That's why we introduced P.T.O.—our Price-at-Time-of-Order purchase policy—last November. We decided it was time for the steel industry to join the 20th century. Wheeling P.T.O. guarantees your price-at-time-of-order for six months—no matter what. Unless prices go down—then your price goes down, too. Sounds tailor-made, doesn't it? Our new customers say it is. Have you looked at Wheeling lately?

Wheeling

Welcome to the steel industry. That's exactly what steel buyers do—order at one price then pay another (higher)—when the goods are delivered.

Ridiculous?

Yes.

That's why we introduced P.T.O.—our Price-at-Time-of-Order purchase policy—last November.

We decided it was time for the steel industry to join the 20th Century.

Wheeling P.T.O. guarantees your price-at-time-of-order for six months—no matter what.

Unless prices go down—then your price goes down, too.

Sounds tailor-made, doesn't it? Our customers say it is.

Have you looked at Wheeling lately?

That ad is well written, crisp, clean, well laid out and well thought out—and very enticing. It solves a problem that has plagued purchasing agents and other executives in manufacturing ever since we've *had* manufacturing. According to Wheeling, "many customers have applauded our P.T.O. efforts and continue to do so. The president of the National Association of Purchasing Agents has made it a battle cry—and all of his speeches refer to it."

Two More Great Ads

Two other ads in this campaign are memorable; almost impossible to pass up and not read. Copy goes like this:

REMEMBER THE FIRST TIME THE
STEEL INDUSTRY RAISED PRICES...
AFTER YOU PLACED AN ORDER?

That policy, which has been penalizing steel buyers since day one, was simply one of the bleaker facts of life—till

November 1965.

That's when we introduced our revolutionary Price-at-Time-of-Order (P.T.O.) purchase policy.

Wheeling P.T.O. guarantees your price-at-time-of-order for six months—no matter what.

Unless prices go down—then your price goes down, too.

Wouldn't you rather do business this new, 20th Century method?

There has to be a first time for everything.

Our number is (304) 233-2200.

Have you looked at Wheeling lately?

A great ad, light, colloquial, and so human you can almost see the copywriter chortling at his typewriter, certain he's done what he set out to do—write a great ad. Bet the telephones at (304) 233-2200 got a real workout.

And, then, to prove that a good ad person is a salesperson—and a psychologist with a keen insight into human nature—Wheeling then ran the following copy:

WHY THOSE DIRTY

A lot of people had warm pet names for Wheeling when we introduced our revolutionary Price-at-Time-of-Order (P.T.O.)

Why those dirty

A lot of people had warm pet names for Wheeling when we introduced our revolutionary Price-At-Time-Of-Order (P.T.O.) purchase policy last November.

Remember? *Wheeling guarantees your price-at-time-of-order for six months—no matter what. Unless prices go down —then your price goes down, too.* And a lot of new customers called us to say they liked the P.T.O. idea. Many old customers called and said, "good show," and instantly signed up for new orders. Why don't you call us . . . anything you like. But call us.

Have you looked at Wheeling lately? **Wheeling**

The Wheeling campaign drew many "fans." Thousands wore "Hustle" buttons in their lapels, and thousands more wrote in to request reprints of the ads for their walls. Readership studies of the ads recorded high scores.

purchase policy last November.

Remember?

> *Wheeling guarantees your price-at-time-of-order* for six months
> —no *matter what. Unless prices go down—then your price goes
> down, too.*

And a lot of new customers called us to say they liked the P.T.O. idea.

> Many old customers called and said, "good show," and instant-
> ly signed up for new orders.

> Why don't you call us...anything you like? But call us.

> *Have you looked at Wheeling lately?*

Reaction to this campaign in the business community ranged from
benign approbation to highly complimentary to downright admiring.
Wheeling said, "Our sales organization was highly complimentary
and continues to be." Well and good, for advertising should stimulate
the sales force; it's a fringe benefit, but a necessary one.

"Customers wrote in and congratulated us," Wheeling said,
"several hundred letters. We've sent out 3,000 to 4,000 reprints to
hundreds of people who wanted 'Hustle' for their walls and to stimulate their sales organization or company people. We've handed out
50,000 'Hustle' buttons, are on the second 50,000, and have difficulty
keeping them in stock.

"Right now we're just getting readership studies. To date: top
readership awards in *Purchasing* and *Purchasing Week*, in *Design
News*, and in *Engineering News-Record*. The New York Ad Club
saluted us with a brand-name luncheon and testimonial on Wheeling's
'outstanding advertising and marketing program.'"

Wheeling's campaign was also selected as the industrial-advertising
campaign of the year by *Industrial Marketing* magazine, and Wheeling's president, Mr. Morris, was chosen Adman-of-the-Year—only
the third time a nonadvertising executive was so honored.

Mr. Avrigean, director of advertising, added: "For more substantial evidence of performance: We are averaging 200 inquiries a week,
and have for many, many months, from all parts of the ad program
(there are roughly a dozen product programs, plus an 'umbrella' program, Hustle). Since the first of the year, we have tabulated approximately 200 new customers—people who hadn't done business with us
in the last two years. Their orders amount to $2 million. This is only
for the steel company, not for the corrugating company, a division doing roughly ⅓ of our total volume. The guess at corrugating is at least
300 new customers, and another $2 million in sales.

"While advertising can't claim all of this $4 million in additional
sales, the ad program, our new P.T.O. policy, and company publicity

were the only things that changed in our overall marketing program prior to and during this period.

"Frankly, this program is simply more proof to me that when you run advertising that *says something* and direct it at audiences whose needs you understand, results are inevitable."

Mr. Avrigean summed it up nicely, except to add that Wheeling's success with this campaign is also due to precise and realistic advertising objectives—and to a great campaign!

Why Set Advertising Objectives?

Few quibble with the concept that advertising, if it's to accomplish its objectives, must have objectives. But equally few establish them. Less than 10 percent of all industrial companies have a formal, written marketing plan. It naturally follows that only this same small segment of industry has firm, well-defined marketing objectives, advertising objectives, and advertising strategy. The others don't. They follow, the 10 percent leads.

Most industrial companies are simply not advertising or marketing oriented. They attach such a small importance to the function that management is unwilling to allocate sufficient time to the planning function so that advertising can contribute its full potential.

Vague notions and good intentions suffice, and somehow they muddle through. Others emphasize catchy slogans, cute ideas, and intriguing themes for their campaigns. And because advertising is part art, part science, with many intangibles, occasionally one of these intuitive advertisers hits upon a real gem of an idea and makes it pay off big. Some gamblers do in Las Vegas, also—and just about as often.

Planning Gains Followers

On the whole, however, corporate management during the past few years has become increasingly enthusiastic about introducing the management-by-objective technique into just about every area of business. This applies to many areas where it was formerly thought impossible to realize benefits from application of this scientific-management philosophy, with advertising in particular singled out. As a consequence, advertising professionals in agencies and advertiser companies have been busily examining various methods of improving and measuring advertising effectiveness and efficiency. This is not difficult when advertising is developed and used to achieve specific objectives, nor is it difficult to determine advertising's contribution to the total marketing effort.

Merely having objectives acts as a creative catalyst, for they aid, rather than impede, those who actually create the advertising campaign and the individual advertisements, literature, sales aids, and other promotional material. Furthermore, the advertising manager who has firm objectives is able to evaluate the creative efforts and thinking behind them much more objectively, and to provide proper direction for those in this area more easily.

If ads are pretested one against the other, or if various slogans, themes, headlines, copy approaches, product features, and user benefits are pretested so that the most effective may be used, specific objectives make development of definitive survey questions and subsequent interpretation of results both easier and more valid.

Since objectives either suggest—or actually spell out on occasion—the audiences advertising must communicate with if it is to succeed, media selection is simplified. Merely having objectives does not result automatically in a detailed media analysis and schedule, of course. The final choice cannot be dictated by any plan or set of objectives regardless of how well thought out they are. Selection of media is one of the responsibilities of the advertising manager.

Another important advantage that accrues to the ad manager who has specific objectives is that it is possible to measure, accurately and precisely, the effectiveness of an advertising campaign. If you make a bench-mark study before a campaign breaks, you then have a record of your public's attitude toward, awareness of, and comprehension of your product(s) or service(s). When you're introducing a new product a study is obviously not necessary, but a study after the campaign has run and the product is launched reveals just what it—and you—accomplished. Many ad managers find such studies extremely helpful in selling management on advertising.

How to Set Advertising Objectives

No two companies are alike, nor are their problems and aspirations. Procedures for setting advertising objectives are much the same from one company to another, or from industry to industry, for that matter. Steps usually taken are:

1. Gathering information.
2. Developing tentative objectives.
3. Expressing the objectives.
4. Gaining management approval of objectives.
5. Distributing the approved objectives to proper people within the company and in the advertising agency.

In some highly organized companies the mere setting of objectives has become an objective in itself, complete with elaborate ceremonies and much hue and cry, somewhat akin to fertility rites at the time of a full moon in a pagan society.

Some companies have detailed checklists with a statement pertaining to every conceivable eventuality. They tend to overemphasize the forest and obscure the individual trees. They make too much out of the basic procedure of pairing marketing and advertising objectives, and the statement of how they will be attained. Even some advertising managers have been known to devote their full time and energies to establishing meaningful objectives, so much so that they never got around to doing much advertising.

Let's take each step individually.

Gathering Information

The ad manager bases the decision and builds the programs on a foundation of facts. Getting the facts and putting them together into a logical, usable format takes a bit of doing as a rule. That's because the advertising manager requires far more information than anybody in the company—even the marketing director—realizes. Much of it is available from marketing management, of course, but must be dug up by the advertising manager. Information essential to setting advertising objectives includes:

1. Market potential, in dollars. Your company's share of this market. Distribution pattern. Product features. User benefits. Competitive information. Analysis of previous advertising your company has done, and *its* objectives.

2. Identification of your prospects. Profile of prospect companies. Identification of buying influences by function, title, and name. Where these prospect companies are located, by state, county, and city. What businesses they are in. Their present attitude toward your company. Their present attitude toward, or opinion of, your product. Their need for your product. Why do these prospects buy—or not buy—your product? What advertising can logically be expected to do to influence them to buy from you, if they are not now doing so?

3. Your company's marketing objectives. If your company has no written marketing plan, help write one, or write one for marketing management's approval; lack of marketing objectives makes setting of realistic advertising objectives virtually impossible.

An advertising manager should never try to second-guess product managers and establish their marketing objectives for them. Most product managers—frequently found wearing the title of marketing manager—are unable to set marketing objectives. These individuals are so technically oriented, knowing as they do a complex line of equipment inside-out, that they are die-hard adherents of eyeball-to-eyeball selling. Setting marketing objectives is outside their experience, despite their being charged with responsibility for all marketing activities for their product in specified markets. They neither know nor understand advertising, nor do they believe, deep down, that it is an effective tool for them.

These unsophisticated product managers *are* capable of setting their marketing objectives—*if skillfully led by the advertising manager.* Ask leading questions and you'll probably get answers which will enable you to write explicit marketing objectives *for approval by the director of marketing, the sales manager, or other final-word executive.* Do *not* assume his or her responsibility in this matter, for to do so puts you in the untenable position of establishing your legitimate advertising objectives based on your illegitimate marketing objectives. Often the director of marketing will be an engineer or other technical person and must be led.

4. Full information on the balance of the marketing mix—plans for the field force. Additions to the field force. Contemplated changes in distribution. Additions to the distribution setup. Any changes in price structure or discount arrangements.

Developing Tentative Objectives

With the required background information on hand, sort it out in your mind, then put it down on paper so it's easily referred to. The ad manager of a major manufacturer organized such information in this way:

(INTEROFFICE MEMO FORM)

Date April 21, 19_____

TO: J. Smith

SUBJECT: Metalworking-market marketing objectives

At a meeting on April 19, you stated your marketing objectives and a suggested communications needs for the metalworking market for our next fiscal year.

The sequence of your comments has been rearranged so that all marketing-areas' marketing objectives are organized in the same manner. This is for the convenience of management, which reviews all of the marketing areas' objectives collectively and individually.

1. Existing situation
   A. *Market*

   The total market in metalworking for our Widget line is $260 million; our present share of this market is $56 million.

   Industries which constitute our market include, but are not limited to, the following:

Aerospace	Aircraft
Automotive	Ordnance
Farm equipment	Mechanical power transmission
Machine tools	Electrical equipment

   Products sold into the metalworking market are as follows:

   1. Standard Widgets $14,000,000
   2. Modified Widgets 4,000,000
   3. Special Widgets..7,000,000

   4. Custom-built Widgets...6,000,000
   5. Automated Widget lines 12,000,000
   6. Complete Widget systems....................................11,000,000
   7. New products 2,000,000

   We are the leader in automated Widget lines and in the controls for them. This market is expanding at the rate of 57 percent a year.

   A broad base in metalworking uses our Standard Widgets; this product's sales volume grows almost in step with the economy as a whole.

   The total market for Modified Widgets is approximately $90 million; we have a bit less than a $4 million share. This is a fertile field for us.

   The market for Special Widgets is probably the widest of all markets we serve. There is hardly a metalworking company in the country that does not have or could not use a Special Widget. Note that when we sell a Special Widget considerable auxiliary equipment is always sold with it.

B. *Products*

   The single item of greatest sales potential is the new Automatic-Automated Widget, to be ready for introduction late this fiscal year.

C. *Buying influences*

   A discussion of buying influences in the metalworking market, as applied to our complete line of Widgets, brought out the belief that it is most frequently a group activity.

   Purchasing and management-level people are seldom determining factors, except in unique circumstances. These people are involved only in a formal sense; in one case it is preparation of the purchase order, in the other it is the approval of an expenditure. The determining group is composed of process engineers, the plant operations group, and product-development engineers. These titles may vary from plant to plant and include others such as factory superintendent or research engineer.

2. Problems

   Since we previously promoted our Numerical Controlled Widget heavily (Machine Tool Show, space advertising) and since have withdrawn further promotion, some uncertainty exists in our field sales organization regarding this unit.

   To overcome our problems of product performance and high cost of sales, it is anticipated that engineering will make a number of modifications.

3. Opportunities

   Automation is the basis of future growth in the metalworking market.

   Use of automation, and particularly numerically controlled equipment such as we manufacture, is growing at a combined rate of almost 70 percent a year. With our reputation for Automated Widgets that really work, we are in a very favorable competitive position.

4. Marketing objectives

   To create a market for our Automatic-Automated Widget and sell $2 million worth this fiscal year.

   To achieve 10 percent more sales in Modified Widgets.

   To double our share of the market for Complete Widget Lines, from $12 million to $24 million.

5. Marketing strategy

   Reactivate the technical sales-training courses used so effectively several years ago. Almost one-third of our present field sales force lacks technical competence in selling Automatic-Automated Widgets.

Automation will have to be sold by personal contact for a long time. Sales of automated equipment result in a number of additional sales of supplementary equipment; in fact, sales of some of our Widget controls are directly dependent upon sales of automated equipment.

Promote our unique technical ability to solve customer problems connected with use of Standard Widgets. Rekindle the enthusiasm of the field sales force, as far as the Numerical Controlled Widget is concerned.

6. Communications needs you requested

There is no need, you feel, to change our present theme of being able to provide the *one* right Widget to solve customers' production problems. You feel this should be retained, but that we should also emphasize the excellent reliability of all of our Widgets.

Awareness and comprehension of our products, and of our technical capabilities to solve customers' problems are your foremost communications requirement.

Develop a color-sound 16mm. movie on automation, featuring the Complete Widget Line installed at Doaks Manufacturing Company, Inc. The film would be used by all of our field sales force with their present projection equipment.

7. Communication-strategy concept

Continue to produce current technical sales literature for field distribution.

Continue space advertising in key media.

Feature more case-history material.

Space advertising to create awareness of the new Automatic-Automated Widget.

Develop a new theme for trade shows.

Exhibit at the national trade shows in which we participated last year; also consider feasibility of exhibiting in local or regional shows.

8. Sales forecasts

Our share of the Widget market will increase to $68 million.

Sales in the automated area alone will increase to $19 million.

Automatic-Automated Widgets to be introduced later this year will account for $2 million.

/s/ Advertising Manager

These data are in the "raw" state, for they have yet to be approved by management. Their accumulation and orderly arrangement make it possible for the ad manager to plan the program with little waste time and motion, particularly if there is responsibility for more than one market, handled by more than one market manager or product manager. Compiled thus, the ad manager can compare apples with apples, rather than unlike items.

You cannot finalize advertising objectives while working with such raw data. You can, however, make a machine copy of this memo, and make marginal notes for your future guidance in establishing your department's objectives.

For example, under Section 4, we find an objective, "To create a market for our Automatic-Automated Widget and sell $2 million this fiscal year." Now, your own market knowledge tells you that the automotive market—specifically the Big Three automobile manufacturers—are the prime market for this production tool. Knowing your customers, and that SIC 3711 is the major group they're in, you check the Standard Industrial Classification Manual for other classifications where this product could logically be used effectively. Subclassification 3714, Motor Vehicle Parts and Accessories, is also a likely market.

Make a marginal note—perhaps in red, or whatever memory-jogging device appeals to you most—that to achieve this marketing objective, your advertising objective is *to create awareness of, comprehension of, acceptance of, and demand for, this new product.* It's early to do this, but one thought usually triggers another, so let your mind run on, making note after note. For example, to reach an audience such as this your past experience tells you, you will want to evaluate and consider certain media. Make this note, too, using only publication names, such as these: *Automotive Industries, Iron Age, Production, American Machinist* and *Factory.* And, since the market is small in terms of the numbers of smokestacks you want to reach, make the notation, direct mail; then product publicity, sales literature, technical literature. These are the how-tos, how you will attain your objective, the tools you will use to communicate with those prospects who represent that $2 million.

Farther down the list of marketing objectives is, "To double our share of the market for Complete Widget Lines from $12 million to $24 million." This is an auspicious objective, but if management feels it is attainable, it is up to you to provide the support program which makes it possible. Again, analyze the market; delve into this with the product and marketing people in charge of Complete Widget Lines. Find out where equipment of this type is sold by examining your list of customers and sales; if the firms in these lines of business have been buying this equipment from you, other firms in similar lines of endeavor are prime suspects to buy more. Pick them out by SIC. Analyze media which will reach the key buying influences. Determine how many prospect firms you have to hit if a rifle approach with direct mail, buttressed by a broad and expanded program of space advertising, is to have sufficient impact to do the job. Ask if inquiries are wanted, and find out whether they will be properly followed by the sales force. See if repeat sales to those who have already purchased Complete Widget Lines are likely. If so, target in with direct mail.

Make your marginal notes on this basis, then determine just what communications functions advertising can perform more effectively, more efficiently, and at lower cost than any other activity. Make no attempt to assign to advertising those tasks that it cannot handle. What advertising can—and cannot—do has been summed up by Du

Pont as follows:

Advertising *can* do these things:
- —Introduce a new product.
- —Give information.
- —Interest prospects.
- —Develop inquiries.
- —Create demand.
- —Help open new markets.
- —Stimulate the trade—agents, distributors, jobbers, jobber salespersons, retailers, and retail salespeople.
- —Test sales techniques.
- —Test its own various types of appeals.
- —Help determine buyer preference.
- —Help make a product competitive in the market.
- —Support sales programs.
- —Open the door to salespersons.
- —Reach pinpointed markets at pennies per reader or listener.
- —Reach mass markets at pennies per prospect.
- —Reduce selling expense.
- —Establish and maintain prestige of company or product or both.
- —Build customer relations.
- —Speed product acceptance.

Advertising can *not* do these things:
- —Sell a bad product—twice.
- —Sell an overpriced or otherwise noncompetitive product.
- —Sell a poorly distributed product.
- —Sell a seasonal product out of season.
- —Sell products to persons having no use for them.
- —Work overnight.
- —Do the selling job alone.

Writing the Advertising Objectives

When writing your advertising objectives, always bear in mind that an unstated objective is to create a frame of mind in the reader of your ads. To do this, write with the *prospect's* viewpoint and desires in mind; determine just what impression you wish to convey, and what you want that person to think after reading your message; how he or she should react if you make a request for action. This is another way of saying you'll come out ahead if you are "you-oriented" rather than "me-oriented."

Be specific. If you want to develop a flow of inquiries, say so—and say exactly how many. A definite correlation exists between the number of inquiries advertising produces and the sales volume of many industrial products. This relationship is so constant that it can be expressed as a percentage with perfectly acceptable accuracy. So, if the sale of one piece of equipment results from every 350 inquiries— and this figure is a valid one for many industries—a legitimate advertising objective is to produce as many *well-qualified* inquiries per ad as possible. There are many ways to assure a continuing high level of inquiries, and they will be covered later.

Another advertising objective that is always present but unstated is to produce a positive mental response to the advertising message. This can, and usually does, take the form of a favorable impression of your product and your company.

Objectives necessarily have to be written to comply with any restrictions placed upon advertising by management. For example, if management selects media—and this occurs with distressing frequency, and almost invariably is based primarily upon "political" considerations—then advertising objectives must be written to reflect this. Too, geographic patterns enter into planning at this time because there may well be areas where your company is poorly represented, or where there is so little potential that no effort has ever been made to exploit possibilities of that territory. If this situation exists, consider the advisability of using regional editions of media; this assures satisfactory coverage of the market where adequate sales coverage exists, yet does not waste money trying to reach steel mills in northern Montana.

The Budget Determines

The size of the advertising appropriation naturally influences establishment of and writing of advertising objectives. If the wherewithal isn't there, the ad manager will be forced to settle for less ambitious objectives. As a matter of good practice, make it firm policy always to develop objectives and work out a sound advertising program *before* working up a budget and submitting it to management for approval. Your chances of having a program approved are infinitely better than those of having a budget approved.

Phrasing of advertising objectives is something like writing the Great American Novel—you can't do it carefully enough to please everybody without some revision. Here, as in the phrasing of the marketing plan, everybody must agree with the objectives and how they are stated.

Questions you will want to consider are: Is each objective stated so that each and every person concerned understands it clearly? Is it so stated that everybody agrees with it? Does the agency understand and agree with it? Is enough information given so there will be no possibility of misinterpretation by those who will actually create the advertising and collateral material?

To get meaningful answers to these and other questions, common practice in many companies is for the ad manager to reproduce his advertising objectives and circulate copies to pertinent personnel—the director of marketing, sales manager, marketing managers, product managers and others within the company; also to the account executive, account supervisor, creative director, and art director at the agency. Then, if no question arises, it is safe to assume the objectives are solid and well stated and that they will act as firm direction in all of the subsequent steps.

A trap lurks, though, and it should be avoided like the plague. All too frequently objectives are established whose prime virtues are plausibility and the ease with which the program designed to achieve them may be measured. Questions, serious ones, have been raised as to the advisability of using so extensively the two criteria most frequently used—awareness and comprehension. Many advertising practitioners are firmly convinced that neither objective in itself, nor, for that matter, the two together, are adequate for products which have previously been advertised and sold. When it comes to new products, it's quite a different story, of course, for creation of awareness and comprehension are two advertising strong-points.

Gaining Management Approval

Once your objectives are well stated and everybody's questions have been answered and changes they suggested have been incorporated, the next step is to do any rewriting required and get them approved by management. Approval of advertising objectives by top management, usually the director of marketing and frequently the president, *before* submission of a formal advertising program greatly eases the birth pangs attending the appearance of the completed program.

To present the objectives for approval, it usually works best to write a short, explanatory memo that (1) relates advertising objectives to marketing objectives, as given in the marketing plan, (2) tells how these objectives fit in with those established for the sales force, and (3) spells out in detail how the advertising objectives mesh with those for other product lines, other markets, or other divisions of the company.

When your objectives are finally approved, perhaps with slight modifications by marketing management, the time has then come to prepare the complete advertising program. Your chances of having it accepted intact are immeasurably improved. The risk of having it totally rejected has been reduced almost to the vanishing point. If the program does meet with some disapproval by top management, it usually is not because of any basic disagreement with the program or the thinking that went into it, but with the cost. What must be done then is to rephrase some objectives, setting goals which may be attained with a reduced investment, then eliminating portions of the program until it falls in line with the appropriation which will be acceptable.

Distributing the Finalized Objectives

Final step in the objectives process is to make copies of the approved objectives and distribute them to those who received the tentative ones. To prevent confusion, state in the covering memo that these are final, that those previously received are to be destroyed.

All concerned are now working toward the same end. Misunderstandings, misinterpretations, and misgivings about directions are eliminated. There's a much better chance of achieving the objectives once they're formal and on paper, and the cost of doing so will be less than under any kind of a hit-or-miss system.

Marketing at Pitney-Bowes

At Pitney-Bowes, originator of the ubiquitous postage meter, a leading manufacturer of machines which automate the mailing of huge volumes of letters and packages, and of sophisticated business machines, the entire marketing operation is planned to the *nth* degree. Nothing is left to chance.

The marketing plan is written in the customary manner, with consideration given to the current situation, competition, new-product introductions, opportunities, anticipated income by product line, gross sales, profitability desired, and the promotional program. Advertising investment is determined by allocation of a predetermined percentage of anticipated sales. Five entire pages of the marketing plan are devoted to problems and opportunities, with firm objectives for each product line.

Sales Matched to SIC Classification

P-B identifies their market through use of a two-digit SIC breakdown of sales; this is watched closely to detect any deviation from traditional patterns. Sales are matched to industry classification. In turn, the reader profiles of various media under consideration are matched to the sales pattern. For the most part key buying influences

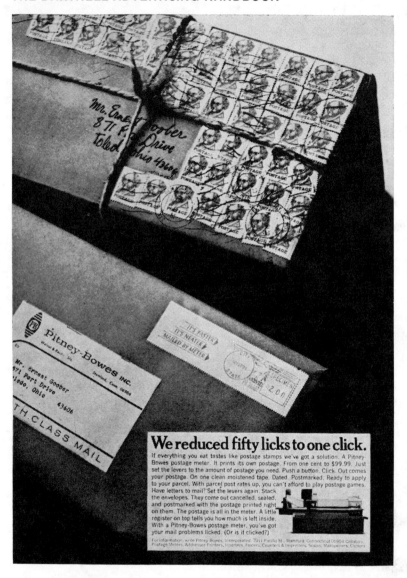

We reduced fifty licks to one click.

If everything you eat tastes like postage stamps we've got a solution. A Pitney-Bowes postage meter. It prints its own postage. From one cent to $99.99. Just set the levers to the amount of postage you need. Push a button. Click. Out comes your postage. On one clean moistened tape. Dated. Postmarked. Ready to apply to your parcel. With parcel post rates up, you can't afford to play postage games. Have letters to mail? Set the levers again. Stack the envelopes. They come out cancelled, sealed, and postmarked with the postage printed right on them. The postage is all in the meter. A little register on top tells you how much is left inside. With a Pitney-Bowes postage meter, you've got your mail problems licked. (Or is it clicked?)

For information, write Pitney-Bowes, Incorporated, 7911 Pacific St., Stamford, Connecticut 06904. Collators, Postage Meters, Addresser-Printers, Inserters, Folders, Counters & Imprinters, Scales, Mailopeners, Closers.

are determined by querying the field sales force, as well as by field trips by members of the advertising department.

One of Pitney-Bowes' striking four-color ads is shown nearby. It appeared in *U.S. News & World Report*, which was selected to reach top management executives. The striking visual compares and compares fast—it is immediately obvious that using Pitney-Bowes' postage meters saves time, saves money, eliminates stamp-stocking, and results in a much more businesslike package. Copy reads:

> WE REDUCED FIFTY LICKS TO ONE CLICK.
> If everything you eat tastes like postage stamps we've got a solution. A Pitney-Bowes postage meter. It prints its own postage. From one cent to $99.99. Just set the levers to the amount of postage you need. Push a button. Click. Out comes your postage. On one clean moistened tape. Dated. Postmarked. Ready to apply to your parcel. With parcel-post rates up, you can't afford to play postage games. Have letters to mail? Set the levers again. Stack the envelopes. They come out canceled, sealed, and postmarked with the postage printed right on them. The postage is all in the meter. A little register on top tells you how much is left inside. With a Pitney-Bowes postage meter, you've got your mail problems licked. (Or is it clicked?)

Interesting, informative, and persuasive—and it reflects the corporate objective of enhancing Pitney-Bowes' position of leadership in metered mail, and the communications objective of creating awareness of and comprehension of the benefits of metered mail. It's easy to see why Pitney-Bowes leads its industry.

Following is a brief condensation of one portion of the Pitney-Bowes marketing plan, that dealing with corporate and communications objectives. The original document contains specific figures, dates, means of attaining objectives and other hard information of a competitive nature.

STATEMENT OF OBJECTIVES

I. *Corporate Objectives:*

Maintain and enhance Pitney-Bowes' position of leadership, as *the* creator and major producer of postage-meter mailing systems. And, in so doing, build an appreciation of, and a desire for, Pitney-Bowes as the source for equipment for the efficient, businesslike handling of mail and other paper.

To broaden Pitney-Bowes' reputation *as a major producer* of office equipment.

Specifically to create a favorable awareness of P-B equipment for:

    a. Mechanical addressing.

    b. Electrostatic copying.

    c. Counting and imprinting.

    d. Folding and inserting.

    e. Weighing mails and parcels.

    f. Related accessories, furniture, attachments, etc.

To enhance Pitney-Bowes' reputation for quality and good service.

To promote Pitney-Bowes' sales force morale and involvement with the company as whole.

To increase Pitney-Bowes' dollar sales over the previous year.

II. *Communications Objectives:*

Enhance the call efficiency of salespeople, thus reducing the cost of selling, and crea a favorable climate for the sale.

Create awareness of and comprehension of the major benefits of metered mail, ther by stimulating an awareness of Pitney-Bowes, the originator of metered mail, as an e pert source of equipment for office efficiency.

Continue the promotion of the small office market as the best means to develop broader mass market.

Help develop an interest in and awareness of the relationship of combinations Pitney-Bowes' equipment among P-B salespeople, their customers, and prospects.

Develop an awareness of and understanding of P-B copiers, SES, Tickometer folders, and inserters among existing customers.

Maintain Pitney-Bowes' position of dominance on the sale and rental of postag meter mailing machines.

Improve Pitney-Bowes' position against competition in nonmeter lines such folders, inserters, scales, and addresser-printers.

Develop inquiries for the sales force.

Simplifying the Planning Process

Setting objectives takes time and it requires thinking. There isn't enough time in the day for most of us to get the administrative work load done right—and thinking is hard work.

The planning job is greatly simplified and handled in less time if it's well organized. That means standardization achieved through well-planned forms which make gathering adequate information easier, and which preclude overlooking important data. Among the best and most complete are those used by Worthington Corporation, one of the leading producers of equipment used for the control and handling of liquids and gases, and for the conversion of energy to useful work. Worthington products include air conditioning, refrigeration equipment, pumps, compressors, locomotives, turbines, valves, controls, motors, and many other industrial items.

Domestic operations include nine divisions and two subsidiaries, organized within five separate groups. Each has a high degree of autonomy and has its own marketing (or sales) personnel. However, a centralized advertising department has responsibility for most of Worthington's advertising and sales-promotion requirements. Headed by the advertising manager, there are account managers for each of the divisions, as well as an account manager for export operations. The account managers must develop and implement promotional plans for all advertising and sales-promotion activities for the product groups which are assigned to them.

The thoroughness with which Worthington plans its promotion programs is shown in the reproductions of various planning forms.

On the first page, or identification sheet of the planning form, space is provided to state either the product line or market area, together with the time period to which the plan applies, and the division or company. Approval of the plan is indicated by the signatures of the division manager and of the advertising and sales-promotion manager; only when both have signed is the plan implemented.

Page 2 of the plan determines immediately whether or not a written marketing plan has been prepared for the product line or market. If not, customer need for this product is stated. Sales goals for the current year, the program year, and two years hence are given, as is a breakdown of sales by industry. Worthington's sales to each of the five industries are estimated, as is the share of this particular market which Worthington can logically expect to secure. Finally, profitability —good, fair, or poor—is stated, again by industry. This facilitates management decision as to the advisability of investing in the promotional plan. The last item is a situation analysis which is merely a recap of the competitive situation.

Page 3 includes in section (b) the account manager's estimate of prospects for the product or market. Additionally, a summary of the advertising and sales promotion of major competitors is given; this includes the type of promotion on which they rely, the theme of their program, and a close estimate of the dollar expenditure which each makes, broken down by business press (including management and news publications).

Page 4 makes it easy—and necessary—for the account manager to list product and service features vital in planning an effective promotion. These are broken down as exclusive and nonexclusive, and the *customer benefits* for each are given. This information is required to develop a copy platform, discussed later.

Plan pages 5 and 6 list "inhibitors" which must be overcome in order to achieve set objectives and sales goals. These inhibitors are the result of experience. Frank answers are a tremendous help in developing a promotional program to overcome hurdles which must be eliminated before.

The plan's page 7 defines programs in other Worthington divisions which might influence this specific plan. Comments of the advertising and sales promotion department are summarized, also.

Data on page 8 makes it possible to pinpoint specific areas which need shoring up, and provides a guide to management in allocation of effort and investment in personal selling by the sales force, and by impersonal selling—by advertising and promotion.

Page 9 states both long-range (3 years) marketing goals, and short-range goals (for the program year). Worthington defines a marketing goal as "the total business effect of all efforts to maintain or improve market penetration, reputation, competitive position, sales efficiency, or marketplace profit." The company also says that "specific sales volume figures are not the marketing goal—they are the result of it."

Also stated here are specific sales-promotion objectives which may be the same as short-range marketing goals; if so, this is noted. Final information is required at stages in the sales-promotion program, complete with target dates and a notation as to the individual(s) responsible.

Page 10 lists critically important information—advertising objectives, with emphasis on *auditable* objectives; strategy, with a rationale of how objectives are to be achieved; other support required, with explanation; and auditing steps, so that it can be determined whether or not objectives were achieved. Worthington's advertising department has a firm policy to audit the degree of achievement wherever this is possible. This usually falls to the account manager.

Page 11 gives a budget breakdown for each plan, separated by fixed budget and variable budget items.

Page 12 summarizes the budget for each plan, and includes various account numbers, budget items, and a monthly and total annual budget figure.

If a number of campaigns are to be run in the same year for different product lines, or to different markets, Worthington prepares a separate plan for each. Forms are usually updated each year, or oftener if changing market conditions warrant.

Worthington management feels, and correctly so, that the importance of gathering and recording basic marketing information cannot be overstressed. The more that is known about the product, the competition, and the market, the easier it is to develop an effective plan and pinpoint communications needs — and fill them with advertising objectives that contribute toward achievement of all marketing objectives.

Worthington's planning forms may be somewhat more detailed than the advertising manager of a smaller company needs, but they can readily be altered and adapted to almost any company, for the basic information they record is needed by *all* ad managers.

G-3545
Page 1 of 12

Advertising and Sales Promotion Plan

Product/Market Program —————————————————————

Period Covered —————————————————————————

Division or Company ————————————————————————

Approved ———————————————————— Date ——————————
(Division Mgr.)

By ——————————————————————— Date ——————————
(A&SP)

G-3545
Page 2 of 12

I. Does a product/market plan exist for this product(s)?

Yes _____   No _____

(If "No," complete the remainder of I)
(If "Yes," move on to II)

Customer Need for this Product: _____

_____

_____

_____

_____

_____

_____

_____

_____

_____

SALES GOALS:

Current year:

Program year:

Two years hence:

INDUSTRIES	Estimated % of Total Product Purchased by This Industry	% of Worthington Sales of This Product to This Industry	Estimated Worthington % of Available	Profitability (Good, Fair or Poor)
1.				
2.				
3.				
4.				
5.				

II. a) *Situation Analysis:* Copy from Marketing Plan Facts Section, adding supplementary A&SP comments and analysis.

G-3545
Page 3 of 12

b) *General Outlook:* Extract from Marketing Plan; supplement as necessary for A&SP purposes.

III. *Competition Advertising:* List below the basic type of program and promotion theme reflected in each competitor's programming. Also, give closest estimate of current annual business paper (including Management and News publications) investment for products such as those covered by this plan. Use same listing as included in marketing plan.

Competitor A _____

_____

_____

Competitor B _____

_____

_____

Competitor C _____

_____

_____

Competitor D _____

_____

_____

Competitor E _____

_____

_____

_____

_____

IV. *Product and Service Features:* (Only key points important to promotion programming)

Exclusive:	Customer benefits:
1.	
2.	
3.	
4.	
5.	
6.	
7.	

Nonexclusive:	Customer benefits:
1.	
2.	
3.	
4.	
5.	
6.	
7.	

G-3545
Page 5 of 12

8. What "inhibitors" in this product/market area are at work which must be overcome?

INHIBITORS	Applicable to our area? Yes or No	Explain specific plans to improve in this area
a. Absence of customer-oriented planning		
b. Inadequate marketing objectives		
c. Internal communication failure (Sales, Engineering, Headquarters)		
d. Inadequate distribution		
e. Lack of innovations (product or packaging)		
f. Budget deficiencies in communications		
g. Failure to dominate in external communications media employed		
h. Insufficient knowledge of customer motivation		
i. Too generic an advertising claim or appeal		
j. Inadequate picture of market and customer opinion		
k. Failure to merchandise or "follow-through"		
l. Too much concern with price		

G-3545
Page 6 of 12

INHIBITORS	Applicable to our area? Yes or No	Explain specific plans to improve in this area
m. Poor division communications to salesmen/distributors		
n. Giving advertising jobs it cannot do		
o. Placing management responsibility for communications too high (or low) in organization		
p. Absence of built-in measuring systems in plans and programs		
q. Failure to define and manage the industry/product image		
r. Imbalance between communications . . . space, literature, etc.		
s. Copying competition in communications activities		
t. Failure to update or train marketing organization		
u. Failure to build extra benefits or quality image of product		
v. Internal policy gets in the way of promotion		
w. Inadequate knowledge of competitive strengths		
x. Inadequate sales tools		

G-3545
Page 7 of 12

VI. Multidivision or Market Programs that might influence this area of promotion activity:

VII. Pertinent A&SP Research - Summary:

Fill Out This Page to Illustrate Areas of Greatest Promotion Need and Opportunity

VIII. We view *total selling* as the use of personal communications (salesmen) plus mechanized communications (promotion). Selling (or quota achievement) is also conceived as a series of tasks which are somehow accomplished in the field. These only involve confirming that previous purchases were satisfactory—or may include finding prospects, negotiating, closing orders, etc. We have listed these tasks for you. (Change them, if you disagree with the list.) We ask you then to *estimate* the necessary effort in selling (time, money, and people) warranted for accomplishing each of the tasks *for this specific marketing area* . . this, in the interest of not overgeneralizing. Division and Field Sales personnel should, of course, participate in deciding the correct statistical pattern. All of the percentages of "Total Selling Process" have to add up to 100 percent—the total time, money and people applied to sell in these particular circumstances.

FOR SALES THROUGH DISTRIBUTORS

(Percentage of total volume through distributors—%)

	Column 1	Column 2 % of Total Selling Process Must add to 100%
	SPECIFIC MARKETING TASKS	
Franchise Development		
1. Making Distributor Contacts		( )
2. Developing Company/Business Image		( )
3. Product/Market Education		( )
4. Negotiate-Enfranchise		( )
Serving/Motivating Distributors or Dealers		
5. Aid for Management Procedures		( )
6. Financial Aid		( )
7. Inventory Control Aids		( )
8. Provide Customer and Market Acceptance		( )
9. Sales Training		( )
10. Job Closing Aid		( )
11. Joint Customer Service		( )
Distributor/Dealer Effort		
12. Making User Contacts		( )
13. Developing User Interest		( )
14. Developing User Preference		( )
15. Making Proposals		( )
16. Closing		( )
17. Account Service—Keeping Sold		( )
	Total	100%

DIRECT SALES

(Percentage sold direct—%)

	Column 1	Column 2 % of Total Selling Process Must add to 100%
	SPECIFIC MARKETING TASKS	
Routine Day-by-Day		
1. Finding and contacting new prospects		( )
2. Developing and maintaining reputation among customers and prospects		( )
3. Familiarizing customers and prospects with the details of products		( )
4. Informing customers and prospects about new product developments		( )
5. Once a sale is made, keeping the customer satisfied		( )
Specific Job Handling		
6. Developing interests in specific products or services		( )
7. Contacting additional buying influences within the customer company		( )
8. Influencing specification of your products		( )
9. Making specific proposals		( )
10. Following engineering details		( )
11. Negotiation		( )
12. Closing		( )
	Total	100%

Persons contributing to this analysis

Division _____ Field Sales _____

G-3545
Page 9 of 12

IX. *Marketing Goals:* (refer to Product Marketing Plan)

A marketing goal is the *total* business effect of all efforts to maintain or improve market penetration, reputation, competitive position, sales efficiency or marketplace profit. (Specific sales volume figures are not the marketing goal —they are the result of it.)

Long Range: (3 years)

Short Range: (program year)

X. *Sales Promotion Objectives:* (If same as short-range marketing goals, write "same." If "none," so indicate.)

*Sales promotion is the coordinated use of several marketing functions to achieve a relatively short-range result. The effort may be either internal or external . . . and should be noted in the Product Action Plan.

XI. Sales Promotion Program (from Action Plan)

STEPS	DATE	RESPONSIBLE

G-3545
Page 10 of 12

XII. *Advertising Objectives:* State specific and *auditable* communications objectives as they relate to previously stated sales promotion program—*State the reasoning that led you to decide on these objectives.*

_____

_____

_____

_____

_____

_____

*Who - What - How Much?

XIII. *Strategy:* What is the basic idea behind your proposed communications action, to achieve objectives?

XIV. *Any other support needed* to make this program work? Is it budgeted or agreed?

XV. *Auditing Steps* (what, when, by whom, for how much?)

G-3545
Page 11 of 12

Plan of Action and Budget

Fixed Budget: (Those items which must be produced regardless of promotion programming)

ITEMS	Required by	Cost
Total _____(A)		

Variable Budget: Costs directly related to achievement of Promotion Objective)

ITEMS	Required by	Cost
Total _____(B)		

Total Direct Cost (A) and (B) _____

Multidivisional Costs _____

Administrative Cost _____

Total A&SP Cost _____

G-3545
Page 12 of 12

Advertising and Sales Promotion Department
Direct Portion Account 49

Promotion Program for Period Covering _____

No.	EXPENSE	Total Monthly Budget	Total Annual Budget
75	Space		
76	Production		
77	Telephone Directory		
78	Bulletin Production Sales Promotion Material		
79	Direct Mail Printing		
80	External House Organs Incl. Postage		
81	Visual and Audio Aids		
82	Postage, Boxing—Shipping Literature Requested		
83	Nonco-op—Distributor Aids and Services		
84	Co-op—Distributor Aids and Services		
85	Photographs—Originals and Prints		
86	Exhibits and Displays		
87	Signs and Maintenance		
88	News Publicity—(Exclusive Photos)		
90	Research Incl. Postage		
91	Calendar—Special Corp. Promotion Projects		
92	Staff Projects		
93	Agency Fees and Supplies		
94	Charged to Other Departments		
	TOTAL		

Chapter 5

COPY—AS A CONCEPT

Y OUR prospects are almost as familiar as your next-door neighbor now that you've identified, located, analyzed, and profiled them. You know them, how they think, how they buy, and why they do what they do.

Well and good, because the time has come to stop hiding your light under a bushel. Now's the time to think about saying something to them—something that, hopefully, will exert a positive influence on their future actions as far as your product or service is concerned.

At this time you get together with your advertising agency account executive and discuss copy. Chances are, if the agency is right for you, the agency will do the actual writing. Many industrial ad managers write their own ads however—some from preference, others because of fiendish product complexity, and some only on an emergency basis when the account executive-copywriter is ill, or handling another job. To be able to understand and evaluate and pass judgment on copy, you should have some background information on it, the words in print that your prospects will read. Copy isn't to be considered lightly.

"To think about saying something" isn't a mere phrase, because copy is more than mere words on paper. Copy, good copy, is a concept. It is an abstraction—an idea. The idea may be yours, the sales manager's, or the agency's. That's of little consequence. What is important is to realize that it is a one-of-a-kind inspiration which was conceived to solve a specific communication problem, to communicate one particular piece of intelligence about one certain product to one audience that is meaningful to you, at a time of your choosing.

"Hopefully" because there's more than a kernel of truth in the remark made by Charles F. Adams, former executive vice-president of D'Arcy-MacManus & Masius advertising agency, when he said, "When you sit down to create an ad, the odds are one to three that you will do more damage than good."

Saying something constructive about your product to your prospects doesn't seem hard to do. It should be the simplest thing in the world. After all, you are intimately acquainted with your product, your market, and the buying influences to whom your message is directed. And all of us talk, most of us too much. We have conversations constantly with those around us in business, in our social lives, and with our families. We use words, familiar tools whose use comes easily to us. If there's any one characteristic which can be attributed to every advertising person, it is that he or she is articulate. Ad people have a unique understanding of, appreciation of, and inordinate fondness for words that are encountered in no other segment of the business world.

Since ad people are such expert word mechanics, it should logically follow that advertising copy (so named almost a hundred years ago by some long-forgotten typesetter to whom every collection of words was "copy") should almost write itself. After all, it's necessary only to shut the door to bar distractions, warm up the typewriter, and whip out an ad destined to become a classic that's oh'd and ah'd over by future generations of advertising neophytes.

Talent Comes From Within

Seldom is it that simple, however. Neither Clio nor Erato—nor any other mythical goddess charged with inspiring budding poets, copywriters, and ad managers—can be depended upon to deliver a massive dose of inspiration on schedule just so you can achieve objectives and meet closing dates. The ability to produce good advertising, sales literature, good sales letters, and a house organ that's a pleasure to read—or any other communication which customarily falls into the advertising manager's bailiwick—comes from within the individual. He or she must draw upon his own resources.

It is usually understood that there are six essential attributes the successful practitioner of industrial advertising should possess, whether copywriter, ad manager, or a combination of the two as is often found. These are:

1. *Competitive instinct*

The advertising manager-copywriter (or copywriter-advertising manager) must delight in being a keen competitor. He realizes instinctively that he is personally in direct competition with his counterpart in a competitor company, and he acts accordingly. He knows that it is mandatory that he outperform and outproduce this unknown individual to make his company's advertising more effective than that turned out by the competition. He must relish being a key element in the marketing arm of his company and find a large amount of inner satisfaction in helping his company achieve at the expense of the competition. Somebody is going to get a larger share of available business than the others, and the topflight ad man has a burning desire for it to be his company.

2. *Imagination*

The ad manager must be somewhat of a paradox; he or she has to be practical and level headed, but also imaginative. He should be a source for ideas. He should innovate, experiment, and, as Webster says, "form mental synthesis of new ideas from elements experienced separately." Some decry imagination in advertising when, in truth, imagination liberally used and well seasoned with the salt of practicality results in outstanding advertising that contributes immeasurably to a higher level of economic activity.

3. *Willingness and ability to think*

On the surface, naming this attribute seems trite. But thinking, *really thinking*, requires more effort than many people are willing to exert. Even the good minds subconsciously flinch at the prospect of having to think through a knotty problem, and they go through intricate and tortuous nonproductive motions trying to convince themselves that they are thinking, when in fact they are merely indulging in mental gymnastics. Self-discipline of the highest order is required to think when it is required. There are innumerable ways to avoid thinking—sharpening a pencil, putting a new cartridge in the ballpoint pen, cleaning the typewriter keys, answering the day's mail, phoning a friend, calling the agency about something trivial. Only the perceptive person *knows* when he or she is really thinking, and only the honest one admits it when not. Thinking is basic to good advertising because advertising is largely problem solving. It has been said that to think a problem through to a solution, it is necessary to do three things: Identify the problem, find out the facts, and, finally, come up with an idea. The experienced ad manager knows when he or she is using time well—when it is time to sit back, pull out the sliding leaf on the desk where the internal telephone numbers are taped, prop the feet up and relax—and think. Sound advertising is based on sound thinking.

4. *The ability to write*

Clear thinking results in good writing. Good writing is more than words grammatically arranged, more than abilty to compose catchy phrases, or the knack of creating an effect. The ability to write is part intuition, so strong that when a good selling proposition is conceived it is *recognized* instantaneously; it is part discernment, so that the extraneous and the trivial are rejected without wasting time; it is part sound judgment and knowledge of good business practice. And it is, of course, being able to express thoughts so that they interest others, so that others *want* to read what you have written, thus enabling you to implant the idea which you had originally and which you want prospects to retain.

5. *Curiosity*

There is no substitute for curiosity, no stronger words than "I wonder," or "What if...". A mind that probes off the beaten path, that questions, that doubts, that demands to know why, that refuses to accept the easy and the pat and the trite, that tempers known "facts" with a healthy dash of old-fashioned skepticism, that takes the Missouri attitude of "show me"—that is the mind most likely to conceive an entirely new and tremendously effective plan. Reach, ask, reject the obvious, search for something elusive, something that seems unattainable, but which is there in every situation. It can make the difference between acceptable and good, between good and outstanding.

6. *The ability to visualize*

This is an ability that every successful ad person has, and has to spare. It consists of thinking in terms of the whole, rather than segments or component parts. In the case of an advertisement, it means thinking in terms of the complete ad—layout, copy, illustration—rather than considering copy only. Visualizing the end result inevitably results in a better ad, one with more impact, or a better piece of literature. For only by doing this, either consciously or subconsciously, can the mind channel itself in the right creative direction and organize the thought sequence in logical order. A few pencil lines scribbled on a tablet, with copy blocks and the headline roughed in, are an aid in thinking visually, as a whole. The so-called "thumbnail" or "copywriter's rough" doodled out to organize thoughts is more than exercise.

7. *The ability to project*

This is nothing more than being able to identify with those with whom you want to communicate. Fortunately, almost everybody except the self-centered introvert has this ability to some extent. Nurture it, for it is a key to advertising *for* the prospect instead of *at* him or her. There's a world of difference.

Think as Your Prospects Think

Where many copywriters fumble, where both ad managers and agency personnel go off onto a tangent, is that they fail to shift mental gears. Nothing else will do except that the person writing the copy must cultivate a certain frame of mind—actually be a quick-change artist with thought patterns—in order to think from the *prospect's* viewpoint, rather than from his or her own, or from that of the company or clients.

Stop for a minute when you sit down to write an ad. Do nothing but think. Forget for the time being what you want. Disregard your desires and put the all-important prospect in the center of your thinking. Concentrate. Make the situation real for yourself by making the prospect come alive. Think back on what you've learned about him or her, where he works, what his habits are when he makes a purchase of a product for a company. Visualize that individual as a person with normal human wants, needs and desires. Project yourself right into that mind so that you actually think of your product in terms of what it means to the prospect, of what it will do.

Do this and you've become prospect-oriented, reader-oriented—which is exactly what you must accomplish if your advertisements are going to be read. When the typical prospect is reading a trade publication which just happens to contain your ad, he or she couldn't care less about you, your product, or your company. Perhaps the prospect isn't even aware that they exist. The prospect is concerned exclusively with himself, his company, and his job—and with products or services which he or she believes can help upgrade job performance, or which will solve a problem on the job. Your advertisement must persuade the prospect to believe that your product does exactly this.

McGraw-Hill proved this in a Reader Feedback survey which asked readers to select for extensive comment *one* ad in the issue of the magazine being evaluated. Readers were asked to select an ad which "describes a product or service, or gives information that may be helpful in your work." A high proportion of the top-ranked ads were selected for comment on this basis—a much higher proportion than the difference in readership scores alone would warrant. This shows that top-rated ads spoke to the readers in terms of job interest. Results showed that 61 percent of the top ads were selected for comment as "helpful in your work" as against 11 percent of the bottom ads.

This is so elementary it's scarcely worth mentioning—except that a surprisingly sizable percentage of today's industrial ads fail, and fail miserably, on this score. The reason for this is because the person who wrote them—and the ad manager who approved them (perhaps one and the same individual)—overlooked this basic premise. He or she had the wrong concept of the tack to take.

Another score on which ads fail is equally inexcusable—they talk product features. This is fine and dandy around the office where everybody regards the product as approximately equal in importance to the arrival of a first son and heir. But talking features is anathema to an ad. Engineers, product managers, draftsmen, and the mail boy enthusiastically discuss features, but advertisements subordinate features to discuss user benefits. Or, they talk features and promptly translate features into benefits. They do if they're successful ads, that is.

What benefits me is what the reader is interested in. He or she simply doesn't care whether or not the Joseph J. Doaks Company's widget has a shaft of heat-treated chrome-molybdenum steel, 1½ inches by 17¼ inches, and that this is the longest, strongest plunger shaft in the entire widget industry, and the only one in the industry made of this expensive alloy.

Instead tell a case-history ad that the heavy-duty plunger in this widget reduced downtime 27 percent for the XYZ Company, saving $57,986 in time and maintenance in only nine months and you've touched the reader. That's a user benefit he or she can fondly clutch to his heart because he's been having trouble with the plungers in widgets of another manufacturer—or he's afraid he might have trouble, or possibly he's farsighted enough to look ahead and plan to protect the continuity of production by installing the widget that will prevent this loss to the company.

Put interests first and your message will get through. Every time.

Three Kinds of Ads

As every ad manager knows, there are only three kinds of ads:

1. Good ads.
2. Ads which never should have been approved and never should have run.
3. Indifferent ads.

Ads in the first category were conceived and written by competent personnel who knew what they were doing, and why they were doing it. Those in the second category were done by incompetents who perhaps should have been apprentice plumbers. Those in the third were done by tired copywriters, copywriters who had only a superficial interest in their jobs, or those who were content to slide by and turn in a perfunctory performance. No ad that is *almost* good should ever get past the copy and layout stage—if it gets that far.

Even poor ads serve a useful purpose, though—as horrible examples. The author has no intention of denigrating or embarrassing any advertiser, so to discuss examples of poor ads objectively the advertisers and their products will, for the most part, be afforded the protection of anonymity. When this is done and the company name must be used, it will be called "Smith." Products, when identifiable, will be

Smith Widgets or a variation which is suitably descriptive without being too specific.

Making your ad stand out from the herd so that it will be read is quite an accomplishment when the average business individual is assaulted with more than 1,600 advertising impressions *each day*. To succeed in the face of such odds requires a high degree of ingenuity—of creativity, to use an overworked word. There's a difference between legitimate creativity, however, and merely being offbeat for the sake of offbeatness.

Recently one advertiser confused creativity with being different without a valid reason for doing so. The one-page, two-color ad features illustrations of seven—yes, seven—dancers, including a close-up of a hula dancer's navel. The headline is feature-oriented, written either by or for the manufacturer. It reads: *Even a dancer doesn't have all the moves of Smith's ram & saddle turret lathes.* Let's assume for some unknown reason that this little gem might possibly have stopped a reader and enticed him or her into pursuing the subject further; perhaps he's a terpsichorean by avocation. However, the body copy continues in the same unrewarding vein: *Ballet or belly. Ballroom or bar. Even a dancer would have trouble keeping up with all the motions possible from Smith's ram & saddle turret lathes.*

That's not reader-benefit copy, reason-why copy; it doesn't involve the reader, it fails to reward for spending valuable time with this ad. It's a poor ad in an ill-conceived campaign that should never have seen print. But the sorry aspect is that this campaign cost just as much as one that would have produced positive and tangible results for this advertiser. The basic concept was wrong.

Another, taking the coy approach, features an illustration of an awesomely endowed cutie in a stretch swimsuit leaning indolently against a driftwood stump on a deserted beach. Headline is: *Do ceramic problems have you STUMPED?* (That stump supporting the curvesome cutie had to be explained, apparently.) Body copy is almost a classic example of extreme self-interest; it ignores reader benefits, fails to examine the product from the reader's viewpoint. It goes: *Our products are chosen for quality, uniformity, and speed of delivery. For greatly increased strength and thermal shock resistance in their most economical form, it's easily blended Smith Substance or Smith Stuff. Much less of our products is required to give you the high alumina body content you desire. If it is a ceramic or refractory problem, let Smith Substance correct it. We make shipments in any manner you desire.* End of copy.

There is an unsupported claim of using less of the product (and the ad *actually* says "our products"), which the reader might possibly infer would result in lower costs, along with the assurance that shipment will go forth by the specified carrier. Not much in those unspecific and uninspired statements to persuade a prospect to use Smith Substance rather than something currently being bought, and it's due to lack of empathy with the prospect. The ad is written from the seller's viewpoint with the seller's desires in mind. Chances are few got as far as the bottom of the body copy, however, for they're given nothing to make them want to read that far.

Dissection of a complete ad, cliché by cliché, written for Lindberg Hevi-Duty by a former agency, shows how dreary and dull ad copy can be when it's written by somebody who lacks the basic knowledge of what copy should—and can—do. The original version of the ad on semiconductor diffusion furnaces read:

Within easy reach . . . new production records!

Like to set a few production records? Then take a good look at the Lindberg Hevi-Duty Mark III Diffusion furnaces. They're setting all kinds of records every day.

The reason? Three independently controlled, stacked furnaces that fit ever-so compactly in the floor space of one. Anyone of average height finds even the uppermost furnace within easy reach. Some people say the Mark III conserves valuable floor space like a miser. Two Mark III's can even be placed back to back.

Because each furnace is controlled independently, it's possible to simultaneously set up to three different process temperatures. And operation is simple. Even major temperature changes can be handled by the nontechnician.

The Mark III furnace profiles are guaranteed to ± ½ °C over a length of 22", from 800° to 1300°C, with almost incredibly precise repeatability.

Cabinet temperature outside? Remains at a safe-to-touch room temperature. Thanks to double-shell construction, new insulating characteristics, and three-way cooling system.

What's more, the exclusive "Disposa-Core" lets you quickly and economically replace coil-and-insulation sections whenever necessary.

Lindberg Hevi-Duty has the largest coast-to-coast staff of sales and service engineers to assure you of complete installation and start-up service, to guarantee equipment operation.

Want the complete Mark III story? Write Lindberg Hevi-Duty. (Single- and two-stack furnace models are available.)

Here are the fatal flaws which would have assured almost no readership of this ad:

Within easy reach . . . new production records! Headline is weak, needlessly verbose.

Like to set a few production records? The rhetorical question is permissible and effective in places, although it shouldn't be overdone.

Take a good look. Nobody is interested in taking a good look at anything just because they have been admonished to do so in an advertisement.

They're setting all kinds of records every day. What kinds? Where? Even on Sunday and holidays?

The reason? Another rhetorical question.

ever-so-compactly. Precious and cute. And it's even hyphenated.

uppermost. This is a coy way of saying what the copywriter actually meant—top.

Some people. What people? Where do they work? Are they acknowledged experts in this field? Does their word carry weight? Are they respected? This is the phony-testimonial approach and it always sounds the death knell for copy believability.

even. Try reading the sentence without it and see the difference.

Possible to simultaneously. Adhering slavishly to the rules of grammar is stultifying, but split infinitives grate on many people. Avoid them.

Even major temperature changes can be handled by the non-technician. This comment is not strictly a critique on copy—but this statement is a technical error and would have been recognized as such by the average reader of this technical journal. The copywriter *must* present facts correctly.

Cabinet temperature outside? Another rhetorical question.

safe-to-touch. Cute, "addy." People simply do not talk like this, except possibly at an afternoon tea attended by beaming dowagers.

Thanks to. Nobody says "thanks to" in an ad—not since approximately 1920, at least. It's a cliché and reflects a lack of thinking.

double-shell construction. Technical error; should be triple-shell. Facts must be correct. Everybody makes mistakes, but in the marginal agency they're part of the scheme of things.

whenever. Putting on the dog weakens a statement. Be simple and direct.

Lindberg Hevi-Duty has the largest coast-to-coast staff of sales and service engineers to assure you of complete installation and start-up service, to guarantee equipment operation. Sentence is too long. Too big a mouthful. Also, a manufacturer's field personnel do not guarantee equipment—the company does. There's a vast difference. Failure to make a correct statement on such an important subject indicates fuzzy thinking. There's no place for it in advertising—particularly in copywriting.

Want the complete Mark III story? Is there no end to the rhetorical questions? (It can become habit-forming.) (Single- and two-stack furnace models also available.) This is known as P.S.-type copy; it is basically feminine and should be avoided in advertising directed to industrial buyers. "Available" is a fine catalog word, but it is a cliché and merely proves the copywriter is either too lazy to select a better way to express himself, or is incapable of doing so.

For comparison, the ad is illustrated (page 209) as rewritten for a leading electronics magazine. This version, written by the ad manager, shows that an industrial ad can be reader-oriented, can talk user benefits, and can be informative and interesting at the same time.

Note that the headline is stronger—despite use of the rhetorical question! It makes a point and a promise fast. The reader is involved and because a benefit wanted and needed is promised, the reader is lured into reading the body copy. Body copy tells how to realize the benefit which interests him or her; no analogies such as "just as" or whatever, no beating around the bush. Reasons why are presented immediately.

A few specific comments on the copy:

No need to recruit labor from the Tall Girls' Club. A touch of humor breathes life into a potent sales point. It translates a product feature into a user benefit—ease of operating this diffusion furnace by the average female employee. This a competitive advantage and users of this equipment are fully aware of it.

As frugal with floor space as a miser is with money. Vivid and highly descriptive. This kind of analogy makes an indelible impression. Also, note there is no vague reference to

New production records? Easy to reach!

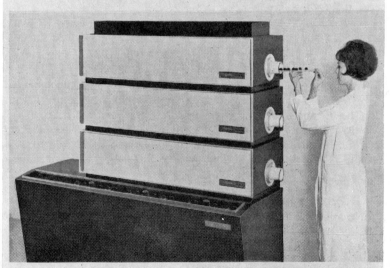

All you need is Lindberg Hevi-Duty's new Mark III Diffusitron furnace. It has three tubes, each with a separate control to do three different jobs at the same time.

Top tube of the Mark III is only 64¼" from the floor. No need to recruit labor from the Tall Girls' Club.

Lindberg Hevi-Duty's three-stack design is as frugal with floor space as a miser is with money. The Mark III is compact, can be installed back to back. Or flush against a wall, if you want.

You operate the Mark III Diffusitron merely by dialing the temperature you want. It's that easy.

Profiles are guaranteed ± ½°C over a length of 22", from 800° to 1300°C. With precise repeatability.

And the operator doesn't need asbestos gloves with Lindberg Hevi-Duty's Mark III. Cabinet always stays at room temperature. That's due to triple-shell construction, new and better insulation, and a three-way cooling system.

Lindberg Hevi-Duty's exclusive "Disposo-Core" lets you replace coil and insulation sections when necessary. Quickly, easily. No long-drawn-out down time.

Sales and service engineers everywhere give you skilled installation and start-up service. And if you need them, they're there. Want the whole story on the Mark III — or on single- or two-stack furnaces? Drop us a line. You have nothing to gain but profit. Lindberg Hevi-Duty, Watertown, Wisconsin 53094.

LINDBERG HEVI-DUTY T.M.

DIVISION OF SOLA BASIC INDUSTRIES

This is the Lindberg Hevi-Duty ad that was rewritten and rescheduled by the ad manager after the text had been oriented toward the potential purchaser rather than representing the manufacturer's views. User benefits are stressed in an interesting way, and the reader becomes involved because the benefits promised are bound to be of importance to him in his work.

unknown people, no pretentiousness about using the word "conserves."

You operate the Mark III Diffusitron merely by dialing the temperature you want. It's that easy. This is straight talk. No nonsense, no nontechnician gobbledygook. The simple, declarative sentence is strengthened by a change of pace—the very short sentence.

And the operator doesn't need asbestos gloves...cabinet always stays at room temperature. An extremely strong statement that is believable because the reason why follows immediately afterwards.

...exclusive Disposa-Core lets you replace coil and insulation sections when necessary. Quickly, easily. No long drawn-out downtime. That product feature and its user benefit come through loud and clear. It's like money in the bank compared to loss of production. Manufacturers understand this kind of talk because they are vitally interested in tool and equipment reliability.

And if you need them, they're there. Simply stated, vastly reassuring, and convincing.

Drop us a line. You have nothing to gain but profit. A bid for action and a potent promise.

The ad is replete with vivid word pictures, colorful, readable, inherently interesting to those in the business of manufacturing semiconductors and integrated circuits because it is reader-oriented. Copy should read as if it literally flows from the typewriter, even if every word, every phrase, every analogy was practically the result of blood, sweat, and tears. If it's worked on, it will.

The Question of Honesty

Honesty is not the best policy—it is the *only* policy.

The veracity of statements made in ads is not under discussion—being fair and honest with your readers is. The fastest way yet devised to lose a prospect's confidence, perhaps irretrievably, is to trick him or her into reading your advertisement by traveling under false colors.

There's no disputing the fact that the advertisement must attract the attention of the reader. It must arouse and maintain interest long enough to read and understand the message, otherwise the money invested in production and space is a total waste because the ad failed in its purpose.

But this can be done honestly, everything aboveboard. Fortunately, there's an elemental truth not known to—or believed by—most industrial advertisers. The truth is that the vast majority of all readers of

Air is cheaper than water

Sure, a ship's freight bill is lower. But indirect and hidden charges can cost you more in the long run. Just look:

TWA compares the cost of a 435 lb. machine parts shipment from Chicago to Zurich.			
Via Surface:	**Time: 20 days**	**Via Air:**	**Time: 15 hours**
Packaging	$ 48.00	Packaging	$ 9.00
Insurance	36.00	Insurance	12.00
Inland freight (Chicago-N.Y.)	22.00	Inland freight	—
Documentation	22.00	Documentation	1.00
Ocean freight	51.15	Air freight	176.12
Customs clearance	20.00	Customs clearance	10.00
Inland freight (Genoa-Zurich)	49.00	Inland freight	—
Interest charges	19.60	Interest charges	—
	Cost: $267.75		**Cost: $208.12**

$59.63 and 19 days saved by air! And that's just the beginning.
You can reduce your inventory and warehousing costs.
Give better customer service.
And increase your sales in time-limited situations.
The speed of air also cuts your investment in goods in transit, increases capital turnover and holds obsolescence to a minimum.
Get all the details. Call or write
your nearest TWA Air Cargo office.
Nationwide, worldwide...depend on TWA.

business publications read advertisements *because they want to*. They want to because in these advertisements is information they need, information that is important to them. They are not serving you by reading your ad, they are serving their own self-interest.

211

A good example is TWA's dramatic all-type ad shown here.

The stark simplicity of the ad in a field where everything is contrived, designed, deliberate, and studied produces an impression of immediacy, importance, and honesty. Invariably it produces results. And the arresting, provocative headline in big, bold type, the abundance of white space, and an exceptionally clean layout all combine to demand readership by those responsible for specifying shipments.

TWA itemizes every cost element of both surface and air shipments to lend credence to their statements. By using one specific commodity flown between two given points as a sort of case history, TWA proves that air shipment—supposedly the premium-priced way to move freight—actually costs less when all pertinent factors are taken into consideration. It amounts to $59.63 less, with a bonus of 19 irreplaceable days thrown in for good measure. Time is a pretty difficult item to which to attach a price tag, but in today's competitive economy it is certainly a significant factor in total costs of operation of a business. Then add reduced inventory, lower warehousing costs, lower investment in goods in transit, increased capital turnover, and minimum obsolescence. TWA's proposition is almost irresistible.

According to Lawrence V. Stapleton, former vice-president of advertising and sales promotion of Trans World Airlines, "Air Is Cheaper Than Water" has proved to be a superior ad that works very hard for TWA Air Cargo. An Ad-Chart survey of readers of *Iron Age* magazine shows that it scored an outstanding 64.1 percent Noticed, and that 58.3 percent of the interviewees contacted by the rating service stated they found the ad Very Informative. Only a negligible 4.2 percent felt that it was only Somewhat Informative. (Survey terminology is capitalized.)

And a Mills Shepard survey of the ad as run in *Purchasing Week* showed that 64 percent of the sample interviewed Remembered Having Seen the ad, while 38 percent Read Partially, and a full 25 percent Read Thoroughly.

Some verbatim comments made by those interviewed by Mills Shepard follow.

"I discussed this ad with our traffic manager and he sent for more information."

Supervisor, Electronics Buyer

"I sent this ad to our shipping department as a reminder that fast shipments via air freight are practical and the head shipper agreed."

Purchasing Agent
Electronics Company

Ceiling Unlimited

Air freight volume will double in the next three years, with no end in sight. Reason: more and more companies are seeking new ways to reduce overall distribution costs or gain a marketing edge.

Not only are more businesses turning to air freight every year, but more each of businesses. They're using it more consistently, shipping bigger loads. One attraction is that using air freight may prove the means to reduce field inventories, lower packaging costs, reduce the capital tied up in transit. Another appeal is the marketing edge: with jet-speed delivery comes greater customer satisfaction, faster replacement of distributors, greater flexibility to explore new markets. United delivers to more U.S. markets than any other airline, with the kind of concern it takes to get an important shipment there safely. And at United, it's always ways handle with extra care.

United Air Freight

HANDLE WITH CARE

the big birds fly the friendly skies of United Air Lines

"We discussed at length the chart shown in the ad and since then we have used TWA for flights."

Purchasing Director
Manufacturer of Brick Block Concrete

"After reading the ad, I sent out a shipment TWA for trial."

General Purchasing Agent
Manufacturer of Crankshafts

"I checked their air rates because of the center of the ad information. I have sent out shipments TWA and was satisfied."

Buyer
Manufacturer of Awnings

One of TWA's most important advertising objectives in air cargo is to communicate the advantages of air versus surface, and to illustrate the cost efficiencies that go even beyond the cost of a specific air freight shipment. Traffic and purchasing people are very important to TWA, and they tell their story in a select list of magazines that reach these buying influences effectively. They add, however, that it is quite possible that top management is actually the single most important group in the long-range development of air freight. The carrier has regular advertising schedules in such management publications as *Fortune, Business Week,* and *The Wall Street Journal.*

United Takes Another Route

Although both companies obviously have the same ultimate goal—to capture a larger share of an expanding air freight market—United Air Lines takes a different approach than TWA. United's striking two-color, two-page-spread ad is illustrated on page 213.

The illustration does a good job of showing the product—as much as a service can be shown, at least—and of arresting the attention of readers. Night photographs, with their massive, dominant black areas, always rate near the top of the heap in interest. Perhaps this is because so many millions of people are casual photographers who automatically think of picture-taking in terms of either sunlight or flash. When confronted with a punchy, contrasty night photograph, few can resist giving it a second—or third—glance.

Copy, instead of hitting home at one strong central point as does TWA's, extolls instead the virtues of air freight in general, and United Air Freight secondarily. This adds up to *two* ideas in one ad, when every ad should concentrate on just one. Copy reads:

CEILING
UNLIMITED
Air freight volume will double
in the next three years,

with no end in sight.
Reason: more and more
companies are seeking new ways
to reduce overall distribution
costs or gain a marketing edge.
Not only are more businesses
turning to air freight every year,
but more kinds of businesses.
They're using it more consistently,
shipping bigger loads. One
attraction is the cost saving:
air freight may prove the means
to reduce field inventories, lower
packaging costs, reduce the capital
once tied up in transit. Another
appeal is the marketing edge:
with jet speed delivery
comes greater customer
satisfaction, faster restocking of
distributors, greater flexibility
to explore new markets. United
delivers to more U.S. markets
than any other airline, with the
world's biggest freight lift.
And at United it's always
handle with extra care.

Deft use is made of United's consumer slogan, "Fly the friendly skies of United" by the carrier's air freight arm, for it is transformed into, "The big birds fly the friendly skies of United Air Lines." This provides strong corporate identification and capitalizes on United's position as the industry leader.

In addition, the air freight operation's slogan, "handle with extra care," is the tag line in the copy block, and it also appears prominently in red—the only spot of second color in the spread—in the signature area.

United's marketing objective in the air freight area is almost classically simple: "United hopes to build the air freight market by providing a satisfactory product to the shipper at a profit for United." To do so, United is of the opinion that top management is the single most important group of buying influences to whom they must communicate. The carrier has singled out, through research, the executives—by title—whom they have to reach. They are: President, financial vice-president (or controller), marketing vice-president, sales vice-president, and operations vice-president.

United stated: "We would like to increase both the number of shippers and the kinds of shipments we receive. In order to do this, we address ourselves both to management, *who makes the original decision to try air freight,* and to traffic management who makes the decision as to which carrier to use after the initial decision to ship by air has been made."

United wants to tell management the reasons for making an air freight decision. These include less capital tied up in traffic, less inventory and warehousing, faster shipping during peak selling seasons, and better service to customers.

Current top markets for United Air Freight include automotive parts, perishables such as produce and flowers, aerospace equipment, and, oddly enough, printed matter. Relative importance of these prime markets was determined by market research and an analysis of sales records.

Although there has been no measurable response to this ad, it has been surveyed by Daniel Starch and Staff and placed well into the top-readership quarter of all ads in that issue of *Business Week.*

Other media include Fortune, Wall Street Journal, U.S. News & World Report, selected to reach top management, and *Traffic World, Air Transportation, Purchasing, Purchasing Week, Distribution Age, Traffic Management, Pacific Air & Truck Traffic,* and *Transportation & Distribution Management*, these latter to tell purchasing and traffic management executives about United Air Freight.

If Ads Are Good, They Are Read

Powerful though this ad obviously is, nonetheless it lacks something almost intangible—perhaps the persuasiveness, the dollars-and-cents "proof" of TWA's ad. There is little doubt that, of the two ads, TWA's outpulled United's in readership and outproduced it in results. And it did so at far lower cost. TWA's ad required no expensive night photograph which could easily have cost $500—or even double that— no expensive half-tone engraving; it used half as many colors, and half as much space.

That people in industry want to read trade publications and their advertisements is again proved quite conclusively by a study conducted by McGraw-Hill Publishing Company. A survey was made to study the readership of "business, industrial, trade and technical publications." Personal interviews were made by McGraw-Hill Research with 1,330 individuals in the metalworking and chemical processing industries. Principal functions and size of plant groups were proportionately represented in the sample.

Sought to Avoid Bias

In order to avoid bias, the interviews were conducted under a name having no connection with any publishing company or publication. The source of the list of plants was the McGraw-Hill Census which encompasses almost all of industry.

The question, "Are you spending more, less, or about the same time reading such publications as you did three or four years ago?" was answered by two groups—those who had changed jobs and those who did not change.

Fifty percent of those who changed jobs spent more time reading business publications; 20 percent spent less; 30 percent spent the same amount of time reading.

Among those who did not change jobs, the results showed that 27 percent spent more time; 18 percent less time; 55 percent spent the same amount of time.

The conclusion is obvious. In today's highly mobile society where more individuals occupy different positions each year than remain in the same slot, business publication reading is regarded as a necessity. It is so important because it is a part of a continuing educational program which makes it possible to keep pace with technological changes. Even among those who resisted the lure of greener pastures, 82 percent spent either the same amount of time, or more time, on business reading. Knowledgeable executives usually consider the person who does not read business publications as narrow, unambitious, and ill-qualified for advancement.

Interviewers asked the same people another question: "Do you feel you rely on them (business publications) for information more, less, or about the same as you did three or four years ago?"

Among job changers, and this includes those individuals who changed companies as well as those who transferred or were promoted to a more responsible position within their original companies, 49 percent placed more reliance on the business press. A scant 12 percent placed less, while 39 percent relied to the same extent.

Top Executive Opinion

In a newspaper supplement produced for the American Business

Press, a number of top executives of major corporations said they "couldn't do without" business publications—for both informative reading and effective advertising.

Russell De Young, former board chairman of Goodyear Tire & Rubber Company, said, "Speaking from personal experience, I can say that no person in management could perform a job effectively, or hope to progress, lacking the information and knowledge available through well-edited, perceptive business publications." Goodyear subscribed to some 400 different business publications for the benefit of its executives and staff. In addition, many other publications are received by Goodyear people.

Robert S. Stevenson of Allis-Chalmers Company was quoted as saying that business publications "serve us in two ways. The first is that they provide authoritative and knowledgeable information relating to a specific business—a type of information just not available from any other source. The second value is that of providing a specific vehicle for us to use in advertising to our customers." Communication is a two-way street.

Noting that his firm does not major in the business of providing goods or services for the general consumer market, Mr. Stevenson added, "It is quite inefficient and overcostly for us to consider advertising in the mass media...if we did use those media, we would spray our message over too much territory, wasting our efforts and investment on many who could not possibly be customers, and, of course, the cost per useful contact would be outlandishly high.

"In other words, we would be shooting with a shotgun when we really need a rifle. Business publications provide those rifles and as a result we can buy directed coverage. For that reason we are good customers."

Business publications are read because they are an indispensable tool. Most top managements—particularly in progressive companies which outpace their industries—urge, and many insist, that all of their technical and management personnel read the business publications in their fields. It is an anachronism cherished by those who haven't had an original thought in years that business publications are not read.

And in the right environment—editorial that is essential to their self-interest—97 percent of business publication readers read the advertisements. It's up to you to make your ads so interesting and so informative that they will achieve high readership. And do it without subterfuge.

What You Owe the Reader

Although it's not often considered this way, the plain fact is that you're asking a favor of the recipient of a magazine every time you insert one of your advertisements. This shouldn't be done unilaterally. Your ad, merely by being there, implies an obligation on your part to compensate the reader for what he has freely given you of his own volition—his time. Make his investment worthwhile. Don't waste it.

You owe the reader:

1. *Information*—concise, precise, specific.
2. *Truth*—no puffery, no exaggeration, no playing fast and loose with facts.
3. *Clarity*—no obscurity, no gimmickry.

These three debts you repay to the reader in exchange for his time eliminate the old saw about the trouble with magazine adertising: That people who live in cities don't believe it, and people who live in small towns don't understand it.

Information

If your selling proposition is right and the concept of the person who created it is right, a good industrial ad should exert such a strong appeal that recipients of business publications will want to read it. The illustration specified by the copywriter should pique the reader's imagination. Then, the headline, which must telegraph what you want to say, should arouse enough interest to entice him or her into the body copy.

Marsteller Inc., one of the country's largest industrial advertising agencies, has this to say about campaigns, ads, and copy. They must have, and do, the following:

1. Campaign identity.
2. Orderly arrangement.
3. One dominating element.
4. Focal point.
5. Identify subject at a glance.
6. Functional layout.
7. Functional color.
8. Be direct.
9. Short, short, short.
10. Simple typography.
11. Single idea.
12. Offer reward.
13. Reader involvement.

14. Don't brag.
15. Buyer language.
16. News, information.
17. Drama.
18. Be specific.
19. Be friendly.
20. Advertiser identification.

The one thing the reader expects from an industrial ad is information. Give it in terms of self-interest, and it will be read. Deprive him or her of it, or beat around the bush and talk in generalities and he'll do one of two things—skip over your ad entirely, or read part of it and immediately forget it. The reader has other things to do with time, such as reading a competitor's ad which *does* reward for his or her time.

An example is the ad (see next page) for an industrial degreaser made by a company whose name is not the "Smith" given in the text. The illustration has little inherent interest, and isn't even remotely related to the product. The headline reads: *You can't drive a spike nail with a tack hammer!* The phrase "with a tack hammer" is underlined to emphasize these words, apparently to explain the illustration. Headlines and/or illustrations that have to be explained to readers are woefully weak.

So far, there's not much to lure the prospect into reading the selling message, but things get worse. Body copy continues: *Driving a spike with a tack hammer would be a very tedious, time-consuming, thankless, profitless job.* That's something short of a grabber for an opening paragraph, but it does give the reader the idea that continuing to read this ad could well be a very tedious, time-consuming, thankless, profitless project. Then the second paragraph: *Whatever the task, it is essential that we use the proper tools to achieve the desired result.* Still no concrete information, no news, no dramatic statement, no reader involvement. There is proof of fuzzy thinking on the part of the copywriter who should have been aware that if the reader is not offered a benefit in the headline, it is imperative to do so immediately in the body copy.

Body copy continues: *For example—some metalworking manufacturers still degrease small parts in old, hand-operated degreasers when they could save a lot of time and money with a new Smith Degreaser.*

Thousands and thousands of parts can be degreased at amazingly low costs in this modern, efficient machine. And there is a varied choice of models to fit different production requirements. All Smith machines will handle a wide variety of parts.

**YOU CAN'T
DRIVE A SPIKE
WITH A
TACK HAMMER!**

Driving a spike with a tack hammer would be a very tedious, time-consuming, thankless, profitless job.

Whatever the task, it is essential that we use the proper tools to achieve the desired result.

For example—some metalworking manufacturers still degrease small parts in old, hand-operated degreasers when they could save a lot of time and money with a new

Thousands and thousands of parts can be degreased at amazingly low costs in this modern, efficient machine. And there is a varied choice of models to fit different production requirements. All machines will handle a wide variety of parts.

Whatever your metal cleaning need—call in the man from the   Industrial Division. Chances are he will give you a practical and economical way to make the job much easier and more profitable.

]II'TI'I:I

CHEMICAL INDUSTRIES, INC.
P.O. BOX 501, DEPT. MP-666, DETROIT, MICHIGAN 48232

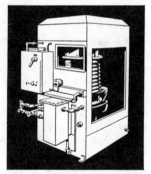

Degreasers are built in four basic sizes with capacities ranging from 1,000 to 12,000 lbs. per hour. Exclusive construction features a spiral trough elevator which carries the parts from vibrating hot solvent bath to controlled vapor spray to pressure steam drying.

Whatever your metal cleaning needs—call in the representative from Smith's Industrial Division. Chances are you will get a practical and economical way to make the job much easier and more profitable.

221

It's not until the caption under the line drawing of the product that specific information is found. Caption reads: *Smith Degreasers are built in four basic sizes with capacities ranging from 1,000 to 12,000 lbs. per hour. Exclusive construction features a spiral trough elevator which carries the parts from vibrating hot solvent bath to controlled vapor spray to pressure steam drying.* And even then, only product sizes are given, discounting discussion of a product feature without exploiting the user benefit.

The ad is pedantic and condescending in tone, vague and non-specific, self-oriented, and does not reward the reader for his time. It is also a waste of money.

Unfortunately, this ad is typical of far too much industrial advertising seen in the business press. It is a prime reason for management's questioning advertising's effectiveness.

Kimberly-Clark's dramatic ad is in vivid contrast to the pallid generalities in the preceding ad. Kimberly-Clark's bold headline is as shocking as a cold shower to members of a society conditioned to regard cheap as synonymous with worthless or inferior. It tantalizes the reader and few can resist looking at the illustration. When they do, they immediately receive another shock—the incongruity of a 53-cent price tag attached to a dirty, discarded shop towel. This, in turn, leads to the advertiser's provocative statement: *shop towel analysis can be a shocker.* The stage has been set. The reader has been lured into reading further.

Body copy immediately involves the reader. *Have you ever figured out what it costs you when a three-dollar-an-hour worker leaves the job to go get a three-cent shop towel? We call it "walk time," and it can blow up the cost of such a simple item as a shop towel to enormous size.*

The answer is an inexpensive disposable wiper that can be dispensed right on the job. Like one of ours. We make a broad line of sturdy, versatile wipers that come bundled, boxed, band-wrapped, or whatever is most efficient. And our distributor salespeople, who have just finished a six-week course in Wiping Analysis, can make sure you get the right wipe in the right package for the right job. See your Kimberly-Clark man, or write Kimberly-Clark Corporation, Neenah, Wisconsin.

The ad is simple and straightforward. It has a strong central idea—a concept. The selling proposition is sound. The ad is informative and rewards the reader for his or her time. It offers an important user benefit, reduced costs, and it does so believably and logically. And it inspires confidence in the salesperson who will call on a sizable number of the readers of this ad, making the job easier, reducing the

CHEAP

shop towel cost analysis can be a shocker

Have you ever figured out what it costs you when a three-dollar-an-hour worker leaves the job to go get a three-cent shop towel? We call it "walk time," and it can blow up the cost of such a simple item as a shop towel to enormous size.

The answer is an inexpensive disposable wiper that can be dispensed right on the job. Like one of ours. We make a broad line of sturdy, versatile wipers that come bundled, boxed, band-wrapped, or whatever is most efficient. And our distributor salesmen, who have just finished a six-week course in Wiping Analysis, can make sure that you get the right wipe in the right package for the right job. See your Kimberly-Clark man, or write Kimberly-Clark Corporation, Neenah, Wisconsin.

THE KIMBERLY-CLARK FAMILY OF INDUSTRIAL WIPERS

TERI*TOWELS KIMTOWELS* KIMWIPES* KAYDRY* LITHOWIPES*

amount of time spent on each sales call, thus reducing the cost of selling. This Kimberly-Clark ad is a fine example of what industrial advertising should be—and what it should do.

Note that there's a built-in invitation to read. Clean layout, a single idea, helpful information, dramatic presentation, short copy, simple typography, a direct approach that doesn't fritter away the reader's time and strong advertiser identification.

The layout makes effective use of a proved principle—that a reader's eye is trained to start at the top of a page and proceed downward in a clockwise direction. Thus, each element of the ad follows in logical sequence, aiding assimilation of the advertiser's message.

Lighthearted Information

Although they are physically dissimilar in layout, illustrative technique, typography, and even in the size of space used, Mathatronics' ad (page 244) adheres to the principle that an industrial advertisement's reason for being is to give information to the reader. It does so in a deceptively lighthearted way that makes it a pure joy to read.

Headline is: *Can an engineer flunk Fortran and still find happiness?* Body copy, unjustified (uneven margins) left and right, continues with subheads breaking up the copy block—letting in air, as it is called. It reads:

Happiness is

finding a digital computer with a simple keyboard,
whose language is algebra.

Happiness is

having 48 to 88 individually addressable storage registers
plus 5 separate registers for arithmetic manipulations,
480 steps of program memory,
and/or 18 optional prewired programs of 48 steps each,
right in your own department.

Happiness is

not spending a million dollars for a digital computer,
or $50,000 or $20,000, or even $10,000.

Happiness is

getting 8 or 9 significant digit accuracy
with a 2 digit power of ten exponent,
automatic decimal placement,
paper tape readout,
100 column number capacity.

Happiness is

getting intelligent accessories,
like a paper tape punch and reader,
or a page printer.

Happiness is
a Mathatron 8-48 plus the new
Auxiliary Program Storage.
MATHATRONICS, INC.

To the average reader—all of us noncomputer types, that is—the term "Fortran" in the headline might seem not to communicate. But this is the language of the buyer and is common terminology in many scientific disciplines. Fortran is a language which translates human language into computer language. It must be learned in order to communicate with a computer and it is the *last* thing an engineer or scientist is interested in. This would be analogous to a medical student having to learn Latin when his real interest is in medicine.

A major user benefit of the computer offered by Mathatronics is that it requires no machine language such as Fortran. The instrument understands and generates on simple algebraic input which is the established working tool of the engineer.

That the ad *does* provide information of importance to readers is proved by one method of measurement—response. This ad and one similar ran in several electronics, computer, and engineering magazines for a year. Number of insertions varied from six to 12. The two ads consistently pulled an average of 800 inquiries per month, with letterhead inquiries, usually considered of higher caliber than bingo-card response, accounting for at least 10 percent of the total. This ad delivered the message.

Mathatronics' objective is not to generate inquiries, however, for the company actually has more than can be handled effectively. Rather, the advertising goal is to attract attention to a relatively unknown—due to its newness—product, and to a small company which is competing successfully with giants in this market. Mathatronics sells through dealers and representatives, making it virtually impossible to correlate the effect of advertising and sales. However, sales doubled, so *something* contributed!

This two-thirds page ad has everything going for it. Given the right concept, the strong central idea, pertinent information of a highly technical nature is fed to readers in a palatable way, in the readers' language. This is another ad that more than paid its way.

Truth

It's unpalatable, but it's a fact of life that a vast number of people —including those from business and industry—question advertising's truthfulness. This is detrimental to business and detrimental to advertising.

THE
ADVERTISING CODE
OF AMERICAN BUSINESS

1. Truth ... Advertising shall tell the truth, and shall reveal significant facts, the concealment of which would mislead the public.

2. Responsibility ... Advertising agencies and advertisers shall be willing to provide substantiation of claims made.

3. Taste and Decency ... Advertising shall be free of statements, illustrations or implications which are offensive to good taste or public decency.

4. Disparagement ... Advertising shall offer merchandise or service on its merits, and refrain from attacking competitors unfairly or disparaging their products, services or methods of doing business.

5. Bait Advertising ... Advertising shall offer only merchandise or services which are readily available for purchase at the advertised price.

6. Guarantees and Warranties ... Advertising of guarantees and warranties shall be explicit. Advertising of any guarantee or warranty shall clearly and conspicuously disclose its nature and extent, the manner in which the guarantor or warrantor will perform and the identity of the guarantor or warrantor.

7. Price Claims ... Advertising shall avoid price or savings claims which are false or misleading, or which do not offer provable bargains or savings.

8. Unprovable Claims ... Advertising shall avoid the use of exaggerated or unprovable claims.

9. Testimonials ... Advertising containing testimonials shall be limited to those of competent witnesses who are reflecting a real and honest choice.

Developed and initially distributed by: the Advertising Federation of America; the Advertising Association of the West; the Association of Better Business Bureaus, Inc.

The Advertising Code of American Business, initially developed and distributed by two advertising organizations and now widely disseminated by the Association of American Advertising Agencies, is illustrated.

Point number 1 in the Code, that advertising shall tell the truth, is understood and accepted wholeheartedly by every industrial advertising manager today, almost without exception. Understood, but not as widely accepted, is point number 8 in the Code—that advertising shall avoid the use of exaggerated or unprovable claims, and use of big, bombastic words and phrases. Braggarts are not believed. The day when a gullible public could be talked into buying Old Doctor Janco's Snake Oil as a cure-all for dandruff, gout, and consumption is long gone, and happily so.

The sad fact remains, however, that advertising as a whole, and this doesn't exclude industrial advertising where the credibility gap is significantly narrower than in the consumer field, has an unfortunate penchant for exaggeration and manufacturer brag-and-boast. In leafing through a couple of trade publications, these examples were found:

Headline in a one-page, two-color ad for a machine tool: *PROVED PERFORMANCE! THE MOST CONVINCING REASON TO BUY A SMITH AUTOMATIC TURRET LATHE.* Copy then goes: *Time after time the Smith has proved it cuts costs for both long and short production runs.* The statement is not documented in any way, no reason why it might be true is given, it is completely unsupported. Believability suffers.

A different ad, also two-color, one-page, in *Factory* magazine proclaims: *Greater Choice of Lifting Speeds and Drum Capacities... That's What Makes the Big Smith Model 3 Hoist Different From Others!* Copy then says: *Take a close look at the clean, functional design of this Smith Hoist. See how the Motor, Drum, and Gear sections are assembled in a "straight line"—not a "box" like some other heavy-duty hoists. Because of this, many drum and motor combinations can be brought together within the basic Smith hoist design to give you the lifting speed and drum capacity that's just right for your handling requirements. That's what makes the Smith different from other heavy-duty hoists!*

Let's start with readership. Readership always goes down when legibility goes down, and capitalizing every word in the headline creates a jumpy appearance that repels the eye. Good typography is the least expensive part of advertising. Poor typography, perhaps the most expensive.

As for content, the headline is strictly brag-and-boast, self-serving, and therefore unconvincing. It fails to persuade because of unsupported claims. The reader quite logically interprets this as exaggeration—and thus is created another skeptic who questions all advertising copy.

Body copy proceeds to insult the readers' intelligence by putting quotation marks around terms that the average reader of *Factory* readily understands. Talking down to readers alienates them. Credit readers with having the intelligence to get the message if it's expressed in language familiar to them.

Proceeding, the copy then offers platitudes instead of information, discusses features instead of benefits. It continues for another long paragraph, then closes with an admonition to see the Smith distributor nearest the reader. If anybody read that far, that person must have been whiling away the waning hours of a quiet Friday afternoon when his vacation started at 5 o'clock.

Then there's the two-color, one-page ad run by an instrument company. Seemingly it *invites* skepticism, at least from those who are not addicted to a current TV situation comedy. Not everybody is, and those who aren't will skip this ad as fast as they can turn the page. The headline is: *Would You Believe This Steroid Analysis?* Reader reaction to that one is a laconic nope.

And Chevrolet, who should know better, makes a pitch for a larger share of the fleet market with this appeal: *Your company's Chevrolet: easier to own because it's easier to sell. This year, more than ever, Chevrolet's the first-choice car. It's bigger looking. Solid feeling. Better looking, inside and out. There's even more value built in with features like...* ad nauseam. Generalities, vague and imprecise, ghost comparisons, no meaty information, and absolutely no feel for the market. Somebody should tell the copywriter that fleet cars are all easy to own because the companies buying them have the wherewithal to pay, and it's a deductible expense. "Easier to sell" may well be true, but who would object to some supporting facts—such as statistics from wholesale used car markets in four geographical areas? Then the time-worn ghost comparison technique—bigger looking than what? Perhaps a Volkswagen? Better looking, inside and out, than what? More value built in than what? Would this bear the scrutiny of a strict value analysis by a corporate purchasing department? This ad, to be persuasive, needs less puffery, less brag-and-boast, and some solid facts. Acceptance of the concept that advertising copy must communicate, must inform, would help a lot.

On the other hand, advertisers with real savvy realize that making a strong statement, then backing it up with proof, makes a powerful presentation of their sales proposition.

IBM provided a good example in a recent spread ad in *Modern Casting*. Left page is in four-color and shows a dramatic photo of white-hot molten metal being poured from the ladle; inset into the upper, dark area is a four-color closeup of the scrap metal that comprised the charge being poured. Headline says: *With the savings from melt charge calculations alone, Georgia Iron Works justifies its computer*. Since calculating the proper proportion of different types of metal for each charge is, after all, a small work load for a modern computer, IBM goes into a straightforward case-history copy approach that carries real conviction. It reads: *Danforth W. Hagler, vice-president of Georgia Iron Works, estimates it would take about 95 man-hours to calculate the least-cost mix for a typical charge. Much too long and expensive to be feasible. But with an IBM 1130 computer, they are now able to perform all of their charge calculations, using less than 1% of the computer's time—and realize enough savings on charge materials to make the 1130 pay its way. This means that the other 99% of the computer's time they get as a bonus*. Typical uses, including shop order reporting, price evaluation, scheduling, production control, cost account and sales analyses and forecasting are then given to illustrate the bonus uses of the computer. Following a paragraph about Georgia Iron Works, IBM adds. *The computer can be an invaluable tool for foundry management. Call your nearest IBM office and learn how. Like Dan Hagler did*.

This is sincerity and believability. There's a refreshing absence of braggadocio and no exaggeration. Just the plain, unvarnished truth. No advertising manager quotes a customer and gives the customer's name and company as a reference unless the facts are exactly as stated. It's too easy to pick up a phone.

Diametrically opposed to exaggeration is an extremely effective technique—deliberate understatement. It is actually whispering instead of screaming. An example is Lindberg's Hevi-Duty spread ad on valve aluminizing equipment. Lindberg Hevi-Duty has an unusually strong story to tell here, one that is, perhaps, truly unique. As far as is known, there were only 21 valve aluminizing lines in the entire free world at the time this ad was prepared.

Instead of strutting and chest-thumping and proclaiming how wonderful it is, the company soft-pedaled its position and let the sheer force of quoted numbers tell the story. This was, incidentally, at a time when a would-be competitor was proudly announcing to all and sundry that it had just produced a valve aluminizing line.

On a more prosaic product Lindberg's Hevi-Duty low-key approach could be disastrous. But here the situation is different. The buying influences in the handful of establishments who could possibly be

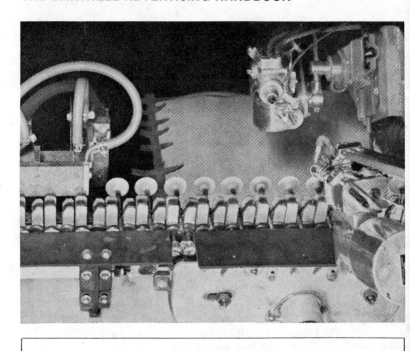

One firm turned us down.

But we've learned a thing or two from our 21 other valve aluminizing lines around the world.

Like how to get fast production. And control coatings precisely. And most of all, we've acquired a thorough understanding of how to design a valve aluminizing line that keeps producing.

Lindberg Hevi-Duty can design for you a line that coats up to 6000 valves an hour. And keeps that pace. You can have equipment tailored to fit your production space. You can have a line that's automated as much or as little as you like.

Are you thinking of a valve aluminizing line? With two others in process, we'll soon have 23 lines. Can yours be our 24th? For more details, write to us at 2450 W. Hubbard Street, Chicago, Illinois 60612.

LINDBERG HEVI-DUTY
DIVISION OF SOLA BASIC INDUSTRIES

Here is the ad for Lindberg Hevi-Duty valve aluminizing equipment, discussed in detail beginning on the opposite page. The low-key approach is justified by the fact that this is a small and highly specialized industrial area with knowledgeable buyers.

classed as prospects *know* how many installations of this type exist, and who built them. It is a close-knit industry.

Headline of the ad is: *One firm turned us down. But we've learned a thing or two from our 21 other valve aluminizing lines around the world.* Body copy is pithy and succinct and plays it straight: *Like how to get fast production. And control coatings precisely. And most of all, we've acquired a thorough understanding of how to design a valve aluminizing line that keeps producing.*

Lindberg Hevi-Duty can design for you a line that coats up to 6,000 valves an hour, and keeps that pace. You can have equipment tailored to fit your production space. You can have a line that's automated as much or as little as you like.

Are you thinking of a valve aluminizing line? With two others in process, we'll soon have 23 lines. Can yours be our 24th? For more details, write us...

The full page, closeup illustration of the business end of the aluminizing gun is stark and simple and it's successful in stopping the reader's eye. Layout is clean and free from clutter, it has inviting white space, and the typography is legible and tasteful.

Underplay it, speak softly—and watch your readership ratings soar!

Clarity

Nobody works at ad reading.

The readers of business publications are busy men. They are unwilling to inconvenience themselves to receive your message. They will not invest extra time to interpret or decipher a message that is not immediately clear. Clarity costs nothing; lack of clarity costs everything, for lack of readership, the one essential, accompanies it.

Automation magazine quoted Stephen Spender, British poet and thinker, who wrote in *The Saturday Review* that "It seems to be universally recognized that everyone should learn to read and write. Not to be able to do so is illiteracy. Little importance is attached to what you read and how you write. The idea that writing is not just a physical attainment, like using a knife and fork, but is communication —and that everyone should be concerned with it to the degree that he has experience and ideas to express—is regarded as eccentric.

"One has only to look at the essays of most sociologists (and almost all business writing) to realize that writing, the language of communication, is often the last thing people who have very important things to tell about the state of our society have taken trouble about. We enter the era of mass communication when the study of the traditional—and ultimate—means of communication, the English language, is looked at as a matter concerning only literary specialists."

Mr. Spender's comments could be shrugged off, even though, upon reflection, we remember that teen-agers in high school cannot spell, nor can college students write a grammatical essay. The comments may well seem out of context in any discussion of industrial advertising, of advertisements prepared at considerable expense by specialists in the art of communications. Obviously all ads should be so crystal clear that the message is transmitted and absorbed at once.

It is little short of amazing, however, how many incredibly vague, ambiguous ads appear in the business press, ads whose message is murkily obscure, whose product is difficult to identify, and even the name of the advertiser must be searched out.

An example of this type of ad appeared in an issue of a metalworking book and is reproduced on the following page.

Granted this ad has shock value. Nobody overlooks the large type, the taking-a-swipe-at-management headline which enjoyed a brief burst of popularity. Then there's the cute, simple copy written for cute, simple people—who promptly ignored it. There just wasn't anything there for them. No reader involvement, product identity, product benefits, information, or drama. Even the advertiser identification is weak—there is no logo. Most of all, though, the ad suffers from lack of clarity due to not having a strong, central idea.

Anaconda Aluminum's ad is even shorter, but is a vigorous, striking ad which succeeds on every score where the other failed. The large four-color illustration is dramatically simple, direct, and to the point. Its presentation of the selling message is unusually effective.

The copy, all headline, *This is an ad for Anaconda Aluminum* casually places the company name in the headline without being ostentatious about it. It identifies the product and, combined with the illustration, promotes a major product benefit.

The mental transition of going from the illustration to the headline, then to the thought of "paint wouldn't blister and peel if the siding were of Anaconda Aluminum. Downspouts of Anaconda Aluminum wouldn't rust. Nails of Anaconda Aluminum wouldn't rust, either." Readers, mostly homeowners, easily identify with the situation shown in the ad. It is immediately clear what is being said to them. They can visualize themselves with this problem and, if the product solves the problems in homes, it is logical to assume that it would solve rust and corrosion problems at the readers' companies.

The impression is made quickly, but strongly. This is an ad that enjoyed excellent readership and it is a campaign that, if continued, will exert a strong influence on awareness of Anaconda Aluminum as an excellent company from whom to buy ingot, sheet, and other aluminum products for industry.

Our founder had holes in his head.

Big holes and little holes. Medium holes, round holes, square holes, diamond holes, straight, oblique, and herringbone holes—the best holes in the world.
And we've been making all those holes ever since Eli Hendrick founded us in 1876. If you want the best holes in the world, come to us.
And, if you have holes in your head that even we haven't thought up yet, that's all right. We're very open-minded.
Hendrick Manufacturing Company, Dundaff Street, Carbondale, Pennsylvania

That clarity, or the lack of it, affects readership is unquestioned, but the degree to which it does so is largely open to question and to individual interpretation. A paucity of information exists on the subject. You can determine for yourself how readership nose-dives when clarity is lacking, merely by analyzing any business publication whose readership is measured by Starch/Inra/Hooper. The actual study results are sent to the advertiser accompanied by a marked copy of the magazine studied. Each studied ad has affixed to it a number of little stickers. These stickers have percentgage figures on them, showing the percentage who noticed the ad at all. Further breakdowns are given and will be disccused later on.

You'll find, in almost every instance, that ads which excel in clarity—those which are well laid out, those which do not contain too many elements, and those which have a strong central idea and are well written—excel in readership.

Research Proves the Point

This is borne out also by an analysis of the results of Ad Chart studies of a large number of business publications. Invariably when an ad is not arranged in an orderly fashion, or when it presents a multiplicity of thoughts with no dominant one, that ad rates poorly. This holds true for analyses of the findings of other readership services as well.

Other factors in addition to copy affect clarity—layout, typography, and illustration chief among them. These will be discussed in subsequent chapters.

McGraw-Hill Publishing Company has done considerable research on the subject of clarity, and in its Laboratory of Advertising Performance the company reports that advertisements with high readership ratings were consistently easier to read than ads with low ratings.

To carry out the survey, 100 one-page advertisements with the highest readership ratings and the 100 ads which rated lowest were selected from all other one-page ads in 10 issues of *Factory* during the period which was studied. Readership ratings were established by McGraw-Hill's Reader Feedback Service.

Ads were analyzed to determine if reading ease of the main copy block differed significantly in the group of high-rated ads, as compared to those which achieved low readership.

McGraw-Hill adapted a formula developed by Dr. Rudolph Flesch and described in his book, *The Art of Readable Writing*, and applied it to each of the ads in the high and low groups. The result was definite: The higher the reading ease score, the higher the readership.

The Flesch Reading Ease Scores of all of the ads were charted to compare them to each other and to editorial material in *Factory* magazine. The 100 top-scoring ads averaged out with a score of 48; the bottom 100 with 39—almost 20 percent difference. Editorial mat-

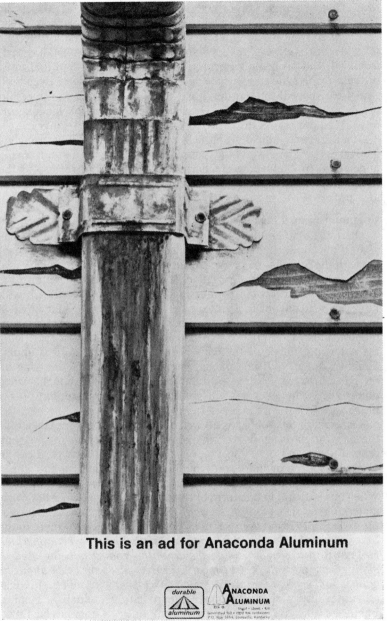

This is an ad for Anaconda Aluminum

durable aluminum

ANACONDA
ALUMINUM

This is the Anaconda Aluminum ad analyzed previously.

ter in *Factory* scored 51 on the Reading Ease chart, quite close to the 100 best-read ads.

It is interesting to note that McGraw-Hill made a point of the fact that the ads were designed to supply information to managerial, technical, and professional people who read *Factory*—and that most of these readers have a college education or its equivalent. Even with readers of this educational level and position in industry, readership of ads went up when they were clearly written in as simple language as possible to put across the idea the advertiser wanted to convey.

Other research indicates that lack of clarity cripples advertising effectiveness in three ways: (1) use of words which are not easily understood by the average reader of the publication, (2) use of the wrong word, and, (3) fuzzy phraseology that just does not convey the idea properly.

Communication's the Goal

There is no acceptable excuse for any of these shortcomings. The goal of the copywriter is to communicate an idea, not to impress people with the fact that he or she has an unusually large vocabulary and is an accomplished sesquipedalian. The ad that should require the average reader to consult the dictionary *won't send him there*. It will, however, send anyone to the next page and a competitor's ad may just happen to be there. In general, it is advisable to use the shortest, commonest, most descriptive word that does the job without sacrificing the color and flavor of the copy. Use of the wrong word is unpardonable. The advertising manager must demand precise thinking on the part of the copywriter—or organize his or her own thoughts when doing the writing. This will automatically eliminate any fuzzy phraseology.

Research on this subject is all well and good, but it is the consensus that lack of clarity in advertising is the result of not having a strong central idea—and of failing to consider copy as a concept. Leafing through a dozen or more trade publications in each of a half-dozen different fields every month makes this conclusion unavoidable. When ads crop up, in one form or another, like the one for a basic raw material that says: *Sh-h-h...Smith Product's part of the process. Many Smith Product users say a lot by not talking...* and then, in the first paragraph of the body copy, *You almost have to be a Sherlock Holmes to discover how and where Smith Product is being used in many plants these days. Chemical Engineers just won't talk about its application to improve processes or develop new products.* Predictably, the illustration is of two men in hard hats, presumably Chemical Engineers (the advertiser's capitalization), one of whom has his finger to his lips, going sh-h-h to the other.

IT CAN'T BE DONE!

It can't be done! No, sir, it can't be done. You don't get labeled *the action company* by saying maybe, or we'll try, or perhaps, probably or possibly. In other words, no pussyfooting. And, Norplex hasn't! Doesn't! Won't! Norplex acts . . . now . . . with complete customer service. No maybe about it . . . when you want price and grade information . . . or research and development action on special grades . . . or immediate shipment of standard grades. Norplex has a complete range of over 75 standard grades of industrial laminates . . . plus glass and paper epoxy and paper phenolic copper clad grades . . . for all kinds of electrical, mechanical and chemical applications . . . manufactured to meet or exceed all NEMA and MIL-P specifications.

WRITE TODAY . . . for your copy of the complete Norplex Catalog . . . sheet sizes and specifications on the complete line of laminates from Norplex.

The Action Company In Laminated Plastics
NORPLEX CORPORATION, LA CROSSE 17, WISCONSIN
Formerly Northern Plastics Corporation

An example of what the author calls "the feline school" of advertising. What makes the technique dubious is that the reader is required to wait for the product benefits until the purpose of the illustration and headline is explained by the word, "pussyfooting." Many readers won't wait.

Intentions of the ad manager or agency copywriter who created this ad were undoubtedly of the best. But can it honestly be believed for one minute that readers, as busy as they are and with the number of advertising impressions rising constantly, will take the time to ferret out the process? And what process? Or that readers will exert the extra effort of wading through paragraphs of inanities to find out why they would have to be a Sherlock Holmes—and they may not want to be Sherlock at all—to discover how and where Smith Product is being used in such a manner that it presumably benefits somebody in another company?

Then there is the feline school of advertising, most of which is as hazy as pea-soup fog. Consider the ad with the illustration of a meowing cat, and the headline *IT CAN'T BE DONE!* Copy goes, *It can't be done! No, sir, it can't be done. You don't get labeled the action company by saying maybe, or we'll try, or perhaps, probably, or possibly. In other words, no pussyfooting.* And so on and on and on. But the pussyfooting *did* explain the illustration. See next page.

Another ambiguous feline ad has the headline, *What do cats and waterless sand with Activall* have in common?* This is explained by the subhead saying, *you're right, they both have nine lives!* This startling bit of intelligence leads to the body copy where we learn that: *Don't mess around. Some cats will put anything in a sand pile!* Readership stopped there, of course. And it never was made very clear what that Activall mentioned in the headline is, was it?

Beware the Off-Beat Ad

An abortive effort to be creative is a final hindrance which frequently makes clarity impossible. Some advertising people—on both advertiser and agency sides of the desk—are imbued with the idea that an ad has to be gimmicked up, it has to be off-beat, to succeed. They'll go to almost any lengths to keep from presenting the product story simply and logically, without pretense or phony frills. Little does it matter, apparently, that the resulting ad isn't read—or readable. This precociousness, this immaturity, this grandstand play to attract the attention of other advertising practitioners costs advertisers vast sums annually in ineffective ads and an incalculable amount in sales which never materialize for this reason. Although not as prevalent in industrial advertising as it is in the consumer field—remember the Renault campaign of a few years ago, in which dozens of typefaces appeared in one ad?—nonetheless perverted creativity rears its head all too often.

Another attempt to be creative, to be different at any cost — including readership—is the advertiser who had the headline of the ad set backwards. Note that it isn't set so that a fast trip to the washroom

What
do
cats
and
waterless
sand
with
Activall*
have
in
common
?

you're right, they both have nine lives!

Don't mess around. Some cats will put anything in a sand pile! But you don't have to add water or anything like it. Just Activall.* Works so well you can make nine consecutive castings without adding a doggone thing. Saves money, too. Up to 50% on sand costs. You can put the difference in the kitty. Write for details: P.O. Box 6504, Houston, Texas 77005. *Magcobar Activator for Waterless Bentonite-Sand Molding System.

where there's a mirror available will help. Nor will holding the page up to the light and reading through the paper, if that's possible. The type is actually set backwards so that it can be read if anybody is willing to spell out each word to himself, writing it down on a handy tablet until the complete three-line headline is transcribed. Headline says: *Can*

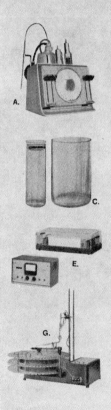

you imagine the time it would take for a researcher to get much-needed information from a textbook printed like this? Can you imagine the time it would take a reader to flip the page? It's unfortunate, too, because this catalog-type ad is unusually clean and airy for one which shows as many products as it does. It would have done the job, except for that headline.

Be Selective

This is in no sense a suggestion that the genuinely creative idea, the fresh approach, the new and compelling way to state a thought should be discarded. Rather, when writing an ad you should train yourself to be highly selective, to discard the ideas which lack merit because there are plenty more where they come from! Occasionally a gem of a idea is born, as in the case of the fine ad run by Simonds Abrasive Division of Wallace-Murray Corporation.

Some products are inherently easy to dramatize due to their end use or the place in which they are used—such as an item of equipment for pouring molten metal in a foundry, for example. Others, more prosaic, demand more of the writer if they are to be presented them in an aura of excitement so that readers of business publications will find the ad attractive and want to read it. The grinding wheels manufactured by Simonds Abrasive Division are an example of the latter type of product.

There are few ways to make a snagging wheel—one used for rough grinding operations to remove excessive material from foundry castings—have much visual appeal. They all look alike, and, quite likely, even users have few reasons to prefer Brand X over Brand Y.

The creative platform for Simonds wheels says, in part: "Take a relatively undramatic product—abrasives—and present it in a highly unusual and imaginative way. Each advertisement to be built around an idea so attention-getting and provacative that it will stand out from the mass of competitive ads—and from noncompetitive ads, for they also compete for readers' time. Regardless of what technique or method is used to get the readers' attention, it must be a functional one. It must be something inherent in our product or our message. Not merely a gimmick that has nothing to do with what we're trying to say, or trying to sell."

The ad pictured on page 242 is a stopper. The yellow and black sign is actually the headline, and the basic concept is so forceful, so vivid and compelling that it simply cannot be bypassed. How many signs state the speed limit as 142 miles per hour?

This speed, in miles per hour, is merely the surface feet per minute at which the wheel is rated expressed provocatively so that it stands out from all of the other ads in the book, as the advertiser's copy platform stated.

The sign headline is quickly explained by a subhead that reads: *AT 12,500 S.F.P.M. HERE'S WHAT YOU GET FROM SIMONDS SNAGGING WHEELS.* Body copy is terse, fact-filled and convincing. It starts out *Metal removal costs drop as much as 60%. Grinding*

AT 12,500 S.F.P.M. HERE'S WHAT YOU GET FROM SIMONDS SNAGGING WHEELS.

Metal removal costs drop as much as 60%. Grinding time drops as much as 30%. Wheel life goes up as much as 35%.

These are the kind of reports we get back from customers who give Simonds YA Borolon wheels with fiberglass reinforcing a trial. YA Borolon is a specially developed aluminum oxide abrasive with 40% zirconium oxide additive. It produces the results at high speed. The fiberglass reinforcing makes sure you can do it with safety.

Simonds reinforced High Speed snagging wheels are available for all types of 12,500 S.F.P.M. snagging grinders. Before you standardize . . . try Simonds. See what they can do for you. And see what Simonds Superior Service from a fast, local distributor can do for your grinding room efficiency.

Typical Simonds High Speed Wheel 30" x 2½" x 12" for 12,500 S.F.P.M. floor stand grinders.

SUPERIOR SERVICE THROUGH LOCAL DISTRIBUTORS — TECHNICAL KNOWHOW, FAST DELIVERY

West Coast Plant: El Monte, Calif.—Branches: Chicago • Detroit • Los Angeles • Philadelphia • Portland, Ore. • So. San Francisco. Shreveport—In Canada: Grinding Wheel Division, Simonds Canada Saw Co., Ltd., Brockville, Ontario • Abrasive Plant, Arvida, Quebec

time drops as much as 30%. Wheel life goes up as much as 35%. These aren't figures which Simonds tosses around lightly, for the ad goes on to explain that speed had been increased from 9,500 S.F.P.M. to 12,500 S.F.P.M., and the Simonds wheel could stand the gaff because it has fiber glass reinforcing, a specially developed aluminum oxide abrasive with 40% zirconium oxide additive. That's good writing—giving the user benefits, then building in believability by giving the nuts-and-bolts reasons why.

Simonds had a Starch study made of the ad as run originally with minor copy changes and it scored well. The ad as a whole achieved a 29 percent noted rating, seen-associated 21 percent, and various elements ranging from 29 percent on the sign to a low of 4 percent in the slogan copy across the bottom. A creditable performance due to a good basic idea, and to such clarity that the ad almost telegraphed its message.

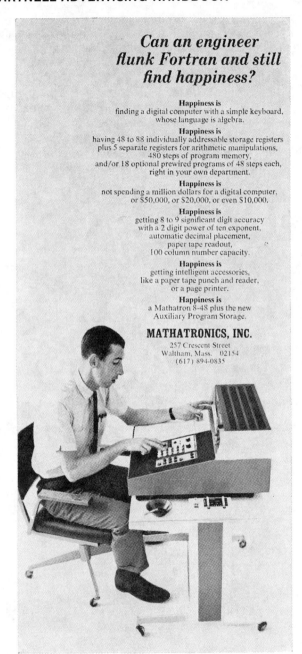

Chapter 6

THE COPY PLATFORM

T HE COPY platform contains all of the guidelines which the copywriter must have to write effective selling copy. It is concrete, specific, and formal because it is written. Because it is written, there are no vague generalities.

The written platform, or plan, contains among its ingredients all of the many things which it is mandatory to do—slants, approaches, directions. It contains an irreducible number of sacred cows near and dear to the heart of somebody up there in the corner office. A small herd must be included more often than not, if for no other reason than that it's desirable for everybody to hold his job. They can and should be accorded only a once over lightly when used, and as seldom as possible at that.

Also in the platform are clear and firm instructions *not* to discuss certain topics deemed detrimental to the company's competitive position or its image. These verboten topics are usually based on one of several things: A product weakness as compared to similar products in the marketplace, lack of distribution in certain geographic areas, a price disadvantage, unfavorable dealer discount structure, inability to produce the product as quickly as competitive companies can, and, usually, one whim. This last consideration can be considered to carry the most weight when it belongs to top management.

A carefully thought out and clearly written copy platform accomplishes a number of things, all of which are desirable. It makes your work easier. It saves time. It clarifies your thinking. It organizes your thoughts. It enables you to direct your agency more effectively. It is an invaluable reference for agency personnel assigned to your account. And, like a written marketing plan, it *forces* all who work within its framework to be precise. The written copy platform is the antithesis of the half-formed, poorly expressed thought, of the ill-conceived concept. As an instrument to upgrade copy quality, it is in a class by itself.

Furthermore, the written copy platform puts all concerned on record, for it is formal evidence of an agreement as to the purpose and scope of a campaign or an individual advertisement. Depending upon the company, those involved with it may include the advertising manager, the director of marketing, the sales manager, product managers, engineering management—and even the president. Naturally, agency personnel will be involved, including the account executive, account supervisor, group vice-president, copywriter, art director, media director, plans board, or other review group.

Producing a formal copy platform is not "made" work, however, nor is it a bureaucratic exercise merely for the sake of going through motions. With a platform everybody's job is easier. There is a drastic reduction in nonproductive effort. Wheel spinning is largely eliminated. That's because the game—and the rules by which it is to be played—are clearly defined for all to see and understand.

A desirable fringe benefit accrues, for getting entire campaigns (as well as individual ads), approved by the chain of command is greatly simplified.

Finally, and perhaps the most important benefit realized from the copy platform, you'll find development of a campaign is infinitely easier. A campaign, unlike a mishmash of separate ads done one at a time, haphazardly and with little overall planning, is a series of ads with a strong, unifying theme. A campaign is developed to achieve stated objectives. All of the ads in a well-conceived campaign are similar in appearance, of course. They share a basic concept as well as bear a strong family resemblance as far as layout and typography are concerned, and are immediately recognized as individual elements in a campaign.

What the Copy Platform Should Contain

The platform will obviously vary considerably due to differences in the product or service which is to be advertised. This variation shows up most strongly in the sections of the platform dealing with the product or service, while the balance of the platform is equally applicable for a manufacturer of bulldozers, babbitt, or bolts. All companies must accomplish the same basic objectives with their advertising if it is to make a significant contribution to the company's marketing success, for, product and market differences aside, all businesses have similar problems and similar competitive hurdles to overcome.

Essentials for the copy platform are:

1. Objectives of the campaign.

2. Objective for each individual ad.

3. Universe—a brief description of the market, the buyer influences with which the campaign and the individual ads must deal.

4. Media to be used.

5. Schedule—frequency of advertisement insertion in each medium.

6. Short statement of the company's position in the marketplace and its reputation.

7. Price range of product and comparison with prices of similar competitive products.

8. Channels of distribution, including the number of dealers and/or distributors, their strengths and weaknesses, and how cooperative they are.

9. When the product is purchased, seasonal patterns, and historical patterns.

10. How the product is purchased and increments in which it is marked—gallons, pounds, bales, individual units, and so on.

11. Why the product is purchased.

12. What action the ads are expected to produce.

13. Central idea or theme of the campaign.

14. Slant, or approach, to be taken; this could be problem-and-solution, question-and-answer, case history, testimonial, editorial, narrative, etc.

15. Format; this could range from four-color, multipage inserts down to fractional-page black and white ads, with illustrative techniques described.

16. Product features in order of importance, and features *not* to mention.

17. User benefits which result from the features.

The copy platform is not a duplication of the marketing plan, nor is it a lengthy, verbose document which will repel so rapidly that it's filed away and forgotten fast. It performs a necessary job. Let's see why these 17 elements are essential in a solid, complete copy platform.

Objective

A campaign—and an individual ad—must have an objective to accomplish before it has a prayer of a chance of returning one cent of its cost to the advertiser.

Copy is a component of the complete advertisement, just as a caption and the illustration are. However, copy has a different job to perform. Captions and illustrations have as their function the attracting of the reader's attention, of arousing interest, of stopping and drawing him or her into the copy. From then on, the copy carries the complete burden of persuading the prospect to accept the advertiser's viewpoint.

There are many reasons—actually objectives—for which copy is written, but this primary one should be remembered: *It is the primary function of copy to persuade the prospect to accept the advertiser's viewpoint.*

Other functions can be to introduce a new product or a significant improvement in an existing product. Only advertising can spread the word across the nation, or around the world, about a new development quickly and economically to a universe which may encompass hundreds of thousands, even millions, of prospective purchasers. Copy in an advertisement is able to make these prospects aware of the new product and make them understand its significance in terms of what it means to them. Copy can create an awareness of product features and user benefits and how the product should be used to produce these benefits.

If copy is well written, interesting, and informative, it can produce tangible results measured by response from readers of the publications in which the ad appears. Copy can cause people to react as you want them to, people far away with diverse interests and backgrounds.

Different products are introduced successfully into different markets by advertisers with varying objectives; one advertiser, for instance, may want response in terms of inquiries which will be followed up by either the dealer organization or field sales force. Another may desire only to increase awareness of the company, trademark, product, or a radically different process.

When the economy as a whole is volatile and there is an inexorable trend to government-induced inflation, advertising copy can do much to remove the curse from an across-the-board price increase. This is particularly important in a basic raw material, and is an objective of the steel industry, among others. Such nonproduct, nonselling copy in an ad is actually a public relations effort, despite its being in a paid message form.

And, in time of war, even a "limited" one, many products critical to the defense effort are in extremely short supply for the general business community. In these circumstances advertising can do much to help retain the goodwill of industrial buyers, irked at not being able to place an order and get normal delivery, by telling them—reminding, actually—why.

Copy can do a tremendous job of building awareness of a new or expanded warranty policy. When capital equipment is involved, this is an unusually potent sales point and one which, although something of an intangible, is of great importance to the purchaser. Advertising copy did a great job for Dodge trucks in explaining the industry's first long-term warranty on the vehicle's power train, and what this meant to the truck user.

These are a few valid objectives for a campaign or for an individual advertisement. You undoubtedly have others equally good.

When writing an ad, or giving directions to your agency, you'll find it good practice to write down the objective for this specific ad. It's remarkably helpful to write down what you want the ad to accomplish for your company and what you want the prospects to do after having read it. You'll have to bear in mind, of course, that pie in the sky is unattainable, and that no ad can produce for you the world with a white picket fence around it. Be realistic so that the ad can attain it. This means that your ad cannot be all things to all readers, or even hope to be.

Be specific, stick to a strong central idea and exploit it for all it's worth. You can include a wrap-up, or summary, of additional product features and benefits, of course, but to do so at the expense of weakening the core idea is to welcome failure with open arms. Multiple ideas always result in dilution of copy effectiveness. Magazine editors, hard-nosed and real experts at evaluating copy, have long stressed the fact that a magazine article must be built around one central idea. *One central idea.* They know it is impossible to develop fully two ideas in a single article, even one of 7,500 to 10,000 words. And it's simply beyond the realm of reason to expect to be able to do so in an industrial advertisement considering how few words you're permitted.

Universe

You'll want to include a short statement in the platform about who you want to read your ad. It's an important element of the platform. A condensed personality profile of the individuals to whom the ad should be slanted is desirable. This profile should include titles or job functions of the buying influences, their educational level, whether they specify or recommend specific brands of products and /or specific purveyors, whether they approve purchases, if theirs is the ultimate decision, and the stage in the purchasing process in which they enter the picture. This, of course, will be from Stage 1 through Stage 7, as previously discussed.

Include also a short statement as to the type of company to whom you're most likely to sell. This will probably mean one of a specific size in terms of number of employees and gross dollar volume.

The profile is simplified if it is charted as shown below. This pyramid chart was originally developed by Bramson Publishing Company and is used with their permission. It can be used for any number of products in any number of markets where buying influences might vary; simply check off the appropriate group and include this as an appendix in the copy platform.

Position of your key buying influences in the pyramid obviously will affect the way the ad is written. A glaring error which will nullify your ad completely is to write an ad slanted toward foremen and supervisors in the same language as one directed toward the president—and vice versa. The two groups won't both read one ad because the appeals would be wrong. User benefits would be different because you'd talk profit to the president and easier production or a similar benefit to first line management. Difference in the level of sophistication also is too great for there to be much reader involvement regardless of the difference in the factors which motivate different levels of managers.

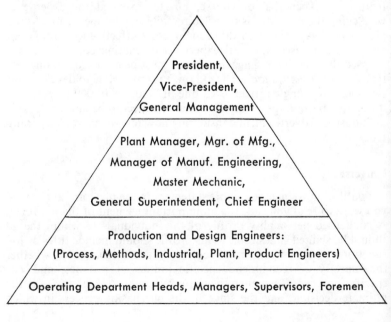

President,
Vice-President,
General Management

Plant Manager, Mgr. of Mfg.,
Manager of Manuf. Engineering,
Master Mechanic,
General Superintendent, Chief Engineer

Production and Design Engineers:
(Process, Methods, Industrial, Plant, Product Engineers)

Operating Department Heads, Managers, Supervisors, Foremen

Media

Media in which the ad will appear should also be in the copy platform. Certain publications almost demand a certain slant due to their audience composition. Although it's not always the case, different media usually call for different ads if each is to achieve its greatest potential readership.

Schedule

The schedule—the frequency with which the ad will appear (if it is to run only one time in a publication or is to be repeated in selected media)—and the months of the year in which it runs are important to the copywriter. A short statement with the schedule in tabular form is a good planning tool for the ad manager.

Company Position in the Market

There is no need to go into a lengthy discussion here, but this is a subject which could influence the writing of the ad. It is simple enough to extract a short paragraph from the marketing plan, or condense a section into a few short sentences for the copy platform. Competitive position influences copy approach, and this information should be at the copywriter's fingertips without having to search through a lengthy dissertation to determine just what it is.

Price

Price of the product being advertised, particularly in comparison to similar products produced by others, is necessary information when an ad is being written. This holds true even if price is not given in the ad. If the price varies considerably depending upon the number of optional features the customer selects, a price *range* should be given and compared to a price *range* of competitive products.

It may well be that your product is priced substantially higher than your competition. If so, there's bound to be a reason which justifies this position and this reason can frequently be turned into an advantage, instead of a disadvantage, in an advertising campaign. Industrial buyers are not gullible; they recognize that getting exactly what you pay for is a fact of business life. They don't expect something for nothing. When giving this information include the dealer or distributor discount structure.

Prices, incidentally, are not company secrets, nor are dealer/distributor discounts. This information is widely circulated and rare indeed is the heads-up manufacturer of relatively expensive equipment who doesn't have a complete catalog and price book of the major competitors' lines. They're easily gotten from friendly dealers, "acquired" at trade shows, or are a fringe benefit which somehow happens to coincide with hiring a salesperson or executive from a competitive company.

Distribution

Channels of distribution must be given in the copy platform because they, too, can influence the slant of an ad. From the price section of the platform the person writing the ad can quickly tell if there are advantages in the price or in the discount structure to exploit—since this information is given with comparisons to competitive products.

Discuss the distributive process in a sentence or two, give the size of the field sales force compared to that of competitors. Point out any major geographic strengths or weaknesses.

When Purchases Occur

Most industrial products are purchased all year around. With some, however, there is a strong seasonal pattern. An example is Freon gas sold by Du Pont to automobile manufacturers for use in automotive air conditioners. Auto builders' purchasing departments place blanket orders well in advance of anticipated use, then schedule shipments against the original order. This means that Freon is sold not in the hot summer months, or even in the late spring, but when winter is waning. Construction materials, including structural steel, are traditionally sold around the first of the year for delivery in late March, although the building season varies in different areas of the country.

If there is an historical pattern—such as machine tool orders being preceded by a rise in carloadings—or some other reliable barometer, this information belongs in the copy platform. Every iota of information which helps the person behind the typewriter contributes toward more effective advertising.

How Purchases Are Made

State how the product is purchased, what unit of measure applies, such as gallons, tons, yards, pounds, kegs, or similar units. Give the size of the average sale. Also give the largest and smallest sales over the last 12 months, and the smallest profitable sale. A brief table giving a statistical analysis of the previous year's sales in percentages according to the number of units sold per individual sale is helpful.

Why Purchases Are Made

This is the time to draw upon the sales manager's knowledge of the product and reasons why prospects' decisions are made the way they are—if you feel even slightly unsure of your ground in this area. And even if you *are* sure, a discussion may turn up reasons why your product is purchased that you've never thought of. Communication between various departments and advertising is almost never what it should be. Others do not realize what can help the advertising manager can help them.

Purchases are made for objective reasons, carefully and logically reasoned out by the industrial buyer. The most important are:

1. *Quality.*
2. *Delivery schedule.*
3. *Price.*

That is probably their order of importance too, although this can vary according to the state of the economy and product availability. In times of scarcity of your product, price would definitely come last. On the other hand, in a recession with its buyers' market, price would move up into second place—but never into first.

Those are the basic reasons for specifying one make over another, or one purveyor over another, that the buyer *thinks* he is basing his decision on. There may be hidden reasons why he makes the decisions he does, however. These may not even be recognized by the buyer. And even if they are, he or she may not admit them. These are decisions made subjectively, emotionally, despite the industrial buyer's lack of personal involvement with the product because he or she does not consume or use it.

One study in motivation research in industrial buying showed that fear was a factor in a surprisingly high percentage of industrial purchases. This included fear of switching from a familiar supplier with whom the buyer has dealt for some time; fear of changing from a product which is known from past experience will perform satisfactorily—even if there is reason to believe the alternate product may be superior—and, underlying all others, fear of making a wrong decision and thus incurring the disapproval of superiors.

If your product is not very well known, if your company is relatively small and you're bucking giants in the marketplace, your advertising must reassure buyers that when they select your product they're making a wise decision.

Another emotional factor influencing purchases is pride, which is acutally the desire to attain personal prestige. This is evidenced by a decision to buy from the largest and best-known source in the industry because that is obviously what the majority of other buyers do. There's safety in numbers.

Ambition motivates many who influence industrial purchases. The desire for self-aggrandizement, to advance within the company, to achieve more than others do, is a potent factor in the makeup of many individuals—most, in fact. It frequently leads to the "safe" decision to avoid mistakes, or the selection of the "best" supplier.

The basic instinct for self-preservation plays a strong role, too, and is similar to the desire for self-aggrandizement; the emotional considerations are almost identical. In both cases it is up to the advertiser to satisfy the emotional yearnings of such individuals, to reassure them that when they buy your product they are acting in their—and their company's—self-interest.

Response

Every industrial ad should close with a request for action, just as every good salesperson always asks for the order. Not to do so is a wasted sales call—either in print or in person.

The bid for action should be carefully thought out and a decision made as to what response you want from the reader of your ad. You may, for instance, want a quantity of bingo-card inquiries. If such is the case, have the publication print on the bottom of your ad, *Circle No. 000 on the Reader Service Card for more information.* Then, when the cards with the key number assigned to you are returned to the publication, or to the book's inquiry-handling service, you will be notified of the names, companies, and addresses of each inquirer who is interested in your product. This generally produces a sizable volume of inquiries if your selling proposition, the message, and the media are right.

Or, you may want to make an offer—free literature, a pocket calculator of the slide-rule type, a wall chart converting fractions of an inch to decimal equivalents, an actual sample of your product (offers are discussed more fully later on), or a proposal to go into a prospect's plant and analyze the equipment requirements or production processes—at no cost, of course. Each of these offers can be counted on to produce a volume of inquiries.

On the other hand, your ad may deliberately be very hard hitting and competitive. It may be written so that it directs the prospect to consider both your product and similar ones produced by other companies—and to compare them in detail. Hopefully, this will be to the detriment of the competition. It will be if the ad is well written and the facts are marshalled correctly.

In any event, the individual ads can be tailored to produce the response that you decide upon. What that will be depends upon your coverage in the field by your sales force, your distribution, availability of your product, production backlog, and many other factors.

Theme

A campaign isn't a campaign without a theme. It can't be. A theme is an absolute essential. It is the theme which transforms a random assortment of individual ads into a cohesive, unified whole, making a neat, logical package.

The theme, however, is *not* the subject of either the campaign or of any individual ad except in rare instances where an advertiser feels the theme needs explaining. And, if it needs explaining the theme is somewhat less than appropriate.

The subject is the product or service which is being advertised, made more desirable by the theme's presenting its user benefits from the viewpoint of the prospect.

A few of the better known campaign themes used by industrial companies follow. Although not all themes are stated, they all refine the selling message and condense it to a few compelling words that are easy to understand and easy to remember. The one central thought each presents runs through all of the ads in the campaign. This thought is repeated time and time again, exerting a progressively stronger effect upon the reader with each repetition.

Almost all currently successful advertising campaigns are built around a strong central idea or theme. The theme is usually repeated in advertising directed toward consumers, either print or broadcast, if the company markets products directly to consumers. Many industrial companies advertise to both—General Electric, for instance. It appears in sales literature, the theme follows through in sales presentations and audio-visual presentations. It unifies the entire promotional effort.

The most trusted name in electronics
   Radio Corporation of America
You expect more from Standard and you get it!
   Standard Oil Division, American Oil Company
You can be sure if it's Westinghouse
   Westinghouse Electric Company
Hertz rents Fords and other good cars
   Hertz Corporation
The airline built for professional travelers
   American Airlines

Leader in adhesive technology
H. B. Fuller Company

It pays to do business with the airfreight specialist—
Tiger International

Wherever you look. . .you see Budd
The Budd Company

Machines that make data move
Teletype Corporation

You'll find our brand all over the West
CF&I Steel Corporation

The big birds fly the friendly skies of United Air Lines
United Air Freight

The discovery company
Union Carbide

Standard of the plotting industry
California Computer Products, Inc.

The better ideas are at UOP
Universal Oil Products Company

Tested. . .trusted products since 1868
Eaton Yale & Towne, Inc.

Have you looked at Wheeling lately?
Wheeling Steel Corporation

Progress is our most important product
General Electric Company

Look ahead—look south
Southern Railway System

Going in new directions with new ideas
Boise Cascade Corporation

Serving man's basic needs worldwide
Worthington Corporation

Where the big idea is innovation
United States Steel

Ford has a better idea
Ford Motor Company

We don't stop with paper
Crown Zellerbach

You can take the pulse of progress at
Republic Steel Corporation

Gulf makes things run better!
Gulf Oil Corporation

For companies going places!
Mack Trucks, Inc.

Preferred performance
Sealed Power Corporation

Themes are deceptively simple. They look easy to create. Most, however, came into being only after company marketing people and their agency counterparts racked their brains for countless hours. It's not uncommon for hundreds, even thousands, of ideas to be suggested, carefully written down, and sifted through in the final selection process. Sometimes data is fed into a computer in hopes the output of its semiconductors, integrated circuits, and other electronic hardware will result in the birth of a revolutionary new product name, which, in turn, will lead to development of a theme to end all themes.

Sometimes, though, you can't plan these things. They're like Topsy —they just grow, or just evolve. Once in a while inspiration strikes like a bolt out of the blue and a new theme pops full-blown into someone's mind—probably while he's shaving or reading the paper on the 5:15. And the chances are that this theme will be just exactly right, that it's one that neither people nor computers can top.

How to Bag a Theme

Actually, though, it is not necessary to wait for inspiration to strike. Inspiration can't be scheduled. A suitable theme can be stalked and bagged if you know where to hunt for it. The most logical place to start is with the product itself.

Ask yourself, what makes this product different? What makes it better? What sets it apart from similar products? Why is it more desirable from the prospect's viewpoint? What will it do for him or her that competitive products won't, or can't, do? What is the one best reason you can think of to buy it?

List your questions on a legal-sized tablet. Rule it off, include as headings your product and similar ones produced by major competitors. Ignore cats and dogs such as regional manufacturers if you have national distribution unless they are unusually tough competition in the area they have staked out. Answer these questions, plus others that will occur to you, for each competitive product—by model number, perhaps—and briefly write down the answer on the pad. Be objective, be honest. This is no time to let emotion and loyalty to good old Ajax Company influence you.

If nothing revealing results, go a step further. Chances are you either have, or have access to, detailed analyses of competitive products. Every company has them—or should. They're lovingly compiled and tabulated by a statistician in the market research or sales department, generally carried out to the fourth decimal place, and then distributed to key individuals inside and the entire field sales force. Emphasis is usually placed on specifications of the products; in the case of mechanical equipment, for example, sizes of various components, capacities, horsepower, and similar methods of comparison are used. Examine these carefully, compare them with your own product. You'll find a number of areas in which yours is definitely superior.

Let's take a hypothetical road grader for the sake of illustration. Now, the fact is that one road grader is very much like another. Rated capacities, power output, size of hydraulic equipment, blade size, cab comfort and what have you are remarkably uniform. Industry doesn't build too many Edsels—of the kind that fly or the kind you drive—and stay in business. Competition serves to assure a remarkably uniform level of high quality.

Our road grader, however, may excel slightly—but only slightly—in several areas. It may, for instance, have an engine with somewhat larger piston displacement; its blade may be an inch or so wider, or deeper; the cab may have a little more elbow room for the driver, or a bit better visibility. Any or all of these product features can be translated into user benefits of real significance to prospective purchasers.

The Rating Game

So, how do we develop a theme? Perhaps by rating, or grading, all competitive road graders. Stress the areas of your grader's superiority. Hammer home the fact that you graded the grader, that you made a thoroughly objective comparison. This can also infer that manufacturers of competitive graders were afraid to do this. Handled properly, you can come up with a catchy, memorable theme that has real impact. Although none of these is such a theme, they do give the general idea of the thought process involved in theme development. *The Grade A Grader. The grader that earned an A grade. The top-graded grader.* Some similar theme can lead to quite a campaign in which the theme—that this grader was graded on features, on performance, on long life, on freedom from maintenance, on high-residual value at trade-in time, and so on—is natural and believable. The old ploy of comparing, in the ad, grader A, B, and C with yours could be employed. Or you could be bitterly competitive and actually name the other graders and give their scores; when writing an ad like this, be absolutely certain that you have your facts right.

In this case, the theme resulted from product superiorities that came to light when the detailed specifications of the hypothetical grader were compared to those of competitive machines. A different tack could have been taken by comparing performance of this grader with others. When products are this expensive, it is common practice for manufacturers of such equipment to go into the marketplace and buy a number of competitive units. These are then tested in the company's proving grounds under typical operating conditions, then returned to the manufacturer's research department for disassembly and a thorough study of how they are built. This gives the sales and marketing departments a wealth of competitive information that's almost impossible to come by in any other way. Reassembled, the equipment brings a good price—almost as much as the manufacturer paid, as a rule—on the used equipment market because it has had so little use.

Such tests quickly point up a difference in performance of your product and those of your competitors. More miles per gallon, more work per hour, bigger loads, faster cycle time, or some other vitally important user benefit usually results. The advertising manager should always be on the list of those receiving reports on such tests.

Where it's not feasible to purchase, test, and disassemble competitive products, a thorough analysis of competitive literature acquired by or through sympathetic dealers or distributors can show where you have a competitive edge. Literature on industrial products is replete with performance data—what the product will do for the purchaser. Compare these statistics with those for your product and you'll probably discover several areas where you have a decided advantage, either in performance or in versatility. This latter can be presented as giving the purchaser more for the money, since if equipment doubles in brass and handles two jobs, there might well be no need to invest in supplementary equipment which might be idle a good part of the time.

Availability As a Benefit

Availability plays a critically important role in the sales picture of many industrial products. In automotive replacement parts, for example, mere availability to the purchaser is credited by many leading companies with exerting a decisive role in a high percentage of purchases. With adequate or better distribution, a manufacturer has a potent sales point—and all the more so if this broad distribution goes hand in hand with better service. International Harvester Company ran a trade campaign for IHC motor trucks some time ago in which some of the ads ended, *Branches and dealers everywhere.* There is simply nothing to be said on the subject which can begin to equal this statement—much less top it. The other builders of heavy-duty trucks must have been envious. Harvester had the final word.

Company capability can result in an effective advertising theme. If the company is the recognized leader in its industry, with a product line bigger and broader than that of its competitors, this can lead to a theme of total capability. This was used with excellent results by Lindberg Hevi-Duty for some time in all of its promotions to five major markets ranging from the semiconductor industry to the foundry field.

Or you could make your product stand out and develop a catchy theme if you do more merchandising to a dealer or distributor group than any of your competitors, thus helping them sell your product to a manufacturer who incorporates it into the end product. This is particularly effective if you market a product which competes vigorously for a market composed of such manufacturers—acetates and other fibers used in clothing, chemicals, building materials, and so forth. Many companies run campaigns which are almost institutional, or corporate, in character, yet their primary objective is to stimulate demand by the end manufacturer for their component or their raw material.

No product is so pallid or so deficient in believable superiorities that a memorable advertising theme cannot be developed if all factors are considered. The greatest theme ever developed may not come to you immediately, and you shouldn't expect it. But, with work, a good one will emerge.

Many companies have themes because they are recognized as vitally necessary for continuity and cohesiveness, but they are not actually used in print. Even if one doesn't appear in every industrial ad you notice, you can accept as fact that the campaign has an umbrella theme—if the campaign is a good one.

18 Basic Themes

In its Laboratory of Advertising Performance, McGraw-Hill published data on basic copy themes. To find out what themes were being used most effectively by industrial advertisers, the publishing company made an analysis of the highest ranking ads in 21 different McGraw-Hill publications. Results are:

1. *Corporate:* Including promotion of logotype or trademark, primarily to enhance the company's reputation and aid in its recognition.

2. *Public or Industry Service:* This type of message is essentially

noncommercial in nature and is designed to give the reader information which would help him or her.

3. *Announcement:* This large category includes introduction of new products, services, product features or user benefits.

4. *General Description:* This narrative-style of advertising usually makes a relatively broad statement about the quality of the product.

5. *Unique Product Features:* Unique is the key word here, because this type of ad discusses exclusive features of a product or product line.

6. *Product Line:* A catalog-type ad showing the number of different items produced by the manufacturer.

7. *Catalog:* Similar to the above type of advertisement, but more detailed so as to include sizes, dimensions, materials, specifications, and so on.

8. *Testimonial:* A case-history ad in which a user's good experience with the product is described, usually in his own words.

9. *Specific Problem Solved:* How a product solved a specific problem, usually with emphasis on the company's overall problem-solving ability.

10. *Product Performance Facts:* Features and user benefits of the product.

11. *Suggested Product Application:* Ways in which the product may be used are discussed and illustrated.

12. *Product Test Results:* A graphic representation of the results of using the product.

13. *Safety:* How the product, when used as directed, reduces or eliminates hazards to factory personnel, or to the public as a whole.

14. *Modernization:* How the product prevents obsolescence; keeps an operation competitive with modern equipment.

15. *Savings, Economy, or Profits:* The pocketbook appeal. Ads stress how the product eliminates unnecessary labor or superfluous operations, reduces maintenance costs, amortizes itself quickly.

16. *Teaser:* A campaign that whets the reader's appetite by arousing his curiosity.

17. *Tie-in:* Relating the product or service to a current event to secure higher readership.

18. *Reader Action:* A campaign designed specifically to produce a desired reaction on the part of the reader. This could be returning a coupon, sending for literature, telephoning for a price quotation, asking for a salesperson to call, or a similar response.

Slant

How a campaign is slanted, or how it is aimed, will be determined by the product itself, the audience for the campaign, the type of buying influences who must be communicated with and a number of other factors. Some are inherent in the marketplace.

The slant, or approach, should be stated in the copy platform after careful consideration of campaign identity and advertiser identification. You won't want to slant one ad one way, then switch to an entirely different slant in subsequent ads. To do so sacrifices campaign identity and dilutes identification of your company as the sponsor of the ads.

The decision isn't always an easy one to make—and sometimes, unless the right decision seems very obvious—it's best not to make it immediately. Instead, write some ads and make rough layouts (copywriter's roughs) using different slants. Once something is down on paper, you can then evaluate its effectiveness much more easily. This isn't wasted effort, for it will save time later on.

Most common approach for all business publication ad copy is straight narrative style. This is simply telling your story in a straightforward manner, presenting your facts one after the other as attractively as possible. It is, perhaps, easiest to write and is equally appropriate for new product announcement ads as it is for products which have been on the market for some time. General description, product features, problem-solving ads and many others fall readily into this category. Unless another approach is strongly indicated, the narrative style is probably the best.

There's also the popular problem-and-solution slant which results in excellent reader involvement because *everybody* has problems, and those in industry tend to fall into well-defined patterns. This type of ad usually enjoys high readership, assuming the problem is a universal one.

Another way to involve the reader is to use the time-proved question-and-answer approach. Similar to the problem-and-solution type of ad, it assures good reader involvement and good readership—if the question(s) is well chosen. Incidentally, the correct form *is* problem, solution—question, answer. It is *not* problem, answer—question, solution. This mistake crops up constantly, even in ads by huge, sophisticated companies. It's extremely bad form.

Case-history ads have been around since the dawn of advertising itself, but they continue to be persuasive and believable—perhaps even more today than in the past. When a firm runs a case-history ad the reader can accept as gospel the statements made about the product. It's common practice—and good practice—to give the name of the firm using the products, the location of that company, and usually the name of the individual involved with the product. He or she will be the person either specifying it or using it, probably the latter. In a surprising number of cases, the reader does what the ad makes easy for him—that person picks up the phone and verifies the statements made in the ad. This is done not because he or she doesn't believe the advertiser's statements, but because he wants the reassurance of somebody who is presently using the product successfully. Since no advertiser would feature anything other than a highly satisfied user of its products, it becomes obvious why generations of ad managers hold the case-history ad in such high esteem.

Testimonial ads are similar to case-history ads, although usually based on either a well-known individual who is making the statement, or on a giant company whose name is a byword. Famous names add authenticity to an advertiser's claims.

An editorial approach is frequently taken, sometimes with the advertisement looking much like editorial material in the medium in which it appears. It's a mistake to make it resemble editorial matter too much, for the reader might get the impression you're trying to deceive him. The editorial ad usually runs to long copy which, in the case of a complex product, is desirable because it gives ample room to explain various features and specifications. Either in spite of the long copy, or because of it, the editorial-type ad invariably rates high in readership.

The newsletter is another highly effective approach—*if* it honestly contains newsworthy material of genuine interest to the reader. If it doesn't, he or she will turn the page so fast that even the name of the advertiser may fail to make an impression. An ad of this type is no place for a collection of rehashed publicity releases. The newsletter format, well done, can do a highly effective job for the advertiser over a lengthy period of time. The famous Rockwell Report has proved this over a number of years. This campaign has consistently rated near the top of the book in the publications in which it appears, and has done so ever since it was launched.

Format

Include a brief discussion of the format for the ads in the copy platform, along with a short statement giving the rationale for the selection. For example, the format might be four-color inserts, perhaps multipage; two-color spreads; black and white spreads; black and white pages; or fractional pages. Also note here the illustrative technique which you've decided to use, and say why. Before making a final decision, review once more photography, line drawings, illustrative art, cartoons, and so on.

Product Features

A listing of product features in the copy platform is desirable—unless it results in a document longer than the Oxford Unabridged Dictionary. If such is the case, or if it even comes close, you'll want to consider including only the exclusive features of your product, those which the competition lacks.

Be sure to include a separate short paragraph listing the features which are *not* to be discussed.

User Benefits

Benefits of the features are the real meat of the copy platform. Discuss them factually and fully, but briefly. Think as the prospect thinks, look at the product as he would. Don't attempt to write ads here, but do be constructive and promotional in tone. Explain what your product does for the user, exactly how it saves money, increases production, reduces maintenance, results in better quality of the end product, eliminates an entire operation, makes possible lower tooling cost, makes the plant secure against fire or theft, or what have you.

Relate user benefits to features, stress those which are unique to your product and nobody else's. Give the copywriter some real meat that he or she can get his teeth into so that a campaign can be created with the broadest possible appeal—yet one which zeroes in on target.

This section is the one most important part of the copy platform, so think through carefully all of the user benefits that you, sales, marketing, and engineering can come up with. List them in descending order of importance. Don't feel that just because the product has been on the market for some time that everybody knows all about the benefits to be derived from using it. Everybody in your company is familiar with all of them, but those in your universe—all of the countless prospects out there—certainly aren't.

How to Compile Source

"Source," in the lexicon of the advertising manager, is the vast mass of reference material about the product, its production, its price, its distribution and selling that must be on hand before any writing can be done.

Seemingly, there's no end to the amount of source the ad manager, or the agency copywriter, finds he or she needs before it is possible to sit down and produce the first word of an ad, a piece of sales literature, a film, or any other promotional material. Experience proves this true. It is very easy to have too little.

Having insufficient source for ready reference invariably results in padded copy, in puffery replacing hard facts—facts that are highly pertinent from the prospect's point of view. From the advertiser's point of view, it means an ad that is almost certain to fail to do its assigned job.

First thing to do after you've firmed up your copy platform is to plan how you'll line up your source material. Compiling enough applicable information about the product appears to some advertising managers to be a formidable task. It needn't be, however.

You know from your copy platform the type of information that's needed. You know the things you are obliged to include, as well as those which can't be mentioned. The project of compiling source is simplified if you look at it this way:

The logical place to start is with the product. It's something you know—or should know—inside out; it's something you've already analyzed when you were preparing the copy platform. Quite frequently the product itself will suggest a course of action in developing individual ads, or, for that matter, an entire campaign. Most products, especially in the capital equipment field, are rich repositories of ideas for individual advertisements. Exploit this opportunity that is available only to you.

Take a tablet, legal size is best, and rule in three heavy vertical lines with a "squeakie"—a felt marking pen. Head one column "Features," the second, "User benefits," and the third, "Ideas." The ideas, of course, are possible approaches for ads. You'll be surprised how fast they flow.

The Creative Process

List all of the ideas that come readily to mind, even those that seem too offbeat to be used. None should be discarded out of hand. The creative process is unique in all the world, unique with each individual. There's no telling what inapplicable idea can trigger one that is a real gem.

Chances are you'll immediately come up with a number of ideas. Don't force the process. Nobody has an inexhaustible supply of brilliant thoughts—at least, not at any one time. When the flow of ideas dries up, accept it. But leave room on the tablet for additional thoughts which will come to you at unexpected times.

Now that you're organized and this far along, have a shirt-sleeve discussion with the sales manager. Ideally, that person should be your equal on the organizational chart and you should establish rapport with him or her. Also talk with the engineering manager, the one in charge of manufacturing or production, and, perhaps, the top research and development person.

Conserve your time and theirs by drawing up a list of questions to which you need answers. Do it before scheduling the meetings. The list won't be complete by any means, but it can serve to channel the conversation in the direction you want it to take. During the discussions your questions will suggest others to you and to the technical people. Questions stimulate thoughts that may be completely different from any that had occurred to you beforehand, but one of them may be the spark that ignites your thought processes and leads to a new approach as fresh as a bright blue morning after a long wet week.

Explain your problem to these specialists, show them how they fit into the picture. Be frank and open, confide in them. Tell them you need their help, that they are the people who can supply information vital to you so that you, in turn, can help advance the company's entire marketing program. By doing so, you give them a sense of participation and it is one they will derive pleasure from because they will be active in an area which they considered outside their province.

Remember, it is human nature to want to help others if asked properly. And it is a universal truth that people with specialized knowledge take pride in using it, in showing somebody how much they know. They are flattered at having the opportunity and, even if they don't show it, gratified at being able to expound on their favorite subject. Like all the rest of us, they want to be appreciated and want to show others how much they can contribute to the company—particularly outside their primary job function. Your coming to them shows that you recognize their ability.

It is likely that these department heads will delegate some of the more routine portions of these source-gathering sessions to certain key individuals on their staffs—marketing managers, product managers, or engineers, for example—who are close to day-to-day problems.

How to Deal With Technicians

A word of caution here. Be diplomatic when talking with these technical people. *Don't* be condescending. In most instances you'll find technical people are as different from advertising people as day is from night. Their basic thinking process is completely unlike yours. The way they approach a problem, the way they regard the product is foreign to the copywriter. Possibly you'll be better off if you draw them out, let them talk about the product in their own language, and at their own pace. This is slower than you think, for these technical people are deliberate and phlegmatic. An advertising individual characteristically mentally sorts and discards the relatively irrelevant and concentrates on and retains certain key points, unconsciously, perhaps. But the technical people, certainly those with an engineering background, don't. To them each and every little product feature is a rare jewel to be dwelled upon to the point of belaboring it to death. They are constitutionally unable to skim lightly over minor matters and concentrate on the truly significant. All you can do in such instances is to be courteous, listen, and remember that technical minds work in weird and wondrous ways. And there's always the chance that the engineer to whom you're talking may have conceived the original idea for many of the features that are being discussed.

Despite what you may consider—and rightly so—verbosity, rambling, and inability to differentiate between the important and the inconsequential, act interested—*be* interested—in what he or she is saying. Never by word nor attitude let slip the fact that you feel, as most advertising people do, that these technical people are a breed apart, that they inhabit their own special little dream world where they're out of touch with what happens outside the confines of their laboratories, drafting departments, or blueprint rooms. There'll be times, many of them, when you'll be sorely tempted to end a long-winded, repetitive monolog with a pointed question. Resist it.

Try to talk in his or her language, not yours. Ask questions about competitive products. Compare them to yours, feature by feature. Although advertising and marketing personnel are in a much better position to evaluate products in terms of their potential and competitive strength in the marketplace, engineers are usually better qualified to do so as regards quality, significant features, overall design, and construction. The fact that their viewpoint is vastly different from yours, and possibly more objective and less emotional, enables them to broaden your outlook and make it possible for you to examine the product from another vantage point.

All the while you're talking with the technical people continue to use your ruled pad of features-benefits-ideas, in addition to taking notes of the gist of the conversations. A small tape recorder, or a portable dictating machine, is invaluable. It frees you from the burden of trying to imitate a court reporter, as well as from having to attempt to decipher your scrawl afterwards. Use a machine now on hand, or get approval to buy one for the advertising department. You'll use it in your own plant, and if it's one of the truly portable ones, it will more than pay for itself when you take it into the field where your product is in use.

When you've established a good working relationship with the technical people, you'll have valuable allies. In addition to supplying you with the source you need, they can prevent embarrassing—and costly—errors from creeping into your copy. Give them the opportunity to review it for technical accuracy before releasing an advertisement for insertion in a publication.

Everyone's an Expert

One thing to bear in mind, however, is that everybody considers himself an advertising expert. Advertising is so simple and easy and deals with such commonplace things as the product and pictures and words that everybody automatically becomes qualified to be a copywriter. And everybody is a copy chief, capable of editing and rewriting your copy—even if they can't write a literate, simple, declarative sentence without becoming entangled with semantic grotesqueries to the point of absurdity. Also, everybody is an art director and a media director.

Resist letting technical people make changes in copy unless there is a technical error. Refuse, in fact, but do so as tactfully as possible. You need these technical experts, so be sure to motivate them to *want* to help you by your being properly appreciative for their contributions. We'll get into how to get ad approvals later on, in greater detail.

Make it standard operating procedure to build goodwill for the advertising department by thanking the technical people for their assistance. Lay it on a bit thick, tell them that without their help the ad, or the sales literature, or whatever is involved couldn't have come to fruition without them. And, to build a checking account upon which you can draw in the future, write a memo of thanks with a carbon to the man's superior.

Ultimately there will come a time when you've just about exhausted the amount of source which can be compiled inside the company—except for incoming reports of activities on the outside. Almost all industrial companies publish an inexpensive rundown of incoming orders, unusual sales activities, or a mere list of equipment sold during the preceding month; this is usually mimeographed or multilithed in the internal reproduction department.

Purpose is to keep the field sales force, dealer organization, or representatives informed as to what is selling where, new applications for a product, and acceptance of new products. Generally this morale-booster is just that because common practice is to describe the product very specifically by model number, describe what it is used for, then give the name of the salesperson who closed the order. Everybody dotes on recognition, salespeople to a greater degree than most.

This "Business News," "Sales Bulletin," or whatever it is called is a prime place to secure product source material, especially if you plan a case-history campaign, or one featuring specific applications for a complex product. Keep a file handy of this internal publication. Then, knowing the approximate lead-time your company requires to produce the product from date of sale, you'll know about when shipment should be made to the customer. If you want to get straight product photography while it's still on the production floor, this will trigger action on your part at the appropriate time. Then, once shipment has been made, you can follow up for an application story.

Detailed data on your product's performance on the job can be almost as difficult to come by as your first million dollars. Or, it can be so simple that it is mere routine.

If you've checked off the equipment in which you're most interested—from the listing of new business—you can then contact sales or marketing to be certain that these specific units are of interest to them as far as promotion is concerned. This is wise because it sometimes happens that specials, or modifications, are not something management wants to emphasize.

After that, it's a simple matter to calendarize the products, setting up shipping dates, and then followup dates at which time you can contact the proper field rep or district office to get customer clearance. Name of the correct individual in the customer establishment for advertising to contact must come from the field. It's then easy to write, phone, or wire to obtain permission to have photos taken and feature their equipment your company manufactured in ads, house organs, publicity releases, and so on. Many customers want to approve copy, many don't. It depends upon the individual and upon the relationship with the sales rep or dealer.

Good Customer Relations

Human nature being what it is, many customers want to be featured in case-history or testimonial ads. Psychologically, this is due to their desire to be recognized as experts who want others to realize how astute they are to have selected the equipment which they bought from your company. It is reassuring to them to see their firms, and perhaps themselves personally, in your print advertisements. This is good after-the-sale salesmanship, too, to enable them to enjoy this warm feeling of having made a wise selection. It is not unknown for a case-history ad to influence a repeat purchase!

Field reps, district managers, dealers, and distributors recognize this, although they may not have reasoned it out in exactly this manner. They do know, though, that their customers desire recognition, and because the salesperson sold the product to them, they want to see the customer and the equipment publicized. In addition to keeping the customer happy and sold, it gratifies them.

Encourage salespeople to report to you good advertising "suspects." Many companies with which the author is familiar have an established policy of offering a tangible reward for such above-and-beyond-the-call-of-duty efforts by sales reps. This usually is a cash bonus, $25 or $50, a savings bond, or, in one instance, a $100 hat. The hat has a universal appeal to successful and affluent sales reps. Few of us enjoy the luxury of wearing a $100 hat!

Remember, salespeople are salespeople. They are intimately acquainted with the product and its applications, and they are extroverted, personable, and persuasive. Seldom, however, does one happen along who is qualified to develop a good case history, hire and supervise a top-notch professional photographer, and supply to you all of the background information necessary for creation of an informative, convincing ad.

Sales reps are unable to separate the wheat from the chaff. They are actually emotionally involved with their customers and with the product. They tend frequently to identify themselves more with the customers than with their companies because their livelihood depends, after all, on customers—more than with a sales manager in the home office half a continent away. Too, it's a rare salesperson who really understands advertising's functions, much less what is needed to produce an ad.

Don't expect your salespeople to be able to gather advertising source for you—even if they have the time, which is unlikely. You can hire any of a number of photojournalism reporting firms to do the job for you, as will be discussed at greater length later.

Go Out to the Boondocks

Or, you can perform the hat trick. This is best of all, and consists of nothing more or less than getting up out of a comfortable swivel chair, locking the desk, putting on your hat, leaving the air-conditioned office and getting out there in the boondocks. There you'll come face to face with the most important individual you're likely to encounter in your advertising life—the person who specifies, buys, and uses your product.

Be prepared when the sales rep introduces you to the customer. Have a checklist with you of all pertinent topics you want to discuss. These might include miles per gallon, weights hauled, material handled, sizes of loads, frequency of trips, feeds and speeds, flow charts, process descriptions, and so on, depending on the type of product. Try to determine what primary benefits the customer enjoys as a result of using your product. These could be cost reduction, decreased maintenance, faster production, improved quality control, reduction of rejects, or similar ones.

The author has developed and worked with many checklists for a variety of industrial products. Because of product differences, none bears much similarity to the others. All have in common the fact that they stress features translated into user benefits, and all have space for direct quotes from the customer.

Take the battery-powered dictating machine or tape recorder with you. This will avoid the traumatic experience of taking brief notes on a complicated operation and getting back to the office only to find you can't rely on your memory quite as much as you'd anticipated. It's always embarrassing to have to phone the customer to remind you what the two of you discussed. With the handy little machine, you can have your secretary transcribe *exactly* what you want, including comments made in the same sequence as your checklist, direct quotes which can be attributed to the customer, remarks made by maintenance superintendents and others important to you.

Back before the day of the ubiquitous transistor-equipped electronic gadgetry, the author spent many an evening in motel and hotel rooms transcribing the day's notes before the semilegible scrawl transcribed itself into Egyptian hieroglyphics. It's never sport after a hard day.

Final source needed is photography of the product, unless it has been decided to use art. This is a topic all by itself, and will be discussed in the chapter on illustration.

Chapter 7

HEADLINES

S INGLE out one component of an industrial advertisement as the one most important and the headline wins hands down.

It is the illustration, however, which initially attracts the attention of the reader in most instances and stops him for that all-important fleeting moment. If the illustration is compelling enough, if it is pertinent and related to what you have to say, it will accomplish its assignment—*which is to secure readership of the headline.*

That done, your ad then has its first, and perhaps only, opportunity to achieve its ultimate objective. If the headline makes a strong appeal and makes it fast, if it arouses sufficient interest, your prospect will then proceed to read the body copy of the ad, giving it a chance to persuade him to accept your viewpoint about your product or service. The ad will have registered a positive impression and strengthened to some extent the acceptance of your product, thus paving the way for a salesperson to make a call and make a sale.

According to Dr. Daniel Starch, pioneer in measurement of advertising readership and effectiveness, the headline is one of the most potent psychological factors which influence readership of an advertisement. And McGraw-Hill, in its Laboratory of Advertising Performance, reports an analysis of several thousand industrial advertisements with different types of headlines. One conclusion was reached immediately: It was strikingly apparent that headlines per se increase readership significantly. Some types of headlines exert a greater positive effect than others, of course, as we shall see.

Indeed, many veteran industrial advertising practitioners are of the considered opinion that the headline constitutes at least *three-quarters* of the benefit the advertiser realizes from running his ad in business publications. A vast mass of research bears them out, for study after study has shown that if an ad is merely "noted," and not "read partially," the headline is the element recalled by almost 75 percent of those interviewed. This means, then, that almost 75 percent of the investment made in producing the ad and in the space it occupies *is made in the headline.*

The say-nothing headline has no place in industrial advertising. The headline couched in vague, general terms, the headline that is unrelated to your product and the story you want to tell about it, should never see type. And the headline that, through borrowed interest or some other illegitimate device, misleads the reader into thinking your ad will interest him or her—and then fails to do so—does your company a distinct disservice. No industrial advertiser has money enough to waste, and such headlines are just that—waste.

Readers of business publications have no interest in the nondescript, nor do they have time for fuzzy thinking or vague generalities. Generalities are pallid, specifics are vivid and fact-filled; they put color and life and vigor into your headlines by giving information slanted toward the reader's self-interest. And make no mistake about it, readers are vitally interested in facts about products which might help them on the job. They want concrete information about products—yours among many, incidentally. Fail to give them something solid in the headline, that they can get their teeth into, or promise to do so, and your ad has fallen flat on its face.

Du Pont says that the headline should:

1. Assist the illustration to select the desired audience.

2. Present sales points in terms of reader benefits—clearly, directly and specifically expressed.

3. Induce reader interest and stimulate further reading.

4. Repeat the product story told in the illustration.

5. Appear in display type, upper and lower case.

6. Be isolated from other elements for ease of reading—it should not be overprinted.

7. Avoid: "teasers"; rhyming, double-meaning, coined words; metaphors.

8. Contain *main* appeals.

9. Avoid tricky headline treatment: change in style, size and color of type; wavy or zigzagging headline; printing on tint block.

These salient points represent the viewpoint of just one company, of course, but they are almost all important. And Du Pont has done reasonably well in business by adhering to them.

Classes of Headlines

Headlines come in assorted sizes, shapes, and lengths. They vary in format and in content, as well as in the approach to a problem common to all advertisers. Good headlines share three main characteristics. They are:

1. Clear 2. Appropriate 3. Interesting

For ease of discussion and illustration, headlines can be grouped into four broad classifications. These are:

1. Direct 3. Combination
2. Indirect 4. Virtually useless

Twenty-three basic types of headlines comprise all except a few scattered mavericks within these four major classifications. They are:

A . *Direct*

1. Command	5. Reason why	8. Dialog
2. Specific fact	6. How to	9. Comparison
3. News	7. Testimonial	10. Prediction
4. Statistical		

B . *Indirect*

1. Question 3. Emotional
2. Teaser 4. Slogan

C . *Combination*

1. Cumulative
2. Headline comprises headline *and* body copy

D . *Virtually Useless*

1. Negative	4. Precious	6. Say nothing
2. Borrowed interest	5. So what?	7. Brag and boast
3. Irrelevant		

Let's discuss these 23 types of easily recognized headlines and look at examples of some of the more important. Then we'll consider why some are inherently stronger than others, where and why they excel, and why other types should be avoided like the plague.

The Direct Headline

Ernest Hemingway is credited with having said, when commenting on the then current literary style—or lack of it—that, "Nobody seems able to write a simple, declarative sentence."

The same statement applies also to present-day industrial advertising. It suffers from a dreary lack of imagination which, in turn, results in appallingly dull fare which enjoys little readership—or from an almost frantic desire to look, sound, and *be* different—primarily, it seems, for difference's sake.

Nowhere is this more evident than in ads in the lesser trade publications. In fairness, they can't be held up as typical of all industrial advertising because of their containing a preponderance of small-budget advertisers who presumably have less know-how than do larger advertisers. All the examples which follow are drawn from major business books, so they *do* typify contemporary industrial advertising.

The direct headline, in all 10 of its sub-types, is simply a headline that is informative. It is informative because it makes believable statements about a product, statements that impart information important to the reader. Following is a critique of each of the 10 in turn, with examples of the more widely used ones.

Command Headlines

Figure that in 15 seconds!
  Friden, Inc.
Stop worker resistance to wearing gloves
  The Wilson Rubber Company
Put power in your hands with Skil
  Skil Corporation
Grab hold of Allflex. . . it handles easier!
  Raybestos-Manhattan, Inc.
Put more power where the power starts with heavy-duty engine parts
  Gould National Batteries, Inc.
Get the facts on Naylor pipe. . . send for this booklet
  Naylor Pipe Company
Drill it with Blue Dragon Power Ring 200
  J.K. Smit & Sons, Inc.
Put power flexibility in your plant
  Anaconda Wire and Cable Company

Not all great headlines by any means, but each has something in common with countless others of this same general character in magazines serving hundreds of different industries. These command headlines are simple, easily understood, and they have strong reader involvement. Readers feel involved because "you" (the reader) are either the given subject of each headline, or are implied. Then follows an action verb which demands reader response.

If the headline commands the reader to do something that he or she recognizes as being in his or her self-interest, you're on solid ground with this type of headline. The reader realizes you're interested in his or her welfare. But where an ad is obviously self-oriented, as in the Blue Dragon ad, there is better than an even chance that the reader will ignore the admonition completely and turn to somebody else's ad that *is* interested in him or her.

Skil's fine ad shows a number of high-quality power tools in a wide variety of situations and, combined with the headline, offers the reader a reward for spending time reading the ad. The transition from reading about and seeing different applications for Skil power tools to considering them for use in the plant is an effortless one for the reader, as it should be.

Gould has a quality story to tell, and tells it well indeed. The ad is convincing enough to warrant use of the command headline. Gould avoids the pitfall of commanding the reader to read the ad, then to take action, and failing to carry out its end of the bargain by not rewarding the reader. Doing so results in a disgruntled prospect who harbors a subconscious resentment toward your company, and loss of readership of subsequent ads in the same campaign—and perhaps longer.

An outstanding example of the command headline—and one which combines the strength of the command with the power to arouse the curiosity of the teaser headline—is the fractional-page ad with the almost unbelievable headline *THINK RATS*. This ad run by Ai-Research Manufacturing Company, a division of The Garrett Corporation, appears to violate the rule that an unappetizing subject is not presented in a headline. In this instance, however, "rats" is an abbreviation—or, rather, the initials—of the company's Ram Air Turbine Systems. Small space is used logically, cleanly, and to excellent effect. AiResearch reports they initially looked with disfavor on the ad because they felt queasy about the headline, but decided to run it and see what the reaction would be.

Combination of the striking headline in huge display type, highly informative copy, the graph showing performance characteristics of the equipment and the photo produced a flood of inquiries—more than from any other ad the company has ever run. And this from an advertiser that habitually runs full-page ads in a number of media!

Obviously, the headline alone didn't trigger such response. But the shocking command headline *did* produce high readership as proved by reader response. And this is the function of the headline, after all.

Specific Fact Headlines

$28.10/M sliced from the cost of Rival Electric Knives by TRS rivets and riveters
Townsend Company

THINK RATS

...for emergency power.

You never know when you'll need emergency power for electrical or hydraulic systems—but you'll know it's instantly available with Garrett AiResearch Ram Air Turbine Systems (RATS) on the job.

RATS can be stored internally or mounted in external pods, ready to pop into the airstream at high or low speeds, at high or low altitudes, ready to generate from 150 watts to 30 kw electrical power. (The unit shown below provides ac and dc power, plus hydraulics compatible with the aircraft's prime system.) RATS provide efficient mechanical power, too, with ratings from 1/8 to 100 shaft horsepower.

Get all the facts on high performance, low drag, excellent power-to-weight ratios, and other RATS design features. Write: AiResearch Manufacturing Company, 9851 Sepulveda Blvd., Los Angeles, California 90009.

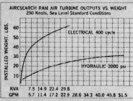

AIRESEARCH RAM AIR TURBINE OUTPUTS VS. WEIGHT
250 Knots, Sea Level Standard Conditions

AIRESEARCH RAM AIR TURBINE SYSTEMS
GARRETT

New Kenloc 5° positive rake insert has 8 cutting edges
Kennametal, Inc.

Blanchard grinds 3½ hours off end-column machining time
The Blanchard Machine Company

Every car in the Indy 500 was Fram equipped...your trucks deserve the same protection
Fram Corporation

This Transferline machine is triple-tooled to turn out dozens of different hydraulic brake hose connections at 3,100 an hour
Gilman Engineering & Mfg. Co.

A CL&T Cintimatic slashed the scrap rate on this part from 35% to less than 1%
Cincinnati Lathe and Tool Co.

Each of these headlines attracts *quality* readership because of the specific facts—of interest to those reading the ad—otherwise, they wouldn't be reading it. Readers are qualified prospects because they qualify themselves; this is especially true when the subject which the ad will discuss is mentioned prominently in the headline. Uninterested readers of the book who are not concerned with products of this type will merely pass on to editorial material, or to an advertisement about some product in which they are interested.

Polaroid's specific fact headline, *200X in 10 seconds*, is as specific as can be—even to showing the results the user will obtain in that minute time span. The promise of no more long-drawn-out waiting to see if the photomicrograph turned out well is enough to trigger a call from the metallurgist or other technical expert to the purchasing agent —Polaroid's goal. The ad is clean, the headline packs a lot of punch because of its promise, and the copy fills out the picture interestingly. No wonder Polaroid has grown by leaps and bounds! (See illustration, next page)

News Headlines

New tool for quantitative analysis of the crowded high frequency spectrum
Hewlett-Packard

Nexus devises 6 new operational amplifiers...each of which may bring a little happiness into the life of a hard-pressed engineer
Nexus—a Teledyne Company

New NDT system checks 250 bars an hour for both surface and internal defects
Automation Industries, Inc.

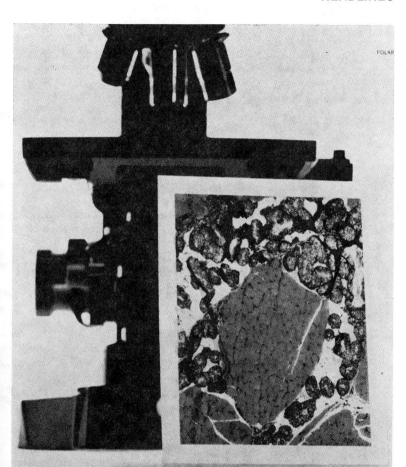

200X in 10 seconds

With a Polaroid Land camera back and Polaroid Land film, you can see your photomicrographs 10 seconds after you take them.

You are always sure of your picture. If you don't get exactly the picture you want the first time, you'll know immediately, and can take another then and there.

You don't have to waste any time in a darkroom only to find out the picture isn't right—that illumination, or filtration, or focus, or field coverage is not perfect. And you never run the risk of having to repeat a difficult and time-consuming photomicrographic setup at a later date.

Because 10-second photomicrography has proven itself an invaluable laboratory tool, Polaroid Land camera backs (or the Polaroid 4x5 Land Film Holder) are offered as standard equipment with most well known photomicrographic instruments.

Land camera backs are available for our roll or pack film formats. The 4x5 film holder, of course, accepts our 4x5 sheet films.

There are two basic Polaroid Land films for photomicrography, and they are available in all formats. There's a panchromatic black and white film, rated at A.S.A. 3000, which lets you shoot at low light levels with fast shutter speeds, and gives you a finished print in 10 seconds. And there's Polaroid color film which gives you an accurate full-color recording in 60 seconds.

The system is well worth looking into, don't you think? We'll be happy to supply more information. **Polaroid Corporation, Cambridge, Mass.**

This modular control center can be assembled, wired and installed in less than 3 days
Allen-Bradley Co.

Methods of carburizing alloy steels
Bethlehem Steel

Polaroid's new close-up camera does all the figuring and focusing for you. Then delivers a perfect close-up in seconds
Polaroid Corporation

New Life Line Globar elements last 50% longer, cost not a penny more
The Carborundum Company

Uniformly coats, but doesn't close the eye of a needle
The Glidden Company

Pittsburgh Corning, the insulation people, announce Celramic-Board, the first roof insulation able to "breathe" without loss of insulating value
Pittsburgh Corning Corporation

To date, 44 Spectrovacs have been ordered by leading metal producers!!
Baird-Atomic

The profusion of new headlines is easily explained. Most new-product ads—accepted even by confirmed skeptics as a desirable function which advertising performs with dispatch and efficiency—fall within this type. So do genuine technological breakthroughs. And new applications for existing products. Improvements made on products which have been on the market for some time. An expanded or revised warranty. A more liberal service guarantee. Easier financing. Lower interest rates. Legitimate announcements made most easily by industrial advertising are probably more numerous than an entire chapter in this book could list. Headlines of the news type always enjoy much higher-than-average readership—unless their effectiveness is diluted by vague language or failure to make the user benefit crystal clear.

Hewlett-Packard's headline is the most widely used type for announcements. It starts out with a straight-from-the-shoulder statement that the company has developed a new product, then gives the application for it. Simple, easy to write, no nonsense. This headline is admittedly old hat, but it is not hackneyed. Instead, it exploits full advertising's unique ability to tell a lot of people about the new tool in a big hurry.

Nexus' fine headline is loaded with reader interest because of a highly technical new product livened up with a delightful light touch seldom seen. This headline communicates with *people*—as well as engineers to whom it was directed, who are, after all-people, too. A sure hand on the typewriter produced this headline.

"If it's new to me, it's new" is the way most readers react to industrial advertising. Allen-Bradley's news-type statement about a product which may have been on the market prior to this ad nonetheless gives news of interest to users of control centers. They can see at a glance that this product may solve a perplexing problem for them. Bethlehem's all-text ad falls into this class, also.

You're fortunate indeed when you have a truly interesting announcement to make. A hard-hitting news headline has you halfway home if you make it clear, concrete and informative.

Here's the newest in structural beams: Koppers fiber glass reinforced polyester is the great headline of Koppers' fine ad. Containing the magnetic "newest" in the first line of the headline gets the ad off to a good start, almost assuring readership of the entire headline. Then comes the company name in the headline so the headline is credited to the right firm. Following comes fiber glass, which has assumed almost magic properties in the public mind, as has polyester to a lesser extent. As you'll note in the reproduction nearby, the ad can't miss. Powerful headline, pretty girl convincingly holding the product (which would be heavy, heavy, in a competing material), dress of the newest (newest again!) modern print, and those ultramodern mesh stockings, clean layout, and lots of white space attract the eye. The complete ad is informative, attractive, tasteful—and it has impact.

This is one of a series of ads Koppers beams to managers in business and industry, each of which is devoted to a single product. Koppers has established through research that its previous communications level was not high enough—prior to this campaign.

Objective of the ad is to launch the new product in very positive terms, to create awareness of the fact that Koppers possesses the capability to manufacture structurals, and to generate interest among business executives and motivate them to "do something" after having read the ad.

Ad Inspired Inquiries

The "something" could take the form of a direct inquiry, a call to a Koppers sales office, clipping and routing the ad to an associate, or placing an order. Koppers says that over-the-transom inquiries for additional information following appearance of this ad is almost three times higher than from other ads in the campaign.

Fiber glass structurals are a completely new product for Koppers, and an ancillary objective of this ad and its companion promotional campaign is to help find and define the market where the product has the most potential. By careful analysis of inquiries (received in the

Here's the newest in structural beams: Koppers fiber glass reinforced polyester

The 4½-foot I-beam the girl's holding weighs less than 17 pounds, yet it has tensile and compressive strengths (longitudinal) of 20,000 psi. It's eXtren* fiber glass reinforced polyester, and no other structural material can match its combination of corrosion resistance, strength, light weight and electrical insulation. Koppers makes beams, rods, angles, tubes, bars, and sheets. Right now these structural shapes are solving problems in the chemical processing and electrical industries, and they could be the answer to your requirements for a strong, lightweight, corrosion-resistant material. Write Koppers Company, Inc., Room 1424A, Koppers Building, Pittsburgh, Pa. 15219.

*eXtren is a trademark of Universal Moulded Fiber   C-6
Glass Corp.—a Koppers subsidiary.

Koppers

thousands) the company can pinpoint the industries by S.I.C., and the prospects by title and function, as well as some of the end uses for the structurals.

Koppers uses the news headline ad for new-product introduction and future sales followup most effectively.

Statistical Headlines

The man who said, "Who needs a 5-year or 50,000-mile engine and drive train warranty?" never broke his cylinder block, cylinder head, engine internal parts, or his intake manifold, water pump, or his flywheel, flywheel housing, clutch housing, or his torque converter, transmission case or its internal parts, or his transfer case, drive shaft, center bearings, or his universal joints, driving axle, or differential, or his drive wheel bearings. We hope his luck holds out.

Dodge Division, Chrysler Motors Corporation

Weighs 86, lifts 1600

Sky Climber, Inc.

This one lifts 35-ton loads and travels permit-free—Koehring truck crane is 8' wide, 12'5" high

Koehring Division, Koehring Corporation

This is compaction—49,000 lbs. of dynamic force applied 20 times per second!

Hyster Company

Cleco's new W-1200 will tighten 1¼" A-325 bolts to 71,700 lbs. tension in just 4 seconds

Cleco Division, Reed International, Inc.

Mister, if you want rugged, dependable power to move 3,000 gpm of water; provide 125-cfm, 200-psi air power; pump 40 cu. yds./hr. of concrete 100 ft. up or 500 feet horizontally; automatically slice miles of concrete; then the 60-hp WISCONSIN is your engine

Wisconsin Motor Corporation

Crucible Verasteel slits 10,000 tons of alloy and stainless sheet at a 40% reduction in tool costs

Crucible Steel Company

Maybe the longest, but certainly one of the best statistical headlines is the explanation of its warranty by Dodge. This was an unusually difficult copy problem to solve because warranties traditionally are phrased in legalese and set in 4-point type almost impossible to read except by the eagle-eyed. A crisp, clean layout and fine typography teamed up with this fine headline concept. Of note is the fact that this is a true statistical headline, yet it contains only two references to specific figures.

On the other hand, Wisconsin Motor Corporation's long but informative headline is loaded with statistics in the form of performance figures. The various applications, or jobs, the engine can handle are of interest to contractors on construction jobs. The facts are there, clearly and forcefully put. If only the headline is read, Wisconsin's ad is still a success.

Cleco's headline is shorter, but still fact filled. This is exactly the kind of information a prospective purchaser wants—and needs—to base a purchase decision on.

Shortest of all is Sky Climber's succinct headline. It contains two of the most pertinent statistics about the product, states them fast and unobtrusively, then gets out of the way so the reader can proceed into the body copy for additional facts.

Statistical headlines are inherently interesting. They can do a real job of capsulizing the highlights of your story. Make sure, however, the statistics are those of highest interest to the reader, and that they're also ones which present the product most favorably.

Reason-Why Headlines

Five reasons why more aluminum is held in Tercod Bowls than in any other type

Electro Refractories & Abrasive Corporation

Here's why plant engineers have replaced nearly 200 roofs with corrugated roofing of Crucible stainless steel

Crucible Steel Company

Why name contractors name P&H

Harnischfeger Corporation

Should a miner 67 years old change his name? We did. And here's why.

American Zinc Company

Why do you suppose we keep the ball joint as simple as we can?

TRW Michigan Division, TRW, Inc.

Readers like reason-why headlines because it tells them whether or not the body copy will interest them. It's a timesaver. If the headline indicates that the copy following is of interest, or that it will help them, they'll read further.

For example, every management man in a nonferrous foundry is interested in a bowl that holds more molten aluminum than the ones he is now using. For this reason, Electro Refractories and Abrasives Corporation's ad with the reason-why headline is a well-conceived ad. The headline tells the reader what the body copy will tell him, and promises specific facts—not puffery.

The same holds true for the headline in Crucible Steel Company's powerful ad. NO maintenance man with an interst in his job could

The shots you goof.
The best reason
for 10-second photography.

Everybody makes mistakes. But when you're using Polaroid Land photography you don't suffer for them.

Say you're shooting a photomicrograph and the exposure is off. Or the filtration. Or the position of the slide. You'll know it 10 seconds after you snap the shutter—when you see your Polaroid print. You can then make your correction and take a perfect picture right away. While everything is still set up.

This nice advantage comes with all Polaroid Land films. And there are quite a few to choose from. There are black-and-white emulsions rated at A.S.A. 3000, 400, and 200. They're the ones that develop in 10 seconds. There's also a black-and-white film that gives you a positive and a true film negative outside the darkroom in 20 seconds. And, of course, there's Polacolor film which gives you a full-color recording in 60 seconds.

Sorry we can't make you infallible. We can only offer you the next best thing. "Polaroid" & "Polacolor" ®

Polaroid Corporation, Cambridge, Mass.

Addressed to industrial users, this Polaroid ad goes right to the heart of an industrial photography problem and clearly explains how the product can be of use in overcoming that problem. The illustration is most pertinent.

possibly pass by this ad without reading it. Most likely replacing a leaky or weak roof with one of stainless steel hasn't occurred to the majority of industrial maintenance superintendents, primarily because of the relatively high cost of the material. Crucible's headline causes them to wonder, first of all, just why their counterparts in other companies chose stainless steel. Then it arouses enough interest to assure readership of the balance of the ad.

No Automatic Readership

Just because a headline is of the reason-why type doesn't automatically result in readership so high it warms the cockles of the heart. If the reason why applies to a subject of little inherent interest, the ad will promptly tally up an abysmally poor score. No type of headline can persuade readers to read about something they couldn't care less about.

Harnischfeger's ad couldn't help but suffer for that reason, and American Zinc's received even less readership. Reasons why a firm, even if it *is* 67 years old (and who cares?) changes its name elicit a long, lengthy ho-hum unless the campaign announcing the change is truly outstanding. Few are.

TRW's ad, on the other hand, proceeds to give a convincing product-superiority story, and for that reason the headline contributed to a successful ad.

The Polaroid ad reproduced here is a classic example of a well-thought-out reason-why headline—and ad. *The shots you goof. The best reason for 10-second photography.* As fine a reason why the industrial camera user should use a Polaroid as can be found. And the illustration is a beautiful marriage of headline and illustration. Copy is terse, informative—and mighty convincing.

How-to Headlines

How to make one Sarco "25" valve body do any of 7 different control jobs
Sarco Co., Inc.

To cut heating and cooling costs, and reduce noises, insulate sheet metal ducts with G-B Ultralite
Gustin-Bacon Manufacturing Co.

How to save money and avoid headaches in transformer and inductor design.
Ferroxcube Corporation

How to succeed in Higher Profits without really trying on a Cleereman Layout Drilling Machine

Cleereman Machine Tool Corporation
>*Six ways Addressograph helps keep 700,000 items shaped-up when they're shipped out*
>Addressograph-Multigraph Corporation
>*Four ways to view displays with Tektronix Type 564 split-screen storage oscilloscope*
>Tektronix, Inc.
>*Four foundry execs tell how their companies saved from 27% to 44% on Worker's Compensation insurance costs.*
>American Mutual

The two little words "how to" are among the four or five most powerful words in the English language for use in headlines. Every management person is a part of management for one reason only: He or she is able to solve problems. Otherwise that individual would be a clerk or a janitor or a draftsman.

When you run a headline of the how-to type, you're promising the reader then and there that you're going to tell how to solve a problem—hopefully one that's been bothering—with your product or service. Helping solve a problem hits him or her right where he or she lives in the business world. Assuming your solution, based on your product, is applicable and pertinent, this is a type of headline that comes as close as any to assuring excellent readership.

How to reduce inventory, freeing capital and effecting a savings, is the promise held out in Sarco's headline. After all, if one Sarco "25" valve body is flexible and versatile enough to do seven jobs, it can easily solve inventory, storage, and application problems. Sarco pulled 'em in with this headline.

Cutting costs interests everybody, as does a reduction in noise. Gustin-Bacon's product should be right down the alley of the maintenance man with heating and cooling and noise problems. Note that this is a true how-to headline, but the word "how" isn't used; it isn't essential that it appear, although a headline is stronger with "how" than without it.

Addressograph-Multigraph's headline promises it will tell how to make order out of chaos six ways with its equipment—and with 700,000 items involved, that's quite an order.

Long though it is, American Mutual's headline contains a pocketbook appeal, a testimonial, and is a how-to headline—much more you can't ask for. It has built-in believability and inherent interest.

A.B. Dick's all-type ad with a how-to headline is as fine an example as has come down the pike in many a moon. The office copy machine market is a jungle with dozens and dozens of firms large and small completing for a larger share. Some are giants, like Xerox, others

How to fight
the cost per copy war.

*With all the cost per copy attacks and
counter-attacks it's often pretty hard to know who's
offering you the best way to make your copies.*

*We don't claim to always have the best answer, but
we can make it easier for you to decide who does.*

*Only A.B. Dick offers you all the copying and
duplicating methods. So we're not for (or against)
copiers or mimeographs or offset machines. Or any
of the other ways to make copies.*

*That's why you can depend on us to show you
a true picture of the cost per copy for each method.
And then let your needs decide what's best for you.*

*In the cost per copy war we have the
ultimate weapon:*

Objectivity.

AB DICK®

ELECTROSTATIC COPIERS • OFFSET • MIMEOGRAPH • SPIRIT • AZOGRAPH • PHOTOCOPY • VIDEOGRAPH • FOLDERS • PAPER • SUPPLIES
A. B. DICK COMPANY, 5700 WEST TOUHY AVENUE, CHICAGO, ILLINOIS 60648

smaller but with products equally satisfactory. Some have a breadth-of-line story to tell, others concentrate on one single type of machine and sell it hard.

The persuasive ad illustrated here hammers hard at the most significant factor in selling a copy machine—cost per copy. For copy machines, like autos, have as the prime consideration not the original cost, but the cost of running the things.

Headline of A. B. Dick's ad is: *How to fight the cost per copy war.* Body copy is so logical, so simple and convincing that the entire text follows.

*With all the cost per copy attacks and
counterattacks it's often pretty hard to know who's
offering you the best way to make your copies.*

We don't claim to always have the best answer, but

*We don't claim to always have the best answer, but
we can make it easier for you to decide who does.*

*Only A.B. Dick offers you all the copying and
duplicating methods. So we're not for (or against)
copiers or mimeographs or offset machines. Or any
of the other ways to make copies.*

*That's why you can depend on us to show you
a true picture of the cost per copy for each method.
And then let your needs decide what's best for you.*

*In the cost per copy war we have the
ultimate weapon:*

Objectivity.

A.B. Dick approached its advertising campaign with several thoughts in mind. First of all, there exists a great deal of confusion regarding the multiplicity of copiers and duplicators on the market in the minds of prospects—ranging from a one-man dentist's office to the largest corporation in the country. So many manufacturers with so many different machines and different systems make it extremely difficult for a conscientious buyer to be sure that the ultimate selection is the best.

As a result, A.B. Dick—the only company in the industry to offer all of the major copying and duplicating processes—decided that its unique position gave it a competitive edge nobody else could have: complete objectivity.

With this in mind, the company decided to prepare advertising that was not only very honest, but unusually straightforward in style and presentation. Furthermore, Dick wanted ads that looked different to separate themselves from the herd. Obvious approach was to have the typical pretty blond girl sitting on, leaning on, looking at, or operating a typical machine in a typical office setting. That particular type of ad has been done to death by scores of companies in this and allied fields.

The all-type ad was decided upon as the one best solution to putting across the A.B. Dick story in the strongest possible manner. That the how-to headline and the logical, objective approach had paid off is borne out by readership ratings by Starch and others. In the first issue of *Business Week* in which this ad appeared, it was the sixth best read ad in the book of this same size, and the cost ratio was 225. A measurement by Gallup and Robinson indicated an achievement approximately double the average *for this type of product.*

A sound selling proposition, an outstanding product line, believable copy—preceded by an intriguing how-to headline—is performing well. All are mutually dependent upon the other to some extent, of course.

Testimonial Headlines

> *"The rotary worktable on our Scharmann horizontal has cut operation setups from three steps to one"*
> Scharmann Machine Corp.
>
> *"Most of the time my 295B's haul just as much dirt as my twin-engine, four-wheel drives. More, altogether, because the 295's haul it faster."*
> International Harvester Company
>
> *"The steering of this machine is excellent. . . "*
> Manitowoc Engineering Company
>
> *"We've had no breakdowns. . . since Torc-Pac's were installed in 1963"*
> U.S. Industries, Inc.
>
> *"Just wish we'd known about the Bobcat sooner!"*
> Melroe Bobcat

These testimonial headlines are all from case-history ads, of course, and are direct quotations from statements made by individual customers or individuals in customer companies. In each one, except for the U.S. Industries ad, the quotation was identified with a specific person in the ad, along with the title or job function. U.S. Industries chose to quote the company rather than an individual.

Best thing the testimonial headline has going for it is that it is so believable. The advertiser is not making any glowing statements about the product; a third party—theoretically a disinterested one with no ax to grind—does this for him. In this way the headline gains credence. Too, the reader finds it easy to identify with the product user who is making the statement. In many tightly knit industries, he or she may well know that person through the trade association.

When you get a really good direct quote from a customer you'll have a hard-working headline. You may even have to help the customer a bit to make sure the quote is up to par by putting words in his or her mouth; you can say them, then ask if that isn't right. When the customer agrees he's said it, you can quote. This is technically honest, but shouldn't be relied upon to any great extent or your ads will all end up sounding like the same person did all of the talking—you.

Frequently after a get-acquainted session with the customer, and perhaps a good long lunch, he or she is relaxed enough to regard you as a friend and loosen up. Then's when the colorful, colloquial quotes come rolling out—and you'd better be ready to write them down or record them fast. Somehow they always bring to the printed page a sense of immediacy, of hearing the gospel truth, of learning something about a product that should be remembered.

One of the finest, most colorful testimonial headlines in the author's experience was that for a four-color insert ad prepared for the truck fleet publications for the old Diamond T Motor Truck Com-

pany. This headline quoted a California dump truck operator who said, without prompting, "These trucks don't owe me a penny." The ad, incidentally, enjoyed excellent readership, partially because it started off with talk that truckers understood.

International Harvester's quote headline is particularly good. Care was taken that it was good, that it understated originally just how good the performance of the machines was—then followed up with the second punch—the fact that these machines actually out-perform larger ones. This headline carries great conviction.

All of us can hear somebody say he or she wished he or she had known about something sooner—probably after a less than satisfactory experience with a competitive product. That makes Melroe's headline about its Bobcat unusually effective, with the bonus benefit that there's an implied statement of outstanding performance.

With a major user benefit—freedom from maintenance expense—in the headline, the Hendrickson ad reproduced here is a good example of a fine testimonial headline.

"After 1,800,000 miles of hard use, our nine HENDRICKSON Suspensions are as good as new!" The illustration reinforces the headline, showing as it does, a tractor with rear axles on different taxes due to uneven terrain; mud on the tires and thrown mud on the front fender belong in this type of photograph.

Hendrickson's body copy adheres to a rule from which you should never deviate—when you quote a customer, immediately give the name, firm and address. It starts out: *"We've never had a breakdown due to suspensions," states Jim Bobb, owner of the Queen City Grain Company, Cincinnati, Ohio. "In fact, after 200,000 miles each on our nine Hendrickson-equipped Ford tractors, we're still running all the original beam end and center bushings in these suspensions."* Copy continues with facts about Queen City's operation, including weight of payload and so on.

Get a statement like that from a satisfied customer and run it in your testimonial ad and you have something with real credibility. Prospects believe such headlines and ads because they know they *have to be true*—picking up the phone to call Jim Bobb in Cincinnati about his Hendrickson suspensions is the easiest thing imaginable. No advertiser would stick a neck out even a little bit in a testimonial headline.

True, testimonial headlines have been around since shortly after the dawn of time, but they are just as effective now as they were decades ago.

Dialog Headlines

> *"We're a little short on working capital." "Ever considered reducing your steel inventory and depending more on steel service centers?"*
>
> Steel Service Center Institute

> *"Right, George. We figure now is the time to invest some of our profits in more Aro Automation Tools for our drilling, tapping, and assembly operations. They'll give us a boost in production, improve quality control, and trim our labor costs. Then when business isn't all milk and honey any more, and we have to fight for our orders, those Aro Automation Tools will give us a competitive edge."*
>
> The Aro Corporation

As a rule, a fatal flaw is automatically built into the dialog headline. Quoting a "conversation" between two executives rendered in charcoal art imparts an air of unreality to the headline. It's immediately apparent that these are not real people talking, they're make-believe, a figment of the imagination—the advertiser's imagination. They're suspect. Logical inference is that the situation itself doesn't exist, that the problem posed is fictional, and that the solution is a contrived one to benefit guess-who—certainly not the reader. Steel Service Center people didn't help the cause of service centers with this ad, but there's every reason to believe that their reasoning is right, up to a point. If they take the same premise and find real, live customers who have realized the identical benefits they're talking about by purchasing steel from their Steel Service Center—and then quoting them, and identifying them—they'll have an ad with believability.

And the phone conversation between a nonexistent Arrow Collar-type drawn with phone in hand and an insipid grin as he talks with an equally nebulous George, also lacks conviction. This is too, too. Aro invites disbelief, invites readers to flip the page as quickly as possible and does nothing to encourage them to think well of either Aro products or the company. Had its men quoted a similar—but not so verbose—conversation which transpired before purchase of their equipment, then did a followup after the equipment was at work, they'd have had something. Naturally, the individual would have been identified, the company would, and it would have been located. Facts and figures about lower production costs, reduced maintenance and so on would put icing on the cake. The ad would have been believable.

Don't confuse the dialog headline with the testimonial headline just because both use quotation marks. There's a world of difference between them and just as much difference in what they can do for you.

Comparison Headlines

This 988 does the work of two machines. . . cuts handling cost per ton 36%
Caterpillar Tractor Company

One way to increase your frequency range. A better way from Sierra
Sierra Electronic Division

Motor lamination production upped from 150 to 250 per minute. Speed and productivity increased 66⅔%.
The Minster Machine Company

Half the plies. Twice the service.
B. F. Goodrich Industrial Products Company

Comparing the product—by inference with competitive ones, or with older models of the same product prior to improvements—results in dramatic headlines that press a point home to readers quickly and positively. This holds true if the comparison is a valid one, but not if apples and oranges are compared. An attempt to trick the reader with a phony comparison will surely backfire and reflect adversely on the advertiser; people are pretty sharp. After a new product introduction, for example, a logical followup could be one of comparison of new and old so that improvements, benefits, and features can be incorporated into the headline.

"Does the work of two machines"—Caterpillar's comparing its new model wheel Loader with the older units is about as strong a statement as is possible to make. Run this type of headline and you instantly cause huge dollar signs to flash in front of the eyes of readers using this type of equipment. The benefit of savings in equipment, in labor, and in maintenance comes through loud and clear. The headline leaves the impression that Cat equipment can bump up the profit picture for contractors; if they read nothing but the headline and noticed the signature or logo, the ad has accomplished something positive.

A basic mistake was made by Sierra, though. One illustration in the ad shows a balding tuba player sitting on a stage ready, apparently, to perform for a large and distinguished audience. The other shows Sierra's wide-range wave analyzer. Comparing the two is not cricket. This attempt to borrow interest from a subject totally unrelated to the problem at hand—and actually comparing them—defeats the ad. Only tuba players, who comprise a small percentage of the population, would find the advertisement inherently interesting.

Minster Machine Company's comparison of new equipment and

that formerly used by a good customer sells hard, as does B. F. Goodrich's comparison of a new BFG conveyor belt with a competitive one which gave poor service. The competitive brand was not named. Used properly, comparisons convince.

Undoubtedly the finest comparison headline—and entire comparison ad—to appear in the business press one year was Firestone's in *Commercial Car Journal*, a leading truck fleet publication.

Headline is: *one Duplex tire and rim replaces. . . 13 dual tire and rim parts*. Our illustration of the spread ad in black and white shows, on one page, the revolutionary new Firestone Duplex truck tire and rim; on the other page is the multiplicity of parts, 13 in all, needed to do the job of the simpler Duplex. Graphic, persuasive, convincing.

Body copy is well written, ties in smoothly with the attention grabbing headline. It goes:

Here's what you do without when you go with Firestone Duplex truck tires: 2 dual tires, 2 tubes, 2 flaps, 2 rim bases, 2 lock rings, 2 side rings, and a spacer band.

Eleven fewer parts to buy and stock. Eleven fewer parts to replace. Multiply that by the number of dual tires you're running now and you'll get an idea of just how much Firestone Duplex tires can be worth to you.

And Firestone Duplex tires have other ways of outdoing duals. Duplex tires provide maximum mobility and flotation —especially in soft, sloppy going. Where duals put down a pair of slim tracks, a Duplex gives you one big, wide, flat "footprint." That's why the Firestone Duplex goes where duals fear to tread.

You make fewer trips to the fuel pumps with Duplex tires. There's less rolling resistance. Your fuel mileage is up as much as 10 percent. There's less wear and tear on brakes, too. Drums have greater air exposure. And they stay cooler. The linings last longer. So does your maintenance budget.

But the Duplex tire does more than just save money for you. It helps you to make more money—by reducing axle weight up to 300 pounds per axle! That, of course, means bigger payloads on every trip, including trips to the bank. And you'll make more trips on Duplex tires with long mileage Sup-R-Tuf rubber.

Ask the tire experts at your nearby Firestone Dealer or store about new Duplex truck tires and the low-cost Duplex Changeover Plan. And remember, always specify Firestone tires, rims, and wheels on new trucks and trailers.

Look at the points Firestone makes—all user benefits: (1) Fewer parts to stock, less investment in parts inventory; (2) better flotation, a potent point for operators of dump trucks, ready-mix trucks or other units which encounter mud and snow off the highway; (3) better fuel mileage; (4) longer brake drum and brake lining life; (5) lower tare weight up to 300 lbs. per axle. This means, for example, that in a tandem-axle trailer pulled by a tandem-axle tractor, that this weight savings could amount to 1,200 lbs. A common rule of thumb in the trucking business is that a pound saved is equal to a dollar a year in increased revenue. Without belaboring the point—admittedly there are variables in the rule which are not always possible to define precisely—Firestone makes it easy for truckers to compute their own extra earnings with Duplex tires; each of them knows how the earnings formula applies to a specific operation; (6) longer tire life with Sup-R-Tuf rubber; (7) a trucker won't run up a bill rivaling the national debt by switching over to Duplex tires, due to Firestone's Duplex Changeover Plan.

All of these benefits are telegraphed in the headline, shown in the two photographic illustrations, then fleshed out in the body copy. This is thoroughly professional, effective industrial advertising.

Prediction Headlines

If your plant electrical system can not be economically expanded Davey Permavane natural gas-driven compressors will solve your compressed air problems
Davey Compressor Co.

Capacity in flat rolled steel will increase 30% at Granite City
Granite City Steel Company

The 1980 trains may ride a little smoother, last longer between maintenance jobs because of the researchers in Building No. 3 in Sandusky, Ohio
New Departure • Hyatt Bearings
Division of General Motors Corporation

Dictaphone Corporation will save enough on this one part to pay for a new Brown & Sharpe No. 3 Ultramatic within one year
Brown & Sharpe

You'll find a plus in buying raw materials from the company that manufactures its own oxo alcohols
Enjay Chemical Company

More work gets done when your Towmotor truck operator gets "shiftless"
Towmotor Corporation

A fine opportunity exists to get the one most important user benefit into the headline when the prediction headline is used. Believability is its long suit, and it is particularly effective if a logical explanation of why the prediction is made follows immediately in the body copy. If no explanation is forthcoming, or if the explanation itself lacks in the convince the reader that your company plays footloose and fancy-free with the truth.

Predicted user benefit promised in the headline must materialize and you should be able to cite chapter and verse at the drop of a hat on where, when, and how it has benefited others. Do that and the prediction headline will cause readers to regard your product favorably.

Brown & Sharpe's predicted cost reduction, enough to amortize the machine tool within one year, is an excellent example of how this type of headline should be used. Note especially that this prediction is a true prediction, not a vague hope, and that the customer is named. A year after installation of the machine—when it has performed as predicted—a compelling case-history ad, referring back to this ad, and restating the savings realized will have tremendous impact.

Be Positive

Hedging the bet, or in this case the prediction, is basically poor policy. New Departure • Hyatt Bearings' headline would have been considerably stronger if it had substituted "will" for "may" in the headline. As it now reads, there seems to be some uncertainty in the advertiser's mind as to whether or not the prediction will come true. Obviously the same doubt—or more of it—exists in the minds of the readers. Chances are they wonder why the manufacturer isn't sure enough of his product to make a firm statement. Residual impression may well be that if the company isn't sure of itself, that's no place to take one's problems.

The word "will" does not have to appear in a prediction headline. Towmotor's headline is a true prediction type, although it also is a statement of a specific fact. Use of "shiftless" in quotation marks requires no explanation of a labor saver in a society conditioned to expect an automatic transmission in every car; the very fact that this situation exists does much to strengthen Towmotor's claim. Everybody knows that automatic transmissions take work out of driving a car, so it's logical that it would do the same in a lift truck.

Just because a headline contains a prediction doesn't mean that every recipient of a trade publication in which the ad appears will consider it of earth-shattering import. Granite City Steel's headline is weak because it is self-oriented and is of interest primarily to those at Granite City Steel Company. There's no user benefit given, no promise of one, nothing is done to draw the reader into pursuing the copy which follows.

INDIRECT HEADLINES

If you like to live dangerously, use the indirect headline. When you do, you're going for broke.

The direct headling, as we've seen, invariably produces an impression about the product or service. At its most ineffective, if the business reader absorbs only the headline, the ad has been only partially successful.

But the sole function of the indirect headline is to induce readers to do one thing: continue reading. You're putting all of your "begs" in one "askit." If your headline is punchy enough to succeed in its purpose, your ad will receive readership far above the average. However, if it fails, you'll probably get next to no readership and you can scratch the number of dollars invested in ad production and space cost.

Sometimes, however, an indirect headline which asks a question can still make a name or brand impression on the reader. The prospect will at least be aware that he or she saw the name of your product. This, however, is the exception. Let's take a look at some indirect headlines.

Question Headlines

Which plate size is best for electron micrographs?
RCA Scientific Instruments
How did we get to be Number 2 in integrated circuits?
Motorola Semiconductor Products, Inc.
Looking for a weather-proof, crack-resistant, chemical-resistant stack paint? And an off-shade lemon yellow for an office?
Devoe Paint
Pioneering? You don't have to have someone re-invent the wheel
Micro Switch
What new motor line has the lift-off top?
Allis-Chalmers
Is the d-c unit substation you're considering worth its salt?
I-T-E Circuit Breaker Company
What will make the biggest change on the interchange in '80?
FMC Corporation
What cable jacket material has the toughness Grumman wants for its A6A Intruder? For its E2A Hawkeye?
Pennsalt Chemicals Corporation
Who could keep bringing new efficiency to oil control better than the people who introduced it originally?
Sealed Power Corporation

Each of the above question headlines risks everything on its ability to whet the appetite of the reader, to arouse his curiosity sufficiently to make him read the body copy. Note that the name of the advertiser is not given; the product itself is scarcely mentioned, except in a generic way. And in Micro Switch's ad no hint whatsoever is given of the topic of discussion in the body copy. Others are a bit more specific, but rely mainly on luring the reader into the text. This is risky business.

Following, though, are question headlines in which either the advertiser, the product, or the problem being considered is included in the headline. Despite this, these headlines are indirect.

Why can you depend on MSA for safety eyewear? For the same reasons you depend on MSA for gas detectors.

Mine Safety Appliances Co.

What in the world is Raytheon doing at 50 fathoms?

Raytheon Company

Tire makers use cords of rayon, nylon, polyester, cotton, glass and steel...so why do they specify rayon for their new radial tires?

American Viscose Division

When does it pay to purchase a Trackmobile?

Whiting Corporation

Why saddle a $40,000 turret lathe with a job an $18,000 Blanchard grinder can do better...and for less?

The Blanchard Machine Company

Question headlines can undoubtedly produce exceptionally high readership, but before deciding upon one, sit back and reflect and consider carefully whether or not you're willing to stake everything on one turn of the card. Perhaps you have too much at stake, too small a budget, or just aren't ready yet for such strong medicine.

On the other hand, it has been conclusively proven that ads which rank at the top of the heap in readership ratings state or imply a user benefit—or ask a question about it which stimulates interest.

Could be the decision making will be a bit easier if you'll do this. Read each of the above question headlines, plus any ready at hand in trade books, and ask yourself what your response would be if you were a reader-prospect. Very possibly in a number of instances your immediate response will be negative—who knows? I couldn't care less! Why don't they tell me instead of giving me the printed third degree?

If most question headlines cause you to react this way, probably you'd better steer clear of them. But if they intrigue you, if they stimulate a desire to learn more, if they're tantalizing and provocative and they stir the mental corpuscles around, this reaction will be reflected in copy you write, the direction you give to your agency, and your presentation of your product. Should that be the case, a bang-up ad should emerge from your typewriter—at least the odds are in your favor!

Two Outstanding Examples

Jones & Laughlin Steel Corporation used the question headline with great effectiveness in two separate campaigns, examples of which appear on pages 302 and 303.

First campaign is to promote J&L Cold Finished Bars to users of this type of steel, and to producers of screw machine parts to whom it is raw material. Objectives of this campaign to cultivate screw machine parts producers by promoting their interests and the importance of the industry.

Communications objectives were to emphasize the quality of Jones & Laughlin Cold Finished Bars, and to stress the importance of this bar quality in obtaining the best service and reliability from screw machine parts.

For this product, J&L communicated with buying and production influences in the screw machine industry, such as purchasing agents, design, production and quality control engineers and others, within the preselected S.I.C. classifications.

What makes your screw machine parts producer turn gambler? is the provocative headline of this striking four-color spread insert ad. An aura of realism is a strong point of the ad; the facial expression of the "gambler" couldn't be improved upon, the cigar and the glass and the eyeshade belong and nothing is out of character—even the screw machine parts fail to strike a jarring note because they, too, belong, due to having been mentioned in the headline. This set the stage for their inclusion in a striking photograph. Complete body copy follows to illustrate a perfect marriage between headline and text.

He's a reliable guy, really.

And he does a great job for his customers who buy screw machine parts.

In fact, that's part of his problem; he does such a great job. He bids as close as possible to his cost for your benefit.

But he runs certain risks in his operations. Risks that his bar stock may not be uniformly machinable. Or that his bar stock is at the lower end of its machinability range instead of at the midpoint or higher.

That's where J&L cold finished bars come into the game. Their reliability and uniformity take the guesswork out of high speed machining.

No one has done as much research in machinability as J&L —research which has achieved uniformity in bar machinability on the high side of the machine range, for every grade of bar. There's no gamble on bar uniformity with J&L cold finished bars.

This four-color insert appeared in *Steel, Purchasing Week, American Machinist, Automatic Machining, Production,* and *Automation.* Readership surpassed the competition, held up well when compared to products with greater and more widespread inherent interest. *Steel* was discontinued several years ago.

The steelmaker's campaign for its extensive line of stainless steel also utilized question headlines with outstanding results. Shown is another four-color spread, an insert ad which had great impact due to superb photography and printing, clean layout and typography— and the question headline.

It reads: *Do you want to reflect the whole truth, or just a glimmer of it?* Then, the text: *Beautiful stainless steel finishes from J&L run the gamut from bright annealed JalGLEAM® (left), that accurately plays back every detail of light, color and form, to nonreflective Grain Line® (right), that joins in a soft, subtle relationship with its surroundings. ☐ Different as an apple from an orange, each finish appeals in another way. One excites with its bright, straight-forward gleam; the other intrigues with the glimmer that is caught in its fineline, straight-line pattern. ☐ But these are only two of the many stainless steel finishes available from J&L. ☐ If your product or structure calls for stainless in an alternative mood, call on J&L for that too. J&L has all the answers in practical, carefree, durable—and beautiful—stainless steel.*

The sharp, citrus smell and tangy taste of the Delicious almost exude from the pages. Color fidelity is beyond reproach—this insert is of such superb quality that the Printing Industries of America, Incorporated, presented its coveted Certificate of Award to J&L and its printer.

That's one reason, of course, why the ad did so well when directed to architects, designers, and metalworking buying influences. Jones & Laughlin's communications objective of presenting the company's stainless steels as a modern, clean, durable, corrosive-resistant, and desirable product—and to show the range of reflectivity—were

303

achieved through a question headline that literally *pulled* readers into the ad, by top quality printing, and by persuasive, informative body copy. Just how well it did is shown by the Starch Advertisement Readership Service rating.

Percentage of Readers Who Have

Noted%	Seen-Associated %	Read Most %
65	51	19

Jones & Laughlin's competition rated 5 percent and 9 percent in Read Most in the same issue of *Machinery* in which this study was conducted.

Ad-Gage study of *Machine Design* showed that this insert ad was the best-read ad in the magazine, and it received an Award for Top Performance.

Concept, headline, copy, photography, printing, typography, and layout are all outstanding. And attention to small details resulted in a winning ad that more than paid its way.

Teaser Headlines

Movies in flight: No fighter pilot should be without them.
International Telephone and Telegraph Corporation

Go five miles and turn right
J. Bishop & Co.

Blabbermouth
Consolidated Electrodynamics

The story of the man-made diamond
General Electric

I was a nobody
United States Steel Corporation

Make us prove it
Chas. Pfizer & Co., Inc.

The teaser headline is even more nonspecific than the question headline. Complete reliance is placed on its ability to arouse enough interest to secure text readership, and this fails to materialize in most instances. Assess the teaser headline as a stockbroker would if shares in a company were under consideration, and the judgment simply has to be that it is strictly speculative.

If you're having trouble getting rid of all of the money allocated to advertising, if you don't *really* care whether or not your advertising produces results, if you're not held responsible by management for a return on the advertising investment, or if you just don't give a damn, by all means use the teaser headline.

Otherwise, don't touch it with a 10-foot pole.

Blabbermouth—now that's a great headline. No question, it's modern, colloquial, slangy, friendly, in the vernacular, common as an old shoe, and unpretentious. Fact remains, however, that it fails spectacularly to communicate one fact about either the product or the company. When not an iota of information is available, just how is the unwary reader to determine if he might, or might not, be in the market for any electrodynamics—particularly electrodynamics manufactured by Consolidated Electrodynamics? Incidentally, just what is an electrodynamic? Something to hush a blabbermouth with?

Nor does *I was a nobody* present data galore about the specific product U.S. Steel is promoting at the moment, and *Make us prove it* probably elicited a singularly universal response—the turned page.

All might have aroused the curiosity of some readers, but only a mighty tiny percentage of them. Could be that some were intrigued enough to pursue the matter to the bitter end, but then, some people read dictionaries and telephone books for recreation. There's no accounting for tastes.

Remember, *at best,* teaser headlines are a calculated risk. Objectively evaluated, you have more chance of winning the Irish Sweepstakes every year then you do in producing an effective ad with nothing but teaser headlines on every attempt.

Most of us prefer better odds. So, if the budget is small, if costs keep rising, and you're under pressure to produce, go some other route. Leave the risk-taking to the giants who can afford it.

Martin Marietta Corporation won on such a long shot, because of a teaser headline. Meshing nicely with a striking stop-motion illustration, this layout ties two pages together better than most, and eye-catching white space provides another reason for good readership of the ad illustrated nearby.

Martin Marietta is a major producer of crushed and graded rock for construction. Because rock is solid, a quality construction material for roads, airfields, jetties, and so on, the headline becomes a teaser with relevance.

**For a smooth
ride, put rocks
in the road.**

Almost $7 billion will be spent this year to stretch the U.S. road network to 3.7 million miles. Roads are built up with rock, up to 15,000 tons of it every mile. The Rock Products division of Martin Marietta supplies a good deal of this rock

For a smooth ride, put rocks in the road.

Almost $7 billion will be spent this year to stretch the U.S. road network to 3.7 million miles. Roads are built with rock, up to 15,000 tons of it every mile. The Rock Products division of Martin Marietta supplies a good deal of this rock from on a hundred major plants around the country. But rock for roads is just part of the story.

People are inclined to take rock for granted, as just something lying around underfoot. Yet commercial-type rock remains one of the most extraordinary materials available to man. Nothing else offers such an ideal combination of strength, hardness, durability and low cost.

That's why rock products now constitute a $2 billion annual market, and have become the added foundation for practically everything.

In its many varied roles, crushed stone, gravel or sand as rock aggregates give concrete its strength and bulk.

Rock jetties hold back the sea. Rock ballast supports the traffic on highways, railroads and airport runways. (What else but rock would take the landing impact of 150-ton jets?)

Of course, your road is partly used in the random form in which nature supplies it. It's of such density and hardness that it must be blasted into manageable chunks for processing.

It is then fed into giant crushers, washed and precisely graded for size, and carried through miles of conveyor belts, until it is finally stored in orderly piles waiting for transport.

Martin Marietta has automated many of these operations, so that one man can often push buttons which direct huge and complicated machinery spread over acres of plant.

In the rock business, planning ahead, decades ahead, is a requisite part of marketing. Certain sections of the country might be having a construction boom twenty years from now. Who will be needing millions of tons of processed rock? Once we've made our predictions, our geologists begin exploration.

Martin Marietta Business produces and market cement and concrete additives as well as rock products. We are, in fact, among the largest producers of these basic construction materials.

As for rock, there's a kind of down-to-earth glamour in digging deep into a $2-billion annual market and market.

MARTIN MARIETTA

from over a hundred major plants around the country. But rock for roads is just part of the story.

. . . Construction rock is rarely used in the random form in which nature supplies it. It's of such density and hardness that it must be blasted into manageable chunks for processing.

It is then fed into giant crushers, washed and precisely graded for size, and carried through miles of conveyor belts, until it is finally stored in orderly piles waiting for transport.

Martin Marietta has automated many of these operations, so that one man can often push buttons which direct huge and complicated machinery spread over acres of plant.

. . . Martin Marietta divisions produce and market cement and concrete additives as well as rock products. We are, in fact, among the largest producers of these basic construction materials.

As for rock, there's a kind of down-to-earth glamour in digging deep into a $2-billion annual market.

Corporate in nature, although a product ad, this spread established Martin Marietta's being in the rock market, and a capability to supply quality rock from more than a hundred shipping points—no small consideration for something as heavy as rock—and the fact that it also produced other allied construction materials.

And there's not one slap at (you'll pardon the word, Martin Marietta) asphalt, nor is there any discussion of the fact that concrete—as most of us know—is the best, longest-lasting material for roads.

Teaser headlines are too risky to rely upon, they shouldn't be used, but occasionally, as in this instance, they come on strong.

Emotional Headlines

Helping people with heart problems to a new lease of life
Hewlett-Packard

To your bookkeeper, who may be terrified that we're going to automate her billing department
Friden, Inc.

Till death do us part
Mobil Oil Corporation

Generally accepted is the fact that industrial purchases are the result of a liberal helping of logic and a detailed analysis of all alternative actions. Emotions, so the theory goes, have absolutely no part in the decision making.

Theory is fine and dandy, but frequently it bears little relationship to things as they actually are. Management people in industry who buy for their companies are just that—people. They're just like the rest of us. They are not bloodless robots or three-eyed creatures from outer space, and they don't push a button to turn off their emotions when they walk into the office at nine each morning. Instead, they react emotionally and viscerally. However, the advertising manager cannot overtly appeal to their emotions in an ad. Doing so covertly, however, occasionally leads to exceptionally powerful advertisements.

Hewlett-Packard's great spread ad is an excellent example. On one page is a four-color illustration of an appealing 3-year-old boy in a hospital bed—and a small child seriously ill tugs at every heart-string. The headline, combined with the illustration, has a dual appeal—pity and curiosity. Hewlett Packard capitalized on this and proceeded in a full page of copy to tell its product story of how their electrocardiographs, sound amplifiers, vector cardiographs and other instruments enable doctors to perform near miracles and cure, or control, a number of conditions formerly thought hopeless.

Emotional appeal in the headline and illustration handed this advertiser an oversize prescription of readership.

The middle-aged woman bookkeeper in Friden's fine four-color ad *looks* worried, so reinforces the headline. The photograph used was taken in a typical office setting. Principal purpose of the ad is to appeal to the emotions of all business executives because Friden recognizes that displacement of people—especially longtime or middle-aged employees—by machines is probably the most difficult situation which has to be faced when a company automates a portion of its operations. Nothing is more distasteful than to have to terminate employees.

Friden handles the situation logically and persuasively by pointing out that the company's 5010 Computer doesn't *displace* people—it makes them more productive, thus making it possible for them to find greater job satisfaction.

The message is directed to management, of course, and quite obviously succeeds in its objective of stimulating thought about modernizing the accounting function. Subconsciously, the prospect of having to dispense with old and faithful employees may well have caused postponement of the decision to purchase new equipment to accomplish this objective by many companies. This ad lays to rest that unpleasant prospect—and paves the way for sales of a lot of Friden Computers.

A Classic in Safety

Classic—and in a class completely by itself—was Mobil's safety-oriented campaign. Designed to communicate with both the industrial buyer and the consumer, the campaign was one of the rare ones of recent years to influence such a broad universe so effectively.

One of the basic communications objectives of the campaign was to project an image of Mobil Oil Corporation as a compassionate, public-spirited company and, in so doing, enhance Mobil's position with present customers and acquire new ones—preferably in large numbers, of course. This applied equally to the suburban housewife ferrying the kids around in the family station wagon and to the fleet operator who bought tens of thousands of gallons of gasoline and diesel fuel at one time, as well as to the plant engineer responsible for purchases of lubricant to keep the machines running and fuel oil to heat the factory.

A theme suitable for such a disparate universe wasn't the easiest thing to find, and after considering and rejecting uncounted possibilities Mobil decided upon safety. Safety was chosen due, in part, to the tremendous amount of publicity automotive safety had received as the result of the federal government's intrusion into auto makers' design prerogatives.

That Mobil was genuinely interested in helping its customers help themselves was apparent to all who read its ads. Partly due to the subject matter itself, as well as to the company's sincere desire to help reduce the carnage on the nation's highways, the campaign produced a massive response.

Mobil was deluged with requests for permission to reprint this ad in mass media—major consumer magazines, newspapers—and in trade publications, house organs, etc. Permission was happily granted, of course, resulting in Mobil's receiving millions of dollars' worth of additional exposures—including editorial comment—at absolutely no cost to the company.

This great ad was so timely, so well written, and of such intense interest to parents of driving teen-agers that the copy is quoted here in its entirety, while the ad itself is illustrated nearby.

Till death us do part.

It may be beautiful to die for love in a poem.

But it's ugly and stupid to die for love in a car.

Yet how many times have you seen (or been) a couple more interested in passion than in passing? Too involved with living to worry about dying?

Till death us do part.

It may be beautiful to die for love in a poem.

But it's ugly and stupid to die for love in a car.

Yet how many times have you seen (or been) a couple more interested in passion than in passing? Too involved with living to worry about dying?

As a nation, we are, allowing our young to be buried in tons of steel. And not only the reckless lovers—the just plain nice kids as well.

Everyone is alarmed about it. No one really knows what to do. And automobile accidents, believe it or not, continue to be the leading cause of death among young people between 15 and 24 years of age.

Parents are alarmed and hand over the keys to the car anyway.

Insurance companies are alarmed and charge enormous rates which deter no one.

Even statisticians (who don't alarm easily) are alarmed enough to tell us that by 1970, 14,450 young adults will die in cars each year.

(Just to put those 14,450 young lives in perspective: that is far more than the number of young lives we have lost so far in Viet Nam.)

Is it for this that we spent our dimes and dollars to all-but wipe out polio? Is it for this that medical science conquered diphtheria and smallpox?

What kind of society is it that keeps its youngsters alive only long enough to sacrifice them on the highway?

Yet that is exactly what's happening. And it's incredible.

Young people should be the best drivers, not the worst.

They have the sharper eyes, the steadier nerves, the quicker reflexes. They probably even have the better understanding of how a car works.

So why?

Are they too dense to learn? Too smart to obey the obvious rules? Too sure of themselves? Too un-sure? Or simply too young and immature?

How can we get them to be old enough to be wise enough before it's too late?

One way is by insisting on better driver training programs in school. Or after school. Or after work. Or during summers.

By having stricter licensing requirements. By rewarding the good drivers instead of merely punishing the bad ones. By having uniform national driving laws (which don't exist today). By having radio and TV and the press deal more with the problem. By getting you to be less complacent.

Above all, by setting a decent example ourselves.

Nobody can stop young people from driving. And nobody should. Quite the contrary. The more exposed they become to sound driving techniques, the better they're going to be. (Doctors and lawyers "practice," why not drivers?)

We at Mobil are not preachers or teachers. We sell gasoline and oil for a living and we want everyone to be a potential customer.

If not today, tomorrow. And we want everyone, young and old, to have his fair share of tomorrows. **Mobil.**

We want you to live.

As a nation, we are allowing our young to be buried in tons of steel. And not only the reckless lovers—the just plain nice kids as well.

Everyone is alarmed about it. No one really knows what to do. And automobile accidents, believe it or not, continue to be the leading cause of death among young people between 15 and 24 years of age.

Parents are alarmed and hand over the keys to the car anyway.

Insurance companies are alarmed and charge enormous rates which deter no one.

Even statisticians (who don't alarm easily) are alarmed enough to tell us that by 1975, some 15,000 young adults will die in cars each year.

(Just to put those 15,000 young lives in perspective, that is far more than the number of young lives we have lost so far in Viet Nam.)

Is it for this that we spent our dimes and dollars to all but wipe out polio? Is it for this that medical science conquered diphtheria and smallpox?

What kind of society is it that keeps its youngsters alive only long enough to sacrifice them on the highway?

Yet that is exactly what is happening. And it's incredible.

Young people should be the best drivers, not the worst.

They have the sharper eyes, the steadier nerves, the quicker reflexes. They probably even have the better understanding of how a car works.

So why?

Are they too dense to learn? Too smart to obey the obvious rules? Too sure of themselves? Too unsure? Or simply too young and immature?

How can we get them to be old enough to be wise enough before it's too late?

One way is by insisting on better driver training programs in school. Or after school. Or after work. Or during summer vacations.

By having stricter licensing requirements. By rewarding the good drivers instead of merely punishing the bad ones. By having uniform national driving laws (which don't exist today). By having radio and TV and the press deal more with the problem. By getting you to be less complacent.

Above all, by setting a decent example ourselves.

Nobody can stop young people from driving. And nobody should. Quite the contrary. The more exposed they become to sound driving techniques, the better they're going to be. (Doctors and lawyers "practice"; why not drivers?)

We at Mobil are not preachers or teachers. We sell gasoline and oil for a living and we want everyone to be a potential customer.

If not today, tomorrow. And we want everyone, young and old, to have his fair share of tomorrows.

MOBIL
We want you to live

Create an ad or an entire campaign with emotional headlines that ring true and you can have an all-time great. Beware, however, of the maudlin and the overly sentimental tearjerker. Motives show through. Ads are not opaque—they're far more transparent than many an ad person realizes.

Slogan Headlines

Progress is our most important product
 General Electric Company
You can be sure if it's Westinghouse
 , Westinghouse Electric Corporation
Ford has a better idea
 Ford Motor Company
When you care enough to send the very best
 Hallmark, Inc.
The quality goes in before the name goes on
 Zenith Corporation

These are typical and familiar themes—and occasionally they show up as the headline of an industrial advertisement. None will be quoted here because, even when paraphrased, they're too easily recognizable. In the past several months, however, the author has culled from business publications 14 such ads.

Using a theme or a slogan for a headline is a mistake. Presumably you've already drummed home the slogan into the reader's subconscious, so there's no earthly reason to use it for the headline in an ad. Besides, the typical slogan is too vague and nonspecific to make a really effective headline. It doesn't say anything of interest, and it doesn't promise specific benefits. Resist the temptation to do so, even if such a nonheadline headline would bring smiles of rapture to the faces of the powers that be within your company. Make your advertising money work, make it produce. Repetition of a slogan isn't the way to do it.

COMBINATION HEADLINES

Combination headlines are just what the name implies—combinations of one or more other types of headlines, or headlines that combine separate elements into a different type of headline than any of those previously mentioned. They are currently in vogue.

Cumulative Headlines

Use Nalgene laboratory bottles for just about any application.
Every one of them will bounce.
The Nagle Company, Inc.
Knock off 35% of shielding material costs with Hipernom. And
   stay competitive into the 1980's.
Westinghouse Metals Division
Bans backlash!
   Our new safety shut-off handle protects the operator . . . helps
   him tighten fasteners securely and uniformly
Gardner-Denver Company
Population explosion.
   Our innovators in switch design have produced more than
   200,000 different types. That's a lot of switches.
The Arrow-Hart & Hegeman Electric Co.
The Victor Digital Printer, just $335.
   335?
Victor Business Products
Parts like these produced in 1/3 to 1/6 the previous time.
   Up to 11.5 hours' saving per piece on N/C Omnimil Machining
   Center at Royal Oak Tool & Machine Co.
Sundstrand Machine Tool

Characteristic of the cumulative headline—or the supplementary headline, or the one-two punch headline, as it's sometimes called—is the fact that the two or more elements of the headline are physically separated from each other in the ad. This is, of course, done by the art director when the ad is laid out, although the copywriter who writes it usually instructs the art director to do so. This device tends to build interest with each segment of the headline, thus drawing the reader bit by bit into the body copy after he or she completes reading the various elements of the headline.

A cumulative headline enables the copywriter to get more information, news, statistics or benefits into the headline than would be possible if some other type of headline treatment were used. And the cumulative headline undeniably has great impact, what with the staccato statements hitting the reader in rapid succession.

Use the cumulative headline, by all means, if it enables you to tell your story easier and faster and better.

Headline for Nagle Company's ad is a vigorous combination of a command reinforced with the specific-fact subordinate headline. Effectively used here, you'll note, because the specific fact explains why it is in the reader's self-interest to obey the command.

The Arrow-Hart & Hegeman Electric Co. uses a cumulative headline that is composed of a teaser headline followed by a specific-fact headline. In this case use of the teaser is quite permissible since readership of body copy does not depend entirely upon reaction to the teaser.

A specific-fact headline followed by a short question headline used by Victor Business Products to make its point that the Digital Printer wasn't inordinately costly. The point was made swiftly and surely, leaving the reader to find out why the unit wasn't priced higher.

American Optical Corporation exploits the possibilities inherent in the cumulative headline to the fullest, as you'll note in the ad shown on the next page.

Can you recall these details . . .
when examining these?

Compare them simultaneously with AO's Duo-Star Microscope.

What could be more natural—or beneficial to American Optical Corporation—than to ask a question, split into two parts, while illustrating the user benefit derived from the product? The question and the extreme closeups team up to almost force a reader to admit to himself that he can't remember every tiny detail, even if it's important that he do so. The human mind doesn't function that way, and American Optical is astute enough to point it out. And to do it very convincingly.

Then comes the payoff—the statement of specific fact that *you,* the implied subject of the third portion of the cumulative headline, don't have to have a memory like an elephant to avoid making a mistake. American Optical's unique Duo-Star Microscope enables you to avoid guesswork without fiddling around with back-and-forth specimen changes.

This advertisement by the former American Optical Company explores the possibilities of the cumulative ad to the fullest. The copy and illustration set up a problem in microscopic analysis and then systematically supply all the arguments for the superiority of the Duo-Star microscope in dealing with the problem.

315

Layout is unusually clean, simple and uncluttered. Normally, half-tone illustrations in odd shapes (other than the conventional square or rectangle) are inadvisable. Here, however, because of the product itself, the round shape is exactly right because that is what the user of the product sees. Any other shape would have been wrong.

This ad telegraphs the facts, the user benefits, and what the body copy will contain even faster than a telegram could!

HEADLINE-IS-ALL-OF-THE-COPY HEADLINES

> *We have a new plan to help you make lube "pros" out of your oilers and cut maintenance costs. It's called Gulf LubeChek and requires practically no effort on your part. Your Gulf Sales Engineer is anxious to tell you about it. Call him at your nearest Gulf office. Or, if you prefer, write us direct for the free brochure which fully explains the plan.*

Gulf Oil Corporation

> *If you process at least 100 tons of steel per month, or 25 tons of aluminum or any other metal—we can provide you with documented proof that you should be using a Warner & Swasey coil conversion system.*

Warner & Swasey

For some time, the all-headline ad has enjoyed a burst of popularity, and justifiably so. Assume that you have only one or two major points you want to make—such as getting names in response to an offer of literature, or to have the reader pick up the phone to ask a district office for information—this can work well. The most significant user benefit can be communicated to an unusually large universe this way, for these ads usually are well read.

Gulf's ad quoted above is a spread; the left-hand page contains a bleed illustration of a lube "pro" wearing his Gulf button, while the right page is the one which carries the message to Garcia and everybody else. It's all in display type, which has great fascination for the average reader. The only other element in the entire spread is a coupon to be clipped and mailed—if the reader doesn't pick up the phone. The ad does a fine job of getting the message across when the product is of negligible interest, at best.

Although Warner & Swasey's ad contained a keyed schematic drawing and an admonition to write, wire, or phone, the long headline *is* the ad. The machine tool builder carefully qualifies readers by the "if you process" lead-in to make certain that only those who measure up to the criteria established by Warner & Swasey's sales department actually read the ad. These are quality readers, quality prospects for W&S—the ones it must talk to.

Large type is eye-catching, it's easy to read, and because of its dominance the reader unconsciously infers that the message is of more than ordinary importance. In this way oversize type frequently contributes to better than average readership.

VIRTUALLY USELESS HEADLINES

Incredibly, advertising's role, the contribution it can make to marketing success, and how the individual ad performs its function still are widely misunderstood—or simply not understood at all.

Only possible explanation for this is that hundreds of industrial advertisers habitually waste their money, three-fourths of it at least, by creating and running ads with useless headlines.

Such ineffective ads may be even worse than merely ineffective—they conceivably exert a negative influence. Instead of just failing to make any impression whatsoever on the reader—the prospect, that is—they may, indeed, make a poor impression because the ad presented either the product or the company in a derogatory manner.

Let's look at the six types of headlines that are useless at best, harmful at worst.

Negative Headlines

Your stock is bound to drop
   Detroit Diesel Engine Division, General Motors Corporation
The Company that Bought these Furnaces Wanted Its Money Back
   Sunbeam Equipment Corporation
Don't don't don't buy a high frequency AC calibration source . . .
   Holt Instrument Laboratories
"We have learned through bitter experience that Allen-Bradley resistors are unmatched for reliability"
   Allen-Bradley Company
Pssssst. Wanna get some nice cards free?
   Brown Company
What They Don't See Can Hurt You!
   R. E. Dietz Company
This Ad got us in deep trouble
   North American Manufacturing Company

317

We're not so nutty
Prestole Fasteners

We can really get you into hot water
Lauda Circulators

You'll miss the "whole"
Joslyn Stainless Steels

*Finally it's become impossible to describe a new machine in a
few words*
Link-Belt Speeder

When you pay over a grand for a tire, it better not go up in smoke
UniRoyal

*We wouldn't blame you if you never bought another new part from
us . . . now that our own brand X is here.*
Reliabilt (authorized rebuilt Detroit Diesel parts)

Including a negative word, phrase, or thought in a headline is a
perfectly legitimate ploy, but it's a mighty hazardous one. When hurriedly scanning the ad, the reader can easily take with him the negative
thought—not the positive one you want to convey.

The Detroit Diesel ad, for example, has a headline that's enough to
chill your soul if you own so much as a single share of stock in any
company. Read the headline and the logo, or signature, and the
thought which immediately leaps to mind is that somehow or other if
you buy a Detroit Diesel engine your stock will decline in price. You'll
lose money. *Your* money. Happy prospect, eh?

Sunbeam's headline is, if possible, even worse. Assuming that all of
the countless readership studies have some degree of validity, that
headline readership is the *one* thing you can count on getting, this ad
does the advertiser a grave disservice. *The Company that Bought these
Furnaces Wanted Its Money Back,* then the signature, Sunbeam—and
what impression does the reader retain from having skimmed this ad?
That of a company which builds such miserably poor products that its
customers clamor for their money back. Steer clear of headlines such
as this; they're too easily misinterpreted so as to distort the message.

Poor taste makes Brown Company's headline distinctly negative.
Pssssst. Wanna get some nice cards free? is innocuous in itself,
although hardly inspired. Possibly the headline is passable, except that
it teams up with the illustration all too well. That shows a seedy,
sinister, mustachioed, bearded hippie with hair longer than General
Custer's *before* the battle, leering into the camera; his hand is reaching
inside his coat for, one gathers, filthy post cards to peddle.

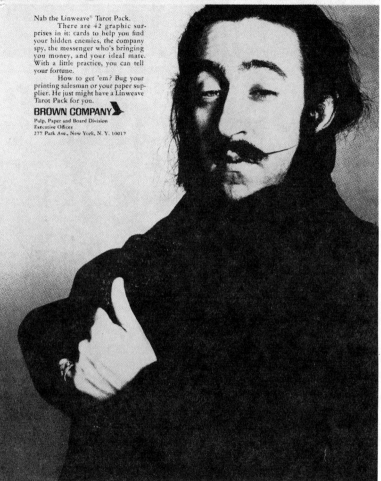

Pssssst.
Wanna get some nice cards free?

Nab the Linweave® Tarot Pack.

There are 42 graphic surprises in it: cards to help you find your hidden enemies, the company spy, the messenger who's bringing you money, and your ideal mate. With a little practice, you can tell your fortune.

How to get 'em? Bug your printing salesman or your paper supplier. He just might have a Linweave Tarot Pack for you.

BROWN COMPANY

Pulp, Paper and Board Division
Executive Offices
277 Park Ave., New York, N.Y. 10017

The power of the word "free" is lost completely in this ad—which is a born loser. It's illustrated nearby.

Don't don't don't buy Holt Instruments is the message flashed by the headline and logo in that company's ad. Hardly one they wanted to convey, of course, but the negative used not once, but repeated two more times, is overpowering. It's more than enough to damage Holt, perhaps indefinitely, in the minds of those who skimmed the display type in this ad.

no! no! Miss K*...
that's _not_ what we mean by WOOD BLOCK
factory floor MAINTENANCE

Our heroine is "all gummed up" and rightly so because she's being too literal. We have no pat process for removing gum, but we sure know how to keep wood block floors in business for a long, long time. Kreolite End Grain Wood Block Floors are our "babies" ... we've been manufacturing, installing and maintaining them for over 55 years (many of the originals are still performing as usual). We know that it's very easy to keep them working for the life of the building, and we'd like to show you how. Old floors that look like new are our best salesmen. So-o-o, let us help you cut costs and improve working conditions. Call EV 2-3411, or send this coupon for advice and counsel.

We've got a slide film that'll painlessly show you how!

There's absolutely no excuse for letting your wood block factory floor deteriorate ... it's just a matter of knowing how to maintain it and that's where we come in. A Jennison-Wright Sales Engineer in your area is ready and willing, in fact, anxious to show you our new enlightening sound strip film "Tender Loving Care for Wood Block Floors." Even if you don't have wood block floors—see this film and we'll give you odds you'll want them.

JENNISON WRIGHT

KREOLITE **WOOD BLOCK FLOORS**
TOLEDO, OHIO | *Inquiries Limited to Continental U.S.A.*

☐ Please send "Low Cost Maintenance" folder and new area marking formula folder
☐ or better yet, send a factory trained Jennison-Wright Wood Block Flooring Expert

Name_____ Company_____ Address_____ City and State_____ Zip Code_____

No! No! Miss K* . . . that's not what we mean by WOOD BLOCK factory floor MAINTENANCE is the headline of Jennison Wright's ad illustrated here. Negative, dangerously so. The reader in a hurry can easily read it like this: *No! No! not wood block factory floor . . . MAINTENANCE.* That's three negatives in a row, followed by the dirty word, maintenance, in capital letters. This implies that it's prudent to avoid wood block factory floors, that if you have one installed all you end up with is a headache caused by excessive maintenance. And even the curvesome cutey in the cartoon can't offset that negative impression.

A connotation of deliberate prevariation—or, at the very least, of flirting with the truth—is created by North American Manufacturing's negative headline. Merely stating that *This Ad got us in deep trouble* is distressing enough; nobody is interested in the other fellow's trouble. There isn't sufficient time for a reader to delve into why somebody he doesn't even know has trouble. If there is a surefire way to guarantee nonreadership, this headline does it. Then, to top off a futile attempt, "Ad" is capitalized in an effort to lift the headline and the ad out of the realm of the generic and into the exalted status of enduring literature. For some reason, this particular piece of prose didn't quite make it.

Link-Belt Speeder's inability to articulate significant facts about its new machine is touching. However, it leads to the inescapable conclusion that there can't really be much to say about it. Never, never confide to the reader that you're so overcome with emotion when you even think about the new Widget that you're all choked up, that words escape you. Doing this in print isn't a headline or an ad—it's a true confession; if this is what's wanted, follow the old formula of sin, suffer, and repent; type the manuscript neatly on blue-bordered paper and submit it to one of the pulp confession magazines. Possibly a check might accidentally come floating back, computed on the basis of a half-cent a word. Keep the hearts and flowers and hauntingly sad violins out of the business press.

Mistake made by UniRoyal is that its headline talks about an expensive tire going up in smoke caused by friction—and that hurts where it *really* hurts, in the pocketbook—and the illustration used ties right in. It shows a tire caught in the very act of destroying itself by—you guessed it—going up in smoke. Now, if the body copy isn't read, and it might not be, UniRoyal has left the impression that its most costly tires are prone to self-destruction. This is not exactly a positive approach to wooing additional customers, or of cementing relationships with present ones.

Borrowed Interest Headlines

up! up! up!
Armour Industrial Chemicals
Bet you didn't know that U. S. Grant & J. S. McCormick were inaugurated together
J. S. McCormick Co.
"Le bain a tout faire"
Gilson Medical Electronics
Just imagine a billion spark plugs
The Prestolite Company

Dead center!
Welch Drill Bushing Company

Come and get it!
American Cyanamid Company

In "The Great Relay Race" you're a winner every time!
Eagle Signal

Et tu, Brute!
Jo-Line Tools, Inc.

The Case of the Flying Stamping
The Crosby Company

If you're a "far sighted" bird, you'll insist on A. O. Smith quality
A. O. Smith Corporation

A lot of fight comes in a small package
Tulsa Products Division

A good decision
The Fremont Flask Co.

For some obscure reason that's difficult to fathom, a few ad managers and copywriters adopt a defensive position about presenting their product to their public. Apparently they feel that readers are not interested in it, making it necessary to disguise what they're up to, what they're going to talk about. They have an urge to make it appear that they're on the verge of discussing something entirely different from the product.

This is the borrowed interest gambit, an exercise in circumlocution—both verbally and visually. Symptoms which make diagnosis of this malady simple are a headline which has little or nothing to do with the matter at hand, usually accompanied by an illustration which is equally inapplicable.

Relying on borrowed interest is a tricky thing; basically, it's dishonest because an attempt is made, consciously or unconsciously, to fool the reader. And there's always a construction job to be done, a bridge to be built between the subject from which interest is borrowed, and the product or service. Most attempts to do this are clumsy and contrived and few readers proceed past this point.

Shortly after World War II, the borrowed interest approach was enthusiastically endorsed by a number of unsophisticated industrial advertisers. Eventually they saw the folly of their ways, and the borrowed interest headline fell from favor. Unfortunately, it didn't fall far enough, for it continues to crop up even today.

Let's examine a few ads of this type whose headlines were given above.

up! up! up! Armour's headline is accompanied by an illustration of a cute little four-year-old girl either bouncing on a trampoline or thrown high into the air by her doting father. She's appealing, her expression is appropriately gleeful, and she's quite obviously having fun. And who can deny that four-year-old girls, in common with those 20 years their senior, are of universal interest? The little ones touch the heart and bring a smile to the lips. But Armour isn't selling little girls' dresses, skirts, hair ribbons, or what have you; the body copy following the borrowed interest headline is so boring, so self-serving, so inept that it's a wonder it ever saw the light of print. Copy starts: *We're growing . . . bursting our seams . . . jumping* (see, the little girl was jumping—that explains why she's there at all, particularly up, up, up) *to meet your needs. We are expanding our facilities and all units are working at increased capacity to serve you better. Serving as we do more than 15 basic industries, we have heard often that our line of*—and so on, ad nauseam. Switch names, product lines, and logos and this collection of trite clichés could have been run by any advertiser who wanted only to see the firm's name in print. Few readers found any incentive to go past the point in the ad where the quoted copy stops, if they even went that far. And that's debatable.

You know, there's no disputing J. S. McCormick Company's headline. They are absolutely 100 percent right. The author confesses to *not* knowing that J. S. McCormick Company and U. S. Grant were inaugurated together. However, there's some consolation. If we exclude those few people at J. S. McCormick and its agency who chose this desperate approach (complete with a woodcut illustration of the late President), chances are those who were aware of this startling bit of intelligence could be counted on the fingers of one hand—with a few fingers to spare. Copy goes: *It's true. U. S. Grant started in Washington about the same time J. S. McCormick Company started in Pittsburgh. So?* So, who got past the "so?" But it turns out that J. S. McC. hedges a bit in the body copy since that says the President and the company were inaugurated *"about the same time."* Now, inaugurated together and at about the same time are a horse of another color. This is reaching far too far. In an attempt to lure a few history buffs or admirers of an heroic general and great President, the ad stretches the truth, then immediately contradicts itself. The number of readers who went on to learn that there was an expansion of Our Plant, and how hard J. S. McCormick Company has worked over the years were few and far between. Who cares?   Consider for a minute, then make a guess. How many buying influences in industry are multilingual? How many, narrowing this down further, read French?

Consider for a minute, then make a guess. How many buying influences in industry are multilingual? How many, narrowing this down further, read French? With no crystal ball handy, a guess would be 5 percent to the first question, one-fifth of 1 percent to the second. This means, of course, that Gilson automatically beams its headline only to this minute segment of its universe—and despite the illustration of a pert French maid in which there *is* interest—the ad was a waste of money. No illustration of an irrelevant person who has nothing to do with the product can begin to compensate for casting aside three-fourths of the ad's ability to produce an impression.

Reliable estimates place the number of gun owners in this country around the 90-million mark. A tally of hunting licenses sold by all of the states disclosed that some 27 million Americans take to the field each year, gun in hand. Add the serious hobbyists, arms collectors, target shooters, and trap and skeet enthusiasts, and the total is impressive. So Welch Drill Bushing people aren't as far off in their borrowed interest headline as they could be, especially so since the illustration is of one of their small products superimposed in the center of a target with three bullet holes in a typical triangle group, framed by a rendition of a Colt Army Model 1848 cap-and-ball revolver. Welch has going for it the average American's traditional love of guns, plus the cherished right, unique in all the world, guaranteed by the Constitution, that all of us may own and use guns for legitimate purposes. Even so, the bridge between a brief discussion of the antique arm and the product is contrived and pretentious.

Vintage airplane buffs might be attracted to the photograph of the 1911 Cessna after reading about the flying stamping in Crosby's ad, just as ornithologists and random bird-watchers might pore over A. O. Smith's headline and four-color photo of a singularly determined looking eagle. And animal lovers in general might glance at Tulsa Products Division's illustration of the ferocious-looking wolverine seemingly on the verge of attacking something—perhaps a doe and fawn.

All of these headlines and copy approaches are essentially self-defeating because of the basic premise that the product is not of interest to the reader. Or the assumption is made that he or she doesn't want to read about it because he'd rather read about eagles or wolverines or old Colts. Both are wrong.

Torrington's ad, illustrated nearby, is something of a shock, and it's also out of context. The Torrington Company campaigns have been excellent over the years. Especially noteworthy is the current campaign on the ability to produce small, intricate parts at lower cost than can most end users. It's noteworthy, persuasive, and undoubtedly effective.

Things are looking up at Torrington.

Right up into space!

Because one of the latest and most remarkable Torrington Bearings is helping to condition our Astronauts for their trip "out there" and back.

The Astronaut you see here is whirling around on a contour couch at the end of a fifty-foot arm that revolves around a central pivot and goes so fast it can create pressures of 20 to 30 G's.

It's the centrifuge at the NASA center near Houston. In it, our Astronauts will be readied for the sustained forces that are exerted on a space vehicle when it brakes during re-entry into the earth's atmosphere.

The gondola is gimbal-mounted on four Torrington

Spherical Roller Bearings, 18.11" I.D., 24" O.D. by 5.14" wide. Ordered by The Rucker Company which built the centrifuge for NASA, these bearings were specifically designed and made for the job. But what an assignment!

The extended length of the arm, the unusual strains placed on the bearing, the extreme misalignment and the tremendous speeds generated presented a whole new set of problems and specifications to Torrington.

If your problem is "way out," we'll give it a whirl at our Bearing Divisions, South Bend, Ind. 46621 or Torrington, Conn. 06790.

THE TORRINGTON COMPANY 100TH YEAR

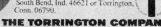

The Torrington Company, maker of small, intricate parts for industry, has been noted for excellent advertising campaigns for many years. Here, however, difficulties were encountered when the "borrowed interest" technique was tried. The illustration is compelling, but does not go with the body copy beneath.

In this ad, however, it takes the borrowed interest tack. *Things are looking up at Torrington* is the headline, with an illustration which appears to be—unless you read as far as the third paragraph of body copy—a rough-looking individual about to do someone bodily harm. In the third paragraph we find that this is not the case. The man shown is an astronaut enduring the stress of 20 to 30 G's, hence his anguished (not threatening) expression.

In addition to borrowing interest which Torrington can never completely make its own, the headline is negative. Implied is that it's high time things look up at Torrington before something terrible happens.

Shy away from the borrowed interest headline. Interest can't be appropriated permanently, there's every chance of losing the reader in the bridge between the nonsubject and the product-subject of the ad, and that you can't afford to do.

Irrelevant Headlines

G-Whiz
International Equipment Company
Varoom
Belden Corporation
What's up?
The Mitre Corporation
Happy landings
United Air Freight
Is your wife cold?
National Fuel Oil Institute

Although the number of irrelevant headlines is relatively small, it's not small enough. After reading the above, do you have the faintest idea of what the product or service is?

Headlines must communicate, and those don't. Any valid relationship between headline and product is strictly coincidental.

Take *G-Whiz*, for example—and it's set in huge display type. Supposedly this should interest the reader, at least those prospects for an ultracentrifuge, in one of the gadgets that can "take you into areas of biological research where you've never gone before." Somehow or other, the headline doesn't exactly say that unless there's a highly technical G-Whiz effect on specimens whirled at great speed. International Equipment Company would have fared far better in the battle for readership if a product benefit—or even a hint of one—appeared in the headline.

And Belden just doesn't say anything in the irrelevant headline, *Varoom*. If it were accompanied by an illustration of a slightly blurred

Indianapolis racing car flashing down the straightaway in an ad run by the manufacturer for a component part which was subjected to great stress and strain, it might have some relevance. For wire used in magnets, lawnmowers, and material-handling equipment, huh-uh. Not even for the neighbor's threshing machine barbering his lawn at 7:30 a.m. on Sunday.

What's up? could apply to baseballs, airplanes, or arrows, but hardly to a team of engineers who are discussed, not shown, in an all-type ad. And *Happy landings* could be relevant to a relaxed vacationer at the airport, ready to take off for Hawaii; to a businessman, briefcase in hand, hurrying to get into the company jet; or to a fighter pilot taxiing down the strip on a mission. But not to *air freight.* Inanimate objects cannot have either happy landings or unhappy landings since they're incapable of experiencing emotion.

In a class by itself is, *Is your wife cold?* This headline appearing over the signature of National Fuel Oil Institute could have just as easily been run by a dedicated group of psychologists, psychiatrists, and gynecologists dedicated to fighting emotional and physical causes of frigidity through mental therapy or, perhaps, surgery. If such were the case, and if the ad appeared in a medium read almost exclusively by young married adults, it could be both relevant and appropriate. As is, the headline is not relevant—but it *is* vulgar and tasteless and crude. Advertising hinting of the gutter should be refused by media, for it accomplishes only one thing: It hurts advertising in general.

Spend your budget money to talk about user benefits and about the product. Going off onto a tangent and talking about a subject foreign to the one you should discuss is unforgivable.

Precious Headlines

Today, the big deal in construction is the Giesel-powered truck.
The what-powered truck?
White Trucks

Time you stopped horsing around?
The Fellows Gear Shaper Company

This boom hoist out boom hoists all other boom hoists!
Northwest Engineering Company

We're not fishing for a compliment. . . we're just "bassking in our glory"
Alloy Metal Abrasive Company

Quit tooling around.
Michigan Tool Company

Don't be "hoodwinked"
Kewaunee Mfg. Co.
What makes SAMI run?
United States Shoe Machinery Corporation
We'd rather freight than switch!
Missouri Pacific-Texas & Pacific

Coined words always require an explanation. Explaining what a coined word means is a fast way to accomplish two things: (1) cause readers not really interested in the coined word to skip over the ad, and (2) encourage nonproductive verbosity through a long-winded explanation which shouldn't have been necessary in the first place.

White Trucks, Division of White Motor Corporation, accomplishes both with one "swell foop." All truck operators and a large segment of the general public are thoroughly familiar with Rudolf Diesel's ultraefficient engine which operates on low-cost fuel oil rather than on more highly refined and more expensive gasoline. The diesel engine has earned an enviable reputation and widespread acceptance because of its cheaper fuel, as well as because of its longer prime of life and greatly reduced maintenance cost. White's attempt to link a new gasoline engine with conventional electrical ignition with the economical diesel which fires from compression is too precious for words.

And it fails to achieve its objective, which obviously is to promote acceptance and demand for the company's new 250-h.p. Mustang gasoline power plant. White could have used the powerful word "new," followed by the name of the engine, its displacement, and a user benefit, and harvested a bumper crop of readers and prospects. For some reason, however, it didn't. More's the pity.

Time you stopped horsing around? in Fellows' headline is followed, predictably enough, by horses pulling a wagon—but the product is plastic. No user benefit, no product feature, but a mighty precious play on words.

This boom hoist out boom hoists all other boom hoists! My, my, we *are* precious, aren't we?

For a manufacturer of fume hoods to demand that readers not be "hoodwinked" is going pretty far. But to then insult their intelligence by putting the term in quotation marks to make sure they understand the little joke is mighty, mighty precious. The same space and the same production investment could have presented a user benefit—and the advertiser's name—at the same cost.

Literary allusions are undesirable because not everyone is familiar with the passage, or the work, referred to. And if they're not, they skip the ad because the headline makes them feel like a clod. Many have read Budd Schulberg's hard-bitten novel, *What Makes Sammy*

Run? But more people, many more, haven't. Granted, the headline is cute, primarily because the Semi-Automatic Multiple Inserter abbreviates to SAMI—close to the name of Schulberg's protagonist. Even if the spelling were exact, it's poor policy to allude to fictional characters. Some people might not find them admirable. Some people might find them detestable, in fact, and there was much to detest about Sammy Glick. It's not quite the same thing as tying in a promotion with Santa Claus, for example, or dropping Uncle Sam's name when mentioning customers.

Referring to another product's slogan, as Mo-Pac did when the carrier casually adapted Tareyton cigarettes' campaign theme, can be disastrous. To those unfamiliar with the original slogan, this headline is meaningless. And what conceivable good can accrue from a meaningless headline? When a copywriter is desperate for an idea, when the creative stream has ceased flowing, when the well of ideas has dried up, that's when another product's headline, theme, or slogan is filched. Trying times shouldn't ever be that trying.

United States Shoe Machinery Corporation's headline—a headline that is both headline and body copy is exquisitely precious—so precious, in fact, that it stands alone. It must be quoted in its entirety. It reads:

> *See the turning spindle on the other lathe.*
> *See the tracer slide under the spindle.*
> *See the chips fall and stop the slide.*
> *Hear the spindle to PR-R-R-KLONK!*
> *Hear the angry machine fixer.*
> *Hear the boss howl.*
> *See the turning spindle on this lathe.*
> *See the tracer slide over the spindle.*
> *See the chips fall free.*
> *See the smiling machine fixer.*
> *See the happy boss.*
> *See the profits grow.*
> *See DBM.*
> *Try a Detroit Tracer Lathe—for better profits.*

See Spot. See Spot run. See Spot run, Dick. See Spot run, Dick and Jane. Color precious ads juvenile.

So-What Headlines

> *This Smith Widget Line adds vigor to a growing industry in a grow-*
> *ing country.*
> Smith Precision Widgets, Inc.

329

The name of the game is Experience
   Pittsburgh Steel Company
Magnecraft Relays go industrial
   Magnecraft Electric Co.
Supermarket
   Turco Products
et cetera, etc., etc.
   HPM, Division of Koehring Company
From the shadows of the past...
   Revere Copper and Brass, Incorporated
When you have work to fasten automatically
   Precision Welder & Flexopress Corporation
Safe, efficient paint handling
   Cleveland Tramrail Division
Buy job-mated hoists
   Shepard Niles

When a headline instantly and automatically evokes a "so what?" response from the reader, it certainly hasn't aroused his interest or done much of a selling job.

...adds vigor to a growing industry in a growing country. So what?

The name of the game is Experience. So what? (Not even *what* game?)

Magnecraft Relays go industrial. So what?

The so-what reaction is one you can do without. As almost anyone would say, and perhaps this sums up the so-what headline as well as any other comment, "Blah."

Try on a headline for size if you're the least bit unsure as to whether or not it's of the so-what variety. Read it to yourself a couple of times, read it aloud, repeat it a few times. Evaluate it objectively, and if it produces a so-what response, waste no time in consigning it to the round file—but don't use it.

An unusually tasteless example is shown. *Dyna-Quip is in a family way*, the headline states. Nothing in the headline to pull a reader into the copy, but it's replete with precious little things like *When we gave birth to the first...our brain-child...multiple birth...quite a family going for us...our Free Catalog filled with pregnant ideas*—and Dyna-Quip capitalized Free Catalog. This advertiser has managed to transform something joyous and beautiful into locker-room snickers. All for what? A so-what!

Say-Nothing Headlines
   It's taking the world by storm
   General Electric

Dyna-Quip is in a family way

so, we're proudly passing out Free Catalogs of our new, complete fluid power component line! When we gave birth to the first completely new design in pneumatic quick couplings in over 50 years, your enthusiasm for our brain-child encouraged us to try again.

This time, it was a multiple birth . . . a complete line of fluid power components.

By adding "that something extra" to water and steam couplings, hydraulic couplings, hose fittings and adapters, general purpose hose, self-storing hose, ball valves, snap valves, blow guns, filters, regulators and lubricators . . . we feel we have quite a family going for us,

Write for our Free Catalog filled with pregnant ideas on how to improve your fluid power systems.

dyna-quip

A DIVISION OF STILE-CRAFT MANUFACTURERS, INC. • 1801 Lilly Ave., St. Louis, Mo. 63110

Author Stansfield's analysis of this ad begins on the opposite page.

The shape of things to come
Drake Manufacturing Company

Simple Folks
State of Georgia

*If you make automobile trim (or other aluminum products) better
make them with HOWMET aluminum*
Howmet Corporation

A winning team in the war against downtime!
International Research and Development Corporation

You've got to be an expert to see what TRW makes.
TRW

What would you do without your Authorized SKF Distributor?
SKF Industries, Inc.

Production increases can now be made in the twinkling of an eye
Hobart Brothers Company

Saying something of genuine importance about a product with which a person is intimately acquainted should be the easiest thing in the world. On the other hand, writing a headline that doesn't actually say anything, stringing words together grammatically and logically but without meaning should take a bit more doing.

Many advertising managers and so-called copywriters manage this, though, as a perusal of the preceding headlines and riffling through any decent trade publication proves.

For some obscure reason, some copywriters strain to be obtuse. Maybe a deep-seated personality problem enters into it. These individuals may have a feeling of inadequacy, a pressing need to prove beyond a shadow of doubt that they are more astute, more perceptive, more of everything than all of us in the common herd. Then again, it could be they merely don't understand advertising; or they're not cut out to be writers; or they're immature. Too, they may be searching without success for a sound selling proposition, or the problem wasn't thoroughly explained to them, or they may not give three whoops whether the headline is effective or not. You'll find all of these personality types in the advertising field, working right beside the real pros.

Regardless of how and why it originated, the say-nothing headline is a flop and a serious mistake in judgment. Comments on a few of the above say-nothing headlines are:

General Electric's statement that *It's taking the world by storm* doesn't say anything, doesn't sell anything. It what? Why is it doing so? No information, no enticement to read further, no strength. And no headline.

Our best salesman is an mpty disp ns r.

(The other guy's.)

With some suppliers, it's a toss-up whether you run out of patience before you run out of towels. With Brown Company's Service Products distributors you won't run out of either.

The reason? Our men are hand-picked. They're aggressive. They know your needs. They're committed to the policy that no order is too tough.

Need NIBROC® towels or tissues fast? Or any other related products that will make your job easier and more efficient? Our area distributor will work overtime, if necessary, to deliver your supplies on time. And in good condition.

You'll find our NIBROC absorbent products top quality—and our distributor's service unbeatable.

So count on your local Brown Company Service Products distributor to keep your dispensers full.

He'll do it. We'll do it.

Service Products Division / **BROWN COMPANY**
Kalamazoo, Michigan 49004 / Executive Offices: 277 Park Avenue, New York, N.Y. 10017

The shape of things to come. What shape? What things? Where are they? What are they good for? When will they come? What will they do for the reader? How will they help in the job? How do they get here? What price are they? How are they sold—singly, in pairs, by the pound, by the gallon, in gross lots, or? Drake's headline leaves a few questions unanswered because it says nothing. Unanswered, also, is the question of why a reader would read the advertisement.

And Howmet didn't say *why* you'd better use its aluminum. There's only the veiled threat that you'd *better* use it, with the implication that there's an or-else somewhat less than pleasant.

When the clichés go marching in, International Research's say-nothing headline is bound to be out in the front ranks. "Winning team," "war against," and similar trite couplings of tired words have moss on them. Use such worn-out phrases to say nothing and you'll get exactly that, as far as readership is concerned.

What would you do without your Authorized SKF Distributor? That's a tough one to answer. The only rejoinder that comes readily to mind is: "Just exactly what I'm doing right now." Somehow or other, the author has gotten along in this world all of these years without ever once having come into contact with an Authorized SKF Distributor—and seems little the worse for it as far as can be determined. You can rely upon the average business reader to think like that, too.

At first glance Brown Company's headline appears to be of the cumulative variety, composed as it is of two parts. Closer examination of the headline, however, discloses that this headline is actually a say-nothing headline.

Initially, this was probably a pretty decent ad. Good, that is, until somebody decided to be ultracreative and illustrate with missing letters that something missing isn't too desirable.

Only thing, when a headline reads: *Our best sales rep is an mpty disp ns r.* the reader won't exert himself enough to fill in the missing letters. Give a reader a puzzle to solve, a task to do, or otherwise make work out of reading an ad—and he or she doesn't. That person will skip over the ad almost invariably because the business reader doesn't have time for fun and games. Of prime interest are ads that telegraph a benefit that will help. Fail to flag the attention in this way and you've lost a prospect.

Second portion of the headline (*The other guy's*), was probably noticed only by a tiny portion of those exposed to this Brown ad. Too bad, too, because the body copy does a persuasive job of selling Brown's services and its towels. It deserved to be read.

Brag-and-Boast Headlines

We are No. 1 in RF Voltmeters and you better believe it!
  Boonton Electronics Corporation

Ampholine—The New Dimension in Protein Separation
  LKB Instruments, Inc.

For the medical student only the best is good enough
  E. Leitz, Inc.

Tougher products for the surfers—thanks to AMOCO IPA
Amoco Chemicals Corporation

Miles from nowhere. . . only the best in valves is good enough
Jenkins Bros.

Thoroughbred products with a winning tradition verify Eaton Yale & Towne capability
Eaton Yale & Towne, Inc.

Morse means "the most" in cutting tools
Morse Twist Drill & Machine Co.

At whatever stage of your project you need a cabinet, your most reliable choice is EMCOR
Ingersoll Products

Wotan Horizontal Boring Mills are setting new standards for accuracy and performance. . .
Wotan Division of Hunter Douglas International Corporation

Hamilton Standard leads with electron beam machines for all types and conditions of production welding
Hamilton Standard

Brag-and-boast headlines are so patently self-serving that they lack credibility. Readers ignore them in droves. Readers read what appeals to them, and that doesn't include hearing somebody pat himself on the back. As stated before, headlines have appeal for business readers because they find in them a benefit resulting from use of the product. Nobody, but nobody, is the least bit interested in listening to an unknown party brag about how smart he is to have developed such a magnificently superior product, or about how the company is so infinitely better than any other company. There's always the unseen, but nonetheless present, capitalization in most brag-and-boast headlines where the product appears to be capitalized even if it's not, as if the word were coming down from on high direct from some omniscient being who's letting the reader in on a good thing as a personal favor and with the purest and most unselfish of motives, of course.

We are No. 1. . .and you better believe it! And just what happens if the reader chooses not to believe it? This is salesmanship in print?

Only the best, only the best. Come, come E. Leitz. Your reputation has been firmly established for more than 30 years; the superb Leica camera, unexcelled optics in microscopes, binoculars, and other instruments have solidified your preeminent position in the industry for you. Superiority of Leitz products is accepted without question. Brag and boast like this ill becomes you. And it's not necessary.

335

Jenkins Bros. headline would have been far more effective if, instead of merely bragging and boasting, it had said something like this: *Jenkins valves on this oil company's header, 57 miles from the nearest town, have required no maintenance since installation 11 years, 7 months ago.* Some interesting story about Jenkins valves has to be there if they actually are the best—or even nearly that good. Had the company searched out that story and told it factually and interestingly, and with a benefit the reader could visualize as helping him or her, the ad would have triggered more than yawns and turned pages.

Being customer-oriented rather than self-oriented prevents brag-and-boast headlines from getting farther than the typewriter. Cultivate the mental attitude that causes you to ask yourself, "Now what does the prospect want to know about my product? What benefit will appeal most to him or her?" Do this and you'll write headlines that do what you want them to—drag the reader into the body copy.

No-Headline Ads

Since the headline accounts for a full 75 percent of the readership of the ad as a whole, on the surface it would seem that no advertiser would run an ad with a virtually useless headline—or (horrors) with no headline at all.

Things are not always as they appear to be on the surface, however, for many advertisers commit the cardinal sin of producing headlineless ads. Why they do this is a moot point. Chances are it's because they think—mistakenly—that their ad, lacking a headline, will stand out from all of the other ads in the book, thus garnering great flocks of readers who might otherwise have passed their ad by. This is a costly fallacy.

Sun Oil Company's two-color spread ad, headlineless, is well written, the selling proposition is sound, there's a story to tell about the product, use of the second color only in the logo is restrained and dignified. As a whole, the ad is well conceived, based as it is on the concept that "a good lubricant's only *half* the story." Sunoco know-how, Sunoco ability to help the customer is the other half of the ad's story.

The device used to attract attention—cutting the pages in half, with white space above the illustration and copy—is legitimate and it accomplished its purpose. The ad does strike you, it has great impact.

Apparently, however, neither the copywriter nor the art director could solve the problem of just how to get a headline in a spread ad which has the top one-third of it consigned to oblivion. A shame, because this ad could have been great with a little more thought and creative time put in on it.

A no-headline ad by the Sun Oil Company—analyzed on previous page

337

If any one thing can be certain in an uncertain business, it's that ads sans headlines will receive substantially less readership than ads with headlines—even poor ones. Why make it tough on yourself?

Headline Length

There's an old saying to the effect that a person's legs must be long enough to reach the ground. Few are inclined to dispute this. Almost the same thing applies to the headline, although there is opposition to this statement. The headline, too, should be long enough to do the job —but should be neither arbitrarily shorter nor unreasonably longer. No reason which will stand up under serious scrutiny exists for anybody to assume a dictatorial attitude about length of the headline, either in favor of short or long.

On the contrary, all available data bear out the contention of most of us that length of the headline has remarkably little to do with how well read it is. Content determines that.

McGraw-Hill reports in its Laboratory of Advertising Performance on a study made by the publisher's Reader Feedback rating service on 4,993 industrial advertisements. Objective was to determine, among other things, whether headlines must be short as a highly vocal group of advertising men proclaim. Exponents of short headlines scored such a hollow victory that not one loud, exultant hurrah echoed from their camp. Results of the study show that headline length influenced readership to this extent.

Words In Headline	Number of Ads	Index of Average Reader Feedback Score
1 - 3	661	127
4 - 10	3,136	126
More than 10	1,130	126
No headline	66	100

So, we see that headlines composed of three words or less collected for themselves the tremendous amount of 1/127th extra readership as compared with headlines of *more than* 10 words—headlines which obviously could contain more information and do a better job of attracting favorable attention of prospective purchasers of the product.

Ignore injunctions against the long headline. This is not to advocate long, rambling, verbose headlines whose outstanding characteristic is that they're long. But if the situation calls for a lengthy headline, don't hesitate to use it.

Factors other than length influence readership of headlines, and of complete ads, as we shall see in subsequent chapters.

Chapter 8

BODY COPY

THE illustration, if it's well conceived, striking, and pertinent, has by now stopped the reader—at least momentarily. Fleeting as this moment is, it's long enough to arouse sufficient interest for him or her to take the next step. This is the critically important one of reading the headline.

This sequence of events is based, of course, on the premise that you're preparing a conventional ad with illustration, headline, and body copy, rather than an all-copy ad. When using the all-copy approach there's naturally one less step in the process.

At this time, the headline—the single most important element in the ad—is able to build upon interest generated by the illustration and, in turn, perform its job. That is to entice the reader into the body copy. The headline is a good one if it does this, regardless of whether it's deathless prose or not.

Even if the headline *is* the most important element of the ad, we must nonetheless recognize that it gained this distinction due to its dominant position and its unique function, to gain readership of the text which follows. For when all is said and done and the money has been invested and the ad has appeared in publications on schedule, in all except a tiny handful of ads the effectiveness of the ad rests pretty largely upon the readership the body copy received.

We've all heard the old clichés that business people are too busy to read ads, and so on. Supposedly, as the pace gets more frantic and more and more demands are made upon our time, we don't read much of anything, much less business publications.

This is dead wrong.

Contrary to uninformed opinion of behind-the-times management of unsophisticated industrial companies (opinion invariably based on personal prejudice and reinforced by lack of exposure to effective industrial advertising and the other marketing services), advertising copy *is* read, and read thoroughly.

There's simply no disputing this. Readership of industrial advertisements has been thoroughly documented, probed, analyzed—and proved—in countless major studies made over the years. Studies were made by publishers and agencies, who admittedly have an ax to grind, as well as by individual advertisers and various independent research organizations. They have no ax to grind. This fact of business life is questioned only by the naive or the incompetent.

The Desire to Achieve

We're lucky. Every industrial advertising person who writes or approves copy has a very potent ally working for him—the fact that the people he or she wants to talk to read business publications because they consider this a vital part of a continuing educational program to enable them to handle their present job and qualify for a better one. The desire to achieve and to advance is one of the strongest you'll encounter in industry, or, for that matter, in with the male and female of the species.

When we're talking to such readers they are in a businesslike frame of mind. They're in the mood to learn. Furthermore, they have both the need and the desire to acquire information about products which can help them, and they're eager to absorb what you want to tell them about your product if you relate it to their interests, their problems, and their needs.

Our typical prospect is quite receptive, something like the well-heeled individual who wants a new car and enters a dealer showroom *wanting* to be sold. The automobile sales rep's job is ridiculously easy when he has a prospect with this mental attitude. And having tens of thousands of prospects with this same outlook makes your job as ad manager—and/or copywriter—simple, too. Industrial advertising, after all, is merely salesmanship in print. This makes the writer the first sales rep from the company to contact the prospect with a specific selling proposition. You're halfway home free when your prospect wants to buy. All you have to do is show why he or she should buy your product instead of a competitor's.

Oddly, only a small percentage of all industrial advertisers take full advantage of their prospects' desire to be sold. The majority kick opportunity in the teeth. They write and place ads so vague and inept and dull that the impression they make has about as much substance to it as a tendril of fog at dawn.

While it is a marketing function to assign specific, measurable tasks to advertising in support of the written marketing plan, it is advertising's responsibility to handle these assignments with the greatest possible efficiency. The burden, in the final analysis, rests on the advertising manager who relies on heavy artillery in the battle for prospects' minds—copy.

This burden isn't a burden in the sense that it weighs heavily or unpleasantly on the industrial advertising manager, however. Exactly the opposite is true because it presents the opportunity to solve problems and to express himself or herself with copy that is interesting and informative, lively and logical, pithy and persuasive.

There's a great deal of satisfaction in writing industrial advertising copy. Creating tight copy is rewarding and fulfilling. The writer derives a unique sense of accomplishment from the knowledge that the output is the end product of an orderly, organized mind, of a person who analyzed and solved a problem, and who knows *what* should be done and does it the way it should be done. He realizes also that he alone in the company has the ability to handle this important job.

This ability to adhere closely to a strong core idea, to discard the irrelevant, and to ignore that which is not truly pertinent, sets the advertising individual and the copy apart from product-oriented, engineering-oriented associates. Usually they're so bogged down in minor details and unnecessary technicalities about how the widget operates and what it should be used for that they're simply unable to grasp the fact that prospects must be told *what the widget will do for them.*

To produce results, copy must do seven things to and for the reader. These are:

1. Create interest.
2. Inform.
3. Involve the reader.
4. Help.
5. Convince.
6. Persuade.
7. Induce a response.

Let's take a look at each of these seven musts and see how they relate to each other—and to an effective ad.

Interest

Ideally, advertising copy should be inherently interesting—interesting, that is, to the average reader of publications in which the ad appears, as well as to those who are your most logical prospects. Face it, though: Just because your company manufactures a valve or turret lathe or a widget doesn't automatically make this fact interesting to the reader who isn't economically or emotionally involved with the product. Your ad about the product isn't intrinsically interesting. It's up to you to make it interesting.

As far as the reader is concerned, you're on the spot. You're on trial—or your ad is—right from the opening sentence in the lead-in paragraph. You remain on trial through the body copy to the signature at the bottom right-hand column of type.

It's here, in this first sentence of body copy, that you have a moral obligation. You must follow through on the promise, express or implied, in both the illustration and the headline. They promised the reader a reward for investing time in your ad. You've had it if you fail to live up to this promise and do it immediately. The reader remains a reader, but of another ad. Not yours.

For some unknown reason—probably because they've found they can get by with it—only advertising copywriters consistently produce a high proportion of vapid, inane, uninteresting copy. If these same writers wrote material for sale, instead of for a salary, they would be forced to punch up their copy and make it come alive. Any popular magazine offers a number of examples of copy on a wide variety of subjects that are genuinely interesting from the first line of the lead-in paragraph.

Take the opening sentence of an article on the mysterious billionaire, Howard Hughes, in the old *Saturday Evening Post*, for example. It reads:

> *7000 Romain Street is in that part of Los Angeles familiar to readers of Raymond Chandler and Dashiell Hammett: the underside of Hollywood, south of Sunset Boulevard, a middle-class slum of "model studios" and warehouses and two-family bungalows.*

Every mystery story addict, TV watcher, and moviegoer is familiar with Chandler and Hammett. "Underside of Hollywood" is a promising phrase, as is "model studios." You can imagine what goes on in *them*. The neighborhood comes alive with this colorful description, and so does readers' interest. Obviously the editors' did, for the article sold.

Or:

Forty minutes after the assassination of President Kennedy, Mrs. Helen Louise Markham left her second-story flat at 328 Ninth Street in the Oak Cliff section of Dallas and walked over to catch a bus.

This lead sentence from an article in *Esquire* comes as close to guaranteeing readership of an article as any 35 words possilby can. There's an aura of suspense, a feeling that something important is to be disclosed for the first time. The casual reader of *Esquire* is compelled to read on, especially since there are so many unanswered questions about the Kennedy assassination and so much legitimate criticism of the Warren Commission and its report.

Then in *Outdoor Life:*

After stalking that bull elk for nearly a mile, we now had him coming toward us.

Name three sportsmen who could pass that one by! Name two. Even one.

Fortune magazine has a lead-in that goes:

The mightiest rocket in the Western world, perhaps in all the world, stands poised to invade the starry seas of space—a rocket whose size and power will unlock fantastic new possibilities in the exploration of the solar system.

That's topical, taut, downright interesting. The article was read.

But, a distant voice complains, those are professional writers. They have to produce salable material. True enough. They do—or end up with a mailbox full of rejection slips. You don't have to be a full-time author to know how difficult it is to cash rejection slips at the local bank.

Copy Review Important

The obvious question is, why shouldn't the same high standards apply to copy written about an industrial product? Because the product lacks the inherent interest, the drama, the mass appeal of Raymond Chandler, of Howard Hughes who discovered Las Vegas, of elk hunting, the Kennedy assassination, the hippies, or space exploration?

That may be partially true. But never lose sight of the fact that readers of trade magazines (called "books" in the trade), are doing what they're doing because it's in their self-interest. These trade publications are intensely interesting to readers because they affect their ability to handle their jobs. Products advertised in these "books" relate to everyday problems of the readers. They must solve these problems in order to hold their jobs, and to advance. What could have a stronger sense of immediacy? What could be more interesting?

One reason industrial advertising copy isn't better than it is, is because there's nobody to judge whether it's good, bad, or indifferent. Agency copywriters, some of them anyway, submit their output for review—and possible rejection—by an account executive, account supervisor, copy chief, or the creative director. Theoretically this prevents poor, off-target copy from seeing the light of type. This system also acts to prevent the client's learning that all agency wordsmiths are not hypercreative types who exude a steady stream of superlative ideas.

Furthermore, such copy is again reviewed by the advertising manager. Presumably it is routed to the marketing director and/or the sales manager for approval. This, too, should prevent hopelessly inadequate copy from being printed.

In practice, however, many agency account executives write copy for their clients, get it finish typed without submitting it to anybody for their opinion, then blithely trot off to the client to get an okay. And the advertising manager who, depending upon the established procedure, or who's out of the office on business travel, or how many upper echelon people are on vacation at the moment, may decide to accept or reject it without consulting anybody.

And if the advertising manager is also the copywriter, as he or she frequently is in most smaller industrial companies, he or she will write, revise, edit, and finally approve his or her own copy. He or she then proceeds to have the ad produced and placed. No checks, no balances, no outside viewpoint. It's all about as objective as a horseplayer's hunches.

But even if copy is routed to a designated committee of company executives, little likelihood exists that any one of them is qualified by either inclination or training to judge copy. As long as the product is mentioned by name, and the copy doesn't cast aspersions on the product, company, J. Edgar Hoover, or the United States flat, it will receive the benign approval of all involved. Then tally up another collection of worn and weary words worth precious little to anybody, especially the company that pays to see them in printer's ink.

Later on we'll go into how copy *should* be approved.

In the meantime, though, let's look at some lackluster copy and see why it falls flatter than a bride's biscuits:

> *The International Loadstar dump truck has the strength to move mountains of dirt, rocks, gravel, anything you want to haul. Plus the sure-footed agility to climb over the roughest terrain.*

That's the complete lead-in paragraph of the copy in a black-and-white spread ad as run by International Harvester. International dominates the heavy-duty truck market, of course, a fact known to all who are remotely likely to buy a dump truck. Hence International has no need to exaggerate—which, when you get right down to it, is what the reference to moving mountains is. We all know that no dump truck yet built is literally able to move mountains—even one mountain, for that matter. IHC would have been ahead of the game if they'd added interest by stating the cubic yards, or payload weight, the Loadstar can handle. Specifics are interesting, generalities uninteresting.

People aren't hopelessly provincial any more, and most of us have seen terrain that no dump truck, even a Loadstar, could climb. Had International said something like, "easily climbs a 17% grade with a

GVW of 72,000 lbs.,'' they would have aroused sufficient interest to make prospective purchasers of dump trucks want to read further. Perhaps the worst thing about this lead-in paragraph is that it could have been written exactly as it now is—but about *any* make of dump truck.

Mason Color and Chemical Works, Inc. ran an ad with a four-color illustration which was beautifully done. The fine illustration was nullified by body copy which was absolutely devoid of interest. Starting out, it reads:

> *When the quality of your work demands the finest ceramic colors, extra-finely ground for smooth, uniform firing—try our line.*

"Quality" is a word that's so loosely bandied about today that it has become almost meaningless. "Finest" is merely another superlative that readers have trained themselves to ignore. "Extra-finely"— just *how* fine is that? And how smooth, how uniform? The clincher that gives interest the *coup de grace* is that self-serving "try our line."

A two-color, one-page ad of United Transformer Company is far from exciting, starting as it does:

> *Over 30 years of experience in the design and production of special filters have resulted in UTC being a first source for difficult units. Present designs. . .*

Readers are not interested in UTC's—or anybody else's—30 years of experience, or the fact that the company considers itself the first source. Readers want to know what the product or the company will do for them. Chest thumping neither attracts prospects nor motivates them to read dull ads.

> *Before you decide that your hydraulic power requirements are "special," check Bellows-Valvair's new modular "packaged" power packs. More and more applications can now be handled by these cost-saving units.*

This lead-in fails to arouse interest, it fails to create a sense of excitement, it fails to give a reader the feeling that, at long last, here's a product that might bail me out of the trouble I have on Assembly Line No. 3! Not only does it not generate interest, it goes so far as to repeat, almost verbatim, the headline in the first paragraph of copy. Headline is: *More and more applications can be handled by Bellows-Valvair "packaged" power units.*

Instead of senseless repetition, Bellows-Valvair would have been better off to have given two or three dramatic applications of the packaged power units, then told how they upped production, reduced costs, resulted in better quality, or whatever their most important user benefit is. Then readers who probably hadn't even considered whether or not their power requirements were "special" would have read the ad. That way they'd have known that B-V has the product and know-how they need. As is, this doesn't come through.

And from Louden Machinery Company we find:

> *Transporting the correct batches of dry-bulk ingredients to the proper mixers for a variety of packaged dessert products was a recent problem confronting the engineers of a prominent food processor.*

All right, so the customer's name isn't given; we've all encountered obstreperous customers who resolutely refuse to let their company be identified because it's against Company Policy—with upper-case C and P, so it sounds like invoking the name of deity.

That doesn't mean, though, that the first sentence has to be 31 words long. Or that words such as "ingredients" and "confronting" and other three- and four-syllable words must follow each other in relentless succession. This makes for difficult reading; reading that lacks interest, reading that lacks readers.

Had Louden said something on this order, readership would have been substantially higher:

> *A leading producer of packaged desserts had a sweet little problem. He had to move big batches of dry-bulk ingredients to a number of mixers—on schedule and to the right ones, of course. Not much demand for a mixture of butterscotch and chocolate. Here's how we gave him his just desserts...*

Specifics were studiously avoided by The Metal Removal Company in a fractional-page, two-color ad on carbide tools. They said:

> *Metal Removal Company solid carbide tool technology offers opportunities for faster, better, and lower cost production with maximum accuracy and using standard machine tools.*

A mouthful, that. And because it doesn't really say anything, doesn't give a solid user benefit that is significant to the reader, it is devoid of interest. How much better the ad would have been if Metal Removal's copy had given some concrete facts; as we all know, carbide tools outwear and outperform tools of alloy steel. Had the copy given some facts on tool life and production rates, then discussed the fact that no modifications need be made on existing machine tools, it would have interested a vast audience of metalworking people who need this product.

Centuries ago man ground some earth and mashed some berries and colored his works of art. Color was vital then. . . it is vital today. And because color is important to man, color is important to Harshaw. We've spent more than fifty years making colors.

The Harshaw Chemical Company may harbor the impression that this copy is interesting prospects, but it's difficult to see just how. Vague generalities and a self-administered pat on the back for having been in business for more than 50 years do not present user benefits of interest. And, somehow or other, the impression persists that color is important to Harshaw because it is important to "man"—not because Harshaw makes a profit in supplying the material to gratify that urge for color. Surely Harshaw isn't a nonprofit institution.

Grim as these examples of uninteresting copy are, they're happily not typical of all industrial advertising copy. Ad copy can be just as dramatic, just as gripping as a well-written magazine article bylined by a big-name professional.

For instance, consider this:

Your guards see a lot, but they miss a lot, too. A guard can see only one area at a time. He would like to see more. Like around corners, behind walls. And be in several places at one time. Now, with Motorola Closed-Circuit Television, he can. Here's how.

This lead-in paragraph follows a striking illustration of a close-up of a factory guard's face, eyes anxiously searching the black night, and the headline, "If he can't see it, he can't guard it."

With rioting, fire-bombing, and looting the order of the day, it's an unusual executive in industry who's not deeply concerned about the security of a plant. Motorola capitalizes on this universal concern, identifies the problem, and in the first short paragraph promises a solution. A spot illustration of a guard watching two closed-circuit television screens shows how the system works, adds believability to Motorola's description of its product.

In a striking two-color ad a famous refrigeration company exploited the business community's awareness of what was rapidly becoming a national problem. Body copy read:

Problem: 70% of California's water is where 77% of her people aren't. Solution: Direct the flow form North to South through rivers, canals, concrete aqueducts, pipelines, and dams. A $2.6 billion project that's computer controlled.

The problem-solution approach to copy has high interest and is particularly effective when the problem is universally recognized as being a serious one. Copy goes on to tell how they produced a system that was helping alleviate the problem, and that other states were watching with great interest the progress California was making. This copy received high readership, and not only from California residents:

> *During the Arab-Israeli war, U.S. carrier-based planes scrambled over the Mediterranean.*
>
> *Their mission was peaceful, but watching Russians had no way of knowing this.*
>
> *Within minutes, though, Soviet Premier Kosygin knew it. The White House chose to assure him of it over the Washington-Moscow Hot Line.*
>
> *It was the first time the Hot Line had ever been used during a crisis.*

International Telephone and Telegraph Corporation, manufacturer of the teleprinter which transmits messages directly from the White House to the Kremlin, was incredibly lucky in having such a vitally interesting topic to discuss. Once readers were drawn into the ad by the action-packed photograph of a jet fighter being catapulted from a carrier deck, and by the headline, "The day the Hot Line got hot," there was no backing out before IIT's story was told.

Few advertisers are blessed with such a spine-tingling situation, but they *can* make their story and their product interesting if the copy is fresh and vivid. There's always a way.

For example, Kaiser Aluminum & Chemical Corporation developed a unique procedure for handling payment of routine invoices, and told about it this way:

> *The idea is to give our suppliers "instant money" instead of endless paperwork. In the past five years we've sent out more than 700,000 signed blank checks—to pay for everything from typewriter ribbons to transportation service— without a single instance of misuse!*

Kaiser has much going for them in the lead-in into this skillfully written piece of copy. The thought of instant money is enough to intrigue almost everybody, of course, but the idea of actually mailing signed blank checks is unique in business. Then, when Kaiser says they cut down on the blizzard of paperwork, everybody takes note. All of us desk-bound people take a kindly view toward that.

Then add the fact that Kaiser reinforces our faith in our fellows by pointing out that not once did a heart full of larceny crop up to abuse an honor system, and readers will want the full story. Kaiser gives it to them, explaining how they send a purchase order and a signed blank check in the same envelope. Excellent image-building for Kaiser. Any company that thinks this way is obviously a progressive firm, one with which it is desirable to do business.

Specifics arouse interest, and Hyster Company makes the most of this proved principle. Copy in this four-color spread ad begins:

> *Hyster's new C450A Embankment Compactor changes the whole compaction profits picture—by doing a better job faster than ever before. It compacts a full 80-inch swath in a single pass. Compacts to required densities at rates up to 2500 cu./yds./hr. Slams 330 tamping feet into the job with the authority of 330 h.p. twin-diesel power. Snakes around slower equipment at 17 mph. Climbs 35 percent grades. Handles as easily as a compact car.*

A long one, but that's a lead-in paragraph with meat in it. Every contractor who sees the illustration realizes instantly why Hyster's claim of compacting an 80-inch swath *twice* in a single pass is absolute fact, for the new machine has two drums with *twice* as many tamping feet as the traditional single-drum compactor. The succinct, fact-filled copy is interesting because Hyster is reader-oriented, not self-oriented. What the reader wants to know—what the machine can do for him—is right there where it reaches him fast. You could say, it's what's up front that counts.

Copy That Demands Reading

Chromalloy American Corporation's compelling ad is another that *demands* readership. Photography is superb, the headline is exciting and has high interest and strong emotional appeal. The ad, illustrated on the following page, says:

Somewhere in this jungle,
there are 19 Viet Cong and a downed American flier

> *Mission: find the flier, and get him out alive.*
>
> *How?*
>
> *The pilot carries a tiny electronic strobelight. Its 25-mile flash guides the helicopter right to him— without tipping off the Viet Cong.*
>
> *The 'copter swoops down, lowers a chair. And the pilot switches to a*

Mission: find the flier, and get him out alive.

How?

The pilot carries a tiny electronic strobelight. Its 25-mile flash guides the helicopter right to him—without tipping off the Viet Cong.

The copter swoops down, lowers a chair. And the pilot switches to a miniature two-way radio whose 100-mile power guarantees clear communication with his rescue crew. Fast talk—and skill—will bring him through

the trees, limbs and life intact.

The radio, and the strobelight, saved 454 lives in Viet Nam last year.

Both are the inventions of Chromalloy American's ACR Electronics Unit.

ACR also devised the first camera to produce films of outer space.

And designed the recovery marker lights for NASA missiles.

And conceived a portable lighting system that can beacon an airport

runway within 5 minutes of electrical failure.

And created the rescue light now required on every commercial airline life jacket: a 1-inch light, activated by water, with 2-mile visibility.

ACR Electronics is one of 24 units of Chromalloy American.

Inventiveness is something they all have in common.

Somewhere in this jungle, there are 19 Viet Cong and a downed American flier.

Chromalloy American Corporation

Illustration, headline, and copy combine to demand attention.

> miniature two-way radio whose 100-mile
> power guarantees clear communication
> with his rescue crew. Fast talk—and
> skill—will bring him through the trees,
> limbs and life intact.

The radio, and the strobelight, saved 454 lives in Viet Nam last year.

Both are inventions of Chromalloy American's ACR Electronics Unit.

ACR also devised the first camera to produce films in outer space.

And designed the recovery marker lights for NASA missiles.

And conceived a portable lighting system that can beacon an airport runway within 5 minutes of electrical failure.

And created the rescue light now required on every commercial airline life jacket: a 1-inch light, activated by water, with 2-mile visibility.

ACR Electronics is one of 24 units of Chromalloy American.

Inventiveness is something they all have in common.

That's an outstanding presentation of an interesting and vitally necessary product, with a smooth transition into a strong corporate story. We'll all read about a product which can save even one life. But one that has already saved 454 young lives in the dark and bloody jungles of strife-torn Viet Nam in just one year can't be ignored.

Chromalloy American tells the story with a fine economy of words, then gets in mentions of other divisional products and indicates the size of the entire corporation. Few readers deserted Chromalloy American before absorbing all that the company wanted to tell them. As a result, Chromalloy American comes off as a vital, vigorous, inventive company with forward-looking management. CA's ad is honestly interesting.

Almost all industrial advertisers present products of genuine merit to readers. They should interest them. That some do and some don't can be attributed to *what* is said about the product and *how* it is said.

How is considerably more important than what—for, in the final analysis—if your ad is uninteresting it will receive mighty little readership. If you simply can't make your ads interesting, you'll be better off to save time and energy and run just one ad. Set it in 32-point type and use an inspirational message such as:

Compliments of Smith Widget Manufacturing Company

At least, this wouldn't bore anybody.

Surprisingly, dull ads aren't easy to write. Skim any number of trade journals and tick off mentally the ads that interest you, even if you're not in the market for the products. Note especially ads from industries which are traditionally dull and dreary—such as the foundry industry or the industrial heating equipment industry.

For the most part, ads for products used in these markets reflect a deep-seated desire to avoid the pertinent in favor of unimportant little details. In the foundry industry, for example, you can almost see the involved workings of the Germanic engineer's mind as he strives mightily to see how he can reject a new concept, to develop valid reasons why a new product or new method described in an ad will not—cannot—work in *his* foundry. He'll do almost anything to justify clinging to the old tried-and-proved ways and things familiar to him, just as they were comfortingly familiar to his predecessors for decades. Writing these innocuous platitudes required just as much research, fact gathering, and effort as would writing something with sparkle.

Writing dull ads for products used in such industries is done because it has always been done—and because backward management will approve them.

Approximately the same expenditure of time and effort is required to develop an effective campaign and write ads that interest people. The main difference you'll find is that writing a dull ad is drudgery. You don't finish the job with a sense of achievement. Put a little—just a little—extra thought into it, however, and you actually impart something of yourself to the ad. You flavor it with your personality, so that it has freshness and vitality and interest.

Who wants to appear pallid and plodding and pedestrian?

Never hesitate to inject colorful thoughts and expressions into your copy. The different—and better—way of saying something is usually interesting. This is what distinguishes Shakespeare from Spillane, what transforms a prosaic monolog into copy that's light and lively.

Invest some extra effort. Any product or service can be made interesting if you'll refuse to let go of an ad until you've found the one approach that's fresh and different, until you've created the spark that ignites the readers' imagination.

Build in interest, then watch the return.

Information

The *one* thing readers of industrial advertisements want above all else is information.

Feed them information that's pertinent, information that relates to their main interest—their jobs—while they're reading trade journals, and your ad stands a better than even chance of being read despite any minor shortcomings it might have.

To business readers, pertinent information is information about a product that can help them solve a work-related problem.

The controller, for example, might find his accounting department bogged down trying to work up the monthly profit-and-loss statement for management. A new system for handling paperwork, or a new calculator or adding machine which performs work faster and easier would be a boon. And, by the same token, the plant manager might have a bottleneck in the sheet metal shop; a new power shear or cut-off saw which turns out more work in less time would enable someone to meet stepped-up production schedules. Give either of these harassed decision makers the information they need in order to specify your product and you've taken the first step in making a sale.

Just what specific information belongs in an ad should be ridiculously easy to decide. After all, there's the copy platform. It contains guidelines. Listed in it are pros, cons, sacred cows, and the things that are never mentioned except in a hushed voice behind a closed office door.

Naturally, not every ad in a campaign can include every iota of information in the copy platform. But the campaign as a whole must include all of it within a specified time, usually a fiscal year.

Pinpointing specific facts which must be communicated to your universe shouldn't entail much effort. But for some reason or other many advertisers—far too many—feed too bland a diet to prospects for the ads to be palatable.

When you're considering what product information you want to put in ad copy, list each feature *and user benefit* you want to talk about. Make the list complete. It's all right if it's as long as a wet week; you can always blue-pencil things which are relatively minor. You'll be sure to include everything that belongs in the list if you mentally analyze your product—and compare it with competitive ones.

Then go a step further. Cultivate an empathic mood—put yourself in the reader's place and try to *anticipate* just what it is that he or she wants to know and what questions your ad will leave unanswered. If you're thorough and if you're honest with yourself, there'll be questions. Chances are there will be several, one or two of major importance. Remember, your prospects for whom the copy is written are unfamiliar with your product in varying degrees. Some may never have heard of your brand or of your company, and they may even be unaware that either your product or similar competitive ones exist.

Ask yourself exactly what information you—as the reader—must have in order to arrive at a well-reasoned decision to seek more information about your product from a salesperson, and how he or she would justify purchasing it to those in the company. Be meticulously exact in this analysis. Be very specific. At this stage of the game fuzzy thinking cannot be tolerated. It can't help but result in an ad which fails to inform. That way lies lost sales.

Let's look at a few ads currently running, such as Instron Corporation's spread in *Metal Progress*. The first two paragraphs of the body copy go like this:

> *New higher capacity instrument incorporates closed loop control, dynamic response, modular design, advanced programming capability.*
>
> *Here is a new Universal Testing Instrument with the versatility and precision needed to provide materials researchers with the means for accurately determining basic physical properties, as well as achieving a better understanding of more subtle characteristics—in a wide variety of new and improved materials.*

Now, these high-flown words are fine for engineers who don't really communicate with words if they have access to blueprints or charts or graphs. And the tone is nice, with "higher capacity," "incorporates," "modular design," "advanced programming capability," and "versatility" following hard on the heels of the other.

Copy written in this engineerese is, if you'll stop and analyze it, puffery. It doesn't inform. No actual product superiorities or user benefits are given. No real reason exists for anybody to spend time reading this ad. It is uninteresting and uninformative.

Then there's the C. M. Kemp Manufacturing Company ad:

> *Creative Engineering slanted to the creative engineer concerned about Systems for the generation of Inert Gas, Nitrogen or gas atmospheres. What is Kemp's approach? Simply this: Kemp uses its special product knowledge and unique field experience as a basis for selecting, developing, and combining components into a system that performs at maximum efficiency. This creative engineering can save you up to 75% of your costs. Kemp's record for increasing its customers' product quality and production rates is unmatched in the gas generation field.*

Again, no pertinent information is given to the buying influences the ad is trying to influence. Aside from telling one and all how good

Kemp is (and this "information" will be regarded as suspect because it comes from you know who), no information is given to help the reader.

A surefire way to prove this is to substitute Smith Widget Manufacturing Company for the C. M. Kemp Manufacturing Company, then substitute Widgets for Systems, and so on. The ad would have been just as ineffective if written for and run over the signature of any other company in any other industry. This is the way all companies like to think of themselves. But readers couldn't care less.

You'll find a plus in buying chemical raw materials from the company that has one of the nation's largest polypropylene plants. Discover all the advantages of doing business with Enjay Chemical Company.

That's all the copy in this one-page ad except for a tedious listing of products Enjay manufactures—and this includes the headline. It's so sketchy as to information that its effectiveness is very doubtful.

If your work involves olefin polymerization, check Stauffer. We have a complete line of titanium and vanadium catalysts—liquids and solids, organic soluble and insoluble, different valence states. We're . . .

Some information there, of course, because Stauffer managed to state what they have for sale. But there's no information of any kind as to why a reader should have any desire to specify Stauffer, why he or she would fare better if he used Stauffer chemicals instead of any other brand.

Another ad in the same vein reads:

Extraordinary. That's the word for Witco's Emcol surfactants. Because nearly all of them were formulated for out-of-the-ordinary problems that customers asked us to solve. After 30 years of solving them, it's no wonder you find us with such a wide range of extraordinary Emcols . . .

. . . and on and on and on. This is another ad that doesn't really give information relevant to the readers' interests. Readers aren't about to wade through several paragraphs of self-praise and recounting how long the firm has been in business to find helpful information.

From Union Carbide comes the next gem of noninteresting noninformation. Following is the entire text from a one-page, two-color ad in *Foundry* magazine:

This new Ucar graphite symbol assures you that all the skills and experience that created National electrodes will continue to serve foundrymen around the country. Wherever

355

At left, a monotone of the first page of the four-page, full-color ad for Baker lift trucks. Six teaser illustrations lead the reader to turn the page to an inside spread full of information.

At right, the back page of Baker's four-page ad series. Listing the dealers makes it easy for readers to respond to the ad, and also serves to increase the loyalty of Baker dealers.

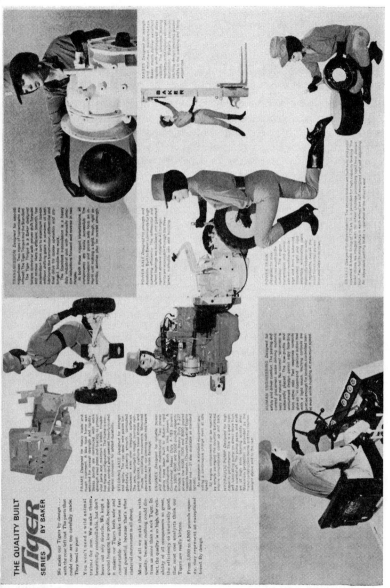

The second and third pages of the Baker lift-truck ad contain specific data about the "Tiger," but the demonstrating "Tiger girl" enlivens the layout.

> *you see this new red and blue design, you can be confident*
> *of consistent leadership in product quality and perfor-*
> *mance. Total product control from raw materials to finished*
> *product. Comprehensive carbon and graphite research,*
> *development, and manufacturing facilities.*

So who read it? Who was influenced by it, who was motivated to pound on the desk and demand, by George, that the purchasing agent purchased only National electrodes henceforth?

We've already discussed how to identify and define the market for a product and how to pinpoint the various buying influences throughout prospect companies. Baker Division, Otis Elevator Company, a leading manufacturer of lift trucks, has done a noteworthy job in this area for some years now.

When the time came to develop a new advertising campaign, it was only natural that Baker should ponder about what information should be presented to prospects—and how to verify unquestionably that information benefiting both prospects and Baker was included.

Baker decided to find out. Hunches have no place in today's industrial advertising, so Baker's director of advertising went to the people whose opinion means the most—prospective purchasers of Baker lift trucks. A detailed questionnaire was sent to 4,997 known buying influences, who had been identified by name and title earlier, when the company analyzed its market.

The survey was spread over 26 SIC categories. A return of 2,341 questionnaires, for a 46 percent response, in effect gave Baker that same number of assistant advertising managers. This advisory staff prefers the following approaches in Baker ads, which is merely another way of saying how they want information dished out to them. The kind of information desired follows:

    33 percent—mechanical details

    23 percent—situation ads

    16 percent—corporate ads

    24 percent—some of each

    2 percent—none of above

Baker paid heed to the unpaid assistants. Some ads of the nuts-and-bolts type were prepared, situation ads were produced, as well as combinations of the two.

Not too surprisingly, a number of those who completed the questionnaire appeared to like girls. Feeling that this is no accident and no idiosyncrasy confined to a handful of respondents, Baker decided to feature girls in some of their ads—a radical departure from lift-truck advertising in general, which heretofore had never admitted publicly that there was anything in life sexier than a bright yellow lift truck, even if some of us *do* know better.

Result is a four-color, four-page insert (see pages 354-355). It is chock-full of precise and detailed information a prospect needs to evaluate product quality intelligently. And it makes it easy to relate Baker's lift trucks to his or her operation.

The front page sets the stage for the spread which follows, showing as it does an even half-dozen teaser illustrations, all in full color, as well as a tightly cropped picture of a Tiger Series Baker lift truck. The jewelled open-end wrench and a tool box full of hand tools painted a delicate, feminine pastel, combined with the small picture of an unusually attractive young lady wearing a Baker "B" make this page impossible to pass by. It leads unerringly to the meat of the ad on the inside spread. First-page copy reads:

Follow the track of the cat to quality . . .

Introductory copy in the spread goes:

We make our Tigers by design . . . with the roar left out. The parts that could roar are too carefully made. They tend to purr.

You won't need a wild animal trainer for one. We make them beautifully controllable, but don't leave out any muscle. We kept a ground hugging low profile, because it makes our Tigers both safe and comfortable. We make them fast and powerful, because that's what material movement is all about.

Most of all we make them with quality, because nothing could distress us more than a sick Tiger. In fact, the quality is so high, the reliability of all components so great, the efficiency so unusually good, that most cost analysts think our Tigers are really kittens. From 3,000 to 8,000 pounds capacity, they represent an exceptional breed. By design.

That intro copy is friendly, low-key, colloquial, and it sells. Following is detailed nuts-and-bolts copy which explains exactly why Baker's Tigers are a different breed of cat. Typical major subheads and copy read as follows:

FRAME. Designed for heavy loads and rough treatment. A box-type frame was selected for overall strength and rigidity. Stress points are reinforced with extra strength steel plate and bracing to protect vital parts and maintain a stable, trouble-free frame configuration. The frame is electrically welded, shot-peened, heavily coated against corrosion for added durability.

POWER AXLE. Designed for strength and durability. Built to Baker's demands for high-operating efficiency. The differential and wheel bearings are enclosed and gasketed against abrasive materials. All components are accessible through the three-piece, malleable-iron axle housing.

BRAKES. Designed for dependability. The service brakes are hydraulic and pedal operated. A brake lining of 125 sq. in. is provided for high-capacity braking. The brake drums are integral with the wheel castings, promoting rapid heat dissipation. Two full floating shoes in each wheel are self-energizing and self-adjusting. An adjustable parking brake is operated at the driver's seat.

Fact filled and informative, that copy is. And it's just plain intriguing, what with the continuity provided by effective use of "design" and "designed." The eye-catching layout and restrained use of background tint blocks complement the illustrations of the worker assembling a Tiger, each adjacent to the proper copy block. Incidentally, little doubt can exist as to the gender of the mechanic; no real-life production worker ever encountered by the author wore coveralls this fetchingly.

Baker signed off with a concise bit of copy which struck precisely the right note. It says:

This is our Tiger. We designed it and built it with care. For you it means the greatest value in the fork lift field. For us it means pride in setting the standard for the industry. Write Baker and we will send you additional information we think you will find valuable. Or call your local dealer listed at right. He'll be pleased to assist you.

Listing dealers makes it easy for readers to respond to the ad with a phone call, of course.

This ad has consistently earned unusually high readership ratings, frequently standing at the top of the list. The only formula it relied upon to achieve this success is to give the readers the information that Baker thinks they need—and which they say they want. Nothing complicated about that.

Another of Baker's four-color, four-page inserts, this one on the company's electric-powered Bobcat line of lift trucks, is reproduced here. Again the front page does nothing more than arouse reader interest and act as a lead-in for the spread. That's where the solid product information is given.

The Bobcat fork lift truck is dramatized by being pictured in a jungle setting with a snarling Bobcat peering through the foliage. Copy is not as nutsy-and-boltsy, instead stresses the advantages the user realizes with Baker's double guarantee of 180 days or 1,000 hours of operation. This, Baker says, is twice the industry average, hence a potent sales point.

Back page features a four-color photograph of the bottom of the Bobcat—which couldn't have been too easy to take. Again, dealers are listed to trigger response.

In a campaign aimed directly at management, Baker emphasizes that their Bobcats and Tigers are:

> *. . . nimble beasts . . . quick as their namesakes and beautifully balanced, with stability unexcelled . . . low center of gravity and wide tread design keep them superbly sure-footed, whatever the load . . . driving motions easy and natural, never awkward . . . easy, safe, boarding from either side . . . driver visibility is unimpaired . . . positive action controls . . . stability and safety in design.*

All of this is to allay management fears of fork lifts, the materials handling tool that's indispensable but universally considered hazardous. This attitude by top management men could easily swing the purchase decision Baker's way.

Elements unifying the campaigns are repetition of the slogan, "Track of the Cats," continued stressing of the identifying names Bobcat and Tiger, and Baker's beautiful brunette. Nobody objects to *her*.

Just how effective an advertising campaign is as far as sales volume is concerned is a moot point. More on this later. That Baker's advertising is successful is beyond question, however. Since the company first defined its market, then gave qualified prospects the specific information they need to make buying decisions, Baker's sales volume has doubled—then redoubled.

Cull out the unimportant, discard the irrelevant, and present information in your ads that you'd like to see there if you were in the reader's shoes.

Then your advertising campaign can make a contribution to sales success on the order of Baker's.

Another intriguing opening page for a Baker ad features a close-up photo of tracks of a bobcat and tracks of a Baker Bobcat. Again the reader is led deftly into spread pages of the ad.

Again, dealers are listed on the back page of the ad so as to become targets of any inquiries. But the detail photo of the undercarriage of the Bobcat also gives selling points.

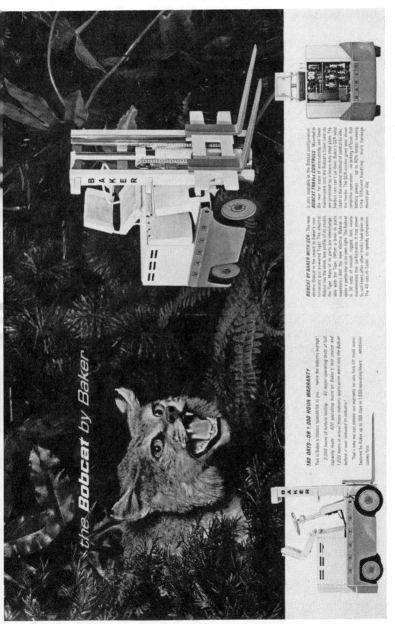

Spread pages this time concentrate on product's user benefits and guarantee.

Involvement

The reader feels a sense of personal involvement with your copy *when it tells how to solve a specific problem through use of your product or service.*

Involvement occurs because the reader is able to identify with the product or service, or, in some instances, with the selling proposition. Copy which involves the reader does exactly what a well-trained salesperson does—it imparts suggestions which the reader recognizes as being in his or her self-interest.

The one best way to achieve good reader involvement, a must if your copy is to be effective, is for you to take the first step. That's acquiring a feeling of empathy with the prospect.

Note especially that the word is *prospect,* not prospects, plural. Project yourself. Put yourself into this individual's position, mentally seat yourself behind his or her desk, feel with his or her feelings as much as it is humanly possible to do so. Use your imagination. Make a determined effort and you'll find that you're automatically beginning to think in terms of what you and your copy can do for Mr. Prospect.

With a little practice, it's easy. You've already identified all of your prospects by name, job function, title, company, location, and SIC classification. This enables you to select a real flesh-and-blood person if that helps you think of him or her as a living, breathing individual. All of this background information about the prospect gives you some pretty penetrating insights into needs and thought processes.

Oversimplifying a bit for the sake of illustration, we know that engineers are, by and large, unimaginative and almost painfully literal. And they almost completely lack the ability to visualize. Copy slanted toward them must of necessity include many more relatively insignificant details than you'd ordinarily want to put in one advertisement. But if all of these little details aren't there, you've left too many unanswered questions. This quickly dilutes involvement because engineers can't make the mental transitions required to fill in minor information gaps.

Since you know your prospect so well, write directly to him or her—not to some hazy group of faceless beings in a never-never land that exists only on the paper of a circulation statement. And by all means resist the temptation to lecture or preach. There's no place in industrial advertising copy for a soapbox or a pulpit.

Writing to a person, as opposed to writing to people, imposes a certain discipline on the copywriter, one which is willingly accepted because of its help.

Talk to "You," Not "They"

Imagine, for example, that you're talking to one of your best friends about the product your company manufactures. You're describing it, stressing how it's better than similar competitive one's on the market. You're telling what it will do. Naturally, you're enthusiastic and it shows. You are fully aware of his or her involvement with your story from facial expressions, nods of understanding, smiles and gestures. Unfortunately, you aren't able to establish this intimate a rapport with your reader prospect, but you can and must feel an affinity with that person.

This relationship you've cultivated will help you write copy which involves the reader both logically and emotionally.

Personal-appeal copy, rather than mass-appeal copy, imparts a special flavor to the ad which heightens the reader's sense of involvement. A hypothetical ad, again using the Widget for the product, might well read this way if the copy is based on mass appeal:

Production people who are responsible for keeping assembly lines humming know the importance of Widgets that work every time. Smith Widgets don't let them down because . . .

On the other hand, personalized copy for the Widget would start out this way:

You can avoid lost production due to faulty Widgets by switching to Smith Widgets. Smith Widgets have oversize, hardened shafts and tapered roller bearings, in contrast to all others which have small, soft shafts and ball bearings. Smith Widgets take the load better, cut your costs, and boost your production.

There's a world of difference. Stray from this concept and copy immediately loses its sense of immediacy and its vitality. Generalities creep in to replace specifics. There's no bite, no vigor.

On land, in the air, and on the sea . . . Hitchiner investment castings are proving their value in weight reduction, strength, corrosion resistance, and functional adaptability.

Certainly there's nothing in that lead-in paragraph of a one-page, two-color ad to cause the reader to feel an overpowering sense of involvement. That's because this is mass-appeal copy, general and nonspecific and not even very interesting.

Some well-done catalog-type copy appears in a two-thirds-page ad by Clarage Fan Company in *Factory* magazine. However, it never really gets off the ground as far as reader involvement is concerned. Body copy is messily executed by the headline and illustration; shown is a frowning, aggressive looking man pointing his finger at the reader, for all the world as if he'd caught you with your finger in the till. Headline reads: "We want you! . . . to order Clarage ventilating equipment''—and, believe it or not, the quotation marks and exclamation point are the advertiser's. Phony involvement is worse than none at all.

Copperweld Steel Company starts a two-color, second-cover ad in *Production* this way:

> *Heavy feeds at high machining speeds require steel that is uniform in cross section. To manufacture cluster gears, the Power Take-Off Division of Dana Corporation specifies Aristoloy 8620H cold-finished bars.*

This is hardly individualized to involve the reader, but it is positive, specific, and it drops a respected name and thus builds in believability. The copy, though, as it continues is pedantic and preachy.

And The Cross Company started its two-color, spread ad by saying:

> *In general terms, this 22-station Transfer-matic is used in the foundry to prepare rough cylinder block castings for the machine shop operations.*

Highly important, highly visible space is thrown away by saying ''in general terms.'' Reader involvement is negligible because there's nothing in which to get involved. Few of us can get all misty-eyed over something that starts out, ''in general terms.''

However, if Cross had begun the copy something like this, for example, readership—due to reader involvement—would have been much higher.

> *Are you satisfied with the way you're now preparing rough castings for the machine shop? Is this part of your operation costing more than it should? Here's how you can. . .*

And so on to involve the reader right from the start. Never make the fatal mistake of throwing away those critically important first few words. If they don't ''pull,'' your ad is a lost cause.

How AT&T Uses Advertising

Two outstanding ads as far as reader involvement is concerned were created for American Telephone and Telegraph Company. They appeared one after the other.

A particularly knotty problem faced AT&T, whose objective is to induce salespeople, district sales managers, home office sales managers, and marketing directors—and any others responsible for sales volume in industry—to make more long-distance telephone calls.

The company presents a very persuasive picture and advances a hard-headed dollars-and-cents reason why their selling proposition is sound.

The first ad starts with the headline:

They don't call it a waiting room for nothing

The illustration shows a bored salesman resignedly cooling his heels at the end of a long row of chairs in a reception area, obviously at the tag end of a succession of callers.

Body copy continues:

There's a better way to cover small accounts you "can't afford" to see. It's called Long Distance. A planned schedule of calling leaves no sales stone unturned. You can serve small accounts, large ones, and develop new prospects. Think of the waiting you save! Take a new look at Long Distance. Call your Bell Telephone Business Office and ask for a Communications Consultant to get in touch with you.

The "waiting room" ad is reproduced on the following page.

As a follow-up, the second ad shows the same salesman after moving up the interminable row of chairs, still bored, tired, unproductive.

Headline of this ad says:

Ah, but there is a way to cover small accounts profitably. It's called Long Distance.

Body copy continues:

It's the way to give small accounts the importance they deserve at a selling cost you can afford. At the same time, Long Distance enables you to serve the big accounts and cultivate new prospects as well. Call your Bell Telephone Business Office and ask that our Communications Consultant get in touch with you. Take a new look at Long Distance.

Everybody who's even remotely connected with sales identifies with this universal problem—that of having a salesperson (or a whole staff of them) whose calls cost an average $106.91, sitting idle and unhappy about a situation beyond their control. The problem's a common one, and as field costs inexorably creep up—salaries, fringes, car leasing, commissions, every one of dozens of expenses incurred keeping salespeople out in the territory—it becomes more pressing.

AT&T involves the reader right up to the presidential level, and does so immediately with its expressive visual and its short, persuasive copy. The company follows through by stressing the benefits the phone user derives by covering *all* prospects, small and large, and of developing new prospects by long distance.

Frosting on the cake is AT&T's promise of help by a communications consultant, who is presumably a highly knowledgeable individual when it comes to special telephone plans such as the WATS Line, which gives heavy long-distance users more for their dollar. This bid

They don't call it
a waiting room for nothing

There's a better way to cover the small accounts you "can't afford" to see. It's called Long Distance. A planned schedule of calling leaves no sales stone unturned. You can serve small accounts, large ones and develop new prospects. Think of the waiting you save!

Take a new look at Long Distance. Call your Bell Telephone Business Office and ask for a Communications Consultant to get in touch with you. **AT&T** and Associated Companies

Ah, but there <u>is</u> a way to cover small accounts profitably. It's called Long Distance.

It's the way to give small accounts the importance they deserve at a selling cost you can afford. At the same time, Long Distance enables you to serve the big accounts and cultivate new prospects as well. Call your Bell Telephone Business Office and ask that our Communications Consultant get in touch with you. Take a new look at Long Distance.

AT&T
and Associated Companies

for action gives AT&T a chance to do some personal selling, something that's not easy to do when the product is already in service, and is as ubiquitous as the telephone.

Reader involvement is built into Friden's two-thirds-page ad in *Space/Aeronautics*. It goes like this:

> *This engineer is winning a $5 bet. Someone gave him the following problem: Find the length of side "a" of the illustrated triangle (dimensions given). He laughingly said he could do it with his hands tied behind his back. Someone bet him $5 he couldn't. He will win the bet in 30 seconds using the new Electronic Calculator by Friden with automatic square root. The Model 132 stores intermediate answers and displays them on a TV screen in four visible registers. As he works through the problem, these answers drop into the working register automatically. There's nothing to write down. Square roots are derived with just a touch of a button.*

The headline about the $5 bet infers something of both personal and professional interest. Personal because betting involves a challenge and the prospect of personal gain—and it usually isn't done on company time. Professional interest may be assumed because the headline talked about engineers. Too, the ad wouldn't be in a business publication if it didn't concern readers' job interests.

The illustration shows two laughing engineers in shirt sleeves, leaning over and timing with a stopwatch as one of their colleagues, hands tied behind his back and pencil in his mouth, pushes buttons of a Friden Calculator. It's natural and believable, and accordingly results in immediate reader involvement. Every engineer is able to put himself in this situation as he absorbs Friden's product message.

When Bendix Automation announced nine new numerical controls, the body copy of the ad opened with:

> *Because one is designed specifically for your kind of machining. And that puts an end to the compromises and limitations of numerical controls that try to please everybody. It also means, dollar-for-dollar, you're getting more control and more machining capability than N/C has ever offered before.*

In all of industry, is there a harassed production executive who hasn't at some time or other thought his problems were unique? Who hasn't moaned about the fact that machine-tool manufacturers and those who produce numerical controls try to be all things to all persons while they blithely ignore *his or her* production bottleneck? This ad recognizes this attitude and this problem, and the copy involves the reader *with* a problem—and who doesn't have one in this day of increasingly complex technology?

Both Friden's and Bendix's ads contain two elements which ensure immediate reader involvement: A core idea of interest to the reader, and product information which promises to solve a problem.

Practically no industry, with the possible exception of the foundry industry and one or two others, has clung so tenaciously to yesterday's obsolete approaches in marketing and advertising as have manufacturers of machine tools. These industries, along with the industrial heating equipment industry, just can't seem to abandon the moss-covered concept that their goal in life is to sell hardware, hence their objective is to tell their universe that they make hardware.

Advertising managers in these industries undoubtedly realize the weakness of this antiquated concept, and they know full well that it accomplishes one undesirable objective: It makes their company and their industry look backward and outdated to prospects in industries to which they sell.

Realizing this and convincing management of it are two different breeds of cat, though.

A Classic From Cincinnati

It's partially for this reason that The Cincinnati Milacron Company's* four-page, two-color ad in *Production* magazine is like a breath of spring after a blizzard-filled winter. Primarily, though, it's because this outstanding ad is a classic example of a hardware manufacturer's understanding that selling hardware is almost as much a thing of the past as a quill pen. Today, the company competing well in the capital equipment field is the company that sells solutions to problems. Not hardware.

Considerable courage was required to approve this ad. The entire first page contains no company or product identification, except in a general way. Copy on page one reads:

"Sure, your machine cuts metal. But what else can it do for me?" As a production manager, you're probably looking at today's machine tools in a new way. Sure, you know that new machines will turn out more parts per hour to closer tolerances than your old ones can. But you're also looking for solutions to problems like these...

With that tantalizing lead-in, the second page of the ad spells out knotty problems found in almost every metalworking plant in the country. Short, fact-filled body copy then solves each problem directly below each subhead and spot illustration.

"We just don't have enough floorspace."
With floorspace at a premium in almost any manufacturing plant, you're looking for single machines that will turn out the work of two or three old ones. Cincinnati's champion

* Now Cincinnati Milacron

space saver is probably the TWIN GRIP centerless. If you're doing thrufeed grinding now with a line of three machines, you can probably do that same job with one Twin Grip. That's a 66% reduction in floorspace. Tolerances and production rate are also usually improved.

"I've got to find ways to reduce lead time."
Production men are continually being challenged to shorten the time between design and delivery of a new product. Sometimes the only answer is a whole new machining concept, like numerical control. One manufacturer is combining a dozen different machining operations on propeller control housing with NC, making them three-at-a-time on a Cincinnati 30" NC Hydro-Tel. Setup time is reduced by an average of 60% and machining hours have been cut 65%. His lead time for these operations has been cut by 30%.

"I have to produce a greater variety of parts every year."
As the customer demands more and more product variations, you find yourself doing a lot more job-shop-type work. Lot sizes may be 25-150 with a lot of milling, drilling, tapping, and boring. A Cincinnati Cim-X machining center was designed for this kind of flexibility. Separate heavy-duty milling (7½ hp) and drilling spindles, plus an integral 72-position index table give you the ability to handle most multiple-setup machining jobs in a single setup. Both NC and manual versions available.

That's page two, with three major problems which plague metalworking production analyzed and solved with Cincinnati products.

Page three continues:

"I simply can't find enough skilled men."
In times when skilled labor is scarce, modern machine tools let semiskilled workers turn out "skilled" work, freeing up your skilled men for more critical jobs. For example, our Hypowermatic belt-type milling machines with Telematic (pegboard) control often combine two or three difficult milling jobs into a single operation. The operator simply loads the part, whether it's a shotgun barrel or crankshaft, and pushes the cycle start button. Telematic then takes the machine through its complete automatic cycle.

"I also have to solve warranty problems."
Profits already made can disappear when warranty costs get out of line. Many Cincinnati's can help prevent excess war-

Here the first page of a four-page ad for the Cincinnati Milling Machine Co. tackles the tough job of dealing with technical benefits. Note that first page names no company, nor is product identified.

Concluding page of the ad, after disposing of the problem of inventory, suggests, "Let's Talk," then gives phone numbers of field representatives so that interested prospects may call.

373

ranty expense. For example, in a car's automatic transmission is a valve spool smaller than your little finger that meters fluid to change speeds. If it hangs up, the whole unit must be taken apart for repair, perhaps at your expense. Our Centuramatic centerless grinders grind these critical spools to close tolerances (.0003 size, .000050 roundness), assuring smooth operation of your transmission through a great many warranty periods.

Finally, page four gives one more problem and solution:

"Our in-process inventory is a lot bigger than it should be."

Semifinished parts tie up your company's capital and take up floorspace that could be used productively. One tractor manufacturer had to keep large lots of drive housings in process at all times, tying up three milling machines, because there were seven different surfaces to machine on four sides of the part. Now in-process inventory can be reduced at least 25% because all of these operations can be handled in smaller lots on one heavy-duty Cincinnati Verci-power with a rotary table and Telematic control. In the bargain, over-all costs are cut by 18% and quality is improved, since all surfaces are machined in one setup.

Then follows a strong bid for immediate action. It's headed:

Let's talk.

This is punched up with an illustration of a telephone off the hook, all ready for somebody to pick it up and call Cincinnati. Body copy reads:

Manufacturing problems of all types often get solved when your engineers and our engineers get together. The Cincinnati-Heald Engineer in your area is trained to assist you with inventory, floorspace, lead time, skill, flexibility and warranty problems. He can call on reinforcements for additional help on specialized problems. Call your Cincinnati-Heald representative today. One visit could suggest a solution to your toughest production problem.

Cincinnati makes it easy for readers to respond by listing the telephone numbers of their representatives in major cities from Boston to Syracuse, complete with the necessary area codes. After all, many prospects in smaller towns would call the Cincinnati representative in the metropolitan center nearest them, which might well be in a different state; the area code would naturally be different from the caller's.

This fine four-page ad makes it obvious that Cincinnati is thoroughly familiar with the various stages in the purchasing process. Some of the problems they cite go all the way back to Stage 1, Incre-

Two pages of spread dealing sympathetically with prospect's problems Cincinnati Milling ad, and offering solutions to each problem discussed.

ment 1, of the process—origination of the idea to make a purchase. Other problems they use continue on through Stage 4. It's noteworthy that Cincinnati concentrates on problems in Stages 1 through 4, which is where advertising is most effective; and, of course, these are the stages in time when a Cincinnati salesperson has probably not yet made contact with most of the buying influences involved in the contemplated purchase.

This is unquestionably a highly effective ad. Cincinnati knows how to achieve strong reader involvement, and they did just that. Nothing was stinted in the manufacture of this ad—deliberation, reflection, or projecting the writer into the prospect's mind. The finished product proves it.

Helping the Reader

There's an old truism to the effect that an effective ad is composed of only two elements, no more, no less.

These are a problem—the reader's—and the solution—which, coincidentally, just happens to be the advertiser's product. It's wonderful how things work out.

And more than a kernel of truth lies in the old saw that all you have to do to build a booming business is to recognize a universal need, then fill it.

Equally true, although cynical enough to have been coined by Malcolm Muggeridge, is the old advertising proverb that if you tell the reader you're going to help him or her, you're well on the way to selling something.

Helping the reader is consanguineous to informing and involving him or her, of course, but with a subtle little difference. All of these actions depend upon presenting problems and solutions, as well as providing information that's pertinent and interesting to the reader. When you help by discussing how he or she can solve his or her problem through choosing the proper type, model, size, formulation, horsepower, specifications, or other criterion depending on the product, he or she considers the message a valid one and will believe it.

Furthermore, if you proceed to offer additional help by suggesting how the reader can use your product most efficiently, how it is compatible with present equipment, how it can be maintained, how it can be installed, how to break it in—then you have a prospect who regards your company and your product favorably. You've helped. The reader is appreciative.

Let's see how some advertisers help readers, and how others don't.

One who misses the boat is HPM Division of Koehring Company, whose ad's headline is:

One who misses the boat is HPM Division of Koehring Company, whose ad's headline is:

Very big on getting the job done

This startling bit of intelligence is immediately followed by body copy that's of precious little help to anyone. Here's what it says:

> *A special purpose HPM hydraulic press isn't necessarily completely custom. We've built too many. Your special pressure forming problems could be one of the many we've solved for others. You benefit from this wealth of experience in time and engineering costs. HOP gets the job done. In plastics with a broad line of screw injection machines that lead the industry in high-speed production. In die casting of nonferrous metals with the famous...* and so on.

This copy doesn't help the reader—it's self-oriented, long on air of elevated temperature and braggadocio.

ACCURACY

Shrieks the headline in type a full 5 inches high in Consolidated Electrodynamic's ad for analytical instruments. It is followed by body copy which does nothing to support the promise shouted by the headline. Complete body copy reads:

> *CEC Direct Reading Emission Spectrometers provide the most accurate information on dynamic background correction, dark current correction, optical interlock and other features which contribute to emission spectrometer accuracy. Call your nearest CEC Field Office, or write to...*

There's no help there, only the sketchiest information to trigger a response.

Binks Manufacturing Company's ad in a metalworking book starts the body copy with leaders, like this:

> *...but there is one company—and only one company—which offers you a selection of all systems. That company is Binks.*

The copy didn't end there, it brags on and on. That's probably as far as 999 readers out of 1,000 pursued the matter, however. Right from the start the copy made it painfully obvious that there would be little, if any, help toward solving the readers' problems in that ad.

Incidentally, it's not considered good practice to use both leaders (...) and dashes (--) in the same ad, particularly if the copy is relatively short. There's no hard-and-fast rule, but it's a question of taste.

The basic mistake made by Stackpole Carbon Company, Electronic Components Division, is an almost interminable recounting of past triumphs which the company has achieved. Naturally, it immediately evokes a reaction of: "But what have you done for me recently?" Body copy starts out:

377

In 1965, Stackpole began supplying Automatic Pincushion Corrective Cores, a major advance, for color television. 1964 saw the introduction of Stackpole 90° color components including Flyback, Yoke, and Convergence Cores. As far back as 1954, these same components were introduced for the 70° color Deflection Systems. The list of contributions Stackpole engineering and production knowhow has made to the growth of color in television is long and varied. . .

Ancient history is of somewhat less than nominal interest to readers of business papers, and in the electronics industry things that happened last year—or even six months ago—are very old hat indeed. Stackpole wasted expensive space, space that was strategically located in the ad, to talk about dead issues, instead of telling readers something which would help them.

Right on target is Statham Instruments Connector Division's ad for the company's Mini Connector. It wastes no time getting to the point and loses no readers with a long preamble. Body copy gets into the story like this:

Statham's Mini Connector weighs in at a trim 2 grams. Mini boasts a body diameter measurement of 0.290 inch and a total mated height of less than 0.75 inch. Mini is the smallest hermetically sealed high-temperature connector available in 1-, 2-, 3-, and 4-contact configurations. Mini's body and pins are stainless steel. Each pin is individually insulated with Statham's exclusive "Stacer" ceramic. Mini thrives in climates of -320°F to + 750°F, and can withstand thermal shock from the upper to the lower extreme without damage or degradation. Consider these intrinsic features—small size, big performance, closed entry socket, weldability, and hermeticity. Then consider Statham's Mini Connector; the world's lightest heavyweight. For more information. . .

And write to Statham they did, for here is help aplenty for the engineer engaged in miniaturization. Statham's ad manager is fully aware that, as competitive as the electronics market is, the ad had to help the buyer if it was to help Statham.

Standard Pneumatic is frank and open in stressing the fact that its product would help the user. Body copy follows:

Here's an automatic screwdriver designed to help your operators work at top efficiency all day. It's the lightest, handiest, most efficient fractional horsepower screwdriver in the world! Smooth running and quiet, it will deliver as much as 100 in.-oz. torque on only 3.2 CFM of air. You can specify a torque-peak clutch for three torque ranges from 1 to 100 torque-peak clutch for three torque ranges from 1 to 100 in.-oz. for precise torque control...If your assemblers must work with #00 through #6 fasteners, we can help their efficiency. For more information...

That's help, a promise that assemblers will be more efficient; any production man quickly translates that into "more production, lower costs," and other benefits.

An unusually effective campaign based on helping the reader is being run by Handy & Harman, a leading manufacturer of brazing alloys. Format is the familiar one of posing a problem, asking a question, then explaining how to solve it through use of Handy & Harman's product. A typical ad is shown nearby. Clean layout, rebus illustrative technique (which will be discussed in a following chapter), attractive typography, and tight, well-written copy combine to make an ad that scored up near the top in readership in the magazines in which it appeared.

A continuing theme sets the stage for the question-type headline. Both theme line and headline are given below, just above the body copy which is a pleasure to read.

Problem in production design:

How would you make a part that "can't be made?"

They throw you a curve.

> *They hand you a sketch of a metal part whose conformation defies normal machining methods. To top it off, they want you to plan production of 50,000 of those parts.*

> *And, as a gentle hint, they suggest that you keep costs down.*

> *Here's what the part is supposed to look like:*

> *(sketch)*

> *Looks simple, doesn't it? And maybe you picture a machinist cutting bar stock to length and turning the diameters on a lathe or screw machine.*

> *But you look once more. You notice there's a rectangular shape protruding from the smaller diameter. And you realize that no lathe you ever saw could turn that "interrupted" diameter.*

> *Vague thoughts run through your mind. An indexing head operation? Ro-*

They throw you a curve.

They hand you a sketch of a metal part whose conformation defies normal machining methods. To top it off, they want you to plan production of 50,000 of those parts.

And, as a gentle hint, they suggest that you keep costs down.

Here's what the part is supposed to look like:

Looks simple, doesn't it? And maybe you picture a machinist cutting bar stock to length and turning the diameters on a lathe or screw machine.

But you look once more. You notice there's a rectangular shape, protruding from the smaller diameter. And you realize that no lathe you ever saw could turn that "interrupted" diameter.

Vague thoughts run through your mind. An indexing head operation? Rotary table? No, they eventually run afoul of the same problem—the juxtaposition of two "contradictory" shapes.

Maybe some kind of exotic contouring machine? No good. Even if it could work (and your shop owned one), you'd be in for some fancy tooling. And you're supposed to solve this problem economically.

By now you're beginning to get a little irritated. You take a trip to the water cooler and come back for a fresh look at the problem.

Wait a minute. This miserable part is really *two* parts, isn't it? Look at it this way:

At last you're getting somewhere. You'll make the round part on a lathe and the rectangular part out of flat stock—the natural way.

And you'll join them.

Any problem joining them? None at all. Just mill a slot in the small diameter, push in the flat block—and braze.

Insert and braze

You wind up with a strong metal part, fabricated at the lowest possible cost. The finished assembly would look like this:

Is production brazing practical here? It is. You'd probably have the pre-assembled parts conveyorized past a bank of fixed burners, which would heat the assemblies.

The brazing alloy could be applied on a production basis, probably in the form of metered amounts of brazing paste automatically dispensed to the joint area.

Now, this example is admittedly an oddball. Most metal parts *can* be made by "normal" fabrication methods. But the question is—how economically?

Very often, metal parts can be made better and cheaper as *assemblies* than as monolithic parts. Particularly where the "part" is characterized by widely-differing configurations, thick and thin sections, rounds and flats and so on.

We'd like to pass along to you some ideas on brazing these assemblies. As a leading manufacturer of brazing alloys, we've learned a good deal about the kind of problems brazing can solve.

So we wrote a booklet, "Brazing Ideas," that suggests just where brazing can do a job for you—and where it can't. The booklet is written in plain

English and illustrated with the kind of doodles you make yourself.

If you like ideas, you'll like "Brazing Ideas." Write for a free copy.

HANDY & HARMAN

850 THIRD AVENUE, NEW YORK, N.Y. 10022
OFFICES: CHICAGO, CLEVELAND, DALLAS, DETROIT, LOS ANGELES, PROVIDENCE

Question-type headline is used effectively by Handy & Harman.

tary table? No, they eventually run afoul of the same problem—the juxtaposition of two "contradictory" shapes.

Maybe some kind of exotic contouring machine? No good. Even if it could work (and your shop owned one), you'd be in for some fancy tooling. And you're supposed to solve this problem economically.

By now you're beginning to get a little irritated. You take a trip to the water cooler and come back for a fresh look at the problem.

Wait a minute. This miserable part is really two parts, isn't it? Look at it this way:

(sketch)

At last you're getting somewhere. You'll make the round part on a lathe and the rectangular part out of flat stock—the natural way.

And you'll join them.

Any problem joining them? None at all. Just mill a slot in the small diameter, push in the flat block—and braze.

(sketch)

You wind up with a strong metal part, fabricated at the lowest possible cost. The finished assembly would look like this:

(halftone)

Is production brazing practical here? It is. You'd probably have the pre-assembled parts conveyorized past a bank of fixed burners, which would heat the assemblies.

The brazing alloy could be applied on a production basis, probably in the form of metered amounts of brazing paste automatically dispensed to the joint area.

Now, this example is admittedly an oddball. Most metal parts can be made by "normal" fabrication methods. But the question is—how economically?

Very often, metal parts can be made better and cheaper as assemblies than as monolithic parts. Particularly where the "part" is characterized by widely differing configurations, thick and thin sections, rounds and flats, and so on.

We'd like to pass along to you some ideas on brazing these assemblies. As a leading manufacturer of brazing alloys, we've learned a good deal about the kind of problems brazing can solve.

So we wrote a booklet, Brazing Ideas, that suggests just where brazing can do a job for you—and where it can't. The booklet is written in plain

(sketch)

English and illustrated with the kind of doodles you make yourself.

If you like ideas, you'll like Brazing Ideas. Write for a free copy.

According to Starch and other readership surveys, Handy & Harman's ads in this campaign received unusually high readership—and unusually thorough readership.

They were conceived to appeal to the engineer, who delights in any kind of mechanical puzzle or quiz. These production engineers absorbed Handy & Harman's message completely, and responded in large numbers by writing for the cleverly executed booklet, *Brazing Ideas.* Naturally, this provides a constant flow of sales leads for Handy & Harman's sales force, as well as proof of advertising effectiveness in disseminating exactly the information about brazing that Handy & Harman wants prospects to have.

Conviction

Copy must convince the reader that claims made for the product are the truth.

Copy must convince the reader that claims made for the product are the truth.

This point is so essential it bears repetition. In an era of constantly increasing advertising pressure on readers of the business press, convincing them of your veracity sometimes isn't the easiest thing in the world to do. But it *must* be done.

The task is made easier by the fact that business readers want information about products that are new to them, hence they are more than willing to be receptive to the claims you make. Even so, we must recognize that the truth is not what we say it is, but is what readers believe it to be. Thus, when a product claim is advanced it should immediately be supported with proof of truth—proof acceptable to the average reader.

Even then you'll never achieve 100 percent believability, you'll never convince all readers of your truthfulness. Of interest is that some research shows that *no* ad will ever be entirely believed because of its basic purpose—to cause people to change their minds.

Claims should be made—and supported with proof—*within the framework of the reader's past experience*. Every statement you make in your copy, all of the facts, figures, performance data, comparisons with previous models of your product or with current competitive products, should be presented so the reader can sit back and assess your claims from personal experience—and from what he or she readily accepts as truth.

Convincing copy never results from use of "than-what" comparisons. Readers have no reference point when "than-what" comparisons are used. For example, Cleco Pneumatic said in a recent ad:

> *Extra strength in the ratchet parts keeps the tool on the job longer.*

This is a "than-what" comparison. The obvious question in the reader's mind is, *longer than what?*

Winter Brothers Company's ad in *Production* magazine on Skew-Shear taps contains two "than-what" comparisons. It said:

> *In many cases Skew-Shear taps have lasted 2 to 3 times longer. And even greater increases are not at all uncommon!*

Two or three times longer than what? Even greater than what?

Then there's this one:

> *Less worker fatigue, higher productivity, and fewer rejects due to misaligned parts at assembly.*

Less worker fatigue than what? Higher productivity than what? Fewer rejects than what? Smith Widget Manufacturing Company courts outright disbelief at worst, a condescending ignoring of obvious unsupported puffery at best. Even if the "than-what" comparisons merely resulted in the latter attitude, could the company's advertising manager actually believe that this ad was doing a job?

What countless "than-what" comparisons actually accomplish is to lessen the effectiveness of *all* advertising. Don't use them. Don't permit your agency to.

And don't wander afield. Be precise and, above all else, be specific. Use actual instances in your copy—real, honest-to-goodness things, facts, companies, figures, people. They convince readers of the truth of your claims.

For example, Precision Welder & Flexopress Corporation started their ad in *Production* magazine by saying:

Precision Palletron lowers assembly costs.

That's a positive statement, a good claim, and it's a user benefit that every production head would dearly love to see happen on production lines. Precision Welder & Flexopress quickly followed up with actual figures which prove to one and all the point they make:

This Precision Palletron assembly system for automobile starter motors handles 18 components and subassemblies at 5 manual, 3 semiautomatic, and 8 automatic stations. It can assemble 400 motors an hour.

The illustration complemented the copy, with the end result that PW&FC achieved conviction in their ad—a vitally necessary step toward making a sale of some expensive equipment.

Testimonials are always convincing, especially so when the name, title, firm, and address of the person being quoted is given. Use them freely. If the opportunity arises, quote expert testimony of acknowledged leaders in the field—men whose names are known and respected carry much weight. More often than not they will permit quotations about your products, assuming the product is performing properly, or did what you said it would do for them.

If your product has received official recognition, such as winning a blue ribbon at a design show, receiving approval by the National Association of Electrical Manufacturers, or the blessing of Underwriter's Laboratories, don't be a shrinking violet. Mention this in your ads, and mention it frequently. This carries conviction.

There's the name-dropping technique that's effective if the names you drop are either very big or are newsworthy in themselves at dropping time. Rocket Research Corporation did this quite nicely in a striking four-color ad in *Space/Aeronautics* magazine which said:

Twelve Rocket Research monopropellant hydrazine rockets will provide precise attitude control propellant settling, and velocity addition control for the Titan IIIC Transtage. Each employs a blow-down pressurization system providing about 25 lbf thrust...Rocket Research has received more than 30 contracts for hydrazine propulsion systems, developed

rockets from .02 to 300 lbf; developed, manufactured, quali-
fied, and delivered control rockets to NASA, Navy, Air
Force, and industry.

The fact that Rocket Research Corporation's hardware has met the exacting standards set by some of the most finicky buyers in the world, and that their propulsion system's reliability is so outstanding that a total of 12 of their units will control yaw, roll, pitch, velocity, and other flight characteristics in some of NASA's most important space projects is a real endorsement. And they're sharp enough to parlay this into an ad that's long on conviction.

Addition of "and industry" at the end of the copy adds just the right touch; this could easily encompass every firm in the country from AT&T to Smith Widget Manufacturing Company. Dropping names like these can't help but convince readers that Rocket Research Corporation's statements are true, that it manufactures outstanding products, and that it's a good company to do business with.

The reputation of the advertiser aids in convincing readers of the truthfulness of the statements in an ad. So does calling attention to widespread acceptance of the product, a permissible bit of chest-thumping.

For example, Worthington Corporation ended an ad in *Factory* magazine by saying:

. . . in the Worthington line that covers all plant air require-
ments. And its dependability has made it the most widely ac-
cepted name in industrial air supply. Worth remembering
when you expand.

The Worthington name alone lends credence to what has been said in the ad. And when Allen-Bradley tells about the enthusiastic acceptance the company's Modular Control Centers have earned—and supports it with believable statements from eight users who point up different user benefits—that's convincing.

Let's look at two examples of ads which do much to convince the reader that he can rely on statements the ads make.

First is a classically simple, tasteful, black-and-white, one-page ad run in *U.S. News & World Report* by Carrier Air Conditioning Company. The advertiser relies on the headline-is-the-copy technique and on a continuing campaign of succinct, convincing statements based on a premise which the reader has been conditioned all of his or her life to accept as absolute truth.

Layout is clean, simple, uncluttered and replete with plentiful eye-catching white space. The grace and charm of the Taj Mahal enhance the concept the copy advances—that low bidders usually are low bid-

**If low bidder had built
the Taj Mahal,**

would it still be a monument
to excellence? We suspect not.
Craftsmanship, in architecture as in
air conditioning, can seldom be shortcut
in the name of price. Quality, in the form
of craftsmanship, is another reason
why more people put their confidence
in Carrier than in any other make.

Carrier **Air Conditioning Company**

ders because of product shortcomings. All of us have been familiar all of our adult lives with various cartoons, caricatures, and jokes about the two bums on the park bench, one telling the other how *he* always used to be low bidder.

Carrier makes excellent use of that part of the reader's past experience with highly readable copy that goes:

> *If low bidder had built the Taj Mahal, would it still be a monument to excellence? We suspect not. Craftsmanship, in architecture as in air conditioning, can seldom be shortcut in the name of price. Quality, in the form of craftsmanship, is another reason why more people put their confidence in Carrier than in any other make.*

The ad does double duty with equal effectiveness: it tells Carrier's quality story to the buying influences in business and industry, and it tells it also to these same individuals *as homeowners and consumers.* This fringe benefit of a campaign aimed primarily at business and industry is of significant, if secondary, value to Carrier.

Norton Company's superb four-color spread is just about as convincing as it's possible for an ad to be. Honesty and sincerity come strongly through the copy, as it should in every well-written ad. It reads:

> **If a wheel fails,**
> **we not only know**
> **why, we know who.**
> **It isn't easy**
> **to be Norton.**

> *When a Norton wheelmaker weighs out and mixes your wheel's abrasive and bond according to its personal prescription, he signs his number on that wheel's traveling pedigree form. And the form stays with the wheel through every step, collecting the identity of every man who has a hand in its making.*

> *That way you get the right wheel, made right, every time. But if a wheel isn't right, we know why and who did it.*

> *You get that kind of care at Norton whether you order one wheel or a thousand. Although we started the abrasives industry by inventing the first modern grinding wheel in 1877, we've stayed first only because we work at it.*

> *It isn't easy to be Norton.*

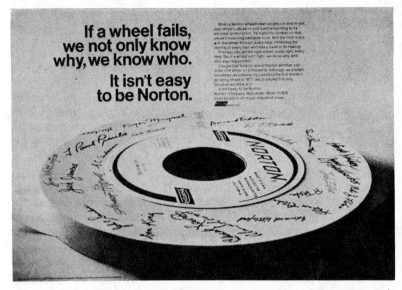

Coming through unmistakably is Norton's message that Norton is Number One in its industry—that, in fact, Norton *started* the industry. Product quality is superb, the ad implies without actually saying so, because of the unusual degree of personal responsibility assumed by all *who had a hand in its making*.

Norton's story is all the more convincing due to its soft-sell approach which tacitly admits it is possible for a Norton wheel to be other than perfect—although, after reading this ad, it would seem highly unlikely.

The tag line, *It isn't easy to be Norton*, repeating the second half of the headline, is a delightful touch. It does more than its share to convince the reader of the truth of Norton's claims.

Persuasion

Industrial advertising uses print almost to the exclusion of all other media. Consequently, the classic definition of advertising attributed to the late copy great, Claude Hopkins, who coined it before the day of electronic intrusion into our private lives, is perhaps the best one yet stated. According to Mr. Hopkins, "advertising is salesmanship in print."

When we accept this as a valid definition, there's only one conclusion which can be drawn: Advertising's most important function is to do exactly what a skilled salesperson does—persuade. Persuade others to accept ideas, his or her viewpoint, his or her advice and suggestions. Obviously, this is to buy the product.

Any of the seven Type IV headlines, the virtually useless ones discussed in Chapter 7, and the body copy which accompanies them as inevitably as night follows day, is destined to be about as successful as the Edsel or the F-111 jet fighter.

Only copy which is completely committed to furtherance of this primary objective—to present information intriguingly and provocatively so the reader is persuaded to take the action the advertiser desires—merits getting outside the advertising manager's office.

Needless to say, a high percentage of all industrial copy fails to persuade, despite belonging to classifications of copy types which are legitimate and desirable.

This may be because the words "persuade" and "persuasion" are misunderstood, although it's somewhat unlikely. To clear up any misconceptions, let's see what one impeccable source, Webster, has to say on the subject.

"Persuade" means: 1. To induce (one) to believe or do something; to argue into an opinion or procedure. 2. To use persuasion upon; urge.

"Persuasion" means: 1. Act of persuading. 2. Power or quality of persuading. 3. State of being persuaded; induced opinion or conviction. 4. A creed or belief, especially religious. 5. Jocular kind; sort; as, the male persuasion—syn. belief.

From all of that we can cull out something acceptable, such as the first definition of persuade: *To induce one to believe or do something.* This is much to be preferred over the latter half of the first definition. The mere thought of copy presenting information argumentatively is enough to give one the vapors.

As far as persuasion is concerned, the act of persuading is applicable to well-written advertising copy, particularly when it is coupled with inducing an opinion or conviction. This, after all, is the one prime criterion by which copy must be judged: Will it affect the opinion of the reader and cause him or her to change attitude enough so that he or she will want to purchase the product? All else is secondary.

Whether or not copy is persuasive isn't the easiest thing to judge. For one thing, the decision is frequently—usually, in fact—a subjective one. There are few fixed guideposts, except that copy must, as we've said, interest, inform, involve, help, and convince if it's to achieve its one objective: To persuade.

Viewed in that light, AC Spark Plug Division of General Motors' two-color (red and black) spread ad printed in *Commercial Car Journal* fails to persuade. Let's look at the copy, then see why it doesn't succeed.

AC has nothing to do with downtime

*When your fleet is equipped
with the Full Time Fire-
power of AC Fire-Ring Spark
Plugs, you'll be minimizing
downtime; downtime that
costs you money.*

*Because self-cleaning ACs
mean sure performance at all
speeds, in all kinds of
weather, under all types of
driving conditions.*

*You can cut downtime
even more by installing AC
ACron Oil Filters, too. They
eliminate virtually all engine
wear caused by contaminants.*

*Get AC Spark Plugs and
Oil Filters for your fleet.
With the complete AC line,
you'll really profit by having
nothing to do with downtime.*

Consider this ad in relation to the attributes effective copy must possess. First, let's take interest. Granted, downtime is the bugaboo that's the bane of every truck operator's life. A truck down is a truck that's not earning its keep, a truck that's increasing costs and cutting into profits. That's elementary.

Every operator is as much opposed to downtime as a man of the cloth is opposed to vice. AC is on firm ground by starting out with a basic premise with which nobody will disagree. That's the gambit known as earning their confidence by making an irrefutable statement, getting 'em on our side by saying things that cause nodding of heads.

Fine and dandy, but the massive disclaimer in the headline is hardly necessary. AC didn't stand in the dock accused of being in cahoots with that wicked old enemy, downtime. The headlined denial is just a little too pious and, at the same time, self-defeating because the immediate reaction to it is, "who says they do?"

Body copy is something less than intensely interesting, even to a man whose livelihood depends on having his trucks pile up mileage, not repair bills. It's pedantic; it preaches as it plods along.

Nothing new is presented, nothing fresh, nothing really solid that the reader can get his or her teeth into, then sit back, scratch his or her head, and ponder. As far as factual, helpful information is concerned, there's remarkably little there. In the first paragraph, AC claims truckers minimize downtime if they use their plugs—then they restate the obvious that downtime costs money. This is belaboring the subject to death, but it's probably due to some ivory-tower copywriter just learning that such a thing exists.

AC still doesn't offer any proof; no information is given to support their statement. If somebody happened to read as far as the second paragraph, he or she would probably jerk bolt upright in sheer amazement at receiving a piece of information applicable to his or her job interests—that AC spark plugs are self-cleaning. Even that's not explained, however, evidently on the assumption that the reader knows all about how spark plugs clean themselves. This is taking too much for granted.

Then, stating that AC spark plugs mean sure performance at all speeds, in all kinds of weather, under all types of driving conditions *really* covers the waterfront. However, this doesn't actually *mean* anything except that these trite words are strung together exactly as words in spark plug copy have always been strung together since the advent of the internal combustion engine. They're equally applicable to all brands of spark plugs, of course.

Next, AC informs one and all that you can cut downtime even more (which is an excellent example of a "than-what" comparison) by installing AC ACron oil filters, too, because they virtually eliminate all engine wear caused by contaminants. This presents just about as much information as the first two paragraphs—next to none.

And precious little information is in the bid for action and the "snapper"—although it *does* clarify headline (never, *never*, NEVER, *NEVER* feel the need to clarify a headline!) a bit. But does it inform, or does it explain the copywriter's play on words?

Reader involvement? Vapidity never results in deep personal involvement.

What help is there in this ad for the reader? Well, the illustration shows what a spark plug and an oil filter look like. Although he or she presumably in the business of operating a fleet of motor trucks, he might not have known. As far as helping on the job, huh uh.

Inspire conviction? For obvious reasons we can skip discussion of this vitally important attribute copy must have.

Ah, now comes persuasion. And persuade. Fine, strong words and the prime criterion by which to judge copy. Here again is the definition which we accept for these words, as applied to copy: "To induce one to believe or do something; to induce an opinion or conviction." This copy never comes close to persuading the reader to continue buying AC spark plugs if he or she now does, or to switch to ACs if he or she is currently using another brand. He or she hasn't been told why he or she should.

Neither an emotional nor a logical reaction is evoked by this copy because it is not firmly committed to persuading the reader to take action by presenting the subject matter so intriguingly and provocatively that he or she finds it difficult to rationalize doing otherwise. Ineffectual copy like this takes a small but sure toll against all advertising. Bore people long enough and they'll overlook you completely.

The CB&Q Is Convincing

Advertising copy *can* persuade by being informative, helpful, intriguing and provocative. The Chicago, Burlington & Quincy Railroad proved that while promoting a service that's little different than that offered by competitors.

The Burlington and its agency faced one of the facts of business life: That empty freight cars are neither objects of art nor objects of interest—until a shipper needs them right now.

To set itself apart from the herd, the Burlington wisely decided upon a copy approach that gave the railroad a fresh, forward-looking, vigorous image and a distinct personality. Personality automatically accompanies use of names of actual key employees who help shippers get better service, enabling the Burlington freight customers to think of the railroad as people, not tracks and cars and locomotives. This results in good reader involvement and gave the copy a chance to persuade—which it did.

A typical CB&Q ad is shown on the page 394. Copy starts with the shocking headline:

Art MacDonald says this railroad specializes in empty promises!

Next part of the cumulative headline takes the curse off of the opening teaser and entices the reader further into the ad:

Who does he think he is?

Then, in the final segment of the headline we find:

*He's one of the hard-driving wheels
on the Burlington Railroad.*

In dialogue form, quoting Art, the body copy says:

*"We not only promise empties," Art insists, "we go all out
to deliver. That's why we're likely to have more cars on
hand when our customers want them."*

*As Burlington's service and car utilization director, it's
Art's job to track down empty cars. To get them right back
into service. And to help our customers use these cars most
efficiently.*

Unloaded cars just sitting around benefit no one.

*So Art has set a deadline for their return. As empties begin
beating the deadline, he shortens it. And demands even
quicker turnaround time.*

*Tough challenge? Sure. But we've developed a few short-
cuts.*

*Like a computer that tells us instantly which cars are moving
and which aren't. Where they're going. What they're carrying. And when they're unloading.*

*So instead of cars sitting around on some siding gathering
rust, they're out working where they belong.*

*Art has good reason to boast about faster return of empties.
But one thing's certain.*

Its's no empty boast.

The selling proposition is sound, a user benefit is given in the first
paragraph, and it is backed up with good reason-why copy. This is an
ad that is believable—and that's persuasive. If you were a manufacturer on one of the Burlington's routes, wouldn't you be inclined to
try Burlington facilities because of their approach to giving you faster
service?

The Goodyear Tire & Rubber Company's striking four-color spread
ad shows how persuasive copy can be for a specialized industrial product. Written in terse, tight style that's almost telegraphic, this fine ad
reads:

There are 30,000 ways to cut costs with Goodyear rubber engineering

*This is how they cut costs at Lake Okeechobee:
Giant rubber suction hose—business end of world's
largest automated dredge—outwears steel 8 to 1.*

Art MacDonald says this railroad specializes in empty promises!

Who does he think he is?

He's one of the hard-driving wheels on the Burlington Railroad.

"We not only *promise* empties," Art insists, "we go all out to *deliver*. That's why we're likely to have more cars on hand when our customers want them."

As Burlington's service and car utilization director, it's Art's job to track down empty cars. To get them right back into service. And to help our customers use these cars most efficiently.

Unloaded cars just sitting around benefit no one.

So Art has set a deadline for their return. As empties begin beating the deadline, he shortens it. And demands even quicker turn-around time.

Tough challenge? Sure. But we've developed a few shortcuts.

Like a computer that tells us instantly which cars are moving and which aren't. Where they're going. What they're carrying. And when they're unloading.

So instead of cars sitting around on some siding gathering rust, they're out working where they belong.

Art has good reason to boast about faster return of empties. But one thing's certain.

It's no empty boast.

Burlington Lines: Chicago, Burlington & Quincy Railroad; The Colorado and Southern Railway; Fort Worth and Denver Railway.

A dangerous flirtation with a compelling but negative headline works out well for the Chicago, Burlington & Quincy Railroad because the copy quickly recovers a positive approach and talks convincingly of shipper benefits. Negative headlines, however, should be used with the greatest of care.

*First 600,000 tons of abra-
sive sand and gravel ruined
steel swivel joint. So company switched to flexible
12-ft. length of 31" diameter Goodyear hose. It con-
nects drill head to dredge,
pumps 4500 tons an hour
nonstop. After 2½ months
on world's largest irriga-
tion-flood control job, hose
has pumped 5 million tons,
now looks good for 22 million
more.*

*Goodyear can help you cut
costs: With rubber products engineered to work
harder, last longer on little maintenance. And replace
more expensive materials. Goodyear has engineered
rubber products to meet 30,000 different specifications. The right one could cut your costs. Call your
Goodyear Distributor. He's backed by a rubber
engineer who understands your business . . . the
G.T.M. (Goodyear Technical Man). Or write:
Goodyear Industrial Products . . .*

Goodyear wisely relies on the basic pocketbook appeal and gives valid reasons why users of Goodyear products produce more at lower cost.

"Business end of the world's largest automated dredge" is colorful, highly descriptive, and just plain interesting. Everybody is curious about almost anything that's in a record class as to size, performance, or what have you.

"Outwears steel 8 to 1" lays the prime user benefit right on the line. A mathematician of Einstein's genius isn't required to see that Goodyear's rubber hose which handled 5 million tons and still looks good for 22 million more, compared to a steel swivel joint that bit the dust after a mere 600,000 tons, is by far the better buy. Specific facts are presented provocatively. The copy is designed to convince and per-suade and *sell*.

50 Years For the Same Theme

Goodyear's campaign has been running for more than 50 years. During this half-century the campaign has been refined, of course, but

The Goodyear Tire & Rubber Company is proof that an organization can use the same ad campaign for half a century and still develop creative copy themes. Campaign is planned carefully to appeal to all in Goodyear "universe."

it retains its basic approach, founded on research—readership studies and analysis of creative approaches told Goodyear this was the tack to take.

The same headline, "There are 30,000 ways to cut costs with Goodyear rubber engineering," is in its fourth year with no apparent loss of readership, proving one again the truth of the old saying that advertisers get tired of their compaigns long before readers do. In fact, many advertisers discontinue campaigns which are becoming more effective with each advertisement merely because they have wearied of seeing what are, to them, the same old ads.

Goodyear's campaign consistently appears near the top in any readership studies performed by the publications. Usually they are in the top three, and frequently are Number One. In four studied issues of one national trade magazine, Goodyear recently had the highest *Noted* score in the book on three ads, the second highest on the other one.

Success of this campaign hinges on communications objectives which can be realized. Goodyear's case-history campaign is designed to:

1. Create a favorable image so that Goodyear representatives will encounter a favorable selling climate when calling on prospects.
2. Present Goodyear product quality so convincingly and persuasively that prospects will accept the fact that Goodyear products will cost less to use in the service to which they are put.
3. Enhance Goodyear's reputation for leadership among prospective customers, distributors, and their sales staffs.

Among the buying influences in Goodyear's universe are maintenance people, foremen, plant engineers, design engineers, purchasing agents, managers, and top management.

Goodyear reaches this diverse group of influences through several business publications, including *Iron Age, Plant Engineering, Mill & Factory, Purchasing, Business Week,* and several general news publications. Among these are *U.S. News & World Report, Time,* and *Newsweek.*

Inducing a Response

An ad that fails to induce some kind of reader response is worthless.

However, this emphatically does *not* mean that every reader of every industrial advertisement must race through the copy with a mounting sense of excitement, throw the magazine hastily aside and

Give us four hours,

and we'll give you a frank analysis
of your best way to melt.

For new foundries or old. And without bias—because we're the only ones who sell all furnace types.

We'll look, we'll ask, and we'll dig. What will you melt now, and five years from now? What charge materials are available, and where'll you store them? What metallurgical properties do you need, and will they change? Our analysis goes on and on.

Then we'll evaluate induction channel, induction coreless, medium fre-

quency, resistance, arc, and fuel-fired furnaces. With no holds barred. And we'll recommend what we think is best.

Let's make a date. Call Roger Hatfield at 414/691-7000. Or write to him at 961 Hart Street, Watertown, Wis. 53094.

OTHER DIVISIONS: ANCHOR ELECTRIC · ENGINEERED CERAMICS · HEVI-DUTY ELECTRIC · NELSON ELECTRIC · SOLA ELECTRIC

breathlessly place a phone call to the advertiser requesting that a salesperson rush to see him or her immediately to accept a six-figure order which he'll force the salesperson to write up.

Things just don't happen that way very often.

Sometimes, though, an advertisement is read by the prospect in just the right climate, at exactly the time when the need is greatest and he or she *does* respond that way.

An example is the Lindberg Hevi-Duty ad shown nearby. The ad's illustration is a dramatic, extreme close-up of a safety-glassed, hard-hatted engineer in a foundry. A ladle of molten metal is in the background for authenticity. Purpose of this ad is to induce a response—preferably a telephone call.

Perhaps this doesn't appear to be too compelling an ad, at least to those outside the foundry industry. But to the foundry owner or superintendent in a dilemma about the type of equipment to buy, it is. He knows, through association with his counterparts in an unusually tight-knit industry, that Lindberg Hevi-Duty *is* the only manufacturer to offer every type of melting furnace, just as the ad says.

The ad's logic is unassailable. The advertiser's claim that he or she can give the foundryman an unbiased evaluation of the one best method for him to use, with consideration given to many factors which influence the decision, such as fuel costs, quality of melt, charge materials, air pollution, and so on, is unquestioned. The ad copy reads as follows:

Give us four hours,
*and we'll give you a frank analysis
of your best way to melt.
For new foundries or old. And without
bias—because we're the only ones who
sell all furnace types.
We'll look, we'll ask, and we'll dig.
What will you melt now, and five years
from now? What charge materials are
available, and where'll you store them?
What metallurgical properties do you
need, and will they change? Our analysis
goes on and on.
Then we'll evaluate induction channel,
induction coreless, medium frequency,
resistance, arc, and fuel-fired furnaces.
With no holds barred. And we'll recommend what we think is best.*

> *Let's make a date. Call John Blank*
> *at 123/456-7890. Or write to him at . . .*
> *With no holds barred. And we'll recom-*
> *mend what we think is best.*
>
> *Let's make a date. Call John Blank*
> *at 123/456-7890. Or write to him at . . .*

The bid for action is a strong one. There's a sense of immediacy due to giving John Blank's name and phone number. This induced the response the advertiser wanted—written and long-distance-telephone inquiries. Sales engineers from the advertiser's office staff promptly followed up on these inquiries. The ad, which appeared in the primary metals edition of *Iron Age,* and in *Foundry* magazine, *has produced several dozen inquiries from prospects upon whom the advertiser's sales force had not previously called. A number of inquiries have been converted into actual sales—to the tune of several hundred thousand dollars.*

Useful life of this ad is far from over. The advertiser continues to run it, and it is still producing a very gratifying volume of inquiries. It's quite possible that this one ad may unearth hidden prospects to whom a million dollars worth of equipment will be sold—all for the nominal expense of producing a one-page, black-and-white ad, and for a few thousand dollars invested in space. This is yet another example of how advertising lowers the cost of selling.

Naturally, the response induced by an ad must be one that is favorable to the advertiser. Not all industrial advertisements are designed to pull inquiries, though. Some go even further—they're written so that the reader response is to write and mail a check for an item that's within the price range of an impulse purchase—and some items sold to industry are just that.

Much more frequently the response that's wanted is a request for a piece of literature. The advertiser mails this material to the inquirer, and also feeds the respondent's name to the field sales force for a follow-up sales call.

A good industrial ad, regardless of the response desired, will always include a bid for action. This is similar to a good salesperson always asking for the order after making a sales presentation. Fail to do it and you have an ad that's a lost cause.

Reeves Vulcan Division missed this point in a one-page ad in *Commercial Car Journal,* the magazine of fleet management. Copy-cat copy starts with a headline influenced by consumer advertising—also of the "the-the" school which labels the product, preferably in outlandishly oversize display type, with a name which theoretically denotes its function. In this instance the headline is:

The
Protector

And the body copy then proceeds to tell us about the tarpaulins Reeves manufactures for "rag-top" trucks and trailers:

You need protection from wet freight claims. And the best protection you can buy is a tarp made of Coverlight. Coverlight is the only tarp material with exclusive Ripstop construction for twice the tear strength of conventional tarp materials.

And Coverlight is not affected by soil, solvent, oil, mildew, or dry rot. It's lightweight and permanently waterproof. Available in vinyl, neoprene, Hypalon, and Hypalon/neoprene combinations. In a wide range of weights and colors.

Smart fleet owners specify Coverlight for open tops, tail curtains, pickup covers, and winter fronts. And The Protector always acts like a hero.

Only in six-point type, way down at the bottom of the ad where it's easily confused with a slug-line, does Reeves indicate that letters or phone calls wouldn't be returned to sender, or be refused. There's no bid for action at the close of the copy; it's far too easy for the reader to infer that nothing is desired from him or her.

And Cummins Engine Company—whose name doesn't even appear in their black-and-white spread in the same publication—makes the same basic mistake. This ad blunders badly by using a dramatic photograph of a corral full of horses. The saddle stock is milling around, facing all different directions, and a realistic haze of dust hangs over the scene. So far, all this is well and good—but the two-page, bleed illustration of the Western corral never is explained, nor is it really tied in with the copy.

Cummins also committed the unforgivable sin of omitting a headline, thus losing the major portion of the immediate impact on the reader. This also obscures what the product is, what it's used for, or a user benefit, as well as doing a dandy job of hiding the identity of the advertiser. Copy starts right out, in the absence of a headline, this way:

You say 210 horsepower isn't enough? And 220 won't do the job either?

Okay, Cummins closes the horsepower gap. With the NH 230.

401

Now, you know who Cummins is. And you know all about engines named NH. So we'll skip the usual adjectives.

The news is, if you need 230 horses or so, now you can get them from Cummins. Conveniently harnessed in the most economical package in this horsepower range.

There may well be 230 horses in the illustration, although a diligent tally of horses' heads and horses' other ends leaves some doubt about this. But the advertiser assumes much too much. There undoubtedly are truckers who have used no other power plants except Mack Thermodyne or Maxidyne engines since starting in business, hence are completely unfamiliar with Cummins engines.

Assuming they know Cummins engines are built to develop 210 or 220 horsepower is taking an awful lot for granted. Neither can they be expected to know the horsepower range of competitive engines; this is something of vital interest to the manufacturer who is reaching for a competitive advantage—but not to the reader.

Granted, the name Cummins will undoubtedly be recognized, but recognition is hardly reward enough to justify production cost of the ad, plus some $2,000 worth of space for every insertion.

Only in the final paragraph is it evident that this is an ad written to introduce a new product—a new 230-horsepower engine. Presumably it's a diesel engine, since Cummins concentrates on diesels, although this, too, is left for the reader to assume.

Additional omissions—there is no signature, no company name, no telephone number, no address, no advertiser identification, no headline, no bid for action, no logotype. In all likelihood, no reader response, either.

The copywriter went to great lengths to make the message as obscure as possible under the impression readers will exert themselves to assimilate information the advertiser wants them to acquire.

Wrong. They won't do it.

The Concept Is All

Underlying every piece of copy, good or bad, is a concept—the basic idea of what the words in print should convey, and what the ad is designed to achieve. If the concept is good, chances are the copy will be, too.

Let's now look at copy—an entire integrated campaign, in fact—which was conceived to achieve just one critically important objective: To induce reader response.

First, though, before we read copy and examine ads and what accompanies them, a bit of background on the competitive situation faced by the advertiser, Fairchild-Davidson, Division of Fairchild Camera and Instrument Corporation, is in order.

In its industry Fairchild-Davidson is in direct competition with a well-known, well-entrenched competitor who is a giant in the field. This competitor is blessed not only with a long-established position, but with a name that's thoroughly familiar to the majority of the prospects. This meant, of course, that Fairchild-Davidson had to solve the problem of bringing their field salespeople face to face with many more prospects than they were now seeing in order to demonstrate their equipment.

Demonstration is the key to the sale, and Fairchild-Davidson simply was not as well known in the duplicator field as was the competition. This meant that quite often Fairchild-Davidson didn't get an opportunity to demonstrate their product when prospects were in a buying mood.

Apparent to Fairchild-Davidson advertising management was the fact that the only way to receive more opportunities to demonstrate was to issue a challenge—through advertising—that was big and brash and bold. It had to have teeth and claws in it. The buying public, of course, sees such a challenge as a form of dare, so accepts the advertising exactly the way the advertiser wishes it to.

First ad in this great campaign is illustrated. Fine, colloquial, hard-hitting copy is set off to good advantage by clean layout, an amusing spot illustration, and good clean typography. Copy gets right to the point:

**The Fairchild-Davidson Gambit:
We'll pay you $25 if you see
our offset duplicator, and then
buy somebody else's.**

The quizzical looking individual is saying:

How's that again?

You read it right.

We'll give you our check for $25 toward the purchase of any other offset duplicator you select. Provided you've looked at ours first.

That's not as wacky as it sounds.

It's worth the $25 to us just to get the chance to show you how the Fairchild-Davidson can help you cut costs and boost production.

As things stand now, we don't always get that chance. Because we're relatively new to office duplicating, we're not the first name a businessman thinks of. Sometimes they don't even think of us at all.

But the satisfying thing is, more than 50% of the companies who do see our demonstration, and who buy a press, buy ours.

$25 says you will too.

Look for the Fairchild-Davidson listing under "Duplicating Machines" in the Yellow Pages. Or get in touch directly with Paul Smith at 123/456-7890.

(He's the one who signs the checks.)

Frank, engaging, intriguing and provocative. And it was followed up with equally interesting ads, all of which stress the money angle.

The headline of the second ad in the campaign reads:

Our great "get-acquainted sale": $25 off any competitive offset duplicator if you still want one after you've seen the Fairchild-Davidson.

Caption for the spot illustration of the F-D duplicator is:

Old Irresistible.

And the body copy:

Hurry! Supply of competitive machines is limited! Buy now and save!

Actually this $25 gambit of Fairchild-Davidson's isn't as kooky as it sounds.

You see, we're relatively new to offset duplicating. Even though we offer some impressive advantages in the way of increased production and decreased costs, many businessmen still haven't heard of us.

But of those companies who do see our demonstration, and who buy an offset duplicator, more than 50% buy ours.

So what we're really after is your attention.

After we've gotten it, if you can still resist, we'll cheerfully shell out $25 toward your purchase of Brand X.

Look for the Fairchild-Davidson listing under "Duplicating Machines" in the Yellow Pages. Or get in touch directly with Paul Smith at 123/456-7890.

Our competitors know of this ad.

The concept is great, really creative, and the quality of the copy throughout the campaign is uniformly high, as you'll note from the small illustrations of four of the Fairchild-Davidson ads. Each adheres to the "Gambit" theme, of course, with individual approaches and a sure-handed light touch that's a real pleasure to read.

Fairchild-Davidson kicked off the campaign at a national sales meeting, where it received an immediate and enthusiastic response from all of the company's branch managers and field sales distributor supervisors. Concurrent with the sales meeting, kits announcing the new campaign were sent to all branch salespeople and distributors throughout the country.

Included in the merchandising kit was a 33⅓ rpm long-playing record which explained the whole campaign from concept to execution on one side, then requested the listener to flip to the other side and "hear music to gamble $25 by." Also in the kit were ad reprints, samples of the initial direct mail units. "Gambit" certificates in a "Gambit" wallet, a complete rationale on the program in black and white, and a comprehensive rundown of the greatly expanded media schedule that would be used throughout the year.

Three mailings were made to support the "Gambit" campaign. The first mailing was simply a letter introducing the "Gambit" concept, with an ad reprint of the first advertisement, along with Fairchild-Davidson's standard business reply card.

405

We'll contribute $25 to our competitor. In your name.

(And they're not our favorite charity.)

It's something less than lovingkindness which prompts the Fairchild-Davidson $25 gambit.

We're doing it for our health.

Not enough of you businessmen know of the remarkable advantages offered by our offset duplicator. Particularly the way it squeezes more production out of each working day.

(Although more than 50% of the companies who do see our demonstration, and who buy an offset duplicator, buy ours.)

So we hit on the idea of paying you $25 toward your purchase of a competitive machine. Should you still want one. After seeing ours, that is.

That way, if we don't score, it won't be because you never heard of us.

If the spirit moves you, look for the Fairchild-Davidson listing under "Duplicating Machines" in the Yellow Pages. Or get in touch directly with Paul Hill at 212 PL 9-6800.

FAIRCHILD DAVIDSON We have one consolation if we lose.
Our $25 is tax deductible.

This is the largest-selling offset duplicator in the country.

We'll bet you $25 you won't buy it.

No.1

Once you've seen ours, that is.

Take a good look at No. 1 and at the Fairchild-Davidson. Ponder a bit.

Then if you still want to go ahead and buy No. 1, we'll help you. To the tune of $25.

There's a method in our rashness. We're relatively new to office duplicating. So we're not the first name you business people think of.

In fact, some of you never think of us at all.

But it's gratifying to report that more than 50% of the companies who do see our demonstration, and who buy an offset duplicator, buy ours.

We'll wager $25 you're another.

Look for the Fairchild-Davidson listing under "Duplicating Machines" in the Yellow Pages. Or get in touch directly with Paul Hill at 212 PL 9-6800.

FAIRCHILD DAVIDSON (If we get to be No. 1, the whole deal is off.)

Does Avis pay Hertz?

Then what's with this $25 bit of ours?

Fairchild-Davidson is probably the only company in existence that offers to shell out $25 every time it loses a sale to a competitor.

Even Avis doesn't go that far to catch up with No. 1.

It could hurt if our offset duplicator wasn't pretty exceptional.

But it is. And not just on our say-so. More than half the companies who see our demonstration, and who buy an offset machine, buy ours.

Our only problem is that, since we're relatively new in office duplicating, not enough of you businessmen know of us yet.

So to get your attention, we're willing to stick our neck out. See the Fairchild-Davidson. See the others. Then, if you buy one of the others, we'll give you a $25 check toward its purchase.

Look for the Fairchild-Davidson listing under "Duplicating Machines" in the Yellow Pages. Or call Paul Hill at 212 PL 9-6800.

FAIRCHILD DAVIDSON (If we get to be No. 1, the whole deal is off.)

If you see our offset duplicator and buy it, you get to wear this medal.

Otherwise, we will.

It's a medal for heroes, sort of.

We'll pin it on ourselves if you buy any other duplicator after you see the Fairchild-Davidson. Because we'll have handed you $25 toward the purchase of the other fellow's machine. A noble, if carefree, gesture.

I LOST $25

But if you buy our machine, you win the medal. To commemorate the way you lost $25 but won the war for flawless duplicating.

What are your chances of being decorated?

Well, look at it this way. More than 50% of the companies who see our demonstration and who buy an offset duplicator, buy ours.

Our only real problem is that, since we're relatively new to office duplicating, not enough businessmen know us. Hence our $25 gambit.

If you aspire, look for the Fairchild-Davidson listing under "Duplicating Machines" in the Yellow Pages. Or get in touch directly with Paul Hill at 212 PL 9-6800.

FAIRCHILD DAVIDSON (If he doesn't answer on the first ring, be patient. He may be busy counting his medals.)

The letters and the entry certificate are shown nearby. The certificate has space for countersigning by appropriate branches or distributors to validate the prospect's having seen a demonstration. To qualify for the $25 check, the winner of the $25 check has to show a valid purchase order for a competitive duplicator—indicating that he wasn't sold by Fairchild-Davidson.

Direct Mail Letter #1
National and Local
(also enclosed is Gambit Reply
Card and Reprint of Ad No. 1)

Dear Sir:

We mean it. We'll send you a check for $25 if, after seeing a demonstration of a Fairchild-Davidson offset duplicator, you decide to buy somebody else's.

Obviously, we believe we've got some pretty top-rate equipment and we're willing to risk $25 to prove it. If you're in the market to buy an offset duplicator, you're probably planning to see several different makes before making a final decision. All we ask is that you come see one of our offset duplicators as well. See what our simultaneous two-sided printing, roll paper conversion, push-button automation can mean in your particular situation. If then, you still buy someone else's, we'll pay $25 toward its purchase.

That's the gambit.

If you'd like to know more about Fairchild-Davidson or our line of duplicators first, that's fine with us. Just check the appropriate box on the reply card and drop it in the mail.

But whatever you do, remember you've nothing to lose and $25 to gain.

Very truly yours,

–Paul H. Till
General Sales Manager

Fairchild-Davidson, a Division of Fairchild Camera and Instrument Corporation, 5004 E. Jericho Turnpike, Commack, L. I., N.Y. 11725

As of this writing only four $25 checks have been issued *nationally.* Fairchild-Davidson's sales staff sells well, apparently.

Subsequent mailings also were sales letters, but the enclosures were fresh and varied. Among them was the little brochure explaining what "Gambit" means, according to Webster and according to

Direct Mail Letter #2
National Only
(Also enclosed is Gambit
Certificate and Reply Card)

Dear Sir:

As further proof of the sincerity of our offer, enclosed you will find a Fairchild-Davidson $25 Gambit Certificate.

It officially qualifies you to (1) see all the competitive offset duplicating equipment available, (2) see Fairchild-Davidson's, and then (3) decide.

Should you decide to buy ours, like most people who see it in action, we'll be delighted. But if you buy one of theirs, we fork up $25 toward its purchase.

Fair enough?

Look for the Fairchild-Davidson listing under "Duplicating Machines" in your Yellow Pages, or fill out the reply card. When you see the Fairchild-Davidson, the demonstrator will validate your certificate.

Then we'll see what we shall see.

Very truly yours,

Paul H. Till
General Sales Manager

Fairchild-Davidson, a Division of Fairchild Camera and Instrument Corporation, 5004 E. Jericho Turnpike, Commack, L. I., N.Y. 11725

Fairchild-Davidson. It, along with a miniature chessman with "OK" on a rubber stamp at the bottom, and a button which proclaims "I LOST $25.00—FAIRCHILD-DAVIDSON." They're shown nearby. All attracted the attention of prospects.

To supplement the program, Fairchild-Davidson ran a special three-month promotion, "The Great Fairchild-Davidson Gambit Sweepstakes." In the sweepstakes, which broke at the National Association

OFFICIAL ENTRY BLANK

The Great Fairchild-Davidson Gambit Sweepstakes

Simply fill in the information requested below, then check the rules governing "The Great Fairchild-Davidson Gambit Sweepstakes" on your copy of the "Official Entry Blank." It's as simple as that.

NAME _____ TITLE _____

COMPANY _____

ADDRESS _____ PHONE _____

CITY _____ STATE _____

5311

My entry is governed by the rules printed below, and on the reverse side, and is subject to State and local laws.

Interested in:

☐ Dualith 400 ☐ Dualith 600 ☐ Dual-A-Matic 720
☐ Dualith 500 ☐ Dualith 612 ☐ Dual-A-Matic 760
☐ Dual-A-Matic 580 ☐ Dual-A-Matic 620 ☐ Roll Convertor
☐ Dual-A-Matic 560 ☐ Dual-A-Matic 660 ☐ 3000 Collator
☐ Dualith 500 TL ☐ Dualith 700 ☐ Supplies

Comments: _____
_____
_____
_____

(SHOW) (SIGNATURE)

Home Office Copy

gambit according to Webster:

gam·bit (*gam'bit*), *n.* in chess a strategy in which a pawn or other piece is sacrificed to gain an advantageous position.

gambit according to Fairchild-Davidson:

gam·bit (*gam'bit*), *n.* in offset duplicating, a ploy to demonstrate our machines while risking the loss of a sum of money if the prospect sees our demonstration and buys someone else's. Otherwise known as the Fairchild-Davidson $25 Gambit.

of Photo-Lithographers trade show in Washington, D.C., the advertiser awarded a Jaguar XK-E to the lucky winner. We've all seen useless trinkets and genuinely useful giveaways handed out at trade shows, but a Jaguar!

Space ads, such as the one illustrated, promoted the sweepstakes—and since the Jaguar was illustrated and discussed, whetted the appetite all of us have for something for nothing. Direct mail reinforced the space ads. The Jaguar was shown at all trade shows in which the company exhibited during that three-month

The Great Gambit Sweepstakes:

See a demonstration of the Fairchild-Davidson offset duplicator. You could win a snazzy new Jaguar. (Plus $25).

It could be yours.

We're convinced the Fairchild-Davidson duplicator will do a better job for you than any other machine. In the full range of duplicating needs. Reproducing business forms, computer printout, price lists...even printing sales literature in colors.

That's why we are continuing our Gambit offer: $25 toward your purchase of a competing offset machine if you see a demonstration of *ours* and then buy *theirs*. And now adding to it a chance to win a Jaguar.

As an added attraction, we'll show you how to cut paper costs 17% to 34% with our new Roll Converter. And a way to imprint bulky catalogs, wafer-thin envelopes and most everything between with our exclusive top-loading feeder.

Just for seeing a demonstration, your Fairchild-Davidson dealer will enter you in the Gambit Sweepstakes. First Prize is a Jaguar X-KE 2+2 (retail list price $6300). Next 100 prizes: 100 games of "Gambit".

How can you lose? Only by not calling your Fairchild-Davidson dealer for a demonstration. Give him a ring today (he's in the Yellow Pages under

FAIRCHILD "Duplicating Machines").

DAVIDSON Wouldn't that Jaguar look great in your driveway?

(Sweepstakes closes midnight December 8, 1966. Winners will be selected and notified by December 15, 1966. Offer void where prohibited by law. All federal, state and local regulations apply.)

Fairchild-Davidson, a Division of Fairchild Camera and Instrument Corporation, 5004 E. Jericho Turnpike, Commack, L. I., N.Y. 11725.

period. To say that this created a stir in the industry is an understatement.

Eligibility for both the sweepstakes, as well as for a $25 check, was established by the prospects seeing a qualified demonstration of the Fairchild-Davidson duplicator in a local showroom.

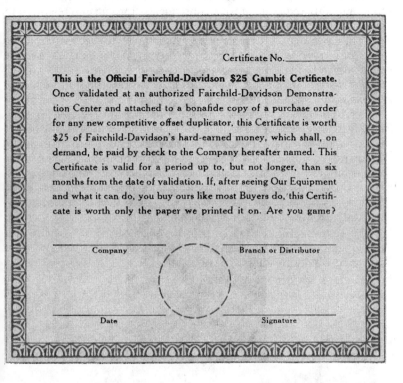

Certificate No._____

This is the Official Fairchild-Davidson $25 Gambit Certificate. Once validated at an authorized Fairchild-Davidson Demonstration Center and attached to a bonafide copy of a purchase order for any new competitive offset duplicator, this Certificate is worth $25 of Fairchild-Davidson's hard-earned money, which shall, on demand, be paid by check to the Company hereafter named. This Certificate is valid for a period up to, but not longer, than six months from the date of validation. If, after seeing Our Equipment and what it can do, you buy ours like most Buyers do, this Certificate is worth only the paper we printed it on. Are you game?

Company _____   Branch or Distributor _____

Date _____   Signature _____

Media used for the space advertising program in a typical month included the following publications: *School Management, Administrative Management, In-Plant Printer, Business Management, Business Automation, Financial Executive, Inland Printer, Modern Office Procedures, The Office, Reproduction Methods, Business Week, Reproductions Review, Dun's Business Month, Graphic Arts Monthly,* and *Printing Impressions.*

Fairchild-Davidson wanted to induce a response from readers of its ads. To succeed in raising sales, the advertising had to produce. So what did the "Gambit" campaign actually accomplish?

Just this, in Fairchild-Davidson's words: "To say that the 'Gambit' campaign has been a rousing success would be putting it mildly. The number of telephone inquiries received from all over the country during the first several weeks of the campaign forced us to print a telephone inquiry form that our various sales department employees could use in obtaining the required information to process these leads.

"We have a number of case histories where signed purchase orders for competitive equipment were subsequently torn up and rewritten to specify Fairchild-Davidson equipment.

"The campaign, to date, has been so completely successful that *we are now 40 percent ahead of the sales forecast for this period—and are so completely backlogged on machine orders that we are quoting 90-day delivery on all equipment. Prior to this campaign we were able to make same-day deliveries.*"

Fairchild-Davidson's files show that the company received approximately a 30 percent increase in inquiries compared to the same period a year ago. This is well and good—but the relationship of inquiries compared to conversions to sales jumped dramatically. This is explained in part by the fact that the company received appreciably better cooperation from the distributor sales organization, as far as follow-up calls on leads were concerned. This is due, of course, to enthusiasm aroused by the entire campaign.

Thought, careful analysis of the sales problem, and creativity produced this copy, this campaign, which achieved exactly what Fairchild-Davidson wanted.

It induced readers to respond—and to buy.

Chapter 9

BODY COPY—STYLE

HARD-and-fast rules almost always lead to inflexible, hidebound thinking that effectively stifles creativity.

Quite possibly those who believe—or profess to believe—that the fewer the rules the better, as far as copy is concerned, are right in their thinking. The fact remains, though, that there are some elements of style with which you must be familiar if you're to turn out consistently good copy.

Some of them are almost painfully obvious, so much so that it's not really necessary to discuss them. Riffling through the business press proves conclusively that some of these elements of style are not known, or they've been forgotten, or they're ignored. One cause is as bad as another, because any of the three can lead to some gruesome ads.

Style, in this chapter, doesn't mean a definite *type* of copy. Rather, the word is used in the newspaper manner, or in the way in which it's used in journalism schools to tell how something should be done. In this case, style means how copy should be written as far as the following 13 points are concerned:

1. Long copy versus short copy.
2. Copy must be in the vernacular.
3. Organize ideas in logical sequence.
4. Stick to the core idea.
5. Use short words.
6. Use short sentences.
7. Use short paragraphs.
8. Be specific.
9. Avoid participles.
10. Avoid superlatives, avoid exaggeration.

11. Refine your copy.
12. Make copy visually attractive.
13. Make the tone suitable.

Let's look at each element individually.

Long Copy Versus Short Copy

The controversy about copy length rages just as fiercely today as it has at any time during the last half-century.

There's simply no meeting of the minds, no unanimity of thought on the subject. Each viewpoint—that copy *must* be just as short as it's possible to make it, or that it's quite permissible for copy to be as long as is necessary—has its staunch adherents. They resolutely refuse to embrace the opposing philosophy.

The hue and cry about copy length has even involved entire agencies to the extent that the law is laid down as to approximate copy length. Some agencies are known as short-copy agencies, others as long-copy shops.

The scale is tipped, however, in favor of those who believe unreservedly in not skimping on words that explain the product and the user benefits—even if the short-copy cult has increased its membership in recent years. There's one sententious slogan that can't be refuted for advertising in general, and especially for industrial advertising: The more you tell, the more you sell. That little gem has been the watchword for many highly successful industrial advertisers for decades.

We've all encountered our share of doubting Thomases with little or no faith in advertising. They maintain that long copy stands little chance of being read. If you'll poke and prod a bit, these same doubters will admit they don't believe, deep down, that *any* advertising copy receives very much readership. Oddly enough, these nervous Nellie doubters are more often than not practitioners of advertising, in one capacity or another. They're frequently introverts. Their attitude toward advertising copy reflects a negative outlook toward almost everything in life. Advertising just happens to be handy, so it's included in the long and dreary list of things they either question or disparage.

Throughout much of the business world, especially in those industries which are less sophisticated than the more fast-moving ones, and particularly those which have a large proportion of engineers in top management, this doubt permeates the upper echelons.

Sometimes the nuts-and-bolts types are almost pathological on the subject. One president of a well-known industrial company, himself an engineer, is known to have remarked that he "hasn't read a magazine or a book in 20 years." He added, "All I read is my mail."

Now, this gentleman didn't adopt this antiquated attitude just to hear himself sound silly. He actually believes that the business press isn't read, consequently advertisements contained in it are not read, either.

This naivete′ was extremely widespread 25 or 30 years ago, but fortunately for industry it has disappeared to some extent as management has become more well rounded, rather than being specialists in one narrow field.

Long Copy Wins in Readership Study

McGraw-Hill has done extensive research on readership of long copy, as opposed to short copy. A thorough analysis of 4,993 ads in four McGraw-Hill publications made by the publisher's Reader Feedback readership service shows that contrary to what the copy length alarmists say, long copy receives *better* readership than short copy in business publication advertisements.

Not readership that's just as good, but *better*.

A total of 263 ads with 350 or more words of copy received a Noted score of 109, while 4,730 ads with less than 350 words of copy received a Noted score of only 100 on an index base.

All of these ads were one page, run-of-publication, bleed and non-bleed, black-and-white or two-color. They appeared in 68 issues of four publications. In some instances ads in categories not pertinent to the analysis were omitted—such as ads with no main copy block. McGraw-Hill held more than 6,800 interviews with readers of *American Machinist, Engineering News-Record, Factory,* and *Textile World* to study readership. The question asked to secure the Reader Feedback score was: "Did you read this advertisement?" (By read, we mean read enough to get the main idea.)

Analysis of 1,125 ads in two publications measured by Starch disclosed that 123 ads of more than 350 words received a Noted score of 103, and a Read Most score of 106. This compares to 1,002 ads with less than 350 words which achieved a Noted and Read Most score exactly the same—100.

Make Each Ad Complete

Play it safe and make each ad complete in itself. You may not get a second chance at some of the readers before they buy.

Industrial advertisements are read for information. The more information you present—if you do it interestingly—the greater your chances are of selling your product. This is not an endorsement of long, dull, dreary copy that's been puffed up with a deadly parade of inconsequentials, however. Instead, it is a strong suggestion to use as many words as are necessary to promote your product. The dividing line's pretty fine, but you'll find it if you try.

Copy in the Vernacular

If copy is to communicate its meaning quickly and clearly and unmistakably, it must be written in the vernacular of the day. There are no two ways about it.

This means copy must be expressed in the idiom of the group to whom you're directing your appeal.

Use of stilted style, literary allusions, or pretentious phrases assures next to no readership.

Flee from pedantry, ostentatiousness, formalism, and didacticism.

Just for a fleeting instant give the impression in copy that you're lecturing—like a learned professor in rimless eyeglasses, upraised finger waving in the breeze as he talks down to a captive audience of more or less interested students—and there'll be a mass migration to the next page.

Be superior, condescending, or patronizing, and again you've alienated your readers. They'll not read this ad, perhaps they'll harbor a subconscious resentment which will cause them to ignore future ads in the campaign—and possibly even in other future campaigns for your company.

Readers are like elephants when it comes to memory. They may not remember specifics, but they remember an attitude they've formed. Completely changing an attitude toward a company and its products can be an expensive undertaking, one that can't be done overnight. Don't risk causing resentment—which poor copy can do.

As long as we're being negative at the moment, here's another don't: Don't be coy or cute or precious. And don't force your style. Be natural in your writing and realize that it's inevitable that the personality of the writer will show through in the copy. Let it. If copy lacks the stamp of the writer's personality, chances are it also lacks flavor and vigor and it will read like an annual report—as dry as dust.

The one best way to learn how the buying influences who can give (or withhold) the nod of approval to your product think, feel, and talk, is to do as the author's good friend, Wim van der Graaf, Du Pont ad man, advocates: *Perform the hat trick.*

The hat trick is easy to learn, for it consists of arising from one's posterior, pushing back that comfortable chair behind the desk, crossing the office and putting on your coat and hat—then getting out where the products are bought and used. While you're out there, cultivate people who can make or break your advertising program by deciding what to buy—or what not to buy—including your product.

Ask Questions and Listen

Establish as close a rapport with these readers of your advertising as you can. Loosen up a little, use the expense account, pop for lunches, and encourage those you're entertaining to talk. You *listen.*

Ask questions about the product you're advertising and about competitive products. Use a list which you drew up before putting on your hat. This will help you avoid those uncomfortable silences while you rack your brain trying to think of another intelligent question. The list of questions, or checklist if you will, organizes your work and thought sequences, and enables you to cover all of the ground you need to.

Frequently your prospect won't mind if you make notes of the conversation. Some people, perfectly articulate and expert in their field, freeze up at sight of note taking or tape recording. If this happens to you, resign yourself to the inevitable and try to remember pertinent points; make careful note of them as soon after leaving the prospect as possible.

Use Colloquialisms Correctly

Learn the colloquialisms common in the industry to which you're selling, then use them in copy.

A word of caution, though: The best way in the world to look just plain silly and fall flat on your face is to misuse the colorful, highly descriptive slang and nicknames found in every industry. Check them out with one of the technical people before your copy gets any further than the yellow-paper stage. Don't ask them to approve content or concept, merely the terminology. In a short time you'll be on sure ground and writing as if you'd spent a lifetime in a field about which you actually know little.

Using the vernacular breathes life and flavor and authenticity into your copy. But be careful not to overdo it. You'll find industry slang and nomenclature a highly effective way to set the stage for a straight product story if you use it right.

Idea Sequence

Disjointed, disorderly copy that rambles and is full of random thoughts in no particular sequence is either the product of a copy cub, or of a poorly organized writer. There are a few of them around.

The competent copywriter, however, is one of the best organized individuals in the business world. He or she has to think through each of his or her ideas, evaluate them as to relative importance, sort them out, and then present them in logical order so that each is reinforced by the one which follows it.

This results in copy which builds on interest already aroused by the illustration and the headline, copy which moves steadily to a proper climax at the end of the ad.

First thing which must be done when writing copy, of course, is to follow through on the promise you made in the headline. Don't let the reader down. To do so is to lose him or her.

For example, if your headline was a command, tell the reader immediately why he or she should do as told to do. If you used a question headline, answer the question at once. If you have a news headline, as in a new-product announcement, don't procrastinate—get right into the story of the new product at once. Never mind all of the puffery about how long the company has been in business, how eager it is for more business, or what have you.

When it's organized properly, a well-written advertisment can, with complete justification, be compared to any number of other logically constructed works—a song, short story, play, or novel, for instance.

The comparison may be drawn because each adheres to the same basic principles. The songsmith, the writer of fiction, and the advertising copywriter must keep within certain prescribed boundaries imposed by the rules of logic.

Music, for example, is so constructed that it has what amounts to a lead-in paragraph of sound. Its ideas are developed so that each capitalizes on those already developed. And, gradually, the theme is completed so that the only logical thing is to proceed into a crescendo to signify completion of the story, much like an ad's closing sales points and bid for action. Consider Ravel's *Bolero*—or Woody Herman's *Apple Honey*. Play one or both and listen to the headline-introduction, copy-melody, and the bid for action-crescendo. You'll see the analogy is a legitimate one.

Orderly arrangement is an integral part of the scheme of things. It is accepted without question. Deeply ingrained in all of us is the subconscious expectation that everything we listen to, everything we read—including advertisements—will be orderly and rational and logical with a distinct, readily apparent beginning, middle, and end.

Build on Basic Premise

It's neither good advertising writing, nor good writing of any kind to put what obviously is a concluding thought or argument at the beginning of an ad. The correct way is first to establish a basi premise, then build on it. Trot out product advantages, marshal features and user benefits—particularly benefits—one after the other. Reach a peak with such irrefutable logic that the bid for action *belongs* there, so that without it the reader would sense an incompleteness.

Just as undesirable as peaking without a bid for action is to put the bid at the start of the ad. It's out of place, illogical. It doesn't belong there because there has been no build-up, no valid reasons have been advanced to justify asking the reader to do as you want him or her to.

Use Copy Platform as Guide

Your copy platform is the guideline as to what ideas you'll want to discuss, of course. Keep it handy. Refer to it, then simply list the ideas—topics, that is—you want to discuss in any given ad. No need to write a lengthy outline, just a one- or two-word heading for each idea is sufficient. Arrange them in numerical sequence, or a-b-c-d.

When an ad is organized in this manner *before it's written*, there's little likelihood that the copy will wander off on a tangent or have the ideas in illogical sequence.

Note in The Torrington Company's striking ad the simple, orderly presentation of ideas which build upon interest aroused by the dramatic close-up photo. Copy reads:

> Are you still
> making small
> precision
> parts (like these)
> yourself?

Pity. It's really a shame. Especially when you consider that Torrington can supply you with shafts, spindles, pivots, dowels, and taper pins—virtually any cylindrical part you need. In any shape or hardness, with diameters ranging from .375" down to .010". And tolerances tailored to your needs, too—even as close as $\pm$ .00015"!

We will make these for you in multithousands or multimillion lots. And we'll do it faster, cheaper, and easier than you can do it yourself. You see, we have all the facilities for the production of these parts—the tooling, the grinding, the hardening, the micropolishing—all under one roof. Each operation is automated and quality carefully checked. As a result, we can give you a superior product at a surprising low price.

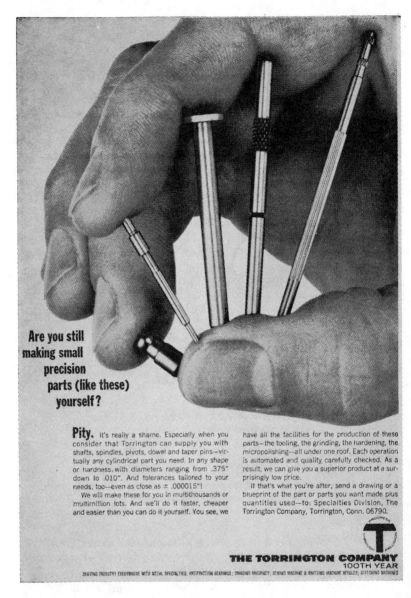

Are you still making small precision parts (like these) yourself?

Pity. It's really a shame. Especially when you consider that Torrington can supply you with shafts, spindles, pivots, dowel and taper pins—virtually any cylindrical part you need. In any shape or hardness, with diameters ranging from .375" down to .010". And tolerances tailored to your needs, too—even as close as ± .000015"!

We will make these for you in multithousands or multimillion lots. And we'll do it faster, cheaper and easier than you can do it yourself. You see, we have all the facilities for the production of these parts—the tooling, the grinding, the hardening, the micropolishing—all under one roof. Each operation is automated and quality carefully checked. As a result, we can give you a superior product at a surprisingly low price.

If that's what you're after, send a drawing or a blueprint of the part or parts you want made plus quantities used—to: Specialties Division, The Torrington Company, Torrington, Conn. 06790.

THE TORRINGTON COMPANY
100TH YEAR

SERVING INDUSTRY EVERYWHERE WITH METAL SPECIALTIES; ANTIFRICTION BEARINGS; SWAGING MACHINES; SEWING MACHINE & KNITTING MACHINE NEEDLES; STITCHING MACHINES

Torrington told them they shouldn't dilute their efforts doing the job of a specialist, told how good Torrington parts are, why they're good, why they're priced right—and ended up with a bid for action that resulted in action. The ad is persuasive, convincing, and logical. Hard combination to beat.

If that's what you're after, send a drawing or a blue-print of the part or parts you want made plus quantities used—to: (address)

Stick to the Core Idea

Only one core idea, call it a central theme or a basic premise if you like, can be communicated effectively by a single piece of advertising copy.

One, just one.

Naturally enough, this means that you have a decision to make before writing copy for an ad. Crystal-clear in your own mind must be the core idea, which is the most important thing about the product— or your selling proposition—you want to implant in the minds of those who read your ad.

A single piece of advertising copy can't be all things to all men, nor can it even come within shouting distance of attaining the nonattainable. This includes your audience, readers of the publications in which your ad will appear, as well as product managers, market managers, the sales manager and others within your company—including top management.

The importance of clinging to the core idea in an industrial advertisement isn't generally appreciated—or understood—in industry. More often than not, the pressure to touch all bases, to cover every conceivable sales point, to list features galore and include everything in the ad from trivia to a lengthy dissertation on *A History of How This Widget Is Engineered, And Why*, comes from within the ad manager's company.

If you cave in and accede to the blandishments of the nonadvertising professionals who seemingly *always* want to emasculate copy by rewriting it in engineerese to make it "more general" or "more universally applicable," you can be absolutely certain of accomplishing one thing: You'll end up with a vague bunch of generalities, couched in cliche's, and a diluted selling proposition which has neither impact nor interest.

Avoid destruction of good copy. Avoid failure to reap the benefits good copy can produce for your product in the marketplace *by selling sound copy.*

Explain it. Believe in and rely upon repetition, just as you do in advertising, to gain acceptance of what is to many a unique new concept—that an advertisement can communicate just one core idea. Go over this again and again and again, each time you present copy to be checked for technical accuracy, for review, or for approval.

Without launching into a lengthy harangue or an intricate explanation of advertising theory, tell your people how the copy adheres to sound advertising practice. Briefly explain what it is and the reason for it. Then stand up on your hind legs and defend your copy, refuse to let it be chopped to pieces.

Use Short Words

When you're writing copy, resist the temptation to be a sesquipedalian. Sesquipedals invariably distract many readers and frequently alienate a large number of others.

A sesquipedalian, of course, is a hapless individual with an unconquerable penchant for using long words, and a sesquipedal is one of the tongue-twisters with which the person is enamored.

Oddly enough, many industrial copywriters exhibit the same weakness which makes much business writing an impenetrable morass. They write, but they don't communicate.

For some obscure reason, a feeling of insufficiency, perhaps, they feel compelled to prove their erudition by organizing an awesome parade of formidable words and trotting them all out for all to see. They give the impression that *they're* under the impression that use of multisyllable words will overwhelm the reader and persuade him or her to accept what the writer says as gospel truth, or else they will browbeat him or her into believing.

But there's not a chance.

We in industrial advertising like to fancy ourselves professional communicators. As such, we must realize that the average person to whom we're writing is more intelligent, better educated, and better equipped to understand what we're writing than is the average American.

That's because we're directing our message to technical and management people in industry who have the advantage of more education and a broader experience than the factory worker or cab driver.

The fact remains, though, that these people, for the most part, are relatively unskilled with words. Technical people—chemists, engineers, research scientists, metallurgists, and so on—are simply not involved with words to the extent that the advertising person is. They think, talk, and write in a jargon peculiar to their specialty in order to communicate with their colleagues and business associates.

Maybe they *do* communicate. But the tortured thought processes which result in the semi-incomprehensible technical papers presented in an endless succession of annual meetings of various technical societies is indeed weird and wondrous.

The intellectual fare of the technical people is composed of gobbledygook disguised to look like writing, done, for the most part, by their counterparts in other companies. It is published in the technical journals they dote on. These journals usually are dull in both content and format, have very few illustrations, and a dreadful gray sameness in page after page of solid type. They thrive because they publish these pseudointellectual exercises in obscuring the meaning of what the technical person turned "writer" is trying to say. And this takes a bit of doing, but this material is presented with an impeccable editorial deadpan expression. Another reason these publications thrive is because advertising managers and agencies cannot read them to evaluate them, so assume that just because *they* can translate the gibberish only with extreme difficulty that the technical people *can*—hence their advertising belongs where it will be read by the technical types they want to talk to.

One thing too many ad persons overlook is that even technical people are people. And this is still an English-speaking country. Well-written English communicates even to the far-out eggheads who consider a sliderule thrilling reading.

Short words put your message across better, even if you're not writing to the technical person. Top management in industry is different, some ad people think, from the technical persons who report to them. But look around you in your own company. Chances are if your firm manufactures a highly engineered product, or one that is made for a specialty market, you'll find the same type of people in all of the paneled offices right up to the corner one with four windows. Executives who head industrial companies are usually ex-technical persons themselves, or ex-accountants who graduated to controller, then moved up the ladder to the top spot.

The nontechnical persons have a broader outlook and more diversified experience, of course, but the fact remains that they're little, if any, more word-oriented than they were when they started in business. The trend in industry is for top management to be composed of generalists, so there's hope that advertising can contribute more each year.

When you keep the words short you're helping your advertising copy do its job.

Ways to Measure Reading Ease

Research has proved that ads relatively easy to read receive higher readership than those which are more difficult. In its Laboratory of Advertising Performance, McGraw-Hill reports that the 100 one-page ads with the highest readership ratings—and the 100 with the lowest —were selected from among all similar advertisements in 10 issues of

Factory magazine. Readership ratings were those determined by McGraw-Hill's Reader Feedback Service.

These ads were analyzed to determine if ease of reading of the main copy block differed significantly in the high-scoring group, compared to the low-scoring group. The reading ease formula developed by Dr. Rudolph Flesch, which appears in his book, *The Art of Readable Writing*, was applied to the main copy block in each ad in the 100-ad sample of high and low scoring ads. The result was as expected: The higher the reading ease score of an advertisement, the easier it is to read.

The 100 best read ads averaged a numerical score of 48 on a scale which ranges from zero (very difficult), to 100 (very easy). The 48 score of the best read ads was about halfway between the two extremes, in the area about midway between "fairly difficult" and "fairly easy."

The 100 ads which had the poorest readership averaged a score of 39, which is "fairly difficult."

Dr. Flesch's formula is based on the average length of sentences and the number of syllables per 100 words.

Only 8 percent of the high rated ads fell toward the difficult end of the scale (21 to 30 in score), while 22 percent of the poorly read ads were in that group. Toward the easier-to-read end of the scale (61 to 70 score) 12 percent of the high rated ads appeared, while only 1 percent of the poorly read ads were found there.

Except for ease of reading, the two groups of ads were comparable. The ads didn't differ significantly in the number of words in the main copy blocks, so copy length definitely wasn't a factor which influenced readership ratings.

Interestingly, the principal editorial material in a typical issue of *Factory* was checked for reading ease, using the same formula. Thirteen articles averaged a Flesch Reading Ease Score of 51, quite close to the 48 averaged by the best read ads.

Any number of formulas have been devised to classify advertising copy (and other written matter) as to form, content, and the ease with which it may be understood. If you'll familiarize yourself with one or two of these formulas, then use them to analyze and evaluate your copy, you'll find it will help you produce copy that conveys its meaning quicker and with less chance of its not being understood—or not being read.

Formal structure of written material is analyzed, in a broad sense, by the frequency with which frequently used, readily understood words appear. Of all words in the English language, only a tiny fraction are used in daily conversation and in writing which communicates instantaneously, as an advertisement must.

Gunning Fog Index Good

Similar to Flesch's Reading Ease Score is the Gunning Fog Index. This evaluation procedure is based upon sentence length and the ratio of words of three or more syllables to shorter words. Actually, a percentage is used in calculating the Fog Index, or the fog level as it's commonly called in advertising. In addition to providing a guideline for the advertising manager, Gunning indicates the number of years of formal education required to comprehend typical writing, with scores based on his percentage figures.

Using typical examples, you can easily determine the complexity of writing which will be readily comprehended by the buying influences to whom your copy is directed. Gunning recommends that you don't write over the heads of those with 12 years of education. You may prefer Gunning's method because it is somewhat easier to apply than Flesch's. The Gunning method is explained in *How to Take the Fog Out of Writing* (Dartnell).

Flesch also devised a terribly complicated formula for determining the amount of human interest in any particular piece of copy. This is so involved that it is almost useless for the advertising manager who wants to do just one thing: Tell, as closely as possible, whether the ad's content contains sufficient meat that it will appeal to most readers.

A better way, and one that's much easier to apply, to analyze the content of copy is Bernard Berelson's Content Analysis method. It is particularly appropriate for use with advertising copy.

Content Analysis involves determining the frequency with which certain elements—words, sentences, symbols, for example—occur, then computing their dependence upon each other. In this way, according to Berelson, you can make an objective breakdown of the copy and arrive at an accurate evaluation of its probable effectiveness. Many advertising agencies habitually use the Content Analysis method of evaluating copy to find out if it measures up.

When it comes to determining how easy it is to comprehend the entire piece of copy, two methods are most widely used. Most common is the recall and feedback technique, in which readers are interviewed and asked if they remember having noticed or read advertisements in the issue of the publication being studied.

The "Nonword" Phenomenon

Speaking of using short words, one pitfall into which many of us fall almost as a matter of routine is that of using nonwords. The non-word isn't a figment of anybody's disordered imagination. It occurs with dismaying frequency in industrial advertising (which may have fathered it).

Nonwords are the brainchildren of frustrated technical people, for the most part, people who feel a faint stirring somewhere deep within themselves to prove that they're creative. This unfamiliar urge is welcomed with broad smiles as they gleefully tack fancy names, usually nonwords composed of segments of two or three honest-to-gosh words, glued together so they delight the eye and ear of their originators—and are utterly incomprehensible to readers, and even to those perfectly familiar with the product.

There's no intent to arouse the populace to take up arms and march in righteous indignation against those who want to assign a perfectly acceptable name to a product. After all, there's precedent aplenty for naming products—all the way from the ubiquitous Parker Jotter to the Rolls Royce Silver Cloud you ride in if you're doing a little bit better than the average ad professional.

Well-chosen names are catchy, memorable, easily written, and easily understood. They actually say something positive to the prospect. And they make promoting a product easier for the ad man and make choosing it easier for the buyer.

What you don't want to do, however, is make the mistake made by so many companies—letting the engineers assign a coined, nonword name to the product or some feature of it. This frequently happens when the product is being designed or engineered—and the name sticks to it all the way from the drawing board, through the tool room, during prototype production, and on up into the upstairs offices where marketing planning goes on.

By that time the nonword name which doesn't say anything to anybody adheres to the new product with leech-like tenacity. It's an oversized albatross around the ad manager's neck. Usually it's deliberately misspelled, cutely so, if an actual word is used.

Short Words

Short words are powerful words, and some of the most potent ones you can use—should use—whenever the opportunity arises are these:

Free	*Cut*	*Facts*	*Here*
New	*Compare*	*End*	*Find*
How to	*You*	*Stop*	*Now*
Easy	*Your*	*Put*	*Try*
Fast	*Learn*	*Wanted*	*Check*
Quick	*Earn*	*Improved*	*Gain*
Offer	*Plug*	*Get*	*Profit*

Power words aren't all one syllable, but they're commonplace, easily understood words that never slow down reading. Greatest grabbers of attention for headlines are the first two—*free* and *new*. Both give a promise in one short word—something for nothing, to which none of us is the least bit averse, and the implication that the something new is actually something better, something that will help the reader. The others are promise-words, action-words, motivating-words that produce a response. Use them well and wisely and they'll produce for you.

Short Sentences

The average person in industry is addicted to using long sentences.

We've already touched briefly on the fact that long sentences make copy difficult to read, just as long words do. As a rule, when you encounter one you'll find the other, because both are cherished by the same type of writer.

A good rule is that a sentence should never be longer than 15 words. Sentences of 15 words or less enable a writer to say exactly what he or she means. Succinct writing helps the reader. It is simpler and easier to read, so it is read.

Adhering slavishly to the 15-word rule isn't a panacea. It's not a secret formula for success. In fact, it's a pitfall. Follow it religiously, make every sentence 14, 15, or 16 words long, and you'll have copy so unbelievably monotonous there's an odds-on chance it'll put you to sleep while you're writing it. People in droves will skip it, even if they won't stop to reason why.

Just for the fun of it, write a short piece of copy on any subject or product that pops into your mind, even a hobby or favorite sport. Write about 10 or 12 sentences and deliberately make them all approximately the same length, about 15 words. This may require a bit of doing. But when you're finished, read what you've written and see how stilted it sounds and how incredibly dull it is. You'll notice immediatly that it's completely lacking in the spark that would make a total stranger want to read past the first three or four sentences.

There's no question that short sentences are desirable in advertising copy. To overcome the monotony of sameness, vary the length. One short, one long—but not alternated so often that you create *another* pattern which repels the mind and eye.

Also, it's desirable to alter the basic structure of your sentences. You'll find, for example, it's best to have a number of simple sentences one after the other. Then break the pattern by inserting a complex sentence and follow it with several simple ones. A compound-complex sentence relieves tedium, and, if followed with an extremely short sentence is visually attractive. An extremely short sentence is visually attrative. It telegraphs a single thought. It punctuates. It creates a bridge. The short sentence channels thoughts straight into the next sequence of ideas, and emphasizes the most important. Use it.

Almost all of the ads illustrated and quoted as good examples of how copy should read use short words, short sentences. And they have varied sentence length and structure to avoid a humdrum sameness.

In a way, copy is much like music. Copy should have a definite beat, a rhythm that you can almost feel. Many people are under the impression that only poetry has rhythm. This isn't so.

On the contrary, good copy should have a beat, a bounce, a cadence that can be felt. One way to write copy that moves rhythmically is to tap it out on your desk with a pencil, just as if you were a drummer in a jazz band.

Short Paragraphs

Sparkling copy with everything going for it can be killed deader than the Edsel by improper paragraphing.

Paragraphing doesn't even have to be improper in a sense that's ungrammatical, or that the breaks come at just the wrong times in the sequence of thoughts. Merely having the paragraphs too long can ruin an ad. Readership goes down fast as paragraph length goes up.

Overly long paragraphs are as grim and forbidding as a Mexican jail. They never fail to give the impression that their contents will require vast effort and grim, single-minded concentration by the reader to wade through and assimilate the information they contain. As the art directors and typographers are fond of saying, long paragraphs look "soggy."

By this they mean there's so much type with so little "air"—or open white space left by the paragraph breaks—that the type seems to be set solid. Type set solid represents hard work. It's reminiscent of a textbook on a dull subject, or of some impossibly tedious memorandum from the engineers about product features.

You can avoid having ads that cause readers to beat a hasty retreat to the sanctuary of more easily read ads by writing short paragraphs.

Short paragraphs open up a copy block.

They make it inviting.

When judiciously mixed, short and long, the copy looks as if it would be fun to read.

And read it is, read by almost 17 percent more readers than is soggy, visually unattractive copy. Numerous studies over the years have left no doubt on this score.

Be Specific

Generalities in copy are like dead mackerel in the moonlight. They glitter, but they also smell.

Vague, half-thought-out ideas and a school of nonspecifics waft toward the reader an unprepossessing aroma of something he or she instinctively realizes he or she will want to avoid because there's nothing in it for him or her.

A number of times we've touched briefly on the importance of being specific. This can't be stressed too hard. Nonspecifics say nothing of any interest to anybody except the advertiser. And there are many ways a person can talk to oneself without paying for the privilege.

Avoid Participles

Participial writing is weak writing.

A participle, according to Webster, is a word that partakes of the nature of both a verb and an adjective. An English verb has two participles—(1) the present, in which words end in *ing*, as in writing, talking, analyzing, and evaluating, and, (2) the past, or perfect, variation of the word; usually this version ends in *ed, d, t, en,* or *n,* as in posted, worked, proved, kept, written, proven, taken.

One major indictment which can be laid at the door of the participle is that when participles are used, verbs are not. Without verbs, writing is wishy-washy, weak, drab, and passive.

Verbs are action words. They are inherently strong and masculine. They connote doing something, taking a course of action, making decisions, moving, giving the heave-ho to the status quo. Verbs strengthen copy. They impart a sense of immediacy, heighten interest, arouse curiosity to see what is going to *happen* next. Verbs impel people to react to your copy—to do what you want them to.

Let's look at a few participles and participle-filled ads and see why the copy is weak and without vigor or bite.

In *Foundry* magazine The Fremont Flask Company starts an ad:

> *Foundrymen are discovering that this newly developed Guide is reducing scrap from shifts as much as 40% on perennial difficult jobs.*

Style is mass-appeal, impersonal, short on reader involvement; there's no *you* in the first sentence of the copy, only the all-inclusive foundrymen. Also, "are discovering" and "is reducing" is weak writing. How much more impact the copy would have had if it had started:

> *You'll find this new Guide is a money-maker. It reduces scrap from shifts up to 40%—even on the tough jobs.*

Or we go a step farther and improve it still more. Compare this version with the pallid original:

> *You can reduce scrap from shifts up to 40% with this new Guide.*

Verbosity is out. Instead of 21 words, there are 13. And the opening sentence says the same thing, but says what the advertiser *wanted* to say, not to be confused with what he *thought* he'd said.

Furthermore, the copy is punchier, more direct, and more easily understood. That's because those participles aren't there to becloud the issue in a haze of foggy prose that doesn't say anything.

With the opening set right, all that remains to be done is to explain why this new Guide reduces scrap. That done, the copy will be believed and the ad will score points with readers.

The Cult of the Superlative

Face it: Everything your company manufactures is *not* unequalled, revolutionary, unexcelled, unique, the world's best, finest yet, the most outstanding, sensational, fantastic, unbelievable, amazing, or the absolute living end.

It's very possible the product you're talking about in your copy simply doesn't qualify for even one of these overworked superlatives. But even if it honestly does—in your opinion—can you convince readers of this? If not, you've lost ground by making a claim that, to the reader, is sheer puffery.

For far too many years now we've all been assaulted by a barrage of superlatives and exaggerated claims for everything from typewriter ribbons to putty knives. Far too few claims were ever proven to satisfaction of the objective reader—and he or she is the person who *wants* to be sold.

If the claim concerns something outside the personal experience of the reader, if it's made about a product with which he or she is unfamiliar, if it's blatantly obvious that the claim is made to benefit the advertiser, or if the copywriter simply threw in superlatives to "strengthen" the ad, it's a lost cause you have on your hands. Reconcile yourself to it.

As the late, great jazz trombonist Jack Teagarden sang in one of his classic recordings back in the '30's " . . . don't start lying, I never cared for fiction . . . speak real clear, don't want no friction with your diction."

No reputable company would dream of deliberately misrepresenting its product in an advertisement or in sales literature. However, excessive use of superlatives and/or gross exaggeration certainly *looks* like unmitigated prevarication to the reader, so the result is about the same. Tax his or her credulity and you've probably lost him or her as a potential customer. The business world is made up of well-informed, well-read individuals who have a vast experience with almost every product on the market, even with those very similar to the revolutionary, supersensational, all-new Widget of Tomorrow that's being introduced today just to give the lucky customer a break. The business-press readers can't be snowed. This is not 1890.

Incidentally, when using an absolute term or a very specific item of information in an ad, you must be certain that it is correct. Many an industrial advertising manager has found to his or her regret that use of such terminology opens a Pandora's box of messy ills in the form of possible legal action by a dissatisfied purchaser of the product. This character can be depended upon to triumphantly produce the very ad that *promised* in print exactly what he or she feels he or she didn't get.

Be particularly careful about use of words like these:

Never	*Certain*
Foolproof	*Positive*
Fail-safe	*Always*
Can't fail	*Invariably*
Impossible ·	*Will*

Refer to the instruction manual, descriptive plates giving rated capacities, engineering drawings, and other reference sources that are beyond question for your information. Even then, check it out with the technical people for accuracy.

Even a tiny connotation of something undesirable can set the legal eagles loose to pounce upon an innocent, unsuspecting advertising manager, even though he or she is pure in heart as all ad managers are.

Refine, Hone, Polish Your Copy

All of the really competent copywriters—whether agency men or members of an industrial advertising department—have one thing in common: They are unabashed users of very large wastebaskets. And at the end of a typical day's writing, these wastebaskets are filled to overflowing, so there's a small mountain of crumpled yellow paper in the corner of the office behind the typewriter stand.

This is because the human mind, though a magnificent mechanism, is far from perfect. Thought processes leave much to be desired, as do powers of concentration. The copywriter doesn't live who hasn't found—on far more occasions than most like to admit—that the mind wanders and little things can distract so he or she is unable to concentrate on the task at hand. Rough copy, which is the copy in its raw state before being worked over, reflects this human failing.

It rambles. It's verbose. The message isn't compressed into the tightest, most concise statements the writer can put down on paper. Organization of the copy leaves much to be desired. Sequence of thoughts isn't the most logical, nor does the copy progress smoothly with well ordered precision from one point to the next, building and heightening interest as the time for the bid for action approaches. And frequently the fog level's high, words are impossibly long, paragraphs are only a whisker shorter than these in *War and Peace,* and gobbledygook that doesn't really say anything to anybody has crept in.

Few writers are able to concentrate enough to "write on the white." Writing on the white is merely writing carefully polished, finished copy on paper that'll be used to submit the copy to the powers that be for comment and approval. The mind refuses to discipline itself enough to make this possible.

Writing "On the White"

After almost two decades in the advertising business, and after working with scores of copywriters, some very gifted indeed, the author knows only *one* who can write on the white consistently. Dick Perry, copywriter, playwright, scriptwriter, novelist, author of numerous arrticles and short stories written for the mass media, with whom the author worked some years ago in a Chicago agency that's now a thing of the past, enjoyed this rare gift. Perry was a prolific producer. He pondered, paced, and planned, then pecked at incredible speed with two fingers. His copy required virtually no rewriting, no deletions, and no revisions.

And J. Woolsey Stanton, marketing genius in package products as well as items sold to sportsmen, and sometime author of tales for the fish-catching and coon-chasing books, is also blessed with being able to write and not rewrite. Stanton, one-time publisher's representative, claims to be able to think a piece of copy throught from start to finish and then type it off—not write it—as conceived with every word, every thought in apple-pie order. The author has seen much of his writing, and it's fresh and sprightly and inventive.

However, we ordinary mortals usually find it necessary to doodle out a plan for each piece of copy. Naturally, this involves determining the core idea that is to be conveyed to the reader, then casting about with the aid of various and varied incantations, rituals, and sorcery just this side of voodooism for the *one* best way to express it to the individual who influences the purchase of the product. Again, note that it's individual, *not* individuals. Remember, too, you're not selling the product or its features, you're selling what it can do for the buyer and his company. You're trying to bring prospect and product together so that a purchase results.

Next step, then, is to write a rough draft following the outline you've prepared and including all of the information you've determined is advisable to put in the copy. It follows, of course, you're bearing in mind the concept of the entire ad—illustration, headline, copy, and rough layout as well as the media in which the ad will appear.

Incidentally, it is the copywriter's responsibility to specify the illustration; he alone is able to determine what it should be because he is the individual who's creating the ad, who's responsible for its success or failure.

Welcome Good Ideas

Often, however, the art director, account executive, or some other person involved in your advertising program will contribute a worthwhile suggestion that will improve upon the original idea. After all, rewriting and expanding upon what's already been done comes considerably easier than does creation of an entire ad right from scratch.

Good copy being as difficult to get on paper as most of us find it is, and idea is welcome from any source. Nobody has a corner on them. The one criterion for assessing ideas is that they must be good. Creativity by committee seldom results in copy with vitality and bite, though, so don't learn on a crutch. Copywriting is a lonely job and it's hard work. It's accomplished without benefit of communal fun and games. When all's said and done, copy is the distillation and refinement of ideas of one person charged with writing it.

In the rough draft try to be as fresh and original as possible in wording and phrasing your thoughts about why the prospect will want the product. Never for an instant lose sight of the fact that you have no inalienable right to bore the reader. He or she won't stand for it.

On the other hand, you have a moral obligation to your company *and* to the reader to feed information in a form that's palatable and acceptable. This doesn't mean your copy must entertain. If you set out to entertain, all's lost. Copy that only entertains may produce a pleased little smile here and there, but it certainly won't produce a lasting impression about—or desire for—the product.

There are many mechanical techniques for copywriting. An Ivory-soap-like percentage—roughly 99 44/100—of all advertising persons who put words on paper do so with a typewriter. This includes presidents of major agencies, creative directors, and directors of advertising who administer multimillion dollar budgets. Those who don't type handicap themselves needlessly.

Touch-Typing Gives Advantage

The writer who types, preferably touch-types (it can be learned at any age, in business school in just one or two nights a week for a few months) has a distinct edge on those who don't. He or she is equipped to retain those fast-flowing thoughts which race through the creative head, to get them on paper fast. Ideas and figures of speech are transitory things at best, and many with charm and vigor and impact are lost irrevocably because they weren't captured and put on paper before they got away in the unexplored recesses of the mind.

Learn to type. Your copy will improve measurably in both quantity and quality. And you don't have to be writing all of your company's space advertisements to benefit from typing. The average industrial advertising manager communicates on paper constantly—internally with product managers and marketing people, externally with a dealer or distributor organization and field sales force. Almost everything that leaves the advertising department is in written form and the better the writing the more effective a job is being done.

Naturally, you won't want to type your own letters. They're better dictated if only for the sake of time saved. Usually they're fairly routine, but occasionally a very important letter comes along that you'll want to rough out on the typewriter, then polish with a pen before giving it to your secretary for finish typing. You'll find this letter far more precise in wording and feeling than if you'd dictated it.

Too, when you type you'll find your work easier. The sheer physical job of writing by hand with a quill pen, or even something as relatively up to date as the centuries-old pencil, is laborious. Tediously putting down one word after another, instead of capturing entire phases, analogies, thoughts, concepts smoothly and quickly with a typewriter, stifles creative thinking. An advertising manager who relies on a pencil becomes little more than a clerk. It is almost enough to preclude producing sparkling copy for all but a few highly individualistic, unorthodox copywriters who make a fetish of belonging to the feet-on-the-desk, Turkish-water-pipe, aren't-I-brilliant-because-I-don't-cut-my-hair schools of what is, to them, apparently an art form for the ultrasophisticated urbanite.

A scant few copywriters think clearly enough to dictate, almost invariably to a dictating machine to avoid the distraction of having another person watch them struggle for expression. Their secretaries then type a rough draft for them, triple-spaced to allow room for blue-pencilling and revising. This procedure wastes time, however, for it ties up two people to do the work of one, and can be depended upon to complicate the task and cool the flow of ideas as time is wasted waiting for transcriptions.

Revision and editing of the rough draft is the next step. Shortening, tightening, and honing is the primary task; the advertising copy must be shortened in almost every instance to reduce it to the bare essentials. Excess verbiage wastes critically important space, wastes the advertiser's money on inconsequentials, and wastes the reader's time—if he or she will give it to you under such circumstances. All of these wastes have to be avoided, the last one most of all. Readers will not fritter away time on witless wanderings in copy. To retain their interest, copy has to be concise.

Weigh Each Word

As discussed, copy length *per se* is seldom of critical importance. Both short and lengthy copy can be equally effective if properly written. What is essential, however, is that every single word of copy carries its weight, that it have a legitimate reason for being. There never is room for extraneous words for which there exists no real need.

A classic example of exquisitely honed copy is Lincoln's Gettysburg Address. In just 272 emotion-filled words of quiet dignity and lasting beauty, Lincoln expressed the hopes and aspirations of a bitterly divided nation in its hour of agony. Perhaps never again will so few words make so indelible an impression.

Each sentence should be studied, each word weighed to consider just how much it contributes to the total effect of the copy. Consider synonyms, keeping in mind there's a delicate and subtle nuance of thought between most of them. Choose the one that's precisely right to reflect the exact thought you want to convey. For example, the Grand Tetons are not beautiful—they're majestic. The Black Canyon of the Gunnison isn't striking—it's magnificent, awe-inspiring, breathtaking. A product may not be strong or husky or large, but it may well be massive. Choose words with great care.

Experiment to see if one carefully considered word can't be made to do the work of several; if so, there's no doubt it will be vastly more effective. One word communicates more clearly and puts across the meaning much faster. Be sure to use power words.

Often you'll find that one rewritten sentence can replace two or; one paragraph, after tightening and revising, can replace two or even three. Experienced copywriters have said for years that it's almost always a good idea to discard the first paragraph of copy because, unless the writer is unusually adept, it usually consists of generalities or at best an introduction to what the writer really wants to say. Space is too expensive for such luxuries.

Once copy is shortened and tightened as much as possible, sit back and read it. Read it slowly and carefully for both context and for tone. Check all facts and figures. Make sure you're right. Good copy is spare and lean with no superfluous words, but it *doesn't* read as if the copywriter had strict instructions not to use a single unessential word, much as though he was personally paying for a transoceanic cablegram at a horrendous word rate. If it's too terse, too telegraphic, the flavor isn't right and the reader is repelled because he or she gets the impression somebody's forcing something on him or her.

Copy that tight is too tight. But relieving the feeling of being hammered at by an overwhelming procession of facts aimed menacingly at the reader is accomplished merely by reintroducing some of the words which personalize copy—*you* and *yours,* for example, and by adding a few transitional words in carefully chosen places. We'll look at some examples shortly.

Copy must relate to the reader's interests—and, as we've discussed, this boils down to a simple matter of economics in most cases. If the copy proves it will be to the reader's advantage to buy the product, probably because it has been economically justified, you have a reader who's pretty well persuaded that your product is for him. You must be thoroughly familiar with prospects' interests, needs, and problems, of course, in order to produce copy which relates to them and which will convince them.

Check, too, for interest. Be as detached and dispassionate as possible. Read the copy to make absolutely sure that it looks at the product from the reader's point of view. Make certain the reader's interest is first and foremost—not the advertiser's. Above all, though, try to make it friendly and inviting and rewarding to read. Interpret product benefits so the reader finds it easy to identify with them and *desire* them.

Although tightening copy by shortening it has been stressed, *never* cut copy fo fit a layout. Layouts are made after copy is written—copy written to an arbitrary length merely to fit into a preselected space stultifies itself almost without exception.

Let's look at two excellent ads written for the farm industry. They show how copy can be short and tight, but still appeal to the reader's interest. The ads appeared in *Successful Farming* magazine.

The end to your manure handling problem

2 COMPLETE CLAY LIQUID MANURE SYSTEMS

*One man hauls 2-months' manure from
400 hogs, or 1-month's manure from 80
cows in less than one day! Conserves
fertilizer value of manure; reduces fly
problem; haul once a month or as weather
and your schedule permit.*

*"Honey Wagon" has pump in tank which pro-
vides vacuum to load from pit; pressure to
spread load in field in 7 minutes or less.*

*Auger Agitator chops up big solids and straw
in pits; homogenizes liquids and solids for
fast, easy spreading.*

*Trailer-Mounted Chopper-Agitator-Pump loads
top-loading "Slurry Surrey," chops up straw
and solids in pit.*

*NEW CATALOG—FREE PIT PLANS FOR HOG,
BEEF, DAIRY SET-UPS*

(coupon)

That's a hard-working one-third-page ad. There's not a single wasted word in the copy, not an excess thought. User benefits come through with no danger of being misinterpreted—and the bid for action makes an offer to induce reader response, as it should. Clay Equipment Company without doubt receives a gratifying volume of inquiries from this fractional-page ad.

Ralston Purina Company's powerful four-color spread ad, shown on the next page, also ran in *Successful Farming*. The dramatic close-up of the well-groomed, healthy-looking young pig busily engaged in his or her favorite pastime—which involves the advertiser's product, happily enough—is appealing to farmers and nonfarmers alike.

On the face of it, this seems like an odd statement. However, the author is assured by James Wettersten, General Electric market research executive to whom he is indebted for a number of thoughts on this marketing service, that there is an unorganized but very active group of pig buffs in the country. Frequently they band together to pursue their hobby of pig-watching, just as binocular-equipped bird-watchers traipse through the countryside in the spring of the year indulging their interest. In the spring, pig buffs can be seen leaning on fences intently watching young pigs eat; so there's every reason to assume the photo would appeal to them, as well as to farmers in general. Many pig buffs get pass-along copies of farm books. They'll read Purina's ad, and although they don't buy pig chow, many are dog owners—and Purina also makes a very fine dog chow. This is a minor residual benefit from the ad for Purina, of course, but not one to be written off as of no value.

Purina takes full advantage of the power words with the most impact to get every bit of benefit from the ad. The most powerful word that can be used, "free," appears only slightly smaller than a barn, spread as it is entirely across the page containing the copy. Note, too, the positive, image-evoking power words skillfully sprinkled through

the copy: *offer, present you with, at no extra cost, take advantage, learn, pays off,* and, again, *free.*

Probably not one reader who read this issue of *Successful Farming* thoroughly failed to notice this ad if he opened these two pages; if he riffled through the book and didn't separate them, naturally he missed the ad. Body copy is well written and enjoyed good readership. It reads:

Start your next litter

FREE

Special March offer at your Purina dealer's

From March 6th through March 18th only your Purina dealer can present you with your choice of a 50-pound bag of Purina Baby Pig Chow or Purina Early Weaning Chow Free, with your order of ONE TON of any Purina Hog Chow products for delivery within that period. If you order two tons you get two 50-lb. bags of Purina pig starter at no extra cost, and so on.

Take advantage of Purina's pig starting offer! Learn what so many folks have already found out. Purina starters give pigs grow-and-go power. High fortification for disease protection and high nutritional levels provide "built-in" livability. Pigs go for them, too. Cost is low—about ½-cent per pig per day from the time pigs are one week to three weeks old . . . that's the critical period when extra disease protection and high nutritional level really pays off.

This offer is available to participating Purina dealers everywhere. Place your order now for delivery between March 6th and March 18th . . . and start your next litter FREE . . . on Purina. See for yourself how your pigs thrive and grow!

Purina's selling proposition is simple and easily understood and will be accepted by the reader as being in his or her interest. This copy was refined until there's not a waste word, not a thought that doesn't belong. It's an excellent example of lean, spare copy that exploits to the fullest Purina's offer. The company got its money's worth from this ad—and then some.

The advertiser received quite a bit of recognition among farm advertising groups. In the national N.A.A.M.A. awards contest Purina captured:

1. Regional Award of Merit for the hog campaign in color.
2. Regional Award of Merit for the hog campaign in black and white.
3. Regional First Prize for a single ad in color, up to spreads.
4. Award of Merit as runner-up to the national winner in Chicago in single ads in color, up to and including spreads.

That's quite a few "bingles" for one ball game.

Make the Copy Visually Attractive

Appearance of the completed industrial advertisement depends largely upon the person who wrote it.

Let's back off a bit and admit there's no denying that most ads consist of an illustration, copy, and a layout that brings order into chaos. Also that art or photography has to be purchased, type has to be specified, and the ad has to go through a rather involved production process. Everybody concerned contributes.

But there are those even in good agencies and well-run advertising departments who feel the writer's job is to write, period. They're of the opinion that the writer has no business "intruding" in other areas once his or her part of the job of manufacturing an ad has been completed.

This attitude is extremely shortsighted. It can easily result in weakened, watered-down ads that have little of the freshness and vitality of the original concept.

When all's said and done, the copywriter, whether advertising manager, account exective, or a writer in an agency copy pool, *is* intimately involved in the appearance of the finished ad. It's the writer who determines the illustration, the format, number of colors, and size of space for the ad—within a prescribed overall cost, of course. In a forthcoming chapter will be a discussion of just how illustrative techniques are selected and how specific layouts are arrived at.

Right now, though, the main concern is to produce a visually attractive piece of copy.

The first thing the writer does when settling down at the typewriter is to outline the ad to be written . That's basic. This will indicate approximately how much space will be required for what he or she is going to say. Depending upon the budget and upon communications objectives for both the campaign as a whole and for this individual ad in particular, he or she may specify a fractional page, full page, spread, special pull-out insert, gatefold, or perhaps a multipage insert—possibly perforated so it can easily be torn out and retained for reference if the reader is so inclined.

One thing is as certain as rising space costs: If copy is visually unattractive, readership plummets.

Be Concerned About Type

Of course, the copywriter usually doesn't specify what type face is to be used, the point size of the type, or the leading between lines—that is, the type isn't "spaced," as this is called. However, the experienced writer with good business sense (and the good ones *do*

have it) is often more of a both-feet-on-the-ground type of person than is an agency art director or an artist in an independent studio which the advertising manager may use. So he or she is vitally interested in the appearance of the ad—which he or she, perhaps more than anybody else involved in producing it, considers to be *his* or *hers*.

441

A purely selfish reason exists for this concern, in addition to the writer's professional concern. If the ad receives poor readership, the person who conceived it and wrote it is the ultimate recipient of the buck that is passed. He or she can't deny fathering the ad, and nobody enjoys having his or her judgment or ability questioned.

In many smaller companies the advertising manager is a complete one-person department and advertising agency. He or she conceives, writes, lays out and produces ads from start to finish. This ad manager is especially concerned that his or her output measures up to high standards.

Always, though, the writer provides either graphic or written direction to the artist to guide him or her in reflecting the writer's concept of the ad. Later we'll see how this is done, but right now let's consider what it is that makes copy visually attractive or unattractive.

We've briefly discussed word length, sentence length, and paragraph length. And we've touched upon how they influence the ease with which the copy may be read. Type set solid with few widows—short lines at the end of a paragraph—with little or no leading, and with long paragraphs repel the eye. People instinctively avoid such copy as either uninteresting or difficult to read.

3M Company doesn't have quite as much to say, but they, too, relied on borrowed interest in an ad which is unusually effective because it is so easy to read. The ad appeared in *International Science & Technology* magazine. It is shown on page 441.

A fine example of visually attractive copy is that in Ingersoll Milling Machine Company's whimsical four-color spread, shown on page 443.

The spread is tied together nicely by having a slice of the illustration carry over on the page containing the copy. The illustration itself is delightfully light touch; it's nice to see an industrial advertiser who doesn't take himself so seriously he's positively grim about the whole thing.

Headline starts out in a light vein, but has some hard sell in it, too, reading as it does:

**Ingersoll won't sell you EDM unless you
let us come in and show you how it works.
You wouldn't want a monster on your hands.**

Good psychology, that. The headline contains the advertiser's name; the much-used observation that if they read *only* the headline they'll receive an impression about company and product has much merit. It also contains the abbreviation for the product—electrical discharge machine; the fact that the advertiser wants to help the reader (good word) who's a prospective purchaser of the equipment; and the fact that it's complex enough to warrant this extra service. People tend to relate complexity with omniscience, or with an almost uncanny ability to accomplish the near-impossible. Sometimes this is all for the best.

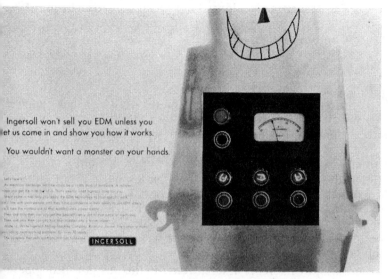

Ingersoll won't sell you EDM unless you let us come in and show you how it works.

You wouldn't want a monster on your hands.

Body copy reads:

Lets face it.

An electrical discharge machine could be a costly blob of hardware. A monster. Unless you get the most out of it. That's exactly what Ingersoll does for you.

We'll come in and help you apply the EDM technology to your specific work. We'll live with your people until they have confidence in the ability to use EDM wisely. We'll take the mystery out of that sophisticated power supply.

Then and only then can you get the best efficiency out of that piece of machinery.

Then and only then can you turn that monster into a money-maker.

Write us. Write Ingersoll Milling Machine Company, Rockford, Illinois. The company that's been licking metal-working problems for over 70 years.

The company that sells solutions, not just hardware.

That's mighty potent copy. It's readable because it's good copy, first of all, but also because it's visually attractive. Note how much leading—or line spacing—there is. And short paragraphs make it light and airy. And how the copy fits logically and neatly into a vast area of white space. This spread was designed to be read, and it received one of the highest readership ratings in the book.

All of us like attractive things. Make your copy visually attractive and you'll show readership heels to competitive ads that don't measure up to yours.

Make the Tone Suitable

Tone is a nebulous thing.

It's hard to put a precise definition on the word. When it's applied to a sound, either vocal or one made by a musical instrument, tone refers to pitch or quality. In the spoken word it can refer to pitch or accent. But when we mention tone in a discussion of writing—copywriting—tone refers to a style or manner of expression.

Actually, that's narrowing it down a bit too much. Tone, as used here, refers also to the character of the copy. To its mood, to the feel of it. And it can also apply to how the copy is slanted, how it attacks the problem of communicating with the reader and telling him or her the essential information he or she has to have to make a rational decision as to whether he or she is interested in buying the product.

Tone also, by inference at least, refers to the way in which appeals are made—whether they're cold-blooded, logical, and dispassionate. In copy this could well mean a dry-as-dust presentation of charts and graphs and a tabulation of how the product can be used in 1,478 different ways to do a given job. Now, this may all be very helpful to the reader. If he or she reads it.

Appeals to the reader can just as well be based on emotion, perhaps more effectively so. We've seen how Mobil Oil Corporation's great ad tugs at the heart strings because it appeals largely to the emotions, and how Chromalloy American's emotion-charged copy enthralls the reader so he or she perfectly willing to read the body copy to absorb information the advertiser wants him or her to have—even after the appeal to his or her emotions is past.

Tone means not only the rhythm with which you march your words across the page, the sentence length, symmetry, paragraph length, or other specific factors. Tone of the copy, if it's right, breathes life and feeling and human warmth into company and product and gives both personality. It hits the reader right where he or she lives, it involves him or her so that he feels an affinity for the advertiser and the product. Temporarily, at least, he feels a kinship with the advertiser.

No One Approach Best

No tone is better than any other for all advertisements written to all audiences at all times. Nothing can be all things to all people. The skilled copywriter varies the tone to suit the circumstances. Actually, at any time the writer has a wide choice of tones; with complete justification he or she can adopt a modest, unassuming attitude which will completely disarm the reader and smooth the way for him or her to accept everything the ad says as truth, absolute truth.

Avis, for example, doesn't really want to convey the message that it is only Number 2 in the car rental field. What it wants readers to remember is that if they go to Avis, chances are they'll receive a car that's cleaner, in better mechanical condition than cars rented from its giant competitor, and that the car will be full of gas and oil. Also, that Avis people try harder so that when you go to Avis you can reasonably expect to receive better service—with less waiting, less red tape, less chance of being disappointed.

At other times the writer is perfectly justified in taking an authoritative tone. If, for example, a company has a unique selling proposition, if it leads the industry, the situation may be exactly right for assuming the position of *the* authority, the leader to whom customers and prospects should rightly look for the final word on the subject. Naturally, this doesn't mean to brag and boast and send up meaningless smoke signals all over the sales hills; that avails the advertiser nothing. A total capability story, for example, if it's true in the most literal sense of the word—and if the universe is at least partially aware that it's true—can provide an extremely effective podium for the advertiser to talk from.

What copy says is important, there's no disputing that.

But how it says it is equally important.

On the surface, it is difficult to understand why all industrial ads are not interesting. They should be. After all, two competent advertising persons can be given the same products, same universe, and the same selling proposition. Both are accustomed to thinking objectively, to analyzing the problems involved in promoting the product, and in developing logical, workable solutions to them.

Given an ad to write, or a campaign to develop, one will retire to his or her office, close the door, and ultimately emerge with platitudes that don't hurt anybody's feelings, but which fall lamentably short of arousing any real interest in the company or its products.

The other, though, quite likely will put forth about the same amount of effort and in approximately the same amount of time or words will produce copy with bite and impact and an oversize measure of reader interest. The difference is in the tone.

Both may have said essentially the same things about the product. But the second one was able to impart freshness and vitality and sparkle to the copy through some mental process which hasn't yet been isolated, analyzed, and labeled by the psychologists. *How* he or she expressed his or her thoughts made the difference between wishy-washy words and vibrant, lively copy bound to succeed.

Many tones, many styles, slants or whatever you want to call the approach to copy can be right for many different advertisers. The one cardinal sin is to have such a complete absence of tone that the copy is flat and flavorless and devoid of any personality which separates it from other people's copy for other products.

Types of Advertisements

The industrial advertising man isn't usually concerned with advertising that is arbitrarily broken down into classifications according to the medium in which it appears—outdoor, radio, transit, television, and mail order. (Direct mail advertising, as opposed to mail order advertising, *is* of interest to the industrial advertising practitioner and will be discussed separately.)

Attempt to classify advertisements and the first thing that's apparent is that the classifications overlap. However, if the hybrids and other ads that are anomalous are disregarded as representing only a minute fraction of all industrial advertisements, there remain only 14 basic types of print ads you encounter with any degree of frequency. All others are offshoots. Naturally, this is excluding corporate ads, which are a breed apart and will be covered in a separate chapter.

The workhorse types of industrial ads are:

1. New product	8. Inquiry
2. Product description	9. Catalog offer
3. Product performance	10. Newsletter
4. Product line	11. How to do it
5. Problem solving	12. Trade ads
6. Case history	13. Institutional
7. Testimonial	14. Comic strip and cartoon

Copy will vary quite considerably from one type of ad to another, of course, because each ad is created to do one specific job. Each job, or communications objective, differs radically from some of the others. Some types of ads may call for unusually lengthy copy—for example, to introduce a complex new product for which the reader example, to introduce a complex new product for which the reader will expect a complete technical description and detailed construction specifications. Other copy may be very short; most will fall somewhere between the two extremes.

Let's look now at each type of industrial ad and consider its strengths and weaknesses and the job it does best.

New Product Ads

Here's a little exercise just for the fun of it: Pick any new product that's just been developed, either by your company or one you're familiar with. Look it over carefully, analyze what it has to offer to buyers, consider the price, competition, and all of the other factors you can dream up. Then hazard a guess as to what degree of success the new product will achieve in the marketplace when it's introduced.

Without even knowing what the product is, or to what market it's going to be sold, one thing is morally certain: It stands less than a 50-50 chance of living out a normal life expectancy.

More than half of all new products developed by American industry lose money and languish away while anguished progenitors in the companies who had a hand in fathering them wonder just what happened, and why.

Answers are as many and as varied as are the companies that go through this painful experience. Far too many firms conceive of a Great Idea, pull out all stops and burn the midnight oil to develop a new product for a silly reason—such as having something new to show at a trade show, for instance.

There's too little thought given to what is going to be done with the product once it becomes an actuality and just how it is going to be marketed. In the majority of cases little or no attempt has been made to research the market for the product to see if a real need for it exists, to determine what similar products it will have to compete against, to learn prices of those competitive products, how they are distributed, their share of the market, and whether the total market for the product is growing, stable, or declining.

A Great Little "What's It"

One company did this recently, with an open, childlike faith that things would work out. It proceeded to develop an amazingly intricate and sophisticated little piece of equipment to do highly specialized research work for metallurgical laboratories. Giving credit where credit is due, the product is an excellent one, and it is unique.

The innocent soul in charge of its development very properly went all of the way and hired a capable industrial designer to design the exterior shell, rightfully feeling that it should be first class in appearance so it would have every chance of succeeding. The designer did an outstanding job and the finished unit is a joy to the eye.

The only flaw was this—the product people and the engineers became so wrapped up in their pet project and so enamored with glowing thoughts of how the new Widget would enhance the company's image that they overlooked one relatively minor thing. Nobody stopped to figure out what the product would be used for—specifically, that is.

In due time it was completed with much overtime and doubletime in the shop and then rushed to the company's booth at the National Metal Show and Exposition. There it was proudly displayed, powered, ready to operate, and with one of the engineers from an outlying plant where the product was developed on hand at all times to explain all about the fascinating new Widget. The dewey-eyed product person charged with responsibility for the new product had given the engineer instructions to sound out attendees of the show to see if *they* could figure out an application for it.

He did—they couldn't.

After the show was torn down the product was lovingly crated and shipped back to the satellite plant where the product people have their offices. There it sat, undergoing tests and more tests and more tests. Everything worked perfectly, there was never a malfunction of any kind. Everybody was tremendously proud of the product and a gleam of ecstasy appeared in their eyes whenever it was mentioned. This was their esoteric baby.

They even entered photographs and a description of the product, along with a few guesses at some of the fantastic things it could do in a "design" contest held by one of the trade publications. And, wonder of wonders, the product was one of a hundred or so winners in the contest, thus showering great honor upon its developers. The contest was primarily to promote the publication, however, not the "winning" products.

Fifteen months after its introduction to those who supposedly constituted the universe for the product, it still remained in all of its pristine beauty in the research and development area of the plant where it was born. Nobody quite knows what to do with it. Some unfeeling individuals have been heard to mutter that it is in their way. Others had to dust it. Still others tripped over it.

However, it was finally decided that it might not be a bad idea to see if someone could find out just what applications the product was suited for—and to determine if a market for it actually existed. At last, real marketing thinking!

Accordingly, a graduate student attending a nearby university was hired to "research the market" for the product. He willingly accepted this subsidy out of the blue and there the matter rests—many months later. It's assumed that sooner or later the student will submit a report and recommendations for marketing the product—unless he first acquires the advanced degree upon which he's working and departs for parts unknown.

In the meantime, back in the product manager's office, all is not at a standstill as far as marketing the product is concerned. He or she has selected media in which to advertise it! Now, if the prospective purchasers of the Widget just happen to be in markets reached by the media given the product manager's stamp of approval, the product might eventually get off the ground.

This story is all too familiar, although not many companies are as inept as this one.

The New-Product Path

Back before Johannes Gutenberg invented movable type some time between 1435 and 1445, disseminating information to widespread audiences was almost impossible. In that era a new product was discussed by individuals, and if the tailor with an improved waistcoat wished to annouce his revolutionary method of manufacture, or style, he wrote an announcement with a quill pen on a piece of parchment and put it in the window of his shop—sans benefit of Scotch Tape. Thus passersby could read the notice—at least, those who could read *could* read it—and the word was spread in this fashion.

To try to introduce a new product to industry today in this way, or in any way except paid space advertising, is next to impossible. To be sure, the staunch disbelievers in advertising can develop a better Widget and wait for the world to beat a path to their plant door. But the wait may be a bit long.

Also, the fantastic, revolutionary, sensational, precedent-shattering new Widget can be developed, then the entire field sales force of 71 men can be called in for a special rah-rah-rah sales meeting to hear the virtues of the Widget extolled to them for long, boring hours. Then they can be given a hearty pat on the back and sent forth with instructions to sell, sell, sell.

Of course, a dollar or two is invested in bringing all 71 bodies in from widely scattered locations, the company loses sales while the sales reps are not covering their territories and the home office staff devotes its time and energies to planning and handling the meeting, ignoring routine duties which make money for the company.

Then, if this sales force bears any resemblance to other companies' sales forces selling capital equipment similar to the new Widget, they will make approximately 400 sales calls per sales reps per year. This figures out to 28,400 total calls by all 71 of the sales reps in the course of a year.

If this sales force is selling to the metalworking market, for example, with some 33,000 establishments with 20 or more employees, they could spread the word about the new Widget to all of these establishments in only 14 months. They'd see only one buying influence per establishment, for the most part, but we could assume that at least half of these influences might logically be expected to discuss the new Widget that Smith Widget Manufacturing Company has developed with at least one other influence.

Weak part of this anticipated reaction, however, is that we know for a fact that when capital equipment is concerned, a minimum of *five* buying influences are involved in a purchase—and usually more. The frustrating thing is that our sales reps can't get in to see these other influences. So what do we do without space advertising?

The Message Can Get Through

That's simple. We'll use direct mail. We can make up a mailing list composed of names supplied by the field sales force, to start with. But wait—isn't it barely possible they'll give us names of people upon whom they call? And this we don't need. So we can go to D&B, or to a list broker, and get additional names. But then there's no assurance that we'll reach even a fraction of the decision makers who can make or break sales for the new Widget. It's a physical impossibility to identify them without a lengthy research project designed for this one specific purpose. And the company can't afford to wait that long for sales of the new Widget, not if the sales forecast is to be achieved—and management is sticky on *that* subject no matter what the company's name is and what it makes.

But if we advertise our great new Widget to the metalworking market, suddenly many scores of thousands of buying influences know all about it over night. People in prospect companies from chairman of the board and president and vice-president of manufacturing, works manager, master mechanic—all of them know about it in a relatively short span of time.

It's quite true that each and every one of these people who are important to the Widget's future won't read the announcement advertisement. Every recipient of the media used won't read every issue. A certain percentage of them—perhaps as high as 25 percent—might skip this issue for one reason or another. But if you use more than one book, or if you prove your perspicacity by maintaining continuity of advertising and repeating the announcement ad, those who missed the most important thing to you in the business world will receive your message when the next issues come out.

If you're concerned that all of the influences you want to reach won't receive *any* business publications, relax. Almost all magazines enjoy a pass-along readership—usually around three per copy—within companies that receive them. This is a bonus the advertiser doesn't pay for, but it's one that's important to him or her nonetheless.

Only space advertising can carry a message to a widespread and diverse market so that businessmen throughout industry all know almost simultaneously what information about your product you feel they should have. It can't be done by smoke signals, by riders on horseback, by skywriting, by mail, or any other method at a price industry can afford to pay.

Another thing: A product is new more than once. It's new many, many times. That's because, while those who live with the product day by day think of it as old hat, untold thousands of prospective purchasers in the marketplace don't know of its existence. They may not realize that any such product has been produced by any company, or they may have an inkling that such a product is on the market but not be aware that your company manufactures it.

A Market Changes Constantly

This is not contradicting what was just said about advertising's ability to announce a product to the majority of your buying influences simultaneously. On the contrary, it merely points out that the marketplace is fluid, in a constant state of flux. Buying influences who can give the nod to your Widget were with another company just yesterday, or they've just been advanced and have new responsibility including specifying or approving purchases. These influences are not static. They change constantly, up to 40-50 percent a year due to death, retirement, promotions, job changes, mergers, and what not. The marketplace is dynamic. To maintain your position in it—or to better it—you must communicate constantly. Nothing is more true than the old saying, "Out of sight, out of mind."

Then again, the product may well be new to people even if you advertise it consistently, month in and month out. People who read your ads *think* they are about new products. This is known as the if-it-is-new-to-me reaction, or the if-I-had-only-known response, or the

I-buy-from-them-but-I-didn't-know-they-made-Widgets statement.

This last frequently happens to multidivision companies when a certain group of buying influences have long been accustomed to specifying the product of one division, but are completely unaware that a sister division produces a product that's complementary to the one they use. They've been going to a different corporation entirely for their requirements of that product. Advertising can do much to increase a corporation's penetration in a given market with products of another division that are not well established there.

Research shows the new product announcement is one of the best-read types of advertising. The word "new" is a potent one. There's the connotation of something improved, vastly better than any product that's ever preceded it, one that will go far toward solving whatever problem it's applied to. And readers of the business press, like all other humans, have their fair share of curiosity. Something new is something all of us want to read about, whether it's something that will help us on our jobs, or something that will make leisure activities more fun.

Run a new-product-announcement advertisement and you're off to a good start at getting more than your pro-rata share of readership, other things being relatively equal. The other things naturally include copy that's provocative in approach and tone; a stopper of an illustration that refuses point blank to let the reader give it short shrift; a fresh layout that piques the imagination; and, of course, media that are right so your message reaches those people who are most important to you.

A new-product-announcement ad run by Clark Equipment Company, Construction Machinery Division, measures up to all of those criteria and then some. This great ad, actually a multipage insert, introduces the company's new Michigan tractor shovels with great impact. The ad was produced by Clark's agency, Marsteller Inc.

Objectives of the ad were:

1. To introduce the new Series III Tractor shovels as highspeed, high-production equipment for heavy construction.

2. Reinforce the prestige of Clark-Michigan as the leader in the tractor shovel field.

3. Arouse interest in the new tractor shovels among Clark-Michigan distributors and prospects with aggressive, new, headline-copy technique.

Let's look at the ad, then go into the rationale of making the announcement this way, the media used, and results produced.

First we see a teaser ad, but not merely a teaser designed only to tease. Shown in the four-color illustration of the full page ad is the business end of a Michigan tractor shovel, digging, flying dirt providing a dramatic sense of motion, of things happening fast and furious. Copy reads: DIG

The new Michigans dig like no tractor shovels ever built before.

On the next right-hand page in publications carrying the ad, we see another four-color page. Illustration is of the Michigan's Bonus Bucket heaped full, *really* full, of a mixture of rock and dirt. It's a heavy load and it looks like it. Copy reads: HEAP

The new Michigans heap like no tractor shovels´ ever built before.

On the next right-hand page of the books we find a closeup of the bucket loading a dump truck. Mechanical details of the hydraulic pistons and lifting mechanism are shown to good advantage. Copy reads: LOAD

The new Michigans heap like no tractor shovels ever built before.

Then, on the next right-hand page is another four-color illustration of an obviously bustling Michigan tractor shovel slightly blurred by motion, disappearing to hunt up some more work to do. Big, fat tires kick up dust so the speed of the unit is apparent to the reader. Copy reads: GO

The new Michigans heap like no tractor shovels ever built before.

When the reader flips the page after this terrific build-up, he finds the wrap-up, a great color photograph of a new Michigan loading a tractor-dump trailer in some scenic country. Even the little things are correct here. For instance, the truck driver was undoubtedly fascinated by the preparations of the photographer; truck drivers always are. But here he's looking at the action, the loading, *not* at the camera. This is relatively inconsequential, considering how small he appears in the completed illustration, but it's a detail that contributes its small share to complete authenticity.

Headline of this fine spread naturally continues with the established theme; it says:

The new Michigans heap like no tractor shovels ever built before.

And the body copy also builds on the interest generated by the single-page inserts, because the key words—dig, heap, load, and go—

are in upper-case letters, boldface type, and break the copy naturally where these key user benefits are discussed. It says:

> This is the Michigan—5 new rigid-frame and 2 new articulated models from 1 5/8 to 7 yds—designed and "task-matched" to fit your loading jobs. And one thing's certain: you've never seen anything like the way they go after these jobs.

> **DIG** Ever see material explode into a bucket? That's how Michigan Bonus Buckets load—maximum bucket speed and rollback angle with "straight-up digging action" **throws** material in.

> **HEAP** 45° rollback from ground to carry—and in less than a second. Result: one quick pass heaps a bucketful in as little as 4 sec. And Michigans **hold** that load—over rough ground.

> **LOAD** New hydraulics zip the bucket to full height up to 53% faster—as fast as 6 sec. The bucket's up long **before** the Michigan reaches the side of the truck—and back down again before you return to the pile. And Michigan's controlled dumping can be as fast as 1.2 seconds!

> **GO** The new Michigans are rock-stable because wheelbase and weight distribution balance perfectly. They operate as easily as your car. And visibility is great—you can even see **behind** the bucket when it's on the ground.

> See the new Michigans. You've never seen anything like them before.

Incidentally, this campaign is a radical departure from long-copy case histories Clark has traditionally run. Clark decided to use this striking consecutive-page technique to get the impact it was felt the ads must produce in order to assure a successful introduction of the new line of equipment.

Prime-user benefits—the superior digging ability, loading ability, load-gathering ability (heaping), and stable mobility of the new tractor shovels were naturals for the individual inserts. In fact, these four major benefits suggested the format. And the advertiser had the opportunity in the wrap-up to get into some specifics—solid nuts-and-bolts information and performance data.

Consecutive right-hand pages (rather than left-hand pages) were chosen because it's traditional in the advertising field to believe that right-hand pages receive higher readership than do left-hand ones. Perhaps they do. This will be discussed later.

The new Michigans dig like no tractor shovels ever built before.

First right-hand insert.

The new Michigans heap like no tractor shovels ever built before.

Second right-hand insert.

The new Michigans load like no tractor shovels ever built before.

Third right-hand insert.

The new Michigans go like no tractor shovels ever built before.

Fourth right-hand insert.

Above are the first four right-hand, four-color inserts of the Clark-Michigan advertisement. The conclusion was a four-color spread, illustrated on the following page.

455

The announcement ad ran in the following 17 trade magazines:

Engineering News-Record

Western Construction

Pit & Quarry

Contractors & Engineers

Rock Products

Construction

Construction Bulletin

Construction Digest

Construction News

Constructioneer

Dixie Contractor

Michigan Contractor & Builder

New England Construction

Pacific Builder & Engineer

Rocky Mountain Construction

Texas Contractor

Western Builder

The decision to use consecutive right-hand-page inserts and a wrap-up spread was made purely on the basis of grabbing the full, undivided attention of readers of those key books. This is an extremely competitive market for the sale of equipment, and for advertising advantages as well. Most of Clark's competitors use four-page inserts in just about the same media listed above. To make Clark's ad stand out, something more than a four-page, four-color insert was called for.

In any event, the ads received some of the highest readership ratings ever achieved in the construction equipment field. Studies made by John T. Fosdick Associates of the ad that appeared in *Contractors & Engineers* showed that it received noted scores of 58 percent one time, and 62 percent for another insertion.

Ad-Gage readership surveys of *Pit & Quarry* magazine reported scores of 31 (3rd highest) in one issue; 29 (highest) in another; 26 (6th highest) in another; and 34 (highest) in appearances the ad made in that book.

In studies made by McGraw-Hill's Reader Feedback Service in *Engineering News-Record*, the following scores and comments resulted:

56 Percent Saw—"I think that he is trying to present the fact that this equipment substitutes for a power dragline or shovel and is less costly."

Engineer, Government Agency

"It's like the TV ads. You think 'loader' and then Michigan 175 comes to mind."

Project Superintendent

"It's a good ad. The picture is attractive, and you can't help but stop to look at it."

Superintendent

62 Percent Saw—"This ad gives a description of what their machinery will do—in less time, at less cost. The loader here is one that might be particularly suited to what I would want on my jobs."

Superintendent, Construction Company

60 Percent Saw—"The ad has a good picture; it tells the message. Those of us in this business know exactly what it's saying."

Supervisor, Area and Utility Engineering

"I noticed that this equipment is larger. With this Clark equipment, I can get the job done faster."

President, Road and Sewer Construction Company

Readers—*prospects*—saw and read this fine ad in unprecedented numbers. And, perhaps almost as important, Clark dealers were highly enthusiastic about the kick-off for the new tractor shovels. They reported many customers' mentioning it to them, indication that the ad made a strong and lasting impression. At least it lasted long enough for them to remember to comment on it to the dealer the next time they met. This may have been days, weeks, or even months since they read the ad.

Isn't this what a new product announcement ad *should* do?

Product Description Ads

The average industrial prospect isn't some kind of a fearsome monster lurking in a murky lair somewhere. Nor is he or she a robot or some kind of a way-out kook.

The prospect is a flesh-and-blood person with perfectly normal feelings and interests and a personal share of curiosity. One thing shared with the prospect for any kind of merchandise—industrial or consumer—is that he or she is interested first and foremost in himself or herself. Uppermost in his or her mind is what the product will do for him or her and the company.

Unquestionably these industrial prospects for your product use more cold-blooded logic when they evaluate a product than does a consumer. And they customarily make a hard-headed analysis of the product, comparing it point by point with competitive ones. For this reason, when you're describing your product in copy for an industrial advertisement it pays to give all of the facts and figures and nuts-and-bolts information the reader will need.

Despite this attitude of the industrial prospect, it doesn't pay to confine your ad to a colorless presentation of a mass of cold statistics. Remember you're talking to a human, not a computer, and you'll find he or she reacts to emotional appeals, to a clean layout, punchy headlines, first-rate photography, attractive typography, and copy that sits up and sings. Give these in good measure and you'll have an ad that does a real job for you.

Naturally, the ad should counter the negative influences working against the sale. In a survey McGraw-Hill made among sales reps selling to industry it was determined that the sales resistances most frequently encountered are:

Price 63%
Lack of familiarity with the product 26%
Resistance to change 24%
Competition 18%

All other resistances were far down the scale in comparison to the four listed above, and they were relatively unimportant.

A good product description ad can do much to counter every one of these objections. Offhand, price would seem to be an insurmountable obstacle for an advertisement to overcome. After all, no amount of advertising can produce an immediate effect on price—but a well-written product ad can describe the product in such a way, and from the reader's viewpoint, and can make the user benefits so desirable that price becomes a minor consideration. By and large, industrial buyers are far more concerned with quality, service, delivery, and reputation of the seller than they are with price. This is assuming, of course, that the price is within reason and that superior quality of the product justifies charging it.

Lack of familiarity with the product is a pathetic reason for a sales rep's difficulty in making a sale—or for his losing it. Certainly this is an area in which advertising can lay to rest this sales resistance effectively and economically. Describe your product and tell what it will do for the buyer—time and time and time again—and this stumbling block will disappear to a large extent.

Everybody is more or less bound by inertia. People don't willingly change direction or do things differently unless they're acted upon by an outside force. There's this to consider, too, when thinking about prospects' resistance to making a change: Your prime prospects may now be buying a product very similar to yours, but one that is actually inferior. Your product may well have more features, better construction, superior materials, a better finish, better engineering, and it may produce more for the user at lower cost.

On the fact of it, this would seem to be an ideal situation. When it exists, all your sales force has to do is march into buyers' offices, explain the facts, whip out an order form and pen, then sit back and watch the commission checks roll in.

Unfortunately, life isn't that simple. There's a great deal of doubt about what *really* motivates people in industry who have the authority to make a buying decision. Pocketbook appeal is vitally important, of course, as is the ability of the product to solve a specific problem such as increased production, less maintenance, using less floor space, and so on. All are perfectly valid reasons to buy a product, or not to buy it if it doesn't measure up to the company's requirements in some respect.

But isn't the prime motivation, once a decision to buy has been made, one to buy the *safe, known product*? Specifying the safe product would not subject the buyer to criticism in the event something unforseen should go wrong, or if the product didn't work out as well as anticipated for some reason. The buyer who specifies the product with which all concerned in the purchase are familiar has, in effect, played the old Army game. He has passed the buck as far as accepting responsibility for his decision is concerned. He has delegated a pro-rata share of the responsibility to all of those who participated in making the decision.

Here advertising can contribute immeasurably by making the advertiser's products and company name known, familiar, accepted, and safe. Advertising can make a massive contribution by helping achieve acceptance for a product, so that it will never be considered unsafe, something to be avoided, something dangerous, and so be ruled out of consideration when a purchase is contemplated.

Industry would be amazed if the dollar volume of sales lost because products weren't considered "safe" could be measured. Non-believers in advertising would have conniptions.

Every advertisement puts the advertiser's best foot forward—or it should. But an informative, tightly written product description can stress the product's strong points, concentrate on those which are exclusive with this product, and create desire for it by making apparent its superiority over competitive ones. In this way advertising counters the competition and helps lay to rest the influence competitors wield with prospects, making it much easier for sales reps to book more orders, and do it in less calls.

The fine product description ad run by Vickers Instruments, Inc. in *Metal Progress* magazine does an excellent job of describing product features and construction of a complicated piece of equipment. It is reproduced nearby.

Small captions identifying key points are reversed out of the black background, and matched up with appropriate features of the metallograph to point them out to the reader. Copy is short and bulleted and to the point. It reads:

The Vickers fifty-five metallograph
gives you these exclusive performance features:

- *MICROPLAN FLAT FIELD OBJECTIVE LENSES*

- *AUTOMATIC INTEGRATING PHOTOGRAPHIC TIMER actuates motorized focal plane shutter to expose film up to 5" x 7" (Speeds 5 ASA to 3200 ASA)*

- *MOTORIZED 35MM CAMERA actuated by Timer Unit for fully automatic film operation.*

- *OPTICAL BELLOWS gives continuous variation of screen magnification from 24X to 2800X without changing eyepiece or moving screen.*

- *MAGNIFICATION INDICATOR — semiautomatic read-out of total screen magnification.*

- *COMBINATION MOVEMENT ROTATING STAGE with both gliding top plate and micrometer actuated traverse motions.*

- *PNEUMATIC LOADING MICRO-HARDNESS TEST-ER—desired load automatically applied at correct rate for load selected.*
PLUS UNIVERSAL HIGH-PERFORMANCE OPTI-CAL CAPABILTY—Microscopy of all types—incident, mixed, and transmitted light—bright field, dark field, oblique—polarized light—phase contrast—macro ex-amination and photography 5X, 10X, 15X.

That copy certainly familiarizes the prospect with features of the Vickers machine.

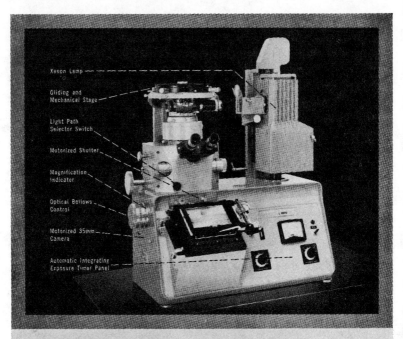

Product Performance Ads

Quality and performance of the product is the single most important factor in selling to industry.

462

An excellent opportunity is provided in the product performance-type ad to tell the reader a rousing quality story. You can impress upon him or her the superiority of the product and the characteristics which make it excel, with no chest-thumping, no boasting.

Furthermore, you appeal to his or her primary interest—himself or herself—by telling what the product will do for him or her. Product performance ads appeal to the reader's self interest, hence enjoy better than average readership. And they automatically enable you to produce reader-oriented copy.

There's high inherent interest in this type of ad because readers of the business press are educating themselves, and they have a lively interest in products and processes which might help them solve a problem confronting them in their company—or which might prevent one from cropping up.

Copy for a product performance ad may discuss features of the product, of course. But it also, and more important, tells what the product does, how it does it, how well it performs its functions, its operating speeds or other characteristics, reliability, maintenance requirements, installation procedure, and other information peculiar to the individual product. All of this is necessary to present it in a favorable light and to give the reader enough information on which to base a tentative buying decision, or to induce a response such as having him write for literature or request a sales rep to call.

Just because copy must give nuts-and-bolts information doesn't mean it has to be as dull and unimaginative as a seed catalog. Selecting the *right* information that will appeal most to the reader's needs and interests makes it easy to write an advertisement that's interesting and highly readable. Product differences dictate to a large extent how technical copy should be, although distribution pattern, size of field sales force, and other factors also enter in.

Let's look at three typical product performance ads—three because each varies from the other in the amount of information given to support claims made.

First is Pacific Plantronics, Inc.'s appealing ad from *Dun's Review* —appealing because who can resist stopping and looking at an illustration of a lovely young miss, hair tucked up, clad only in a large towel, fresh from her shower? Mighty few indeed, and most of these are ready to retire so you can forget about their influencing purchases for very long. The ad is shown.

Copy of this fine ad strikes just the right tone. It reads:

118 lbs. (2 oz.)

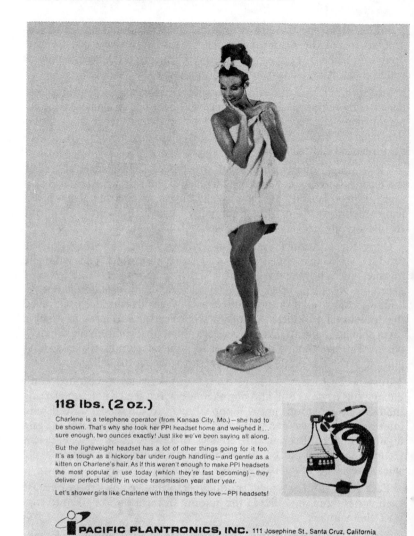

118 lbs. (2 oz.)

Charlene is a telephone operator (from Kansas City, Mo.)—she had to be shown. That's why she took her PPI headset home and weighed it... sure enough, two ounces exactly! Just like we've been saying all along.

But the lightweight headset has a lot of other things going for it too. It's as tough as a hickory bar under rough handling—and gentle as a kitten on Charlene's hair. As if this weren't enough to make PPI headsets the most popular in use today (which they're fast becoming)—they deliver perfect fidelity in voice transmission year after year.

Let's shower girls like Charlene with the things they love—PPI headsets!

PACIFIC PLANTRONICS, INC. 111 Josephine St., Santa Cruz, California
Distributed by: AUTOMATIC ELECTRIC CO • GRAYBAR Electric Co., or Contact Your Local Telephone Co. Business Office.
Licensee: S. G. Brown Ltd., Watford, Eng. — a Hawker Siddeley Co.

Charlene is a telephone operator (from Kansas City, Mo.)—she had to be shown. That's why she took her PPI headset home and weighed it . . . sure enough, two ounces exactly! Just like we've been saying all along.

But the lightweight headset has a lot of other things going for it too. It's as tough as a hickory bar under rough han-

dling—and gentle as a kitten on Charlene's hair. As if this weren't enough to make PPI headsets the most popular in use today (which they're fast becoming)—they deliver perfect fidelity in voice transmission year after year.
Let's shower girls like Charlene with the things they love—PPI headsets!

Illustration and copy are tied together logically and attractively. First paragraph explains why the illustration is a towel-clad Charlene and establishes a climate of believability for a major product benefit all at one time. Other benefits follow in the second paragraph—lightness of the headset is hit again, the fact that the headset is not fragile, that switchboard operators like it because it doesn't muss their hair (as tough as good employees are to get today, keeping them happy is vitally important), and that they deliver superb fidelity over a long prime of life. Final paragraph is a delightfully light touch and gets in one more appeal, one more plug to buy the product.

The spot illustration shows the entire product, including the parts that don't go on the girl's head. It reinforces the copy and makes the product come alive.

Product Line Ads

There comes a time in the life of every industrial advertising professional when it seems he or she doesn't have much of anything to say. There's a lull in activity. He or she has no sensational new products to announce. Products which have been advertised have been on the market for some time. So long, in fact, they have been just about milked dry as far as different copy appeals are concerned. This is a logical time to consider preparing a product line ad.

Product line ads serve many useful purposes. First of all, they create an awareness in the reader's mind that the company manufactures an unusually broad line of products, ranging from the smallest shown in the ad up to the largest. A broad range can be impressive.

Many a reader might not have been aware of this range. He may have turned to the company to buy one or two items in the line, but remained blissfully—but unprofitably—unaware that the company also produced items he was buying from another source.

For a customer with a long and satisfactory experience with one product from the company, considerable brand loyalty has been built up. Other things being equal, chances are this satisfied customer would like to buy related items from the company *if he or she knew it produced them.* One product strengthens the sales of another.

In addition, the product line ad creates an awareness of the company as one with the capability to engineer and produce a complete line. A broad product line gives a company stature. Although the "image" business may be overworked and an image actually be a nebulous thing, don't discount it entirely. A company's reputation as a leader, as one with know-how in depth, as a thoroughly reliable source, is second in importance only to product quality and performance when it comes to selling to industry. Anything that enhances the company's reputation is like money in the bank. Remind an industry from time to time that your company offers every type of widget in existence and the payoff comes in additional sales.

Product line ads in regular issues of media normally used in reaching the industrial universe usually do an effective job. They are especially effective in annual issues—so called "Buyer's Guide" issues—and in directories such as *Thomas Register of American Manufacturers, MacRae's Blue Book*, and the various publications of trade associations. In directories the ad gives basic product information which remains "alive" until the next edition of the directory, usually a year.

Problem-Solving Ads

Everybody in industry who has any responsibility has problems connected with his or her job, and everybody wants to solve them.

Extend a helping hand in an ad—hold out a promise of solving a problem that's bothering the reader and he or she will pore over every word you have to say. He or she will read and reread what you say about the problem, about your product, then it will be evaluated based on past experience.

The approach is an excellent one. You should, however, be sure to give yourself every break by selecting a problem that's relatively commonplace so that a high percentage of readers can identify with it. If you choose some far-out problem your product can solve, one that won't be encountered again until the year 2,000, the "hooker" is too hypothetical and the average reader won't give your ad a second glance. Your sales manager knows what problems prospects encounter regularly; this is fed back by the field sales reps.

The problem-solution approach is a time-tested one that's just as potent today and just as interesting as it was when the first industrial advertisement appeared a half-century or so ago.

Identify and describe a problem with which the reader is familiar, then show how use of your product will solve it, and he or she is psychologically conditioned to accept as truth everything you say from that point on. One follows the other just as naturally as night follows day. Base your case on a problem that's pertinent and timely, make it one the reader either has encountered or is likely to, then show your familiarity with it in the copy. Then you're on solid ground.

Readership of a well-done problem-solution ad is usually several percentage points higher than a straight product description ad.

The Dow Chemical Company has an entire campaign based on problem solving; two of the ads are illustrated above. They appeared in *Reinforced Plastics, International Science and Technology,* and in *Materials in Design Engineering* magazines.

Headline is the same for all ads; the subhead varies with specific applications for Dow's line of epoxy resins in order to stress its prime user benefit.

Let's look at the copy of one of these ads:

 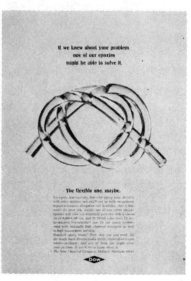

If we knew about your problem,
one of our epoxies
might be able to solve it.
The fire-retardant one, maybe.

It's a brominated epoxy resin with high physical and electrical properties. And if that won't do your job, maybe one of our other unique epoxies will. Like our extremely pure one with a viscosity of 4,000—5,500 cps. and 20 ALPHA color max. Or

> *our epoxy novolac resin with unusually high chemical resistance as well as temperature stability. Or our extremely flexible resin.*
>
> *These are just a few examples. We make a full line of standard resins, too. All are tough, hard, dimensionally stable, chemical resistant, solvent resistant. And one of them just might solve your problem. If you'll let us know about it.*

The Dow Chemical Company has developed an unusually good line of epoxy resins which include most of the standard "commodity-type" epoxies plus several others with unique properties. The market for standard epoxies is fairly well known. However, the unique-property epoxies have yet to establish themselves into well-defined market patterns—so this campaign was developed.

There are three primary objectives for the campaign:

1. To increase awareness of Dow's total line of epoxy resins with emphasis on the unique-property resins.

2. Increase awareness of specific properties of Dow's unique-property resins.

3. Produce inquiries to help determine the degree of interest that exists in various segments of the market.

The campaign has been a success. It has produced hundreds of inquiries to be followed up by Dow's field salse force. The sales force is enthusiastic about the campaign and feels it is completely compatible with selling efforts.

Unfortunately, Dow has the same problem most industrial advertising managers have—establishing a positive correlation between the advertising campaign and sales growth. Dow *has* seen significant sales growth in the epoxy area, but cannot attribute any specific percentage to advertising. The advertising has disclosed that one of the largest and most fertile markets for Dow epoxies appears to be among molders of reinforced plastics, so future advertising programs will put more emphasis in media directed to that market.

Case History Ads

Case history ads give you a double-barreled bonus: They receive higher readership than the average product advertisement, and they are believed implicitly. A combination like that is hard to top.

The reader feels an affinity toward the advertiser and the product featured in a case history advertisement because it is an easy matter to project himself or herself and the company into the situation that's illustrated and described. Only a simple mental step is required to visualize a piece of equipment in the plant, doing the same job that it does for the firm described in the ad.

Chances are the reader has virtually the same problem in his plant (if you've selected it to make sure it's a universal one) and it takes no budding genius to deduce that if a certain product solved a particularly knotty problem at one factory, it surely can in another.

Then, too, there's a theory that many industrial advertising persons have shared for a long, long time. No research study has been done to confirm it—or to disprove it, for that matter—but the feeling is too widespread to believe it's altogether lacking in credence. This is that the reader derives a certain sense of satisfaction out of reading that his or her counterpart in another company has experienced difficulty. He or she finds this comforting and reassuring. It inflates the ego and contributes to the sense of well being. Naturally, he or she goes on to read how the problem was solved just in case he or she ever encounters it, and so absorbs the product message.

It's human nature for one to have a deep interest in reading about the trials and tribulations of others, and to find out how they overcame their troubles and solved their problems. After all, this is the basic raw material from which all fiction is constructed, be it a play, short story, novel, movie, or TV epic. Retain this inherent interest in a case history advertisement where you can show the reader a solid, dollars-and-cents reason why he or she should use your product, and you will have him or her hanging on each and every word as if they were sparkling gems, too precious to take a chance on losing.

The reader is perfectly willing to accept the case history ad at face value. It has a ring of sincerity that can't be faked. Statements in the copy are presented by somebody with identifiable, and in a frame of reference that is acceptable. And it isn't the advertiser who's making the claims.

Instead of having some unknown advertising manager or agency copywriter trying to force-feed information which he or she may or may not want, the reader realizes that copy in a case history ad is a report of the facts; it is based on an unbiased individual's experience with the advertiser's product. Furthermore, the reader knows that verification of the facts is merely a matter of picking up the phone. He or she is fully aware that no advertiser in his or her right mind would dream of stretching the truth in a case history ad because the customer's name and company is given.

Built-in believability of the case history ad makes it terrifically potent. If more advertisers were aware of its greater impact and greater readership—which means greater effectiveness, of course—there would be far more case history advertisements in the business press than we now see.

Have Copy Verified

When you're writing copy for a case history ad, try to retain the flavor of the remarks the customer made. After all, you're quoting him or her and putting his or her reputation on the line. Send the copy to the customer to read for content and accuracy; have him or her check facts, figures, performance data, production rates, maintenance costs, and other technical material to be sure it is absolutely correct. When you write him or her, make it clear you don't want the copy rewritten. You don't want approval of how you write—merely *what* you write.

You can do this tactfully without ruffling feelings. Then, when he or she is satisfied that the copy is "correct," ask him or her to initial and date a carbon or Xerox copy of it and return it to you with a covering letter stating that it meets with his or her approval, and that your company has permission to use it in advertising.

This is a formality in most instances, but should anything ever arise of a legal nature, your company attorneys will regard you as a hero—as will your management. When an ad is being prepared there's no telling whether the equipment may explode in use, or disintegrate, catch fire, injure workmen, or what have you; having copy initialed and formal, written permission to print it can be of utmost importance in such event.

It's always a good idea to show a picture of the customer who's being quoted in the ad. This increases believability and helps the reader by making it immediately apparent this is not a hypothetical story, the copy is talking about a real flesh-and-blood person and company. A fringe benefit is that all of us have a certain amount of vanity and we like to see our names and pictures in print. *Always* have a signed, witnessed model release from any recognizable people in your pictures. Pay the customary dollar for the signature to assure its legality, and make sure the signers are of legal age.

Speaking of pictures, think back for a minute to a group picture in which you appeared. When it was shown to you for the first time, what was your immediate reaction? You looked for yourself. Or, if a group photo was taken in which a friend or customer appeared and you gave them their copy of the photo, didn't they remark at once, "This is good of me," or, "This isn't too good of me." Almost everybody is self-centered to the extent they enjoy seeing themselves in pictures. Customers are no different.

You'll find, if you develop a case history campaign, that you have a bit of difficulty at first in securing enough material—information and photographs. After awhile, however, when the campaign has been running for six months or a year customers will volunteer, perhaps through your field sales force or your dealer organization, to let you feature themselves and their equipment in your ads.

Case history ads accomplish another very desirable objective, too. They firmly cement a good relationship between customer and company. When a customer has been featured in one of your ads, he'll usually become one your hardest-working unofficial sales reps. He identifies with your company and takes great pleasure in telling others in his line of business how good your product is, based on favorable experience with it. There's no way to measure this residual benefit from a case history campaign, but it's there and it's giving your company advertising that money couldn't buy.

A typical case history advertisment is illustrated nearby. This ad of Lindberg Hevi-Duty's was written by the author. It received a distinguished award, a large and impressive walnut plaque suitably inscribed, from *Ceramic Industries* magazine because this ad received the highest readership of any ad in the magazine for the calendar year in which it appeared, as shown by Cahners Publishing Company's Ad-Ed Audit readership study.

The ad is built on a sound foundation. Uniformity of ceramic products as they are removed form the kiln after firing is a major problem for most manufacturers in that field. If the temperature of the kiln is not completely stable and uniform, product size and quality varies and reject rates shoot up—and profits nose-dive. That the firm featured in the ad fired alumina ceramic pieces within ±.003 (that's three thousands) of an inch, consistently, seven days a week, month in and month out, speaks well for the equipment.

Added authenticity and human interest is built into the ad through use of a small spot illustration of the president of the customer-company and his plant superintendent. Pictures with people in them always attract more readers than illustrations without people.

Copy is believable because it tells the story from the customer's viewpoint, rather than from the advertiser's. It reads:

Meet a man who fires alumina ceramic pieces within a ±.003 inch tolerance . . .

He's D. M. Roberts, president of Roberts Engineering & Mfg. Company, Corpus Christi, Texas. He manufactures high explosive "grenades" used to perforate oil wells.

Meet a man who fires alumina ceramic pieces within a ± .003 inch tolerance...

He's D. M. Roberts, president of Roberts Engineering & Mfg. Company, Corpus Christi, Texas. He manufactures high explosive "grenades" used to perforate oil wells.

The two halves of the ceramic grenade must fit together *perfectly* to protect the explosive charge until it is detonated. Maximum as-fired tolerance on critical dimensions is ± .003 of an inch.

Alumina ceramic is the ideal material for these sophisticated grenades. Under explosive force it reduces to sand and does not impede oil flow.

Mr. Roberts must have a kiln he can rely on — one with dependable temperature stability and uniformity.

He gets just that with his Lindberg Hevi-Duty Gas-Fired high temperature Car Tunnel kiln. It's been in service three years now, and it works 7 days a week, 24 hours a day. Reject rate of grenades is insignificant.

Lindberg Hevi-Duty has *total capability* in supplying heat to industry. Chances are that Lindberg Hevi-Duty has already solved your problem — or can, and quickly.

For kilns for firing ferrites, electronic ceramics, whiteware, refractories or what have you, write us. Let us study your needs. The address is Lindberg Hevi-Duty, 2450 W. Hubbard Street, Chicago, Illinois 60612. Department CI351.

The two halves of the ceramic grenade must fit together perfectly *to protect the explosive charge until it is detonated. Maximum as-fired tolerance on critical dimensions is* ±.003 *of an inch.*

Alumina ceramic is the ideal material for these sophisticated grenades. Under explosive force it reduces to sand and does not impede oil flow.

Mr. Roberts must have a kiln he can rely on—one with dependable temperature stability and uniformity. He gets just that with his Lindberg Hevi-Duty Gas-Fired high temperature Car Tunnel kiln. It's been in service three years now, and it works 7 days a week, 24 hours a day. Reject rate of grenades is insignificant.

Lindberg Hevi-Duty has total capability in supplying heat to industry. Chances are that Lindberg Hevi-Duty has already solved your problem—or can, and quickly.

For kilns for firing ferrites, electronic ceramics, whiteware, refractories or what have you, write us. Let us study your needs. The address is . . .

This case history ad is typical of the type in that it gives the name of the individual whose experience is being talked about, his firm name, and the city the customer company is located in. This proves to the reader's satisfaction that the facts are exactly as stated.

This was a highly effective ad. When an ad tops all other advertisements in a book in readership over a year's time, it *has* to have something going for it.

Testimonial Ads

The testimonial ad is a kissing cousin of the case history ad.

And the testimonial ad shares the strengths of the case history ad—excellent readership and believability. Major difference between the two is that in the testimonial ad the customer or user of the product is doing the talking, rather than being quoted.

In actual practice the advertising manager or agency copywriter frequently "helps out a little" by strengthening the customer's remarks, or by making them more grammatical. Often it's necessary to rewrite what the customer said, almost entirely. This is permissible and it's often desirable as long as there is no distortion, no deviation from what the customer actually said.

Many people freeze up when they realize they're going to be quoted. They find it next to impossible to utter more than a mono-syllabic grunt, or at most a deadpan yes or no. For some reason or other the reaction is much the same as the one that occurs when a person unused to having a picture taken sits for a formal portrait, or has a professional photographer take a head-and-shoulder closeup for use in an advertisement. He or she freezes, becomes extremely self-conscious and the mental processes almost grind to a screeching halt.

If this happens to you when you're gathering background material for a testimonial ad, you're going to have to put words in the customer's mouth. This isn't as dishonest as it might appear. You're undoubtedly thoroughly familiar with the customer's operation, having heard about it from the sales manager, district sales manager, or dealer. What you need now is for the customer to commit that the facts *are* the facts—and give you permission to use them over his or her name.

Ask questions, plenty of questions. When the customer nods yes, or shakes his or her head no, probe a bit and find out why your supposition is true or untrue. Generally you can count on people unfreezing if you'll be considerate and friendly and genuinely interested in what they're doing. Then the little gems will come trickling forth, the direct quotes in regional colloquialisms that add flavor and color to the copy. Get them down on the tape recorder just as the customer says them—either in his voice or in yours. But get them.

Not all customers are shrinking violets, of course. Many, particularly Southerners, are so loquacious your major effort will be to sort out the wheat from the chaff when you write the ad. It's always preferable to have too much source material than too little, though, so never dry up the fountain that's providing you with the wherewithal for your copy. Encourage the person to talk and keep talking, all through lunch, for as long as you consider it necessary to secure sufficient material.

Again, before you set type on copy, be sure to clear it with the customer—and in the case of a large corporation, with the public relations people or whoever has this responsibility assigned to them. When you're quoting somebody directly a mistake is a serious thing and can be embarrassing for all concerned. Having written clearance and copy approval in the file is something like life insurance; it can't be overdone.

Inquiry Ads

Far too many industrial advertisers judge the effectiveness of their advertising programs solely by one criterion—how many inquiries are produced.

This is a mistake. It's unfortunate for advertising and unfortunate for the advertiser. Although there's invariably a signature and address at the close of the copy in the ad (except for the Cummins ad discussed recently), and usually a bid for action, most industrial ads are not designed specifically to produce inquiries. Probably nowhere inadvertising is there more misunderstanding than there is on this score.

Readers respond to an advertisement—they inquire, as it's put — primarily because they want additional information about a product they feel might be useful to them. Or they inquire because they've been assigned the responsibility of collecting information on all similar products prior to having somebody upstairs making a purchasing decision. Or they want literature to enable them to compare products themselves.

Or they're inveterate literature collectors.

Literature collectors are the bane of an advertising manager's life. One time when the author was at the old Diamond T Motor Truck Company, there occurred an encounter with one of the most avid collectors extant. It was like this.

As a matter of policy, all incoming inquiries from space advertising, sales promotion, public relations, shows and so on were carefully and systematically screened. A naturally competitive spirit and a hunger for sales combined with a well-developed sixth sense and much practice made it possible to sense with some degree of accuracy those inquiries which were probably the hottest. No claim whatsoever is made for anything approaching perfection, nor for being able to weed out the out-and-out nixies.

One morning just before 9:30 coffee, while still not fully awake, a particular inquiry rang a mental bell most clamorously. The name of the inquirer was familiar! This was, without doubt, one of the hottest prospects to come down the pike of recent moons. The inquiry was carefully put aside for immediate action—immediate as soon as the rest of the inquiries were screened and coffee break was over.

Then, heavens to Betsy, what should show up in the balance of the day's inquiries except *eight* more inquiries from this same worthy gentleman! Two came from publicity and the others from space ads in six different books; somehow one book duplicated, it seemed.

All of the inquiries were concerned with three different models of motor trucks. In itself this wasn't unusual because all were quite similar and could easily have been used for the same application.

Obviously these inquiries had to be handled right then and there.

The customary snap-out inquiry form wasn't good enough for this prospect. He was too hot. It was too easy to sit there (before coffee) and visualize him sitting in *his* office (also before coffee, of course) just panting in his eagerness to give the company's local dealer an order for an entire fleet of trucks. And the models he was interested in were very near the top of the line. This could be a *really* big sale.

Visions of a large and highly profitable sale directly attributable to advertising danced through the author's head. Nothing would do except to dictate a special letter—and an extremely cordial one at that—to the inquirer, send it and appropriate sales literature by airmail, with blind carbon copies to the district manager and the local dealer to whom the inquirer was referred.

Then all that remained to be done was sit back, take care of routine and anxiously await the long distance call—or an airmail letter at the very least—from the happy dealer thanking the good old advertising department for the lucrative lead.

But nothing happened, nothing at all.

Finally, consumed with curiosity, a memo went out to the district manager. It should have evoked an immediate response, since it was a little bit plaintive. No reply, so the only possibility to be considered was that the district manager was making a lengthy swing around his territory and wasn't up to date on happenings in this particular city.

Nothing from the dealer either, so, consumed by curiosity, a call was made to the dealer. He laughingly thanked advertising for helping him, then explained the inquiries had all come from a 12-year-old whose father was a mechanic at a competitive dealership down the road a mile or so. Out of curiosity, the dealer traced down the whys and wherefores and found the mechanic was in the habit of taking home back issues of trucking publications when the office staff finished with them. His young son was enamored with trucks and soon found out that mailing bingo cards with his home address and a fictitious firm name swamped him with pretty literature. When his father found out that sales reps were wasting their time, he put a stop to it.

This isn't to denigrate inquiries. Inquiries are a valuable source of high quality sales leads. Handling inquiries is a subject all in itself and will be discussed in a forthcoming chapter.

Catalog Offer Ads

The catalog offer ad is essentially an inquiry ad. Inquiries are just as welcome and they're followed up by the advertiser's sales force just as assiduously as if the ad were designed specifically to elicit a response.

Important difference, though, between the two types is that the advertiser who uses the catalog offer is primarily interested in having information about his product in the hands of his prospects. He wants them to be aware of his product so that when they decide to buy—presumably at some time in the future—they will refer to it.

As a rule, catalogs that are offered in ads are "complete line" catalogs. They're packed with such a wealth of information, data, and specifications on such a wide variety of models that it would be a physical impossibility to mention even a fraction of them in an ad — perhaps even in an entire year's campaign. Back tables and shelves behind the purchasing agents' desks are crammed with thick, bulky highly informative catalogs to which they refer constantly in the course of a day's work. Merely having the catalogs available is analogous to having merchandise on display in a department store.

Objective of the ad is to announce availability of the catalog, create additional awareness of the company, and to make certain that a group of buying influences—determine by the media selected—*wants* the catalog and *requests* it.

Then, when the field sales force follows up and a sale doesn't result immediately, nobody's surprised or disappointed. But the advertisement has nonetheless achieved its objective because the catalog is where the advertiser wants it to be. And chances are good it will stay right there until it is superceded by a new issue of the catalog, and that it will be "working" all the while.

Many advertisers customarily offer a less elaborate piece of literature to solicit inquiries in different types of ads. Others offer catalogs—expensive to produce, handle, and mail—on a highly selective basis on the theory that the product must have exposure and this is one way of getting it. Seldom does it pay to run an ad offering a piece of literature on a single new product; just as many inquiries—if not more—will result from using publicity to do this job. Other methods of geting additional mileage from literature will be gone into in the chapter on that subject.

Newsletter Ads

Newsletter ads average around 25 percent higher readership than ads that are more ad-like.

Near relatives of newsletter ads—advertisements which closely resemble editorial matter in publications in which they appear—can be counted on to garner higher readership, also. In the business press this edge in readership is generally considered to be around 5 percent, although some studies have indicated it to be considerably higher; in mass consumer media it has been found that editorial-type advertisements receive as much as 50 percent more readership than obvious paid ads.

This is not to infer there's a dislike for, or rejection of, advertising by readers of business publications. On the contrary, good business paper advertising is read thoroughly, and even poor advertising is read. It's just that newsletter ads are eye catchers. They stop the reader right in his or her tracks with a strong implied promise that if he or she will but take the time to read the ad he or she will receive an abundance of interesting and helpful information. Actually, the reader is more inclined to read than he is to pass by. Newsletter ads, by their very nature, have a strong sense of immediacy, of containing something timely and fresh. They have the ability to involve the reader very rapidly.

Newsletter ads excel in being readily adaptable to either corporate or product advertising, and to fit into almost any given situation. All that's required is subject matter that's honestly interesting to those to whom you want to talk. And this is important: *The subject matter must be of genuine interest to those to whom you want to talk.*

Fill a newsletter ad with glowing accounts of how ground was broken for your new plant, internal promotions, how great business is, how much sales are up over the comparable period last year, installation of a gigantic new gizmo machine in Plant No. 1, and so on and on, and you'll have a newsletter ad that will lull even a seasoned insomniac to sleep, but fast.

On the other hand, make it sprightly and brisk and write with the reader in mind and your newsletter ad will perform a service *for the reader* as well as for the advertiser. The reader recognizes this, which is why he or she is willing to invest time reading what you have to say. He or she believes he or she will receive needed information from the ad or he or she wouldn't be "in" it.

One thing, though: Be sure to identify your advertisement as an advertisement, or the Federal Government's watchdogs will be baying at your heels. It's considered by the bureacratic types to be a "deceptive practice" not to identify ads as ads, if there's any possible doubt about it.

How to Do It Ads

Few things in advertising arouse as intense interest—and do it as quickly—as telling the reader you're going to tell him or her how to do something.

This applies equally to the reader as a member of the business community and as an individual human being. "How to" are magic words. They're semaphoric. Run them up in display type and it's like running up a brightly colored signal flag. They inform the reader in no uncertain terms that this advertisement is going to show him or her a new way of doing something, and chances are it's a lot better than the way it's been done it all along. The automatic reaction is to assume you'll tell him or her a better way to do it so he or she will produce more, save more, or reap some other desirable benefit. Otherwise, why spend money on it?

By this time the reader's curiosity is aroused and he or she mentally prepared to accept as absolute fact the product story that follows. At the very least, the reader will listen to it with an open mind.

The how-to-do-it approach is particularly effective with engineers and technical people, who are constantly searching for ways to improve the product or production process. After all, their primary job responsibility is to find better ways to accomplish specific tasks. When you show them you can help them, you're almost home free.

The how-to-do-it ad is very similar to the problem-solution ad; however, the problem-solution approach is generally broader. How-to ads zero right in on a narrow, well-defined target. They're limited, as a rule, to describing how use of the product for a specific purpose will achieve a desired result.

Waldes Kohinoor, Inc.'s excellent two-color ad, illustrated nearby, is a true how-to-do-it ad, even though the "how to" words are not used as such; the headline instead starts out "how *do*."

This is an ad that has just about everything going for it. The technical people are shown cut-away drawings, closeups showing how the retaining rings are installed eliminate any question in that area. And the copy is nutsy-and-boltsy enough to endear it to even the most literal engineer who questions everything he or she encounters in life. Copy reads, in part:

How do you lock shaft components under spring pressure?

TRUARC PRONG-LOCK retaining rings simplify design, eliminate costly parts and machining, speed assembly!

(Illustrations)

Locks positively on shaft, serves as spring and shoulder.

The Truarc Series 5139 Prong-Lock is a radially-assembled retaining ring which serves as both a spring and a positive-locking fastener. It derives its name from two prongs on the inner circumference of the open end. Before the ring can be installed, it must be flattened to permit the prongs to enter a groove on the shaft. When the prongs clear the groove, the ring springs back to its bowed form and the prongs lock around the shaft. The ring must be flattened again before it can be removed.

The Series 5139 can be used to replace nuts and lock washers, cotter pins, rivets, screws, and other fasteners. It

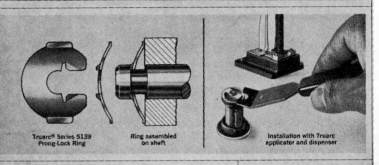

eliminates springs and bowed washers and can be installed on grooved shafts which do not require costly drilling or threading. The ring has high thrust-load capacity and, because of its positive-locking qualities, can be utilized as a shoulder against rotating parts. The bowed design provides resilient end-play take-up and compensates for tolerances in the assembly.

The Series 5139 is available in nine sizes for shafts .090" to .441" dia. It can be installed and removed quickly with the Truarc applicator shown above or with a screw driver. The dispenser illustrated—used with stacked rings—is designed for high-speed assembly.

Also shown are two typical uses for Waldes Kohinoor's retaining rings, and a wrap-up offers a free copy of a new 128-page *Truarc Technical Manual.* The advertiser does what many more industrial advertisers should do, but don't—it calls attention to the company's Yellow Pages listings, and to the fact that the complete catalog is in *Thomas Micro-Catalogs.* This is a separate subject, and will be covered in the chapter on media.

Trade Ads

Major objective of so-called trade ads is to gain greater distribution of the product—more outlets, greater acceptance on the part of those who resell the product.

This is usually a dog-eat-dog field. Most advertising designed to increase distribution is pretty strident and hard-sell copy Restraint is just about an unknown word, for everybody strives to shout a little louder than the next advertiser.

An unusually well-conceived campaign, and one that has been outstandingly effective in the terms all advertisers want—increased sales—was developed by Marsteller Inc. for the Residential Lighting Division, Thomas Industries, Inc.

This company sells home lighting fixtures. Largest and most lucrative segment of the market for its Moe Light fixtures are new homes. At one time the bulk of the company's sales consisted of low-priced fixtures that were easily installed. Moe Light had widespread distribution and enjoyed excellent acceptance with electrical contractors; the contractors at that time usually selected the brand of light they wanted to install and home builders were content to accept that fact.

Unit sale—fixtures per house—was low, but the company had an acceptable portion of the market, and it was a rising market. Home building was booming and every year it went up, Moe's sales rose.

Then, later on, tastes changed. Home buyers were no longer content to accept nondescript styling. What's more, this change in taste coincided with a sharp drop in new home starts and the market for Moe fixtures shrunk. Moe Light couldn't anticipate a rising sales volume merely because the total of new houses kept rising.

At this time style came to the forefront, with price and ease of installation relegated to the sidelines. Also at this time the home builder decided he'd better start making buying decisions to make it easier to sell his customers.

Moe Light's sales edged up, but were well off the boom rate management had become fond of. As far as share of market was concerned, Moe held its own; but that was little consolation in a declining market.

Agency Gets the Problem

The problem was put to the Marsteller Inc., agency: What could be done to reverse the trend toward a lower dollar volume, and to break Moe Light away from sales fluctuations caused by the size of the total market? After all, a company with plenty of marketing savvy should be able to *increase* its sales in a declining market, rather than sit glumly around resigned to taking it on the chin with a vague hope that things would get better.

Marginal companies should take the brunt of an industry slump, leaving the leader, or leaders, relatively unhurt—or in even better position than before the downturn.

First thing Marsteller recommended was a research project to find out exactly what attitude builders in general had toward Moe Light. This was vitally necessary if meaningful marketing objectives were to be established and a communications program developed to achieve them. If the foundation isn't right, there's little likelihood anything built upon it will be, either.

The study was made and Moe Light was rated a poor second in three important areas: (1) product quality, (2) product development, and (3) product style. Both client and agency evaluated the results of the study objectively and both agreed that it was undoubtedly correct. Moe Light *did* lag.

Then, working together, Moe Light and Marsteller set four marketing objectives:

1. To improve styling and increase the price range.
2. To develop a special sales group to handle sales to the residential lighting market.
3. To do everything possible to gain the favor of the home builder.
4. To get increased distribution in lighting fixture showrooms.

Improving the styling of the entire product line was a time-consuming job, and a great deal of money was poured into the project. The line was also broadened to enable Moe Light to compete in areas where the company had previously not been represented. Poor designs were discarded; poor sellers were scrapped.

Ready for Action

With the product restyled, with fixtures for every price range, and with an eager, beefed-up sales force, the company was ready to exploit all of its efforts. At this time firm communications objectives were developed. They were simple, but were what the company needed. Objectives were:

1. To build greater awareness of Moe Light as a brand.
2. To create an image of Moe Light as the industry style leader in the residential field within 36 months.
3. To give sales reps the backing they needed to enable them to contact builders with an effective presentation.

To help turn the tide that first crucial year, Moe Light's space advertising campaign had as a theme "two ways to win a woman," naturally using the redesigned and greater choice of fixtures to show the builder he'd gain a competitive advantage with Moe Light. Media chosen were three magazines for builders, all monthly publications. One book had 10 spreads; the others ran the same spreads on an every-other-month basis.

Moe Light dominated the market, as far as advertising was concerned, with those 44 pages in four-color. One of the four-color spreads from that first year's campaign is illustrated nearby.

Photography is superb, the mood is one of grace and charm, and the tone of the copy is just right. It reads:

TWO WAYS TO WIN A WOMAN: VINTAGE RIGHT . . .
OR MOE LIGHT

Moe Light colonial lanterns give her something special to remember about your houses. For more ideas on how to win a woman with lighting, write to Moe Light Division . . .

Where men clamber around in an attic nodding sagely as they pound roof joists with their clenched fists, women notice and remember little touches that contribute so much to a gracious appearance. Moe Light is on firm ground with this appeal.

At the end of a year this campaign had helped Moe Light, but not enough. Attitude of builders, as determined by another study, still showed Moe in second place in two of the three areas, but by not nearly as much. And in one important area—new product development—Moe was tied with its major competitor due primarily to stressing new fixtures in the advertising campaign. Solid progress had been made.

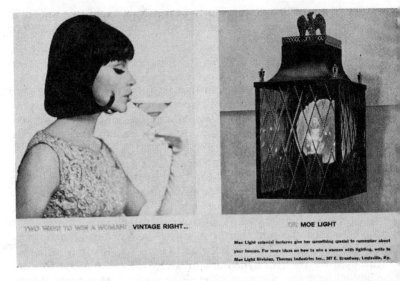

TWO WAYS TO WIN A WOMAN! **VINTAGE RIGHT...** **OR MOE LIGHT**

Moe Light colonial lanterns give her something special to remember about your houses. For more ideas on how to win a woman with lighting, write to Moe Light Division, Thomas Industries Inc., 207 E. Broadway, Louisville, Ky.

Again the product line was overhauled, revamped, and upgraded. Moe retained the same communications objectives for the next year, and the ads preserved continuity by retaining the same basic format. This year, however, the theme changed slightly and famous women in history were used. the excellent photography and quality four-color reproduction continued to be used. One of the ads in that campaign, featuring Queen Isabella, reads:

If Queen Isabella were here today . . .
She'd want Moe Light in her library

A Moe Light pulldown adds a touch of royalty to dining rooms and living rooms too . . . gives modern-day queens something special to remember about your homes. For more ways to add extra appeal with lighting, write to Moe Light . . .

A followup survey was taken after this campaign had been running for a year; Moe Light was solidly established in builders' minds as the leader in product quality, product development, and in product style!

A four-color, spread ad from the current campaign—which still retains the same successful format—also is shown.

Sell the fashionable homemaker
with fashionable Moe Light

She's as style-conscious of decor as she is of clothing. She'll decide whether to take a second look at your model home. So

If Queen Isabella were here today...

She'd want Moe Light in her library

A Moe Light pulldown adds a touch of royalty to dining rooms and living rooms too . . . gives modern day queens something special to remember about your homes. For more ways to add extra appeal with lighting, write to Moe Light, Thomas Industries Inc., 907 E. Broadway, Louisville, Ky.

Sell the fashionable homemaker

with fashionable Moe Light

give her something special to remember: a Moe Light chain-hung styling with brilliant suede blue shade and black-silver finish.

For more ideas on how to sell the fashionable homemaker, write to Residential Lighting Division . . .

485

This is a near-classic example of what can be accomplished with carefully planned market research to establish very specific communications objectives. They, in turn, were the groundwork for a spectacularly effective advertising campaign that exerted a tremendous effect on sales and profits.

There was no head-in-the-sand groping or hoping here. Moe Light and its agency faced up to facts—which many advertisers steadfastly refuse to do—then determined exactly what was needed to reverse a trend and put the advertiser out in front in its market. This they proceeded to do with never a misstep.

Incidentally, here again is proof that a market can be "bought" with advertising, and at not very great expense. Once you have the "trade" solidly sold, increased distribution automatically follows and sales don't merely go up—they zoom!

Institutional Ads

Institutional ads that are run in the trade press are *not* corporate advertisements. Instead, they are a weak and wishy-washy form of industrial advertising.

Copy appeal in the typical institutional ad is basically wrong. The premise on which it is based is faulty. The thinking that went into the ad probably was fuzzy. Copy, which should be based on telling the reader reasons why he or she should buy the product—in terms of features translated into user benefits—goes off onto a tangent. It's vague and nonspecific, and usually of mighty little interest to the reader because there's nothing in it for him or her.

The institutional approach isn't to be damned in total, however. There may very well be perfectly valid reasons for using it. For example, it's quite conceivable that if a company dominates an industry its primary communications objective may be to keep reminding readers of this pleasant little fact.

Does the Customer Care?

If that's the case, the inference may be drawn that the company achieved this position of dominance for a good reason—product superiority. After all, no company becomes a leader and stays in the number one spot unless it has something nobody else has.

A danger, though, is that ads may harp continuously on product attributes that are meaningless to the customer. They may not really say anything to him. Quality, dependability, productivity, performance, purity, consistency, uniformity, full strength, strict quality control, and other equally nebulous words appear in ads of this type—and they've been so overworked they were ready for retirement on a pension a half-century ago.

Another danger is that it's so infernally easy to fall into the trap of bragging and boasting. Armour Abrasives Company in a recent ad illustrated a roll of belts of abrasive paper in a bank vault; the headline proclaimed: *On the surface, all abrasives look alike. But Armour gives you what your customer demands . . . consistent finish. It cost us $3,000,000.*

Customers don't care about this.

Moreover, if you take the institutional approach there's the ever-present temptation to hold yourself up as the knight in shining armor, a sort of metal-clad Jack Armstrong whose motives are unsullied. A dirty word like profit would never pass his lips.

And even worse, you could be a (ugh) bore. Being cruel to one's aged mother, beating one's wife, starving one's children—even kicking one's dog—could, if the perpetrator were suitably and sincerely sorry, be forgiven. But in advertising the unforgivable sin is to be a bore. It can't be swept under the rug, ignored, simply not discussed, or forgiven. Ever.

One sure way to bore the reader so that he or she shudders and turns the page for succor is to run an ad with a picture of Our Factory—unless it's for sale, of course. This applies equally whether it's a new factory, or an old one. Worse yet is to show an addition to Our Factory. Our Factory is of interest only to the powers that be who own the place. Period.

The reader doesn't really care one whit if the product is produced in a pup tent, a cave once inhabited by prehistoric man, or in the lair of a purple people-eater. This simply does not concern him or her.

Yet another way that's guaranteed to cause the reader to flee in panic is to run a picture of Our Founder in an ad. Now, there's surely a place for such a portrait. Generally this gentleman was a hard-bitten, rugged individualist of the old school who forged ahead despite some pretty trying times. He carved out a sizable empire under adverse circumstances when the dollar amounted to something—before the advent of mini-money that's not backed by anything other than a politician's promise. You know what *that's* worth. Give Our Founder credit. He didn't turn pleadingly to Washington (D.C., not George), hand out, begging for a handout. Back in the days when many of today's well-known businesses were struggling little companies whose owners wondered if they'd be able to meet the week's payroll, the man who founded one believed in self-reliance; he had no thought of ap-

487

propriating the next generation's income which had been confiscated from the present generation to be squandered by an all-powerful bureaucracy—even if it had existed then.

Place for such portraits is in the company conference room, the president's office, or even in the reception area. There it's appropriate and speaks well for the stability of the company and its ability to change with the times. It provides recognition for an unusually dynamic person.

Comic Strip or Cartoon Ads

Favorite reading fare of the *majority* of the people in this country is the ubiquitous comic strip.

Whether he's a fan of 'Lil Abner, Dick Tracy, or Terry, the average American regularly reads the comics with mingled amusement and affection. Most people have a favorite character whose activities they follow with great interest.

Life, Time, Fortune, and any number of other literate magazines edited for literate people have run lengthy feature articles on comic strips and comic strip characters. *Life* had a multipage article on good old Charlie Brown, Snoopy, Lucy, Linus, and their cohorts in *Peanuts* and, incidentally, on the philosophy of Charles M. Schulz, creator of these beloved, vividly real little characters.

Indeed, Charlie Brown graced the cover of *Life*—in color. And Charlie and his beagle, Snoopy, who regularly battles the bloody Red Baron in a flimsy Sopwith Camel, and who has the most vivid imagination in the entire animal world, are nationwide favorites of all ages. They appear on sweat-shirts worn by teenagers, college students, and authors.

In a previous article, *Life* came to the conclusion that the comic strip constitutes the most significant body of literature that's read by an overwhelming majority of the American people. Kids and blue-collar workers and advertising professionals and other executives—even Presidents—read the comics.

On the surface, it would seem that an advertisement that adopted the format of the comic strip would have a decided advantage over others when it comes to securing readership. You can't argue with acceptance. Look how popular sex is.

This is quite true in consumer advertising when the ad appears in broad media reaching great masses of people. Here the comic strip format comes into its own. It's known and accepted by countless millions in Sunday supplements and in the comic sections of the newspapers.

Effectiveness of the comic strip format in industrial advertising depends to a large extent on the company running the ad, the product advertised, and the universe.

United States Steel's fine comic strip, illustrated nearby, is from a highly successful campaign. The one-page ad was in two-color, with the second color (red) reserved only for the advertiser's USS logo and the product, Alloy Steel Bars.

This ad was written with a deft touch and a sure hand. There's just a hint of a gentle spoof, of a good-natured bit of leg pulling, yet the copy in each of the comic strip boxes is down to earth and presents solid user-benefit information about the product. It reads:

> *Emily . . .*
> *take a letter.*
> *Yes, Daddy.*
> *Dear U.S. Steel . . . your technical*
> *service representative called as*
> *promised, and looked into the*
> *alloy bar grades we were using.*
> *Very pleasant, capable fellow.*
>
> *He proposed a Carilloy FC grade*
> *that will probably save us $16,000*
> *a year on sprocket and gear*
> *machining.*
>
> *And he proposed a way that will*
> *enable us to standardize on*
> *just two alloy bar grades for our*
> *entire pinion operation.*
>
> *Speaking of proposals,*
> *I wonder if he would be*
> *interested in marrying*
> *my daughter . . .*

Then, in the lower right-hand box, United States Steel really packs in product information. A very strong bid for action is made by assuring the reader a U.S. Steel technical representative is as close as a phone—and that he or she is a trained problem-solver who's ready, willing, and able to put specialized knowledge to work for the reader. This copy block reads:

> *Call a U.S. Steel technical service representative about your*
> *use of standard and specialty alloy bar steels. He may be able*
> *to save you money: for example, with a Carilloy FC grade for*
> *heavily stressed machine parts. USS Carilloy FC Bars give up*

A comic strip ad for the United States Steel Corporation not only tells an amusing, warmly whimsical story, but also manages to pack a lot of good product information about alloy steel bars into the space.

490

to three times the tool life and 50% better machinability than standard steels with comparable hardness. Whatever your needs, you'll find that U.S. Steel can furnish a complete range of alloy steel bars—AISI and SAE standard grades as well as nonstandard grades and other steels with special properties; such as USS "T-1" Steels, maraging steels, 9% nickel and other quenched and tempered steels. U.S. Steel's modern heat-treating facilities for rounds and flats closely control heating and quenching to insure proper structure, hardness, and related properties required by subsequent machining, forming, or service applications. USS Alloy Bars can also be furnished ultra-clean through both the open hearth and the electric furnace VCD processes.

Get all the advantages: quality alloy steel bars; competent metallurgical and technical service; the industry's most extensive research and development program; and conveniently located service and production facilities . . .

USS ran this ad in *Iron Age, Production, Materials in Design Engineering, Purchasing*, and in *Machine Design*.

Well read, believable and informative, this campaign is doing a great job for United States Steel. It's possible that a comic strip ad directed solely to engineers and egg-head scientists might lay an egg, but a good comic strip campaign directed at the right segment of management in industry can do an effective job.

Chapter 10

THE ADVERTISING MESSAGE

John S. Wright*
James R. Bostic**

AT a time when increased productivity is so vital to American business, companies should carefully review their existing processes for advertising message development. More effective message formulation can help achieve greater customer and market leverage which will, in turn, substantially improve the company's measured return on its advertising investment. The Association of National Advertisers (ANA) holds that the value of an excellent advertising message be 10 times (or more) greater than a mediocre message. This is true whether the measuring stick is in terms of consumer attitudes, preference for the product, or final sales results. In general, every advertiser pays the same amount for similar time or space in advertising media, thus the effectiveness of the message can itself be an important source of competitive advantage.

Yet no clear-cut management science of advertising message development exists in the business world today. Decisions concerning the advertising message are often made in a subjective or arbitrary fashion with little more than personal feelings and opinions as guides. Advertising is one of the last bastions of the truly intuitive manager in many companies. Few areas of marketing have spawned so many self-appointed experts, and advertising message development is often characterized by considerable lost effort and wasted dollars. However, better methods, as described below, are being developed and implemented, so that advertising message creation becomes creative problem-solving just as amenable to systematic approaches as other problems. Once the full import of the advertising decision is realized and some of its mystique is brushed aside, message development should become more businesslike.

---

*Professor of Marketing, Georgia State University

**President, IVECO Trucks of North America, Inc.

Advertising's Role in the Marketing Mix

Understanding how the advertising message works to influence consumer perceptions and preference—and thus to effect increased market leverage—depends first upon an appreciation of the role of advertising in the marketing mix. The marketing mix can be defined as that combination of active ingredients—including *product* (design, quality and performance), *price; positioning; promotion* plus *distribution* processes and channels—which affect the company's pace of doing business, as reflected in its rate of new customer acquisition, old customer retention, market penetration growth, etc. Thus, marketing encompasses all those activities involved in ascertaining and analyzing customer needs and wants and then moving products from the factory to the marketplace. This process is shown in the accompanying diagram.

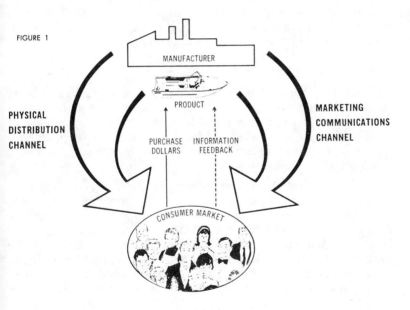

FIGURE 1

The flow of product from the manufacturer to the customer, along with accompanying forecast, order, production and shipping documentation, pricing data and terms, as well as legal title to the product, moves through the physical distribution channel, while the

493

flow of consumer information about the product, including advertising, publicity, engineering releases, merchandising materials plus sales aids and training is carried by the marketing communications channel. (See Figure 1.) Two separate items flow back from the customer to the manufacturer. First is the incoming flow of dollars to pay for the products purchased and provide profit for the manufacturer; the second is information feedback about product acceptance and use, sales volumes and share results, and changes in market and consumer reasons for buying or not buying.

Advertising's place is clearly within the marketing communications channel. Its basic task is to convey information to the consumer about the product in order to convince him or her to buy or to choose it instead of a competitive product. The advertising message must bring company strengths and product attributes into sharp focus for the prospective buyer, and then dramatize specific benefits to be realized through product ownership and use. Advertising must inform, persuade and remind the customer about specific product attributes in a way that is attention-getting, interesting and memorable. The advertisement works as a carrier of the selling message without being so intrusive as to overshadow the basic product-selling story itself.

The Importance of Advertising Planning

Advertising without planning is like running a giant manure spreader; the advertising agency throws ideas out the back faster than the client can shovel money in the front. Advertising for the sake of advertising is wasteful, whereas advertising that meets specific objectives is an investment in future sales. Like any investment, it will have a yield which can be measured.

Specific Objectives. A statement of specific advertising goals or objectives is a fundamental part of any sound advertising investment plan. These objectives provide focus and direction for advertising message development, insuring that (1) the message is on target for the intended market segment, (2) promises made are consistent with the product's capability to deliver, and (3) the reasons given for buying fit the needs and motives of potential customers. Advertising objectives also provide a ready means of evaluating the effectiveness of the advertising investment.

Advertiser-Agency Collaboration

It is axiomatic that effective advertiser-agency relationships produce effective advertising; yet the task of structuring and maintaining a productive decision/work environment in which needed synergy can take place is often difficult. Advertising which produces market results is most often the result of client/agency *interaction*. Message development should be viewed as a collaborative process in which both partners have important contributions to make. In such a relationship, the advertiser's responsibility is to provide all relevant facts and strategic direction, including specific definition of products, markets and the competition, consumer demographic and psychographic data, buyer behavior research and purchase motive analysis, as well as an explicit marketing and communications strategy statement. Correspondingly, the agency is responsible for message concept and execution, including development and recommendations of the specific vehicles, format, language and visual ideas which best fit the target reader or viewer and best fulfill the chosen strategies.

Proper care and feeding of the client/agency work relationship to assure open communication and collaboration pay dividends in the form of more effective advertising.

Product Position

The linchpin between client-supplied facts and direction and the agency's creative concept and executions is the product position, developed jointly by advertiser and agency. Product position is defined as "the basic thought or idea which advertising must communicate to target prospects in order to:

- set the product apart from alternatives being considered, and;
- provide a purchase rationale which relates product advantages and benefits to specific consumer buying motives."

Well-conceived positioning provides a viewpoint for the advertising message which self-selects the most likely prospects, then convinces them that this product provides a better fit to their needs than competitors can.

Creative Blueprint

As a final step before beginning to prepare the advertising message, a creative blueprint is developed. This document draws upon the information and direction provided in the written advertising plan, as well as the shared experience of both client and agency, in order to summarize to whom the advertising message should be directed, what the characteristic product uses and buying motives of this consumer group are and what type of information is most relevant to their buying decision. Information on the advertising tone is also included. This statement is sometimes called the "copy platform."

It is highly important that agreement on the basic elements of the advertising plan exists between advertiser and advertising agency, for the advertising plan charts the course of the creative team.

The Copywriter's Contribution

Advertising messages are developed through the joint efforts of a copywriter and an art director. The copywriter frames the message and develops the best way to say it. He or she takes information about the product and finds a way to enhance the consumer's interest. He or she provides the consumer with a specific purchase rationale. Although there are as many ways to write successful advertising copy as there are advertising copywriters, a few fundamental principles apply to advertising message development:

Know the product, its market, users and competition. The copywriter should become immersed in information about the product and its users. Only when he or she fully understands buyers and their motives, and can put himself or herself in their place, will the copywriter be ready to write an informative, persuasive advertising message.

Understand the advertising objectives and the advertising plan. Unless the copywriter knows where he or she is going and the route to take, he may never reach the goal—an effective advertisement. Advertising objectives and strategy, specific reasons for buying, the product positioning statement and the creative blueprint are the road maps. If he or she is in agreement with all of these guidelines, it is even better; but understanding them is fundamental to the development of a sound advertising message.

Start with the advertising concept. Every copywriter should tackle each advertisement with the approach used by researchers, scientists and inventors, leaving wordsmithing for later. The approach includes these steps:

Study the problem carefully from all angles.

Test alternative hypotheses; determine what is right and wrong with each approach.

Develop a "best" creative solution by deciding which alternative seems to be "on target" with no legal, technical or policy problems; select the one bearing the potential to become great advertising.

Write in the idiom of the customer. Use language that the prospective buyer understands and feels comfortable with; tell what is needed to know if he or she is to decide to buy your product; talk in terms of needs and motives.

Avoid the gimmickry and faddism of creative cultists. Tricks and sensationalism destroy the credibility of advertising messages. Customers look for honest product stories. Being honest does not necessarily mean being dull; the copywriter must find—or create— interest in the product and feature this interest in the advertisement.

Remember that the copywriter's contribution in large part depends upon the objectives set for the campaign and the informational inputs provided. The quantity and quality of alternative creative solutions that are able to be generated are a key factor in eventual success. Finally, judgment in selecting the "best" solution is also critical.

The Art Director's Contribution

The art director, the other half of the agency's creative team, provides visualization, continuity and graphic substance to the advertisement. Specifically, his or her function is to use such visual elements as color, form, texture, contrast, motion, graphics in such media as film, photographs, artwork and videotape to provide information on how the product looks, how it performs, what kind of people use it and the kind of situations where the product is most often found. Thus, visualization helps position the product.

Getting the attention of readers and viewers is also the art director's job. Visual elements are employed to help pull the consumer into the message and to interest him or her in the product.

A few basic principles apply to the art director's task of executing the visual portion of advertisements:

Understand the advertising objectives and the advertising plan. These basic documents contain valuable information about what specific settings, product use situations, and visual elements should have the most impact on readers and viewers.

Know the visual idiom and context of the consumer. Successful art directors understand how the potential buyer perceives himself or herself in a product-use situation; art directors also know how the consumer wants others to see him as he uses the product. Visual mistakes, caused by art directors who do not fully understand how the consumer views the advertised product, are "tuned out" by intended recipients of advertising messages.

Work with the copy content. The art director builds upon the framework established by the copywriter. Copy springs from the product itself and from the advertising plan, and the visualization comes from what is said about the product in the copy. It is essential that visual elements enhance, amplify and build upon the basic copy platform. For that reason, the copywriter and art director are in close communication in the concept stage of message development.

Eight Rules for Getting Better Advertising

Effective advertising messages contribute to the success and profitability of most business firms. Businessmen, therefore, desire to know as much as possible about how better advertising can be developed. Following these eight guidelines will accomplish a great deal:

1. State your advertising goals. Unless an advertising message is directed toward the accomplishment of specific company and product advertising goals, it must stand or fall only as a work of art, not as a business investment.

2. Gather the facts. The advertising message should be planned far in advance of the time that the first piece of paper is rolled into the typewriter. The starting point is gathering all pertinent facts and information about the product, consumer, competition and sales trends. At this stage market problems and opportunities are identified; key factors bearing on the product selling situation are examined. No matter how they are listed, the facts fall logically as follows:

    a. *operating climate*—the prevailing business conditions surrounding the product selling situation

    b. *problems* pertaining to the product's current position in the marketplace

    c. *product strengths and opportunities* which can be capitalized on in the advertising. This element is called the "situation analysis."

3. Position the product. Because this extension of the situation analysis is so vital, it is given as a separate and distinct step. The situation analysis leads directly to the question: "In the whole marketing arena, what is the best place for our product?" In turn, positioning is answering the question: "What kind of products and services do we offer, and to what kind of people?"

Product positioning is important, because of today's marketplace few products are for everybody. The trend is toward segmentation with specific products for portions of the market. By positioning a product against a selected body of potential users, it is easier to convince them that the product is ideally suited for their needs, providing a better solution to their problems than the offerings of a competitor. It will be easier to design more direct advertising messages which communicate with the selected market segment.

4. Develop a creative blueprint. Answers to six questions provide a blueprint for the creative effort:

    a. What business goals do we seek to accomplish?

    b. What kind of persons do we now sell to?
       What kind of persons should we sell to?

    c. How does that person now think, feel and believe about our product, our company and our competition?

    d. What do we want that person to feel, think and do?

e. What key thought can we put into that person's mind to make him or her think, feel and believe or do that?

f. What tone of voice will get that person to hear and believe us?

5. Obtain agreement on advertising concepts. Be certain that the advertising decision maker concurs in the choice of the "best" creative solution from those developed, screened and analyzed by the creative team. He or she should be brought into the picture early in the game.

6. Set out to create advertising that informs, persuades and reminds in a way that is attention-getting, interesting and memorable. Great advertising messages spring from an appetite for greatness. Set out to get the very best from the creative team. Don't settle for anything less than their very best effort.

7. Check the advertising message. Make certain the message meets the AIDA test. Good advertisements create Attention, Interest, Desire and Action. Each advertisement should be checked to see that these elements are present. This point is demonstrated in the accompanying illustration. (Figure 2.)

8. Test the message. Always test the finished message (art and copy) with a sample of the audience for whom it is intended to be sure that it is "on strategy," clearly communicates the product position, and provokes the intended reader or viewer response.

How Planned, Goal-Oriented Advertising Works

An excellent illustration of carefully planned, goal-oriented advertising is that appearing in mass consumer media under the sponsorship of the Starcraft Company.

The company is a leading manufacturer of leisure and recreation products. In two of its product areas, aluminum boats and camping trailers, Starcraft is the first-ranking brand. Starcraft has been quick to recognize that future product sales in the rapidly expanding industry will be closely linked to precise consumer marketing analysis, establishment of a meaningful brand identity and specific product positions. Careful advertising planning and coordination are also key elements in the success pattern of the firm.

Definition and development in advertising of a summary statement or "triggering device" is vital to the program. Such a statement reminds consumers of the company's leadership in: (1) design ingenuity, (2) human engineering, (3) finest quality materials, (4) craftsmanship in construction, (5) superior product performance, (6) service and warranty assurance and (7) support by Starcraft's well-earned reputation.

499

The term "Starcraftsmanship" has been coined to accomplish this goal, since it literally links the name Starcraft with the word craftsmanship and tends to pre-empt the craftsmanship claim as an exclusive for Starcraft.

As stated in the company's written communication plan, the advertising must:

". . . identify Starcraftsmanship both as the company's philosophy of doing business and as a term associated with all Starcraft products."

" . . . define Starcraftsmanship to encompass the catalog of values, including superiority in design, engineering, materials, construction, performance and service."

" . . . provide concrete examples of what Starcraftsmanship means to the buyer, in terms of specific consumer benefits."

" . . . meld the Starcraftsmanship concept with the particular product the reader or viewer is interested in to create a strong and exclusive reason to buy a Starcraft-branded product."

Exactly how the advertising fulfills these requirements is shown in the accompanying aluminum boat advertisement.

1. The *headline* contains three specific consumer benefits which help to define and substantiate Starcraftsmanship—big family cruisers, "trailerability" (unique in big family cruisers) and a 15-year warranty (a Starcraft exclusive).

2. The *body copy* continues to define Starcraftsmanship in terms of specific consumer benefits, which result directly from the company's superiority in design, engineering, materials and construction.

3. The *illustrations* serve a number of related purposes: to attract the reader's attention and help him to relate to the romance of the end-use activity, to supplement copy development and provide further documentation of the Starcraftsmanship story (performance plus roominess and comfort), and finally, to link the Starcraftsmanship story to *all* company products.

4. The *closing statement* sums up the Starcraftsmanship process as a concrete reason to buy a specific Starcraft-brand product, then asks the reader to take action, in this case, writing for a boat catalog and the name of his nearest Starcraft dealer.

Implications

The advertising message is the spearhead of the total marketing effort. Its job is to reach consumers with pertinent facts and information about the product and to help convince them to buy. Smart advertisers think of advertising as an investment in future sales and use effective advertising messages to improve the yield on their investment.

A planned, systematic approach to message development can: (1) yield high levels of consumer awareness and purchase consideration; (2) work in combination with other ingredients in the marketing mix

Giving you a big family cruiser that's trailerable <u>and</u> warranted for 15 years.

That's Starcraftsmanship.

The Starcraft 21' Islander I/O above — roomy enough for 10 people and with a cabin complete with upholstered cushions and backrests — was towed to the launching ramp. At highway speed. On a conventional boat trailer. Behind a car no different from your own. **That's Starcraftsmanship.**

Starcraft makes it possible because every Starcraft aluminum boat is made of special 5052 Marine Aluminum alloy. That means it's really light weight, so besides easy trailering an aluminum Starcraft performs with more speed, better gas mileage and maneuverability than a comparable boat made of anything else. And it'll take the saltiest, most polluted water with only a yearly waxing to keep it looking new. **That's Starcraftsmanship.**

Starcrafts do so many things well because we build them that way. They have the industry's first one-piece bottom and a few other secrets we picked up from the aerospace industry. Like a hull unitized to exterior keels and interior "Z" ribs and stringers with solid aluminum rivets. The few hull seams that are necessary are triple sealed. It's so well built that we warrant it for 15

years against metal fatigue, cracks and popped rivets (under normal recommended use) and for 24 months against defects in workmanship and materials. **That's Starcraftsmanship.**

Starcraft doesn't forget that the interior of a boat has to be lived in, not just look good. So the interior is covered with a special vinyl that resists

Pick any Starcraft and leave the rest of the world behind.

everything from ultraviolet rays to chocolate ice cream. The windshield is safety glass. The cabin door is lockable. Positive foam flotation is standard on every Starcraft as is BIA certification in compliance with federal safety regulations. But just as important to a family man, there are over 1400 Starcraft dealers across the country. So even if you're a long ways from home you're never very far from a reliable Starcraft dealer. **That's Starcraftsmanship.**

You're probably getting a pretty good feel for **Starcraftsmanship** by now. It's just simply that when you make and sell more aluminum boats than anyone else you learn what people want, and so you take a little extra care to make them better or roomier or more convenient or less expensive or longer lasting...then boaters who own Starcrafts are happier. And that makes us happy. **That's Starcraftsmanship.**

If you like, we'll see that you get a free 1972 Starcraft Marine catalog and the name of your nearest dealer. Just write and ask Starcraft Company, Dept. B-5-A, Goshen, Ind. 46526.

STARCRAFT
A BANGOR PUNTA COMPANY

The Starcraft Company coined the word "starcraftsmanship" to link the company name and "craftsmanship" in the consumers mind.

This IVECO ad for diesel trucks combines forcefully the four important points of an effective ad (see page 503).

to increase sales and market share and (3) contribute significantly to the improved productivity of the company's marketing program.

All Good Ads and Commercials Create: ATTENTION, INTEREST, DESIRE and ACTION

1. Attention—A good ad must divert the attention of the reader or listener from what he or she is doing to what your ad is selling.
2. Interest—Then tell your story in a way that sparks interest.
3. Desire—Deliver consumer benefits in such a way that the consumer says "That's for me!"
4. Action—Make the reader or viewer react to your message and take action! Give urgent reasons.

Remember: Advertising can put prospects in your showrooms but it takes good sales follow-up to close the deal.

Suggestions for Further Reading

Philip Ward Burton, *Advertising Copywriting,* (Columbus, OH: Grid Publishing, Inc., 4th ed., 1978).

W. Keith Hafer and Gordon E. White, *Advertising Writing*, (St. Paul, MN: West Publishing Company, 1977).

Claude Hopkins, *Scientific Advertising,* (New York: Chelsea House Publishers, 1980).

H. Gordon Lewis, *How to Make Your Advertising Twice as Effective at Half the Cost,* (Chicago: Nelson-Hall, 1979).

David L. Malickson and John W. Nason, *Advertising—How to Write the Kind That Works,* (New York: Charles Scribner's Sons, 1977).

David Ogilvy, *Confessions of an Advertising Man,* (New York: Atheneum, 1963).

Rosser Reeves, *Reality in Advertising,* (New York: Alfred A. Knopf, 1961).

C. Dennis Schick and Albert C. Book, *Fundamentals of Creative Advertising,* (Chicago: Crain Books, 1979).

Vic Schwab, *How to Write a Good Advertisement,* (New York: Marsteller, Inc., 3rd ed., 1976).

John S. Wright, Willis L. Winter and Sherilyn K. Zeigler, *Advertising,* (New York: McGraw-Hill Book Company, 5th ed., 1982).

Sherilyn K. Zeigler and J. Douglas Johnson, *Creative Strategy and Tactics in Advertising,* (Columbus OH: Grid Publishing, Inc., 1981).

Chapter 11

ILLUSTRATION

PEOPLE like illustrations. They find them interesting. They enjoy looking at pictures. There's something about looking at pictures that enables people to dream and yearn and project themselves into another time, place, or situation. Pictures appeal to the romantic hidden away in all of us.

This fascination with pictures is due, in part, to their being so easily understood. Pictures communicate ideas quickly and easily, so there's almost no chance of misinterpretation of the thought behind them. Partially because of this, pictures have been an integral part of every culture and society since time began.

You can remember fine art from ancient Egypt, from the Ming Dynasty of China, and you're aware that in Europe caverns have recently been found whose walls are lavishly decorated with lively animal portraits painted by skilled Magdalenian artists who worked 10,000 years before the birth of Christ. Theory has it that these ancients produced art so profusely for two reasons: A desire to beautify their quarters, a feeling that's inherent in the human animal, and to propitiate the spirits of animals they painted. This was, perhaps, done to cast a spell, or weave some magic that would enable the painters to achieve victory in the hunt. Colors were carefully blended of mineral oxides and charcoal, and animal fat was blended in to serve as a binder.

Many intriguing examples of similar artistic efforts of Cro-Magnon man painted some 25,000 years ago are in an excellent state of preservation.

A few years ago the author and his family took a fascinating trip back into antiqity, although of a later era, by browsing through a number of cliff dwellings in the colorful canyon country of the Southwest. On the stone walls of many of these long-abandoned homes, beautifully preserved by the high, dry desert air, are illustrations—not mere drawings, but wonderfully detailed and skillfully executed illustrations—of scenes from the contemporary life of the

Pueblo artists. Animals long since extinct, exotic tribal customs, and curious religious ceremonies are depicted with charm and precision.

These priceless paintings, part of our national heritage, were done long before Columbus—or was it Leif Ericson?—discovered America, yet this Indian art is as vivid and fresh as if it had been done just yesterday. They give us an enthralling glimpse into life as it was lived a thousand years or more ago.

Pictures exert an even greater attraction for people today than in the past merely because there are so many more of them—pictures as well as people, that is. Through the years as printing and other reproduction processes improved, it has become increasingly easy for the great mass of people to enjoy pictures. For many centuries art was found almost exclusively in churches and in the castles and mansions of the very rich.

The Trend Toward Illustration

However, the printed page, the ubiquitous camera in the hands of the tourist, movies, and the electronic monster that mesmerizes people with pictures of sorts, all combine to make our society picture-conscious and picture-oriented to a degree scarcely possible to foresee.

In advertising an occasional all-type ad sans illustration scores a resounding success in readership and reader response. If the advertiser's selling proposition is unusually clear-cut and so well defined there's no possibility of its being misunderstood by anybody with anything approaching average intelligence, all's well and good, as far as the all-type ad is concerned.

On the other hand, there's no questioning whether or not there should be an illustration in your advertisement. Incidentally, in the advertising field the illustration is always referred to as the "illustration"—not as the "picture."

The illustration works in harmony with the headline and the body copy to communicate your message. Key word here is that the illustration *works*—it doesn't merely occupy expensive space on the page. An appropriate illustration with real impact hammers home your idea a lot faster than anything else that's ever been devised. If the illustration isn't appropriate, and if it doesn't have real impact, what is it doing in the ad?

When it comes to catching the reader's eye and attracting attention in that crucial instant when a glance flashes across your ad, the illustration has no competition.

There's no reason to believe that The Sterling Remedy Company's all-type ad, illustrated nearby, didn't receive good readership, or that

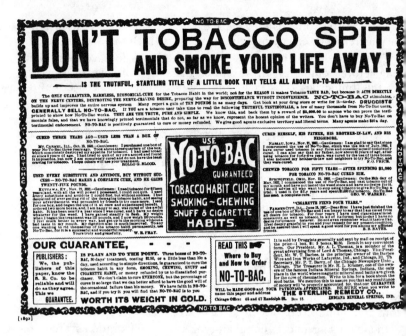

[1892]

reader response wasn't up to the advertiser's expectations.

This classic, circa 1892, appears in *Those Were the Good Old Days*—a "happy look at American advertising, 1880-1930." It was published by Simon and Schuster, and this ad and the two following are reproduced by permission of the author, Edgar R. Jones.

Sterling's ad was written too soon to capitalize on the public's growing awareness of the link between lung cancer and cigarette smoking, so the ad had to do all of the selling job for the product, aided only by an intuitive knowledge that the habit is harmful.

The headline says:

DON'T { TOBACCO SPIT
{ AND SMOKE YOUR LIFE AWAY!

Subhead following is designed to intrigue the reader, to make him or her want to know more, thus assuring good readership of the body copy. It says:

IS THE TRUTHFUL, STARTLING TITLE OF A LITTLE
BOOK THAT TELLS ALL ABOUT NO-TO-BAC

Body copy starts out:

The ONLY GUARTANTEED, HARMLESS, ECONOMI-CAL CURE for the Tobacco Habit in the world; not for the REASON it makes Tobacco Taste Bad, but because it ACTS DIRECTLY ON THE NERVE CENTERS DESTROYING THE NERVE-CRAVING DESIRE, pre-paring the way for DISCONTINUANCE WITHOUT IN-CONVENIENCE. NO-TO-BAC builds up and improves the entire nervous system. Many report a gain of TEN POUNDS in as many days. Get book at your drug store or writer for it—today. DRUGGISTS GENERALLY SELL NO-TO-BAC. If YOU are a tobacco user take time to read the following TRUTHFUL TESTIMONIALS, a few of many thousands from No-To-Bac users, printed to show how No-To-Bac works. THEY ARE THE TRUTH, PURE AND SIMPLE. We know this, and back them by a reward of $5,000.00 to anyone who can prove the testimonials false, and that we have knowingly printed testimonials that do not, so far as we know, represent the honest opinion of the writers. You don't have to buy No-To-Bac on testimonial endorsement. NO-TO-BAC is positively guaranteed to cure or money refunded. We give good agents exclusive territory and liberal terms. Many agents make $10 a day.

Testimonials and case histories were recognized effective as far back as the 1890's when this ad appeared, for the advertiser devoted almost one-third of the space in this ad to five testimonials. A typical one follows:

CURED THREE YEARS AGO—USED LESS THAN A BOX OF NO-TO-BAC

Mt. Carmel, Ill. Oct. 10, 1892—Gentlemen: I purchased one box of your No-To-Bac three years ago. Took about three-quarters of the box, which completely destroyed my appetite for tobacco. I had used tobacco since nine years of age. I had tried to quit of my own accord and found it impossible, but now I am completely cured and do not have the least craving for tobacco. I hope others will use your treatment.

ROLLO G. BLOOD

Then comes a money-back guarantee that's straightforward and ap-parently made in good faith. In the bid for action there's a kicker, though, because The Sterling Remedy Company says:

READ THIS
Where to Buy
and How to Order
No-To-Bac

It is sold by Druggists generally and sent by mail . . . the Treasurer is Mr. H. L. Kramer, one of the owners of the famous Indiana Mineral Springs, Indiana, the only place in the world where magnetic mineral mud baths are given for the cure of rheumatism. Write to him for a book about the mud baths.

Even the publisher of the newspaper in which the ad ran got into the act; included in the ad is a box with copy that says:

PUBLISHERS:
We, the publishers
of this paper, know
the S.R. Co. to be
reliable and will do
as they agree. This
we
    GUARANTEE

That's hard sell so hard that diamonds are soft in comparison.

Of interest is the business proposition—"many agents make $10 a day." Now *that* might well beat the advertising business!

The copy, as hard sell and apparently effective as it is, speaks in a muted whisper compared to the all-type ad which follows. First, however, the question that's bound to occur to everybody is: Did The Sterling Remedy Company market a product with merit? Did it work? Is the user benefit valid?

These things are sometimes a bit difficult to check out after 76 years, although the author *did* verify that Rollo G. Blood did *not* smoke at the time of his death, nor did he for several years before. A long distance phone call to Mt. Carmel, Illinois, put the author in touch with a Mrs. Marguerite H. Stansfield, and through her a Miss Mabel Jacquess; although neither of these ladies is a professional investigator, both are life-long residents of Mt. Carmel. They talked with friends and acquaintances of the late Mr. Blood and found that he stopped smoking once and for all in 1892, as the ad stated. Mr. Blood was well known in the city, having lived across the street and several houses south of the hospital; his family owned and operated a brickyard just north of their home, and in digging clay for bricks dug what became "Blood's Pond" where local children ice skated.

Since this testimonial was legitimate, it's safe to assume the others were too. It's inspiring to know that truthfulness in advertising prevailed that long ago.

In 1895 The Brandreth Company ran an ad, illutrated nearby, that promises the moon with a chain-link fence around it. It reads:

Salva-cea!
What are its uses?

SALVA-CEA will cure Bruises and Contusions—Daniel Thomas, of Sing Sing, N. Y., had the third finger of his right hand crushed by a heavy log falling on it; the nail was torn off and the end of the finger was reduced almost to a pulp. Salva-cea was applied, and not only did the pain, which was intense, quickly subside, but the finger healed perfectly.

SALVA-CEA will cure Eczema—A child of Victor Savage, of Monroe, Mich., was covered with sores on one side of the body, and had been in that condition for a year. It was an unusually bad case of eczema, yet in one month's time was perfectly cured by Salva-cea.

SALVA-CEA will cure Earache—Peter Venior, also of Monroe, Mich., says that his children have in the past suffered greatly from this painful complaint. He tried Salva-cea, putting a small quantity in the ear and covering it with cotton. The result was instant relief, and now the moment the children are threatened with a return of the pain they come to him, sure of immediate cure.

SALVA-CEA will cure Piles—Testimonials from many persons show that Salve-cea is a specific for this almost universal complaint. Itching piles are immediately relieved and quickly cured.

SALVA-CEA will cure Colds and Rheumatism—A small quantity occasionally snuffed up the nostrils will cure a cold in the head in less time than anything yet discovered. A gentleman to whom it had been recommended for a cold, when asked if it did him any good, answered, "To tell the truth, I did not use it for my cold, but look at that!" at the same time holding his hand over his head. He went on to say that for three months he had been troubled with rheumatism in his shoulder, so that he could not put on his coat without assistance, yet six applications of Salva-cea, well rubbed in, had given him complete relief.

SALVA-CEA will cure Chilblains, Neuralgia, Headache, all Itching, Chafing, Coughs, and Fever Sores, and is, in fact, a

Salva-cea!
(TRADE-MARK.)

What are its uses?

SALVA-CEA will cure Bruises and Contusions.—Daniel Thomas, of Sing Sing, N. Y., had the third finger of his right hand crushed by a heavy log falling on it; the nail was torn off and the end of the finger reduced almost to a pulp. Salva cea was applied, and not only did the pain, which was intense, quickly subside, but the finger healed perfectly.

SALVA-CEA will cure Eczema.—A child of Victor Savage, of Monroe, Mich., was covered with sores on one side of the body, and had been in that condition for a year. It was an unusually bad case of eczema, yet in one month's time was perfectly cured by the use of Salva-cea.

SALVA-CEA will cure Earache.—Peter Venior, also of Monroe, Mich., says that his children have in the past suffered greatly from this painful complaint. He tried Salva-cea, putting a small quantity in the ear and covering it with cotton. The result was instant relief, and now the moment the children are threatened with a return of the pain they come to him, sure of immediate cure.

SALVA-CEA will cure Piles.—Testimonials from many persons show that Salva-cea is a specific for this almost universal complaint. Itching piles are immediately relieved and quickly cured.

SALVA-CEA will cure Colds and Rheumatism.—A small quantity occasionally snuffed up the nostrils will cure a cold in the head in less time than anything yet discovered. A gentleman to whom it had been recommended for a cold, when asked if it did him any good, answered, "To tell the truth, I did not use it for my cold, but look at that!" at the same time holding his hand over his head. He went on to say that for three months he had been troubled with rheumatism in his shoulder, so that he could not put on his coat without assistance, yet six applications of Salva-cea, well rubbed in, had given him complete relief.

SALVA-CEA will cure Chilblains, Neuralgia, Headache, all Itching, Chafing, Coughs, and Fever Sores, and is, in fact, a universal external remedy. One great advantage is its speedy action. Only a few applications are needed in order to bring both relief and cure.

SALVA-CEA will come into general use as soon as its value becomes known. It will, in fact, be considered a household necessity, and the only regret of those who ascertain its merit will be that they did not know of it before.

Price, 25 and 50 cents per box. At druggists, or by mail.
THE BRANDRETH Co., 274 Canal St., New York.

[1895]

---

universal external remedy. One great advantage is its speedy action. Only a few applications are needed in order to bring both relief and cure.

SALVA-CEA will come into general use as soon as its value becomes known. It will, in fact, be considered a household necessity, and the only regret of those who ascertain its merit will be that they did not know of it before.

Price, 25 and 50 cents per box, druggist, or by mail.

Chuck out that penicillin, discard all of the numerous . . . . myacins, stop production of sulfa, give the heave-ho to the wondrous array of wonder drugs. Your doctor can prescribe and bring on the Salva-cea! At last, a cure for the common cold that's also pure magic on those common aches and pains that beset and bedevil the hard-working advertising person!

A question comes to mind, though: Where, oh where, was the Food and Drug bureaucracy?

There's no disputing that The Brandreth Company sells Salva-cea mighty hard, and does it without benefit of an illustration in the ad. What kind of illustration would they have used, though—a before-and-after photo of that wildly inventive chap who used a cold remedy for rheumatism, leaping into the air and kicking his heels while he chortles with glee at being able to put on his coat unaided? Now, *that* would be an illustration!

Usefulness of the illustration was recognized by forward-looking, aggressive advertisers of that era, though, as Schiele & Company proves with their ad shown nearby.

There, flying gracefully around in a moon-drenched sky, are a pair of the most angelic looking angels to appear in anybody's ad before or since. Of course, there's reason to believe there's an ulterior motive for invoking the aid of assistants to Diety. It so happens the angels are wearing such rapturous expressions because they are proudly holding one of Madam Dean's Spinal Supporting Corsets for some reason or other—perhaps because the corset is the advertiser's product.

Copy hits just about as hard as in the two illustration-less ads. It reads:

MADAM DEAN'S SPINAL SUPPORTING CORSET

They support the Spine, relieve the muscles of the back, **brace the shoulders** in a natutral and easy manner, imparting **graceful carriage** to the wearer without discomfort, **expanding the chest,** thereby giving **full action to the lungs,** and **health** and **comfort** to the body. Take the place of the ORDINARY CORSET in every respect, and are made of fine **Contil,** in the best manner, in various styles and sold by agents everywhere at **popular prices.** Mrs. Wm. Papes, Keota, Iowa, says:—I have been an invalid for six years, have travelled extensively for health, yet never received as much benefit as I have in a few weeks wear of your MADAM DEAN'S CORSET. I am gaining strength all the time, and could not do without it. It has proven to me a **godsend.**

FREE—Our book entitled: "Dress Reform for Ladies" with elegant wood engraving and Biography of **Worth, the King of Fashion,** Paris: also our **New Illustrated Catalogue** sent free to any address on receipt of two 2-cent stamps to pay postage and packing.

AGENTS WANTED for these **celebrated Corsets.** No experience required. Four orders per day give the agent **$150 monthly.** Our agents report from four to twenty sales daily. **$3.00 Outfit Free.** Send for terms and full particulars.

Schiele & Co.

Those are claims that are claims. Boldface type pops out the major user benefits—support the spine; brace the shoulders; graceful carriage; expanding the chest; full action to the lungs; health; comfort;

MADAME DEAN'S SPINAL SUPPORTING CORSETS.

They support the Spine, relieve the muscles of the back, brace the shoulders in a natural and easy manner, imparting graceful carriage to the wearer without discomfort, expanding the chest, thereby giving full action to the lungs, and health and comfort to the body. Take the place of the ORDINARY CORSET in every respect, and are made of fine Contil, in the best manner, in various styles and sold by agents everywhere at popular prices. Mrs. Wm. Papes, Keota, Iowa, says:—I have been an invalid for six years, have travelled extensively for health, yet never received as much benefit as I have in a few weeks wear, of your MADAME, DEAN'S CORSET. I am gaining strength all the time, and could not do without it. It has proven to me a godsend.

FREE Our new book entitled: "Dress Reform for Ladies" with elegant wood engraving and Biography of Worth, the King of Fashion, Paris; also our New Illustrated Catalogue sent free to any address on receipt of two 2-cent stamps to pay postage and packing.

AGENTS WANTED for these celebrated Corsets. No experience required. Four orders per day give the agent $150 monthly. Our agents report from four to twenty sales daily. $3.00 Outfit Free. Send for terms and full particulars, SCHIELE & CO., 390 Broadway, New York,

[1885]

Ad illustrations of the 1800's were wood engravings like this

popular prices. Hard to fault those without coming out strong against Flag and Motherhood.

Mrs. Wm. Papes explains the illustration, although it's not an appropriate illustriation that requires explaining in the testimonial. Her statement that the corset has proven a *godsend* to her obviously caused the copywriter to pause and reflect on his choice of an illustration. His conclusion: Who can top God? So, we have angels because we all know what *they* look like.

Here again—and back in 1895, at that—is the tried and proved formula for triggering a response: Offer a piece of literature about the product or about how it will benefit the reader. Then sit back and convert the inquiries to sales.

Distribution might have been better for Madam Dean's Supporting Corsets, as evidenced by the offer of lucrative territories for agents—complete with a $3 outfit given to new agents absolutely free. And who could sneeze at congenial work with congenial customers?

But selling 20 corsets a day!

Since the late 1800's a higher percentage of advertisements—both consumer and industrial—use illustrations each year. The ad without an illustration is the exception today, possibly accounting for the effectiveness of certain individual ads or campaigns that go the all-type route.

The Writer Specifies the Illustration

At first, at least, the new advertisement is practically the sole property of the advertising manager and the copywriter—unless they're one and the same individual.

The writer lives with his or her baby. He or she meditates, cogitates, and usually procrastinates during its incubative period, waiting for the germ of an idea to flower into a complete creative concept instead of merely knowing that the writer is under the gun to produce a new ad about the new Widget in time to get it produced and placed before deadline.

Usually the process works two ways, depending upon the individual and the background. The ad person who's mostly writer is strongly word-oriented; he tends to think of ideas in terms of headline and copy approaches. Frequently, when doodling and mulling over random thoughts while getting ready to write an ad, the writer receives a complete ad in close to final form as far as concept is concerned—and this includes headline and body copy—almost from out of the blue.
that way on the surface because the writer's subconscious takes a number of different approaches into consideration, tries them on for

size and rejects those that are unsuitable. This process of trial and error continues, sometimes for a period of days, until exactly the right approach is found. Suddenly, there's the ad!

There's the ad in word form, that is. Headline. Copy approach. Slant. Tone. It's all there except for one essential ingredient—the illustrative idea. That's where the rub comes in with many writers and advertising managers. Skim through a number of trade publications serving any market and make note of the illustrative ideas that *really* come on strong. Chances are you'll be able to number those from a half-dozen books on the fingers of your two hands—and maybe on one of them if you're fairly critical.

However, if the same product, selling proposition, and marketing problems are presented to an art-oriented advertising practitioner to solve—an art director, for example, or an account executive whose background lies in the art end of the business—exactly the opposite is true, as a rule.

This art-oriented ad individual generally comes up with compelling illustrative ideas, ideas that often are highly creative and original, ideas that are completely fresh and new in this particular market. And maybe new in any market, for that matter. Mostly they're good ideas, too, although some will naturally be discarded as unfeasible or so far out they can't be used.

The point is, though, that ideas are thoughts on the ways to *show* the reader the advertiser's message, rather than *tell* him or her. Not that the art-oriented ad person is wrong—he's not. But he or she's only half right. He's developed only half of an ad because he simply hasn't thought through the problem in its entirety, at least as far as the copy is concerned, although he's probably developed a headline idea. For the most-part, it isn't in usable form because it's only a basic idea—not words that have been refined and rewritten and reworked.

Infrequently does the ability to create with equal facility in both copy and in illustration occur in one individual. Most seasoned advertising men do both very well, but not equally well. One's more work than the other.

The fact remains that the ad is initially the copywriter's. It's his or her responsibility and it's necessary to specify the illustration.

If you're the advertising manager and you're writing the ad, you're not expected to be an accomplished artist or a top-flight illustrative photographer. However, you should direct the agency account executive, or the studio with which you work, by telling exactly what the illustration should consist of.

Note that "exactly" was used. This is because you can't leave room for guesses or stabs in the dark. Spell out in detail precisely what it is that you want to see in the ad, then forget the details. You can't dictate nuts-and-bolts mechanics of how the illustration is to be created, physically created. The subject in the illustration far overshadows in importance how it's portrayed.

The Deadly "Dry Spell"

Sometimes the writer gets stuck. Absolutely stuck. There's an awful and inexplicable dearth of illustrative ideas. The creative well seems to have run as dry as the Sahara.

Once, when the author was considerably younger and working as a copywriter with an old-line, 4A agency, a dry spell occurred. This was the first one. I was distressed and disturbed; nothing seemed to go right. Words wouldn't come, much less scintillating, sparkling, shining illustrative ideas. The first afternoon passed with no output; even staring fixedly out the window at the ants a couple of dozen stories below didn't help. No ads.

The next day, after a good night's sleep, the well was still dry. Ideas refused to come. That was when panic came close to setting in. Could it be possible that a copywriter couldn't come up with anything new and different? Couldn't words be strung together interestingly enough to keep from boring the person who strung them? Could it be?

Well, that was Thursday. The obvious thing to do was be sick on Friday, to relax completely, go out to the rifle range and happily punch holes in small groups at 200 yards until a sore shoulder showed the fun was at an end for the weekend.

Next Monday output was 16 ads—in one day. All complete, all with provocative illustrative ideas, all proofread on the yellow and ready for finished typing. Every one of those ads hit print just as written.

Speed with which a writer works is a highly individual matter. Some writers are prolific. Thoughts and ideas flow fast, seemingly without end. Others take more time—they're deliberate, they procrastinate more, interruptions cause them to lose a train of thought more easily. But all have the same problems and getting stuck at times is one of them.

Don't let it worry you too much when it happens—and it *will* happen. When it does, walk around the office for a while. Go to the water cooler and have a drink. Take a stroll to the company cafeteria and have a leisurely cup. Kid your secretary. Bother your assistant. Check up on your clerk. If some or all of this doesn't help visualize a terrific illustration, let your subconscious take over.

Don't take your plight too seriously. Remind yourself that, after all, the illustration is only a vehicle to convey the appeal you want to make in the ad. It's not a life-or-death matter; there's no law on the books that says it has to spring full-blown to mind, all in vivid, glowing color, complete down to the last little detail.

You're after a picture of something, nothing more nor less. That something may be the product, a benefit realized by using the product, details of construction of the product, a reason for buying the product, or something similar to convey the basic idea of the advertisement as a whole. The illustration should complement the headline and body copy, of course, but it doesn't have to parrot either one.

Chances are if you're stuck for an idea you can talk your way out of it. Talk with others about the problem, that is. Discuss it with your account executive, the art director, a layout artist—even with your secretary. There's no telling where the bit of help you need to nudge your mental processes will come from.

Advertising, whether in an agency or in an industrial advertising department, tends to attract highly articulate visual thinkers, people who are considerably more imaginative than run-of-the-mill employees working in other capacities. Don't overlook them—use them. They'll be glad to listen to you, and you, in turn, should listen to their suggestions. Don't discard anything out of hand. Even if an idea isn't the greatest that ever came down the pike, there's always the possibility that it will trigger one that is.

Purpose of the Illustration

Business has always been competitive, but it's becoming more bitterly competitive each year.

As this trend continues, advertising pressure on readers of business publications has increased steadily and relentlessly. There are no signs of its diminishing. In fact, just the opposite holds true. As the level of marketing sophistication rises, more and more industrial companies are becoming increasingly aware of the major contribution advertising can make to their overall marketing activities.

Consequently, each individual ad has more pressure on *it*. Each ad has a bigger job cut out for it. Each advertisement must work harder, must produce more than ever before. This means, of course, that the components going into each ad have to be of higher quality—illustration, headline, body copy.

Each of these elements depends upon the other. Each is a link in the chain of reader reaction to the ad. Sequence of ad reading is: (1) looking at the illustration, (2) reading the headline, and, (3) reading the body copy. Let just one element fall down and the ad suffers; it lacks credibility in the reader's mind as he or she realizes instinctively that something's amiss—even though he can't quite put his finger on just what it is. Lacking credibility, the ad has failed to convince the reader of the validity of the advertiser's claims. This means the ad has failed to make a *sales* call in print; it merely made a call, an incomplete one, one that borders on being futile.

Most of the burden is carried by the illustration. If it doesn't stop the reader long enough to cause him to read the headline, all's lost. Get out the white flag and wave it. Little will it matter if the headline is the greatest ever written, if it's loaded with user benefits and promises the reader everything he's ever desired in his wildest imaginings.

Your illustration must contribute to the strength of the ad as a whole. It can't freeload. To justify itself, the illustration must do one or more of the following:

1. Capture the attention of the reader.
2. Identify the subject of the advertisement.
3. Qualify readers by stopping those who are legitimate prospects, letting others skip over your ad if they are so inclined.
4. Arouse interest in reading the headline.
5. Create a favorable impression of product or advertiser.
6. Clarify claims made by the copy.
7. Help convince the reader of the truth of claims made in the copy.
8. Emphasize unique features of the product.
9. Provide continuity for all advertisements in the campaign through use of the same illustrative technique in each individual ad.

No one illustration is going to do all of those, but every illustration must do one or more.

Types of Illustrations

A real fun experience if you approach it with an objective in mind is to leaf through a dozen leading trade publications, preferably from a number of different fields. Ignore the editorial material and concentrate on the ads.

Amazing is the only word that comes readily to mind—or even comes close to describing the inventiveness of the advertising people who conceived, created, and produced the ads. Simply amazing.

What makes the experience memorable, rather than an academic exercise, is not merely looking at the illustrations in the ads, but taking a few seconds—or, in some cases, minutes—to try to recreate the mental processes of the copywriter at the moment the illustrative idea occurred. Try this and you'll find yourself thinking in ways you never dreamed of. The sensation is an odd one.

Illustrations run the gamut from those that are downright ridiculous to some that are little short of sublime. When you're flipping through the magazines haphazardly there appears to be neither rhyme nor reason for many of the illustrations.

And something else that immediately comes to mind is that the subjects of the illustrations are almost limitless; they defy hasty attempts to categorize them into neat little groups or classifications, all neatly labeled. This holds true unless each individual illustration is regarded *not* as an illustration complete in itself, but as a *type* of illustration— one that has many kissing cousins in other advertisers' ads.

Twenty-one basic types of illustrations just about wrap up those used most commonly in industrial advertisements. In various forms they appear and reappear year after year. If treated imaginatively and with good taste, each type of illustration can be effective indefinitely. Let's look at the classifications, then at examples of each. Types of illustrations are:

1. Package containing the product.
2. Product alone.
3. Product in use.
4. Product feature(s).
5. Explanation of feature(s).
6. User benefit.
7. Comparison of products.
8. How to use the product.
9. Storytelling.
10. Implication.
11. Humor.
12. Borrowed interest.
13. Contrast.
14. Curiosity arousing.
15. Charts and graphs.
16. Cutaway or cross section.
17. Symbolism.
18. Negative appeal.
19. Make-believe figures.

20. Abstraction.
21. Rebus.

Package Illustration

Sometimes it's just as important to the advertiser to illustrate the package in which his product is sold as it is to show the product itself. This is particularly true in highly competitive fields where the difference between competing products is either slight, or when it's difficult to convince prospects that the difference that does exist is significant.

In the automotive aftermarket, for example, this situation is frequently encountered. This is due to the distribution system of the industry; manufacturers don't sell direct. Manufacturers sell to warehouse distributors; these WDs then sell to jobbers; the jobbers, in turn, sell to dealers; dealers, as the term is used in this industry, are actually automobile dealers, repair garages, fleets, and so on. Each performs a service, each has salespeople out on the street selling to those next in line in the chain.

Competition for the sales force's time—and to motivate them to push one manufacturer's line at the expense of another—is intense, to say the least. At the warehouse distributor level there's relative indifference about brands and manufacturers. The WD will buy anything he's reasonably confident his sales reps can move at a profit. Brand loyalty is a foreign concept to him. On down the ladder, though, manufacturer sales reps are increasingly preoccupied with development of brand loyalty and constantly engage in "missionary work" to help jobber salespeople on calls to dealers. It is here, on the lowest level, that a product either catches fire or fails miserably.

For some years Sealed Power Corporation emphasized its package for the company's line of stainless steel piston rings. This was done in all advertising directed toward jobbers. "Look for the familiar red box," Sealed Power said in every ad—and the box was illustrated big and bold and in red, its actual color.

The War for Shelf Space

Competition for shelf space in an automotive jobber's place of business is also pretty rugged. When a dealer or a garage individual comes in to buy parts for a particular vehicle he's working on, he frequently has no preference as to what specific brand he'll buy. Often he's inclined to accept the recommendation of the counterman—the inside salesperson. This individual as often as not tallies up a tidy little income on the side in the form of "spifs"—which are nothing more nor less than bribes from a manufacturer to push *his or her* brand of parts at the expense of others. In the case of a set of automotive valves, for instance, the counter salesperson might be paid 75 cents per set to push the brand made by Smith Valve Company, Inc.

One way to counter competition's spifs is to offer bigger and better spifs yourself. This tactic can become costly indeed as the war escalates. Only so much can be given away without a jump in selling price, which is an additional competitive disadvantage. Or the manufacturer can, through advertising and strong selling, create brand preference and brand loyalty.

To the mechanic—visualizing a set of automotive valves is the easiest thing possible. That's because he or she doesn't see the shiny new valves in all of their pristine beauty floating in a cloud-filled sky; *he sees the package the valves come in.* Maybe it's red or blue or brown or black. But whatever the colors or the shape, this buyer visualizes the package. The package is the product.

When a person enters a jobber's establishment he or she may well be undecided about what brand of valve to buy. The only thing sure is that it's for a 289 cu. in. Ford V-8 engine. While waiting to be waited on, he or she eyes shelves laden with neatly stacked fast-moving items handy and up front where the counterpeople can grab them quickly to speed customer turnover.

This is when the moment of truth arrives for many a manufacturer. Smart marketers faced with similar conditions have distinctive boxes. The manufacturer's name is prominent, it's in type large enough to be read from the customer side of the counter. It has the logo big and bold enough for all to see and identify.

The Timken Roller Bearing Company's fine four-color spread ad illustrated above is basically a package illustration. It is from *Commercial Car Journal* magazine. The copy approach is from the safety angle with the left page devoted to a testimonial given by the president of a large trucking company that consistently wins awards for an excellent safety record. The trucker uses Timken Roller Bearings in vehicles with outstanding success in terms of bearing life—which can be translated into cost per mile, and in freedom from accidents caused by bearing failure.

The stark, simple right page of the spread has a hand—a greasy, mechanic's hand—holding the package in which he or she receives Timken bearings. This is the package seen on the jobber's shelf, this is what is visualized when he or she thinks of wheel bearings.

Timken capitalized on the high interest everybody has in highway safety to gain readership, then strengthened product identification and brand recognition with the illustration of the box. A well-done ad.

Product Alone

Time was when an industrial advertising manager, faced with having to show the product in a new ad, invariably specified that it be shown in use. This was done without question, without second thought.

After all, it was a time-honored tenet that the product was *never* shown all by its lonesome in an illustration unless it was for a catalog or a piece of sales literature. It was unthinkable to show the product alone in an ad. It bordered on blasphemy. Thinking was, if just the product was shown the illustration couldn't help but be trite, static, and boring. Nobody but nobody in industry would condescend to give it a second glance, and probably not even a first one, either.

A bulldozer, for example, obviously should be shown gouging out a cut for a new interstate highway; a transverse profilometer would naturally be trailing a test vehicle; an electric typewriter or an electronic calculator might be illustrated in a typical office setting. All of this was done in the name of realism with an uppercase "R." Nobody wanted to give the impression he or she was being crass enough to show a product. That would be gauche' .

Product-in-use illustrations are effective, there's no denying that.

However, there are times when it's advisable to show only the product—all alone, sans background, without benefit of a sexy model or carefully constructed set that simulates a working atmosphere. With no background or other elements in the illustration, there's nothing to distract the reader by diverting his eye from the product.

Consider the new product ad, for instance. The reader is not familiar with the product because he or she never seen it before. He doesn't know what it looks like. He doesn't know how it differs in appearance from the old model it replaced. He doesn't know how it appears compared to competitive products. And he has no mental impressions of the product to enable him to form an opinion or attitude toward it.

Show an illustration of the product alone and it instantly telegraphs to the reader what the ad's all about, and what the product looks like. Until recent years, the external appearance of an industrial product was considered relatively inconsequential. If the thing worked, what did it matter what it looked like?

A Change in Thinking

Now, however, that thinking has fallen by the wayside. It is generally accepted that appearance of the product is highly important. Despite the fact that buying decisions are theoretically based on value analysis and are made logically and unemotionally, appearance can be the decisive factor in a sale—to a much greater extent than most buyers will admit. Other things being even close to equal, it's an odd sort of individual who won't choose a product whose appearance is esthetically pleasing over one that's unprepossessing. If the product is genuinely pleasing in appearance—and many of today's machine tools and control panels and electronic instruments are beautiful due to growing reliance on competent industrial designers—the smart manufacturer exploits this advantage for all it's worth. And it's worth plenty.

When you have a smart-looking piece of equipment, a simple, straightforward picture of the product all by itself conveys the impression you want the reader to get faster than almost any other type of illustration.

Product in Use

Readership studies have quietly laid to rest the old dogma that products *must* be shown in use if the ad is to be read.

However, just because it's not obligatory to show the product in use, there's no need to have the pendulum swing to the opposite extreme and have every illustration look like an imitation of a Volkswagen ad.

Frequently you'll find the best way of conveying a sense of immediacy, a feeling of reality, of causing the reader to project himself or herself into the illustration and identify with the product is to show it being used.

When you're going to use a product-in-use illustration, probably a photograph, take pains to make sure it's authentic. Nothing repels a reader as fast as an illustration that's obviously phony. Do a poor job of staging a photograph and you've lost a lot of prospects.

Many fine product-in-use photographs are set up in the photographer's studio—most of them, in fact, when the product is small enough to be transported, or would logically be used indoors. However, if your product is a dragline or a trencher or a tank trailer, you won't disassemble it and put it back together in a studio just for the sake of staging a picture. It's easier to move a photographer over to a 40-story building in which your super-deluxe dual-glass windows are installed than it is to bring the skyscraper to the photographer. And the cost is usually lower.

A dramatic illustration of the product in use—or even a carefully staged photograph that looks authentic—instantly shows the reader what the product will do for him or her. An illustration is quick to explain itself, quick to tell the reader there's something in it for him or her if the copy is read.

A good example is the striking four-color spread run by Trojan Division, Eaton Yale & Towne, in *Construction Methods and Equipment* magazine. The ad is shown on the following page.

This illustration has great impact. You can almost hear the engine as the mechanical monster scoops up a giant-sized bite of dirt and rock. How much more effective this illustration of the loader is than it would be if the equipment was just sitting idle, motionless, and not working.

Users of construction equipment of this type can easily visualize their own operators in the driver's seat, they can see in the illustration that this is a huge unit that's capable of handling big jobs fast. The illustration is so credible and just plain interesting that the reader feels compelled to read at least the headline. Once that step is taken, a sizable percentage will proceed into the body copy.

Show Heavy Equipment in Use

This color photograph has stopping power in spades. No amount of photos of construction equipment taken out behind the manufacturer's factory can begin to convey the "feel" that an on-the-

job shot can. Equipment of this type is the exception to the "rule" that it's not necessary to show the product in use. On the contrary, heavy equipment should *always* be shown being operated. Construction men and contractors expect it. Fail to give them something they've been conditioned to look for and to get, either consciously or subconsciously, and you've made a negative impression.

Product Features

One of the most widely used illustrations in industrial advertising is one showing features of the product. This type of illustration accomplishes a number of the nine purposes of an illustration that have been discussed.

Strength of the product features illustration lies in its ability to clarify copy claims. It proves again the truth of the old Chinese cliche' that "one picture is worth ten thousand words."

When the reader turns to an illustration of product features he or she sees immediately just what the feature is that the manufacturer feels is so important, and he's able to relate this to the job even before the copy explains it in many instances.

An illustration of a feature of the product, or of several features permits focusing of attention on specifics the advertiser believes will have the most influence on desirability of the product, hence on sales.

Some products by their very nature are strictly utilitarian—so much so that despite a coat of paint, or a little chrome plate here and there, or some brightly colored plastic knobs—there isn't much the product's maker can do to cause the heart of the beholder to do ecstatic flip-flops.

Few garbage cans for the plant cafeteria, sold to industry through the maintenance superintendent who's in charge of janitorial services, among other things, are particularly lovely. However, the manufacturer of a garbage can that's constructed better than others on the market doesn't have to be a nonadvertising shrinking violet who won't tell industry his product is superior.

Perhaps he spot-welds a reinforcing gusset under the side handles of his product.

This would naturally make the can last longer and prevent handles from tearing or bending the metal when a heavy load is lifted by the mechanical arms of a hydraulic device used to hoist the can and dump the contents into a truck. This would make an excellent feature illustration, of course.

And the top of the can could have a roll-over edge that's larger and heavier than those of the competition. The handle on the lid could be double thickness with an extra spot weld. Or a cross-section of the metal could show corrugations that are deeper than other cans, stiffening and strengthening the can. An extreme closeup might show the galvanized finish is thicker than normally applied to prevent rust and corrosion.

The illustration for this brand of garbage can might well show the can as a whole, then closeups of the various features, perhaps with key numbers or letters to which the copy could refer.

Despite the fact we're all out after the competition tooth and toenail, we must realize most products offered for sale are good. They're good or the companies producing them wouldn't remain in business. You can sell a poor product once through hard-sell advertising and high-pressure salesmanship, but you can't do it twice. Once burned, forever warned.

Even if all products are good, none is perfect. Some are better than others in almost every respect—sometimes, but not often, significantly so—but every product has a weakness or two that's not discussed outside the company. Furthermore, some products that might not rate right up there with the very best in the marketplace still excel in certain features, or for specific applications. Even those acknowledged as resting on the pinnacle of near perfection have features that are better than the product as a whole. These are the ones you'll want to show and talk about.

Spotlight these features, select those that are unique with your product, those the competition can't match, then talk about them in your advertising. Show them in the illustrations. You'll find that you can exploit just a few features—even one that's really significant—enough to carry the product story. Readers usually assume that a product is superior in most respects if it is in one and you can convince them of this. It's up to your ad to do this.

User Benefit

The benefit the company derives from the product is infinitely more important to the industrial buyer than is the product itself, of course. After all, he or she doesn't personally consume the product; it isn't used to gratify any personal tastes or desires or ambitions.

For this reason the user-benefit illustration is an excellent one for industrial advertising. This type of illustration immediately answers the reader's question, What's in it for me?—meaning, of course, the company. Nobody is remotely interested in a turret lathe *per se*. No turret lathe is a thing of beauty, none stirs men's souls, nor did any ever inspire a poem or a revolution. It's what the turret lathe produces and how fast it produces that's of interest.

It follows, then, that if you can develop a creative illustrative idea that sells the squeal instead of the pig, you're well on your way to a highly effective advertisement. Frequently you'll find it easier to illustrate a user benefit than a feature, explanation, comparison, or what have you.

This all boils down to a basic tenet of industrial advertising: The reader is looking for a *reason why* he or she should buy the product that's advertised. Show in the illustration the reason why he or she should, tell why in the headline and in the body copy, and you have a presold prospect whose sales resistance is significantly lower than before he read the ad. The ad has made a partial believer. Your sales reps will find completing the process easier because of the advertising.

Many manufacturers of products such as rowboats, yachts, travel trailers, trucks, jet airplanes and overhead doors are vitally concerned with the weight of the finished product. Lightness in weight is synonomous with extra quality and extra earning ability in many instances. Yet these same manufacturers are faced with opposing demands of building to a minimum weight and, at the same time, producing a product that will stand the stress of exceptionally severe service.

This is where aluminum comes in. Although aluminum has many other desirable characteristics—it won't rust, it requires little maintenance, it doesn't have to be painted—its lightness is probably the attribute that's most salable. Nobody except one former defense

Are kids stronger today? No. Boats are aluminum.

You don't have to be a weight-lifter to carry an aluminum boat.

An 11-year-old can hold up his end with ease.

Aluminum is so light (one-third the weight of steel) and so strong (some aluminum alloys are stronger than structural steel), the role it plays in all forms of transportation keeps getting bigger.

Today's jetliners are 75% to 85% aluminum. There are 2,000 *tons* of aluminum on the S. S. *United States*, world's fastest ocean liner.

The most modern railroad cars are aluminum. So are the newest buses, trucks, mobile homes, travel trailers.

Aluminum makes automobiles look better, perform better, wear better.

Aluminum is a wonderful homebody,

too. Aluminum siding is rustfree, practically maintenance-free, and hardly ever needs painting.

A great deal of the frozen food you buy comes packaged in aluminum. And every woman knows how good aluminum foil is.

Aluminum is big today. And it's going places. Come on along.

May your future be as bright as aluminum's.

The Aluminum Association

The mark of aluminum; symbol of the world's most versatile metal. © The Aluminum Association 1966

chief ever deliberately selected a heavy fighter-bomber for the armed forces, for example. But, then, he's not there any longer.

Accordingly, when a new campaign to extoll the virtues of the light-weight metal was being created for The Aluminum Association, it was only logical to consider the user benefits that are most important. Lightness was selected as the major one.

The ad from *Modern Metals* magazine, illustrated above, is a little gem. There's sunlight and warmth and a lighthearted feeling about this wonderful illustration, and a pure joy in being alive. Lightness of the boat is strikingly apparent, as is the smallness of the two happy boys. Also apparent is that they're not struggling with something beyond their capacity; otherwise they'd look strained and tense, boys being boys.

But they're just as pleased as punch about getting the boat out on the water for a trip, and this comes through in this fine photograph. Having the oars in the boat is proper, of course. They belong there. But having the dog in the boat is an inspired touch! It's the clincher that ends all arguments. The dog rules out any possible question in the reader's mind about the weight of the boat.

This illustration is such a happy thing the reader *can't* pass it by without looking at it and smiling. Only an unfeeling individual could then refrain from reading the headline. And the headline alone puts the name of the product (aluminum) in the reader's mind, even if the body copy isn't read in its entirety. But the body copy is so well written, so loaded with information that's honestly interesting, that it enjoyed high readership.

Come up with an illustrative idea this good for your user-benefit ad and you'll have a sure winner.

Comparison of Products

Carefully done, a photographic illustration comparing your product with a competitive one is a potent piece of salesmanship.

Note especially that *photographic* illustration is specified for this purpose—not artwork of any kind. Photography is realistic, art is impressionistic and subject to interpretation, or even to distortion.

The reader knows this. Everybody's a photographer these days. Everybody accepts a photograph as being an impartial, unbiased representation of an object exactly as the eye sees it. When you show your product and another one side by side in an illustration, making mighty sure they're unretouched, the reader believes without question. Make the mistake of retouching the photo, though, and more likely than not it'll look as phony as a three-dollar bill. Then you'll have a reader you'll have a tough time *ever* convincing.

Another thing: If your product's superiority is plainly evident in the photograph, copy claims are automatically changed in the reader's mind from mere claims to statements of fact. Some advertising managers are blessed with products that *look* so superior there's no great need to belabor the point in copy. When the photograph makes this obvious it speaks for the manufacturer and the reader tends to accept this almost as a testimonial or endorsement given by a third party. We should all be so lucky!

There's a danger inherent in using the products-comparison illustrative technique, though. This is that you might end up looking as if you're slamming the other person's product. This is poor practice, as any good salesman will admit. Take a slap at another product in a negative way and you actually accomplish just the opposite of what you intended to do. You call attention to your competitor and his product, and you make yours just a little bit distasteful because your ad engages in name-calling.

This is no argument against the highly competitive ad. Far from it. Avis did itself nothing but good by mentioning Hertz; Braniff's determined attack on the plain plane acknowledged the unspeakable, that other airlines existed and that they have planes in the air. Yet Braniff's traffic climbed enormously. You can use brass knuckles and name names if the tone of your ad—illustration *and* copy—are positive and if it leaves a good taste in the reader's mouth rather than alienating him and possibly turning him to your competition. Some ads do just this.

How to Use the Product

Readers read business publications to educate themselves. When you use an illustration that shows how to use your product, you're helping them along. You're educating them.

There are two main classes of illustrations that show how to use a product. The first is a highly detailed thing which generally is similar to photos found in an instruction manual—perhaps complete with diagrams. It's designed to teach the reader how to do something; drive a bulldozer, fly a jet airplane, handle a punch press, operate a tape recorder. Frequently the illustration will show a hand moving various levers, punching buttons, and moving other controls. This is primarily a how-to-do-it type of illustration and it is directed to personnel farther down the pecking order than the buying influences most industrial ads are prepared for.

Many manufacturers use this type of illustration to instruct the actual operator of his equipment how to get the most out of it, as well as to show the executive how easy it is for his people to familiarize themselves with it. This implies there is no need for a lengthy and costly training program for shop employees if the advertiser's widget is purchased and installed on the assembly line.

The other class of how-to-use-the-product illustration is educational also, but it is concerned with showing how the product can be used to achieve a desired objective. For the most part, advertisers taking this tack concentrate on processes, how to produce products using their process, raw material, or equipment. They're not concerned with illustrating how the product operates, in the case of mechanical equipment, for example.

A good example of this latter class of illustration—and they're far more rare than a photograph showing how to perform a simple, repetitive task—is in the unusually striking four-color insert ad run by Alcan Sales Inc. in *Metal Progress* magazine. It's on the next page.

Alcan's illustration establishes a mood by showing a very old and much used blacksmith's anvil; a horseshoe being made; tongs, hammer, and leather bucket. The setting is perfect right down to the tiniest detail, such as the dirt floor and roughhewn board wall. Alcan then injected a note that's as up-to-date as next year's calendar.

Contrasting with this colorful old-fashioned setting, both in shape and material, as well as by having the extruded shape in a "cold" tone as opposed to the "warm" tone of the setting, is an intricate aluminum extrusion. Of course, Alcan markets aluminum, and this ad is part of a campaign designed to stimulate basic demand.

Copy points up the versatility aluminum makes possible, the "impossible" shapes extruders routinely produce, and that the industry finds aluminum saves money in many uses.

The illustration has great impact and did more than its share toward the ad's success.

Storytelling Illustrations

Ever since childhood the reader has been conditioned to read, enjoy, and accept the picture story.

Readership studies show that ads with more than one illustration are, on the average, read by around 15 percent more people than are those with just one illustration.

Arrange your pictures so there's a logical sequence, so they tell the reader a story either by themselves or with the help of the copy, and readership climbs rapidly. Two kinds of reading matter that *must* communicate quickly to wide masses of people with various levels of education and basic intelligence—comic strips and instruction manuals—both rely on the picture story. Both use captions, "balloons"

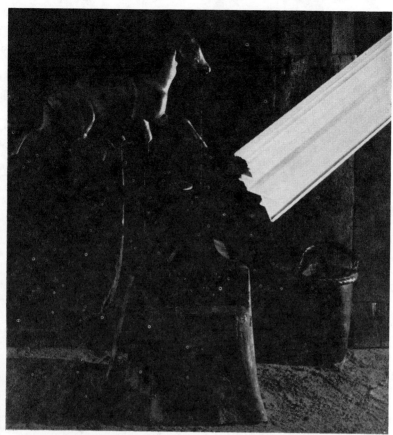

"Impossible" design shapes are possible with aluminum extrusions

with dialogue in comic strips, to augment the pictures. But the pictures nonetheless carry most of the load.

A Picture Story Ad

Plan a picture-story ad and you're on firm ground. This is especially true when the message to be conveyed is complex and not easily il-lustrated with just one or two illustrations. Some subjects won't com-press into an arbitrary one-picture illustration; they require the greater latitude that can be achieved with a number of illustrations.

Take Sperry Rand, for instance. A major communications objective for the company in its campaign directed to the business community is to create awareness of the fact that the company is synergistic. Web-ster defines synergism as: "Cooperative action of discrete agencies (as drugs or muscles) such that the total effect is greater than the sum of the two or more effects taken independently—opposed to antago-nism." Synergistic is merely serving as a synergist—cooperating, that is.

The three-dollar word is a "hook" to pull the reader into the ad by arousing curiosity, and to permit the company to be reasonably modest while patting itself on the back by telling the business commu-nity how great it is. Copy tone is light and factual. Reading is higly in-teresting.

The picture story in the powerful four-color spread ad from *Business Week* is an example of the impact this type of illustrative technique produces. This is reproduced on the following page.

Each of the illustrations "carries" well; none is small or insignifi-cant. The box of blueberries—you can almost *taste* them, the color is so superb—is almost 7 inches across; the giant thumb measures just about the same.

This is an excellent concept for this ad. Each illustration cooperates with the others to strengthen the impact of the whole. The illustrative idea itself is synergistic, as it was intended to be.

Caption of the thumb illustration is: *We shrink. At Sperry, we've developed complex electronic circuits smaller than a match-head.* And between thumb and forefinger is a tiny integrated circuit, that minia-ture marvel of this age of electronics.

The farm illustration is captioned: *Chop. This piece of New Holland farm machinery cuts and chops silage crops in one fell swoop.*

From the computer's caption the reader learns that: *Seat. Airlines use our Univac computers to reserve your seat, schedule your crew and even see that your steak is aboard.* (This is reassuring; the author has always had a secret horror, never mentioned until now, that some-day on a trip to the West Coast the airline might forget the food.)

Plot. Sperry gyrocompasses and autopilots work beautifully together to hold your ocean liner on course. No matter what. That's the caption beside the ship.

And by the luscious looking blueberries we read: *Pick. Today,*

blueberries are picked by machine—one of thousands powered and controlled by our Vickers hydraulic systems.

Body copy ties in beautifully with the headline-picture-story format. It starts out: *We do a lot of different things at Sperry Rand. And we do each one better because we do all the rest. That makes us synergistic. Like 2 and 2 adding up to 5.*

And the kissoff says: *At Sperry Rand, everything hangs together. That's why we're synergistic.*

All of which adds up to an unusually persuasive, convincing story, as well as to an exceptionally hard-working marriage of illustration, headline, and body copy.

Sometimes you're faced with the problem of showing elapsed time, a variety of locations, a sequence of events which are closely related to each other and must be shown, a radical change in equipment used in a specific place, or a progressive alteration in the appearance of something in process—a skyscraper under construction, for example.

The picture-story illustration is made to order for these and similar situations. You can take a leaf from the ad manager of a major airline who frequently illustrates happy tourists boarding one of his or her airplanes, sightseeing all over the globe, then returning home—tired, sated with exotic sights, and impoverished. This last is understood, but not illustrated, of course.

533

Implication

Ofttimes you'll encounter a situation where you can *tell* the reader how great your product is, how adaptable it is to a variety of applications, how much more it will do than a competitive item—but you find yourself right up against it as to how to illustrate this.

Maybe you're not slipping. Maybe you've not run out of ideas. Perhaps the primary idea you want the illustration to put across is one that cannot be illustrated. Possibly the idea is too complex, or too abstract to permit a good visual presentation.

In this case you'll frequently find you're better off to come up with an illustrative idea that *implies* the benefit the reader will realize from use of your product, rather than settling for an illustration that does less than a creditable job of showing him or her. After all, the reader does have imagination. He's able to make the mental transition from the implied benefit seen illustrated and adapt it to personal circumstances—if it's a logical implication, and if the illustration hews close and hard to the benefit without getting way out in left field.

When you illustrate an implied benefit a whole new area of illustrative subject matter is opened up. And techniques that are regularly used to excellent advantage in consumer advertising but are seldom seen in the industrial field may be used with outstanding effectiveness. Despite what we, who feel a deep fondness for industrial advertising, claim we prefer to think, the fact remains that the level of sophistication in consumer advertising is much higher, particularly in illustrative and layout techniques.

With the implied benefit illustration we can legitimately borrow some of the flair and style and feeling of the best that consumer advertising has to offer. We can adapt and mold to suit ourselves and to mesh new and improved techniques into what we now do.

Humor

Humor is one of the most controversial subjects in industrial advertising.

Advertising agencies, some of the large, successful ones, have as a firm agency policy that humor is never used. Never. Official policy is that it's unsuited for an industrial advertisement. Others, just as large and just as successful, believe implicitly in humor as a highly effective device for attracting reader attention—favorable attention, of course —to the advertisement.

Industrial advertisers themselves are divided on the subject. Many who have run highly effective campaigns based on humor are unalterably of the opinion that humor sells, and sells hard. They have facts, figures, and a wealth of accumulated information to back up their arguments, making them almost impossible to refute. It's always hard to argue with success.

On the other hand, there is an even larger number of industrial advertising managers who are vociferously opposed to humor in any shape or form in their ads. They don't hesitate for a minute to hold forth at length, usually for as long as anybody will listen, on the "fact" that "humor isn't for industrial advertising; fun and games are fine in their place, but it's someplace else."

These industrial ad managers who cast aspersions on humor at the drop of a hat are actually calumniators who are making an unwarranted attack on a form of communication that really carries the mail. For the most part, ad managers who launch into bitter diatribes against humor start out by citing chapter and verse of arguments against humor; they cull up from the depths of their memories every antihumor statistic they've ever heard or read, some going back a couple of decades.

They don't hesitate to quote McGraw-Hill's highly respected Laboratory of Advertising Performance analysis of the effect of humor on readership. It documents the results of a study of 5,502 industrial advertisements whose readership was determined by the publisher's Reader Feedback system. The ads appeared in *American Machinist, Engineering News-Record, Factory*, and in *Textile World*. According to the study, ads without humor scored 22 percent higher readership than did ads with humor.

Interesting, though, is that of all these 5,502 ads only 176 used humor as an attention-grabbing device. And there's no indication whatsoever as to whether the ads that did use humor did so in an effective way—or whether it was pure cornball.

Analyzing what these antihumor advertising managers *really* mean when they're holding forth against it points up that they're invariably talking about competitors' ads—ads that in their heart of hearts they instinctively feel are performing ably. Fact is, most industrial advertising managers haven't had any past experience with using humor in their ads. It's human nature to be wary about the unknown and to hesitate to leap aboard a bandwagon whose horsepower isn't known. But the mark of a professional is that he or she maintains an open mind. To do otherwise irrevocably closes many avenues of communication. The ad person suffers, as does the company or agency.

One thing about using humor, though: It must be funny—*really funny*. Humor that's not genuinely funny, humor that falls flat because instead of being funny it's corny or precious or contrived will fail faster than you can say The Dartnell Advertising Manager's Handbook.

And, because the ad manager's usually too close to the trees to see the forest, he's often unable to evaluate whether a humorous illustration is humorous or not; too often he conceived the idea himself and finds it next to impossible to judge it objectively. It's odd, too, because an advertising manager whose judgment and ability to analyze any other type of illustration is beyond reproach encounters difficulty here. Probably this is because humor is a subjective thing that appeals to the emotions. And it's highly personal. What's uproariously funny to one person leaves another as cold as a loanshark's heart. Each of us regard most things differently and our senses of humor are as different as day and night. Best to get other viewpoints if there's any doubt in your mind about the humorous illustration.

Another word of caution about the use of humor: Be sure, absolutely sure, that it's pertinent. In some way or other the humorous illustration must be involved with the product or the benefit the ad is to promote. If the illustration is totally unrelated to the product or its use, the reader is left in the lurch; he or she has no idea of the message the illustration was supposed to convey. And because he or she has no idea, the impression of the product—if he retains one after looking at an irrelevant humorous illustration—is nebulous and vague and can just as easily be negative as positive.

Borrowed Interest

Some advertising individuals don't consider the borrowed interest illustration a separate and distinct breed of cat.

Their argument, and admittedly it has merit that's hard to put down, is that *any* illustration other than one showing the product alone is of the borrowed interest variety. Otherwise, they ask, what is anything other than the product doing in the illustration if it isn't to borrow interest from something the advertiser isn't selling—that is totally unrelated to what he or she's really interested in?

However, since one of the primary functions of the illustration is to attract the attention of the reader, something must obviously be done other than merely showing the product, especially if that product is lacking in strong inherent interest. Many products are of that type. They lack interest. They're not particularly pleasing esthetically, or they're simply so prosaic that to show an illustration evokes a ho-hum attitude, boring the reader so much he promptly turns the page. No amount of devotion to company or *esprit de corps* or gung-ho attitude on your part is going to change that one little bit, even if your livelihood does depend on increasing sales of the good old widget.

Some Products Not Photogenic

Suppose, for instance, your product is a nail, saw blade, file, wet mop, lubricating grease, putty, paper towels or something similar. You can't honestly think for a minute that a disinterested reader is going to be anything other than disinterested if you pop a picture of a lump of putty in front of him or her, can you? Even if it *is* your product?

It follows, then, that you have to borrow interest from something else if your illustration is to stop and entice the reader into your ad even as far as the headline. As noted, there are 21 basic types of illustration, 11 of which have been discussed. Any of these, under the right circumstances, will do the job. Now, however, let's see just how we go about borrowing some interest from something not directly connected with the product, but related to it. (Bohemian advertising managers will please forgive the use of the word "borrowed." There's no way around it.)

Let's say your company manufactures bearings. You could feature an illustration showing a product that incorporates bearings, maybe lots of them. SKF Industries, Inc., did this very successfully with a dramatic full-color spread ad in *Business Week*. The illustration, a color photograph, was taken from high in the air; the nose of a naval jet fighter plane was in the immediate foreground and far below and about the relative size of a bar of soap in a bathtub was an aircraft carrier upon which it was going to land. The illustration was colorful, action-packed, exciting. It served the purpose of stopping the reader admirably well.

And the product was there, even if it wasn't visible; a caption on a subordinate illustration on the copy page told the reader that SKF bearings were on the U.S.S. Enterprise's rudderposts. This is excellent placement, incidentally, for this information. Captions invariably receive far more readership than any other element of the ad except the headline.

Or you could do as Electro-Mechanical Products Division, Stackpole Carbon Company, did in a one-page, four-color ad. The product is a minature rotary switch; it's hardly enough to cause the reader to get into a lather just from seeing it. But Electro-Mechanical Products showed the switch partially buried in sand on a deserted beach at sunset, partially awash, and with an ancient rusty ship's fitting beside it for atmosphere. This illustration borrows interest from a circumstance, a locale, and a prop. All are contrived, but all are interesting and pictorially appealing.

Then, if you happen to produce space-age materials, you could use what's fast becoming an illustrative cliché, an illustration of some space hardware screaming through the frigid night of outer space. Overworked, of course, but much more interesting than an illustration of a space-age bolt all by itself.

Contrast

Sharp contrast is always an eye-catcher.

Contrast stops the reader because it's interesting by its very nature. The device arouses curiosity. The reader instinctively wants to find out *why* the contrast between two objects is shown in the illustration. He or she wants to know *why* one item appears as it does, why it differs so radically from one that's apparently very similar. He wants to know what this difference means personally and corporately.

For example, suppose you're in the valve business. Your company installed some very large and expensive valves in the boiler room of a major utility company long before you come on the scene, approximately 40 years ago. These valves have given yeoman service all of these years with no corrosion, no leakage, no maintenance problems.

However, 20 years ago one of your competitors managed to get a foot in the door at this utility (obviously by bribing the purchasing agent) and installed the same number of valves in the same kind of service. Fortuitously, the valves are side by side. Your company's valves are of much higher quality, however, and appear to be in as good condition today as when they were installed four decades ago. Competition's valves are of vastly inferior quality, however, and have almost had it. They have required all sorts of maintenance over the years; they leak, the metal was too soft and become badly chewed and worn, and they *look* bad.

Here's a natural illustration showing the contrast between your high quality valves and competitive ones that failed. The appearance alone will stop the reader who will wonder about the difference, what happened to the competitive valves, why some look good and some don't. It will be obvious in the illustration that the valves have had the same general use and were exposed to exactly the same conditions because they're alongside each other. Headline and copy can hammer hard at the benefits the user will receive from using your valves, and it will do so believably. The illustration has set the stage for this.

Drill Presses, Electrodes, What Have You?

Or the illustration could show two drill presses next to each other, both at work. One could be using a new type of hardened drill with a special carbide tip comparable to a diamond in hardness. Both are drilling into identical pieces of steel, but the carbide-tipped drill has

Shorted 16 times   # Shorted once

You can spark out an ECM
electrode without getting burned. The
difference between left and right is our ECM
machine's new electronic control system. It spots
shorting conditions well in advance, then stops the
machine. Even if the electrode touches the work, you're still
safe. Because the current breaks in 5 milliseconds. The system would
pay for the machine if all it did was prevent spark-outs. But
it goes even further and allows you to safely use the
maximum feed rate. And the more you feed, the ·
fatter you get. For more details, write Ex-Cell-O
Corp., Lectra-Form Dept., Detroit, Mich.
48232. A short note will do.

EX-CELL-O CORPORATION

produced more hole by about 50 percent than the old fashioned drill, and in exactly the same time, too. The contrast in the amount of work done, very evident in the illustration, interests readers enough to pull them into the headline. It could be a testimonial from the general foreman, production superintendent, or other first-line manufacturing executive to the effect that a company saved X-number of dollars and X-number of machine hours in a specified period of time due to use of the new carbide-tipped drill.

There's no end of good illustrative situations like this. Smart advertisers take full advantage of the comparison technique to boost readership of their ads and stress user benefits of their products.

The illustration in Ex-Cell-O Corporation's striking two-color ad from *Production* magazine is an excellent example. It is shown above.

Graphics are unusually powerful. Eye-catching white space initially attracts the reader's eye. Then the short, punchy one-two headline and the vivid contrast of two identical parts—one perfect, the other obviously at the ragged end of its tether—pulls the reader into the copy with a force that is almost irresistible. He or she simply *has* to find out why one electrode, shorted 16 times, shows no ill effects while another electrode that's identical was shorted just once and is ready for the ash can.

This is realism that cannot be questioned. The photograph is unretouched and the reader accepts it at face value. the mood has been set, the reader has been pulled into the copy and eager to learn more about an electrode that can save money. Ex-Cell-O goes on to explain in the body copy just why its new ECM machine doesn't wreck electrodes when they're sparked, making possible savings from prevention of spark-outs that can pay for the machine.

Although the ad as a whole is well done, the excellent illustration with the contrast between two identical parts can claim most of the credit for stopping the reader.

Arousing Curiosity

The word "curious" implies a desire to learn. In the case of the reader of business publications it is particularly apt, for, as we've seen, this reader is being educated to improve performance on the job.

And "curiosity," of course, means that which is curious—or designed to excite the attention. It isn't some kind of stuff used to kill cats.

A curiosity-arousing illustration in an industrial advertisement has one prime purpose: To excite the reader, to create desire so strongly to find out what the purpose of the illustration is that he or she finds it almost impossible to refrain from reading the headline.

Whether curiosity actually killed the cat is a moot point. One thing is certain, though: Curiosity is a very strong emotion, one that most people cannot shrug off lightly. Given a reasonable opportunity, people gratify their desire to assuage this feeling for, unless it is appeased, they know full well from past experience they harbor a sense of frustration. Even Alice during her trip to the never-never land of New York City—or was it Wonderland?—was in an emotional tizzy when she became "curiouser and curiouser" and lacked the opportunity to gratify her yearning for learning about the strange sensation which possessed her.

Use a provocative, curiosity-arousing illustration in your advertisement and the reader responds immediately. He or she wonders why you show it. Or if the object illustrated doesn't explain itself, he or she'll wonder why you used it. Then, if the headline provides an explanation that satisfies an innate sense of logic by bridging the gap between the unexplained illustration and the body copy, your ad has every chance of being well read.

The young lady as used by Bostitch, Inc., a Textron Company, well-known fastening methods manufacture, *is* enough to arouse the reader's curiosity. The ads are shown together nearby. First question that comes to mind is, "What is she doing there, taking a bath in an ad?" Second question which follows hard on the heels of the first is, "And just what kind of bathtub is *that?*"

Both headlines—Bostitch used two, to test which one produced the better response—continue to whet the curiosity, talking as they do about "packaging hot water at a heartwarming profit." Only when the reader has been enticed into the body copy, and the illustration and headline work well together to assure that this happens, is the mystery unfolded.

Body copy tells the story of a manufacturer of water heaters who found himself in hot water due to a bottleneck in his crating department. A Bostitch man solved his problem pronto by designing a new shipping carton; it reduced packaging materials cost by 50 percent, desirable in itself. Better yet, the Bostitch man solved *his* problem by switching the manufacturer to Bostitch staplers to assemble the cartons and thus boosted packaging speed 500 percent, ending the bot-

HOW TO PACKAGE HOT WATER AT A HEARTWARMING PROFIT

BOSTITCH HELPS PACKAGE HOT WATER AT A HEARTWARMING PROFIT

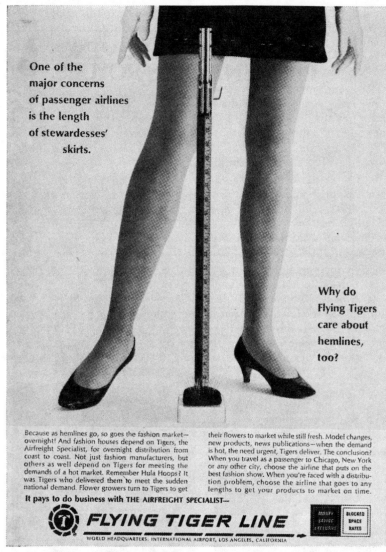

tleneck. This enabled water heater production to be stepped up 133 percent to keep up with sales.

One version or the other of the two ads ran in *U.S. News & World Report, Newsweek, Purchasing Week, Factory, Mill & Factory, Handling & Shipping, Modern Materials Handling, Materials Handling—Engineering, Package Engineering,* and in *Modern Packaging.*

Flying Tiger Line uses a strong combination of a curiosity arousing illustration of a pair of luscious legs and a two-part headline to stop the reader right in his tracks. The compelling black-and-white ad appeared in *Business Week* magazine.

First reaction of the reader is, "My, what luscious legs!" Next, he settles down a bit and thinks, "You mean the skirt's going to be shorter yet?" Then, "What's this bit with the Flying Tiger Line—they don't have stewardesses?"

By this time the reader's thoroughly hooked, so he or she proceeds on to the body copy to learn that Flying Tiger Line is the stand-by of famous fashion houses which depend on speedy, economical air freight to keep the pipeline to the marketplace filled with the latest numbers—which are actually perishables when you equate demand with feminine capriciousness.

Naturally enough, it follows that if the Tigers can perform so ably for fashion, they can come to the rescue of any troubled manufacturer who finds that time is a critically important factor in his distribution process.

This ad is unusually persuasive and convincing, and it got the chance to persuade and convince because the illustration delivered the readers. Sic 'em, Tiger!

Charts and Graphs

With an appropriate chart or graph you can summarize a complex mass of numerical data so the reader can grasp it at a glance.

Engineers and others accustomed to analyzing complicated performance figures for components being incorporated into a finished assembly are vitally interested in these data. They find them greatly simplified and much easier to grasp when presented in the form of a chart or graph. The advertiser's message is presented succinctly and in much less space than copy could explain such detailed information.

McGraw-Hill's Laboratory of Advertising Performance ranks charts and graphs third from the top in readership. This isn't because charts and graphs have high interest for the average reader, but because they satisfy one of the reader's most important objectives in reading business publications. Charts and graphs present useful information, stripped of all except essentials so the reader can evaluate without fuss or fanfare.

The technical reader has a gut-feeling about this. He or she believes that the advertiser who presents charts and graphs is taking an approach toward the product that is open, frank, and unbiased. He's not trying to con the reader. Believability of charts and graphs is excep-

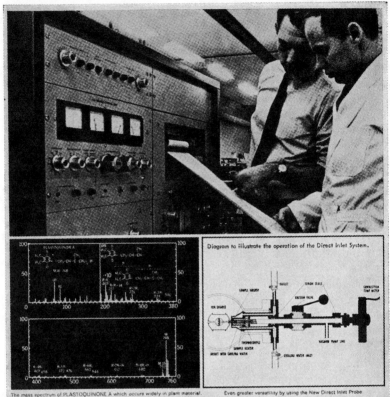

tionally high. Technically-oriented readers have a basic distrust of much advertising because it relies heavily on *words* to disseminate the message. Words are something the technical man would just about as soon do without, unless they're spoken ones. Show something in a way that he or she's accustomed to working with when doodling with a product or its development and you immediately have a person who's prepared to believe what you have to say. Obviously you can't step out of the pages of the book with a slide rule clutched firmly in your hand, nor can you wave a blueprint in the reader's face. But you can do what is considered the next best thing: Show what you have visually with a chart or graph, or both.

It's not advisable to rely completely on charts and graphs, however. Research shows that most industrial advertisements using charts and graphs are strengthened when the illustration also contains a photograph or artwork *in addition to* the chart and graph. This permits the advertiser to show the product, show how it's used, illustrate important features, or do whatever else is called for to arouse reader interest in the ad.

Effectiveness of this combination is exploited with considerable skill in the LKB Instruments, Inc. ad illustrated nearby. This black-and-white ad discusses the first commerical instrument to integrate a gas chromatograph, a molecule separator, and a mass spectrometer. It's little short of amazing this hasn't been done before, come to think of it.

The ad has an attention-getting photograph in which the two men are so interested in the information coming from the instrument that you almost wish you could look over their shoulders.

Then, in reverse (white on black) is information portrayed graphically—far too much to explain in copy; it is crystal clear here, though. On the right is a diagram illustrating the operation of the equipment's direct inlet system, also easily understood by the technical audience to whom the ad is directed.

Copy does a good job of suggesting applications and performance characteristics of the instrument, and it makes a strong bid for action.

Technical people dig charts, graphs, diagrams, schematics, and so on. Give them what communicates with them.

Cutaway or Cross Section

An average reader of a trade publication is not blessed with either X-ray vision or extrasensory perception. More's the pity. However, if he or she were, he'd not be reading trade publications where your ads run—he'd be hanging onto a table in Las Vegas.

When you're faced with presenting a complicated mechanical product that's all neatly housed in a very solid metal case that's impossible to see through, yet you want to explain all of the intricacies and

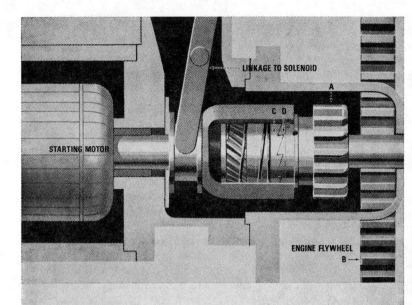

A Bendix starter drive won't kick your flywheel in the teeth.

This is the Bendix® Positork® starter drive. It offers performance that's far superior to sprag-type designs, that's for sure. Positork's unique indexing ability automatically aligns its pinion teeth (A) with flywheel teeth (B). Only then does cranking action begin. After the engine fires, a unique separator mechanism automatically disengages dentile clutch teeth (C) and dentile pinion teeth (D). There's no chance of damage caused by prolonged high-speed pinion overrun.

What about grease seals? Spline covers? Positork doesn't need them. Price? Less than competitive models. Positork is for all your heavy-duty construction equipment, large industrial engines and large over-the-highway trucks, gasoline or diesel. For complete details, write: The Bendix Corporation, Motor Components Division, Elmira, New York 14903.

wonderful workings of the contraption, you could write a learned dissertation only a whisker shorter than the one Tolstoy titled *War and Peace*. Even then, chances are you'd fall short of something that satisfied either you or the reader.

Yet you can't merely photograph the thing because all you'd end up showing is its shape, with the exterior nice and smooth and painted and mighty unmechanical looking. This wouldn't do any good, or very little anyway. Nor would merely showing what the contrivance *does* be an acceptable solution.

There's a way out, though, so don't despair. One thing you can do is to show a cutaway view of the device. This is simple to do in either one of two ways.

You can have a product actually physically cut—have the outer wall sliced away with a grinder or power saw to expose the workings of the mechanical marvel. Then all that remains to be done is to have the working parts photographed when they're exposed. This usually works out very satisfactorily. Many well-done industrial advertisements use this type of illustration. Old though the technique is, it results in excellent illustrations of engines, transmissions, and similar items.

An example of the cutaway illustration is the Bendix starter drive in the black-and-white ad run by Bendix Automotive, division of The Bendix Corporation, in *Automotive Industries* magazine; it's shown nearby.

This artwork depicts the relatively complicated mechanical assembly just as if the housing of the Bendix Positork starter drive unit had been carefully cut in half just as you'd cut a ripe cantaloupe to get at the good eating. Then, by keying the different elements, A, B, C, and D, copywriting and explaining how the unit operates is greatly simplified.

Studies show that cutaway illustrations consistently rank at the top as far as readership is concerned. Using a cutaway illustration almost guarantees readership, if such a thing is possible.

Another technique that's highly self-explanatory is the cross section. This is particularly effective when the advertiser wants to discuss the composition of a product. For example, the manufacturer of bar steel might want to tell the reader that the molecular structure is consistent from the exterior surface of the bar all the way to the center. To illustrate this, a bar could be sawed, then photographed to show the manufacturer's claim is based on more than fond hopes and desires.

Yet another excellent method of illustrating that which cannot be readily seen is the X-ray view, or the so-called phantom view. They're very similar but not quite the same. In the case of the actual X-ray, the illustration is photographic, of course. Phantom views are usually artwork.

Either is highly effective when the advertiser knows it's necessary to show the reader the internal parts of the product. This may be done to show either how it operates, or how it's constructed. Many advertisers take this tack in order to show how their products— usually small in comparison to the completed assembly—are used by manufacturers of the end products.

Symbolism

Sometimes your illustrative idea is too broad, too all encompassing, to be shown—or even implied. Such ideas call for an illustration that symbolizes them.

The symbol selected for use conveys the meaning the advertiser wishes to implant in the reader's mind. Industrial advertising is directed to an extremely large universe where levels of sophistication vary widely, as does ability to interpret what is seen. Ability and willingness to interpret ranges from the low of the extremely literal engineer up to the high represented by top management who have broad educational backgrounds; these individuals are often widely read, cultured, and possess vivid imaginations. Due to this vast difference, the symbol used must be one that is quickly grasped by the lowest of the common denominators. Never, however, illustrate down; never condescend.

It's absolutely essential that the symbolism be understood by the reader, however. Should you have any question whatsoever on this score, try the illustrative idea on for size. See what your secretary, your lunch friends, the sales manager, a publication representative who calls, a company engineer, think about it. If all of them grasp it quickly, so will the reader. However, if a few of them seem somewhat puzzled and require an explanation of just what it is you're trying to do, be wary. Better search for another symbol, one that's more appropriate, because this one is destined to fail to communicate.

The symbolist—that's you when you're using a symbol—frequently creates unusually dramatic illustrations, especially if it is done within the frame of reference of the average reader, but still uses flair and style.

Some typical symbolic illustrations, and what they symbolize, follow. With a little thought you can come up with many more that are far more imaginative, of course.

1. Skull and crossbones . . . . poison.
2. Cross, on a road sign . . . . railroad crossing.
3. Mars (the god) . . . . war.
4. Democratic donkey . . . . wild spending.
5. Eros (the god) . . . . love, usually not platonic.

6. Trojan horse ....deception.
7. Dog................................man's best friend.
8. Boatman at River Styx ....death.
9. Bearded gentleman in bed
   sheet with scythe ....the passing year.
10. Red-clad horseman with scabbarded rifle
    in snow-covered mountains ....rugged he-man.

The connection between the symbol and the idea should be readily apparent so the reader will cross-reference the two immediately.

It's when the illustrative idea symbolizes a concept, rather than a tangible object, that you have to tread lightly and be mighty sure you're not too far out in left field to be understood.

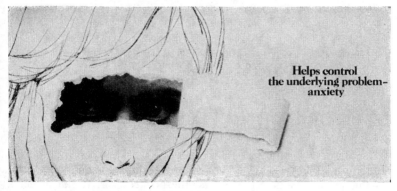

An unusually sensitive and touching symbolic illustration created by a gifted visualizer appears in Wallace Pharmaceuticals' tasteful spread ad shown above in full and sectionally enlarged.

Unfortunately, the copy cannot be reproduced so that it is legible; the ad appeared in a publication edited for the medical profession.

The advertiser does not want lay people to read about Miltown, a tranquilizer well known to apprehensive advertising men, which is available only by prescription. The ad as a whole is shown, though, because the spread is so well balanced with fine legibility in the copy page and with the spread tied together by having a small, subtle portion of the art carried over onto the right-hand page (see top photo, page 549).

A close-up of the artwork also is shown. It is an exceptionally creative combination of pencil drawing and four-color process photography, reproduced offset. The woman's eyes were either photographed in color through the torn pencil rendition, or more likely, were combined by paste-up of the two different illustrations during makeready when it was being prepared for the camera for offset lithography reproduction.

Symbolism in Wallace Pharmaceuticals' impressive spread is perfect, letter perfect. Total effect of the unusual technique is to portray vividly an apprehensive patient who suffers the anguish of anxiety. Doctors being human, there's every reason to feel this illustration communicates with them as professionals, as well as on an emotional basis. When you develop an illustrative technique that communicates objectively and subjectively, guard and cherish it and use it time after time after time. Such illustrations are few and far between.

Symbolism is a touchy area. Good symbolic illustrations are outstanding. Poor ones flop resoundingly.

Negative Appeal

The negative appeal frequently involves use of the scare technique— the look-what-can-happen-to-you-approach.

Because the reader finds what the advertiser shows is distasteful, it's possible for the illustration's negative appeal to backfire with disastrous results. The reader may retain only the negative impression produced by the illustration and from then on take a dim view of the product that was advertised.

Used properly, however, the negative appeal shows a situation the reader is anxious to avoid. It's one that will cause personal distress. It can hit in that tenderest of spots, the pocketbook. It can affect a career adversely. If the product being advertised promises that the reader won't encounter such unpleasant situations, and if the ad convinces of the truth of the claims being made, the advertisement that uses the negative appeal is frequently extremely effective.

An illustration for safety shoes in an ad, for instance, may show a worker grimacing in pain, standing on one foot holding the other in both hands; nearby is a heavy object on the floor. This is certainly negative. It conjures up all sorts of dire happenings—employee compensation claim, lost production by a key worker, trouble with the union about a temporary replacement worker, increased insurance costs and so on. None of them are very appealing.

Or the illustration could show the interior of an office, charred papers strewn about, files gaping open with contents burned and water-soaked, a safe sprung open and scorched by intense heat. This is exactly the type of illustration Shaw-Walker, largest exclusive makers of office equipment, used in its striking two-color, one-page ad from *U.S. News & World Report.* The ad is shown on page 551. This sickening scene is realistic, believable, and downright frightening. Everybody is familiar with statistics that prove that very few businesses reopen after a major fire—at least, in medium to small companies.

Shaw-Walker's illustration is exceptionally lifelike because of restrained and effective use of the second color—brown. There's just enough brown to make things look charred and scorched; you can almost smell the wet, smoky odor such a fire causes.

When business personnel see an illustration like Shaw-Walker's, they imagine the results of lost accounts receivable; or of having to duplicate thousands of hours that have already been expended in doing work that's now lost forever.

Make-Believe Figures

Fantasy is fascinating. Fantasy has universal appeal. In each of us there's at least a little dash of Walter Mitty, a touch of the romantic, a bit of the escapist. Unexpressed, but nonetheless there, is a twinge of desire to get away momentarily from the humdrum and indulge in an occasional flight of fancy.

Few indeed are those of us who no longer delight in the sight gag. The sight gag was ancient and hoary and securely established long before Mack Sennett's time, long before the Keystone Kops took a single pratfall. Comedians from Bob Hope back to the court jester knew it as a sure-fire formula to earn an appreciative laugh—and to establish a rapport with the audience.

Perhaps the world changes, but people don't. In industrial advertising the time-proven sight gag, refined and polished and going under a variety of names, is used with telling effectiveness. Use it and you appeal to the desire of the average reader for something that will briefly lift him or her up and take out familiar surroundings and give free rein to imagination.

When you do so, you entertain. But this is not the purpose of industrial advertising, even though some misguided members of the smart-aleck school seem to think so.

By entertaining in the illustration you capture the full attention of the reader. You not only have undivided attention, but you have it when he or she is in a receptive frame of mind, assuming your illustration is fresh and appealing.

Make-believe figures in advertising have real appeal. You remember the insurance company whose campaign featured the little man with the key protruding from his back so he could be wound up; the Volkswagen ad with the key to wind the bug up, proving it doesn't *really* have to be pedaled; the delightful little puppet, Speedy Alka Seltzer; the Jolly Green Giant; Rockwell's brawny T-shirted mechanic; Hastings piston rings' soft-hearted tough guy; and many others of similar persuasion.

These make-believe people assumed real identities and personalities. Used time after time in campaigns, they identified the product in the reader's mind and invested it with attributes attributed to the imaginary character. In one-shot uses, for the illustration of a single ad, the odd, grotesque and far-fetched can capture much interest and produce very high readership.

The weird and wonderful little bearded Viking in Standard Pressed Steel Company's skillfully executed black-and-white ad from *Iron Age* is an example of delightful whimsicalness and a fine flair for illustration.

Layout of this fine ad is clean and orderly, typography is good and readable, and the advertiser's logo and products are shown to excellent advantage. All in all, this is a good ad, better than the average

Not a cliché ad showing the typical "tired businessman" worrying about deliveries—instead Standard Pressed Steel Company used this fey little figure representing a Viking. Eyecatching is a guarantee of such creative use of illustrations.

you'll find in any representative trade book. But there's nothing outstanding about the ad except the illustration. It is superb. It lifts the ad up out of the ordinary. It does a great job of doing just what the illustration is supposed to do—stopping the reader.

Visualize the ad if Standard Pressed Steel Company had done what undoubtedly came to mind. The company could have used a tired cliché—the inevitable close-up of the worried businessman, forehead creased by concern over a problem the advertiser's product can solve. This has been done to death for so many decades the reader has developed a conditioned reflex which causes fingers to grasp, the hand to move, and the page to turn.

Instead, SPS used a fresh approach that probably required a little more mental effort, but it paid off with much higher readership.

Abstraction

Abstract art in advertising illustration is not complex, but very simple. It is nothing more nor less than a device the advertiser has embraced to capture the reader's attention. The abstraction was created for an agreed-upon price by a commercial artist who had an assignment with a deadline.

There are those who won't take kindly to this. They prefer to regard an abstraction in different terms. They believe, or profess to believe, one of two things: (1) That the advertiser has, for altruistic and humanitarian reasons known only to himself or herself, included in the abstraction a hidden message of tremendous significance, or (2) unknown to the advertiser, a struggling genius, unrecognized and unknown, has incorporated a profound meaning into the abstraction so that suffering humanity can be enlightened and enthralled.

Oddly, though this visual Holy Grail may be discerned only by the truly discerning. Although remarkably few of us are discerning to this degree, the ability to read meaning into an abstraction has nothing whatsoever to do with snobbishness. Some have it, others don't. It's that simple.

An abstraction can have grace and charm and it can have force and vigor. Feeling in the headline and copy can be reflected by movement of lines of force and mobile representational masses that capture the dynamics of the message.

Celanese Chemical Company has a well-known and well-read campaign running in management publications based on highly impressionistic abstract art. An example of this four-color bleed campaign that appeared in *Business Week* is shown nearby.

chemical attraction

Attracting people with vigorous imagination is the powerful force in our continuing successful growth as a chemical company.

So we search for exceptional people. Provide a climate in which ideas are nurtured. Shared. Rewarded. We charge them with responsibility for their professional growth. And ours.

They've made us the foremost producer of acetic acid and formaldehyde. A world-wide supplier of basic bulk chemicals. Plus some very specialized ones.

We combine their technical contributions with constantly expanding physical resources. New equipment, machines, technologies. This combination makes it possible to improve market service in existing product lines and to explore new areas of chemistry. So we can serve the markets of the future.

Our search has produced sound, practical results. Exceptional people. Products. Profits. Which means exceptionally fine service to all of our customers. Celanese Chemical Company, 522 Fifth Avenue, New York, 10036. **CELANESE**

Celanese®

Objectives of this campaign are:

1. To project the image of Celanese as a modern, progressive, well-run company whose future growth is inevitable.

2. Increase favorable awareness of Celanese as one of the major bulk chemical producers, with strong production technology, modern manufacturing facilities, and a highly skilled, experienced sales force.

3. Portray Celanese as a good place to work, in terms of its dynamic growth and forward-looking personnel policies.

4. Increase awareness of specific products, and their advantages.
5. Continue to stress the broad line of bulk chemicals not available from Celanese.
6. Strengthen Celanese's reputation for R&D capabilities.

These are all legitimate communications objectives, of course, and well within the ability of advertising to deliver.

That Celanese uses abstractions and impressionistic art effectively is beyond question. Celanese ads have consistently been in the top sixth in Starch readership surveys. Bench-mark studies and followup surveys have shown that the company's audience has increased by about 10 percent in its recognition of Celanese as an entity of the sort defined by the company's objectives.

What's more, the company has experienced a large and unforeseen demand for reprints of the abstract illustrations. Requests came in in such quantity that Celanese couldn't supply ad reprints to each inquirer; also, an ad was hardly the right thing to send to an inquirer. He or she had already seen it.

So Celanese had a black-and-white merchandiser printed; it served to recap the advertisements and illustrations, with legible copy. Also, an explanation of the rationale behind use of the abstractions was given on the inside fold. It explained:

The art of managing and integrating the scientific disciplines of marketing and technology is the core of our operation at Celanese. It has continuously generated our progress. It still does. It always will.

In seeking appropriate graphics to communicate the essentials of our philosophy no ordinary form would do. The search bypassed the commonplace and moved toward the experimental . . . the bold.

Abstractions were developed to symbolize dramatically, the interdependence of our creativity and science. The result: Variations within a geometric theme that consistently states our belief in disciplined freedom.

Gallery prints of these abstractions are herewith presented along with reproductions of the advertisements in which they were used. We hope they will be of aesthetic as well as practical interest to you.

The merchandiser and eight four-color reproductions of the abstract art, on heavy paper and suitable for framing, were mailed to the inquirer in a neat double-pocket folder.

If you have precise objectives, abstract illustrations will deliver a well-defined audience. And if you don't have precise objectives, why don't you?

Rebus

The rebus ad is an advertisement using a particular illustrative technique, but it's also using a particular layout technique. Many seasoned ad people don't or can't differentiate between the two and tend to use the name "rebus" interchangeably; actually, there's no reason why they shouldn't.

A rebus ad is an ad that usually has fairly long copy. Instead of the type being set solid, however, or set solid and broken up with subheads, the rebus ad has the copy opened up with small line drawings, or, less often, with half-tones. It makes for a highly effective advertisement, one that has much to recommend it.

Readership studies show the average rebus ad, if it's well written and thoughtfully illustrated, frequently gets as much as 40 percent more readership than a conventional ad with one or more illustrations. Explanation for this attractiveness of the rebus ad to the reader is just that—it is attractive.

The small illustrations open the ad up. It is inviting to the eye. There's a fresh feeling, as if something nice were about to happen. The copy looks shorter than it actually is, and it looks easy to read. The small illustrations make it look as if they were carefully chosen. Small illustrations—often anywhere from six to 12 or even more in a one-page advertisement—add a sense of drama to the ad. They provide continuity and act as an incentive to the reader to continue reading all the way to the end of the copy. The reader tends to think of the rebus advertisement as a related series of events in type, something like a picture story or a comic strip that builds toward a climax at the end. To him or her, stopping reading before completing the ad would be to deprive the sense of suspense the ad generates; it would be similar to turning off the television while Matt Dillon is pinned down by a fusilade of fire from a band of desperados—unthinkable.

Sherwin-Williams uses the rebus technique with a fine sense of the dramatic and with admirable restraint. Its fine ad that appeared in a metalworking magazine is shown nearby.

Copy is pithy and punchy and is supported throughout by the rebus illustrations. The illustrations themselves are deceptively simple little spot drawings, pen and ink, which heighten the feeling of action and contribute to an overall impression of something pleasurable happening.

When you ask us for a finish, the finish we come up with is THE finish.

And here's how we reach the finish,

You call us in and ask us about an acrylic or vinyl or alkyd finish for your aluminum or steel product.

Nothing specific yet. (Some of our competitors recommend one or two finishes before they know all of your requirements.)

You tell us what characteristics you'd be willing to give up in order to gain others.

You tell us how important you think it is in your case to get exceptional formability, hardness, flexibility, pressure-marking resistance, economy of cost, etc.

For example, you might want a finish with excellent color retention more than you want a finish with excellent chemical resistance. (Common sense tells you that you can't always have everything.)

Then we recommend a vinyl plastisol or an alkyd amine or a solution vinyl or a vinyl organisol or a thermosetting acrylic or a fluorocarbon or a silicone-polyester finish.

We engineer them in any combination to satisfy any of your specific requirements.

What it comes down to is this: While we don't recommend a finish in the beginning, we do at the finish.

By then, we know it's the *one* finish for your product.

Now, begin. Write Chemical Coatings Division, The Sherwin-Williams Co., 101 Prospect Avenue, Cleveland, Ohio 44101.

We'll start from there.

Note that as the story unfolds, the final, complete illustration takes form. This subtle technique acts as a gentle hint to the reader that he or she is expected to read all of the copy, and that if he fails to do so he won't benefit from having read what he did. Everybody has a subconscious desire to see a project completed, and so it is with the line illustration of the can of paint.

As the reader gets deeper into the copy he or she subconsciously feels that is contributing toward making the illustration complete. This is one of the rewards received here, that and information that is useful.

There's inviting white space aplenty, the layout is clean and simple, and the only spot of color is in Sherwin-Williams' red logo on the paint can in the lower right hand corner. The *completed illustration* shows the advertiser's logo. This is a very delicate psychological boost for the Sherwin-Williams logo and company name. It leaves a definite, positive impression about the company and its products in the reader's mind—as was intended.

Qualities of Good Illustrations

Invest an illustration that's exactly right for your advertisement with attributes of people and you should have a graphic combination of Jack Armstrong and Mr. Clean.

Illustrations are supposed to be nice-guy representations. They never bore, they never repel. They're always in good taste, or should be, at least. Illustrations are never blatant, cheap, or tawdry and they never show anything likely to offend even the most sensitive member of any ethnic or religious group—or even a stern-faced, flinty-eyed stuffed-shirt who's opposed to almost everything. To commit any of these cardinal errors is to risk alienating the reader, perhaps forever.

To be really cogent and to exert the greatest possible influence on the reader, the illustration should possess in generous measure four major qualities: Stopping power, believability, balance, and good composition.

Let's look at each one, one at a time, and see just what's involved in achieving these qualities.

Stopping Power

Some have it, some don't. Different types of illustrations have the ability, the power, to stop readers with varying interests and pull them all into the headline and body copy. Engineers, for instance, are inordinately fond of cutaways and cross sections; they also dote on charts and graphs with figures and lines substituting for words. Run an ad like that and they'll eat it up.

Whatever illustration is used in the industrial advertisement must excel in ability to cause the reader to stop, look—and then look again. It must interest enough to cause the reader to read the headline. It must telegraph that something of more than passing interest follows, and it is in self-interest to find out what it is. The examples we've already seen have this ability for the most part.

In industrial advertising the audience for your ads is mostly male. Granted, more women are becoming involved in buying decisions in industry, especially if style and color are highly important. Women also exert influence if they happen to be the wife or partner or owner of a business. Today though, it's not safe to ignore this universe when considering the illustration. You should deliberately use illustrative matter that would appeal to both sexes.

To stop any audience you may use the following list of subjects:

Other men	Entertainment
Business	Adventure
Home	Travel
Sports	Machinery
Outdoor life	News
Automobiles	Humor
Animals	Do-it-yourself
Clothing	Sex
Science	Hobbies

Here are a few illustrative facts of life that aren't widely recognized, judging by industrial advertisements currently running in the business press.

Crowds repel people, as far as an illustration in an ad is concerned. Your illustration has far greater appeal if you concentrate attention on one person, or a small group.

Do not, however, use an extreme closeup of one person; enlarged pores, blackheads, wrinkles and other evidences of mortality that we all have are repulsive to most people. Readers flee in droves from such illustrations.

Avoid graphic clichés—a jumble of type faces; scissors cutting a dollar bill in half to illustrate cutting costs; a piggy bank to indicate savings; illustrating the earth to denote a world of ways to do something; the model with the fatuous grin pointing to the product; a police officer scowling threateningly to indicate the reader should stop doing whatever it is he's doing that doesn't involve the advertiser's product—such as using a competitive product; and *never* show a picture of The Factory unless you're trying to sell it.

There's no disputing that the four basic necessities of man are: Shelter, food, self-preservation, and sex. Every person on earth possesses these four drives, but in varying degrees and order of importance.

Research shows that people prefer pictures of people with whom they can identify. In movies and television shows, men prefer to watch actors and women would rather watch actresses because each can identify with his own sex.

Here's an engineer's magazine even your wife will love

It's the *portable* chart paper magazine from our new Mark 250 Strip Chart Recorder. Now you can take the record home with you, or any place for that matter! Manual turning knobs let you roll the chart forward and back. Later, you can re-record on the same chart for side-by-side comparison. Chart take-up is automatic. And you can reload the magazine in seconds. (Many users get an extra magazine . . . study one while the other is in the recorder.)

But the world's slickest chart magazine is just one of the Mark 250's great new features. Step response over the full 4½-inch span (10% to 90%) is 40 milliseconds . . . records up to 100 cps . . . flat to 10 cps full scale! Choice of 21 interchangeable preamps. Pushbutton selection of 12 chart speeds. Crisp, clear, rectilinear presentation. Patented,

pressurized inking system. Owners say there's no other strip chart recorder in the same league.

Words just don't do it. You have to see a Mark 250 to understand why it's called "the first strip chart recorder for the perfectionists of the world." A call to your local Brush Sales Engineer brings a Mark 250 right to your office or lab. Go ahead. Even *our* wives will love you for *that*. Clevite Corporation, Brush Instruments Division, 37th & Perkins, Cleveland, Ohio 44114.

CLEVITE
brush INSTRUMENTS DIVISION

Exactly the same thing holds true for illustrations in advertisements. In consumer advertising women exhibit an overwhelming preference for illustrations of other women. Next, they prefer illustrations of babies. Men are far down the list. Just the opposite is true for men, as would be expected. Studies show that the illustration that attracts the greatest interest is one showing another man, or a small group of men.

An illustration of a product with people in it will always out-pull one without people. Show a male audience an illustration of the product with a believable looking man in it and it is far and away the most effective technique. Most research shows approximately 10 percent higher readership of an industrial ad with this type of illustration than one with the product alone.

At last we come to sex. Now, the fact is that sex appeal is definitely *not* a figment of a disordered imagination. Sex appeal is for real. Sex exists. And it *is* appealing. Furthermore, it's highly unlikely that sex will disappear, despite the blue-nosed attitude of some Puritans who oppose it as they oppose most of life's other little blessings. It's quite safe to assume that sex is here to stay, and when you use sex in an illustration you can do so secure in the knowledge you're not using something that will soon be passe'.

Use sex with a deft touch—in the illustration of your industrial advertisement, that is—and you'll have an illustration with all of the tremendous impact and stopping power of "The Nailer" which Modesty Blaise uses with such devastating effectiveness.

Every red-blooded man is attracted to the movies' sex kittens; Bridgitte Bardot isn't really much of an actress, but who cares? Marilyn Monroe didn't win Oscars on the strength of her Thespian ability alone; nor did male TV addicts delight in the *Beverly Hillbillies* solely because Elly Mae endorsed blue denim by wearing jeans all of the time; and *The Great Race* is truly a hysterically funny movie, but Natalie Wood fetchingly clad only in unmentionables failed to detract one whit from it. Only the pixilated or the peculiar would want to delete *those* scenes.

Shown with taste, sex in the illustration can arouse such intense interest that it cannot fail to stop the reader and deliver him, fully charged with anticipatory interest, into the headline and body copy.

Brush Instruments Division, Clevite Corporation, used sex with impressive results in its ad from *Research/Development* magazine illustrated nearby. Think for a minute: Name three men you know under the age of 85 who can pass by that illustration without taking a second look, without reading the headline, and without proceeding into the copy. Never mind—name just *one*. This is quite obviously a situation into which the reader relishes projecting himself.

But Brush didn't just throw a little sex into the illustration promiscuously (you'll forgive use of the word). To have done so might possibly have alienated a Puritan. No, Brush did it right—note that

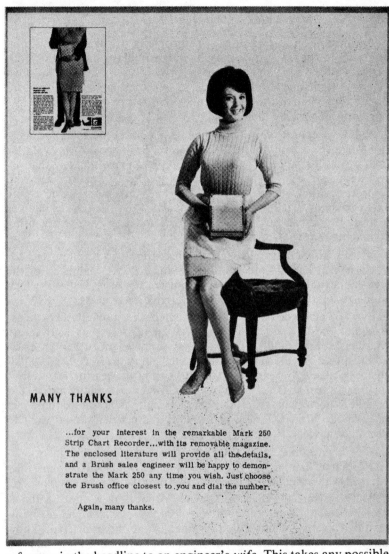

MANY THANKS

...for your interest in the remarkable Mark 250
Strip Chart Recorder...with its removable magazine.
The enclosed literature will provide all the details,
and a Brush sales engineer will be happy to demonstrate the Mark 250 any time you wish. Just choose
the Brush office closest to you and dial the number.

Again, many thanks.

reference in the headline to an engineer's *wife*. This takes any possible curse away from the enticing scene because the faceless gentleman is greeting his wife—not a warm-hearted secretary, friendly receptionist, or lonesome neighbor.

According to James W. Graham, marketing services manager at Brush, the rationale for the ad is that just because a man is an engineer does not mean he is isolated from human emotions and appeals. The advertiser is aware that technical journals should provide the serious editorial diet that will aid in growth and discipline of the engineer.

Inquiries are answered with appropriate technical material and covered with the "front view" reply piece. Brush produced this because so many letterhead inquirers asked to see the "other side" of the model. And aren't they happy they did! This is smart promotion, and the company gets the last inch of mileage out of the advertisement.

However, Brush's purpose in marketing communications is first of all to attract the reader, then educate the reader about Brush products, and ultimately to sell the reader on the idea of requesting a demonstration. The advertiser wants him or her and the company to know about Brush so that the doors will open a bit easier when a Brush sales engineer calls.

Communications objective is to draw attention to the company's new Mark 250 Strip Chart Recorder, and since one of the hottest features of the recorder is the highly portable chart magazine, this method of illustrating it was conceived.

The ad *did* stop readers. Its first appearance pulled several hundred inquiries. And customers came into Brush's booth at the I.E.E.E. Show in New York City *talking about the ad*. The impression this ad made lasted.

A young fighting man in the Marine Corps who "reads everything he can get his hands on" wrote from Vietnam to praise Brush's illustration and to thank the company for making his nights a little shorter. He'd gotten hold of a friend's copy of *Scientific American* in which the ad ran. Of course, he wasn't too interested in the copy, and he wasn't buying any recorders right at the moment, but his reaction proved the illustration appeals to every man from engineer to fighting man in a dark and bloody jungle halfway around the world.

Sex can do a job for you that nothing else can. It's unique in its appeal. Use restraint in illustrating it, however. Don't overplay it because a heavy hand spells ruin.

Believability

Illustration, like copy, must be believable if it is to succeed in convincing the reader of the truth of the claims made in the advertisement.

Naturally, this doesn't apply to illustrations with make-believe figures, cartoons, humorous situations, or other legitimate devices which exploit the built-in appeal of fantasy. The reader easily recognizes this type of illustration as a device used to inject interest into the ad, and accepts it in that spirit.

But an illustration that looks phony for some reason or other will alienate the reader—and it won't waste any time in doing so. The product may be used ineptly, for example, by a professional model who has no idea what it actually is, what it's supposed to do, or how it's supposed to be used.

This situation should never exist. Part of the advertising manager's responsibility is to supervise photography or to pass on the validity of illustrative art from pencil sketch to finished art. He must weed out jarring notes. Otherwise, the illustration is stamped as staged and unrealistic. Not only does this fail to convince the reader of the truth of statements made, but it insults his intelligence. Never forget the reader may be even more familiar with the product than you are!

Or the model may be the wrong type, again grating on the reader's sensibilities. The Arrow-collar model, handsome and well groomed, would be exactly wrong seated in a heavy-duty truck cab or working with greasy hands at a machine tool. Little things—a model in improper clothing, clean fingernails on a mechanic's hands, failure to wear safety glasses or safety shoes—any one of a hundred minor details can ruin the illustration as far as believability is concerned.

So, too, can retouching if it's carried too far. Almost every photograph used as an illustration for an industrial advertisement must be retouched to some extent. Slight imperfections in the product—a ripple in the sheet metal, a rough spot on a cast housing, a dust ball in the paint, an unwanted reflection—any of these may necessitate retouching. How much retouching is done and how it's done are of great importance. A heavy-handed retouching job can make the illustration look like "boiler plate"—stark whites and jet blacks, lines so straight and well defined they're simply out of this world, surfaces so inhumanly smooth and perfect the mind immediately rejects them as impossible, tiny details overemphasized. This is retouching that shrieks "phony" in a loud, strident voice.

Some retouching is almost always called for, however, and good retouching actually improves the picture. It does so without being obvious, though. The reader never notices skillful retouching because it blends in with the picture; it's so unobtrusive and self-effacing and soft-spoken that it contributes without intruding. You always make a mistake when trying to save a dollar by buying retouching that's anything short of first class. Retouching done by a first-rate craftsman can run from $25 to $150 or more per black-and-white photograph. That's a lot of money, but compared to the cost of producing a 7x10 black-and-white ad and the thousands of dollars in space cost to run that advertisement, retouching is insignificant. Don't try to economize there.

Believability suffers also when the general impression the illustration creates is one of doubt or skepticism. Many things can contribute to the uncomfortable feeling that something's not quite right. Props—the objects used to impart atmosphere to a picture—must be well chosen and must be exactly right, not almost right. One wrong note there and the entire illustration collapses and is branded false by the reader. Backgrounds must be in character and contribute to the illustration as a whole. Great care must be taken to achieve 100 percent believability; 99 percent isn't close enough.

Always strive for believability. Don't settle for less than perfection. Partial believability is as useless as none at all, something like a woman's being partially virtuous. There's little demand for half measures in a number of commodities.

Balance

This isn't a discussion of layout; that subject will be discussed in the next chapter. However, the illustration must be planned to achieve an attractive balance in order for the ad as a whole to be aesthetically pleasing.

Achieving precisely the right balance between illustration, headline, copy, logo, spot illustrations, product listings, slug lines containing names of other divisions of the company, and all of the other many sacred cows included in much industrial advertising is a delicate and fragile task.

There's much room for personal opinion, preference, prejudice, and plain old-fashioned whim. This is especially so because there's not necessarily a right or wrong way, there are no hard-and-fast rules. The matter is subjective and the instances are many in which circumstances alter cases.

The fact remains, though, that most of the time the illustration should be of ample size in comparison with the rest of the advertisement so that it's quickly seen and easily interpreted. Properly it should be the dominant element in the ad—although there are any number of excellent examples in any major trade publication where this requirement has gone by the wayside. Unquestionably it is desirable that the illustration should attract the reader's eye through sheer size alone—although this is not an inflexible rule.

Most products fit well within conventional formats, so that the complete illustration in the advertisement is a square, or a horizontal or vertical rectangle. Most of the examples reproduced thus far in this book fall within one of those categories, although there is no hidebound dictum that this *must* be. Sometimes a product is of such a shape that it literally defies attempts to confine it within so-called standard formats. If such is the case, there's every reason to outline it or to have it photographed in highkey so the product "floats" with neither background nor floor visible. It can then be dropped into the available space in the ad in such a way that it is shown to best advantage.

Good Composition

Getting the proper spatial relationship, showing the product so there's a good balance and the right "feel" to the ad is primarily a function of the art director at the agency, or an art studio with which the ad manager works. However, many smaller industrial advertisers use neither an agency nor a studio and it's up to the advertising manager to do all of this. Best guideline is good taste and a questioning attitude. Constantly ask yourself whether the ad looks right, whether it's appealing and attractive enough to ensure visual effectiveness.

The illustration is specified by the person who writes the ad—advertising manager, account executive, or copywriter. The writer is able to visualize the complete advertisement; he or she can conjure up in the mind's eye the ad with the illustration properly in place, type set, and the advertiser's logo dropped neatly where it's supposed to be. The ad may not spring full-blown into mental imagery in glowing color, but assisted by a copywriter's rough or thumbnail sketch, it's there nonetheless.

Just because you're able to see the ad before it has actually taken shape doesn't necessarily mean you automatically assume an art director's title and ability, nor do you acquire an artist's or photographer's knowledge of how a picture should be composed. You should, however, be familiar with general rules of good composition so you'll be able to judge work shown to you for approval. Easiest thing to do is to select competent artists and photographers. Then part of your job will be simplified because you'll have no poorly composed work submitted for review.

Whether it's art or photography, the illustration for your ad should have a strong center of interest. This means that the product should dominate all other elements in the picture, or else the person using or operating it should be the center of interest.

A center of interest becomes dominant through its placement in the picture area. If the subject of the illustration is, for instance, far from the reader's point of view, the inference is it's of less interest than some object nearer to the reader.

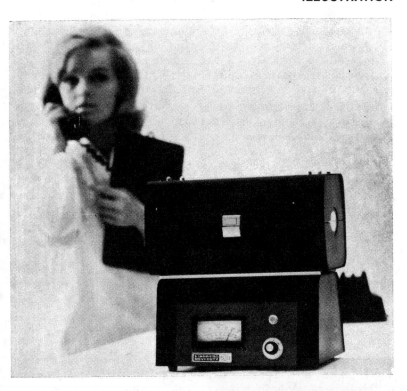

Two photographs illustrating selective focus and the use of this technique in industrial advertising. Above, the photographer focused sharply on the Lindberg Hevi-Duty instruments. This put the model in the background slightly out of focus, thus keeping her from distracting the eye from the product. At the right, the tubing and connections in the foreground were important to the ad story, therefore the background was not focused upon sharply.

An artist or photographer also punches up an object by lighting. The eye automatically is attracted to the lightest area of a black-and-white picture, particularly if it is immediately adjacent to a dark area for vivid contrast. Careful control of the lighting in an illustration can concentrate attention where the advertiser wants it — on the product.

Selective focus is also an excellent way to confine attention to one small area of a photograph. This technique was used in a fine back-and-white photograph used by Lindberg Hevi-Duty for an advertisement and for sales literature. Note that the product is razor-sharp, while the model in the background is deliberately subdued by being thrown out of focus. This and another example of how selective focus pulls the eye directly to where the advertiser wants it is shown nearby. Los Angeles photographer Jason Hailey took the second example, deliberately throwing both the immediate foreground and the background out of focus so the heart of the picture would pop out and make a strong impression on the reader.

The subject of the illustration should never be centered. If it is centered, it's perfectly symmetrical. In perfect symmetry lies boredom.

Illustrations should be composed by what photographers and artists call "the principle of thirds." This is an effective guide to good composition. The principle of thirds states that the object which is to be the center of interest should be located in the picture area so that it is approximately on one of the interesting lines that divide the picture into thirds, both vertically and horizontally. This is illustrated in the sketch with the centers of interest shown by round dots at intersections of the lines.

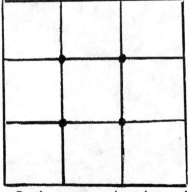

The sketch illustrates the "principle of thirds" which is found within the composition of every good illustration. A photograph on the following page also demonstrates this principle.

On the next page is a photo taken by the author in British Columbia, along the Athabasca River, some years ago. It illustrates the principle of thirds, for the rustic little cabin is approximately one-third

of the way up from the bottom of the picture area, and about the same distance in from the left hand side. The tree on the left frames the picture, while trees on the right lead the eye to the center of interest, the cabin. The same principle applies whether the subject is a turret lathe, a putty knife, or a bulldozer.

It is *not* needless to say that an effective illustration should be free from clutter, extraneous objects, unexplained items, and other elements that do nothing except detract from the illustration. It is necessary to say this because illustrations found in a vast mass of the industrial advertisements produced today *are* cluttered—so much so they distract the eye and prevent the illustration from doing its job. Eliminate an element and you invariably strengthen the illustration. Simplicity is the keynote. If in doubt about whether or not to include something—don't. There's no need to illustrate this; look through the trade publications for your industry and see for yourself how unappealing many illustrations are simply because of this failing. And it's so useless.

There should be good contrast in the illustration. Contrast in size, distance from the reader, color if color is used, good tonal gradation in black-and-white photographs—the range of tones from pure white to jet black—to separate the planes and the objects from each other. If, for example, a photograph was taken in black-and-white of a mechanic wearing a typical light blue work shirt, operating a milling machine that's painted a light grey, and with the control panels, the bins holding the work, and other elements painted medium green or buff, this photograph would be a confusing mass—a confusing *mess* —of middle tones. Everything would be the same dreary light gray, nothing would stand out, nothing would contrast with anything else. The picture would be devoid of inherent interest, drama, and appeal.

Although you're not expected to be either a great artist, magnificent photographer, or highly qualified art critic, use judgment—select pictures that have impact. If they have impact to you, if they're clean and free from distracting elements, if you've hired a good man to produce them for you, chances are they're more than adequate for the job.

Art or Photography?

Upwards of three-quarters of all illustrations used in industrial advertising today are photographs. Various types of art make up the balance.

The photograph excels in believability. Readers are familiar with photography, they accept it as representing the product as it actually appears, and they realize that a photograph represents reality. A photograph of an object can't be taken unless the object exists. There's no question of whether a product is under consideration, is being developed, or whether it actually has been produced. If a photograph of it is shown, that product is here and here right now. No two ways about it.

When art is used, regardless of how well done it is, how beautiful the technique, the reader is always aware that art is interpretive. The art illustration of the product or situation is the result of a man's interpretation of it, of his idea of how it should be shown to produce the effect the advertiser desires. This makes the reader *dependent* on the artist to some extent and he or she realizes this—and resents it subconsciously. He recognizes that he is unable to make a decision by himself about a product as it's shown because an unseen artist has injected himself into the situation. This puts the reader at a psychological disadvantage. He is aware of this disadvantage and he doesn't like it.

Despite photography's credibility and widespread acceptance, some campaigns call for art; photos would be inappropriate and they couldn't possibly produce the impact that art does. Examples will follow.

Types of Art

In the meantime, let's look at different types of art and the advantages of each.

If you've decided to use art for illustrations in your advertisements, it's necessary to be specific about the type you'll use. This includes whether the art will be interpretive, or realistic, just as there are a number of different techniques—each called a "medium." Sometimes a medium is particularly well suited for doing a specific job or type of job, as will be seen from the brief discussion of each which follows.

Oil and Acrylic Paintings

The oil painting is a heavy medium and is the old stand-by when something solid and dignified and distinguished is desired. Acrylic is

Hustle Muscle!

very similar to oil and has the same character; however, it is somewhat more translucent than oil, enabling the artist to paint over some colors with others and still see the original color through the overlay. This is highly desirable. Acrylic paint dries very fast and doesn't stay tacky as oil does. This is a desirable quality also in an advertising illustration, which is frequently finished, then put directly into production. Because acrylic drawings dry fast, they're less likely to incur accidental damage.

In the four-color spread advertisement illustrated nearby is a striking example of a combination medium. The Great Northern locomotive was drawn by the tremendously talented Tom Fawell, West Chicago, Illinois, artist, for Electro-Motive Division, General Motors Corporation. These impressive ads run in a number of railroad publications, and in *Fortune*.

Fawell's first step is to make a pencil sketch for approval by the Marsteller Inc. agency art director. When it has been approved, reflecting any changes that are desired, a comprehensive chalk sketch in color is prepared for submission to the client and to the railroad.

Then the work begins—from 60 to 90 hours per illustration. The artist first paints the illustration in acrylic, finishing it completely in this medium, and waits for it to dry. He then paints over the acrylic paint with either tempera or casein to incorporate fine detail impossible to achieve with the heavier medium.

The original drawing is made in 20″ by 30″ size. Colors used are those of the individual railroad which is the subject of the illustration, although the artist has some leeway to change them slightly in the interest of creating a more attractive illustration if he deems it necessary.

The diesel-electric locomotive is accused by many railroad buffs of destroying the glamor and romance of railroading. They remember with fond nostalgia the day of the steam locomotive when people had time to be friendly and engineers waved at small boys alongside the tracks as they passed through sleepy little towns.

One purpose of this campaign is to restore some of that glamour and air of excitement through a colorful advertising program. Each advertisement in the campaign features a different railroad, and all are, of course, customers of General Motors' Electro-Motive Division. The original art is mounted, framed and presented to the president of the railroad. These executives are always delighted and flattered to receive the art and they hang the paintings with pride in their offices. The program has brought Electro-Motive much goodwill.

This is important because Electro-Motive has approximately 85 percent of the locomotive market. A great deal of additional penetration into the market would be difficult to achieve, but it is vitally important to the company that it retain customer goodwill and thus help retain the dominant share of the market it enjoys.

Oil and acrylic paintings are expensive, make no mistake about that, expecially when they're done by top talent. However, they reflect enormous prestige and project and aura of quality that is inherent in the medium.

Tempera Painting

Tempera is a heavy, solid medium with paint of great opacity much like oil. Primary difference is that the color is mixed with water rather than oil, although it has the same body and thickness and exhibits the same characteristic brush marks and strokes as oil. Some artists dilute it so that it appears much like water color, however, when the occasion calls for it.

The average individual cannot tell the difference between thick tempera and oil. Most artists prefer tempera to oil for advertising illustrations because it dries very rapidly, speeding their work. A high percentage of advertising illustrations that the public thinks are oil paintings are actually tempera, for tempera imparts the same dignified, desirable impression of a quality illustration of a quality product that has long been associated with oil.

Tempera looks exactly like oil and will reproduce just as well, but will probably cost somewhat less because the artist can work faster.

Watercolor

Watercolor isn't seen too much any more. It has just about disappeared from the industrial advertising scene.

Watercolor has various tones when reproduced in black-and-white, of course, just as oil, acrylic, and tempera paintings do. However, the color is not laid on as thickly as with the heavier mediums and the color is weaker to start with. Fine detail is not possible with watercolor. What's more, the reader does not receive an impression of stark realism from a watercolor illustration because it is quite obviously an interpretation by an artist.

There's a place for watercolor in advertising illustration, though, because it has considerable charm and grace and appeal. To illustrate a consumer advertisement, particularly for an item sold to a feminine audience, watercolor is frequently effective.

Even in industrial advertising, watercolor can be employed with telling effect if it's used by a sensitive and highly talented artist. The

Used to be, all hell broke loose when the computer couldn't compute. Vice presidents went off the deep end. Costs rocketed. Hands shook. Voices got shrill.

Quietly to the rescue: The St. Paul Insurance Companies, with a policy covering disablement of computers. ("Externally caused, fortuitous disablement.") The reception astonished even us. Problem-solving policies like this one, never written before, have helped make The St. Paul quietly notable.

Got no computer? Be calm. You can still have the advantage of our experience (a century or so), our solvency, our creativity in fitting a policy to a problem. We write all kinds of insurance: personal, casualty, even life. It's good insurance, and you get good value for your money.

Note to V.P.'s in Charge of Computers: The name of this policy is "Electronic Data Processing." If some inner voice tells you to get on the stick and find out about it before your boss does, call or write. (Look in the Yellow Pages.)

We've been called The World's Quietest Insurance Company, probably because we didn't advertise for about 100 years. Our agents and brokers will talk, though. Try them!

THE ST. PAUL
INSURANCE COMPANIES

Serving you around the world . . . around the clock

St. Paul Fire and Marine Insurance Company
St. Paul Mercury Insurance Company
Western Life Insurance Company
St. Paul, Minnesota 55102

medium is most useful when no attempt is made at a literal rendition of a product or an object, but a stylized, individualistic approach is taken. Such is the case with the outstanding illustration used by The

St. Paul Insurance Companies in its forceful one-page black-and-white ad shown nearby.

This rib-tickling illustration of an ailing computer is a delightful thing. Art is wonderfully light hearted and appealing and cannot fail to stop the reader. This outstanding illustration was painted in watercolor by the late Boris Artzybasheff. Mr. Artzybasheff will be remembered for numerous covers of *Time* magazine, all of which had a remarkably sure touch and an inspired sense of humor.

Crowning touch is the comical little angel with a bouquet of dollar signs flying to console the computer.

This art was produced by a master and is very close to perfection. It is brilliant in concept and in execution and performs its job in a highly workmanlike manner.

Watercolor is not especially suited for hard mechanical products as a rule, nor for scenes which show heavy masculine objects such as factory assembly lines, machinery, construction sites, or metallic parts.

Wash Drawing

Wash drawings approach quite closely the realism that distinguishes the photograph illustration, although they lack the ability to delineate fine detail.

Basically, a wash drawing is merely a painting done in one color—usually black or brown in various shades, although the color is invariably reproduced as a black-and-white illustration. Wash permits the artist to control shadings and contrast quite precisely, providing high-quality half-tone reproductions.

When an advertising manager is faced with the task of illustrating an "impossible" scene or product, often the first thought is to turn to a wash drawing. As far as the product is concerned, it might be a battery of equipment installed in a customer's plant, each piece either painted differently or marred by use so it wouldn't be at all attractive in a photograph. For a photographic illustration to be made, the equipment would have to be cleaned with a solvent to remove all of the accumulated oil, grease, and other film, then repainted so that it puts its best foot forward. All of this preparation is expensive in time and actual labor. Furthermore, it's quite possible it would result in lost production for the customer, making his approval of the project a pretty difficult thing to come by.

There's a way out, though. A good wash drawing of the product in use would be almost as realistic as a photographic illustration and the reader would accept it as depicting things as they actually are. This would solve the ad manager's problem. Even if a campaign relies on

photographs for the illustrations, the wash drawing wouldn't appear too much out of place if there was no way around using it.

Dodge Trucks, a division of Chrysler Motors Corporation, uses wash drawings in its entire campaign. A typical spread ad with a wash illustration is shown on page above.

Basic technique in this case is a posterized-graphic one to produce strong, flat shapes in wash. It is felt this style enhances the Dodge Truck "Toughness" campaign. Imparting as it does a feeling of brute strength and power, the medium is well suited for the product.

While no attempt has been made to show fine detail, the truck cab in the tilted position nonetheless shows accessibility of the engine-transmission-radiator area so the reader is able to visualize how easy the truck is to service. The illustration projects a feeling of massiveness and strength. The "ad work" illustration on the opposite page has a fine flair and feeling to it, almost photographic in quality.

Line Drawings

If you're looking for sharpness and clarity of detail, line drawings excel.

The line drawing is always done with pen and ink in stark, contrasty black and white with no shadings of grey. Line is direct and uncompromising. Each little detail is shown faithfully and literally. Em-

"One Man Gang" Materials Handling System DOES A HUNDRED JOBS

SCRAP AND SALVAGE

HOT MATERIAL AND DUST

ONE OF THE
DEMPSTER DUMPSTER
SYSTEMS ®

LIQUIDS

BULK REFUSE & WASTE

RAW MATERIALS

One-Man, One-Truck, DEMPSTER-DUMPSTER System STORES ... COLLECTS ... TRANSPORTS Material

■ For storage and transport of materials ... in-plant or over the road ... check the Dumpster containerized system. A low-investment hoisting unit mounted on a truck serves any number of a wide variety of standard or special-purpose containers.

While materials accumulate at many points in your plant, the "busy-beaver" Dempster-Dumpster works continuously picking up containers, hauling, dumping and returning "empties" ... all without waiting for time-consuming loading or unloading. Small wonder one Dumpster outworks five conventional trucks!

Write today for a no-obligation survey by your nearby Dempster Materials Handling Consultant, or we will be happy to send a free, informative brochure.

DEMPSTER BROTHERS, Inc., Knoxville, Tenn.

Dempster Brothers, Inc. Dept. FM-11
Knoxville, Tennessee

Please send: Consultant ☐
                        Brochure ☐

Name_____Title_____

Company_____

Address_____

City_____State_____

A "clutch" of line illustrations.

phasizing a particular part of a product or a specific feature is easily done by having the artist use broader pen strokes or by having less white space—or more white space, depending upon the object involved—between the strokes.

Drawing in line usually costs less than drawings with middle tones. Line reproduces with exquisite fidelity and line drawings are favorites of printers because of the ease with which they are handled.

Line drawings have additional appeal because of their flexibility. The line technique may be used for a relatively complicated illustration, or it may be used for a number of small spot illustrations used to show individual product features. Line illustrations may be greatly reduced in size with absolute assurance they will reproduce well and retain all of the detail the artist included.

The one-page black-and-white ad illustrated on page 579 was run by Dempster Brothers, Inc. in *Factory* magazine. It is a good example of effective use of simple line drawings. Illustrative material consists of a very realistic wash drawing of a truck equipped to handle the Dempster-Dumpster materials handling system, combined with line-drawing spot illustrations to point up individual features of Dempster Brothers' system and its various applications.

Line is also used for the exploded view that's used occasionally in advertisements and very frequently in instruction manuals and parts manuals. The exploded view illustrated just below is typical, and is very well done. It is the work of Russ Eales, of Eales-Attaway Art Associates, specialists in highly technical illustrations for complex mechanical and electronic equipment.

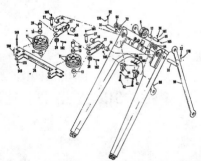

To the layman, the exploded line drawing at right is a bewildering jumble. But to the engineer it is a beautiful picture—one which he can assemble in his mind's eye.

Cost of art for an ad like Dempster Brothers' is well within the budget for the average industrial advertiser. He realizes other benefits from the art besides its use in the ad, of course, for it is equally applicable for sales literature, instruction manuals and similar uses. Too, line art doesn't date itself, so has a long life.

Pencil, Crayon, and Charcoal

Neither fish nor fowl are pencil, crayon, and charcoal. They are

Relax. You've only got two kinds of air pollution problems.

Inside and outside

AAF will help you put an end to both of them. Air pollution problems are many things to many people. A small machining operation throws oil mist and filings into the air. A battery of furnaces covers a community with smoke and fumes. The list is almost endless. But AAF's *complete* line of dust and fume control equipment assures you the best solution to any specific problem. Never any danger of trying to fit your problem to a limited product line or vice versa.

In fact, there's a good chance we've already solved many problems similar to yours. When a new puzzler pops up, AAF's unequalled experience in all types of air decontamination pays off big. Make us prove it.

First of all, get AAF's *Dust Collector Selection Guide.* Ask your AAF representative for a copy, or write: Robert Moore, American Air Filter Company, Incorporated, 266 Central Ave., Louisville, Kentucky 40208.

American Air Filter
BETTER AIR IS OUR BUSINESS

part way between line art with its complete absence of middle tones and the full range of tones of oil painting or photography.

Good detail may be captured with these processes, although they are chosen primarily for the freedom of expression they give the artist, and for the special impressionistic feel a skilled artist can produce.

When used in its simplest form, pencil comes very close to giving the same effect as line art in ink. The excellent humorous sketch in American Air Filter's black-and-white ad illustrated nearby shows how expressive this medium can be. This illustration combines the hardness of line art with the softness of pencil with appealing results. There's almost the feeling of an editorial cartoon about the clever illustration of the hard-working little sales engineer atop the tall chimney; subconsciously the reader notices this, although he doesn't stop and hang a name on the feeling he gets from the illustration. He does, however, react favorably to this type of illustration. It strikes a responsive chord because of the pleasant emotional reaction it produces.

Pencil Is a Flexible Medium

Pencil is an unusually flexible medium. Artists using it can give free rein to their imaginations and make full use of their creative ability. Using pencil, an artist can recreate history and capture the feeling and mood and air of excitement that's always present when great events are being shaped.

The illustration in the black-and-white ad run by Basic, Incorporated for its line of refractories is a case in point.

This striking series of illustrations was used in a corporate advertising campaign and for product advertising as well. *Fortune* magazine is used for the former, metalworking books for the latter.

Illustrations were done by artist Paul Calle, one of the country's leading illustrators. To produce this fine pencil illustration, the artist gave the smooth side of a piece of masonite a random thick-and-thin coating of casein. He then drew the illustration on this surface, using various hardlead pencils.

That most people are intrigued by high quality illustrations has been proven to Basic, Incorporated by this campaign, according to Arthur P. Clark, director of communications. He noted that the company doesn't have a single customer who doesn't know as much about the products as the company itself. As a consequence, Basic's advertising is largely institutional, and is designed to sell company image rather than products *per se.*

A primary objective of the corporate campaign—and the product campaign as well—is to place reminders of Basic's goodwill in the offices of customers and prospects.

Secret ingredient used to do this important job is a handsome portfolio titled "The History of Steel." The portfolios that bring such a

If you would like a large tone art print of this illustration, please write.

First Man-made Iron

Four thousand years ago, the Egyptians produced iron in a blast furnace that was a mound of earth filled with iron ore and charcoal. Only within the last hundred years has iron, refined into steel, become the universal metal. Over half of this time, Basic has provided refractories essential to steelmaking.

BASIC
REFRACTORIES
845 HANNA BUILDING
CLEVELAND, OHIO 44115

large volume of requests are offered in a one-line picture caption in very small type below the illustrations.

Clark reported over a thousand inquiries in response to the company's first ad in *Fortune*, with subsequent ads producing a similar response. Letterhead inquiries are regularly received from top executives in companies to whom Basic wants to sell; the art prints are framed and exhibited in countless walnut-paneled offices throughout heavy industry.

Requests for reprints from the first ad—from *Fortune* and from the trade publications in which it appeared—totaled more than 4,000. This phenomenal response is due to three things: A striking, compelling illustrative technique; subject matter of inherent interest to the public as a whole, and to Basic's universe in particular; and a well-known company with an established position making an offer of an item of real value at no cost to the inquirer. This formula cannot be topped.

Fine art prints in the portfolio Basic offers are richly printed on a heavy, attractively textured stock, already matted with a well-proportioned border, ready to be framed.

One illustration shows an ancient artisan checking the quality of a famed Damascus blade. Steel was first produced in Hyderabad about 400 B.C., where skilled artisans combined black magnetite sand, bamboo charcoal, and the leaves of aceous plants. This charge was then sealed in a clay crucible and smelted to yield buttons of metal which were alternately melted and cooled to form two- to five-pound pieces known as wootz cakes.

This high grade steel was discovered in India by Persian merchants and carried to Damascus where armorers heated and hammered the cakes into the legendary Damascus blades. After annealing, these blades were quenched in a live slave, according to legend; the red-hot blade was thrust to its full length into the bound body of the slave so the body temperature would quickly bring the blade to the proper temperature to impart the desired metallurgical qualities. The system worked to perfection, but the rate of attrition of slaves was rather high—one blade, one slave.

Blades were then drawn to the desired hardness. Polishing and etching them then served to bring the distinctive "damask" pattern to the surface. When finished, these blades were so supple they could be bent from hilt to tip and still take a cutting edge that has never been surpassed.

Almost all of Basic's customers and prospects are aware of this fascinating bit of steel-making history, yet until now none of them has ever had access to a fine piece of art depicting it.

Crayon is frequently combined with other mediums, wash, for example. When this is done crayon still retains the vigor to enable it to reproduce with almost line-drawing strength and character. These combination drawings are often made dry, without water, with the water-soluble crayon producing an effect similar to wash when water

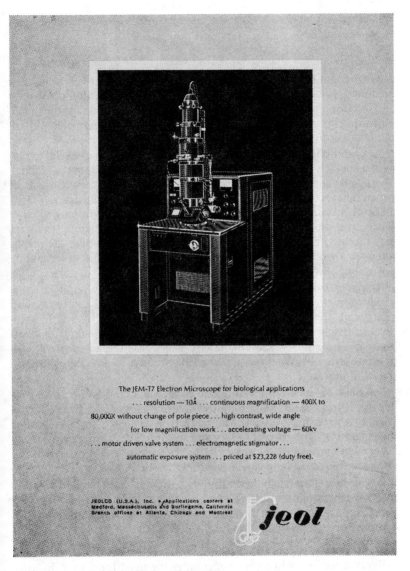
is brushed over the completed work.

Charcoal is at its best when used for work calling for broad, full-toned illustrations in which fine detail is not desired. The medium is bold and vigorous and has a fine flair with great appeal to the masculine audience.

Neither crayon nor charcoal are used to any great extent in industrial advertising.

Scratchboard

This medium is a breed apart, almost unrelated to other art mediums. It is actually a modern imitation of an old white-line wood-cut. Although an artist can create a scratchboard illustration much more quickly than a wood-cut can be made, great care is required nonetheless. It is a demanding medium.

A scratchboard illustration is done with black ink on a special paper with a surface specifically made for this art form. Black ink is applied liberally to almost the entire picture area, except for any well-defined broad masses that are to appear white in the finished illustration. The artist then uses X-acto knives, paper clips, pieces of barbed-wire fence, and an amazing assortment of scraping and etching tools to pick, scrape, gouge, and chew away the black ink. Where the ink is removed a white line or area remains—just as if the artist were making a wood engraving.

The scratchboard illustration imparts a feeling of quality to the product in the advertisement. It is so distinctive and different that readers are greatly attracted to it. Readership of ads with scratchboard illustrations is usually quite high despite the fact that the large mass of black causes some readers to regard the technique as funereal and overpowering. The fact remains that the product looks solid, substantial, and desirable.

On page 585 is an interesting one-page, black-and-white ad run by Jeolco. It has a scratchboard illustration that imparts an air of dignity and great precision to the JEM-T7 Electron Microscope the company manufactures for biological applications. The tiny, many-sided "stars" are typical of the scratchboard technique and most artists include one or more in every illustration.

A good scratchboard illustration usually runs from around $800 to $1,500, depending upon the amount of detail involved, the location, and just how busy the artist happens to be at the time he receives the commission.

Clip Art

Every once in a while you'll encounter the need for a spot illustration, possibly of an offbeat subject or one with a definite feel, possibly an old-fashioned technique. More often than not the budget is limited and doesn't contain the wherewithal to hire an artist to do the job, especially since the illustrative idea itself frequently is an afterthought dreamed up to "put more punch in the job."

Despair not. There's a solution to your problem. You *can* afford first-class professional art of excellent quality for a few cents.

The way out of your dilemma is found in books of original art produced for sale to advertisers and agencies by a number of reputable art studios around the country.

Clip art is reproduced in book form—usually loose-leaf for ease of use—on high quality enamel paper. Most advertising men actually clip it from the book with scissors and give the piece of art to the engraver, hence the name, "clip." Of course, the entire book could be sent with other material, layout, type, photos and so on, but this would entail needless extra handling of the book with possible damage or loss, and also would tie it up and make it unavailable just when you might need it again without delay.

Books of clip art, usually grouped by subject matter, are available from a studio the author can recommend as producing excellent work at a price you can't turn down. This is:

The Dick Sutphen Studio
Box 628
Scottsdale, Arizona 85252

This studio offers the following volumes at this time and at the following prices, although it constantly produces new art to reflect topical happenings, changing styles, and so on.

Antiques, Filigree, and Rococo $19.95
Copyright Free Cartoons $34.95
Designing Devices $24.95
Old Engravings and Illustrations. Volume
      One: *People* $24.95
Old Engravings and Illustrations. Volume
      Two: *Things* $24.95
The Cartoon Clip Book $34.95

The Dick Sutphen Studio requires a check or company purchase order. All orders from non-rated firms must be prepaid or will be shipped COD. Please enclose $1.00 per book for postage and handling.

Let's take a more detailed look at some of Sutphen's books to see what's in them.

In *Antiques, Filigree, and Rococo*, there are hundreds of beautifully executed steel engravings. The subjects are almost limitless, and include antiques of all kinds, frames, tapestries, mosaics, lacework, borders, plaques, trophies, ornamental ironwork, and so on. Pages of the book are printed on 80-pound matte-finished enamel to assure the very finest reproduction possible. The book comes to you in a vinyl-covered ring-bound notebook. Pages are easily removed or clipped.

Volume One: People contains, in part, the following:

People in routine situations from colonial times to 1907, in period dress.

People in wild situations.

Artists.

Cowboys and Indians.

Military, Revolutionary War through the Civil War.

Foreign military.

Farming.

Sculpture, including the world's most famous sculpture.

Ancient times, people and situations.

Medieval times, knights and heraldry, costumes and situations.

Religion, from Christ's birth through the crucifixion.

Famous people.

Anatomy.

Volume Two: Things contains the following:

Architecture from ancient times to 1907, including world-famous architecture, old castles, street scenes, and interiors from prison cells and opera houses.

Furniture and room settings.

Mechanical things.

Nature, including landscapes, storms, flowers, and plants.

Transportation, balloons, boats, trains, and so on.

Horse-drawn vehicles.

Military weapons large and small, including naval battle scenes.

Animals including birds, fish, and insects.

Miscellaneous including money, commercial props, household items, and so on.

These two volumes from Sutphen add to rather than "me too" the existing books of this kind. There's no need to request permission to reproduce any of the illustrations. All of them are yours to use as you see fit without permission or payment to anybody.

Since Sutphen has grouped art by subjects and titles, you can purchase only what you need at the time; there's no need to make a major investment in art that's inapplicable to your product or needs. And considering that you get hundreds of pieces of art all ready for the camera and that each can be reproduced as often as you wish, the art is the best buy you're likely to encounter in years.

Incidentally, the author has never met any of the Sutphens, has no interest in the studio and no ax to grind; this isn't a "plug" but is recognition of good art at a price that's really right.

Photography

There's probably no product or process in existence that has been perfected to the point where there's absolutely no room for improvement. Everything changes and usually for the better. Technology is in a constant state of flux. New products, new developments, and better ways of doing things are introduced so often in so many highly specialized fields that even the technician man in industry has a difficult task confronting if he or she to keep current about advances in a discipline.

Photography is no exception. Comparing J.M. Daguerre's tintypes to today's fantastically fast films—both black-and-white and color—is much like discussing the Wright Brothers' venture at Kitty Hawk in the same breath with a moon probe, complete with soft landing and thousands of pictures flashed back to earth across a quarter-million miles of cold, black, empty space.

Photography has not been perfected in the sense that it is static. Just the opposite is true, for the art—and it *is* an art just as much, if not more, than it is a craft—is constantly updated and improved with a flow of radical new tools, materials, and techniques from the laboratories of Kodak, Du Pont, and General Analine & Film to broaden photography's scope.

Today, photographers routinely take outstanding pictures of what were, just a few years ago, "unphotographable" subjects. They do so under conditions that previously would have caused them to throw up their hands in abject despair. Film speeds make possible high speed action shots, even in color, under existing light conditions that would have tried photographers' souls a decade ago. And extremely fast stop-action stroboscopic photographs of bullets in midair, blades of a turbine spinning at 10,000 rpm, and laboratory experiments that cannot even be seen with the naked eye are now commonplace.

Only photography can capture and show minute detail so crisply and sharply and clearly that the reader needs no explanation of what he's seeing—such as this picture of an exquisite, graceful old flintlock, bullet pouch and powder horn hanging on square nails on a wall of an old log cabin. This photograph was taken by the author in color for a magazine cover, and was also shot in black-and-white at the same time. Notice the texture of the logs and clay "chinking"; only photography can show this. And only photography can faithfully reproduce thousands of individual items in one picture, each of which

At right, an ordinary camera catches every detail of the flintlock musket and fittings on the grained walls of a log cabin. Below, a photomicrograph reveals the molecular structure of a basic metal—image enlarged 600 times.

stands out separately and distinctly, whether it's a photomicrograph of the molecular structure of a cell or the structure of a basic metal enlarged 600 times.

What's more, photography stands alone when it comes to carrying conviction. Readers, most of whom are snapshot artists, know from their own personal experience that a photograph shows something just as it appears to the eye.

Only photography can record faithfully the serene beauty and the clean sparkle of fresh snow under a brilliant blue sky at 11,000 feet, as in the photo on the next page. Here, photography captured every tiny detail of this magnificent panorama high atop the Beartooth Plateau, right down to each tiny tree far below on the shores of this lost lake. Photography reveals the texture and the subtle shades of different strata of the rock; the vivid realism of photography projects you right into the scene. The author took this photograph one cold day in mid-July.

Illustrations such as this are reader stoppers because everybody is interested in beautiful scenery; borrowing interest from nature herself can lead to an effective illustration for an industrial advertisement.

Photographs have the capability of imparting credibility, believability, to the illustration. There's a sense of reality and immediacy about a photograph that is lacking in other mediums. The photo is factual and literal and it instills confidence in the reader. He accepts the product that's shown photographically and automatically transfers some of this belief and trust to its manufacturer. It's difficult to attach a price tag to this.

The camera is a tremendously flexible tool. A really good photographer is more artist than craftsman, more illustrator than technician. He or she is incredibly versatile. From the camera comes everything from an extremely literal picture of the product alone, stark in its simplicity, to highly imaginative interpretive scenes from history, recreated and staged to perfection. Thus the camera which uses tiny fractions of seconds as *its* tool can also ignore time—even hundreds or thousands of years of it, at will.

Range and scope of the camera almost stagger the mind, for it can be dramatically incisive and cut right to the heart of the matter by excluding all extraneous detail, or it can generalize and capture breathtaking panoramas that encompass an entire mountain range, or, in the case of a camera carried into orbit, tens of thousands of square miles of the earth's surface—or even an entire galaxy in the heavens.

In the right hands the camera has no limitations.

A Better Selling Job

Furthermore, photography excels in the one most important function of an advertising illustration: *It outpulls and outsells art, any type of art.*

Photography delivers more readers to an advertisement than art does. Each reader tends to examine the photographic illustration at greater length and with greater interest than if it were art. This has been proven in study after study, as well as by hundreds of individual advertisers who used two illustrative techniques for the same ad—a photograph, and the same scene exactly but shown with art. Then, by split-running the ads in the same publication, they were able to determine *exactly* how much readership each received, and how many inquiries each technique produced.

This takes all of the guesswork out of the subject and makes it easy to arrive at an objective evaluation of the two mediums. Split runs, which will be discussed at greater length in the media chapter, are merely regional editions of publications; advertisers are permitted to use different plates (different ads, that is) in various editions for a very modest extra charge. This enables them to run two ads simultaneously over the same quality circulation list for test purposes, and to present different messages to different segments of the total market.

Greatest difference in readership of ads with photographs as compared with ads with artwork illustrations is reported by McGraw-Hill's Laboratory of Advertising Performance. According to LAP, "less realistic illustrations" produced an average Reader Feedback Score of 8 percent, whereas ads for the same product, manufactured by the same company, scored 16 percent when the illustration was a photograph of the product. Exactly double. That's quite a difference.

Over the years, advertisements that the author has produced for clients and companies have consistently scored higher readership ratings when photographs were used for illustrations. There have been exceptions, but these were rare. In instances when artwork produced higher readership it was due primarily to greater inherent appeal of the product, as well as to an almost unlimited art budget which made it possible to buy the work of top-flight illustrators.

Black-and-White Photography

Photography divides itself neatly and simply into two classes—black-and-white and color. Each will be discussed separately, black-and-white first because it's used more often.

When you have black-and-white photography taken of a product, the product you receive from the photographer is the familiar black-and-white print, usually an 8- by 10-inch glossy. And it *is* called a print, not a picture. A picture is what is shown in the print—a product, scene, building, or person.

The print is merely a piece of paper, coated on one side with an emulsion which contains light-sensitive particles of silver. In the single-weight glossy you'll encounter most frequently, the sheet of photographic paper costs the photographer approximately 10 cents, depending upon the quantity in which he buys. Yet he may well charge you anywhere from $10 to a thousand dollars or more for extremely complicated pictures; more on this later.

Naturally, the difference between the cost of the piece of paper and the finished product which will be used to illustrate your advertisement represents the photographer's cost of doing business—equipment, transportation, rented or purchased props, model fees, know-how, and salary. Some photographers have been known to consider this last item one of the most important, but there are crass, commercial types wherever one goes these days.

This glossy black-and-white print didn't spring full-blown from the photographer's mind, nor did it come directly from his camera. As a rule a great deal of hard, exacting, and highly technical work precedes this last step in the photographic process. The photographer, with anything from one to a small army of assistants, makes a setup—that is, he stages the photograph to be taken. A fantastic amount of care and attention to minute detail is called for. Nothing is overlooked. Nothing *can* be overlooked, for the camera lens is all-seeing and reveals any mistakes that have been made with pitiless exactness. The lens is ruthless. Setups may involve anything from a room setting to a grand ballroom full of people dressed in formal attire, or 50,000 flashbulbs strung on wires around a mile-long curve in a railroad track in the mountains to be fired just before a train comes. Or it may be a relatively simple arrangement of lights used to photograph small objects in a studio.

The product itself is combed, curried, brushed, polished, washed, painted, touched up, coated with dulling spray or what have you; highlights are either reinforced artificially, or are knocked down depending upon the circumstances. Unwanted reflections or shadows are killed. If the photograph is taken in the studio, rather than out of doors, giant floodlights and spotlights are arranged with incredible precision to light the product to best effect. This in itself may require hours or even days of a photographer's time and that of assistants. And even before the set is lighted it may have to be built specifically for this one photograph.

Then, once the entire scene is lighted to perfection and there are no stray highlights or unwanted shadows, no flare or glare, the photographer at last puts film in the camera and shoots the picture. He or she exposes the black-and-white film to light through the lens for a carefully determined length of time, usually a fraction of a second, timed with great precision by the camera's shutter.

Film is then processed in a darkroom through developer, shortstop, and fixer before it becomes a negative. Following an hour's washing in vigorously running water, the negative reveals the picture in various tones of gray ranging from a pure black to a clear white, exactly opposite the way the tones appear in brightness to the eye.

Final step in the process is the easiest—that of making the print from the negative. This negative is printed either by direct contact with the paper if it's a large negative, or by projection—enlargement of the image through a lens—if the negative is small.

Glossy Prints Preferred

You'll find it's usually best to get a glossy print from which to reproduce. This is a print that has been dried, after the fixer is washed out, with the face of the print in contact with either a ferrotype tin or a highly polished drum of a gas-heated or electric print dryer. This leaves a coat of gloss on the dried photographic print.

Photoengravers who make the plates from which printing presses produce magazines prefer the glossy print for illustrations, although this is probably due mostly to habit of long standing. If much retouching is to be done on the print an engraving of equally good quality may be made from Kodak Illustrators' papers—Illustrators' Azo for contack prints, or Illustrators' Special for enlargements. These papers are identical except for the difference in emulsion speed (sensitivity to light) necessary to make them suitable for the two different printing methods. Illustrators' paper has a fine-grained luster surface that is ideal for retouching or other art work; it is preferred by retouchers for its superior tooth. They can, however, work equally well with glossy paper simply by rubbing it with lava stone or other mild abrasive to give it tooth so the retouching colors will adhere.

Contrast in black-and-white photography may easily be varied considerably by the film that's used, for the slower films with fine grain are inherently contrastier than high speed films. In addition, use of specific emulsions on photographic paper permit the photographer to control contrast further.

Paper contrast is determined by the grade number of paper used. It ranges from very soft, Number 1, to extremely contrasty, Number 5. By matching the paper contrast grade to the tonal gradations of the negative, the photographer can produce a print of normal contrast despite any minor shortcomings in the negative.

Even greater control is provided by Du Pont Varigam paper, and by

Kodak Polycontrast. Both are very similar in that contrast is controlled by various filters which change the color temperature of the light source, allowing only the desired color of light to reach the emulsion. A skilled craftsman can even use two or three different contrasts on the same piece of paper, in the same print. Possibilities for control and for producing special effects are endless.

Occasionally the "wrong" contrast paper is deliberately used to produce a desired special effect; in posterization, for example, the photographer may be instructed to produce extreme contrast in the negative by using a "hard" developer on a hard or contrasty film. Overdevelopment builds up what is normally considered excessive contrast very quickly. Then when the negative is printed on a hard, contrasty paper, a picture is produced with almost no middle tones between a stark white and a jet black. This procedure frequently results in highly daring dramatic illustrations, although it's largely impressionistic and designed to attract attention rather than depicting the product or scene faithfully. No fine detail is shown, of course.

Black-and-white photography has much going for it. To start with, black-and-white film is fast, fiendishly so, some of it. Speed of b/w film—as it's frequently abbreviated—ranges from around 25 to as high as 1,000 on a scale established by the American Standards Association. This matters little to you as an advertising man, except that availability of film to your photographer that's so fast it can do a workmanlike job under extremely adverse lighting conditions is something to keep in the back of your mind.

Resolution, the ability of a film to record extremely fine detail, decreases as film speed increases. There's no getting something for nothing, even in photographic processes. As a rule, you'll probably want to discuss resolution with your photographer; highest possible resolution, consistent with sufficient film speed to do your work, is always desirable. Along with high resolution goes fine grain, which means the silver particles in the film emulsion do not clump together in large grains, thus impinging on peak resolution and sharpness. When you get the best resolution, fine grain automatically accompanies it.

Instruct your photographer about permanence. Most commercial and illustrative photographers worth their salt "fix" photographic prints so they're as permanent as the paper they're printed on, and this is measured in generations. However, some volume workers cut corners and make prints designed to last a few months, or a few years at best. Talk this over with him or her and give instructions that your prints are to be made for posterity. Cost is the same to you, a few extra minutes in the hypo bath and wash water is all that's required of the photographer.

Getting the "Feeling" You Want

Black-and-white photography is a rich and versatile medium.

The range of middle tones between white on the one hand and black on the other is long and varied and interesting. Tonal gradation reveals and enhances every subtle nuance of difference in color, shape, form, and texture of your product. A b/w photograph taken by a sensitive photographer is mellow and deep and expressive and it can interpret a mood or a feeling, or it can be brutally frank and as literal as an engineering drawing or a bill of materials.

You can get *exactly* the feeling you want in a photograph if you make it crystal clear to the photographer *exactly* what it is you're looking for. Most photographs that are unsatisfactory for their intended purpose aren't suitable because advertising did something less than a satisfactory job of issuing instructions. When working through an agency art director this hazard is avoided because art directors and photographers speak each other's special language.

The black-and-white photograph is easily retouched, which helps you hold production costs down. Usual method is for a retouch artist to use an airbrush, smoothing out rough spots, "repainting" the product where paint has been scraped or gouged, removing extra highlights, lightening shadows, removing an unwanted background, "sweeping" the floor or asphalt parking lot or removing a skid from under the product, or picking up trash from an outdoor scene. In this way telephone poles, unwanted people, cars, or whatever else that's unsightly can be deleted.

There's almost no end to the cleanup work a good retoucher can do. A good rule of thumb, though, is that you're better off with the least possible retouching; an over-retouched photograph is said to have a "boiler-plate" appearance, meaning it looks painted and artificial.

Cost of retouching can run from $35 or $50 on up to $400 or $500, depending upon the complexity of the job, how fast you push the artist to get it done, and what he thinks the traffic will bear. The law of supply and demand applies here, too.

Photographic negatives remain the property of the photographer unless this matter has been discussed and agreed upon to the contrary. Although negatives remain in his possession, you're naturally at liberty to order additional prints at any time. Price is usually nominal. When a photographer surrenders negatives to you, it is customary to add on a modest extra charge for each negative, called a surrender fee;

often, though, when the customer is from another city a photographer automatically gives the negatives along with the first prints at no extra charge.

Negatives should be handled with extreme care. They are easily damaged on both the fragile emulsion (dull) side, as well as on the backing (shiny) side. Best practice is to file them in heavy kraft negative envelopes made for this purpose; they're special and have a special glue that doesn't bleed through the paper and damage negatives in this way. Write the date, subject, photographer's name, name of customer who owns the equipment shown, the address, and other data on the envelope.

Facts like this can easily slip your mind, and a year or two later you can find it embarrassing. File by a negative number, cross-indexing with a permanent photograph book of the three-ring binder type with glassine pages containing a print, or file by model number of product, date, or some other system. Whatever system you use, stick with it. Don't jump from one system to another. And write down the system you use in the book of photographs so that when you're on vacation other people looking for a photo won't be at loose ends.

An excellent system is to have photographers make "file card prints"—contact prints or small enlargements—and put these in a small file in an established sequence. Give the file card prints and the negative envelope the same number, of course.

A system that has worked well for a number of advertising managers is to number the negatives like this: First digit is the month, second digit(s) the day of the month, then the year, then a letter for the individual exposure taken on that date, and another digit or alphabet letter to show to what series of pictures the foregoing refers.

For example, take the following negative and photograph number: 11178C3. This tells us immediately that the photograph was taken on November 17, 1968, the "C" shows that this negative is the third (A-B-C) one taken of the subject, and that this was the third subject photographed that day. Every subject fits into this system, and the file card prints can then be filed either according to this number, or by subject.

Black-and-white photography is relatively inexpensive and can do yeoman service for you. Buy well, and use it liberally. It sells hard.

Color Photography

Unless instructed otherwise, when you hire a photographer to photograph your wonderful new Widget in color, you won't receive a print.

Instead, you'll be presented with a positive transparency, in full color, with each tone and value just as the eye sees it. This transparency is not a reproduction of any kind, but is the actual film that was exposed in the camera—after it has been processed, of course.

You'll receive it in a transparent plastic jacket to prevent its being scratched or fingerprinted. Fingerprints are the mortal enemies of *both* black-and-white and color photographs, negatives, and transparencies. Grease in the skin etches into sensitive emulsions, leaving a big, fat fingerprint the FBI can use to identify you with—right smack in the middle of the print.

Depending upon the size of the camera the photographer used, the transparency will range in size from 35mm. to 8 by 10 inches, or even larger. You'll be ahead of the game if you specify 4- by 5- inch negatives; this is the preferred size because it's large enough for high quality reproduction, yet small enough so that cost is held to a minimum because the photographer does not have to waste time manhandling bulky, expensive equipment on the job when it's not really needed.

Four-color separations are made directly from the transparency for four-color printing. This offers savings in time and cost of production. No intermediate print is required unless, for some reason or other, extensive color retouching is required. If such retouching is done, you may be better off to have the photograph retaken rather than invest in expensive art—which is what retouching actually is— than to run the risk of having an unnatural-looking end product.

To retouch the color transparency itself, the retoucher need have the soul of an exceptionally gifted artist and the eye of a pronghorn antelope. Dye transfer prints in full color can be made, however, and these can be retouched more easily. They're frightfully expensive, though, and can play hob with a budget.

Modern film, such as Kodak Ektachrome, is beautifully lifelike and has marvelous color fidelity. Color film has been improved so much so fast that it's truly one of today's technological marvels. As recently as just before World War II, color photography and color printing in magazines was the exception and was seldom seen in industrial advertising; it was reserved for those with massive budgets with which to advertise cake mixes and cosmetics and toothpaste to hordes of more or less eager consumers. Today, though, color photography and four-color reproduction are commonplace in industrial advertising.

If you have a specific reason for wanting a color print you can have your photographer shoot the product in Ektacolor film and then have a color print delivered to you along with a color negative. This negative will have the colors reversed—that is, primary colors will appear in their complementary colors. Red will be green, green will be red, and so on through the scale. In addition, a typical Ektacolor negative has an odd brownish-buff-gray cast. It's a distinct breed of cat all by itself, but yields results that are very fine indeed. Photographers like to use Ektacolor because the film has much greater latitude—that is, the exposure need not be quite so precise and there's more room for error without resulting in inferior quality in the print.

A color print is relatively easy to retouch, much more so than retouching an Ektachrome transparency, primarily because it's so much larger and because the retouching is done on paper rather than film.

Separations for four-color printing can be made from color prints made from Ektacolor negative film, or from dye-transfer color prints made from Ektachrome transparencies. Dye transfer is much the better of the two. A print made from either process is an additional reproduction step, however, and with each process there's a slight but inevitable loss of quality. Best four-color printing results from separations made directly from the transparency.

Almost every good commercial and illustrative photographer shoots both black-and-white and color today as a matter of course. There's nothing esoteric about having color photography done, although most photographers charge more for color on a per-picture basis because their costs are higher—and also because they know they can get it.

The photographer's thinking is that if an advertiser has a budget that permits advertising in color, he or she should have one that will purchase photography that costs more than mine-run black-and-white. And you can't really blame the photographer for thinking that way.

Then there's the fact that the photographer works harder when shooting color. For example, lighting is more critical in both intensity and in balance between highlight and shadow, and color temperature —degrees Kelvin, after the British Lord of the same name who first discovered how to measure color temperature—must be precisely controlled and balanced for the particular emulsion number of the color film that's being used. This requires tests before hand to ascertain if filtering the film is required to alter the color balance for most pleasing rendition. This costs the photographer in time and money.

When you're having color photography done, *always* have black-and-white pictures taken at the same time whether you see an immediate need for it or not. Of course, it's possible to have a color-corrected black-and-white negative made from either the color transparency or from the Ektacolor negative and then have black-and-white prints made in the usual fashion. But the prints are never quite as good. They always seem to lack a little something. A slight loss occurs when the additional step is taken because the print is one more process removed from the original picture. Nothing comes free in the graphic arts.

Colors used in color photography should be warm, that is, toward the red end of the spectrum. Warm colors attract, cool colors can be passed by by the reader. Red is an exciter color; this explains the old-time advertising man's cherished slogan, "I don't care what color it is, just so it's red."

Choice of Colors Critical

Although people are attracted to vivid colors, it's terribly easy to go overboard. Use taste and judgment. Avoid the muted, the cool, and the overly subtle. Naturally, the subject matter will to some extent dictate the colors and whether they'll be warm or cool, as will the product itself. A hard-and-fast rule hasn't been laid down, but a good guideline has.

Color film is not nearly as fast as black-and-white film, which means you'll either have to have more of your color photography done out of doors, or in a studio under high-intensity lights. Speed of color film ranges from around 32 to 100 ASA, much less than black-and-white and much more critical as far as the correct exposure is concerned. The photographer doesn't have much margin for error when working with color. Furthermore, color film will not handle as great a range of contrast—the difference between the darkest part of the picture and the lightest—as will black-and-white film.

Resolution of color film is exceptionally good, and the grain is very fine. There's never a problem on either score. Color film will show with great fidelity and high resolution the tiniest little detail just as it appears to the eye.

Kodak and other manufacturers of color film make a point of printing a disclaimer on the box containing the film. It's to the effect that the manufacturer does *not* warrant the colors in the film against deterioration or change. The fact is, colors used in the manufacture of color film are inherently unstable over a prolonged period of time, although the author's good friend Ed Wiegand, an unusually sensitive and expert photographer, has any number of color transparencies taken during World War II that are apparently in as good condition today as when they were taken more than a quarter-century ago.

Just how well the colors stand up and for how long depends to a great extent on the storage conditions; high humidity and high temperatures are the mortal enemies of color film. That's why you'll find color film of knowledgeable amateurs and professionals alike stored in the refrigerator.

If you're having photography taken for "the record" and it's important that it last indefinitely, have it done in black-and-white.

So You Can't Use Photography?

Sometimes you're trapped into artwork. A situation exists about which you can do nothing. Photography is out of the question, so there's no use sitting around moaning about your fate. The thing to do is call in an artist, or have your agency contact one to render something you'd actually rather illustrate photographically.

Maybe, for example, you want to illustrate a famous event that's already transpired. Granted, you can't very well send a photographer back into history to take pictures of George Washington crossing the Delaware or of the Pilgrims landing on Plymouth Rock. And mighty few photographs of Custer's Last Stand are floating around; Sitting Bull must have forgotten to ask his public relations counsel to arrange for photographic coverage of the event. If your heart is set on this type of illustration, art it will have to be.

But just because you can't hire and send a photographer someplace doesn't mean that perfectly good, usable photography doesn't exist, and that you can't benefit from it. Many times stock photos that are available from a number of sources will do your job just exactly right. Later we'll go into this subject more thoroughly.

Collins Radio Company went more than 30 years into the past for the arresting illustration nearby. This illustration shows the communications center used by Admiral Richard Byrd on his Antarctic expedition in 1934. At the time the picture was taken, the temperature near this desolate spot by the South Pole was a slightly chilly 82 degrees below zero.

Copy in Collins' ad points out that this was actually an environmental test laboratory for the company's radios that were used by the Byrd expedition, and that they functioned perfectly and reliably and consistently.

Naturally, Collins' advertising manager wasn't along on the expedition; he didn't snap the picture with his trusty Brownie. But he did go to a source such as a stock photo house or the Bettmann Archives to get a photograph that works hand in glove with the intriguing headline.

Or perhaps you'll encounter a set of circumstances like this:

1. The equipment cannot be shown due to military security.

Collins' first environmental test lab

The time is 1934.

The place is near the South Pole.

The tent houses Admiral Richard Byrd's Communication Center — equipped with Collins' Radios.

The temperature is −82 F.

Communication with the outside world is reliable and consistent.

Today, of course, the environmental testing facilities are much more sophisticated.

But the results are just the same.

COLLINS

COMMUNICATION / COMPUTATION / CONTROL

COLLINS RADIO COMPANY / DALLAS, TEXAS · CEDAR RAPIDS, IOWA · NEWPORT BEACH, CALIFORNIA · TORONTO, ONTARIO
Bangkok · Beirut · Frankfurt · Hong Kong · Kuala Lumpur · Los Angeles · London · Melbourne · Mexico City · New York · Paris · Rome · Washington · Wellington

2. The technical operation of the equipment could not be described in the copy, nor could features of the product be described—for the same reason, of course.

603

3. End results of use of the product couldn't be shown, also for reasons of military security.

4. Use of the equipment couldn't be mentioned in connection with the war in Vietnam, site of the product's primary application.

This was the knotty situation facing Texas Instruments and which led to the striking illustration in the ad from *Space/Aeronautics* magazine shown on page 605.

A liberal dose of ingenuity solved the problem without fuss or fanfare. A plastic model of a McDonnell Phantom II jet fighter plane was used to cast a shadow on a small section of an aerial photograph of a Vietnamese rice paddie; the shadow on the photograph was then photographed and a print was made. Lo and behold, finished art, ready to use in the ad!

Nothing violates security and no secrets were given away, but the illustration has all of the impact and stopping power of the real McCoy.

There's no intent to deceive the reader, no deliberate attempt to infer anything that isn't true. Texas Instruments built both the infrared mapping and low-altitude radar for this reconnaissance plane, this electronic equipment is in service in Vietnam, it's doing an outstanding job just as the copy says.

This just goes to prove that some things can't be photographed, yet a photograph of them can be used to illustrate an advertisement.

Despite customer restrictions or obstacles of other kinds, advertisers must capitalize on the timeliness of illustrative material. Look long and hard and you'll find a way to get photographs of the unphotographable.

How to Buy Art and Photography

When the time comes to purchase art or photography, you've undoubtedly already made up your mind which it is to be.

Your decision will have been made after considering media—whether the advertisement is for a trade publication, a chamber of commerce annual extolling the virtues of your city, or whether you're producing a direct mail piece. Also considered is the question of realism; just how realistic is it necessary or desirable to be? And is it possible to use photography if that's the way you're inclined? Most important consideration, though, is to continue using the same illustrative technique that's been used thus far in your campaign. This maintains campaign identity and aids in reader recognition of your ads as being yours.

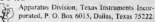
Let's take art first, and assume you're buying it yourself rather than having your agency or a studio handle this task for you. (You *do* save the commission or markup, of course.)

If you've decided on art, you've also undoubtedly made at least an initial selection of what medium you feel is most suitable—oil or acrylic, tempera, line, pencil, and so on.

Now the thing to do is to choose the artist who can produce the kind of art you need at a price you want to pay in the length of time you can allot to the job. You can feel perfectly free to call your agency about this; it's a fact of life that many advertising managers buy some services direct without funneling the job through the agency. This is done to save money, naturally. Ask your account executive, who will ask your art director, or phone yourself if you're well acquainted.

Explain what specific type of art you have in mind and ask for the names and phone numbers of three or four artists who are well qualified to handle your commission. Chances are the art director will have a number of names on the tip of his tongue.

Shown nearby is the American Association of Advertising Agencies' "Standards of Practice in Handling Artwork." Everything said, except point number eleven, applies just as much to an industrial advertising manager in dealings with artists as it does to agencies. What the standards of practice actually boil down to, if you'll read them closely, is fair, honest, businesslike dealings between art buyer and artist. This is what everybody wants, of course.

You'll find that artists—and photographers—are some of the finest people you'll meet in your business life. Chances are some of them will become personal friends over the course of years. Do right by them and they'll more than reciprocate by giving you more and better work than you have a right to expect for the price.

Photographers Also Specialists

Photographers also have sample books, usually duplicate prints or color transparencies of work they've done for other customers. When you're thinking of assigning a job to a photographer with whom you haven't worked before, always ask to see a sample book. This will enable you to evaluate ability and judge whether or not the work is of the type you can use.

Just as artists tend to specialize in either a certain medium or a specific type of subject matter, so do photographers. The major breakdowns in photographic specialties are portrait, commercial, and illustrative. The last two usually overlap, of course.

An industrial advertising manager is usually pretty certain of getting something less than top quality commercial or illustrative work if he goes to a portrait photographer. This isn't to denigrate portrait photographers as a class of highly skilled photographers; they are, but in their own field. You're much better off to hire the type of photographer who specializes in your requirements rather than hoping a specialist in another field can adapt to something he or she has deliberately chosen to avoid.

STANDARDS *of* PRACTICE
in HANDLING ART WORK
American Association of Advertising Agencies

THESE STANDARDS are predicated upon the belief that adherence to a code of fair practice, agreed upon in advance, will contribute to the welfare of the Advertiser, the Creative Craftsman and the Agency and will reduce the opportunities for misunderstanding and inefficiency in handling Art Work.

1. An artist or photographer should not be asked to speculate with or for an advertising agency, or asked to do work on any basis which entails the possibility of loss to him through factors beyond his control.

2. An artist or photographer should not be expected to suffer any loss that is due to poor judgment on the part of the advertising agency.

3. Dealings with an artist or photographer should be conducted only through an Art Director or art buyer who is the authorized representative of the advertising agency.

4. Orders to an artist or photographer should be in writing and should include all details for which the supplier will be held responsible. The price, whenever possible, and delivery date should be set at this time and included in the written order.

5. Changes or alterations in drawings or photographs that are demonstrably made necessary by mistakes on the part of the artist or photographer should not be paid for by the advertising agency, but the supplier should be compensated for major revisions resulting from a change in agency plans or instructions.

6. If the purchase price of a drawing or photograph is based upon limited use, and later this material is used more extensively than originally planned, the artist or photographer should receive additional remuneration.

7. If comprehensive layouts or other preliminary art work or photographs are published as finished work, the price should be adjusted to include additional compensation.

8. If preliminary drawings, photographs or comprehensives are bought from an artist or photographer with the intention or possibility that someone else will be assigned to do the finished work, this should be made clear at the time of placing the order for preliminary work.

9. Work stopped by the advertising agency for reasons beyond the control of the artist or photographer after it has been started should be paid for on the basis of the time and effort expended.

10. Should an artist or photographer fail to keep his contract with the advertising agency through unreasonable delay in delivery, or non-conformance with agreed specifications, it should be considered a breach of contract by the artist or photographer and should release the advertising agency from responsibility.

11. There should be no concealed charges in art work as billed by the advertising agency.

12. No personal commission or rebate should be asked or accepted by the art buyer from an artist or art service.

In small towns and out in the hinterlands this is particularly true when the nearest major city is a considerable distance away; here you'll find the local photographer is almost always primarily a portrait man because that's where the necessary volume comes from if he's to make a living. Often the local portrait photographer can do a creditable job on a commercial assignment, especially if it's fairly routine. Almost all of these dual-purpose operators have their studio cameras, big and bulky to impress the local citizenry, as well as the famous Speed Graphic for use on location. Note especially, however, that these jacks-of-all-photographic-trades can handle portrait and commercial work—*not* illustrative photography of the caliber required for advertising use, especially if the subject matter is complex or will be greatly enhanced by an interpretive treatment.

Photographers, the good ones, are just as much artists as are those who work with oil or pencil or charcoal. The day of the technician clicking a shutter and proudly proclaiming a picture is long past. A good commercial or illustrative photographer is a sensitive visualizer who puts the stamp of personality on his or her work, who imparts a definite flair to the finished print or transparency.

Usually you can find a photographer who's right for you by using the same process used in finding an artist. Ask your agency, ask the studio you've dealt with, ask your printer, or just start phoning.

When you're faced with having your product photographed out of your city, however, perhaps in a far distant location, the problem is a bit different. Just finding any commercial photographer can be a chore—and then there's the fact that if you do your photographer-selecting on a hit-or-miss basis you stand about one chance in three of getting exactly the kind of photograph you want.

Often you'll find it's well worth the price of an airplane ticket, a night in a motel, and a few meals for you to go to the scene and supervise the photography yourself. When you compare these relatively minor expenses with the photographer's invoice, cost of producing an advertisement, and the space it will occupy—not to mention the result it is expected to produce—this is inconsequential.

There's an easy way to choose a photographer in a distant city, though, and that's to use the *Directory of Professional Photography.* The Directory is published primarily as a service to the members of the Professional Photographers of America, Inc.—the PPofA, it's called. However, the ultimate service is provided to three specific groups: Buyers of photography; suppliers of photographic goods and services; and the professional photographers listed in the 218-page directory.

The directory is essentially a buyer's guide—a where-to-find-it in the sense that buyers of photography can search for and find photographers in almost any geographical area, or in virtually any photographic speciality.

Of special interest is the *Qualified Listing.* To earn this classification, photographers must have submitted samples of their work to a PPofA Board of Review. It isn't just handed out hither and yon. Those studios and individual photographers who are Qualified are listed alphabetically within cities and states, making it convenient to locate a really good photographer near the job. It's a great little time-and telephone-bill saver.

The author has used the PPofA Directory with great success for a number of years. In almost every instance, even before the advent of the Qualified Listing in 1958, the resulting photographs were of acceptable quality—or better.

Choosing a Qualified photographer has boosted even that excellent batting average. Every single Qualified photographer the author has hired—and this has been in every section of the country, in major cities and out in the boondocks—has delivered work of superior quality without exception. There are no plumbers in the Qualified section.

Establishment of the Qualified Listing has eliminated the bugaboo of hiring blind, of not having any assurance except that from a disembodied voice on the other end of the telephone, and of worrying about the quality of the photographs which will arrive in the mail. Advertising managers can rely on the Qualified photographers found in the directory to do a bang-up job every single time. Naturally, they'll need instructions from you, what to be sure to do, what to be sure not to do, camera angles, preferred backgrounds, whether or not people are to appear in the pictures, and so on.

Classified By Code

The PPofA directory is highly useful in another way. It enables you to choose a photographer who specializes or who has had considerable successful experience in the area in which you're most interested. There's a classification code for this purpose, simplifying use of the book. Various classifications are:

Ae . . . . . . Aerial photography, obliques and verticals.

AM . . . . . Aerial mapping with specialized aerial cameras and facilities for scale production and mosaics.

An . . . . . . Animal photography; specialists in livestock and pets.

Ar . . . . . . Architectural photography; fine quality work for architects, builders and suppliers for national architectural magazines—not ordinary exteriors and interiors.

AS . . . . . . Art studio; layouts to finished art.

Ba . . . . . . Banquets or large groups; specialists in this field.

Bi . . . . Biological photography; specialized work for the medical profession.

CAPS . . . Advertiser in the Directory.

CB . . . . . . Commercial photography, general; black and white only, normal exteriors, general publicity, small groups, meetings, copies, products in use, studio set-up products, catalogs.

CC . . . . . . Commercial photography, general; color and black and white, normal exteriors, general publicity, small groups, meetings, copies, products in use, studio set-up products, catalogs.

Color. . . . Studio Operating exclusively in color. Does not solicit black-and-white work.

Cr . . . . . . Criminal; photography, photomicrography, and radiography, as practiced in criminal investigation.

Cx . . . . . . Commercial photography, occasional; the average picture that any photographer can be expected to make with ordinary equipment. Most studios in smaller cities, unlesss exclusively portrait, are so listed.

DP. . . . . . Direct color and processing.

DT. . . . . . Direct color for trade; prints and film processing for other studios.

En . . . . . . Enlargements and blowups; made for other studios.

Fu . . . . . . Furniture; experienced in photographs of furniture for sales use of furniture manufacturers with studio facilities for same.

HS. . . . . . High speed motion pictures and stills; specialists with proper equipment.

I. . . . . Industrial illustration; large industrial installation, interiors, exteriors, with or without models, machines in operation, large machinery on location, creative work for advertising and publicity.

IA . . . . . . Illustrative and advertising photography; creative work with or without models, in studio or on location, making sets, furnishing props, etc.

IM . . . . . . Industrial motion pictures; complete production, including editing, titling, sound, etc.

La . . . . . . Lantern slides; only for exclusive slide studios or quantity producers.

Le . . . . . . General legal; experienced in photographs for use in court.

L-F . . . . . Legal-forensic; specialists in having knowledge of evidential photography used in casualty, liability and negligence trials with competency to testify on technical considerations involved in making, processing and properly presenting evidence photographs.

Ma. . . . . . Marine photography; specialists only in photographing boats, races, and so on.

Mi . . . . . . Microfilming; only if microfilm equipment is owned by the studio.

MP . . . . . Motion pictures; taking only, but can furnish finished product.

P . . . . Portraiture; including studio, home, passport, school, groups, children.

PE. . . . . . Photoengraving; only when plant is conducted in connection with studio.

PF . . . . . . Photofinishing; when performed as a sideline to the studio's major types of work.

Ph . . . . . . Photostats; rectigraph and similar photography, not ordinary copying.

PJ . . . . . . Photoreporting; photojournalism in telling a complete story with a series of photographs.

PM . . . . . Photomurals; equipped to handle complete job at listed studio, including mounting, also on location installations.

PP. . . . . . Print production, quantity; prints and postcards.

PR. . . . . . Public relations and publicity; experienced in posing and handling people, knowledge of publication media requirements.

PW . . . . . Photofinishing, wholesale, including mail order and fine grain work.

q . . . . Qualified; see yellow pages (in PPofA Directory).

SE . . . . . . Conventions and special events; expositions, meetings, and conventions.

SF . . . . . . Slidefilms; the complete production of sequences.

SP . . . . . . Stock photographs; studio maintaining cataloged stock prints for sales.

SR . . . . . . Sound recording studio; for slides and motion pictures.

ST . . . . . . Scientific and technical; specialists in such techniques as photomicrography, and metallography, persons and organizations equipped and offering these services.

Th . . . . . . Theatrical photography; specialists in "show business."

The *Directory of Professional Photography* is available without charge to legitimate buyers of photography. Write:

Professional Photographers of America, Inc.
1090 Executive Way
Oak Leaf Commons
Des Plaines, Illinois 60018

The News Services Available

Another way to get fine photographs in out-of-the-way locations is to call on a service that specializes in serving advertisers and agencies regardless of how remote.

For example, Wide World Photos, Inc., 50 Rockefeller Plaza, New York, New York 10020, maintains staffers—competent photographers and frequently skilled reporters to work with on case histories—all over the United States and throughout most of the free world.

Let's say you want to have one of your automated widgets shot in North Africa. You'd arrange with Wide World to have a local man shoot it, carefully following your directions about camera angle, direction of light, special care to be taken about showing or not showing certain features; this photographer would also be guided by a rough layout you would supply, as well as any other instructions you feel desirable. Wide World handles all details and gets sharp, clean, well-composed photos by airmail a few days later and forwards them to you, along with an invoice.

And the invoice isn't the rub. Rates for foreign photography are usually very modest; the minimum charge for up to five negatives is $75—although you can usually depend on paying about double the minimum, plus mileage, model fees, prop rental, and other extras that are found even in your home city. Extra negatives are $15.00 each.

This is a far cry from the tab you'd expect to pick up if you sent your local photographer to Casablanca, considering the time and expenses involved! Even the airplane ticket would play hob with the budget for months to come.

In addition to this service, Wide World has on file a number of stock photos available to you at low prices.

An unusually efficient photographic service is provided by Compix —the commercial photography division of United Press International. Headquarters is at 220 East 42nd Street, New York, New York 10017.

Compix, or UPI, as it's frequently called, also has branch offices in Boston, Chicago, Cincinnati, Dallas, Detroit, Philadelphia, Pittsburgh, Minneapolis, New Orleans, San Francisco, and Washington, D.C. Foreign offices are in London, Paris, Rome, Milan, Frankfurt, Tokyo, and Montreal.

On-location assignments are handled economically by strategically located photographers; they're in many other cities and countries besides those listed, of course, although work is assigned from the nearest office. These photographers are capable individuals who can photograph almost anything to your exact specifications, and to your layout if you supply one. Their work is usually somewhat better than average.

Compix also has a very efficient field photo and reporter service which involves a team effort by a photographer and a reporter. These teams are available in almost every city of any size throughout the world; they make it remarkably easy for you to get good coverage of your product's performance regardless of where it's installed.

These knowledgeable teams practically put the reader at the scene of the application of your product. Standard service supplies you with six to eight photographs, a 1,500-word written application story gathered by a skilled industrial reporter and rewritten by experienced editors, as well as an interview questionnaire report on the key people located on the site.

LogEtronics Photoprint Service—which is a coined name that doesn't communicate, even if the service does do good work—is also offered by Compix.

This is simply giving the advertiser bulk prints from the original negative (no copy negative!) with excellent quality, usually as good as that of hand-processed prints, and at a price that's competitive with bulk-process rates. In addition, Compix has a new "Pushbutton" rush distribution service which provides same-day distribution of captioned LogEtronics prints to the nation's top 100 newspapers. This can get tremendous coverage in the press for your news releases if something really hot warrants it.

Besides offering the services of photographers who are skilled journeymen, Compix has what it calls the "Signature Group of Photographic Illustrators"—a network of 14 of the country's most talented illustrators—who are on call to Compix when something truly outstanding is needed.

And if you're stuck for a photographer and need one fast, Compix will send a man in to do your product shots for catalogs and advertisements. UPI photographers are experienced in both consumer products and industrial equipment and can work with a minimum of supervision, in case you're going to be out of the office for some reason. This can be a real boon when a vacation is coming up at the same time a new product is scheduled to be born, and your regular photographer is on vacation, out of the city on assignment, or sick. Compix also offers stock photographs from decades back; almost everything imaginable is in its files.

One thing: When dealing with any of these services, be sure to stress the fact that you require model releases. North Africa is too far away to be worrying about getting the signature of some Arab for one dollar.

Price Range Suggested

When you've found the photographer whom you want to do your photography, discuss the price and come to an agreement with him. In many cases it won't be an absolutely firm price and it's to your advantage that a specific figure isn't set. Most photographic jobs involve some intangibles that can't be foreseen by either you or the photographer.

Ask a photographer for a firm price and he will of necessity quote you the maximum price based on anticipated labor involved and assuming the worst about unforeseen circumstances. Instead of establising an exact figure, agree on a price *range* with minimum and maximum figures. Photographers are just as hungry for a dollar as any of the rest of us, but they're a very decent and likable group as a whole.

After you've worked with a local photographer for a while it won't be necessary to get a quote and an agreed-upon price range before assigning every job. This need be done only when the project is unusually complex, when extensive time and travel are involved, if expensive props must be rented or built or purchased, or if the assignment is so different and demanding that the photographer must rent or buy specialized equipment to handle it. This latter situation occasionally crops up and is not one in which the photographer should be penalized by expecting him or her to absorb unusual costs, even if he were willing to do so for the sake of good business relations.

Prices of photography vary widely, as much as 300- to 400 percent according to different geographical regions. In the Northeast, Midwest, and California they're highest, with the South the lowest, followed by the Southwest and the Pacific Northwest. In general they reflect the cost of living of various sections of the country and the prevailing wage and salary structure.

The Professional Photographers of America does not set any price guidelines for member photographers, feeling that this is strictly up to the individual or to the studio owner. Photography, like any other goods or service, is priced according to the law of supply and demand. If it's overpriced, advertisers will switch to artwork until the price becomes what they consider is right.

Some regional associations, however, have prepared suggested price ranges or published estimating manuals to help advertisers—and agencies, too, for that matter—arrive at an informed guesstimate of what it will cost to have the widget's picture taken.

Layout Is Helpful

So that both artists and photographers will have some firm direction, you should always give them a layout to work from to show the final use to which their work is to be put. The artist, of course, will use it to make a rough pencil sketch for approval before proceeding with his work. The photographer, though, does both his preliminary and finished work at one sitting, so it's even more necessary in his case.

Even a "copywriter's rough"—doodled by the advertising manager, account executive, or art director, will be of great assistance. Show the photographer past advertisements from the same campaign, give reprints of them so he or she can see the shape and format into "live matter" in the photograph must be confined.

Then sketch out what you're looking for in the photograph, discussing it with the photographer at the same time. If you're working by mail or long-distance telephone, you'll have to be a lot more explicit the first time around because you won't have the verbal give-and-take you enjoy with a local individual with whom you're familiar.

Stock Photos

Yes, Virginia, there *is* a pot of gold at the foot of the rainbow for advertising men looking for a top quality photograph when they have neither time nor much extra money in the department budget.

This pot of photographic gold is called "stock photos."

Stock photos are instant photos. They already exist, there's no waiting to get them, no hiring of models or photographers, no praying for sunlight, no frantic search for exactly the right scene to photograph, no worry about the season of the year.

All you have to do is pick up your phone, or write an airmail letter to have a good selection of high grade photographs on your desk a day or two later.

Probably the best source in the country for quality stock photographs is this one:

> The Photography of H. Armstrong Roberts
> 4203 Locust Street
> Philadelphia, Pennsylvania 19104

This company has been in business since 1920 and is thoroughly reliable and reputable.

Roberts' rates are realistic and a price quotation accompanies each approval selection. Rates are based upon the reproduction rights needed, of course. In most cases, Roberts issues an invoice-license to reproduce the picture for specified media, with the transparency to be returned after separations are made. Transparencies are also available on an exclusive basis, either in a certain field, or for a specified period of time, or for outright purchase of all rights. A quotation on any basis you prefer will be made upon request.

Roberts' camera covers almost every conceivable subject. People, of course, account for the bulk of the pictures because people are interested in people. The butcher, the baker—where's that other tradesman?—or members of their families from the moment of rising in the morning, brushing teeth, having breakfast, off to school, shopping, at work, going to bed. All are there.

All such daily activities on every day of the week, all through the year, every age group, in all seasons, at work and at play; Roberts shows people in every activity from babyhood through the retirement years. Photographs are dramatic and realistic, well-lighted and well-posed. And the pictures, *with model releases on file*, are available to you immediately.

Almost as varied are the photographs Roberts has of places. With coast-to-coast coverage of points of interest in the nation, including typical scenes of each state, you can choose industry, farmland, forests, waters, or mountains. Similar substantial coverage of foreign countries is also available.

In addition to offering excellent black-and-white prints, Roberts has a large and growing library of color transparencies, mostly 4 by 5 in size, mounted for viewing ease and protection of the transparencies; each is numbered for positive identification and orderly presentation.

Selections, based upon your specifications, will be sent for 10 days on approval. The only obligation you incur is to handle the transparencies carefully and return any you do not accept promptly, well protected and by insured mail or registered with an appropriate valuation declared.

So you'll obtain the most useful selection, it's advisable to supply to Roberts as much information as possible about your requirements. For example, most transparencies will crop either vertically or horizontally, although some, because of subject matter, will not.

How to Get Greater Impact Into Illustrations

There is no magic formula that will assure a constant flow of fresh ideas that results in powerful, effective illustrations that excel in stopping power. Developing really good illustrative ideas is much like writing copy—it seldom comes easy.

One thing is obvious, though: The reader must find the illustration interesting. This means that more likely than not he or she will skip over one that's been done to death in one variation or another. And he'll ignore one that doesn't offer some incentive to read the ad or reward the time spent. You can't serve up a bland illustrative diet when your competitors are offering seven-course visual offerings.

Numerous studies have proven that you *can* deliberately set out to produce an illustration specifically to garner more than your share of readership—and pull it off. A few ideas that will work follow. Mull them over and they should trigger plenty more.

Then, there's the use of type itself as an "illustration." When this is done the type is actually a design element, as well as the medium that conveys the message. Two ads from an unusually bold campaign run by Fairchild Semiconductor, Division of Fairchild Camera and Instrument Corporation, a leader in its industry, are illustrated nearby.

Ads are two-color, red and black, with the large firm name printed in black, and partially cut off.

Few industrial advertisers have either the inclination or the intestinal fortitude to chop up the company name this way. And few should, unless they're in the happy position that Fairchild is in—unquestioned industry leadership. Occupying this position makes it possible to be bold and brash without looking presumptuous.

Even when it's shown only partially, and with the firm name in the tiny little type tucked away in an inconspicuous corner, there's no doubt that the name of Fairchild comes through loud and clear. And it makes a vivid impression on the reader's mind. This is particular-

ly so because Fairchild had enough self-confidence to run the ad. Few indeed are the advertisers who would have had the courage to do so.

Short copy in one ad asks this simple question:

> How many semiconductor manufacturers
> delivered more than one million
> integrated circuits last month?
>
> One.

Then the name, Fairchild, minus only the "d" and a small part of the "l," literally leaps up off of the page at the reader. He simply cannot ignore it, nor can he overlook it.

The other treatment asks the reader a provocative question:

How many integrated circuit manufacturers shipped more units last December than all others combined? One.

Again the name "Fairchild," abruptly chopped off after one leg of the "h" is shown, dominates the spread and immediately telegraphs the message. Nobody in the electronics industry—customer, prospect, or competitor—could possibly harbor any doubt about what company was doing the talking in this ad.

Primary objective of this striking campaign was to emphasize Fairchild's leadership and dominance of the industry in the manufacture of integrated circuits. The campaign exploited a positive asset that Fairchild's competitors would give an eyetooth to have, of course.

This illustrative technique rests on a strong foundation borrowed from tactics used by consumer advertisers. If your company's position is as well-established in your industry as Fairchild's, it's a ploy you might want to consider. However, if your company doesn't actually dominate the industry *in the mind of the reader*, this is the road to disaster.

Sure way to get an extra helping of attention from the reader is to take the offbeat path. Be different in your illustration. Don't settle for the tried and proven, the stodgy, the static picture of Our Product shown before a nice, clean, even-toned background.

Chapter 12

LAYOUT

THERE's nothing complicated about layout, nor is there any form of voodoo or black magic or anything else mysterious. Yet it's in this stage of its evolution from idea to completed selling tool that an advertisement most frequently hears the mournful tolling of the death knell to its effectiveness.

A layout must present the advertising message forcefully and attractively, and it must have an orderly structure.

A layout is merely a guideline, a blueprint, a road map, an architect's drawing. A layout is an idea drawn on paper. It performs the same functions for people in the advertising business that these other forms of layouts do for those engaged in other crafts. Just as the civil engineer uses working drawings to determine the path and grade of a new interstate highway, the advertising manager uses a layout to spell out in detail the precise placement of every element in his or her particular advertisement.

An element, incidentally, is a complete entity in itself, and is almost always one of several in the ad. The illustration, for example, is an element. So is the headline, each column or block of body copy, each spot illustration, the logo, and so on. We'll go into this more later on.

To be effective, a layout must be tasteful. *There is no substitute for good taste.*

It is immediately obvious that this is getting into a highly subjective area. What is one person's meat is another person's poison. Nobody can fault you for preferring one thing, while the author happens to prefer another—and neither of us is right or wrong. The man in the next office may have bought a shocking-pink car at one time (a few actually were sold, you know, back in '56); to him, it was the most beautiful, inspiring, delightful set of wheels that ever left Detroit. Most people were in complete agreement in their reaction to the color—*urrrrp!* But that still doesn't make them right and the buyer wrong.

There's plenty of room in advertising, just as there is in any other field, for different viewpoints. And there's more than one way of performing creative chores such as writing, making layouts, and what have you. Many are just as persuasive and forceful, perhaps equally so, as if they were done in any of several other ways, and many are in such impeccably good taste that no justifiable criticism can be made on that score despite the vast difference in approaches.

Given a forceful, tasteful layout, the climate is established in which the selling message can be presented with peak effectiveness.

However, if the layout is plodding and unimaginative, the ad will lack force and vigor and vitality. It cannot do as good a job.

But if the layout is tasteless and crude and vulgar, if it offends the sensitive and shocks the perceptive, the ad is doomed to be completely unsuccessful.

Happily, though, what is tasteful and what is tasteless isn't entirely a subjective thing. There are many ground rules that help you hew to the tasteful, effective side of the layout street and keep you from wandering off into a morass of wasted time and effort and money. Now that we know what layouts are, we'll go into some of them.

Why a Layout Is Needed

The copywriter is the first person to face up to the fact that a layout is needed, and he or she is the first to do something about it.

Usual procedure when writing an ad, a piece of sales literature, a brochure, or what have you, is to make a "copywriter's rough." The copywriter's rough is simply a hastily drawn layout in very crude form and often in greatly reduced size. It shows how the copywriter feels the various elements in the ad should be arranged.

In addition to showing a suggested arrangement, the copywriter's rough serves an even more important purpose—that of establishing the relative importance of each element in the ad, and how much space in the advertisement each should occupy. For instance, if several different widgets are to be illustrated, the copywriter's rough would show which widget should be dominant, which ones should be subordinate, and to what degree.

The copywriter is qualified to perform this important task of assigning space in the advertisement according to the importance of the different elements because he or she has access to far more information than an art director or layout artist. He or she knows the product, its functions, and its user benefits; he or she knows the market into which it is to be sold, and he or she knows the influential buyers with whom the ad must communicate.

As a rule not too much of this information is readily available to the person who lays out the ad, nor is this individual greatly interested in it. It's outside his or her province. For the most part, art directors and layout people are a step or two removed from contact with the advertising manager and manufacturer marketing people, although in the really good advertising agencies they become involved in client problems and client thinking because it's mutually beneficial.

The person who writes the ad transmits directions and instructions by making a copywriter's rough, sometimes called a "thumbnail" because it's actually a rough layout in miniature. A typical copywriter's rough of a one-page ad with illustration, headline, three copy blocks, and logotype of the advertiser is shown life-sized beside a matchbook cover.

Small it may be, but a copywriter's rough (left) is invaluable to the artist.

It's quite obvious why the term is used; most copywriters are not artists and when they attempt to draw something the result is apt to be little short of ludicrous. Frequently they'll label each element so the layout artist will be able to identify it. What's more, such layouts are called thumbnails because the average writer, when thinking of making a copywriter's rough, immediately decides to make it in reduced size. Perhaps this is to compensate for his or her deficiency in the art department, or perhaps it's because it's less work; in any event, most copywriter's roughs of a one-page ad are about half the size of a playing card. And small and rough as they are, they're still a good guide for the artist. The artist always welcomes them and feels almost lost when he or she doesn't get one. Many art directors complain bitterly that the copywriter is deliberately making it difficult if they're not supplied with a copywriter's rough. It pays off in better ads to do so, and it also pays off in better-natured art directors.

One of the most important reasons for making a layout is so the advertiser can visualize the completed advertisement when it's still in process. A drawing or rendering of the completed ad bears such a close resemblance to the finished product that even a poor visualizer can see enough to have an informed opinion of whether or not this ad will express the thought he or she wants to convey. If it doesn't, or if by making a change here and there the idea can be expressed more forcefully, little is lost at this stage of the game.

Working with a copywriter's rough, the artist can "rough out" a layout in just a few minutes for advertiser comment or approval. If changes are to be made they can then be reflected in the next rough. Or, if the layout is close enough to what is wanted in the completed ad, any modifications can be incorporated into the next stage in the layout, which will be discussed later.

When there is a layout to see, the advertiser isn't working in the dark. He or she is not asked to approve something as nebulous as an idea expressed in words. What the advertiser is to evaluate has been put on paper so it can be seen and studied and considered at leisure.

Make any changes you want to make in the advertisement *now*—not later. After the layout stage is past, changes are terribly expensive and wasteful.

The layout serves also as a guide for the photographer or artist who will create the illustration. When this person has the layout, he or she can see the exact size and proportions of the finished work he or she is to produce, and how it will appear on the page. This is of inestimable help because it comes as close as possible to ensuring work that will measure up to expectations and satisfy all concerned. Photographers and artists usually take the layout or a photocopy of it with them to use as a reference when making the illustration.

By using the layout as a guide it is also possible for all production people to estimate the cost of producing the advertisement. They can show it to the typographer, for example, and let the typographer see how much space so many words of copy are to occupy, thus enabling the typographer to submit a very close estimate of his or her charges.

And when getting bids from printers, the layout is also used. Printers are accustomed to working with layouts since they are always ready long before the final keyline and finished art are available. If production people had to wait until all camera-ready finished material was on hand, the pace would be impossibly hectic; they couldn't work ahead and save precious days when they are most needed.

Printers, working with the layout, can tell quite closely how much stripping time, how much extra camera time, how much retouching time, and how many extra operations they'll have. Estimates based on good layouts are remarkably close to actual invoiced charges in most instances.

Types of Layouts

Some industrial advertising departments are as fully staffed with artists, production people, and traffic people as an advertising agency. These departments are capable of handling every step of the manufacture of an advertisement, from original idea to getting material ready for the engraver.

However, the typical industrial advertising manager usually has either an agency perform the art and production functions, or hires a studio to handle the mechanics. The art studio—in many instances actually a small, specialized advertising agency—concentrates primarily on production of collateral material: sales literature, brochures, booklets, films, and the like. Many have branched out as their business has grown, and offer a complete advertising service including media analysis and purchasing of space in publications. Also offered, of course, are copywriting, layout, and production.

A good, reliable studio that can produce finished art of good quality and do so in a minimum of time is a jewel to be guarded and treasured. Many times you'll have jobs that must be "banged out" fast, and they're really too small to make them profitable for your advertising agency. Yet art is required, and there's type to spec, layouts to be made, keylines to be done, and so on. This is probably work that you either cannot do, or simply do not have time to do.

When this situation arises, the studio is the obvious answer. It's good practice to put the bulk of your business through one studio so that your business is valued there, although it's equally good business to get competitive quotations on some jobs just to keep everybody on their toes and to assure yourself your business isn't being taken for granted—and that the price stays right.

Layouts are presented in three forms: Rough, ruled comprehensive, and type comprehensive.

The rough layout is just that—a crudely drawn indication of what the final advertisement will look like. Usually it's done with either the ubiquitous squeakie (felt pen), or with chalks of differing shades of

gray and black. Whatever the medium is used, the rough layout reflects the artist's thinking—not his or her ability to render an illustration. It should be accepted for just what it is, and the rough should be judged by what it shows, rather than how it shows it. You're not paying for an El Greco now, and you shouldn't expect fine art.

A typical rough layout, this one done with a squeakie, is shown. Note that the headline, subhead, and logo are indicated, rather than

624

being lettered in. This is sufficiently indicative of how the advertisement will look, and there's no use in having an artist waste time lettering on a rough. Frequently this is called "Greeking in" the printed matter—possibly after the Greek alphabet which, to most people who aren't Greeks, looks like Greek. Copy blocks, three of them, are indicated by rough lines.

While it's still inside the agency the rough is usually submitted by the artist to the chief art director, the creative director, or to the account executive handling the account—frequently to all three, and often to the copywriter as well. If it reflects the thinking of all of those inside satisfactorily, the account executive may want to show it to the client. Or the account executive may pass judgment on its merit, depending upon how familiar he or she is with the account, his or her relationship with the client, and whether or not the account executive believes the rough represents what the advertiser wants—and should have. Sometimes these two aren't the same thing at all.

The next stage is to make a ruled comprehensive layout, commonly called a "comp." A typical comp layout is shown nearby.

Instead of rough doodling that indicates merely the vague outline of the elements in the illustration, and the other elements in the advertisement, the comp has been drawn with some care.

A photostat of the photograph which will illustrate the ad (called a "stat") has been made to the exact size the engraving will be and carefully pasted into place where the halftone will be in the completed ad. This shows the advertising manager how it looks and will later be given to the engraver for guidance.

Copy blocks are indicated quite close in size to what they will be in the actual advertisement, and the logo has been roughed in. Note, however, that the headline and subhead, while lettered in in a close approximation of the type face to be used, do not use the exact words which will be set in type. Artists and art directors are notorious for misreading or mislettering headlines and subheads. If it's critical that the exact wording appear, their work should be carefully checked. However, since the type will occupy approximately the same amount of space, the precise words don't really matter.

Interestingly, the mat around the ad is always made *exactly* one-half inch too wide to fit into an account executive's attaché case. This is standard in all agencies and may well be a part of a worldwide plot hatched by artists to bedevil account executives. This is the one essential that artists never fail to get exactly right. This forces the account

625

Switching to powder metals?

we'll help you lower processing costs

executive to go to the mailroom, wrap the layouts, and carry an extra item when going to call on the client. Even if it's empty, the account executive cannot leave his or her attaché case behind; without it he or she is not really an account executive. The account executive would be like Linus without his blanket. For the account executive, happiness is having an attaché case to carry.

At this stage of the game the advertiser can see just what the forthcoming advertisement is going to look like. There isn't so much in-

vested, though, that a change can't be made. If changes must be made, this is the last opportunity to make them without running up production costs and wasting money.

The final stage in layout is to go to the type comprehensive. Such a type comprehensive is shown nearby.

This consists of the ruled comprehensive layout, with stat still in place, but with type set and pasted down. Except for the stat's mediocre quality—stats compress the tonal range of art or photographs, show less middletones and thus appear more contrasty than the original subject matter—the ad appears much as it will when an engraving has been made and proofs have been pulled.

The Touchy Problem of Changes

Here again, the advertiser can still push the panic button and make a change, of course, if it's absolutely essential and there's simply no escaping it. However, type has been set and any changes now will necessitate all new type; patching is not always possible because of a difference in the weight of the impression of type set at various times. Also, agencies like to set type all new when a client has made a last-minute change because this tends to teach the indecisive client a costly lesson. Henceforth, the client will probably remember it and not cause the fuss and furor that inevitably results when changes have to be made and the deadline is near and everybody had considered this job completed.

The habit of looking at type comps is a bad one to get into. It's almost as vicious as smoking cigarettes, although not quite, and equally costly. The type comp represents an extra step that causes your invoices to climb amazingly. It stands to reason, when you stop and think about it, that when a job has to be handled at the agency or the studio that somebody's going to pay for it, and this is an extra handling. Then your account executive has to hop in a cab and drive out and show it to you, or rent a car, or—horrors—mail it to you. This runs up the cost of doing business with you.

Actually, a rough will suffice in most cases for you to pass judgment on an ad. And certainly a ruled comprehensive layout is adequate to enable you to visualize what the completed ad will look like, and it will be sufficiently close to let you explain to the sales manager, marketing manager, or product manager what they're going to get to carry the message to the marketplace. Train your people internally to expect nothing further after they've seen a ruled comp layout. You'll spoil them if you let them know there's an additional step; as soon as they find out, they'll want to take it up with you. And as sure as the sun rises in the East, they'll force you to make changes when type's been set.

Properly, however, you should clear retouched photos with your product and sales staff if there's any doubt in your mind about whether or not they show the product to best advantage, or if a technical question arises. Technical people can also pass on art, but from a technical viewpoint; they shouldn't be encouraged—or even permitted—to render any verdict on either art or photography as far as technique is concerned. This is your province. You're the expert here. Just because all engineers are draftsmen doesn't automatically qualify them to pass judgment on art or photography.

You'll find you're far better off if you don't even intimate you want any kind of opinion. Once you have ad reprints you can then drop any number of gentle hints about what a fine piece of art it is, or how good the photography is. After all, you didn't give birth to the art or photo, so you can legitimately brag on the work of others—almost, at least.

If you're going to make your own layouts, you'll find you're better off to go the thumbnail route as a method of developing ideas. Thumbnails are excellent time savers for they can be doodled out almost as fast as ideas come to mind.

However, when you decide you've come up with *the* idea, or with one you want to pursue further, by all means make a full-sized layout. Only when it's sized up to the approximate dimensions in which it will appear in the publications can you judge accurately whether or not it measures up to your standards and meets with your approval.

Chances are you'll find that thumbnails are a bit deceptive. What looks just great when it's matchbook size frequently falls apart—fails to "carry" when it's "up."

Cost of Layouts

Layouts don't come free to an industrial advertising manager. Almost every industrial ad manager who's on a commission basis with an agency, rather than an agreed-upon fee basis, pays for layouts. Copy is free if it's written by an agency, but not the layout. Agencies regard copywriters and account executives as necessary personnel, but for some reason or other, artists, layout people, and art directors are considered overhead personnel who must be charged off against what they produce; this work is billed to clients.

Most agencies are very fair and layout charges and turn a legitimate profit for this work, one they're entitled to. Nobody is in business for his or her health. Some agencies, though, particularly the marginal ones which specialize in mailing lists at inflated prices and similar bits of larceny, make it standard operating procedure to gouge the client with puffed-up layout charges. The art department in these so-called agencies has become a profit center. This shouldn't be.

What you'll be charged for layout naturally depends to a large extent on how much work went into the layout. This includes initial "think time" for the layout artist, time actually spent working, and normal agency markup or profit.

The more changes that are made, the higher the price that's paid. Every change involves time spent by the account executive and the layout artist as well as others involved in the account. Changes are costly little items, so try to get your own thinking tidied up before giving instructions to the agency.

Definition of Black and White

When an ad is in black and white, it's a one-color ad. This means simply that black ink has been printed on white paper. Granted, neither black nor white are actually colors in the true sense of the word, but for practical purposes in the advertising industry they're considered colors.

This page you're reading is in black and white—black type on white paper. The use of two "colors," however, doesn't make this page a two-color page. It's a one-color page because the basic color of the stock—the paper—doesn't count as a color. Only the different colors laid down by the printing process are counted as colors when describing an advertisement.

For an additional charge you can have your advertisements printed in brown ink—or red, purple, chartreuse, blue, green, orange, or whatever silliness occurs to you. But as long as the publication's printer laid down only one color of ink, you still have a one-color ad.

However, you have a two-color advertisement when your ad is printed in the publication's basic ink color—black—and another color is added. Let's assume you're going to run your ad in two colors, and the second color is that old exciter, red. (As the older generation of industrial advertising people used to say, "Let me have any second color, as long as it's red.") So now you have a red and black ad—the second color is usually given first when discussing a two-color ad—on the basic "color" of paper that publications use, which is white. Although you actually have a red, black and white ad, it nonetheless is still a two-color ad, not a three color one. Remember, the color of the paper doesn't count.

By the same token, a three-color ad is one in which the basic black ink is used, plus the addition of any other two colors. Used functionally, three colors can do a tremendously effective job. Used decoratively, however, with color splashed around indiscriminately just because the money's in the budget to pay for it, three-color ads are ghastly monstrosities that nauseate and repel.

Shy away from using three colors unless there's a very logical reason for doing so—*a very logical reason*. They don't come along very often, and happily, happily you don't encounter too many of these gruesome three-color monstrosities. They're horrible horrors.

Later on in this chapter the four-color process will be discussed.

Fundamentals of Good Layout

A layout starts with a blank piece of paper. Whether an advertisement is a rousing success or a dismal failure depends to a large extent on what the layout artist does with this piece of paper.

He can be given an illustration that's so well conceived and so beautifully executed that it almost brings tears to the eyes and really motivates the reader to want to stop and read every last word of copy; and he can be handed copy that softly sings a siren song of such persuasiveness that the reader is morally convinced the product is even *better* than the advertisement will admit in all of its modesty.

These two elements *are* essentials, of course, but not one bit more so than a layout that's equally good. It's all too easy to arrange a fine illustration and sparkling copy so that the various elements clash and distract and fail miserably to communicate a single salient fact to the universe because the ad is so uninviting.

This is a major sin committed unknowingly by far too many advertising managers of small industrial companies; these ad managers frequently are what amounts to one-person agencies for their companies, they specify and purchase the illustration, write the copy, and make the layout. Frequently these talented individuals do a remarkably competent job, but layout is usually the area in which they're weak.

Most advertising people are word-oriented rather than design- or art-oriented and their work suffers in effectiveness due to inept layout more than any other area. Working with a good agency, a competent art studio, or even with a free-lance artist would avert disastrously poor layouts and do more than anything else to boost the productivity of the advertising program.

A good, clear visual interpretation of the selling concept increases readership tremendously.

To enable the advertisement to succeed, the layout must let the various elements of the ad work together to do the entire job—the illustration, subordinate illustration, if any; headline, subheads, if any; charts or graphs, body copy, logotype, and any other elements or devices the ad includes.

A good layout helps the other elements do an effective job, whereas a poor layout hinders them and makes it difficult—if not impossible—to accomplish the objective of getting readership.

To enhance the effectiveness of the other elements, layout needs to have four "musts." These qualities must be present in each and every layout, not just one once in a while. They are:

1. It must be attractive.
2. It must have "feel."
3. It must have balance.
4. It must have individuality.

Early Decision Needed

The time to decide if you want—or need—a highly individualized layout and visual approach is when you're in the process of planning a new campaign. At that time you, your account executive, copywriter, and art director can get your heads together and kick around a succession of ideas until you achieve unanimity of thought and come up with *the* idea for the forthcoming year.

Any number of routes may be chosen—some good, some better—and hopefully the one that's the very best for your circumstances at the specific time it's selected will get the nod.

Don't make the mistake of being drastically different merely for the sake of difference itself, however. Do so with solid reason. If your reason is right, your advertisements that bear little resemblance to all of the other advertisements in the books you use can get tremendous readership and do an outstandlingly effective job for you.

What a Layout Does

Every industrial advertisement in every trade publication published has one thing in common with every other one: Both occupy space. And this space must be divided so that the ad makes a maximum impact on the reader. This means, of course, that each element of the advertisement has to be allotted an amount of space deemed sufficient for it to accomplish its objective.

This apportionment of space would be greatly simplified if hard-and-fast rules for proper division of space existed—or, for that matter, if there even was such a thing as a "proper" division of space.

Guidelines exist; a layout must be attractive, it has to have feel, balance, and individuality. Too, it needs a sense of proportion so that the different elements will have a relationship to each other that is esthetically pleasing. This is, when all's said and done, what separates most successful advertisements from the also-rans. Industrial ads that didn't quite make the grade failed because of poor layout more often than any other reason.

Space in the advertisement is never divided equally so that each element is given exactly the same area. To do this would unfailingly create a static, dull, dreary, uninteresting ad. It would be an ad without a fluid sense of motion. Excessive symmetry is not good.

Instead, space is divided so there are dominant and subordinate elements, so the white space that remains plays a key role, so the layout does its job to best effect. The layout must produce an ad that is harmonious and appealing to the eye. This is its critically important job.

First of all, one-page, black-and-white advertisements and some tow-color ads will be discussed. These are, of course, the most widely used forms of space advertisements in the business press. Fractional pages will also be gone into, although not to as large an extent.

The Classic Layout

Various names are attached to the so-called classic layout. One that crops up more often than any other, and one that instantly identifies the classic layout to the layout artist, art director, or studio, is "Ayer Number 1."

Advertising legend has it, rightly or wrongly, that the classic layout was originally one of a number of basic layouts, all identified by number, developed by N. W. Ayer & Son, Inc., one of the country's largest and most successful old-line advertising agencies. The classic layout is supposed to have been developed several decades ago. Through long usage in both the consumer and industrial fields, it has proven itself to be what is, without question, the one layout that deserves the name classic.

Readership studies have proven repeatedly over the years that this is the one layout that is fairly certain of success. Use this layout for your advertisement and you have an edge going into the great game of enticing the reader to read your ad in preference to all of the others in the book.

The classic layout has ideal proportions, an innate sense of structure and nearly perfect division of space so that values are precisely as they should be for the ad to have an optimum chance to accomplish its objective. Naturally, if *all* ads were laid out in the Ayer Number 1 format, advertising would be incredibly monotonous. But in the business press where everybody tries to out-scream everybody else, where clatter and clutter abound and there's apparently either a desire for tastelessness—or an inability to produce tastefulness—the classic

The 9¢-an-hour inspector

It's the ST-1 closed-circuit television camera from Diamond Power.

It checks conveyor belts for fast, full, economical operation. Inspects products for minute flaws. Or monitors material flow from receiving to shipping.

The ST-1 does all this, and more, with up to 800-line horizontal resolution. Picture clarity more than double that of home television.

This inspector is tough. The ST-1 is all silicon transistorized for long life under almost any conditions. It endures heat up to 140 F. Its thick steel housing is pressurized to keep out dust.

It has solid state sweep failure protection, built-in electronic light compensation, and wide tolerance circuitry for maximum picture stability—features not found in ordinary cameras.

You can get more than a camera from Diamond. With controls and accessories you can add-on, adapt or ruggedize the Diamond camera for close-ups, 360° inspections, or extreme environments.

Nine cents an hour puts the ST-1 on your payroll. That will write-off capital costs in three years, and pay for maintenance and electricity too.

Diamond Power Specialty Corp., Lancaster, Ohio.

Diamond Power

layout is a sight for eyes grown tired of layout anarchy.

Let's look at a beautifully done industrial advertisement with the classic layout and dissect it to see why it's good and what its strong points are.

This deceptively simple one-page, black-and-white ad run by Diamond Power Specialty Corporation, a subsidiary of The Babcock &

Wilcox Company, is an extremely attractive advertisement that appeared in the trade press.

It's a bleed ad; the illustration goes off the page on the top and on both sides. As the advertisement appeared in the publications, the illustration is 7 7/8 inches deep; this leaves a whisker less than 3 1/4 inches for the headline and body copy. These proportions are highly pleasing and there's a serene sense of logic and order and well-being imparted by the ad. Very obviously it is a well constructed ad that's laid out for one prime purpose—to communicate. That it does exceedingly well.

The large photographic illustration of the closed-circuit television camera manufactured by Diamond Power is shown at work on an assembly line, checking conveyor belts. The illustration is the dominant element in the ad, and rightly so, because its function is to stop the reader, to attract the reader's eye, to keep the reader from continuing on through the book. This layout makes it possible for the illustration to accomplish this crucially important task.

Headline is easily read, of a tasteful size, and is set in lowercase type except for the lead capital letter; this is the easiest to read and attracts the greatest percentage of readership.

Copy is laid out in two blocks. Readership studies prove this arrangement attracts the eye more readily than any other. Type arranged in illogical blocks, or scattered at random (at least to the unanalytical reader) throughout an ad decreases readership very appreciably.

The signature is quite similar in weight and size to the headline, resulting in a neat, businesslike appearance that's absolutely devoid of pretense or ultrafancy logotypes that probably do more to confuse the reader than they ever do to increase advertiser identification.

The one-page, black-and-white bleed ad run by Eastman Kodak Company in *Editor & Publisher, Industrial Photography, Infinity, National Press Photographer, Photo Methods for Industry, The Professional Photographer,* and *The Rangefinder* is illustrated later.

Clean and simple and uncluttered, this layout is a close relative of the Ayer Number 1. Kodak's ad differs only in that the headline is offset to the left and the body copy is laid out in three blocks rather than two. Also, the signature and logo appear at the bottom of the third copy block rather than being centered at the bottom of the page.

Many art directors prefer to block the type in three columns. This enables it to be set approximately 40 characters wide, which is the optimum for ease of reading. Having one additional column of type increases the number of elements in the advertisement from five to six, but that's of little consequence when an ad is as beautifully simple and tasteful as this one of Kodak's.

Free with Kodak boxtops

Service, that is. Most photographers think of Kodak Technical Service as a kind of insurance. If you are turning out work in really large volume, Kodak Service is insurance against down-time that could wreck production schedules. If the finished print is intended to reflect in high degree your personal creativity, Kodak Service is insurance that the print will give you back what you put into it.

Kodak representatives and dealers who bring this Service to you are the underwriters of this insurance. They see that you get the latest news about the newest methods and materials. The Kodak man, particularly, is a top-flight representative of the world's foremost photographic engineering staff. Through him, on a person-to-person basis, you share in the important findings of the Kodak research

and development laboratories.

Add it up. It's all included—when the box you buy is labeled "Kodak." Professionally, you can't afford less.

Kodak

EASTMAN KODAK COMPANY
Rochester, N.Y.

Clean, simple, uncluttered— those are the benchmarks of a classic ad. The Kodak layout at left is another example of what is called the Ayer Number 1 treatment.

Merely having type in three copy blocks frees some space between the illustration and the headline, and between headline and body copy. This means there can be some attractive white space up there to make the ad look inviting and easy to read; this space is not available when the type is set in two columns because it must necessarily run deeper, assuming the same measure, of course.

The photography in Kodak's illustration is superb, as is to be expected. Every tiny detail is shown crisp and clear and razor sharp. Gradation of tones is long, the white shirts of the two men are not "burned up," and there's detail in the shadows even in a halftone reproduction. Too, the picture is exceptionally well composed.

The direction the two men are looking automatically guides the reader's eye to the heart of the picture where the negative is being retouched, and from there directly to the headline. This is why the headline is offset to the left, incidentally, to take full advantage of the eye path of the reader.

Much thought and a great degree of knowledge of human nature went into Kodak's fine ad. Note that once the reader's eye follows the path established for it, it goes to the headline where the power-word, "free," immediately lures him into the body copy.

This tasteful and pleasing ad did a highly effective job for Kodak.

Space Divided Horizontally

Divide space exactly in half, or so nearly in half that it appears to be equally split, and you have a dull and dreary sameness in the layout.

In nature, for example, nothing is perfectly symmetrical. No two trees are exactly the same height, no two boulders exactly the same size and shape, no two rivers exactly the same width, no two mountains of equal mass. Even people's faces have distinct halves and when compared by means of split photographs flopped and pasted together show that symmetry, perfect symmetry, is nonexistent.

Any attempt to achieve precise uniformity in a layout by allotting an identical amount of space to various elements in an advertisement, or by splitting it equally between illustration and copy-headline-signature-logo will result in a visual Donnybrook, each element striving to achieve dominance, but none succeeding. The ad will not succeed, either.

Following is an ad of T. B. Wood's Sons Company which is an example of how space may be divided horizontally.

Space appears to be almost evenly divided in T. B. Wood's Sons Company's one-page, black-and-white ad from *Factory* magazine.

Space is almost equally divided between illustration and copy in this advertisement. Had the illustration been deeper on the page—or even shallower—the impact of the ad would have been stronger. Even balance is static.

Wood's MCS Variable Speed Drive takes the "crimps" out of production

To the eye, space seems to be divided so that the illustation cuts the ad almost exactly in half, although use of a ruler shows that it is dominant by a scant quarter of an inch. Coming as close as it does to achieving a static equality, the advertisement lacks impact and appeal and a feeling of excitement, although the advertiser's product seems to be excellent, the headline promises a user benefit, and the copy comes through with an explanation of the benefit and offers a strong selling proposition. If only the illustation had been deeper—or even shallower—the ad would have been stronger.

An advertisement laid out with an illustration that occupies less than half the depth of the page is also shown. Illustration for the 7x10 black-and-white ad is 4 7/16 inches deep, leaving room for a caption, stacked (two line) headline, a subhead, three blocks of copy, logotype, and slugline listing other divisions of Lindberg Hevi-Duty's parent corporation. Sluglines, incidentally, are dearly beloved by management, which is under the impression they are *read*. Frequently a listing of products as long as a dreary winter is offered to the reader in a slugline in hopes that the reader will rush right out and buy other products of the company.

Sluglines are inelegantly referred to in the advertising business as "garbage." Although it's almost impossible to do, try to dissuade management from cluttering up your ads this way. Little benefit accrues from addition of garbage to an ad—but another element is added to detract from the layout.

Space Divided Diagonally

Not too many industrial advertisements use the layout device of dividing space diagonally. This is, perhaps, because it's a bit more difficult for the layout person who's accustomed to thinking primarily in terms of things horizontal or vertical.

Diagonals are dramatic. They express movement. When a diagonal division of space is employed, a flowing feeling and an atmosphere of excitement is imparted to the layout. This signals the reader that something a bit out of the ordinary is occurring in the advertisement. It makes the reader want to see what's happening.

Whereas the horizontal line represents rest and tranquility, the diagonal is exactly the opposite.

Diagonal lines are especially effective in layouts for advertisements for hard goods with moving parts—machinery of all types, for instance, ranging from machine tools to shoemaking machines to earthmoving equipment. The reader receives the implication from diagonals that the ad concerns a product with power and strength and vigor, one that will produce and accomplish.

Space Divided Vertically

If you take a 7x10 space and divide it into equal halves, vertically, it's just as dreary and dull and unappealing as if the layout had cut the space in half horizontally.

However, if you offset the copy to one side or another by devoting a major portion of the space to the illustration—or even do just the opposite, for that matter—you neatly avoid bisecting the ad in half. And you automatically create an interesting situation due to the inequality of the segments of space.

In addition, the layout with space divided vertically achieves a certain measure of individuality because the overwhelming majority of all industrial advertisements are laid out so the space is divided horizontally. What's more, vertical lines suggest power and dignity, something like the giant redwoods in Muir Woods, north of San Francisco. A connotation such as this can increase readership. The reader doesn't stop to rationalize why the layout creates this impression, and isn't consciously aware that it does—even if it does.

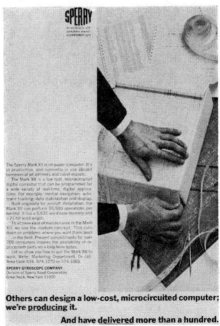

Here is strong vertical division of space. The eye-travel path of the reader begins with the Sperry Gyroscope logotype, then goes into the illustration, and finally moves up the left-hand side of the layout into the body copy. Use vertical division of layouts carefully —they are a definite break with tradition.

Others can design a low-cost, microcircuited computer; we're producing it.

And have delivered more than a hundred.

Keep in mind, however, that every illustration cannot arbitrarily be drastically cropped so that it becomes an effective vertical with proportions of roughly two and one-half to one, as far as length-to-width is concerned. If you're planning a campaign laid out so that your illustrations will be verticals, with the space divided vertically, be sure the illustrations reflect this and are not adaptations of illustrations that would actually look better if horizontal. This could result in ads that are very weak indeed.

An ad from *Space/Aeronautics* magazine shows how space should be divided vertically so that the illustration dominates the copy space. In this two-color ad run by Sperry Gyroscope Company, Division of Sperry Rand Corporation, the duotone illustration is 3 15/16 inches wide, while the copy space is 3 1/16 inches wide, giving it a pleasing four-to-three ratio.

Note that the illustration was *planned* to be a strong vertical; there's no impression of anything missing of left out, despite the tight cropping of the illustration to include only the man's hands. Interest is concentrated on what the hands are doing, what they're holding, rather than on the unseen figure to whom they belong.

In Sperry Gyroscope's advertisement, the reader's eye goes first to the Sperry logo in the upper left corner of the ad. It then proceeds down through the illustration, reads the headline, and then goes up the left side of the page into the body copy. This is the normal clockwise pattern and normal point of eye entry.

Some very effective ads have resulted from dividing the space vertically. For the most part, however, you're bucking tradition, you're up against the lifetime habit of expecting to find material on a printed page arranged so that it's divided horizontally. This can cost as far as readership is concerned. Unless there's a compelling reason—such as product shape, perhaps—to divide the space vertically, you're better off not to.

Both tradition and habits of a lifetime are not to be lightly regarded. On the other hand, there is no rule or regulation that says you have to take them as law, written or unwritten. Produce a well-conceived campaign with solid objectives and strong individual ads and it really matters little how the space is divided. The important thing is the overall effect the ads produce on the reader.

Fractional-Page Ads

Budgetary woes dictate use of fractional pages on occasion, especially for minor markets or products of minor importance in the overall sales picture.

No truer words were ever said in all of advertising than those uttered by some long-forgotten ad sage who said, "The bigger the ad, the more it's read."

A one-third page ad will receive more readership than a one-sixth-page ad; a two-thirds-page ad will likewise be read by more readers than the one-third unit; a page attracts more people than a two-thirds-page ad does; a spread gets more attention than does a one-page ad; gatefolds, popouts, and multipage inserts do still better—but more on this later on.

If the money isn't there, though, there's nothing else to do except to be philosophical and practical and run fractionals, as they're called. A consistent program of fractionals with regularly scheduled insertions keeps the advertiser's name and product in front of prospective purchasers.

This is vitally important because the reader has a remarkably short memory. Run a page now and then, disappear for months at a time from key business publications while hoarding the precious dollars in the budget to make another ego-soothing splash of a page or a spread, and you're diluting the impression your advertising has worked so hard to make. When your company isn't in key publications, your competitors *are*. They're making points, building identity, creating brand preference, and preselling their products.

There is no substitute for continuity.

It's better by far to appear regularly in publications you know reach your universe, and do it with fractionals, than it is to go the in-again, out-again route.

Sporadic advertising actually accomplishes remarkably little except to give the powers that be within the company the feeling that, by golly, our firm is full of vigor and vitality and it's proceeding under a full head of steam. Advertising spasmodically *does* accomplish a negative goal: It lulls management into a false sense of security because it's under the mistaken impression that advertising is working for the company, when it is not. Unless advertising is constant and continuous, it's doing no such thing.

The immediate question here, however, is how should fractionals be laid out in order to attract as many readers as possible?

Research has proven quite conclusively that a vertical division of space is the best choice to make in business publications of standard size, where pages are ordinarily laid out in three columns. Most books do, though, have a part of their editorial pages laid out in both two columns and three. This provides flexibility in accepting advertisements of varying sizes, as well as giving visual relief from a format that could become tiresome.

If you're considering a one-third-page ad, you can buy space for a vertical one-third page—frequently called a one-column ad, although this terminology isn't as specific as referring to what fraction of a page is being used—as shown in "C" of the sketch, below. This is a vertical format. However, the same amount of space at the same price—one-third of a page—is also shown in "D," although this is almost a square format. The one-column fractional shown in "C" will receive much more readership, other things being equal.

Then, too, you can buy a half page. This half page of space can be

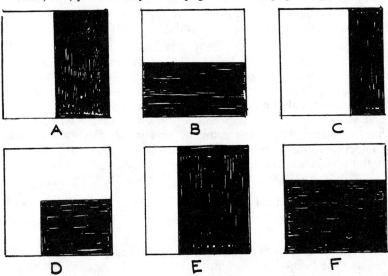

purchased as either a vertical half as shown in "A," or it can be a horizontal half as in "B." Cost is exactly the same, but there's no problem in making the selection. A vertical half page will receive almost 25 percent more readership than will a horizontal half. Just why there's such a large difference isn't entirely understood, although it's well-known that the reader's eye tends to scan the top half of a page first, then drifts downward, looking for something attractive to pursue further.

The largest fractional page offered in standard size business publications is the two-thirds page. Here again, it can be specified as a vertical segment of the page, as in "E" or as a horizontal two-thirds, as in "F." Use "E" and get much more readership for the same money.

Incidentally, most first-class business books will make a determined effort to make sure that editorial matter occupies the other column of a two-thirds-page ad, thus, in effect, giving the advertiser the benefit of having the entire page for his or her advertisement. This is called dominating the page. Evidence exists to indicate that a good, strong, two-thirds-page ad will receive more readership than it can rightly expect, due to people reading the editorial matter, then automatically continuing on into the advertisement. This is a fringe benefit you can count on with the two-thirds-page fractional.

Bleed

When an advertisement's live matter extends flush to the edge of the page, rather than stopping short about one half inch, it is said to "bleed" off of the paper. It is then called a bleed ad.

Bleed ads are much bigger ads, and they look like it even if they are on the same sized page in the same publication. For example, we measured ads in an issue of *Production* magazine. Tinnerman Products, Inc., had a one-page, black-and-white ad directly opposite a one-page, black-and-white ad run by Laminated Shim Company, Inc.

Tinnerman's ad is a nonbleed ad, so it measures 7 inches by 10 inches; it's a 7x10 ad, that is. It has 70 square inches of available space for illustration, headline, copy, signature, and logo.

Laminated Shim's ad, however, is a bleed ad and it measures 8 3/16 inches by 11 3/16 inches, which is the trim size of the book. It has 96 square inches of space for the advertisement—37 percent more.

Bleed is no exception to the rule that most things in life worth having have a price tag attached to them. Most publications charge a premium price for bleed, usually 15 percent of the basic page rate. Even at a 15 percent bump in price, though, bleed is a tremendous bargain. Getting 37 percent more of a product—whether it's space or what have you—for 15 percent more money can't help but be a bargain.

However, when you're buying something such as space to use to communicate with a vast audience, value must be based on effectiveness. A massive amount of research has been done on the readership of bleed ads compared to nonbleed ads. McGraw-Hill analyzed 7,548 advertisements that appeared in 135 issues of the company's magazines over a 10-year period. More than 13,000 readers were personally interviewed. Bleed advertisements had better readership than nonbleed ads in 68 percent of the cases.

Readership Up 25-35 Percent

When a bleed ad *doesn't* outperform a nonbleed ad, the reason lies elsewhere, not with the fact that it's a bleed ad. Most readership studies put the increase in readership between 25 percent and 35 percent—which is certainly a good return on a 15 percent greater investment in space dollars.

That bleed outpulls nonbleed ads so substantially is due in part to the additional space bleed makes available for the illustration. The larger the illustration, the better the chance of attracting the reader's attention, of arousing the reader's curiosity, and enticing the reader into the ad. When an illustration bleeds, there's an inviting feeling of roominess, of a complete lack of crowding of any elements of the ad. Bleed is the best buy of any of the space "extras"—such as preferred position (excepting second and fourth covers) and so on.

Layout artists and art directors like to work with bleed space. The much larger size of the overall advertisement gives them more latitude, more elbow room. Elements of the ad must still be arranged so they're esthetically pleasing and in such a way that they will attract the reader's eye, of course, but more often than not bleed permits a feeling of airiness, or roominess, to be imparted to the ad in measure entirely out of proportion to the 37 percent increase in available space.

Most bleed ads bleed off of the page in three directions only—top and both sides, as does the Lindberg Hevi-Duty four-color advertise-

The Lindberg Hevi-Duty ad at left bleeds at the top and both sides, allowing the illustration to come up big and bold. Ad industry research shows that the use of bleed pages increases readership more than the extra cost of such media space.

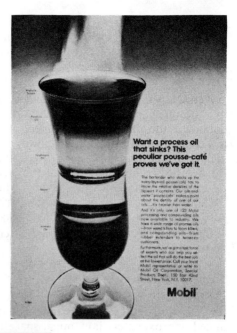

Full bleed, where the ad goes off the page at top, bottom, and both sides, makes a dramatic impact. Note that the flame in the illustration bleeds off the top of the page and the glass bleeds off the bottom, creating a vertical division of space.

The impact of bleed is intensified by the dramatic camera angle used for the illustration in this effective ad for Ford. The dark tones of the low-key photo are overcome by setting the headline in reverse and by putting the body copy against a white background.

645

ment illustrated nearby. This is a typical bleed layout, with illustration approximately 8 1/4 inches wide and 7 inches in depth. Bleed enabled the advertiser to use the extra space to make the illustration bigger and bolder and to boost its stopping power. Copy is printed normally in black type on the white stock.

Another way to lay out a bleed ad is shown in Ford Motor Company's powerful advertisement. Here the dramatic illustration really dominates the ad, as it was intended to. Combination of an extremely low camera angle, rough, off-highway roadbed, and the vehicle on an incline all contribute to a sense of action and excitement. Ford's truck catches the eye immediately, then the gaze drops to the headline which is reversed out—that is, having white type against the dark background. Copy is set in a small panel and it's printed in the customary black against the white background for good legibility.

Bleed buys a lot for you—impact, attention, extra readership. It's a best buy.

Element Placement

Now that you've made a decision as to whether the space will be divided horizontally or vertically—or diagonally—and have determined approximately how much space is to be allotted to each element, the time has come to look at factors which influence placement of the elements.

Elements, and the white spaces between them, must be placed so that their relationships with each other contribute to a harmonious whole. The end result must appeal to the eye. The ad must be inviting. It must appear easy to read. Show the reader an ad that looks as if it would require hard work on the reader's part to wade through it and you've lost yourself a potential prospect without ever having had the opportunity to talk to him or her in print.

The reader is not viewing the ad from a great distance, like looking at the patterns fields and cities and rivers make when seen from a jet airliner at 39,000 feet. He or she doesn't have the advantage, if advantage it is, of being able to back off from your advertisement to see if the pattern it makes from a distance is one that's pleasing or not.

And the reader's not omniscient, either. The reader is unable to judge immediately whether or not an advertisement is of interest because he or she cannot examine the entire ad at one time. The reader has to scan it, look over the elements, and then make up his or her mind if this is something in which his or her time will be well invested.

Location of the elements within the ad will determine to a large degree to what extent your ad is read.

This is the merchandiser Celanese Chemical used to display and offer reprints of its abstract ad art.

Fortunately, though, you don't have to fly blind and place the illustration, headline, copy, and logotype by guess and by golly. Many studies have been made to determine where the reader's eye spends its time. This has been done on a large scale with concealed motion picture cameras equipped with telephoto lenses to bring the eye of volunteer subjects up close so it could be determined with certainty at all times, by frame numbers on the film, at what portion of a page the subject was looking. By giving these subjects magazines in which all material had previously been cross-referenced with film frames, researchers obtained excellent insight into the reading habits of different classes of individuals.

Educators and the armed forces have also gotten into the act in an effort to devise methods of improving the clarity of instruction material and to develop material that is easier to read and quite a bit easier to assimilate.

It has been found that the reader's eye is naturally attracted to the top of the page because, ever since kindergarten, we have been trained to regard what is at the top as the beginning. In other cultures, where writing proceeds from bottom to top, this would, of course, be just the opposite. The reader has long been accustomed to looking at the top of the page first, because this is where he or she "starts."

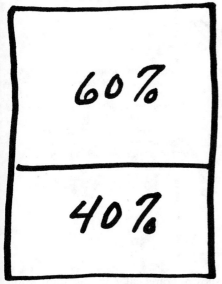

Ad research shows that the dominant element in an ad — almost always the illustration—belongs at the top of the page. This is where 60 percent of the "eye dwell" has been shown to be located in eye-travel studies.

Time spent by the reader's eye has been divided approximately as shown in the 60-40 percent diagram, although no attempt has been made to locate the dividing line with great precision because no definitive study has been made that is accepted by all communicators. For all practical purposes it's enough to know that 60 percent of the reader's eye time is spent in an area that comprises roughly 55 percent of the page—the top portion. Below that line, the eye lingers 40 percent of the time.

This is enough to dictate that the element of strongest inherent interest—almost always the illustration—should be located in the upper portion of the page.

The all-revealing motion picture cameras also disclosed the percentage of time the reader's eye spends in each quarter of the page. Divided into half, of course, it's 60 percent in the top half of the page; but when the top part is divided in half, vertically, it was found that 40 percent of the eye time was put in on the left half of the page, and only 20 percent on the right.

Time devoted to right and left halves of the bottom portion of the page showed the same tendency. Here, the left half received 25 percent of the total of 40 percent of the time spent below the dividing line, while the right half received only 15 percent.

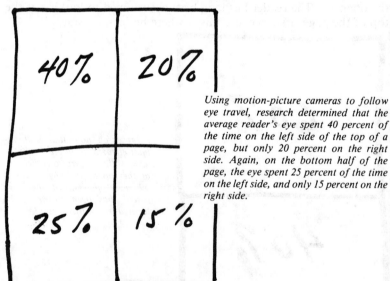

Using motion-picture cameras to follow eye travel, research determined that the average reader's eye spent 40 percent of the time on the left side of the top of a page, but only 20 percent on the right side. Again, on the bottom half of the page, the eye spent 25 percent of the time on the left side, and only 15 percent on the right side.

Eye-dwell percentages are shown graphically in the illustration above.

Layout should be greatly influenced by the amount of time the eader's eye dwells in each section of the page. Elements of greater importance should obviously be placed so that the reader is likely to devote more time to the area in which they are located. Lesser elements can be positioned so they do not infringe upon the critically important 60-65 percent of the top-left, bottom-left space and thus reduce the effectiveness of the entire ad.

A word of caution on this subject, though. It would be a mistake to adhere slavishly to what these research data suggest. Factors which influence layout and element placement are too numerous and vary far too much from one advertisement to another to force an art director to rely entirely on theory at the possible expense of the effectiveness of the layout as he or she intuitively feels it should be.

With this basic information on the habits of the reader, you're in a better position to place elements logically and objectively rather than resorting to hunch and hope.

Eye Path of the Reader

The reader's eye enters your advertisement in the upper left quarter of its area. The reader's eye stops for the first time approximately

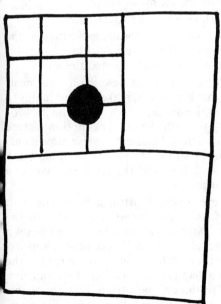

Lines divide the "most looked at" area of this rough chart into thirds. At any one of the four inner intersections is a place for the reader's eye to start making a detailed examination of the ad's contents. In this case, the point where the large dot appears was selected. From this point on the eye scans the ad clockwise.

where the large dot is in the diagram nearby. Note that this is not only in the upper left-hand quarter of the page, but it is also at the approx-

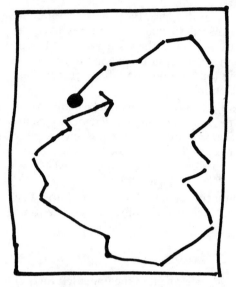

The clockwise scanning of the ad is only the initial path, leaving the reader's eye about where it started. Then, if interested, the eye starts making a detailed examination of the contents of the ad. It darts and roves until it reaches the body copy, then settles into the normal back-and-forth pattern of reading.

imate location of one of the intersections of lines dividing an area into thirds, as discussed in Chapter 10. This is helpful in planning an illustration, of course, as well as in laying out the advertisement.

Depending upon the layout of the ad, the normal movement of the reader's eye is then in a roughly circular pattern, clockwise, until it returns almost to the point where it originally entered the ad.

Most studies indicate that the eye does not describe a nice, neat, round path around the ad, but that it wanders, makes jagged jumps to various elements—or even to white space, which is a total lack of elements—as it pursues its way through the ad. The motion picture camera, set on slow motion, shows these lightning-fast eye movements very clearly, and also emphasizes that the eye path is anything but a smooth and steady one. In general, however, the eye does travel in a clockwise pattern in most instances.

A rough indication of this eye path is illustrated here. The path shown, starting at the point of entry into the ad as indicated by the large dot, is just the *initial* path. After the average reader completes a clockwise visual scanning of the ad, the reader's eye then is approximately where it started. At this time, if the ad interests the reader, the reader's eye then starts making a detailed examination of its contents. There's little rhyme or reason to the eye path from then on; at this time the reader's eye wanders. it darts up and down, roves from side to side, then gradually settles into the familiar back-and-forth pattern of reading as it moves into the copy.

Reflecting a lifelong habit, the reader's eye customarily leaves the advertisement after reading is completed at the lower right hand corner, just as if a book were being read. After all, this is where one completes reading a page, an ad, or what have you.

Advertisements should be laid out so they take advantage of the normal eye path. Layout can make the ad both easier to read and more interesting.

Guiding the Reader's Eye

A layout contains lines to guide the reader's eye, even if the guides are not carefully ruled and printed in ink on the paper. Horizontals, rest; diagonals, movement; verticals, power.

Recall the fine advertisement that Kodak ran for just a moment. The two technicians were looking at a negative, and the direction of their gaze then carried the reader's eye directly to the headline; immediately below the headline was the first block of body copy. The reader's eye was directed straight to it. It wasn't left to wander around alone, unaided. Kodak took no chances; it didn't want the reader lost, it wanted that advertisement read.

The eye is naturally attracted to the largest mass in a given space. Two drawings nearby show three masses of approximately the same "weight," or darkness, but of different sizes. In each instance the eye immediately is attracted to the largest mass, then to the next largest, and so on. This holds true whether the largest mass is at the top of the ad, on the right, left, or at the bottom. However, in a third arrangement the eye is attracted to the largest mass, but it is *directed* to the next largest mass (here it's supposed to be a spot illustration).

The headline's first line of type has been screened back so that it's approximately 50 percent, thus it has less weight and carrying power than the lower line which is printed in solid black. This, together with the fact that the subordinate illustration is considerably darker than the main illustration, compels the reader's eye to go there immediately after it skims the illustration and headline.

So, although the reader's eye habitually follows a well-known path, it can be manipulated to focus it on portions of the advertisement that we want to stress. The reader finds it easier and more natural to conform to what is easiest, due to habit, although the reader can be made—forced, actually, although there's a nasty connotation about the word—to look where the advertiser wants the reader to look. This is done through various layout devices.

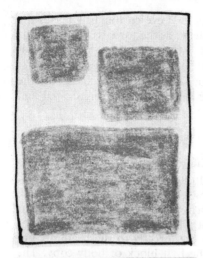

How the eye can be manipulated with layout techniques is shown in these illustrations. The drawings above show how the eye is attracted first to the largest mass, then the next largest, etc. At left, the eye is attracted to the largest mass, but redirected to a smaller mass because that area is stronger and bolder in color.

Eye-Steering Techniques

Among the devices that can be used effectively to guide the reader's eye is one that's as old as advertising itself—the pointing finger. Bourns, Inc., does this to lure the reader into the headline in its black-and-white bleed ad from *Electronics* magazine (page 653).

Usually it's not necessary to use any kind of guidance system, inertial or otherwise, or it shouldn't be, at least. The headline should pop right out, almost jump off of the page it's so readable and attractive and inviting. Bourns must have had a mental reservation about the

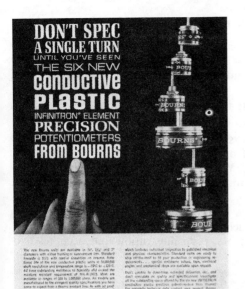

Even though the pointing finger has been overdone in advertising, the device was given a refreshing new twist here. The finger keeps the eye on the headline, which many might try to resist because of the mixture of typefaces. The pointing finger here is not the usual "Uncle Sam Wants You" approach.

jumble of type faces in the stacked headline, however, and felt the necessity to do something—maybe just about anything except setting the headline in one face so it could be read easily—to get the reader to read the headline and the advertiser's name.

Then there are ruled lines. They're a layout person's stock in trade when he or she can't think of anything really creative, and typographers carry them in stock just as they do the letters of the alphabet. Lines can be inserted judiciously to separate various elements and mark a trail for the reader's eye to follow, something like hacking a piece out of a tree every hundred yards so you'll be able to find your way back to the game you've downed when you return with the pack horses.

Also, the direction in which people in the illustration are looking causes the reader to look in that same direction. There's the intimation that the model must be looking at something that interests him, so the reader automatically becomes interested, too. The layout should be planned to take advantage of this device, for it works remarkably well. Everybody's usually curious about what somebody else is looking at.

653

Large Illustrations Pull Better

Have your illustration large enough to occupy two-thirds of the area of your advertisement and it will receive 18 percent more readership than it would if it were smaller. This was proven in a McGraw-Hill study of 5,398 ads.

This means, of course, that in a standard 7x10 ad the illustration should be 6 2/3 inches deep and 7 inches wide.

Naturally, you can't always use the classic Ayer Number One layout and never deviate one iota from it. Situations arise in which the classic layout won't do the job. You may, for instance, want to do a complete-line advertisement. Or the before-and-after illustrative technique may be called for. A number of smaller illustrations that show various features of a new product might be required. Then again, there might be so much to say that copy length alone precludes having space enough to devote to an illustration that occupies two-thirds of the page.

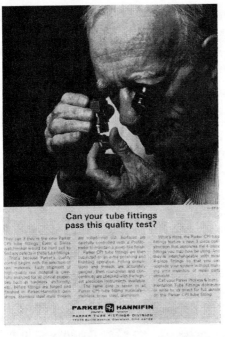

Can your tube fittings
pass this quality test?

PARKER HANNIFIN

Here the layout artist was well aware that the big illustration pulls the reader into an ad. A banked headline is large enough to start—not startle—the reader into the body copy. Type is clean and bold but not overpowering.

Type and Logotype

Type is far more than a necessary evil, something that has to be in your ad to convey your message. Weight, form, style—all contribute to the impression your advertisement makes.

Choice of typeface and the way it's handled exerts tremendous influence on the layout of the ad, determines whether or not the ad is readable, whether or not it's interesting looking—and whether or not it will be read.

A powerful illustration will overshadow a weak typeface, one that doesn't "carry" well, so the copy appears weak and gray and lost and lacks appeal. When copy has no visual character, no strength, it's pale and pallid so that readers avoid it in vast numbers without realizing why.

On the other hand, it's terribly easy to select a typeface so wrong for the advertisement that it weakens it and detracts from it. A typeface that overshadows the illustration, for example, does this because it has too much weight. The dividing line is fine indeed, and both good taste and good judgment are required to refrain from overstepping it in either direction.

A thorough study of typefaces (there are almost 6,000 different ones in existence, although only a comparative few are in general use) is interesting and well worth one's time.

Right now, however, it's desirable to mention a few ways in which type can be laid out so that your advertisement will receive maximum readership—and also to discuss briefly some pitfalls to avoid. The author is indebted to International Paper Company for making available much helpful information on this subject, and on paper and printing. Especially useful is the company's *Pocket Pal,* a graphic-arts digest for printers and advertising production managers. It is available upon letterhead request from:

International Paper Company
77 W. 45th St.
New York, New York 10036

Usually the advertising manager relies on the experience and judgment of his or her art director at the agency, upon his or her art studio—or upon a printing salesperson or representative of a typographer. This is good practice. These individuals live with type day in and day out, and they're expert in choosing the right typeface for the job at hand. As a rule, there isn't enough time for an advertising manager to become a typeface expert unless the manager pursues it as a hobby in his or her leisure time. Some do.

You should, though, be aware that type not only puts words on paper in front of the reader, but it also implies certain qualities and characteristics are possessed by the product with which it's associated. For example, Black Letter or Text is commonly associated with the church, old manuscripts, and wedding invitations; it's frequently called Old English.

Jim Crow, Gold Rush, and P.T. Barnum are faces that are strongly suggestive of the immediate post-Civil War era; they're strong on flavor, but very dated and of little use except in instances when you want to telegraph the impression you're discussing something from that period, or if you're setting the stage for something. This is mood type.

Many advertising people feel the sans serif typefaces, such as Futura and Grotesque, that are used in so much industrial advertising today, somehow connote something mechanical and complex and metallic. These are said to be "nutsy and boltsy" faces.

At the opposite end of the scale are the serif faces. These typefaces suggest elegance and dignity, solidity and integrity. They are at the top of the list when it comes to legibility. Baskerville and Garamond are two excellent faces with much character. They are among the most beautiful.

Actually, however, there are seven main groups of typefaces. They are as follows:

Oldstyle Roman. This group of faces was derived from early Dutch, Venetian, and English typographic designs. It looks better in mass, on the page, than it does when you examine it letter by letter. Legibility is excellent because the letters are open, wide, and round, and have pointed serifs that provide a pleasing contrast between heavy and light strokes. Caslon and Garamond are examples of this face. This book is printed in Oldstyle.

Transitional. This family of typefaces was designed to be a lighter, more refined type than Oldstyle Roman. There is a greater contrast between the hairlines and the main strokes, and the face has long, rounded, curved serifs. Most pleasing characteristics of Oldstyle Roman have been retained. Century and Baskerville are examples.

Modern Roman. The term "modern" doesn't actually refer to a period in time, but to a style of type that was designed almost 200 years ago. Characteristics of the group are greater contrast between thick and thin strokes, square serifs, and rounder, more mechanically perfect curved letters. Bodoni and Scotch Roman are examples.

Sans Serif. This comparatively new face has gained widespread acceptance only in the last 50 years—and in industrial advertising it has swept the country in the past 10 or 15 years. Letters have no serifs and with few exceptions are optically evenly weighted. Because of lack of contrast between the letters, sans serif faces are less legible than either oldstyle or modern. In addition, they are colorless and tiresome and repel the eye after seeing them in ad after ad after ad, on a monkey-see, monkey-do parade of metooism. You'll note that editorial matter in well done trade publications is *not* set in sans serif type—publishers want magazines to be read. News Gothic, Futura, and Grotesque are examples of sans serif type faces. They have their place in some headlines and subheads. The chapter titles of this book are set in Helios Bold.

Square Serif. This contemporary type style became popular in the 1930s. Letters have square, or blocked, serifs and generally are evenly weighted. Many of the square serif types are quite geometric in design. Some, however, have roman characteristics of a transitional type face. Clarendon and Stymie are examples.

Script. This typeface simulates handwriting or hand lettering. It is of limited use and should not be used for body copy. Often you'll find it in invitations, announcements, or other places when a special effect is wanted. Typo Script and Commercial Script are examples.

Black Letter. Sometimes called Text, this group of faces is fashioned after the hand-drawn letters of early scribes whose job it was to copy manuscripts before the advent of printing. There's usually a religious flavor about it. It's used for certificates, diplomas, and wedding invitations. Otherwise, it isn't used very much, primarily because it is old-fashioned and almost impossible to read. Old English and Engravers Text are examples.

With the help of your art director, select a typeface that's right for your campaign, your product, and your company. Then stick with it. Don't deviate from it; don't hop, skip, and jump from a serif face to a sans serif face and back again. This way lies loss of campaign identity and reader confusion. It's as bad as having a radically different layout for every individual advertisement.

A few tips on type handling that will boost readership of your ads follow:

In an industrial advertisement type should not be set in a measure of more than 40 characters—more than 40 characters in width, that is. People read by letting the eyes take "bites" of type; some people absorb entire phrases and clauses at one bite, others who read more slowly look at each individual word. When you have a line of 40 characters in width the average person takes this in with three or four bites, or eye movements. Don't consider this a commandment that can never be violated, but it's a good rule of thumb to go by if you want to have your copy read.

How much you'll get into a line of 40 characters naturally depends upon the size of the type. Type size is measured in "points"—each point being approximately 1/72 of an inch. This means, of course, there are 72 points to the inch. All printers, typographers, and artists think of type in point sizes, whether in foundry or machine composition type. Typefaces are available ranging from 4 to 144 points, but you'll encounter sizes from 6 to 72 points most often. There is little need for tiny type or the monstrously large.

Other things being even relatively equal, the most readership accrues to the person who uses nothing smaller than 10-point type—and 12 point is even better. The average reader isn't like the average industrial advertising manager; the average reader doesn't have a magnifying glass in the center drawer of his or her desk. And even if the average reader did, he wouldn't get it out to read an advertisement with type set so small that a magnifying glass would be necessary.

Line spacing also affects readership. The amount of space between lines of type is called "leading." It's pronounced "ledding," like "bedding." Although there is no hard-and-fast rule to follow, a few things should be borne in mind.

Leading is measured like type—in points. If you have one-point leading, for example, you've allowed an extra 1/72nd of an inch between the lines. Two points leading provides 2/72nds of an inch extra space. Use two-point leading in all advertising body copy and you'll reap a reward of 10 percent *extra* readership. Use of proper leading is one of the easiest ways there is to lure more readers into your body copy because it makes the type so attractive and inviting. It looks easy to read and pleasant to read.

Too much leading can make copy very hard to read, however, so don't overdo it. A point or two is sufficient.

This page has body copy set 10 on 11, as it's expressed. That means that the type is 10 point in size, with an extra point of leading.

The wider the measure of text composition, the more leading is needed between the lines to make it easy to read. If, for some good reason, you're going to have body copy set wider than 40 characters, be sure to have additional leading. Otherwise you'll end up with copy set solid so that it repels the eye.

The first paragraph should be short, as discussed in the chapter on body copy. This pulls the reader's eye into the copy.

And speaking of paragraphs, have then indented, Indented paragraphs attract more readers than do flush paragraphs by some 10 percent. There's no earthly reason to make your advertisement's job more difficult by not indenting, is there?

However, if you can't convince an art director that paragraphs should be indented without having a major skirmish that would result in what the art director would consider an affront, make sure there's additional leading between paragraphs to separate them. Otherwise the reader will be confused and not follow the transition in thinking as different subjects are discussed in different paragraphs.

Having *no* paragraphs is a sin so horrible it won't even be discussed. *Don't do it. Don't ever do it.* Not if you want your advertisement to be read by anybody except the typographer, the art director, the account executive, the agency proofreader, the agency production manager, your secretary, and yourself. That would make it rather an expensive ad.

The one-page, black-and-white ad illustrated nearby was run by Protective Lining Corporation in *Food Engineering*. The illustration is quite good, the product is shown to excellent advantage, and the illustration is the dominant element because it was allotted sufficient space to produce a real impact on the reader. Furthermore, the company's selling proposition is sound and the copy is well written, colloquial, direct, and to the point.

This is a good ad—*except.*

It has a major weakness, however, and it's a fatal one. Type is set 6 1/8 inches wide—about 115 characters in width. (You count the periods, apostrophes, and spaces as characters, incidentally.) This is far too wide. Type in such measure is uninviting. It repels the eye. The reader automatically thinks that there's too much copy there, it must be boring because it's set solid like school books of two or three decades ago, and the lines have a tendency to "swim" or waver because they are too wide. This causes the eye to shift momentarily—actually for a fraction of a second—to a line above or below that which is being read. This causes loss of comprehension of the message, confusion to the reader, and a why-bother-with-it attitude.

What's more, there are no paragraphs and there's precious little leading, if any. Protective Lining Corporation has 16 lines of copy there, and the eye is presented with a solid mass of words with no relief whatsoever. It's too much to take in stride—or even out of stride, for that matter.

A good ad with but one serious flaw—the body copy is set in far too wide a measure and is not broken by paragraphs. Typographers say a line should contain at most an "alphabet and a half"—which is 39 characters. The lines in this copy contain an average of 115.

Learn to Love Widows

As has been discussed, short paragraphs open up copy, make it airy and appealing—and make it read. Widows, left-over words at the end of a paragraph that appear as just one or two words on a line, also open up the copy. Some years back it used to be considered the height of bad taste to have widows, and copywriters labored long and hard "filling out" lines so they would be flush and even on both right and left. However, because widows let in air, they actually result in additional readership.

This is quite true, despite the fact that *Life* magazine made heroic efforts to kill every widow, and pretty largely succeeded, especially in captions and short copy blocks of less than 500 words. Love and cherish widows—those in type, that is—and you'll have ads that invite the eye, and readership.

Despite the reader's having been accustomed to thinking of type as being justified on both sides, flush right and left, that is, quite frequently type is set "ragged right." That is, it is unjustified on the right. This adds interest to an advertisement and imparts individuality to the layout. Actually, it acts as a design element in many instances and can lead the reader's eye to the place the advertiser wants it.

Caps and Lowercase

Headlines should be set in lowercase type, with the possible exception of the first letter. Many seasoned art directors who have made a lifelong study of the subject refuse to use *any* capital letters in the headline unless they're used on a proper name or the firm name.

No doubt exists on the question—lowercase letters are much more easily read. Even in a Roman face, the most easily read, having both uppercase and lowercase letters in the headline slows the reader down, prevents the message from telegraphing itself and delays absorption of the meaning. And when a face like News Gothic is used in both uppercase and lowercase, reading is difficult indeed. The worst possible choice for a headline is News Gothic Condensed, because the message becomes lost with unbelievable speed. Refrain from making it hard for the reader to read.

This line is set in News Gothic Condensed.

Here's a hypothetical example. No, it's not actually hypothetical, for this very headline really appeared in a 1968 issue of *Production*. Only the advertiser's name and product is not given.

To Maintain Our Record
of "Immediate Shipment"
We Have Built This Plant

Then, the body copy of this advertisement is very short and general and advertiser-oriented. Naturally, it ran under a picture of Our Factory, highly retouched and looking about as real as an unretouched photograph of the man in the moon.

Whatever Your Requirements,
We Are Equipped in this Largest
Exclusive Widget Plant to Provide
Stock Shipments of Your Widget,
Feed Finger, Pad, and Yo Yo Needs.

Always Smith Quality
The Best

You can see how hard copy is to read when excess capital letters are thrown around with abandon, for reasons known only to the advertising manager. Perhaps for the same reason some people aim the little finger like a cannon when they're holding a cup at a tea in high society. They want to prove they're genteel.

Too many capitals in the headline is all that Author Stansfield can find to fault in this ad. But readership studies have shown that it would require more time and effort to read it than had it all been set in lowercase except for the first letter.

Quality Need Not Be Expensive

Some people would have you believe that to buy the best, you must pay the most. This is not necessarily true. Price is only a measure of value—never a substitute for it.

At Stackpole, the real value of any resistor is determined by a combination of its performance record and its price. Perhaps this is why so many of our customers continue to specify Stackpole resistors year after year to maintain top performance for established products and for their new ones, too. Such confidence and loyalty cannot be based on price alone.

Uniformity has become the accepted characteristic of Stackpole resistors. Unique production methods, coupled with in-depth experience in manufacturing and testing are your assurance that Stackpole resistors will give you absolute performance. The resistors you order today will be identical in every way to your last order.

Most leading manufacturers of electronic equipment have long recognized Stackpole resistors for reliability.

Whether it be the rugged demands of portable television or the critical tolerances of space age communication and tracking equipment, Stackpole resistors deliver the performance you expect—the kind of dependability that builds a reputation for your products.

Why continue to pay a premium for quality? Let us prove that you get value from Stackpole. Quality resistors, economically priced, are delivered promptly and backed up by our complete corporate facility. Next time, specify Stackpole. There's a family of fine resistors available in sizes of 2, 1, ½ and ¼ watts. For samples and additional information, write: Stackpole Carbon Company, Electronic Components Division, Kane, Pa. Phone: 814-837-7000 — TWX: 510-695-8404.

The Logotype Identifies the Advertiser

Time was when the advertiser's logotype was of considerably greater importance than it is today. Several decades ago, for instance, the percentage of illiterates in the population was many times higher than it now is. The logo at that time identified the company for those who couldn't read, and presumably strengthened the identification and image even for those who could. There's not nearly as much need for logotypes today as there was in the past, but anybody who thinks he or she will see the decline and fall of logotype is very much mistaken.

Cynics have long recognized that there's a very strong bond between the advertiser and his or her logo. This cunning little design has been invested with near-human properties. It's regarded as highly valued property, to be cherished and protected from any except those who have the honor of *owning* it.

Agency people in general, and layout artists and art directors in particular, harbor a mighty cynical attitude about the logo. Among themselves they always proclaim that if the ad has nothing to say, the selling proposition isn't good, the product is almost impossible to promote for any one of a number of reasons, the copy approach leaves something to be desired, or the illustration isn't everything it should be, there's a magic formula for satisfying the advertiser (regardless of whether the advertisement is worth three whoops or not).

All that has to be done is to bump up the logo size. Make it the dominant element in the ad. Show it big, *really BIG.*

This attitude is wrong. But the thought behind it shouldn't arbitrarily be shot down in flames. An advertiser wants identification—and needs identification.

Logotypes are usually shown at the bottom of the advertisement, below the copy block, and most of the time appear in the lower right hand corner, the point of exit for the reader's eye. This is done on the assumption that the last impression the reader will receive from the ad is the identity of the advertiser. The reader won't be left wondering just who in blue blazes manufactures that wonderful little widget he or she read about the other day in—what was the name of that magazine?

There's much to be said for this theory. The reader's eye *does* generally depart for other parts from the bottom right hand corner of the ad. A logo there *is* noticed most of the time. The reader may or may not remember it, or—as complicated and far-fetched as many logos are today—he or she may or may not be able to interpret it and ascribe it to the company that fathered it. Be that as it may, the bottom fraction of the ad is the proper place to put the logo; that way it doesn't do a disservice to the advertiser by cluttering up his or her ad and adding a distracting element.

Name and Logo Together

Then there's the use of the company name *and* the logo as a design element, often to tie the two pages of a spread advertisement together. This device is frequently used in industries that are frantically competitive, where product differences are relatively insignificant, or are unusually difficult to present convincingly to the reader.

Nothing is inherently wrong with this device, and there's no question that if it does nothing else, it will succeed in identifying the advertiser and making at least a "name" impression on the reader. Naturally, if this is the only impression the ad makes—merely being noted for the name—that's a pretty expensive piece of space. Any number of advertisers are apparently unwilling to take even a tiny little chance on having anything more than the name read, however. They want to be sure of that one thing.

Giddings & Lewis Machine Tool Company's attractive four-color

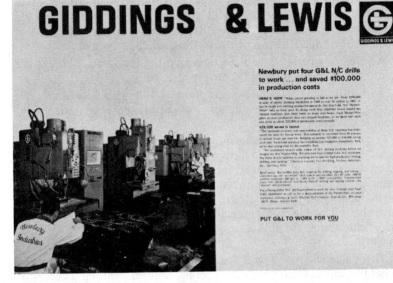

spread is an example. Name and logo act as a unifying force to identify the ad instantly as a spread so that no reader can possibly make a mistake and think the illustration is editorial, the other page is an ad, or some similar boo-boo. Despite the massive type at the top of the pages, there's no oppressive feeling, no connotation of things being crowded or hemmed in. This is due, no doubt, to the presence of so much attractive white space.

Giddings & Lewis is fully aware of the importance of white space and doesn't feel an unconquerable compulsion to cover every fraction of an inch of space with ink as so many industrial advertisers do. It's refreshing.

If you have a sound, logical reason for bumping up the firm name or logo, by all means have at it. Go right to it. There's no real need to, however, because almost all research on the subject indicates that the reader will identify the advertiser even if the advertiser's name is set in type the size of that used for the body copy.

Indeed, some research leads one to believe that having the advertiser's identity shown in inordinately large type actually causes some readers to skip over the ad and the name without devoting enough attention to it to hang a mental name tag on the company that's picking up the tab for the space.

Being too large can be self-defeating. You're better off to stick with the conventional, rather than trying to burn up the track and leave all other advertisers in a cloud of dust.

Mostly it won't work.

How to Use Second Color

When space is purchased in a business publication, that publication agrees to print the advertisement that's to go in it. But the publication's responsibility is limited to printing the ad in the basic color of ink the book uses—black.

Rather frequently you'll encounter books that have special news sections or editorial sections devoted to current price structures prevailing throughout the industry, or something on that order. And these special sections may be printed on a colored stock; usually it's a very light color, perhaps buff, green, or blue.

Although the book may print on colored stock in black ink, oftentimes a very dark ink of the color of the stock will be used—dark brown on buff, for instance, or dark blue on light blue stock. When this is the case the ads appearing in this special section will be printed with the ink color used for the editorial material as a matter of course. This is attractive to readers and does not increase cost of production for the publisher.

So what is a second color? It is any color that appears in the advertisement in addition to the basic color in which the publication is printed, usually—but not always—black.

Incidentally, when writing informally about a two-color advertisement, such as in an agency media schedule, a note to an agency by an advertising manager, or an internal memo within an agency, two-color is frequently abbreviated and written "2/c." Without the quotation marks, of course.

Happily, advertisers can't pick any color out of the rainbow and specify this as the second color for their ads. If this happened, business publications would be so garish and tasteless as each advertiser clamored stridently for attention that one's stomach might stage an instant revolution at the sight when leafing through pages.

The American Association of Advertising Agencies, in cooperation with American Business Press, has established standards for second (and third) colors. This information is given in a booklet entitled *Recommended Standard Second Colors for Business Publications.* You may get a copy of this helpful booklet at no charge by writing to either of the following—letterhead, of course:

> American Association of Advertising Agencies
> 666 Third Avenue
> New York, New York 10017

American Business Press
205 East 42nd Street
New York, New York 10017

Prior to 1951, most business publications offered at least one second color which was designated "standard." Inasmuch as each publication determined what its own "standard" would be, there was naturally a considerable difference in hue and shades of the various colors that were offered.

Both advertisers and agencies recognized the problem and urged that business publications attain a greater uniformity in colors. Accordingly, a joint committee was formed which represented the American Association of Advertising Agencies, Associated Business Publications, and National Business Publications.

This committee selected standard colors for industrywide use, and recommended that all business publications adopt them.

A joint committee representing the AAAA, American Business Press (formed as a result of the merger of Associated Business Publications and National Business Publications) and the Magazine Publishers Association met during 1965 to review previous recommendations on color. Not only were improvements in design and illustration made, but several hues were also changed quite significantly.

It should be stressed that this standardization effort in no way was intended to influence a publication as to the number of colors it offers as standard, nor with respect to its policies on special matched colors which some advertisers demand.

Before choosing the standard colors, the joint committee studied samples of second colors submitted by 326 business publications. The most popular colors were red, offered by 312 publications; blue, offered by 293; green, offered by 282; yellow, offered by 277, and orange, offered by 261.

One of the samples of each of these five colors was selected and approved by the joint committee.

These five standard colors can be duplicated by any business publication. Inks that will reproduce them may be obtained from any of the leading ink manufacturers; any printer can get them. Scientific specifications of the standard colors permanently identify them. You may send to the AAAA for a list of their ink specifications.

Color Loses Its Novelty

Color is far less of a novelty to the reader than it used to be, so an ad with color in it doesn't automatically draw the reader's eye like a magnet picks up iron filings. In fact, the trend is so much the other way that if it continues not too many years will pass before the black-and-white ad will be a novelty, one that will pull in readers merely because it represents something seldom seen. Industrial advertising will then have gone full circle.

To show how the use of color has grown by leaps and bounds (it's more than doubled of recent years), a tally of all ads of one page or more (fractionals weren't counted because they would have weighted the results) in an issue of *Iron Age* showed the following: 41 black-and-white ads, all either one page or spreads. However, appearing in the same issue were a total of 66 ads of two, three, or four colors; all were full pages or spreads. That's a three-to-two ratio of color over the traditional black and white. Whether or not you receive extra readership as a reward for having invested a few more dollars for a second color depends almost entirely on how it's used.

When color is used functionally and selectively and with restraint to accomplish a specific objective, it can produce excellent results that far outweigh the additional investment involved.

Here are some of the things, not necessarily all, though, that the second color should do for your advertisement. If it doesn't do *any* of these, don't use it. Save the money and put it into more space. It should:

1. Call attention to your illustration.
2. Indicate or suggest action.
3. Relate the headline to the illustration.
4. Relate the copy to the headline.
5. Separate the product from the background in the illustration, or separate a special feature of the product from the rest of it.
6. Show the color of the product if it is important in its sale; for instance, in a sporting magazine blaze orange was used in an illustration of a hunting jacket because this is the safest known color.
7. Highlight key words in the headline and possibly, though far less likely, in the body copy.
8. Be used for subheads to break up large blocks of copy.
9. Show structure, shape, or design of the product.
10. Dramatize how the product works.
11. Point out what the product produces.
12. Show how the product should be installed.
13. Point up the simplicity of maintenance.

14. Define an eye path the reader is to follow.
15. Separate elements of graphs or charts.
16. Identify the company—Kodak's yellow is an example.

Functional use of a second color unquestionably results in higher readership. In a study that McGraw-Hill made, the average Noted scores of advertisements in *Power* magazine were 19 percent higher than scores of black-and-white ads that were comparable in all other respects.

In Read Most, though, was where the payoff came when a second color was used functionally. The 68 ads studied achieved 32 percent more readership than did black-and-white ads.

This is very comparable to the extra readership that accrues to bleed ads. The difficulty is that far too many industrial advertisers fail to differentiate between mere *use* of a second color and its *functional* use. It's entirely possible, too, that they may not know there is a difference, and believe that because they are using a second color this surge in readership is something their ads are bound to get.

The use of a second color, by and large, isn't something the industrial advertising manager should become enamored with. Quite likely he or she has no real reason to use it. It's more than possible his or her ad would be stronger without it. One large agency, Marsteller, Inc., customarily recommends against using it. When an agency recommends against something that would increase its billings, it has the client's welfare at heart—and it's mighty sure the recommendation is to the client's advantage.

Functional use of a second color—you could call it *logical* use with just as much justification—tells all and sundry that color is used properly. It *looks* right. Compared to ads that look for all the world as if they'd been in the path of a derailed freight train whose ruptured tank cars dumped ink promiscuously all over the landscape, the ad with functional use of color is restrained and sensitive and effective. The difference is strikingly apparent.

The Use of Yellow

The nosedive in readership of an advertisement with copy overprinted on a strong color is due to lack of legibility. The reader finds it so incredibly difficult to read an ad of this type that the reader simply skips over it without consciously considering just why he or she does so.

Type printed over a solid yellow or orange can be read reasonably well because the color is light enough in tone and the apparent depth of tone is considerably less than that of the black type if it were regarded monochromatically with appropriate filters. Screen the yellow or the orange back and it's more legible yet, although overprinting nonetheless results in a decided reduction in the number of those who will read the ad.

Tint Blocks Overpower

Using tint blocks of the second color is almost as discouraging to better-than-average readership as is use of a solid second color. This is because ads employing this technique are confusing to the reader. The reader doesn't know where he or she should enter the ad. The reader can't tell what he or she is supposed to look at first. Even if he or she figures this out, the confusing use of color doesn't let the reader's eye follow the natural path, clockwise, around the ad that it normally would if the color weren't there to distract the reader.

Then, for good measure, throw in the fact that type overprinted on *any* color of tint block—and this includes a light screen of black, which is gray, of course—is more difficult to read than that same type printed on white. This gives you a situation that is wide open for improvement. Much improvement.

Four-Color Advertising

Four-color refers to a process, although it's a term commonly used to describe an advertisement, piece of literature, calendar, envelope stuffer, or what have you that's been printed in full, natural color so that it looks just as the eye sees the object that's shown. Full color results from four separate impressions made on the paper by the printing press.

Four different colors of ink are laid down—yellow, blue, red, and black. When one is on top of the other, the result is color as the eye sees it, although in some instances when a dramatic effect is desired, the result is color as the camera sees and captures it in the color transparency. The transparency may have been deliberately exposed so as to imprint an off-color or ethereal effect, or an impression of something weird or wonderful or exciting.

You can have four-color ads by taking two entirely different routes. What you get, as far as quality is concerned, and how much it costs varies considerably depending upon which way you choose to go.

One route is four-color ROP (run of publication), which will be discussed now, and the other is the four-color insert, which will be gone into shortly.

Undoubtedly you've noticed the tremendous increase in four-color pages in the major business publications, both in editorial pages as well as in advertisements. This is due to the fact that publishers are doing everything possible to produce a more attractive package for advertisers, one that will be more attractive for readers and hence increase advertising effectiveness.

Such prodigious use of color—and it continues to proliferate in most of the better business books—is economically possible because these publications are now printed by web offset, an extremely fast, efficient method of producing quality printing at fantastic speed and lower cost.

Advent of web offset has made it feasible for publishers of business magazines to reduce drastically the price of four-color advertisements. This benefits everybody concerned. Readers prefer and are attracted to four-color material, so they're happy about the whole thing. Publishers must have high readership, readership that can be documented, in order to sell space in their books, so the trend toward more and more four-color printing is all to the good as far as they're concerned. And advertisers benefit greatly from both higher readership of editorial copy and from higher readership of their ads.

ROP Color Comes of Age

Some years ago the quality of publication-printed color left much to be desired. Most of it was somewhat better than comic pages, but nonetheless was dull and flat and lifeless looking, without the vigor and bite the really good four-color reproduction has. Since web offset, though, ROP color has become better accepted due to lower cost and greatly improved quality. ROP color today is not as good as the individually-printed four-color insert or piece of literature you prepare with tender loving care and admonish a printer to labor mightily on, and it probably never will be. But it *is* good, though, and certainly is no longer to be considered either experimental or risky to use. Quality control of the final printing job of the good business magazines is excellent. When you buy ROP color you can be the next thing to absolutely certain that you'll receive an attractive ad.

As one large advertising agency noted, it's indeed an old question that keeps cropping up with relentless regularity—what is the value of color in advertising? More specifically, just what is it that a four-color ad can accomplish that the same ad in black and white cannot seem to accomplish?

Inherent in the question is the implication that black-and-white advertising may really be more efficient in terms of readers reached per dollar invested.

Researchers have reviewed all available published information on the use of the four-color process in advertising, but there's remarkably little that can be classified as solid fact when viewed dispassionately. Much of the incremental benefit claimed for four-color advertising is in the area of intangibles, such as "impact," "prestige," and "implied image."

We in advertising recognize the merit of these intangibles, but they are indeed difficult to justify to management when making a budget presentation. In order to do this, they should be measured definitively, although to date this has not been done.

Other accepted benefits of using four-color advertising are equally difficult to pin down. These are:

1. Memorability—greater retention value.
2. Realism—product or stituation appeal.
3. Identity—when used as a characteristic of a certain product or company.
4. Psychological implications—warmth, coolness, and other factors that the reader associates with a product or company.
5. Intrinsic appeal—beauty, personal involvement.

Actually, there's no end to such a list. It could go on and on. However, definitive *quantitative* measurements of the effects of using the four-color process in advertising have been limited pretty largely to two areas: Inquiry production and readership scores.

Daniel Starch & Staff performed a massive analysis of 5,000,000 (that's five *million*) inquiries and found that color produced 53 percent more returns per 100,000 circulation than did black-and-white advertising.

Furthermore, Starch conducted an analysis of the effects of size and color variables on ad recall, based on 3,819 ads in seven different product categories in *Life* and *Post*. These were consumer ads, to be sure, although there is no reason to feel that results would have been significantly different had it been in the industrial field. Results showed:

	1 page	2 pages
Black-and-white	100	100
Four-color	153	150

It's quite interesting to note that the 53 percent advantage for four-color advertising in the one-page ad is identical with the advantage for color disclosed by the analysis of inquiries.

Similar studies seem, for the most part, to center on a figure of approximately 50 percent as the relative advantage of four-color advertising over black-and-white advertising. This is borne out by analysis of two years' of readership scores in *Time* magazine, as reported in Starch Ad-Norms.

During this two year period Starch studied nearly 5,000 ads of all size and color combinations in *Time,* certainly a large enough number to permit averaging and comparing readership of specific combinations without sacrificing reliability. Among the 5,000 ads studied, 3,305 were one page or larger in size, split as follows by color: Four-color, 1,554; black-and-white, 1,751.

A comparison of Noted scores shows a 43 percent higher average for the four-color advertisements. However, it's when comparing Seen-Associated—which includes whether or not the advertiser's name registered and made an impression on the reader—that the four-color ads came into their own. Here, four-color ads rated 52 percent higher. Read Most scores showed the least variation, as might be expected, because thorough readership is more a function of content and inherent interest than of physical format. Four-color ads scored 21 percent higher than black-and-white ads in the Read Most category.

Regardless of the analysis applied, Starch's figures lead to the inescapable conclusion that the four-color process produces at least half again as much response to an advertisement as does the black-and-white process, when used in increments of one-page or larger ads.

Interestingly, ads of less than one page seem to utilize the four-color process even more effectively than do larger space units. Four-color ads increased recall by as much as 85 percent over black-and-white ad levels, according to Starch.

However, McGraw-Hill reports that an analysis of *all* run-of-publication advertisements in *Business Week* (except second, third, and fourth covers) for an entire year, involving more than 7,500 personal interviews, advanced a potent argument in favor of four-color ads. Both bleed and nonbleed ads were studied. Four-color pages had an average Noted score 77 percent higher than black-and-white, while spreads averaged 63 percent higher. In both cases the increase in readership was much greater than the increase in cost.

Inserts in Full Color

One of the first questions that arises when you're planning a four-color advertising campaign is, "ROP color or inserts?"

Inserts are frequently referred to as "furnished inserts" because they usually are supplied to the publication by the advertiser, already printed and ready to put into the book.

The most important consideration of all is readership, of course. As we've already noted, four-color ads as a group receive more than 50 percent higher readership than do black-and-white ads.

Four-color inserts tend to receive higher readership than do ROP color advertisements, although this depends to a large extent on the individual ads involved. Many intangibles occur that make direct comparison more subjective than is desirable.

For instance, ads about products of high inherent interest will always be better read than advertisements for sweeping compound or salt to melt snow on the company's sidewalks and driveways. Numerous ROP four-color ads consistently out-pull four-color inserts for this very reason.

What's more, there is always a difference in the creative approach used by two different advertisers. This is impossible to standardize, even if it were desirable to do so. But the fact remains that this sharp variation in the "quality" of the creative approach and of the advertisement itself is a factor that can produce either unusually high or unusually low readership—either with or without color.

In general, though, and this can be accepted as a rule of thumb, one-page four-color inserts receive the highest readership of any kind of advertisement that you can produce.

One-page four-color inserts have approximately a 5-percent to 10-percent edge on ROP ads of the same size, other things being relatively equal.

Under your direct control, when you use the furnished insert, are creative approach, quality of the illustration, quality of the copy, and quality of the printing job. Excel in every area and run a truly great four-color one-page insert ad and what can happen to you? Your biggest competitor picks this exact time to kick off a new campaign that produces tremendous impact. Your insert that would have easily shown its heels to every other ad in the book still looks good by comparison with all ads, but it may have suffered considerably at the hands of the competitive ad. This you cannot control, of course.

Always remember, too, that a dull, uninteresting, poorly conceived four-color ad won't receive even one little bit more readership than will a dull, uninteresting, poorly conceived black-and-white ad.

Granted, the Noted score may be higher with the four-color ad that's a crushing bore, but the Read Most certainly will not.

One thing that's not to be overlooked is the fact that the advertiser who pays the price to furnish four-color inserts can tip the scale in his or her favor.

Heavier Stock Permitted

Inserts automatically attract more attention than publication-printed ads regardless of the number of colors involved. That's because most publications will accept inserts on paper that's much heavier than that used in the magazine. *Iron Age's* rate card, for example, shows that the book accepts inserts with a maximum weight of stock (paper on which the insert is printed), basis 25x38, four-page inserts or less—100 pounds coated, or 80 pounds uncoated. For inserts of more than four pages, or fractional-page inserts of more than two thicknesses, the maximum weight is 80 pounds for coated stock, and 60 pounds for uncoated.

Since an insert is usually heavier and thicker than the rest of the pages around it, the book "breaks" to your insert ad—that is, it opens to the insert when the reader casually starts flipping pages. The reader's fingers automatically turn to your ad, and you know from your own experience how likely you are to read something that's stopped you in such preemptory fashion.

This is giving your advertisement every break—actually, one more than it could rightfully expect unless the insert was used. This holds true even for a single-sheet insert, but even more so for multipage inserts with their increased weight and bulk.

The Agency Markup

One last thing, and this is controversial to say the least. When your agency produces four-color inserts for you, it naturally marks up the printing, separations, type, keyline, and whatever else is involved in the job to the tune of 17.65 percent. This is proper and it compensates the agency for the time and effort and expense involved in supervising your work.

A few agencies habitually gouge their clients in this area and mark up incoming invoices to the agency a full 40 percent—or even more. Some have been known to go the dummy invoice route when padding bills to clients. Two ways to avoid being clipped like this is to have a good idea what things cost, and to deal with an honest agency. Honest ones are in the overwhelming majority.

However, and your agency won't particularly appreciate this, but it will nonetheless purchase space and have inserted in the publications the inserts that you—the client—had printed and produced. You can save 17.65 percent here if your agency relationship is less than it should be and you don't really think it can be ameliorated to any great extent, or if you have made this agreement with the agency beforehand strictly due to budget limitations. Both situations exist, and inserts are advertiser-produced and agency-placed as a common practice, usually for one of the two reasons above.

One place you could run into trouble in printing your own inserts is in the variation of sizes that different publishers require for different magazines. Careful tabulation of the finished sizes and producing to a common-denominator size—after discussing this matter thoroughly with your printer—eliminates this bugaboo. It's mostly clerical detail to start with, although size differential can wreck an insert program unless it's taken into account early in the program. Your printer can trim to proper size, even leaving flaps on some inserts if necessary, and ship the correct sizes to the proper publications. If your printer goofs, it's his or her responsibility to get reshipments made. Be sure to have this understanding in writing before undertaking an insert program.

The furnished insert is the one best way to go first class, and the best method ever devised to attract the most possible readership to an advertisement. If you can justify advertising to your management, you can certainly justify use of four-color inserts.

Spreads

The larger the advertisement, the more readers it attracts.

Spreads—ads of two pages, facing each other—invariably attract much more readership than does a one-page ad. They cost a bit more, too. Twice as much, in fact.

Therefore, it's only logical to assume that if you invest twice as much in space, you're entitled to receive twice as much readership— right? But it doesn't work out that way.

Daniel Starch has found that readership for black-and-white ads averaged 19.8 percent in certain publications, whereas the typical spread advertisement received only 31.5 percent; this is a far cry from twice the readership of the one-page ad, since that would actually be 39.6 percent.

And when it comes to four-color ads, Starch found that typical one-page adertisements in books being studied received 35.2 percent readership, whereas four-color spreads received but 53.2 percent. Doubling of the one-page ad readership would have resulted in a score of 70.4 percent.

What's more, McGraw-Hill has found in 5,400 personal interviews with readers of 14 of this company's publications that the average readership for 2,936 one-page advertisements is 16.7 percent, while the readership for 212 spread ads is 22.9 percent. Doubling the one-page readership rating would have resulted in readership of 33.4 percent. The spreads, received only 73 percent higher readership.

There's this to consider, though: McGraw-Hill research also pointed out that both pages of spread advertisements—when considered as individual pages—received more readership than did one-page ads. The left-hand page of spreads checked by this study received 24.4 percent readership, while the right-hand page received an even 24 percent readership. None of the spreads studied had a layout with one full page given over to the illustration with the copy occupying the other page.

On a readers-per-dollar basis, spreads certainly are not the best buy, although many valid reasons exist to justify running spread advertisements. The first, and usually considered the most important, is dominance. Dominance impresses the reader, it attracts the reader, it stops the reader, it gives you a jump on your competition, and enables you to put in a stronger pitch for your advertising program with your management and your sales force.

In almost every major business publication, the *average* ad is a one-page ad. But who wants to be average? Average implies mediocrity. You'd be incensed indeed if somebody said that you are an average advertising manager, or an average account executive, or that you work for an average company, your product is average, or you have average intelligence.

So why tie yourself down to an advertisement that, at best, can be only average?

Visually, the spread is the perfect unit of advertising space because it's the *whole* that the eye sees. When your advertisement occupies the whole, you're not competing for the reader's attention with the advertisement or editorial copy across the gutter. You have the reader's entire attention.

As a matter of fact, the idea of the visual whole is so simple that few advertising people think of it in this way. They don't realize that anything less than a spread is actually fractional space. Usually we think of one-thirds, one-halves, two-thirds, and so on as fractionals, but not full pages. However, unless we're talking about the back cover position, a single page is only one-half of the whole that the eye sees.

Another thing about spreads: You get the chance to tell your story without crowding. You have room to move around. The layout artist has the opportunity to get in those strong heads and large illustrations *plus* a lot of copy. And the layout artist does so without jamming things together so tightly that only you and the president of the company are willing to read the ad—if he or she will struggle through it.

Furthermore, spreads exert a strong psychological effect on the reader. The spread looks important. It compels attention. It's difficult to pass by. The spread creates a feeling of bigness and progressivness and it automatically makes the advertiser appear to have more stature. Instinctively the reader feels that this is a company that occupies an unusually strong position in its industry.

Then, too, there's something a lot of advertising people tend to underestimate, and that's the feeling of pride that outstanding advertising generates throughout the entire company, all the way from the board chairman down. Salespeople especially can be motivated to produce more because the company's advertising enthuses them and makes them downright proud of the company for which they work.

Let's look now at how space is usually divided in spreads. Illustrated nearby are eight spread "layouts" to show the most common divisions of space. The illustration, of course, is the dark area that's been doodled in with artist's chalk. Also obvious is that the author will never become an art director—at least as far as producing finished art or comp layouts is concerned.

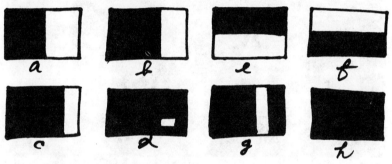

These eight divisions of space are:
- a. One page devoted to illustration, the other to copy.
- b. One and one-third pages devoted to illustration, the copy in the balance of the space.
- c. One and two-thirds pages devoted to illustration, copy in one column.
- d. Illustration is full bleed and covers all of the two pages; copy is set in a panel against the page's white background.
- e. Illustration occupies the top half of both pages, copy is on the bottom portion.
- f. Illustration occupies bottom half of both pages, leaving the top for copy.
- g. Illustration is full bleed on both pages except for a panel the depth of the page, usually one column wide, in which copy is printed.

h. Illustration is full bleed on both pages; copy is overprinted, usually in a light area of the illustration.

Business Week magazine carried B.F. Goodrich Company's excellent ROP four-color spread illustrated nearby. The spatial division is five-sixths for the illustration, which is a dramatic photograph of a B.F. Goodrich conveyor atop Oroville Dam (California), one of the largest earthfill dams in the world; this leaves one column for copy on the far right. It's a wonder this dam was not built in Texas,

considering it is so big and overshadows many other dams. You can't win them all, though.

Progress report from B.F. Goodrich overprinted in italics in the upper left corner of the left-hand page helps assure high readership. There's an implied promise of something newsy and interesting and informative about it, and this is the first page the reader's eye stops on.

Having the illustration carry over onto the right-hand page is another device to boost readership. The reader's eye automatically looks at the entire illustration, and when it does it's attracted to the white space in the upper right, above the column of copy; it then drops into the copy.

The headline is a delightful light touch, for it reads:

> We're part of
> the biggest dam
> project California's
> ever seen

The accompanying copy is replete with a case history full of facts and figures and user benefits. It really does right by B.F. Goodrich.

This layout is clean as a whistle and is an excellent example of how simplicity can contribute to an unusually effective spread advertisement and a great campaign.

Combustion Engineering's magnificent four-color ROP spread ad from *Business Week* is a real stopper. The cool green of the trees, the blue of the rushing mountain stream, the blue sky with a puffy white cloud, and, in the distance, the faintly-purple, snow-covered peaks all add up to a scene so restful and tranquil that it's a rare executive indeed who can ignore this beautiful spread.

The headline, *Air, land or water, CE helps keep it clean*, meshes wonderfully with the illustration, for it shows a lovely scene that's clean and unspoiled by beer cans and candy wrappers strewn all over the landscape by tourists in undershirts and shorts.

Again, one-third of the right-hand page is reserved for a column of copy, but in this instance Combustion Engineering used a device that's almost guaranteed to keep the reader's eye from straying. The panel with the copy is set in from the edge of the page, permitting the arresting illustration to bleed on all four sides of the pages.

Everything's right about this ad: Terrific illustration, fine layout, four-color process, headline tied in with the illustration, serif typeface, good copy. This is money invested to produce a return.

Try a Good Layout (Almost) above All Else

While the reader's eye goes to the illustration first of all, it's the layout that he or she actually sees when all is said and done. This is so even though he or she doesn't necessarily realize there is such a thing as a layout.

Try in every single advertisement for cleanliness, simplicity, freedom from clatter and clutter, and for a layout that lets the advertisement achieve the objective established for it. It isn't always the easiest thing in the world, but it can be done if enough effort and thought are invested.

There's no need to launch a lengthy dissertation on things you should do; they've been covered before this. Bear one thing in mind, though, that there is no established formula, no set rules, no hidebound do-it-this-way-or-else dictums laid down by anybody.

A layout exists only to produce an effective ad.

If it does that, there's no reason to criticize because it happened to have six elements instead of five, or because one person is shown more than once, or what have you.

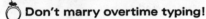

In advertising as in other arts, it's OK to break the rules when you know what the rules are. In this layout containing 16 elements, a chaos of clutter could have resulted. But so effectively was the theme developed that it's a good ad in spite of the rules.

Dura Business Machines, Division of Walter Kidde & Company, Inc., proved this very thoroughly with its strong black-and-white ad from *Business Week*. If you count individual elements, you end up with an amazing 16, 11 more than the classic number.

This should, by rights, produce the most cluttered up mess it's possible to create. But Dura's ad, while it breaks all of the rules of layout, is nonetheless very readable and highly effective.

It benefits from repetition of the overworked blonde secretary whose love life suddenly becomes so smooth she receives a huge diamond—all because a Dura 1041 electric typing system with Edit Control made her work life so much smoother.

Don't hesitate to innovate.

Be sure at the same time to temper creativity with taste, an inclination to be flamboyant with discretion, and the desire to be completely different with a large dash of prudence.

Let the layout work for you, not against you.

Chapter 13

CREATION

A CHAPTER in this book titled "creativity" had been promised to Dartnell, but at the last minute the author's stomach staged a one-stomach revolt and proved unable to tolerate this particularly vulgar debasement of the English language—in display type heading a chapter, at least.

To the advertising person who unabashedly loves his or her chosen field, words are wonderful things, to be fondled, arranged and rearranged, admired and treated with tender, loving care. Both written and spoken English is in a constant state of flux, of course, and that's as it should be if the tongue is to reflect sweeping changes in our culture.

Deliberate mongrelization of the tongue is too much to tolerate, though, especially when words are apparently coined in desperation due to an inability to express one's self. When advertising people who are supposed to be articulate stoop this low it is truly deplorable. It is consanguineous to engineers' tagging inoffensive new products with nonword nonsense names, although a major difference exists: Engineers don't know any better, advertising people do.

"Creativity" is a cliche' that's much admired and vastly overworked. It's bandied about hither and yon on the slightest pretext, or, as often as not, with no pretext whatsoever. It is universally regarded as an excellent topic to kick around while wearing an erudite expression and a faintly supercilious air.

"Creativity" is lovingly discussed and examples are held up for all to admire throughout ad-dom, for all the world as if this non-word referred to a very special charisma bestowed from on high upon a fortunate few, thus enabling these favored ones to achieve upon a level we peasants can never even aspire to.

In the frenetic world of consumer advertising where lofty thoughts about cake mixes and hair spray and dog food and underarm deodorants are regarded as Pronouncements, a premium is placed on the offbeat and the kooky.

Much of the advertising that results from such thinking is superficially intriguing until upon closer examination it becomes painfully apparent that the wild "mod" layouts and jumble of typefaces and psychedelic colors and way-out copy with "high camp" puns and "in" slang have next to nothing to do with the product, they don't *say* anything, and they are totally unrelated to the advertiser's marketing objectives.

Then dawns the realization that such advertising actually is a massive put-on. It is intended to communicate only to bearded, beaded flower-wearers, those who affect bearskin vests and World War I army blouses, and other real cool cats in competitive agencies. This "advertising" was created by spoiled adolescents to achieve *their* primary objective—having fun and games and impressing the absolute living hell out of their contemporaries. And, to a somewhat lesser extent, to build up a sample book to prove to one and all how bright and precocious and terribly, terribly clever they are. They used the client's money to show themselves off, of course.

Strictly from Squaresville is the grim thought of producing advertising designed to exert a positive influence on sales (how crass and commercial can you get?), or stooping to cranking out advertising that talks intelligently in terms of their own self-interest to mature adults in Keokuk, Wichita and Pueblo who are neither turned on nor dropped out.

They Forgot the Name of the Game

The creativity cult has forgotten completely, conveniently ignored, or never knew that the name of the game is selling more of the product at a profit and reducing the cost of selling.

Perhaps the preceding has been an exercise in digression. At the present time it's the height of good taste and the in thing to do to follow the thundering herd of industrial advertising people and pan most consumer advertising—and in the very next breath shout from the roof tops that industrial advertising is not phony like *that,* that industrial advertising gives the reader facts and figures and information that he or she needs about the product.

Industrial advertising doesn't wear a hat to these ostrich-like ad people whose heads are buried in sand up to their armpits—it wears a halo. And industrial advertising people never go swimming—they walk on water.

Before getting any farther into this, though, let's get onto firm ground with solid rules that don't have to be made up as we go along.

First of all, let's see just what "creativity" is. Until the most recent (and most controversial) edition of Webster, there was no such word as "creativity." There is another word, though, that's both accurate and descriptive when it's applied to the process of producing a campaign or an individual advertisement out of nothing except thoughts and experience and, perhaps, hunches; it applies, too, to the analytical process by which knotty marketing problems are solved and programs developed. The word is "creation."

Webster says that *creation* is: "(1) Act of creating, or fact of being created, specifically the act of causing to exist, or fact of being brought into existence . . . and (2) Act of constituting or investing with a new character, title, or the like (3) The presentation of a new conception in an artistic embodiment (4) Something which is created."

Definitions (1) and (3) obviously apply, except when we're talking about the end product itself, the campaign or advertisement—or, for that matter, a layout, an illustration, a piece of copy, or a marketing plan.

Furthermore, Webster says that one definition of *create* is: "To produce as a work of thought or imagination, as a work of art." And *creative* means: "Having the power or quality of creating." This last, it would seem, is close to the intended meaning of what we still insist is a nonword, "creativity."

Far too many practitioners of industrial advertising are perfectly content to remain in peace and quiet with their heads buried in sand, neither knowing nor questioning whether their output and that of their agencies is good, bad, or indifferent. They are satisfied with drifting aimlessly without a communications plan—and very probably without a written marketing plan, as a rule—and continue to produce, approve, place, and pay for advertising that hasn't a chance in a million of achieving its objective because no objective has been set for it.

Objectiveless advertisements in trade publications probably account for at least 90 percent of the total of all pages sold. Many examples have been discussed and illustrated so far.

This is much like the product manager who is in charge of several other product managers in a small satellite plant of a medium-sized corporation. This person, in a meeting in the vice-president-marketing's office with the advertising manager, the sales manager, and three agency people, said that the marketing objective for the year was *to sell more*. The pathetic thing was that the head product manager was serious; the manager had no marketing objectives; the vice-president of marketing had no marketing objectives, no written marketing plan, hence didn't realize how naive this sounded. The advertising manager and the agency people were aghast. Speechless. Even the Wizard of Oz couldn't have miraculously created a more inane remark if he'd tried.

The really sad thing, though is that management of these industrial companies doesn't really give three whoops either, becaue for far too many years too many industrial advertising managers either haven't had the guts to get up on their hind legs and explain advertising to management—to *sell* it—or else they've tried, found they were talking to closed minds as solid as a brick wall, and given it up as a hopeless job.

This is a far cry from being a one-way street, though. While it's quite true that industry's advertising manager hasn't contributed his full potential, it's usually because he hasn't been permitted to. And it's equally true that he is frequently the one lonesome individual in the small-to-medium-sized company who has even the haziest idea of what the marketing concept is and what it can help accomplish if it's embraced enthusiastically.

Surrounded by engineers and other technical men, the advertising manager is often in the unique position of being able to guide the company's marketing activities. He doesn't do it in his name or over his title, of course, but manages to accomplish this through the sales manager or the engineer who has miraculously been transformed into a marketing executive through a change in title. Industry is full of these. Most of them have never even *heard* of a marketing plan.

More often than not, though, management is so archaic and deeply rooted in nuts and bolts and in the dim, dead past, that the advertising manager who persists—for the good of the company—to try to plant ideas and stimulate thinking about updating the company's marketing efforts finds himself a thorn in the side of these throwbacks to the era of selling hardware.

These inept throwbacks invariably come up with a bright idea—such as preferring to sell "standard" or "price book" products to "save engineering cost." This self-defeating policy which passes for thinking in such circles is a fantastically costly one. It completely ignores the wants and needs of the marketplace. Incompetents who pursue such a seller-oriented policy can guide their companies only one way—down.

Babes in the marketing woods that they are, these misfits from some engineering department have yet to learn that the day is long since past when the seller can dictate what will be sold.

Shocking as it may seem to them—if they were to hear somebody say it—the success of a venture rests in the hands of the buyer, the failure in the hands of the seller.

Advertising managers who meekly give up and sit back and accept inadequate budgets because this enables management to "increase profitability" instead of "wasting money on advertising" do their companies a far graver disservice than do those who make a determined effort to bring the throwbacks into the twentieth century, but don't quite make the grade. Abandoning the field to the engineers and nonmarketing technical people has cost industry untold billions in lost sales that can never be recovered.

An Advertiser's View

One top management man who is both knowledgeable and concerned about industrial advertising is William F. May, chairman of the American Can Company.

In the keynote address he gave at the 44th annual conference of the Association of Industrial Advertisers,* Mr. May said, in part, "We have a strong tendency to seek change and newness. At the same time we have an inclination to sameness and conformity that can clearly be seen in the trends of advertising over the years.

"Look at today's advertising. This is the year of the big, bold headline or half-page color photograph with copy block underneath. These are recent sameness patterns. You can find more if you go back over the years.

"If the agencies and American business can achieve change in advertising, followed by conformity, why is it so difficult to achieve better advertising?

"I'm talking primarily now about the *look* and the *language* of industrial advertising. The style in which the reader receives it. I'm aware that some of today's advertising, particularly industrial, is quite technical and is read for the information it contains. But does the majority of it *have* to be repetitive and dull?

"I believe there is too much sound and fury surrounding today's advertising that doesn't contribute a damn thing. There seems to be a tendency to try to talk the problems of the profession to death.

"If you were to agree with me that advertising is fast approaching the point where it's inundating the prospective customers, that a large percentage of today's advertising is dull and unattractive and that its critics are constantly increasing in numbers, wouldn't you also agree that basic remedial steps are *all* that is necessary? And I don't mean a full-blown debate that explores in depth the economic, the social, and the cultural aspects of advertising.

"What I do mean is a return to the 'ITT' of advertising.

"That's spelled with two T's and, prosaic as it may seem to some,

*Now Business/Professional Advertising Association.

stands for intelligently-conceived, truthfully-written, and tastefully-presented.

"Possibly you are as bored as I am with the literally millions of words that are written about what should be done to improve advertising and the infinitesimal amount of attention and ultimate action these words seem to generate.

"This has made me aware, as you assuredly are, of the lexicon of today's advertising world. It has all the earmarks of a foreign language. I believe it was Aldous Huxley who said that 'words are indispensable but also can be fatal.'

"A perusal of a number of publications in the field disclosed the following terms: qualitative values, product differentiation, ethical and social responsibilities, behavioral science concepts, linear programming, societal expectations, factor analysis, and statistical decision theory.

"I have no quarrel with application of scientific judgment to the creative function, nor with the development of copy based on scientific judgment, so long as the finished product isn't as a teenager might put it: 'From Dullsville.'

"I also took a look at some of the letters-to-the editor columns of some of the more prominent advertising publications. If they accurately reflect the interest of a segment of the advertising profession, it is easy to understand the lack of attention given some of the more basic aspects of the profession.

"The corresponding professionals seem to be more interested in expressing views on why the XYZ 'look' is just a flash in the pan; on an abhorrence of colored airplanes; on the sheeplike tendencies of some advertising agencies; on a casual remark made about Texas in an advertisement; on use of the words 'junk mail'; and on the thought that business and industry will never consider you people mature and responsible professionals if some of the advertising columnists didn't stop referring to you as 'Madison Avenue Ad Boys.'

"This interest on the part of advertising professionals may have prompted a responsible writer of an equally responsible advertising magazine recently to make a statement that should be of interest to this group. He said: 'What's mostly wrong with industrial advertising is that *it is monumentally boring.*'

"As head of an industrial organization that spends $23 million a year on advertising and promotion, with a good chunk of it in the industrial area, that statement interests me. And I assure you that I do not believe the responsibility for doing something to improve industrial advertising lies exclusively with agencies or the business publishers.

"Business and industrial advertisers must accept their share. Certainly any major advertiser should be capable of looking at a proposed campaign and determining if it is intelligent, truthful, and tasteful. If he can't he shouldn't be advertising—he shouldn't be managing.

"At the American Can Company, advertising plays a prominent role in our marketing approach—one that we anticipate will increase as our organization continues to grow and diversify. We have taken advertising fully into our plans in conjunction with the recent corporate restructuring of the American Can Company that has resulted in our organization being completely market-oriented.

"Approximately two years ago we were completely decentralized as a company, functioning under the divisional concept. Today we operate as one company, completely market-oriented instead of product-oriented. Every aspect of our business, with emphasis on advertising, reflects this fact.

"Let me again emphasize what I said earlier. I believe in advertising. I have great respect for the talents and capabilities of the advertising professional who has played such a major role in creating this mass consumption society.

"If I've conveyed anything in this brief discussion, however, I hope it's that the buck for 'ITT' advertising stops with the advertiser. If the advertiser doesn't insist on high standards for advertising, no amount of regulation, policing, codes, or conversation will bring it about.

"The primary impetus for 'ITT' advertising, however, can come from only one source: The advertiser. It's his money, his product, his reputation, and his business that is on the line every time he advertises. If mangement of American business must be more knowledgeable about the basics of advertising, it will have to learn. As I said earlier, the major advertiser who can't determine if a campaign is intelligent, truthful, and tasteful shouldn't be advertising."

Now They Sell Systems, Solutions

Industrial advertising *per se is not* monumentally boring, however, Only about 95 percent of it is.

Yet only a decade or two ago the picture was even dimmer. Back then every advertiser had had drummed into him from the Year One that *Everything Had to Be Told.*

Industrial ads were replete with dry-as-dust exposition about every tiny little detail of the product, its engineering, its construction, its materials, and so on ad nauseam. And every last nit-pickin', cotton-pickin' iota of information conceivably related to the product was there in five- or six-point type. Engineers in the company advertising the product loved it.

Things have changed, though, and for the better, praise be.

For one thing, industry today no longer sells hardware. That is, the industrial companies that pace the pack, those that outstrip all of the others in their industries, sell systems and solutions to problems and automation.

Either gone or rapidly disappearing is the seller of standard price-book widgets. Whether such companies survive depend upon management's waking up to the fact that it does *not* determine what will be sold. This is the prerogative of the buyer, one he or she isn't about to abdicate. The 1890's are long gone, and it's doubtful if they will return.

Of course, management of these backward little companies can continue to instruct the field sales force to sell standards, to concentrate on price-book equipment. This they'll do despite reduced commissions until a better opportunity arises in a modern company, then no more sales force. Such managements grudgingly accept orders for what the buyer wants, but don't actively seek to sell such products.

In the meantime, guess what the competition back at the ranch is doing? What any alert, up-to-date company should be doing—determining just what it is that's wanted in the marketplace, then advertising exactly that very line of products aggressively, selling in increasing volume, and making nothing but money. It's all so very simple.

Gone, too, is the buyer who formerly said, "I need a drill press to drill holes in this part." Instead, today's buyer says, "How can I put these holes in here the cheapest way? Punch them? Drill them? Die cast a part with the holes already in? An investment casting?"

Cincinnati Milacron Company formerly sold milling machines, and did quite well at it, too. Now, though, the company sells solutions to problems—solutions based on use of its machining systems. In this and similar ads the copywriter is writing to the buyer, not to the seller.

A few years ago that was kind of a revolutionary concept in itself.

Only the advertiser is interested in the trivia of detailed descriptions of the nuts and bolts that go into the product.

Just what is selling solutions to problems? Isn't this merely another way of saying it is the marketing concept—of selling what the buyer wants and needs, not what the seller wants the buyer to have?

Isn't it at least 30 years behind the times to talk seriously of selling so-called standard widgets, or price-book widgets, to hold down the engineering costs, thus making more profit? Or maybe 40 years? Doesn't the customer pay the engineering costs—isn't he perfectly willing to do exactly this if the seller solves his problem, thus enabling him to achieve *his* marketing objectives?

And isn't it quite true that companies which have taken the biggest bite of their markets for themselves—IBM, Xerox, Polaroid, General Electric, and so on—haven't those companies stopped thinking of themselves as manufacturers, don't they regard themselves as problem-solvers?

New Directions Set

The marketing concept has given "creativity" in industrial advertising a real shot in the arm. New meaning, new purpose, and new direction are apparent in the advertising of companies that understand it and which have embraced it. Their advertising is vigorous, vital, compelling, persuasive—and quite effective.

Every dollar invested in advertising pays them a handsome return. What's more, it has shown up the vast bulk of industrial advertising for what it actually is—dull, stuffy, pretentious, self-serving and a relic of the dim, dusty, dead past.

If Mr. May is right—and *leading* industrial advertisers and *leading* industrial advertising agency men agree that he is—just why is it that so many industrial companies are perfectly content to plod along with advertising that is dull and pedestrian and pedantic and tiresome; advertising that makes no impact, advertising that produces no strong impression, advertising that is forgotten a moment after it is read, if read it is at all?

Certainly it's not that industrial advertising is placed in the wrong medium. The better business publications unquestionably reach the people who make the decisions about whether or not to buy our products, and these decision-makers read these publications.

The medium is right, the audience is right and the product that we present is one they need. This vast universe needs what advertising does for it, needs information only advertising can present.

And advertisers realize the necessity to motivate the people to whom their advertising talks if they are to broaden the market for their products or make a greater penetration into the one that exists.

If we grant that this hypothesis has any validity whatsoever, there's quite obviously a missing ingredient. Could it possibly be that advertising's approach is wrong? Could it be that both the ridiculous hysteria that characterizes the worst consumer advertising and the monotonous drivel characteristic of *most* industrial advertising are at fault? That it isn't the medium, it's not the universe, it's not advertising *per se*?

The Weak Link

This means, then, that the creative approach to industrial advertising is the weak link in the chain. For want of an approach that is genuinely creative, original, fresh, inspired, imaginative—rather than a tired rehash of all that has happened in the past—industrial advertising finds itself in the untenable position of failing to achieve its objective of informing and stimulating and motivating.

A woefully weak creative approach for most industrial advertising is responsible for the waste of hundreds of millions of dollars that are invested—squandered, actually—every year.

Squandered, not invested, because if the creative approach is a pallid echo of past pallid echos the advertiser is not casting bread upon the waters. With pathetic naivete' he or she is pouring money down a bottomless hole with a childlike expectation of receiving a return. There's little likelihood that this will happen.

When psychologists and other experts who profess to know what makes the individual think and react and do so predictably discuss the creative process, or "creativity" as they seem to prefer to call it (they're so erudite it almost sounds like a genuine word-word when they use it, rather than a nonword word), the high-flying terms really proliferate.

Conceptual fluency, reality, orientation, rationalization of self-motivation, societal expectations, want-need trauma, autonomous action, behavioral science concepts, relativistic, innovative function, linear programming, authoritarianism, heterogeneous, and rushing torrents of similar words flow forth to obscure what may be recognized, but most assuredly isn't said.

This unspeakable thing that's automatically swept under the carpet is that in every discussion of the state of the industrial advertising art, either overlooked or left unsaid is the fact that most industrial advertisers are as pure and innocent as newborn babes. They have no written marketing plan, no formal communications plan, they do not realize that their advertisements are tired and tiring and tiresome, nor do they have an inkling that they are not being read.

This sad situation can be attributed primarily to four things. First, a self-oriented, product-oriented attitude, rather than an awareness that success accrues to the marketing-oriented. Second, a barnacle-encrusted belief that all the reader of the business press wants is facts, and lots of 'em. Third, a reliance on the dicta of the motivation analysts and the dogmas of the market research team. There is no denying the necessity for either, of course, nor is this to advocate plowing blindly ahead, guided purely by hunch, hearsay and hope. An insight into the involved process most individuals use to arrive at decisions, and of the major factors which move them to action, coupled with solid, verified facts about products and product features the marketplace demands, provide vitally necessary background information for the creative individual. Fourth is a dismaying lack of quality in the creative approach.

Both the analyzers and researchers attempted to usurp both the advertising function and the creative function in many companies. They attempted to dictate not only the tack to be taken, but *how* it was to be taken.

This resulted in some pretty esoteric formulae for advertising in general, industrial advertising in particular, and rigid rules from which no deviation was permitted in creating communications plans, advertising campaigns, individual advertisements—and even the components in each and every advertisement, layout, illustration, copy, and signature.

Needless to say, the result was invariably a fiasco. Having the creative approach dictated by noncreative people is folly. It can result only in a shambles.

Many industrial companies that should have known better wasted time and money and effort—and lost sales—by producing a spate of technically superb but terribly sterile campaigns for a number of years. A few are still at it, although these campaigns have apparently accomplished little.

The "Hot Creative Shops"

All the while there has been an increasing amount of discussion and analysis of the creative function and of creative thinking. Already the pendulum has swung sharply; the slide-rule-and-formula approach is almost a thing of the past.

This is due not to the fact that industrial marketers very suddenly grew tired of hard facts or developed an aversion for cold statistics, but to the formation and rise to prominence of the "hot creative shops"—advertising agencies that justify their existence by developing fresh, original, daring campaigns for both consumer and industrial clients. These campaigns were a roaring success, by the way. They caused advertisers to think.

There's no scoffing at agencies that started with nothing and a couple of years later billed $50 million a year. And there's no denying that agencies—hot creative shops, all—such as Doyle, Dane, Bernbach; Wells, Rich, Greene; Rink, Wells Associates; Jack Tinker & Partners; Carl Ally and others of that caliber have been fantastically successful in attracting new business.

Their success is due not to scintillating personalities or wearing tiretread sandals, but to producing highly creative advertising *that sold the product*.

Adult urban males on the managerial and executive level are the recipients of more than 1,600 advertising impressions each and every day. And there is no indication whatsoever that this burden on advertising—or on its targets for that matter—will be smaller in the years ahead. In fact, just the contrary is true. There is every reason to think that it will increase, although it is difficult to see how many more impressions could be registered than now are.

This imposes another burden, that also grows larger and heavier with each passing year, on the creative quality of industrial advertising. For, much as we would like to think otherwise, there comes a time when the business world is bombarded with so much advertising that much of it is pretty largely ignored due to its sheer volume.

As this happens—and it is happening right now—the only way the advertiser can realize a return on his or her investment, the only way the advertiser's communications objectives can be achieved, is through a rejection of hidebound thinking and embracing a creative approach that will get the advertiser's advertisements read.

What is involved in the creative process? Actually, it's deceptively simple, or else it's deceptively simple to oversimplify.

Ideas Come From Facts

Creative ability is essentially the ability to solve problems. When applying it to the advertising individual, implied is the ability not only to solve the problem, but to solve it in a unique way, a way that's different from any solution ever before devised for the same or a similar problem.

What this means, of course, is that the advertising individual who desires to create advertising that stands out, advertising that is better and more effective than other advertising, has to do home work and do it well. He or she must do his or her research and read the research that's been done by others. He or she has to know the product intimately and be thoroughly familiar with the markets for it. Furthermore, the advertising person has to be aware of changing conditions in the marketplace, he or she has to know the objectives set forth in the company's marketing plan, and he or she has to develop a communications plan that's right—then keep it in mind.

The Honeywell Philosophy

As Dean B. Randall, vice-president-communications, Honeywell, Inc., said in *Marketing Forum*: "At Honeywell each division of the company performs seven steps that the company is convinced produces exciting advertising. These are: (1) A thorough fact-finding process involving marketing, sales, advertising and the agency is conducted, and a "fact book" on each product or family of products is produced; (2) Define the market in writing. What industry? Who is the key buying influence? Where is the 20 percent that buys the 80 percent?; (3) Define the selling proposition in writing. What are we selling? Why would a buyer select us? What are our pluses? What are the competition negatives?; (4) Write objectives for each ad; (5) Prepare the advertisement; (6) Present a written media plan; (7) Propose methods for measuring results. Propose something. Even if we decide not to measure, we at least have agreed it's measurable."

Except for number 5, "preparing the advertisement," Honeywell's philosophy on the precreative portion of producing a campaign or an ad is that all concerned must ground themselves in facts and more facts so that every iota of information is available to the creative person. This enables the creative person to opt for any idea or any approach with unruffled equanimity, with perfect aplomb, comfortably aware that nothing is lacking as far as basic background information is concerned.

But that's the crux of the creative process—developing an idea. The truly creative individual and the seasoned advertising professional—all wrapped up in one bundle—has conceptual fluency, as the psychologists are inordinately fond of saying. This means, simply, that copywriters and to a somewhat lesser extent art directors and layout artists are perceptive and sensitive and have the mental makeup that enables them to produce an almost constant flow of ideas. Many of the ideas are unusual and daring and different, some too much so; many are good, many must be discarded. But all are as original as anybody's idea can be; everything is rooted in something, of course.

Optimum conditions favorable for problem solving, which is merely developing ideas, according to the Yerkes-Dodson Law, occur when the individual's motivation is neither extremely high nor extremely low. One tends to stifle the ability to develop creative solutions, the other encourages a don't-care attitude. Both prevent a steady flow of good ideas, while moderate motivation acts to increase the productivity of the creative individual and results in a large number of ideas that are "keepers."

Time and time again it has been proven that far more good ideas are produced than are recognized as being good. Indeed, studies have made it very evident that certain ideas are advanced, either discarded or ignored, only to be brought to light again and then recognized as ideas of exceptional merit. This can be called the Slapped Forehead Syndrome, particularly when accompanied by a cry of, *egad, that's it!*

Actually, the creative process in advertising bears marked similarity to that encountered in the fine arts or in science. All have one thing in common: The act of creation contradicts the rules of logic. The majority of the really significant advances in science, the most magnificent examples of fine art—and the most memorable advertisements, as far as that's concerned—have been due to an idea that occurred as the result of intuition.

Use that word carefully, though.

Engineers, if told this, would immediately raise a great howling hue and cry to the effect that you simply cannot engineer a better widget by relying on intuition. They'll proclaim loudly that it takes a slide rule and formulae and equations and mathematics and trigonometry and calculus and blueprints and protractors and triangles and hundreds of hours in drafting time.

This may well be true.

But who conceived the original idea about the better widget in the first place? Who determined there was a need in the marketplace for the better widget? Who researched the marketplace to ascertain how much demand existed for it? And who specified what form the new widget was to take, what features it should possess to make it more desirable, to make it better?

The engineers?

Unlikely.

The basic idea that this widget was needed to fill an existing gap in the product line and that it was necessary for the company to market it rather than continuing to rely on standard price-book widgets undoubtedly originated with a marketing person—more often than not the sales manager, marketing director, or advertising manager.

A Victory for Intuition

At Bausch & Lomb, leading producer of superior quality optical goods—microscopes, binoculars, precision scientific instruments, and so on—the originator of Bausch & Lomb's famous externally adjusted telescopic sight for big-bore sporting rifles was the company's advertising manager. Undoubtedly, when the concept of external adjustments was advanced, it was viewed with considerable scepticism simply because all other manufacturers produced internally adjustable 'scopes.

This advertising manager, J. F. Brandt, persisted, however, and by sticking to his guns ultimately was responsible for development of the BALvar 8 and other members of the family of the finest 'scope-sighting system (scope, clamp-ring assembly, receiver mount) yet devised for high-power sporting rifles. Bausch & Lomb's 'scopes are more rugged, more fog-free and less prone to accidental damage because of the solid-tube construction that external adjustments make possible. Sturdier elements and construction may be used in their manufacture because there are no holes in the tube for internal-adjustment controls with all of their attendant problems.

One of B&L's company engineers undoubtedly *could* have developed this idea, and it's even possible that it occurred to one or more of them at some time or other. But the fact remains that it was not recognized as a superior idea; and this engineer, if one did indeed conceive of the idea, didn't know how to determine its practicality as far as sales and marketing were concerned.

An unrecognized good idea has less merit than one that is somewhat better than mediocre, but whose potential is grasped immediately for obvious reasons.

Intuition has led to a scientific theory that exerts a profound effect on the fate of the entire world today; Albert Einstein's theory of relativity which made nuclear energy possible. Einstein himself later said, "The really valuable factor is intuition," when discussing his development of that revolutionary concept. He added, "There is no logical way to discovery of these elemental laws. There is only the way of intuition, which is helped by a feeling for order lying behind the appearance."

And Darwin credited an intuitive realization of the fundamentals that led to his theory on survival of the fittest. He explained later, "To my joy, the solution *occurred* to me."

Other brilliant creative thinkers in the sciences, literature, and in the field of advertising also credit intuition with playing a large role in the formulation of some of their most successful ideas.

The late Leo Burnett, who headed the giant Chicago advertising agency that bears his name, said in the old *Printers' Ink* that a "wee voice" guides the creative advertising man. "In the lonesome caverns of his mind, and in his private viscera, he develops a *thing* of some kind—an idea, a technique, a phrase, a graphic design, whatever. It strikes him as appropriate to the problem he's trying to solve—it seems accurate and sound, and hopefully *new* and *fresh* and *desirably different.* He may not quite know where it came from, but here he is with a *creation.* "

Printers' Ink added, "Advertising, as everyone reminds everyone else, is a dollar-and-cents business. Its objective is sales, not the development of scientific theories or the enjoyment of perceivers. The *substance*—what's being said—is more important than how you say it. There's ample evidence that this attitude is dead wrong."

The outstanding creative idea in advertising is different from any other idea ever conceived. Substance may be similar, but how it is expressed and how it is shown makes it as different as night and day. Being different is what makes it creative, what sets it apart from all of the kissing cousins that look something alike and sound something alike.

Because the really good creative ideas *are* different, they're regarded with deep suspicion by noncreative people in advertising agencies whose burning desire it is not to rock the boat by offending the client—and by the noncreative client who may never in his or her life have produced anything more creative than pages for a parts manual.

These noncreative people are superbly equipped to produce anything you can think of *except an idea.*

When they encounter a good idea, they take a very dim view of this offspring of the creative person, much as you'd regard a small green three-eyed man with antennae sprouting from the top of his head if you opened your garage door some morning and there he stood, all 3 feet, 5 inches of him.

This is because the noncreative types find it exceedingly difficult to identify with the person who has ideas. They simply do not understand that ideas can be the result of anything else except black magic—or of that semiobscene intangible, intuition.

They are unable to rationalize the fact—and barely able to accept it—that the creative individual's intuitive solution to the problem, his better idea for an advertising campaign, a single advertisement, or even an illustrative idea or a piece of copy, is other than a forehead-slapping, "egad" type of inspiration.

The Discipline of Intuition

Noncreative people are constitutionally unable to conceive of the rigid discipline the creative person has subjected himself or herself to all of his or her working life, as well as the vast amount of research, self-analysis, trial and error, and past experience that makes possible the realization that this particular intuitive idea is, after all is said and done, the one that solves the problem best.

This is because if the creative idea *is* new and different—completely new and different—there is nothing they can subject to objective analysis. It's impossible to poke and pry and pick out an element of the idea here, and one there, and then run them through a computer to determine what the success ratio was in the past when these various elements were present to either a greater or lesser degree.

Indeed, they find the entire process mystifying. They take solace only in the fact that the creative person's intuition did not result in recommendation of something so far-fetched and blue-sky that they are unable to understand its rationale. If presented for approval properly, with patient, humble explanations, accompanied by both the agency's and the advertising manager's blessings, the idea often—but by no means always—finds acceptance, grudging though it may be.

Unfortunately, though, no creative individual bats 1,000. Even the best, the most prolific, and highly respected creative advertising people with a long string of successes come forth with a resounding flop on occasion.

When this happens, the "I-told-you-sos" may not ring from the rafters, but they're there nonetheless. Then it's up to you to mend the fences and rise up on your hind legs and defend advertising.

Nobody comes into this world with any kind of a guarantee, not even of living to the ripe old age of five. Nor does the creative person, the agency, nor the advertising manager offer an ironclad guarantee that an idea will inevitably achieve meaningful results. Such an assurance would be nothing more than pure fraud if one stooped low enough to offer it in a weak moment.

The problem, it seems, is to encourage creative thinking, to refrain from accepting the fact that committees pass on both creative ideas and on finished copy, and to bear the following in mind:

HOW TO STIFLE "CREATIVITY" WITHOUT REALLY TRYING

1. Never rock the boat.

2. Always take the line of least resistance.

3. Don't ever suggest, even in jest, measuring what the advertising program has accomplished.

4. Always submit budget requests based on a heavy media schedule in books you know the president and the vice-president of marketing like.

5. Avoid mentioning objectives; chances are the word is unknown, but don't take a chance.

6. Read the riot act to your agency frequently. Make it toe the line. Let it know *you* give the directions, you make the decisions.

7. Discourage agency people from contacting either management or your field sales force. They might cause somebody to think like a marketing person. That would cause a giant flap throughout the organization.

8. Jump up and shout, *"Yes, sir!"* if your president lays down the law that your company is going to concentrate on selling standard price-book widgets to save engineering costs. Your next year's statement may look good, and maybe you won't be there the following year.

9. Refrain from coddling the agency. Crack the whip. This business about needing two weeks to produce an ad is for the birds. They can do *yours* overnight. After all, you can stop right now and write one immediately. And they can always get an extension from media.

10. Be sure to doodle out a "suggested" layout for your agency. Two-color, small illustration, lots of tint blocks and reverses, long copy, sans-serif type, and get the logo up BIG. The president likes that. Don't let 'em go off on any tangents.

11. Lay down firm guidelines. Make sure the agency knows that you want to see pet expressions that "communicate" in every ad. And let there be no mistakes, technically. All of your competitors have ads that are technically correct, so make sure yours are full of nuts and bolts and dimensions and tolerances and weights, all correct to four decimal places.

12. Resist any and all suggestions of a fee for the agency, or of additional compensation for research, redoing layout, or other extra work. Doesn't the agency get the same as all other agencies—15 percent from media?

13. Dissect every piece of copy word by word.

14. Then submit all copy to a copy committee. Make sure all of the engineers read it, and that engineering is well represented on the committee. It wouldn't do to let anything wrong slip by and get into print.

15. Stand up for your rights. Don't let your agency push you around. Never let them throw a group of ads at you at one time; chances are they're just trying to get out of work by having them all look alike and all having a single theme. This is obviously done to save the agency's time making layouts and writing copy.

16. Always keep the agency guessing. Throw in some veiled threats every time you talk, even on the phone. Let 'em know that other agencies are soliciting your account, and that they've given you some pretty good ideas. This will keep your agency on the ball and prevent your receiving second-rate thinking.

17. Make the agency give you new thinking as often as you can. This business of running a campaign more than one year is from hunger, strictly.

Before looking at some examples of creative thinking and creative problem solving, it's appropriate to consider what Marsteller Inc. has to say about the advertiser who tires of his advertising. In a mailing piece, this great industrial advertising agency said:

BORED WITH YOUR OWN ADS?

Everyone is usually enthusiastic about a new campaign.

The sales idea seems sound, the approach good, the format powerful, the copy alive. "Best campaign we've ever had," everyone says.

Then succeeding ads in the campaign begin coming through. First in layout. Then art. Then brown prints. Then proofs. Then preprints. And finally in the publications. Did you ever stop to think how many times you see every ad?

At first the only evidence of boredom is a lack of expressed enthusiasm. But then there are murmurs, faint but growing louder. "Wonder if we don't need a fresh approach?" "How about a change of pace?" It builds up into a kind of pressure that too often bursts forth in the form of a decision: "Let's do something different."

So the campaign is dropped. It is dropped in spite of a fact so well-documented and so often repeated that it has become a cliché: By the time an advertiser is thoroughly fed up with his campaign the buying public is just becoming really conscious of it.

And along with the campaign are dropped all the cumulative values it may have built up: readership, impact, recognition. The new campaign must start from scratch.

This is obviously wasteful, but it happens all the time. How do you prevent it?

We know of one very practical method. It is based on common sense, it is simple, and it works.

First, in advance of a campaign, provide for evaluating the results. *Your yardstick will, of course, vary with your campaign and its objectives—inquiries, readership, direct sales, etc.*

Second, watch *results carefully from ad to ad. Is the trend up or down?*

> *Third (and this is extremely important), keep everyone concerned in your company* informed *about results.*
>
> *If results are good, there will be very little agitation for "something new and different." It is very difficult to get bored with success.*
>
> *If results are bad, the campaign* ought *to be dropped.*
> *Either way, you're making your advertising dollars work harder. You're investing them not on the basis of internal company opinion, but on the demonstrated reactions of potential customers.*
>
> *And it's only* their *votes that can be tabulated on the cash register.*

This is another way the death knell frequently tolls for a creative idea that could have accomplised much for a company—scuttling a campaign long before its useful life had run its course. It happens all too often in industrial advertising, more's the pity. When you have a good campaign running, explain it, defend it, sell it, preserve it.

Thinking creatively leads to a *different* solution to a problem, one that's never been thought of or used before, It will be unique in both concept and approach, as well as because the problem itself is frequently analyzed from an entirely different vantage point, much as if the creative individual took a mental walk around it and attacked it from an angle never before considered.

Take railroad cars, for instance. The railroad car definitely isn't a glamor item, yet North American Car Corporation's entire business consists of renting and leasing tank, refrigerator, covered hopper, stock, box, and gondola railroad cars to industry, usually for a long period of time.

Railroads own railroad cars, of course, in which they haul freight belonging to customers. But these shippers with problems peculiar to certain industries or to certain segments of industries frequently have highly specialized requirements as far as cars are concerned; railroads can often provide the special cars such shippers demand, but sometimes only after waiting for the appropriate car to be emptied, or to be returned from another trip. This is time-consuming and costly because the shipper's product piles up in the factory, shipping dates aren't met, promises to customers aren't kept.

As a consequence, many companies own their own railroad cars, while others find it more economical to lease specialized rolling stock from firms such as North American Car Corporation. Cost of rental or lease is a tax-deductible item of business expense, of course, and may well be more advantageous in many circumstances than amortizing the purchase price of a car or number of cars over a period of years.

Even so, it's not exactly the easiest thing in the world to take a product that's inherently less than lovely and transform it into something that, while not beautiful, is desirable.

A Challenge Is Met

This is the problem that account executive-copywriter Wim van der Graaf faced when he landed the assignment to develop a new campaign for North American Car Corporation.

One approach would have been to show an illustration of a railroad car and run a headline saying, *We rent railroad cars*, or something similar. Not very creative, however, and the advertisement immediately would have evoked a so-what, shrugged-shoulder response and next to no readership—unless somebody just happened to be hard up for a railroad car right at that particular moment.

Or a box or refrigerator or covered-hopper car could have been shown sitting on a siding with a headline proclaiming, *You can lease me*. This is a little bit more buyer-oriented, less self-interest on the part of the seller, but something less than a stopper either in the illustration or in the copy approach.

What was obviously needed was to set the product and the service and the company apart from similar products and services offered by competitors, for they, too, lease railroad cars and they're all built by the same car makers, they'll all transport the same number of pounds, gallons, or cubic feet of freight—and they're hauled by the same locomotive with the same horsepower over the same tracks. Cars leased by the competitors didn't haul merchandise any faster, the ride wasn't any smoother, and the cost was undoubtedly remarkably close to a Mexican standoff.

First thing required for a memorable campaign was a unifying theme to weld it into a cohesive entity rather than a series of individual advertisements. This required looking at the problem—actually, looking at North American Car's business—from a different angle. A fresh, creative evaluation of NACC's operations brought to mind, perhaps intuitively, that the company actually operated in a logistical capacity. Logistics was the key to the new campaign.

North American Car promptly defined logistics for its prospects in ads in *Traffic World, Railway Age, Traffic Management, Chemical Week,* and in *Oil, Paint & Drug Reporter.*

A black-and-white spread told readers that many dictionaries disagreed on the proper definition of "logistics," some still stoutly insisting it was the art of supplying military troops in the field with the necessities of life and with material and equipment to enable them to carry on military operations.

The company, however, grabbed *el toro* by the horns and proclaimed that logistics is the carrying out in an orderly manner a massively complicated program, the art of managing materials; the skill of delivering the goods where wanted, when wanted, at maximum profit.

North American Car didn't hesitate to state that it acted as supplier, inventor, designer, and catalyst in the development of new and better ways to improve the logistics of business—and to put more profit in distribution systems. The stage was set promptly and properly.

A highly imaginative campaign followed. One of the first one-page black-and-white ads is shown on the following page.

This advertisement violates almost every rule in the book as far as layout is concerned. Illustrations are small; captions are a headlong flight into frivolity; on first consideration neither illustrations nor captions appear to be relevant as far as the product or service is concerned; there's a jumble of typefaces and body copy is set in a simulated typewriter face that's really a bit too light to carry well; and nonexistent characters converse with each other about the product-service being offered, thus sacrificing believability.

All of this is true enough.

The next observation, though, has to be that this is an inspired solution to North American Car's communications problem. Creating a situation as a platform from which to talk and populating it with people who *could* easily exist in the business community personalizes the message and enables the reader to identify with them.

Miss Friday quickly accumulated a following of loyal fans, and well she might for she is as cute as a button and she imparts a tasteful dash of that wonderful ingredient, sex appeal, to the ads.

Unquestionably this is a great campaign and the individual ads are also great. It's highly creative, daring, imaginative, different. It has a fine flair, flavor and a delightful light touch.

Furthermore, the approach is unique in this field. That a unique campaign could be produced is due to the copywriter's taking a fresh look at what the advertiser offers for sale and a fresh look at the problems encountered in the marketplace. The gifted copywriter automatically does this; the capable copywriter occasionally does; the also-ran copywriters almost never do.

Initial impression of the advertisement as a whole is that the layout is unusually clean, and that there are almost acres of nice, clean, inviting white space to make the ad attractive to the eye. The smaller top illustration is properly located to take advantage of the reader's

<u>MEMO</u> <u>ON</u> <u>LOGISTICS</u>:

Re: Sag Junction Terminal

To: Mr. McCall   From: Miss Friday

I was so excited when you asked me to take personal charge of this important research project. I just know you won't regret giving me this wonderful opportunity. After all, a secretary is as distribution minded as anybody!

I did as you said, and got a map from Charlie in Traffic. He's nice. There it was —Sag Junction Terminal near Lemont, Illinois—right in the middle of the Tri-State Tollway, U.S. 66, the Cal-Sag Channel, the Illinois Waterway, and surrounded by railroads. All just a short shopping trip from Chicago's loop.

Thank you for letting me use your expense account. After I called the limousine service in Chicago, I discovered I only had $2.27 cash. The chauffeur remembered you from last year's convention, so I just signed for it. I also figured I'd need an outfit for this safari. Nothing special, you understand, just a few casual things and some boots.

Let me tell you about the darling little hat I got when I arrived at the Sag Junction Terminal. It's a cute little hat with a visor. As you can see from the picture, these are safety minded people.

This research project may take a little longer than I thought, even though I have the limousine to drive me around. Before I give you a complete report on all the facilities, I want to check where all those pipelines go. Whether all those tanks are being used. Just what all that steam from the steam house is for. I wonder how they remember just what is in each of those storage tanks...they all look alike. I'm sure I'll have a lot more to report tomorrow.

Your girl,

Friday

The hat was cute, safe, too.

Nothing special on the expense account... just a few casual things and boots.

If you can't spare your best secretary, send yourself, or write to Terminal Services Division,

NORTH AMERICAN CAR CORPORATION
77 South Wacker Drive, Chicago 6, Illinois

LOGISTICS *is our business*

known eye path, as is North American Car's campaign theme, as well as the headline.

Copy in this first ad in the campaign is so fine, it sets the stage so skillfully, it deserves to be carried here. It reads:

THE DARTNELL ADVERTISING HANDBOOK

MEMO ON LOGISTICS

Re: Sag Junction Terminal

To: Mr. McCall   *From: Miss Friday*

I was so excited when you asked me to take personal charge of this important research project. I just know you won't regret giving me this wonderful opportunity. After all, a secretary is as distribution-minded as anybody!

I did as you said, and got a map from Charlie in Traffic. He's nice. There it was—Sag Junction Terminal near Lemont, Illinois—right in the middle of the Tri-State Tollway, U.S. 66, the Cal-Sag Channel, the Illinois Waterway, and surrounded by railroads. All just a short shopping trip from Chicago's loop.

Thank you for letting me use your expense account. After I called the limousine service in Chicago, I discovered I only had $2.27 cash. The chauffeur remembered you from last year's convention, so I just signed for it. I also figured I'd need an outfit for this safari. Nothing special, you understand. Just a few casual things and some boots.

Let me tell you about the darling little hat I got when I arrived at the Sag Junction Terminal. It's a cute little hat with a visor. As you can see from the picture, these are safety-minded people.

This research project may take a little longer than I thought, even though I have the limousine to drive me around. Before I give you a complete report on all the facilities, I want to check where all those pipelines go. Whether all those tanks are being used. Just what all that steam from the steam house is for. I wonder how they remember just what is in each of those storage tanks . . . they all look alike. I'm sure I'll have a lot more to report tomorrow.

Your girl,
Friday

If you can't spare your best secretary, send yourself, or write Terminal Services Division,
NORTH AMERICAN CAR CORPORATION
(address)

LOGISTICS *is our business*

That's as fresh as a morning breeze off a mountain lake. It's sprightly, lively, and appealing. It *sounds* feminine and has just exactly the right amount of flightiness as the captions make clear. The top one says, *The hat was cute, safe, too.* And the lower one reads, *Nothing special on the expense account . . . just a few casual things and boots.*

There was a mighty deft hand on that typewriter.

The second ad in this appealing campaign follows Miss Friday in her adventures and discoveries at Sag Junction as she has a ball unearthing a number of solid-selling propositions about North American Car's giant facility. For some reason or other, barge captains, tank truck drivers, and miscellaneous employees around the place welcome her enthusiastically—almost with open arms, you might say.

Three illustrations instead of two this time, each of which makes it apparent that Miss Friday is a Miss and not Joe Friday in disguise. Again light-hearted captions arouse the reader's interest and curiosity and pull him or her right into the body copy. It shows an exceedingly sure touch and an understanding of human nature. The copy reads:

MEMO ON LOGISTICS

Re: On the spot at Sag Junction
To: Mr. McCall   *From: Miss Friday*
What a spot to be in! I don't mean the spot you are in . . . trying to move all your production into the Mid-America market; I mean the spot Sag Junction Terminal is in to move it for you! I decided to check available transportation to Sag Junction Terminal personally, so I took the barge today. Can you imagine me, like Cleopatra, floating down the Cal-Sag Channel on a barge? I really saved the expense money though, and the captain even served coffee.

When I docked, I got a ride with a real nice truck driver. I know you don't approve of a young lady hitch-hiking, but I just couldn't walk—the place is too big.

Many things here are automatic. The driver even muttered something about how he would like to see them try to automate truck driving. Frankly, I wouldn't tempt them. You never know what these logisticians will do next!

After the truck driver dropped me off at the track, the train track, I mean, I found out that North American Car Corporation not only leases automobile rack cars, they lease almost any kind of railroad car including the two North American Car tank cars you can see whizzing by in the background.

The thing I like most about Sag Junction Terminal is that you can get here any way you want—water—rail—highway.

MEMO ON LOGISTICS:

Re: On the spot at Sag Junction

To: Mr. McCall   From: Miss Friday

The captain even served coffee

The tank cars are North American

The truck driver was nice

What a spot to be in! I don't mean the spot you are in...trying to move all your production into the Mid-America market; I mean the spot Sag Junction Terminal is in to move it for you! I decided to check available transportation to Sag Junction Terminal personally, so I took the barge today. Can you imagine me, like Cleopatra, floating down the Cal-Sag Channel on a barge? I really saved the expense money though, and the captain even served coffee.

When I docked, I got a ride with a real nice truck driver. I know you don't approve of a young lady hitch-hiking, but I just couldn't walk—the place is too big.

Many things here are automatic. The driver even muttered something about how he would like to see them try to automate truck driving. Frankly, I wouldn't tempt them. You never know what these logisticians will do next!

After the truck driver dropped me off at the track, the train track I mean, I found out that North American Car Corporation not only leases automobile rack cars, they lease almost any kind of railroad car including the two North American Car tank cars you can see whizzing by in the background.

The thing I like most about Sag Junction Terminal is that you can get here any way you want—water—rail—highway. You can even fly in by helicopter! There's more space here than I could cover today. More about space in tomorrow's report.

Your girl,

Friday

If you can't spare your best secretary, send yourself, or write to Terminal Services Division,

NORTH AMERICAN CAR CORPORATION
77 South Wacker Drive, Chicago 6, Illinois

LOGISTICS *is our business*

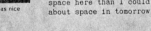

You can even fly in by helicopter. There's more space here than I could cover today. More about space in tomorrow's report.

Your girl,
Friday

If you can't spare your best secretary, send yourself, or write to Terminal Services Division,

NORTH AMERICAN CAR CORPORATION

LOGISTICS *is our business*

This copy is fresh and believable and typically feminine. The writer was a real professional, so knowledgeable about what he or she was doing and about the audience and how they would react, that he or she intuitively knew it was the right thing to do to have the little non sequiturs in the copy.

After the truck driver dropped me off at the track, the train track I mean, humanizes Miss Friday, breathes the breath of life into her, makes her seem so real that it's actually straining the imagination to believe that she doesn't actually exist as a real flesh-and-blood secretary having fun doing a special job for her boss.

Copy makes it very obvious that North American Car Corporation has the cars, the storage facilities, the mass of equipment and the technical know-how to offer a superior logistical service. It makes the company's statement—made by Miss Friday—that the men she talked with are logisticians one the reader accepts.

Readership of this exceptional campaign was unusually high. The advertiser reaped an oversize return on its investment in terms of prospect interest and in strengthening the company's identity.

And North American Car's final words in every ad in the campaign are nothing less than perfect. The bid for action—*If you can't spare your best secretary, send yourself, or write to Terminal Services Division, North American Car Corporation.*

Superb!

Another Flight of Fancy

Eastern Air Lines' great black-and-white spread advertisement from *Business Week,* shown on page 709, proves the copywriter took a flight of fancy to develop a highly original advertisement for air freight.

Selling a service in industrial advertising isn't the easiest thing in the world to do. Whether advertisers like it or not, the fact remains that competitors are not all miserable, uncouth ruffians who offer such a terribly inferior product for sale that it should be legislated off the market. In truth, whatever the industry, product or service, any number of competitors are pretty decent guys who market a product that is almost as good as the one the advertiser offers, and in some instances and some ways, sometimes a better one.

Advertising must make the advertiser's product *seem* more desirable.

For instance, any number of excellent airlines offer air freight service; in fact, most airlines delight in hauling freight along with the passengers on every scheduled flight. This is almost like finding money in the gutter because few of today's big jets are loaded near rated capacity when they take off. Hauling freight doesn't consume any additional fuel to speak of, it requires no additional personnel to fly the beast, no extra stewards or stewardesses to serve coffee, tea, or milk, or otherwise coddle the freight. And freight never hijacks a plane and takes it to some other destination.

Then, too, there are the air freight specialists such as Slick Corporation, Tiger International, and numerous smaller operators who prefer freight to people and do a mighty fine job of it. This is very tough competition for the scheduled passenger airlines to buck. The freight carriers are aggressive and make a determined effort to keep those airplanes full, for they have no herd of passengers milling around the terminal waiting to board, thus paying for the fuel, salaries, depreciation, landing fees, maintenance, etc.

Showing a nice, clean 727, 707, or DC-8 in an advertisement, even in living color with a gorgeous sunset, along with a headline proudly proclaiming that Wild Blue Yonder Airlines hauls air freight if you want to ship it, by cracky, lacks a little something. The approach isn't quite as creative as it might be.

And having an illustration of a nice, colorful topographical map with lines drawn neatly on it and little top-views of the airplanes—perhaps as viewed from a satellite in a low orbit—has been done to death, too. This is no solution, unless there's a story to tell that's so sensational it would almost make the papers as news, not as an advertisement. Those are few and far between.

Eastern Air Lines, though, came up with a different twist in its ad.

Eastern's illustration showing dots for cities, all identified, with the headline, *We connect the dots for a living*, is just whimsical enough to have lots of reader appeal. This is another case of the advertiser proving the business world isn't all grim and competitive and hard-sell.

The advertiser tells its story in a straightforward manner, selling the fact that Eastern has more flights to more cities in the eastern half of the United States than does any other airline, and that it now flies nonstop to Seattle-Tacoma and to Portland, as well as to other farflung places—and it does so very persuasively.

Copy ends with this bid for action: *So if you're planning to ship freight to any dot on the map, give us a call. We'll tell you how we can help.* Only two words with more than one syllable.

Eastern Airlines chose a most creative way to talk about air freight.

This is a highly creative, effective approach to selling a service that isn't very easy to sell—or to illustrate. Eastern did well by itself.

The Product Is Service

Another service that practically invites a hackneyed approach to advertising is the food-service business. After all, food is food, we're all perfectly familiar with it, we encounter it three times a day and have all of our lives. There's almost nothing we don't know about it, or will admit that we don't know about it, at least. Every man or woman fancies himself or herself a suave, sophisticated gourmet.

The food-service industry is rife with advertisements that are nothing short of works of art. Magnificent meals on fragile china with a small fortune in sterling carefully placed on snowy-white linen are photographed with great skill and reproduced with exquisite fidelity in four-color inserts. And you can't quibble about it—this shows the product as the advertiser visualizes it in fond imaginings and as he or she wants prospective buyers to think of it.

Then again, the advertiser may have decided to get really wildly creative and *not* show the luscious meal ready for consumption, but show instead the high quality food before it's prepared—raw steaks, fresh vegetables with little droplets of dew still on them; when in the eyes of the potatoes, they're actually dewy-eyed. Such ads are also very old hat.

What all food-service management firms actually offer to their clients and would like to sell to their prospects is not food *per se,* strange as it may seem. The "product" that is up for sale is ser-vice—purchasing, accounting, preparing, portioning, training of per-sonnel, supervision, professional dietary planning of meals, and so on and on.

Almost no food-service management firm, with the exception of Szabo Food Service, Inc., one of the leaders in this booming industry, realizes or recognizes this, according to Raymond F. Neuzil, Szabo vice-president and director of corporate communications.

Because Szabo does, the company was able to develop a particularly creative, highly effective advertising campaign for its Hospital Ser-vices Division. A typical one-page two-color (red and black) advertise-ment is illustrated.

This ad is beautifully simple and tasteful. Only a spot of second col-or is used—in the lipstick imprint on the cup. Because of its subtlety, the illustration achieves tremendous impact and works very closely with the headline.

Although it's 196 words long, the copy is informative, interesting, and very convincing. It reads:

Sorry,
this just isn't our cup of tea.

Cups like this shouldn't get beyond the dishwasher. And when Szabo operates your dietary department, your personnel are expertly trained to see to it they don't.

Training your employees . . . is *only one of the important features of Szabo's total dietary management program. In addition, Szabo, through its resident food-service director, handles all the time consuming details connected with staffing, employee relations, purchasing, record keeping, and inventory control. This leaves you more time to devote to your prime responsibilities.*

These are but a few of the meaningful advantages enjoyed by Szabo's clients throughout the country. Important, too, Szabo provides timely executive supervision of your dietary department by knowledgeable staff supervisors, including ADA dietitians. Also, significant savings in dietary budgets are brought about by Szabo's operating know-how and massive purchasing power.

In short, you enjoy all of the advantages of a highly professional dietary management program—yet you retain complete control.

To learn how Szabo does it, ask for our free 8-page booklet, "Professional Dietary Department Management—A Key To Better Patient Care." There is no obligation, of course.

This excellent creative approach was made possible by a critically objective analysis of what the advertiser's business really consists of, and how it might best be explained and made desirable to this segment of its market.

Szabo's fine campaign has enjoyed outstanding readership, as well as producing a substantial volume of inquiries. Inquiries are of unusually high quality and a number have been converted into sales. This is industrial advertising that is creative—industrial advertising as it should be done.

Teflon—Challenge to Du Pont

E.I. Du Pont de Nemours & Company faced a marketing problem that required creative thinking to solve during its introduction of Teflon, which is Du Pont's registered trademark for its TFE and FEP fluorocarbon resins and nonstick finishes.

Sorry, this just isn't our cup of tea.

Cups like this shouldn't get beyond the dishwasher. And when Szabo operates your dietary department, your personnel are expertly trained to see to it they don't.

Training your employees . . . is only one of the important features of Szabo's total dietary management program. In addition, Szabo, through its resident food service director, handles all the time consuming details connected with staffing, employee relations, purchasing, record keeping and inventory control. This leaves you more time to devote to your prime responsibilities.

These are but a few of the meaningful advantages enjoyed by Szabo's clients throughout the country. Important, too, Szabo provides timely executive supervision of your dietary department by knowledgeable staff supervisors, including ADA dietitians. Also, significant savings in dietary budgets are brought about by Szabo's operating know-how and massive purchasing power.

In short, you enjoy all of the advantages of a highly professional dietary management program—*yet you retain complete control.*

To learn how Szabo does it, ask for our free 8-page booklet, "Professional Dietary Department Management—A Key to Better Patient Care." There is no obligation, of course. Szabo Food Service, Inc., Hospital Services Division, 4242 South First Avenue, Lyons, Illinois 60534.

(ⵤ) Szabo Food Service, Inc.

Regional Offices: Chicago • Cincinnati • Denver • Indianapolis Los Angeles • New York • Seattle • Winston-Salem

The product discussed here, in a generic sense, is cookware treated with Teflon.

When such cookware was first introduced on the consumer market, there was a brief sales flurry followed by an abrupt downward sales trend even before national distribution was achieved. There was every indication that Teflon utensils would join the slag heap of unsuccessful products that are so prevalent on the American market.

The relatively short history of Teflon cookware dramatically reveals the forces of competition at work and the need for adequate market planning and control. Importance of advertising research is also highlighted, as well as benefits attained when a judicious mixture of promotional approaches is applied to a chaotic marketplace. Reflected, too, is the need of constant evaluation of advertising strategies in light of changing conditions brought about by forces at work in a competitive distribution system.

There are many uses for Teflon resin, especially in industrial and military markets which are superficially treated in this case study. No attempt has been made to evaluate the full market potential for the entire range of Teflon products or the promotional programs that have been undertaken outside the cookware field. The degree of success or failure in promoting Teflon-treated kitchenware represents only one aspect of the overall demand for the product. Teflon has achieved success in other markets and offers a rich potential for further development in the years ahead.

Teflon, Du Pont's family of fluorocarbon resins and materials has an extremely low coefficient of friction which is comparable to rubbing two pieces of ice together. Teflon is almost completely inert to most chemicals, does not enter chemical reactions with food and water, is nonflammable and retains its functional properties in a wide temperature range—from well below the temperature of dry ice to temperatures in excess of 700 degrees Fahrenheit.

Du Pont, as a major chemical firm, is primarily a supplier to industry rather than a producer of end-use goods for the consumer market. Although the company does produce some consumer goods, the bulk of Du Pont sales are made to other manufacturers and fabricators who, in turn, use Du Pont chemicals and derivatives in their production processes.

Du Pont produces and sells Teflon plastics, finishes, fibers, and other derivatives to industry. In this position, as a producer of basic industrial materials, often of an extremely sophisticated nature, it follows that Du Pont has a dual role to play.

Through its basic research program it not only unlocks the door to chemical secrets, but then must develop efficient production processes within the Du Pont organization to turn out these products. However, this is only the first step.

No new product necessarily finds a ready-made market breathlessly awaiting its arrival on the scene. Industry must first be made aware of the existence of the product through a communications program.

In effect, a basic innovator such as Du Pont must undertake an educational program to inform industry that a new item is not only commercially available, but also how the item can be used. It is also necessary to explain what fabrication processes are involved, and how the product might be incorporated in existing or potentially existing technology to bring about improvements in efficiency.

For example, Du Pont developed Teflon and then set about to find a practical means of producing Teflon resins on a commercially feasible scale. Within the Du Pont laboratories there was also much experimentation to develop an efficient process for applying Teflon finishes to various surfaces (steel, glass, aluminum, and others).

Du Pont supplies Teflon in two liquid forms: as a "raw material" of particles of resin suspended in an aqueous solution, and as a completely formulated finish.

This distinction is more than academic, for it must be borne in mind that nothing sticks to Teflon. How, then, could Teflon be made to adhere to a surface? Teflon finishes were the answer to this contradiction. After this process had been largely perfected, Du Pont naturally could have followed one of two basic courses.

It could have invested in plant and equipment and gone into the business of applying Teflon to other materials in response to industry needs; or it could pass along its know-how resulting from research to other companies. They, in turn, would enter the application business. The latter course was followed because it was in line with Du Pont policies and tradition.

Through technical releases, personal visits, and other means, data were circulated to industry. With Du Pont encouragement more than two dozen firms became custom applicators of Teflon.

After Two Decades—"Nowhere"

However, almost 20 years after Teflon resins were first discovered in its laboratories, this Du Pont trademark was still relatively unknown in the U.S. consumer market. For all practical purposes no Teflon-treated consumer items had yet appeared in domestic retail stores. All Du Pont promotion and advertising had been directed to the industrial market. Teflon, unlike Dacron, Lucite, Mylar and many other Du Pont trademarks that are household words, was virtually unrecognized by the consumer. On a somewhat modest scale entries had been made into both the industrial and military markets, and experimentation was continuing to broaden usage and to find new applications.

During the early part of the 1950's the unusual "nonstick" properties of Teflon had led to some experimentation to determine whether or not it was feasible to apply it to food processing equipment and cooking utensils. A few manufacturers had shown some interest in the product, and early research generated sufficient interest for Du Pont to consider the safety of cookware treated with Teflon and to determine whether Federal Food and Drug Administration clearance was necessary.

Extensive experiments conducted by Du Pont and independent laboratories showed that Teflon coated utensils were safe for conventional kitchen use. Du Pont took the matter up with FDA, which issued a statement to the effect that pans coated with Teflon are safe for conventional kitchen use.

It was at this time that French and Italian firms achieved quite a good sales success in the European market. The two firms exported to the U.S. market, which led to consumer demand here because Teflon made possible fat-free frying—low cholesterol dieters welcomed this development with open arms.

Importers were unable to meet demand for the coated utensils, Du Pont was selling Teflon finishes domestically to all buyers, and soon a number of U.S. firms were producing similar cookwares. Burgeoning demand led to appearance of "shabby" frying pans coated with Teflon as certain manufacturers (both U.S. and European) cut corners by using metal of too light a gauge, and applying Teflon finishes improperly or by using the raw liquid Teflon. This inevitably led to a deterioration in the Teflon marketing situation as purchasers of inferior utensils coated with Teflon became dissatisfied.

Finally, sales of Teflon to housewares manufacturers fell almost to zero. Du Pont had to reevaluate its position.

One possible approach was to do nothing. Du Pont could have abandoned this particular market because Teflon sales in other markets continued to increase very nicely. However, the manufacturer realized that (1) logically, Teflon had properties which could demonstrably improve most kinds of cookware from the user's viewpoint and (2) technically, there was absolutely no reason why Teflon finishes could not be properly applied to these items.

Du Pont determined to see what, if any, steps could be taken to revitalize the market.

Emphasized Another Benefit

There still existed an uncertainty at this time about two major dimensions of the problem. One involved consumer attitudes and the other related to the efficacy of Du Pont's undertaking a consumer-oriented advertising and promotional program on behalf of Teflon. Unavailability of empirical data as to consumer attitudes and on the degree of risk in launching an advertising program made obvious the fact that field research was needed.

When this was completed the validity of the "no-fat cooking" sales appeal was seriously questioned, and it had been used exclusively up until this time. It was decided to drop this appeal and substitute the more universal appeal of "ease of cleaning" due to Teflon's nonstick surface. This opened up a far larger market than ever had existed in the health-conscious segment which had bought Teflon coated cookware until this time.

A marketing program was developed and explained to key segments of the cookwares trade to enlist their support and cooperation. Du Pont assured its customers that Teflon was here to stay, that it has a universal market, and that problems were being solved.

The program presented by Du Pont and its advertising agency, N.W. Ayer & Son, was built around six points:

1. Changing the creative strategy behind the promotion from a health appeal to no-stick cooking, no-scour cleanup. This was an appeal that could be directed effectively at all consumers, rather than just those interested in weight reduction or low cholesterol.

2. Offering a certification mark or "quality seal" to the industry. This showed that Du Pont was assuming a completely new role. No longer did the company simply operate as a supplier to the housewares industry. The seal was to go only to those manufacturers who applied Teflon to cookware according to Du Pont specifications.

   Du Pont would set standards and would police quality through frequent spot checks of the product output of those who were awarded the coveted seal.

   Any manufacturer who did not coat according to Du Pont specifications would be denied use of the seal.

3. Development of new colors for Teflon and stressing their availability.

4. Expanding the coated cookware line to include a wider assortment of utensils.

5. Providing useful product information to the trade, especially designed to educate retail sales clerks so they could promote

Teflon to the consumer with greater effectiveness.

6. Launching an advertising campaign in a number of test markets. Details of the program follow.

The need to advertise the concept of "easy cleanup" and to promote the Du Pont Quality Seal appeared logical. However, there was a reluctance on the part of Du Pont top management to commit huge sums to support those efforts without facts on which to base judgements. The author has yet to encounter a management that did not exhibit this same idiosyncrasy, incidentally!

No one really knew if advertising Teflon in the national market would be successful either in generating demand from consumers, or in remedying a demoralized trade situation. What's more, this approach represented a drastic departure from the past. Although Du Pont had tentatively decided to play a more active role in marketing Teflon in the consumer market, the company nonetheless was basically a supplier to other manufacturers.

And the cost of Teflon incorporated in finished utensils represented only a small fraction of overall unit production costs or selling prices. For example, a pan made with Teflon that sold at retail for between three to 10 dollars had less than 2 percent of the selling price invested in the Teflon.

This meant that a question remained: What level of Du Pont advertising was necessary to move finished cookware, and would the funds needed to do an adequate promotional job in the consumer market be prohibitive from Du Pont's point of view?

At one time providing cooperative funds to the cookware industry was considered, but Du Pont decided not to make co-op money available. It was felt that a unified Du Pont-controlled program would be far more efficient in redirecting the basic appeal away from "no-fat" and to promoting the "quality seal" approach.

Consumer education was vitally important, and Du Pont was fully aware that Teflon had failed up until now due to lack of control of market development. Du Pont's own advertising, bought and paid for and managed by the company, was the only logical means available to bring about an orderly reintroduction of the product into a shattered market. Once this decision was made, approval was given by Du Pont's top management to move ahead with advertising research to provide a better factual basis on which to proceed.

Why Television Was Chosen

Advertising research that was undertaken was simplified by the decision to use television as the prime medium. This was based upon a number of considerations, chief among them that the merits of Teflon could best be shown by a demonstration. In-store demonstrations conducted earlier had been successful when imported coated products first reached the market. Television was chosen with the full knowledge that print media are more easily merchandised to the trade, for the objective here was to cause consumers to act; if this objective was accomplished, it was believed trade problems would practically solve themselves.

Advertising research involved testing three levels of advertising effort during two 11-week periods. By means of an experimental crossover design, it was possible to test at national levels of $1,000,000 (10 one-minute commercials in the fall and seven one-minute commercials in the winter), $500,000 (five and three), and $250,000 or a "promotional" campaign (five and none). Thirteen cities were used for test and control cities.

Due to certain retailers refusing to cooperate in the research venture, measurement of sales was based on telephone interviews with 1,000 female heads of households, randomly selected, in each of the test markets and during each of the test periods during both fall and winter.

Research indicated, among other things, that:

1. Sales of cookware finished with Teflon could be increased with a proper level of advertising.
2. Test markets where advertising on TV was carried on at lower levels showed no discernible effect on sales.
3. Promotional effort in test markets at the one-million-dollar level resulted in the doubling of sales as compared with the lower level or of the no-advertising test markets.
4. There was strong evidence of a "carryover" effect of advertising in test cities where promotion was carried on at the million dollar level of expenditures.

One critically important element was omitted in the test design. Normally, the national television effort would be the subject of a trade advertising program to retailers. Without retailer backing, particularly by department stores, neither a test nor the projected national program could be expected to be operational.

Enlisting the cooperation of the retailer was left entirely to the participating cookware manufacturers. Here Du Pont was overly optimistic; word filtered down too slowly from the manufacturers' organizations to the retailers in the test markets.

Accordingly, Du Pont used its own personnel plus a special outside group to contact key outlets on an emergency basis to acquaint retail buyers with the advertising program; this had to be done to get them to stock sufficient coated cookware in their outlets.

These and other research data provided Du Pont with a solid basis for planning a national advertising effort. There had always been a supposition that advertising could work; now there was evidence as to how much of an investment would be needed in the national market to make advertising work profitably.

In the meantime, research was undertaken to determine the consumer attitude toward products finished with Teflon. This was done by mailing 734 Teflon-coated cooking utensils to a consumer test panel—one to a home. A mail questionnaire was used to solicit response at the end of five months; a return of 624 showed that consumers consider nonstick cookware desirable. Ease of cleaning was the most often noted advantage. It appeared obvious that consumers appreciate the merit of the product once exposed to it. This research also indicated that advertising at a realistic level would be able to tap the market potential.

At this time Du Pont management approved a budget of approximately $1,000,000 to promote Teflon to consumers via television, and to the trade in trade publications; in addition, certain specialized vehicles were chosen to carry messages to two additional key groups—doctors and home economists.

Daytime TV was to be used to concentrate coverage on women who were considered the primary target and to take advantage of the economy of daytime television to permit an adequate degree of frequency. The campaign was conceived as follows:

ADVERTISING OBJECTIVES	To educate consumers to the benefits of Teflon when used on cookware and bakeware.
CREATIVE STRATEGY	To demonstrate the ease and convenience of cooking with Teflon, summed up by a "no-stick—no-scour" theme.
AUDIENCE	To reach a broad cross-section of women.
	To concentrate efforts on daytime television—television because of its ability to demonstrate the benefits of Teflon, and daytime television in particular because of its economy in reaching women.
TIMING	To key the weight of advertising effort to the seasonal ups and downs of cookware sales at retail.

In addition, during the first few weeks participation spots were purchased in new nighttime television shows to provide extra reach at the start of the advertising program, and to create additional merchandising impact on the trade.

Net result was a total of 115 daytime-participation one-minute commercials from mid-September to the end of the calendar year. During an average week seven to eight commercials were aired over network television. In addition to these sustaining commercials, eight one-minute commercials were purchased on nighttime network television during the first part of the program.

The trade was recognized as a very important target for Du Pont advertising. past experience pointed this up, and it was also reflected in the proposal of N.W. Ayer, Du Pont'a agency, to management.

Strategy underlying the trade program was highlighted in the agency presentation:

The retailer is important to Du Pont, for his willingness to stock, display, and promote cookware finished with Teflon is an important influence on sales. And as distribution improves, so does the effectiveness of Du Pont's advertising.

Outlook for Teflon at the retail level now seems encouraging. Reports from the field and a recent trade show indicate the trade is willing to take a second look at Teflon. But some deep-rooted prejudices against Teflon must be dispelled before the outlook can be called exciting. Hopefully, we will begin to move in that direction . . .

> . . . as the retailer begins to feel the response *in his own store* to Du Pont's television advertising,

> . . . as the retailer is exposed to Du Pont's continuing advertising program in the trade press, and

> . . . as he or she becomes more aware of the Teflon-coated lines and promotion plans being offered by cookware resources.

Notwithstanding this limited success, we think consistent trade advertising should play an important role because:

> . . . Most of the trade is likely to miss DuPont's daytime television advertising, so it must be continually merchandised to them through trade advertising;

> . . . Many retailers may feel Du Pont's efforts are merely a promotional shot in the arm; through trade advertising Du Pont's long-range commitment to Teflon will be stressed and made crystal-clear.

> . . . And finally, trade advertising will enable Du Pont to keep the retailer abreast of Teflon development, such as success stories, new products that become available, new colors, etc.

Copy approach, as envisioned by the advertising agency, was to "present the facts quickly and clearly, with as much detail as needed to get the dealer to apply the Teflon program to his own sales situation." Pocketbook appeal was built into the copy platform, of course.

Copy would stress the following facts uncovered during the advertising research project:

1. All cookware sales went up 20 percent in the test markets.
2. Cookware finished with Teflon accounted for almost a third of total sales in these markets.
3. Teflon television commercials would reach some 90 percent of the nations's housewives an average of nine times per month for four months during the kick-off campaign.
4. The Teflon "quality seal" would be available on the products of at least 10 top manufacturers, and these manufacturers would be identified in trade promotions. (It's interesting to note that several months later some 28 manufacturers representing 80 to 90 percent of the total output of metal cookware production were making at least some utensils coated with Teflon and were carrying the Du Pont seal on their qualified merchandise.)

As stated by Du Pont's agency, the copy approach to the trade would be essentially "news, presented factually with authoritative-looking layouts in one-page size, with credence lent by the name of Du Pont."

Open With "Pocketbook Appeal"

On page 723 is the hard-hitting two-color advertisement to the trade that appeared in *Hardware Retailer* and *Housewares Buyer*, both monthly publications, and in *Hardware Age*, a bi-weekly, as well as in *Housewares Review*, also a monthly.

This ad makes very effective use of the pocketbook appeal. The headline, *New Du Pont Teflon Program Increased All Cookware Sales 20 percent in Multi-City Test*, immediately causes dollar signs to flash in front of the reader's eyes, as well as arousing curiosity to see just *what* this program of Du Pont's is that it can do this for one of its profitable lines of merchandise. Subhead, *This Proven Campaign Goes National September 4*, is timely, topical, and pulls the reader into the body copy.

Body copy hammers home that cookware finished with Du Pont Teflon snared 35 percent of total cookware sales—sales that were up 20 percent and that Teflon means quality cookware. Copy also stresses the support Du Pont TV advertising will give to the retailer, and that the entire promotional program isn't something that's being gone into with fingers crossed and dewy-eyed optimism, but that it is a proven program that has already worked in test cities. Selling theme—"No-Stick Cooking with No-Scour Cleanup" is explained and given believability by stating it is the opinion of consumers who tested Teflon finished cookware, not the advertiser's.

Another exciting trade ad is headlined, *How Du Pont Teflon captured 35 percent of total cookware business . . . while boosting ALL cookware sales 20 percent.* This advertisement again lists the manufacturers who earned Du Pont's Quality Seal and presents the central selling theme. Copy then proceeds to describe the consumer TV promotion and an arrow points to the kick-off date for the consumer campaign and makes a bid for action by the retailer.

Quality Seal Always Stressed

This ad is clean and attractive and well laid out; the inviting white space, coupled with the feeling of motion and excitement produced by the large symbols, pulls the reader right into the ad.

Rigid factory control program assures you Du Pont quality in cookware finished with TEFLON is the headline of another good ad (not illustrated).The Quality Seal itself is the illustration, circled with an attention-grabbing circle, rough and crude to impart a sense of immediacy and excitement to the advertisement. This ad does much to remove the curse from Teflon that any dealers might associate with the substandard merchandise that was marketed in the product's early days before Du Pont launched this program. Again, leading manufacturers of cookware who earned the right to display the Quality Seal are listed.

Another trade ad in the campaign has a primitive abstraction for the illustration and the headline: *New selling idea for cookware finished with Du Pont TEFLON attracts over 90 percent of women.* It leads into a very convincing discussion of the selling theme and of how Du Pont can be so sure its appeal is right, the very best one that can be used.

The next Du Pont ad again headlined the pocketbook appeal, as well as merchandized to the hilt its consumer advertising program. Headline reads: *Du Pont TV advertising produces profitable retail results for cookware finished with TEFLON.* Body copy plays up profit first of all, then introduces the facts that back up Du Pont's statement. It is very logical and believable, and accomplished its objective of increasing trade awareness of Du Pont's efforts in the consumer area.

During this period N.W. Ayer recommended to Du Pont a space advertising program directed to the medical market; it was to be based on the health angle of cooking with utensils finished with Teflon. This selling theme had been used in the early days when Teflon achieved

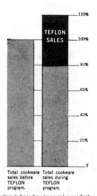

One of the first Teflon ads aimed at retail dealers by Du Pont.

something less than a tremendous sales success.

Six ads were run in *The Journal of the American Medical Association.* Copy stressed the health appeal and contained a coupon offer for product literature and a Teflon-coated fry pan on a reduced price basis. These six advertisements produced some 2,600 requests for booklets and cookware from doctors. Because of this success and the interest the ads generated, it was recommended and approved by management that the program continue.

Additional ads stressed Teflon's role in low-calorie, low-cholesterol diets.

One of these excellent ads is shown. Copy appeals to the doctors' main "job" interest—welfare of their patients. User benefit of the product, elimination of fats and oils when preparing fried foods, is stressed, as is the power word, "new."

723

Lets you give patients new diet freedom. Now, thanks to a new development by Du Pont, your dietary patients can be allowed to eat fried foods without worry. TEFLON® TFE fluorocarbon resin, a new finish for frying pans and other cookware, permits frying without fats or oils. With the addition of this frequently forbidden category of foods, diets become less rigid, more easily followed.

Pans finished with TEFLON are so slick, hardly anything sticks to them. Fried eggs, for instance, slide easily from the pan even though not a single drop of butter, fat or oil is used. Housewives are also pleased to learn that these non-stick pans are easy to clean. A quick rinse and wipe is all that's needed. Never any scouring. The special TEFLON finish is available now on cookware produced by a number of manufacturers.

It's easy to prove the value of TEFLON. Du Pont would like to prove to you that cookware finished with TEFLON can perform a significant service for you and your patients. The coupon below offers you any or all of the following: a supply of folders, containing facts about cookware finished with TEFLON, which you can give to your patients; a regular or an electric fry pan with a TEFLON surface (offered at manufacturer's cost) for your personal use and/or experimentation. If you already have a frying pan finished with TEFLON (many doctors do), please feel free to order a supply of descriptive brochures.

®TEFLON is Du Pont's registered trademark for its TFE fluorocarbon finish.

E. I. du Pont de Nemours & Co. (Inc.)
Div. MJ 4-13, Room N-2507
Wilmington 98, Delaware

Please send me:
☐ A supply of folders containing facts for me and my patients about cookware finished with TEFLON.
☐ A 10" fry pan with a TEFLON surface, a $5 retail value, at manufacturer's cost of $3. My check is enclosed.
☐ An 11" electric fry pan with a TEFLON surface, a $20 retail value, at cost of $10. My check is enclosed.

Name_____

Address_____

City_____Zone_____State_____

REG. U.S. PAT. OFF.

BETTER THINGS FOR BETTER LIVING ... THROUGH CHEMISTRY

Du Pont's advertising program was so successful that manufacturers producing utensils finished with "Teflon" were over-sold and had such large back-orders that this special-market campaign was delayed and finally canceled before its second year.

The trade media schedule follows:

Publication	Space Unit	Frequency	Unit Cost	Total Cost
Home Furnishings	2 pp. fcg. B&W	4X	$1,845	$18,204
Daily (Tabloid)	7x10 unit B&W	22X	492	
Department Store	2 pp. fcg. B&W	2X	1,350	8,100
Economist	1 p. B&W	8X	675	
Hardware Age	2 pp. fcg. B&W	2X	1,020	6,120
	1 p. B&W	8X	510	
Hardware Retailer	2 pp. fcg. B&W	2X	1,060	6,360
	1 p. B&W	8X	530	
Housewares Buyer	2 pp. fcg. B&W	2X	830	4,980
	1 p. B&W	8X	415	
Housewares Review	2 pp. fcg. B&W	2X	820	4,920
	1 p. B&W	8X	410	
Chain Store Age	2 pp. fcg. B&W	2X	1,530	9,180
(Variety Store Edition)	1 p. B&W	8X	765	

			Total Space	$57,864
			Preparation	15,500
			TOTAL	$73,364

Another special promotion was undertaken, this one directed to home economists. It was designed to acquaint them with the "No-Stick—No-Scour" benefits of cookware finished with Teflon, and also to put into the economists' hands both "Teflon" teaching materials and cookware finished with "Teflon."

Advertisements were produced and run in *What's New in Home Economics* and in *Forecast for Home Economists.* This approach was an initial means of reaching consumers, although indirectly; when the extensive consumer campaign was launched, the promotion to the home economists was discontinued.

The headline, *What's new in Home Economics from Du Pont,* is reversed out of the illustrative area just where the eye normally enters the advertisement. It arouses interest and curiosity, and when the illustration makes it plain how remarkably easy it is to clean a greasy pan with only a simple rubber spatula, the ad really had the reader hooked. The reader can hardly refrain from reading the subhead, *TEFLON Finishes for NO-STICK, NO-SCOUR COOKWARE.* By this time Du Pont has telegraphed its message with an interesting illustration and the provocative subhead. If the reader proceeded no further, he or she still was made aware of Teflon and of its primary user benefit.

What's New in Home Economics from Du Pont

Home economists were the next target for Du Pont's Teflon campaign. This ad stresses the benefits of Teflon cookware to homemakers, and offers a "professional discount."

TEFLON® Finishes for NO-STICK, NO-SCOUR COOKWARE

Even burned food won't stick to the super-slick surface of cookware finished with Du Pont TEFLON*. Lets you cook, bake or fry the stickiest of foods...then clean the pan with just a quick wash and rinse. No scouring pads. No scouring powder. Calorie counters can fry in pans finished with TEFLON, while using little fat or oil (or none at all), and still get fast, easy cleanup.

Free teaching aids, explaining how to take advantage of the work-saving and dietary benefits of cookware finished with TEFLON, can be ordered by coupon on page 000. You can also order professional discount schedules from several manufacturers with this coupon.

Look for this seal on: Fry Pans, Saucepans, Griddles, Casseroles, Muffin Pans, Roasting Pans, Cookie Sheets, Cake Pans, and many other items.

Better Things for Better Living . . . through Chemistry
* TEFLON is Du Pont's registered trademark for its TFE-fluorocarbon resin

Body copy stresses ease of cleaning, that even burned food won't stick to the superslick surface of cookware finished with Du Pont Teflon. In addition, copy mentions the reduction in calories possible with cooking done with no fats, no oils.

Free teaching aids are offered, as is a discount from several manufacturers—a professional discount, it's pointed out.

Du Pont's "quality seal" is displayed prominently just above the company's logotype. Such close association provides a favorable "rub-off" onto the "quality seal" from the logo.

Four smaller illustrations in the next advertisement highlight the user benefits of the amazing Teflon finish. In the upper left, there's a fresh egg casually being poured from the skillet—no sticking, no having to use a spatula to pick it up, and no fats or oils used in frying. Upper right illustration shows a housewife easily pouring muffins out of the pan, no sticking, no paper cups, no having to run a knife around each individual muffin and pry it loose from the pan. And look how clean the pan itself is! The two lower illustrations flash across the message that cookware finished with Du Pont Teflon almost cleans itself so little effort is required.

Another ad stressing the user benefits of Teflon cookware. While still directed to home economists, the campaign is now developing a definite consumer orientation.

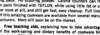

**Cooking and baking utensils finished with TEFLON®
give you NO-STICK COOKING with NO-SCOUR CLEANUP!**

Even burned food won't stick to the super-slick surface of cooking and baking utensils finished with Du Pont TEFLON*. Lets you cook, bake or fry the stickiest of foods ... then clean with just a quick wash and rinse. No scouring pads. No scouring powder. Calorie counters can fry in pans finished with TEFLON, while using little fat or oil (or none at all), and still get fast, easy cleanup. Full lines of this amazing cookware are available from several manufacturers. More will soon be on the market.

Free teaching aids, explaining how to take advantage of the work-saving and dietary benefits of cookware finished with TEFLON, can be ordered by coupon on Page 000, as well as professional discount schedules from several manufacturers.

Look for this seal on: Fry Pans, Saucepans, Griddles, Casseroles, Muffin Pans, Roasting Pans, Cookie Sheets, Cake Pans, and many other items.

Better Things for Better Living ... through Chemistry

*TEFLON is Du Pont's registered trademark for its TFE-fluorocarbon finish.

Now, if we'd had cookware finished with Teflon in the Army in World War II, life would have been much easier! The pots-and-pans detail, always one of the worst for less than eager KP's, would have been one of the easiest, better even than egg-cracking or head-counting.

Headline of this ad is: *Cooking and baking utensils finished with TEFLON give you NO-STICK COOKING with NO-SCOUR CLEANUP!*

Body copy advances the easy-clean, low-calories story quickly and convincingly. Again, the "quality seal" appears just above and to the right of the Du Pont logotype. It's in good company.

As plans were finished and approved, it became possible for Du Pont advertising management to prepare a budget covering the introduction of Teflon, both for the first half-year, and for the following 12 months. Included was television advertising to consumers, trade advertising, and promotions to special target groups—the medical profession and home economists.

Furthermore, direct mail pieces had to be prepared in order to satisfy the requests of coupon respondents, and for other purposes. Plans were also made to participate in trade shows. The "quality seal" had to be designed, produced, and disseminated to manufacturers whose processing methods met Du Pont's high standards. Literature was needed for sales clerks.

And as Teflon became available in more colors, a color-card became necessary to help purchasers make a selection. Publicity releases were prepared, and the costs of research activities had to be met. The budget included these, plus other related functions needed to produce a unified program.

A condensed version of the budget is shown below:

TEFLON-COATED COOKWARE ADVERTISING AND SALES AIDS BUDGET

	Introduction Year	Second[1] Year
Total Consumer Advertising	$652,100	$1,145,000[2]
Retail Trade	51,300	75,400
Professional Trade	27,100	11,000
Advertising Research	40,800	26,500
Direct Mail and Printed Matter	24,800	14,000
Exhibits	3,000	3,000
Travel and Operations Expense	24,700	20,000
	$823,800	$1,294,900

There is no grand finale to this well-planned product introduction, for it succeeded just as it was supposed to do. As the program got into high gear the volume of sales of Teflon to the cookware industry increased each month during the first two years, and it continues upward. There is every indication it will continue to do so, for as more manufacturers are approved and the number of coated utensils rises, so, naturally, do Teflon sales.

Teflon became a hot item in the housewares field. The display of confidence in the product by major utensil producers helped to generate interest in other areas. Waffle irons, ice cream scoops, and even a Teflon-coated rolling pin have been introduced into the market. And one manufacturer produced an electric oven with removable Teflon-coated wall panels to make it easier to clean; other manufacturers were exploring the possibility of using Teflon for such products as range hoods and soleplates for irons. Teflon-coated safety-razor blades also appeared on the market.

---

[1]Introduction year figures are based on eight months of actual expenditures and four months forecasted expenditures. Figures for all of second year are forecasted amounts.
[2]Difference in TV budget results from full second year national TV advertising versus only last half of introduction year on national basis and first half with test market costs only.

New Markets Appear

Use of Teflon isn't confined to products for the kitchen, or for the home, however. At least one manufacturer is exploiting Teflon's slickness to make work easier for the home handyman and for the professional carpenter; this toolmaker is producing a handsaw coated with Teflon. This eliminates binding and a large part of the work, for a reduction in friction naturally means less physical effort is required.

Interestingly, sales predictions made on the basis of Du Pont advertising in test markets largely materialized on the national scene.

Unquestionably the market for coated cookware had been revitalized. Consumers were purchasing Teflon finished merchandise in large quantities; manufacturers had greatly expanded, or were in the process, their offerings featuring Teflon; retailers and jobbers were once again excited over future prospects and acted accordingly; new applications were being found for Teflon; the Du Pont "quality seal" had been instrumental in bringing about high quality standards; added advertising support by the trade reinforced Du Pont's continued national promotional efforts. Teflon was becoming a readily recognized household word.

The continuing research program indicated that 52 percent of all cooks in test markets covered by TV commercials were aware of Teflon. This figure was approximately the same throughout the national market.

Du Pont pulled Teflon out of the doldrums and reestablished it—successfully—with creative thinking. Well-conceived market research, sound planning, and effective advertising. These are the necessary steps in any successful promotional program.

Chapter 14

MEDIA

"**M**EDIA" is the plural of the word "medium." Media are *not* a group of turban-swathed mystics who claim to be intimately familiar with the supernatural and who, after peering intently into the depths of a crystal ball, pass on messages from those who are dead.

Rather, media are vehicles that carry messages. Typical media are jungle drums, skywriting, a chit impaled on a forked stick, smoke signals, the heliograph, the semaphore, and pennants fluttering from a ship's mast.

In industrial advertising when we think of the best possible medium to disseminate the message we've put in our advertisements, we ignore the marginal media mentioned above and think instead of a business publication—or a number of business publications.

The business press is the most efficient and economical means yet devised to reach the untold tens of thousands of hidden buying influences throughout industry—and of reaching the largest possible number of primary buying influences.

As industrial marketers have become more sophisticated and increasingly aware of the necessity of an effective, productive communications program, the value of the business press impressed itself on them more and more. Approximately 55% more advertising dollars are invested in business publication advertising today than 10 years ago. More than 1,450,000 pages of advertising are run annually in the business press.

Advertising managers and industrial advertising agencies have as a secondary goal the creation and placing of the best advertising they're capable of producing. The goal that's always uppermost is increasing sales and reducing the cost of selling. This is what industrial advertising does if the program is well-planned and well-conceived.

Space advertising in the business press isn't accepted on blind faith. It isn't endorsed, recommended, or purchased just because somebody claimed it was the thing to do. No space program was ever launched by an advertising manager who knew what he or she was doing merely because the competitors did it.

To achieve its present place in the mixture of media and techniques that comprise the arsenal at the disposal of the well-armed industrial marketer today, space advertising in the business press had to earn its position by proving its worth.

Advertising people are curious by nature. They're questioners. They accept very little without analyzing and evaluating and comparing with the tried and proven from past experience.

For example, American Business Press tells about the direct mail lists that were compiled from sales call reports by American Hard Rubber Company. All 2,937 customers and prospects on the list were asked to supply the names of others in their companies who would be interested in the company and its products.

A total of 402 replied and named 232 new people who, in their opinion, had buying influence and who should be on the mailing list.

American Hard Rubber then surveyed these 232 people to see if they were being reached by the company's business publication advertising; 93 percent of those who replied said they read one or more of the publications in which the company advertised. The conclusion was obvious: even though the company had not known these influences, they had an opportunity to know the company.

Some Research Studies

Time after time research conducted by industrial advertisers—not by their agencies, or by any outsider with an ax to grind—prove beyond a shadow of doubt that people in industry who are contemplating a purchase look first to business publications for product information.

The Du Pont study on the influence of industrial advertising asked this question: "How do you obtain information about industrial supplies and equipment?" 78 percent said from business publications; most of the rest said from direct mail.

The American Screw Company asked industrial buyers how they first heard of the Phillips recessed-head screw. Of all, 71 percent said through business publication advertising; 23 percent named sales reps, direct mail, exhibits and what have you.

In a study covering buying influences in six fields of industry, a manufacturer of heavy equipment asked, "Which of the following has been most helpful in keeping you up-to-date and providing you with information about products?" Business publication advertising was mentioned first by 71 percent, and 19 percent said by direct mail.

A manufacturer of electrical controls recently reevaluated its entire marketing operation. Everything was questioned. No area where waste or inefficiency might exist was excepted without careful analysis to see if improvements could be made for improved efficiency and lower costs. Among other things, space advertising in the business press was thoroughly examined. A study that required several months was performed and an unusually large sample was asked, "How do you get information which enables you to compare competitive products (in our line) before buying?" Of these, 83 percent specified space advertising in the business press; 14 percent said direct mail; the balance mentioned salespeople, trade shows, catalogs and other random answers.

George C. Kiernan, president, George Kiernan Associates, Inc., successor to the Eastman Research Organization, the 38-year-old firm that specializes in editorial research in the business press, wrote a very enlightening article for *Media/scope* magazine.

Among the conclusions reached after a quarter-century's detailed analysis is that business publications are extremely well read, and that they are held in high regard by the business community *if* they are well edited.

If they are well edited—be sure to note that qualifier.

Furthermore, the research expert stated unequivocally that business publication advertisements are read intentionally, not accidentally. And he backed up his conclusion with some meaningful statistics.

For instance, 85 percent of the 9,513 people interviewed in 174 separate Reader Performance Surveys on 45 different business publications had either completed or started their reading of the surveyed issues while the issues were still current. Furthermore, 64 percent of these had completed reading the studied magazines.

A very healthy 51 percent of those interviewed had read both feature articles and the departments of the various magazines.

Of those who had read any part of the surveyed publications, 95 percent read the advertising either "on purpose" (68 percent) or at least "by accident" (27 percent).

In fact, many readers reported having devoted as much time and attention to the magazines' advertising as they did to the editorial matter—31 percent devoted as much, 14 percent more. And a resounding 78 percent of the business publication readers reported finding something in the publications that applied directly and immediately to their work.

The advertising manager and the agency naturally look at each publication analytically—to determine if it has real merit and if it is right for the company and its products, but they don't question the merit of the business press as a whole.

If a member of top management seriously questions readership of the business press in its entirety, this reveals either a personality defect—one that is unbelievably negative—a gaping void in this individual's business education, or a lack of management ability. This person's qualifications to manage are, to say the least, questionable.

The business press is unique. The business publication is the most economical, most influential, most penetrating path to specialized groups. All good selling is specialized, and nothing specializes like the business press.

It is good sense, and good advertising, to cultivate the people who are immediately and directly concerned with the purchase and use of your product in the language, atmosphere, and reading environment of their job interest. Business publications, the working press, provide you with this opportunity.

Each medium of advertising has, or should have, distinctive characteristics—things that make it different and, for certain purposes, better than any other medium. Business publications are unique inasmuch as people read them for the job benefit alone. They are used for profit and not for pleasure. Only in a business publication can you always find your sales prospect with his or her mind on business — when *editorially conditioned* to absorb your business message.

Prime, Low-Cost Audiences

Because business publications serve specialized audiences, their circulations are compact and relatively small. Their rates are modest accordingly. Thus, a campaign of dominance, something strong enough to stir excitement is well within the pocketbook reach of just about every advertiser. This powerful medium is the lowest-cost, least-wasteful of any at your disposal.

Do not, however, let this low cost make a catchall of your business publication advertising program. "Buying across the board" is pretty unsophisticated. The best advertisement you can produce will not achieve maximum effectiveness unless it appears in the *right* business publications to reach your prime prospects.

Shortly evaluation of business publications will be discussed to see just how they're rated and analyzed to determine which is best. First, however, let's take a brief look at just what it is that comprises the business press.

Industrial Marketing magazine, in an issue on the subject, listed more than 3,000 business publications in the United States and Canada. This listing was published as a special supplement to the regular edition of the magazine, and it is both very complete and very helpful. Every industrial advertising man should receive and read this authoritative publication; it is the voice of industrial advertising. Membership in the Association of Industrial Advertisers (AIA) automatically includes a subscription; however, if for some reason you don't belong to AIA, you should by all means subscribe to *Industrial Marketing*. Its articles are timely and helpful and down to earth; there's no blue-sky stuff.

The 3,000 publications listed range from *AAMA Bulletin,* the official publication of the American Association of Medical Assistants, to *Wisconsin Motor Carrier*, official organ of the Badger State's for-hire carriers.

Each of the 3,000 books listed in the guide is under the basic industry which it primarily serves, such as aerospace, construction, transportation, and so on.

Multiple and group publishers with a number of magazines in their "stables," such as McGraw-Hill, Chilton, Cahners, and so forth are listed under the name of the publishing company. Home office address is given, as is the phone number, a complete list of the company's publications, alphabetically; they are, of course, listed fully in the guide in its two sections.

And Standard Rate & Data Service, Inc., 5201 Old Orchard Road, Skokie, Illinois 60077, publishes a massive volume of some 1,400 pages each month. It is titled *Business Publication Rates and Data*; SRDS also publishes *Canadian Advertising Rates and Data.* Companion volumes cover consumer media—magazines, newspapers, TV and radio stations and networks.

This book, usually called merely SRDS from the initials of the publisher, contains not only a listing of business publications, but detailed information that advertisers and agencies require about each medium in order to plan a media program efficiently.

Here's a tip: Most agencies are happy to give this expensive volume to clients at no charge immediately upon receipt of next month's issue. Although some of the information is made obsolete by the newer volume, much of it is not and the industrial advertising manager always finds that a copy of SRDS on business magazines is one of the handiest things to have around the office. All sorts of questions can be answered without wasting time calling the agency.

The thousands of business publications listed in *Business Publication Rates and Data* are not listed alphabetically, but are divided into classification groupings according to the market served. Some numbers are not yet used. Classifications are:

1. ADVERTISING & MARKETING
2. AIR CONDITIONING, PLUMBING, HEATING
3. AMUSEMENTS
3A. APPLIANCES
4. ARCHITECTURE
5. ARTS
5A. AUTOMATIC DATA SYSTEMS
6. AUTOMOTIVE
7. AVIATION & AEROSPACE
9. BAKING
10. BANKING
11. BARBERS, BEAUTY SHOPS, HAIRDRESSERS, ETC.
14. BOATING
15. BOOKS AND BOOK TRADE
15A. BOTTLING
16. BREWING, DISTILLING, BEVERAGES
17. BRICK, TILE, BUILDING MATERIALS
18. BRUSHES, Brooms & Mops
19. BUILDING
19A. BUILDING Management & Real Estate
20. BUSINESS
21A. CAMPS & CAMPING
22. CANNING
25. CEMETERY & MONUMENTS
26. CERAMICS
27. CHAIN STORES
28. CHEMICAL & Chemical Process Industries
29. CLEANING & DYEING
31. CLOTHING & Furnishing Goods (Men's)
32. CLOTHING & Furnishing Goods (Women's)

32A. COAL MERCHANDISING
32B. COIN-OPERATED and Vending Machines
33. CONFECTIONERY
34. CONTROL & INSTRUMENTATION SYSTEMS
34A. CORSETS, Brassieres & Undergarments
34B. COSMETICS
34C. DAIRY PRODUCTS
35. DENTAL
35A. DEPARTMENT & SPECIALTY STORES
35B. DISCOUNT MARKETING
35C. DISPLAY
35D. DRAPERIES & CURTAINS
36. DRUGS, PHARMACEUTICALS
38. EDUCATIONAL
39. ELECTRICAL
40. ELECTRONIC ENGINEERING
41. ENGINEERING & CONSTRUCTION
44. FARM IMPLEMENTS
44A. FARM SUPPLIES
44B. FASHION ACCESSORIES
44C. FEED, GRAIN & MILLING
45. FERTILIZER, Agricultural Chemicals
46. FINANCIAL
47. FIRE PROTECTION
48. FISHING, COMMERCIAL
48A. FLOOR COVERINGS
49. FLORISTS & FLORICULTURE
50. FOOD—PROCESSING & DISTRIBUTION
52. FUNERAL DIRECTORS
53. FUR TRADE, Fur Farming, Trapping

This is a total 173 different categories of business publications, and in many of the categories are 10, 20, 30 or more individual magazines. In group 87, for example, MEDICAL & SURGICAL, there are a total of 213 separate magazines serving this "industry."

These various publications must abide by the following regulations:

CONTRACT AND COPY REGULATIONS

1. Insertion instructions shall be supplied for every advertisement and shall clearly state the following information: name of publication, name of advertiser, date to be inserted, size of advertisement, identification of advertisement (proof of ad to be furnished if possible) plus any special instructions such as bleed, color, etc.

2. No conditions, printed or otherwise, appearing on the space order, billing instruction or copy instructions which conflict with the publisher's stated policies will be binding on the publisher.

3. All advertising orders are accepted subject to the terms and provisions of the current rate card. Orders are accepted subject to change in rates upon notice from the publisher. However, orders may be canceled at the time the change in rates becomes effective without incurring a short rate adjustment, provided the rate has been earned up to the date of cancellation.

4. Orders acceptable for not more than one year in advance.

5. A contract year, or twelve-month period, starts from the date of the first insertion. Twelve-month periods do not overlap: in other words, space counted in one contract period to determine the rate for that period, cannot be counted again toward determining the rate for the subsequent or past periods.

6. T.F. Contracts will be billed at rate earned through the previous twelve months or billed at rate earned through contract year period without incurring short rate, provided that the same frequency is maintained up to the time of cancellation.

7. Space orders wherever possible should specify a definite schedule of insertions, issues and sizes of space.

8. The forwarding of an order is construed as an acceptance of all the rates and conditions under which advertising is at the time sold.

9. The publisher reserves the right to void any contract unless the first insertion is used within three months from date thereof.

10. Contracts may be discontinued by either party on 30 days' written notice.

11. Verbal agreements are not recognized.

12. If more or less insertions are used within one year than specified in the order, charges will be adjusted in accordance with established rates.

13. Cancellation of space order forfeits the right to position protection.

14. The publisher reserves the right to give better position than specified in the order, at no increase in rate.

15. Advertiser and advertising agency assume liability for all content (including text representation and illustrations) of advertisements printed, and also assume responsibility for any claims arising therefrom made against the publisher. It is the advertiser's or agency's responsibility to obtain appropriate releases on any items or individuals pictured in the advertisement.

16. Acceptance of advertising for any product or service is subject to investigation of the product or service, and of the claims made for it in the advertisement submitted for publication.

17. All advertising is subject to the publisher's approval. The publisher reserves the right to reject advertising which he or she feels is not in keeping with the publication's standard.

18. The advertisers' index is prepared under the regulations and policies of the publisher as an extra service to the advertiser over and above the space order. The publisher, therefore, does not assume liability for errors in the index notwithstanding all normal precautions.

19. The publisher's liability for any error will not exceed the charge for the advertisement in question.

20. The publisher assumes no liability if for any reason it becomes necessary to omit an advertisement.

21. All agreements are subject to strikes, accidents, fires, acts of God, or other contingencies beyond the publisher's control.

22. Failure to make the order correspond in price or otherwise with the rate schedule is regarded only as a clerical error and publication is made and charged for upon the terms of the schedule in force without further notice.

23. The publisher reserves the right to limit the size of space to be occupied by an advertisement.

24. Two or more advertisers are not permitted to use space under the same contract.

25. Association advertising ordinarily takes the rate earned for space used by the association advertising alone. Individual members of associations cannot bulk their in-

dividual company space with the association space to earn a bulk rate for themselves.

26. Supplied inserts shall be charged regular black and white space rates plus additional production costs incurred. A charge lower or higher than actual black and white space rates would be considered price discrimination.

27. Agencies are entitled to only one copy of an issue regardless of the number of advertisements placed by the agency in the publication.

28. When change of copy, covered by an uncanceled insertion order, is not received by the closing date, copy run in previous issue will be inserted.

29. The publisher assumes no liability for errors in key numbers, or its Reader Service Section, or advertisers' index.

30. Any deliberate attempt to simulate a publication's format is not permitted, and the publisher reserves the right to place the word "advertisement" with copy which in the publisher's opinion resembles editorial matter.

31. Advertisements offering prizes, or contests of any nature, are accepted provided prior approval has been obtained from the Post Office at place of publication entry.

32. Requests for specified position at R.O.P. rates are given consideration but no guarantee is made unless the position premium has been provided for in the contract.

33. An advertiser requesting that a standard full page plate be printed without the name and page number appearing on the page shall be charged a premium.

34. No allowance is made to advertisers for furnishing complete plates, text and illustrations for their advertisements.

35. Advertisements ordered set and not used will be charged for composition.

A few additional facts about the business press make it obvious that business publishing is a huge industry that serves other industries that go from tiny to tremendous.

For example, last year the editorial pages in all business publications was well in excess of one million. More than 16,000 editors work full time to find, evaluate and interpret information that's useful to the specialized businesses they serve.

No other publications or information media render this type of concentrated service to specific types of business, or to people in specific job categories.

Most top managements, the good ones, urge that all of their technical and management people read the business publications in their fields—and many insist upon it.

Most business publication editorial is engineered to give readers important information fast, to let readers discover quickly what they want to study closely, and what they'd just as soon pass over. Business publications are essential tools. Without them the progress of business and industry, science and medicine would be greatly hindered and slowed down.

Media Evaluation

Progressive, up-to-date management is fully aware of the value of the business press. It realizes its importance as the one most efficient and most economical medium with which to communicate with the vast audience to whom you must tell your product story.

A question that inevitably arises at this stage is: But there are so *many* business publications! How do you choose between them? How do you select the ones that are right for your company, the ones that will do the most to help you achieve your communications objectives? Since any number of magazines are published to serve your industry, and since they compete with each other, how do you determine which are best?

This is quite a problem and it is not one that can be solved by drawing straws, shooting poker dice, or by a few wise words mumbled over the current copy of *Business Publication Rates & Data.*

Objective evaluation of media is necessary so that you can make an informed choice of publications that will do your program and your company the most good. Such an evaluation, using specific criteria, is possible and is relatively easy to accomplish, as we'll see. Once you've evaluated media for one program—perhaps for one given market, or even for one year—this should lead to a formal media appraisal system which you can establish with all of the guidelines and rules firmed up and written down.

There is no magic formula, though, that will enable you to perform the task effortlessly, and this chapter won't qualify you for an agency media director's position; it will, however, point out most of the better means of evaluating media successfully. It will give you a good working knowledge of media so you won't have to rely on direct mail pieces and contradictory claims in media mailings or from media salesmen.

Even before getting into this, though, it's well to examine a problem that's prevalent throughout industrial companies—the existence of anywhere from one to a dozen or more "media directors" in the company or organization.

Every one of these individuals has strong opinions about any number of publications, particularly those published by technical societies to which they have belonged for most of their working lives. This long familiarity with these media makes each of the media directors supremely self-confident. After all, they know their industry, so it naturally follows that they are well qualified to judge the merits of magazines they've seen around for years. These gifted individuals have strong opinions and they don't want to be confused with facts.

An advertising manager faced with this situation—and it's a common one — must be armed with facts and more facts which enable him or her to ascertain that certain publications are desirable and others are not.

Only facts, coupled with an explanation of how media are evaluated, will enable one to scuttle the poor books and use those which should be on the schedule. He or she has to make a viewpoint prevail. After all, the advertising manager is the company's advertising professional; it's his business to be able to evaluate media. And he's responsible for company money and for a program that influences the degree of success the company achieves in the marketplace. This can't be jeopardized by personal opinion founded on instinct and little else.

However, often the "true facts" fail to dissuade many of those in the company who are staunch proponents of marginal publications just because they've "seen them around for years." Although this situation crops up in all kinds of industrial firms, it is much more prevalent in companies in industries that are somewhat less than progressive as well as individual companies whose managements are strongly engineering-oriented.

An explanation for the prevalence of this attitude may be found in a provocative article in *Research/Development* magazine. The author, Harold K. Mintz, is an experienced technical editor-writer, as well as a teacher whose specialty is to teach engineers to write.

In his 13 classes—in that many years—Mr. Mintz was able to analyze a total of 275 graduate engineers from virtually all of the major disciplines of modern technology. These engineers work for 85 different organizations, including private industry, the armed forces, the civil service, "think tanks," and public utilities. Included in the companies represented are such giants as General Electric, Westinghouse and medium-sized companies like Polaroid and Sanders Associates.

These engineers to whom the author taught English held degrees from 57 different colleges and universities scattered all over the country, as well as six overseas institutions. Among them were MIT, Rensselaer, and a number of the Ivy League schools.

Principal objective of the course Mr. Mintz taught was to "sharpen the students' ability to communicate technical information clearly."

A secondary objective was "to escalate some of the engineers—the more literate minority—beyond that modest level so as to write competently."

Of 197 engineers surveyed, 104 took no English courses beyond freshman English. English literature was taken by 35. And 20 studied public speaking. A total of 13 studied engineering writing. Shakespeare was taken by five. And four engineers studied world literature.

Note the heavy emphasis on literature courses, the glaring lack of a composition course, and the negligible number (13) who took an exposition course.

A questionnaire disclosed that the engineers themselves, in a self-critique, recognized the following weaknesses:

Grammar	2
Getting started	5
Spelling	10
Finding information	18
Using artwork	44
Paragraph structure	97
Lack of clarity	101
Sentence structure	109
Organizing information	115
Wordiness	161

These engineers were responsible for writing the following material in the course of their everyday duties on their jobs—writing that required between seven and nine and one-half hours a week; the average being slightly over eight and a half hours per week:

Brochures and catalogs	6
Magazine articles	14
Product description	47
Process description	65
Specifications	83
Proposals	107
Instructions	111
Letters	170
Reports	198
Memos	225

The article in *Research/Development* concludes that "the dilemma of engineers who can't write" may be overcome only by additional education, and that it can be prevented in future engineers by a more well-rounded curriculum to prevent the graduation of inarticulate engineers who are unable to communicate.

What wasn't mentioned, however, is that *most engineers cannot read*, either. Rather, they do so poorly, and this in itself discourages a desire to read and contributes to their not reading. Engineers are not communications-oriented, they are not word-oriented.

Most of you are familiar with what is jokingly referred to as "copy" produced by engineers for product literature, specifications, proposals—even the letter from the company president to employees at Christmas.

To classify this rape of the English language as "writing" is not taking poetic license. It is taking an indecent liberty.

The average advertising manager in a company that manufactures technical products spends a large part of time translating tortured engineerese into English so that it will be intelligible to prospects; if he or she uses engineerese in product literature, for example, without rewriting it, the end result will be dull, plodding, pedestrian, uninteresting, verbose, trite and semiliterate at best. What's more, the literature will certainly not be promotional in tone—as it should be if it's to accomplish its purpose. More on this in the chapter on literature.

The written horrors that leave a large percentage of the industrial companies doing business today in the form of letters and proposals are nothing short of appalling.

Recently a friend who is an advertising manager wrote a memo to his vice-president of marketing, suggesting that certain key personnel take a course in business writing that was being offered by a well-known university in the city. When no reply was received, this ad manager advanced the suggestion personally, along with several particularly horrible examples to point up the desirability of trying to achieve better writing within the company.

The vice-president of marketing, himself a graduate engineer, *did not understand* the necessity for clearer, less verbose, more forceful writing. So he vetoed the idea.

Remember that the individuals who write those amazingly long-winded, involved letters and memos, the people who start a written description of a product by saying, "The widget is essentially . . ." are the media directors you'll have to contend with. They relish poorly written, poorly edited, crudely laid out and cheaply printed publications that pander to the interests of the advertiser rather than of the reader.

They do so not from any ulterior motives, not from malice, but because they are incapable of making an informed, objective analysis of media; they have never been told that this can be done, nor how it is accomplished.

Recently the president of a company that manufactures highly technical capital equipment, some of it with a six-figure price tag attached to it, wrote the company's advertising manager a memo asking why a certain publication was not used in the advertising program.

It seems that the publication's editor-publisher-owner had attended an association meeting—as usual—and as usual had done considerable high-level space selling. This "publisher's" so-called "business publication" is a fantastically profitable venture because it greedily gobbles up advertising budgets and returns nothing to the advertisers. It is the antithesis of a well edited, useful magazine. It is actually a farce and provides no job-help for decision makers. This book will print anything at all that an advertiser sends in as a publicity release, however, including magazines articles—if they can be called that—written by all of the inarticulate engineers in that industry.

This advertising manager then wrote the following memo which ended discussion of the matter, at least for the time being. However, sacred cows in the media pasture are hard to round up and drive to the shipping pens to slaughter.

The memo is genuine, it was actually written to the president of a company that is a major factor in its industry. And the publication, such as it is, still exists. Only the names have been changed.

TO: Mr. Smith   Date: 3-29-80

SUBJECT: Media

Dear Ralph:

I'm glad to have your memo of March 28 about *Commercial Cooling* magazine because it gives me a chance to discuss briefly how media are evaluated.

Ralph, all of us in advertising, whether in an agency or with an advertiser, analyze media thoroughly and carefully and systematically to determine their desirability as far as our company is concerned.

Following are 10 of the points which are basic criteria used to make an objective analysis:

1. Editorial policy.	6. Readership.
2. Editorial content.	7. Market potential.
3. Editorial format.	8. Advertiser acceptance.
4. Circulation.	9. Services to advertisers.
5. Publication image.	10. Space cost.

Briefly, I'll take up each of the criteria as they relate to *Commercial Cooling* magazine.

1. EDITORIAL POLICY

   Commercial Cooling has no editorial policy. It does not define critical issues in the industry, nor does it take a stand on them even if they are vitally important to individuals and companies. *Commercial Cooling* vacillates because in vacillation lies safety. You irritate nobody if you refuse to take a stand.

2. EDITORIAL CONTENT

   Commercial Cooling is what is known in the advertising field as a "pastepot book." That's because its so-called editorial material is largely rewritten after it has appeared originally in legitimate publications, or it is material contributed at no cost to *Commercial Cooling* by manufacturer personnel. The publication has, to the best of my knowledge and that of the agency, *one* editor. No field editors, no Washington editor, no corresponding editors, no other editors.

   In this connection, I might mention that the *one* thing an advertiser buys when he purchases space in a business publication is editorial content. When it's good, the magazine is read, his ad is read and the money is well invested. In the absence of good editorial, money is wasted.

3. EDITORIAL FORMAT

In this respect *Commercial Cooling* is as up-to-date as the Stanley Steamer.

Years ago the offbeat size—digest-sized, square magazines, *Life*-sized magazines and what have you—enjoyed a brief (fortunately) burst of popularity. Some publishers rationalized that their magazine's being off-size made it stand out.

Soon, however, reason prevailed and today almost all of the good business publications are approximately 8¼ by 11¼ inches. This is necessary, Ralph, because many advertisers (including ourselves) print their own four-color insert ads. Without size standardization, business publishing would be a jungle.

Commercial Cooling magazine sells its front cover. Back in the early days of the business press this was considered smart business. It simply isn't done today. Can you imagine *Business Week* or *Iron Age* or *Fortune* or *Factory* with an advertisement on the front cover?

Layout inside *Commercial Cooling* is typical of pastepot books. Deadly dull, no four-color—not even any two-color—in the editorial pages, no white space, no imagination, no vitality, no invitation to read. It repels the eye.

4. CIRCULATION

Next to editorial (policy, content, and format), this is the most important criterion by which value of a book is judged.

Commercial Cooling lags in qualifying recipients of the book, according to its own BPA Statement. The publisher stated that 18.7 percent had not been qualified for three years, and that 81.3 percent were not qualified for two years.

This is not good enough in today's industry with its mobility of personnel.

Additionally, under Section 3C of *Commercial Cooling's* BPA Statement, the publisher would not state the "Mailing Address Breakdown of Qualified Circulation." The publisher did not give the following requested information:

a. Individuals by name and title/or function.

b. Individuals by name only.

c. Titles or functions only.

d. Company names only.

e. Bulk copies.

As a publication to consider seriously, no professional in advertising would give a second glance to a publication with a circulation such as this.

5. PUBLICATION IMAGE

In this instance this is a nebulous thing, although with quality publications it is almost a tangible and it can be measured.

Commercial Cooling's image with nonadvertising people in advertiser companies —primarily company presidents and other top executives—is good. The publisher does *not* call on advertising professionals, either in agencies or in advertiser companies. They are familiar with publications of this type and recognize them for what they are.

6. READERSHIP

Commercial Cooling retains no rating service—Starch, Ad-Chart, Readex, Reader Feedback, Ad-Gage, Mills Shepard, or any other service.

This means the publication offers no proof of readership, either quantitatively or qualitatively. It offers no means of measuring advertising effectiveness. Every legitimate publication does, however, with almost no exceptions.

Ralph, this is opinion, but I think a valid one: I feel quite sure that the readers of *Commercial Cooling* are on *neither* a specifying nor a decision-making level. The publication simply does not have reader appeal for personnel of that caliber.

7. MARKET POTENTIAL

The market which *Commercial Cooling* professes to serve is huge.

8. ADVERTISER ACCEPTANCE

Commercial Cooling enjoys good advertiser acceptance because it is sold to non-advertising professionals. Ralph, here's another opinion: I'd guess that many of our competitors—smaller companies, by and large, you know—do not have professional advertising management.

This function may well be assigned as an "extra" duty to some willing individual who is completely lacking in qualifications. That individual is probably impressed as can be with seeing all of his competitors' ads in *Commercial Cooling*. He is also probably fearful of making a horrible mistake, so readily assumes that the book has merit. I have encountered this situation several times over the years.

It is interesting to note that the company's last three advertising managers all recommended dropping this book, and that our former agency did also. In addition, our present agency states flatly that *Commercial Cooling* is a complete waste of money.

I sincerely hope that all of our competitors continue to pour money into *Commercial Cooling*. This drain on their promotional funds will prevent their investing in publications which would help them achieve their marketing objectives.

9. SERVICES TO ADVERTISERS

Commercial Cooling offers absolutely none, in vivid contrast to every legitimate business publication.

No merchandising. No mailing. No market research. No market analysis. No marketing information. Nothing.

10. SPACE COST

Space cost is low, but is overpriced for what is offered.

Offhand, I can't think of even one business publication that has to be turned on its side to read a conventional 7 x 10 ad.

Ralph, good trade magazines are read and read thoroughly. They are good and getting better all of the time. And as they do, time is running out for the parasitic publisher that has quietly sucked away promotional dollars to no end but his own.

In my years in the advertising business I've seen many *Commercial Cooling* magazines —by one name or another. All of them had just one goal: to make a fast buck for a fast-buck artist. Advertisers wasted money on them, sometimes for years, but ultimately saw the light.

You asked me, Ralph, what to tell the publisher of this book the next time he buttonholes you and tries to get you to have the book added to our schedule. My suggestion is that you ask him to talk to me, or to our agency. You might say that in your organization advertising management's function is to manage the advertising, and that you have more important things to occupy your mind.

You can do this courteously and then you'll have the problem solved by placing it where it belongs—with me.

I hope this has helped, and I'll be happy to go into any of these criteria with you, either in a memo, or personally if you'd like.

Sincerely,

/s/

J.J. Jones
Advertising Manager

This memo made quite an impression. This company president had always thought heretofore that media are selected on the basis of personal likes and dislikes as far as sales reps are concerned, or on what magazine just happened to appeal to the advertising manager. That media could be measured and evaluated was an entirely new concept. This memo, incidentally, ended discussion of this pastepot book.

These criteria will be covered more thoroughly a little later on, but let's first take a look at how business publications present themselves to prospective purchasers of space.

AIA Business Publication Data Form

Until 1967, when the new Business Publication Data Form was developed by the Association of Industrial Advertisers, business publications presented advertisers and agencies with a statement about themselves in a variety of forms.

Audited publications used either a BPA Form or an ABC Form; unaudited publications used one of hundreds of forms of their own devising, printed to look pretty and official and impressive.

All of these forms made a stab at showing circulations, geographical breakdowns of circulation, recipients of the publications, and similar information deemed necessary either to sell space in the particular book to the advertiser or to make forming an informed opinion about the magazine easier.

Business Publications Audit of Circulation, Inc., is the leading auditing service in the business publications field. Business publications use either a BPA audit or one provided by the Audit Bureau of Circulation (ABC). Unaudited publications devise their own auditing procedure.

Most of the unaudited business publications issue statements that make a stab at showing circulations, geographical breakdowns of circulation, recipients of the publications, and similar information that is deemed necessary to sell space in a particular book.

One obvious difference between audited and unaudited books remains, however, that the unaudited publications cannot verify their circulation claims.

There is an ongoing movement among advertisers and advertising agencies to buy space only in audited publications for that very reason. With the continually increasing cost of advertising, advertisers and their agencies want to get the most for their dollar. The only way to ensure that an advertiser is reaching a specific audience is to purchase space only in audited publications.

Controlled circulation publications — those that are sent without charge to a carefully screened list of qualified recipients—as well as a number of paid publications use a form devised by BPA. At the present time, BPA audits some 880 publications and charges from $880 to $3,640 for an audit, depending on the size of the circulation.

BPA primarily audits business publications with all-paid, all-controlled, or any combination of paid and controlled circulation for business, industrial, technical and professional publications. Through its Selected Market Audit (SMA) division BPA audits nearly 50 general interest/consumer oriented publications.

Until recently, ABC only audited business publications with paid circulations. ABC currently audits approximately 260 business publications, as well as newspapers, consumer magazines and farm magazines.

BPA's governing body is composed of 21 members with an equal number of advertisers, agency people and business publishers.

In addition to auditing business publications, BPA offers its members the opportunity to elect to enter its Market Comparability Program.

(As of November 1981, BPA had 105 comparability programs in effect or adopted, with about half of BPA's members participating.) The Market Comparability Program is especially helpful to media buyers that are looking to purchase advertising space among competing publications.

Comparability within a market is achieved by publishers meeting together to draw up comparable guidelines for reporting their circulation figures. The program offers media buyers the opportunity to quickly define the target audience a specific advertiser is trying to reach.

Why aren't all business publications audited? Because many cannot afford to invest the modest sum that would make their product more saleable, perhaps. But more often, because they cannot afford disclosure of information that would reflect derogatorily on them. This is the assumption many veteran advertising agency people make.

Granted, some publications honestly are of the opinion that an audit is unnecessary, and they are unwilling therefore to take the time and provide the documentation an audit requires. Unless the pressure that is currenly being maintained continues, some publishers will continue to have this attitude.

At one time, one of the major obstacles to increasing the number of audited business publications was that a number of the largest and most reputable publications did not understand the need of an audit. This is no longer the case today. The majority now use the audit as an integral part of their selling operation. It is the smaller publications that now must understand the need for and benefits of an audit.

One way to increase the number of audits currently being conducted is for both BPA and ABC to develop a single audit procedure. This was the recommendation put forth by Richard C. Christian, chairman of Marsteller Inc., Chicago, at a meeting of the ABC membership held in November, 1981.

While this proposal is not a new one, BPA has long been in favor of developing a common audit between the two auditing organizations.

Mr. Christian called for both BPA and ABC to continue with their present structures, staffs and symbols, but to agree to change their individual audit reporting rules "so as to be identical in field procedure, language and reporting."

He went on to propose that the Media Comparability Council sponsor a meeting to set up machinery for developing a common audit.

Commenting on Mr. Christian's proposal, Joseph B. Foley, president of BPA said, "I fully agree with Dick Christian's remarks concerning the need for a common audit procedure to be developed in discussion with the Media Comparability Council." Mr. Foley explained that the major difference between BPA and ABC continues to be the reporting of the business and occupational breakouts.

BPA has been an active member of the Media Comparability Council since its inception.

In addition to the development of a common audit, Mr. Christian stressed the need for publications to enter the Market Comparability Program, which provides a means of collecting information and presenting it in an uniform manner so that buyers can make valid comparisions of the recipients of all publications in a given industry or market.

"Too often, in these programs, not all the eligible publications have been represented," Mr. Christian said. "To be blunt about it, the Market Comparability Program has been a BPA operation. With only a few exceptions, ABC members have elected to stay out."

"BPA has a longstanding mandate from its board of directors to effect joint comparability," Mr. Foley said. "Before we begin a new comparability program, we offer ABC the opportunity to jointly sponsor it."

Both BPA and ABC forms are still used because both organizations still audit publications used by industrial advertisers.

Some agencies do everything they can to prevent clients from using unaudited publications. Marsteller Inc., for instance, always specifically calls it to a client's attention in writing if an unaudited magazine is on the media schedule for some reason or other. And Meldrum & Fewsmith does not recommend unaudited business publications "unless we can't get coverage in certain fields." For years that agency has attached stickers to all media contracts that go out of the agency saying, "Audited circulation is a keystone of confidence. We need your help."

Granted, some publications, and very high quality ones at that, honestly are of the opinion that an audit is unnecessary, therefore why go to the trouble and waste of money that an audit entails? Unless pressure from advertisers is brought to bear, publishers will continue to have this attitude. The *Journal of the American Medical Association,* for example, is unaudited and it may well have the largest income from sale of advertising space of any specialized business or professional publication anywhere.

In the case of this highly respected journal, failure to have an audit does not cast suspicion on it. The fact remains, though, that when reputable, responsible publications achieve such acceptance and operate so successfully without an audit, they tempt lesser publications to do the same. And it is the lesser publications upon whom prospective advertisers look askance due to lack of an audit.

Indeed, Phillip Gisser, AIA president and director of marketing services of U.S. Industrial Chemicals Company, a National Distillers division, has made a proposal to the AIA board of directors—that the board urge its members to drop out, for one month, of all publications that do not offer an audit, according to *Media/scope,* the magazine that serves the buyers of advertising.

Media/scope added that: "Industrial advertisers need a single audit of *all* business publications. Until and unless they get one audit, they will not be able to apply modern methods of media analysis—computerized or otherwise—to the task of selection of publications."

There's better than an even chance that industrial advertisers will have the single audit. This will be a massive step forward. It will benefit good publications, it will force less desirable ones to improve, to measure up to set standards—or go out of business.

There's no doubt about the desirability of the single audit. Among other things it would solve a problem that has become more pressing each passing year—development of a standardized form that would permit comparing competing media. It has become increasingly difficult to do this due to the manner in which information is presented by many publications, as well as the fact that some desirable information is either obscured or not presented at all.

The AIA Model Form

Accordingly, AIA, through its Media Comparability Committee, devoted many months of effort toward the development of a data form that would solve the problem by eliminating the shortcomings of existing forms—BPA, ABC, and the multitude dreamed up by publishers. Result was the AIA Business Publication Data Form. AIA expects publishers to update the form every year so it is always current.

The AIA has this to say about its new Business Publication Data Form:

> "This form is designed to be used in conjunction with *Standard Rate and Data,* publisher's rate card, circulation audit (or statement of circulation) and other available data. Its purpose is to assist advertisers and agencies in their media analysis by helping publishers to present pertinent information in a concise and orderly manner.

> "This Business Publication Data Form is sponsored and approved by the Association of Industrial Advertisers, Association of National Advertisers, American Association of Advertising Agencies and American Business Press. It may be used in conformity with the bylaws and rules of the Audit Bureau of Circulation and the Business Publications Audit of Circulation by member publications.

> "Registration of this form at AIA Headquarters does not constitute validation of the information contained herein or endorsement of the publication by any sponsoring association. No attempt has been made to value-judge the items herein or place them in any rank order. Responsibility for proper use of this information rests entirely with the media planner."

Research/Development's AIA Form has been expanded, as is permissible, from a basic 8 pages to a full 20 pages to include information the publisher feels it desirable for advertisers and agencies to have.

Incidentally, AIA requires that all publishers fill out the form *completely*, and where a question is not pertinent to enter "Does not apply" or "Not available" in answer to this question.

Reference will be made to this AIA Business Publication Data Form from time to time in this chapter as different topics are discussed. The reader is advised to write for the data form of a publication in which he or she is particularly interested and spend some time analyzing it.

Editorial Policy

If a business publication is to be of any genuine value to both the readers in the market it serves and to its advertisers, it must have definite, specific objectives.

The publication should define its responsibilities to its readers and describe very clearly and concisely its editorial character.

Doing this is quite similar to an industrial company's development of a written marketing plan and establishment of formal communications objectives. Without a formal plan and objectives, the manufacturing company drifts aimlessly.

A typical page from an AIA Form. Data are on Research/Development magazine. Incidentally, the old AIA changed its name to Business/ Professional Advertising Association in 1974, but most of us think of it as AIA, new name notwithstanding. BPA initiated an "Audit of Responsibility" on R/D's circulation to make sure every recipient of R/D actually works in the area defined in paragraph 1 of the BPA statement. Due to R/D's strict qualification form, the book immediately qualified for this special Audit of Responsibility—the only book in its field to so qualify. This means the advertiser's message goes only to prime buying influences. No waste circulation to pay for.

4   RESEARCH AND DEVELOPMENT

12. CIRCULATION TO FIELD SERVED ANALYZED BY PLACE OF DELIVERY:

Number of copies

Home	1,896
Business Establishment	68,215
Newsstand sale	0
Other (explain below)	0

Source and Date of Above Information: Publisher's circulation count.

Is this information: Audited? _____ (show symbol) Unaudited? ✓

For Items 13 and 14, publishers participating in BPA Comparability Programs should fill in market and date. This publication conforms to the uniform business occupational breakdown, which was developed by the BPA advertiser, agency and publisher committee for the _____ market on _____
DOES NOT APPLY   (date)

CIRCULATION TO FIELD SERVED ANALYZED BY BUSINESS CLASSIFICATION AND OCCUPATION, TITLE AND/OR FUNCTION:

13.
14.

Occupational Title or Function	BUSINESS CLASSIFICATION				
	Industrial Laboratories	Independent Labs. & Consultants	University or Colleges	Government Laboratories	Hospital/Medical Laboratories
Corporate Officers	2,845	1,689	85	122	64
R&D Executives	5,112	791	600	680	216
Project Managers	16,591	1,458	6,133	4,167	1,539
Professional Staff	15,348	1,434	4,952	3,925	746
Technical Personnel	584	75	144	140	43
Librarians	154	16	22	34	2
Other Personnel	339	12	18	29	2
Percent	58.4%	7.9%	17.0%	13.0%	3.7%
Total	40,973	5,475	11,954	9,097	2,612

Source and date of above information: BPA Publisher's Statement, December 1973.

Is this information: Audited? YES (show symbol) BPA Unaudited? _____

GEOGRAPHICAL BREAKDOWN OF CIRCULATION TO FIELD SERVED (REGIONS, STATES, PROVINCES, FOREIGN, ETC.) SHOW UNITS REACHED:

15.

Area	Total Circulation	UNITS REACHED**					Total Units
		Industrial Laboratories	Independent Labs & Consultants	College/University Laboratories	Government Laboratories	Hospital/Medical Laboratories	
039–049 ME	141						57
030–038 NH	236						112
050–059 VT	104						29
010–027 MA	3,687						1,239
028–029 RI	280						108
060–069 CT	1,551						525
New England	6,000 8.6%	1,384	343	176	102	71	2,076
100–149 NY	7,258						2,472
070–089 NJ	5,102						1,518
150–196 PA	5,536						1,586
Middle Atlantic	17,896 25.5%	3,731	820	473	323	229	5,576
430–458 OH	4,090						1,176
468–479 IN	1,290						411
600–629 IL	4,065						1,340
480–499 MI	2,185						705
530–549 WI	1,003						414
East No. Central	12,623 18.0%	2,731	392	433	236	254	4,046

Without editorial objectives and goals, as well as a precise definition of its responsibilities and a sound editorial philosophy, the publication lacks viability. Without them its sole apparent reason for being is to make a profit. Making a profit is both desirable and necessary. But pursuit of profit, if stressed above everything else, will prevent a publication's achieving stature and acceptance and respect in full measure from both its universe and its advertisers.

All of us have encountered fast-buck books and thin, marginal magazines whose position is precarious at best. These are the publications whose reason for being is to make a fat profit, if humanly possible, for a money-hungry publisher, or whose reason for being hasn't really been thought through. Such books drift and imitate—they never lead and innovate.

Steer clear of both classes of publications, for to use either is to squander the budget dollars with little hope of realizing a return from the investment.

If you're in doubt about a publication's purpose in life, ask its representative the next time he or she calls on you. Remarkably few publications have put their objectives into print—although the worthwhile ones have. And these good magazines provide this formal, written rationale of what they strive to be and hope to accomplish to their representatives so they can give it to you. It's something you need, something you have every right in the world to request.

Publication X is edited as a relatively independent weekly intending to merit the attention and respect of mature adults in commerce, industry, and public affairs.

Generalities as weak and wishy-washy, and perhaps wistful in a pathetic sort of way, as in the above, are a reliable tip-off to editorial matter with about as much impact as a ping-pong ball falling out of a basement. Publications that make statements like that, and there are more than you'd believe until you check for yourself, simply do not merit serious consideration for your media schedule.

On the other hand, when a publication can make a simple, relatively short statement that makes sense and denotes a sense of purpose as does this one from *Production* magazine, it obviously knows what it wants to do:

It is the purpose of Production *to recognize and to fulfill the special needs of engineers and managers who are concerned with improving manufacturing efficiency, costs, and quality in production metalworking plants.*

Editorial Content

Regardless of how wonderful it may sound, editorial policy is a collection of pallid platitudes unless it's translated into vigorous, timely, interesting editorial material that makes the reader *want* to read it.

The attitude—or philosophy, more accurately—of the publisher is reflected in the content of the magazine. Take the statement made by the publisher of *Iron Age,* for instance, and then compare it with any issue of the book. Philosophy and attitude come alive before your eyes. Let's see just what *Iron Age* has to say on the subject:

EDITORIAL PHILOSOPHY

Iron Age serves metalworking as a primary communications force—pulling this vast industry together and fostering its efficiency and advancement.

The most valuable contribution of the *Iron Age* is its outside view of the metalworking industry, coupled with nonbiased, interpretative reporting of the significant events which shape it. *Iron Age* provides:

- News features about management, finance and labor.
- Technical articles on significant advances in metalworking processes.
- Timely market and price information.

Also to be considered and tabulated and compared with competitive publications are cold statistics. For example, you'll want to know exactly how many pages were in the average issue of the book for the past year—both in editorial and in advertising. Any publication you use or are considering using should be looked at from this standpoint.

When you're either analyzing one publication or comparing one with another, it's always helpful to list the titles of feature articles from one issue selected at random. This enables you to assess the relevance of the articles to the publication's editorial objectives and to its audience—and to your products, naturally.

What cannot be learned about a publication from any tabulation of facts, a perusal of the table of contents, or a mass of dry statistics, is the *feel* of a leading publication in its field.

This is a very special character imparted to a business magazine by a number of factors, each significant in itself, although none is of overriding importance, unless, perhaps, it is the reflection of the personality of the individual at the helm.

In the case of *Commercial Car Journal,* the magazine of fleet management, this may well be editor James Winsor's almost incredible depth of knowledge about the fast-changing trucking industry that the magazine serves.

Commercial Car Journal not only serves its readers by helping them solve day-in and day-out operating, personnel, and maintenance problems, but it also reports and interprets legislative trends and the impact they inevitably will make on trucking operations. This influences the equipment required to take advantage of them, of course, as well as labor contracts, financing, and every facet of the business.

The magazine speaks authoritatively, and it is a respected spokesman for the industry. *Commercial Car Journal* has no official status as an association organ, but it has industry-wide respect that means as much, or even more, perhaps.

That the magazine could achieve such a position and maintain it for decades is due, in part, to Chilton Company's policy of investing in its properties so they become leaders in the industries they serve. Of course, this is self-serving to the extent that space in publications with genuine prestige is easier to sell, but it also benefits the advertiser whose message appears in conjunction with editorial material with built-in believability and acceptance.

CCJ's years of leadership are due also to the editorial staff's understanding of the trucking industry, an industry to which, when all is said and done, they are personally dedicated to helping. Personal involvement, publisher permission to *build* a publication rather than merely harvest the profits, has resulted in a magazine of such stature that when it speaks editorially the trucking industry, the unions, and the government listen to what it has to say.

Exceptionally fine editorial content has helped *Commercial Car Journal* rise to the top of the heap and stay there. An example of the hard-hitting business press journalism for which CCJ is famous is the following article. It was written by Neil R. Regeimbal, the magazine's Washington Feature Editor. Title of the article is: "CARGO THEFT —They Steal by Night." Part of this provocative, stimulating article is reprinted by courtesy of the Chilton Company.

CARGO THEFT
They Steal by Night

**The inside story
of a billion dollar rip-off**

I can steal one of your tractors.

I can hook it to one of your loaded trailers and steal a complete, loaded rig out of your terminal and get away with it.

It doesn't matter whether you're a common carrier or a private operator. It applies to almost anybody.

The grim truth is that I can steal a rig in any major U.S. city where trailers are loaded and unloaded.

I have "stolen" rigs to demonstrate to my own satisfaction how easy it can be done. And I could have sold the load just as easily as I stole it.

The assignment was not inspired by journalistic sensationalism. The wholesale theft of trucks and their cargoes is a pressing problem that has become more acute each year. *What* was happening was not new. *How* it was happening needed a critical analysis and an objective report to the industry so that remedial action could be taken to ameliorate an intolerable situation.

As the direct result of the article, many segments of the trucking industry have mounted intensive antitheft campaigns. The writer, Editor Neil Regeimbal, was invited to address the Board of Governors of the Regular Common Carrier Conference, the American Trucking Associations Terminal Operations Council, the ATA Industrial Relations Committee, and the New Jersey Motor Truck Association. More than 100,000 reprints have been distributed, or published in other noncompetitive magazines. A followup article reporting progress was scheduled.

This is representative of the caliber of editorial content—and editors—that the best business publications have, and the respect with which top magazines are regarded by leaders of the industries they serve.

A price tag cannot be put on an editorial climate such as this.

Questionable Practices

When you run across a publication that devotes one-fourth to one-third of its editorial space to new product announcements and announcements about the availability of new literature, stop, look, and look again. Unless it's a new-product type of publication, you've come across a book that lives on handouts from manufacturers who scurry hither and yon in search of every last bit of ink they can get—as free publicity is termed. Such announcements require very little editing—and frequently are given none—little technical knowledge, little industry knowledge, little effort, and little investment in people and research.

This does not apply, of course, to tabloid-type new products publications. They serve a legitimate purpose and have as their reason for being their ability to disseminate this type of material and present it to their readers in an orderly fashion with most of the puffery edited out.

Something else: Many publications are special-issue prone. They'll devote an entire issue of the magazine to a certain subject with what is to most advertisers, dismaying frequency. Often there's a valid reason for having a special issue—intense interest in an esoteric new process, a development that has wrought a radical change in an industry or production method, such as numerical control in the machine-tool field for example, or other legitimate, newsworthy subject.

On the other hand, most advertising personnel suspect the special issue is a gimmick designed solely to increase sale of space in that particular month. Sometimes the special issue just happens to be published in a month that's normally slow for the publisher. This is lucky for him or her, of course.

A legitimate topic for a special issue is the one major trade show of the year for a major, specific market, or the annual convention of a society that represents the decision-making element in an important field, or something on that order.

This is something you'll have to judge on the individual merits of the magazine you're analyzing, and of that special issue. Beware, though, of the book that publishes one special issue after another; more often than not this is merely a thinly disguised attempt to entice advertisers into buying more space than they normally would have scheduled.

Another practice that is ethically questionable is publishing a magazine 13 times a year. Some publications attempt to whipsaw advertisers into buying space in a special issue by not giving the customary frequency discount unless that special issue is used. This attempt to blackmail the advertiser into buying something he really may not want and may not need is, happily, fast disappearing. Most legitimate publications and reputable publishers have long since discontinued this shady practice. Those that haven't should be viewed with a jaundiced eye. Even with two jaundiced eyes if you can stand the strain.

The American Association of Advertising Agencies has this to say about business magazines that are published 13 times a year: "Some publishers who have only 7- and 13-time rates make it obligatory to use a directory or special issue in order to earn the lower rate in regular issues. In order to make best use of directory or special issue space, it is often necessary to prepare a special advertisement appropriate only for that particular publication and that particular issue.

"Publishers who quote such extra-time rates are urged to offer the customary 6- and 12-time rates in addition. Even more equitable would be the use of the customary 6- and 12-time rates with the extra space for the directory taking the 6- or 12-time space earned by the regular space program."

It's just about an even bet that when you unearth a publication that publishes 13 times a year, and that bases its frequency discounts on a 7- or 13-times basis, you'll also find by doing a little digging that this book plays footloose and fancy-free with the truth in a number of areas.

Some marginal publications make it a practice to charge the advertiser for editorial cuts—engravings—used for illustrations of products announced in the magazine's new products section. This is not strictly a dishonest practice, although it is one that no worthwhile publication engages in. When you run across this, best thing to do is steer clear of that publication. Remove it from your publicity list and by all means don't even consider it for your media schedule for a minute.

Another practice of some business publications of less than debatable merit is not allowing agency commission. Incredible as it seems, a few actually exist in the face of accepted practice of almost a half-century. Invariably, when you run across one of these, you'll find upon analyzing it that the magazine obviously disallows agency commission because it is afraid to have agencies examine it.

Most such marginal publications never have representatives call upon agencies—if they have representatives, that is—because these knowledgeable advertising people would instantly recognize such a publication as an out-and-out fraud. Most such books publish only pirated material, have no art director, but rely instead on the printer who sets type and drops in halftones; typically it has no four-color editorial section, and sometimes doesn't even have two-color editorial pages. Flee as a bird from any of these.

Yet another shady practice that was devised purely to sell space is that of presenting a so-called "award" to a company—either for one of its products or to one of its better-known executives. This is usually done in hope of receiving additional advertising space, or else the "award" is made when space in a book has been discontinued or greatly reduced. As transparent as the practice is, some managements have been known to be overwhelmed at the honor; often the advertising manager is promptly instructed to waste scarce space dollars on the questionable book. This should be resisted strenuously.

Editorial Format

Don't discount appearance when evaluating media. Readers don't.

A smartly turned out publication invariably is one in which both the publisher and the editors take pride. It's a publication in which an investment has been made and is being made. Attractiveness is dear.

On the other hand, it is ridiculously easy to grind out a pastepot publication; all that is required is to employ part-time hack writers to filch articles from leading publications, rewrite them using the same hard facts, then rearranging the sequence of thoughts so the legitimate publisher can't file suit for plagiarism. One "editor" can thus assemble the book and make a crude dummy.

Then, with copy in hand, the publisher of the schlock book trots off to a cheap printer, has him set type and print the thing, has a mailing service mail it, and he's in business. He's a business publisher.

Schlock books, such as our hypothetical *Commercial Cooling*, are characterized by deadly-dull, dingy, drab, dreary pages singularly unappealing and unattractive. They march in a monotonous parade of black-and-white, one boring page after another. Type is invariably set in two sterile columns. There is no ROP four-color, not even any editorial second color, as a rule. Everything is done as cheaply as possible to avoid making an investment. The publisher of the pastepot magazine has the philosophy of the slum landlord who won't invest a nickel to improve property; he just lets it run down while milking every last red cent out of the operation.

Such magazines have no layout, no attempt at art direction; halftones, almost always squares or rectangles, are dropped in place by the printer. There's no white space to alleviate the monotony because white space is paper on which ink could be laid—either "editorial" or paid space advertising.

What's more, the publisher of the marginal business magazine seldom, if ever, uses artwork; that has to be bought and would eat into the return on investment—if you can call it that.

Needless to say, such publications are "edited" for the advertiser, not for the reader. Just as water seeks its own level, though, as industrial management becomes more knowledgeable about advertising the worthless publications and the parasitic publishers will slowly disappear.

Circulation

A trade magazine can have the finest imaginable editorial content and be so beautifully put together that it simply takes your breath away, but if its circulation isn't such that it reaches most of the prospects you must talk to, the book is of no value to you.

How a publication gets readers, both for paid and controlled circulation, is an important consideration you'll want to look into. Paid circulation books—the good ones, that is—offer enough to the reader so that subscriptions come in over the transom, or are readily obtained by the publications' circulation staffs.

Good business magazines receive subscriptions without offering an 85-foot, twin-diesel-powered yacht, six months for two with all expenses paid in Acapulco, or a 90-day safari in Africa with a choice of white hunters as inducements to part with a few dollars that will go on the expense account anyhow.

Books that have to offer a bribe to subscribe, including a drastic reduction in price so that it's put at a ridiculous level, are books whose publishers are having a hard time making them appear attractive to readers.

You're perfectly entitled to ask how publications get their circulations, and, indeed, this is a question you *should* ask.

Additional information you'll be interested in because it is a tip-off as to the desirability of the publication *as judged by the reader* is the rate of subscription renewals; percentage of subscriptions sold at full price vs. a cut-rate inducement; percentage sold in quantity to distributors for their customers; percentage sold in quantity to an association or trade group for its membership; percentage of subscriptions in arrears over the last five-year period; and how long a subscriber is "carried" after the subscription expires.

Besides this information, ask the percentage of subscriptions sold to individuals as opposed to those sold to companies; find out if subscriptions are sold for one year, or for shorter or longer periods. One year is customary; less than that assures far too much reader turnover, longer than that would indicate that the magazine is giving something away merely to achieve a large circulation, and the readers may not actually be readers—they may merely be recipients. When it comes to controlled circulation—unpaid, that is—ask how the circulation list is built, what methods and sources are used to change the circulation.

The Numbers Game

It's an unfortunate fact of life, however, that it's much easier to tell that one publication has a 10 percent advantage in total circulation than it is to analyze the *quality* of the circulation, or the quality of the editorial. The numbers game—forcing circulation up artificially—results in much higher space cost for the advertiser with no higher readership among individuals who can make buying recommendations or decisions. As a rule the second and third ranking publications serving a market are the ones tempted to play the numbers game and force up circulation; after all, they have to have some apparent advantage to tout.

From the AIA Form you'll be able to determine the total number of copies of the publication sent to qualified individuals. Notice, too, this is broken down by copies addressed to individuals *by name* and copies addressed to a title or job function only; the mail person in most companies usually isn't an M.I.T. graduate, and some things can reasonably be expected to perplex. Names of individuals within the company, he or she understands; functions of these same individuals probably mean about as much as would a dissertation on the gold drain to an unclothed Ubangi.

Naturally, you want to be sure your advertising messages will be read in the geographical area of the country most important to your sales efforts; always analyze a magazine's circulation geographically. Oddly enough, some magazines that claim to cover a given market thoroughly have excellent coverage in some sections of the country, but are very spotty in others. If it happens that a certain publication is spotty in an area of critical importance to your company, perhaps because of distributor strength, unusually strong product acceptance, or some other good reason, this could very easily make the publication exactly wrong for your company and exactly right for your most vigorous competitor.

Universe coverage is a question that should be raised when analyzing any publication's desirability. Only if the magazine covers the overwhelming majority of the establishments that comprise your universe will you want to consider it seriously; marginal publications always fall short here, as do regional publications, of course, although in some instances the regionals have considerable merit if they reach a particularly strong market in their section of the country—and it's of prime importance to you.

The Company Mailing List

Incidentally, it's the advertising manager's responsibility to see to it the company's key people receive the major magazines in its industry. Subscription expense is always a legitimate expense-account item, and key personnel should subscribe to paid-circulation books; in the case of controlled-circulation magazines, the advertising manager should have the agency ask the publisher to add the names.

Even district sales managers out in the field should receive the most important magazines. That's because, first of all, it's advisable for them to see your advertisements in the magazines—instead of merely as preprints or reprints. Secondly, these are the future sales managers and marketing directors in your company; their familiarity with the business press will make your job easier in future years.

One thing, however, is definitely very undesirable and should be discouraged vigorously. This is for business publications to put every dog and his brother in the company on their promotional mailing list. All this accomplishes is to get the natives all stirred up unnecessarily.

Thing to do is to insist to the media representatives who call on you that they instruct the home office to delete the superfluous names from the magazines's promo list—not from the publication list, but the promo list. Magazines are very familiar with this problem and will accede to your wishes. You can't blame them for trying to make their names familiar with everybody who conceivably could influence a page or two of space for them.

Publication Image

"Image," in the communications field, is a word that means many things to many people. It's one that's pathetically overworked.

Advertising people who have nothing to say can usually be depended upon to launch into lengthy harrangues about image, or even to make formal speeches about it if the occasion arises.

It does all too frequently.

Properly applied to media, or to a specific medium, rather, image simply means the opinion the magazine's universe has of it, how it's regarded, how it's thought of.

Books such as *Fortune, Iron Age, Business Week, Production, U.S. News & World Report, Barron's* are acknowledged leaders in their fields. They're respected; looked up to; quoted; considered authoritative; relied upon; influential; believed. All of these attitudes and more contribute to publication image.

Publication image, according to Marsteller Inc., is the third dimension that must be evaluated correctly in order to increase the effectiveness of client media dollars. The agency carries on continuous research to develop additional qualitative media yardsticks so that editorial material and publication image may be analyzed more scientifically.

First dimension is circulation, of course, and the second is the editorial job done by a publication.

Some years ago the agency developed useful, workable criteria to measure both the first and second dimensions—prior to working on the third dimension of publication image, how the reader regards the magazines that are read.

Perhaps the most popular method for measuring business publication reader reaction is the magazine readership, or reader preference study. Thousands have been conducted.

If the questionnaire is well-designed and the mailing list is good, such surveys can be very helpful. More on this a little later, though.

Where readership studies fail is that they don't give all of the necessary information about *why* a reader reads a certain publication, why he prefers it, why he considers it "most useful"—which is a question often asked.

Marsteller's research technique was deliberately designed to be relatively simple so that technique wouldn't obscure results. The way the study was conducted makes it possible for any advertiser or agency grounded in the most basic research techniques to conduct the same type of research.

After going into editorial objectives with publishers, Marsteller then attached the problem of editorial recall and impact. The author is indebted to this fine agency for its assistance and for background material on this subject. The entire Marsteller media department was especially helpful.

The problem was identified as: Could you, as a reader, identify the newspaper you read every morning by its appearance, format, and method of presentation, if its name were not visible? Or could you have identified the format of *Life, Time,* and *Post*? How about the marketing and advertising publications most of us see —*Advertising Age, Sales & Marketing Management* and *Industrial Marketing*?

If you are a *real reader* you probably would not have too much difficulty in doing so.

In order to test this theory, and to get some additional ideas to add to its store of knowledge regarding the measurement of editorial quality, the agency undertook what it calls Editorial Recall and Impact Research.

The study was carried out by personally contacting a representative sample of individuals in a major industry and finding out what they thought of the leading business publications serving their industry—what they thought about the subject matter of the articles in the publications, from the first impression (physical appearance) standpoint.

Good editors strive to turn out a publication containing articles which literally *ask* to be read. Marsteller was trying to find out if it's possible to put one book ahead of another because of success, or lack of success, an editor has in achieving this goal.

Marsteller researchers analyzed a total of one year's issues of the publications to be studied so that the article, format, and so on that was most typical of the books could be selected. Representative ar-

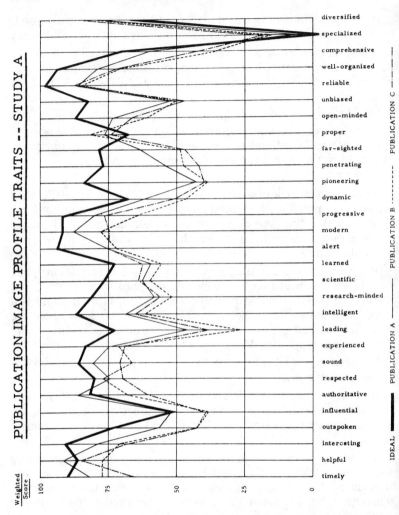

PUBLICATION IMAGE PROFILE TRAITS -- STUDY A

diversified
specialized
comprehensive
well-organized
reliable
unbiased
open-minded
proper
far-sighted
penetrating
pioneering
dynamic
progressive
modern
alert
learned
scientific
research-minded
intelligent
leading
experienced
sound
respected
authoritative
influential
outspoken
interesting
helpful
timely

PUBLICATION C ——— |
PUBLICATION B ---------- |
PUBLICATION A ———
IDEAL ▬▬▬

Weighted Score

100   75   50   25   0

ticles from the publications were clipped and all identification from each publication was removed. Interviewers went into the field armed with the articles and a questionnaire. People interviewed were individuals in a field with a common job function—those who theoretically would be most likely to read the publications being considered. The agency's analysis follows:

PUBLICATION IMAGE PROFILE STUDY—CONCLUSIONS

1. Readers do form images of the publications they read.
2. These publication images are definable.

3. These images can provide an additional qualitative dimension to the advertising buyer.

4. The individual importance and strength of specific character traits contributing to a publication's overall image tend to vary by the reader's job function.

5. A combination of specific character traits contributes to the general atmosphere, mood, or frame of reference within which a reader reads a publication. An advertiser's knowledge of this publication image assists not only in media selection, but also enables to adjust the product or corporate presentation to that image for the best result.

6. Some publications, which have developed weaknesses in circulation and editorial, have previously established such strong positive images that these present limitations are often overlooked. Consequently, such publications are being carried by the impetus of past reputation.

7. There appears to be a correlation between the strength and sharpness of a publication image and the strength and rating of a publication on readership, reader preference, and editorial studies which this agency has previously conducted.

SUMMARY OF GENERAL CONCLUSIONS

1. There are real differences in editorial character of business papers and they are roughly measurable, so long as conclusions are not based on a single factor.

2. Editorial evaluation measurements, even if they are inadequate but so long as they are not empirical, force the space buyer to examine editorial on an organized basis and are therefore desirable.

3. Measures of editorial objectives, character and performance can very definitely increase the effectiveness of business publication selection.

4. Few advertisers and agencies currently use a qualitative measure on editorial, and few business paper sales reps are really trained to interpret it.

5. Business publications have definable images based on specific character traits. Knowledge of such images helps the advertiser in media selection as well as in the presentation of the advertising message.

The image of a publication affects not only readership of editorial material—which, after all, is what you're *really* buying when you plunk down the dollars for space—but there's also a rub-off as to the credence the reader places in everything read in the publication.

This includes the advertising.

Publications with all of the attributes the reader wants and looks for unquestionably are the best vehicles to carry your advertising message. When it's viewed in this way, image isn't such an intangible after all.

Readers

In its circulation statements and in accompanying material, the first rate business paper is able to describe accurately and concisely the *type* of reader it attracts, and to define its readers as a group.

Sometimes after you've finished analyzing them, there are two or even three publications in a given field that all have approximately the same "score." Making a selection of just one, if that's all the budget will permit, is exceedingly difficult.

However, it is absolutely essential that you select the best publication(s) to carry your advertising messages to the maximum possible number of interested prospects for your product.

To do this, you need to know one thing: Which publication among those on your list of possibles is preferred by the readers you're trying to reach? Which publication is most read, which one means the most readership for your advertisements?

Going to Your Prospects

If you've reached an impasse as far as making the final decision is concerned, there's only one way open to you that will let you get the information you need to make an objective decision—assuming you've analyzed all prospective publications thoroughly. That's to go to your prospects and ask them what their preferences are.

The advertising manager of Lindberg Hevi-Duty was faced with this situation when planning a campaign directed to buying influences in the metalworking market. The company was planning to advertise to support its marketing objectives for heat-treating furnaces.

This ad manager's dilemma was compounded by the fact that a number of very fine publications serve the metalworking market, and choosing between them was not the easiest task ever attempted.

All prospective publications had been analyzed and a tabulation of the score each received on each specific criterion had been duly entered, weighted as experience dictated, and the sums totaled. Cost was considered last, of course.

At this time it was decided to do a readerhip survey to determine just what publications the universe actually preferred.

This survey did not fall into the trap that so many do, however. It did *not* fail to seek the attitudes of *prospective purchasers* of the manufacturer's line of heat-treating furnaces and accessories. This is often a weakness that seems to be inherent in most advertiser-conducted readership surveys.

Far too many advertisers make a survey over their own mailing list. Naturally, it consists primarily of customers and hot prospects compiled over a period of time from leads from the sales department, the field sales force, lists of visitors to the company's booth at trade shows, and similar sources.

When this is done the manufacturer making the survey ends up talking to himself because the questionnaire reaches only those who are presently familiar with the company and its products. The sample is not representative of the universe. Absent from the list is the vast army of companies and individual buying influences who have little or no awareness of the manufacturer and his products because they buy from competitor companies.

Overcoming this weakness is simple, though, and is accomplished merely by using a nonweighted mailing list. In Lindberg Hevi-Duty's case it was the Dun & Bradstreet list; very obviously some present customers would be on this list, but so would even more prospects who had never bought anything from Lindberg Hevi-Duty.

Names from the Dun & Bradstreet list were selected at random on an every *nth* name basis; the list was on IBM cards purchased by SIC classifications. A representative mix, as far as company size is concerned, was then selected, and care was also taken to assure a good geographical spread.

Questionnaires were individually addressed to 1,000 top production men in metalworking firms that do on-premises heat treating. Typical titles included vice-president, manufacturing; vice-president, production; director of manufacturing; works manager; plant manager; and others on that management level.

The company's advertising manager wrote the following letter and had it reproduced by multilith with a signature in blue ink on the company's letterhead:

Mr. R.W. Wilberforce
Vice-President, Manufacturing
Smith Widget Manufacturing Company
123 Any Street
Podunk, Iowa 12345
Dear Mr. Wilberforce:
Will you take two minutes to help us?
We want you to see our advertising, so we need to know if we use magazines that you read.
Simply check the ones you read on the enclosed questionnaire.
Then put it in the enclosed stamped envelope and drop it in your "out" box.
There's no need to sign your name, and no need to identify your company.
Many thanks . . . and have a cup of coffee on us!
Cordially,
/s/
R. Howard Sanderson
Advertising Manager

The letter is short, straight to the point—and only small words are used in short sentences and short paragraphs. It is extremely easy to digest; there's no struggling over involved thoughts.

And the return envelope was *stamped*—not an envelope with the company's postage-paid indicia. Using a stamped return envelope invariably boosts the returns from a mailing. There's something about seeing a stamp on an envelope that triggers action. Maybe it's because people cannot bring themselves to throw away a stamp, nor do they find it easily ignored. This is a point to remember when you're interested in pulling a good return from a mailing—and the cost is little more.

A shiny, new quarter was Scotch taped to the covering letter for "coffee money" and as an incentive to reply. This gimmick also always increases the returns on a questionnaire type of mailing. The quarter is exactly right, incidentally; you cannot really compensate an individual for time because it was company's time being invested. Too, an attempt to do so would run the cost sky high.

Some researchers have tipped on half-dollars. There is no indication that enclosing more money produces more returns. Buying somebody a cup of coffee is a friendly gesture and is well received.

The questionnaire is of the aided-recall type to make it easy and fast to check off the publications the recipient read. Included was the now-defunct *Steel*. The questionnaire read:

PUBLICATION PREFERENCE QUESTIONNAIRE

1. Please check which publications you read regularly (3 out of 4 issues).

American Machinist	*Machinery*
Automotive Industries	*Metal Progress*
Factory	*Metal Treating*
Industrial Heating	*Modern Metals*
Iron Age	*Precision Metal Molding*
Light Metal Age	*Production*

2. Now, please *circle* the *one* publication you find most useful and helpful in your work.

3. Which *one* activity is most closely related to your work:

Company management	Plant operation or Manufacturing
Purchasing	Metallurgy
Engineering	Other (specify)

4. Your title, please..

5. Total employment at *this* plant: Less than 250   More than 250

THANK YOU . . .
AND ENJOY THE COFFEE!

Out of 1,000 questionnaires mailed, Lindberg Hevi-Duty received a return of 597—just a bare whisker under 60 percent. Anywhere from 15 to 40 percent is considered a worthwhile return and is statistically valid, so Lindberg Hevi-Duty's return was exceptional.

When tabulated the average respondent read 3.6 publications regularly, which were in addition to daily newspapers and consumer magazines, of course. The results showed the following:

RANK BY READ REGULARLY (3 out of 4 issues)

RANK	PUBLICATION	TOTAL MENTIONS
1	*Iron Age*	451
2	*Steel*	388
3	*Factory*	292
4	*American Machinist*	262
5	*Production*	246
6	*Machinery*	219
7	*Modern Metals*	87
8	*Metal Progress*	81
9	*Automotive Industries*	58
10	*Industrial Heating*	47
11	*Metal Treating*	46
12	*Precision Metal Molding*	41
13	*Light Metal Age*	24
14	*Several miscellaneous books*	7

The shift that took place between mentions for Read Regularly and Most Useful are interesting indeed.

Iron Age placed first in both, of course, and by a substantial margin at that.

Fourth-ranking *American Machinist* climbed to second place in the Most Useful category, indicating an exceedingly high quality of editorial content; almost always magazines with outstanding editorial rank up near the top of the ladder when this question is asked.

Industrial Heating magazine, which ranked 10th in Read Regularly, received only three mentions out of a return of 597 when publications were ranked by Most Useful, so it dropped to the last on the list. And *Production* magazine, fifth in Read Regularly, climbed to fourth in Most Useful. *Factory* exactly maintained its status quo, third in both questions.

The Most Useful category looked like this when tabulated:

RANK BY MOST USEFUL

RANK	PUBLICATION	TOTAL
1	*Iron Age*	92

2	*American Machinist*	78
3	*Factory*	70
4	*Production*	59
5	*Steel*	54
6	*Machinery*	21
7	*Modern Metals*	18
8	*Metal Progress*	10
9	*Metal Treating*	6
10	*Automotive Industries*	5
11	*Precision Metal Molding*	3
12	*Industrial Heating*	3

JOB FUNCTIONS OF RESPONDENTS

RANK	FUNCTION OR AREA	TOTAL
1	Plant operation or manufacturing	183
2	Company management, not specified	162
3	Purchasing	33
4	Engineering	29
5	Metallurgy	15

SIZE OF COMPANY OF RESPONDENTS

Less than 250 employees 349
More than 250 employees 248

Many advertising managers consider there is a factor present that cannot be controlled, weighted, or otherwise compensated for when making a readership survey—and that is frequency of issue of the publications involved.

On the face of it, it's quite obvious that a weekly publication will make *more* impressions on the reader than will a monthly publication. For this reason a poor weekly may receive more mentions than a good monthly.

Read Regularly is considered a significant question, and it is one that certainly indicates where your advertising will stand the best chance of being seen and read. It cannot be overlooked.

Which publication do you consider most useful is, without doubt, the key question in the survey. It measures attitude, or image. What's more, it tells without equivocation which publication the respondents prefer over all others because they consider this publication to be the most help on the job. This is unquestionably the one publication in which they place the most faith—which means that this is the publication with the editorial climate that's ideal for your advertising.

Market Potential

One major factor influencing selection of media is the potential of the market that a given publication serves.

For example, most advertisers intent on marketing to the metal-working market are much better off to use broad horizontal publications such as *Iron Age, American Machinist,* and so on in an effort to reach as many buying influences in the marketplace as possible with their advertising messages.

Within the metalworking market media are any number of vertical publications that concentrate on one narrow segment of this vast industrial complex. A publication can be outstanding in its field, have editorial that's unquestionably first rate, circulation clean and well-directed to reach the people the magazine is edited for, and have a publication image that makes it come off like a printed Western sheriff saving the heroine from villains who were going to do her in and steal her ranch.

Let's take *Wire & Wire Products* magazine, a vertical publication that serves a segment of the vast metalworking market; it has this editorial objective:

> *A technical monthly edited for those in the wire industry whose interests concern the manufacture of wire rod, bar, wire, fabricated wire products, electric wire, and cable. Subscribers are presidents, vice-presidents, works managers, superintendents, engineers, chemists, and purchasing agents. Contents are of interest to those concerned with manufacturing, and material and equipment procurement. News articles relate to personnel changes, new products, new developments and book reviews. Editorial articles cover new products and equipment, processing techniques, safety, plant management, production controls, material handling, statistics, etc.*

There are hundreds and hundreds of business publications that serve highly specialized portions of various broad markets; they do their job so well for the most part that the advertiser who sells *only* in these narrow, well-defined markets does well to use such books. Their coverage of the specific area they've staked out for themselves is usually excellent. Their editorial is geared to fit the individual with specialized interests in a specialized market and it does so without wasting time on trying to be all things to all men. Price of these vertical publications is almost always less per page than that of horizontal books because total circulation is usually always much smaller.

However, if you're selling a certain type of steel to almost every SIC within the metalworking market, for example, it takes a whopping big budget to use *both* horizontal and vertical publications. Not too many industrial advertisers have sufficient wherewithal to do this. Assuming a shortage of funds hampers your plans for including every medium that's good and that serves all, or a significant portion, of your market, just how do you go about determining the market potential for a given publication in order to analyze its desirability?

Every legitimate publication will supply you with a statement or description of the industries or fields it serves, usually broken down by SIC, and frequently by SRDS Business Publication classifications. This will enable you to determine just where it fits into the scheme of things in reference to your overall picture. Market data in your files and that given to you by the publication makes this easy.

Using this information, you can determine the size of the total market by number of establishments and where these smokestacks are located.

Working with information such as that supplied in *Iron Age's Metalworking Marketguide*, you can spot the total dollar volume of goods and services produced by the entire industry, that of individual states and counties, as well as the number of employees per establishment within the geographical area(s) in which you're most interested.

This enables you to ascertain with good ball-park accuracy the dollar volume output of individual establishments, using number of employees as a basis for making the estimate. All that's required is to determine dollar volume output per employee, then do a little multiplying—or have your secretary do it, better yet.

Leading business publications usually report—at least annually—the anticipated dollar volume of expenditures for new plants and for equipment of specific types used in the production processes found within each industry. This is yet another way to guesstimate the size of the market these publications serve.

Information leading publications present is remarkably accurate, incidentally, and is usually based on field research and government figures, along with those released by trade associations, state chambers of commerce, and similar sources. You can rely upon it with only slight mental reservations because, after all, nobody knows a market as well as the best business publications that serve it.

What's more, the really good management-oriented business publication such as *Iron Age* always uses its prognosticative prowess to keep readers informed about market trends—industry growth; forecasts, immediate and long-range outlook; week-by-week recapitulations of significant events such as changes in government or military procurement policies; customer buying patterns; changes in weekly output of both ferrous and nonferrous metals; fabricators' workloads; changes in inventory; drastic changes in unit-size purchases and their frequency; labor outlook; various factors affecting distribution.

Carefully analyze this mass of available information in your spare time and you can pinpoint practically to the silverless quarter of a non-goldbacked dollar the size of the market and its potential for your company. And you can do this for all of the markets to which your company sells, then use this information to aid you in selecting the proper media mix to communicate most effectively with your universe.

Advertiser Acceptance

Anybody can make a mistake and purchase the wrong product—whether it's a chrome-laden automotive monster that turns out to be the worst lemon ever to leave Detroit, a television set that requires so many service calls the neighbors think the TV repair person's truck belongs to a close friend who calls often, or a magazine that doesn't deliver the goods for an industrial advertiser.

Chances are, of course, you'll never buy that make of car again, sooner or later you'll trade off the never-ending service calls on a new TV, and you'll cross off your schedule the book that didn't produce.

Not only is this human nature, it's also sound business judgment.

For this reason, you can form a pretty sound initial impression of a publication merely by judging it by the company that keeps it.

If a magazine paces the pack, if it leads its competitors in total advertising pages year after year, there has to be a reason. The collective judgment of many hundreds of advertising managers and media directors and account executives has said, in effect, that this is the best book in the field in their considered opinion.

When you're considering adding a publication to your schedule, take several recent issues and leaf through them. List the advertisers. Look for your competitors. They're not always right, but if they're there and the other advertisers that use the book are substantial, successful firms, chances are the magazine is worth further evaluation. Frequently it's very revealing to phone the advertising manager of companies that use a publication you're evaluating. Naturally, you won't phone direct competitors because they have no desire to help you. But the advertising manager of a company that's not a competitor, but sells to the same market, more often than not will prove to be a veritable fountain of wisdom.

Notice that telephoning is suggested, not writing. Most people will open up on the telephone and volunteer all sorts of interesting and informative and helpful information they usually wouldn't take the time to give you in a letter. They might not care to put it down in black and white. The phone lets you take advantage of this facet of human nature.

These knowledgeable ad managers will give you their opinion of a book—its editorial, its circulation, its image as far as they've been able to determine it, and most important, what results their advertising has produced. Whether they're after inquiries or a check by return mail, don't question the validity of their objectives; after all, companies are different and communications objectives are all over the lot. And it's not their objectives you're really interested in as much as whether the magazine helps these advertisers achieve them.

One time the author telephoned the advertising manager of Fisher Scientific Company, Lewis McKinstry, about media. Fisher markets instruments, apparatus, furniture, and chemicals for laboratories—it's a laboratory supply house, in other words, and about the biggest in the country.

Fisher's ad manager was interested primarily in inquiries for the company salesmen to follow up on. And the firm for which the author was working was interested in inquiries, also, so there was much to talk about.

From a program that he had run for several years, McKinstry reported that *Chemical Engineering* magazine produced 1249 inquiries, *Science* magazine produced 898, and *Analytical Chemistry* brought in 486. Fisher had used another magazine in the research field, but dropped it because it failed to produce inquiries in volume, and the inquiries it did produce were questionable as far as quality was concerned.

Decent thing to do after such a conversation as this is to write the ad managers a letter thanking them for their time and help. And if your company is one that goes the gimmick route, send them an 8-foot steel tape, Zippo lighter, cuff links with the company emblem engraved on them, tie bar, or something that shows you appreciate the courtesy.

A half-dozen such calls will prove very revealing, particularly if you take pains to select dissimilar firms, yet companies that might well have advertising objectives similar to yours. Be sure to include a good geographical spread, round out the size of the companies and the products to get a representative group of advertisers in the magazine.

This method of determing what others think of a publication has been extremely helpful to the author and a number of friends over the years. Invariably the collective judgment of other advertising managers has shown much merit.

Although inquiries are probably not your primary objective, inquiries nonetheless are important when it comes to comparing two competing publications that appear to be close rivals for your space dollars.

Bingo Cards vs. Letterheads

When comparing inquiry production, ask the publications how many inquiries they produced in each of the last five years. They'll give you this information, and most will break it down, bingo cards versus letterheads, although the vast majority of letterhead inquiries go directly to the advertiser. Some do go to publications, though.

Keep in mind there are ways to produce an artificially high volume of inquiries. Most publications run the traditional Reader Service Card in the book with key numbers corresponding to advertisements and editorial publicity listed for the reader to circle those he's interested in. This makes it relatively easy for a number-checker to send off for huge quantities of literature and ask for all sorts of information in which he or she is only remotely interested. This cannot be avoided and is a fact of life that has to be lived with.

Some publications bind in several bingo cards so pass-on readers can also send them in. This raises the book's total number of inquiries by several hundred percent, but it also raises the question of just how valuable such inquiries are.

Still other magazines publish separate bingo cards, sometimes containing capsule descriptions of products and processes, for each item in the magazine. When the publication also binds in a postage-paid envelope, as some do, this usually results in a very large return of the cards, although inquiry quality is open to question.

Inquiries will be covered as a separate subject in the next chapter.

Something else to consider when you're evaluating media is the apparent difficulty, or the lack of it, that a magazine might encounter in selling its premium-priced space—those preferred positions that smart advertisers gobble up and retain in the best books for years at a time.

Almost all leading business publications today have a minimum amount of four-color reproduction that includes the cover (not sold in publications worth running space advertising in), back cover, second cover, and third cover.

As a rule of thumb you can assume that if there's a large turnover in advertisers in these preferred positions, something's amiss. If this space is producing as it should, advertisers wouldn't renounce their right to retain it. Preferred positions in top ranking books have a waiting list of advertisers who are eager to buy.

What's more, if a magazine prints four-color covers and then runs black-and-white advertisements on its fourth cover, that's another tip-off that the publication is short on advertiser acceptance. No industrial advertiser is going to shortchange himself by running black-

and-white in premium-priced space when for just a few dollars more he could have quality four-color ads. And quality is consistently good in the best business publications; their production people and web-offset presses combine to produce mouth-watering color quality. This is a showcase for the magazine and no publication will accept less than the very best. The advertiser will get attractive appearance on the covers regardless of cost.

When a book with a four-color cover is running black-and-white ads on the fourth cover—and they may change, one advertiser then another very frequently, or even from month to month—you can suspect with reason that publisher is giving that space away at the same price as an inside page. He or she is doing so just to get somebody, anybody on that fourth cover. You can't very well run a "house" ad there.

Also ask to see the results of buying studies that the publication has made—and remember the good ones have several that will be interesting to you. They were made, in almost every instance, by outside research firms and they document action taken by readers of the magazine, frequently those who inquired via bingo cards. They prove, too, that magazine readers have the authority and the jobs that enable them to buy and to specify—vital if your advertising is to be effective.

Proof of readership as determined by readership studies performed by a recognized research firm is also an essential you'll want to review thoroughly. Leading magazines use recognized services—sometimes their own, such as McGraw-Hill's Reader Feedback, or Chilton's Ad-Chart—but always ones that are accepted and respected in the industrial advertising field.

Services to Advertisers

Publications with something to offer—as far as editorial and circulation are concerned—invariably offer a wide range of services to their advertisers. Marginal and less than marginal publications seldom do.

Important among these services are merchandising and direct mail; they will be discussed in subsequent chapters.

Leading publications offer a vast amount of market research, as has been mentioned. Those that do not are usually publications that are marginal at best, worthless at worst.

One mark of a publication with an excellent circulation is it has acquired a truly encyclopedic knowledge of its market in the process of building its circulation. The publication committed to making a genuine contribution to the market it serves always starts by becoming intimately familiar with that market, every aspect of it. It probes and digs and analyzes; its appetite for facts and information is insatiable. And this information is yours either free or for a very modest fee. Avail yourself of it.

Research in the marketplace which would help the advertiser sell his product is extremely important to that advertiser. Few indeed are the industrial companies with market knowledge even approaching that of the the leading magazines in their industries. Quite often publication information constitutes the bulk of hard-core data that are available to smaller companies without research departments of their own.

Iron Age, for instance, has gone farther than the government; it has broken down and defined industry finer than the customary four-digit SIC. *Iron Age* has classified all of the metalworking industry by six-digit SIC. This greatly simplifies market identification and location for the advertising manager, as well as for the sales manager who finds it exceptionally helpful in planning.

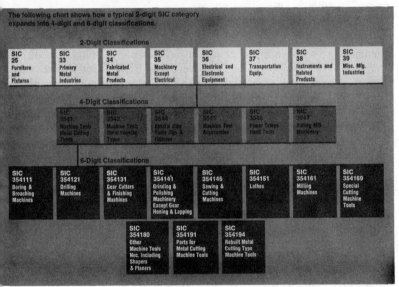

The following chart shows how a typical 2-digit SIC category expands into 4-digit and 6-digit classifications.

An outstanding reference to the metal trade is the *Iron Age Metalworking Marketguide*. This highly valuable book provides a statistical summary of *Iron Age's* continuing census of the metalworking industry. Included in the *Marketguide* is the following absolutely essential information:

- Description of the metalworking market—detailed information on the size and scope of the market and its relationship to all other manufacturing markets.

- Description and explanation of the SIC system.
- Market tools and how to use them.
- National two-digit SIC analysis.
- National four-and six-digit SIC analysis—showing count of 214 product groups at the four-digit level, and 1,427 different products at the six-digit level.
- State summary of plants and employment.
- Metal Service Center data—state summary and employment information on 1,717 centers.

All of these data, stored by *Iron Age* in a computer *Metalworking Data Bank*, is available in numerous forms at surprisingly low rates considering the value and accuracy of the data. This kind of information is basic to the success of your market and media plan. How many thousands of man-hours would it take to develop through your company's facilities? Think that one over.

Most of the better business publications make available to their advertisers a copy service that's used by those advertisers who don't have agencies and who want professionally written copy; there's usually no charge for this service. What's more, most business publishers have translators who will translate English into whatever language the export publication is printed in; as a rule there's no charge for this either.

A number of business papers maintain files of photographs that may be of help to their advertisers, and they also have bulging files of case histories gathered by their editors when they're on field trips. Advertisers whose equipment is mentioned are generally welcome to these data, and it's almost always accompanied by photographs of good quality. This can save time and expense in gathering case history material for a campaign.

Some publications of editions are broken out geographically; they're called "regional editions." *Iron Age*, however, goes one major step beyond this. It also offers 13 Mini-Zip areas, corresponding to the 13 prime metalworking centers. This allows national advertisers to direct separate selling messages to as many as 13 selected market areas in the same issue. For regional advertisers, usually those with limited distribution or who sell only in a limited geographical area, it thus becomes possible to single out individual zones, or use combinations, to match sales, distribution and expansion potential area by area. In short, *Iron Age's* Mini-Zips add another important element to the flexibility of marketing communications.

Using only one edition enables you to test copy and other components of an ad—as well as the basic selling proposition and the copy appeal that the ad advances, as well as the appeal of the product itself, and it does so inexpensively.

Split runs are also broken out according to SIC, as *Iron Age* does with its Primary Metals Edition. This portion of *Iron Age's* circulation goes only to SIC 33, the basic ferrous and nonferrous metal producing mills and foundries; it provides exceedingly fine coverage of these establishments. Quite often *Iron Age*, although edited for the entire metalworking market, enjoys higher readership in metal producing mills and foundries than will monthly magazines edited specifically for them. This is because *Iron Age* is a weekly and presents timely news of the market, along with significant trends that enable management to plan its activities with greater effectiveness.

When you have a sticky problem and need some help, ask the best business publication that serves your market—even if the problem doesn't directly involve space advertising.

Chances are the book will be able to come through for you, that it will do so in an incredibly short time, and that the cost to your company will either be nominal, or nothing at all. Business publications are very service-minded—at least, the good ones are.

Space Cost

Many of the better things in life are cheaper by the dozen, and space in business publications is no exception. In fact, space in the business press goes other things one better because it is also cheaper by the *half*-dozen.

Except for a few marginal publications that publish 13 months of the year—attempting to coerce advertisers into using a special issue that may hold little interest for them by giving only one-time, 7-time, and 13-time rates—business publications give what is called a "frequency discount" to their advertisers.

Frequency discount is simply a reduction in the per-page price as more and more space is purchased. Another term for this reduction in price is "earned rate"—which means the advertiser has earned a lower price or rate through the amount of his or her purchases.

Cost of space hinges on circulation, of course, and the larger the circulation the higher the per-page price you'll pay. Some books force circulation by using massive drives—by direct mail, sales reps, dealer-distributor organizations, and by offering the book at trade shows, industry association meetings, and just about every other conceivable place—all to boost circulation.

These same publications frequently seem to make only a nominal effort to qualify those whom it solicits; net effect of all this promotion is to dilute the value of the circulation, while at the same time charging more for it. They can get by with this because the numbers are larger, that is, the circulation is larger—hence leading to the name of this practice, the "numbers game."

It is inevitable, of course, that circulation of legitimate publications that do *not* force circulation will also rise; this reflects the larger size of the business community, growth of the gross national product, and the population explosion of the country as a whole.

This is all well and good and publications whose growth is gradual and parallels that of the industry they serve cannot be questioned on this score. It is only when the circulation of a publication is swollen by leaps and bounds—say, 10, 15, 20 percent at one swell foop—that a jaundiced eye should be cast upon the book's policies.

Just a little bit hard to swallow is the glib explanation the publisher invariably advances under these circumstances—that "Book X now covers an even *greater* percentage of the market for your widgets" and so on and on.

One question that may logically be asked at this time when you're talking to the magazine's representative is, "And just who the hell needs this additional circulation?"

Doesn't it stand to reason that if the book was giving you as much coverage in the market as it could economically provide without turning over every log in an effort to flush out an additional relatively logical recipient for the magazine, that it's a bit odd that circulation should leap ahead like a missile being launched from its pad? And that this many truly qualified people could be found all at one time is even odder?

Space cost is boosted substantially to pay for both the promotions that "found" the additional "qualified" readers, as well as to pay for this extra circulation. The advertiser pays for both, of course. No altruistic publisher picks up the tab out of the goodness of heart. You can be sure of that.

Best way to tell if circulation of a book you're using or considering using has taken any of these numbers-game jumps is to look at its AIA Form and examine the circulation figures for the past five years. Gradual growth is fine, sharp surges of 15 percent or more are highly suspect.

Also in the AIA Form are space costs—rates—for the publication for the last five years. Rates of business publications in general have gone up over the years, just as everything else has gone up. There's a fixed relationship, however, between space cost and circulation; this varies with individual publications, but it's there and can be determined with a little pencil-and-paper work.

The Cost Per Thousand

Something else to consider is the cost per thousand, often abbreviated as "CPM." This is the circulation divided into the cost per page of space. CPM is a tremendously handy unit of measurement in consumer publications where circulation is circulation, all of it just about the same as far as quality is concerned.

However, in the industrial area it's relatively easy to increase circulation beyond the requirements of the market that's being covered by the publication—particularly in smaller, highly specialized, vertical markets.

If undue emphasis is placed on CPM, the obvious thing that will occur to publishers is to boost circulation (and raise rates, of course) so that cost per thousand comes down—even if rates do go up.

Playing the numbers game and indulging in circulation races with competitive books can result in oversaturation of the market for the publication; there is a limit, after all, to the number of readers who are really and truly buying influences in any market or for any product.

Reaching down the ladder on the corporate table of organization— or reaching too far up it, for that matter—to snare some additional recipients of the magazine accomplishes one thing as sure as you sit there reading this: It raises the cost of doing business.

This added cost is not going to be absorbed out of profit. It's going to be passed on to you know who. And when all is said and done, if a publication's circulation is good, if the editorial is excellent, if the book is useful to you, if it reaches the people you want to talk to, if it does so without straining to reach every single peapickin' individual in the universe, that's all you can logically expect.

After all, you don't buy circulation. You buy readers.

Cost per thousand of a given publication should be reasonably well in line with competitive publications, but don't base a buying decision solely on CPM.

As a matter of interest, cost of advertising in business publications has risen more than has cost of using consumer magazines, daily newspapers, or spot radio. Only the bright-eyed electronic monster has surpassed business publications in having an insatiable hunger for advertisers' dollars; spot TV has risen to 323 on the cost index.

There's no indication the business press rates will either level off or get out of the upswing they're in. Cost of publishing has risen steadily and continues to do so. Salaries are up and continue to go up as inflationary pressure raises the cost of living.

Paper, too, has steadily posted higher prices and this trend appears to be one that will also continue. Printing costs have gone up more than 47 percent in the last 10 years.

And the government itself, through that vast, archaic organization of bureaucratic dinosaurs, the post office, has hit the business press a body blow with dismaying frequency.

In the face of financial facts of life like these for publishers of business papers, only a dewy-eyed optimist would predict stabilization of rates in the business press.

Media Representatives

Chances are, some of the best friends you'll make in the advertising business will probably be media representatives. As a group, they're fine people, knowledgeable, informed, helpful—downright nice guys.

Like attracts like in this field as it does in any other. Almost invariably the leading publications will have better sales reps than will lesser magazines. Water seeks its own level, and there's no changing that.

The typical media representative—the space rep, as he or she is often called —is actually a fairly outstanding individual. He or she knows the publication backwards and forwards. There's remarkably little the rep can't tell you about it off the top of his or her head. And not only does he or she know the magazine, the product, but also knows the market it serves inside-out, backwards and forwards.

A really good space rep is a gold mine of information; he or she sees so many people that trends are detected while they're still not sharply defined. And on top of everything else, he or she is usually a pretty good advertising person.

Although it's from the agency point of view, Marsteller Inc. has formalized a procedure and questions that should be asked when a media representative is being interviewed. That agency's how-to-do-it point of view follows:

HOW TO INTERVIEW MEDIA REPRESENTATIVES

1. Could you make available circulation galleys for a particular company?
2. Please relate your publication's audience to my client's products.
3. What is your total market, and what percentage of this total market do you cover?

4. What is your editorial objective?

5. For whom is your publication edited?

6. Can you show me some articles from your publication that would interest my client's prospects? Which of these articles have produced the most reader reaction? Why?

7. A hypothetical question—if you were, I, Mr. Space Representative, which of your competitors' books would you add to the schedule after yours? Why? (Or, what's the second best book in the field?)

8. What do you think of my client's campaign in your publication?

9. In your opinion, Mr. Space Representative, what advertisers in your magazine are doing an outstanding job of advertising? Which campaigns are getting particularly good results? Why?

10. Would you please point out the competitive differences between publications in your field?

11. What is your volume of requests for editorial reprints? (Be wary of individual requests versus total number of reprints sent.)

12. What kind of merchandising program do you offer advertisers?

13. Does your publication have a policy concerning advertising quality control—truth, taste, etc.?

14. In what way is your publication contributing to the industry? Do your editors take stands on controversial issues?

15. When did you last visit my client?

16. Occasionally request that the representative summarize the arguments in letter form, specifically relating his or her story to your individual client.

One of the best checklists to rate salesmen is one that the late G.C. Buzby, board chairman of Chilton Company, presented to his own staff. It follows:

The buyer speaks (of sales reps)

How much does the rep know about my company, product, my marketing posture? Has that rep ever called on any of my distributors, dealers, or users? Is there *really* interest in my problems or does he or she expect me to be interested in?

Does the rep give me the impression he or she knows my

market and my place in it? Is he or she selling a marketing service with full understanding of the function of media advertising, or is the rep just peddling space?

Does the rep come to me with a standard pitch which he or she grinds out for everybody, or has that rep tailored the approach to my situation, my interests, and my objectives?

When the rep receives a contract from my company, does he or she consider the case closed until he shows up 11 months later for the renewal? Or does the rep realize that when he or she gets the order, the responsibility just starts?

Does the rep tell me the same story over and over and then wonder why I don't want to see him or her? How often has the rep written me between calls, passing out information helpful to me or a clipping from the magazine, or even some competitive magazine?

If the rep were in my position, would he or she place advertising in the publication? Really? Does he know why? Has it been thought out?

On the occasions I've called on the rep for information or services, how promptly and effectively has been the response?? Has the rep followed up on these requests?

How well does that person know his or her own publication? Does the rep read every issue? Does he or she ever call on any of the subscribers and readers? Does this result in case histories which are of interest to me?

When I make a reasonable request for market information or help, does the rep go back to the publisher and knock himself or herself out getting the answers or does he armwave me?

Does the rep slug the competitors trying to prove that they are robbers and thieves and that that particular book is the only good one? Does he realize that some of them are good friends of mine?

Does the rep waste my time with long-winded anecdotes, painful pleasantries and bum jokes, or with sales calls that have no aim or purpose except to generate a call report to the boss?

How courteous and pleasant is the rep to our receptionist, my secretary, and others in my company with whom he comes in contact?

Does the rep try to be a hero by telling five or six agencies that my account is ready to be plucked—especially when he or she picked this up as an unfounded rumor?

Does the sales rep think he or she can buy my business with alcohol and outings or does he know that the old gladhanded prince of a good fellow salesman is passé? Mind you, I don't mind a lunch or a cocktail now and then while we talk business.

Does the rep know that by a strange quirk of nature I like to be sold? I don't really like to give business to people who haven't earned it.

One very good bit of advice is: See media representatives. Don't make the mistake of regarding their calls as useless, time-consuming and nonproductive. Good reps have something to say, and it's a really rare advertising manager (or account executive) who doesn't learn something from them.

Do not, however, encourage calls made merely for the sake of the rep's conscience. This merely wastes your time and that of the representative. Make it known you *want* to see media representatives when they have something significant to tell you. Don't be the unapproachable, unseeable advertising manager whose switchboard or secretary fends off all callers because he or she is "too busy."

Granted, there will be days when you're writing, when you're working on an especially important report, when you're planning a new campaign, when you honestly cannot spare time to see reps. Have your secretary explain the circumstances and apologize for you.

Quite often you'll find it is helpful to expose other people in the company to the space sales rep—at least to those from leading publications serving markets in which you're most interested. These representatives not only help you sell the medium for which they work, but they help sell advertising in general.

Furthermore, the well-informed representative—and all of the good ones are well-informed—can often impart specific market information to your people that they can use. This can be done without being patronizing or making the product manager and the market manager feel that they are being force fed information *you* want them to have.

Also mentioned was "competitive information"—details or clues as to what competitor companies are up to. Reps see many people within an industry and most advertisers are something less than reluctant about picking up competitive information these media people might have.

The Media Plan

For a company to spend money on advertising without having firm, well-defined, written objectives makes about as much sense as failure to adopt the marketing concept.

These two failures usually go hand in hand, however, and the company whose management is determined to sell standard pricebook widgets is generally the company whose vice-president of marketing calls the advertising manager in when the new fiscal year rolls around—then innocently says, "Your budget for next year is $000,000. Now, I like Book B, you know, and Book D, and Book F and such-and-such trade shows (they're usually in swinging cities, of course). Why don't you develop a program for me, using these magazines and these shows, plus any others you think belong, and I'll pass it along to our fearless leader for approval?"

Such childlike faith that this course of action will accomplish anything positive is, unhappily, much more common in industry than we'd prefer to believe.

Developing a media plan involves some of the world's hardest work —thinking.

Despite the mental agonizing and the effort entailed, having a plan is essential if the advertising dollar is to be invested rather than spent, and invested so it produces the highest possible return.

Marsteller Inc. says its eight-step checklist enables it to develop a media plan that's exactly right for any specific client, and all without fuss and furor. The checklist reads:

THE MEDIA PLAN

Here's a checklist of eight steps important in the analysis and selection of industrial media:

1. *Marketing objectives.* Absolutely necessary to build the industrial media plan. Marketing objectives put us in the right ball park.

2. *Communications objectives.* Must be specifically oriented to the marketing objectives and given priority by their relevance to each marketing objective. Communications objectives define the *boundaries* of the ball park.

3. *Circulation.* Numbers and characteristics of those numbers are always a fundamental factor. Audited figures from ABC and BPA are the media buyer's fact source.

4. *Editorial.* Evaluation of the editorial content and quality is also essential. This analysis yardstick gets the most lip service and least actual application of any media technique.

5. *Readership.* What we buy from a medium is readership. The measurement of this critical factor is dependent partly on the effectiveness of the medium itself and partly on the creative message used. Readership measurement methods are still primitive in many respects.

6. *Publication image.* This relatively new media yardstick often tips the scale to one book when all other factors seem equal. A publication image has a "rub-off" effect on the advertiser. Therefore, the two images had better be compatible.

7. *Media strategy.* This will often in itself dictate or at least narrow the final selection. Strategy concerning frequency, dominance and impact, national versus regional coverage, horizontal versus vertical industry reach, are all important factors. So, too, are such elements as product market share, competitive pressures, and marketing strategy.

8. *Budget.* Budget limitations often dictate the advertiser's ability to employ a balanced communications mix and/or to apply extra impact through any given media.

When all is said and done and the media plan is finally developed, what it really does is to show how publication space can best be used to help achieve the company's marketing objectives—and what additional media such as direct mail, trade shows, merchandising, and so on can do to augment the basic program. In industrial advertising, space advertising is the one basic, fundamental tool we can't dispense with.

A trend today is to have more and more internal media specialists in the industrial companies. These specialists work with agency media people, rather than relying entirely on the agency for media selection as was common several years ago. In smaller advertising departments, the advertising manager is usually the media specialist, as well as the specialist in almost everything else, of course.

When all of the chips are down and the schedule is almost ready to be typed, a decision still has to be made. Will media recommended by either the agency and/or the internal media specialist be used, is there a conflict of opinion, or are more suitable media available and more advisable?

This decision will be made by the man who's responsible for the company's money—the advertising manager, the advertising director, or whatever title the top ad person in the company wears. Specialists recommend, and rightly so, but the advertising manager has the ultimate responsibility. And he or she usually has a more complete picture of all of the various forces exerted on and in the marketplace, as well as a *feel* for the market that cannot be imparted to media people.

Computerization of media data and greater comparability are worthwhile goals, of course, and the computer is playing a bigger and bigger role in media selection. Its importance has been growing year by year.

Monthlies Versus Weeklies

This is one of the moss-covered questions that always arises when making media decisions, and it is certainly one that should have been quietly laid to rest lo, these many years ago.

The Basford agency in New York made some very revealing comments in its assessment of this question that seem to analyze the situation as well as it has been done.

If an advertiser is going to run only six advertisements in a publication during a year, will he or she be better off using a monthly, or a weekly? Suppose he's able to schedule only three ads, then what?

This question, or one very much like it, was asked of Basford several times a year. The agency checked into it carefully, and the answer appears to be that frequency of issue should *not* be a prime consideration. Media should be selected on the basis of its *circulation, rates, and editorial content*—these three considerations only, according to Basford. (No mention was made of publication image.)

Contrary to what many advertising men think, if a reason cannot be found to choose one publication over another except frequency of issue, it is just as well to select the one that is issued *most* frequently.

Offhand, this might seem contrary to good sense. However, when the problem is considered in this light, it takes on an entirely different aspect:

1. Does an advertisement have a better chance of being seen in a weekly or a monthly?
2. Will a series of advertisements, if they all *are* read, make more of an impression on a reader if they appear, let's say, in every other issue of a monthly, or in every eighth issue of a weekly?

George Kiernan, who is head of George Kiernan Associates, Inc., formerly the old Eastman Editorial Research, and others who do editorial research, says there are wide differences among publications in how many issues a typical reader reads—but the differences stem from how "vital" or interesting the books are, not from frequency of publication. A good weekly will be just as thoroughly read—and just as many issues will be read—as a good monthly.

Readers spend more time per issue, but less time per page, on a good thick issue than on a good thin one. Since good weeklies are usually thinner than good monthlies, there may even be some advantage to the weekly. The fact that a monthly "sits around" for a longer time than a weekly is not valid; the page on which an advertisement appears doesn't get exposed any more often.

Inquiry records show that inquiries come in just as long from a weekly as from a monthly, showing that life of the two kinds of publications is the same. McGraw-Hill's Laboratory of Advertising Performance reports both weeklies and monthlies secure reader action for two or three months. For example, only 63.5 percent of the reader actions had occurred at the end of four weeks for the monthly, and only 75.3 percent for the weekly. By the end of eight weeks, the monthly figure is 95.8 percent and the weekly 94.4 percent, showing weeklies and monthlies have a very similar length of life.

From the standpoint of an ad being seen, then, there are very real differences between publications—but these differences come from how well the publication meets the readers' needs and interests, not from its frequency of issue.

How about the impression a *series* of advertisements makes? Is the impression stronger when ads appear every other month in a monthly magazine, rather than every other month in a bimonthly or a weekly?

No evidence has been found that this makes the slightest bit of difference. When you stop to think about it, this is only logical. The reader you are trying to reach will be exposed to hundreds—thousands, really—of ads between one appearance of your advertisement and the next appearance, whether your ad appears in a weekly magazine or in a monthly one.

Almost certainly, if the reader sees one of your advertisements today, and another one two months from now, that person won't even remember *where* he or she saw today's ad. And that person couldn't care less. Only the advertiser, not the reader, worries about things like that.

Is there any evidence to support all of this? Emphatically yes!

Some business publications have been such good advertising buys that they became very fat, in both income and in physical format. They then increased their frequency of issue in order to reduce their thickness. There was no change in editorial content or approach.

In every case where this has happened, so far as is known, advertising readership scores and inquiries per advertisement have gone just one direction—up. This has probably been because the resulting issues were thinner, but it supports the case for giving at least equal consideration to the book with the greater frequency—assuming circulation, rates, and editorial content are equal.

Directories

In addition to trade publications, other print media used widely in industrial advertising are directories.

These massive publications—frequently several heavy, thick volumes one could slip a disc just lifting—contain detailed listings of tens of thousands of individual manufacturers and their product lines, as well as paid space advertisements run by many of these companies.

Directories are the purchasing agent's right arm. The PA knows that almost anything an industrial company could conceivably purchase is listed in one or more of these directories, complete with product description, sometimes prices, and always the names and addresses and phone numbers of the makers of these products.

When the purchasing agent knows who makes the product, it's a very simple matter to look in the local phone book for a logical office of the manufacturer, for its rep, or to write, phone or wire asking to have a sales rep call.

Untold millions of dollars in sales result each year merely from a listing in the various directories. Especially when the product is one that is used or consumed in manufacture, or is used for plant or equipment maintenance, most purchasing agents buy by directory description and issue purchase orders without ever having seen that particular manufacturer's representative or sales rep; these PO's often say "advise price" instead of giving an existing price because it may not be known.

In the case of capital equipment, however, the purchasing process is very different as we've seen. Even when expensive capital equipment is involved, however, use of directories is advisable. It is insurance that your company will not accidentally be overlooked by a buyer or purchasing agent with an information-gathering assignment which includes compiling a list of prospective vendors.

Actually, the directory publishers do all of industry a favor by publishing. Listings are often given at no charge for the basic product line or lines. Advertisers in the directories usually receive bold-face listings, additional listings, and a much finer breakdown of product lines with listings under a number of different product classifications; this is an incentive to take a space advertisement in the directory, of course.

The average directory has an unbelievably long life span. Most of the major directories are issued annually, but it is not at all unusual for advertisers to receive queries—or even actual orders—from buyers who are referring to a directory that is anywhere from two to 10 years old. This situation is particularly prevalent overseas, especially in countries that are not highly industrialized.

Undoubtedly one of the best known and most widely used of the industrial buying guides is Thomas Register of American Manufacturers. The original edition of Thomas Register was published for the years 1905-1906; it weighed a pound and a half, contained slightly over 1,200 pages, and "rented" for $10. Thomas Register has been published regularly since then, although during World War II it was published at 18-month, rather than 12-month intervals due to a paper shortage.

In 1982, the 72nd edition of Thomas Register was produced. This edition weighed over one hundred pounds, contained over 27,000 pages, and cost $145 for the 17 huge volumes shown.

Thomas Register gives the specifier and buyer in-depth information in a three-part system. The first nine volumes are classified by products and services. They contain nearly 55,000 specific product and service headings with more than 1,500,000 listings of qualified sources. Supplementing these listings are tens of thousands of ads providing detailed information. These advertisements help the buyer decide which of several qualified vendors to contact.

The next two volumes (#10 and #11) provide profiles of 115,000 companies, alphabetically by name. Included are addresses and phone numbers, along with locations of distributors, plants, service/engineering offices, divisions and subsidiaries. The company profiles often include the complete product line, brand names, corporate affiliations and the asset value.

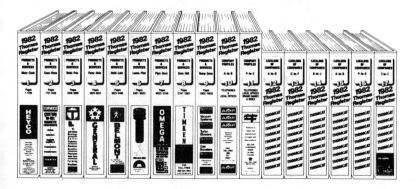

Also included in volume #17 is the Inbound Traffic Guide. This guide, introduced in 1980, is used by buyers to help to determine the best shipping mode and carrier for factory inbound shipments.

Surveys show that Thomas Register is referred to more than 300,000 times a day—75,000,000 times a year, and is used regularly by more than 1,500,000 people throughout the world.

Another very fine directory, and one which tens of thousands of buyers and purchasing agents swear by, is MacRae's Blue Book. It is published in five huge volumes; a line conversion illustration of the five volumes is shown here.

MacRae's Blue Book is an industrial directory/catalog service produced and published annually in February. It is directed to purchasing agents, plant engineers and top management, and is distributed to approximately 25,000 of America's leading specifiers of goods and services. Although its circulation covers the gamut of industry, the majority (approximately 80 percent) is in metalworking—S.I.C.'s 33-39.

Listed alphabetically are around 50,000 company names with addresses, telephone numbers, capital asset listings, plus branch and sales office locations and their telephone numbers. Also included is an index of trade names.

Space is relatively inexpensive in directories, and your advertisement lives for at least a year—often for many years. All of this is yours for the price of one insertion, one production cost. Directories are excellent buys, and as many should be used as the budget permits.

Chapter 15

ELECTRONIC MEDIA ADVERTISING*

ELECTRONIC media advertising (commercials), which is currently composed of radio, television and CATV (cable TV) messages, has a uniquely Western World beginning and is a total product of the 20th century.

Today, the electronic media spans most parts of the globe, and commercials can be heard in hundreds of dialects, with announcers speaking the tongues of their listeners loud and clear.

It wasn't always this way. Radio broadcasting started shortly after World War I, from KDKA Pittsburgh and WWJ Detroit. In 1922, the first commercial was broadcast over a limited distance, sponsored by a real estate firm in Jackson Heights, NY.

Relying heavily on ad lib and innovation, the first radio commercial totally lacked the later organized format of copywriting and production. The first commercial sound effects were used for the Clicquot Club (soda water) Eskimos in the early 1920s.

The growth of radio was impressive in those early days. Some milestones included:

— An experimental network over telephone lines in 1922
— World Series broadcast by WJZ (now WABC) New York and WGY Schenectady
— Joint hook-up between WEAF New York (now WNBC), KDKA Pittsburgh and KYW Chicago (now Philadelphia), to carry talks made at a dinner in New York in early 1923
— In 1926, NBC starts a network with 24 stations
— In 1927, first coast-to-coast hook-up.

FM and television broadcasting emerged from their experimental stages just before U.S. entry into World War II. Wartime restrictions retarded expansion of radio facilities, although the emergency produced new techniques and apparatus that are in use today. In the decades that followed, broadcasting expanded domestically, and today, with the development of communication satellites, new possibilities for internal relay have evolved.

*Contributed by Robert N. Robinson, President, WHHY Radio, Montgomery, AL

To truly understand the rapid growth of radio in those first decades, let's look at some statistics:

OFFICIAL COUNT of U.S. BROADCASTING STATIONS
(from records of FCC)

Jan. 1, 1922	30
March 1, 1923	556
Oct. 1, 1924	530
June 30, 1925	571
June 30, 1926	528
*Feb. 23, 1927	723
July 1, 1928	677
Nov. 9, 1929	618
July 1, 1930	612
July 1, 1931	612
Jan. 1, 1932	608
Jan. 1, 1933	610
**Jan. 1, 1934	591
Jan. 1, 1935	605
Jan. 1, 1936	632
Jan. 1, 1937	685
Jan. 1, 1938	721
Jan. 1, 1939	764
Jan. 1, 1940	814
Jan. 1, 1941	882
Jan. 1, 1942	923
Jan. 1, 1943	917
Jan. 1, 1944	912

Radio commercials during those early broadcasts were quite different from today's smooth, professional efforts. For one thing, there wasn't any limit on their length. The duration of the message usually depended on the stamina of the announcer in the 1920s. They were not limited to 30 or 60 seconds. There was little or no station planning. Government regulations were unheard of. They could run as long—or short—as the station wanted. And with competition from other stations limited or nonexistent, the station didn't worry about losing its audience—it had it all.

Rather, the main competition to the commercial was the advertising dollars being spent with local newspapers. It wasn't until the late

*Federal Radio Commission takes over regulation from Department of Commerce.

**Federal Communications Commission replaced Federal Radio Commission July 11, 1934.

1970s that AM radio found itself with another competitor for listeners and advertising dollars—FM radio.

In the 1980s, FM radio is moving past the 50% mark in audience and advertising dollars over AM radio. Radio advertising is continuing to set new peaks in dollar volume years after the impact of television advertising, with all its audiovisual strength, was met and lived with.

Radio exhibited quite a deal of strength when pitted against the emerging television industry during the 50's, 60's and 70's. New programming, together with the versatility of auto, portable and home listening, gave radio advertising an exclusivity untouched by other media in audience reach. People worldwide were on the go, and radio went with them. Radio jingles often became as popular as the latest tunes.

Retailers and manufacturers quickly bought radio commercials in greater and greater quantity. By the late 50's, advertisers were spending a half billion dollars to send sales messages through more than 3,300 radio stations. (Now advertisers are spending an estimated $3.6 billion on AM and FM radio, reaching 99% of Americans through over 12,000 stations in 50 states.)

Television's rise led radio time salespeople to use new figures in promoting their product, pointing out that in the early 1950's, over 41 million radios were used in homes, and a few years later, 38.5 million were installed in cars alone (1957). Radios totaled 150 million by this time, and the tremendous new ability to reach consumers wherever they were resulted in impressive advertising revenue growth for radio.

If you are considering radio commercials for your enterprise, you should know and understand some of the basics. They are:

1. *Radio Rate Cards.* Radio rate cards are radio's price list for commercials. There are three basic units sold in radio: 60-second; 30-second; and 10-second announcements. Some stations sell only 60's and 30's. The general industry practice is to price 30's at 80% of the rate for 60's. And 10's are priced at approximately 50% of the minute rate.

In addition to buying an announcement, you can buy various programs such as newscasts, sportcasts or even special features. When you study a station's rate card, you'll see it divided into different time classifications. These depend on the time of day. The terminology used for these classifications isn't currently standard throughout the industry. But, here's a system recommended recently by an industry-wide committee that is useful as an example:

Time Slot	Abbrev.	Times of day
A.M. Drive	(AMD)	5:00 a.m. - 10:00 a.m. Mon-Sat
Daytime	(DAY)	10:00 a.m. - 3:00 p.m. Mon-Fri
P.M. Drive	(PMD)	3:00 p.m. - 7:00 p.m. Mon-Fri
Evening	(EVE)	7:00 p.m. - 12:00 Mid Mon-Sun
Overnight	(OVN)	12:00 Mid - 5:00 a.m. Mon-Sun
Weekend Drive	(WKD)	10:00 a.m. - 7:00 p.m. Sat & Sun
Sunday A.M.	(SUN)	6:00 a.m. - 10:00 a.m. Sunday

Some stations call 5 a.m. to 10 a.m. their Class AAA time, or something else, but the point is that most stations vary their rates by the time of day. In general, those time periods with the largest audiences are assigned the highest cost. Also available at many stations are "package plans," which enable you to buy a combination of announcements, chosen from a number of time slots, at a package price.

2. *Dos and Don'ts of Buying Radio Time.* As with any purchase, there are certain factors you should consider before buying. Experienced time buyers suggest the following:

A.   Don't rely on just your taste alone. Customers often prefer formats that won't appeal to you.

B.   Know the product and its competition. Study audience surveys available from local stations to see which are strong with customers.

C.   Provide as much advance notice as possible to stations about your schedules. This lets them provide you with their best at all times.

D.   Consider using radio on a long-range basis to enhance continuity in any campaign you are mapping, and to secure the best availabilities.

E.   Verify your buys in writing. Utilize a signed contract, with instructions on how many spots, which days and which copy.

F.   If you require verification that your announcements ran (for co-op advertising, for example), let the station know exactly what you need when you finalize the buy—things like exact times, spots run, notarized scripts, station affidavits, invoices, air-checks . . . whatever. This is much easier to accomplish if the station knows your needs in advance.

G.   Listen to your spots on the air and encourage your staff to do likewise.

H.   If your method of selling allows it, track the success of your campaigns by asking customers if the commercials were heard and influenced them.

I.   Learn from experience. Plan your next campaign to take advantage of past experience with the station's pulling power, time slots, item selections and impact schedule.

3. *Selecting the Station that's Right For You.* Radio is a selective medium that reaches different kinds of people through different programming. Consider stations in your market on the basis of the kind of audience they deliver, the size, and whether or not it will be interested in your product.

Almost every city has a choice of AM and FM stations, and usually they cover the following formats: (A) Middle of the road, (B) News, (C) Conversation, (D) Country music, (E) Contemporary, (F) Progressive rock, (G) Classical, (H) Ethnic, (I) Variety, and various combinations of those already mentioned. For awhile, there were disco stations, but they have faded fast. In the future, there will be stations featuring new sounds we can't even imagine.

The price you pay for commercials is related to the size of your market, the number of people the station reaches, the make-up of the audience (age, income, family size, etc.), and the selling power of the station's on-air personnel.

4. *Some Tips on Writing for Radio.* Since radio is a medium that reaches people while they're doing other things—yard work, driving, cooking, hobbies—in effect, your sales message is reaching an audience of "half listeners" and you must keep this in mind when writing commercials.

Most likely you'll succeed if you follow these tips:

A.   Write conversationally. Radio is a human being talking to another human being, not a novelist or poet writing to a reader.

B.   Talk about benefits. Listeners like to hear what they'll get from your product or service . . . and fast. Stress economy, health, quality, dependability, rapid service, etc.

C.   Be direct and go straight to the point. Short sentences are better because they can be absorbed easily through the ears.

D.   Repeat your store name, or product name, the price, the comparative advantages and the benefits as many times as possible to register the points you wish to make.

E.   Provide listeners with a single idea to carry them. Details should be kept to a minimum.

F.   Try out your script before airing. Read your copy over. Even better—have someone else read it. Or read it into a tape recorder. This way you'll hear any phrases that are awkward, hard to read or unbelievable.

5. *Steps to Capturing Your Listener's Attention.* You want your messages above the "ho-hum" and humdrum of your competition. You'd like them to be unique and attention getting. Here are some hints to accomplish these:

A.   Give the listener variety and he or she is likely to be attentive, wondering what's coming next. Do so by using various combinations of jingles, dialogue, straight announcements, sound effects, music, etc., all in one commercial. It'll be a miniature show.

B.   Don't let your commercial sound like an interruption from the regular programming and you'll do better. How? Integrate commercials with weather reports, time checks, musical styles or even the call letters.

C.   Change gears and move ahead. Just because you've hit upon a magical jingle is no time to sit still, presenting it at one tempo again and again. Instead, see that it gets as many treatments as the imagination and good taste allow.

D.   Consider testimonials. It's possible you could develop them yourself, using a person who visits your store or uses your product. Such things, properly handled, captivate your audience. They can identify—then buy.

E.   Use local and regional radio personalities, if their images fit your product or service. Radio listeners are accustomed to accepting the word of commentators who bring them the news. That same voice and the authority that goes with it could benefit your sales message.

Now that you have a good working knowledge of radio, let's turn our attention to television. In 1946, television burst on the American scene faster than its most optimistic boosters had believed possible. From a dozen TV stations and a few thousand receiving sets, the industry grew to 450 stations and 34 million receivers, serving an estimated 100 million persons by 1955. In the process, it grew from a money-losing industry to an important factor in the success of the nation's economy.

Time sales, a growing giant in the advertising business, by 1957 was grossing $868 million dollars. Of that, $394 came from networks, $300 million from national spots and about $174 million from various local advertisers.

ELECTRONIC MEDIA ADVERTISING

Television's rapid growth was to occur between 1964, when it recorded $1.67 billion in advertising dollars and 1975, when it notched $4.72 billion. By 1980, it had zoomed to $11.3 billion. Radio recorded $3.6 billion in sales in 1980.

Television commercials create demand for all kinds of merchandise. On television, an advertiser can show how his product looks and what it does. Home demonstrations to millions occur at one time. Television advertising is so far reaching that sponsors spend several hundred thousand dollars for one 60-second announcement, broadcast during a Super Bowl football game, World Series game, or other maximum audience program. Advertisers judge advertising expense by the total cost of sending a sales message to one prospective customer. If millions of viewers see a television show, the average cost of reaching one person or prospective customer is relatively small. This is called C.P.M., or Cost per Thousand.

Advertisers prefer their messages on programs that maintain high ratings. Ratings, or audience measurements, are determined by market research agencies which take a sampling of the home audience's size. The show is given a high rating if the sample indicates it attracts a large audience.

Prime time advertising is the most expensive to buy because it occurs between 7 and 10 p.m., where the largest audiences are encountered. Television prime time differs from radio prime time in several ways. Generally, radio prime time is from 6 to 10 a.m. Monday through Friday, with 3 to 7 p.m. Monday through Friday being a secondary radio prime time. Radio announcements are more costly in these two periods than at other times such as 10 a.m. to 3 p.m. and after 7 p.m. at night. Radio rates are generally from five to six dollars a minute in the smallest markets, and several hundred dollars for each minute in the large major markets. Radio advertising rates are generally less than those of television, ranging from 20% to 50% less.

For example, a $50.00 radio rate for a 60-second spot in AAA time (6 to 10 a.m. or 3 to 7 p.m.) would probably cost $250.00 on prime time television, 7 to 10 p.m. Monday through Friday. However, rate comparisons are difficult to make, because of varying business conditions and other market variables.

Both radio and television sometimes have additional charges for advertising other than times charges; generally for 10-, 30-, or 60-second spot announcements and programs. Many times additional charges are made for talent used in production of announcements or programs. Engineering costs and telephone line charges are added for remote broadcasts. Use of production studios, usually on television, can result in talent and production charges.

799

First radio and then radio and television combined have brought political campaigns closer to the voters than previously. Candidates easily reach many prospective voters, utilizing radio or television. Both have added to political campaign cost. In fact, buying television time frequently becomes a candidate's biggest campaign expense.

Charges for political advertising are closely regulated by the federal government through the Federal Communications Commission (FCC), established in 1934. Within a few weeks of the election, a station must charge only its lowest rate to a candidate. Most radio and television sales managers consider legal advice from their Washington attorney invaluable in interpreting the latest FCC rules regarding the sale of radio or television time to political candidates or parties.

Since the early 1970's, radio has usually sold only spot announcements to political candidates and parties.

A growing source of television revenue comes from religious programming. Commercial religious programming is usually found on Sunday morning radio or on TV from 6 a.m. till noon. In many cities, one or more radio stations is classified as religious. WHHY features local and taped programs, selling 15 to 30 minutes of broadcast time to preach or sing, and sometimes both. The period from 11 a.m. to noon on Sundays on most radio and television stations features a remote broadcast from a local church. Charges may involve only the cost of telephone line charges and equipment. However, as operation costs rise, many station owners and operators are charging for time as well, although some times are discounted.

Network and taped religious shows have been on the broadcast scene for almost as long as the media have existed. Many a preacher's fame has grown because of exposure to radio and television audiences. Millions of dollars a year are spent on radio and television by churches and religious organizations.

Dozens of Protestant and evangelical denominations are principal users of paid religious air time. In recent years, religions have built large networks to spread the Word as they see it. These programs are sustained by large and small donations sent by listeners.

AM and FM radio licenses are owned and operated by churches and religious organizations tax free. These stations are required to operate fairly and impartially, just as their counterparts are operated. Some religious station licenses have been revoked for not complying.

The first television stations occupied channels one through thirteen: the Very High Frequencies (VHF). Later, higher channels were called "Ultra High Frequencies" (UHF). VHF channels are preferred because of greater power and coverage and better dial position.

By 1957 America had 497 VHF stations and 111 UHF stations operating for the full year. By 1978 the total was 513 VHF stations and 201 UHF television stations. Of the 714 stations, 596 were affiliates of the three major networks, 103 were independents, 74 were independent UHF stations, and 29 were independent VHF stations. Fifteen were network owned and operated, known in the industry as O and O's.

The 45th annual report of fiscal year 1979 from the Federal Communications Commission showed 714 television stations, with 693 reporting total broadcasting revenues of $3.985 billion from 290 different markets. This excluded 21 satellites that filed combined reports with their parent stations. It included specialty stations such as ones featuring religious formats.

Let's look at the costs involved in advertising on television. The average 30-second, prime-time network television announcement costs about $85,000. Spots on top rated series can cost in the range of $165,000. Low-rated shows have spots that average about $55,000.

An estimated 100 million persons watched the 1980 Super Bowl telecast. Thirty-second announcements during that event cost $234,000. Thirty-second announcements on individual TV stations range from $15,000 in top rated specials in major markets to as low as $10 in the second hundred markets.

By comparison, radio spots run from $600 or more in major markets to less than a dollar in smaller towns.

A national buyer may buy the top ten TV markets. The top 10 A.D.I. (Area of Dominant Influence) markets have 32.87% of the total TV households—24,910,200 households out of a total of 75,793,500 households.

A TV network spot announcement in New York City, the number one A.D.I. market, costs a high of $10,000 for a 60-second spot. The cost of a TV spot announcement is generally determined by the station's share of the audience. The share is determined by such factors as the number of CATVs carrying its signal, programming power, tower height, promotion/market size. In television, power greatly determines the cost of a spot announcement and A.D.I. TV households reached.

In the 49th A.D.I. TV households market of Birmingham, AL, the cost of a network spot announcement on the UHF TV station with lesser coverage is 25% of the cost of a network spot announcement on a competitive network TV station, $450 to $1,800.

TV network spot rates fall drastically from the $10,000 cost in New York City with its more than 6 million households to $5,000 in Los

Angeles, the number two market. Dallas-Ft. Worth commands a rate of $2,050 as the tenth market in the U.S.; Atlanta, GA, earns $1,700 per network announcement for being the 16th market; Portland, OR, the 24th market, garners $1,250; Columbus, OH, the 35th market, receives $1,300.

The 55th market, Little Rock, has a spot rate of $750. Other markets and their network spot rates are: Omaha, 65th, $1,050; Jackson, MS, 80th, $900; Austin, 99th, $250; Las Vegas, 126th, $375.

Locally, costs of radio and television advertising is usually lower because of greater frequency, longer contracts and lower costs in selling the advertising. Network radio 60-second rates range from a high of $600 in New York to $225 in Dallas, $240 in Atlanta, $80 in Little Rock, $50 in Jackson, MS, $68 in Austin and $45 in Las Vegas. Thirty-second rates are usually 75% to 80% of the 60-second rate.

Some radio and television stations sell 10-, 15- and 20-second announcements. Fifty percent of the earned 60-second rate is the factor usually used to determine these less-than-standard length spot announcements.

Television and radio time is sold by salespeople representing an individual station, a regional group under single or multiple ownership or a network of stations. These representatives call on an owner, a manager or advertising manager of a business or businesses, or an agency time buyer representing an account. The salesperson is either male or female, since most radio and TV station sales staffs now include women.

These salespersons arm themselves with rate cards, showing rates based on frequency and times. They also carry with them a contract, to be completed at the close of a sale. Another item in their kit: a sheet showing times of day and names of programs with announcements available in or around the programs. From the buyer's standpoint, statistics showing a station's ratings are a valuable tool that efficient salespeople utilize in selling to them. Demographic strengths in various time periods, metro or TSA (Total Service Area) can be used to guide the buyer to the audience he or she desires from men, women, adults or teens, or as the seasoned buyer knows, 12 + teens, 18 to 49 or 25 to 54-year-old age groups.

Other tools of the station salesperson are coverage maps, station fact sheets which might include a description of physical and technical facilities, production facilities, copy deadlines, amount of news carried and when, tower height, transmitter power, etc. Pictures and profiles of station personalities are also helpful in cementing signed contracts for commercials. Enterprising salespeople often bring success stories from other clients with them. They often bring special spots to the client for approval. In TV, the salesperson usually brings the client to the station to watch and listen to the offering.

TV and radio salespeople usually work on a 15% to 20% commission. However, the TV salesperson with a higher rate and a greater volume is usually compensated at the rate of 7½% to 15%. In making a sale, the radio or TV time salesperson usually follows these steps with regard to the sales contract:

1. The sales contract is signed, including the schedule of times and days for the advertising to run.

2. If copy is unavailable from the client, facts are obtained from the client and sent, in turn, to a copywriter. The copywriter prepares the proposed commercial(s) for the client's approval. Occasionally, the client films his or her announcement for TV, or tapes it for radio. This is usually a local practice and is seldom done on network or with national spots.

Copywriting is such an important phase in the creation of a commercial that it bears special study at this point. Remember, the few seconds of a TV commercial can represent hours or days of concentrated effort on the part of several creative copywriters.

The TV commercial allows the advertiser to not only tell a customer about products, but also to display a product or service—to show it in use. The main purpose of a TV commercial is not to entertain the viewer but to sell him or her. Studies show there is no correlation between people liking commercials and being sold by them.

In preparing a TV commercial, a copywriter and an art director work together much as they do in preparing printed ads. The copywriter writes the proposed script that tells the product's story. He or she times the commercial to the right length. The art director then sketches in the action on a chart showing the visual action, the spoken words and the sound effects of the commercial, step by step.

After securing approval from the client, it is ready for production. Television commercials, unlike radio commercials, must rely on words and pictures to tell the story. The function of the words is to explain what the pictures are showing. A picture without sound to sell it is useless. Most effective TV commercials are built around one or two specific points, simply stated.

Too many ideas or facts in a commercial will leave the viewer confused and unmoved. The points of most commercials are to deliver the message in a way that will be remembered the next time the viewer is shopping, and to repeat the name of the product or service throughout the commercial, to make sure it is remembered.

In a TV commercial, you have 30 to 60 seconds to make the sale. Start selling in the beginning and never stop is the advice most experts suggest. Remember the average consumer sees thousands of TV spots in a year. A commercial like all others is apt to be unnoticed. A good TV copywriter will look for the different approach that will make your commercial stick in the viewer's mind and cause constant recall. A good commercial will increase the consumer's interest in buying your product.

We would be remiss if we didn't now turn our attention to cable television. Cable television was initially developed in the 1940s to provide television in communities where terrain or distance prevented television reception. Antennas were placed in areas having good reception to pick up broadcast signals and distribute them by cable, for a fee, to subscribers. The multiple channel capacity of cable television systems make many services available. Most systems offer 12 or more channels of programming. Some dual channel systems are technically capable of offering as many as 72 channels. Future plans envision systems with over 100 channels.

Many systems provide specialized channels for movies, sports, entertainment features, wire service news, weather, stock market reports, FM radio and children's programs. Recently, cable subscribers received the first televised gavel-to-gavel coverage of U.S. House of Representatives proceedings. The increased use of TV satellites by television stations and other program suppliers has led to the rapid development of subscriber pay cable services.

Two-way communication services, many of which are now technically feasible, allow subscribers to shop, order facsimile newspapers, conduct banking transactions from home, or receive security alarm and utility meter-reading services. Many systems also originate their own programs and/or provide access channels for use by educational or local government entities or for leased purposes.

Cable television advertising has experienced steady growth over the past three decades. In 1950 cable systems were serving some 14,000 television subscribers in only 70 communities. By the end of 1979, more than 14 million television subscribers in almost 10,000 communities were enjoying its benefits. Pay cable services were provided to 2.1 million subscribers by 900 cable systems in more than 3,000 communities. Pennsylvania has the most cable systems, and California has the most subscribers.

Although most cable systems began in small communities, the systems spread to communities large and small. Of all homes passed by cable systems in January 1979, 54% subscribed. Operating revenues totaled more than $1.5 billion. Pay cable revenues yielded

$192 million, or 13% of the total. Average monthly subscribers rates for basic service was $7.03. For pay cable service the rate averaged $8.60.

Ogilvy & Mather makes the following estimates for the future of cable TV:

Year	Number of Homes Passed by Cable TV	Number of Subscribers
1982	43,700,000	23,600,000
1983	49,400,000	27,900,000
1984	55,300,000	32,800,000
1985	60,700,000	37,400,000
1986	64,500,000	41,600,000
1987	67,500,000	45,600,000
1988	69,800,000	49,500,000
1989	72,100,000	53,200,000
1990	74,500,000	56,800,000

As you can well imagine, advertising is a growing part of the cable industry. The greatest changes in the coming decade will be the tremendous new revenue source coming from advertising. Cable has the advantages of television in providing sight, sound and motion to mass audiences. Cable is like radio, though, with a multitude of channels to make the medium cost effective.

At the end of the 1970s, American business had spent more than $50 billion to direct its messages to the public through advertising. The middle 1980s should see advertising expenditures rise to $75 billion, according to knowledgeable analysts. Currently in its infancy, cable receives a very small part of the overall advertising budget of the nation's advertisers. Total cable industry advertising revenues registered $35 million in 1980, up from $2.5 million in 1977. In contrast, the newspaper industry registered advertising revenues of $14.6 billion in 1979, television $10.2 billion, radio $3.4 billion and magazines, $2.9 billion.

The list of many large national advertisers utilizing cable is impressive. The target for future local cable advertising sales will be local business, top local advertisers, and local businesses with cooperative funds available from national manufacturers. Other prospects include purely local businesses now using radio and newspaper.

Many cable systems hire radio sales executives to sell for them. These individuals take a rate card based on radio prices and inform their clients that they are getting radio combined with television for the price of radio commercials alone.

One striking fact about cable advertising: the experimentation going on. As operators and advertisers test various approaches, national advertisers reach cable viewers through the satellite-distributed programming services.

A Bristol-Myers spokesman explained his company's reason for investing $25 million over 10 years on cable News Network advertising. A 30-second commercial broadcast once a week for a year on a major network would cost $3 million, or about $57,000 per showing. On the cable News Network, the client gets a 30-second commercial 40 times a week, which figures to approximately $1,400 per showing.

National advertising is sold on cable programming networks and delivered by satellite to systems by Block Entertainment Television, C.N.N., Cinema Satellite Network, C.B.S. cable, E.S.P.N., Las Vegas Entertainment Network, Modern Satellite Network, Satellite Program Network, V.P.I. Newstime, U.S.A. Network, Video Sports Network and W.T.B.S., channel 17. In some parts of the nation, cable systems are working together to sell regional advertising.

One of the largest independent cable systems is Gill Cable in San José. With 80,000 subscribers, Gill offers three program channels devoted to national, regional and local sports on one channel, movies on another, and Cable News Network (C.N.N.) on the third, to 300,000 subscribers of 60 other cable systems in the San Francisco Bay area. Gill handles the advertising, sales and service for the Interconnected Network, offering advertisers a large audience reach.

Then there's local level advertising. Many systems provide some coverage of local events. They are selling announcements and sponsorships of these programs to local businesses. Other cable operators offer varying blocks of time from two to 30 minutes, to advertisers who demonstrate products, a concept sometimes called informercials. System operators are starting to designate channels or programs for cable catalogs, where retailers show products and consumers order by phone.

Broadcasting magazine predicts cable television advertising could grow into a robust medium. The most knowledgeable estimates, according to *Broadcasting*, are that cable advertising expenditures in 1980 of $35 million should rise to about $350 million by 1985. By conventional media standards, over $350 million dollars is less than a staggering amount.

The most loyal cable advocates concede cable will cause hardly a dent in radio-TV broadcast advertising revenues, even in the next decade. In California, Paul Kagan, a respected financial seer dealing with cable, pay and commercial television, feels commercial television is not threatened by the new technology, and the American home is not destined to be equipped with computer terminals providing informational services, even though many others predict these things.

He also says no communications medium has yet totally replaced a predecessor medium. Even the telegram continues to exist. Says Kagan, "I don't foresee anybody obsoleting anybody." To some extent they can change places with another medium, becoming more important than the other, which is exactly what happened with radio and television.

In 1979, after 30 years of cable penetration of markets to the point where 20% of all American homes subscribe to cable television, television stations are selling at record prices. The top television station in a major market today is valued in excess of $100 million dollars. Recently, the FCC issued results of an economic inquiry into what would happen to radio and TV revenues once cable came of age. They decided there wasn't anything to worry about. Commercial television audiences are not shrinking—even if the new technology is stealing some viewers—because the number of home television sets is constantly expanding.

What about pay television? Will people like watching television programs without commercials so much they will shun commercial stations? Mr. Kagan says no. He says nobody has ever said you shouldn't see television with commericals in it. People say there are too many commercials, but they don't say they never want to see a commercial. You can always have programming interrupted by commercials.

In any event, consumers could probably never afford (on a pay television basis) to underwrite the large amount of programming now made possible via advertising.

Chapter 16

INQUIRIES AND INQUIRY HANDLING

F EELINGS about inquiries, either pro or con, are inclined to be strong among members of the industrial advertising fraternity.

Few shades of gray are recognized or acknowledged. Inquiries are regarded as either black or white. There is virtually no middle ground. And there is remarkably little fence-straddling.

On the one hand, there's a large and highly vocal group that is unalterably of the opinion that inquiries are the most rapturously wonderful thing to come down the pike since the invention of the wheel, and they don't hesitate to say so.

When these advertising men receive their monthly quota of inquiries from one of the publications on their media schedule, they tend to exhibit what has been called the Inquiry Syndrome; they writhe rapidly in their chairs, wiggle their toes in their shoes—and sometimes without shoes—and otherwise make it obvious they are experiencing an ecstatic sensation beyond description. Furthermore, they feel what is apparently a deep moral obligation that approaches religious fervor to rise up on their hind legs and defend inquiries against all attackers—and attackers *do* exist.

Then, on the other hand, there's the opposite camp (the word "camp" is used here not as a measurement of in-ness or out-ness)—those who strongly espouse the opposing philosophy.

They are equally outspoken, of course, and never hesitate to blurt out to one and all that inquiries are nothing more than a major nuisance, that inquiries are actually of very little tangible value (if any, their tone of voice and curl of lip imply), and salespeople never follow up on them. So why bother?

As with most other questions, there is a certain amount of merit to both viewpoints.

And a fact of life that cannot be ignored, regardless of which group you gravitate toward, is that inquiries are like dandruff.

They are not going to just go away.

Despite personal feelings in the matter, irrespective of whether you are passionately fond of inquiries, detest the sight of the things, or are somewhere in the middle of that relatively small gray area where opinions shade off into a neutral tone that's neither black nor white, inquiries are going to be around for a long, long time. Longer than any of us, in fact.

Three perfectly logical explanations exist for the strong feelings about inquiries which pervade industrial advertising:

1. Ad people who cherish inquiries and watch them appear in increasing numbers are those who *know* what inquiries mean to them. They know how to produce inquiries, how to handle them, and how to get the most out of them. These industrial advertising practitioners can predict within a fraction of a percentage point just what incoming inquiries mean to their companies in terms of sales volume.

2. Advertising personnel who denigrate inquiries simply do not understand them. They do not realize that inquiries enable them to search out a market, determine the specific segments of a market wherein their product has the greatest potential, and, finally, determine the buying influences within that small part of the total market who are willing and eager to buy their products. Furthermore, these advertising personnel who customarily downgrade inquiries lack basic knowledge in handling them — and this includes establishment of a basic system, screening, tabulating, follow-up, and other facets of the function.

3. Those with no strong feelings on the subject tend to view inquiries as routine paperwork that gives them something to do—some paper to shuffle. These are the ineffectuals within the advertising community; for the most part they hold down a desk in backward companies that are not marketing oriented and hence place little importance on the advertising function because *it* is not understood. For this third type of advertising manager inquiries are about the only concrete, tangible thing that can be produced in the way of hard data to justify either his or her existence or that of advertising. As a consequence, he or she is more pro than con, although this is a sad justification for inquiries, the job, or for advertising itself.

However, when all is said and done, inquiries do present conclusive evidence that somebody out there read your advertisement. This is something positive in itself. And even more important, the ad motivated the reader to respond, to take the action you wanted. He or she contacted your company as your ad urged.

Typical Reader Action Audit of inquiries generated.

50 Million Inquiries Can't Be Wrong

Each year, *Industrial Marketing* reported, industrial advertisers generate more than 50,000,000 (that's 50 *million*) inquiries via the business press. *IM* said the figure was established by the prestigious Center For Marketing Communications.* The Center was the highly competent research arm of industrial advertisers.

A bit more about the former Center For Marketing Communications: Industrial advertisers who believed in advertising (they're the *leading* advertisers and the *leading* companies in their industries, for the most part) found they could increase advertising's effectiveness by using research done by CFMC. In one year, for example, the Center scheduled eight major studies:

1. Optimum distribution of the marketing dollar.
2. Characteristics of effective industrial catalogs.
3. How to develop marketing information on limited budgets.
4. Better use of publication reader service information.
5. Measuring effectiveness of industrial direct mail.
6. Merchandising advertising.
7. Standard functional classifications for industry.
8. Role of communications in introduction of new products.

ARF's address:

Advertising Research Foundation
3 E. 54th Street
New York, N.Y. 10022

Research made prior to writing this chapter put the author in touch with agencies and advertisers in Chicago, New York, Philadelphia, Los Angeles, and elsewhere, as well as with major business publishers throughout the country. The figure that recurred time and time again in correspondence and over the telephone is 70 million—sometimes as high as 75 million. It's a figure that is virtually impossible to establish with any assurance of being absolutely right, of course, or of being within plus or minus 10 percent.

Shown nearby is a miniature marked copy of *Product Design & Development* showing a typical spread with the number of inquiries generated by both editorial matter and advertisements. This is called a Reader Action Audit.

The new-product tabloid, published by Chilton Company, is strictly a new-product publication; it has a controlled circulation of 125,000 and is sent primarily to executives and engineers responsible for the design and modification of durable goods in 20 SIC groups.

*Absorbed in 1977 into the Advertising Research Foundation.

Where Inquiries Come From

A massive survey was performed by *Product Design & Development*. In the tabulation of results are listed 250 industrial companies in various industries throughout the United States, complete with the number of inquiries each company receives from all sources. Given is the source of inquiries for each firm, as well as a number of other facts relating to inquiries. This study is, perhaps, the most definitive of its type made to date.

According to *PD&D*, the source of inquiries of these 250 companies, in percentages, breaks down as follows:

Advertising	43.5%
Editorial mentions (publicity)	21.1
Normal operations	19.3
Direct mail	12.6
Other	3.5

Percentages will vary, of course, depending upon the companies surveyed; factors that affect the percentages would include company size, pattern of distribution, size of sales staff, communications objectives, and many others—in addition to a vast difference in products.

The percentage of inquiries also varies tremendously according to the type of advertisements that are run. Ads designed deliberately to pull inquiries usually succeed in producing them in quantity if they're created by knowledgeable advertising personnel.

For example, you can run a coupon in your ad and increase the amount of response by 300 percent. The coupon waves a flag in the reader's face and practically shouts the fact that the advertiser wants response, that the advertiser will do something for him or her—send literature, send a sales rep, analyze the reader's plant's requirements for a certain widget, or whatever is offered in the ad.

ITT Semiconductors, Division of International Telephone & Telegraph Corporation, ran a three-color ad in *Electronics* magazine that is a real reader stopper. It is illustrated nearby.

Red and blue reproduce the familiar air mail symbol in three languages and immediately impress upon the reader the fact that this is no ordinary advertisement. ITT Semiconductors is obviously talking about an urgent matter.

Copy is anything but heavy-handed, and is certainly straight to the point. It shows an excellent knowledge of problems electronics manufacturers encounter, and an equally fine knowledge of human nature and how people react. Copy is printed in black.

"AIR MAIL" is overlined in red and underlined in blue to carry out the theme and to induce the reader to respond right now, without wasting another minute—even before he or she finishes reading the article in which he may have been engaged.

ITT Semiconductors used good judgment in having the coupon large enough to write upon; although all coupons inform readers a response is wanted, they are irked by little coupons on which they cannot write a short name such as Vincent J. Gruzczyznski, and a short title like Assistant Chief Engineer, Electronic Components—and still have room to get the firm, city, address, state and zip code in. Make it easy for a prospect to inquire and your inquiry rate will go up.

This advertisement doesn't make a plea for inquiries just for the sake of receiving inquiries, you'll note. It tells the reader to attach blueprints so that ITT Semiconductors can demonstrate how its products qualify for a place in *his or her* products. This makes it very obvious this ad is not directed at the literature collectors and the idly curious, but to bona fide prospective customers.

A.W. Cameron, ITT Semiconductors' advertising manager, reported receiving 203 inquiries from the specific issue of *Electronics* from which this ad was clipped. For competitive reasons the conversion rate is not available, but from the slant of the ad and the proposition offered to the reader, chances are more than good that a sizable percentage of those 203 inquirers became new customers of ITT Semiconductors.

This is an excellent example of using advertising and the inquiries it generates to flush out new prospects.

Just the opposite of ITT's fine advertisement, which was designed solely to produce inquiries, is Microdot's long-copy ad from its great "Connector Thing" campaign. Shown is another of these great ads that consistently pull inquiries by the hundred—even by the thousand —month after month after month. Readership of these ads is fantastically high and response, in terms of inquiries, is an ad manager's dream, according to Leon Levitt, manager of advertising and public relations at Microdot.

And the zany replies from nonzany buying influences flooded Microdot with quality inquiries that meant sales. No coupon, a kooky kind of offer, a light touch that entertains as it informs—that's Microdot's formula. It works for Microdot, but it certainly is not for everybody. There's a time and a place for the light touch, just as there's a time and a place for the straightforward, no-nonsense appeal for reader action. Both work.

Companies with an annual sales volume under $1 million and those with sales over $20 million tend to generate a higher percentage of inquiries from space advertising than do companies between these two sales ranges. But when the annual sales climb up around the $100 million volume, many industrial companies put more money and more effort into publicity as a percentage of the total promotional budget than do their smaller competitors.

Top company on the inquiry tally in *Product Design & Development's* study was Aluminum Company of America with an average of 12,000 inquiries per month. Second highest was Indiana General Corporation, manufacturer of magnets and magnetic equipment, with 3,500 inquiries coming in every 30 days.

Low in the survey was Rotary Seal Division, Muskegon Piston Ring Company, maker of mechanical face-type seals for rotating shafts, which receives 35 inquiries per month.

Most industrial companies surveyed by the magazine receive between 250 and 300 inquiries per month as a result of *all* activities, including normal operations.

Of the companies in *PD&D's* study, 9.3 percent received from 0 to 50 inquiries a month, and 2.8 percent tallied up an inflow of more than 2,000 per month. The other 87.9 percent of the companies are somewhere in between these two extremes.

Incidentally, in *PD&D's* survey "other" includes miscellaneous promotional activities such as press conferences, trade shows, 100th anniversary celebrations, and similar cats and dogs.

The overwhelming percentage of incoming inquiries received in the typical industrial advertising department come in as a result of readers having returned a "bingo card"—otherwise known as a Reader Service Card, Reader Inquiry Card, Business Reply Card, or some other such name. Almost all business publications include one of these postage-paid cards with numbers keyed to advertisements, editorial matter, or publicity.

Shown are bingo cards from *Research/Development, Iron Age, Production,* and *Product Design & Development.* All have certain features in common; numbers referring back to products about which the reader has read, blanks to solicit information about inquirers, an offer to send a qualification form to the inquirer so he or she can receive the magazine—if qualified under the requirements of the magazine's circulation policy—and so on.

By checking numbers on the incoming inquiries from the publications the advertiser can easily determine whether the inquiry is the result of the reader's responding to a space advertisement, or to editorial matter or publicity.

For the most part, industrial advertisers receive more than 90 percent of all of their inquiries on bingo cards—the ones that come through business publications, that is. Business publications do generate letterhead inquiries and telephone inquiries with both space advertising and editorial—and publicity, too, for that matter—to make up

THE connector THING

A periodical periodical designed to further the sales of Microdot Inc. connectors and cables. Published entirely in the interest of profit.

Everybody wins! Play Microdots Historical Spaghetti Grams

In the words of Virginia Woolf, it's time for fun and games.

For this new national pastime, you simply need a smattering of history, mythology and current events. And some information about Microdot's cable products. We'll supply you with the latter. For the rest, go listen to Walter Cronkite.

We got started on this activity while we were sitting around one evening with a bottle of Slivovitz (we ran out of Scotch), trying to think of memorable ways to remind you of the various unique features of Microdot cables. Like—

Like our Mini-Noise cable – reduces noise voltage from shock and vibration by a factor of more than 100 to 1 compared to untreated cable. This makes possible the transmission of extremely faint signals through coax cable without audio frequency noise. Off-the-shelf.

Like our microminiature coax cable – uses a fine silver-plated copper steel-covered wire. You get 50 ohm impedance, and even with the addition of dielectric, outer shield and protective jacket, the nominal O.D. does not exceed .080". And we can get that O.D. down to .025" in a range of hundreds of different cables.

Like our new complete in-house capability to produce precision quality multiconductor cables, which includes twisting, extruding, shielding and jacketing – the whole deal. All under one roof. And we can cable hundreds of conductors into one unit.

Like we're the only one to produce a high temperature, low weight, low capacitance coax cable through the use of a cellular Teflon dielectric. Especially suited to the requirements of video tape recorders.

Like Microdot's Twinaxial cable – to be used when you need to send two signals from a single source which must both terminate at the same point. No need to use two coax cables; therefore lower cost and greater flexibility.

Now when you think of cables, you think of cablegrams. And when you drink a lot of Slivovitz, it sort of takes you back through time and you come up with stuff like this:

WIN YOUR OWN CABLE FORK

Low noise Spaghetti-Gram:
"You lose. Signed, Calvin Coolidge."

High temperature Spaghetti-Gram:
"Julius, honey, ain't nobody home tonight but me. Signed, Cleopatra."

Miniature size Spaghetti-Gram:
"Cancel that order for bras. Signed, Twiggy."

Dual shield Spaghetti-Gram:
"I can lick any guy in the joint. Signed, Brunhilde."

Large size multiconductor Spaghetti-Gram:
"Send more elephants. Signed, Hannibal."

Get the idea. You can use any of the features of any of our cable products, such as low noise (Mini-Noise), special requirements (Multiconductors), high temperature, low weight, and, of course, small size. You don't really need the Slivovitz. It works well even with Sanka.

About the fork

No, Melvin, we won't explain the relationship between cable and spaghetti. We call it a cable fork, and if you don't want to use it for eating cables that's your problem. The manufacturer describes this handy gadget as a "revolutionary breakthrough that leaps forward from antiquated hand labor to the modern machine age!" We won't try to top that. We'll just explain that you stick it into the pasta and then turn the little handle to save getting spaghetti all over your celluloid collar.

Want one for your very own? Okay. Just send us a Microdot Spaghetti-Gram scribbled on company stationery and taking off from any of the product features we've discussed. We'll send you a beautiful cable fork along with more literature on our cable products than we care to mention.

But hurry. We've already run out of Slivovitz. It won't be long before we run out of cable forks. (That means offer is limited.)

MICRODOT INC. 220 Pasadena Avenue South Pasadena, Calif. 91030.

Mini-Noise is a registered trade-mark of Microdot Inc. Cable Fork is open to question.

the balance.

On the surface all such inquiries might seem to be of the same approximate quality, although publications go to some lengths to enable an advertiser to determine to some extent how hot inquiries are—and to give the ad manager some means of measuring their value.

For example, *Product Design & Development* asks for the telephone number and extension number of the inquirer on its bingo card. Now, it certainly stands to reason that if a person is merely a literature collector, or is idly curious about a product read about in PD&D, he or she probably will omit the telephone number because it will encourage a salesperson to contact him or her.

Yet, more than 80 percent of all inquirers who return bingo cards to *Product Design & Development do* give phone numbers and extensions. These busy people are also serious people.

Few industrial advertising managers depreciate bingo cards. The cards are truly ubiquitous today, and are used by almost every business publication of merit. Those books not willing to make the investment in handling the returned cards and those unwilling to pay the nominal price to index advertisements and key them for bingo card response don't use the cards. Such publications are almost always marginal and don't belong on your schedule anyway.

Another practice held in low esteem throughout the advertising community is that of printing page after page after page of "summaries" or brief product descriptions—even brief descriptions of *advertisements*—and calling this "editorial." Some publications do this and even have blanks inquirers may fill in with their names, firms, and so on; when these are mailed to the publications they are handled much like the conventional bingo cards.

Presenting the casual reader with page after page of such enticements to respond usually succeeds only in triggering response from pass-on readers and others too far down the pecking order to be classified as legitimate buying influences.

Good "Books" Do Generate Quality Inquiries

Nobody wants inquiries to result in sales any more than the publishers of quality business magazines. Many of them go to great lengths to help raise the level of inquiries, both in quality and in quantity. Frequently this involves considerable research and extra effort that is costly, but reputable publications are more than willing to make the effort.

A vast difference exists in the number of inquiries certain classes of products generate, of course. Capital equipment will, if other things are relatively equal, pull fewer inquiries than will component parts for OEM use. Unless it's new equipment and unless it's truly revolutionary—something like numerical control for machine tools when introduced several years ago—capital equipment won't pull as many inquiries for the simple reason fewer pieces of it are sold. And there are relatively fewer buying influences to respond to the ad.

Letterhead inquiries tend to increase in percentage as the volume of inquiries rises. For example, say a certain ad for a product produces 100 inquiries a month on the average. That ad will probably generate three or four letterhead inquiries each month, certainly not more unless it's an unusually strong ad, the selling proposition is outstanding, or the product is nothing less than sensational, fantastic, revolutionary, unbelievable, and terrific. Not too many products are all those.

But if an advertising campaign consistently generates, say, 500 inquiries a month, the volume of letterhead inquiries should be more than five times as high as that produced by a campaign that resulted in only 100 monthly inquiries. The percentage in the 500-per-month program might run from 5 up to 10 percent, or even more.

Letterhead inquiries are generally conceded to represent a greater sales potential and a higher caliber of inquirer because a letter requires more effort than does circling a number and tearing a card out of a magazine—if for no other reason.

Telephone Inquiries Grow

A third way that inquiries come in—and it's one that is growing faster than Topsy ever dreamed of—is the telephone. More and more advertisers are urging the reader to pick up the phone and call them in the advertisement's bid for action. This means of getting inquiries is proving productive beyond the wildest dreams of most industrial advertising managers. This, of course, is greatly due to the prevalence of 800 numbers and the fact that many firms now have WATS lines.

Telephone inquiries are usually not from the curious with nothing else to do at the moment, nor are they from minor draftsmen, literature collectors, or mail boys.

When Lindberg Hevi-Duty started listing telephone numbers and the names of the company's product people in its advertisements some years ago, the response was little short of amazing. Since doing this, hundreds of thousands of dollars in sales have resulted from advertisements that asked the reader to phone—because readers responded just that way. They called, gave the listener their problem, and usually had a salesperson on the way to their office to discuss the matter further within hours. This method of generating inquiries works, and it delivers high quality sales leads.

One thing that should be done when a telephone inquiry comes in is to make sure—always make sure—to find out where the caller saw the product advertised. Get the name of the publication. This information is vitally important when it comes time to evaluate media and determine the effectiveness of the advertising program as a whole. Most of your product managers and marketing people will keep a simple tally for you if you explain why it is so necessary. Giving them a simple mimeographed form to use helps get the information for you.

Another way of keeping a record is to list a fictitious name, or one that's semifictitious. You can, for instance, make sure that product manager Steve Salisbury gets all incoming inquiries for a new automatic widget he's responsible for. His correct name, Steve Salisbury, can be listed in Magazine A; however, in Magazine B he could be John Salisbury; in Magazine C, Ralph Salisbury, and so on. This always works out very well because all Mr. Salisbury has to do is just what comes naturally for most of us—when answering the phone, say "Salisbury," or "Salisbury speaking."

This shows the inquirer is talking with the right man, the one the advertisement asked the reader to call. This puts the burden on Mr. Salisbury only to keep a tally of all the Steves, Johns, Ralphs, Georges and what have you; there's no need for him to cross-reference to a magazine. That job can be done in the advertising department when he reports monthly that Steve Salisbury received 17 phone calls, George got 9, Ralph had 23, and so on. The system is simple to put into effect and easy to keep going. You have only to supply the company's Steve Salisbury with each of their "names" and a simple form.

The switchboard operator has to be instructed to ask for him by name, however, or to keep a tally herself. This is done in most companies by asking the caller, "Which Mr. Salisbury did you want, sir?" The inquirer assumes several brothers or several people work for the company with the same surname—a frequent occurrence.

Ways to Increase Inquiry Volume

The following subjects have been touched upon briefly elsewhere, or will be, but it's desirable to summarize them very briefly so these factors that exert such an influence on the volume of inquiries will be at your fingertips.

Four-color ads achieve something better than a 50 percent increase in readership and they consistently produce at least 50 percent more inquiries than do black-and-white.

Make an offer to the reader, use the word "free"—and bump it up in size so it's really prominent—and your ad will produce approximately four times as many inquiries as it would have without the offer and use of the magic word. Naturally, you can't offer free milling machines and stay in business very long, but you *can* offer a free piece of literature on milling machines, or an analysis of how your new machine could up production and cut costs on the reader's production floor.

Use a coupon in your ad, and preferably more than a little token coupon so there's room for the reader to write, and you'll increase your inquiry volume by more than 300 percent.

Increase the size of your advertisements and the amount of inquiries goes up to direct proportion, although not in the same proportion. A one-page ad, for instance, will not produce twice as many inquiries as a one-half-page ad, nor will a spread produce twice as many inquiries as a one-page ad. Rather, when you double the size you can reasonably anticipate receiving about two-thirds more inquiries than the smaller ad has been pulling.

Try to get your advertisement in the front one-third of the publication and you'll have a slight edge and garner a few additional inquiries because of higher readership in the front of the book—although not nearly as much so now as a few years ago.

Run nothing except outstanding advertisements that rate near, or at, the top of the heap in the readership ratings, and that ad will produce more inquiries by far than an advertisement that wasn't as well read.

The trick, of course, is knowing how to produce a winner every time!

Issue Life and Inquiry Life

Daniel Starch has reported in *Media/scope* that roughly half of all inquiries produced by a monthly magazine that was studied were received during the first month after it was distributed, and that approximately the same percentage of inquiries was received from a weekly magazine during the first week of issue.

In McGraw-Hill's Laboratory of Advertising Performance, the Columbia Ribbon and Carbon Manufacturing Company, Inc., reports running a campaign consisting of 14 one-third and two-thirds page advertisements in one calendar year in *Business Week* magazine.

Inquiries came in for an average of 7.6 months after the issue of *Business Week* was mailed to subscribers. All advertisements were couponed and key addressed so the company was able to make a thorough study of each ad and each publication in which it appeared.

Longest life of an issue was 19 months; inquiries were received that long after the magazine was mailed; shortest life span was one and two-thirds months.

Interestingly, a further check on Columbia Ribbon and Carbon's inquiries showed that 69.7 percent were received from top management or purchasing titles. According to the manufacturer, almost half of the sales leads (48.4 percent) were classified as "excellent, good, or fair" in quality.

In the case of annual publications such as *Product Design & Development's Product Encyclopedia, Vacuum Technology Buyer's Guide, Thomas' Register, MacRae's Blue Book,* the Conover-Mast *Purchasing Directory,* and so on, inquiries come in over the transom for *years* after publication. Technical publications of this type are usually filed in the department that uses them, and/or in the purchasing department. Issue life is simply fantastic. Everybody has favorite stories of inquiries from old, old directories.

Tally Incoming Inquiries

The first thing to do when inquiries come to your company from business publications is to make certain the mail room realizes their importance and doesn't delay delivery to the advertising department.

Inform the head mail room person that inquiries are *not* third class mail, that they are *not* to be delivered when the mail boy doesn't have anything else to do, that is if your company customarily divides mail deliveries by class of mail—or by appearance, in some instances.

Then, when the inquiries are received in the advertising department, they should be tallied up immediately. You'll probably find it easiest and most convenient to keep a record of all incoming inquiries by publication; naturally, a master record kept by your secretary will reflect the source of inquiries. You may, however, want to keep a record yourself that contains other information—information to which you refer frequently.

A form that worked well for clients of O'Grady-Anderson-Gray, Inc., advertising agency in Park Ridge, Illinois, was given to the author by old friend Bill Cason, president of the agency. It's simple enough that it can be produced in the company printing department, or on the office multilith machine. Have it set up so spaces are correct for the typewriter in case you decide to have your secretary handle it, and also so there is adequate room to contain figures that don't necessitate use of a microscope to decipher.

You'll undoubtedly want to keep a record of product model number and so on that drew the inquiries, although the ad number and key number from the publication would provide that information with cross referencing.

Depending upon your method of distribution, you likely will find it advisable to show on your running record the geographical area or sales territory which produced the inquiry, as well as the territory that is tops in inquiry activity, and to which dealers or distributors the inquiries were referred.

Some advertising managers find this information extremely helpful to have available at a glance when they're planning media schedules, particularly when reviewing regional publications.

A separate tally, similar to the one for your ad inquiries, should be kept for inquiries produced by publicity. Break this tally down by

MAGAZINE INQUIRY REPORT

PUBLICATION	PRODUCT	TOTAL INQUIRIES	RUNNING TOTAL

book, month, and key number, also, as well as by product and model.

Incidentally, *Product Design & Development's* study of 250 industrial advertisers shows these firms keep a record of inquiries by source for the following reasons:

Media evaluation	74.6%
Advertising response	27.2%
Cost analysis	26.2%
Product interest	16.2%
Salesperson follow-up	3.5%

This totals more than 100 percent because many companies give more than one reason for breaking out inquiry sources.

Ideally, when tallying inquiries, the SIC of the inquirer's company should be entered on the tally form in a column provided for this purpose. This is a tremendous help when determining where new, untapped markets exist and identifying markets that offer the most potential. Too many industrial advertising managers neglect to do this. It is one of the most important breakdowns they can supply to management.

About as often as not letterhead inquiries mention the magazine in which the inquirer saw your advertisement. When this is done there's no problem in keeping the tally accurately. Roughly half of the time,

MAGNITUDE _____ MONTH, YEAR _____ AD NO. _____

AD HEADLINE _____ AD KEY NO. _____ AD SIZE _____

LITERATURE SENT _____ PRODUCT _____

DATE	1	2	3	4	5	6	7	8	9	10	11	12	13	14	15	16	17	18	19	20	21	22	23	24	25	26	27	28	29	30	31	TOTAL	RUNNING TOTAL
JAN.																																	
FEB.																																	
MAR.																																	
APR.																																	
MAY																																	
JUNE																																	
JULY																																	
AUG.																																	
SEPT.																																	
OCT.																																	
NOV.																																	
DEC.																																	

DEALER FEEDBACK	JAN.	FEB.	MAR.	APR.	MAY	JUNE	JULY	AUG.	SEPT.	OCT.	NOV.	DEC.	TOTAL	RUNNING TOTAL
SALES														
DEMONSTRATIONS														
FUTURE PROSPECT														
NIXIES														

however, the inquirer will merely say he or she has seen your widget advertised, would like more information on it, and to please send a piece of literature posthaste.

Such an inquiry is potentially just as valuable as if the inquiry had mentioned the name of the book a dozen times—and you'll want to handle it just as quickly. Simply maintain a record of unidentified inquiries, so headed, and you'll find this presents no problem.

Efficient publishers clip either a tear sheet of the ad, publicity article, or what have you, directly to the inquiries. It's good policy, it makes a favorable impression for the book (which the publisher is trying to sell) and it helps you.

Maintain Your Own Cross Index

In addition, you should have a department clerk go through each publication when the advertising department copy arrives; the clerk should cross-index every reference to your company—in advertisements, editorial, publicity. It's also a good policy to do this for major competitors also, then, when the vice-president of marketing calls you unexpectedly and asks you if you know anything about such and such in some magazine or other, you can pat yourself on the back—you know all about it. And without a lengthy search, either. That really gives the impression of a well-organized department.

You'll want to key all of your advertisements so the name of the magazine, month of publication, and the ad number can be determined by checking the key number that appears on bingo card returns.

And there's the old dodge of using a variation of the firm's street address. Suppose, for instance your company is located at 4401 West Industrial Street. By varying the address—4400, 4402, 4430, 4440, 4460, and so on and on—it's very easy to determine the publication involved, the subject of a news release, the product discussed in an advertisement, a specific trade show, or even the company from which a questionnaire is being returned. Your local post office will cooperate and have all mail routed directly to your company despite any minor differences in the address; a couple of theater tickets a couple of times a year, or some similar small but welcome gift, will help.

Data you compile about inquiries concern not only the advertising department, but are an invaluable source of marketing information for the sales department, production, marketing, and others, including top management. They reflect very accurately the amount of interest that exists in various products or product lines; they enable management either to put a push behind products that have either slipped, or haven't caught on, or to make a reasoned, well-informed judgment as to the advisability of withdrawing them from the market.

One last thing on which a record should be kept, and most industrial advertising managers need no urging about this, is known conversions to sales. A compilation of all of the sales traced directly to inquiries, complete with dollar amounts, sales territories, names of district managers, and similar helpful information will make a hero of you when you submit the memo to management. This should be done on a fixed schedule. It shows that all of that money spent on advertising is not wasted, and it shows good management of the advertising department. And it shows that sales are the most important thing to you, just as they are to the sales department.

Handling Inquiries

Handling of inquiries by industrial advertisers ranges from very simple systems to some that are almost incredibly complex.

There's usually a reason for the existence of a system, any system, or at least a rationale of why the system that's used is used; how it evolved from the one that formerly was used. This isn't double talk, for most industrial advertisers have found inquiry handling is a far more complicated subject than it appears to be on the surface, and methods of handling inquiries have undergone a metamorphosis.

Let's back up for a minute and see just what we're talking about. *Product Design & Development's* survey of inquiry-handling systems, the definitive one on the subject, lists the following percentages of companies as receiving this quantity of inquiries; quantities given are undoubtedly projectable across industry as a whole, with the possible exception of companies manufacturing capital equipment—and even they probably fall pretty much in line with these findings:

Question: What is the number of inquiries received each month from all sources?:

Quantity	Percent of companies receiving this quantity
0 to 50	9.3%
51 to 100	15.3
101 to 250	21.4
251 to 500	28.4
501 to 1,000	16.3
1,001 to 2,000	6.5
Over 2,000	2.8

So more companies receive between 251 and 500 inquiries per month than any other quantity, although one company in six receives between 500 and 1,000. Handling this much paperwork poses a problem in itself.

But handled they must be, and the sooner the better. Never for an instant lose sight of the fact that when you receive an inquiry from a prospective customer via the bingo card route—or even a letterhead inquiry—*the chances are your competitors also received an inquiry from the same individual.*

That's right—your competitors also received that selfsame inquiry from that same person.

Too many industrial advertising managers fall into the self-oriented trap and regard inquiries as something uniquely *theirs*, that *their* advertisements and *their* publicity shook those prospects out of the bushes for the sole use of *their* company.

At the risk of sounding iconoclastic, there's comment that has to be made:

'Tisn't so.

More than 64 percent of inquirers who circle your number on a bingo card also circle one or more numbers belonging to your competitors. If not in the same magazine, then in one that competes with it. These inquirers ask your competitors about a product directly competitive with your beloved widget. Horrible, isn't it?

Don't let this dash cold water on your enthusiasm for your advertising program and for advertising *per se*, however. It's very likely that your ad *did* shake the prospects out of the bushes, that it *did* convince them your product would likely solve their problems, and that they honestly *are* interested in more information about it.

What your advertisement also did, though, was to wake up the prospect to the fact that other manufacturers produce competing widgets. And because industry usually does not leap to have purchasing agents write purchase orders without an information-gathering period, followed by one of evaluation of all available products, doesn't necessarily mean your advertisement hasn't accomplished anything except to alert your competitors to the fact that here's a bona fide, live prospect.

In all probability your ad triggered the response from the inquirer— and as a result your company has the inside track when a sales rep gets down to brass tacks and asks for the order after a presentation or proposal.

Fine and dandy as this is, it shines a bright light on a situation many industrial advertisers ignore. This is that inquiries are woefully mishandled.

Inquiries *are* woefully mishandled.

But isn't this paradoxical, for isn't advertising created, produced, and placed in the best media to do just two things: (1) Inform prospective customers about your product, and (2) induce them to respond to the advertisement as you want them to?

Isn't it?

Yet industry as a whole fails miserably to take the first step to make contact with a prospective customer after he or she has taken that first step to contact the seller.

This failure, incredible as it is, can be laid right at the doorstep of either naive' marketing management or an inept advertising manager.

When I was advertising manager of a large truck manufacturer, an unexplained mystery was the fact that no inquiries came in. I found that all inquiries from advertising and publicity were routinely sent to the sales engineering department. The engineers didn't know what to do with the inquiries, so they threw them away. *They threw them away!* To the engineers' pleasure, I took inquiries henceforth—then sent literature and a salesperson.

Time Is of the Essence

Promptness is vitally necessary because the inquirer's inquiry has already been in the pipeline for anywhere from a few days to several weeks; most progressive business publications forward all inquiries to advertisers once a month as a rule, although some forward several times a month if the volume warrants it.

You can assume the average length of time that elapses between the reader's filling out and mailing the bingo card and the receipt of literature about the product he's interested in is four weeks. Add to this any delay in the advertising department and you can see how even a hot prospect has plenty of time to cool down—or to be sold by a competitive salesperson!

In its survey *Product Design & Development* also asked the average time between receiving and handling inquiries. Results are:

Average time	*Percentage of companies*
1 day	9.0%
2 to 4 days	32.1
5 to 7 days	39.5
8 to 14 days	16.5
Over 14 days	2.9

Despite the majority of companies' handling inquiries in five to seven days, this is very casual treatment indeed of a potentially large volume of "extra" sales. Unless some kind of emergency exists within the advertising department—illness, an unusually heavy volume of work due to a major trade show, being in the throes of new-campaign planning—every incoming inquiry should be transformed into an outgoing reply, complete with literature, within 48 hours. And this doesn't mean 48 working hours in the office—it means two working days.

If the advertising department cannot handle what is bound to be a normal work load and get the inquiries handled in this length of time, it is understaffed and a request should go in immediately for an extra person—or two—to bring personnel strength up to an adequate level. Ignore the problem and you'll always find yourself in a bind.

As a rule, if the inquiry level is less than 1,000 a month one clerk can easily handle this load. This would include all internal paperwork in connection with the inquiries except screening; this should be done by either the advertising manager or the assistant. The function is far too important to delegate to subordinate personnel.

Product Design & Development explored this facet of inquiry handling in its survey. Answers to the question, "How many people are required to handle your inquiry system?" showed the following:

People required	*Percentages*
Less than 1	5.6%
1 to 2	43.6
2 to 3	31.6
3 to 4	12.0
4 to 5	5.1
5 or more	2.1

Interesting thing here is that most companies say it takes from one to two people to handle their inquiries, and the biggest percentage of companies surveyed by *PD&D* receive between 251 and 500 inquiries per month. This shows either poor systems or lack of organization.

Incidentally, *Product Design & Development* also asked whether an outside firm was used to handle inquiries. It develops that 13.6 percent of the surveyed companies do use an outside firm, whereas 86.4 percent do the work internally. This reflects the fact that it's the consensus of most advertising personnel that handling inquiries is a function that belongs inside the company where it can be controlled better and supervised more closely.

Another way a high percentage of industrial firms misuse inquiries is to handle them well and reasonably promptly, then mail the reply by third-class mail. With the postal situation as deplorable as it now is—and with no improvement in sight—answering an inquiry by third-class mail is tantamount to presenting your competition with first crack at an eager group of prospects.

First-class mail and airmail are slow enough; but if the material you send in response to inquiries is sent either of these ways you're fairly sure it will be delivered anywhere in the country in five or six business days.

On the other hand, third-class mail can easily consume 10 days or two weeks once the material leaves your office. Post office policy seems to be to handle third-class mail when there's spare time, when the mood strikes the workers, or when enough mail users complain loudly.

Using first-class mail increases costs, but postage seldom accounts for more than 15 or 20 percent of the total cost of handling inquiries—if that much. Skimping on postage can easily result in loss of an incalculable sum in sales. It isn't worth it. Use first class or airmail.

Physical Method of Handling

Long gone are the days when a business person expected a reply written with a quill pen, or, for that matter, even an individually-typed reply.

With the paperwork load getting heavier in the business community every year, almost everybody in industry is accustomed to forms of one type or another. We've all been taught to cringe in mortal terror at the mere thought of stapling or mutilating an IBM card that sometimes accompanies business invoices—and even monthly bills received at home. Labor- and time-saving forms are an integral part of everyday life and are no longer regarded as slighting the person who receives one.

Advertising managers surveyed by *Product Design & Development* reflect this acceptance of the ubiquitous form. When they were asked, "What type of form is used in your inquiry handling system?" the following was disclosed:

Type of form used	*Percentage using it*
"Snap-out" form	31.7%
Personalized typed letter	26.1
Reply card or reply form	12.2
Printed form letter	11.7
Multicopy internal forms	9.1
No forms used	9.2

Amazing is the amount of personalized, typed letters; this requires a tremendous amount of time and the expense of typing a letter over and over again is unbelievable, what with clerical salaries higher today than secretarial salaries were a few short years ago.

Also nothing short of astounding is that a total of 18.3 percent of these industrial companies used either multicopy internal forms, or no forms at all. When the internal forms are used, the inquirer receives nothing in the mail except a piece of literature—no thank you for your interest, no nothing. Can't help but make a poor impression. The inquirer feels the company isn't interested in him or her.

However, 9.1 percent of these firms at least bucked the information about the inquirer on to their sales force with a copy of the internal form. But the 9.2 percent of those advertisers who used no forms apparently mailed literature and then dropped the matter right there with a dull thud.

And 3.9 percent of the surveyed firms did not report sending names of inquirers to their salespeople for followup. This is indeed difficult to understand. The reasoning there is too elusive to surmise. One thing it *does* prove is the day of miracles is not past—companies not seeking any additional sales are doing business today. Must be pretty soft.

The "snap-out" form used by more firms than any other surveyed by *PD&D* has come into its own in recent years. Use of this handy little form greatly simplifies handling of inquiries and facilitates prompt mailing of material to the inquiring party.

A typical snap-out form is that used by Lindberg Hevi-Duty; it is illustrated nearby.

Let's take a look at this form since it is typical of those used by many companies throughout industry.

On the top sheet is the company logo and address on the left side, with a place for the inquirer's name, title, company, address, city, state and zip code. Left half of this top sheet is detached and becomes a mailing label for the envelope of literature; it is gummed on its reverse side. This saves the clerk much time and additional typing.

The right half of the top sheet is filled in with the name of the publication from which the inquiry was received; it is clipped to the literature mailed to the inquirer. Note that on the bottom there is room for the numbers of the pieces of sales literature so there's a permanent record in the advertising department, and the salesperson receiving a copy of the form is also aware of what was sent.

Paper is thin, and a very thin carbon sheet is between each form.

The second sheet, the sales rep's copy, is rather a deep yellow. On it is a carbon of the inquirer's name, firm and so on; a record of what magazine produced the inquiry; what literature was sent; plus room for the sales rep's evaluation of the lead. Space is also provided for entering the date the individual was contacted, equipment needs, and whether he or she is a live one, somebody to see again in the future, or other—"other" is a polite way of saying literature collector.

Next in line is a pink copy with exactly the same information on it, but it's marked "follow-up copy." This is for the advertising manager's use as a tickler file to make sure sales reps are following the leads sent to them. The tickler file can be set up so that all inquiries

UARCO BUSINESS FORMS
CHICAGO

FROM:

LINDBERG HEVI·DUTY S‖B
DIVISION OF SOLA BASIC INDUSTRIES
2450 WEST HUBBARD STREET • CHICAGO, ILLINOIS 60612

DATE:
Dear Sir: Here is the information you requested concerning

As described in

For further information or to have your name added to our mailing list, please fill in and return the attached card. Our nearest sales office is listed below; they will be pleased to be of service to you.

We appreciate your interest.

TO .

LINDBERG HEVI·DUTY S‖B
DIVISION OF SOLA BASIC INDUSTRIES

LIT. SENT:

EVALUATION:_____Individual contacted:_____Date:_____

	Equipment Needs:	☐ Immediate	☐ Future	Other:_____
	Did contact result in:	☐ Quotation	☐ Sale	What type equipment?_____
	Is this a potential account?	☐ YES	☐ NO	

COMMENTS:_____

ADD TO MAILING LIST – CHECK AREAS OF INTEREST

		☐ Ovens
☐ Heat Treat Furnaces	☐ Pilot Plant Equipment	☐ Induction Heating Equipment
☐ Vacuum Furnaces	☐ Laboratory Equipment	☐ Gas Process Equipment
☐ Kilns	☐ Melting Furnaces	☐ Semiconductor Equipment

·SALESMAN'S COPY

not reported on will automatically come up; at this time they can be copied and the copy mailed to the salesperson with a handwritten note in red ink asking for a report. This can be set for every 30 days, 60 days, 90 days, or whatever length of time you feel is desirable.

Final copy, which is yellow, is the file copy; it stays in the advertising department. It, too, contains the same printed information and has space for inquiry evaluation to make tabulation every 90 days an easy matter.

Last form in Lindberg Hevi-Duty's snap-out form is a postage-paid reply card. Carbon on it is placed so that only the individual's name, firm, and address is typed when the departmental clerk handles the inquiry initially.

The inquirer is given a number of options, as you'll notice, including having his or her name added to the company's mailing list; stating interest in a particular type of equipment; asking for additional information about a specific product or product line; a quotation; or, praise be, asking for a representative to call. The card is addressed to the advertising department.

Return of the card from an inquirer automatically qualifies him or her as an honest-to-goodness live prospect, at least live enough to be called on. The field sales force is notified immediately as cards are received and requested to make an immediate call. These inquiries are treated like money in the bank!

In general, the letter method of handling inquiries is both more costly and less efficient. If your volume of inquiries is very low, perhaps it is adequate; however, when it rises to several hundred a month you'll be far ahead of the game to use snap-out forms.

Most business printers, such as Uarco Inc. and others can produce a snap-out form that will be exactly right for your needs. Cost is modest, and you'll be money ahead to purchase an estimated year's supply at one time. Cost per thousand comes down sharply when volume goes up, just as it does in all printed matter.

You can also buy "canned" snap-out forms—one basic design that many advertisers use and like—from Sales Essential Mfg. Co., 10555 Lunt Ave. Rosemont, IL 60018. This form contains carbon paper, of course, and the following:

1. Thank-you page to go to the inquirer.
2. Gummed label.
3. Sales rep's copy.
4. Sales department copy.
5. Follow-up copy.

Handling Inquiries Outside

For most industrial advertisers the physical handling of inquiries is not such a huge project that it constantly taxes the capacity of the advertising department's manpower. Most advertising managers get inquiries in and the appropriate material out to the inquirer without too much trouble. Seldom is more than one pint of blood lost in the daily process.

When inquiry volume consistently runs into the thousands every month, though, it is often considered advisable to have the routine work farmed out to a specialist—an organization that makes a living handling inquiries.

This is true especially when inquiries surge sharply up in volume, from a routine 500 a month to three, four, or even five thousand. As infrequently as this happens, it still occurs with *predictable* frequency —such as when a major push is put on a product, introduction of a new product line, or a major trade show coincides with another major promotion.

A solution that's proved right for many industrial advertisers is to retain a firm such as Sales Development Service, a division of Chilton Company.

Sales Development Service is dedicated to increasing marketing effectiveness through sales leads—and the proper handling of them. The company noted there is a dramatic rise in inquiry activity during the past few years; this obviously indicates that manufacturers place a growing importance on their use.

These sales leads—inquiries—quickly lose their value unless the follow-up on them is executed properly and promptly. This is where Sales Development Service comes in, for S.D.S. is organized to process all types of inquiries at a very economical rate—and usually in much less time than most manufacturers are now processing them. Sales Development Service has highly automated systems, in addition to data processing equipment for handling statistical information.

Using this efficient system, inquiries can be processed within 48 hours or less. In addition, tabulated reports of all inquiries by name, products, and source of inquiries will be available for the advertising manager each week.

This inquiry handling system is broken down into five main elements:

1. *Personal reply*. A personally addressed and typewritten letter is enclosed with the appropriate literature forwarded to the inquirer.
2. *Complete listing*. A listing of all inquiries received during the current period sorted by your sales territory or territories. Three copies of this report will be submitted to you for sales follow-up. Carbon copies may be sent to field sales offices, distributors, or representatives if you wish.

3. *Tabulation by source.* A tabulation of inquiries broken down by source is provided. This report can be used as a measure of evaluating the inquiry pulling power of different media.
4. *State breakdown.* A tabulation of inquiries broken down by state is supplied; you can use it in evaluating your sales territory distribution.
5. *Tabulation by product.* A breakdown of inquiries by product category will help indicate your company's sales effectiveness for each different product line or individual product.

For complete information on Sales Development Service, write to:

Manager
Sales Development Service
Chilton Company
Radnor, Pennsylvania 19089
Telephone: (215) 748-2000

A similar inquiry handling service was offered by Hitchcock Publishing Company. Here's the way it worked:

The advertiser receives inquiries from the magazines in which he or she advertises as usual, and then forwards them to Hitchcock. Here they are turned over to specialists in inquiry handling to be keypunched.

Each advertiser using Hitchcock's inquiry handling service has supplied appropriate product literature, catalogs, envelope stuffers and so forth that are to be mailed to the inquirers. This material, along with a custom-printed inquiry form produced by Hitchcock's printer for each different advertiser, is inserted into the envelope and mailed.

The advertising manager receives a monthly tabulation of all inquiries handled, listed by publication that produced the inquiry, by issue of the publication, and a tally of total inquiries handled.

In addition, the advertiser is supplied with a list of names of the inquirers; these can be broken down in any desired manner for ease of handling internally—such as adding to a mailing list, or using in special promotions.

Average handling cost per inquiry at Hitchcock at that time was 59 cents. This included 22 cents postage, but did not include the cost of the envelope in which the material was mailed; most advertisers prefer to supply their own, although Hitchcock could have had them printed, of course.

Publishers themselves find inquiry handling is such a perplexing problem *they* farm the job out! If handling 500 inquiries a month seems like a chore, imagine the job that *Product Design & Development* has in handling 912,373 inquiries a year, plus more than 100,000 additional ones from the *PD&D Product Encyclopedia*!

Of course, Chilton is in the inquiry-handling business and is staffed and equipped and computerized to take this massive load in stride. Many smaller publishing houses, as well as many individual magazines, simply are not set up to cope with such a volume; and many have no desire to do so. After all, magazine publishers are publishers. Inquiry handling is one business, publishing is another.

Nielsen Clearing House, a Division of A.C. Nielsen Company, is the mecca many publishers with well-developed Reader Service systems turn to when they bog down in a sea of inquiries.

Established in 1962, Nielsen Inquiry Service (a part of Nielsen Clearing House) has refined the inquiry handling process down to a scientific system that's perfect to the last dotted "i." Today some 200 publishers and more than 300 leading business magazines have contracted for this efficient and cost-reducing service.

Thomas E. Fitzgerald, Director Marketing Services said: "Our system can prequalify the leads for the advertisers as well as provide the data needed to enable publishers to prove advertising in their publications is effective." For detailed information, contact Thomas E. Fitzgerald, 1900 North Third Street, Clinton, Iowa 52732; phone (319) 242-4505.

How It's Done at Westinghouse

Sales leads: Profits or problems? Let's hear from John L. DeFazio, marketing communications representative, Electronic Components and Specialty Products, Westinghouse Electric Corporation, whose major product is semiconductors.

Mr. DeFazio developed what is widely considered to be the most effective inquiry handling system in use in industry today. The following discussion of how inquiries are regarded and of his system of handling them at Westinghouse is based on a very enlightening phone conversation with Mr. DeFazio, and on remarks he made at the Scientific Apparatus Makers Association meeting in Miami. His help was graciously given and is gratefully acknowledged.

Inquiries developed by advertising, publicity, trade shows, and so forth mean many different things to different people and companies. They can, for instance, be the lifeblood of a selling program, a source of sales leads when the inquiries are properly screened, an aid to product literature distribution, a measure of advertising effectiveness—or merely a bothersome mishmash of slips of paper sent to the mailroom and then promptly forgotten.

There's another way to look at inquiries; they can be regarded as a vitally important pipeline in the flow of ideas, ideas that play an absolutely indispensable part in the sale and distribution of industrial products. From this viewpoint, inquiries form a circle.

The circle starts with readers—or inquirers—seeking information. They're asking for ideas and are using the established inquiry system to get them.

Funneled through publishers, readers' inquiries—requests for information—are distributed to the source of that information, the advertisers.

To complete the circle, the information then goes back to the reader who made the request.

Another significant meaning and interpretation can be made about inquiries. They are very likely the means by which the market is trying to talk to the manufacturer and the dealers. If only the manufacturer and dealer would listen, they would learn much about the changing needs and problems of the market. This would profit both of them.

The role of inquiries from the point of view of the industrial marketer is that communication from the marketplace via inquiries can be valuable in two entirely different ways. One is the provision of immediate or future sales leads. This is well known, though oftentimes neglected.

The other, less known, use of inquiries is as a tool for marketing intelligence. Looked at in this light, each inquirer is someone in the marketplace with a problem.

By accumulating records of these problems over time and judiciously interpreting the records, some advertisers have developed extremely worthwhile information about new markets, new product applications, and have been able to test advertising effectiveness.

Such intelligence has been used successfully to aid sales forecasts, production scheduling and to meet future market demands. Successful new products have been developed from this same information.

As academic as it is, perhaps it's worth stressing again that the keystone of modern marketing is to begin by the manufacturer's finding out what the customer—or prospect—needs to solve problems.

Once this is learned, the other elements of marketing fall naturally into place. A product is developed by the manufacturer to fill these needs. The characteristics of the product are communicated to the customer or prospect by the manufacturer through advertising, and a distribution system is set up to get the product into the hands of the prospect.

However, the complexities of the industrial marketplace are such that many roadblocks—marketing problems—retard the carrying out of this inherently simple process. Probably the most formidable is in the area of communications.

The worst and most serious marketing problem is communication from the customer to the manufacturer.

Because of this, it is safe to say that many manufacturers—most of them, probably—have a very faulty knowledge of what their potential customers need, or who and where these prospects are.

Developing this information is the responsibility of the manufacturer.

Here lie lost opportunities and the main source of the high cost of selling (and buying) industrial products.

And never forget for an instant that the success of a firm rests in the hands of the buyers of its products, its failure in the hands of the seller.

Anybody can produce standard price-book widgets. Having enough marketing savvy to determine what the marketplace wants, and then producing *that* and selling it at a profit requires a mind that exists in the twentieth century. This is where the Neanderthal managements succeed in looking incredibly inept.

Advertising as an Investment

Westinghouse has developed a system that closes the information gap involving inquiries between the company and its potentially interested customer-prospects. The system enables Westinghouse to retrieve vital marketing information from "hidden" data in the inquiries it receives.

According to Mr. DeFazio, *it is essential that industry accept the fact that advertising is an investment, not an overhead.*

Few thing are as difficult to accomplish, however, as determining just what you receive in results from the money invested in advertising and communications. Yet it is vital that precise results from the communications program be documented, because advertising has become one of the biggest—if not *the* biggest—of the controllable expenditures in the corporate budget.

Advertising *is* an investment; *apply* advertising and communications as an investment; *prove* it as a return on investment. Live with this principle and you'll find your entire program more meaningful.

Communications may be taken for granted, but a prospect cannot become a customer for a product he or she does not know exists. By the same token, a prospect cannot become a customer until he has sufficient information about a product to determine how it might solve problems on the job.

"Sales seek individuals, not companies," Mr. DeFazio is fond of saying. Advertising and marketing managers concern themselves with SIC's and companies, but sales managers and sales reps must know the *people* who specify and buy in the company.

Although this is elementary, it is often overlooked when advertising programs or communications projects of one type or another are being planned.

All of this brings us to the crux of the matter, and Westinghouse's John DeFazio put his finger on one problem that's universal—failure to handle inquiries promptly, and attaching too little importance to them. He said, "Inquiries demand immediate action, undivided attention."

Too often overlooked is that today's sales accrue as the result of yesterday's work. And tomorrow's results depend on what we do today. Convince yourself of this by picking up a handful of old inquiries —*letterhead inquiries*—12 or 18 months old. Review each one. You may be shocked to find many problems and ideas that are today's successful new products discussed in them.

But what was done with those inquiries at the time?

Were they really followed up vigorously, was everything possible done to solve these prospective customers' problems at that time?

It's highly unlikely.

But it's in this area where some research effort could produce vital intelligence for the marketing and sales plan—as it has done at Westinghouse.

"Get objectives in writing that can be measured. Always 'keep the monkey on management's back' by asking for their measurable objectives by priorities, specific markets, the job function to be reached, and appeal to each function," DeFazio said.

And he's unquestionably right because by doing this the advertising manager can *prove* without a shadow of a doubt that advertising is an investment with a measurable return.

But he or she can prove this *only* if objectives are firm, in writing, and measurable.

As pro-advertising as those of us are who *know* what industrial advertising can accomplish, nonetheless when a company drifts without marketing direction the money spent on advertising would probably produce more of a return if it were invested in hiring a marketing vice-president to replace the engineer in that spot right now—or even adding additional salespeople to the field force.

In no way is this intended to be an anti-advertising diatribe. Rather, it is an indictment of inept management of a fantastically high percentage of industrial companies doing business in this country today.

Managements that are engineering-oriented, production-oriented—and even sales-oriented—but ignore the marketing concept, ignore marketing as an activity vital to their companies, ignore development of a written marketing plan, ignore setting marketing objectives, ignore development of a written communications plan, ignore setting communications objectives, ignore the role marketing communications alone can play, are incapable of managing effectively.

They should be replaced with top people who would *demand* and *get* smart marketing as the *only* way to improve significantly the company's position in its industry.

"Lost Business" Reports

The relationship between inquiries, negotiations, and sales must be established very precisely. Again, "keep the monkey on the back" of sales management by asking for *accurate records of negotiations activity by product*. Insist also on a system of "lost business reports." This will enable you to develop important intelligence about what occurs between the negotiations and sales stages.

What can be done between the inquiry to negotiations stages? Work out a system to determine what transpires during this time and you'll be able to prove a return on advertising investment.

To do this, it is essential that you accept only objectives that advertising can perform—such as securing a greater share of mind, creating interest, motivating distributors, supporting the sales organization. Such objectives will show that *advertising can measurably increase negotiations activity.*

Educate your people, your immediate management group, your sales force, anybody else who'll listen to you, about the role of marketing communications. Advertising is an investment, so let's treat it as such and prove it is just that.

Educate everybody that advertising cannot directly sell the product, even if an occasional order does come in over the transom due to advertising. Don't stress these sales because you'll be stressing a role that industrial advertising isn't supposed to play.

Never forget for an instant that the important role of marketing communications is measurably to increase negotiations activity. Advertising can take full credit for digging up new prospects and putting them in touch with the company—and it should.

If sales do not result, you can still prove you met your communications objectives successfully—and management will have to look elsewhere to determine why. Always tie the advertising and communications program and budget to negotiations activity only. Converting negotiations to sales is the responsibility of the sales force. That is beyond your control.

Westinghouse's Mr. DeFazio says there is a "communications flow" that consists of separate phases. These follow, and here he is quoted.

"There are three communications steps to a sale. The first is the inquiry step where the inquirer (prospect) asks for more information, such as, what is it? What can it do? Give me a price list? Why is it better than a competitor's product? And so on.

"The second step, the negotiations step, is the bartering step with the inquirer seeking more specific information, such as, can you meet this spec? What is my discount? Delivery? And so on and on.

"The third step is placing the order. Steps two and three are talents best cultivated by sales reps. Get the sales reps to concentrate on the negotiations step and processing the order and you have accomplished maximum sales rep's efficiency."

These are the two major ways in which advertising reduces the cost of selling, of course—by bringing prospect and salesperson together in the first place, and by enabling the sales force to sell more in the same amount of time.

The inquiry step in the sale is best handled by company or division headquarters, in the advertising department.

Certain inputs are essential for the process, Mr. DeFazio said. "Now for the inputs. You create interest—which are the inputs—four ways. By advertising, publicity, trade shows, and annual catalogs and directories. At this state I'm not talking about a manufacturer's or distributor's catalog, but rather about an annual such as *Thomas Register* or *Sweet's Catalogs.*"

Created interest generates raw inquiries. Convert raw inquiries to verified, or qualified, inquiries and in the process a certain percentage of hot leads is the fallout.

At Westinghouse, even qualified inquiries are not sent to the sales force, but are sent to a product expert at the appropriate plant. This is to avoid the back-breaking administrative exercise that ensues because the salespeople cannot answer every question the inquirer asks.

We've all seen far too many instances where the field sales force has had to "get on the horn" to the inside product people when actually in the company of a live prospect. This is disruptive, time consuming, and does not do anything to inspire customer confidence in the salesperson.

Westinghouse product experts spend at least a half-day a week telephoning all hot leads; after discussing the matter with the inquirer, the product man determines the next step. If the lead is really hot, a sales call is warranted.

Another important reason Westinghouse product experts handle qualified inquiries by phone is that the product expert is the one who needs all of this information and intelligence to keep abreast of all new developments. Westinghouse has found it is an effective and economical way to get the most accomplished in the shortest period of time and with personnel used with greatest efficiency. This method is considered *extremely* important at Westinghouse.

Verified prospects make up Westinghouse's Prospect Mailing List. Regular mailings are made to keep the prospects advised of the latest product information, new prices, new applications, and so forth. Technical data sheets, brochures, price sheets, catalogs, and other material is mailed to these verified prospects quite frequently.

It's impossible to overstress the importance of this activity to Westinghouse. These verified prospects are the best and primary return on the investment. Mr. DeFazio advocates making at least 24 mailings a year to them—if the list is kept virgin-pure. When it is, the mailings are rifle shots, as opposed to the shotgun activity of arousing interest.

The customer mailing list at Westinghouse's Semiconductor Division is made up by salespeople who submit names of people on whom they call at each customer establishment. The customer mailing list breaks down as:

   60—70% purchasing agents
   20—30% design engineers
    1— 5% R&D

On the other hand, the prospect mailing list from verified inquiries breaks down just the opposite; it looks like this:

   60—70% research and development
   20—30% design engineers
    1— 5% purchasing agents

For all practical purposes this means that the customer mailing list actually makes up the buyers, and the prospect mailing list makes up the specifiers. Having this information gives Westinghouse marketing people a wonderful understanding of today's business—and an excellent insight into tomorrow's.

"Tap the static that goes on between each step and you are really on your way for real growth in your markets," Mr. DeFazio said. "The marketer of tomorrow will be one who masters this technique.

"The static between inquiry stage and negotiations reveals new market trends. The static between negotiations and sales steps can determine sales forecasting, lost-business reports, and marketing intelligence by products."

At Westinghouse it is emphasized that there are only two ways to increase sales volume.

One is to increase and improve the conversion rate of negotiations to sales; this can be done either by making sales aids available to the sales force, or conducting sales or product training for the sales force.

The other way to increase sales volume is to increase the negotiations base, and to increase the negotiations base the inquiry base must be increased. It's that simple.

Of course, the manufacturer must develop the need in the marketplace, it must have the right product, at the right time, and at the right price. Furthermore, distributors must know their conversion rate of negotiations activity—that is, quotes, bids entered, proposals, or whatever it's called in each industry. And he or she has to have the sales force well-trained by the manufacturer about the product if they're to operate at peak efficiency.

Three-Stage Data Processing

Proof of the pudding at Westinghouse is provided by the data processing inquiry system developed by Mr. DeFazio to be a basic means of establishing the fundamental relationship between marketing communications and sales.

The data processing inquiry system was designed to get product information to a prospect; to get more information on prospect needs; and to follow up with personal selling to produce sales.

Inquiries are handled in three stages. The first stage is called the raw inquiry stage; this division of Westinghouse pulls more than 20,000 inquiries a year. The second stage is the process of verifying, or qualifying; it reduces the raw inquiries to 8,500 in number. The last stage is referred to as the "hot" lead stage; here the total quantity is only 750.

Interestingly, the ratio of raw inquiries to hot sales leads is 40 to 1—2½ percent.

Here's how Westinghouse semiconductor's system works.

First step is to answer *immediately* all raw inquiries generated by advertising, publicity, or trade shows by sending information requested; along with a letter of transmittal and a questionnaire reply card.

The questionnaire reply card is the second stage of the system—the verification or qualification process.

When Westinghouse processes a raw inquiry, a source code is entered in area "A" on the questionnaire card; it identifies where and how the inquiry was generated. Thus the company can specifically identify the specific advertisement and the publication that produced the inquiry, the publicity release, and the publication or the trade show.

This verification procedure is very similar to most systems used by controlled circulation magazines. The card requires information in considerable detail concerning the inquirer's job function, product interest, and data about his company, whether the application is commercial or military—and boxes to check for "have your sales rep phone" or "have your sales rep visit me." When the inquirer completes and returns the card, he or she is considered a qualified prospect.

A customer or noncustomer code is assigned in area "B" on the card, and all of the information is punched on data processing cards. The information loop, for all practical purposes, is closed. Westinghouse now has a complete record of an inquiry from the time it originates until—or if, that is—it becomes a sale.

Third stage of inquiry handling comes about when processing the questionnaire reply card. Should the inquirer complete area "C"— asking for a salesperson to phone or visit—this information is immediately reproduced on the Inquiry Follow Form and sent out within 24 hours of its receipt to the salesperson handling that particular area or account. This is the hot lead stage, the *only* time a salesperson is asked to follow up with a prospect immediately.

"I believe there are basically five important by-products accomplished with this inquiry handling system," said Mr. DeFazio.

The first is a virgin-pure mailing list that is effectively offering economy because of its selectivity—sending out information only to those who are genuinely interested. The system is also easily maintained on a current status, with a known turnover rate of approximately 40 percent a year.

This is remarkably close to what is considered the normal attrition rate of personnel, as far as remaining on one job in one company is concerned; this figure is generally considered to be approximately 35 percent. Which means that 35 percent of your prospects are no longer prospects at the end of a year because they're someplace else, in another position, in another company. They may, however, be prospects there as well.

Second important result of Westinghouse's system is the identifiable sales efficiency. The system has done away with cold calls and replaced them with hot leads. It isn't very difficult to guess which the salespeople prefer. Phone numbers are listed on the form so Westinghouse salespeople are encouraged to make quick contacts.

Over the past five years, it has been shown that three out of four of the hot leads have led to immediate negotiations or a sample order. *Every* hot lead has been qualified *by Westinghouse sales reps*—not by the advertising people—as a good prospect. In every case, the sales rep assigned a full-line catalog to the prospect. This catalog definitely is not handed out to literature collectors.

Every three months, a galley run-off of all verified inquiries is assembled for each salesperson by accounts in his or her area. This galley shows new prospects in the area. Sales reps and their inside back-up salespeople have a tool that helps give them a better "commercial" feel of the area, since the galley also includes job functions of the inquirers.

Again, the salespeople realize the contribution of marketing communications because they can also save valuable time during customer calls by phoning new prospects listed in the organization—all from their reception room phone. This obviates scheduling additional, separate calls and eliminates much back-tracking and duplicated effort by the sales force.

The third important benefit realized from Westinghouse's system is the reports that show market trends by analyzing the information furnished on the questionnaire card.

Also on a quarterly basis, Mr. DeFazio receives an incremental report and a cumulative summary report from the system. The reports are broken down by all field sales areas with a complete listing of customer versus noncustomer potential by product interest, product application, and industry group.

Over five years the reports reveal inquiries from noncustomers—fine prospects to *become* customers—have never been less than 80 percent of the total. Proof to top management that advertising is an investment, or that the communications program has met its objective of creating interest in the product. This is proof that cannot be disputed.

And it is obvious to all that advertising extends the reach of the salesforce and flushes out prospects they never knew existed!

What's more, the quarterly incremental report detects new markets or accelerating market trends. The summary report displays gradual market shifts by areas, by products, and by industry.

Fourth important result of the system is the invaluable marketing intelligence feedback found in the sales rep's hot lead reports. This information and intelligence is used to produce new products, learn of new product applications, new customer contacts, and new product lead time for sales.

By having every inquiry customer or noncustomer coded, Westinghouse is able immediately to match all purchase orders entered for the first time by a new customer with any inquiries received from his or her organization. Not only can it be shown that inquiries definitely lead to sales, but Mr. DeFazio and his staff can accurately measure the time it takes from the inquiry stage to the actual sale—and do it by product line.

As an example, it was found that the minimum time sales could be expected to be made following inquiries was six months. By plotting the negotiation activity curves recorded by sales management and superimposing them over actual sales curves, it was immediately apparent that negotiation preceded sales by three months.

All industrial advertising managers should explain the time lag between advertising and measurable results to their managements. Recognize, though, that the time between inquiry and sale varies tremendously depending upon the product. In the case of major capital equipment used for a manufacturing process it can be months, even a year or more. A management sitting in walnut-paneled offices with bated breath, watching the sales curve and expecting it to surge instantaneously and miraculously just because the company started an intensified advertising campaign, is a management doomed to disappointment. And when this happens, this is a management doubly hard to convince about advertising's effectiveness and advertising's contributions to attaining marketing objectives.

The last important thing in the way of beneficial results produced by the inquiry handling system at Westinghouse is ease of evaluation of the marketing communications program. This analysis matches what was planned and expected from an advertisment in a given publication or trade show with actual readout results.

A media evaluation report provides a total of 12 areas for evaluating the effectiveness of advertising copy, as well as the media themselves; it is very easy with this system to determine both the quantity and the quality of inquiries of all of the publications on Westinghouse's schedule.

Cost of Handling Inquiries

The industrial advertising manager who *knows* for sure exactly what it costs the company to handle the average inquiry received from a trade publication is a member of a minority group so small it couldn't even organize a first-class riot. This group could hold its annual convention in a broom closet, with no crowding, no jostling, nobody cramped, and with no feelings of claustrophobia.

INQUIRIES AND INQUIRY HANDLING

Inquiries can have value. They are used effectively by thousands of companies, including many of our industrial giants such as Westinghouse, as well as by many of the smaller companies most of us have never heard of. They are used as sales, marketing, and promotion tools, and in dozens of other ways.

Also, though, there's no getting away from the fact that inquiries are expensive. If you're advertising manager of a typical industrial company and you're doing a better than average job of follow-up on your inquiries, that job is costing money—lots of it.

Furthermore, it's a pretty safe bet you're spending at least one dollar to handle each and every inquiry, and this figure is so low it borders on the absurd. Mighty few companies can handle an inquiry for this sum today; most companies spend something between $1.50 and $3.00 to handle one inquiry, but this figure does *not* include:

1. Cost of generating inquiries—via advertising, direct mail, publicity, trade shows, or what have you.
2. Cost of literature and/or samples sent to inquirers.
3. Postage—and it's going up so often it's difficult to remember what it costs any more.
4. Cost of salesmen's followup calls.

However, for most companies the cost *does* include:

1. Typing the label.
2. Getting the material in the mail.
3. Simple recordkeeping.

If you're doing the job for *under* a dollar, you are a financial genius on the order of J. Paul Getty, H.L. Hunt and Hugh Hefner. Your management should cherish you and give you much tender loving care and frequent salary adjustments, always upwards. And on your part, you should cherish the inquiry handling system you've developed and give it plenty of tender loving care. Don't change it in even the tiniest way for the world.

The truth is, though, that many good, large, sophisticated companies that spend hundreds of thousands of dollars to generate inquiries and tens of thousands to handle them haven't the foggiest idea what the whole thing costs. They'd stomp off in high dudgeon if told so except in the pages of a book, though. The truth always hurts.

Although the following chart won't pinpoint to the nearest mill what it costs your company to handle an inquiry, it will nonetheless give you a good, ball-park figure. And it may prove to be a real eye-opener!

Charge or function	Monthly cost
1. Your time (only what you spend on inquiries).	$ . . . .
2. Your secretary's time (ditto above).	. . . .
3. Other supervisory or executive time—such as your assistant, for instance.	. . . .
4. Their secretaries and/or assistants.	. . . .
5. All clerks, typists, messengers, etc., and this includes the mail boy, the labor used to haul your literature in and out of the supply room, and so forth.	. . . .
6. Warehousing and inventory control.	. . . .
7. Mechanical costs, including collating, stuffing, metering, bagging, labeling, etc.	. . . .
8. Supplies and service, including letterheads, envelopes, inquiry forms, labels, telephone, typewriter ribbons, paper clips, and so on.	. . . .
TOTAL	

Once you've tallied all of this up if you really want to be accurate, as well as fair about the whole thing, you should by rights add a fair share of fringe benefits to the labor costs you used above. Also standard overhead items—rent, light, heat, taxes, maintenance, watchman, etc. And maybe even a few cents for recruiting and training.

Tally up the total monthly cost, then divide by the average number of inquiries you process in a month. If that figure comes to less than a dollar per inquiry, you win a gold-plated key to the executive washroom.

There's another little item to be added in before we complete all of the addition—that's whatever it costs you to prepare and print each copy of that brochure, catalog, or booklet you sent out to inquirers. Don't forget to add in all labor, overhead, and so on to the cost per piece of literature. Finally, add in that little item of postage.

Screening Inquiries

Not every industrial advertiser has either the budget or the manpower to set up an elaborate and highly effective inquiry handling system like that used by Westinghouse.

Every industrial company, however, should screen its inquiries and refrain from feeding its sales force a huge mass of raw inquiries. Nothing discourages a salesperson faster—and actually turns him or her against both inquiries and advertising—than sending him on one wild goose chase after another when all that is accomplished is wasting time, wearing out a car, and handing some literature to junior drafts- man, mail boy, or other literature collector.

Detailed examination of the replies from all of the companies surveyed in *Product Design & Development's* massive study on in- quiries reveals that, for the most part, screening of inquiries is remarkably casual. Little importance is attached to it. This may well be because of a chronic shortage of manpower in the typical industrial advertising department, although it may also reflect a near-total lack of understanding of *why* inquiries should be screened.

Let's see how some individual companies do their screening of in- quiries.

Hunter Spring Division, Ametek, Inc., receives more than 1,000 in- quiries each month. This company makes little effort to screen them, and answered *PD&D's* question by saying, "Segregation by product and territory; inquiries from competitors are considered separately; 'casual' foreign inquiries where we cannot sell are discarded." Hunter Spring Division sends 99 percent of all incoming inquiries to its field sales force. Individual salespeople are to use their own judgment about whether or not to follow-up. The company added that let- terhead inquiries are considered important and well worth follow-up effort; bingo card inquiries are a good source of names and companies worth pursuing.

Anaconda American Brass Company is the recipient of more than 1,000 inquiries a month; they are sorted as to product, geographical location, manufacturer, or student by "a senior employee familiar with our products." Sixty percent of these inquiries are sent out to the field sales force.

Hamlin, Inc. receives a substantial number of inquiries each month; upon receipt, they are counted and recorded in a log covering each advertisement or publicity release *by magazine.* They are then coded as to the sales representative (territory) who handles them. The original is sent to the mail room and the label is affixed to an envelope containing the proper product literature and a cover letter showing the name, address, and phone number of the appropriate representative. These envelopes are prepacked and coded with the number of the representative, so all that remains for the mailperson to do is match code numbers on the labels to those on the envelopes. The duplicate label that comes in from the publication is sent to the rep for follow- up activities. Hamlin added that several publications do not send duplicate labels, making extra work; for this reason Hamlin has decid- ed not to advertise in them! No effort is made to screen inquiries.

Barber-Coleman Company, manufacturer of AC motors, DC motors, relays, actuators, valves, impressors, control systems and so on, receives around 1,000 inquiries a month—with 850 the result of advertising, 150 editorial mentions (publicity) and 50 from direct mail. The only screening that is done is to remove competitors, catalog collectors, and some foreign countries. Salespeople get 100 percent for sales followup—and interestingly, the company states that approximately 5 percent are "hot leads"; this is just about *double* the usually accepted percentage of hot leads as determined by both industrial companies and insurance companies who have analyzed their inquiries.

Blue M Electric Company, manufacturer of electric ovens and furnaces, temperature/humidity environmental cabinets and so forth, gets an average of 250 inquiries a month from advertising, 250 from publicity, and another 100 from direct mail. Inquiries are screened to weed out competitors and, when possible, literature collectors. That little qualifier, "when possible" is Midwestern humor at its best. Blue M's sales force receives all inquiries for follow-up at its discretion. Salespeople are obliged to follow up and submit a report within 30 days of receiving inquiries, however, so their discretion is limited.

Gates Rubber Company, Industrial Division, manufacturer of industrial hose, V-belts, and automotive products, answers all inquiries and encloses a postage-paid reply card with the appropriate literature, along with the inquiry-handling form. Return of the reply card, which contains a questionnaire, qualifies the inquirer as a live one—and Gates averages a 12 percent return of cards. Inquirers who do not use the card are also referred to the field sales force, but to be followed up with discretion. Naturally, all of the hot leads—the qualified inquiries —are followed up immediately.

Most industrial advertisers use mail, via the ubiquitous post-paid reply card, to screen inquiries and to determine who among all that mass of paper work is an honest-to-goodness prospect and who should be contacted by the sales force.

With the cost of an industrial sales call running around $106 and climbing every year, it is mandatory that these inquiries be screened some way if the sales force is to operate efficiently and not dissipate its efforts. And since advertising's prime function is to lower the cost of selling by making the salespeople more efficient and productive, it certainly will not do the job by dumping a mass of names on a salesperson's desk, muttering darkly, "Go, man, go."

One way to determine just who is a live one and who isn't is to run two boxes in ads that are couponed. One box says, "I'm interested." The other one says, "I'm serious." This automatically qualifies inquiries immediately with no additional steps required. People are honest about checking the boxes and this system has worked beautifully for several industrial advertisers who use it. It sorts out the wheat from the chaff fast.

The Telephone Screen

A faster way than mail to qualify inquiries is by telephone. With WATS lines (Wide Area Telephone Service) being used by more and more companies, the long-distance call is not prohibitively expensive for routine use. When sales reps follow only hot leads their sales shoot up amazingly, and use of the telephone provides plenty of hot leads plus all of the application information sales reps need to close sales with less calls. This method of screening inquiries truly reduces the cost of selling and does it *now*.

John O. Cook, formerly advertising and public relations manager of Marbon Chemical, Division of Borg-Warner Corporation, reported that his company screens 100 percent of its incoming inquiries by telephone in an effort to qualify them for personal sales followup. A phone call and an individual's time together cost a little less than $106, which is the sales rep's cost to do the same job—not taking into account the lost time for the sales rep if the inquiry turns out to be a dud. Marbon Chemical values inquiries and considers them highly important. And effective use is made of them.

Johns-Manville used the WATS line to follow up on inquiries that resulted from an 8-page insert advertisement for Dutch Brand electrical tape. The calls made a tremendous impression on startled inquirers who found it a little hard to believe that a major company like Johns-Manville was calling *them* long distance after they'd inquired about one of the company's products. The inside salespeople who did the calling were able to qualify inquirers with great precision as to product application, the brand of tape they were currently buying, and much additional marketing information. Distributors received the data unearthed by the telephone calls and made effective use of it.

The telephone survey to determine the intent of inquirers is extremely helpful, and it is a great aid in media selection. It pinpoints intent to buy and enables the advertising manager to predict with reasonable accuracy the dollar volume of sales that can be expected from a given number of inquiries. Publications vary widely in the quality of inquiries they produce, as some telephoning will point out.

A telephone method is Chilton Company's Wide Area Telephone Service (WATS), used for many purposes, only one of which is follow-ups. Chilton uses professional interviewers to find out if inquirers received the information they requested, the type of work they are engaged in, the use they have in mind for the product, and so on.

Both telephone methods have their advantages. Inquiry Evaluation is favored where an understanding of highly technical information is of critical importance, and Chilton is chosen when questions that are relatively standard are involved—such as in a sample survey to be tabulated.

A number of business publications have been doing inquiry follow-ups for advertisers; sometimes for promotional reasons, sometimes to uncover new applications for products, and sometimes to dig up other data. The fact remains, though, that the company that systematically analyzes this type of follow-up is in the minority.

The same may be said as far as evaluating raw inquiries in the advertising department is concerned, as we've seen from the typical companies surveyed by *Product Design & Development*.

One problem quite prevalent in smaller companies is that the advertising department, which normally handles this work, must choose between holding up the inquiry for analysis and getting the information to the inquirer and the field sales force in a hurry.

Work is being done by publications to upgrade inquiry handling. At McGraw-Hill, for example, where service bureaus do most of the work, the company's own computers now produce reports and labels for some of the company's magazines. A spokesman for the company said, "We're wondering whether we couldn't turn over punched cards or tape to the advertiser and let him or her do the rest—send out the material, analyze the inquiries, or whatever. This may be a problem for the small guy who can't handle computerized information, but there may be answers to that, too. Actually, we think we haven't even scratched the surface of processing inquiries."

Conversion Into Sales

This is the bugaboo of most industrial advertising managers. They're all intent on "proving that advertising sold X number of dollars worth of widgets."

Fallacy here is that these advertising managers are going to much trouble and great lengths to prove something that's unprovable—because 'tain't so. Unless the advertisement made a direct plea to send in a check or money order for an item bought by mail (mail order), advertising doesn't sell.

Industrial advertising *presells*, it puts the buyer and the company's salesperson in touch with each other. As Westinghouse says, it "increases the negotiations activity." And this includes submitting a proposal, putting in a bid, and so forth—whatever your company calls it.

Advertising can and does put a large number of buyers and salespeople in touch with each other and thus produces a substantial volume of sales; but the sales were made and closed by the sales reps, not by the advertisements.

Of course, it's quite true that occasionally an advertisement will result in an over-the-transom order for a piece of equipment. All of us have had this happen a number of times, although such an occurrence is certainly an exception to the rule. When an ad does produce a sale, or bring in an order without a sales rep's having been involved, don't rush frantically hither and yon calling it to everybody's attention.

Those who don't understand the function of industrial advertising —which is to reduce the cost of selling by enabling the sales force to sell more in the same amount of time—will inevitably view such a sale as something advertising should do *more often.*

They may very well ask you, or at the least wonder to themselves, why you go through all the back-patting routine just because "advertising has done what it's supposed to do—sell." Encouraging this attitude can do you nothing but a disservice in the long run, and it can undermine what little faith exists in advertising among members of management of industrial companies.

New customers shaken out of the bushes by advertising are not merely inquirers, as many industrial advertisers know—they're prospective customers, prospective buyers. When they inquire about a product they want information on which to base a buying decision. Inquiries handled promptly and properly and with proper product information sent to the inquirer are frequently like money pouring in straight out of the blue.

How to Get the Most Out of Inquiries

There's no magic formula, no pie-in-the-sky when it comes to milking the largest possible dollar volume of sales out of the maximum number of clean inquiries your advertising-communications program can generate.

Notice that *clean* inquiries are specified. Clean inquiries come from publications with proven performance when it comes to converting inquiries to sales. Far too many magazines sell circulation—circulation that has been forced past the point where the universe has been saturated. This inevitably results in a larger volume of inquiries, but many of them will be from Indians too low on the corporate totem pole to be honest-Injun buying or specifying influences.

You're much better off with fewer inquiries of higher quality—cleaner ones, that is.

And don't let your enthusiasm run rampant and your hopes fly high due to a large number of created inquiries. These are inquiries that some publications produce by multiple listing of products; first, for example, may be an advertisement you run. Then comes a publicity release about the product which coincidentally appears in that same issue. After this comes a wrap-up of some offshoot of the bingo card, cloaked in sanctimonious pseudo-editorial language, all ready to clip and shoot in for more free literature. Such inquiries don't produce much in the way of sales as a rule.

Instead of concentrating with grim tenacity on producing the most possible inquiries, publishers rather should try to screen inquiries for advertisers.

A ridiculous mistake made by many advertising departments is to forward literature to an inquirer and send a copy of the inquiry-handling form to the appropriate salesperson—but neglect to tell one little thing. Such as what product or model of the product is involved. This leaves the salesperson in the dark, unable to tailor a presentation for this particular prospect. So simple, yet it happens so often. And it reduces the value of the inquiries.

Other industrial advertising departments generalize too much. On the off-chance of selling somebody something, just anything apparently, a footlocker full of literature on every product the company has manufactured in the last 60 years is sent to any and all inquirers. This leaves *them* out in the cold because nine times out of 10 the literature is not specific; it doesn't present the one product they're interested in, it doesn't discuss the one application they have for it. This cools prospects off fast.

Few industrial advertisers give prices, apparently feeling that charging a fair price for a well-made product is inherently unfair and that the industrial buyer isn't able to judge value received with any great degree of exactitude.

This is a false assumption. Surveys have shown that more than two-thirds of all industrial inquirers have expressed a desire for price information—yet it's almost never supplied.

Don't harbor the impression that a salesperson can "soften the blow" of what your product costs. If the quality is there, if your company reputation is up to par, and if delivery is made when it's promised, price comes afterwards; it won't scare off the prospect. More than likely quoting at least a ball-park price will increase the returns on your inquiry qualification cards by approximately 20 percent. Try it and see.

It's a known fact that mention of price increases readership of ads. McGraw-Hill's Laboratory of Advertising Performance reported two instances. In the case of power supplies, price mention increased the Seen rating of ads by 80 percent and the readership *more than two and one half times*. With test and measuring equipment and instruments, Seen was up 19 percent and Read was up 31 percent when price was given in the ad. Inquiries go up as readership goes up, of course.

Generate inquiries, screen them, handle them fast and properly and they'll produce sales. Fumble any one of the steps and you're shuffling paper.

Because the following article by Paul Daugherty is so relevant to this chapter, we have persuaded *Industrial Marketing* to allow us to reprint it *in toto*.

How Your Inquiry System Can Help Pick Trade Media

Media evaluation is one of the most difficult areas in which to gain objective information. Keeping ad response records by state, Standard Industrial Code (SIC) and number counts provide some data. Readership, did-you-buy and other advertising follow-up studies from trade magazines also contribute. But bias, timeliness, sample size and infrequency limit usefulness.

So every year the same questions reappear. Which magazines should we choose? Do the present ones on our list reach the right people? How many ad respondents are really prospective customers? Which magazines provide the highest quality responses?

It seemed to us that ad respondents could contribute to the decision-making process beyond being just a name on a list. In thinking about did-you-buy and readership studies, the names on our response lists appear to be just as valid a circulation sample as used in magazine-sponsored studies. We would also have the advantage of a greater sample group size and the opportunity to continuously study all the magazines in our program. So we implemented a program which revised our ad follow-up card into an ongoing market/media evaluation research project.

The redesigned card tells us a variety of information: the product produced at the respondent's plant; if the respondent uses a product we make; how much of that kind of product he or she purchases to determine an account's potential; the exact application for our product; the usual are-you-in-the-market/do-you-want-a-salesperson-to-call; and finally, what three trade magazines are read regularly.

Value Judgments

That information is compared with information from ad response lists. For instance, once a month we list all respondents by state, noting for each person the magazine that generated the reply. As the list is prepared, we judge the respondent's potential as a customer. The decision is based on information gathered from the ad respondent's reader service card or coupon and from directories. While it may sound subjective, it is usually quite easy to make an accurate determination. Our initial assessments have not been off more than 2% or 3%.

From that we prepare a tally chart for each magazine:

- Magazine name—75 responses
- Possible users—15
- Probable nonuser—60
- Definite user
- Definite nonuser

Our ad follow-up card is enclosed in all literature mailed to respondents in the United States and Canada. We type the person's name, company and address on the card, mailing again once or twice at 30-day intervals as needed.

As cards return, we refer to the state summary to find which magazine generated each person's response. At that point each person is either deleted from both our state and SIC summaries or designated a potential user. We then refer to the magazine tally and place the prospect in the correct definite user/definite nonuser catagory. At the end of a month our tally sheet yields data as in Figure 1.

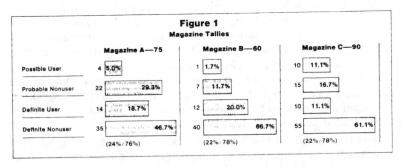

Figure 1
Magazine Tallies

	Magazine A—75	Magazine B—60	Magazine C—90
Possible User	4 — 5.0%	1 — 1.7%	10 — 11.1%
Probable Nonuser	22 — 29.3%	7 — 11.7%	15 — 16.7%
Definite User	14 — 18.7%	12 — 20.0%	10 — 11.1%
Definite Nonuser	35 — 46.7%	40 — 66.7%	55 — 61.1%
	(24%/76%)	(22%/78%)	(22%/78%)

By comparing user to nonuser categories, we arrive at an overall evaluation of the quality of ad response and also compare magazines.

In magazine A, 24% are in the user category; in both B and C, 22%. Among all respondents we have had an average 61% card return rate from the beginning of the program. Individual magazines have approximated that, from a low of 59% to a high of 65%. More importantly, however, our probable user/definite user rate is averaging 26% overall, in a range of 22% to 33%. In other words, one out of four people on average responding to our ads has been a good prospect.

Recently, we began tracking the respondents who are currently in the market and also those who wish to have a salesperson call on him, for each magazine. In the past we kept gross totals only—21% currently in the market, 15% who wish to have a salesperson call. But the new method should provide one additional evaluation benchmark.

Duplicated Reach

The last question on our postcard is an unaided recall readership question. Realizing that this readership study is biased in favor of the magazines with the heaviest ad responses and, therefore, the heaviest circulation representation, we insert the readership question to learn if magazines we are not currently using consistently appear, and to confirm that people are actually reading regularly the magazines from which they respond.

As in traditional studies, each magazine wins the readership of its own circulation list. However, this multiple monitoring program shows relationships we did not realize previously.

For instance, we have long used two major magazines to cover a particular market. Our past studies said both had high readership. But the new method of analysis indicates that one of the two magazines has an unexpectedly large percentage of its circulation duplicating the other magazine's circulation—but does not have the sole readership of the other. If that trend continues, then our media selection may change.

Refinements can be incorporated into the study. If the quantity of response for a given ad is great enough, one could compare the usage/nonusage rate or the number currently in the market to the ad program as a whole, or to other individual ads. One can keep readership records for potential customers by individual markets or even by job title.

If one is willing to assume that the ad respondent or the company is a potential customer, then one should gain more information to maximize market penetration. Information about ad respondents maximizes the efficiency of the marketing program. The information reduces guesswork in decision making.

Chapter 17

READERSHIP MEASUREMENT

DETRACTORS of advertising—and industry harbors an over-
abundance of them—are wont to declare whenever the opportunity arises (they'll even *make* the opportunity) that advertising is an
inexact art; it is not a science, it is created by hunch and hope, and it is
largely intuitive. That last word is a dirty one, by the way, and is supposed to be a real crusher.

These detractors immediately add, as if this eliminates all questions
as to the validity of their antediluvian babblings, that nobody has yet
proved the effectiveness of industrial advertising.

Its only staunch upholders are the company's advertising manager
and his agency counterparts, and they have, after all, a personal stake
in advertising.

Maybe, say the dinosaurs who achieved management status by pure
chance and by constantly looking backward, never forward, as well as
by always keeping a closed mind, we're actually squandering all of
that money to run advertisements nobody reads!

When that remark is made you can see past the horror-stricken
look—without benefit of X-ray vision—the slide rules sliding in those
engineering minds as they compute the profit the company *could* have
shown if only that wasteful advertising had been entirely eliminated.

This is a wonky argument indeed.

Without going into how to justify advertising to management at this
time, let's look instead at methods of determining the actual readership your advertisements received, and how you can put this information to good use in your planning and in your creative activities.

Having firm data also enables you to refute the "advertising isn't
read" chant from the walnut-paneled offices.

Readership of your advertisements is measured regularly by
organizations whose specialty this is. They use a carefully controlled
sample, usually a given number of people, from the circulation of the
publications whose readership they measure. The information they

develop is solid. It's authoritative. It is statistically correct within a negligible margin of error. Readership isn't a dream or a hope or a yearning, it's something definite that has been proven. It simply cannot be questioned.

These measurements, called readership studies, are conducted by both independent research organizations who are paid either by the advertisers and/or the publications, or entirely by the publications.

In addition to telling how well read advertisements are, readership studies tell *why* some ads are well read and others get the back of people's mental hands—if the results are carefully analyzed.

Such reasons why ads perform as they do, why people are attracted to them and read them provide the background information that leads to guidlines the ad manager and agency people can follow. Such guidelines greatly reduce the chances of producing an ad that "bombs out," as the teen-agers are wont to say.

Perhaps the most valuable benefit of all from readership studies, though, is the fact that they make possible an honest, objective evaluation of advertisements you're currently running. Studies enable you to see if your ads are achieving the communications objectives of your program, or coming close to it. Regardless of what the objectives are, your ads must be *read* before they stand a chance of achieving them.

What's more, readership studies make it possible for you to analyze the strengths and weaknesses of *your competitors' advertising.*

Naturally, this is not to suggest that your copy borrow, "improve upon the technique," or otherwise scuttle your own program and adapt a competitor's to your company and your product. If your competitors happen to be running a particularly effective campaign, it behooves you to know about it. Never react to competitive advertising, however. Doing so puts you on the defensive.

The intelligence you garner from close examination of the analysis of your competitors' ads cannot help but be very revealing about their communications objectives, and perhaps it will even enable you to make an informed guesstimate as to their marketing objectives.

And examining the readership ratings your competitors achieve will give you a good clue of how close they're coming to achieving what they set out to do.

Business Magazine Readership Studies

At one time there were almost 300 leading business publications offering nearly *five times* that many readership studies to their advertisers. Some publications offer readership studies by more than one research organization.

One prominent construction book, for example, has studies conducted by Daniel Starch & Staff made in February, March, April, May, August, and November. In addition, the publication is studied by Readex in January, March, April, May, October, and November. This gives advertisers an opportunity to compare the results of studies taken independently of each other. It is a very desirable cross check. Corroboration of an advertisement's performance by a different service results in a high degree of validity.

And *Purchasing* used Readex for six issues, Starch for another half-dozen.

Using two different firms is expensive for publishers; for that matter, using even one research organization to conduct studies is costly. But it is worthy of note that the *leaders* in business publishing offer this service to their advertisers.

They have nothing to fear in having advertising readership disclosed; marginal publications seldom offer such services, perhaps for this reason. Readership of advertisements is contingent upon readership of editorial, and this is where the marginal publications falter badly.

By rights, every issue of a monthly publication should be studied, at least 13 issues of a biweekly should be studied, and the figure should climb to a minimum of 26 times for a weekly magazine.

This is particularly true because publishers understandably put an extra sales push on studied issues, using the study as an inducement to persuade advertisers to buy space in those issues. What this accomplishes is having advertisers tending to concentrate their ads in studied issues to the exclusion of nonstudied ones immediately preceding and following.

As a consequence, studied issues are usually fatter by far than are regular issues. Traditionally, ads have encountered harder going in fat issues than in thin ones due to the intensity of the competition for the readers's time. Using studied issues when there are only a few during the year could thus place the advertising manager in the untenable position of deliberately selecting issues that he or she knows ahead of time will be less productive for the company.

Upshot of this is that the publisher who is ostensibly doing the advertiser a great big favor by providing the readership service in the first place, actually does his advertisers a disservice by forcing them unwittingly into issues where the competition is much greater.

The *only* way out of this built-in booby trap is for industrial advertisers to clamor long and loud for more studied issues.

How Readership Studies Are Conducted

A discussion of the major services follows, along with a brief description of how the studies are conducted. All of the studies discussed are continuing studies, not occasional ones or one-time-only efforts.

Measuring readership of industrial advertisments in the business press has approximately a 20-year history. During this period some 25-30 different services have sprung up, encouraged by the intense interest industrial advertisers have exhibited in determining how well-read their ads are.

Statisticians and psychologists continue to probe and experiment for new and better tools with which to measure readership, and to interpret the results once they have them.

An area in which a glaring weakness exists and in which there is a dearth of information is in projectability of the results of the studies. So far few, if any, of the services have proven to the satisfaction of hard-nosed skeptics among us that the results of the surveyed sample of a publication's circulation can be projected across the entire circulation with anything approaching 100 percent accuracy—or even 90 percent, for that matter.

In addition, more information as to *why* readership ratings result as they do is needed; this calls for additional research.

Starch Readership Services

Starch Reports will be discussed first because Daniel Starch pioneered in measuring advertisement readership in the business press. Starch Reports are available from Starch/Inra/Hooper, 566 East Boston Post Road, Mamaroneck, NY 10543. Starch Readership Service measures the reading of advertisements in the business press using a standard technique developed by Dr. Daniel Starch and his staff in some 40 years of continuous experience in readership studies.

Objective And Value of Starch Reports

The purpose of Starch Reports is to show to what extent respondents have seen and read the advertisements in each study issue. The Starch Readership service has these main objectives:

1. To provide advertisers and agencies with a continuous check on the readership performance of their print advertising. The

ever-changing interplay of competition for reader attention creates the need for a continuous flow of research.

2. To base this research on a large number of studies so that findings do not merely reflect single issue situations but in combination provide a significant barometer of print advertising performance in general.

3. To focus attention on the inherent strength of print media so that advertisers and agencies can make the most effective use of their opportunities.

Starch data makes it possible to determine which kinds of ads attract the most reader interest. The continuous analysis of Starch Readership data help point the way to creating more effective advertisements.

Sample

Starch Reports utilize a minimum sample size of 100 readers per sex. It has been established that at this sample size, major fluctuations in readership levels stabilize.

Adults, 18 years and older, are personally interviewed face-to-face for all publications except those which are directed exclusively to special groups, i.e. for young girls, etc. For these publications, only the appropriate age group is interviewed.

Interviews are assigned to parallel the geographic circulation of each study publication. The quota for each interviewer is small in order to minimize interviewer bias. Between 20 and 30 urban localities are used for each study issue.

Interviews are distributed among people of varied ages, income levels and occupations so that collectively each study is broadly representative of the publication's audience. For select business, trade and professional publications, interviewing assignments are also designed to parallel the circulation by Field of Industry and Job Responsibility. For publications having small circulations, subscriber lists are used to help locate eligible respondents.

Starch Readership data are based on interviews with issue readers. Starch studies are not designed to measure the total number of readers of a study publication and consequently, the data are not projectable to the entire circulation.

Selection of Advertisements To Be Studied

The length of an interview is held to 90 items or less in order to prevent respondent boredom. When an issue contains more than 90 items, only selected advertisements are studied. Advertisements are selected for study on the basis of advertiser and agency interest in Starch data. When it is necessary to study more than 90 items, an additional sample of respondents is interviewed. Each respondent is questioned on only a portion of the total items in the issue. In this way, it is possible to report on more than 90 advertisements but not interview any one person on more than 90 items.

Interviewing Methodology

Starch Readership studies employ the "recognition" method. With the publication open, the respondent tells to what extent he or she had read each ad prior to the interview.

Before going into the field, interviewers obtain a copy of the publication and code each advertisement to be studied according to detailed instructions from the Home Office. A different starting point in the publication is assigned to each interviewer so that each advertisement appears with equal frequency toward the beginning, middle and end of the interview.

Carrying a coded copy of the study issue, interviewers locate eligible readers of the issue. An eligible reader is one who meets the age/sex/occupation requirements set for the particular publication and has glanced through or read some parts of the issue prior to the interviewer's visit. If a person is not sure from looking at the cover that he has read a particular issue, he is allowed to glance through the publication or look at the Table of Contents. If there is any doubt about whether or not the issue has been read, no interview is conducted.

Once issue reading is established and the respondent's cooperation obtained, interviewers turn the pages of the publication inquiring about each advertisement being studied.

For each advertisement, respondents are first asked, "Did you see or read any part of this advertisement?" If "Yes," a prescribed questioning procedure is followed to determine the observation and reading of each component part of the advertisement. (Illustration, headline, signature and copy blocks.)

After these questions are asked, each respondent is classified as follows:

"Noted" Reader: A person who remembered having previously seen the advertisement in the issue being studied.

"Associated" Reader: A person who not only "Noted" the advertisement but also saw or read some part of it which clearly indicated the brand or advertiser.

"Read Most" Reader: A person who read half or more of the written material in the ad.

After all ads are asked about, interviewers record basic classification data on sex, age, occupation, marital status, race, income, family size and composition so that sampling can be checked and cross-tabulations of readership can be made. Readership and demographics are recorded on standardized questionnaires which are returned to the Home Office for tabulation by electronic computer.

Basic Form of Starch Reports

Reports are compiled issue by issue and include three features:
1) Labeled issue
2) Summary Report
3) Adnorm Tables

How To Use Starch Readership Reports

Over the years Starch Readership data have consistently shown that the best scoring advertisements outperform the poorest ads in the same product category and size and color groupings by significant margins. Properly used, Starch data help advertisers and agencies to identify the types of advertisement layouts that attract and retain the highest readership and those that result in average or poor readership.

To realize the greatest potential from Starch Readership Reports, data for individual ads should not be used for sharp comparisons but should be regarded as broad indicators subject to modification with the addition of more data. The Starch Readership Service has been designed to be both inexpensive and reliable for use on a continuing basis. Therefore, it is possible to accumulate, study and analyze a large mass of readership data. The value of Starch data compounds when used over a period of time to track advertising performance.

Comparison is the keynote in using Starch Readership data:
1. Compare current advertisements against those of competitors.
2. Compare current campaign against previous campaigns.
3. Compare current campaign against competitors' previous campaigns.
4. Compare current advertisements and campaigns against Starch Adnorms tables.

It is especially important to compare advertisements with identical or at least similar product interest levels. Average the figures for several insertions rather than use the scores for single advertisements.

Look for recurring factors in order to establish significant trends.

What factors distinguish the high scoring advertisements from the low ones? Using the data on the component parts, try to see what factors work best in converting headline readers to thorough readers. The objective is to isolate the high scoring techniques. Study advertisements for theme and method of treatment. How do display advertisements compare with editorial-type insertions? Does the direct or indirect approach work best?

The use of Starch Readership Reports provides a practical and economical method of studying the readership performance of advertisements, as well as a means of suggesting changes for improving readership levels in the future. Remember, however, the more broadly based your conclusions are, the sounder they are likely to be.

A Word of Caution

Advertisement readership scores such as those provided by Starch are only relative measures of advertising performance. The level of such scores can vary significantly from issue to issue, and from publication to publication. In addition, no readership service measures or pretends to measure how many of those who received a copy of the publication actually read it. Therefore, readership studies cannot and should not be used to compare publications.

Additional Starch Services include Hitchhike Questions, Starch Impression Studies, Adnorms Report, General Magazine Ad-files, Readership Analysis, Working Women Readership Studies and Tested Copy.

Anaconda's High-Rated Ad

How Starch annotates studied ads is shown by Anaconda American Brass Company's outstanding one-page four-color ad. This ad, which appeared in *Production* magazine, scored an exceptionally high Noted rating of 64, as will be seen from the large sticker at the top of the ad—the one headed "Ad as a whole."

Seen-Associated rating for Anaconda American Brass Company's great ad is an unusually high 47, and Read Most is 14.

This ad topped all other studied advertisements in this issue of *Production* in all three degrees of readership. This ad beat all others in attracting readership, even four-color spreads.

And when it comes to delivering a large number of prospects on a readers-per-dollar basis, Anaconda's advertisement really produces measured against this criterion, also. Cost ratios, according to Starch, are as follows: Noted, 181; Seen-Associated, 171; Read Most, 175.

THINK COPPER

READ
3

AD AS A WHOLE
Noted Assn. Read Most
64 47 14

SEEN
64

READ
41

You'll net greater durability and fatigue resist: with modern coppermetals

Today's fatigue-resistant coppermetals are design-d to resist stresses and strains either indoors or out . . . stand up against conditions that often cause other metals t̶ ak away at the point they're most needed.

TEXT READ
NONE   MOST
17   14

Think of the durability and fatigue resistan metals. Then think of their other practical qualities, such as conductivity, machinability, bility, corrosion resistance and the wide range of colors and finishes available. Then call us.

For High Performance Alloys Think...

SIGNATURE
46

ANACO
AMERICAN BRASS C...

This means the ad worked a bit over three-fourths again as hard as the median for the book.

Because it is a four-color advertisement, the ad would have been expected to produce approximately 50 percent more readership than would a comparable black-and-white ad, of course. But this ad did even better.

Not illustrated is the back-up of the four-color ad, this page in two-color, orange and black. This also achieved usually high readership. This is due in part to a rub-off effect from the preceding four-color ad which really pulled the readers in, as well as to the fact that the advertiser gave the reader product benefits and solid nuts-and-bolts product information. And even with all of the individual elements in the ad, layout is clean and attractive—and the advertiser used a highly readable serif type face that's easy on the eyes.

One-Color Ad Scores Well

Let's look now at the number one black-and-white one-page advertisement in the same issue of *Production,* Kimberly-Clark's fine ad illustrated nearby.

The ad as a whole received a Noted score of 35, Seen-Associated 28, and Read Most 10. Compared to the issue median of 21 percent Noted, this ad lured a full 60 percent more readers than did the ad that ranked right in the middle.

It's apparent from the scores on various elements of the ad that readership was thorough and that interest for the reader was sustained from illustration to signature. Every element held up its end and contributed to the total impact.

Kimberly-Clark Corporation's excellent ad ranked 17th in the issue of studied ads, Starch said. Considering that this compares a one-page black-and-white ad with spreads, two-color spreads, and one-page four-color ads—as well as four-color spreads—this is bragging performance, nothing less.

Even more noteworthy, though, and of greater importance to the advertiser is the terrific job the ad did of delivering an unusually large number of readers per dollar.

Cost Ratios of Kimberly-Clark's black-and-white ad were extremely high—highest, in fact, of any studied advertisement in this issue of *Production* with the exception of one two-thirds page two-color ad on saw blades and drills. What makes the performance of Kimberly-Clark's ad especially impressive is that it is for a product of low inherent interest. Despite a heart full of love for the homely disposable paper wipes that bring in the salary, even industrial marketing manager T. L. LaPin admits the product lacks inherent appeal—although Kimberly-Clark's *selling proposition* is superb.

Here are the Cost Ratio figures for this ad: Noted, 189; Seen-Associated, 193; Read Most, 238. Hard-working advertising dollars, those!

Although this builder of executive jets

saves a small fortune by using our disposable paper wipers instead of cloth,

True, the money is not to be sneezed at. Savings of over $5,000 shop towels is definitely a more. Our towels are inert, ive, clean, and fresh. They ngs, cuttings, or paint chips—things that can infest even a newly-laundered cloth towel.

So our wipers are perfect for all manufacturing that cannot tolerate contamination of any sort. And this holds for everything from jets to jellybeans.

If you too have a critical wiping operation, why not call your local distributor or write us at Neenah, Wisconsin? We know what counts.

that's not what counts.

KIMBERLY-CLARK FAMILY INDUSTRIAL WIPERS

WELS® KIMWIPES® KAYDRY® LITHOWIPES® TERI®TOWELS

Write, wire or call Commercial Products Department
KIMBERLY-CLARK CORPORATION
Neenah, Wisconsin 54956 · 722-3311 (414)

This one-page black-and-white ad by Kimberly-Clark Corporation outscored two-color and full-color spreads in the same magazine.

Starch always includes directions on how to use and interpret the study in every copy that's sent to a client; it's a handy memory refresher. Also available on request from Starch headquarters or one of the many local offices across the country is a variety of literature explaining the Starch system in more detail, and with many helpful suggestions for making more effective use of the research material once you have it. You'll probably find it interesting.

Ad-Chart Awareness Study

Ad-Chart Awareness Studies are available from Ad-Chart Services, Chilton Company, Chilton Way, Radnor, Pennsylvania 19089.

Reports must be ordered directly from Ad-Chart Services, and they must be reserved in advance of the study. Cost is $50 per report. The reports are mailed from seven to nine weeks after issue date.

Ad-Chart Awareness and Advertising Management studies are an advertising measuring tool which gauges communication in selected business publications by means of:

1. Scientific probability sampling methods.
2. Personal interview of qualified primary readers of the magazine by trained personnel.
3. Carefully designed, pretested questionnaires.
4. Exact coding and tabulating procedures.

The studies reflect "how informative" an advertisement was to issue readers. Also, a highly useful separate section of the report lists both readership and information scores for those readers *who claimed purchasing or specifying influence in individual product or service categories.* These are the individuals to whom your message is primarily directed; these are the individuals who can make or break your company's sales.

Using Ad-Chart Awareness and Advertising Management studies helps the advertising manager answer the following kinds of questions:

- To what degree was my advertisement noticed and read?
- How informative did the readers find my advertisement?
- How well did the readers who claimed purchasing or specifying influence in my product category read my advertisement? How informative did they find it? Is there any difference between the scores of total respondents and those who claimed purchasing or specifying influence?
- What are the job titles, job functions, or job responsibilities of the reading audience?

- What is the effect on readership of a long-term advertising campaign?
- How did my advertisement's readership scores compare with the scores of other advertisements of the same size, and same color, and of the same type? How did it compare with ads in the same product category? (These would be ads run by competitors.)

Studies are based on a minimum of 100 personal interviews of primary readers—not pass-on readers. Respondents are scientifically selected by means of a probability sampling procedure unique among reader measurement surveys. The sample represents the major characteristics of the publication's circulation, including geographic location, type of industry or business, and job title or job responsibility of respondents.

All personal interviews are conducted by professional Chilton Research personnel. The reader must first verify the claim that he read the issue. He is then taken through the publication (page starting points are varied to minimize position bias) and asked to indicate the extent to which he saw and read the advertisements under study, and how informative he found them.

Profile data on each respondent are also obtained.

Coding, tabulation and preparation of reports are under the direction of Ad-Chart Services.

What the Report Contains

An Ad-Chart Advertising Management report consists of three sections:

I. ANALYSIS OF RESPONDENTS provides the following basic profile information about the readers interviewed:

1. Respondents' job titles and functions.
2. Respondents' number of years in specific industry.
3. Respondents' claiming purchase influence in each product category.

II. READERSHIP AND INFORMATION INDEX OF TOTAL RESPONDENTS provides quantitative information on reader traffic and information scores:

1. Readership scores for advertisements divided into "Noticed," "Started to Read," and "Read Half or More" percentages.
2. Scores ranked by advertisement size and color within each product category.
3. Informative scores for advertisements.

III. READERSHIP AND INFORMATION INDEX OF RE-SPONDENTS CLAIMING PURCHASE INFLUENCE IN PRODUCT CATEGORIES provides quantitative information on reader traffic and information scores:

1. Purchase influence readership scores for advertisements divided into "Noticed," "Started to Read," and "Read Half or More" percentages.
2. Scores ranked by advertisement size and color within each product category.
3. Informative scores for advertisements.

Definitions of Report Terms

Product Category—Division into which the product or service advertised is placed according to use and function.

Advertiser—Name of manufacturer or company.

Page—Page number in issue where advertisement is found.

Size/Color—Shown by following code: P-page; BW-black-and-white; 2C—two-color; 3C—three-color; 4C—four-color; INS—insert; BLD—bleed; SPRD—spread; ROP—run of press.

Averages for Product Category—Average percentage scores of all advertisements in product category. Advertisements are ranked within each product category according to size and color.

Questions frequently asked about Ad-Chart Awareness and Advertising Management studies are:

How does Ad-Chart differ? Ad-Chart is not just another readership study. Rather, it is a management and marketing tool for advertisers and agencies. Readership information is only one part of an Ad-Chart report.

Some of the ways that Ad-Chart is different include the following:

A. National probability sample of magazine's circulation.
B. Results scientifically projectable to primary reading audience. (This is one of the possible shortcomings of other studies.)
C. Telephone screening determines current issue readers.
D. Valid, time-tested questioning technique.
E. Personal interviewing.
F. Only primary readers interviewed.
G. Readership and informative scores *for purchasing influence respondents*, as well as total respondents.
H. Number of items studied per issue limited to reduce respondent fatigue.

What are the advantages of Ad-Chart probability sampling? Professor George Katona, of the University of Michigan Survey Research Center, says, "For reliable, scientific investigations, aimed at a predetermined substantial degree of precision, there is no substitute for probability sampling." This is from his work, *The Psychological Analysis of Economic Behavior.*

Ad-Chart respondents interviewed are subsampled from a probability sample of a magazine's primary circulation, reflecting in miniature all of the major characteristics of the circulation.

These include geographic distribution, SIC, age, education, job title, job function and purchase influence in the case of business magazines. Appropriate demographic and marketing characteristics are also reflected for circulations of consumer magazines.

The most prominent advantages of an Ad-Chart probability sample are:

A. Projectability of results to total primary reading audience of a specific issue at the time of interviewing.
B. Accurate representation of actual reading patterns and market characteristics, at a fraction of the cost of a census-type survey.
C. Quick determination of changes in the character of the reading audience.
D. Objective evaluation of advertising performance and effectiveness.
E. Consistency in reporting results over time.

Is a sample of 100 really large enough? This question is asked frequently about Ad-Chart, as about other readership studies. In the case of Ad-Chart, the answer is an unequivocal *yes*, considering the normal needs of the user.

As a true probability sample, the Ad-Chart sample accurately reflects the percentage distribution of the major characterisitics of a magazine's circulation—including readership—with an average sampling variation of less than four percentage points.

Composed of at least 100 completed personal interviews, an Ad-Chart sample is subsampled from a substantially larger probability sample of recipients of the publication.

Actually, the proportion of total circulation names drawn into an Ad-Chart sample is higher than the proportions used in many widely accepted government surveys.

The Ad-Chart probability sampling technique, based on a high completion rate, has proven to be reliable over hundreds of studies.

Moreover, since separate samples are used for each Ad-Chart study, the major characteristic results attain even more reliability over time.

What does an Ad-Chart Awareness Report include?

A. Full disclosure of methodology and procedures used.

B. Profile and marketing information about respondents interviewed.

C. Readership and information scores for 50 advertisements, presented by product groupings, of total respondents.

D. Readership and information scores for all respondents claiming purchasing influence, by product category.

Why Scores Are Higher

Why are Ad-Chart scores higher? The quality of Ad-Chart research reflects reading of an advertising and editorial message that is much closer to reality.

Quality controls, including a national probability sample, telephone screening for verified readers, and *personal* interviews with primary readers only, partly account for higher scores. Valid readership research, for example, has shown that primary readers read more intensively than do secondary readers.

Another factor is the number of advertisements and editorial items studied. Many readership services study as many as 125 items per issue; Ad-Chart limits items to 60. Thus, respondent fatigue is minimized and a more accurate response is obtained from the studied items.

In every Ad-Chart Awareness and Advertising Management study is a checklist to help the advertising manager make the most of the information the study provides him. This reads:

USE THIS CHECKLIST TO HELP ANALYZE YOUR AD—CHART SCORES IN THIS ISSUE OF *IRON AGE*

☐ Carefully check profiles of readers (white pages) to determine if publication is delivering the kinds of readers you desire.

☐ Compare your ad scores (yellow pages) with those of competitors.

☐ Compare your ad scores (yellow pages) with the averages for product categories.

☐ Compare your ad scores (yellow pages) with the averages for all ads of the same size and color on the green page.

☐ Compare readership scores to total respondents (yellow pages) with purchase influence scores on the blue pages.

- [ ] Compare your purchase influence scores (blue pages) with those of competitors.
- [ ] Compare your purchase influence scores (blue pages) with averages for product category.
- [ ] Pay particular attention to all your "informative" scores and relate them to your ad objectives.
- [ ] Have Ad-Chart complete a special breakout showing readership and nonreadership of your ad by corporate officials, engineers, department heads, etc., or perhaps by number of years in the field.

Manville Ratings

This study is available from Richard Manville Research, Inc., 211 E. 43rd St., New York, New York 10017.

The Manville Ratings are based on approximately 100 personal interviews with a cross section of a magazine's readers. These are "randomly drawn from the subscription lists in urban markets." Cities are preselected. A new sample is selected for each issue studied. No sample names are repeated. No home subscriptions are included in the sample.

Measurements are obtained for:

1. Percentage of readers who saw the ad.
2. Percentage of readers who read the ad.
3. Percentage of readers who read one-half or more of the ad.
4. Attitude-Change Score: An index score which attempts to measure the change in the reader's feelings toward the product as a result of exposure to the ad.
5. Manville Effectiveness Ratings: A composite index obtained by multiplying the Seen Score by the Attitude Change Score.

Attitude Change was measured as follows: For each ad read, respondents were asked, "In what way, if any, has your opinion *of this product* changed as a result of seeing this ad?" The scale is a numerical rating ranging from plus 4 to minus 4.

In a recent letter to the author, Mr. Manville observes—and it's very difficult to refute his contention—that "There is no necessary correlation between an ad which scored a high 'noted' score and ads which were effective. By 'effective' we mean an advertisement that increased the favorable attitude *towards the product*. Note that we are not measuring the ad, but the mind of the reader."

And the weight of logic is on Mr. Manville's side when he says, "We have dozens of case histories to show that ads which scored high in 'noted' scores, scored low in persuasiveness.''

Noted and Persuasiveness do not necessarily go hand in hand like two lovers in the spring, but the fact remains that *to get the chance to persuade, the advertisement must first be noticed by the reader, it must stop him, interest him and he must read it. All of this precedes the act of persuading him.*

Perhaps in no other area of industrial advertising does as much confusion exist as in making use of the readership ratings that advertisements we've created have received.

Most industrial advertising personnel need a registered, well-trained guide to lead them through the bewildering labyrinth the various services have created due to a complete lack of comparability.

As Roger Barton wrote in *Media/scope,* ''One of the factors that militates against the use of advertising readership studies on a comparable basis is differences in methods and findings that are found among the more than two dozen rating services.

''For instance, the average noted score for a one-page black-and-white advertisement studied by one service is 18 percent, that produced by another service 55 percent, and that by a third 33 percent.''

This wide variation in what is considered ''average'' is indeed striking when it is seen in tabular form. Below is a list of the averages established by some of the leading services:

Service	What is Measured	Average Rating of a One-Page, Black-and-White Advertisement
Starch	Noted	18%
Mills Shepard	Remembered Having Seen	31
Ad-Chart	Noticed	55
Reader Feedback	Saw	33
Readex	Interest	12
Ad-Gage	Interest	5.9*
Advertising Impact Measurement	Read	34

Comparing the scores an advertisement earned in different publications that were studied by competitive services means nothing if the raw figures are compared because they are obviously apples and oranges, hence are not directly comparable.

Attempting to compare them can be very deceptive and lead to erroneous conclusions—particularly as regards how well-read various advertisements actually are. This is due in part to the methodology of various services, as well as to the fact that some ratings are for *interest* and others are for *readership.* There's a vast difference between them.

---

*This figure is based on 49 studies conducted for *Foundry* magazine at this writing. The figure varies slightly from one issue to another, although seldom more than .2 percentage points.

The only way in which the ratings become meaningful is if they are both compared to the average score for the particular issue of the publications that were studied. An ad is either average, above average, or below average. No figures can dispute this.

Advertising scores, as provided by the various readership services, have just one main purpose for being. By providing a yardstick, they encourage advertisers and agencies to prepare more effective ads.

Until something is measured it is pretty hard to make it better—or to know how to, that is.

So observed the Advertising Research Foundation some years ago when considering the question of readership scores. The extreme difficulty of comparing and interpreting the scores caused the problem to be considered initially.

Too many questions remained unanswered. What, for example, does a score of 15 mean? Is it good, bad, or indifferent? And how good, bad, or indifferent?

The Letter Grade Ad Scoring System

The Advertising Research Foundation was quick to point out there is yet another complication. For reasons as yet unknown, the *level* of scores will vary from issue to issue of the same publication as rated by the same service. Usually this variation is only a few points. However, it is not at all uncommon for the average score for one-page ads to vary all the way from 11 to 22 during the course of a year. In one issue of a book the Center analyzed, a score of 22 would be just average; in another issue of the same publication it would be one of the top ads in the book.

Inconsistency was the name of the game.

So ARF determined just what it was that caused the discrepancies. It quickly found that different practitioners of industrial advertising had developed their own individual ways of interpreting scores. One way is to use issue medians, as discussed. Median scores are calculated for different-sized ads, and then individual ad scores are reported as so many points above or below the median.

However, there are several stumbling blocks in such a solution to the problem. First, it involves much time-consuming work. Second, there may not have been enough advertisements of a given size or product group in the issue to have the medians mean anything. Finally, users of the data are prone to exaggerate the significance of small differences from the median—if an ad is merely one or two points above the median, they are apt to assume immediately that it is an excellent ad, or vice-versa.

ARF's Project Council for Analysis of Advertising Readership Studies worked assiduously for a year and a half on ways of cutting through this confusion, and some time ago it introduced the Letter Grade Ad Scoring System.

This system, which is outlined below, surmounts most of the difficulties previously mentioned, and the reports based on it have been found to be easily understandable and meaningful to the users of readership scores.

As a matter of interest, it hs been found that more than 80 percent of all industrial advertisers with budgets of more than $100,000 are consistent users of readership studies. Firms with lower budgets are occasional users, although a large number of smaller advertisers never avail themselves of the wealth of information at their fingertips—usually free for the asking. This may well be because of the confusion and lack of comparability of scores.

A total of 78 business publications have announced they will supply Letter Grade scores on ads; this is in addition to the readership ratings they normally make available to advertisers. In addition, a number of other magazines will give you Letter Grade scores *if you make the request*. Ask for them—they cost nothing and are immensely useful.

Essence of the Letter Grade Ad Scoring System is to rank ads as follows:

A—Ads that compare with the top sixth of all ads in the past year.

B—Ads that compare with the next sixth.

C—Ads comparable to the middle third of all ads in the past year.

D—Those in the next to bottom sixth.

E—Those in the bottom sixth.

Besides the basic A, B, C, D and E scores with which we've all been familiar since grammar school days, the very best advertisements are so outstanding they deserve special attention—so a special A+ classification has been established for these ads that are in the top 5 percent of all advertisements.

Readership By Prospects vs. Readership By Total Audience

Most industrial advertising managers, and agency people, too, for that matter, are preoccupied with readership ratings. They are beset with the obsession that their ads *must* achieve outstanding readership ratings; otherwise, they seem to feel, it is a reflection on their honor, their character, and their loyalty to flag and country.

Everybody concerned is hypnotized by sheer numbers, with quantity, with a burning desire to out-achieve all competitors in the great game of readership ratings. They are enamored with high ratings. Entirely overlooked is that the ads may be absolutely terrific, so great that the magazine's audience simply cannot refrain from reading. In fact, *most* of the audience reads the ads even if they have not one whit of interest in the product, don't need it, don't want it, can't use it, can't specify it, can't purchase it.

This is plain silly. It's carrying the matter far too far and attaching far too much importance to the ratings an ad receives.

It's much better to attract the attention of those who are legitimate prospects, those for whom your product solves a problem, those who can specify and purchase it.

This holds true despite the fact that your advertisement itself should qualify the readers so that those who are not prospects can skip over it, and those who are will—hopefully—read it.

If the advertisement is well-conceived and well-constructed and the right people read it, it can be a roaring success if it achieves only a 12 percent Noted, a 6 percent Seen-Associated, and 3 percent Read Most. If those who are your prime prospects are those who are reading your ads, those are very successful advertisements indeed.

You can determine this to some extent the response to the ads. If your inquiry volume is high, if your negotiations activity is high, if your rate of conversion to sales is high, your ads are working overtime for you.

Readership of the ad by *bona fide* prospects is, of more critical importance than mere masses of readers who may or may not be prospective live customers. And this is undoubtedly one of the more important elements in measuring advertising effectiveness insofar as a readership service can determine it.

Readership Scores and Media Selection

Advertising personnel most familiar with readership studies—and even the various services themselves—strongly urge that readership ratings should not be used in selection of media.

Systems and numerical values used by the services differ too greatly to permit comparing results an advertisement achieved in one publication versus another magazine. An extremely high score in one book does not necessarily mean that medium is better for a given product or a specific advertisement than is a magazine in which the ad received a rating that was something less than sensational.

However, it is interesting to note that the various services have very carefully refrained from accepting as clients magazines that are direct competitors such as *Iron Age* and *Iron & Steel Engineer, Commercial Car Journal* and *Fleet Owner, Scientific American* and *Science & Technology.*

To do so would enable too many partially informed advertising people to leap to too many partially-correct conclusions—as well as too many that have little relevancy to the "true facts" of the matter. Because the fact is using readership ratings to determine that one publication is more desirable than another has little or no place in the scheme of things.

Leading business publications can and do provide proof of readership for the doubters, however, by means of studies of the audiences they reach. This data is competitive only in that it tends to make the publication disseminating it appear desirable; and making yourself look desirable is the world's fastest way to make yourself looked at with raised eyebrows. This information does not compare readership scores of advertisements in one magazine versus another, although probabilities are rightfully discussed. Every advertising manager and agency man has the right to request such information from publications—and *should* request it so as to have all pertinent facts at hand prior to making a decision.

Factors That Influence Readership

In preceding chapters when the creative process was discussed, many factors affecting readership were touched upon because they influence how the ad should be constructed in order to get the maximum return from it.

There are many others, however—actually enough to fill a book almost this size. At this time some of the more important ones bear looking into. This will involve the slaying of a few fearsome dragons that have long threatened the happiness of hapless advertising people who practically cringe when confronted with them. These are negative factors, of course.

Others, while perfectly valid, bear remembering because they exert a positive effect on readership of your ads.

Some that have been kicking around for decades were of unquestioned validity 'way back when—but today is not 'way back when. Tremendous changes have taken place in industrial advertising and in the media in which it appears. Today's business press is well-edited, helpful, interesting, and attractive. It is a far cry from the many drab publications that people in industry were supposed to read 25 years ago "because it is good for you."

Let's examine a few of these factors that influence readership—or that don't influence it.

Front of the Book vs. Back of the Book

Before business publications achieved their present degree of sophistication, advertisers clamored for positions "up front." It was felt that readership fell off rapidly once the halfway point was reached, and that advertisements in the second half of the magazine were, in effect, consigned to some sort of unspeakable oblivion due to their position.

Considerable justification for this belief existed at one time. Readership *did* fall off drastically toward the back of the book. But today more knowledgeable editing spreads interest—and editorial matter—throughout the magazine so the reader no longer lingers longer in the front and middle of the magazine than he or she does toward the tag end.

Marsteller Inc., in its internal house organ *Pubset*, had this to say on the subject:

ADVERTISING READERSHIP, FRONT VS. BACK OF ISSUE?

This question has frequently been asked, so we've checked our library and marketing files with the following results:

1. Several years ago, the Daniel Starch readership research organization searched through researched issues of publications like *Time, Life, Satevepost, Good Housekeeping,* and *McCall's* to find identical advertisements which had appeared at least once in each of three positions in the magazines—front, middle, and back. They found 144 such ads. An analysis was conducted whereby the "front of book" score for each ad was assigned an index value of 100, and that same ad's performance was calculated as above or below 100 in the other positions. The index values were then converted back to readership scores, with this result:

	Noted	Seen-Associated	Read Most
Front	48%	44%	10%
Middle	45	41	10
Back	44	41	11

These data indicate that (exclusive of cover positions) readership is fairly uniform from front to back, at least for the publications included in the test.

2. The Starch organization also did a major analysis of 12 million inquiries. This analysis concluded that "large or small numbers of people read an advertisement dependent on two factors: (1) the natural inherent product and subject interest to the reader and (2) the characteristics of the advertisement itself— what it says and how it says it." Dr. Starch reported "whether an advertisement is within the first dozen pages or the last dozen pages is of relatively minor importance. To be sure, cover positions and pages facing them do have decided attention advantages." He went on further to say that "The front 10 percent of pages show a slightly higher rate of (inquiry) returns, but the difference in position is completely overshadowed by the substance of layout and copy."

3. Audits & Surveys studied an issue of *Life* and an issue of *Look* on a similar basis, and came to the same conclusion in both cases.

4. Cahners' *Purchasing* magazine was analyzed also. A representative issue of the publication had 51 full-page ads (black-and-white and two-color). The readership scores were separated for the first 17, the second 17, and back 17, by positions in the issue, with this result:

	Average Noted Score
1st 17 ads	22.2%
2nd 17 ads	21.1
3rd 17 ads	21.8

5. A contributing editor to *Media/Scope* treated this subject as follows:

"There is sufficient evidence to suggest that reader traffic does not start at its highest point on the first page and decrease continually to the last. There are peaks and valleys which reflect the efforts of magazine editors to maintain good pacing and reader interest throughout the issue."

All of which goes to show that trade publications are read front to back, thus laying to rest another old wives' tale.

One fact that's often overlooked is that "position" cannot help a bad ad or hurt a good one. An advertisement that's inept and uninteresting will not receive high readership simply because it happens to be right up in the very front of the book. It will receive low readership because it doesn't deserve high readership.

And a good advertisement will be read and be read by a sizable portion of the buying influences you're trying to reach if it's *really* a good advertisement, whether it's on Page 2 or Page 176.

Preferred Positions

Preferred positions, such as the inside front cover, cover 3, and the back cover, invariably receive higher readership than do the so-called "inside" positions. That is why they are able to command a premium price.

According to Starch, the back cover (Cover 4, it's often called) of the typical business publication receives approximately 65 percent more readership than does an inside page. The second cover (inside front cover) attracts about 30 percent more readers than do pages in the middle of the book. The third cover (inside back cover) also receives approximately 30 percent more readership than do inside pages.

Starch undoubtedly has a mass of statistics as high as Chicago's John Hancock building to back up his observations. As far as the fourth cover and the second cover are concerned, he's undoubtedly right. However, most knowledgeable industrial advertising men scorn third covers as not worth the extra cost. And it has been the author's experience that this is a "dead" position—one that is not only *not* worth more money, but actually one to be avoided. Ads for my clients and companies have never done well on any third cover in some two decades. This is one man's opinion compared with statistics.

Certain preferred positions inside the book which usually command a preferred-position price *are* good buys and can be depended upon to deliver higher readership than run-of-book positions.

For instance, the first page in the book, the one facing the inside front cover, usually tallies up around 25-30 percent more readers than do random pages inside the publication. But you pay more, too.

Pages facing certain editorial matter inside the book, such as the editor's editorial, for example, are charged for at a premium rate in most instances. But they invariably deliver more readers to the advertisement than it would receive in a run-of-publication position.

In its Laboratory of Advertising Performance, McGraw-Hill reports on an analysis of 89 issues of two of its magazines after 8,900 personal interviews by Daniel Starch & Staff. Involved were nine different advertisers whose advertisements had appeared inside the book and on various covers. Here is the readership they received:

Company	Second Cover	Third Cover	Fourth Cover	Run-of-book
A	27.9%			17.3%
B	25.3			16.1
C	20.8			16.5
D	19.0			14.3
E	16.6			13.9
F		27.0%		19.2
G			28.5%	14.2
H			26.2	23.0
B*			26.0	16.1

Readership advantages for cover positons ranged from 14 percent to more than 100 percent above that received *for the same type of advertisements* inside the magazine. On a 12-time basis, the average cover costs somewhat more than one-third more than an inside page; depending on the ad and on the company that runs it, this extra cost is usually offset by more than that much additional readership.

Advertisers are extremely fond of good preferred positions, and heads-up advertising managers and agencies have more than their fair share of these positions that give increased exposure and readership.

A tip: Get as many second and fourth covers as you can—in the best publications in your field, of course. Even if management wields the ax on the budget at some time in the future, it can frequently be

---

*One advertiser, Company "B," had experience with second covers, fourth covers and run-of-book inside pages.

dissuaded from forcing you to relinquish the cover positions. Once abandoned, they're usually gone forever for all practical purposes.

Cover positions in the leading trade publications have a formal "waiting list" of advertisers who are panting with ill-concealed eagerness to sew them up. The old Diamond T Motor Truck Company, for instance, had a "bid" in for almost 10 years for the fourth cover of *Commercial Car Journal* before it became available.

Right vs. Left

In politics right is right and left is wrong, but we're discussing here the age-old question of right-hand pages versus left-hand pages. This is so controversial that a heated discussion of politics or religion is considered noncontroversial in comparison. Even the experts—or those who claim to be experts—disagree with each other on this.

For example, Starch studies of some publications show that right-hand pages have at least a 10 percent advantage over left-hand pages. This is due, no doubt, to the fact that most of us are both right-handed and right-eyed. As a consequence we hold a magazine so that the right hand turns the pages. And because this is the page that is thumbed to get a grasp on it so it can be turned, the mind automatically tends to concentrate more attention on this page than on the opposite, left-hand page.

Readex ratings of some magazines bear out the conclusion that Starch has reached.

On the other hand, Mills Shepard studies of *Electrical World* indicated that left-hand pages receive 2 percent more readership than do right-hand pages.

And McGraw-Hill's Reader Feedback studies showed left-hand pages in *Textile World* receive 1 percent more readership than right-hand pages.

Probably the truth of the matter is that there's very little difference. Given a choice, though, which you usually are not, take the right-hand-page. You'll be ahead in the long run.

Fat vs. Thin

Size of issue also affects the readership an advertisement receives. Publishers are understandably anxious to pooh pooh the idea that fat issues of books cut readership of individual advertisements, and much research has been done in an effort to produce reliable data to dispel this idea. Most of it is undoubtedly valid, all of it is truthful.

McGraw-Hill states unequivocally that larger issues do *not* limit readership of advertisements. Instead, the publisher contends, the larger issues, if anything, offer a better chance of getting an ad noticed, along with an equal chance of getting the ad read.

A check of 147 issues of *Power* magazine and an equal number of issues of *Factory* showed that larger issues offer equal readership for the advertising and somewhat higher attention-getting values. Ads in seven issues of *Power* that were over 350 pages in length—the book, not the ads—averaged the highest Noted scores (22.9 percent) of any size-group of that publication, and they maintained a Read Most average of 8.7 percent. *Factory's* 10 issues over 400 pages in length scored the highest Noted average (23.4 percent) of any size-group of *Factory*, and maintained a Read Most average of 8.8 percent.

This is all well and good, but the fact remains that advertisements in fat issues of books have *less time spent on each individual ad* than do ads in thinner issues.

The competition in fat issues is greater, too, for there are just that many more ads clamoring for the attention of the reader. This makes the job harder for each individual advertisement in the issue.

And readers do not spend proportionately more time on fat issues than they do reading thin ones. The overall trend is to spend more time reading business publications than was spent, say, 10 years ago. Time spent on various publications differs greatly according to the field, although the average for all business publications would seem to be in the neighborhood of 1½ hours.

That's per issue, and it doesn't change very much whether fat or thin.

Continuity

On-again, off-again industrial advertisers—and there are many of them—accomplish just one thing: They throw away the money they spend on advertising. They don't *invest* it in continuous planned advertising; they *waste* it on sporadic advertising that's done by fits and starts at the whim of top management—or as sales start to decline.

American Business Press put it just about as well as anybody has in quite some time when it discussed continuity in an advertisement. Its ad read, in part:

> *In advertising, you have to be as relentless as a 30-year-old girl looking for a husband.*

That's because prospects simply do not remember your company. There's no earthly reason why they should. The prospect is, naturally enough, self-oriented, not your-company-oriented. You and your company are the farthest things from his mind—unless you deliberately inject yourself there somehow, such as by advertising.

"If there is one enterprise on earth that a 'quitter' should leave severely alone, it is advertising. To make a success of advertising, one must be prepared to stick like a barnacle on a boat's bottom," so said John Wanamaker, merchant, who made a success of his business due in large part to continuous advertising.

One study showed advertisers who appeared in every issue of two business publications averaged 21 percent higher readership than did those who used five issues or less. Advertisers in one monthly business magazine increased their readership scores after becoming 12-time advertisers.

Another study showed that a company increased recognition of its primary message 12 percent by upping its space from 7 one-third pages to 10 pages. A similar company cut its space from 13 to 7 pages and lost 6 percent in recognition.

The Laboratory of Advertising Performance reports on a study of several thousand advertisements and the massive difference continuity makes. Advertisers whose insertions amount to 12 or more pages a year get almost a fourth more readers at only three-quarters of the cost per reader than do those using six pages or less. The figures look like this, using a base of 100 at the low end:

Annual schedule	Scored ads	Readership	Cost per reader
1- 6 pages	1,007	100	100
7-11 pages	871	109	87
12 or more pages	1,567	123	74

These ads appeared in 135 issues of 10 publications studied by Reader Feedback; all were one-page black-and-white run-of-publication ads. Ads were grouped according to the total number of pages used by the advertiser in the publication and in the year in which it appeared, and the average readership of scored advertisements was calculated. The annual schedule was figured on the basis of the total amount of space used in the publication in that year.

Readership averages are based on total advertisements scored and are *not* weighted to give each publication equal representation. Approximately 13,500 personal interviews were made to develop the readership figures.

"Repetition makes reputation," said editor Arthur Brisbane. Right he was, too, for nothing in advertising succeeds like repetition. *Nothing*. Repetition is the essential ingredient for advertising success. It's merely another way of saying continuity, of course.

A common fallacy harbored by many managements of industrial companies is that "everybody knows about our company and the products we manufacture." The engineering-oriented, production-oriented throwbacks to the turn of the century who say this can usually be depended upon to add, "We don't really need to advertise. Why, we're the leader in the widget industry. Nobody will forget us if they need a new widget."

One advertising manager reports a company president who periodically asks him "for an alternative to advertising." A short, honest reply to that request could be: *Liquidate*.

Too often overlooked is the fact that prospects forget a company easily and fast. Readers of a publication in which a company advertises sporadically dismiss that company from their minds when its advertisements stop appearing regularly.

And there is no disputing that you advertise to a passing parade of buying influences, no matter what market. People you've sold move out. They retire. They die. They are promoted or transferred to another plant and/or another city. Stop advertising for a year and you've lost touch completely with at least one-third of the buying influences who "know your company and its products." Stop advertising for two years and more than half of all prospects are unaware of your company.

How efficient is your field sales force when that happens?

Proofs of Continuity's Value

The Scott Paper Company decided to test the effect of different levels of advertising on recognition for Scott as a manufacturer of paper towels for industrial washrooms. So Laboratory of Advertising Performance made a series of recognition surveys in three geograpical areas of the country.

With the cooperation of *Business Week*, Scott ran about twice as many ads in one geographical area as in another. In a third area, no Scott towel advertisements appeared in the publication during the test period.

Recognition among subscribers to *Business Week*—all management people in business and industry, of course—was measured in all three areas before the advertising campaign started. It was measured again afterwards, using a sample of 1,000 names of individual subscribers to *Business Week* to represent a cross section of the audience for each geographical area; returns ran from 37 percent to 43.6 percent.

Using 100 as a base figure representing the level of recognition before the campaign started, it was found that recognition rose to 103 in the low-advertising area after four ads, and to 124 in the high advertising area after eight advertisements ran.

Another reason that continuity is so critically important is that not every issue of a business publication—even the very best ones in your field—is read by every one of your prospects.

A McGraw-Hill study on the subject showed that 95.1 percent of recipients of busines magazines read one out of four issues. It also showed that 49.5 percent read all four issues. Furthermore, the study disclosed that 28.5 percent read three out of four issues. And 12.1 percent read two out of four issues. But more than 95 percent read only one issue out of four—that's the point.

Unless your advertisements appear continuously, there is an excellent chance they'll not be seen by the people who could be most important to you. This is a chance no prudent advertiser takes.

A fringe benefit of continuity is that it reinforces the opinion of current users of your products; through being continuously exposed to your advertising messages, they are *resold* on your products and the value they represent.

How much is this worth? Nobody yet has attached a price tag to this benefit, and it's doubtful if anybody ever can. But this is an intangible you certainly wouldn't care to throw lightly out the window.

Continuity of advertising is essential. It all depends on what you want your advertising to do. You can eschew continuity and let people forget, or you can get them to remember who you are and what you sell by advertising continuously. Advertising continuity in the best business publications serving your market literally keeps your firm name and your products uppermost in prospects' minds.

Readership

One of the best ways to boost readership of all of your advertisements is to *run more than one ad in an issue* of the magazine you've selected as best for your company.

Unfortunately, this highly productive tactic is little understood by the naive innocents who inhabit management chairs throughout typical industrial firms. Nor is its importance realized even dimly by engineers who fancy themselves "marketing experts" in these backward companies.

One Chicago advertising executive tells of the two company presidents and one "marketing" vice-president—an excellent sales manager, he says—who practically throw up their hands in horror, emit little high-pitched squeaking noises and otherwise exhibit every symptom of having conniptions when faced with two company advertisements in one issue of a leading trade publication.

However, running two advertisements in the same issue obviously gives the advertiser twice the exposure that one provides. But it does much more.

Numerous studies have shown that the first ad in the book receives the same readership and Noted scores that it would if it ran alone, as would be expected. The second advertisement by the same advertiser, however, always receives *more* readership than the first ad did, and *more* readership than if it appeared unaccompanied by another ad. A cumulative effect results from having more than one advertisement in an issue.

This cumulative effect is greatly strengthened by the practice of a number of progressive advertisers of using consecutive right-hand pages, such as the Clark Equipment Company ads discussed in Chapter 9. Repetition is one of the pillars of advertising, and repetition of one-page ads on consecutive pages is one of the very best ways of creating tremendous impact in the reader's mind.

Even if multiple insertions do not follow each other on consecutive pages, each succeeding advertisement following the first one in the publication reinforces each of the others. The advertiser gains much in recognition and readership, and intangibly by creating the impression of a leader who dominates the magazine.

Dominating the magazine is translated in the reader's mind to dominating the industry. Such a positive attitude toward a company by its prospects is something everybody wants and only a few advertisers get.

Multiple insertions in the best business publications is a way to get it.

An Ad for All Seasons

Advertising, some "experts" would have it, is read when coyotes bark at the moon—only in certain months or at certain times of the year. This, too, is an old wives' tale. There's nothing to it.

The theory that advertising is not read in December because Christmas is at hand simply doesn't hold water—or snow, either. After all, the first of December rolls around every year and the world doesn't come to an end, nor does all of industry grind to a screaming halt.

But business still goes on. There is no automatic shut-down of productions lines or offices.

The seasonal pattern, if one ever existed, has become a thing of the past. Publishers are understandably anxious to lay to rest the old saw that "nobody reads trade advertisements in December because of Christmas, or in June, July, and August because of vacations."

To help determine whether or not there actually are seasonal trends in reader interest, McGraw-Hill's research department analyzed the reader service response of 10 of the company's magazines for each month of the year.

This analysis compared (1) the number of readers responding to each publication month by month for a full year to determine if there are seasonal patterns to response, and (2) the monthly response in one year compared to the monthly response in the following year.

Results showed there is no general pattern of high interest in one season and low interest in another. Rate of response fluctuated widely between different publications. In one, for instance, April was above average in seven out of ten magazines—but January, June, August, and December showed six highs out of the 10 publications surveyed. And these are supposedly the nonproductive months of the year.

Since every season provides examples of high reader response, the only conclusion to be reached is that an advertisement or an article which offers real help to the industrial reader can and does get a good response in any month of the year. If any seasonal variations do exist, they are not great enough to affect the ability of an editor or an advertiser to get a good response from the publication's readers.

Space vs. Message

Size of space also affects readership of your advertisements, and there's one easily remembered rule of thumb that cannot be lightly dismissed—the larger the space unit, the larger the illustration the ad can have. And it's the illustration that stops the reader in almost every instance. Larger illustrations and higher readership are almost always inseparable.

Larger space means higher attention value. More space gives you room to stretch in, room to tell your story more completely. Larger space produces greater impact.

This is assuming that all factors are equal—which they generally are not. The story is much the same in advertising as it is in boxing. Fight fans are well aware of the truth of the old saying that "a good big man can whip a good little man every time."

In advertising, this holds equally true. However, there's another side of the coin. Dr. Joseph E. Bachelder of the Advertising Research Foundation said in *Media/scope*: "The message in the ad is so important that to a certain extent one is comparing apples and oranges when comparing ads of the same size. A quarter-page ad with a real message and exceedingly well done in a creative fashion can outdo a two-page spread which has nothing to say and uses four color."

Dr. Bachelder is quite right. But the qualifier—*all other factors being equal*—rules out violent fluctuations in the level of creative quality and level of communications thinking.

One study, for instance, indicated that advertisements of the same size had a disparity of readership up to 20 times, and "in one extreme case" the ratio was 50 to 1, *Media/scope* said.

The scintillating advertisements that are truly brilliant in concept and execution will always be with us and they will always receive outstanding readership; so, too, will inept, inane ads continue to clutter up trade magazines and continue to be ignored.

Media/scope drew up a table to show the relative effectiveness of different size space units on an index basis. This is:

1 page	100
1 page, bleed	116-137
¼ page	29
⅓ page	33
½ page	44
⅔ page	64-75
2 pages (spread)	132-150
2 page insert	211-241
3 pages	171
5 pages	163-186

Advantages of use of larger space are born out in McGraw-Hill studies. In its Laboratory of Advertising Performance the publisher states: "Larger advertisements get higher readership. The larger the advertisement, the more readers it attracts. In addition, reader comments indicate that larger space permits the advertiser to get across a more complete message and a better impression of the company."

By all means run the largest ads the budget will permit. However, if you are forced to make the difficult choice of having either continuity or larger size ads, choose continuity. You'll be ahead in the long run running two-thirds page ads every month, as opposed to running spreads three or four times a year.

Concentration

"Listen carefully," ABP said. "That sound you hear, a subdued, saddened wail, is your advertising budget dribbling away. All over the place. On uninhabited wastelands, far-off shores.

"And all the time you wanted your advertising to shout and stomp, grab and get action. What went wrong?

"You were probably playing the wrong game: Scatteration. You should have been playing *concentration*—especially in the leading business publications. Only it isn't really a game, it's smart business.

"Playing the field costs money—wastes it, too. You lose the discounts available to consistent advertisers. And you lose the *impact* of continuity."

And you don't really buy yourself anything by scattering advertisements through a series of marginal publications. Because of circulation duplication, secondary publications usually provide relatively few new readers—and they do so at a cost that is truly exorbitant when it's considered as applying only to the *additional* readers the secondary book enables you to reach.

One or two leading magazines serving a field of business or industry will, on the average, reach the great majority of men who can be reached by *five* magazines—and will reach them at a fraction of the cost of all five.

This principle is called "The Law of Diminishing Returns" by McGraw-Hill, who says it can be demonstrated by finding out what magazines a group of customers or prospects read. By ranking the publications they list in order of number of mentions and finding out how many new readers each succeeding publication adds, it is possible to determine the number of additional new readers and how much it costs to reach them.

The publisher conducted a study in nine fields to determine the cost of adding additional publications to secure unduplicated readers.

Combined cost and unduplicated coverage of five leading publications was:

	Cumulative unduplicated coverage	Cumulative Cost
Leading	66%	24%
Second	83%	44%
Third	93%	65%
Fourth	98%	84%
Fifth	100%	100%

Thus we see the leading publication secured about two-thirds of the coverage at about one-fourth of the cost. The fifth publication added to the schedule performed the ridiculous task of adding only 2 percent additional coverage at 17 percent of the cost of all five publications combined.

Unless your company has money to throw away, it behooves you to recognize that there comes a point where the cost of reaching a few new, unduplicated readers through an additional publication becomes prohibitive.

Repeat Ads

Industrial advertisers (and perhaps consumer advertisers, as well) are maladjusted in one respect. They are out of harmony with their environment from failure to reach a satisfactory adjustment between the desire to see an advertisement achieve complete success and the burning ambition to create a new advertisement that might do more.

Pointing this up is the fact that industrial advertisers get tired of their advertisements *long before readers do.* This applies both to campaigns and to individual ads and is a major reason for a shocking waste of money every year.

This waste occurs because good advertisements are not repeated, or are not repeated enough times. They are not repeated because (1) advertisers are tired of them, and (2) advertisers do not understand a basic principle that ads can be repeated time after time without loss of effectiveness.

One study measured these recognition scores for 70 ads running four times each in business publications: First appearance, 23.5 percent; second, 23.6 percent; third, 24 percent; fourth, 23.5 percent.

Another study zeroed in on inquiries produced by 31 repeated ads, American Business Press reported. First appearance of the ads generated 1,525 inquiries; second appearance, 1,217; third, 1,178; fourth, 1,067. So how do you explain the ads continuing to produce at better than two-thirds the rate as compared to their first time around if "everybody's seen them already?"

An account executive in a major Chicago agency tells of an advertising manager-client who received a terse memo from a product manager complaining on two scores—he ran two advertisements in the same issue of the best magazine to serve the field, and one ad had been run three times before, the other twice before.

This incredible dereliction of duty, according to the product manager, was only slightly less serious than that performed by one Benedict Arnold.

Sad part of the story is that when the advertising manager memoed back to the effect that the company received *more than double* the exposure one ad would have produced due to the cumulative effect, that the medium was the best possible choice, and that repeat ads receive just as good readership as when they're virgin-pure, the vice-president of marketing got in the act. He called in the advertising manager, and in the true spirit of the engineering profession, sided with the product manager.

The Cold Facts

Center For Marketing Communications did a depth analysis of the performance of 80 ads which appeared four times in business publications under tightly controlled conditions. The ads ran in 23 publications during an 18-month period, with 65 advertisers involved.

The Center's conclusion is: "Industrial ads in general can be run *at least* four times in the same publication without material or necessary loss of effectiveness. This study indicates that readers of industrial publications look at and read each of the four appearances in virtually equal numbers. These findings hold true regardless of: (1) The readership service used. (2) The industry covered. (3) The publication in which the ad appears. (4) The type of question asked about readership. (5) The time interval between appearances of the ad. (6) Whether recognition or reading score is considered. (7) Whether the scores are based on personal interviews or mailed questionnaires."

Laboratory of Advertising Performance reports that "Four studies indicate little or no loss of readership for repeated advertisements, no matter what time elapses between the first and subsequent insertions."

Analysis of the readership of 1,600 repeated advertisements that ran up to four times each revealed the following, using an index of 100, according to LAP:

No. of Ads	Insertion	Readership
1,351	1st	100
1,351	2nd	100
197	1st	100
197	2nd	98
197	3rd	97
52	1st	100
52	2nd	103
52	3rd	103
52	4th	111

These and many other studies of multiple insertion advertising readership indicate that:

1. Little or no loss of readership as measured by Reader Feedback is indicated when advertisements are repeated once, twice, and three times.

2. Little or no change in thorough readership, as measured by Starch Read Most scores, is indicated for advertisements repeated once, twice, and three times.

3. Little or no shift in readership, as measured by Starch Noted scores, is indicated for advertisements repeated at intervals from one to 48 weeks between insertions in a weekly publication, or one to 12 months in a monthly magazine.

Chapter 18

DIRECT MAIL

DIRECT MAIL, according to the American Association of Advertising Agencies' Committee on Direct Mail, is "the use of mailed advertising to develop sales directly or indirectly, employing selected lists to achieve the desired circulation."

There are three separate and distinct forms of direct mail used today, the four A's claim. These are:

1. *Mail Media Advertising*—This is simply direct mail which produces sales *through established channels of distribution*. Examples of this form of direct mail advertising are: sales inquiry letters ("lead-getters"), credit-card offers, store-traffic builders, product couponing and sampling. Mail media advertising is directly competitive with magazines, newspapers, television, radio and other media for the advertising dollar.

2. *Mail Order Advertising*—This is direct mail which produces sales *directly with customers and prospects*. Examples are: sale of magazine and newspaper subscriptions, books, merchandise, correspondence courses, and other items sold directly by mail. Mail order advertising eliminates the use of a sales representative or middleman in the process of distribution. The important element is that completion of the sale is accomplished entirely by mail.

3. *Mail Sales Promotion*—Direct mail which stimulates or reinforces sales. Examples are: TV, radio, magazine, or newspaper advertising promotion. Others are: recipe books, instruction manuals, displays, coupons, annual reports, catalogs, external house organs, reference bulletins, etc.

By and large, the industrial advertising manager is primarily concerned with the first form—mail media advertising. Common usage of the term "direct mail" when it's applied to industrial mail programs mean mail media advertising, so in this chapter that is what is referred to henceforth unless otherwise noted.

Direct Mail Has Grown Up

While direct mail is still third in the hierarchy of advertising media it has tremendous volume today. When all of its facets, including mail order promotion, are included it represents an annual expenditure by American businesses of somewhere between three and five billion dollars. There are few businesses, organizations or individuals which do not use the medium in one form or another.

The "unseen medium," direct mail is about a half billion dollars ahead of consumer magazines in annual dollar volume, although consumer magazines are the next largest benefactor from the advertisers' dollars.

Direct Mail Is Misunderstood

More often than not, direct mail is misunderstood throughout industry. It is regarded either as a panacea for all that ails a company's sales, or as a vulgar pretender standing in the wings all ready and willing to siphon off the company's promotional dollars to no good end.

And direct mail is one of the easiest victims of the eager amateur who believes implicitly it is simple and easy to master because, after all, all you have to do is mail something to a prospect. This, of course, miraculously transforms the prospect into a cherished customer who is practically panting with eagerness to part with his or her hard-earned money— preferably in very large sums.

Corporate management in many small to medium-size industrial companies are the amateurs hardest to ignore. Their intentions are good. Although they have only a dim understanding at best of *how* they can use the magic of direct mail, their objective is a valid one—more sales.

These amateurs who tamper with the promotional program are horribly prone to abandon formal marketing objectives (if the company has any) and formal communications objectives (if the company has any) and go blithely off on a wild tangent. Without thought of the consequences they'd scuttle a program when it's half-completed, thus wasting most of the money allocated for it originally, and committing at the same time the worst sin of all—waste of precious time. It can't be replaced.

Most industrial ad people are accustomed to encountering more or less difficulty—usually more—in persuading management to accept the fact there is a certain time lag in every form of advertising. During this period it's all outgo, nothing is income. If only the managements of industrial companies would realize that advertising (in all media) they do this year will affect *next* year's sales—and those of the year *after*. Remarkably little industrial advertising produces measurable results *this* year. If it did, life would be much easier for all advertising managers. And industry would maintain continuity of advertising so as to reap benefits to the fullest.

Unfortunately, such managements know that mail is delivered in a matter of days almost any place in the country, so they also "know" that direct mail "should be used to produce sales now."

It seldom works that way.

Another thing about direct mail is that it is seemingly so easy to measure, particularly when compared to space advertising. After all, it should be a question of arithmetic, shouldn't it? You mail so many pieces to so many prospects and you reap so many orders as a result. This is mail order-type thinking, not direct mail advertising thinking.

Happily, a large portion of the misguided management thinking that reflects this naive attitude has changed as more research has been conducted to place the medium of direct mail where it belongs in the marketing communications media mix.

A Chicago advertising manager told the author of a company president who called him into his office one afternoon and said, "I want an alternative to this advertising we're doing. How about direct mail—we can save some money."

This president was neither more nor less uninformed than his peers in other companies on this score. That direct mail is a "cheap" medium is a fallacy that's even more widespread than dandruff.

Robert Stone, prolific writer on the subject of direct mail, acknowledged expert in this fascinating specialty for decades, and an *Advertising Age* columnist, said: "Direct mail is expensive. One of the most popular misconceptions about direct mail advertising is that it is inexpensive. Nothing could be further from reality. Direct mail is one of the most expensive advertising mediums at the disposal of today's business executive."

Fact of the matter is, the three most expensive ways yet devised by mortals to promote the sale of a product to industry are:

1. Television
2. Salespeople
3. Direct mail

This statement holds true since it is predicated upon the assumption that industry will continue to use direct mail, either in whole or in part, as a substitute or alternative for space advertising in trade publications. The advocate of direct mail, which is a very direct and highly personalized medium, who recommends it as the cure-all for all that ails a company's communications effort—and who recommends it to replace a mass medium—is on very wonky ground indeed. *Use of direct mail for this purpose is indefensible.*

A Most Personal Medium

In his monumental work, *The Dartnell Direct Mail and Mail Order Handbook,* Richard S. Hodgson advanced the thought that the greatest mistake made by industrial advertisers when using direct mail is the tendency to forget that their customers and prospects are people.

Instead, they tend to think of them only as engineers, purchasing agents, production supervisors, controllers, and so on. The fact that a prospect has a functional role in industry (otherwise, he or she wouldn't be there, of course) somehow obviates the necessity of approaching the prospect as a thinking, feeling human being with his or her fair share of emotions, hopes and aspirations.

This, in turn, leads to a gross misuse of direct mail, this most personal of mediums, by neophytes who want to "use up" all of those extra catalog sheets gathering dust in the back storeroom. They profess to see no need to "get fancy" in presenting a plain nuts-and-bolts story, they want to go pore-mouth (as we used to say in turnip-greens and hog-jowls country) about the task of cultivating a prospect's interest and convincing the prospect *this* is the promised land as far as he or she's concerned, *this* is the company to do business with, *this* is the company that's service-minded, *this* is the product he or she needs to solve all of his or her problems large and small.

To do so is a gross error.

Direct mail tyros who adopt this attitude and who try to penny-pinch their way to a curve on the sales chart that would make even the most hard-nosed company controller in all of industry break out in ecstatic smiles are doomed before they start—doomed to failure.

They conveniently ignore the fact that the industrial buyer in whom they're interested is being courted assiduously by other companies selling the same kind of widget. In short, competition has reared its ugly head—even in direct mail.

Industrial buyers, particularly those in metropolitan areas, are barraged with some 1,500 advertising impressions a day from all media. Only a tiny fraction of those messages make a real impression, a positive, forceful impression that can in any way alter the prospect's mind about a company or its products.

Audiences for industrial direct mail are smaller, more easily defined, and hence ideal prospective recipients for effective mailings even when the budget is limited. And competition is encountered from less companies than in the consumer field, although it is no less vigorous.

For this reason many industrial advertising managers using direct mail make the same mistake about this medium as they do about space advertisements. They regard the competition as more direct mail—or space ads—from their competitors. This is a fallacy, and a dangerous one at that.

Never for an instant lose sight of the fact that your competition is the direct mail sent to your prospect by every other industrial advertiser who contacts your prospect. Too, it is *every* advertiser—both industrial and consumer. Every individual has a limited amount of time. Each day contains just 24 hours. Each workday takes a bite of 8 or 9 or even 10 of those hours, no more. And in that given period of time the competition for the full attention of the individual you want to reach is intense.

Six Fundamental Principles of Direct Mail

Now that a few fallacies concerning direct mail have been exposed, let's look at some basic principles for successful industrial direct mail, as given by Edward N. Mayer, Jr., in his *Handbook of Industrial Direct Mail Advertising*, published by the Business/Professional Advertising Association. These principles are:

1. *There must be a need for the product or service being advertised.* However, it is quite possible to create a need by emphasizing a want, or an unfulfilled wish of the people you are trying to sell. But keep in mind that you can't sell electric blankets to people in the tropics; nor can you sell bottling machinery to a plant that manufactures canned goods exclusively.

2. *There must be a need for the product or service being advertised at the particular time it is being advertised.* Although there is very little seasonal appeal involved in the sale of most industrial products, it must be obvious that, even though you make the best snow-removal equipment available, you are not going to be able to arouse much interest for this equipment in the purchasing agent for a plant in Dallas, Texas, during the summer's hottest spell.

3. *The proposition you are making must be attractive to the potential buyer.* Even though your bottling machine or snow-removal equipment is the best available, unless you can find reasons—solid reasons—why your proposition is a fair and attractive one, and your prospect should buy your product rather than your competitor's—you will be wasting your direct mail advertising, and to some degree your salespeople's efforts.

4. *The advertising must be prepared from the reader's viewpoint.* The fact that you have a product or service to sell, from which you are going to derive a profit, isn't interesting to your best prospect. However, the fact that he or she can either reduce his or her costs or make a greater profit through its usage is interesting to that same prospect. You must think of any direct mail advertising you do in the industrial marketing field in terms of how it can talk the reader's language—how it can present your sales story, whatever it may be, in a way that will appeal to the prospect and make him realize that he is the one who will benefit from following your suggestions.

5. *Direct mail advertising, to be effective, must be sent to good prospects.*

6. *The reputation of the advertiser must be good or at least not open to question among the people being solicited.* If there is anything in the history of your company which is detrimental, it will be extremely wise to straighten out your reputation and your market acceptance in the field, if your advertising is to be successful.

Seven Keys to Success

Along with his fundamental principles, Mr. Mayer has given "seven cardinal rules" which he says must be followed to achieve success in industrial direct mail advertising. They are:

1. *Know exactly what you want your mailing to do.* Do you want an order, an inquiry, a chance to have a salesperson call? Are you trying to open up a new territory, introduce a new product, or announce a new use for an old one? Or do you want to do a goodwill or institutional job?

2. *Write your copy so that the recipient will know what your product will do for the recipient!* Have you appealed to his or her selfish instincts or have you used all of your space talking about yourself, your president, and your beautiful new factory? Have you made your copy human and easy to read? Have you given all the information your prospect needs to take the action you desire?

3. *Make the layout and format of your mailing tie in with your overall plan and objective.* Many a potential success has turned into a dismal failure because someone forgot that appearance is an important part of the selling impression.

4. *Address each mailing piece (correctly) to an individual or company who can buy the product or service you have to sell.* The list is the absolute foundation of successful direct mail.

5. *Make it easy for your prospect to send you an inquiry.* Have you included a reply card or return envelope? If you are not looking for direct business, have you listed the places where your product is available?

6. *Tell your story over again.* Very few salespeople make a sale on their first call. It isn't reasonable to expect a single mailing to produce a large return.

7. *Research every mailing you make.* Never take anything for granted in industrial direct mail advertising. Don't even trust your own experience. You cannot rest on your knowledge. Times and results change. What worked last year may not work today.

Functions of Direct Mail

Definitions, rules and sins are all necessary to bear in mind, but just what are the basic functions of industrial direct mail advertising? According to the Direct Mail/Marketing Association—and they should know—there are just six primary functions. These are:

1. *Creating more effective personal sales contracts.* This includes direct mail advertising which creates a specific opportunity for salespeople to call by getting inquiries or leads for personal follow-up. It also means paving the way for salespeople by lessening resistance, arousing interest, educating and informing the prospect before intended sales calls, but without trying to get back an order or response from the prospect through the mail.

2. *Bringing the prospect to you.* This applies particularly to the retail field and to service businesses (like banks) which do not have sales forces. It has other applications, such as getting customers or prospects to visit new plants or special displays.

3. *Delivering background, sales, or public relations messages to customers, prospects, employees, or other special groups.* This includes mailings that are designed as pure advertising. It also covers any prestige reminder or goodwill advertising, employee relations, or anything to influence selective groups along certain lines of thought or action, but without direct response being sought by mail or without any direct personal follow-up intended.

4. *Taking actual orders through the mail.* This function is direct mail selling, or mail order selling, where every step in the sales process, from the initial contact to the final sale, is done exclusively by mail. This applies to publications, business, investment, and news services, as well as to selling merchandise by mail. It also applies to raising funds by charitable and educational organizations.

5. *Securing action from the prospect by mail.* This covers any promotion intended to secure response or action by mail, but not designed to secure an order or result in a personal contact between the prospect and the advertiser. Included in this category would be getting entries in a competition or securing requests for general information literature.

6. *Conducting research and market surveys.* This covers every phase of research, investigation, and fact-finding by mail.

Incidentally, the Direct Mail/Marketing Association is a wonderful source of information of all types about the medium. It is, of course, the advertising trade association for the direct mail medium, hence is authoritative. Member companies of DMMA are usually direct mail practitioners and users, but also include creators, producers and suppliers, as well as many advertising agencies.

The address of the Direct Mail/Marketing Association is:

Direct Mail/Marketing Association
6 East 43rd Street
New York, New York 10017

DMMA's Advertising Agency Committee initiates projects which will assist agency media and account personnel in programming effective mail advertising campaigns for their clients.

A few of the helpful services the Direct Mail/Marketing Association makes available to the advertising community include:

Washington Newsletter. This is a twice-monthly publication of current information on postal and legislative matters which affect business users of the mail. Copies are available upon request.

Library. DMMA's vast library contains more than 2,000 successful direct mail campaigns covering almost all categories of both consumer and industrial advertising, and thousands of loose samples of material used in direct mail. These include such items as reply cards, house organs, annual reports, and so on and on.

Information Service. DMMA is a thoroughly reliable source of information on almost every phase of direct mail. This includes such necessities as reliable list brokers, supplies and services, postal regulations, research data, and so forth.

Direct Mail Institutes. These intensive cram courses in direct mail take from three to five days as a rule, and cover both basic and advanced areas of direct mail, as well as some specialized aspects of the medium. They are held 10 times a year at strategic locations throughout the country.

Annual Conference. Round-table discussions and panel sessions provide a sound source of information on current practices and developments of the art, as well as a report on new techniques.

Workshops. These one-day programs are concerned primarily with specialized interests such as circulation promotion and mail order.

Direct Mail Leaders Contest. This annual competition for superior direct mail campaigns attracts widespread interest and entries from the country's leading advertising agencies and direct mail agencies.

Placement Service Bulletin. This bi-monthly publication emphasizes positions that are open on the middle management level. A nominal charge is made for such listings.

Standards of Practice. The direct mail medium polices itself through the Direct Mail/Marketing Association's Standards of Ethical Business Practice.

The small-to-medium size industrial company is unique in American business today, although more often than not this is nothing to write home about.

With marketing sophistication and know-how at an undreamed of level, the *average* industrial manufacturing company still carries on by muddling through. The *average* company proceeds on hope and hunch and trusts that having good intentions and a firm faith that the world is round will suffice to see it safely through the perils of the sales jungle.

Such a lack of firm policy, it is innocently hoped, will offset failure to develop a written marketing plan and formal marketing objectives. Furthermore, there is the unexpressed but ever-present trust that it will also make up, somehow or other, for lack of written communications objectives and a planned program complete with step-by-step details of how they will be achieved.

Such an attitude is unrealistic and unforgivable when it concerns mass media. It is especially asinine when it concerns a very specific medium such as direct mail. Failure is invited with open arms and a welcoming smile.

Many of these smaller companies—say, up to $50-75 million in annual sales—are being rescued from themselves by larger corporations whose managements *force* their acquired divisions to think in terms of marketing their products, rather than selling them. The days of the hardware salespeople are long past. They're relics of the dim, dead past and never again will they see the light of day.

Direct mail is a highly selective medium. It uses the approach best described by the old cliché, the "rifle approach." The fact that direct mail is not a mass medium makes it all the more essential that adequate planning precede the actual start of a program.

A midwestern advertising manager in a medium-size industrial company who's an old friend of the author's recently wrote deploring the fuzzy-minded top management in his company. The president actually advocates "using direct mail because nobody reads trade publications."

Now, there are reasons aplenty—and good ones at that—for using direct mail. But this is not one of them.

Both mediums have their places. To expect one to be more productive than a well-balanced mixture of the two is naive in the extreme.

Balance Is the Answer

Effective marketing strategy for an industrial company almost invariably calls for a balanced use of *both* space advertising and direct mail. Seldom, if ever, can one medium alone—*either* medium alone—achieve the impact and the effectiveness of a blend of the two.

What's more, use of each medium must be planned so the total effect is synergistic. That is, each medium must reinforce and augment the communications job done by the other so they build upon each other to create a stronger *total* communications impression in the minds of those prospects who have been exposed to the messages than either could produce alone, or even than the two could do if not carefully coordinated.

Involved, of course, is determining which medium is to be assigned certain specific objectives. Direct mail is called for when:

1. Sampling is to be done.
2. When the message is either too long or too complex to be disseminated efficiently in space advertising.
3. When a specific market is to be aimed at so that waste circulation is minimized.
4. When a highly selective, personalized approach is called for.
5. When a localized market area is to be saturated without disturbing the "balance of nature" in other markets or other areas.
6. When timing or frequency of communications is really of critical importance.
7. When communications and market research are to be used simultaneously, such as in establishing demand, determining price structure, developing prospect profiles, and locating specific buying influences by title or job function.
8. When mail order technique is called for; this is to sell the product directly, without obtaining the assistance of dealers, jobbers, or distributors.
9. When inquiries are wanted from carefully selected individuals.

9. When inquiries are wanted from carefully selected individuals.
10. When it is desired to build attendance at a trade show among certain qualified prospects.
11. When eliciting response to build a mailing list is the goal.
12. When merchandising the space advertising program to specific individuals.
13. When responding to inquiries generated by other media, such as space advertising.

Four Basic Types of Direct Mail Campaigns

Once you've established firm campaign objectives, you have something concrete to strive for. There's a very firm, definite goal and specific objectives which should be *measurable*. With measurable objectives, you can then show one and all how much over the target the campaign went, or under it. At this time you'll feel the need to pick one of four basic types of direct mail campaigns to help achieve your objectives. These are:

1. *Persuasive.* A direct mail campaign of this type is usually chosen to produce immediate results—such as mail orders, inquiries for salespeople to follow, or to build a mailing list. A strong bid for action is used and response is made as easy and simple for the recipient as possible.

2. *Informative.* This type of campaign is not developed to produce a large volume of returns, although a response is welcome. Instead, something of an educational nature, such as a catalog, product literature, price pages, or some other similar material are mailed; they are designed so the recipient will want to file them for future reference.

3. *Reminder.* Reminder direct mail is not expected to persuade the recipient to respond, nor is it developed to provide a great mass of background information about a company or product. Instead, it is a form of name-dropping by mail. Its purpose is to keep the company's name and products fresh in the mind of those who receive this kind of communication.

4. *Utility.* Direct mail pieces of this type are often used with the other three forms; they consist of order forms, reply cards, and stamped or postage-paid envelopes, samples of the product, reference charts (such as a table of decimal equivalents and tap drill sizes), folders, three-ring binders in which to file product literature, and so forth.

Characteristics of Direct Mail

The fantastic degree of *selectivity* possible with direct mail distinguishes this massive medium from all others.

Direct mail is the only advertising medium which enables you to aim your message directly at one specific individual, or a group of very similar individuals who share certain necessary common denominators. Using direct mail, you can easily communicate with 33,000 works managers or directors of manufacturing in metal-working establishments, for instance, and not say a single word to anybody else in those organizations.

Almost every adult American has been defined, classified, subclassified and tabulated as to a number of criteria. It's a very simple matter for you to reach any group geographically, by income, by occupation, by SIC, by sales territory, by educational level, by type of residence, or almost any other way you care to make a breakdown.

Computers have eliminated the trial and error and the drudgery formerly associated with direct mail. They spew out information formerly compiled and retrieved at the expense of untold working hours, they address labels, continuous-form envelopes, and almost everything else except one thing—as yet they don't plan the program, and they don't make decisions.

Selectivity is the key that has led direct mail to come into its own as a vitally important medium for the industrial advertiser. With selective direct mail, there is absolutely no waste, no paying for putting your message in front of people who couldn't care less about the product—and it obviates a tendency to generalize in an effort to appeal to varying interests of various groups of readers. With direct mail you talk only to the group you're interested in.

As an example of the selectivity direct mail makes possible, the old Diamond T Motor Truck company used direct mail very aggressively in support of its nationwide dealer organization.

Basis of the program was the Polk Motor Vehicle Registration List which gave the name, address, firm name, and type of motor truck operated by every user of commercial vehicles in the United States for which state license plates had been issued. The list contained no deadwood, no nixies, nobody except bona fide owners, lessors, and other users of heavy-duty motor trucks. These are, quite obviously, the best possible prospects for the sale of additional and replacement vehicles, as well as parts and service.

As could be anticipated, the most active, most aggressive, most successful dealers eagerly participated in the direct mail program on a coop basis; most dealer-distributor programs are cooperatively financed, incidentally, with the manufacturer usually picking up the lion's share of the tab. As a rule, most manufacturers assume around two-thirds of the cost of a cooperative direct mail program, leaving the outlets to assume the balance.

Few Copy, Format Restrictions

Copy can be as long as necessary when you're using the direct mail medium; there is no arbitrary length which must be adhered to because there is no arbitrary format such as a one-page ad, a spread ad, and so forth.

Long copy is particularly well suited for direct mail, and the old saying "the more you tell, the more you sell" was never more true than when used in connection with this medium.

You have the prospect's *undivided attention* with direct mail. You're not clamoring for attention. You're not competing with an advertisement across the gutter from yours, and there's no editorial matter to distract the prospect from what you want to tell him about your product.

The *format* is not limited in direct mail. You're free and unconfined (except by the budget and certain postal restrictions) in the physical appearance of your direct mail pieces.

What's more, direct mail is the only medium that makes it easy and inexpensive to *test* copy, test appeals, test layouts, test type faces and various other elements of the program. All of this can be done with a small sample at very low cost.

For instance, if you're undecided about which of two—or even more, for that matter—copy appeals are more on target, it's a very simple matter to produce the mailer you have in mind just as you have it in mind. Use any complicated techniques you want; die-cuts, pop-ups, and what not. The only change involved is in a piece of type, or all of the type if you want. A split run can be made on the press to provide certain quantities of mailers with the different appeals. They will measure the interest, response, or return—whatever your program is geared to produce.

Flexibility of timetables is inherent in direct mail. After all, you control when it is going to be produced and mailed, and this can reflect any special seasonal needs, a tie-in with space advertising, or reinforcing local dealer advertising.

There is, however, a factor you cannot control. This is the service you receive from the post office. Often this can be predicted with sufficient accuracy in most instances so you won't encounter a problem once your material is mailed.

This doesn't always hold true, though, for it's common gossip that the post office is going from bad to worse. Rates go up in massive 20 percent jumps, while service deteriorates.

But—back to the pluses of direct mail—you can make it easy for the recipients of your mailings to *respond*. Enclosing a postage-paid business reply envelope, a postage-paid reply card, or (and this is best of all when it comes to producing a volume return) a stamped, self-addressed envelope.

Making this enclosure will undoubtedly not increase the weight enough to add to your postage bill. Recipients of direct mail advertising use the postpaid reply route to return order forms, request a salesperson to call, ask for a sample, or whatever it is you've asked them to do. Direct mail advertising that goes out without one of these built-in response producers is pretty largely a mailing that's wasted, assuming a response is desired. Never try to save a few pennies here.

The List

Now that we've looked at this highly selective, highly specialized, highly personalized and highly productive medium from a generalized point of view, let's get into the mechanics of direct mail—and learn how to put it to work for an industrial company.

The list, as the mailing list is usually called, is basic and is entitled to very careful scrutiny.

Your list is a vitally important element and it is impossible to over-emphasize the extreme care with which it should be compiled and/or selected and maintained.

No mailing list floats effortlessly in over the transom, to land all neatly zip coded and broken down by sales territory, on the advertising manager's desk. A mailing list comes from one of two sources: internal or external.

Internal sources are customers and prospects. They shouldn't be combined into one gigantic mailing list because more often than not mailings will be made to both groups, but the messages in most instances are entirely different. Put all names on one list and it is impossible to break them out for various communications specially suited to each specific group.

Actually, the average industrial company should have at least three mailing lists:

1. Customers
2. Prospects
3. Combination of both

Easiest to compile is the customer list. Every firm, almost without exception, has a master record in the sales department or accounts receivable department of all of the firms to which it has made sales.

Seldom, however, can you take the customer list and use it for a direct mail list as you receive it from one of the other departments. For one thing, as often as not the addresses are incomplete; often there'll be a firm name and city, but no individual's name or title, no street address, no state, no zip code. This is perfectly adequate for sales department records or accounts receivable people. They seldom need more.

Since direct mail is above all else a personal medium, though, you'll want to mail to specific individuals and address them by name, title, firm, street address, city, state and zip code.

Internal sources for names of *prospects* are many indeed. They include:

General correspondence

Telephone inquiries

Salespeople's call reports

Employee and stockholder lists

Bingo cards

Trade show registrants

External sources include that old standby, directories. Principle ones of interest to the industrial advertising manager are:

Telephone directories

Yellow pages

Business or industrial directories

Chamber of Commerce directories (local, state)

Dun & Bradstreet Directory

Poor's Register

An unusually complete and helpful source of names and addresses of business directories and associations is in the *Dartnell Sales Promotion Handbook;* it contains more than 50 pages of data, and lists every worthwhile directory in almost every industry.

Of the directories listed above, you'll find Poor's Register most helpful. With industry broken down by SIC's, and names of key executives listed for every firm, firms properly identified as to products, located, and zip coded, this massive directory is virtually indispensable to the ad manager planning a direct mail program.

List brokers are a common source of mailing lists. These brokers are really agents, for they do not own the lists themselves. They handle correspondence and negotiations between list owners and those who rent the lists.

The list broker is a specialist in direct mail and is usually well qualified to judge the quality of a list, and to secure the best possible list for the purpose you have in mind. He or she knows what lists are available, so using a list broker saves much time and trouble. The DMMA describes a list broker as:

> List brokers can be defined as independent agents whose primary function is to arrange rental and addressing transactions between list users and list owners. Brokers represent the list owners, and the commission that they receive from them for their services usually is 20 percent of the amount the mailer pays. The commission is deducted by the broker before payment is forwarded to the list owner.

> Here it should be pointed out that often there is an overlapping of activity in the list business. Some brokers not only arrange for the rental of lists that are owned by other companies, but they also either do compilation work or buy outright certain lists which they can make available for rental.

> Although this may seem confusing, in the course of working with list organizations you are likely to find that each has its own particular specialty. And very often you may decide that it is wise to deal with certain organizations for specific type lists.

For the most part the user rents lists for one-time use through the broker; the broker is reimbursed for his or her efforts by the list owner who realizes a return from his or her investment in time and money spent in compiling the list originally. Most list brokers have capable staffs who are constantly on the lookout for "new" lists, additional information about existing lists and new wrinkles to help users of direct mail make their lists more profitable.

Most list brokers, like most other business people, are honest and aboveboard in their transactions and you will encounter no difficulty in dealing with them. However, as in any other business or industry there is an occasional bad apple; the list broker with a heart full of larceny has given this segment of the direct mail industry a reputation that "it pays to do business with a broker you *know* you can trust," for all the world as if most brokers were out to steal your gold inlays. This is not the case.

Renting Lists

Remember when renting your list that you always do so on a one-time basis. Should the list prove productive for the mailer who rents it from you, he or she is charged each time he or she rents it; the fee does not vary with subsequent rentals unless agreed upon ahead of time. And there exist few reasons for reducing the price of a desirable property which should be constant.

Assuming your list is clean and is made up of buyers—as opposed to prospects, suspects, hopefuls and so on—you can anticipate charging around 6 cents per name, or $60 per thousand names.

On the other hand, if your list consists primarily of prospects, suspects, expires, or other less active names it is obviously less attractive to the mail user and so must be priced lower. Such lists usually rent for $35 to $40 per thousand names, and there is less demand for such lists, too.

List owners usually handle the addressing of material, or supply labels to the list renter. The physical work is seldom performed by the owner of the list; he or she customarily relies upon a letter shop with which he or she does business to handle this. Many list owners return the addressed envelopes, labels, cards or what have you to the mailer for further handling.

Perhaps even more, however, insist on handling the entire mailing; in this case, the cost of folding, collating, stuffing and so on are billed to the mailer in addition to the list rental fee. This is done through the broker. This way the list owner is certain that nobody is going to copy his or her list; if you operate on the principle that you trust others—but not much—it's best to go this route.

When preparing material to be mailed for a list user, make sure the necessary arrangements have been made for a postal permit, that indicia are printed correctly, and other minor details are handled ahead of time to avoid a last-minute, frantic stab at the panic button.

List compilers are specialists in creating high quality lists. Almost any conceivable list is usually available on relatively short notice from the compilers without your having to go to the trouble and expense of having one compiled especially for your company. However, if the exact list you need is not in existence, the compilers will quickly produce one that matches your requirements right down to the last dot on the last "i."

Many of the leading list compilers maintain previously compiled lists, marvelously complete and specialized in almost any category you'd need. Most of these lists are broken down by geographic location, and many by demographic characteristics.

The list of lists is so long it's virtually endless. For example, Fritz S. Hofheimer, Inc., 88 Third Ave., Mineola, N. Y. 11501, phone (212) 674-6420, is a leading source of high quality lists. This company is a member of the Direct Mail/Marketing Association, and of Mail

Advertising Service Association. It is thoroughly reliable and reputable. Hofheimer publishes an annual catalog of lists it offers—more than 20,000 in all! Separate lists are offered for Canada.

Use of Hofheimer's catalog puts fantastic selectivity in the direct mail advertiser's hands. As an example, let's assume you've prepared a lavish, beautiful, and precisely-written brochure, and you want to mail it only to certain carefully selected buying influences. To show the selective reach of these lists, it would be easy for you to mail to the following, although this is a somewhat improbable collection of individuals:

No. of names on list	Name of list	Price per M
67,214	Advertising managers	$32.50
14,147	Bank presidents	30.00
638	Whiskey and brandy distillers	40.00*
470	Prisons and reformatories	25.00*
24,686	Agricultural implement dealers	28.50
5,696	Butter, cheese, and egg wholesalers	35.00
9,230	Dog breeders and kennels	40.00
3,653	Fertilizer manufacturers	35.00
4,863	Camps, logging	35.00
4,507	Gunsmiths and firearms dealers	32.50
42,000	Mobile home owners	30.00
3,862	Monument and memorial makers	35.00
59,800	Socialites	30.00
70,000	Treasurers and controllers, corporate	35.00
4,933	Tree surgeons	35.00
2,194	Venereal disease clinics	30.00
3,393	Water well drillers	32.50
13	Windmill manufacturers	12.50*
10	Yo-yo manufacturers	8.50*
167	Zoological gardens	20.00*
24	Zwieback manufacturers	10.50*

Hofheimer, in common with many other list sources, offers complete mailing facilities and services—folding, collating, inserting, sealing, metering and sorting, all at competitive prices. A sample of your mailing piece or a description of your requirements will bring a prompt quotation for handling an entire job for you.

Incidentally, Hofheimer *guarantees* its lists. This is relatively common practice among the better list purveyors. Statistically, every year

*A flat rate for a small list, not a price per thousand names.

911

more than 25 percent of the country's population undergoes some kind of change—both individual and industrial. Individuals move, change jobs, get promoted, retire, die.

To protect the user of Hofheimer lists against an abnormal number of post office returns, the company guarantees 95 percent deliverability. It makes refunds at the rate of 10 cents per piece, regardless of the class of mail and actual postage carried, for all in excess of 5 percent of the addresses furnished, provided the returns reach the company within 30 days after purchase of the list.

Dun & Bradstreet, Inc. has detailed lists of 300,000 manufacturing establishments, 15,000 mining establishments, 44,000 contract construction establishments, 28,000 transportation, communication and public utility establishments; all are available from D&B on IBM punched cards, magnetic tape, Cheshire labels, pressure-sensitive labels, 3 by 5 cards, tabular listings, and printed tabulating cards.

These D&B lists identify the establishments, give SIC's, full names, addresses, state-county-city geographical code, area code and telephone number, name and title of chief executive, number of employees, sales volume, credit rating, and net worth. Names of other executives in the firm are also available if needed, including the executive vice-president, individual in charge of manufacturing, head purchasing executive, and the treasurer or controller.

SRDS Joined the Mail Media Parade

Something finally came to pass—SRDS (Standard Rate & Data Service, Inc.) entered the direct mail field. SRDS' service, *Direct Mail List Rates and Data,* provides quick, convenient, accurate source information about mailing lists currently available. The three classifications covered are: Business, Consumer, Farm.

The publisher said that *"Direct Mail List Rates and Data* will enable you to select the best prospects quickly and determine immediately the reliability of the list, its source, its cost, and how it can be mailed mechanically."

Standard Rate & Data Service's 60 years of experience, plus full cooperation of the DMAA and the 4A's Direct Mail Committee, went into the production of this reference work. It contains approximately 9,000 list selections and is issued twice a year with up-dating bulletins between editions.

This authoritative guide to direct mail lists is price at $50 for the year, which includes both editions and attendant bulletins. It is available from:

>Standard Rate & Data Service, Inc.
>5201 Old Orchard Road
>Skokie, Illinois 60077   (312) 966-8500

Major Pitfall in List Compilation

A camouflaged booby-trap for the unwary industrial advertising manager about to launch a direct mail campaign is using names supplied by the company's field salespeople and internal product people.

Salespeople and product managers are quite sincere in believing they actually know "all" of the buying influences to whom direct mail should be addressed.

When it's composed of names submitted or approved by the product people and the field sales force, a direct mail list will inevitably consist entirely of the names of people on whom they call, and whom they know. These names should be included, without doubt. But if your list is composed entirely of these names, your direct mail advertising cannot hope to achieve more than a mediocre success.

More than 60 percent of all industrial sales calls are misdirected. And industrial salespeople of capital equipment frequently cannot call on buying influences high enough up the corporate ladder, despite their protestations to the contrary; they claim to be able to "see anybody in the company they want to" because they actually believe it. Unknown, unidentified buying influences are not called on, however.

In addition to names supplied by your people, include the names of key executives you can get from your list source—Dun & Bradstreet, R. L. Polk, or whoever it might be. These prime buying influences quite often are individuals upon whom your salespeople do not call because they are unable to get to them because they do not receive salespeople.

What's more, salespeople and product people seldom appreciate the importance of developing as effective a mailing list as humanly possible, nor do they understand the advisability of including as many names of key buying influences as it is possible to secure. They tend to feel that one or two names within a prospect company are sufficient. Just the opposite is true.

This was strikingly apparent during a recent conversation with an advertising manager friend; he works for a Cleveland company that manufactures capital equipment sold to the foundry industry—and he had encountered this very same problem in his company, it developed. He sent the author a copy of a memo to his product people on this subject; with individual and firm names changed, the memo follows because it illustrates this point so well.

To: Mr. Roger Houston

SUBJECT: Mailing List

Dear Rog:

Last week Bob Morton and I talked on the phone about the mailing list for your new direct mail program.

We do not want superfluous names on the list, so we are going to use a list from the following SIC's:

- 33 21 Gray iron foundries
- 33 22 Malleable iron foundries
- 33 23 Steel foundries
- 33 61 Aluminum castings
- 33 62 Brass, bronze, copper, copper-base alloy castings
- 33 69 Nonferrous castings, n.e.c.

Roger, if we concentrate exclusively on these SIC's, where our market potential really lies, we end up with a net list of slightly more than 3,600 establishments. All have 20 or more employees. Included are both ferrous and nonferrous foundries.

Incidentally, I got a copy of *Penton's Foundry List* to evaluate, and I can see why you like it. It can be very valuable to field salesmen and to sales managers, since it locates and identifies establishments.

For use as a mailing list it is not too practical, however. Too much time and money would be spent identifying and qualifying buying influences. This is not to say we can't do it; we can with, I would estimate, a 75-80 percent correct return.

This would take several weeks, probably up to two months. Cost, I'd guess, would run in the neighborhood of $1,500 to $2,000. This would include questionnaires, followups, phone calls, and verification of returns with internal labor here in the department.

Penton's list is a list of *firms*. Firms are fine, but you do not mail to them. The mail boy always throws your material in the round file.

To be effective and productive, direct mail must be addressed to a specific individual. This is what we have done for other product lines, and is what I recommend we continue to do.

Field salesmen (in *most* companies) tend to denigrate direct mail—and the direct mail list itself—because they do not consider direct mail's objective.

The objective of our program, as established by marketing management, is to make a sales call, by mail, *on executives on whom our salesmen do not now call.* This is what this type of direct mail *should* do.

With the cost of the average industrial sales call at an all time high—now nearly $107 per call—a call by mail for pennies *on a top executive the salesmen do not see is* dirt cheap.

As we discussed the other day, recommendations for our equipment probably start on the operating level. But we must not lose sight of the fact that, when an expenditure of tens of thousands of dollars is involved, top management is going to get in on the act.

Top management must be thoroughly familiar with Smith Widget Manufacturing Company, they must have confidence in us. They will on both scores if we advertise consistently, and if we continue to call on them by mail.

Roger, we can reach them by mail *only* if we use their names on the envelopes.

I've checked our list, and it's highly accurate. I used normal verification methods, without a survey. Dun & Bradstreet's massive reference, *D & B's Metalworking Directory,* Standard & Poor's excellent book *(Poor's Register), Automotive Industries' Marketing Guide,* and so on.

The list is valid, and it's clean as a whistle when you consider that throughout industry average annual personnel turnover, in the class of people we want to reach, is on the order of one-third.

But our list will be even better within the next three weeks because I'm getting the latest revision from D&B; it was compiled within the past month.

I realize, as you do, that no list is 100 percent perfect, the minute it is compiled somebody quits his job, somebody dies, a firm goes out of business, a merger occurs, or a score of possibilities can change the quo of the status.

But the Dun & Bradstreet list is, in my opinion, and in that of our agency, the best there is. It is remarkably accurate. It is the best way to get the names of the four top executives in all of the foundries we want to reach, at a cost that is not prohibitive—and without wasting time.

We can cross-check the establishments against Penton's list, or any other you suggest if it will ease your mind.

But I feel very strongly, Rog, that we absolutely *must* mail to individuals, not simply to a firm. In good conscience I can't acquiesce with any other course, nor can I countenance mailing only to names supplied by product management and the sales force.

If there's real doubt in your mind, let's get together and Indian wrassle. I'll pop for lunch!

Cordially,
/s/
Bud Edwards
Advertising Manager

That advertising manager touched 'most all of the bases on this subject—and he's 110 percent right. He knows his subject.

List Maintenance

Without being iconoclastic about the matter, there are a number of ground rules the industrial advertising manager should follow as far as maintenance of the mailing list is concerned.

Average industrial lists change more than 30 percent per year. Considering a mailing list a static thing is a terrible tactical error. Reconcile yourself to constant maintenance, and budget for it.

Allocate approximately 10 percent of your direct mail budget to list development, procurement, and maintenance. This figure naturally varies considerably, depending upon the nature of your business and the breakdown of your promotional budget. The more you spend on direct mail, the smaller the percentage will be. Skimping here is the wrong place to try to save a dollar.

Rely on outside experts. Except for the giants of industry, very few companies have or can afford full-time list experts in their advertising departments. Rather than attempting to muddle through or make do with something almost right, you're much better off to rely on outside sources for lists—including compiling and maintenance. Cost will be less in the long run.

Too many spoons spoil the soup. Adopt and enforce a strict rule that everybody and his brother is *not* to get his hands on the mailing list, nor is just anybody permitted to add or delete names. Establish a firm policy as to why and when maintenance is to be performed, the kind of names that are to be added to the list, and the person who is to do the actual work, and who is to supervise it. Dilution of responsibility results in dilution of the value of the list.

Be a chronic list questioner. Refuse to accept at face value any list, including your own. The perfect list has never yet been compiled and chances are mighty small indeed that it ever will. The sooner you learn to be skeptical about *all* lists, the sooner you'll be in a position where you can't get burned by a poor one. Numerous good lists exist, of course, but numerous incredibly poor lists are used by mail advertisers who should know better. Make it standard operating procedure to analyze all lists thoroughly and accurately—including your own—before using them.

Lists are like teeth: They should be cleaned twice a year. Normal maintenance should be done continuously without stopping for anything, regardless of how busy the department is. But major cleanings should be scheduled every six months and the list should then be reviewed, analyzed, and checked to make absolutely sure it is as good as you can make it.

Six mailings a year over a sizable list call for mechanical addressing. Excepting First Day Covers and other special mailings, the economics of the situation dictates use of mechanical addressing, although you should analyze this to ascertain whether you're going the right route or not.

The mailing list is the key to success in direct mail advertising. Respect it, cherish it, nurture it. You can't put too much effort, time, or thought into keeping it clean and up to date. The better the list, the better the results. It's that simple. And this is a fundamental truth that definitely cannot be avoided, ignored, or swept under the carpet—even temporarily.

Besides periodic maintenance, it is necessary that the mailing list be updated daily, or as often as mailings are made and returns return. Basis of corrections made this frequently are:

Nixies—This is mail returned by the post office as undeliverable for one reason or another. Personnel changes, mergers, new plant locations, companies now out of business; all these reasons result in a certain percentage of nixies. The cleaner the list is, the fewer the nixies, of course, although there are always a few. They're like death and taxes.

Salespeople call reports—Many aggressive industrial companies have a policy that all new names showing up in salespeople call reports are automatically bucked on to the advertising department to be put on the appropriate direct mail list. Furthermore, these companies have standing instructions to their salespeople to report all new names (plus changes, although this seldom gets done, salespeople despising paperwork as they do) to be added to the list.

Customer notifications—It is not at all unusual for customers to accept the responsibility of sending you changes in their status, address, and so on as they receive mail from you. These notifications should, of course, be acted upon immediately; if these customers are interested enough to help you communicate with them, they're certainly customers you want to take good care of.

Easiest and best list cleaner yet devised is asking the recipients of your direct mail advertising to help you get the job done. Many industrial mail users routinely request change-of-address information in each mailing they make, while others include list cleaners at less frequent intervals—say, three or four times a year.

Other companies make special list-cleaning mailings to elicit information they need to maintain their mailing lists. This may well be the most effective way of handling the cleaning job, although it's also the most expensive way.

Your nearby post office will lend you a hand with a pair of special services designed to update your mailing lists. If you print *Address Correction Requested* on your outgoing mail, you will be notified of the addressee's new address when first-class mail is forwarded. A charge of 15 cents per piece will be made for this service.

Pieces of third- and fourth-class mail bearing the words *Return Postage Guaranteed* which are undeliverable as addressed will be returned to sender upon payment of return postage at the applicable rate. Reason for nondelivery or the new address of the addressee will be furnished for each such piece only when the 15-cent fee for a notice is paid in addition to the return postage.

Paying for returns, unless they number into the thousands, is good policy. It saves future postage, time, materials mailed, and prevents the illusion of accomplishing something constructive if the list is horribly inadequate. If the returns *should* be more than 25 percent of a mailing, the time has long since passed when the list should have been thoroughly cleaned and the time for immediate action is *right now.*

Formats

Direct mail is a highly personal medium. In fact, the personal letter from one person to another is the oldest form of direct mail—and it is still one of the most effective.

In a personal letter you can talk just as frankly and confidentially as if you were actually engaging in conversation with the individual you're trying to convert from prospect to customer.

Failure to personalize direct mail letters lessens their effectiveness very substantially. Even mass mailings are personal communications because they are received in privacy by one person; he or she regards the letter as a communication to himself or herself and to nobody else.

Personalizing, via fill-ins of varying lengths (lines) is no longer prohibitively costly, nor is it too time-consuming for the typical direct mail advertiser to use. Today's techniques result in printed letters that look very much like the real thing; a close match on the fill-in of the address and salutation produces a letter that looks as if it had been individually typed. Cost is a fraction of the fully-typed letter, of course.

Autotyped Letters

The most personal of all direct mail letters are those which are individually typewritten. When the quantity is more than just a few letters, they are usually produced on an automatic typewriter. There is something about the overall impression of a typed letter which brands it as genuine. Even if the recipient does not know the first thing about letter reproduction processes, he or she is quick to recognize an individually typed letter. Such letters create an interesting reaction, particularly in business offices. When a typewritten letter is received, the recipient usually has to make a more complicated decision than is required of a printed piece, which the recipient can simply discard if he or she decides to take no action. But with a typewritten letter, the recipient often feels he or she must dictate or write an answer—even when all that has to be said is, "No, I'm not interested in what you propose."

Many mail order advertisers, who have previously received only an occasional complaint from nonbuying recipients of their usual printed letters, have been surprised to find a substantial number of replies from nonbuyers receiving Autotyped letters—letters saying, "Thanks for telling me your story. I'll keep your letter on file for future reference." And, true to their word, many of these nonbuyers do respond with an order at some future date, presenting evidence that Autotyped letters are indeed filed rather than discarded.

There are certain types of computer letters which closely approximate an Autotyped letter, but the majority of letters rushed through a computer are too obviously the product of an impersonal machine to yield the full personal touch captured by a regular Autotyped letter.

Computer Letters

In recent years, there has been an ever-increasing use of computer-generated letters, including those where the message is created by jet ink imaging. In fact, the advent of computer letters is considered by many direct mail people as the factor which really made mass personalized mailings practical. With today's advanced techniques, the computer letter often has the look of an individually-typed letter. Computer companies are constantly working to improve these.

For long runs, computer letters are considerably less expensive than any other form of personalized letter.

The Chrysler Airtemp Program

Airtemp Division, Fedders Corporation, is a large industrial marketer who uses direct mail created by Graphic Service, and does so to good effect. Airtemp's program, now well established, is designed to attract new dealers for the division's products—room air conditioners, packaged cooling and heating systems, and applied machinery and systems.

This direct mail advertising campaign is a continuing effort directed to target dealers; the company realizes the way to achieve a sizable sales increase is through expanded distribution. Each Airtemp distributor furnishes a list of target dealers in his or her locality and he or she constantly cleans and updates it.

When a new dealer is signed up to sell Airtemp products, he or she is removed from the target dealer list, of course, for any communications the company sends to the new dealer henceforth will be of a different character than the ones created to persuade the dealer to handle the line.

Each of the two-color mailing pieces (blue and black) includes a photograph of Tom Kirby, vice-president, marketing, of the Airtemp Division. This "humanizes" the pieces and shows prospective dealers they are not going to have to transact business with a huge, impersonal corporation. Prospective dealers see a living, breathing person, obviously warm and friendly, a person they begin to feel they know as the series progresses.

Graphic Service imparted more immediacy and produced greater impact by personalizing each individual mailing piece for each individual recipient with a drop-in paragraph or P.S. which tells the prospect exactly who his or her distributor is, where the distributor is located, and what the distributor's phone number is. Let's see what the copy says:

(Page 1)
This name holds
a promise for you . . .
A promise too big
and too important
to overlook

(Page 2)
(logos)

Let me ask you something.

If you were to name the one thing—above everything else—that keeps you in business, what would your answer be?

You bet. *Profit.*

Because nobody—you, us, or anyone—moves, grows, or *stays* in business very long without it. At least, that's what we believe at Airtemp . . . not only for ourselves, but for everyone who is part of us.

In fact, profit is the promise we hold for you as an Airtemp Dealer.

What makes us so sure?

Look at our sales. In the last three years alone sales have actually doubled in every phase of our business . . . in room air conditioners, in packaged cooling and heating units, and in applied machinery and systems. And our sales figures so far this year indicate that the current year will top everything we've done in the past.

Look at our products. Our entire line of equipment is second to none in the industry, and in many instances far more advanced. In packaged units, for example, we offer a broad range of "Pre-charged" models. In water chillers, we stand alone with the smallest, lightest, most compact new chillers ever designed or manufactured by anyone. And our furnace line offers a wide variety of gas and oil-fired units as well as all-electric furnaces.

(Page 3)

Look at our plans. Based on our equipment and its advanced engineering, our expanding sales in every area, *and dealers like you who've made it happen*, we've already completed a $40,000,000 capital expansion to meet what we believe will be our biggest production demands in history.

In short, there is no question in my mind or in the mind of anyone at Airtemp that *Airtemp is going up and we're going to stay*.

We can see it, we can feel it, we can taste it.

Let me repeat: As a dealer who can share in this growth and the *profit* it represents, Airtemp holds a promise for you that you can't afford to overlook, and I urge you, most sincerely, to take the time *now* to get the story for yourself.

W.L. Regan, your local Airtemp distributor, will be glad to meet with you at your convenience and discuss our lines and plans in detail and answer your questions in full.

His number is 786-8710; he's the kind of person you'll like doing business with; and there's no obligation in any way.

Come on. Make this *your* year to grow with Airtemp. We'd like to have you with us.

> Sincerely,
> T.W. Kirby
> Vice-President, Marketing

TWK/gs

We mortals have yet to devise a sounder approach when attempting to enlist new dealers than dangling profit in front of their faces. This mailer did, and did exceptionally well. A mighty deft hand was guiding that typewriter. While it might initially appear Airtemp was bragging a bit on its sales gains, prospective dealers automatically translated this into retail sales with 40 percent markup.

This copy approach is sound and logical and persuasive.

Notice the next to last two paragraphs on page three; these are drop-ins. They make it easy for the prospective dealer to take immediate action by picking up the phone and calling the individual who can "close" the prospective dealer—the local Airtemp distributor. No waiting, no risking having a prospect who's very close to being sold get unsold by delay in contact. This is smart direct mail advertising because it strikes while the iron—the prospect—is hot.

Fedders Airtemp had used the usual collection of trade shows, distributor salespeople incentive programs, publicity, and space advertising to attract new dealers, all with a certain measure of success.

Addition of this personalized direct mail advertising campaign aimed directly at prospects judged hottest by aggressive, on-the-spot distributors *doubled* the number of new dealers signed up in the first 12 months this excellent program was employed. You don't have to be a mathematician to estimate what effect this many additional new dealers had on sales!

A Winner for Victor

Final example of the illustrated-letter mailing piece was also produced by Graphic Service, although this fine direct mail agency by no means limits itself to one format.

Victor Business Products, according to James G. Johnson, Electrowriter sales manager, spent a lot of money on trade shows each year. He said, "When prospects visit our booth, we spend a great deal of time explaining the Electrowriter, what it does, and then point out its uses in the particular field being covered by the trade show.

"What we want is some way to pre-educate those attending the show so they will have a basic knowledge of the Electrowriter and how it can be applied in their business or industry."

It's axiomatic that every exhibitor at every trade show has a burning desire for lots and lots of traffic in the exhibitor's booth. An empty or mostly empty booth is a depressing thing, and it creates a terribly negative impression on attendees at trade shows. Victor wanted not only a heavy traffic flow, but wanted a *knowledgeable* group to see its wares at the International Association of Fire Chiefs convention, where Victor exhibited. The problem was put to Graphic Service.

Graphic Service folks realized instantly that the thing of prime importance was to interest fire chiefs in Victor's Electrowriter Alarm System so they'd be intrigued enough to search out Victor's booth to learn more about the product.

What was finally worked out was a four-page letter that graphically described Victor's amazing new alarm system, and went into quite a bit of detail on how it sends an immediate *written* message to selected fire stations, the police department and to public utilities.

It did the job.

Sales manager Johnson reported, "So often at conventions I've stood in a booth while people stroll by and look in with sort of a blank, hesitant expression, as though they were thinking, 'I wonder if there's anything worthwhile in there?'

"It was a real pleasure at the Fire Chief's convention to have men walk in *knowing where they were going and knowing what they wanted to learn.*

≣ VICTOR

BUSINESS MACHINES GROUP 3900 NORTH ROCKWELL STREET, CHICAGO, ILLINOIS 60618

At right, start of the four-page illustrated letter used by Victor Business Products to arouse interest in product before trade shows. It did the job—nine of every 10 of those who called mentioned piece or brought it with them.

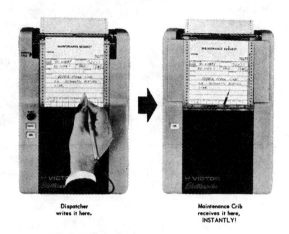

Dispatcher
writes it here.

Maintenance Crib
receives it here,
INSTANTLY!

HERE'S HOW YOU CAN IMPROVE
YOUR MAINTENANCE DISPATCHING
CONTROL WITH ELECTROWRITERS

The units you see above make up Victor's new Electrowriter Maintenance Dispatching System that you can use to transmit <u>written</u> "work orders" to any number of maintenance cribs in your plant in a matter of seconds.

Let me tell you how it works, and how it can benefit you.

"On top of it all, we got much more traffic than we expected."

Victor has used this same kind of a pre-education program for the petroleum industry show, the Midwest Hotel-Motel Convention and the Armed Forces Communication Electrical Association Show. All were highly successful.

That the mail goes to the right people and that it accomplishes its objective isn't open to guesswork or interpretation at Victor. Sales manager Johnson said after the first couple of mailings prior to shows, "These pieces are really getting through. About nine out of 10 people visiting the booth either mentioned the mailing piece early in the conversation, or had it with them."

Self Mailers

Self mailers—pieces mailed sans envelope—are usually closed with

a gummed "wafer" to prevent unfolding in the mail. Self mailers are considerably less costly to produce and mail since no envelope is required, and they can be mailed in bulk.

When an extra heavy stock is used, such as an 80-pound cover stock, a variety of shapes, sizes, folds, and other treatments may be used to catch the eye and add interest to the piece. And when either a colored stock or screenings of second colors are used overall, some truly outstanding self mailers can be produced at remarkably low cost.

The self mailer nearby was created by Derse Advertising Company, Milwaukee, specialist in signs of all types and trade show exhibits. It is 8 inches square. On the outside this mailer looks as if it's printed on a light brown stock, although this is actually brown ink laid down solid on white stock. Colors are brown, black, and red. On the side opposite the address, the theme of the piece is splashed boldly across the mailer—that Derse Advertising Company provides all of the services listed on the other side, all tied up in one nice, neat package. The "string" tieing the package together is a nice touch, and the white wafer sealing the mailer seems to belong there.

Opening just the two flaps of the package gives Derse a generous area for copy space, four black-and-white halftones, and a strong, hard-sell bid for action.

When the top flaps of the package are opened up, there's a very strong and very convincing testimonial based on articles in Milwaukee's two leading newspapers, as well as an endorsement from the Chicago, Milwaukee, St. Paul and Pacific Railroad Company about how delighted William J. Quinn, president of the railroad, was with arrangements Derse made to create a "colorful, well coordinated setting" for the dedication of an imposing new three-story railroad depot.

Catalogs and Price Lists

Catalogs, product literature, and price lists have long been favorite mailing pieces for industrial direct mail advertisers. They're effective, for they put your selling message in front of the prospect just the way you want it presented. There's no deviation in presentation, as there is from salesperson to salesperson.

Mass mailings of catalogs and similar literature are no longer possible for many companies, however. Printing costs, paper costs, production costs, administrative costs—and even that for postage itself—have zoomed in recent years.

Catalogs, up-to-date literature, and prices are still excellent mailing pieces and can still be used without waste *if* your mailing list is clean and well maintained. If it isn't, you shouldn't be using it. When you mail with the assurance that those who will receive your mailings have been qualified, then it becomes obvious the investment may well pay off.

Literature about the company's products may range from lavish, four-color catalogs with hundreds, or even thousands, of pages—or it may be a single-sheet, front and back black-and-white technical story.

Mailing literature pays, and pays handsomely, in increased awareness of the product and the company, in heightened receptiveness to the salesperson's story, and in occasional over-the-transom orders-*if* you put your literature in the right hands. If you're less than 100 percent sure on this score, forget it and put the money into a clean list for future mailings.

Promiscuous, helter-skelter mailing of literature alone, unaccompanied by a covering letter, order form, reply card or some other request for action is also a waste of money in most instances.

Showmanship Formats

One thing in life is as sure and certain as rising taxes: The oddball, the curious, and the unique can be depended upon to attract people's attention.

Human nature varies neither a whit nor a jot (find increments smaller than those!) from Portland, Maine to Portland, Oregon—or anywhere in between. And human nature being what it is, people *like* things and ideas and places that are strictly off the beaten path. They thoroughly enjoy being titillated by the unusual.

A word of caution, though. Showmanship mailings should be wisely chosen so they do not call so much attention to themselves that they obscure the sales message. As with every medium and every technique, there are pitfalls to be avoided. Dick Hodgson, author of *The Dartnell Direct Mail and Mail Order Handbook*, quotes Henry Hoke, editor of *Direct Marketing*, on seven basic problems to avoid in developing showmanship in direct mail. These are:

1. Do not use any unusual or tricky format unless there is a real reason for it. Many advertisers are tempted to use so-called trick mailing pieces simply because they see something similarly clever used by someone else.

2. Be sure of your audience. Use the same good taste and judgment in selecting unusual mailing pieces as you would use in your copy writing to a given audience.

3. Do not use unusual or tricky pieces on the spur of the moment, just to be different. Plan your unusual pieces carefully in advance, along with the rest of your merchandising campaign.

4. Be sure the finished job will look right when it reaches each recipient. Many good ideas go wrong due to amateur handling. For example, in die-cutting, be sure you use the right weight of stock. With tip-ons, be sure they will stay on. In sampling, be sure they are packaged right.

5. Realize that only a limited number of producers are equipped with machinery and experience to handle intricate, unusual formats properly. Some printers have discouraged the use of die-cuts because they are not equipped, or do not know how to handle them. Avoid disappointments by employing experienced production facilities.

6. Appreciate the limitation of tricky forms and abide by those limitations. Follow the advice of experienced designers who usually know what can and cannot be done.

7. A final rule of warning should be printed in large letters, framed and hung in clear view of every planning desk: *Do not make your unusual mailing piece so clever that the recipient will remember your cleverness rather than your offer.*

Hodgson also noted that Kenneth Goode and Zenn Kaufman, in their book, *Profitable Showmanship*, have defined seven general principles about successful business showmanship. These are:

1. *Ideas are born right or wrong.* Showmanship calls for extremes—but the *right* extremes. Doing a thing differently may be doing it worse, no matter how differently! It does not help to be different when all the others are right.

2. *Find yourself a "natural."* The greatest danger in showmanship is the almost irresistible temptation to accept its traditional symbols—often threadbare and tawdry. Take hockey, for example, Red-white-and-blue uniforms look like showmanship. The idea of recruiting a whole Chicago team among American-born boys *is* showmanship.

3. *Think BIG.* Do not waste time on middle-sized elephants. There is no percentage in a "little-bigness," in second bests. If you cannot get a Jumbo, the biggest of them all, don't compromise on a near-Jumbo. Reverse your attack completely and get a *baby* elephant, the smallest of them all. Lacking a whale, turn completely about and exploit a minnow. Take a lesson from the little tourist restaurant buried deep in the Alabama woods which courageously called itself, "Swamp View."

4. *Do it surpassingly.* Sincerity in showmanship includes adequacy! Half a show is *not* better than none. It is worse! Don't ever feel that because you have done your best you have done everything.

5. *Don't compete with yourself.* Do it surpassingly. But do not have more than one *it.* Circuses have six rings to take care of 6,000 customers simultaneously. When the ringmaster seeks the climax of attention, he turns off everything but the spotlight, and speaks alone—quite softly. Advertisers, as a rule, give themselves more competition than their competitors do. You cannot get 300-percent attention by combining three 100-percent features.

6. *Make it crystal clear.* Sincerity in showmanship also includes absolute clarity of meaning. To avoid ambiguity may, in fact, be the greatest function of showmanship. True meanings must explode themselves—immediately, unmistakably, energetically to every mind.

7. *Keep it a game.* The genius of showmanship expresses itself in apt and picturesque play, sometimes quite unconsciously. Make your work interesting to people—and people will make it important for you.

Almost everything is an adaptation. New ideas don't spring forth fullblown from nothing. Something always triggers an idea, something that has already transpired, something that somebody has already done. With thought, however, you can improve upon almost anything that's been done by others. And just because you can't seem to come up with something completely new and different doesn't mean that what you have come up with won't be effective.

Various audiences have been exposed to various ideas, but not every audience has been exposed to every idea.

Letter Gadgets

Something—almost anything, in fact—stuck to a letter attracts the attention of the recipient far faster than a plain letter. Tiny plastic reproductions of everyday items, for example, are ridiculously inexpensive, yet they provide a good place for copy to take off from.

Shown on the next page are a miniature gold-colored hammer to hammer this point home, as well as scissors (which actually work), a crescent wrench, and a monkey wrench. To prove this is not monkey business, these items are placed alongside a penny to show size.

927

Other Tip-Ons

You're limited only by your imagination and that ever-present ogre, the budget, when it comes to tipping things onto your letters and mailing pieces.

Shown is a clever tip-on that really works—an abacus. If the office adding machine, calculator, or the controller's computer breaks down, the abacus could keep your business from going on the rocks. Nobody wants business on the rocks.

This particular abacus works so well it enables the author to handle the expense account without bothering a hard-working secretary. Other tip-ons might be keys, buttons, wristwatch calendars, and so on. All do what they're supposed to do, which is attract attention.

Abrasives, sandpaper, a message scratched on glass with a diamond, cloth, and so forth are all unusual enough to pique the curiosity and cause the recipient of a message on their surface to peek again at the mailer.

Magnification

Take a familiar object and blow it up to an absurd size and it automatically evokes amusement.

The ad manager of a prominent manufacturer of semiconductors had an integrated circuit made of plastic by means of the injection molding process.

Now, the original circuit is about half the size of a sugar cube and about 3/32nd of an inch thick. All of the recipients of his direct mail ads know this full well. What made this mailing stand out more vividly than a sore thumb was that it was 13 inches wide, 18 inches deep, and 4 inches thick! Selected buying influences in some 2,500 establishments received the giant integrated circuit and they practically howled. It was such good-natured fun poked at the industry for constantly trying to make its products smaller and smaller that the mailing won't be forgotten for years.

Miniaturization

Reductions in size always have appeal. One direct mail advertiser recently mailed a tiny telegram, hardly larger than an airmail stamp,

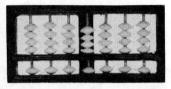

Plastic abacus that really works was used by the author as a direct mail curiosity.

complete with a tiny magnifying glass so the recipients could read it.

And stamp-sized books of hundreds of pages are available from dealers in advertising specialties; they invariably cause much comment and make a very strong impression.

Miniaturization is an excellent route to go because the impression the tiny items make is large, and also because of the kindly bite the post office takes due to the light weight of the items.

Unusual Shapes and Folds

Novel die cuts and unexpected folds are stoppers.

Almost nobody is able to discard a tightly folded oversize flyer, for example, without unfolding the thing just to see what's inside. This is akin to the big-game hunter's desire always to "glass just one more valley" and to go through just one more pass between two mountains to see what's on the other side. Everybody wants to find out what is hidden behind a mountain or an enticing fold or cut shape in a mailing piece.

Useful Items

When you're mailing to an industrial audience, these stouthearted members of industry *who are businessmen and businesswomen first and people and consumers as a very close second.*

Here you can use ballpoint pen refills (available from many sources for 6 cents each for all-metal ones), golf tees, plastic hat covers, combs, folding umbrellas, toothbrushes, shoelaces, plastic raincoats, portfolios, tie bars, or what have you. But don't mail razor blades. Too many people have been badly cut, including a number of small fry.

Advertising Specialties

Advertising specialties are really an extension of useful items; they can be imprinted or unimprinted. But why miss a chance to make another impression, not once but many times?

Ballpoint pens, matches, cigarette lighters for those who don't mind a little lung cancer, tie bars, cuff links, and so on are all attractive, useful and welcome. They can do double duty, too, serving as hand-out pieces as well as items to be mailed. Shown in a photograph are: Diamond T "Old No. 1" cuff links, Diamond T "Old No. 1" tie bar, pearl-handled scissors-knife, pearl-handled money-clip knife, Zippo lighter, stainless steel knife with case, and stainless steel Christy knife with case.

The jewelry, rhodium-plated or gold-plated, was used by Diamond T Motor Truck Company. It was purchased from Leavens Manufacturing Company, Summer Street, Attleboro, Massachusetts, and is of exceptionally high quality.

The money-clip knife was also used by Diamond T, and is available from a number of advertising specialty houses.

The Diamond T pearl-handled scissors-knife is a superb item; it's all stainless steel and brass bound. The author imported it directly from:

> Viola and Company
> Viale Coni Zugna 34
> Milan, Italy

When you're importing, *always* engage a reliable customs broker to handle the paperwork connected with getting the shipment into the country and through customs. You pay for the merchandise with an irrevocable letter of credit in favor of the foreign manufacturer; payment to his or her account is made when he or she presents shipping documents showing the merchandise is aboard a ship. This can be handled through your company's local bank.

Be absolutely *sure* to instruct your customs broker *in writing* to have your shipments insured. You can depend on having the boxes broken into and approximately 10 percent of the merchandise stolen.

Customs brokers handle shipments for a tiny fraction of the total value of the shipment, usually around 5 percent, and take all of the headaches and frustrations out of importing. They're intimately familiar with the government forms; they handle payment of the customs fee and bill you net on this.

Sources of domestic advertising specialty can be found in the *Thomas Register* and other directories, although you might save yourself some time by looking in the classified advertisements in the back of *Direct Marketing*. This is a magazine you should be reading if you plan on doing any volume of direct mail advertising. Subscriptions are $7.50 per year. Address of the publication is:

> *Direct Marketing*
> 224 Seventh Street
> Garden City, New York 11530

Historical Items

For the past few years there's been a noticeable upsurge in interest in things historical and in Americana in particular. Full-sized reproductions of old newspapers, on "antiqued" paper so they look and feel properly old and yellowed, are popular mailing pieces. E. F. Houghton & Company celebrated its 100th anniversary with an exceptionally attractive and nicely bound portfolio of old newspapers, all historic editions such as the April 10, 1865 issue of The Philadelphia *Inquirer* announcing the end of the war with the headline, *Victory! Victory!*

Historical mailers not only attract attention, but they receive avid and thorough readership; and they're frequently taken home, passed around to members of the family, then taken to school by the youngsters. Such pieces are an excellent buy and are highly effective in terms of interest aroused.

First Day Covers

Philatelists and almost everybody else take an interest in First Day Covers—that is, stamps issued and canceled by a specially designated post office to commemorate a historical event.

The beauty of First Day Covers is that although the recipient may not be a philatelist—a stamp collector, that is—almost everybody knows somebody who *is*. Frequently it's one of the recipient's offspring. One sure way to become an instant hero is to present a First Day Cover to a dedicated collector.

You can use regular envelopes, but they lack the impact that specially prepared envelopes developed especially for this purpose have. These First Day Cover envelopes are called "cachets" and are available from a number of sources at a modest price. They are usually beautifully engraved, and often printed in two or three colors. For a source of cachets nearest you, contact your nearest coin and stamp dealer or look in the advertisements in *Direct Marketing*.

The post office is the source of information about future First Day Cover stamps.

Caution: When mailing First Day Covers, do *not* seal the envelopes. Put your letter inside and tuck in the flap. Philatelists will *not* slit open a First Day Cover envelope; to do so destroys its desirability as a collector's item for them.

Handling a First Day Cover mailing program is easy. Simply order cachets from the source you've selected, have them shipped directly to your letter shop, assuming you use one, have them addressed and then have the letter shop ship them in ample time to the postmaster at the city of issue for the new stamp. A postal money order, bank draft or cashier's check for the proper amount of postage must accompany the covers; no company or personal checks are accepted. The post office makes no charge for affixing the stamps and mailing.

Unusual Postmarks

Mailings from odd-sounding places that tickle the fancy and stir the wanderlust are economical, as well as highly popular. They are received with enthusiasm even among those who are only casually interested. Attention is called to the postmark in copy inside the mailing piece, of course, although recipients catch on fast when a campaign is a continuing one, and they look forward to receiving future mailings.

The mechanics of making unusual postmark mailings is simplicity itself, although certain considerations should be borne in mind. You can get an alphabetical index of the *Directory of Post Offices* from the Superintendent of Documents, Washington, D.C. 20402. This manual lists post offices that lend themselves to almost any theme or scheme, whether it be Faith, Hope and Charity, Construction, Economy, Value, or what have you.

Prudence dictates that you verify the post office you've selected is still a going concern. Mortality rate among small post offices today is high.

Write to the postmaster at the town you've selected and request a sample of his or her postmark to be sure it's legible. Sometimes they're pretty badly worn. Then tell the postmaster of your plans and give him your timetable as closely as you can pinpoint it. This is frequently necessary to assure having sufficient labor available to handle your mailing. Your mailing may well be the largest the post office has handled in its entire history.

Be sure to purchase your stamps from the post office you're using. This is common courtesy and will be appreciated by the postmaster; he or she receives credit for stamp sales and wants to make as good a showing as possible. Stamps will have to be applied to your letters or mailers *before* them are shipped to the post office you've selected, however. Even if you buy them from Spotted Horse, Wyoming, the postmaster there will not affix them for you. First Day Covers are the only exception to this.

Although the post office is a government service, nonetheless you've asked a favor of the postmaster who handles your mailing. It's only decent to send a token of your appreciation to him or her after the job is done. And a nice touch is to send a sample of the mailing, along with a brief story about it, to the town's newspaper—or the one nearest the town from which your mail was sent. Give the postmaster a warm mention and you've made a friend for life.

Foreign Mailings

Foreign stamps and postmarks are conspicuously successful in attracting attention. They inject an aura of glamour and romance which produces high readership. Best practice is to use as many stamps as are required for the minimum postage; that is, use stamps of as low denomination as possible to add up to the correct total postage.

Doing this, you receive more stamps for the same amount of money and more attention when the mailing is received. This practice actually makes envelopes or mailing pieces real billboards for your message inside.

Money

This is a favorite subject of many people.

One of the most widely used tip-ons in direct mail is the penny. The penny has much going for it; it's legal tender, few of us can resist it, it attracts attention and causes the letter or mailer to assume much more importance in the eyes of the recipient than its negligible value warrants, it can be put in some parking meters, and it's inexpensive to use. What else can you ask of a penny?

Foreign coins are often available for even less than a penny, and they make an even stronger impression. Obsolete coins are also used with great success. McGraw-Hill made a series of mailings with authentic-looking reproductions of ancient Roman coins; accompany-

ing each was a capsule description of the original coin, its worth when struck, and other tidbits of information. Numismatists were delighted.

Reproductions of Confederate money invariably do an exceptionally fine job of attracting and holding interest. Mailing good-quality antiqued reproductions in a window envelope so piques the curiosity it's safe to assume not one person in a thousand would throw away the envelope unopened.

Both of these items (in fact, a complete catalog of historic papers) are available from this source:

Historical Documents Company
8 North Preston Street
Philadelphia, Pennsylvania 19104
(215) 386-4268

Historical Documents Company offers a substantial list of high-grade documents and reproductions of important pieces of American history, such as the Declaration of Independence. Printed on parchment-like paper and appropriately yellow with "age," the antiqued documents are kept and framed and displayed by many who receive them; they are tasteful and of lasting interest, and they hang proudly in many offices and recreation rooms in homes.

Phonograph Records

Direct mail activity is making itself *heard* around the country these days!

This new direct mail tool is an all-vinyl "Soundsheet'' which weighs just one-sixth of an ounce, yet provides an extremely fine quality high-fidelity phonograph record that can be played on any home or commercial record player at 33⅓ rpm—the ubiquitous LP (long playing) turntable speed.

Developed by Eva-Tone, St. Petersburg, FL, the Soundsheet "has not only proven to be highly flexible in adapting to marketing plans, but has also overcome the high cost of hard records, mailing costs, and handling costs."

Szabo Food Service, Inc., Lyons, Illinois, used three Eva-Tone Soundsheets, bound into attractive "albums," with excellent success.

A sales message can be put on a vinyl Soundsheet and mailed to prospects at a most reasonable cost. Sound fidelity is almost as good as on standard records, and there is no breakage and less shipping weight.

R. F. Neuzil, vice-president of communications, said the records produced a "tremendous increase in awareness of Szabo Food Service as the leader in the in-plant, hospital, and university feeding fields, and created an unexpectedly high volume of inquiries from top executives in leading companies in the industries to which we mailed them."

Dick Evans, president of Eva-Tone, is one of the most cooperative, helpful fellows you'll ever run across, and there's almost nothing he won't do to help you with your direct mail-sound program.

One thing, though: Dick says that while they make Soundsheets from tapes recorded by advertising managers, presidents, sales managers, order clerks, and assorted big butter and egg people, the fact remains that *this is a professional job for a professional narrator. And it should be done in a professional sound studio or radio station.*

Everybody is entranced with his or her own voice on tape or record, just as everybody delights in looking at pictures of themselves. But the ad manager and other executives in the company are just not cut out for this job of narration, despite personal opinions.

Narrators charge from $100 to $2,500 or more for a six-minute record, depending upon the narrator, how busy he or she happens to be at the moment, and how much he or she estimates the traffic will bear.

Eva-Tone will be happy to send you an Eva-Tone Soundsheet Idea

Kit, complete with samples, price lists, suggestions, art-work aids, etc., if you'll make a letterhead request.

Eva-Tone Soundsheets, Inc.
4801 Ulmerton Rd.
St. Petersburg, FL 33714

Special Processes

Offbeat processes frequently make an impression that lasts and lasts —if they're well done.

An old stand-by is the 3-D message for which the reader dons a special pair of glasses accompanying the message. Actually, they're cardboard frames and special plastic lenses, readily mailable without danger of damage. Moreover, because they are not manufactured of the customary optical materials, the price is held down so the industrial direct mail advertiser can afford to buy them in quantity. Most printers can handle the job for you.

Day-Glo ink which fluoresces when viewed by either artifical room lights or by daylight has also been around for a long time now, but its impact, especially on large broadsides, is tremendous.

Vivid colors include orange, shocking pink, red, and chartreuse. Incidentally, printing with black ink on orange Day-Glo stock produces striking browns where the black is laid down, with Day-Glo highlights in the halftones. The effect is unusual, almost weird.

"Smellies" are mailing pieces printed with special perfumes. This is done by making another run through the press and applying perfume through the press fountain, instead of ink. Scents available include barbecue, pizza, grape, bourbon, gin, apricot, pickle, coffee, hickory, spruce, pine, rum, smoke (used with striking effectiveness by insurance companies making mailings about fire insurance), tobacco, and so on and on.

Other special processes include X-ray visuals, which use acetate overlays to expose the internal workings of a mechanical product; invisible ink, and others ad infinitum.

Hard Covers

Many industrial companies budget for reasonably large mailings of thick, comprehensive, expensive catalogs which are almost always paperbound. No valid reason exists, they feel, for a more expensive binding. After all, catalogs become outdated within a year at the most.

For a few prospects whom you're trying to impress, however, nothing can equal a fine binding job. People keep hardbound books.

For such special prospects the author had one client's catalog bound in genuine leather. Top quality cowhide, gold-stamped, was used with telling effect. The catalogs so bound had their tops, edges, and bottoms gold-edged. They were so impressive they paved the way to signing eight new dealers within the first three months after they were mailed. The psychological impression produced by that expensive binding (it *was* expensive, around $60 per catalog) made the recipients feel they were something special, and it did much to lower their sales resistance and to make them favorably disposed toward the advertiser.

Product Samples

Nothing, but nothing, sells as hard as making possible the laying on of the hands.

Chain store retailers found this out many decades ago when Woolworth and others stumbled onto the fact that goods displayed on open counters where shoppers could fondle and feel sold far faster than similar items kept behind glass.

Although the industrial purchase is made more logically and less emotionally than are consumer purchases, the basic principle of putting the product, or a part of it, in front of the prospect and letting the prospect examine it cannot be questioned.

Unfortunately, this is not possible for a turret lathe, computer, road grader, bulldozer or similar large, heavy, expensive product. However, pieces of the product can be used in a direct mail campaign with excellent results. For instance, tip-on a tiny piece of a very large product onto a letter, then tell a strong quality story about this one little part. By inference at least, the recipient will receive the impression you want to give—that the entire product has had similar lavish care lavished onto it, all of which benefits the user.

One manufacturer of powdered metal parts—tiny, intricate, and forced to almost unbelievable precision and small tolerances—tipped on a miniature gear to mailings it made to prospective customers.

The letter, a four-pager, called attention to the complex shape of the part, the different surfaces which would have made machining prohibitively expensive, and to such features as the density and hardness. Finally, almost as an afterthought, the letter mentioned quite casually that the intricate part was quite inexpensive.

A series of these mailings resulted in a continuing flow of highgrade inquiries and requests to quote, or to have a sales engineer call. This advertiser acquired a number of new accounts with this direct mail advertising, and has an even larger number of suspects it is hopeful of closing eventually.

Split Mailings

The effect produced by split mailings, or cumulative mailings as some prefer to call them, is far greater than the impact of each mailing added together. Total impact is akin to that resulting from *squaring* each individual impact, rather than adding them together.

The Chicago office of Marsteller Inc. used the cumulative technique for its client, Clark Equipment Company, with outstanding results.

This $12,000 direct mail program triggered $3.5 million in sales and opened 50 new target accounts with a multimillion potential.

The direct mail campaign which Marsteller conceived was directed to 300 companies who were not buying Clark truck-trailers. One-sixth of the firms have become customers, placing initial orders for more than 700 semitrailers.

Called "Clark Cookout," the program involved six mailings of worthwhile items for backyard barbecues. Each mailing was associated with important product and service benefits of Clark trailers.

Marsteller selected dimensional direct mail for the Clark program for a very specific reason: A small, identifiable audience could be pinpointed, recipients would notice it, and the cost was reasonable for the sales potential involved.

Cost for dimensional direct mail is higher—in this instance $40 for each target account. Marsteller and Clark felt this was reasonable because average annual trailer purchases by these companies are ten units worth $55,000.

First mailing was made on July 1st. A chef's hat, representing both the cookout theme and the male aspects of barbecueing, introduced the program. The theme, "Hold on to your hat," emphasized that other cookout items were on the way. The hat also tells the Clark story that the man from Clark "wears many hats—equipment consultant, financier, used trailer specialist, and expediter."

As with all the program mailers, the salesperson's card was attached. And, the mailer was personally addressed to the prospect at the prospect's place of business.

Five days later the second mailing was made. It was a set of barbecue tools and explained that Clark's full line offered "the right equipment to do the best job." Included were tongs, fork, spatula, and brush.

Four days afterward, a spice set emphasized the *quality* and *reputation* of Clark Trailers by pointing out that whether making trailers or grilling steaks, the little extras mean a better finished product. Copy explained that Clark's reputation resulted from careful attention to detail throughout the manufacturing process.

Mailing number four was also made four days later. It was a *Better Homes & Gardens* cookbook to keynote the theme, "There's no substitute for experience."

Speeding things up a bit, the fifth mailing was made three days later. It consisted of an apron and gloves specially designed for outdoor cooking—to provide prospects with "extra protection and handling ease."

Approximately a week after the prospect received the fifth mailer, a Clark salesperson contacted the prospect with the keystone of the entire campaign. Following the presentation, the salesperson gave the customer a 14 oz. prime-cut porterhouse steak that had just been flown in from Milwaukee. The steak was packed in dry ice to preserve its flavor. Completing the series, the steak emphasized the personal service and attention that Clark provides its customers. And, it gave the salesperson the perfect chance to talk to the prospect face to face.

Following the presentation many salespeople were asked to deliver quotes. Sales didn't materialize instantly, of course. Buying decisions for trailers can take several months and many companies routinely purchase trailers at a specific time each year. However, by the end of the first quarter of the following year, 50 companies had placed first orders totaling $3,500,000.

Gag Mailings

Using gag items in a direct mail program is fun for all concerned, including the advertising manager. Recipients enjoy a chuckle when they open the mailings, and if they're tied in with the product, service, or selling proposition—as they should be—humor can do a job of making a positive impression.

For more than 20 years, Leo P. Bott, Jr. Advertising, an agency in Chicago, has mailed some wonderfully wild and wacky letters with gags, gimmicks, and guffaw-producing items attached, enclosed, tipped-on, inserted, and otherwise accompanying letters.

Among Bott's gags have been a Mexican jumping bean, Spanish moss, excelsior, corset spring, detective badge, false mustache, mask, stereopticon picture, etc. The letters have caused many laughs, much comment, and incalculable goodwill.

Printers send out kooky scratch pads with gags, jokes, humorous drawings, and the recipient's name printed neatly at the top. This never hits the round file because it's personalized, as is all effective direct mail advertising.

Plastic "panic buttons" have been—and still are, for that matter—a popular item. Few and far between are the offices where some individual doesn't have a panic button epoxied to the wall over his or her desk. It's always good for a laugh.

Something, almost anything, should tie the gag in with your product, company, or proposition. It loses effectiveness and produces a "so-what?" attitude if it doesn't. This is where the majority of gag-mailing industrial advertisers fumble the ball.

Teasers . . . the Case of Agent 3.1415

One of the cleverest teaser campaigns was one William T. Dyer, advertising manager of Electronic Products Division, Corning Glass Works, used for a highly refined mailing list of 200 prospects. Objectives of this campaign were to:

1. Isolate and communicate with a key list of specifying influences within the computer industry representing a potential for Corning's thin-film microcircuit business.
2. Identify Corning with the market.
3. Set forth the competitive advantages of Corning's product.
4. Motivate the prospect to take further action.

Electronics Products Division's mailing list was built through recommendations from the field sales force. *However, the list was screened by the division's microcircuit marketing groups for additions, deletions, and changes; they had the final say-so as to what names would be used, and properly so.*

Chances are this is one of the few industrial direct mail advertising campaigns that resulted in an investigation by the FBI. A special agent thought the campaign was exceptionally interesting, and asked for a copy to send to the late J. Edgar Hoover for use in the *FBI Newsletter*.

Twelve mailings were made over a three-month period; they included the following items:

1. Scribbled note—"you are being investigated . . ." This is on a torn piece of brown wrapping paper, "written" in black "ink" and with a stamped logo and signature, TOES, LTD.

2. Scribbled note—"So far, so good! Swallow this. Agent #3.1415 (logo) TOES, LTD."

3. Scribbled note—"You check out OK! Details will follow. Swallow this message. Agent #3.1415 (logo) TOES, LTD."

4. This was a 3-D mailing with shape and weight and form. It was a do-it-yourself Spy Kit containing such items as a water pistol—carefully labelled "Ray Gun"—a black mask, and a package of Tums for "relief of indigestion caused by swallowing all the previous messages." Also in the kit was a message telling the recipient that regular spy

reports would follow. The stage was set. Recipients were hooked. After being teased like that, few could resist wondering what was next.

5. Special Report No. 1, containing a snapshot of the "secret research facility." The report read as follows:

TOES, LTD.

FROM: Special A G ent #3.1415

ASSIGNMENT:The infiltration of all companies engaged in research and manufacture of micro-circuits for the purpose of obtaining daTa relating to the stability of organization and commitxment to micro-electronics field.

FINDINGS: Many cxxxxxx companies not firmly xxxxx committed to manufacture of micro-circuitry. Have wait-and-see attitude which could cause big problems for designers who must have a reliable source of micro-circuits. *However, hoave located one company which shows much* promise. Apparently has total commitment to micro-electronics field. Investment in new facilities totals millions of dollars. Reliable informatns say company was one of first in field and is determined to x continue leadership. Personal investigation indicates xxx conclusively that company is totally reliable and means to stay in micro-electronics. They have already developed highly automated processes which have consistently reduced costs for their customers. Company is in Raleigh, N.c. area. Its top xxxxx secret research facility is humming with activity. A photo of this facility is enclosed. Plan intensive undercover investigation of this company. A full report will follow.

G
Special xxxxx A ent # 3.1415

The tone of the copy in the "Special Report" is exactly right. The misspellings, strikeovers, and crossouts of the "typewritten" copy are deft touches that impart authenticity to the piece. Copy of this report reads:

TOES, LTD.

FROM: Special Agent # 3.1415

ASSIGNMENT:Continuing undercover investigation of Corning Electronics in Raleigh, N.C. to gain information about the way company achieves such high reliability in manufacture of micro-circuits.

FINDINGS: Thexxx enclosed packet of information was intercepted by an accomplice in the Corning plant and turned over to this agent. Information is self-explanatory. Another report will follow.

agent #3.1415
(logo)
TOES, LTD.

FINAL REPORT

TO: All TOES, LTD. Members

FROM: National Headquarters
       TOES, LTD.

Our mission is a complete success.

Special agents working under the auspices of the TOES, LTD. national organization have discovered that although there are some companies which are not totally committed to micro-electronics, Corning Electronics in Raleigh, North Carolina, plans to remain in micro-circuitry.

Investigation also reveals that the company understands designers' needs for high reliability micro-circuits and is qualified to meet all specifications.

Secret evidence accumulated from inspection of plants and questioning of reliable informants indicates conclusively that Corning plans to maintain leadership in micro-circuitry field and will be a reliable source of advanced micro-electronics indefinitely.

The advantage of materials used by Corning and company's experience in handling materials has also been proved conclusively.

This exhaustive undercover investigation was not achieved without some casualties. But they were minor, and all agents will recover. The only disappointment came with the desertion of Special Agent #3.1415 after a brilliant beginning. However, all members of TOES, LTD. have in their possession the special implement obtained for use if Special Agent #3.1415 should be encountered.

Remember that this organization may be reactivated at any time under the name Corning Electronics. This secret stuff has been fun, but now we've gotta let everybody in on the thin-film story.

So how did the FBI become involved?

It seems a nigh janitor at the Corning plant in New York found one of the roughly-typed messages in a wastebasket. The security man to whom he turned it over promptly called in the Federal Bureau of Investigation.

No telling how far it might have gone. TOES, LTD. *must* have been mighty elusive and hard to track down—if the FBI hadn't talked with Bill Dyer, Corning Electrics' ad manager. And the FBI agent had the Spy Kit in hand, so was aware it was some kind of a spoof by that time.

Effectiveness of this inspired direct mail campaign was not left to guesstimate. Corning conducted before-and-after attitude studies to measure results. Proven quite conclusively was that the company attained most of its objectives by enhancing Corning's reputation and brand preference in the industry.

Direct Mail Copy

Much of what has already been said about copy in preceding chapters applies to direct mail just as much as it does to space advertising.

Copy must be written with the user—the buyer—in mind. It must be you-oriented, rather than advertiser oriented. And it is essential that it stress benefits, rather than product features.

In direct mail advertising, perhaps even more than in industrial space advertising, everyone concerned is firmly convinced he or she is a copywriter, possibly one of the great ones—although unrecognized as yet. The fact is, 99 percent of those in responsible positions in industry cannot write a literate letter. Typical letters from industrial executives are unbelievably verbose. And they ramble, digress, repeat, and repel.

Writers of these horrible-example letters are usually excellent *product* people and often strong personal salespeople. But they have no conception whatsoever of what marketing communications can and should do for the company, nor do they know how communications should be employed to best advantage.

Perhaps the oldest and most frequently used formula is "AIDA"—get *attention*, arouse *interest*, stimulate *desire*, ask for *action*.

Very similar to the AIDA formula is the AIDPPC formula developed by the late Robert Collier, one of direct mail advertising's great copywriters. He emphasized the proper sequence of thoughts in all direct mail sales copy as:

Attention	Persuasion
Interest	Proof
Description	Close

Most copy formulas are very similar, and there are literally dozens of them kicking around. Their proud creators have espoused them in everything from books to articles in the trade press to speeches at symposiums and association meetings. Among them are Victor Schwab's AAPPA Formula. These cryptic letters mean:

A—Get *Attention*

A—Show People an *Advantage*

P—*Prove* It

P—*Persuade* People to Grasp This Advantage

A—Ask for *Action*

Direct mail and mail order marketing expert Bob Stone, *Advertising Age* columnist and head of Stone & Adler, has used the following copy formula with success:

1. Promise a benefit in your headline or first paragraph—*your most important benefit.*
2. Immediately enlarge upon your most important benefit.
3. Tell the reader *specifically* what he or she is going to get.
4. Back up your statements with *proof* and *endorsements*.
5. Tell the reader what he or she might lose if he or she doesn't act.
6. Rephrase your prominent benefits in your closing offer.
7. Incite action—*now*.

Bob Stone also quoted 20 checklist points developed by Maxwell C. Ross, today a creative marketing consultant, back when he was director of advertising of Old American Insurance Company. This checklist is reprinted with permission from the March 25, 1968 issue of *Advertising Age*, copyright 1968 by Advertising Publications, Inc.

CHECKLIST FOR BETTER DIRECT MAIL COPY

Copy Technique

1. Does the lead sentence get in step with your reader at once?
2. Is your lead sentence more than two lines long?
3. Do your opening paragraphs promise a benefit to the reader?
4. Have you fired your biggest gun first?
5. Is there a *big idea* behind your letter?
6. Are your thoughts arranged in logical order?
7. Is what you say believable?
8. Is it clear how the reader is to order—and did you ask for the order?
9. Does the copy tie in with the order form—and have you directed attention to the order form in the letter?

Copy Editing

10. Does the letter have "you" attitude all the way through?
11. Does the letter have a conversational tone?
12. Have you formed a "bucket brigade" through your copy?
13. Does the letter score between 70 and 80 words of one syllable for every 100 words you write?
14. Are there any sentences which begin with an article—a, an, or the—where you might have avoided it?
15. Are there any places where you have strung together too many prepositional phrases?
16. Have you kept out "wandering" verbs?
17. Have you used action verbs instead of noun construction?
18. Are there any "thats" you do not need?
19. How does the copy rate on such letter craftsmanship points as (a) using active voice instead of passive, (b) periodic sentences instead of loose, (c) too many participles, (d) splitting infinitives, (e) repeating your company name too many times?
20. Does your letter look the way you want it to? (a) placement of page, (b) no paragraphs over six lines, (c) indentation and numbered paragraphs, (d) underscoring and capitalization used sparingly, (e) punctuation for reading ease.

Stone notes that nine of the points are devoted to the *technique* of writing, while 11 points are devoted to *editing*. He then calls attention to the fact that few amateurs even bother to edit their copy, and suggests this is where the pros and the amateurs part company.

Significant is the fact the first four points of this checklist are given over to the lead. All of the professionals in direct mail advertising copy agree completely on one point: The lead and/or first paragraph determines whether the copy scores a resounding success, or is a gruesome failure and a waste of money.

It is there, right at the start of the sales call by mail, when your prospect decides to stay with you through the message until he or she is asked to take action, or he or she makes the decision to desert you.

As Elmer Wheeler said, "Your first 10 words are more important than your next 10,000."

Ross espoused a principle first stated by Richard Manville, now head of the advertising research firm which bears his name, but at that time an advertising consultant. Manville's principle is simply *to give people what they want in copy*—thus creating copy that outpulls copy which presents things which people do not want as much, or do not want at all.

In his *Advertising Age* article, Bob Stone stressed the importance of having just one idea—which is actually one core idea, or one central idea, as discussed in the chapters on space advertising copy. In copy for direct mail advertising it is even more essential, if possible, that the copywriter should hew to a straight copy line based on one strong idea.

A disconnected series of little ideas, or even a well-connected series of little ideas, will invariably result in copy that fails to make much of an impression. Stone said, "Emphasize many ideas and you emphasize none."

Believability is, perhaps, even more important in direct mail than it is in space advertising copy. You can say, and be completely truthful, "This widget will reduce machining time 20 percent." But people have been bombarded by too many unsupported claims and glowing promises over the years to pay very much attention to such glittering generalities.

But if you say, "Don Olson, plant superintendent, General Steel Company, reduced machining time 20 percent with this widget," you're home free. This is a believable statement.

Just one unbelievable statement can shatter the impression the mailer can make. It can cancel out in one brief instant the effect produced by all the rest of the copy—which might be superb.

Attitude is critical. Direct mail advertising copy *must* be written with a "you" attitude. Direct mail is such a highly personal medium that copy written to a vast mass of recipients will be impersonal. And impersonal copy in a personal medium makes an impression exactly the opposite of the one you want and need.

It has been said that the first question the reader wants answered is:

"What will you do for me if I listen to your story?"

To answer this question, direct mail copy must be you-oriented, not advertiser-oriented.

Use the "Bucket Brigade"

"The 'bucket-brigade' is a series of connectors," Stone said. "Connectors are transitional sentences or phrases which either end one paragraph or begin the next. Used properly, connectors give copy swing-movement, gliding the reader smoothly from one paragraph right into the next."

Examples are: *But that's not all, and in addition, moreover, so that is why, what's more, but there is just one thing, as I say, so mail your order today*—and so on.

Used with economy and taste, the bucket brigade can carry your story and your reader to the conclusion swiftly, smoothly, and as inevitably as night follows day.

When you next receive a dull, uninteresting direct mail piece, analyze it thoroughly. Chances are you'll find it doesn't contain enough of these connecting links to give the copy a fluid sense of movement; it will undoubtedly contain "island paragraphs"—paragraphs by themselves that are usually as dull as they look to the reader.

Too few writers bother to count the number of multisyllable words in their copy; you'll recall this was discussed at some length in an earlier chapter. Just because there's more room to use more words in direct mail copy than there is in space ad copy does *not* justify a long string of multisyllable words.

People to whom you're writing understand these words, of course, they can use them, *but they will not take the time to read them.* Boost the fog level of your copy and readership plummets. Fast.

Avoid starting sentences with articles (a, an, the). Steer clear of the prepositional phrase. Delete wandering verbs; keep them close to the subject rather than separated by a sea of other words. Use action verbs. Excite the reader, don't lull the reader to sleep. Use the active voice, not the passive. Do, don't talk about doing. Don't split infinitives. Many people don't care much, but among those who do you're hurting yourself unnecessarily. Keep your copy from being or looking soggy; open it up, let in some air, use short paragraphs, make it visually attractive.

Most reliable weapon with which to kill copy readability is repeating the company's name so many times and so often the reader is ready to scream.

Naturally, the company name should be mentioned. It's perfectly permissible to put it in display type, even across a spread, and it should be on both the front and back pages of the mailer. Signatures with addresses are proper and necessary.

But if you have even the slightest desire to have your copy read, do *not* for the love of all that's holy repeat the company name every sentence or two.

Copy route, chances are, follows a logical sales formula right through attention, interest, desire, and action. Then, the first draft written, the real pro applies a massive dose of self-discipline. He or she rewrites, polishes, and prunes until he or she is finally convinced the copy is the best he or she can do—that it's really copy he or she can be proud of. It is not at all unusual to rewrite a piece of copy three, four, six, a dozen times or more before it's finally just right.

Impose rigid self-discipline and then work—work hard. There's no other way to turn out copy that measures up to what you consider the very best you can write. No other copy is acceptable.

The Post Office

Only direct mail advertising is at the mercy of the vast, faceless, often capricious—and fantastically inefficient—army of bureaucrats which comprises the post office. And the worst of it have been the almost constant rate hikes in every category, from first class mail to fourth class. Offsetting such huge hikes isn't easy for users of direct mail advertising. Many companies are compelled to become more selective in mailing, and are looking into alternative ways to reduce costs.

One company with a $20 million annual postage bill, *Business Week* reported, schedules "postal cost reduction clinics" aimed at reducing expenditures while operating at normal levels. Some of the suggestions developed: Stationery of lighter stock, faster printing and paper handling, more self-mailers, and piggyback mailings (two or more messages in one envelope).

Zip Code Has Helped Save the Day

Experience with the five-digit zip code now required to follow the name of the state on any addressed mail has permitted sufficient mechanization and/or automation to enable the Post Office to pull itself up by its bootstraps.

Also, zip code is providing valuable clues to the potential of mailing lists. Westport, Connecticut, and Hibbing, Minnesota, for instance, are widely known as communities whose residents rank above the average in personal purchasing power. Research organizations are unearthing information about other communities identifiable by zip codes, as to their desirability or lack of it in providing good prospects for various products and services.

Direct mail advertisers are now required to do much of the work formerly done by the post office since the inception of zip code. Since regulations are constantly being changed or amended, the reader is advised to contact the post office he or she will be using for copies of manuals and bulletins containing up-to-the-minute material. The Post Office has been advocating a nine-digit code in order to exploit speedier service but this idea has met with great resistance in Congress.

Chapter 19

TRADE SHOWS

O F all the tools at his command, the marketing person has none more exciting, more versatile, and more challenging than the trade show exhibit. None offers more scope for the imagination and creativity; none allows more direct contact with the prospect; nor the ability to obtain an immediate impression of how a person is doing. None has the immediacy and the presence of the exhibit.

It is indeed a major medium, although it is such a complex one that it is not easy to obtain figures, especially figures that are universally acceptable. One might start with a study conducted by the industry newsletter, *Tradeshow Week*, which covered the 150 largest shows, in terms of square feet used for exhibits. Ranging in size from the 500,000 square feet occupied by the International Machine Tool Show down to the 41,000 square feet of the two smallest, these 150 shows added up to a total of 17,451,921 square feet of actual exhibit space sold.

The cost of this space to the companies that exhibited at these shows added up to $82,722,000. But according to studies of exhibit costs made by Exhibits Surveys, space amounts to only 18.75% of all costs to exhibitors. This means that exhibitors paid, for their part in these 150 shows, approximately $411,184,000.

But exhibits are put up for people to see, and people came to see these 150 shows and their exhibits. The total attendance was reported as just under 2½ million people. Using figures developed by convention bureaus, these people spent a total of $465,381,000. This makes a total of nearly one billion dollars generated by just these 150 shows.

But, of course, there are far more shows than these. A *SM/Successful Meetings'* figure gave an annual count of shows of 4,500 plus. Most of these are small, but 25% of them attract at least 3,000 attendees. It's difficult to say how much attendance is contributed by the nearly 1,000 shows that are over 3,000 and less than the top 150, nor by the nearly 3,500 small shows, but a total attendance of 20 million people is not unreasonable. Extrapolating this conservatively, you come up with a total figure of more than $7 billion a year!

What is a Trade Show?

This is a large amount of money, no matter how you look at it. What kind of medium is it that generates such a sum of money?

The trade show, with which this chapter is primarily concerned, is only one segment of a form of communication which is based on creating an environment for a visitor. This environment can include graphics, photography, copy, color, sound, motion, demonstration, personal communication, and even techniques that utilize the senses of touch and smell.

The overall exhibit function can operate within a number of formats, not all of which can be legitimately considered as trade shows, although all of them may be given corporate support, may employ many of the same techniques, and may become part of the responsibility of the exhibit manager. Here we are thinking of the various manifestations of trade shows: World's fairs, theme parks, state and county fairs, special interest public expositions, private shows, and regular trade shows.

How to Select Trade Shows That Count

There's certainly no dearth of trade shows.

Just the opposite is true. The average industrial company can pick and choose and be as selective as it wants to be when it comes to exhibiting its products.

Speaking before a workshop conducted by the Association of National Advertisers at Oakbrook, Illinois, Homer Morrison, manager of the advertising department, Union Carbide Company, listed six criteria for selection of trade shows. If followed, they should help increase the return on your trade show investment. The criteria are:

1. The geographic area within a radius of 200 miles of the location of the show should be a fertile marketplace.
2. Determine that the show will provide a personal selling environment in which salespeople can make selling calls on a significant number of prospects who are in the marketplace, and who have some degree of buying influence.
3. Determine that the atmosphere of the show will be conducive to serious business discussion.
4. There should be products or processes that are new (or sufficiently improved) to the potential audience.
5. Total cost of show participation divided by the number of "sales calls" that can be expected to be made should compare favorably with the average cost of making a regular sales call.
6. Total amount to be spent on show participation must not be a disproportionately large share of the total promotional budget.

Firm, formal, written objectives are an absolute essential if a company is to benefit to any great extent from exhibiting at shows.

Enter a trade show without objectives and you're actually without a purpose. About all you can logically expect to accomplish is to prove to attendees of the show you're "still in the widget business." This startling communication can be made to an infinitely larger audience by using space advertising, and it can be accomplished at far less expense.

What's more, it can be communicated to a more highly selective audience composed only of prime prospects and major buying influences by using direct mail. This medium is also more effective and much less costly.

Unless your company has something in the product lineup that's truly new, truly improved, truly exciting, the trade show is a poor investment for it to make. This includes both time and money.

However, if you *do* happen to have a revolutionary new widget, then by all means exhibit at the National Widget Users Exposition and Congress.

So, since you're stuck with having the terrible tab for countless shows taken from the advertising budget, do everything possible to run a tight ship. This means, first of all, establishing firm objectives.

For obvious reasons it is impossible to give a generalized objective, or set of objectives, that would be applicable for every company. Valid objectives for one company might be something like these, which were used by a prominent manufacturer of widgets sold to the metalworking market:

1. Inform a minimum of 600 buying influences of the new automatic widget we now offer.
2. Show this automatic widget, in operation, to these influences.
3. Give each influence a piece of sales literature about the new widget.
4. Get names, titles, firms of those 600 influences for sales followup by the field force.
5. Make a name impression—the fact that Smith Widget Manufacturing Company exhibited—on an additional 1,000 attendees of the show. This could be accomplished by holding a daily raffle with three silver-plated working-model widgets holding two fountain pens as prizes. To be eligible, attendees must register and deposit their names in a barrel in the booth.
6. Make contact with 150 selected old customers, current hot prospects, and others who marketing feels are desirable, and give top management a chance to mingle with them. This can be accomplished by handing out printed invitations to a buffet dinner in the company's entertainment suite. Because attendance is controlled by printed invitations, cost is held in line and guests will be limited to those most important to the company. Invitations (R.S.V.P.) will have been mailed two weeks prior to the show's opening date, of course.

With such specific objectives, it is more likely than not that the company will realize some benefits from having exhibited at the show. Without objectives, everything would have been left to chance.

The Mechanics

Nothing entails so much advance planning as does a trade show.

Be sure to inform people in your company why shipments to the show must be made exactly when and how you specify. Work closely with traffic managers, truckers, airlines, freight forwarders, and others who will handle your equipment shipment en route from factory to show. Make certain they understand it is consigned to you *to be exhibited*, and that they know the dates of the show.

Have your traffic manager stay in close touch with the carriers during the time they have the shipment, and have him or her follow it from place to place with regular progress reports. This is especially essential if the shipment is interlined—handled by more than one trucking company. Trace, trace, trace. Instruct your traffic manager to live with that shipment every inch of the way, every hour of the day until it's delivered to the exhibition hall or to the official freight handlers for the show.

Finally, make certain that all concerned know you're to be kept fully informed of progress—or lack of progress. This latter is even more important because if something does go amiss you can take remedial action.

Exhibition halls are scenes of such chaotic confusion as to stagger the imagination when a major trade show is being set up. The easiest thing in the world is to lose your boxes and crates inside the hall itself, after they're safely out of the hands of the truckers. Aisles are virtually nonexistent, and trying to wend your way through boxes stacked 10 feet high and look for your lost ones among acres of others is enough to try the patience of a saint. Saintly advertising managers are scarce these days.

Smart exhibitors long ago figured out that the way around that problem is to paint their crates and boxes a distinctive color so they would stand out from all of the others. Naturally, red was used with great success. So was orange, yellow, blue, green, gray and black. Finally, though, everybody's boxes and crates were painted and everybody was back at the starting place.

So smart exhibitors again got the gun on their slower compatriots and took to leaving their crates and boxes unpainted. That raw wood really stood out from all of that painted wood. Trouble was, everybody else started doing this about the same time. Full circle.

Best way out of this labyrinth of colors and noncolors is to use something so offbeat nobody else would think of using it. Chartreuse. Shocking pink. White. And, despite disliking the color as a matter of principle, the author used lavender with great success in recent years.

Lavender boxes are just too too distinctive to like, but they really stand out and can be spotted the length of the Cow Palace.

Stripes and polka dots, carefully masked before spraying, can make crates clash frantically from those that are merely wildly colorful. Zigzag stripes of one color, with a background color entirely different, telegraph instantly that your lost crate is over in *that* dark corner.

The Exhibitors Manual

Every exhibitor at a trade show receives an exhibitor's manual from show management. The manual becomes an extension of the advertising manager's person because it is checked and referred to so frequently. The volume provides a checklist of essential things to do and things not to do and serves as a second memory.

Almost every conceivable question that could come to mind is answered somewhere in this manual. The world of conventions and trade shows has many heads-up exhibit management organizations which have been in the business so long they can anticipate knotty questions even before some puzzled advertising manager can ask them.

Service contractors for the show are listed, along with addresses and telephone numbers to make it easy for advertising managers with special problems to contact the correct firms without having to go through exhibit management.

Having a checklist and referring to it daily during preparations for a trade show is an excellent way—in fact, the *only* way—to remember the myriad details you have to handle. Best possible checklist is one you make up yourself. List the things to be done, then in two ruled columns are spaces for dates—one the deadline date by which something must be handled, the other the date on which you concluded arrangements or took final action. This provides a fast, visual reference as to how things are progressing, and pinpoints any trouble areas before the trouble becomes serious.

It's a good idea to mark the deadline dates in a red squeakie, the dates each item was taken care of in blue or black. The color contrast makes your checklist graphic.

Arrangement of exhibits is specified by exhibit management. In general, specifications are quite uniform throughout the country, from show to show, and in all industries. Eight-foot backwalls (except for certain areas of the hall where the booth is erected immediately in front of an exterior wall), are standard. Nothing may project above this 8-foot height except equipment.

One critically important consideration when either planning a new booth or planning to use an existing one is to make absolutely certain it complies fully with all safety regulations and fire ordinances.

Your display house will see to it your exhibit meets established specifications, but be certain to check this. Fire marshals in all exhibition halls everywhere are extremely skittish since the disastrous fire which destroyed Chicago's magnificent lake-front McCormick Place the day before the National Housewares Show was scheduled to open. Fireproof buildings are a figment of the imagination; they do not exist. This tragic fire proved this once again.

So-called exhibitor package plans are proving highly popular with ad managers who have to exhibit at trade shows. What the package plan is, in essence, is having exhibit management combine almost all needed services into one neat bundle with one billing for services rendered.

So exhibit management will have at least a rough idea of what to expect—and what to make available—a form is provided in the manual for each exhibitor to estimate the approximate amount of labor he or she will require to set up the exhibit and equipment. This makes it possible for the various unions involved to supply sufficient bodies to get the job done.

When an exhibitor pays for floor space he or she is offered at no extra charge "standard booth equipment." This invariably consists of soiled draperies to form an 8-foot-tall backwall and 3-foot sidewalls. Using draperies at a show is really going poor-mouth, though. Almost every firm that has two nickels to jingle together has an exhibit booth designed and constructed by a professional display house.

Unless the company has its own furniture for the booth—tables, chairs, settees, smoking stands, coat racks, wastebaskets and so on — these must be rented. These items are delivered right to the exhibitor's booth and the ad manager signs to show he or she has received them. The renting firm picks them up immediately upon conclusion of the show.

Cost is high, of course, because this is trade show country. Furniture is usually of good quality and more than adequate for the purpose.

You'll be money ahead in the long run to rent furniture. If you buy your own there's always the chance you'll want to change color; color can be specified when you rent. What's more, if you buy furniture you have not only the original investment, you also have the cost of custom-built boxes to hold the furniture so it won't be battered to pieces in shipping. And then there's shipping, no inconsequential item in itself. By the time you pay all of this, you've invested more than the furniture is worth.

Return forms well before the show—the deadline is always given in the exhibitors manual—to get all company personnel properly registered. Nothing irritates product people, engineers, and others who normally do not man a booth as much as having to sweat out a massive line to get into a show where their company is exhibiting. Handle this detail well for all concerned, and you'll earn their gratitude.

Hotel rooms for all hands attending the show—booth personnel, visitors, and others from the company—are always a problem. Rooms are always doled out by a convention housing bureau. Check with your product people or whoever you most want to please in your company as to first, second, third, and fourth choices of hotels. Then get your application for room reservations in *immediately upon receiving your exhibitors manual. Fill out this form and mail it immediately if you want to get a hotel of your choosing.*

Housing bureaus always demand to know the names of individuals who will occupy the rooms you are reserving. But here's a tip. Get that reservation request in to the bureau with the *number* of rooms you want. Never mind listing the correct names of occupants—just put down names of people in your company regardless of whether they will attend the show or not. Names can be corrected later.

Booth Location

Maps of exhibit space supplied to each exhibitor by show management enable you to visualize the hall with all booths in place. Such maps make it easy for you to select a space that fits your budget and which stands every chance of attracting a good flow of traffic.

In general you're better off with space somewhat ahead of and to the left of the hall's registration area, restaurant, or central exhibit—whatever focal point exists. People tend on the whole to walk away from such an area, and they tend also to walk in a clockwise direction. Avoid dead ends and physical bottlenecks of any kind.

When you apply for space you're asked to give your first, second, third, and fourth choices. Try to select the space you want with the above in mind. You may want to block your choices together, with your first choice in the middle.

Something else to remember is that show managements always permit exhibitors to specify what companies they do *not* want to be near. This assures an exhibitor he or she won't have his or her bitterest competitor breathing down his or her neck from across the aisle, or next door. Such a situation would severely hamper both companies, of course.

The Booth

Very few companies use the background and sidewall draperies provided by show management. They make a poor impression. They make the company look like one that cannot afford to have a suitable booth built, and this can't help but reflect adversely on the company's products.

If your company has decided it can't live without exhibiting at trade shows, if there's no possible way you can prevent this squandering of money, it's important that you sell all concerned on one thing: *Going first class is the only way to go.*

Naturally, this means you'll eschew jerry-built displays whacked together in your plant's shipping room or carpenter shop.

Trade show booths are frightfully expensive things. Unless you *know* you're dealing with an honest, reputable display house, costs can creep up at an alarming rate.

Much of the cost of a booth, of course, is in the creative work. Concept, design, decorative treatment, and art are not inexpensive. Nor are the huge four-color translites, murals, special illustrations, attention-getting devices, special projection equipment, closed-circuit TV, "in booth" telephone systems and other specialty items.

Rule of thumb when having a new booth constructed is that you can expect to pay between $450 and $600 per running foot. Thus, a 50-foot booth should carry a price tag of somewhere between $22,500 and $30,000. However, it can run much higher if there's any great quantity of intricate and expensive electronic attention-grabbers built in. The figure can easily double itself. What's more, cost of island booths, finished on all four sides and often containing air-conditioned conference rooms and other niceties of life frequently run several times this figure.

When you're in the process of having a new booth built, remember that it must serve two purposes—to be an attractive background for your products and equipment, and to attract prospects *into* your booth area.

The three best traffic stoppers at a trade show are light, motion, and sex.

Insist on having your booth *light, light, light.* It doesn't necessarily have to be painted a light color, although this is usually desirable, but it is absolutely necessary that it have a very high level of illumination.

The booth should be lighter than the general surroundings in the hall, which itself is well lighted.

Motion—perhaps a lighted bulls-eye that revolves, flashing lights, blinking signs, moving machinery, a slide show, motion pictures, blowing streamers—all attract the eye of the show visitor and pull him or her into your booth. Still items are static and uninteresting; moving objects are vigorous, attractive, and appeal to the desire to do something, to move things, to change things, to accomplish.

Individual trade shows have different rules and regulations about what constitutes a "nuisance" and what doesn't, so be sure to check your exhibitor's manual if there's any question in your mind about the legitimacy of what you're proposing to do. If the formal rules don't cover your particular situation, pick up the phone and call exhibit management.

Sex is attractive. Every study made points out that use of comely models in the booth results in higher traffic flow. Here again, use taste and don't be blatant about it. And don't make the mistake of having a bevy of beauties standing around doing nothing except showing how attractive they are.

Put your models to work. Give them a legitimate reason for being there. Have them answer the telephone, run the inquiry-card imprinter, handle registrations for door prizes, take care of requests for literature, demonstrate the product, run the projector, hand out giveaways, and keep the literature supply neat and properly replenished. There is almost no end of tasks a pretty girl can legitimately handle at a trade show—and all the while she attracts the eye of your prospects. They're not immune to a pert face and shapely figure.

You can get a free trade show booth in just about any size you want if you have it designed and constructed in 5-foot modules. Of course, you do have to pay the exhibit house for it, but a modular booth will save so much money during its life as compared to one that must be painstakingly bolted together by carpenters at every show that it's almost like getting it free of charge.

A booth built in 5-foot modules is the most flexible arrangement. Space at shows is sold in 10-foot increments as a rule. This means you can have, for instance, a half-dozen 5-foot modules for a 30-foot booth; but this also gives you a 10-foot booth, a 15, a 20, and a 25.

At the time your display house is building your new booth, instruct them to install electrical junction boxes in every module. This means the "electricians" at the halls merely have to plug in the lines running from the junction boxes—not an individual cord for each light, fixture, translite, or projector.

Having all of this work done by your display house so it becomes a permanent part of the booth is likely to save a minimum of $2,000 over the life of the booth if it's used three or four times a year for three or four years. In addition to saving labor, your booth will require fewer outlets in the halls, each of which has a price tag attached to it.

Evaluating Return From the $$$$$ Spent

Effectiveness of participation in a trade show can be measured only by the number of high-interest prospects to whom sales and marketing people in your company talked. Casual strollers who visited your booth only out of idle curiosity or to ogle the models or to watch the card-sharp perform are worth little or nothing.

But your booth personnel should be instructed to take names of those who are considered genuine, livewire prospects, interested enough in your product to warrant a follow-up sales call.

These names should be guarded closely. The advertising manager will want to add them to the mailing list and ultimately forward them to the field salespersons as soon as proper literature has been mailed. All of this should take place within two weeks of the end of the show. To procrastinate is to lose a possible prospect.

Incidentally, the advertising manager and his or her assistant are *not* booth personnel. Repeat: *The advertising manager and the assistant are not booth personnel.* Neither should be on the roster to do regularly scheduled duty. One or the other should be nearby—at least in the hall—during most show hours in case something arises that must be handled with hall labor or exhibit management. But they have no place standing there trying to sell the product or to smile merrily at prospects and customers. This is the province of the sales or marketing executive in charge of the product line being exhibited, and he or she alone has the responsibility of establishing duty rosters with hours and dates.

Determining exactly how efficient your exhibit and your booth personnel were at the trade show in which you participated is simple enough. All that's necessary is to find out how many attendees at the show had an interest in your product, then find out how many of those interested individuals entered your booth.

The old reliable mail questionnaire is used to develop this information. Select a random sample of 2,000 names chosen on an every *nth* name basis from the roster of attendees who registered at the show. Show management can provide the list of registrants. Prepare a questionnaire and mail it to them while their memories are still fresh, say, not later than three weeks after the show closed. Data developed this way have proven to be projectable.

Auditing Trade Shows

Most of the better trade shows are now audited either by firms of certified public accountants or by BPA—Business Publications Audit of Circulation, Inc.

According to *Clearing House*, publication of the Media Comparability Council, Business/Professional Advertising Association, the Audit Bureau of Circulation (ABC) has audited the registered attendance of a number of trade shows in conjunction with its new affiliate, Audit Bureau of Marketing Services. It is anticipated that this activity on the part of ABC will be stepped up significantly as time passes.

While exhibitors are more than pleased at having BPA and ABC audit trade show attendance, joy does not reign supreme among everybody concerned by any means.

More than a sneaking suspicion remains that most exhibit managements fear what the audits will disclose, fear the consequences of having this impartial, factual information in the hands of exhibitors, fear that facts revealed by the audits will severely hamper their selling activities. As far as trade shows are concerned, it's much easier to sell a pig in a poke than it is to peddle a questionable product.

Trade show auditing is in its infancy. With some 4,500 shows held annually and only a tiny handful audited, the room for improvement is large. Significant is that those shows which are the largest and most important are the ones that have been audited, much like the leading trade publications were quick to produce an A.I.A. form to present information about themselves.

Costs of Trade Shows

Staggering, that's what they are—the direct cost of trade shows, that is. And usually these are the only costs considered. Indirect costs are more often than not several times as high, but equally often they're overlooked or conveniently ignored. Both types of costs will be discussed.

When management of an industrial company is struck with an inspiration to exhibit its wares in a trade show, it's usually after having received a promotional mailing from the show promoter.

This piece lovingly extols the virtues of the trade show. It emphasizes the almost unbelievable number of board chairmen, presidents, executive vice-presidents, plain ordinary vice-presidents, research directors, chief engineers, plant superintendents, directors of manufacturing and others on that level of management who have been sitting around biting their nails all year long waiting impatiently until *THE DAY* finally arrives. *THE DAY*, of course, is the one on which this particular trade show throws open its doors and admits these busy executives so that, once again, they can find out what has been happening in their field.

The promo piece points out that all an exhibitor has to spend is a thousand or two, give or take a little, depending on where in the hall the exhibitor wants to be and how much space the exhibitor requires.

A Typical Problem

Let's look at one company's expenses at the I.E.E.E. Show held in New York City. Here is a case study of what *not* to do in exhibiting at a trade show. It shows how important it is to tally all the potential costs and analyze what results you can expect before signing your entry application. We can assume it's typical for this size company and for the size space the company's exhibition used—30 feet. Best way to go into these costs* is to quote the advertising manager's memo to the company president. It reads:

SMITH WIDGET MANUFACTURING COMPANY

Interoffice correspondence

TO: Mr. Carl Roberts

SUBJECT: I.E.E.E. Show cost

Dear Carl:

As you requested, I'm giving you a rundown on the costs of the I.E.E.E. Show held in New York in March.

Unfortunately, I'm able to give you only direct expenses. I have no way of knowing what indirect costs are; these would, of course, include salaries of individuals while they were at the show and en route, shop time spent readying equipment for the show, time spent in shipping and other plant departments. In addition, indirect costs should include the loss the company incurs from having field men in the booth instead of out selling; this can easily be determined by Sales as a fraction of each individual's annual productivity.

* N.B. We realize all these figures will be out of date when this edition is released but you can extrapolate them.

Space	$ 2,250.00
Al Miller studio, mounting literature	7.88
Models	320.00
Cleaning blazers worn by booth personnel	17.00
Expo decorating	67.20
Cleaning, waxing, mopping, chambermaiding	132.62
Shipping, outgoing	196.57
Shipping, incoming	160.00

Shipping, outgoing, laminar air-flow widget	98.00
Shipping, literature and odds and ends	10.45
Booth photographs	10.00
Prepaid freight on booth by display house	186.91
Freight back to display house, check and store booth	214.39
Riggers, set up	397.88
Phone bill	93.62
Refurbishing of booth...	1,436.17
New blazers and hats for booth personnel.......................	58.29
Electrical service to booth.....................................	151.28
Movie film, extra print for safety's sake	28.00
Special literature on conveyor widget for show	375.00
Snap-out inquiry form...	30.00
Printing district office listings on forms for handout................	256.96
Literature and incidentals shipped to display house.................	12.31
Travel expenses, including plane tickets, of personnel...............	1,169.87
Travel expenses, on expense accounts	2,490.76
	$10,161.16

Several weeks go by before all invoices are received after a show, and before Accounting has all expense accounts, billings from the airlines and so forth—and before all costs are pulled together here in Advertising.

Cordially,
Joseph S. Nocco
Advertising Manager

This company did, in fact, pay only a trifling $2,250 for its 30 feet of corner space at this show in New York's Coliseum. That admittedly *isn't* a huge expenditure. And the company *could* afford it, just as the show promoter said.

What wasn't mentioned by the show promoter is that the rule of thumb commonly applied to trade show expense is that total direct costs customarily run between four and five times the cost of the space. This ration holds for both large and small companies because large companies tend to purchase larger space, show more products, and have more bodies on booth duty, while smaller ones spend proportionately less.

Show expenses, though, are like an iceberg.

Only a tiny fraction of the total is visible above the surface. In this instance the advertising manager, although obviously not privy to individuals' salaries, could, nonetheless, make a reasoned guesstimate that was undoubtedly correct within plus or minus 7½ percent; this expense was put at $12,000.

Furthermore, there was the little matter of lost sales from having a large number of the field sales force in New York, as well as home office marketing personnel. This advertising manager checked on each sales rep's annual sales for the preceding three years, divided this annual figure by 52 and came up with the conclusion the company probably lost a minimum of 100,000 in sales.

During this time under the searing lights and on the hard concrete a total of 142 legitimate contacts were made by booth personnel. However, only *three* out of all those were with individuals on whom the sales force did not call at that time, and they turned out to be junior engineers a cut above the draftsmen level—hardly prime buying influences.

Thus, if we take *only* the direct costs and the indirect costs accounted for by salaries *and ignore lost sales*, we find this company spent a total of $22,161.16 to talk with 142 people to whom it talked frequently, both before and after the show—minus those three young engineers, of course. This figures out to more than $156 per contact—and the 16 cents was also ignored.

Proponents of trade shows, scarcer and scarcer these days, have always admitted when pinned right down to it that trade shows are a legitimate medium of communications *if the cost per sales contact at a show is approximately that of a contact made by a sales rep in the normal course of events.*

Since the cost of the average industrial sales call is $106.90, Smith Widget Manufacturing Company spent over $49 more to make a contact at this trade show than it spends to call upon buying influences in their own offices.

This cost per contact of $156 per individual tallied up by Smith Widget obviously translates into a cost of $156,000 per thousand individuals. What advertising man in possession of even a tiny fraction of his faculties would advocate buying a medium with a cost of $156,000 per thousand?

Final consideration in trade show costs is: What percentage of the total communications budget does the company allocate for shows? If it approaches 10 percent, the time has long since passed when somebody should have taken a long, hard look at what the company has been getting for its money.

If trade shows siphon off more than 10 percent of the average industrial company's promotional dollar, chances are something is radically wrong with the emphasis placed on this communications medium. Consideration should be given to seminars, expanded direct mail advertising, and additional space advertising in trade publications. All do a better job, reach more buying influences and cost less.

How to Make It All Easier

You can lessen the pains and avoid a large share of the frustration of handling trade shows if you'll heed the following:

Fill out your "Empty" stickers before you leave for the show. These go on each and every crate, box, carton, container, case and so on that you'll use to pack up and reship your product, booth, furniture, floor tile and so on when the show closes and you tear down your exhibit. Write exhibit management and request that they be sent to you in your office—and at the same time, get your "Return" labels; these will usually be addressed to your display house, of course. Fill them out before you depart for the show.

Send all of the people in your home office, field force, and others in the company who will attend the show a machine copy of an area map showing the location of the exhibit hall and the hotel where they will stay. Circle the hotel and the hall. Everybody who receives this is grateful.

Send all of your people their copies of the hotel reservations. And you check personally when you get there ahead of them to make sure nothing has gone amiss.

Make copies of all bills of lading for all shipments—equipment, booth literature, and what have you. This makes tracing easier in case anything goes wrong—which it will.

Also have copies of all of the order forms you filled out and mailed to various suppliers of such stuff as furniture, water cooler, electricians, labor, carpenters, porter, janitor, and so on and on. Then, if you get any static in the hall (which you will), you'll be able to prove you ordered material and services as specified.

Check *immediately* upon arriving in the city where the show is to be held to see if your equipment and booth have arrived. If there's the slightest bit of doubt, get on the horn and start tracing *immediately*. Don't let anybody reassure you, don't take anybody's word that the shipment will show up tomorrow, or that it may be in the hall right now. Don't wait, don't hope, don't delay. Don't assume it will show up in time. If you do that, you can be morally certain of one thing—it won't.

Have handy the dimensions and weights of each individual crate, carton, box, case, container, drum and so forth. Your shipping department and that of your exhibit house will have compiled all of this data for you prior to shipping. Truck lines, airlines, and railroads are helpless unless you can supply this information.

Take phone numbers with you. Never does it fail but what something crops up that makes it necessary for you to call your boss, your assistant, your secretary, or somebody else. Take both office and *home* phone numbers. More likely than not whatever it is that makes it necessary for you to call long distance will happen on a weekend when everybody's office is closed.

Two last things: Lock your booth telephone at night.

Repeat: *Lock your booth telephone at night.* You can buy telephone locks at nearby drugstores, hardware stores, stationery stores, and often in the exhibit hall itself. These simple little locks cost a couple of dollars and have two keys. Tell the man in charge of your booth personnel that you have only *one* key. You keep it. Make the last thing you do at night to lock the phone.

Locking your booth telephone prevents all of those unexplained person-to-person calls to Willie Smith in Saigon or Frankfurt or London. They mount up amazingly. The author knows one hapless advertising manager who accumulated more than $700 worth of these calls, all made at night, all made to soldiers in far-flung cities throughout the world.

Final thing to remember: Don't blow your cool.

Chapter 20

LITERATURE

UNQUESTIONABLY one of the most important assignments handled by the industrial advertising department is the production of literature.

For the most part this is product sales literature. However, most advertising departments also create and produce a miscellaneous assortment of other print material including house organs, employee manuals, instruction manuals, company histories, annual reports, and so on.

When McGraw-Hill conducted a survey to determine what sales reps consider the most important selling tool with which they are provided, sales literature on the product won hands down, as reported by the Laboratory of Advertising Performance.

Sales reps of manufacturers selling machinery and equipment to the chemical process industry were singled out and asked the question:

> *Which sales aids are of greatest help in facilitating your general selling approach and in developing the confidence of present and potential customers?* (Check as many as are important to you.)

Predictably, manufacturer's literature breezed into a strong front-running position with a total of 95 percent of the vote. In second place was space advertising in trade and business publications; it had 70 percent of the vote. Considerably down the scale in importance in the sales rep's scheme of things came direct mail, which tallied up 45 percent of their favorable mentions.

Data for the report were developed with the cooperation of 101 manufacturers of machinery and equipment sold to the chemical processing industry. The sales managers of 46 companies cooperated with McGraw-Hill Research by distributing 2,091 questionnaires to their own sales force. In addition, 55 other companies sent in 2,007 names of their sales reps so that they could be sent questionnaires. In the returns were those from direct sales reps, as well as manufacturer's representatives, so the results present a good cross-section of opinion of those selling industrial capital equipment.

What's more, according to LAP, industrial buyers, when asked to rate difficult information sources as to usefulness in supplying facts about products purchased for their companies, rated manufacturers' literature right at the top—63 percent of them stated literature was their number one source of help.

Thus, it's quite obvious there is unanimity of opinion as to the efficiency with which sales literature presents information, and from both sides of the desk at that—sales reps and buyers see eye to eye on this subject. This is indeed convincing.

Manufacturer's literature also serves another purpose which is seldom mentioned to sales reps, although they are, of course, fully aware of it. Collecting information of the three or four leading makes of widgets enables the prospective purchaser of a new widget to make an unhurried comparison of the merits and specifications of each, away from the blandishments and distractions and persuasive remarks of the sales rep.

Actually, there are six primary objectives for sales literature. These are:

1. To support the sales force.
2. To strengthen dealer relations.
3. To intensify the advertising.
4. To help hold old customers.
5. To help win new customers.
6. To help broaden the market.

Advertising Department Does Not Initiate Literature

Although the advertising department produces and frequently creates sales literature, advertising does not and cannot initiate it. To do so would be to assume the prerogative and function of a different department altogether.

Planning literature, that is, foreseeing the need for it, properly is part and parcel of marketing planning. Needs in this area should be spelled out in the marketing plan for the product line involved (or for the individual market, depending on how the company is structured) at the start of the fiscal year.

To expect the advertising manager to be able to "guesstimate" the number of different pieces of literature it will be necessary to produce during the year is absurd. Yet this happens most of the time in most companies.

In order to be able to plan a budget for the advertising department, the advertising manager must know the number of different pieces of literature to be produced, the degree of complexity of each, and the anticipated print run for each.

But it is the marketing and product people who are privy to plans for new products and revamped, renewed, renamed, and facelifted old products for which new sales literature will be needed in the forthcoming 12-month period. Too, they are conversant with thinking of top management on how hard specific products are to be promoted and the emphasis to be placed on all products.

Market management, product management, or sales management requests literature from advertising, usually with a requested needed-by date, guidelines as to how elaborate the piece is to be, any special photographs or artwork, slant of the copy, appeals to emphasize, and quantity needed. All of this must take place before the advertising department can do a good job.

How to Decide What Goes in the Literature

Assuming your company is like most industrial firms, you'll be subjected to pressure that's little short of ferocious to put everything that everybody and his brother can think of in the literature you produce.

The engineers, for instance, will lovingly dwell on the pitch of the thread of the bolts that hold the nickel-chrome, heat-treated steel of the frame of the widget together, and that the gears are helical and have faces that overobfuscate the retuddity with a bright linear kopacetic. And this is just the start of it.

Listen to them, keep on listening, mutter sweet nothings politely, smile toothily, and nod agreeably. But for the sake of sanity, *don't* put everything in the literature that they want. If you do this, nobody will wade through it because the copy will be so boring and tedious. Moreove, your literature will have missed its mark.

The product and marketing people also will talk features to you endlessly. You'd think that because this widget holds 8 cubic yards, or that it pumps 1,567 gallons per minute, nothing else mattered.

One sure way to determine exactly what should be in literature and what shouldn't, is to make an informal survey. Informal doesn't mean having lunch with a few friends or quizzing a few cohorts at the water fountain.

Instead, be a bit more formal than that. Go at the survey just as you would if you were doing some deep digging for market data. And indeed you are because you're determining what it is those in the marketplace want to know about your product. There's no necessity to invest a small fortune in printing, but by all means consider this thing carefully and draw up a questionnaire that's easy to answer, that has boxes to check off, and send a *stamped* envelope (not a postage-paid reply envelope) along with it. And write a covering letter asking for the recipient's help.

Explain in the letter that you're in the process of developing a new piece of literature on your new widget which is just about ready to be announced to a breathlessly awaiting world, and tell the recipient that you'd like to know what *he* or *she* would like to know. Say that his or her help, will enable you to produce a piece of literature to end all pieces of literature as far as answering questions he or she has about the product is concerned.

Send your questionnaire to:

1. Product and market people inside your company.
2. Your field sales force.
3. Your dealers, distributors, representatives, or jobbers.
4. Prospects and customers from those two mailing lists you have.

Don't make a big production out of the questionnaire. But it's best to mail at least 1,500; in addition to your own people and those who handle your product (presumably you can rely on a high percentage of returns from them), mailing to at least 250 customers and an equal number of prospects and dealers or distributors should be sufficient. Those who are really interested in your products will reply, and they're undoubtedly your best prospects anyway, so the chances are their thoughts would be most helpful.

Criticism may be leveled at you for using a questionnaire. You may hear the remark, "We never had a questionnaire before. Why all the fuss? Just put in everything about the widget and let it go at that."

Such thinking is commonplace throughout product-oriented companies with complex and highly-engineered products. They've used old-fashioned "bulletins" so long that nobody in the company actually realizes how poor the sales literature is.

Often overlooked, but a valuable source of information about what should be included in the piece of literature, is what is in your competitors' literature on the same product. Presumably they've given thought to this subject and have researched it. They may not be right, and circumstances certainly alter cases, but this viewpoint represents the combined thinking of dozens of individuals throughout your industry and it is not to be taken lightly.

Questions to ask yourself when planning a piece of literature were spelled out by S.D. Warren Company, manufacturers of fine papers, in its booklet, *The Sales Catalog*. The eight questions asked under the heading, Proper Preparation, are:

1. How are the products used by a potential customer? And how are they purchased?

2. How can the product and accompanying information best be presented and described so that prospective buyers can inform themselves fully? With pictures that display exteriors and interiors—with diagrams—with color? With installation photos?

3. How can the present literature be improved to make it more helpful to the user?

4. What products or models are most frequently purchased?

5. What are the different things that potential customers will want to know about the class of product—applications, ease of operation, construction specifications, economy, comfort, beauty?

6. What uses can be made of the product? Is it versatile? What are all of its advantages (major and minor)? Has the product features that are exclusive?

7. In what circumstances and environment will the literature be used? Will it be kept in a desk drawer or in an office file cabinet or on a shelf? Will it be used by shop mechanics? Should it conform to standards specified by a trade or professional association? What size will best suit the condition of use? What measure of protection is required?

8. What is the forecast on prices? Should price schedules be included, or should prices be issued in supplementary sections?

Since advertising managers as a breed are able to cut incisively to the crux of things rather than rehash trivialities for hours as the technical types are fond of doing, maybe you can save much time and conversation and effort by asking yourself (and maybe others) the following questions:

1. What information about the widget do your prospects and customers really want?

2. Is this the information they actually need to make a buying decision?

3. How should this information be organized to make the most persuasive case for your widget that can be made, and are you certain it is in logical order with nothing of consequence omitted?

4. How should you present your widget—photographically, line art, wash, scratchboard, black-and-white, four-color; product by itself, product in use, installation photographs, cutaway views, or what have you.

5. How detailed should your literature be? Should it be two pages (front and back), four pages, eight, or is it better to produce a complete catalog? What form should it take—loose pages, spiral bound, three-hole punched, side stitched, stapled, paperbound, hardbound?

6. When and to whom should the literature be distributed? How should it be distributed? Correct timing can affect sales and demand, as can the list of recipients and the method of distribution.

The literature you produce is a silent sales rep. It continues to sell long after your prospects have forgotten your advertisements and have dismissed your sales reps from their minds. The power of the printed word in sales literature is mighty indeed.

Product Line Catalog Versus Individual Sales Literature

Perplexing many industrial advertising managers is the age-old question: Should I produce a complete, detailed catalog covering every widget we manufacture, or should I take the alternate approach and produce sales literature for each individual product as a separate item?

Answering that one is easy for many ad managers, especially those whose companies engage in high volume production of standardized items such as components to be incorporated into the end products of other manufacturers. Such products might be screw-machine products, nuts and bolts, fastners, standard hardware, cotter pins, electric motors, pumps, hydraulic pistons, generators, tires, and other items for which there is a relatively stable demand and which do not undergo sweeping changes in approach very often.

For example, a full-line catalog of electric motors might well be in order and it could very easily be the most economical method of presenting a vast mass of product information about many different models to prospective customers. Such a catalog could have photographs and complete technical descriptions of each and every motor in the line, cutaway artwork, overlays, and four-color printing.

In short, the advertising manager for a company like this could logically make a major investment in a selling tool of high quality, secure in the knowledge that tomorrow or next week or next month the product would still look like the ones shown in the catalog. If new motors were developed, supplementary pages could be issued.

Volatility of the market and frequency of changes in the product are the big bugaboos confronting most advertising managers. They make investing in a full-line catalog, often to the tune of $50,000 or more, inadvisable.

In many companies the advertising manager is faced with the problem of producing a piece of literature for one product line only, when the company may manufacture a half-dozen different product lines or more, each for a different market.

All too often this hapless ad manager labors long and mightily, creates strong, succinct, swinging, selling copy; a beautiful, clean layout; and he or she uses superb photography or art; and then rides herd on the printer to assure a faultless job.

Then what happens? Somebody either changed one of the products, the sales manager dropped it from the line because it wasn't selling or there wasn't enough profit in it, or else some engineer developed a completely new widget—all without even a whisper to the unfortunate advertising manager.

Lack of internal communications causes this waste of time and effort and money too frequently in too many companies. Eliminating obsolescence in product sales literature is almost impossible in a fast-paced industry, especially when frequent product changes—such as occur in the electronics industry—create a built-in obsolescence in new literature even before the ink is dry.

You'll never live to see the day this problem doesn't exist, but much can be done to keep it fairly well under control. Most important thing to do is to lay down clear channels of information within your company—perhaps from marketing to sales to advertising to engineering to production, or however the sequence runs in your firm. Make sure, however, that you are on the route list for memos and other written matter concerning all new products and all revisions in existing products.

In many companies there's a product review committee, a new product committee, or some such group. Attend these meetings, or (better yet), get your name on the route list for a summary and save valuable time you can't afford to waste.

An exceptionally attractive and informative product-line booklet was produced by Electro-Motive Division, General Motors Corporation. The company's six-axle, six-motor mainline locomotive, the SD Series, is shown attractively in impressionistic art in color. It is identified on a separate page opposite the illustration. Flip this page and there are specifications for Model SD-45, components included in this model, and a tractive effort curve on the opposite page. All very tidy.

Continue flipping the half-pages and the same information is presented on the other models in the SD Series. Then there's a striking night photograph, in black-and-white for a change of pace, of an SD Series locomotive in actual service.

This page is a fold-out. Printed in black against an olive-green background are line drawings of each model locomotive, with dimensions printed in a darker green. The effect is striking and very effective as well as providing necessary information for those in need of a locomotive.

If specifications were to change because the engineers got to doodling around with the product after literature has been printed—as usually happens—most of the expensive art, type, keylines and so forth could be saved and reused in another printing. This is good planning. Much effort and thought went into this excellent booklet.

To negate literature obsolescence, many industrial advertising managers produce one or more prestige booklets of 12 or 16 pages to tell a corporate or divisional story.

Ringbinder catalog of GM locomotives has expensive art work on full pages by itself. Pages devoted to data are on half-pages (shown below) so that changes can be made fairly inexpensively.

Stress interesting or unique applications of your company's products. Tell about the achievements of your engineering staff, hit on the accomplishments of your research and development people, brag about the skill and depth of knowledge of the field sales force and the enviable position of your company in its industry. Emphasize the quality theme, the capability of your company, and its ability to solve prospects' problems.

Paul Marcott, advertising manager of Bell Helicopter Company, a Textron Company, took this tack with great success in his literature. He could do so because the company's choppers are sold in many ver-

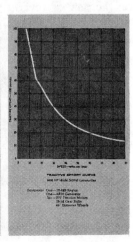

sions in many diverse markets, both military and commercial. This made it impractical to invest in a full-line catalog suitable for every market and application.

A typical production is Bell Helicopter's attractive 28-page booklet; the cover is printed in four-color and shows small spot illustrations of various choppers in a wide variety of applications. Inside pages are printed in orange and black, while the halftones are mostly duotones, a combination of the two colors.

One thing Bell's booklet has going for it is that it's timeless. At the end of the Vietnamese War all that has been said remains just as compelling and just as arresting as the day it was written. Instead of a current document, the booklet discusses recent history. When it's both product- and company-oriented, there's nothing wrong with that.

This multipurpose type of literature makes prestige handout pieces that any company representative can present with pride to a prospect or customer. They dramatize the major role Bell Helicopter is playing in transportation, pipelining, construction, crop-dusting, oil fields, geological exploration, road building, ranching, rescue work, surveying, fire fighting, reforestation, and military service.

Quality can be emphasized, as Paul Marcott did, in photos and art and fine layout, as well as in words—and the obvious quality of the finished literature itself.

Supplementing a couple of basic pieces of prestige literature such as this can be sales literature on individual products. Thus, when a product becomes obsolete, there is no need to scrap an expensive catalog and start from scratch again; simply prepare a new piece of literature on the new or revised product and you're back in business without spending a small fortune.

Although the cover of this Bell Helicopter booklet shows military uses, it suggests civilian applications.

This method may not be ideal, however, due simply to the fact your company wants to make a big splash. Perhaps the competitive situation dictates that to the broadest line goes the major portion of the spoils, a situation encountered with increasing frequency in bitterly competitive markets such as the automotive aftermarket.

If this is the case, the company undoubtedly feels the necessity of putting out a thick catalog to show prospective warehouse distributors, jobbers and dealers that it produces the right widget for every vehicle—and far more different widgets than the competition does. This is the "single source" concept, and it's a potent one.

Ideal solution to this problem is to do as Sealed Power Corporation did, which was to come up with an inch-thick, spiral-bound catalog. Although it's big and impressive and it hammers home to prospects the fact that Sealed Power markets an unusually comprehensive line of piston rings and internal engine parts, the catalog was nonetheless produced by advertising manager George Wickstrom without investing an inordinate amount of money.

This was possible because the catalog is, for the most part, a compilation of appropriate tabular information supplemented by individual pieces of product literature. Literature was produced one piece at a time, as needed. The entire thing was then collated, punched, and bound together.

An essential that musn't be overlooked if you want your catalog to be an effective, persuasive selling tool is a good index. Many companies think they are producing an effective catalog when they are, in fact, producing a pain in the neck for a busy purchasing agent by making it almost impossible to find anything without going through all the pages.

This holds especially true for companies that persist in hanging on a nonword name onto every product they produce. Products should be indexed by their generic names, then if pressure from the technical people forces you into it, you can get in the meaningless names to make them happy. But by all means make it easy for a person to find what he's looking for without wading through what is, to them, a bunch of gobbledygook.

Dividers, tabs, colors, even a simple printed index in the front listing the contents of the catalog, can all enable the user to locate what he's interested in without trying his temper and wasting his time.

Budgeting for Literature

Approximately 20 percent of the typical industrial advertising budget is earmarked to sales literature and catalogs, although in some companies—depending on method of distribution—the percentage goes much higher. Some companies regularly spend 50 percent or more of their promotional dollars this way.

Merely having attractive, accurate sales literature in the briefcase gives the sales rep an important psychological boost. It makes him or her master of any situation encountered, that the "factory" is backing up all the way, and that he or she can cope with any questions a prospective buyer might throw. This one benefit alone may well be worth the total investment made in literature.

Buoying up the sales force's morale is using literature properly, and it is making effective use of the dollars allocated to produce it.

What is *not* using this portion of the budget to best advantage is the practice of producing a new piece of literature at the behest of one individual, or a group of people who want it merely to have—not because an objective is to be met.

When you're working on your annual budget you will, of course, query all of the product managers or market managers, the sales manager, vice-president of marketing, and any others in the company who initiate requests for literature. This will give you a good ball-park figure on how many individual pieces you will have to provide for in the budget. And if you discuss each piece with the individual, you can probably make a pretty close estimate of the cost involved.

It is routine for most ad managers to operate this way, of course. What most *do not* do, however, is to ask their people—in production or sales or marketing—for formal, written objectives for each piece of literature so that they can put it in its proper perspective as far as assigning dollars and cents is concerned.

There's no need to make a big production out of establishing the objective for the literature. A sentence or a short paragraph will do, just so long as it's logical and it represents an objective the literature can achieve.

Ask these questions:

1. What is the objective for this proposed new piece of literature? Just what do we expect from it?
2. What will it contribute to our total marketing program? Can a price tag be put on the contribution the literature or catalog will make?
3. Is the literature or catalog really necessary? Is there an alternative way of accomplishing the same objective, perhaps more effectively and more economically?

Based on past experience, an advertising manager can usually come quite close to the actual cost if he or she is told the company will require 47 pieces of new sales literature during the coming fiscal year, although he or she will require guidance from product or marketing people on whether each is to be a major effort, or if it is to fit into a pre-established format.

Inside or Outside?

Sooner or later the question arises: Should our sales literature be produced in the advertising department, or should it be done by outside specialists such as our advertising agency?

Before the question can be answered it's necessary to evaluate two factors as objectively as possible.

First of these is: Are you really equipped to handle the entire job inside?

Chances are you're exactly like most industrial ad managers. Ad managers are a capable breed. They are able administrators and they have more than a slight touch of genius when it comes to handling the company's money, for they are dollar-stretchers *par excellence*.

Furthermore, almost every ad manager, due to training and inclination, is a skillful editor who can pare and prune away the innocuous and the irrelevant to get to the heart of the company's story in all written matter, be it a space advertisement or a piece of sales literature.

Indisputable, though is the fact that most advertising managers are not top writers. Nor do they really consider themselves writers despite their being the best word-mechanics in their companies. There is a vast difference in the *degree* of craftsmanship of any writing just as there is in the construction of any industrial product. The advertising manager has the perception and the training and the judgment to recognize this, although few others in the company do.

Besides the question of writing skill, there's a second factor—consideration of whether the average advertising manager *has the time* to spend writing literature. Most two-page, two-color pieces of sales literature require at least two days to write, considering the incessant telephone calls and other interruptions. This is after all reference material is on hand, of course.

Usually there's enough work to do on literature without writing it internally. For instance, there's directing the photographer, specifying type, buying type, making or buying layout, proofreading galleys, reading keylines and approving them, reviewing and approving retouching, reading and approving silverprints—all in addition to getting bids from three printers, plus other odds and ends.

Unless you can find an agency or studio that is in business for its health, having your literature produced by an outside source will always cost more—much more.

For example, if you write, lay out, and produce a reasonably simple two-color, two-page (front and back) piece of sales literature, you'll spend about $500 for the complete job—excluding original photography. Also, if any line or schematic drawings are included, these would have to be produced in your engineering department in order to get it under this price. The $500 does, however, include everything except writing and original photography and art; it includes layout, type, etch proofs, keyline, silverprint, and printing a quantity of 3,000 pieces.

Original photography of your widget on which you're producing literature can run from $25 to $10,000—although you'll probably lay out approximately $50 to $75 for it unless there's an unusual amount of setup time or travel involved. Include this and your sales literature ends up costing around $575.

However, if you had the same job done by your agency or by a studio, you could logically expect to be invoiced anywhere from 40 percent to 75 percent more, depending upon the markup the agency or studio customarily charges, how busy they happened to be at the moment, and whether they really wanted the business or not.

Some agencies and studios discourage small jobs such as this, unless there's a steady flow of them, to concentrate almost exclusively on higher-markup collateral material—four-color literature and catalogs, prestige booklets, films, and so on. Average price you can expect to pay for the two-page job in a metropolitan area is at least $500 to $600, and more if the agency supervises or supplies photography or art.

Final consideration when deciding whether to produce inside or go outside is that if you do the actual writing, or if your sales promotion manager or someone else within the department does, you're going to be locked into one man's viewpoint and one man's outlook on life.

What may well be the absolute living end in written persuasiveness and great style may easily be dated and dull tomorrow. And even if this doesn't happen, there is ample reason to question seriously the wisdom of having the stamp of one individual's personality on the company's sales literature year after year.

When an agency or studio creates some of your literature, you avoid this risk. Granted, one individual will write it, but that person is backstopped by other equally competent craftsmen in the agency.

Upshot of this is that the typical company gets, in most instances, a superior end product if it contracts out the writing, layout, and production of sales literature.

Striking a happy medium isn't difficult. You can stretch dollars by doing the simpler jobs internally, and retaining outside experts for those projects that are more demanding. This enables you to function as you should, as a manager; to use your abilities to make and save money for the company.

Copy for Sales Literature

Of primary importance is that copy written for sales literature be informative. When your prospect sits back with his feet on his desk to concentrate on a piece of your literature about your widget, the copy had better come through.

If it's been written with the prospect in mind, if it anticipates the questions he has in mind about your widget, if it gives him specifies on which he can base a buying decision, the literature has accomplished its purpose.

But if the literature fails on any of these scores the money you spent on it has been wasted and you've lost a prospect.

The copy in typical literature from the average company is poor. Much of it commits four cardinal sins:

1. Repeating the company name ad nauseam.
2. Bragging and boasting.
3. Boring hell out of the reader.
4. Not selling the product.

Of course, you've seen far too many examples of the first sin, literature wherein the company's name seemed to appear at least once in every sentence.

Repeating a firm name does *not* strengthen the firm in the reader's mind. It merely slows down his or her reading and dilutes the effectiveness of the copy.

And if you have to resort to brag and boast to describe your product there's one thing you'd better do even before you finish reading this page—look for a job with a company that manufactures better products.

Mull this one over for a minute, for instance. It's the actual lead-in paragraph in a three-color, 22-page booklet into which much money and time was poured. The company name has been changed, but the copy is verbatim otherwise.

Smith's Die Springs represent quality in design, in material, and in manufacturing. Quality controls are strict to assure you of an exceptional Die Spring—unmatched performance.

Now change the name "Smith" to any other company name, and

change the product from Die Springs to Widgets (even capitalized) or turret lathes or bulldozers, and there isn't a company in these United States that can't say the same thing about its products. Too many companies do just that.

And this lead-in on page 2 of an orange-and-black 8-page booklet really waves the company flag for all to salute:

> *Smith-Jones widgets are the end result of continuing research, skilled engineering, and precision manufacturing. This combination, unique with Smith-Jones, invariably produces widgets that instantly become the standard by which all others are judged. Smith-Jones widgets are acclaimed throughout the world as the finest it is possible to produce. Here at Smith-Jones we take great pride in the knowledge that Smith-Jones builds the best and has for more than 40 years. And we look resolutely to the future, determined to continue Smith-Jones' great traditions.*

Retain your lunch, anybody?

Copy *must* interest. Copy must make the product seem desirable by pointing out in a vivid, vital way the benefits the user derives from it. Copy must enable the reader to project himself and his company into the "you" that's in, or should be in, the sales literature copy.

Establish a rule of thumb in your advertising department that nobody ever, under any circumstances, starts writing copy with the words "New Horizons."

Twenty years or so ago, "New Horizons" and "New Directions" and similar vague generalities were the *in* thing. One company outdid all rivals and produced what it fondly hoped would be a prestige 48-page booklet titled: *New Directions and New Horizons.* It is cherished and preserved in the author's files. A carefully worded letter to the company requesting permission to reproduce the cover of that amazing booklet elicited an obviously suspicious response that can be summed up in one word: Why?

Organizing the Material

Half your battle is won if you can assist your product and engineering people in organizing their source material, so it's in the same sequence as information will be presented in the completed sales literature.

Following is a product literature source material outline suggested by James J. Hubbard, formerly an account executive at Marsteller Inc. The outline is logical and workable.

PRODUCT LITERATURE SOURCE OUTLINE

I. GENERIC NAME OF PRODUCT (widget, gadget, and so on).

II. PRODUCT BENEFITS (most important sales points, in order of importance—why the prospects should buy the product).

III. PRODUCT FEATURES (significant design points).

IV. APPLICATIONS (types of jobs and in what industries the product can be used, and why product is good for these applications).

V. PRODUCT DESCRIPTION (nuts-and-bolts description).

VI. DIMENSIONS AND SPECIFICATIONS (including drawings, tables, etc.).

Jim Hubbard then went on to suggest to the client the following sequence of material in the company's sales literature.

I. PRODUCT GENERIC NAME (avoid coined names, nonwords and similar inanities).

II. BENEFIT SUBHEAD (a short headline that tells what the widget will do for the buyer).

III. INTRODUCTION (capsule pitch on how this product can help the prospect, and why the product is good).

IV. APPLICATIONS (be specific, be factual, but be promotional; tell how well the product does the job, why it's better than competitive ones, stress advantages and savings).

V. FEATURES (here, again, be factual but promotional; stress uniqueness of features that actually are unique, emphasize exclusive features the product has).

VI. PRODUCT DESCRIPTION (describe product factually, but inject benefits into description—such as, "Stainless steel case prevents formation of algae which could contaminate the transmitter").

VII. DIMENSIONS AND SPECIFICATIONS (strictly nuts and bolts)?

VIII. BID FOR ACTION (if your literature is to sell, it must do what every good salesman does—ask for the order. The bid for action might be to ask a sales rep to call, phone the nearest district office, fill in and return a tipped-in reply card, ask for a free sample, write for more information and so on; it should be the last element in the literature except for the signature and address).

Make your sales literature copy pithy, punchy, and, above all, promotional. There's no getting around one thing: If literature sells, it's working for you. If it doesn't, it isn't.

Fitting Copy

When writing copy for sales literature, or for any other printed piece, for that matter, never write to fit a layout. Instead, make the layout after the copy is written. What this means, of course, is that copy length is not determined so it will be pleasing to some artist, but by what needs to be said to tell your product story.

Once copy is written, edited, and finish-typed, the layout artist then measures it, or makes a close estimate of how much space it will require after he has specced the type. He needs certain basic information to enable him to accomplish this, however, such as that given in Table

I and Table II on page 981.

Generally a writer starts by making a thumbnail layout, then proceeds to doodle a full-size rough.

Once satisfied with the rough layout, it's a simple matter to compute the amount of type you've selected required to fill each line. Then set your typewriter accordingly.

For instance, if a space 13 picas wide is to be filled with 10-point body type, cast on a 12-point linotype slug (2-point leaded), the table shows there are 2.5 ten-point characters to each pica of column width. Thus there will be 32.5 characters to the line.

Set the typewriter to start at 0 and to stop at 32 on the scale. Or, if you don't want to endure the aggravation of having to punch the margin release every time the carriage comes to the 32 and there are a couple of additional characters to go (which, of course, even out those lines that are a couple of characters short), you can draw a light pencil line down the right-hand margin. Or you can do as many copywriters do, hold down firmly on the period key and give the carriage a few quick turns, rolling the paper farther onto the roller. This leaves a faint vertical line on the paper to show where the margin should be.

Determine the number of lines required to fill the space by measuring the vertical space with a line gauge. Most printers and typographers have a supply of 18-inch rulers especially made for measuring type; they are used as handout pieces to customers and prospects. Your printing or type salesperson will give you one if asked.

This copy-fitting system will do for the average job. For more precise work, many tricky type-fitting systems have been developed. Some call for slide rules, others for IBM computers, and still others for an unbelievable expertise. This author likes the method developed by the International Typographic Composition Association, 2262 Hall Place, N.W., Washington, D.C. 20007.

Based on the most exhaustive study ever made of the frequency of use of the letters of the alphabet, the ITCA Copy-Fitting System is a landmark of progress in graphic arts technique. The results of this research, combined with an analysis of modern-day word spacing concepts, formed the basis of a computer program that delivered extremely accurate character-count information for the more than 15,000 sizes of type.

In sizes ranging from 4-point upward, every type face, old and new, used in the graphic arts was analyzed. This information has been organized into the simplest copy-fitting procedure ever devised. Using it enables the type user to perform any copy-fitting task easily and accurately. Every effort was made to supply a quick, precise solution to the stickiest problems.

TABLE I

Characters Per Pica

Type Size	Average Characters Per Pica
4 point	5
5 point	4
6 point	3.5
8 point	3
10 point	2.5
12 point	2
14 point	1.5
18 point	1

TABLE II

Average characters per one square pica with corresponding average type face required to fill space

Size of Average Type Face Required to Fill	Characters Per One Square Pica
4 point solid	15
4 point on 5 point	12

TABLE II *(Cont.)*

Size of Average Type Face Required to Fill	Characters Per One Square Pica
5 point solid	9.6
5 point on 6 point	8
6 point solid	7
6 point on 7 point	6
6 point on 8 point	5.3
8 point solid	4.5
8 point on 9 point	4
8 point on 10 point	3.6
10 point solid	3
10 point on 11 point	2.7
10 point on 12 point	2.5
12 point solid	2
12 point on 13 point	1.8
12 point on 14 point	1.7
14 point solid	1.4
14 point on 15 point	1.3
14 point on 16 point	1.2

Key to copy-fitting is based on what has come to be called The Gauge—with upper-case letters as a mark of respect and fond affection. This unbreakable gauge of sturdy vinyl has calibrated on it the ITCA numbers and their character counts per pica for all measures up to 42 picas. Also on The Gauge are typewriter-character counters for both elite and standard typewriters. You can get The Gauge from ITCA, or from a local typographer.

Approvals

Essentially the same logic prevails and the same techniques should be used in securing approvals of copy for sales literature as for space advertisements.

Certain additional problems crop up in copy written for sales literature, however. These problems occur merely because there is so much *more* copy in sales literature than there is in a space ad. So there's much more opportunity to put one's foot in the company's mouth. Lawsuits are viewed dimly indeed by most companies, as are advertising managers whose sales literature results in such suits being filed.

For that reason alone approval procedure is important, as we'll see. Cut first, though, let's consider briefly a few rather broad suggestions about the legality of the copy in your literature. These must necessarily be broad because of the tremendous differences in products and their applications; there's wide variance in considerations between copy written to promote sales of bulldozers and for caustic chemicals sold to industry.

About the only way to determine what legal pitfalls exist in your industry is to be guided by past experience, common and accepted practices, rules and regulations and restrictions established by your industry organization—and clearing any questions through channels with your company attorney. Many firms make it standard practice to clear all copy with an attorney before printing literature. They've either been burned before and are now gun-shy on the subject, or are overly cautious.

As in writing any advertising copy, avoid such words as *never, foolproof, fail-safe, can't fail, can't, won't, impossible, certain, positive, always, invariably, inevitably, and will* (consider "may" or "designed to").

There are many other similar words whose use can be inferred as putting the company in a position of making a flat statement, a guarantee, or failing to draw the user's attention to an inherent danger.

Better be safe than sorry about such terms. Perhaps they've been used for years by your company before you joined it. If so, chances are they've achieved acceptance in your industry and nothing untoward will occur from continuing to use them. Smart thing to do, though, is to draw this to management's attention in a memo; inquire about the desirability of requesting legal advice on these and similar terms.

Before submitting copy to those who must give it their blessing, make certain your own house is in order.

This includes, of course, having properly signed, witnessed releases from all identifiable people in the photographs you're using, having reproduction rights to such photographs and/or art, and that all company trademarks, slogans, and symbols are used properly. You'll find it is incumbent upon a company to use such identifying marks in interstate commerce in order to guarantee its exclusive right to the mark, slogan, or symbol.

Don't make the mistake of registering a trademark, using it a time or two and then retiring it only to bring it back into use months or years later and expecting it to be protected. Such marks must be used regularly to remain the exclusive property of the company. Have such trademarks, slogans, and symbols appear in sales literature which has an identifying printing date appearing somewhere in it; this constitutes use, although it is advisable also to use such marks in print advertisements from time to time.

When you discuss guarantees in your sales literature, and many companies do, spell out exactly what is guaranteed—the entire widget, certain component parts of it, the length of time for which it is guaranteed, what "lifetime" means if you use the term, details about who pays shipping expense and/or expense to get an expert into the customer's plant to perform examinations, diagnosis, and repairs; what percentage is charged back to the customer, if any. Also state whether the guarantor (usually the manufacturer, but occasionally a distributor or dealer) is obligated to repair or replace.

Failure to spell out details fully and specifically could easily open the door to a Federal Trade Commission ruling that your company is engaging in unfair and deceptive practices. Moreover, it is not unknown for a company that did not spell out its guarantee to have been ruled to offer an *unconditional* guarantee—and few, mighty few, companies want to go that far.

Almost every warranty or guarantee has some limiting clauses and some conditions of use or maintenance or *something* that prevents manufacturers from being deluged with claims. Be wary about using lightly such terms as "money-back guarantee" or "satisfaction guaranteed" or "performance guaranteed." Such terminology should *always* be cleared with your legal department.

Repeat: *Such terminology should always be cleared with your legal counsel.*

If the price of your product is mentioned, make absolutely certain it is correct and that your company is prepared to sell the product at that price. You can, of course, state that a given price is in effect for a specified period of time only. But if the product is not offered at the advertised price (in advertisements or in promotional literature), you are wide open for a bait-advertising or deceptive practices charge.

Not only must the price quoted for your product be an actual price at which the product can be purchased, but comparisons of your price with prices of competitive products must be accurate and must be stated correctly. If this is not the case it could be assumed there was an intent to deceive the prospective buyer.

To protect your department, get dated signatures of all persons who approve what you've done. A special form can be mimeographed for the purpose. This protects you if there's a major change in thinking after the money is spent and the piece is printed, and it protects you from those who shirk responsibility. A typical copy-approval form is shown nearby.

Never offer to let product or market or technical people review galleys, etch proofs, keylines or silverprints. Inform your people that if, once they've approved the basic material, typos creep in, material is left out, lines are reversed, captions go on wrong photos, and so forth, it's strictly your baby. It's up to you to prevent these gremlins from sabotaging your literature, although the advertising manager doesn't live who hasn't had at least a few typographical errors in his time.

APPROVAL

Please review carefully the attached copy and other material to be used in printed matter No. ....

When you are satisfied that it is technically correct, sign your name and fill in the date in the blank by your title or job function.

Then phone me and I will pick up the material from you.

DATE   NAME

_____   _____ Application or market manager who requested this literature

_____   _____ Product manager

_____   _____ Market manager

_____   _____ Research manager

_____   _____ Engineering manager

_____   _____ Sales manager

_____   _____ V.P. marketing

R.H. Stansfield
Director of Advertising
and Sales Promotion

Proofreading

Because it is the ultimate responsibility of the advertising manager to eliminate all errors before literature is printed, proofreading is critically important. This refers to reading of galleys, type proofs, that is, for both context and for correctness. Best way to proofread is the team method, using a proofreader and a copyholder. If you do this with your secretary or your assistant, you read aloud the copy that has been set in type while the copyholder checks what you are reading, using the original typed copy as reference. Don't leave anything to chance or to interpretation.

When you read the type galleys aloud, read every word and every punctuation mark. With the copyholder-secretary (whom we'll call

Kay) checking the correctness of what you read, you might say, for instance:

> *All upper-case letters for this subhead, Kay. AISI TYPE NUMBERS. Cap T The same stainless type can be made by a number of steel producers, period. Cap I In order to establish standards for comparison and specification comma, the American iron cap A and cap I, Kay, Steel Institute cap S cap I has assigned numbers to the recognized standard types or analyses period. These cap T AISI all upper-case letters, Kay, types are sometimes given trade names by individual producers such as Republic cap R, Kay, "Enduro." Quotes cap E E-n-d-u-r-o period close quotes.*

That paragraph from one of Republic Steel Corporation's attractive booklets shows how proof is read. All numbers, fractions, and other tabular data are spoken out in full, just as they should appear in the printed piece, so they can be verified from the typed copy—which has, of course, itself been read and approved and certified as correct by your technical people.

Typographical errors made by the typographer or type house are reset at no charge, although according to trade custom *no financial responsibility other than this is accepted by typographers. Trade custom also dictates that the customer is responsible for reading all type proofs, or galleys, as well as all corrections that are made. Detecting errors is the responsibility of the customer, and this includes copy which has been accidentally omitted by the typesetter.*

Be especially alert for strictly mechanical errors: Misspellings, transposed letters, wrong fonts (wrong type face, although the letter or figure itself may be correct), bad letter spacing or bad word spacing or improper paragraph spacing. As noted above, these will be reset correctly by the typographer at no charge.

Look, too, for *widows* (type lines consisting of only *part* of a word); they should be fixed by adding a word or two of copy, although the copy doesn't have to be important. It can be merely a conjunction, or substitution of a longer word for a very short one— anything to add a few characters, or to delete a few to get that partial word into the line above.

Also be alert for several consecutive broken words at the end of lines; they detract greatly from the visual appearance of literature and are considered to be in very bad taste. Lines of type that are excessively loose due to improper word-spacing, or inability to break a word properly, should be corrected by minor rewriting.

Lines of type that are too tight—that have insufficient word -spacing—create an uncomfortable feeling in the reader and result in poor legibility. Let in some air by minor rewriting or deletion of an unimportant word or two—such as knocking out an "and" and substituting either a comma or a semicolon.

By themselves these are minor things, to be sure, but added together they are important because they contribute to an attractive, tasteful, professional piece of printed literature that you can be proud of—and that will reflect credit on both you and your company.

Something you'll have to watch with an eagle eye are omissions. Entire sentences or paragraphs are overlooked with remarkable ease by all concerned. For this reason the copyholder's function is critically important.

Another thing that must be checked carefully because it can't be anticipated in typed copy is how words are broken (divided) at the end of the line. Ligatures (characters consisting of two or more characters that are united) constitute another pitfall that should be avoided. For greater legibility and better letter-spacing where thin characters such as "i's" and "l's" and "f's" are concerned, typographic usage dictates that certain combinations should be run together in a single type character rather than be set individually. Thus, such combinations as "fi," "fl," "ffi," "ffl" and so on form single condensed characters, and the proofreader has to be careful that they don't appear as widely spaced individual characters.

Professional proofreaders' marks should be used in correcting type proofs; these marks constitute a language that is understood and used by all advertising people, typographers, and printers in the country. Short and succinct, these marks are a form of graphic arts shorthand used to convey specific instructions.

Layout

Most of what should be said about layout for sales literature has already been said about layout for space advertisements in Chapter 11.

What cannot be overemphasized is an old homily: There is no substitute for taste.

With a combination of a lack of good taste and a lack of a professional hand at the helm when sales literature is being created, visual horrors are produced. They result in a negative impression of the company and its products.

Perhaps the best way to illustrate this, and to point out things to do

THE LANGUAGE OF PROOFREADING

MARK	EXPLANATION	EXAMPLE	MARK	EXPLANATION	EXAMPLE
ℓ	Take out character indicated	ℓ The proof.	¶	Start paragraph.	¶ read [The
∧	Left out, insert.	∧ Te proof.	no ¶	No paragraph; run in.	no ¶ marked. The proof.
#	Insert space.	# Theproof.	⌐	Raise.	⌐ The proof.
9	Turn inverted letter.	9 The pﬂoof.	⌐	Lower.	⌐ The proof.
X	Broken letter.	X ƒhe proof.	⊏	Move left.	⊏ The proof.
⊥	Push down space.	⊥ The proof.	⊐	Move right.	⊐ The proof.
eq#	Even space.	eq# A good proof.	∥	Align type.	∥ Three men. Two women.
⌣	Less space.	⌣ The proof.	=	Straighten line.	= The proof.
⌒	Close up; no space.	⌒ The proof.	⊙	Insert period.	⊙ The proof.
tr.	Transpose.	tr A proof good.	,/	Insert comma.	,/ The proof.
wf	Wrong font.	wf The proof.	:/	Insert colon.	:/ The proof.
lc	Lower case.	lc The Proof.	;/	Insert semicolon.	;/ The proof.
sc	Small capitals.	sc The proof.	∨	Insert apostrophe.	∨ The boys proof.
c+sc	Capitals and small capitals.	c+sc The proof.	∨ ∨	Insert quotation marks.	∨ ∨ Marked it proof.
caps	Capitals.	caps The proof.	=/	Insert hyphen.	=/ A proofmark.
P	Capitalize.	P The proof.	⋀	Insert inferior figure.	⋀ Water, H$_2$O
ital	Italic.	ital The proof.	∨	Insert superior figure.	∨ A^2 + B^2 = C
rom	Roman.	rom The proof.	/	Insert exclamation mark.	/ Prove it
bf	Bold face.	bf The proof.	?	Insert question mark.	? Is it good
stet	Let it stand.	stet The proof.	(?)	Query for author.	(?) was The proof read by
out sc	Out, see copy.	out sc He proof.	c/⊃	Insert brackets.	c/⊃ The Jones boy ...
spell out	Spell out.	spell out King Geo.	(/)	Insert parentheses.	(/) 1
			⊢⊣	Insert 1-en dash.	⊢⊣ The proof
			⊥	Insert 1-em dash.	⊥ The proof
			⊥	Insert 2-em dash.	⊥ The proof
			□	Indent 1 em.	□ The proof.
			□□	Indent 2 ems.	□□ The proof.
			□□□	Indent 3 ems.	□□□ The proof.

and things to avoid, is to look at Horrible Example Number One. This is Lindberg Hevi-Duty's "Bulletin" on that company's semiconductor diffusion furnaces. Let's dissect it element by element and see just why it is so inept and just why it produces a poor impression of the company.

To start with, simplicity is next to godliness in layout for sales literature just as it is in layout for an advertisement. Poor layout can cripple sales literature just as fast it can destroy an ad. Here again, the fewer the elements, the cleaner and simpler and more modern the layout is—and the more effective it is, too.

Reducing the number of elements per page to an absolute minimum, consistent with presenting all necessary information, always results in literature that's inviting to the eye and easy to read. Failure to limit the number of elements results in distracting clutter. It is impossible to generalize on just how many elements should be on one page, but somewhere between two and five are ideal. More than this is self-defeating.

Lindberg Hevi-Duty's bulletin has the following elements on the first page:

1. Name of company in display type.
2. Coined name of product in display type.
3. Unexplained symbol (not a logo or trademark) in the upper right-hand corner.
4. Model numbers of products, also in display type.
5. Generic name of products, also in display type.
6. Halftone of product, complete with a cute little black border around it (somebody was in mourning?).
7. Caption describing this product.
8. Halftone of the other product covered by this piece of literature.
9. Caption describing this other product.
10. A block of copy reversed out of solid blue.
11. Lindberg Hevi-Duty logo.
12. Attached box with initials and symbols in it.
13. Slogan.
14. Bulletin number.
15. Distracting little white line around the entire page.

In addition to being a nightmare of a layout, a jumble of clutter and clatter and a succession of distracting elements, this literature is virtually impossible to read. For some reason impossible to fathom, the layout artist felt constrained to use a light sans serif type face that's not the easiest to read under favorable circumstances. When it's overprinted in black on a solid blue, as it is in the captions here, it is practically illegible unless a major effort is made.

These captions undoubtedly went unread by all except a hardy few. Professional advertising people know the one thing above all others that must be done is to make literature easy to read.

The body copy, set in two paragraphs, is another nightmare. It, too, is in a light sans serif face *and is a full 42 picas wide—seven inches*. There's practically no leading, and the wider the measure the more leading needed for legibility. Reversed out of a solid blue as it is, this type seems to "swim" or "float," and it is only with extreme difficulty that it can be read.

You can guess how hard this sales literature sold.

Shown on page 989 (upper right) is Lindberg Hevi-Duty's newest two-color sales literature. The only color is in the two bars; different colors are used for the company's various product lines that are sold into specific markets. Color coding simplified collation, use and distribution of sales literature to the field sales force, and helped speed it to inquirers.

Note the clean appearance of this sales literature. There's eye-

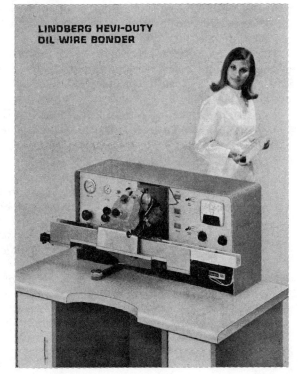

Evolution of a bulletin series. Above, left, an example of the earliest, heavy with clutter and reversed, hard-to-read type. Above, right, an intermediate stage, with better layout. Color is confined to two simple bars. At right, a yet newer bulletin. It marks the final steps toward the impact of simplicity.

appealing white space. The company's logotype is shown prominently. Generic name of the product is in display type, not some nonsense word that means nothing to the prospect. This instantly identifies the literature for both company personnel and for prospects. No longer do they have to wonder what a "Diffusitron" is, or what various "Mark I's," "Mark II's," or "Mark III's" are.

Furthermore, there is no reverse type to strain the eyes and discourage reading of the message.

Lindberg Hevi-Duty literature continued to be refined and improved, as is apparent from the next example.

Simplicity is the keynote of this strikingly attractive cover. Only two elements are present—the company name and product name appear in olive green in the upper left corner, and the photograph of the product, with its pretty "operator" softly out of focus, is the second. The photographic illustration bleeds from both sides, top and bottom. It is, incidentally, superb photography; creator was Spence Zog, ace photographer at Pohlman Studios, Milwaukee, Wis.

The layout (not shown), is airy and open. Tasteful white space, repetition of the olive-green bars that color-code this product line, and the outlined halftone illustrations of the product make the recipient of this piece of sales literature *want* to read what it has to say.

The copy is quoted here because it is a good example of what copy in sales literature should be—promotional and selling, yet factual and informative. It is the antithesis of the rambling copy the company had become accustomed to in its previous literature.

Lindberg Hevi-Duty Model 2212 DIL Wire Bonder

Here's a wire bonder for DIL strips . . . for high production, absolute control, and minimum handling. Companion die bonder available.

Just about everything's automatic that can be automatic on this wire bonding system. You get high production with mechanical indexing and automatic wire feed. Saves time for the operator, of course. The needle is mounted in a low mass, frictionless bearing spindle so you get shockless bonding with no damaged parts. And there's no need to handle parts during processing; the in-line carrier and belt system takes care of storage. Making a setup, or making a changeover for different devices, is easy. Clean, functional design was developed with people in mind—for greater operator convenience, reduced operator fatigue. Easy access simplifies service.

Features

Thermocompression bonding. Fast cycle time for high yield.

In-line carrier and belt system for DIL strips and various flat pack configurations; special belts are available for TO series headers. Protective atmosphere. Multi-level belts. Mechanical indexing, automatic wire feed. Adjustable bonding force. Special tunnel to deliver DIL strips to the bonding station at precisely the right temperature. Pulsed flame cut-off. Optional tailpuller. Superior optical system—Bausch & Lomb stereo zoom. The bonder handles a wide range of wire sizes. It is easy to operate. Reduced operator fatigue.

How the Bonder Operates

Model 2212 console wire bonder has an in-line carrier and belt sytem for DIL strips and flat packs. It delivers parts to the work station through a heat tunnel which has a closely controlled heat profile. Parts arrive at precisely the right temperature. An inert gas atmosphere is preheated and delivered to the work station to protect parts during heat-up, bonding, and cooling.

Bonding is by thermocompression. When the bond is completed the belt is mechanically indexed. The carrier indexes vertically after each of the four belts of DIL strips is prcessed.

When the DIL strip is at the work station the operator uses a micro-manipulator to orient it to put the bonding point beneath the capillary. Then the operating lever is depressed to bring the wire into contact with the bonding area. Only very brief contact is required for a firm bond. Bonding force is adjusted with a precision vacuum gauge on the control panel.

A pulsed hydrogen flame severs the wire when the operator signals, producing a uniform ball for the next bond. A taipuller is available as an option to remove the ball from the last bond immediately after the flame cut-off.

At no time does the operator have to take her eyes from the microscope during the assembly operation.

Wire is fed automatically to the capillary when the operator signals. Wire tension is variable and vacuum controlled. The bonder handles wire from .0007 to .003 in size.

Wrap-up of the product story is given neatly and quickly in a form that's highly readable for a busy man who wants to absorb information without fuss or folderol, without forbidding him to read by setting type 42 picas wide, then reversing it.

Credibility is lent to the whole story by having the model pose just as an ordinary operator would. And the company's logotype appears

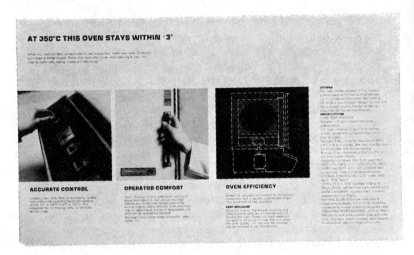

here, near the signature and the customary reminder that the company manufactures many other products in addition to the DIL bonder discussed. Even with all of the nuts and bolts information, the photo, the logo, the color-coding bars, and the signature, there is still plenty of clean white space to make the literature inviting to the eye.

Final example of good layout, and an example of the evolution of Lindberg Hevi-Duty's literature, is seen in a brochure promoting the company's semiconductor oven.

No nonsense words are thrown at the reader to cause him to wonder just what it is the company is trying to say. This brochure pulls no punches. It comes right out, straight from the shoulder, and tells the reader he is going to get helpful and interesting information about a semiconductor oven manufactured by Lindberg Hevi-Duty.

The spread is exceptionally appealing and attractive. Clean and simple and uncluttered, the major use benefit is given in the headline. In the copy block immediately below, set ragged-right, are additional user benefits spelled out in rapid-fire order.

The two photographic illustrations are duotones, a combination of blue and black. Options available to the buyer and the specifications of the standard semiconductor oven are given, neatly listed and logically arranged.

Page 4 is simple and functional and presents necessary performance information quickly and strikingly with two graphs showing recovery rate and heatup rate. Along with the logo and a kissoff, this winds up the company's message about this product.

Use a "Safe" Size?

First thing that pops to mind when planning a piece of literature for an industrial product is to make it that good old standard, accepted, approved, familiar, traditional, customary, usual "safe" size—8½ by 11 inches.

To be sure, three-ring binders, large envelopes in stock, sales reps' sample kits, literature jackets, proposal folders, presentation binders, and other items meant to contain or use literature are designed around this hoary old size. The size has been used for everything from the paper this manuscript is being typed on to the bond paper your outgoing letters are on. And so is most industrial literature in racks and on shelves throughout the country.

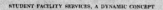

There's no law, though, that says that everything has to be this size. To deviate is not a felony, and it's not even an unwise course of action if deviation is done for a good reason. A good example of an unusually attractive piece of two-color sales literature took exactly the opposite tack: It is an 11 by 8½ inches (width always given first when discussing size of printed matter) booklet. *The Fine Art of Campus Food Service Management—A Vital Force in Modern Education* was produced by Szabo Food Service, Inc., a leader in the mass-feeding market.

Type, most halftones and all solid areas are in a rich, chocolate brown; the second color, used in the logo, the decorative border and in occasional duotone illustrations inside the booklet, is an attractive, warm orange-red. The combination of the two colors has a connotation of friendship and hospitality and happy things in life.

Throughout, in pictures and words, the high quality and personalized service of Szabo's product, which is actually management service, not food, comes through strongly. Shown and described is the custom campus food service Szabo offers to colleges and universities, including candid shots of happy, smiling students who are obviously well fed. The booklet was produced when students went to school to study, rather than to riot. Photographs, incidentally, are by Bill Pease, president and *numero uno* photographer of Images West, Riverside, Illinois. They are excellent in every respect.

In addition to describing the high-caliber management service it offers, Szabo touched on the financial arrangements with institutions of higher learning. It is common practice for colleges and universities to show a profit on student feeding—a profit rebated by the food service holding the feeding contract. Szabo summed up its services on page 7, then listed directors and officers of the company, its transfer agent and its registrar; this quickly tells those who were not familiar with the company that it is large, stable, and reputable.

A fine source for excellent ideas in collateral material, including layout and illustrative techniques, is the better paper manufacturer. Good paper mills make regular mailings to customers and prospects just as all aggressive businesses do, and some of the printed matter they mail is of superb quality. Among the better paper houses are:

S.D. Warren Company	Crown Zellerbach Corporation
225 Franklin Street.	One Bush Street
Boston, Massachusetts 02101	San Francisco, California 94104
International Paper Company	Kimberly-Clark Corporation
77 West 45th Street	North Lake Street
New York, New York 10036	Neenah, Wisconsin 54956
Hammermill Paper Company	Mead Corporation
P.O. Box 1440	Courthouse Plaza, N.E.
Erie, Pennsylvania 16533	Dayton, Ohio 45463
Westvaco Corporation	Nekoosa Papers, Inc.
299 Park Avenue	100 Wisconsin River Drive
New York, New York 10017	Port Edwards, Wisconsin 54469

House Organs

So-called house organs fall into one of three distinct categories:

1. An employee publication for internal distribution.
2. A sales publication produced for a company's sales force.

3. A customer publication, usually called an external house organ.

Again, the author acknowledges with gratitude the help of S.D. Warren Company, paper manufacturer, in permitting use of its excellent booklet, *The Company Publication*, as a good reference work for this portion of this chapter, as well as for quoting certain passages from it. This booklet of Warren's comes very close to being an indispensable tool for an advertising manager tapped to create a company publication, or house organ as we'll call it henceforth.

According to Warren, many businesses have found that company publications can provide the means of communication necessary to establish mutual understanding between management and employees, between home offices and salesmen, between manufacturers and dealers, and between a business and its customers.

Many companies issue two publications—an internal house organ edited for persons within the organization, the other an external edited for people outside the company.

Internal house organs are designed expressly for plant and/or office people, of course; such publications are usually called "employee" publications. Ofttimes such publications are simple and unpretentious and are reproduced on a one-color printed masthead by either multilith or mimeograph. When this is the case, the personnel department usually does the writing or, at least, the information gathering. The advertising manager is much better off not to have a hand in such a publication. Advertising managers tend to be perfectionists, so devote far more time to such publications than they warrant.

The external house organ is directed toward the wholesaler, dealer, or jobber organization, including their sales reps, as well as to retailers and store people. This publication is usually slick, well illustrated, and generally either two-color or four-color, although it can take the form of a tabloid newspaper and be printed in black-and-white.

Still another audience for whom an external house organ is produced is customers. An example of the latter is the *Ford Times*. This is an interesting, well-edited periodical mailed regularly to owners and potential buyers.

Most external house organs fall into a pattern that is slick and professional. Photography is usually much above average and the writing is by full-time editors and reporters.

Internal house organs of many companies have a full-time editor on the staff, usually working under the advertising manager, who devotes most of his time to the publication.

Articles almost always have a company slant, as is to be expected, although most "house magazines" frequently use human-interest articles, travel articles and other mass-appeal material.

One thing to keep constantly in mind when writing and producing an employee publication is that people are interested first and foremost in themselves. Show plenty of pictures of people. People like pictures of themselves. And don't spare the verbal horsepower when describing the accomplishments of both individuals and departments. One of management's objectives in funding any employee publication is to build *esprit de corps*, to increase the feeling of belonging to one big, happy family.

You can turn out a nice looking house organ for employees without investing a fortune—and with a four-color cover, too, by using a *stock* four-color cover. Several firms offer four-color covers already printed, with pages 2, 3, and 4 blank. Your printer can imprint these blank pages in two-color, or in black-and-white. One such source is Monthly Cover Service, 400 N. Michigan Ave., Chicago, Illinois 60611.

Chapter 21

CORPORATE ADVERTISING

C ORPORATE advertising has been around for decades—perhaps as long as product advertising. But it's not discussed very often. It's an unattractive stepchild that's kept hidden most of the time. Nonetheless, corporate advertising takes a very big bite out of the total promotional budget for industry.

Many esoteric articles filled with three-dollar words have been written about the long-predicted demise of product advertising. Seers who write these learned-sounding articles, many of which don't actually *say* anything, are very fast on the draw when it comes to predicting that corporate advertising will ultimately replace product advertising almost entirely. And they say it in the same tone they would use if promising you could rid yourself of athlete's foot or body odor.

The thing for you to do, if you're a devout person, is to pray that this indeed comes to pass; if you're not, next best thing is to cross all fingers and both arms and legs, then mutter an incantation or two, or go through some other personal ritual designed to bring about that which you greatly desire. For, just as surely as you're sitting there reading this, if your competitors all rush to jump on the corporate advertising bandwagon, that will leave only your company advertising its products.

About all you can look forward to then is cornering the market as your sales surge and your competitors' decline.

What Corporate Advertising Sells

Unlike product advertising, which obviously helps sell the product (or service), corporate advertising sells an intangible. It sells an idea, or, perhaps, a series of closely related ideas.

Call the idea "positive attributes" or whatever term you fancy, but corporate advertising is actually selling the advertiser's capabilities, the overall quality of its products, the depth of the company's research and development activities and what they're expected to lead to, the caliber of its personnel, its management, the problem-solving ability of the company's people, its ability to increase sales steadily and to earn a profit while doing so, its dominance of a market, its reliability and stability.

Corporate advertising, like any other advertising, tries to persuade the reader to accept the advertiser's viewpoint. It tries to persuade him or her to share the same favorable opinion of the company.

How much is invested in corporate advertising? That's a question that nobody yet has answered to anybody's satisfaction. But one thing is certain: In business publications edited for the top management "market" and the financial community "market," between 30 and 40 percent of all advertisements of one page or larger in size are *not* product advertisements. Call these by any name you want, but the fact remains they are definitely corporate advertising—advertising that is selling ideas, not products.

Ideas persuasively presented by corporate advertising are critically important because they influence every facet of the company's operations, both at the present time and well into the future. For instance, the "image" of the company in the minds of its many publics can influence the company's ability to function as it must in order to earn a profit. The financial community's opinion of the company determines whether needed financing is available at suitable interest rates and terms, or whether it is available at all in many instances.

The opinion people have of the company determines to a very large extent its ability to attract employees and executives of the caliber necessary for its continued progress. If the company's reputation in its community—and this includes the business community throughout the entire country—is such that it is considered an undesirable company to work for, the company is in deep, deep trouble. It cannot lure top-notch people into its fold. This obviously means the best people will work for competitors.

Furthermore, corporate advertising, while it is not created to sell products, nonetheless exerts great influence on future sales by making the company appear desirable from many viewpoints and making it a positive factor in the minds of its publics. Truly fine corporate advertising by a manufacturer of capital equipment, for example, cannot help but produce a significant effect on future sales by creating a receptive attitude toward both company and products in the minds of executives who will make buying decisions for that product in the years to come.

This is such a tremendously valuable asset that nobody, and no computer, as far as that's concerned, can assigna dollars-and-cents value to it.

Other protective campaigns are undertaken to protect a company or an industry from harassment by government; this is a problem that has become increasingly acute in modern times.

One thing to remember: There's an old saying to the effect that small minds discuss people, good minds discuss events, but great minds discuss *ideas*.

Your corporate advertising is aimed at the best minds in government and industry and finance. It discusses ideas. Make your discussion interesting and you'll plant your ideas in fertile ground—the best minds extant.

Objectives Are Absolutely Essential

Solid objectives that are well thought out and precisely defined are even more essential in corporate advertising than they are in product advertising.

There is no built-in interest in the product itself on which corporate advertising can lean for support. It has to cut the mustard all by itself.

The most common failing of much corporate advertising is that it rambles. It flits hither and yon, it tries hard to touch all bases, it attempts desperately to be all things to all men.

When vague, imprecise, enigmatic corporate advertising fails miserably to present an interesting message, a clear message, a message of importance to a carefully selected universe, you can be morally certain that no firm objectives were set before the ads were produced. Fuzzy thinking right at the start, even before a single word was written, before even a thumbnail layout was doodled out, even before a photograph was taken, doomed the campaign to waste the money invested in it right down to the last red cent.

Formal objectives are the one indispensable ingredient for success in a corporate advertising program.

Repeat: *Formal objectives are the one indispensable ingredient for success in a corporate advertising campaign.*

The objective(s) should be formulated only after very careful consideration. They should mesh neatly with the company's short-term marketing objectives, its profit objectives, its long-range goals. Moreover, objectives should be *attainable*, not some dreamy pie-in-the-sky idealistic wish. Objectives must reflect the company's needs *as determined by top management*. Unlike product advertising, corporate advertising should be based on bed-rock guidelines established by top management because only those executives up in the walnut-paneled corner offices with four windows have sufficient information to make this decision.

As advertising manager, it's up to you to help top management by advising what objectives can logically be expected to be attained, at what approximate cost, and through what methods.

Get the formal objective(s) *in writing*. Writing helps eliminate ambiguities, and it is lasting evidence that this is what management agreed the company needed. Having objectives in writing prevents future misunderstandings and attempts to weasel or hedge. And it permits *measurement of what advertising has accomplished*.

Assuming objectives are attainable through advertising and you accept them on that basis, you must be able to provide to management's satisfaction that advertising measured up to what was expected of it. This means measuring what was accomplished.

On the other hand, if management sets objectives—even though they're in writing—that are not attainable through advertising, it's incumbent on you to explain why the objectives are not acceptable to you and why they must be revised. Never make the biggest of all mistakes and let impossible objectives be foisted on you. That way lies management loss of confidence in advertising—and in you.

Once objectives are firmed up, they provide a foundation upon which to build the forthcoming campaign. Every question that arises during its creation will be considered just one way: In light of the objectives. You'll be able to explain to your agency exactly what your company must accomplish and why it needs to accomplish it. And the objectives will act as a road map to creative people at the agency, enabling them to devote their full time and attention to developing the best possible program to achieve those objectives.

How It's Done at Grumman Aerospace

The most meaningful way to consider the how's and why's of corporate advertising is to dissect what was done by a top-flight advertising professional in a leading company.

It's with sincere appreciation that the help of Norman G. MacKinnon, former director of advertising, Grumman Aerospace Corporation, is acknowledged.

Norm's rationale of his company's outstanding corporate campaign in the aerospace market is so cogent that much of the analysis of Grumman's campaign is in his own words.

Before looking at one of Grumman's corporate ads, let's see what the man responsible for it has to say about the *raison d'etre* of his corporate advertising campaign. Norman MacKinnon had this to say:

"Corporate aerospace advertising is required to create an awareness of Grumman's corporate capabilities and to identify a company in all aspects of the industry.

"Today, the whole industry is faced with greater technological challenges than every before, and there is greater competition for diminishing product lines.

"Aerospace, in my opinion, must make a greater selling effort, and advertising must be applied in greater intensity to support that sales effort in order to keep ahead in an extremely competitive market.

"Our corporate aerospace advertising is designed to create a better understanding and a friendlier attitude towards (the corporation) management and its philosophies. And insofar as Grumman is concerned, our advertising is designed to reflect Grumman management.

"More important is advertising's impact on the future of our company. It's like insurance . . . five, ten years from now, who knows what we might be producing? We must create acceptance for our products no matter what they are, or to whom we are selling.

"Again, if you will excuse another analogy, our advertising is like R&D: If you don't spend money on R&D today, you'll be nowhere tomorrow. The same holds true in the establishment of corporate identity—the company that spends for promotion and advertising shows, just as R&D fundings shows, that it's on the move.

"Aerospace advertising is primarily aimed at keeping the armed services, selection committees, and final arbiters in any defense system *aware.* Objective here is to remind this primary audience of the aerospace producer's capabilities in the systems area involved. Secondary audience is made up from government agencies, legislative bodies, business and finance, employees (morale factor), stockholders, and the tax-paying public in general who have a right to be informed on how his money is being spent in defense and space programs."

Mr. MacKinnon went on to analyze his corporate program as follows:

1. *The objective:*

   Provide an umbrella for our total efforts. Identify our company as a complete independent aerospace producer—as a constantly growing leader in all aspects of aerospace, undersea technology, and commercial transportation.

   Demonstrate our capabilities in areas of national defense policy such as:

   a. Military and technological superiority over any potential enemy.

   b. Attain greater technological reliability.

   c. Reduce present cost of space operations.

   d. Discover new and better ways of performing space missions.

2. *Strategy:*

   Demonstrate total capability for designing, producing, and delivering such weapons systems and space products as spawned by, and as a result of, our individual capability and capacity which can be supported by demonstrable proof of our wide experience, record, and management and work force stability.

3. *Creative strategy:*

   Such an objective as outlined above—total image development—product complex and individual capabilities and resources demands an overall thematic structure, a theme which transcends those individual capabilities, gives form and substance, and provides a base upon which to demonstrate and dramatize them.

   Such a theme was required to voice past capability and, more important, to imply future capability.

   Such a theme was required to be as applicable to management capabilities as it was to technical and production capabilities (we are selling "people" here).

   Such a theme had to be believable, demonstrable, and rememberable.

   The theme had to be easily grasped, easily understood, and easily translated by the audience to *its* needs.

   And such a theme had to be promotable in areas other than advertising.

   The advertising campaign which grew out of the foregoing is:

   > MAN IS THE HEART
   > OF THE SYSTEM . . .
   > GRUMMAN NEVER FORGETS IT.

   We created an advertising campaign which, through emotional appeal, lets the reader conclude for himself that our corporation has all the capabilities necessary to secure, and manage, major aerospace and other systems programs.

   We introduced the human element into our advertising. Because our prime audience for our advertising had either flown, were flying, or had an emotional appeal towards flying, we took advantage of this emotional climate to get across the story of our total capabilities in aerospace.

   We expressed a very real concern for the human element by showing that this was our *primary* concern. In other words, man is the *heart* of the system and Grumman never forgets it. This, then, was our attention getter and this theme carried through all of our advertising and has gained recognition with similar format and continuity.

4. *Reaction:*

   What is the reaction to our advertising? These are typical:

   "One of the most outstanding examples of thoughtful, effective advertising that has ever appeared in the aerospace industry."

   > Robert W. Martin, Jr.
   > Publisher
   > *Aviation Week & Space Technology*

   "Man is the heart of the system is one of the best advertisements I have seen in years."

   > Harry A. Bruno
   > H.A. Bruno & Associates
   > (Public Relations Counsel)

The highest readership score in a typical issue of *Armed Forces Management*. Highest scoring advertisement in *Science & Technology*.

In two recent issues of *Business Week*, Starch readership research showed Grumman's ad was second among 100 studied ads in that issue, first in the other.''

Shown nearby is one of Grumman's exciting, compelling ads—a four-color bleed spread. Skilful montage work shows a typical "pilot" and a military aircraft, both against the wild blue yonder.

Copy is reversed out of the dark blue sky; legibility is greatly helped by using a very readable serif type face. It reads:

A man is still the heart
of the system.
Grumman never forgets it.

The Intruder is two men with a solid-state nervous system. When it's not a fit night out for man or beast, they form a "flying ambush." Through the Intruder's computers and radar they see all, sense all, know all. They find and identify targets in any weather, day, or night.

And their firepower is as deadly as their see-power. Grumman avionics and weapons systems work together like the right hand and the left.

How can they work together so beautifully? Because Grumman is one of the few aerospace companies with the plant, the personnel, and the experience to create and completely integrate both avionics and weapons systems.

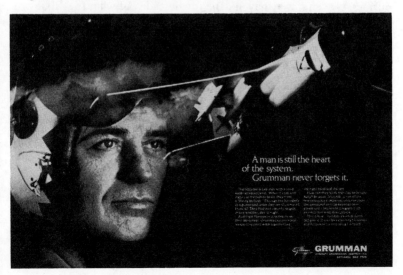

> *This is how Grumman extends the intelligence of man by extending his senses, and his power by extending his reach.*

This is an exceptionally powerful ad. Layout is clean, illustrative technique is gripping, copy is persuasive and convincing. Knowing a Grumman Intruder is up there enables the author to sleep better at night.

Grumman's approach is factual and objective, yet emotional and subjective at the same time. Humanizing the campaign, rather than presenting a mass of nuts and bolts and reasons why Grumman is the best buy, accomplished exactly that in a subtle way. Thinking behind this creative approach and analysis of the communications problems involved was first-rate.

Source of the Impetus Behind "Image" Advertising

So-called image advertising, in which the company itself is the product that's being sold, is due primarily to the fantastically fast-paced technological change in industry.

And mull this one over: More than half of the products that many companies manufacture today were unknown 10 years ago. Yet a handful of years from now most of these highly-touted new products on which all of the tender, loving care and all of those promotional dollars are being lavished will have disappeared from the scene.

Given reasonable success in the marketplace, though, the companies that make these less-than-successful products will still be in business—even if they haven't the foggiest idea of what they'll be producing a decade hence. All of which means that many managements have swung away from product advertising because the product is the thing that's not here to stay.

Hopefully, however, the company is.

And as companies expand and merge and acquire other firms, there is increased emphasis on advertising that enhances the company's image, that makes it more attractive to investors, that broadens its base of ownership, that makes security analysts go into rhapsodies over it, that make it well regarded by those who hold the business community's purse strings, that link its name with not only one product or market, but with a philosophy and an aura of success.

The image of the company in the minds of those diverse and widely separated publics is more than a mere intangible. It is solid and concrete and yes, Virginia, it really and truly exists. It is not merely imagined. You can almost inventory it at so many dollars and cents and list it as an asset in the annual report—or, if it's a sour image, as a liability.

Marketing Forum recently reported on how a strong image sells the financial community on a company. It said:

Strong "image" sells
Wall St.: L&M

A study of "corporate image" as an influence in Wall Street, said to be the first of its kind, found evidence that it has a noticeable effect on price-earnings ratios, share prices, and buy-and-sell decisions of both private and professional investors. The study by Lippincott & Margulies, presented recently in its publication Design Sense, *also indicated that a favorable image has desirable effects in such areas as stock stability, corporate borrowing, and press exposure.*

Conclusions were based, in part, on opinions of Wall Street figures. Dan W. Lufkin, board chairman, Donaldson, Lufkin, and Jenrette, Inc., investment counselors, pointed out that in certain cases image actually outshines stock performance, notably among the giant food companies.

James H. Carey, vice-president, Chase Manhattan Bank, said that image alone was not enough. "It must be honest . . . must project a true picture of business experience, plus such things as quality control and extent of service."

The design firm compared price-earnings ratios of two leading companies in five industries to back up its case. "Theoretically," said L&M, "companies in similar industries with similar general opportunities should have similar price-earnings ratios—if Wall Street did not give weight to the intangible value, or image, of company." The P-E figures, covering 1961-65, showed superior performance by GE over Westinghouse, Scott vs. Kimberly-Clark, Du Pont compared with American Cyanamid, IBM over Sperry Rand and Sears, Roebuck vs. Montgomery Ward.

In commenting on this article, *Industrial Marketing* magazine quoted Lippincott & Margulies extensively, then went on to spot check a broad cross-section of paired companies in what are considered growth industries—such as electronics, chemicals, petroleum, and so on. In each pair, one company advertises heavily *to management*, while the other does little or no "image" advertising. *IM* quoted the following cost-earnings ratios:

Honeywell 23.9
Johnson Service 14.9

Union Carbide............................ 13.09
Chemetron.............................. 9.21
Shell Oil Co. 16.02
Ashland Oil Co. 13.0
Kennecott Copper........................ 10.98
Cerro Corp............................. 6.07
Square D Co............................. 16.5
ITE 12.08

In each example, the more highly valued stock represents the company that has projected its corporate image to other corporate leaders.

Although these pairs of companies are specific examples, they are *not* isolated instances. This list could go on and on and on. Every management is extremely interested in information of this type; gather it and use it to help justify budget requests.

In addition to communicating ideas that interest Wall Street, a company makes itself more attractive in the eyes of all beholders when it uses corporate advertising effectively. This could make the company more desirable as a merger partner, and strengthen its bargaining position.

One thing just as certain as the fact it will get dark tonight is that communicating ideas to maintain, change, or enhance the corporate image must be done deftly. Go at it heavy-handedly and you'll be preachy and pompous and pedantic. Your shirt will be considered to be very stuffed indeed. You cannot carp at the business and financial community, you cannot lecture to it, you cannot talk down to it.

Corporate advertising campaigns *must* be lively and interesting and the message they convey *must* be of genuine interest, free from gimmicks and cynical tricks designed only to get attention. There's room aplenty to be creative and fresh and to get off the beaten path, but do so with a good reason.

The surge in image—corporate, that is—advertising during recent years can be attributed also to expansion of the economy, to dawning realization that corporate advertising is an extra and mighty useful marketing tool, and to the vast changes that have taken place in the structure of industry itself.

Reaction to decades of laxity during which little or no formal attempt was made to communicate with industry's publics contributes to the ready acceptance of and intensity of feeling toward corporate advertising today.

Overreaction, though, can lead a company right down the primrose path of relying *entirely* on corporate advertising for all communications needs. If this route is chosen, sales will suffer as sure as God made little green apples.

A Successful Image Campaign

An excellent corporate advertising campaign, this one well known because it had been running in management publications for 10 years, was the famous Rockwell Report, created for the Rockwell Manufacturing Company, a former division of Rockwell International, by Marsteller Inc. One of these interesting, highly read ads is shown nearby.

Why the "Rockwell Report?" Because Rockwell Manufacturing Company had grown from a one-plant, one-product, one-market company to a diversified enterprise operating multiple plants making many products sold to a large number of different markets.

Future plans called for further growth through diversification. Both the company and its agency, Marsteller Inc., felt the need for an overall corporate campaign that would help each division capitalize on the strength of the company as a whole.

Out of that broad need were crystallized these specific objectives:

1. Make Rockwell Manufacturing Company (whose shares were not listed on any exchange) well known to professional investment and financial men.

2. Show customers, shareholders, investment and financial men the advantages inherent in Rockwell's particular kind of plant, product, and market diversification.

3. Create a corporate "character" or personality for the company by picturing it as a well managed, successful, healthy, enterprise growing soundly through carefully planned diversification.

4. Humanize management of the company by presenting management problems and solutions in terms of everyday experiences with which readers can identify themselves, and do it without bombast and bragging.

5. Capitalize on the prestige of any Rockwell product in any specific field by applying it to other products in other fields. A long-time user of Nordstrom Valves, for instance, is apt to have a higher regard for Delta Power Tools if he or she knows they are made by the same company.

6. Do all of the above at the lowest possible cost in order that the bulk of advertising money can be used for specific product advertising.

The Rockwell Report format, which has become familiar to so

The Rockwell Report is a classic in the annals of corporate advertising. Shown here is a typical issue of the now-famous newsletter.

Rockwell Report

by A. C. Daugherty
President
ROCKWELL MANUFACTURING COMPANY

EXPENSE CONTROL is of vital concern to management these days. At every level, managers are being asked for action programs to maximize short-range profits by tighter controls on costs. The real challenge for a manager is to strike a balance between short-range *corrective* programs and continued long-range *constructive* plans. And further, to communicate this balance to people below him who may only see cause for pessimism in his actions.

For example, our managers have been working hard on controlling expenses this year. But we've invested in four new management development programs for supervisors instituted in 1967. We've been tough on marginal or inefficient producers as identified by a strengthened, improved performance appraisal system. At the same time, this system has provided a sound basis for salary increases and promotions that are comparable with last year's record.

So, while our employees know we take a tough line on inventory control of goods, they see we're putting just as much time and attention into building and improving our "people inventory." And that's the inventory on which the future of the business rests.

* * *

Colonel W. F. Rockwell has been awarded the Decoration of Francisco de Miranda, by decree of the President of Venezuela. The award has been made for his outstanding contribution in stimulating foreign investments for the industrial and economic development of the Republic of Venezuela. The award was presented to the Colonel at the Venezuelan Embassy in Washington, D.C., by the Venezuelan ambassador to the United States, Dr. Enrique Tejera-Paris. Colonel Rockwell has in the past received many distinguished international honors, including the title of "Commandeur de l'ordre de la Couronne" from King Leopold III, of Belgium; the "Cruzeiro do sul" of Brazil; and was knighted by the President of Italy in the order of "Al Merito della Repubblica."

* * *

Have you gotten a Rockwell power tool as a gift yet? If not, it won't be long, for the Premium & Incentive Department of our Power Tool Division reports sharply increased use of power tools as gifts, bonuses, and incentive prizes by business firms. (If you're on the business giving end, you may be interested in seeing a copy of our four-color Premium & Incentive Catalog: send us a note on your letterhead and we'll send one along.) But if you don't get a power tool in your business life, hint around: your wife can pick out your Christmas gift with the help of a knowledgeable Rockwell Power Tool dealer.

* * *

The Rockwell-Edward valves installed at an eastern utility may be the world's largest: 12 feet tall, they weigh 7 tons each, with steel walls over 5 inches thick. The Impactogear handwheels used to open and close them are 6 feet in diameter. Closing these valves during seat tests at elevated pressures required 1,175,000 pounds of thrust on the stem — a thrust equal to that developed by the Titan rocket boosters on the Gemini space flights.

* * *

This is one of a series of informal reports on Rockwell Manufacturing Company, Pittsburgh, Pa., makers of measurement and control devices, instruments, and power tools for 22 basic markets.

Rockwell
MANUFACTURING COMPANY

many millions of businesspeople, was not created, full blown, out of thin air.

Once the objectives of the campaign were established, the big question had to be asked and answered: What kind of campaign would be most likely to achieve the objectives?

To answer that big question, many smaller ones had to be asked and answered. What copy approach and tone? What kind of layout treatment? Photographs or artwork—or nothing at all? Big space or small? Color or black and white?

Eventually, and after a lot of consideration, the "column" technique was selected. These are the reasons why:

Flexibility—several different and often unrelated subjects could be treated in each ad. This was important if the overall company story was to be told.

Informality—reflecting the essential personality of the company and its management.

Authenticity—by presenting each advertisement as a report by, and in the words of, the company president. This would also help to humanize and personalize the campaign.

Even after all of this thinking had been done and all of these decisions had been made, the thought cropped up: Is there enough legitimately interesting material about any company to support such a series over a long period? Won't we run dry?

Actually, the reverse is true. In a growing, dynamic company practically everything is grist for the mill. Every phase of management. Research. Production. Sales. Finance. Community relations. Industrial relations. New products and new uses for old products. There is, literally, no end of things to write about. The main problem is not one of getting material, but of selecting from the wealth that is always available.

Actual selecting was done in meetings between the president, his advertising manager and the agency account executive. In these conferences Rockwell Report subject matter was programmed several months ahead, but was deliberately kept flexible so that subjects of particular timeliness could be inserted as they arose. The account executive from Marsteller Inc. then wrote copy around selected subjects; it was submitted to the president and his advertising manager. Minor differences of viewpoint and expression were worked out, and the result was pretty much as the president would have written it.

Two criteria must be met: First, have something interesting to say. Second, say it as interestingly as possible.

While the format and copy were being worked out, media selection was being made. Rockwell was interested, primarily, in reaching customers and potential customers; shareholders and potential shareholders. For Rockwell, most of this desired audience existed at the decision-making level in practically every segment of industry, business, and finance. From the beginning, the list had been built around a nucleus of management publications.

Readership Grew

When the first Rockwell Report appeared, everyone concerned thought it was sound, but at the same time, everyone realized that it had several possible weaknesses. No striking layout treatment. No dramatic illustrations. No color. Small size—just two-thirds of a page. And a great deal of copy for its size.

The big question was: *Will anybody read it?*

From the beginning, the agency had Starch and other organizations measure readership. From the vast mass of data compiled over the years, several interesting conclusions emerged. For instance, people *did* read the Rockwell Report. The Rockwell Report turned about twice as many "noters" into "readers" as the average ad in the books studied. Actual figures were: Average of all ads, 34 percent; Rockwell Report, 62 percent. That represents those who noted the ads and who also read most of the copy.

Cost Ratio figures were also impressive. In the Starch method, "cost ratios" compared the performance of ads in a given issue of a magazine by relating readership to the cost of the space used. The average of all ads in an issue was designated as 100, and each individual ad was related to this average. The Rockwell Report was always above the average of ads in the same issues of publications studied. Rockwell Report ads produced about *three times more readers-per-dollar of space cost than average ads.*

Moreover, the Rockwell Report quickly went well above average in readership, and it maintained its leadership position for many years. Apparently the series constantly developed and renewed a large following of loyal readers much as newspaper and magazine columns do.

Readership is one thing, response is another. Readers responded to the Rockwell Report; they ordered tens of thousands of reprints—security analysts, other financial people, management men, educators. Requests for additional information on subjects covered in Rockwell ads were received each time one appeared. Finally, a number of direct sales resulted, even though this was corporate advertising.

How to Determine What Your Company Image Is

Top management, and even marketing management of many industrial companies cannot conceive of prospects and customers regarding their company in any way other than favorably. However, much as some outdated top management people would like to emulate an ostrich and keep their heads buried safely and comfortably in the sand, reports filtering in from the field through the sales manager often exert considerable pressure for remedial action. When this goes on long enough, even the engineers in top management and in marketing slots throughout the company can be led gently to accept the advisability of determining exactly *what* the company's image is.

Total image of the company is usually based on many factors; those that follow are the most important and will usually appear in any tabulation of factors influencing company image:

1. Prices
2. Sales contacts
3. Product specifications
4. Delivery
5. Service
6. Reliability of the product
7. Application engineering
8. Technical literature
9. Advertising
10. Manufacturing facilities
11. Breadth of product line
12. Research and development
13. Parts availability

How the company's universe feels about it in relationship to these 13 factors constitutes the company's image. Best way to get an objective analysis of the way the company is regarded is by undertaking a company image study. Personal interviews can be conducted throughout the country using teams of trained interviewers; this is an excellent method, but it is relatively slow and quite expensive. Best way to do an image study is to go the mail survey route.

Using mail to survey prospects and customers is a valid method of making a study *if the mailing list itself is valid.* Make certain your survey mailing goes to *both* prospects and customers.

One large company, which we'll call Smith Widget Manufacturing Company (SWMC) performed an image study quoted here because it is well thought out and obviously refers to a number of areas that are sensitive and need inquiring into by most industrial companies.

TO: Mr. Dave Carew   March 16

SUBJECT: Image Study, Widget Market

As a result of the meeting you attended on March 14, it was agreed that the study should be undertaken to develop information to satisfy the following objectives:

1. To identify areas of strength—and possible areas in which improvement can be attained—in the image of Smith Widget Manufacturing Company in the minds of those in the widget market.

2. To provide a basic framework around which a dynamic marketing program, designed to establish and/or maintain SWMC as the leading producer of widgets, can be developed and activated.

3. To develop specific communications goals, in line with SWMC's short- and long-term marketing plans, around which effective advertising and sales promotion programs can be designed.

4. To establish a bench mark against which the effect of the present advertising platform can be measured in future years.

The specific characteristics of the company to be evaluated by the study are segmented into five groups.

I. GENERAL LEADERSHIP CHARACTERISTICS
   A. Research and development (on new products).
   B. Initiative.
   C. Ability to keep abreast of market needs.
   D. Contributions to the industry.

II. PRODUCT
   A. Product quality.
   B. Maintenance requirements.
   C. Product price.
   D. Ability to meet needs for widgets.
   E. Improvement of existing products.

III. MARKETING
   A. Sales
      1. Sales coverage (contact).
      2. Salesperson's knowledge of customer problems.
      3. Technical capability of salespeople.
      4. Salesperson's knowledge of SWMC's products.
      5. Helpfulness of sales office.

IV. SERVICE
   A. Technical in-plant assistance.
   B. Instructions in use of equipment.
   C. Cooperation and efficiency shown during installation and setup of equipment.
   D. Efficiency in solving equipment difficulties after setup.
   E. Handling in complaints.

V. ADVERTISING
   A. Informative value of advertising relating to:
      1. SWMC products.
      2. Application of SWMC products.
      3. Problem identification (customer's need for equipment).
   B. Informative value of technical literature relating to:
      1. SWMC products.
      2. Application of SWMC products.
      3. Problem identification

C. Amount of advertising.

D. Originality of advertising.

E. Persuasiveness of advertising.

These, then, are the areas that one company decided it needed information about in order to correct problems which had not been identified heretofore.

Always be certain that questions in the questionnaire are "open end" and that they do not identify any one company. Select recipients of the questionnaire from SIC's in which your company is most interested, and mail them to job titles or functions most important to you, although mailing by actual name is better.

Changing the Company Name

In one of their articles *Industrial Marketing* said, "The most expensive mania that modern business has fallen victim to is the compulsion to change the company name."

But *IM* tends to take a dim view of many goings on in the marketplace, especially if the changes are revolutionary, rather than evolutionary. Apparently tinkering with the company name falls into the first category and so incurred the magazine's editorial wrath.

Be that as it may, companies are changing their names at a faster rate than are lissome maidens in the month of June. Despite the complexities inherent in the process—and they range from new business cards and stationery to convincing stockholders of the necessity—more than 150 major firms listed by Standard & Poor's made a change in either firm name or trademark (or both) in a recent year. The trend continues.

The "world's greatest newspaper" (the Chicago *Tribune*) noted with some amazement, that a trickle of firms abandoning old, respected, long-established names for a series of initials had suddenly become a veritable deluge. The *Tribune* proceeded to call attention to the United Gas Improvement Company which suddenly became UGI Corporation, and to General Acceptance Corporation, which transformed itself into GAC Corporation.

Long ago Pittsburgh Plate Glass Company became PPG Industries, Inc., and General Aniline and Film Corporation (that's Ansco, you know) became GAF Corporation. The Thompson-Starret Company took the plunge and switched to TST Industries and Tractor Supply Company became TSC Industries. United Shoe Machinery Corporation, was transformed into USM Corporation, but is now part of the Emhart Corporation.

The rush to clasp a bunch (usually three) of initials in a warm corporate embrace shows no signs of abating, although Wall Street and most individual investors are bewildered, confused, and dismayed. An information gap only slightly smaller than the Grand Canyon has resulted from not being able to remember what the alphabet-soup initials stand for. And pity the poor devil who provides input for the stock ticker?

More than a score of the country's largest firms now use initials for their corporate names. One such is FMC Corporation, nee Food Machinery and Chemical Corporation, whose annual sales have reached the $3⅓ billion mark.

Then there's TRW, Inc., formerly Thompson Ramo Wooldridge, Inc., now in the elite $4½ billion class; interestingly, TRW engaged in a game of mixing up the alphabet when it acquired IRC, Inc., known at one time as International Resistance Company.

Regarded most fondly are three initials, although some of the name-changing companies modestly limit themselves to two—including GF Industries and G-L Industries—while other, brasher, firms take that somewhat inevitable extra step. Among those who took four initials are R.E.D.M. Corporation and BACM Industries. At least one company, UARCO, Inc., manufacturer of business forms, uses *five*.

More than half of the companies in *Fortune's 500* initiated changeover programs in the past 15 years, involving the company name, trademark, or logotype. Some of these companies were reported to be reevaluating their approach for the *second* time, and at least one for the *third*. Management is vitally concerned with broadening the concept of their organizations, of not placing any sort of artificial, arbitrary hindrance in the path of orderly growth.

Let's look at some typical successful companies whose names have been changed, see why the change was made, and how advertising poured communications oil on the troubled waters of transition.

Most frequently encountered rationale for changing the company's name is that the old one was either irrelevant or misleading. What with the fantastic number of mergers which have taken place in the past couple of decades, many companies found themselves in businesses and markets they never dreamed of—and their old, familiar names which they had used for years did not reflect this.

Tennessee Gas Transmission Company was such a firm. The company's reason for wanting to change its name can be *seen* in one of the advertisements it ran when it found itself becoming bogged down in a bottomless morass when it attempted to explain just what it was the company did besides conveying natural gas through a pipeline. Shown below is a typical baby spread of the period, a four-color page and a one-third page in black-and-white.

While the advertisement itself is attractive, the art has strong emotional appeal, and the copy is crisp and well written, the fact remains that the one-third page opposite the full page is devoted to explaining what the company consists of and what it does.

Conrad H. Collier, former director of advertising, said this "bird" ad was part of a campaign that was running before the company

changed its name; the campaign was created to point up the fact Tennessee Gas Transmission Company was a significant factor in three other types of business besides the one highlighted by its name.

As long as the company was engaged solely in pipelining natural gas, its name couldn't be faulted.

But when growth occurred and the company expanded and diversified into areas far beyond its old boundaries, a different picture emerged. The company now has completely integrated oil operations; is a major supplier of packaging and manufactures industrial and agricultural chemicals.

So, as an ad in *Business Week* said, the company adopted a name "general enough to reflect our present . . . and fit our future." Tenneco Inc.—with "lots of elbow room"—was the choice.

One of the corporate advertisements (Mr. Collier preferred to call them "institutional" ads) announcing this landmark change for the company is shown below.

This interesting black-and-white bleed spread appeared in *Invest-*

Hand caught in the act of changing letters was a dramatic way to introduce a new and meaningful name for an expanding, progressive company.

ment Dealers Digest, Financial Analysts Journal, and in Trusts & Estates; the same ad in four color ran in a number of media chosen to reach management in business and industry.

Copy is so lucid and it does such an excellent job of explaining why the name of the company was changed that it is carried here. It reads:

Beginning a new era . . . under a new name

22 years ago, when we began as Tennessee Gas Transmission Company, our only business was transporting natural gas. And today, we operate one of America's largest pipeline networks, delivering billions of cubic feet of nature's finest fuel daily to utilities serving homes and industries in 24 states.

But, over the years, we have grown in other fields and are now active in four basic natural resource areas. In addition to our expanding pipelines, we're in every phase of petroleum as Tenneco Oil Company . . . exploration, producing, refining, and marketing. We're in chemicals as Tenneco Chemicals, Inc. . . . produce a host of chemicals and plastics for industry, farm, and home. We're in pulp and paper, as Packaging Corporation of America . . . from the forest to paperboard to versatile and colorful packages that merchandise the goods of our country.

As a result of these expanding activities we find our name "Tennessee Gas" too limiting. So we have changed it to . . . TENNECO INC.

We leave our old name with regret. It has served us and America well. But with the new comes the promise of even greater growth through four areas vital to the nation's economy—natural gas, oil, chemicals, and packaging.

Tenneco is on the move.

Tennessee Gas Transmission Company is now TENNECO INC. (new logo)

Reader's "eye path" is practically guaranteed to rest upon the bikini, and there is the matter under discussion — the new Tenneco logotype symbolizing fresh company image.

Following these name-changing advertisements, Tenneco Inc. launched a series of institutional ads designed to emphasize the company's new name, and to stress the company's success in four different types of major businesses. In sequence, the ads emphasize these four diversified businesses; the new name; and the new logo-type.

Divisions and subsidiary companies continue to run straight product advertisements, of course.

Shown nearby is a typical four-color Tenneco ad in the new series. Clean, simple, and dramatic, this illustration catches the reader's eye for obvious reasons—and while male readers are looking at the bikini-clad lass, they can't miss seeing the new Tenneco logo she's wearing.

It must be a tremendous relief not to have to run a full column of explanatory copy about what comprises the company.

Audience at which Tenneco aimed with its campaign was the broad mass of "influentials"—that is, the thought leaders and decision makers of the country. The company was particularly anxious to reach the broad financial fraternity of the nation so that the people who really count would know who Tenneco is.

Ad director Collier stressed that these were not "marketing ads." Instead, he said, they were "image ads for lack of a better word." Media list for this campaign was: *U.S. News & World Report, Time, Newsweek, Business Week, Wall Street Journal, Forbes, Financial World, Barron's, Investment Dealers Digest, Financial Analysts Journal, Trusts & Estates, American Banker,* and the *Commercial & Financial Chronicle.* Media are listed in descending order of importance.

Two More Classic Campaigns

Two communications programs stand out from 'most all others in the proliferation of name-change campaigns that inundated business publications of the management genre of recent years. One is simple and was used by a smaller company; the other is more ambitious and was used by a giant.

Forbes magazine reports on the first of these and quotes the following delightful little ad which appeared in the *Wall Street Journal:*

The name we had was pretty confusing:
(The New Haven Board & Carton Company, Inc.)

By the time our telephone operators got it all out, the caller had hung up. If they tried to shorten it, people thought we were a railroad.

Unfortunately, our competitors had grabbed all the really good names. (We thought of calling ourselves "Container & Packaging Corporation of America," but our lawyers felt somebody might sue.)

So, we mulled it and mulled it. We ran contests and put all suggestions into the computer. Everything came up BLAH!

*Then one day our President, Lee Simkins, had an inspiration:
"SIMKINS INDUSTRIES." He tried it out on his family and
they all thought it was swell!*

*A few Executives didn't like it much. After their employment
was terminated, everybody else agreed it was really great.
(Actually, we were all happy the Boss' name was not
Weyerhaeuser, or Potlatch.)*

SIMKINS INDUSTRIES, INC.

packaging

Simkins Industries' modest little ad is a gem. It is as refreshing as
dabbling a pair of tired feet in a crisp mountain stream, especially
after wading through some of the pretentious, self-oriented, self-
conscious copy ground out to explain why companies change their
names.

This sparkling little ad required thought and tact and courage—all
combined with a lively sense of humor, the ability to see an event in its
proper perspective, and the candor needed not to take one's self too
seriously. The last is rare indeed.

Signal Oil & Gas Becomes The Signal Companies

Much different and far more complex was the problem faced by
Signal Oil and Gas Company, giant $4¼ billion Los Angeles-based
conglomerate. Due to an aggressive program of planned growth and
acquisition, the company had undergone radical changes. Its oil and
gas operations, for example, formerly its life blood, accounted for less
than half of the current dollar volume. As a result, the old name was
simply outgrown. It applied to the company as it used to be.

Signal Oil and Gas Company's name-change advertising campaign
was an exceptionally fine example of how such a program should be
handled to arouse maximum interest in the change—both before the
event occurred, as well as afterwards. Let's go into the nuts and bolts
of the campaign itself, as well as the excellent thinking behind it.

The first step toward diversification was taken in 1952. At that time
Signal Oil and Gas Company acquired a substantial stock interest in
American President Lines, a leading Pacific Coast steamship com-
pany.

Even then, Signal Oil and Gas Company took to heart the
aphorisms that to stand still is to fall behind—and that in diversification lies *both* stability and greater profitability. In 1964 Signal entered
the booming aerospace field through a merger with The Garrett Corporation, one of its leaders. Then, in 1967, came simultaneous
mergers with Mack Trucks, one of the oldest and most respected

names in the automotive market, and with Arizona Bancorporation, a Phoenix holding company with profitable investments in a variety of areas, including banks and steel production. Hard on the heels of these desirable mergers came one with Dunham-Bush, Inc., an important factor in the design, manufacture, and distribution of systems and components for environmental comfort, and for food and materials preservation and processing in the commercial, industrial, and institutional markets.

In addition to these factors, management was well aware that continued identification of Signal as an "oil and gas" company was psychologically limiting. Moreover, such obsolete identification imposed an artificial handicap on the company's relationship with the financial community because the name inevitably conjured up an erroneous, incomplete image by failing to reflect the broad-based diversification which had taken place in the past decade and a half.

Worse yet, the "oil and gas" label stuck on there for all to see could be misinterpreted as a deliberate slighting of other important elements of the company, especially Garrett and Mack. The inference could be drawn that they did not loom large in management's plans for the future, when exactly the opposite is true.

The decision to change the name of a 45-year-old company isn't made as casually as choosing the necktie to harmonize with that day's suit, nor is it one that's rushed into. Signal management, in fact, had been considering making a name change for at least two years, although actual planning didn't begin to gel until mid-1967, which was about six months before the board of directors was asked to approve the new name.

First step, as with any other well-managed project, was to establish objectives. These were:

1. To adopt a parent company name which indicates broad diversification.

2. To develop a distinctive trademark or signature (logo) for the parent company.

3. To take full advantage of existing recognition and reputation of Signal and its subsidiaries.

4. To develop a consistent program for identifying subsidiaries and affiliates with the parent company in a way that does not conflict with their individual identities but supports and contributes to the broad recognition of the parent company, particularly in the financial community.

5. To build a parent company identification which adds to the strength and reputation of each affiliate in its respective field.

Responsibility for developing a recommended name—or names, that is—and logo was given to Signal's advertising and public relations agency, The Bowes Company, Los Angeles. Thus was avoided the pitfall of putting the company's future into the hands of one of the glib image merchants and design hotshots who specialize in extracting exorbitant fees from mesmerized managements in exchange for concocting brittle say-nothing names and highly contrived logos which also fail to communicate a single, solitary thing.

These "consultants" are responsible for many of the inanities which, for a fat fee, replaced well-known and highly respected firm names.

How many people in business don't know, for example, exactly what a Citgo is—or an Amex, an Abex, an Amax, for that matter—after untold millions of dollars have been spent to tell them? There are many more "A's," as well as 25 other letters of the alphabet involved in such ill-conceived foolishness.

All too often the name of the game seems to be change for the sake of change itself—and the greater the change and the more incomprehensible the new name is, the greater the fee for giving birth to it. (And the greater the confusion in the marketplace, among prospects, customers, security analysts, investors, brokerage houses, etc.)

Management of The Bowes Company determined to avoid such nonsense. The project began, logically enough, with an in-depth discussion between Bowes personnel (all of whom were intimately familiar with signal's day-to-day operations and long-range objectives —unlike a strange image merchant) and Signal's top management.

Purpose was to clarify the objectives and all pertinent facts and make *sure* both teams were pulling in the same direction. Tugs-of-war are expensive and time-consuming. Resulting information was carefully documented by Bowes for study by the agency's account team and creative staff.

There was complete unanimity of thought on the subject at the agency. All agreed that the name ultimately selected should be easy to use and easy to remember. Furthermore, the chosen name should be one which indicated diversification while simultaneously representing the sum of the parts.

Consensus at the agency was that retention of the word "Signal" would be desirable because it would help maintain corporate recognition. Signal's publics wouldn't be presented with something foreign and unknown, so the task of creating awareness of the new name would be simplified.

Also among the advantages of retaining the word "Signal" in the new name were:

1. It was already well established.
2. The name was legally available.
3. "Signal" is a short name; it is easy to spell and pronounce (in fact, it can't be *mis*pronounced); it is not easily confused with any other commonly used name.
4. Meaning and connotations of "Signal" are both favorable and, coincidentally, have a fairly direct relationship to many of the products and services of the various affiliated companies—without creating any limitations. "Signal" has these various meanings: Sign for action; warning or command; object to be observed; way to transmit intelligence; messages; sounds; impulses; (as an adjective) notable; significant; outstanding; distinguished.

Scores and names were considered, tried on for fit, and ultimately rejected at the agency. Finally, all concerned agreed to recommend two alternatives:

1. Signal Industries, Inc.
2. The Signal Companies

These names were first submitted to Signal's top management, which chose The Signal Companies. Management then presented this name to the company's board of directors, who approved it.

"The Signal Companies" was preferred because it was considered more distinctive than "industries" (half of the cat-and-dog companies in business have renamed themselves Such-and-Such Industries). Moreover, "companies" is somewhat less confining than "industries"; banking, for example, is usually not considered an industry. Also, "companies" conveys a vivid word-picture of individual companies united in approach but individual in types of business and autonomous in managerial responsibility.

Specific reasons for the agency's recommending "The Signal Companies" as the new name for the parent company were:

1. The name is distinctive, yet simple, easy to remember, and not gimmicky or contrived. It rings true.
2. Plural "companies" carries the connotation of multiplicity, broad diversification, and continuing expansion.
3. No limitations as to kinds of companies—whether light industry, heavy industry, financial, service, transporation, or what have you—are inherent in the name.

Legality of the new name was checked prior to submission to Signal management; this included ascertaining whether or not "Companies" could be used alone—and it could not. To comply with Delaware law, the word "Inc." must be included after the name, wherever the full, official designation is required, such as on stock certificates, contracts, and similar legal documents. For the most part, though, the "Inc." could either be omitted or included in very small type.

In international situations, to help identify the company or any subsidiary as an indigenous operation, the customary designations can be added, such as "Ltd.," "GmbH," "S.A." and so on.

Also recommended by the agency was that affiliated companies be identified as "One of The Signal Companies." It was agreed that all subsidiaries should use this identification consistently and uniformly on letterheads, standard forms, and promotional material where appropriate. Continual repetition would have a synergistic effect in building and maintaining favorable recognition for the parent company and its various components.

To provide guidance and assure uniformity in usage of the parent company name and logo, the agency developed a comprehensive style manual with detailed instructions and examples of the identifying line in a wide variety of possible uses.

Signal's new logo, and an attractive one it is, was born in the creative department at The Bowes Company. Major considerations in developing the new trademark design for the parent company were:

1. It must be distinctive, easy to recognize and remember.
2. It should not be identified specifically with any type of operation.
3. It must be flexible enought to have dominance when used alone, but should not compete with identifiction of subsidiary companies, nor should it confuse the viewer.

The new corporate trademark or symbol or logo is shown above. It consists of two half circles, positioned to form a subtle initial "S," within a light-line square frame. The logo may be used in color (left half red, right half green), black and white, or blind embossed.

To summarize, The Bowes Company describes the logo as "simple, distinctive, subtle, contemporary and dynamic." And that's a pretty irrefutable assessment of the new logo, even if it is one of the agency's brainchildren—especially when it's mentally compared to some of the silly abominations hopefully embraced by other corporations in recent years.

Attributes of the new logo are:

Simple. It's free of frills, clean, highly visible, and perhaps best of all, it's not gimmicky.

Distinctive. No other logo is just like it, yet the component parts fit together so logically that it is very basic, easy to remember and to recognize.

Subtle. Signal's new logo avoids the well-worn cliche' of an ordinary monogram or obvious initial. The "S" formed by the half circles is not gross or insulting; it arouses the viewer's curiosity and involves him or her by allowing the viewer to "discover" the "S" for himself or herself, and to relate to Signal on a more personal basis.

Contemporary. The simplicity of the symbol, together with the new corporate name, gives just the right amount of understatement to show corporate self-assurance and a feeling of the "today company." Yet it is not a faddish design that will be soon outdated, nor is it blatant and tasteless and vulgar as are many of the so-called "bolder" approaches which include screaming reverses and pseudo-cultural symbolism which enjoyed a brief vogue.

Unlimited. The logo is not symbolic of any specific type of business or industry, hence does not limit itself. It is readily adaptable to all present or future operations of Signal and its subsidiaries.

Dynamic. This logo is bold, solid, sharp, vigorous. It has substance. And it is easily and quickly read and absorbed and retained. In addition, it benefits from use of basic, familiar human-response colors—red and green. Colors and shapes work well together to attract and hold the eye. The colors, incidentally, might be described as "signal" colors!

Meaningful. The symbol, like The Signal Companies, is made up of separate elements, each well defined and self-sufficient, yet complementing each other as parts of a larger, orderly framework. Together the parts form an upward path between them, symbolic of progress. A feeling of positiveness, conciseness, confidence, and importance is imparted.

Reminiscent of the Signal heritage. The new logo is a logical evolvement from the way the company had been represented in the past. Colors are a soft suggestion of the old Signal stoplight and are retained in the new Signal trademark. They are all part of the subtle background, now incorporated in a new symbol for a new parent corporation.

Practical. The logo can be used in every size, in color, in black-

and-white, in halftone and in line art; too, it can be lighted or painted. Economy is built in because it is simple to reproduce. And it's easy to control. Also pointed out by Signal's agency is that company typewriters could easily be equipped with a key to type the new "S" symbol, thus permitting broadest possible use.

At no time was there any doubt as to the advisability of changing Signal's name, nor was there any fear that such a change would result in dilution of the company's image or in reduced awareness of the company.

Need to make the change was manifest, and it was the consensus that the new name could not fail to strengthen the company—particularly since retention of the word "Signal" obviated the need to reestablish completely the company's identification. It's much better to start with something than with nothing.

Wisdom of retaining the word "Signal" is obvious upon examination of corporate advertising campaigns of companies who adopted a completely new name with no familiar element; many have spent into the seven-figure bracket in an attempt to build awareness of the company to former levels—with conspicuous lack of success. Signal didn't make this costly mistake.

Every step of Signal's name-change program was planned down to the last detail, and some sharp marketing thinking went into it.

Signal began the campaign with one of the most outstanding teaser ads to come down the pike in many a year. This tremendously stimulating and imaginative black-and-white one-page advertisement appeared in *Forbes, Fortune, Business Week* (Pacific Coast edition), four editions of *Time*, and three editions of *Wall Street Journal*. Insertions carried over into December.

If this headline isn't enough to titillate the fancy and pique the curiosity of even the staidest member of the business and financial community, nothing else would. Offhand, you probably can't name anybody who could read the headline and then not proceed on into the body copy. Copy reads:

We've thought
of calling ourselves
Signalgarrettmacktruckarizonabancorporation

Our present name, Signal Oil and Gas Company, gives no hint of our diversification.

It doesn't remind you that we merged with Garrett in 1964, putting us not only in the aerospace business but into the development and production of gas turbines, heat transfer systems and life sciences research.

Joining the conglomerate companies in one impossible combination was an effective way to demonstrate the need for a change in the corporate name, image of Signal Oil & Gas.

We've thought
of calling ourselves
Signalgarrettmacktruckarizonabancorporation

Our present name, Signal Oil and Gas Company, gives no hint of our diversification.

It doesn't remind you that we merged with Garrett in 1964, putting us not only in the aerospace business but into the development and production of gas turbines, heat transfer systems and life sciences research.

You may think of us as solid—"built like a Mack truck", in fact—but from our name you wouldn't know that we recently acquired that very company. Mack Trucks, Inc. is the nation's largest seller of trucks in many heavy duty lines.

And now, by adding Arizona Bancorporation to our action team, we're in banking, consumer financing, leasing, life insurance, prescription drugs and steel production.

For more information on our activities, write us at the address below. Of course our expanding petroleum production and marketing activities are of prime importance. So the "Oil and Gas Company" part still applies.

But "Signal" means a lot more these days.

Signal Oil and Gas Company
1010 Wilshire Boulevard, Los Angeles, California 90017

You may think of us as solid—"built like a Mack truck," in fact—but from our name you wouldn't know that we recently acquired that very company. Mack Trucks, Inc. is the nation's largest seller of trucks in many heavy-duty lines.

And now, by adding Arizona Bancorporation to our action team, we're in banking, consumer financing, leasing, life insurance, prescription drugs, and steel production.

For more information on our activities, write us at the address below. Of course our expanding petroleum production and marketing activities are of prime importance. So the "Oil and Gas Company" part still applies.

But "Signal" means a lot more these days.

Signal Oil and Gas Company
1010 Wilshire Boulevard, Los Angeles, California 90017

That's stage-setting with a mighty sure hand.

Effectiveness of this ad was emphasized by the fact that it hit the editorial jackpot (which naturally warmed the cockles of many hearts at both Signal and its agency) because it was picked up as the lead in both *Time's* and *Newsweek's* stories about Signal's proposed acquisition of Allis-Chalmers Manufacturing Company, Milwaukee-based leader in electrical, construction, and farm machinery, whose annual

We have decided against changing our name to
Signalgarrettmacktruckarizonabancorporation,
but because of continued diversification we are
definitely going to change our name to something
other than Signal Oil and Gas Company.

sales were some $850 million. Publicity like this you can't buy.

Next ad in the campaign was a powerful all-type spread shown nearby. It makes impressive use of what appears to be *acres* of pristine white space to lure readers into the copy. Copy is doubly appealing because it's set in display type, all of it except one line. Typography is clean and attractive, set ragged-right, and well spaced. For a fast change of pace that reaches right out and grabs the reader, the "snapper" is set in very small type in the lower left hand corner of the spread; it delivered readers in droves to Signal's succinct statement about its continuing diversification. It reads:

We have decided against changing our name to
Signalgarrettmacktruckarizonabancorporation,
but because of continued diversification we are
definitely going to change our name to *something*
other than Signal Oil and Gas Company.

Our diversification program includes recent acquisitions of Garrett, Mack Trucks, Inc., and Arizona Bancorporation. Signal Oil and Gas Company, Los Angeles, California.

An unexpected advertising hiatus resulted from a proposed merger with Occidental Petroleum; the annual stockholders' meeting was postponed for one month, also. But the second part of Signal's name-change advertising campaign began as soon as possible thereafter.

First ad in the new series is reproduced nearby. It is highly dramatic. Only color on the left-hand page is the red-and-green Signal logo, while the right-hand page is in four color.

Copy is especially lucid, persuasive and "appropriate." It says:

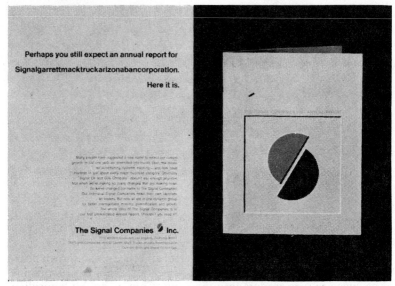

Perhaps you still expect an annual report for Signalgarrettmacktruckarizonabancorporation.

Here it is.

Many people have suggested a new name to reflect our current growth. In just one year, we diversified into trucks, steel, real estate, air conditioning systems, banking—and now have interests in just about every major business category. Obviously "Signal Oil and Gas Company" doesn't say enough anymore. Not when we're making so many changes that are making news. So we've changed our name to The Signal Companies. Our individual Signal Companies retain their own identities as leaders. But now all are in one dynamic group for better management, mobility, diversification, and growth. The whole story of The Signal Companies is in our first consolidated Annual Report. Shouldn't you read it?

The Signal Companies (logo) Inc.

Layout is simple and it takes full advantage of the known eye path of the reader. The combination of a four-color page and a three-color page—with the second and third colors used *functionally*—is sound thinking.

This spread not only announces the company's new name, but it illustrates and offers Signal's annual report. Investors, analysts, brokers, bankers, and others in the business and financial community couldn't help but notice this arresting ad, nor could they refrain from requesting their copy of the report. This spread appeared in the following media:

Fortune

Business Week

Time
New York edition
Chicago edition
Los Angeles edition
San Francisco edition
Washington, D.C. edition

Forbes

Wall Street Journal

Barrons

U.S. News & World Report

Newsweek
New York edition
California edition
Chicago edition

Dun's Review

American Banker

Financial Analysts Journal

Finance

Wall Street Transcript

Commercial & Financial Chronicle

Investment Dealer's Digest

Financial Executive

Financial World

Los Angeles Times

San Francisco Chronicle-Examiner

Phoenix Republic & Gazette

New York Times

Washington Post

Chicago Tribune

Additional ads are being developed to remind readers of Signal's new size and diversity; they will display the new name and logo prominently.

Media are selected to reach Signal's target audience in the business and financial community—people and institutions who regularly make investments, and people who influence the choice of investments. Business and financial publications were chosen on the basis of their coverage of all of these people. A few local newspapers (financial pages) also were chosen because of special local interests.

Cost of Signal's two stage-setting ads run over a two-year period reached a six-figure level for space alone. If all other elements of the program are included, the investment goes into the seven-figure bracket—about par for the course for a company of Signal's size.

The Bowes Company, Signal's agency, is developing a proposal for a name-change study to determine how much impact the campaign has actually produced. This survey would be designed to reveal both quantitative and qualitative recognition.

Important in the overall scheme of things is that the name-change campaign, while significant in its own right, is just one of several means to an end. In Signal's case, the end is a broad-scale awareness in the financial community of the new Signal.

This program includes extensive publicity, personal contacts with security analysts, a stockholder relations program, the annual report, other corporate documents, and media advertising which talks about the new Signal rather than about the new name.

The name change does have extra significance in Signal's case, however, because it not only reflects a very different corporate nature, but opens the way to disseminate just what that difference means to the company and to its many publics.

Radio Corporation of America's name change to RCA, Inc., for example, is much less meaningful because most people already knew that RCA is much more than a "radio" company—and also most people had already thought of RCA as RCA for years; this was like Coca Cola calling its product "Coke."

However, most people did not know that Signal is far more than an "oil and gas" company before the name change, so the new name not only properly identifies the company, but also serves notice the new Signal is a viable company, one that's on the move.

Signal's name-change advertising campaign is superb. It is well conceived and well executed, and it's tasteful. It evidences thoroughly professional thinking at the agency and within the company. Everybody who had a hand in it should be justifiably proud of the end product.

Happily it skillfully avoids the deadfall that has broken the back of many other campaigns designed to do the same job—boring the reader half to death by bragging and boasting and being too self-centered to present information in terms of *his or her* self-interest.

All in all, there's every reason to consider this campaign a signal success!

Sales—and the Corporate Name

What's in a name?

Look at it this way: If there's one word of paramount importance to business today, it's *change*. New products and processes are emerging at an accelerating rate—and, because of them, new and different markets.

The management "decision team," too, is on the move. There are many new faces to see, new people to be sold—and not all of them, by any means, accessible to salespeople.

These facts place an additional responsibility on advertising. Advertising's basic function is to help sell existing products, of course. But it must go beyond that. It must establish the importance and integrity of the *company name* (build an image, if you will) among all of those people who—now or in the future—can play an important part in a company's total successful operation.

Heart of the matter is that the name carry a separate identity all its own, that it produce an instantaneous recognition. It is the badge of identification, of course, but it is more. It is the touchstone of value.

Many companies have had the vision to foresee this technological revolution—the importance of change in our economy—and gear their advertising programs accordingly.

One such forward-looking firm is Cleveland-based Warner & Swasey Company, which is now a subsidiary of the Bendix Corporation. At the beginning of World War II, it recognized that a company's most important asset, an asset that would see it through any change in products or product lines, is a favorable company reputation.

It is with a great deal of pleasure and appreciation that the author acknowledges the help of B. T. Fullerton, former director of marketing, Warner & Swasey Company, in preparing this case history of how advertising imparts prestige to a name.

Back at the start of World War II, Warner & Swasey's vice-president-sales stated, "I don't know what we are going to make when this war is over, but I want such a reputation for this company that even if it is baby carriages, the Warner & Swasey name will sell them."

Today, no baby carriages are in the Warner & Swasey line. But it does manufacture rugged earth-moving equipment, complex textile machinery, and sophisticated new automatic machine tools—and 75 percent of the company's shipments are in the new product lines.

In order to achieve this volume and its place of leadership in its industry, Warner & Swasey developed a highly favorable corporate reputation among all of those countless unidentified people that a company touches or is affected by in one way or another. A consistent and well-conceived corporate advertising program produced greater public recognition, it is true, *but above all else it produced sales.*

Here is how the benefits of a consistent 30-year corporate advertising campaign piled up and up and up at Warner & Swasey.

All of these years, Warner & Swasey has held fast to these basic purposes in this outstanding corporate advertising campaign—which is, incidentally, one of the best known, most admired, most respected, and most widely quoted campaigns ever to appear in publications edited for top management people:

> *A typical Warner & Swasey advertisement talks to a customer or prospect about business—the subject in which he or she is most interested. It talks about the profit-and-loss system, briefly, one point per advertisement, so that even the busiest businesspeople will read (as they do , in amazing numbers).*

> *Finally, the advertisement speaks clearly and convincingly as one businessperson to another and is read and accepted in exactly that understanding way. In thus attracting the readership and attention of management people at all levels, it will stimulate the sale of Warner & Swasey products.*

One medium which has been on Warner & Swasey's schedule for more than a quarter-century is *U.S. News & World Report.* W&S runs 26 pages per year in this leading news weekly and considers it the key publication in its schedule because this magazine reaches more top management people in industry than do others in its field.

Now, newspaper editors are also readers, and they, too, read *U.S. News & World Report* as do many other upper-income, well-educated members of society in general. An uncounted, but very large, number of editors have seen Warner & Swasey's ads in the news magazine and have *reprinted them in their newspapers as editorials*—with proper credit, of course.

And a large percentage of readers of *U.S. News & World Report*

Typical Warner & Swasey ad, one of a long series pulling inquiries and orders in spite of taking a hard-hitting political stance.

who are corporation officials have published Warner & Swasey's advertisements in their companies' house magazines, or have them pinned to company bulletin boards.

Furthermore, members of Congress pass these messages out to a broader constituency by reprinting them in the *Congressional Record.*

There's no doubt that this unique campaign continues to meet the challenge of change by making new friends and reacquainting the old. Reported the company: "Even after more than 20 years of every-other-week appearance in *U.S. News & World Report*, the Warner & Swasey campaign still draws fan mail by the hundreds and thousands from readers of the magazine."

Warner & Swasey advertisements were quoted in full on the editorial pages of daily and weekly newspapers throughout the nation, throughout the year. It was not at all unusual to have 50, 60, 70 or more newspapers reprint the same advertisement at approximately the same time; this included some of the leading dailies in important industrial cities, incidentally, which were prime markets for the company.

Executives at Warner & Swasey who had made a study of the situation estimated these editorials furnished at least an additional 30 *million* circulation to the campaign every year, although they stressed that this was without doubt a very conservative estimate. Privately, the opinion is held that the actual figure was at least 60 million.

Not every letter received at Warner & Swasey was laudatory, by any means. Some were quite bitterly opposed to what they consider the ultraconservative nature of the ads.

Just what sort of pro-American corporate advertising campaign is it that does all of these things: Enhances Warner & Swasey's image, increases awareness of W&S as a leading manufacturer of sophisticated products, builds a reputation for integrity, recognizes the company's massive contribution toward Americanism, and sells the product?

Let's look.

Shown nearby is a typical advertisement from Warner & Swasey's classic corporate campaign which was run in management-oriented publications for some three decades.

Clean and simple and appealing, with plenty of attractive white space, superb typography, and an interesting in-use photographic illustration of the product, this ad did a tremendous job for Warner & Swasey—and for our country. Copy reads:

The bigger the government
the smaller the people

Everybody—labor union member, farmer, veteran, ship-owner, road builder, importer, sheep herder—everybody seems to want special "benefits" from the government. So they demand help, and get a law or regulation. That requires a bureau to enforce it, taxes to pay for it.

That is how Washington bureaucracy has grown to more than 2,000,000 and taxes have grown ruinously high.

Laws and regulations are written by government employees, and Americans are being drowned in laws they don't understand, bureaus they can't grasp, taxes they cannot afford.

Self-reliance (another name for self-respect) is like a muscle —unused, it soon becomes flabby. Our enemies know it, count on it. That is why every time we ask Government for something instead of doing it ourselves, we surrender, we lose, another bit of America.

High precision aircraft hydraulic pump parts being machined on a Warner & Swasey 1 AC Automatic Chucker.

YOU CAN PRODUCE IT BETTER, FASTER, FOR LESS WITH WARNER & SWASEY MACHINE TOOLS, TEXTILE MACHINERY, CONSTRUCTION MACHINERY

Warner & Swasey realizes that the company can prosper and grow and build for the future only if our country does, also. If the country goes down the drain, so does Warner & Swasey. It is that simple. That admirable philosophy led to an ad that said:

How do you get Obliterate on the ballot?

You vote for the best Republican or Democrat, sure he or she will work for what's best for the country, but somehow the bureaus and bureaucrats, the deficits and the debts, keep on mounting.

How do you get a place on the ballot where the American people can vote NO to hazy theories, NO to spending billions we haven't got for too many programs of questionable value, NO to courts more interested in kindness to criminals than laws and protection of decent citizens, NO to those many bureaucrats whose chief aim is to perpetuate their often -useless jobs.

Put places to mark these on the ballot and you'd roll up the biggest patriots' landslide in history. And it's high time.

*Outdoor lift truck, a product
of the Duplex Division of
Warner & Swasey, hauling
prepackaged lumber in
outside storage area*

Other powerful Warner & Swasey ads have been directed at government fiscal policies, foreign aid, domestic spending programs, and similar themes. Warner & Swasey was modest about the splendid contribution it had made toward preserving freedom in America. The vice-president-sales of the company said, "I have not referred to this as an 'institutional campaign,' because the purpose is very definitely to sell machines, and we know it is doing so. Let me put it this way: If an executive committee or board of directors has three proposals presented to it for the purpose of machine tools, and if they pick up the one with Warner & Swasey on the cover first, our advertising has been successful, because that's all we can ask for. *And we know by checking case after case that that has been happening.*

"We have even sold machines almost by mail from this campaign. A man walked into our Atlanta office one day and said he had never heard of our company except through our advertising, and he wanted to give us an order for a turret lathe.

"I believe that a casual purchase item like a tube of toothpaste is bought almost by reflex action. But capital goods like our products, which average more than $20,000 per unit, are very studied purchases. Everywhere we go we know that the people who control these studied purchases *know our company and know us favorably.*

"We have succeeded in reaching the very people our campaign was originally designed to reach—the top executive, the member of the executive committee, and the board of directors—whose favorable nod we must get.

"How do we know this? Through our sales managers and officers it is our business to be in touch with as many customers and prospective customers as we can. We all have the same experience—wherever we go and talk to key executives we are told that our product is being favorably considered or that the sale has actually been consummated *because of the reputation our advertising has built for our company.*

"Through this advertising Warner & Swasey has sat in thousands of directors' meetings, executive committee meetings, production executive meetings, where no Warner & Swasey person could ever sit—but Warner & Swasey, I repeat, has sat there and has spoken forcefully because our philosophy has spoken for us—our philosophy as expressed in our advertising."

Of the thousands of letters Warner & Swasey ads brought in to the company, an important part was from customers and prospects who had been turned into friends by the advertisements. A typical letter follows:

MANITOWOC ENGINEERING CORP.

John D. West
President

The Warner & Swasey Company
5701 Carnegie Aveune
Cleveland, Ohio 44103

Attn: Mr. W.K. Bailey, President

Dear Mr. Bailey:

Thank you for the copy of "More Precious than Gold" [an ad reprint] which you sent on August 10th.

For years I have read your advertising with a feeling of appreciation of your important contribution toward setting the record straight on many national economic issues.

No doubt you have had occasion to question whether this approach influenced the of your fine products. Let me assure you that in the recent case of our purchase of two of your machines, our awareness that we were dealing with a progressive company having strong convictions as to our free private enterprise system, somehow gave me added confidence in your company, and a feeling of sharing in your efforts.

I hasten to say, however, that the technical information supplied by your sales people and our superintendent's enlightening visit to your plant, actually sold the product.

I hope you plan to continue your advertising program along this most interesting and effective line.

Sincerely,

John D. West
President

This is one of the two ways advertising "sells"—by increasing the base of negotiations activity.

Warner & Swasey has received so many letters like this one from the president of a leading manufacturer of heavy crawler-type cranes, power shovels, and draglines that singling out one to quote was a difficult task. As might be expected, the same theme ran through almost all of them: *We bought Warner & Swasey machines because we know and respect your name as the result of your corporate advertising campaign.*

Also running through letters from top executives who gave the nod of approval to purchasing Warner & Swasey products was strong approbation for the company's splendid campaign—*and for Warner & Swasey as a company* for running it.

Chapter 22

MERCHANDISING

ALTHOUGH this is the shortest chapter in this book, it concerns a topic—merchandising—that is of vital importance to the success of your communications program.

Strangely enough, merchandising is usually either completely ignored or else given short shrift by most industrial advertising managers. This neglect may well be due to not understanding merchandising and what it can accomplish. (Would you believe many companies do *no* merchandising whatsoever?)

Just what is merchandising? In the context we're using it here, merchandising includes both the *internal* and *external* promotion of an advertisement and/or an advertising campaign. Let's look into these one at a time, although many techniques are applicable to both as will be seen.

Internal Promotion

Internal promotion sells the concept of the campaign—its strategy, audience, and media—to your sales force, product, and marketing people, to company management, agents, representatives, jobbers, distributors, and others in the channel of distribution.

Merchandising is an extremely effective technique for selling sound advertising. Because it does sell sound advertising it builds internal support for and understanding of advertising, and in turn increases the effectiveness of the sales effort externally.

Merchandising your advertising program internally means you are not content to sit idly by, twiddling your thumbs, and let nature take its course. You do more than merely hope that those with whom you work—*and through whom you sell*—will see your ads in various publications and, hopefully, regard them favorably. When you merchandise aggressively, you're taking positive action to make certain your advertising is seen and read and understood.

Actually, it's just as essential to merchandise your communications program internally as it is externally. So doing can help dispel the negative attitude towards advertising that's unbelievably prevalent in many less-than-progressive industrial companies. There's a widespread feeling in industry that advertising in some unexplained way is something that nice people don't talk about—like B.O., or an uncle who voted for F.D.R.

The woeful lack of understanding of the massive contribution industrial advertising makes, and how it does so, can be ameliorated to a great extent by merchandising your advertising program *and the rationale behind it.*

The following four questions raised by one industrial ad manager in a memo to the boss, a vice-president of marketing, point up the necessity to merchandise the advertising program:

1. How can the advertising department receive proper direction so as to operate efficiently if our people do not understand advertising's basic reason for being?
2. How can we establish realistic, concrete communications objectives when our marketing people have almost no concept of what advertising can—and cannot—do?
3. How can we measure the effectiveness of the advertising program unless we have communications objectives which reflect marketing objectives?
4. How can the advertising department expect our people to understand advertising's role in the marketing-communictions mix unless we explain it to them?

These are pertinent questions that pinpoint the plight of many an industrial advertising manager. He or she is boxed in, can't move, can't plan; all due to a lack of understanding of the function managed. The answer, of course, is a well-executed merchandising program. It should sell the current communications program, *as well as advertising per se*, by tactfully and persuasively educating your people in some of advertising's fundamentals.

Most efficient way to do this is to give examples and illustrations of the things you're talking about. Explain in nontechnical terms. Quote outside experts on various topics.

This is especially effective. Quoting recognized authorities from outside your company is an ideal way to provide basic education in advertising for those who count. Because the experts you quote are *not* in your department and are *not* associated with your company (but your agency *is*), their comments tend to be taken at face value. They encounter no credibility gap.

What's more, this is a custom-built solution to the problem of gathering suitable educational material. You can "borrow" it from any advertising publication you wish and reproduce it *within your company* without finding yourself on the inside looking out for copyright infringement.

And, because you are quoting a disinterested third party, you can present information you know is desirable without embarrassment. The following discussion, *Relating Advertising to Corporate Profits*, enlightened key personnel at Lindberg Hevi-Duty. Reproduced on an inexpensive, one-color (red) masthead designed specifically for the advertising department to use for its educational and merchandising program, the discussion quoted Alan G. St. George, associate market and research director, Meldrum & Fewsmith Inc., as follows:

According to a study done by *Business Management* among 108 company presidents, more than 80 percent felt that an immediate halt of advertising would have little or no effect on sales this year. More than two-thirds felt that an immediate halt would have little or no effect on next year's sales. These feelings lead to one conclusion—top management has little or no confidence in the ability of advertising to contribute to sales efforts or to increase profits.

The survey pointed to a paradox in the attitudes of presidents toward advertising. When respondents were asked, "How does your company measure the effectiveness of its advertising?" almost half named sales results.

This raises what may seem to be a rather academic question. Must advertising necessarily increase total sales volume to be considered effective? No! Of course all advertising has commercial reasons for being: advertising is a major factor in the reduction of selling costs, a reason that should be sufficient to convince management that it is worthwhile even if sales don't increase.

In another study, McGraw-Hill recorded the opinions of 646 top executives, sales managers, and advertising managers about what they felt were the objectives of business-press advertising. The results were as follows:

Task	Percent who rated advertising as important
Introducing new products	93
Creating favorable attitude toward firm	90
Contacting buying influences salespeople do not see	79
Paving the way for salespeople	79
Maintaining the market for established products	70
Reducing the cost of selling	43

Let's take as an example the highest-rated objective, that of introducing new products. Are there any critics of advertising who can deny the efficiency and the economy of introducing a new product to a large number of potential users through this medium? It can take months, if not years, to introduce many industrial products by direct sales calls. In that time valuable sales have been lost, never to be regained.

This, in combination with the $106.00 cost of a direct sales call, should be enough to convince corporate management that advertising does reduce the cost of selling, thereby increasing profits.

Incidentally, there's a woeful lack of authoritative information on just how advertising affects corporate profits, but you undoubtedly tell that by the fallacious opinions you encounter. Ignorance reigns supreme here. An educational effort in this area is highly desirable in almost every company.

When your field sales reps are in your office periodically, make every effort to talk with them. Their help will be of inestimable value because they can clue you in about the sales resistance they encounter, tip you off to worthwhile case histories, and so on.

Get to know as many salespeople as possible. You'll find it easier to "sell" your communications program to them at the annual sales meeting if you do. Incidentally, this should be a major merchandising effort on your part, and that of your agency. Use slides, blown-up ads, banners, a flip-chart presentation, or whatever you feel best to dramatize your ad program and show how it will help the salespeople sell. Be sure *not* to put your foot in your mouth by claiming that advertising "sells." Stress, instead, that it helps salespeople sell, that it enables them to use their valuable time more productively, that it helps them ferret out prospects, that it saves time for them by letting them dispense with introducing company and product because advertising has already taken care of this for them.

Never hesitate to explain, but, heaven forbid, don't be patronizing. Although everybody *thinks* he or she understands industrial advertising, it is probable that you're the *only* person in the company who actually does—and this definitely includes your vice-president of marketing, especially if he's an ex-engineer.

Because advertising is not understood, it is distrusted. For the same illogical reason many in the company look askance at the advertising manager. For isn't he or she the character who spends all of that money; money which *could* have been pure profit?

One advertising manager tells the story of an unusually naive vice-president who reported he had had a complaint that the ad manager was "advertising the advertising department."

Seems that one of the company engineers had risen to the point where he was in charge of other engineers in marketing slots, hence qualified to receive the merchandising mailings. When he saw that it concerned advertising, that it discussed the company's campaign and the reasons why the copy platform was constructed as it was, he immediately lodged a vociferous protest with marketing brass, claiming that this was nobody's business except the advertising department's, and there was no need to trumpet advertising's thinking.

Naturally, this occurred in a backward company unaccustomed to any merchandising. Unfortunately, though, this negative attitude is encountered all to frequently, especially in small to medium-size companies where the level of marketing sophistication is low and product complexity is high. The two seem to accompany each other.

Use of Preprints and Reprints

About the most dismaying position an industrial salesperson can be is to be in the office of a prospect and receive a comment about a product that the company is currently advertising in several magazines, and then realize that he or she does not know *what* product it is.

Keeping key people in the company, including the field sales force, dealers, and others informed about what advertising is doing to help them is one of the most important functions of merchandising.

There's no need, of course, to merchandise each ad individually unless it is a kick-off ad in a new campaign, or introduces the most revolutionary widget ever devised, or something equally sensational. Instead, mail either preprints or reprints (one is before the ad appears, the other after) each month of each ad that runs. It's desirable to capsulize each ad with a brief description, including communications objective, media used, and so on.

Something you can do to make this material more relevant to the sales force is to present it from their viewpoint; relate the advertising to their activities. You could say, for instance, that this single month's advertising makes 2,567,432 impressions on 78,964 individual buying influences, 6,123 of whom are in their *territory*. (Give territorial breakdowns in an attached sheet). Doing so enables sales reps to relate advertising to themselves—which is what they're most interested in.

Media Will Help You Merchandise

You can dramatize your advertising, make it come alive, and give it the full importance it deserves by employing creative merchandising techniques developed by media.

No publication can tell you how to merchandise, of course. You're the best judge of that. But the good ones, such as *Iron Age* and others published by Chilton, will gladly share their vast merchandising experience with you upon request, and assist in the production of certain merchandising pieces. Let's see just what these and other good magazines will do for advertisers.

The publication itself is a great merchandising tool. There's no better way to tell your own people about your campaign than with copies of the magazine itself—with your ad suitably spotlighted. You may order as many copies of the magazine as you need, but as with most publications, this must be done at least three weeks (preferably more) in advance of publication.

Your ad can be spotlighted with bookmarks which tell the recipient of the magazine to turn to page so-and-so to see your ad. *Iron Age,* for example, will imprint a bookmark with a short message and your company name.

Thumbcuts can index your advertisement, just as they do in a dictionary or other reference volume. Because they're unusual and not often encountered in a trade magazine, they're fine attention-grabbers.

Acetate overlays imprinted with your message and firm name in one or two colors, and hinged to the cover of your selected issue of the magazine also make a strong impression.

Plastic bags with a copy of the magazine inserted and heat-sealed may be imprinted with your sales message in one or two colors. This gets the magazine to recipients in first-class condition, incidentally.

Letters, Blowups, Covers

Letters from the publisher—personal letters—can enhance your internal merchandising program. You control the contents of the letters, of course, and the publication prints, signs, and addresses them. Letters are effective to presell in advance of the campaign. Or, you can attach them to copies of the magazine or cover reprints.

Advertising blowups produce tremendous impact. Take even the most unassuming advertisement and blow it up to single sheet size (up to 22 by 28 inches for full page ads, 34 by 22 inches for spreads) and it takes on an entirely new personality. You can't overlook it, and you can't help but read it. Advertisement blowups can carry an imprint such as, "as advertised in *Iron Age.*" Brightly colored mailing tubes and breezy explanatory letters can be an important part of the overall effect.

Various cover folders are available from media, designed primarily for carrying a reproduction of your advertisement with additional areas for your selling copy. The actual cover of the issue in which your advertisement appears may be used.

Jigsaw puzzles never lose their fascination. Your advertisement is seen often—each time the puzzle is put together. *Iron Age* has dies for making puzzles from full-page ads and spread ads. Both types are conveniently packaged in a brightly colored box.

Display cards are available, consisting of your advertisement laminated on chipboard, with an easel backing. They are ideal for displaying your message within view of everyone, and can also be put to good use in a trade-show booth. They also carry the "as advertised in" imprint.

Giant matchbooks are available from *Iron Age*. They are tremendously potent merchandisers that present your advertisement and your message and firm name forcefully, all the while attracting a fantastic amount of attention.

Another impressive merchandising tool is plaqued ads. There are almost as many different ways of dressing up an ad reprint to make a handsome presentation piece out of it as there are business publications that will help you with your merchandising. (*All* of the good ones will.) These handsome pieces are designed to hang on the wall and come complete with all necessary hardware and attachments. They're obviously expensive (some are of solid walnut an inch thick). But if you run a decent schedule in a first-class magazine, they'll usually give you such items free of charge as long as you don't push a good thing too far by asking for too large a quantity, or asking too often. Best thing to do is to ask each magazine you use heavily just once a year, or twice at the most.

Incidentally an ad manager friend had publications he used mail out plaqued advertisements at the rate of one a month—that is, one publication mailed each month to a selected list of names. The plaqued ads were given to this advertiser at no charge, and the publications even packaged and mailed them, paying the postage. Yet several "marketing" people within that company who received these impressive merchandising pieces criticized him vociferously. One complained, "It cost 82 cents to mail this hunk of wood."

When it was explained that this merchandising cost the company not one red cent, these "marketing" people had the unmitigated temerity to suggest the ad manager try to get lower space rates instead of accepting merchandising from the publications. That ad manager said he muttered for days about the "bird-brained engineers who fancied themselves marketing men."

Plaqued ads make excellent displays to dress up district sales offices. They also look good in executive offices, and the reception room or lobby should contain several. Finally, the advertising department should display plaqued ads as part of a continuous program of putting its best foot forward.

Merchandising Allowance

For some reason or other, publication representatives don't offer pie in the sky to every advertiser. Fact is, most publications don't offer merchandising assistance of the no-charge variety *unless they're asked for it.*

Bear in mind the old bromide: The squeaking wheel gets the grease.

Almost every publication charges for extra copies of the magazine, reprints, overlays, blowups, and what have you, although this is not regarded as a profit center by media and every effort is made to hold costs down to a rock bottom minimum.

Nonetheless, almost every publication you're likely to consider seriously will give you a "merchandising allowance" if you ask for it. Depending upon the volume of business you do with the book (which translates into how much space you use each year), your allowance can be sizable. Always check on just what you're entitled to in the way of a merchandise allowance before committing yourself when you're on the fence and two books appear to be a stand-off value. The merchandising can make all the difference.

One proposal that's received widespread comment in the advertising world was made by Keith Gallimore, ad director at Harnischfeger Corporation. *Folio* magazine reported that Mr. Gallimore had suggested to the American Business Press that the money rebated in the form of a cash discount (usually 2 percent) be given instead as a merchandising allowance. This would, in effect, lay on the line exactly what you could expect from media.

This is a sensible proposal, one with much merit because the 2 percent cash discount for paying bills on time almost always reverts back to the controller's dollar-hungry grasp. How many ad managers receive this 2 percent as part of their budgets?

Once taken, it's put back in the company till, gone forever from where it actually belongs—in the funds appropriated for the advertising budget. Incidentally, you can make a strong (but probably losing) case that this 2 percent is really your department's, that it does *not* belong to the controller, and that you should be entitled to get it back.

Folio went on to say that in any event, "The 2 percent and its purpose should be written right into the advertising budget so that after the budget has been okayed, the controller won't expect to get his greedy hands around it later on."

External Merchandising

Since the objective of merchandising is to focus a bright spotlight on your advertising, thus increasing both its readership and its effectiveness, anything you can do to direct the attention of prospects and customers to it gives you that much more mileage from your promotional dollars.

Perhaps the major method of getting this additional mileage is to mail either preprints or reprints (the former produces more impact) of your advertisements to your customer-and-prospect mailing list. Some advertisers mail only the ad itself, although the smart ones use a professionally-written covering letter and include a postpaid business reply card; this is far more productive.

Your literature, catalogs, and other printed matter should retain the same general theme, graphic elements, and other distinctive features and devices used in your space advertising. Here, just as in advertising, constant repetition contributes immeasurably toward making a lasting impression.

Use publications in your external merchandising. Naturally, you can't afford to mail 19,000 copies of the magazine itself, nor would that be desirable. But it's a simple matter to isolate target accounts or key prospects and concentrate on them; investment won't be heavy when you do this, but returns—in sales—*will*. Chances are, depending on the type of business you're in, that your target accounts won't number more than a couple of dozen.

This is where the ducks are, so this is where to hunt them. Expend your merchandising ammunition here, don't scatter it all over the landscape so thinly it makes next to no impression. Concentration in merchandising, as in space advertising, pays off.

Dollars invested in merchandising probably won't total more than 5 percent of your total budget, but used wisely can increase the overall effectiveness of your program severalfold.

Chapter 23

THE BUDGET

ISOLATE one activity and hold it up for all to see as the one calcu-lated to give an industrial advertising manager conniptions—it's the annual wrestling match in which he or she pitted against that hideous ogre, the budget.

Most ad men regard it as like being in a rat race with the odds stacked in favor of the rats.

Ideally, budgeting should be done by politicians. They're born com-promisers, whereas advertising people are essentially pragmatists. There simply isn't the necessary wherewithal to accomplish even a respectable portion of the really important things that need to be done in the communications area. Invariably something has to give, and the *what* is what makes life so miserable for an ad manager at budget time that this person resembles a grizzly with a toothache.

Incidentally, let's clear the air as far as terminology is concerned. The words "appropriation" and "budget" are tossed around for all the world as if they meant the same thing. This is not the case.

"Appropriation," as any accountant or controller will be happy to tell you, actually means the maximum amount of dollars allocated for a specific purpose, whereas "budget" means the nuts-and-bolts details of *how* this sum of money will be used.

How Advertising Appropriations Are Determined

Industrial advertising appropriations (the *number* of dollars, not how they are to be used) are usually established in one of four ways in industry. Three of them are naive, unsophisticated, and ignore all sound principles of good management. Here is how industry does it:

1. By management fiat.
2. By percentage of sales.
3. By the competitive parity method.
4. By the task method.

The fiat, or edict, method of establishing the size of the advertising appropriation is used by almost half of all industrial companies. The company president, the sales manager, or the vice-president of marketing calls the ad manager into the office (or writes a memo) and presents a *fait accompli*. The conversation usually goes like this: "Your 'budget' for the next fiscal year is $000,000. Let me know what you plan to do with it." No reply is needed.

On the surface this seems logical enough. After all, it is management's prerogative to manage, isn't it? And this certainly should include managing the lifeblood of the business—money.

Do a little digging, though, and find out the *reason why* this specific sum was allotted for advertising. Invariably you'll find it is the exact amount management feels it can "spare" and still meet profit objectives. This is negative thinking right out of the last century. *It completely ignores the fact that advertising contributes to profits.*

Usually this situation is encountered in companies whose management is riddled with engineers and ex-engineers. Usually, too, there's a pathetic dearth of marketing savvy, although technical competence is high. This type of company is, above all else, dependable. It can be depended upon to have no formal marketing plan, no formal commnications plan, and the terms "marketing objectives" and "communications objectives" are so much gobbledygook.

"Everyone Else" Advertises

These backward managements are somewhat less than enthusiastic about "sparing" this money to "spend" on advertising, but reluctantly go along with it because almost all other companies (including competitors) advertise. Not to advertise might make them look bad to their peers.

They don't understand advertising, but you can bet your sweet life they *claim* they do. They don't *want* to understand advertising, so don't bother them with facts; their little minds are already made up. They haven't the slightest inkling of what advertising could contribute to their companies, but then, everybody *knows* advertising doesn't produce anything—it's a cost item. Trying to plant an idea in such minds is not sowing in fertile soil.

Setting the advertising appropriation by fiat doesn't consider the needs of the company, or what advertising can and should accomplish—how it should contribute to company profit by reducing the cost of selling. It's an archaic practice, but one that's going to be around for a long time. If you have to, learn to live with it, but continue the educational program you've established.

The practice of setting an advertising appropriation by allotting a certain percentage of sales (usually anticipated sales for the coming year, but not infrequently last year's actual sales) is commonplace in industry.

What it actually is is an attempt to set aside an optimum amount of money for the advertising appropriation, hoping against hope that it will be sufficient to accomplish what needs to be done—*without knowing what needs to be done.*

Establishing an appropriation for advertising by percentage of sales is as unsophisticated as the management fiat route. It ignores company aims and policies, marketing objectives, sales objectives, communications objectives, the competitive situation, the economic outlook, and similar matters that should be analyzed thoroughly before arriving at a firm figure.

Roughly one out of four industrial companies determine the advertising appropriation by the antiquated percentage of sales method. It's a great way to avoid facing reality.

The competitive parity method is a monkey-see, monkey-do performance, which should be discouraged vigorously and vociferously. It is nothing more than attempting to determine what major competitors are investing in their advertising programs, then matching them dollar for dollar.

Such a course of action ignores the fact that companies differ tremendously in products, marketing objectives, strengths and weaknesses in the market, rate of new product introductions, channels of distribution, size and efficiency of the field sales force, company image, and many other considerations.

Any attempt to allocate a so-called "industry average" sum for advertising—despite the fact that these figures are readily available for almost every industry—is a veiled attempt to be average rather than be a leader. How many companies have this as an objective?

Reacting to competitive advertising, rather than acting on your own initiative, is a sure road to failure. This applies just as much to appropriating a specific sum for advertising as it does to copycatting campaigns and a basic advertising philosophy.

About 25 percent of all industrial companies are sophisticated enough and possess enough know-how to work up an advertising appropriation *by the only valid method*—using the task approach.

The task method is the only logical, sensible method of establishing an appropriation because it is based firmly on the premise that enough money must be appropriated to achieve desired objectives. Inherent in the task method is stating objectives.

In most industrial companies, management—or, more likely, sales management—defines the goals, be they a certain dollar volume of sales, introduction of a new product, increased penetration into a certain market, or what have you. Acting on these goals, the advertising manager then sets communications objectives and decides what program will be most likely to produce the desired results.

How the budget is created from the appropriation and how the money is used to achieve the objectives is where past experience and seasoned professional judgment come into play.

The easiest and best way is to budget by objective (task) and assign all necessary money to each objective *by priority assigned by management*. Only top management has enough information about the company as a whole to make this decision.

The most serious error that can possibly be made is that of diluting the pressure put on each objective. If management has a caviar appetite and approves a hot-dog appropriation, it's certain that *none* of the objectives will be achieved if an inadequate sum of money is spread so thin that no real push is put on any one objective. Dollars will stretch just so far. Dilute them too much and they aren't used, they're wasted.

It's critically important that management be made to realize that a weak, wishy-washy attempt to achieve too many objectives with too little money will result in inevitable failure to achieve *any* of them. Management *must* assign priorities to objectives and leave it to advertising management to determine what is needed to achieve them—how much money is required—starting with the most important and working down. When the money is exhausted and some objectives are not budgeted for, it is up to management to decide if it is desirable to appropriate additional dollars to achieve them, or to accept the fact they can't be reached.

How to Present A Budget to Management

Assuming you've taken the task approach to determining what the advertising appropriation should be, all that remains to be done is to budget the allotted number of dollars by objective.

In order to get a budget approved "as submitted," you have to be prepared to outline and define advertising's role and functions and to present the objectives that investment of this money will attain. Merely presenting a breakdown of dollars and where they go doesn't say much, but setting forth objectives does.

Following is the budget presentation used by the director of advertising and sales promotion for the GATX Corporation. Working with various members of the company and its divisions and with the vice-president and account executive at Edward H. Weiss Company, the GATX advertising agency, he prepared the following presentation for the company's program. It is complete, just as presented to GATX management, although various elements are not "priced out" for competitive reasons. Accumulating this information, including internal costs, and presenting them on a summary sheet, presents no problem, however.

In addition to this presentation, the director prepared a slide presentation which highlighted the written portion and included layouts of proposed ads, a review of competitive activity, and a summary of results of past programs—along with a detailed dollar-by-dollar breakdown of his suggested budget.

His suggested program was so on-target and his method of explaining what the appropriation would buy was so clear and forceful that management approved it virtually as presented. A portion of that presentation follows:

FOREWORD

The development and subsequent implementation of an effective advertising, public relations and sales promotion program *must* start from a firm base of clearly defined, reasonably attainable objectives.

The following programs proposed by the Advertising, Public Relations, and Sales Promotion Department were developed from such a base.

CORPORATE COMMUNICATIONS OBJECTIVES

I. To present GATX as . . .

    a. The prime source for the lease or purchase of railroad cars with special emphasis on tank, covered hopper, and other special purpose cars.

    b. The operator (lessor) of the nation's largest and most comprehensive systems of tank storage terminals.

    c. The designer and builder of all types of freight cars—serving both shippers and the railroads.

    d. The fabricator and erector of a wide range of steel vessels, and their attendant "environment," for liquids, gases and dry bulk materials.

    e. The prime source for custom molding of plastics; as well as a marketer of a *quality* proprietary line of plastic products.

    f. The designers, fabricators, and erectors of an extensive line of engineered equipment and systems used in mining, processing, manufacturing, and in the control of air and water pollution.

    g. A company energetically involved in research and development work for both government and industry, along with R&D for its own products and services.

    h. A *growth* company that has diversified and is diversifying along a carefully charted course that will afford the opportunity to better serve its customers and shareholders.

II. To deliver our Corporate "messages" to the many audiences of importance to GATX via the most effective and efficient means at our disposal—publication advertising, public relations, direct mail, brochures, trade shows, company publications, and a variety of other sales promotion tools.

The "audiences" of GATX are defined, in descending order of importance as:

    a. Present and future customers.

    b. Key influences in the financial community.

    c. Present and future stockholders.

    d. Suppliers.

    e. Government officials, educators, opinion molders, and thought leaders.

III. To make certain that our corporate messages are disseminated in a way that will enable us to reach, with greater efficiency and frequency, our present customers and prospects. This primary segment of our "audience" is defined by industry as:

    a. Chemical.

    b. Petroleum.

    c. Petrochemical.

    d. Food.

    e. Cement and nonmetallic mining.

    f. Railroads.

By job function as:

    a. Top management.

    b. Traffic and distribution management.

    c. Engineering and operating management.

CORPORATE MEDIA PLAN

The following corporate advertising media plan was designed to give maximum coverage of our prime audience as defined by Communications Objective II and further spelled out in Objective III.

The media plan allows us, for the first time, to hit *directly* and with *force* our customers and propsects in those industries of importance to the present and future prosperity of GATX.

It will reach top and middle management people in the chemical, petrochemical, petroleum, food, mining and railroad industries. Plus, it will give coverage of traffic and distribution managers across all industries.

The plan is designed to provide frequency, continuity, and impact against the target audiences, at reasonable cost, consistent with our objective.

We recommend the use of the leading publication(s) in the specific industries of prime interest to GATX, to present our corporate messages to the buying influences by industry and/or job function.

Chemical Process Industry and Petrochemicals	*Chemical Week*
Petroleum and Hydrocarbon Processing Industry	*Oil & Gas Journal*
Food Processing Industry	*Food Engineering*
Mining and Cement	*Pit & Quarry* *Rock Products*
Railroads	*Modern Railroads* *Railroad Age*
Traffic and Managers	*Traffic World* *Traffic Management*

To *increase* the penetration of our corporate messages to the required specific industries, as well as give us needed coverage across the entire industrial spectrum, we recommend the continued use of a business management publication, *Business Week*.

Each of the recommended publications has been evaluated in terms of upper and middle management people reached, circulation delivered, editorial environment, and cost efficiency.

While the publications listed cover different industries, they share one thing in common . . . their proven ability to deliver a quality audience—the decision makers that are of primary importance to GATX.

In essence, this plan is one of *high frequency* and *direction* based on carefully defined objectives.

PROPOSED CORPORATE ADVERTISING MEDIA PLAN

Business Week	13 color pages	
Chemical Week	6 color spreads—12 color pages	
Oil & Gas Journal	6 color spreads— 6 color pages	
Food Engineering	6 color spreads— 6 color pages	
Pit & Quarry	3 color spreads— 3 color pages	
Rock Products	3 color spreads— 3 color pages	
Traffic World	6 color spreads— 6 color pages	
Traffic Management	6 color spreads— 6 color pages	
Modern Railroads	6 color spreads— 6 color pages	
Railway Age	6 color spreads— 6 color pages	
Estimated Advertising Space		$370,000.00
Estimated Advertising Production		60,000.00
	Total	$430,000.00

The presentation continued with similar sections covering corporate publicity, financial public relations, etc.

Nearby are two ads from the great GATX campaign. They stress the service the company provides, and also emphasize how GATX can free capital for customers to use to better advantage elsewhere—rather than putting it into rolling stock and terminal handling facilities which, happily, can be leased from GATX.

These fine ads from this outstanding campaign have earned excellent readership ratings. They are doing the job assigned to them and then some.

The manager of the GATX Tank Car Division went on record in writing that this advertising program—and the direct mail program—"helped us maintain a very high lease/sale ratio."

What's more, the Chicago Chapter of the Business/Professional Advertising Association awarded its coveted Silver Award (second place) for excellence for integrated advertising campaigns. GATX also won a Silver Spike Award from the Association of Railroad Advertising Managers, "to recognize those advertisers whose promotion of their own products and services augments the individual and collective efforts of railroad advertisers, thus creating a better understanding on the part of the public of the importance of railroads in the transportation system of America and encouraging the development of additional rail freight and passenger traffic."

Besides all of this, the director received yet another award that same week from *Chemical Week* through Reader Feedback. The GATX ad was "right up there" in the letter grade scores, receiving an A+ rating.

By all means when you have successes like these, mention them in your presentation; they show management how hard your advertising campaign is working, how much benefit it is providing the company.

How to Get Management to Look Favorably on a Budget

According to McGraw-Hill, there are an even half-dozen key points to remember when preparing a budget for submission to management:

1. Educate yourself about the marketing problems confronting management in today's economy.
2. Gather and present evidence to show how advertising can help solve these problems.
3. Help management formulate immediate and long-range marketing policies.
4. Use every opportunity to set forth the fundamental values of your company's advertising in reducing marketing costs, building customer preference and acceptance, protecting and improving market positions, increasing sales, and expanding profits.
5. Develop arguments to demonstrate that your company can't afford to stop or curtail effective product advertising, regardless of current, temporary conditions.
6. Know management objections to advertising—*and* the answers to them.

There are two final things which help assure budget acceptance.

First, don't "go in high." Be forthright and honest. Tell management—probably your boss, the vice-president of marketing—that your budget is an honest one. Impress on him or her that you haven't deliberately padded it in anticipation of having the top brass take a whack at it with a meat ax. Stress that it is realistic and represents what is, in your considered opinion, the least dollars that can be expected to achieve the objectives.

If you submit an inflated budget in anticipation of having it cut, management will surely do so. Then, sooner or later, it will be ap-

Two of the great ads from the GATX campaign, a series which won several awards and a host of letters from industry people praising the general concept. The copy made great sense to railroad people and to people using railroads.

parent to the discerning that you're not *really* unhappy with the cut; furthermore, sooner or later, it will also be apparent that the objectives were achieved, or very nearly so. When this happens it's only a matter of time until you submit a budget, management cuts it; you resubmit, management recuts, you resubmit . . . and the games goes on and on. *You can't win it.*

Second thing to do is indicate an anticipated cash flow so that management knows approximately what to expect—that is, the timing of major expenditures. For instance, your production expense for producing ads will be heavy during the first quarter of the year, and probably completed in the first half. Merely knowing what to expect will make your controller happier and having this goodwill (or as good as you can expect to get) isn't to be regarded lightly. You don't have to tell exactly when each single last penny will be invoiced to the company, but give a good general idea of the *pattern* that's to be expected.

Finally, don't let every cat-and-dog expense in the company be foisted off on you. Stand up on your hind legs and fight against having miscellaneous charges against the advertising budget.

Don't let the company picnic, employee dances, labels and cartons, price lists, market research, the president's wife's flower gardens, sales meeting costs, sales rep's samples, the house organ, the annual report, nameplates, display signs, and so on and on be charged to advertising. This is a deceptive dodge that ultimately will cost the company dearly. Stop it before it becomes an entrenched practice—as it is in many companies today.

The Contingency Fund

One last thing you should budget for is the unexpected. Depending upon the size of your budget, approximately 2½ percent of the total should be earmarked "contingency fund."

The contingency fund makes available dollars to produce that unexpected piece of literature, that unexpected piece of research, that unexpected this or that. One thing you can predict with assurance is the unexpected. It always happens.

When you budget for it you're able to handle it without having to request a supplementary appropriation; always an undesirable thing to have to do.

Don't make the mistake, though, of "giving back" any unused portion of the contingency fund. The controller has no claim to it. Instead, plan ahead to use any unspent dollars where they will do the most good—a few extra pages for space ads for a product that's not moving as it should, an extra direct mail piece and mailing for an ailing product—anything constructive and productive.

APPENDIX

GLOSSARY OF TERMS RELATING TO BUSINESS PUBLICATION AUDITS

Following is a glossary of terms relating to business publications auditing; it was developed by the Association of Industrial Advertisers and is used here with its permission.

ADDITIONS: New names, either of individuals or companies, added to a publication's mailing list.

ADVANCE RENEWAL: A subscription which has been renewed prior to the expiration of a previous subscription.

ADVERTISED PRICE: The basic price of publication. (See Basic Price.)

ARREARS: Subscribers whose names are retained on active subscription list after the period for which they are paid has expired.

ASSOCIATION SUBSCRIPTIONS:

    a. Deductible association subscription.

      Individual subscription paid for out of association membership dues where the recipient has the option of deducting the subscription price from his dues if he does not wish to receive the publication.

    b. Nondeductible association subscription.

      Individual subscription paid for out of association membership dues where the recipient does not have the option of deducting the subscription price from the dues and automatically receives the publication.

AUDIENCE: The total number of individuals exposed to any part of the content of a publication. Synonymous with total audience.

AUDIENCE, PASSALONG: Individuals, other than addressees, who are exposed to some part of the content of a publication.

AUDIENCE, PRIMARY: Individuals for whom a magazine is edited and who are exposed to some part of the content, and who receive it first in order of time.

AUDIENCE, TOTAL: See Audience.

AUDIT: Examination of publisher's records and corroborative data in order to check for correctness of the Publisher's Statements covering the period audited.

AUDIT REPORT: A document attesting to the accuracy and validity of a publisher's circulation claims, not to be confused with Publisher's Statement.

AVERAGE PAID: Average circulation, qualified as paid circulation, of all the issues, arrived at by dividing the total of all the paid copies during the period by the total number of issues.

BACK COPIES: Copies of periodicals of date prior to the current issue.

BASIC PRICE: The price at which a copy or a subscription may be purchased, as opposed to a special price.

BREAKDOWN: The division of circulation as to types of business or industry reached, the functions or titles of recipients, and/or their demographic characteristics or geographical location.

BULK SALES:

    a. Definitions applicable to Audit Bureau of Circulations.

      All copies or subscriptions purchased in quantities of five or more which promote the business or professional interests of the purchaser.

RECIPIENT QUALIFIED: Individuals who receive a publication and who conform to the recipient qualification requirements within the field served.

REFERENCE MEDIA: Books or publications of periodic issue giving statistical data and designed to be kept for reference.

RELIABILITY: In sampling, the degree of the stability any measure found within the sample is likely to have in the universe from which the sample was drawn. Measures of reliability (the measures of stability of the data) are used in market research to determine the point at which a sample is of adequate size to assure that a larger sample under the same procedures would not affect appreciably any values.

REMOVALS: Names of individuals or companies removed from the mailing list of a publication.

RENEWAL: A subscription which has been renewed prior to or at expiration or within six months thereafter.

RENEWAL PERCENTAGE: The ratio of subscription renewals to the total subscriptions possible of being renewed, during a specified period of time.

REPLATE: A change of one or more pages during the printing of an edition or issue of a newspaper or periodical. This procedure generally serves the purpose of adding late news items or of correcting an error in the original copy.

REPORT, AUDIT: See Audit Report.

REQUEST CIRCULATION: See Circulation, Request.

SAMPLE COPIES: Copies distributed free to prospective subscribers or prospective advertisers and copies distributed at shows, conventions or by publishers' sales reps for potential prospects.

SHORT TERM SUBSCRIPTION: Subscription for less than a year.

SINGLE COPY SALES IN BULK: See Bulk Sales.

SPLIT-RUN: The insertion or substitution of different advertising content for a portion of the distribution of an edition or of an issue for either a newspaper or periodical.

SPONSORED SUBSCRIPTIONS: Subscriptions obtained through cooperation between publisher and an organized local civic or charitable organization, members of schools, churches, fraternal or similar organizations, publisher donating a percentage of the subscription price to the organization involved.

STANDARD INDUSTRIAL CLASSIFICATION: A numerical coding system developed by the Bureau of the Budget used in the classification of business establishments according to the principal end-product made or service performed at that location.

STANDARDIZATION: A system for classifying recipients in terms of business or title or function that is uniform for all publications serving the same general field.

SUBSCRIBER: An individual, firm or corporation that orders and pays for a subscription to a publication. (See Subscription)

SUBSCRIPTION: Contractual agreement by an individual or firm to purchase one or more copies of a publication for a given period which conforms to established rules.

SUBSCRIPTION AGENCY: An individual, firm or corporation obtaining subscriptions for two or more publications. Subscriptions (except those resulting from a direct mail effort) produced for one publisher by another publisher are classed in Audit Bureau reports along with those obtained through agencies.

SUBSCRIPTIONS:

Association—See Association Subscriptions.

Bulk—See Bulk Sales.

Credit—See Credit Subscriptions.

Feature Issue—See Feature Issue Subscriptions.

Franchise—See Circulation, Franchise.

Gift—See Gift Subscriptions.

Group—See Group (Mail Subscriptions Special).

Installment—See Installment Subscriptions.

Intermittent—See Feature Issue Subscriptions.

Mail Subscriptions Special—See Group (Mail Subscriptions Special).

Monthly Payment—See Monthly Payment Subscriptions.

Paid—See Paid Subscriptions.

Short Term—See Short Term Subscription.

Sponsored—See Sponsored Subscriptions.

Term Bulk—See Bulk Sales.

Trial—See Short Term Subscriptions.

SUBSCRIPTION SALES REP: One who, as a regular or temporary or part-time vocation, solicits subscriptions for a publication. He or she may receive compensation on either salary or commission basis or both.

SUBSCRIPTION SALES REP'S COPIES: Copies of a publication carried by a subscription salesperson to aid in obtaining subscriptions. (See Sample Copies.)

TERM SUBSCRIPTIONS IN BULK: See Bulk Sales.

TITLE: An appellation given by a firm to certain of its personnel by virtue of their rank or function.

TOTAL AUDIENCE: See Audience.

TOTAL PAID: Total of all classes of a publication's distribution for which the purchasers have paid in accordance with the standards set by the rules.

TRAFFIC, READER: A measure of the number of readers who look at or are exposed to the different pages of an issue of a publication. Usually expressed as number of readers per page.

TRIAL SUBSCRIPTIONS: See Short Term Subscriptions.

TWO-PAY PLAN: Designation of sales plan under which the subscription solicitor collects from the subscriber a portion of the subscription price and the publisher or the subscription agency receives the balance direct from the subscriber. Some publishers refuse to start service until second payment is received.

UNIT: An establishment primarily engaged in one type of economic activity at a single physical location.

UNIT COUNT: The number of units included in a publication's circulation.

UNIVERSE: The total units or individuals under consideration.

UNPAID COPIES: Copies distributed either entirely free or at a price inadequate to qualify them as paid in accordance with established rules.

VALIDATE: To testify, as one in a postion to know, to the truthfulness or reliability of evidence.

VERIFY: To prove to be true; to establish the correspondence between evidence and actual fact.

VOCATIONAL CLASSIFICATION: See Occupational Classification.

WASTE: That part of a publication's distribution considered to be valueless to the individual advertiser because of the absence of any relevance between the advertiser's proposition and the recipient's business interest.

Seven Deadly Sins

In his handbook on direct mail, Richard S. Hodgson quoted from the "Copy Chasers" who write a monthly column in *Industrial Marketing* magazine. The Copy Chasers' comments on the seven deadliest sins committed by industrial advertisers augment the cardinal rules and provide a checklist against which to measure a direct mail program. Sins are:

1. *The sin of being a braggart.* A lot of industrial advertising is like the blowhard—the man who interminably insists that he is better than the next guy. Claiming superiority, in itself, is not necessarily wrong—unless little or nothing is done to substantiate the claim in a friendly, persuasive, and convincing manner.

2. *The sin of talking to yourself*—instead of thinking of the other fellow. The most creative industrial advertising is that which directs its remarks to the interests of the readers—not to the interests of the company doing the talking.

3. *The sin of preaching.* Faced with white paper to fill, some advertisers get a compulsion to lecture. Looking down upon the reader from the high altitude of their superiority, they *tell* the reader—rather than *invite*—to do what they want him or her to do.

4. *The sin of being noisy.* Everybody hates the bugler, but a good many advertisers believe they have to make a big noise in order to get readers to stand at attention. If you have something interesting to say about a subject of interest to readers, there is no need to set your hair on fire in order to catch their eye.

5. *The sin of being messy.* Nobody likes the man who is messy, dirty, or inconsiderate. A lot of advertising, unfortunately, can be so described.

6. *The sin of trying to be cute.* Don't be a smart-aleck in industrial advertising. Deliver your story in as straightforward a manner as possible—and you'll get more applause from your audience than if you put on an act.

7. *The sin of being dull.* Of all the deadly sins of industrial advertising, the worst by far is being dull. Almost all an advertising person is expected to do is to enliven the sales message with a crisp presentation of visual elements and some fast-moving copy.

How Industrial Direct Mail Should Be Used

Guidelines used and accepted by almost every successful practitioner of industrial direct mail advertising have been established by the Direct Mail/Marketing Association.

These guidelines have been proved effective, efficient, and well thought out through the years. Numerous organizations have organized numerous committees to consider and reconsider the subject of direct mail advertising, and to date none of them has either expanded or changed this comprehensive checklist.

DMMA has suggested that it be used to analyze direct mail programs in three main areas:

I. Checking the ways you are now using direct mail.

II. Marking the ways you are not now using direct mail but which could be profitable possibilities.

III. Double-checking those direct mail applications you are now using that could be altered, improved, or increased—for greater results, effectiveness, and efficiency.

IN YOUR OWN ORGANIZATION:

1. *Building Morale of Employees*—A bulletin or house magazine published regularly, carrying announcements of company policy, stimulating ambition, encouraging thrift, promoting safety and efficiency, will make for greater loyalty among employees.

2. *Securing Data from Employees*—Letters or questionnaires occasionally directed to employees help cement a common interest in the organization and bring back practical ideas and much useful data.

3. *Stimulating Salespeople to Greater Efforts*—Interesting sales magazines, bulletins, or letters help in unifying a scattered selling organization, in speeding up sales, and in making better salespeople—by carrying success stories and sound ideas that have made sales.

4. *Paving the Way for Salespeople*—Forceful and intelligent direct mail, persistent and continuous, will create a field of prospective buyers who are live and ready to be sold.

5. *Securing Inquiries for Salespeople*—Direct mail can bring back actual inquiries from interested prospective customers—qualified prospects your salespeople can call upon and sell.

6. *Teaching Salespeople "How to Sell"*—A sales manual, or a series of messages, will help educate and stimulate salespeople to close more and bigger sales.

7. *Selling Stockholders and Others Interested in Your Company*—Enclosures with dividend checks and in pay envelopes, and other direct messages, will sell stockholders and employees on making a greater use of company products and services, and in suggesting their use to others.

8. *Keeping Contact with Customers Between Sales Calls*—Messages to customers between sales calls will help secure for your firm the maximum amount of business from each customer.

9. *Further Selling Prospective Customers After a Demonstration or Sales Call*—Direct mail emphasizing the superiorities of your product or service will help clinch sales and make it difficult for competition to gain a foothold.

10. *Acknowledging Orders or Payments*—An interesting letter, folder, or mailing card is a simple gesture which will cement a closer relationship between you and your customers.

11. *Welcoming New Customers*—A letter welcoming new customers can go a long way toward keeping them sold on your company, products and services.

12. *Collecting Accounts*—A series of diplomatic collection letters will bring and keep accounts up-to-date, leave the recipients in a friendly frame of mind, and hold them as customers.

BUILDING NEW BUSINESS

13. *Securing New Dealers*—Direct mail offers many concerns unlimited possibilities in lining up and selling new dealers.

14. *Securing Direct Orders*—Many organizations have built extremely profitable business through orders secured only with the help of direct mail. Many concerns not presently selling direct by mail can and should do so.

15. *Building Up Weak Territories*—Direct mail will provide intensified local sales stimulation wherever you may wish to apply it.

16. *Winning Back Inactive Customers*—A series of direct mail messages to "lost" customers often revives many of them.

17. *Developing Sales in Territories Not Covered By Salespeople*—Communities unapproachable because of distance (bad transportation schedules, or poor roads), offer the alert organization vast possibilities to increase its sales direct-by-mail.

18. *Developing Sales Among Specified Groups*—With direct mail you can direct your selling messages specifically to those you wish to sell, in the language they will understand, and in a form that will stimulate action.

19. *Following Inquiries Received from Direct Advertising or Other Forms of Advertising*—A series of messages outlining the "reasons why" your product or service should be bought will help you cash in on inquirers whose initial interest was aroused by other media—publications, radio, television, and so on.

20. *Driving Home Sales Arguments*—Several mailings, each planned to stress one or more selling points, will progressively educate your prospective customer on the many reasons why he or she should buy your product or service—and from you.

21. *Selling Other Items in Line*—Mailing pieces, package inserts, or handout folders will educate your customers on products and services other than those they are buying.

22. *Getting Product Prescribed or Specified*—Professionals, such as physicians and dentists, will prescribe a product for their patients if they are correctly educated on its merits and what it will accomplish. Likewise, consumers and dealers will ask for a product by name if they are thoroughly familiar with it. Direct advertising can be profitably used for this purpose.

23. *Selling New Type of Buyer*—Perhaps there are new outlets through which your product or service might be sold. Direct mail is a powerful tool in the development of new sales channels.

ASSISTING PRESENT DEALERS

24. *Bringing Buyer to Showroom*—Invitations through letter or printed announcements will bring prospective customers to your showroom or factory.

25. *Helping Present Dealer Sell More*—Assisting your dealer with direct mail and "point of purchase" helps will sell your product or service faster, step up turnover. The right kind of dealer helps will win hearty cooperation.

26. *Merchandising Your Plans to Dealer*—Direct mail can forcefully present and explain your merchandising plans to the dealer, and show how to put your promotion ideas and material to work as sales-builders.

27. *Educating Dealers on Superiorities of Your Product or Service*—Memories are short when it comes to remembering the other fellow's product or service and its superiorities, especially when you keep telling your dealers the benefits and advantages of your own.

28. *Educating Retail Clerks in the Selling of a Product*—Clerks are the neck of the retail selling bottle. If they believe in a company and a product, their influence is a powerful aid to sales. If indifferent, they lose their sales-making effectiveness. Direct mail that is friendly, understanding, helpful, and stimulating will enlist their cooperation and up the sales curve.

29. *Securing Information from Dealers or Dealers' Clerks*—Letters, printed messages, a bulletin, or a house magazine will bring back helpful data from the individuals who actually sell your product or your service—information you can pass along to other dealers or sales clerks to help them sell more.

30. *Referring Inquiries from Consumer Advertising to Local Dealers*—The manufacturer can use direct mail to refer an inquirer to his local dealer for prompt attention. At the same time, the dealer can be alerted with the details of the prospect's inquiry.

THE CONSUMER

31. *Creating a Need or a Demand for a Product*—Direct mail, consistently used, will stimulate the demand for your product or service, and will remind the customer to ask for it by name.

32. *Increasing Consumption of a Product Among Present Users*—Package inserts, booklets, etc. can be used to educate customers to the full use of the products they buy, especially new benefits and advantages.

33. *Bringing Customers into a Store to Buy*—This applies to retailers; personal, friendly, cordial, and interesting direct mail messages, telling about the merchandise, will bring back past customers, stimulate present patrons, and lure new people to you.

34. *Opening New Charge Accounts*—This also applies to retailers. There are many people in every community who pay their bills promptly and do the bulk of their buying where they have accounts. A careful compilation of such a list and a well-planned direct mail program inviting them to open charge accounts will bring new customers to your store.

35. *Capitalizing on Special Events*—Direct mail helps retailers to capitalize on such events as marriages, births, graduations, promotions, etc. Likewise, letters can be sent to select lists featuring private sales. Other lists and format can cover general sales.

OTHER USES

36. *Building Goodwill*—The possibilities of building goodwill and solidifying friendships through direct advertising are unlimited. It's the little handshake through the mail that cements business relationships and holds your customers. Certain "reminder" forms also can help build goodwill.

37. *Capitalizing on Other Advertising*—Direct advertising is the salesmate of all other media. As the workhorse among advertising and promotion mediums, it helps the sponsor capitalize on the investment in all visual and audio advertising—especially when initial interest can be given a lift and converted into action and sales.

38. *As a "Leader" or "Hook" in Other Forms of Advertising*—Publication space, as well as radio and television commercials, is often too limited to tell enough of the story about a product or service to make a sale. Direct mail provides the leader or hook—in the form of booklets, folders, catalogs, instruction manuals—that other mediums of advertising cannot feature, to stimulate action as well as to satisfy the inquirer with full story of product or service.

39. *Breaking Down Resistance to a Product or Service*—Direct mail helps to overcome resistance in the minds of prospective customers.

40. *Stimulating Interest in Forthcoming Events*—A special "week" or "day" devoted to the greater use of a product; an anniversary, a new line launched by a dealer, special "openings," and scores of other happenings can all be promoted by direct mail to produce sales.

41. *Distribution of Samples*—There are thousands of logical prospects who could be converted into users of your product if you proved to them its merits. Direct mail can help you do this by letting prospects convince themselves by actual test . . . provided your product lends itself to sampling by mail.

42. *Announcing a New Product, New Policy, or New Addition*—There is no quicker way to make announcements to specific individuals or groups, to create interest and stimulate sales, than through the personal, action-producing medium—direct mail.

43. *Announcing a New Address or Change in Telephone Number*—When these important changes are made, a letter or printed announcement sent through the mail has a personal appeal that will register your message better than any other medium.

44. *Keeping a Concern or Product "In Mind"*—Direct advertising includes many

forms of "reminder" advertising—blotters, calendars, novelties. Regular mailings help keep you in the minds of customers and prospects.

45. *Research for New Ideas and Suggestions*—Direct advertising is a powerful force in building sales. Direct mail can be used to find market facts, cut sales fumbling, chart direct, profitable trails to sales. It furnishes all the important tools for sales research, to discover what, where, how, and to whom to sell—and at what price.

46. *Correcting Present Mailing Lists*—Householders have an average annual change rate of 22 percent; merchants of 23 percent; agents of 29 percent; advertising personnel of 37 percent. Keeping a mailing list up-to-date is a most important detail. Direct mail can be employed to keep your list accurate by asking your customer occasionally if the name and address are correct, of if there are others in the organization you should be reaching.

47. *Securing Names for Lists*—Direct mail can help you build mailing lists by securing names of customers and prospects from many sources—such as direct from distributors, sales reps, clerks, stockholders, employees; from people who have access to the names of individuals in specific groups; from recommendation of customers and friends; from special mail surveys, questionnaires, etc.

48. *Protecting Patents or Special Processes*—Shouting forth the ownership of such patents or processes by direct advertising can leave no question in the minds of your customers, present or prospective, as to who owns such a product or process. At the same time, it gives you greater protection from possible infringers.

49. *Raising Funds*—Direct advertising can afford an effective, economical method of raising funds for worthy causes.

Mail-Oriented Agencies

Here are some of the leading specialists in the country in the direct mail medium, and they are the creators of exceptionally fine campaigns—both consumer and industrial.

Ansa-Letter, 200 Hudson St., New York City 10013	(212) 966-4500
Buckley-Dement DM Advertising, 555 West Jackson Blvd., Chicago, IL 60606	(312) 427-3862
Lawrence G. Chait, 430 West Merrick Road, Valley Stream, NY 11502	(516) 825-2699
Dickie Raymond—A Metromedia Company, 485 Lexington Ave., New York City 10017	(212) 682-9100
Franklin & Joseph, Inc., 641 Lexington Ave., New York City 10022	(212) 759-8801
Cliff Kelley, Inc., 2850 South Jefferson Ave., St. Louis, MO 63118	(314) 664-0023
Kobs & Brady Advertising, Inc., 625 North Michigan Ave., Chicago, IL 60611	(312) 944-3500
Herbert Krug & Associates, 500 Davis St., Evanston, IL 60201	(312) 864-0550
Nat Lazar, 1 Jane Street, New York City 10014	(212) 929-7068
Mail and Media Inc., 32-02 Queens Blvd., Long Island City, NY 11102	(212) 784-6800
McVicker & Higginbotham, Inc., 113 Atlantic Ave., Brooklyn, NY 11201	(212) 522-2940
R.L. Polk & Co., 431 Howard St., Detroit, MI 48231	(313) 961-9470

Reply-O-Letter: 1860 Broadway, New York City 10023   (212) 245-8118
148 State Street, Boston, MA 02109   (617) 426-1555

Sales Letter, Inc., 307 West 36 St., New York City 10018   (212) 279-4800

Smith & Hemmings, 2000 Pasadena, Los Angeles, CA 90031   (213) 223-3241

Maxwell Sroge Company, Inc., 731 N. Cascade,
Colorado Springs, CO 80903   (303) 633-5556

William Steiner Associates, Inc., 135 East 55 St.,
New York City 10022   (212) 688-7030

Stone & Adler Inc., 150 North Wacker Drive, Chicago, IL 60606   (312) 346-6100

Sales Problems

According to Jim Smiley, vice-president of Graphic Service, sales problems are very much like construction problems. They fit into certain well-defined groups. These groups, he explains, are as different as sawing wood and pounding nails.

Once they're analyzed and understood, however, and the right kind of program for each is developed, the direct mail advertiser is well on the road to success. The 15 classes of programs Graphic has defined are:

1. *Assistant Salesperson Program.* If you can identify your customers and prospects by name, but feel that your salespeople can't call on every prospect often enough—or if you need to increase sales effectiveness—this is the program you need.

2. *Favorable Opinion Program.* If your salespeople find it difficult to get prospects to be "open minded" toward your company or product—or if you want your prospects to say to themselves, "That's the kind of company I'd like to do business with . . ."—This fills the bill.

3. *Prospect Qualifying Program.* If you want prospects to identify themselves as warm (or hot) prospects for your particular product—or if you want to get leads for followup phone or personal calls—or if you want to supply leads to your distributors or dealers or retailers—this is the ticket.

4. *List Building Program.* If you'd like to promote your better prospects by mail, but have only a general idea of who they are, you need this program.

5. *Door Opener Program.* If you know who your best prospects are but your sales reps, branches, distributors or dealers have a difficult time getting in to see them (either because they are protected executives; are blocked behind a purchasing agent you can't "go around"; or are impatient when your salesperson calls with "nothing new")—or if you want to make it easy for your salespeople to call on new prospects—this is for you.

6. *New Product Program.* If you have a new product to introduce to new markets, or a real change in your product to promote, or other real news to get to your prospects—or if you are moving your current products into new markets—this is the one to do the job.

7. *Traffic Builder Program.* If you have a retail store, or if you are a manufacturer or distributor with a relatively "big ticket" product, sold through retail stores—or if you are showing your product at an important show and want people to come to you—choose this program.

8. *Account Reactivator Program.* If sales to some distributors or dealers have fallen off sharply or stopped altogether, or if you have lost customers and know their names

and addresses—or if charge account customers have stopped buying from you—you need this.

9. *Fact Finder Program.* If you want to know what your customers think of your product; what your distributors think of you; how your product is being used; why people have stopped buying; whether they'll buy the new product you're thinking about; or any other kind of research or survey dealing with facts or opinions, go this route.

10. *"Pure Advertising" Program.* If you want to educate your prospects and customers about the benefits your product has to offer; or if you want them to be sure to think of you when they are ready to buy or to ask for bids—or if you want to make a strong company or brand impression—take this tack.

11. *"Sales Stimulator" Program.* If you want your salespeople to work harder; or if you want your distributor, wholesaler, or retailer's salespeople to mention, demonstrate or sell your product more effectively—or if you want more dealers signed up, or want service personnel to sell your product—you need this program.

12. *"Sampling" Program.* If you have a product that "sells itself" to most users once they try it, and it's the kind of a product that can be sampled, or tried out, this program is tailor made.

13. *Mail Order Program.* If you want to open and stock retail outlets entirely by mail; or get industrial buyers to order direct from the factory; or cover those "open" territories where your distributors are weak or nonexistent—or get ultimate users to send in orders by mail—this program is made to order.

14. *Subscription Program.* If you're selling subscriptions to magazines, or plays, or book clubs, or records or anything else that goes on and on—this is a producer.

15. *Fund Raising Program.* If you are interested in an organization that depends on gifts, or on "memberships," for support, go this way to go over the top.

Each of these problems has a "best" kind of direct mail answer, and the techniques that work for one problem may fail on another. That's one reason why direct mail is so difficult for most people. They often "adapt" successful campaigns which look great and worked fine for somebody else, but don't fit their problems—hence don't do the job.

The analytical and creative thinking at Graphic Service is the product of more than a quarter-century of direct mail experience. Specialty of the house in the organization is ferreting out the problem, determining what it *really* is—sometimes the manufacturer or other client doesn't actually understand it, so an outside viewpoint is mandatory—and then developing the one best direct mail program to solve it. This Graphic Service does exceedingly well from its headquarters at 846 South Main Street, Dayton, Ohio 45402.

List Brokers

Following is a list of active mailing list brokers. Almost every conceivable list for both consumer and industrial direct mail advertising may be rented through these brokers, or your list may be offered through them.

Just as you don't necessarily buy your new automobile from the first dealer to whom you talk, neither should you leap at the first offer from the first broker you talk with. Time spent on writing a few letters, explaining in detail just what it is you need (or offer), on phone calls, or in personal visits, is well invested.

You'll find these brokers are knowledgeable professionals who are anxious to do business with you—and to help you.

Accredited Mlg. Lists, Inc., 3 Park Ave., New York City 10016	(212) 889-1180
George Bryant & Staff, 71 Grand Ave., Englewood, NJ 07631	(201) 688-2651
The Coolidge Co., Inc., 25 West 43rd St., New York City 10036	(212) 730-5660
Dependable Lists, Inc., 257 Park Ave., South, New York City 10010	(212) 677-6760
Alan Drey Co., Inc., 333 North Michigan Ave., Chicago, IL 60601	(312) 346-7453
Guild Co., 171 Terrace, Haworth, NJ 07641	(201) 387-1023
Walter Karl, Inc., 33 Maple Ave., Armonk, NY 10504	(212) 324-3336
Levine Ceil Screened Mailing Lists, 250 West 57th St., New York City 10019	(212) 586-2086
Metromail Corporation, 11 Eisenhower Lane, Lombard, IL 60148	(312) 620-3300
Names Unlimited, Inc., 40 East 34th St., New York City 10016	(212) 725-5522
National Business Lists, 162 North Franklin St., Chicago, IL 60606	(312) 236-0350
R. L. Polk & Co., 777 - 3rd Ave., New York City 10017	(212) 826-0600
Raymond-Loew Associates, Inc., 50 Broadway, New York City 10004	(212) 425-1290
Wm. Stroh Inc., 568-54 St., West New York, NJ 07093	(212) 564-7939
Target Mailing Lists, Inc., 35 East Wacker Dr., Chicago, IL 60601	(312) 782-3810
Yates Mailing Lists, 386 Park Ave. South, New York, NY 10016	(212) 686-3090

For the fun of it, here's a little question-and-answer session on readership; you'll probably find it's fun. It is reprinted with permission from the July 4, 1966 issue of *Advertising Age*. Copyright 1966 by Advertising Publications, Inc.

QUESTIONS
(Answers following)

1. Readership studies are a measure of how well an ad communicates its selling message.
   ☐ True   ☐ False

2. Readership of magazine ads is substantially lower among nonusers of a brand than users.
   ☐ True   ☐ False

3. Half-page horizontal ads are not as effective as half-page vertical insertions.
   ☐ True   ☐ False

4. Men tend to give more attention to pictures of men than they do to pictures of women.
   ☐ True   ☐ False

5. Drawings generally achieve a higher noted score than photographs.
   ☐ True   ☐ False

6. Multi-page ads attract correspondingly more readers than one-page or two-page ads.
   ☐ True   ☐ False

7. In a weekly magazine, about one-quarter of all inquiries produced by an ad are received during the first week after the ad appears.
   ☐ True   ☐ False

8. Generally, ads picturing the planning process or pretrip activities are among the most successful travel ads.
   ☐ True   ☐ False

9. Although the costs of reaching a reader have substantially increased in recent years, the increase has not outrun other business costs.
   ☐ True   ☐ False

10. Food ads with recipes are usually better read than food ads without recipes.
    ☐ True   ☐ False

11. It makes no difference in testimonial advertising whether the testimonial is by a celebrity or not.
    ☐ True   ☐ False

12. Readership scores for half-page full-color ads are about 85 percent higher than for half-page black-and-white insertions.
    ☐ True   ☐ False

13. One of the best ways to get maximum readership for a steamship line is to show lots of water.
    ☐ True   ☐ False

14. Interests of farm magazine readers follow the same pattern as general consumer magazine readers.
    ☐ True   ☐ False

15. The easier an advertiser makes it for a reader to send in an inquiry card, the more likely the reader will study the ad.
    ☐ True   ☐ False

16. Single-column quarter-page ads have a distinct advantage over square-shaped quarter-pages.
    ☐ True   ☐ False

17. Readership scores of half-page advertisements using black-and-white plus one color score about 25 percent better than half-page ads using no additional color.
    ☐ True   ☐ False

18. Single-page advertisements separated by suitable intervals reach a larger number of readers than the same space used all at once.
    ☐ True   ☐ False

ANSWERS

1. *False*. They are a quantitative study and not a qualitative one—they are intended to measure how many people see and read the ad. Much of the criticism of readership studies has stemmed from a failure to differentiate between these two types of studies.

2. *True*. Readership is about 40 percent higher among brand users.

3. *False*. Horizontal ads are slightly more successful in producing readership than are vertical ads.

4. *True*. Men also seem much more inclined to look at women than women are to look at men in ads.

5. *False*. Photographs generally score higher than drawings.

6. *False*. Although multi-page ads attract more attention than do one-page or two-page insertions, they do not attract correspondingly more readers. (In other words, three pages do not attract three times as many people as one page.)

7. *False*. About half of all inquiries produced by an ad appearing in a weekly publication should be received during the first week.

8. *False*. The highest attention goes to those travel ads which picture the travel destination.

9. *True*. Cost-per-reader has increased about 68 percent in the last decade, which is about the same as the increase for general business costs.

10. *True*. The use of recipes generally results in substantially higher readership of food ads.

11. *False*. Celebrity testimonials are far more effective than testimonials by noncelebrities.

12. *True*. Half-page full-color advertisements attract nearly twice as many readers as black-and-white units of the same size.

13. *True*. Many high-scoring ads show the ship itself out at sea.

14. *True*. Men are principally interested in forms of transportation and mechanical things. Women are interested in food, household furnishings, and clothes.

15. *False*. The easier an advertiser makes it for the reader to send in an inquiry card, the less likely the reader will bother to study the ad. Presumably, readers feel the literature would be more complete, and hence why read the ad?

16. *True*. A reader's eyes are more likely to sweep across the upper half of a page and so are more likely to be stopped by a quarter-page that occupies an entire column.

17. *False*. They score about the same. One color plus black-and-white does not attract any more readers than do plain black-and-white ads in magazines.

18. *True*. Except for special overriding reasons, single-page ads are more effective than multi-page or gatefolds using the same total amount of space.

PUBLICATION IMAGE PROFILE TRAITS

TIMELY—provides information of recent developments and new ideas while they are still newsworthy.

HELPFUL—furnishes its readers with information which is useful for the accomplishment of their work.

INTERESTING—engages and holds the attention of its readers.

OUTSPOKEN—expresses its opinions frankly.

INFLUENTIAL—has strong effect on the actions and ideas of its readers.

AUTHORITATIVE—has the stature of experience necessary to present ideas that carry weight.

RESPECTED—is widely recognized for its worth or stature in the business world.

SOUND—is strong and secure. It has a high degree of business health.

EXPERIENCED—has gained through actual experience a first-hand knowledge of its field.

LEADING—is ahead of almost all others in its field.

INTELLIGENT—is brilliant, resourceful and mentally keen.

RESEARCH-MINDED—studiously investigates the facts before writing its articles or reporting the news.

SCIENTIFIC—displays expert knowledge of its subject matter in the writing of its articles.

LEARNED—has unusually wide and deep knowledge of its field gained by study, research, or experience.

ALERT—watches for new ideas and new developments in its field.

MODERN—is up-to-date and belongs to the present time.

PROGRESSIVE—accepts and uses new ideas in order to move forward.

DYNAMIC—is energetic, forceful, and enthusiastic.

PIONEERING—has a reputation for being the first to explore and use new ideas and new developments.

PENETRATING—has the power to see below the surface and to understand and explain that which is not readily evident.

FAR-SIGHTED—has a reputation for seeing trends and predicting events before they are obvious to others.

PROPER—acts in strict accordance with the standards which are considered correct for a business magazine.

OPEN-MINDED—is happy to receive ideas or new arguments.

UNBIASED—is free from undue or improper influence.

RELIABLE—merits confidence or trust. It is believable, truthful and accurate.

WELL-ORGANIZED—arranges its material so that it is convenient to read.

COMPREHENSIVE—thoroughly covers all subjects that are of importance to its readers.

SPECIALIZED—stresses one specific area of interest in particular.

DIVERSIFIED—covers a number of different areas of interest.

INDEX

A

Abstract illustrations, 554-558
AC Spark Plug Div., General Motors
    Corp., 390-392
Ad chart awareness study, 869-874
Adams, Charles F., 199
Addressograph-Multigraph Corp., 287
Ad-Gage Reports, 457-468
Ads
    average, 676
    black and white, 630
    bleed, 643-646
    cartoon/comic strip, 488-491
    case-history, 262, 468-473
    catalog offer, 476-477
    charts and graphs use in, 543-545
    clock-wise scanning, 650
    close with action request, 254
    and continuity, 641
    editorial approach in, 263
    feline, 237-238
    fractional-page, 640
    Hendrick Manufacturing Company, 233
    honesty in, 210
    how to, 478
    inducing response to, 397
    information, truth and clarity in, 219
    inquiry, 474-476
    inserts, 672-674
    institutional, 486
    kinds of, 204
    lighthearted information in, 224
    newsletter, 263, 477-478
    off-beat, 238
    one-column, 642
    outline, 440
    page domination in, 643
    picture story, 531-533
    pointing device, 653
    preferred positions of, 881
    problem-solving, 466
    product line, 465
    question-and-answer approach in, 262
    and readership ratings, 675
    rebus, 558-560
    repeat, 892
    schedule of, 251
    size of, 641-643
    testimonial, 263, 269, 473-474
    trade, 481
    two page spreads, 675-679
    up front position of, 880
Advertiser-agency collaboration, 494
Advertising
    appropriations, 1046-1049
    blowups, 1042
    budget, 179, 1046-1055
    concepts, 499
    corporate, 34-35, 582, 997-1036
    creativity in, 681-729
    definition of, 388
    electronic media, 793-807
    facts, 498
    goals, 494, 498
    guidelines for better, 498-499
    house-agency, 25
    long-range plans, 999
    measurement of, 1038
    message, 492-503
    objectionable, 58-62
    objectives, 171-198, 494, 999
    planning, 494
    research, 54
    specialties, 929-931
    sporadic, 641
    types of, 446
    what can & cannot be accomplished
        by, 178
Advertising Age, 41, 897
Advertising agencies, 40-82
    client relationship with, 79
    compensation of, 42-47
    income, 43-45
    markup, 674
    media commission, 45-47
    medium-size, 41
    organization chart by functions, 64
    organizations, 44, 47-65